Parameters of Power

Canada's Political Institutions

Fifth Edition

Heather MacIvor
University of Windsor

D1377208

NELSON / EDUCATION

NELSON / EDUCATION

Parameters of Power: Canada's Political Institutions, Fifth Edition
by Heather MacIvor

Associate Vice President, Editorial Director:
Evelyn Veitch

Editor-in-Chief, Higher Education:
Anne Williams

Acquisitions Editor:
Bram Sepers

Marketing Manager:
Ann Byford

Developmental Editor:
Heather Parker

Photo Researcher:
Beth Yarzab

Permissions Coordinator:
Beth Yarzab

Production Service:
Macmillan Publishing Solutions

Copy Editor:
Erin Moore

Proofreader:
Barbara Storey

Indexer:
Maura Brown

Senior Production Coordinator:
Ferial Suleman

Design Director:
Ken Phipps

Managing Designer:
Franca Amore

Interior Design:
Suzanne Peden

Cover Design:
Peter Papayanakis

Cover and Part Opener Image:
Courtesy of Robin Kelsey

Compositor:
Macmillan Publishing Solutions

Printer:
Webcom

**Library and Archives Canada
Cataloguing in Publication Data**

MacIvor, Heather, 1964–
    Parameters of power : Canada's
political institutions / Heather
MacIvor. — 5th ed.

Previous eds. written by Keith
Archer . . . [et al.]

Includes bibliographical references
and index.

ISBN 978-0-17-610538-9

1. Canada—Politics and
government—Textbooks. I. Title.

JL65.P37 2009   320.971
C2009-900070-9

ISBN-13: 978-0-17-610538-9
ISBN-10: 0-17-610538-7

BRIEF CONTENTS

TABLE OF CONTENTS

PART II: THE CANADIAN *CONSTITUTION*   63

CHAPTER 3: CONSTITUTIONS   65

CHAPTER 4: FEDERALISM AND INTERGOVERNMENTAL RELATIONS   81

CHAPTER 5: FROM MEGACONSTITUTIONAL POLITICS TO NONCONSTITUTIONAL RENEWAL   133

TABLE OF DOSSIERS

CHAPTER 12: ELECTIONS AND VOTING 419

CHAPTER 13: ADVOCACY GROUPS AND THE CANADIAN POLITICAL SYSTEM 479

CHAPTER 14: THE NEWS MEDIA 507

PREFACE
Heather MacIvor

What is the purpose of a first-year textbook? The most obvious is to provide more information than the instructor can deliver in class. Another is to generate discussion in the classroom or tutorials. Ideally, a textbook will excite students' interest in the subject matter by presenting up-to-date information and ideas in a clear and easily accessible way. A fourth purpose is to expose students to some of the primary source documents in the discipline; for example, the appendix to this book reproduces the *Constitution Acts* of 1867 and 1982. Finally, a first-year textbook should organize a mass of complex information within a coherent framework of analysis, to assist the instructor in presenting the material to students who may lack any background in the subject matter of the course.

This fifth edition of *Parameters of Power*, like its predecessors, has been crafted with these purposes in mind. The framework of analysis grounds political institutions in their social and cultural context, highlighting the reciprocal relationship between the political system and the society that it serves. This book explains the ways in which political institutions shape the behaviour of political actors, by setting incentives and embodying social norms. It also shows how changing political values in the electorate, and conflicts between new and established subcultures, can create strong pressures for institutional reform.

CHANGES TO THIS EDITION

In response to instructors' requests, the structure is considerably different from the previous edition.

Many of the chapters are shorter and more tightly focused. They have been rearranged into four parts, to improve the cohesion and flow of the material. There is a new chapter on the courts, separate from the discussion of the *Canadian Charter of Rights and Freedoms*.

The content has been updated to reflect recent developments in Canadian politics, including the following topics:

- the January 2006 federal election, which brought a Conservative minority government led by Prime Minister Stephen Harper to power (replacing the Liberal minority government of Paul Martin);

- although the October 2008 election and the December 2008 prorogation of Parliament occurred shortly before this book went to press, some references have been included where appropriate;

- the Harper Government's institutional reform agenda, including changes to the appointment of senators and judges, fixed election dates, and the *Federal Accountability Act*;

- the 2002–04 Sponsorship Scandal, which helped to defeat the Liberal Party of Canada after more than a decade in power;
- Justice John Gomery's Commission of Inquiry into the scandals;*
- the resignation of Liberal leader Paul Martin, the 2006 leadership convention that chose Stéphane Dion to succeed him, and the unorthodox elevation of Michael Ignatieff to replace Dion; and
- the fading impact of 9/11.

Students will benefit from the pedagogical features of this fifth edition, which include:
- at least one updated feature report in each chapter, called a "Dossier," which discusses a current Canadian political issue or institution in some depth;
- a clear and accessible writing style, using everyday language and examples to clarify abstract and challenging concepts;
- "Learning Objectives" at the beginning of each chapter, which flag the most important themes in that chapter and help you to read more efficiently;
- "Discussion and Review Questions" at the end of each chapter, to focus your studying and generate debate;
- a "Glossary of Key Terms" at the end of each chapter, which defines the words presented in **boldface** throughout that chapter;
- a "Suggested Readings" section, featuring both print and website information sources, to kickstart your research projects or just point the way to more information about intriguing topics.

THIS TEXTBOOK AS A LEARNING TOOL

Students who approach the study of Canadian politics for the first time are sometimes overwhelmed by the unexpected complexity of our laws and institutions. If you are a first-year student, or a more advanced student with little previous background in the subject matter of this book, don't panic! The structure of each chapter is designed to guide you through the material as painlessly as possible. Here are a few pointers to help you get the most out of this book:
- Before you begin to read each chapter, take a few minutes to orient yourself to the material. Read the chapter title, the headings in the table of contents, and the "Learning Objectives."
- Think about how the material in that chapter fits with what you already know.
- If your instructor has provided you with a lecture outline or some other kind of guide to the key themes in the chapter, refer to that information; otherwise, turn to the "Discussion and Review Questions" near the end of the chapter. *To read effectively and efficiently, you must begin by knowing where you're headed and what you need to look for along the way.*
- As you read, remember two key rules:
  — Do *not* highlight whole pages, or even whole paragraphs; use a highlighter to emphasize just the key words or phrases, not to turn the entire book into a fluorescent rainbow.
  — *Always* take notes of what you've read; if you write or word-process a brief summary of each chapter, in your own words, you will understand and retain the material far more effectively, and you will find it much faster and easier to study for tests.

---

*In June 2008, the Federal Court of Canada rejected Justice Gomery's factual conclusions about the role played by former Prime Minister Jean Chrétien and his Chief of Staff, Jean Pelletier, in the Sponsorship Scandal (Dossier 8.2). The court did not criticize Gomery's overall analysis of Canada's political institutions, the lack of accountability in the executive branch, or the excessive power of Canadian prime ministers in general. Therefore, the ruling does not affect the credibility of those aspects of Gomery's work that are cited in this book. See *In the Matter of the Right Homourable Jean Chrétien v. The Honourable John Gomery et al.; Jean Pelletier v. Attorney General of Canada et al.*, 2008 FC 802; accessed at www.canlii.org, June 2008.

- Learn to distinguish between the really important points in each chapter, as identified by your instructor, and those that require less time and effort to understand. Do *not* read a textbook like a novel, in which every word must be given equal attention. If you try to do this with all of your first-year textbooks, you will never get your reading done. Instead, practise reading critically and analytically. Use the pedagogical tools in this book to guide you through the chapters, picking out what you need and mastering those elements.
- Keep up with your assigned reading. You can't make the best use of your class time unless you have read and understood the assigned chapter(s) before you show up. And don't try to skim a chapter right before the class—you will only confuse yourself and start to panic. Take the time you need to really understand each chapter, or at least those parts that you need to know.
- When you finish reading each chapter, test yourself by jotting down answers to the "Discussion and Review Questions." Then turn back to the "Learning Objectives" to see how many of them you have already met. If you find that you are stuck on a particular point, go back and reread that section of the chapter. By the time you finish this process, you should be well prepared for classroom discussion and testing.

Above all, I hope that this book will accomplish two things. First, I hope that it will inspire students to learn as much as they can about Canadian politics. This does not necessarily mean majoring in political science (although that would, of course, be an excellent idea!), but it does mean reading a good daily newspaper—many are available for free online—and staying informed about current political developments. Second, if you are not already an active, engaged citizen, I hope that this book inspires you to get involved in politics. The future of our democracy depends as much on the commitment and energy of young people as the experience and wisdom of older Canadians. Get involved, and use the information in this book as a tool to achieve your goals. Only by understanding our existing political institutions, and evaluating the various arguments for and against their reform, can we make a positive difference for the entire community.

SUPPLEMENTS TO THE BOOK

TEXT WEBSITE. This website is intended to enhance the teaching and learning experience for instructors and students. Browse our extensive and helpful resources at www.parametersofpower5e.nelson.com.

INSTRUCTOR'S MANUAL. This comprehensive guide is organized to provide chapter outlines, overviews, and instructional tips. Available only as a downloadable supplement on the text website.

TEST BANK. This resource includes a variety of questions (multiple choice, short-answer, and essay questions) from which to construct tests and exams. Available only from your Nelson Education Ltd. sales representative.

ACKNOWLEDGMENTS

I wish to thank the team at Nelson Education Ltd., particularly Bram Sepers and Heather Parker. In this case, my gratitude goes well beyond the usual acknowledgment of professionalism on the part of the publisher: the Nelson Education Ltd. team was exceptionally gracious, accommodating, and considerate. I am also grateful to the anonymous reviewers for their comments on the fourth edition and their very helpful suggestions to improve the fifth edition. The students in my first-year Canadian Politics course at the University of Windsor have been a constant source of inspiration and advice, although they may not know it; their questions and comments have helped me to refine the book and to make it as "user-friendly" as possible. As always, I am profoundly grateful for the love and support of Kendal McKinney. Our Dandie Dinmont terrier, Mazie, does her best to plan her walks around my writing schedule.

I dedicate this edition to the memory of my parents, Murray MacIvor and MJ Walker. They gave me a consuming (and often irreverent) interest in politics, and an addiction to the news. Most important, they showed me that politicians are people just like the rest of us. For their insights into the human side of government and politics, I will always be grateful.

Part I

Political Institutions and Political Culture

CHAPTER 1: Institutions and Politics

CHAPTER 2: Changing Political Culture and Canada's Political Institutions

Institutions and Politics

LEARNING OBJECTIVES

After you finish reading this chapter, you should be able to:

* *identify* the three branches of Canada's national government;
* *explain* the differences between a federal state and a unitary state;
* *explain* how institutions shape individual behaviour;
* *explain* the role of myths and symbols in politics, with original examples; and
* *summarize* the four central principles in the Canadian *Constitution* in your own words.

INTRODUCTION: INSTITUTIONS IN DAILY LIFE

Imagine yourself walking into one of your classes. You enter a large room with fixed rows of desks, all facing the board, screen, and lectern at the front. You choose a seat and pull your notebook computer (or pen and paper) from your bag. As you wait for the professor to enter, you exchange information and opinions about the course with the friend who always sits next to you. When the professor arrives, she places her briefcase on the lectern and takes out some notes. She projects a slide outlining the day's lecture on the screen. You and your classmates write down the outline and then prepare to listen to the rest of the lecture. You know that this professor has strict rules against talking in class, so you try to resist the temptation to share your comments with your friend (although you sometimes give in). You also know that the prof hates it when students walk in late and disrupt the class, so you always make sure to be there on time. When the lecture ends, you put your stuff back in your bag—while the professor does the same—and leave the classroom.

Although you may not know it, you have just participated in an institution. Like all institutions, the university classroom has its own authority structure, rules, rituals, **myths,** and **symbols.** An institution shapes the behaviour of everyone inside it, although in different ways depending on each person's position in the authority structure. In other words, everyone in that classroom is playing a role that is preordained by the rules of the institution and by the architecture of the room itself. The professor plays the role of teacher, dispensing knowledge to the students, who either receive that knowledge passively or become active participants in their own learning. While the screen and lectern are practical tools for teaching, they also symbolize the professor's authority. So do the rows of student desks, which face the source of knowledge (the professor). Everyone has his or her own set of rituals in the classroom, some of which serve the official purpose of the institution (the sharing of knowledge). Everyone understands the myths associated with the lecture: the wisdom and authority of the professor, the students' eagerness to learn. (Please note: The word "myths" does not mean "lies" or "illusions." The point is that the behaviour of the participants in this situation is structured by a set of common assumptions, not that these assumptions are inaccurate.) And everyone understands the rules and expectations of classroom behaviour—quiet attentiveness, punctuality, preparation—even though they may not always follow them. Students know that if they refuse to obey certain rules, such as the due dates for assignments, the professor can punish them with a poor grade. Myth, symbol, ritual, rules, authority structures, and preordained behaviour patterns are the hallmarks of an institution, even one as small as a university classroom.

Like any institution, the degree to which the university classroom fulfills its assigned functions depends on a number of factors. If the professor disregards the rules, rituals, and symbols by persistently arriving late or unprepared, or abuses her authority by favouring some students over others, the class will become alienated and the myths will lose their power. When a professor is incompetent or careless, the **legitimacy** of the institution diminishes and its outcomes—particularly the grades awarded to the students—may be rejected. If the professor's authority is undermined by outside forces, such as the university administration or a government agency, the effectiveness of her teaching may suffer. If the students are unable or unwilling to follow the rules of the institution, they will not play their roles properly and the professor's performance will suffer. And if the institution itself is out of step with the needs and expectations of the students, its myths and symbols will lose their legitimating power and no amount of hard work on the professor's part can restore it.

THE APPROACH OF THIS BOOK

This book is about Canada's **political institutions** and their relationship to the society that they govern. Like the classroom just described, the institutions that make up the Canadian **state** embody unique sets of rules, roles, authority structures, myths, symbols, and rituals. Most of the time, we obey the rules because it is appropriate to do so, and because we believe that the state has the legitimacy to set and enforce them. When the most important rules are broken, the state has the power to punish the offenders. The ways in which we perceive government authority are shaped by the ways in which that authority is exercised. When political leaders fail to deliver the outcomes we expect, or they violate the myths and rituals of governance by abusing their authority, the institutions within which they work lose some of their legitimacy. Even when our institutions work properly, they may be constrained by outside forces or challenged by a shift in public perceptions and expectations of government; in such instances, their legitimacy will suffer. If the loss of legitimacy is severe enough, and it persists for long enough, the entire institutional structure may lose the authority to shape our behaviour.

The differences between political and nonpolitical institutions are not always easy to define. Table 1.1 lists examples of Canada's key political institutions, and contrasts them to social structures that are often considered as "nonpolitical."

On closer inspection, the division between the two lists begins to blur. The definition of "the family" has been a hotly contested political issue in many Western countries since the

TABLE 1.1	POLITICAL AND NONPOLITICAL INSTITUTIONS	
POLITICAL INSTITUTIONS	**NONPOLITICAL INSTITUTIONS**	
The House of Commons	Families	
The Senate	Churches	
The Supreme Court of Canada	Minor Hockey Leagues	
The Cabinet	Labour Unions	
The Federal Public Service		
The Liberal Party of Canada		
Greenpeace		

1970s, as rising rates of marriage breakdown and the increasing participation of mothers in the workplace forced governments to re-examine their assumptions about the relationship between the state and the home. Public policies may encourage or permit the formation of certain family structures while discouraging others (e.g., same-sex marriages). Church congregations may be encouraged by their pastors to engage in political activity, or the clergy themselves may decide to issue public statements on social issues. Minor hockey leagues are directly affected by laws concerning insurance liability, equipment standards, and gender discrimination. Some labour unions are directly affiliated with the New Democratic Party; even those that are not formally tied to the NDP may participate in public demonstrations against particular government actions, or seek to persuade their members to vote in a certain way. In practice, therefore, the distinction between political and nonpolitical institutions is less clear than it initially appears.

Nonetheless, no single book can provide an adequate discussion of every important institution in Canadian society. Therefore, we must distinguish between the institutions that form the subject matter of this book and those that will be mentioned infrequently, if at all. We will do so by focusing on the main purpose or function of each institution. We will define "politics" as *the process of making and enforcing public rules and decisions that affect all or part of a given population.* This is admittedly a narrow definition of "politics," focusing as it does on the institutions described in this book. Other authors adopt a much broader perspective. One classic example is the late Harold Lasswell: "Politics is about who gets what, when, and how."[1] Such definitions raise fascinating questions about power, privilege, and decision-making across the whole spectrum of human experience. On the down side, they obscure the subject-matter of this particular book: the role of specifically political institutions in government and society. So we will adopt a narrower definition of "politics," while acknowledging its limitations.

Therefore, an institution whose main function is to make or to enforce rules and decisions that must be followed by all or part of the population may be considered to be a political institution. The federal Parliament passes the laws proposed by the political executive and drafted by the permanent executive. Once enacted, those laws are applied and enforced by the permanent executive (and by the police and judges, in the case of criminal laws). They may be interpreted authoritatively by the courts. In order to perform their assigned functions effectively, political institutions that exercise authority on behalf of the population must be generally considered legitimate. In other words, their structures and operations must conform to a reasonably widespread set of myths, rituals, and symbols.

At the beginning of the twenty-first century, national political institutions in Canada and elsewhere confront a host of challenges:

- Their perceived legitimacy is declining, as reflected in public-opinion surveys and falling voter turnout.[2]
- Some of their power to make and enforce decisions for their populations is shifting to local and regional governments, international organizations (such as the World Trade Organization), and nonstate agencies.[3]
- Ethnic and linguistic minorities within their borders are demanding greater rights and more autonomy from their central governments, which could lead to the breakup of some existing states.[4]
- New communication technologies are blurring national borders and creating new, non-territorial forms of community over which national governments have no authority.[5]
- The political values and expectations of their populations are changing in ways that conflict with existing political institutions, thus undermining the power of the old political myths and symbols to legitimate the use of lawful authority.[6]

Although these are potentially serious problems, national governments are not an endangered species. Institutions can and do adapt to changing environments. The history of Canada's political institutions is a story of continuous adaptation to changing conditions: the expansion of the federation from four to 10 provinces, participation in two World Wars, the management of recurring economic crises, and the evolution of one of the most diverse populations in the world. There is no reason to suppose that the Canadian state will disappear any time soon. Much depends on the effectiveness of institutional reforms: the degree to which a particular change meshes with the attitudes and values of the electorate, and fits with the rest of the political system. A poorly judged reform can weaken the legitimacy of the political system.

The premise of this book is that political institutions and the societies that they serve continually redefine themselves and each other. As the political attitudes and values of citizens change, partly in response to the performance of their governing institutions, so do the criteria by which they judge that performance. Chapter 2 examines the changes in Canada's political culture since the end of World War II: the growing emphasis on individual and group rights, rising demands for provincial autonomy, Quebec separatism, the redefinition of **"democracy,"** declining deference to political authority, and a pervasive cynicism toward our political institutions and leaders. The ability of our political institutions to respond to these shifts in political attitudes has been diminished by fiscal constraints, the difficulty of amending the written constitution, and the power of new communication technologies to engage citizens across national borders. At a very basic level, Canadians disagree about the goals that our political institutions should pursue and the means by which those goals should be achieved. The recurring bouts of **"megaconstitutional politics"** in the 1980s and 1990s (described in Chapter 5) revealed the depth of those disagreements and the difficulty of reforming our political institutions through formal constitutional amendment.

HOW INSTITUTIONS SHAPE POLITICAL BEHAVIOUR

One of the enduring questions in political science, dating back to the very beginnings, concerns the relationship between the state and the citizens. What sort of state is best suited to a particular population? This question goes beyond the immediate issue of designing political institutions that fit the existing political capacities of a given *demos* (group of citizens), although this issue is clearly important. In the fourth century B.C.E., Aristotle argued that each of the different types of state—kingship, aristocracy, and democracy—was naturally suited to different kinds of people. Consequently, there was no one "best" type of state; each type was suited to particular political and social conditions.[7] In 1762, Jean-Jacques Rousseau advised those who would design political institutions to "investigate the fitness of the people, for which they are destined, to receive them."[8] A century later, John Stuart Mill identified three conditions for the success of any political institution:

(1) That the people should be willing to receive it. (2) That they should be willing and able to do what is necessary for its preservation. (3) That they should be willing and able to fulfil the duties and discharge the functions which it imposes on them.[9]

The twentieth century bore melancholy witness to the truth of these classic insights. In Europe, Asia, Africa, and Latin America, democratic constitutions were imposed on populations that, at that time, lacked the willingness and the capacity to operate and sustain them. In many cases, they quickly degenerated into one-party tyrannies or military dictatorships. Such was the experience of the Weimar Republic, the democratic state established in defeated Germany after World War I. The constitution designed by the victorious Western powers was a model of abstract democratic perfection: a proportional electoral system, opportunities for the electorate to make laws through plebiscites and referenda, protection for individual rights, and a political executive dependent on the support of Parliament. After 14 years, the Weimar Republic collapsed. Adolf Hitler brought his National Socialist (Nazi) Party to power, dissolved the representative institutions, and effectively threw out the democratic constitution. The failure of the Weimar Republic led to the deaths of millions of innocent people, inside and outside Germany. That failure can be partly attributed, not to any particular flaw in the constitution itself, but to the mismatch between institutions and political culture. In 1919, too few Germans were ready to accept the compromises and self-restraint that democracy demands.[10]

While there is little doubt that political institutions must be suited to the political culture of the population, political scientists have not always been content with the status quo. They have asked a further question: Can we create political institutions that will not only reflect, but actually enhance, the political virtues of the people? For Aristotle, man[11] is born with the potential to acquire moral and intellectual virtue. He cannot realize that potential unless he receives a good education and lives under good laws. Education, in Aristotle's conception, goes well beyond the acquisition of facts; it knits disparate individuals into a community, and instills in them the principles of justice that promote the good life.[12] Following good laws creates the habit of performing virtuous acts, which in turn creates a virtuous character.[13] Aristotle defined happiness as the highest human good, and pointed to virtue as the best guarantee of a happy life. Because the moral training of the people is the chief business of those who design political institutions, political science is the "master" science. It gives men the tools to achieve a happy life for themselves and their fellow citizens.[14]

In a similar vein, Mill argued that the chief criterion for evaluating a political institution is its influence on the moral and political character of the people whom it governs:

The first element of good government, therefore, being the virtue and intelligence of the human beings composing the community, the most important point of excellence which any form of government can possess is to promote the virtue and intelligence of the people themselves. The first question in respect to any political institutions is, how far they tend to foster in the members of the community the various desirable qualities, moral and intellectual . . .[15]

The Federal Republic of Germany, founded by the American, British, and French Allies in the Western zones of occupation after World War II, was carefully designed to avoid the failures of Weimar.[16] The institutions established in the Western zones in 1949 were crafted by pro-democratic German politicians, in concert with the occupying powers, to strike a balance between the existing political culture and the requirements of liberal democracy. By the

1990s, survey research revealed that West Germans had adopted the same political values as other Europeans. While this transformation cannot be attributed solely to the political institutions of the Federal Republic, their influence was powerfully beneficial.

After World War II, the focus shifted from institutions to the political behaviour of citizens. Political scientists sought to understand political life as the result of millions of individual choices, based either on deep-seated psychological characteristics or on a "rational utility" model borrowed from economics.[17] Institutions were largely ignored, or reduced to "arenas" where the competition among social and individual interests played itself out.[18] In the 1980s, some political scientists rediscovered the independent influence of institutions on political life. They recognized that political behaviour does not exist independently of institutions; rather, "political institutions define the framework within which politics takes place."[19] These "new institutionalists" define politics as an interaction between state and society, not as the exclusive preserve of one or the other.

Without denying the importance of both the social context of politics and the motives of individual actors, therefore, institutional analysis posits a more independent role for political institutions. The state is not only affected by society but also affects it. Political democracy depends not only on economic and social conditions but also on the design of political institutions. Bureaucratic agencies, legislative committees, and appellate courts are arenas for contending social forces, but they are also collections of standard operating procedures and structures that define and defend values, norms, interests, identities and beliefs.[20]

The "neoinstitutionalist" school has revived the ideas of Aristotle and Mill. "New constitutionalist" thinkers seek to design political institutions that will "develop and strengthen civic virtue and competence."[21] As we saw at the beginning of this chapter (the classroom example), institutions do shape individual behaviour and attitudes in at least three ways:

1. setting incentives for those who operate within them;
2. exploiting symbols to legitimize the authority structures on which they are based; and
3. imposing structured roles and rituals on actors inside and outside them.

Incentives

Institutions create incentives for political actors: they require or encourage some types of behaviour, and discourage or punish others. The effectiveness of these incentives depends on two factors: their congruence with the preexisting beliefs and motivations of the participants, and the clarity with which they are expressed. A student who intends to earn an A in a particular course has a stronger incentive to follow the professor's rules than one who only aspires to pass. But if those rules are arbitrary, incomprehensible, or poorly enforced, the A student may become frustrated and cease to follow them.

Every institution provides a structure of opportunities for those who are motivated to succeed within it. An ideal opportunity structure in a university course provides fair deadlines for submitting assignments, clear rules for classroom conduct and academic work, and the chance to solicit help from the instructor when required. Similarly, political institutions create opportunities and incentives—both formal and informal—for ambitious politicians, as illustrated in Dossier 1.1.

When a political institution channels ambition into behaviour that conflicts with the political values of some citizens, its legitimacy can suffer. For example, the authority of the Canadian Cabinet (the political executive) rests on the continued support of a majority of the members of the House of Commons. Consequently, the prime minister—as the leader of the largest party in the Commons—has a powerful incentive to ensure that his or her MPs remain loyal. That loyalty is secured through party discipline, a system of rewards, threats, and punishments that reinforces the team spirit already present among parliamentarians elected

One of the most important criteria for evaluating a political institution is its success in channelling the ambition of individual politicians to serve the public good. Failure to do so can result in corruption, self-seeking behaviour, and the disregard of the public good. Personal ambition is the product of individual psychology. While often condemned by those who fear its effects in political life, personal ambition is more properly regarded as a crucial resource for democracy. The power of ambition as a motivating force in politics was stated succinctly by Senator Serge Joyal in March 2007: "Le système est fondé sur l'ambition. On aurait tort de le nier. La carrière politique est caractérisée par l'ambition, qui fait marcher tout le système. [The system is based on ambition. One cannot deny this. Political careers are characterized by ambition, which keeps the whole system running.]"[22]

An effective institution "transforms private goals into public morality"[23] by creating incentives for ambitious politicians to serve the common good. If an aspiring party leader, for example, can win a leadership contest by deceit and manipulation, he may well be motivated to engage in campaign tactics that undermine the health of his party. But if such behaviour is likely to be exposed and condemned, with fatal consequences for his campaign, the risks of dishonesty may be too great. "Properly channelled, ambition can be used to curb its own natural excesses."[24]

to represent the same party. A government MP who votes against a budget, or some other key piece of legislation, knows that she is risking her political career. The incentives for government MPs are crystal clear: if you hope to rise to a Cabinet position, you must demonstrate your loyalty to the prime minister (see the discussion of "court government" in Chapter 8). As we will see in Chapter 7, party discipline is increasingly perceived by Canadian voters as a barrier to genuine political representation.[25] But as long as the relationship between our executive and legislative institutions remains unchanged, party discipline will continue to shape the behaviour of our members of Parliament.

Political institutions structure the behaviour of all citizens, not just politicians. For example, it is sometimes argued that institutions that encourage rational, deliberative debate among citizens promote the development of civic virtues.[26] By allowing nonpoliticians to acquire the "habits" of justice and community participation, as Aristotle might put it, these institutions strengthen the commitment to democracy among the electorate. Institutions that discourage public participation, on the other hand, may weaken citizenship and erode the foundations of democratic legitimacy. Critics of representative democracy often argue that Canada's political parties, Parliament, and Cabinet government exclude "the people" from the decision-making process. These critics believe that the introduction of direct-democracy provisions—initiatives, referenda, and recall—would give citizens an incentive to become better informed about politics and strengthen their faith in our national institutions. We will return to this debate in Chapter 2.

Symbolism

Political institutions both embody and create legitimating symbols. They simplify a world of overwhelming complexity, reducing it to predictable routines and a set of shared meanings.[27]

By providing a structure of routines, roles, forms, and rules, political institutions organize a potentially disorderly political process. By shaping meaning, political institutions create an interpretive order within which political behaviour can be understood . . .[28]

That "interpretive order" includes the primary myths, symbols, and rituals that underpin the political system of a given state. (For examples, see the glossary at the end of this chapter.)

There are three important points to make about political myths and symbols. First, the word "myth" is not synonymous with "lie" or "deception." To be credible, and hence influential, every myth (political or otherwise) must have some basis in fact. Otherwise, the gap between myth and reality eventually becomes too great, and the myth loses its power to inspire political action or legitimize political authority. For example, Quebec nationalism is a "myth" because it is a powerful narrative of oppression and resentment against the English-speaking majority in Canada (not to mention the **anglophone** minority in Quebec, which held a disproportionate share of economic power until fairly recently). Nonetheless, it is indisputably true that the French-speaking percentage of Canada's population is shrinking; it is also true that there are cultural differences between **francophone** Quebeckers and other Canadians, which might lead one to conclude that they cannot live together in the same country. Similarly, Albertan alienation from Central Canada is a powerful myth that affects the ways in which residents of the four westernmost provinces interpret political events. When former Prime Minister Chrétien made a speech in Edmonton in August 2001, in which he called upon Albertans to share the wealth from their oil and gas revenues with the rest of Canada, he inadvertently triggered an explosion of anger and fear about the federal government's intentions toward the province. That intense regional sensitivity and antagonism toward the federal government can be puzzling to non-Westerners, who may not be aware of the historical reasons for it (such as a perceived lack of concern for Western interests by governments dominated by MPs representing Ontario and Quebec).

Second, political myths and symbols change along with social and economic circumstances:

> In a fully developed civic culture and polity, politics will in part be a process of forming, choosing between, adapting and revising myths and symbols. It is in the nature of myths that they are selective and only deal with some facts and issues, and ignore others. They are intensely ideological, and each major ideology, including nationalism, Marxism, socialism, liberalism, or conservatism, has a system of myths and symbols associated with it.[29]

Third, each political institution embodies its own set of myths and symbols, which are not always compatible with those embodied in other institutions. The decisions of the House of Commons are legitimated, in part, by the symbols of the national political community: the Crown, the prime minister, the general election in which all Canadian citizens may participate. On the other hand, decisions taken collectively by the first ministers can be legitimated only by the symbols of federalism and provincial rights, which conflict with the idea of a single national interest. Because it divides the loyalties of citizens between two levels of government, federalism necessarily creates conflicting sets of myths and symbols. These may undermine the sense of a unified political community, which Aristotle considered to be an essential part of a good constitution. There are competing myths and symbols in every society, as Dossier 1.2 illustrates.

Even a universal myth, such as the value of voting in a representative democracy, means different things to different people: "membership in a national political community, an instrumental attempt to attain state benefits, a routine obligation of citizenship, a belief in a particular ideology or worldview."[30] Perhaps we should say "a *formerly* universal myth," given the disturbing decline in voter turnout in recent Canadian general elections (the 2006 vote was an exception). If the link between political symbolism and political behaviour is as strong as we have suggested in this chapter, the drop in turnout can be attributed (in part) to a loss of faith in the national political community, in the value of citizenship, or in the meaning of political ideology. There are, of course, other reasons for sitting out an election; we will explore some of them in Chapter 12.

As previously mentioned, "megaconstitutional politics" involves a clash between competing myths and symbols of the political community. As the battle rages, the symbolism becomes increasingly crude and polarizing. During the debate over the Meech Lake Accord (Chapter 5), the struggle to redefine Canadian federalism revolved around two conflicting mythologies: the Quebec myth of "Canada as a duality, a partnership of two founding peoples, with Quebec representing one of the partners" versus an English Canadian myth of "Canada as a partnership of ten equal provinces."[31] The death of the Accord in June 1990 was portrayed in Quebec as a rejection by English Canada of the province and its legitimate constitutional demands, despite the ratification of the Accord by nine provinces (one of which later withdrew its approval) and the federal Parliament.[32] Prime Minister Brian Mulroney became the symbol of support for the Accord and a lightning rod for those in English Canada who believed that Quebec was "getting too much." On the other side, former Prime Minister Pierre Trudeau and Newfoundland Premier Clyde Wells came to symbolize the opposition to the Accord, and they were vilified in Quebec after its demise.

Other symbols that characterized the Meech Lake debate included the West's demand for a Triple-E Senate (Elected, Equal, and Effective);[33] the *Charter of Rights,* which some "*Charter* Canadians" sought to defend against the "threat" of the Accord;[34] and the secretive process by which the Accord was negotiated in April 1987, encapsulated in the phrase "eleven white men in suits." As one of the participants in the process later acknowledged, "The Accord generated such fierce opposition outside of Quebec because it was seen as an attempt to change the delicate balance in the 'symbolic order of Canada' . . . Changes to the symbolic order will be fiercely resisted."[35] Perhaps, but only by those who are indifferent to the new symbols. Gradual change in the symbolic order happens all the time, without a public uproar; only the attempt to impose symbols that conflict with deeply held political values provokes resistance. Such is the quandary of those who would reform Canada's political institutions through formal constitutional amendment.

Structured Roles for Political Actors

The rules, rituals, and norms embodied in institutions tell us how to behave in varying situations. Without them, most human interactions would be chaotic and meaningless. When you register for a particular course, you know what sort of behaviour is expected of you in your role as "student." You probably behave quite differently in your roles as "friend," "sibling," "parent," or "child." Each role imposes particular constraints on your actions, and each entails a set of rules—some of which are imposed without your consent and others negotiated with the people to whom you relate—that make your behaviour fairly predictable. The same is true for your professor, who (in all likelihood) behaves rather differently with his or her friends and family than with students. Without being aware of it, you expect the professor to behave in a certain way—in effect, to "act like a professor"—and you would be shocked and uncomfortable if he or she suddenly started to behave inappropriately (e.g., sexually harassing students).

Political institutions provide scripts for the actors who work within them. They define appropriate and inappropriate conduct for political actors and establish sanctions for inappropriate behaviour. Each political role is defined differently. For example, we expect the leader of a political party to defend his or her partisan position fiercely and to attack the ideas put forward by the other parties. But we would be appalled if the chief justice of the Supreme

Court—whose role requires her to be as objective as possible—did the same. We expect the minister of Finance to announce the details of the annual federal budget in the House of Commons, not in a bar in downtown Ottawa. Some of these roles are defined in the written constitution; others are informal and unwritten, and breaches are enforceable only in the political realm (see the discussion of constitutional conventions in Chapter 3). For example, the governor general has the power under the 1867 constitution to remove the prime minister and govern by executive decree. She does not exercise this power, because the role of the Crown's representative has been greatly restricted by the growth of democratic norms in Canadian society.

CANADA'S POLITICAL INSTITUTIONS

■ The Three Branches of Government: Parliament, the Executive, and the Judiciary

Each of Canada's political institutions performs a unique set of tasks or functions within the state. Political scientists often distinguish among three primary types of function: legislative (making laws), executive (implementing laws), and judicial (enforcing and interpreting laws).

In the Canadian state, the legislative power is shared by the Crown (represented by the governor general) and the two Houses of the federal Parliament: the lower house (the House of Commons) and the upper house (the Senate). The executive power is divided among three separate institutions: the Crown, the political executive (the prime minister and Cabinet), and the permanent executive (the federal public service). The judicial power is allocated to a hierarchical set of courts, some provincial and some federal. At the top of the judicial hierarchy is the Supreme Court of Canada, which is both the final court of appeal and the ultimate authority on constitutional issues.

In the classical liberal tradition, summarized in Dossier 1.3, the legislative and executive powers must be vested in different bodies. To unite the power of making laws with the power to implement them is to invite tyranny. This tradition is epitomized in the American *Constitution*, which vests the legislative power in the two Houses of Congress and the executive power in the president. Neither the president nor his Cabinet Secretaries may sit in Congress, and their tenure of office does not depend on their ability to secure and maintain the confidence of either House.

In contrast, the British and Canadian model of Cabinet–parliamentary government unites the legislative and executive powers in the Cabinet. The prime minister occupies the position at the top of the political executive because he leads the party with the most seats in the House of Commons. His Cabinet ministers must be drawn from the governing caucus (the parliamentary wing of the party in power) in the House of Commons and, to a lesser extent, the Senate. A Cabinet that loses the confidence of the Commons must resign immediately. In effect, the governor general delegates the powers of the Crown to the prime minister; those powers must be relinquished when the legislative branch withdraws its support (although the events of December 2008 suggest that there are some exceptions; see Chapter 8).

Theoretically, the Commons uses its power to remove the Cabinet to keep the political executive accountable to the electorate. In practice, a majority government—a party that holds more than half the seats in the Commons—need not fear a loss of legislative support. Strong norms of party discipline protect a majority Cabinet against fluctuations in political support and the attacks of the Opposition parties. As a result, the House of Commons cannot hold the executive to account unless the governing party holds less than a majority of the seats. Under a minority government—such as the Liberal Government elected in June 2004 or the Conservative Government elected in January 2006—the Cabinet is more vulnerable to

DOSSIER 1.3 The Liberal Approach to Political Institutions

In *The Spirit of the Laws* (1748), the French writer Montesquieu (1689–1755) identified "three sorts of powers" in every government: "the *legislative*; the *executive*, in regard to those matters determined by the laws of nations; and the executive, in regard to those matters determined by the civil law" (emphasis added). Montesquieu also called the last of the three the *judicial* power. The legislative power grants the right to make laws "either temporarily, or for all time, as well as correcting or abrogating those already in existence." Using its executive power, the government "makes war or peace, sends or receives ambassadors, ensures security, and makes provision against invasion." Finally, the judicial power is applied to "punish crimes, or pass judgment upon disputes arising among individuals."[36]

By 1787–88, when the United States *Constitution* was being drafted and debated, the belief that a division of powers was the best safeguard of liberty was taken for granted by the framers. In Federalist Paper No. 47, James Madison relied on Montesquieu's authority to defend the proposed constitution against charges that it united the three powers in a manner that threatened the liberties of Americans. He wrote: "The accumulation of all powers, legislative, executive, and judiciary, in the same hands, whether of one, a few, or many, and whether hereditary, self-appointed, or elective, may justly be pronounced the very definition of tyranny."[37] This formulation has remained influential for more than two centuries.

defections by its members and must make policy concessions to one or more of the Opposition parties in order to remain in power.[38] The implications of a minority Parliament are discussed in Chapters 7 and 8.

Both Houses of the federal Parliament have changed over the years. The Senate, whose members are appointed by the prime minister, has almost as much formal power in the legislative process as the elected House of Commons. But senators rarely veto laws that have been approved by the Commons, because they know that they lack democratic legitimacy. At the other end of the Centre Block, the Commons conducts its legislative business in much the same way as Westminster (i.e., British-style) parliaments have done for centuries. But it, too, has adapted to changing times. Party discipline, which was relatively weak at Confederation, now dominates the institution. While the membership of the Commons resembles the Canadian electorate more accurately than ever before—the numbers of women, visible minorities, and Aboriginal peoples rose in the 1980s and 1990s, although there has been little progress since 2000—the distribution of seats among the four official parties does not reflect the preferences of Canadian voters (Chapter 12). For this reason, among others, the legitimacy of Canada's Parliament has diminished in recent decades. There have been persistent calls for reform of the Commons and the Senate, which are discussed in Chapter 7.

Ideally, the judicial branch operates in isolation from the legislature and the executive. Courts must be independent and autonomous, to the greatest possible extent; otherwise, their fairness and impartiality may be compromised. Nonetheless, the judicial branch both affects and is affected by changes in the social and political environment. The policy influence of the Supreme Court of Canada grew significantly after 1982, when the *Canadian Charter of Rights and Freedoms* was proclaimed into law. Unlike Parliament and the Cabinet, the Supreme Court is not a characteristically British institution. Since its establishment in 1875, its task as a court of appeal in criminal and civil cases has been overshadowed by its responsibility for **judicial review.** Until 1949, the Judicial Committee of the Privy Council in London (JCPC) was the final court of appeal for Canada. The Law Lords on the JCPC objected to the

FIGURE 1.1   DIAGRAM OF CANADA'S POLITICAL INSTITUTIONS

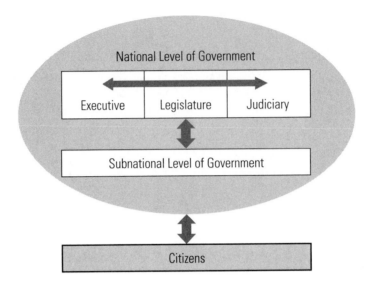

centralizing elements in the *Constitution Act, 1867,* on the grounds that they violated the principle of federalism (Chapter 4). They usually decided appeals concerning the division of powers in favour of the provinces, to the frustration of Canadians who preferred a strong central government.[39] The evolution of judicial review under the *Charter* has provoked new controversies about the legitimacy of the court's interventions into politics and policy-making. We will examine those controversies in Chapters 6 and 10.

Federalism

Canada is a federation, as are the United States, Germany, Switzerland, and many other democratic states. Britain and France, the first European powers to colonize North America, are unitary states (Dossier 1.4). When the future Dominion of Canada was taking shape in the 1860s, the choice between a federal and a unitary structure was a contentious issue. The advocates of federalism prevailed, although they had to accept some unitary elements. The national government was given the power to veto or delay provincial laws, which placed the provinces in a subordinate position and weakened their autonomy within their own areas of jurisdiction. Although these powers fell into disuse in the twentieth century, Ottawa has found other methods—in particular, the transfer of huge sums of money to the provinces—to intervene in provincial policy-making. We will discuss the struggles between the two senior levels of government in Chapter 4.

Federalism illustrates the mutual influence of political institutions and the societies that they serve. Canadian federalism exists, in large measure, because the four founding provinces contained ethnically and geographically diverse populations. Neither Quebec francophones nor the Maritime colonies would accept a unitary state. They demanded a significant degree of self-government within the larger Dominion. Over time, the provincial governments themselves began to shape the political attitudes of their populations. As they struggled with Ottawa over scarce resources—principally tax revenues and policy-making powers—they created new political symbols to increase their legitimacy vis-à-vis the federal government. Provincial governments have also redefined their populations as distinct political communities that can best be served by autonomous provincial states.[40]

In a federation, the power to make binding decisions for the population is divided between two levels of government. The national (or federal) government is responsible for matters of national concern, such as defence, foreign affairs, and currency. The subnational (state or provincial) governments take care of local or regional needs. Each level of government has its own sources of tax revenue, and neither can invade the jurisdiction of the other without express consent. The subnational governments are not subordinate to the national government; their separate existence and powers are guaranteed by a written constitution that cannot be amended without their agreement. Conflicts between the two levels are resolved by the courts, or by the ad hoc processes of intergovernmental relations (Chapter 4).

In contrast, unitary states have only one senior government. The national government may establish local or regional agencies to assist in the delivery of services and the implementation of laws, but these agencies have no independent status and may be abolished at any time. They exist solely to carry out the orders of the central government in the national capital. (Canada's municipalities have a similar relationship to their respective provincial governments.)

In addition to these two ideal types, there is a third category of state: the quasi-federation. In quasi-federal states, the regional governments are both separate from and subordinate to the national government. Their powers can be curtailed by the national government if they exercise them in a way that conflicts with national priorities.

[T]he political language of federalism, and the federal political system with which it is intertwined, have encouraged a politics in which provincial particularisms have been accorded special prominence. Provincial governments, as the claimants for and recipients of federal bounty, have acted as surrogates for the communities they govern . . . The political incentives for the federal government to couch its claims in the language of individual citizen rights and obligations engender a direct conflict with provincial claims on behalf of territorially based communities, the reconciliation of which is worked out in the federal process.[41]

THE *CONSTITUTION*

As we will see in Chapter 3, Canada's *Constitution* is not limited to the written text contained in the Appendix to this book. We must also understand the unwritten conventions by which our political leaders operate, and the courts' evolving interpretations of the entrenched provisions, if we are to grasp the full meaning of our "supreme law."

Where the text of a **constitution** conflicts with deeply held political values, it may cease to operate. For example, the British Crown is technically the source of all executive power and legitimacy in the Canadian state. The Crown's chief representative in Canada, the governor general, could fire the prime minister and seize dictatorial power tomorrow. Such a coup would be perfectly legal under the *Constitution Act, 1867*. It would also be a gross violation of the democratic principles that sustain Canada's representative institutions. Those principles restrict the legitimate use of executive power to a prime minister and Cabinet who enjoy the confidence of the elected House of Commons. Hence, direct rule by the governor general would be unconstitutional, despite its formal legality. Similarly, the December 2008 attempt by the three Opposition parties to form a coalition government and oust Prime Minister Harper's Conservative Government was entirely consistent with the unwritten rules of Canada's constitution; but many Canadians were shocked by what they perceived as an "undemocratic" effort to overturn the results of the 2008 election (see Chapters 7 and 8).

The constitution evolves in response to changing conditions, usually without formal amendment to the entrenched written text. New constitutional conventions develop, gradually acquiring the moral force to restrain the exercise of power by political leaders, and judges interpret the constitution in new ways that recognize and confirm the shifting standards of political legitimacy. However, it would be a mistake to assume that the constitution is constantly in flux. Certain core principles remain intact, although their meaning and their relative influence change as the political culture evolves. A constitution is intended to last for decades, even centuries; but its meaning must evolve to keep pace with changing political attitudes (see Dossier 1.5).

If changing public attitudes shape the meaning of the constitution, the reverse is also true: the constitution influences the ways in which citizens perceive themselves and their relationship to the state. For example, Cairns argues that the *Charter of Rights and Freedoms* has transformed our political culture by redefining particular groups—women, Aboriginal Canadians, ethnic and racial minorities—as state-protected "*Charter* Canadians" with special rights.[42] Many of these "*Charter* Canadians" take a dim view of political processes that exclude their representatives, particularly closed-door constitutional negotiations among the federal and provincial governments. By redefining individual Canadians as "bearers of rights"[43] and endowing certain groups (but not others) with unique constitutional recognition, the *Charter* has eroded the legitimacy of territory-based politics (i.e., the federal system) and made future amendments to the division of powers even more difficult than they would otherwise have been. We will examine Canada's changing political culture in Chapter 2 and recent constitutional controversies in Chapters 3–6.

DOSSIER 1.5   The Principles That Shape Canada's Political Institutions

In 1998, the Supreme Court of Canada identified four central principles that underpin our political institutions: "federalism; democracy; constitutionalism and the rule of law; and respect for minorities" [para. 32]. While these principles are not always explicit in our constitutional texts, they are the "lifeblood" [para. 51] that sustains our system of government. None of the four operates in isolation. Each principle modifies the others, and each must be interpreted according to the historical development of the Canadian *Constitution*.

The justices defined "federalism" as the sharing of power between two sovereign levels of government: the national government and the 10 provinces. The federalism principle "recognizes the diversity of the component parts of Confederation," and "facilitates democratic participation" by assigning specific powers to the appropriate level of government. Finally, it permits "the pursuit of collective goals by cultural and linguistic minorities which form the majority within a particular province" [paras. 58–59].

The principle of "democracy" refers to "the representative and democratic nature of our political institutions" [para. 62]. In other words, Canadian democracy entails the right of the people to choose their legislators—not their *government*, as Prime Minister Harper claimed in December 2008—through free and fair elections. Although the justices defined democracy as "a political system of majority rule" [para. 63], they rejected the argument that "the sovereign will of a people" [para. 61] outweighs the other three principles. Canadian democracy is qualified by federalism, which creates "different and equally legitimate majorities in different provinces and territories and at the federal level" [para. 66]. At the same time, "democracy in any real sense of the word cannot exist without the rule of law" [para. 67]. According to the court, "It would be a grave mistake to equate legitimacy with the 'sovereign will' or majority

(continued)

rule alone, to the exclusion of other constitutional values" [para. 67].

The rule of law gives all Canadians "a stable, predictable, and ordered society in which to conduct their affairs" [para. 70]. It imposes the supremacy of law over "the acts of both government and private persons," and requires that "the exercise of all public power must find its ultimate source in a legal rule" [para. 71]. "Constitutionalism" refers to the more specific requirement that "all government action comply with the Constitution" [para. 72]. Political institutions are strictly limited in their actions by constitutional law: "indeed, their sole claim to exercise lawful authority rests in the powers allocated to them under the Constitution, and can come from no other source" [para. 72]. The importance of this principle is reflected in the special procedures for creating and amending a constitution "beyond the reach of simple majority rule" [para. 73]. In other words, the will of the majority cannot override the principle of federalism or the protection of minority rights. While this might appear to be undemocratic, the justices argued that constitutionalism and the rule of law make democratic government possible by "creating an orderly framework within which people may make political decisions" [para. 78].

Finally, "the protection of minorities" is inherent in both our federal system and the *Charter of Rights and Freedoms*. Since 1867, the Canadian *Constitution* has guaranteed the rights of some linguistic and religious minorities (e.g., Catholics and francophones in Ontario). While past Canadian governments, both federal and provincial, have sometimes ignored the rights of particular minority groups—such as Aboriginal peoples and Japanese Canadians—the *Charter* makes future violations of minority rights illegal unless they can be justified under section 1 (see Chapter 6).

Source: Reference re Secession of Quebec, [1998] 2 S.C.R. 217.

EXTERNAL PRESSURES ON CANADA'S POLITICAL INSTITUTIONS: GLOBALIZATION AND 9/11

Before we conclude this introduction to the Canadian political system, it is important to understand that our political institutions are affected by external as well as internal forces. While these external forces are often lumped together under the heading "globalization," we will distinguish between globalization and internationalization. **Globalization** describes "a technological and economic process" that is

driven by the revolution in telecommunications and computers, massive increases in the movement of capital around the world, greatly expanded capacities for flexible world-wide production sourcing by firms, especially multinational corporations, and environmental spillovers.[44]

Therefore, the term "globalization" does not refer to public policy; it describes a set of forces originating outside the scope of direct government control. However, national governments may try to resist or to reduce the impact of globalization within their territories; for example, a government can impose tariffs on imported goods in an effort to protect domestic producers from foreign competition.

The term **internationalization** is more specific. It refers to "a process by which various aspects of policy or policy-making are influenced by factors outside national territorial boundaries."[45] This phenomenon is nothing new for Canada, whose economy has been based on the export of commodities to foreign markets since the colonial era. What is new is the burgeoning number of **supranational** organizations and agreements. Examples include the border security arrangements between Canada and the United States; the North American Free Trade Agreement (NAFTA) among Canada, the United States, and Mexico; the United Nations, most of whose Conventions Canada is bound to enforce; and the World Trade Organization (WTO). When a national government signs and/or ratifies a treaty with another government (or several), it undertakes to amend its domestic policies in order to implement that treaty. In the process, it may be forced to change its own priorities or to alter the direction of particular programs. In this sense, internationalization narrows the freedom of choice that a nation–state would otherwise enjoy.

Although the constraints imposed on nation–states by globalization and internationalization are real, they are not paralyzing. Contrary to a widely held belief that certain types of policy—particularly tax levels and social programs—are completely determined by world capital markets and multinational corporate interests,[46] the evidence shows that nation–states retain a wide discretion over their fiscal policies.[47] The principal exception is corporate taxation, which has fallen in most Western states in response to the increasing mobility of multinational companies (and the jobs that they provide).

The growing internationalization of public policy-making affects some policy fields (climate change) more than others (social welfare). Globalization also affects different areas of social policy in varying ways. When, in 1995, the federal government cut transfer payments to the provinces (Chapter 4), it was driven by the need to cut the **deficit** and avert the possibility of a severe fiscal crisis. The cuts forced provincial governments to slash their spending on health care, education, and social assistance. However, programs directed toward the labour market—training and retraining, job creation, and enhanced productivity—received increased funding, as the federal and provincial governments tried to ensure that Canadian workers would not be left behind in a more competitive global environment.[48]

In general, the external forces discussed here seem to have affected the process of policy-making more than the content of the resulting laws and programs. As we will see in Chapter 4, globalization does more than transfer power from nation–states to supranational organizations like the WTO and NAFTA. It may also shift power from the national government to subnational governments (provinces and cities)—hence the buzzword "glocalization," which captures both the upward and downward transfers of policy-making authority. However, any reduction in Ottawa's power may be offset by two other developments. First, the national government may be able to use supranational commitments—e.g., the Kyoto Protocol—as a tool to invade the policy fields of the provinces. Second, globalization appears to undermine local attachments to particular geographic regions. If this is the case, then we might expect the political force of regionalism—a contributing factor in the intergovernmental conflicts of recent decades—to diminish.

Internationalization also changes the balance among the three branches of the federal government. Specifically, it reinforces the dominance of the executive branch over Parliament. To the extent that Canadian policy is shaped by supranational agreements among prime ministers, presidents, and Cabinet ministers, Parliament's ability to hold the executive accountable is weakened. The levers of economic policy are still largely controlled by the federal Department of Finance, but they must be operated under some global constraints. Therefore, Parliament's "power of the purse" becomes less effective, and the political parties in the Commons exert even less influence on events than they would otherwise have done (Chapter 7).

Globalization and internationalization have been relatively long-term and gradual processes. A more immediate, and (at least temporarily) more potent, constraint on Canada's political institutions emerged in the aftermath of the 9/11 terrorist attacks. The global "war on terror" and the increased American emphasis on border security have forced Canada (and other countries) to adopt new laws and policy measures to protect their citizens and placate the American government.[49] Once again, both the process and products of policy-making have changed in response to external events, although the substance of policy seems to have been more strongly affected by 9/11 than by the other external trends discussed in this section:

- In the first place, the "war on terror" strengthens the national government vis-à-vis the provinces by raising the salience of national security (a federal responsibility).
- Second, the "POGG (peace, order, and good government) clause"—the section of the *Constitution Act, 1867* that assigns the residual power to Ottawa—gives the federal Cabinet broad "emergency powers" that can be used to invade provincial jurisdictions (Chapter 4).
- Third, the heightened emphasis on national security temporarily strengthened the national executive in relation to both Parliament (which has no formal power over foreign and defence policy) and the judicial branch. As discussed in Chapter 10, the Supreme Court of Canada signalled in the wake of 9/11 that it would defer to the Cabinet in cases involving security policies—even where such policies violated the rights and freedoms protected in the *Charter*. By 2007, however, the court had begun to push back against the executive branch by striking down portions of the security certificate regime imposed on alleged terrorists. The renewed assertiveness of the judicial branch may be explained, in part, as a reaction against perceived abuses of executive discretion by Royal Canadian Mounted Police (RCMP) officers and others involved in the mistreatment of some Muslim Canadians—notably Maher Arar.[50]

As our political institutions adapt to changing external pressures, they may diverge even further from the political values and attitudes of some Canadian citizens. The "antiglobalization" movement reflects a growing unease with the economic consequences of world markets—even as the new communication technologies at the heart of globalization make it easier to organize protests in far-flung cities. The expansion of executive power, at the expense of Parliament and the judicial enforcement of rights, seems to conflict with calls for greater citizen participation in decision-making and the generally positive orientation toward the *Charter*. If the incentives to cooperate with the American government in sensitive policy fields like national security, immigration, and criminal law are believed to outweigh domestic political opinion, Canada's politicians could pay a heavy price. Worse, the legitimacy of the institutions within which they operate could suffer over the long term.

CONCLUSION

The central theme of this book is that institutions shape human behaviour and values, and vice versa. As institutions evolve in response to changing social and cultural conditions, so do the incentives that these institutions create for the people involved with them. The challenge is to ensure that our political system adapts in positive ways, and that it continues to impose incentives that produce constructive behaviour among our politicians.

In formal terms, Canada's political institutions have changed relatively little since Confederation. The three branches of government are much as they were in the late nineteenth century, with the notable exception of the executive branch; its size and activities have expanded beyond anything that the Fathers of Confederation could have imagined. The constitutional division of powers between the federal and provincial governments, which was reasonably well suited to the conditions of 1867, is also intact. In practice, however, the division of policy-making duties between the two levels has mutated considerably over the decades. With the notable exception of the *Constitution Act, 1982,* Canadians have usually relied on nonconstitutional ways to change the rules of the political game.

Such ad hoc adaptations may no longer be adequate. The environment in which our political institutions operate has been transformed since 1867, and our institutions have not always kept pace. The population of Canada is larger and more diverse than ever. Its political attitudes and expectations—shaped by historical events, the rapid diffusion of ideas and information across national boundaries, and the mobilization of regional subcultures—are no longer compatible with many of the myths and symbols embodied in our institutions. Canadians face a choice: to try to restore the legitimacy of our political system by reforming our institutions (either through constitutional or nonconstitutional means) or to make our existing politics and government work better. In either case, we will need a better-informed and more engaged public. It is hoped that this book will contribute to reaching that goal.

GLOSSARY OF KEY TERMS

Anglophone: English-speaking.

Constitution: The supreme law that defines the scope of state power and divides it among the various institutions that make up the state. More broadly, a constitution incorporates both the unwritten principles that guide the execution of public activities (see Dossier 1.5) and the sources of political legitimacy in a particular territory (i.e., myths, symbols, and rituals).

Deficit: An excess of spending over revenues in a given fiscal year. For example, Canada's federal government spent $42 billion more than it took in during the 1993–94 fiscal year. In the 2003–04 fiscal year, the federal government spent $9.1 billion *less* than it received in revenues; this is referred to as a "surplus."

Democracy: Literally, "rule by the people." In practice, "we the people" cannot govern ourselves directly on a daily basis. We elect political leaders to make decisions on our behalf and delegate the power to make binding decisions to them. We have the opportunity to reject those leaders at election time if they use that power in ways of which we do not approve. The problem with this system of representative democracy, according to its critics, is that the people who run our political institutions cannot be held accountable between elections. If they exercise the powers of their offices for their own benefit, instead of the benefit of the electorate, we have no legal recourse.

Francophone: French-speaking.

Globalization: A technological and economic process driven by the revolution in telecommunications and computers, massive increases in the movement of capital around the world, greatly expanded capacities for flexible worldwide production sourcing by firms, especially multinational corporations, and growing ecological interdependence and environmental spillovers.[51] The effects of globalization tend to reduce the social, political, and economic importance of nation–state borders and territorial divisions (e.g., provinces).

Internationalization: A process by which various aspects of policy or policy-making are influenced by factors outside national territorial boundaries.[52]

Judicial review: See Chapter 3.

Legitimacy: The broad base of support within the electorate for the political system as a whole, which translates into acceptance of its outputs (i.e., binding rules and decisions). The exercise of constitutional authority in conformity with prevailing political values (e.g., democracy, federalism, the rule of law, and the rights of minorities) is legitimate;

the brutal exercise of naked power by state authorities is not. In liberal democratic theory, legitimacy is founded on the consent of the governed.[53] While citizens need not necessarily give formal consent to each individual law (a practical impossibility, however desirable it might be in practice), they must implicitly accept the political norms and values embodied in the existing political institutions. Legitimacy is also based on the existence of a shared sense of identity—or, in other words, a political community. If no such community exists, because the electorate is divided into competing subcultures with divergent political values, the legitimacy of the political system is questioned. As its legitimacy weakens, its authority diminishes.

"Megaconstitutional politics": A process of reconsidering not just the technical details of a constitution, but also "the very nature of the political community on which the constitution is based."[54] As the debate widens beyond the political elite—i.e., the First Ministers of the 11 senior governments, their advisers, and academic experts—the emotional temperature rises. Powerful, and often incompatible, myths and symbols are evoked to justify conflicting definitions of the political community.

Myth: A story we tell ourselves to make sense of a confusing and complicated world. It presents a partial account of the past, justifies certain actions in the present, and lays out a particular path for the future. Political myths usually incorporate one or more symbols into a blend of fact and fiction, which is used to evoke an emotional response for or against a particular institution. Example: The Québécois myth of "la survivance" following the English "conquest" of 1759 has become a powerful source of legitimacy for the provincial government in Quebec.

Political institution: An organization, usually grounded in constitutional law (either written or unwritten), that makes and/or enforces binding rules for the population of a particular territory. Its authority rests on its legitimacy in the eyes of the governed—based in some measure on its exploitation of myths and symbols—and ultimately on its monopoly of coercive force (i.e., the police and the armed forces). Canadian examples: the House of Commons, the Senate, the Supreme Court, the federal public service.

The state: The collective term for the political institutions in a particular country: the legislature, the executive, the courts, the armed forces, and the police. The state is responsible for "creating and maintaining internal order," for "protecting its own territorial integrity in the international system," and for making and implementing binding decisions for society "in those areas where private actors are incapable of responding successfully."[55]

Supranational: Literally, "above the nation–state." The term is often used to describe global or regional institutions and agreements like the World Trade Organization (WTO) or the North American Free Trade Agreement (NAFTA). When a national government enters into a supranational institution or agreement, it gives up some of its sovereignty. It accepts the power of the other member states to set policy priorities and directions for its citizens. In exchange, the national government receives an opportunity to participate in the supranational policy process.

Symbol: Any object or procedure—such as an image, a word or phrase, a sound, a person, a historical event, or a set of rules for making decisions—that conveys a particular meaning (either rational or emotional) to those who see or hear it. Often used as a shorthand way to refer to a complex reality. Canadian political symbols include the Maple Leaf flag, *O Canada,* the Peace Tower in Ottawa, the battles at Vimy Ridge and Dieppe, and the *Canadian Charter of Rights and Freedoms.*

DISCUSSION AND REVIEW QUESTIONS

1. What is a "political institution"? How does it differ from some other type of institution, such as a family or a private corporation?

2. In your own words, explain how the incentives built into political institutions shape the behaviour of the individuals who participate in them.

3. In your own words, describe and distinguish the three branches of government. How do Canada's political institutions differ from the classical model summarized in Dossier 1.3?

4. In your own words, explain the difference between a federation and a unitary state. Give one example of each type of state.

5. In your own words, explain the four principles described in Dossier 1.5. Which of the four do you consider to be the most important, and why?

6. List and briefly describe some of the challenges facing nation–states in the twenty-first century. If you were prime minister of Canada, how would you try to respond to those challenges?

SUGGESTED READINGS

Aristotle, *The Politics* and *The Nicomachean Ethics,* various editions and translations.

Harold D. Clarke, Allan Kornberg, and Peter Wearing, *A Polity on the Edge: Canada and the Politics of Fragmentation* (Peterborough, ON: Broadview Press, 2000).

C.E.S Franks, *The Myths and Symbols of the Constitutional Debate in Canada* (Kingston, ON: Queen's University Institute of Intergovernmental Relations, 1993).

Paul Howe and David Northrup, *Strengthening Canadian Democracy: The Views of Canadians* (Montreal: Institute for Research on Public Policy, 2000).

James G. March and Johan P. Olsen, *Rediscovering Institutions: The Organizational Basis of Politics* (New York: Free Press, 1989).

John Stuart Mill, *On Liberty and Other Essays*, edited by John Gray (Oxford: Oxford University Press, 1991).

Pippa Norris, ed., *Critical Citizens: Global Support for Democratic Governance* (Oxford: Oxford University Press, 1999).

Susan J. Pharr and Robert D. Putnam, eds., *Disaffected Democracies: What's Troubling the Trilateral Countries?* (Princeton: Princeton University Press, 2000).

Jean-Jacques Rousseau, *The Social Contract,* various editions and translations.

Peter H. Russell, *Constitutional Odyssey: Can Canadians Become a Sovereign People?*, 2nd edition (Toronto: University of Toronto Press, 1993).

NOTES

1. Harold Lasswell, *Politics: Who Gets What, When and How* (New York: McGraw-Hill, 1936).

2. See Pippa Norris, ed., *Critical Citizens: Global Support for Democratic Governance* (Oxford: Oxford University Press, 1999); Susan J. Pharr and Robert D. Putnam, eds., *Disaffected Democracies: What's Troubling the Trilateral Countries?* (Princeton: Princeton University Press, 2000). As we will see in Chapter 12, turnout was higher in the 2006 election than in the previous two elections; this turned out to be an exception to the general downward trend, because turnout in the October 2008 federal election was the lowest in history.

3. See Matthew Horsman and Andrew Marshall, *After the Nation-State: Citizens, Tribalism and the New World Disorder* (London: HarperCollins, 1994); Susan Strange, *The Retreat of the State: The Diffusion of Power in the World Economy* (Cambridge: Cambridge University Press, 1996).

4. Horsman and Marshall, 171–99; Harold D. Clarke, Allan Kornberg, and Peter Wearing, *A Polity on the Edge: Canada and the Politics of Fragmentation* (Peterborough, ON: Broadview Press, 2000).

5. Cynthia J. Alexander and Leslie A. Pal, eds., *Digital Democracy: Policy and Politics in the Wired World* (Toronto: Oxford University Press, 1998); Strange, *The Retreat of the State,* 7–8; Benjamin R. Barber, *Jihad vs. McWorld: How Globalism and Tribalism Are Reshaping the World* (New York: Ballantine, 1996), Chapter 19.

6. Ronald Inglehart, *Modernization and Postmodernization: Cultural, Economic and Political Change in 43 Societies* (Princeton: Princeton University Press, 1997); Ronald Inglehart, "Postmodernization Erodes Respect for Authority, But Increases Support for Democracy," in Norris, ed., *Critical Citizens,* 236–56; Russell J. Dalton, "Value Change and Democracy," in Pharr and Putnam, eds., *Disaffected Democracies,* 252–69; Neil Nevitte, *The Decline of Deference: Canadian Value Change in Cross-National Perspective* (Peterborough, ON: Broadview Press, 1996).

7. Aristotle, *The Politics,* translated by Benjamin Jowett and edited by Stephen Everson (Cambridge: Cambridge University Press, 1996), 90.

8. Jean-Jacques Rousseau, "The Social Contract," in *The Social Contract and Discourses,* translated and edited by G.D.H. Cole (London: Everyman, 1993), 217.

9. John Stuart Mill, "Considerations on Representative Government," in *On Liberty and Other Essays,* edited by John Gray (Oxford: Oxford University Press, 1991 [1861]), 257.

10. Inglehart and Welzel attribute Weimar's collapse to the economic chaos of the 1920s, which focused the minds of most Germans on physical survival and prevented them from embracing democratic values. Conversely, they argue that the Federal Republic of Germany succeeded because of the *Wirtschaftswunder* (economic miracle) of the 1950s and 1960s, which liberated younger cohorts from material concerns and allowed them to develop post-materialist values conducive to the survival of democratic institutions. (See the discussion of value change in Chapter 2.) Ronald Inglehart and Christian Welzel, *Modernization, Cultural Change, and Democracy: The Human Development Sequence* (New York: Cambridge University Press, 2005).

11. Aristotle did not believe that women—or, for that matter, male slaves—were fully human. Only free men possessed the full faculty of reason, which was the distinguishing human characteristic. While we would now use gender-neutral language to describe human nature, male-specific language is used in this paragraph in order to reflect the exclusion of women from political science until relatively recently. See Heather MacIvor, *Women and Politics in Canada: An Introductory Text* (Peterborough, ON: Broadview Press, 1996), 20–27.

12. Aristotle, *The Politics,* 37 and 74–75.

13. Aristotle, *The Nicomachean Ethics,* translated and edited by David Ross (Oxford: Oxford University Press, 1980), 28–29.

14. Ibid., 18 and 24–25.

15. Mill, "Considerations on Representative Government," 226–27.

16. Eastern Germany was occupied by the Soviet Union. It became the Communist state of East Germany. The two German states reunited in 1990, following the collapse of the Soviet Union.

17. James W. Ceaser, "Reconstructing Political Science," in Stephen L. Elkin and Karol Edward Soltan, eds., *A New Constitutionalism: Designing Political Institutions for a Good Society* (Chicago: University of Chicago Press, 1993).

18. James G. March and Johan P. Olsen, *Rediscovering Institutions: The Organizational Basis of Politics* (New York: Free Press, 1989), Chapter 1.

19. Ibid., 8.

20. Ibid., 17.

21. Karol Edward Soltan, "Introduction: Imagination, Political Competence, and Institutions," in Karol Edward Soltan and Stephen L. Elkin, eds., *The Constitution of Good Societies* (University Park, PA: Pennsylvania State University Press, 1996), 2.

22. Hon. Senator Serge Joyal, *Minutes of Proceedings and Evidence of the Senate Standing Committee on Legal and Constitutional Affairs*, March 22, 2007, 23:55 [author's translation].

23. Joseph A. Schlesinger, *Ambition and Politics: Political Careers in the United States* (Chicago: Rand McNally, 1966), 3.

24. James W. Ceaser, *Presidential Selection: Theory and Development* (Princeton: Princeton University Press, 1979), 14.

25. Paul Howe and David Northrup, *Strengthening Canadian Democracy: The Views of Canadians* (Montreal: Institute for Research on Public Policy, 2000), 78.

26. Benjamin R. Barber, *Strong Democracy* (Berkeley: University of California Press, 1984); James S. Fishkin, *The Voice of the People: Public Opinion and Democracy*, expanded edition (New Haven: Yale University Press, 1997); Stephen L. Elkin and Karol Edward Soltan, eds., *Citizen Competence and Democratic Institutions* (University Park, PA: Pennsylvania State University Press, 1999).

27. March and Olsen, 47–49.

28. Ibid., 52.

29. C.E.S Franks, *The Myths and Symbols of the Constitutional Debate in Canada* (Kingston, ON: Queen's University Institute of Intergovernmental Relations, 1993), 7.

30. Roger Friedland and Robert R. Alford, "Bringing Society Back In: Symbols, Practices, and Institutional Contradictions," in Walter W. Powell and Paul J. DiMaggio, eds., *The New Institutionalism in Organizational Analysis* (Chicago: University of Chicago Press, 1991), 255.

31. Franks, 8.

32. Ibid., 7.

33. Ibid., 21.

34. Peter H. Russell, *Constitutional Odyssey: Can Canadians Become a Sovereign People?* 2nd edition (Toronto: University of Toronto Press, 1993), 143.

35. Patrick J. Monahan, *Meech Lake: The Inside Story* (Toronto: University of Toronto Press, 1991), 258.

36. Charles de Secondat, Baron de la Brède et de Montesquieu, "The Spirit of the Laws," in Montesquieu, *Selected Political Writings*, edited and translated by Melvin Richter (Indianapolis: Hackett, 1990 [1748]), 182.

37. James Madison, "Federalist Paper No. 47," in Alexander Hamilton, James Madison, and John Jay, *The Federalist Papers*, edited by Clinton Rossiter (New York: New American Library, 1961 [1788]), 301.

38. See, for example, the discussion of the 1974 *Election Expenses Act* in Chapters 11 and 12; this legislation was part of the price exacted by the New Democratic Party for supporting a Liberal minority government.

39. See, for example, Frank R. Scott, *Essays on the Constitution: Aspects of Canadian Law and Politics* (Toronto: University of Toronto Press, 1977). For a defence of the JCPC, see Alan C. Cairns, "The Judicial Committee and Its Critics" [1971], in Douglas E. Williams, ed., *Constitution, Government, and Society in Canada: Selected Essays by Alan C. Cairns* (Toronto: McClelland and Stewart, 1988 [1971]).

40. Alan C. Cairns, "The Governments and Societies of Canadian Federalism" [1977], in Williams, ed., *Constitution, Government, and Society in Canada*, 145.

41. Ibid., 163.

42. Alan C. Cairns, "Citizens (Outsiders) and Governments (Insiders) in Constitution-Making: The Case of the Meech Lake Accord," in Douglas E. Williams, ed., *Disruptions: Constitutional Struggles, from the Charter to Meech Lake* (Toronto: McClelland and Stewart, 1991).

43. Ibid., 117.

44. G. Bruce Doern, Leslie A. Pal, and Brian W. Tomlin, "The Internationalization of Canadian Public Policy," in G. Bruce Doern, Leslie A. Pal, and Brian W. Tomlin, eds., *Border Crossings: The Internationalization of Canadian Public Policy* (Toronto: Oxford University Press, 1996), 3.

45. Ibid., 3.

46. Ibid., 8.

47. Christian Lammert, *Modern Welfare States under Pressure: Determinants of Tax Policy in a Globalizing World* (Montreal: Institute for Research on Public Policy, 2004), 5 and 7; available online at www.irpp.org.

48. Keith G. Banting, "Social Policy," in Doern, Pal, and Tomlin, eds., 27–54.

49. Dirk Haubrich, "September 11, Anti-Terror Laws and Civil Liberties: Britain, France and Germany Compared," *Government and Opposition*, 38:1 (January 2003), 3–28; Canada, Privy Council Office, *Securing an Open Society: Canada's National Security Policy* (Ottawa: Her Majesty the Queen in Right of Canada, April 2004), available online at www.pco-bcp.gc.ca.

50. Mr. Arar is a Syrian-born Canadian citizen. In 2001 he was a software engineer based in Ottawa. Arar was wrongly suspected of involvement in terrorist activities, which led to his detention by American officials on a stopover in New York on his way home from a family vacation. The Americans "rendered" him to Syria, where he was tortured and imprisoned for over a year. The story of the Canadian involvement in his ordeal is told in the *Report of the Commission of Inquiry into the Actions of Canadian Officials in Relation to Maher Arar* (accessed at www.pco-bcp.gc.ca, March 2007).

51. Doern, Pal, and Tomlin, "The Internationalization of Canadian Public Policy," 2–3.

52. Ibid., 3.

53. David Held, "Democracy, the Nation–State and the Global System," in David Held, ed., *Political Theory Today* (Stanford, CA: Stanford University Press, 1991), 203.

54. Russell, 75.

55. Alan C. Cairns, "The Embedded State: State–Society Relations in Canada," in Keith Banting, ed., *State and Society: Canada in Comparative Perspective*, volume 31 of the collected research studies for the Royal Commission on the Economic Union and Development Prospects for Canada (Toronto and Ottawa: University of Toronto Press and the Minister of Supply and Services Canada, 1986), 54.

2 Changing Political Culture and Canada's Political Institutions

LEARNING OBJECTIVES

After you finish reading this chapter, you should be able to:

- *define* a political institution;
- *explain* the concept of political culture and its relationship to political institutions;
- *distinguish* between ideology and political culture;
- *define* at least four of the ideologies described in Dossier 2.2 in your own words;
- *identify* two important subcultures in the Canadian electorate;
- *identify* and briefly *explain* three factors that shaped Canada's political culture;
- *explain* how changes in political culture affect the legitimacy of political institutions;
- *identify* and *explain* (in your own words) three explanations for change in political culture;
- *identify* and *describe* two recent debates about the nature and reform of Canada's national political institutions.

INTRODUCTION

Imagine that your entire class—minus the professor—suddenly disappeared from your classroom and reappeared on a desert island. There is just enough food, water, and shelter for everyone to survive for several months. Once you've gotten over the initial shock, you gather in a jungle clearing to figure out how all of you will survive. Who will make decisions on behalf of the group, and how will those people be chosen? How will their decisions be enforced? Should everyone receive the same amount of food and water, or should the hardest-working get more than the others? As the meeting goes on, the group starts to divide into factions. One faction favours equal distribution, while another argues that the hardest workers should be rewarded with more food and water. Some inhabitants propose decision-making by consensus, to the amusement of those who believe that only a single leader can make decisions quickly. Another conflict could erupt between those who want to punish rule-breakers and others who trust their fellows to behave in the best interests of the group. After several hours, the meeting breaks up without reaching any decisions. You face an uncertain future as you wait and hope for rescue.

This little thought experiment illustrates two fundamental facts about politics and government. First, it shows that every human society has to reach a basic agreement about the rules and procedures by which it will operate. Second, it demonstrates the sheer difficulty of doing so. Granted, real human societies do not magically appear out of nowhere; they are united (sometimes divided) by family and tribal ties that can make it easier to recognize shared interests and agree on mutually beneficial arrangements. But regardless of time, place, and culture, different people hold varying and sometimes irreconcilable opinions about power, justice, and rightful authority. When the resulting disagreements cannot be resolved, societies are consumed by civil war (at worst) or agree to a peaceful separation (at best).

As if these deep and lasting disagreements were not enough, younger generations within a given society may hold very different political views from their parents and grandparents. Political beliefs change over time, both for individuals and for entire communities or subcultures. As we saw in Chapter 1, there must be a good fit between political institutions and political culture. Over time, a persistent or growing mismatch between the two threatens the stability of the state. Although there is no sign in Canada of the kind of catastrophic failures that have recently occurred in Yugoslavia, Zimbabwe, or Afghanistan, there is a growing gap between the political values embodied in our institutions and the expectations of citizens. This chapter discusses that particular challenge, along with others arising from recent trends in **political culture**:

- Immigration has produced an unprecedented diversity of national electorates in Western democracies, especially Canada.
- Two long-standing **subcultures**, Quebec nationalism and Western populism, were **mobilized** into intense political activity in the second half of the twentieth century. At the time of writing, however, both subcultures seemed to be ebbing (for the time being).
- Some newer ideologies, such as feminism and **postmaterialism**, question fundamental assumptions about power and authority.
- Advocates of direct democracy argue that citizens should make more decisions for themselves, instead of leaving the decisions up to politicians and public servants.
- Many of our most important political institutions—Parliament, elections, federalism— are based on the representation of geographic communities such as provinces or towns. Recent demands for greater representation of non-territorial interests, notably women, ethnic minorities, and Aboriginal Canadians, have turned our already complex political and constitutional debates into insoluble riddles.

This chapter explores the relationship between the political attitudes of Canadians and the institutions that govern us. It argues that while most Canadians are reasonably contented with our political system, we—like citizens in other Western democracies—are increasingly critical of certain elements of it. In part, this criticism arises from a growing gap between our institutions and the political values of Canadians, especially younger Canadians: "There was a distrust of 'citizen power' at the time our representative democratic institutions were being developed. Today, it is the opposite, as distrust is now directed at the political and bureaucratic elites."[1] Those changing political values are also reflected in recent demands for institutional reform, and in emerging patterns of political participation. The trends in political culture described here underlie much of the analysis in subsequent chapters.

We begin with a general discussion of political culture and ideology, followed by a description of Canada's political culture (more precisely, our principal subcultures) and a comparison of the leading explanations of their evolution. Then we examine current trends in political culture, and evaluate three general approaches to explaining them. The chapter concludes by considering the possible implications for our political institutions.

POLITICAL CULTURE

In Chapter 1, we distinguished between institutions in general and the more specific set of political institutions. We can draw a similar distinction between the broader culture of a specific society and its particular political culture. The culture of a given population is made up of a unique mix of values, attitudes, and rituals. It is shaped by history, economy, geography, **demography**, and religion. Different customs evolve in different societies, in response to both universal human needs (gathering or growing food, rearing and socializing children) and the challenges posed by local conditions (climate, soil quality, access to fresh water). Within that broad culture, certain values, attitudes, and rituals are explicitly political; others are indirectly related to politics.

At the risk of oversimplifying, the *political* aspects of a given culture relate to power, authority, the proper role of the citizen, and the making and enforcement of rules for the entire community. Every human community needs to establish some legitimate authority, however informal or dispersed, to settle disputes and make collective decisions that bind all of its members. Examples range from the *agora* (marketplace) of ancient Athens, in which the citizens gathered to pass the laws by which they were governed, to tribal warlords and European kings who exercised absolute power over their subjects. However, the distinction between political and nonpolitical values and attitudes must not be taken too far. To fully understand the political culture of a society, we must interpret it in the context of the broader culture: basic attitudes about human nature, the exercise of legitimate authority, the "natural" **hierarchies** that divide the powerful (e.g., freeborn Athenian men) from the powerless (Athenian women and slaves), and the major religious doctrines that sanctify authority.

As we saw in Chapter 1, the themes just listed dominated Western political theory from the time of Socrates (circa 350 B.C.E.) until the early twentieth century. The study of political culture enjoyed a revival in the 1950s and 1960s, as political scientists tried to explain why democracy had failed in Germany and Italy before World War II. Why did democratic political institutions work well in some states and not in others? And what, if anything, could be done to prevent future calamities like the fascist regimes that plunged the world into war in 1939?

In their 1963 classic *The Civic Culture,* Gabriel Almond and Sidney Verba argued, "A democratic form of participatory political system requires as well a political culture consistent with it."[2] The authors defined the political culture of a particular country as the pattern of individual **orientations** toward "the political system and its various parts, and attitudes toward the role of the self in the system"[3] among its citizens. Those orientations, which we acquire through a lifelong process of **political socialization**, are divided into three types:

1. *Cognitive (intellectual):* How much do citizens know about the political system as a whole and each of its parts?
2. *Affective (emotional):* How do citizens feel about the various components of their political system?
3. *Evaluative (opinion):* How positively or negatively do citizens judge the different elements of their political system? What criteria do they use?[4]

To fully understand how political culture and institutions affect each other, we will distinguish among five levels of the political system.[5] Beginning with the most general, these are:

1. *The political community:* "A basic attachment to the nation beyond the present institutions of government and a general willingness to co-operate together politically";[6] acceptance of the boundaries of the state.
2. *Regime principles:* Acceptance of the core ideas reflected in the political system (e.g., democracy, minority rights, and the rule of law); citizens' assessments of the fit between the values embodied in existing institutions and their own expectations.

3. *Regime performance:* Evaluations of how a particular political system works in practice. These can be either procedural (e.g., "the system generally treats people fairly") or substantive ("the government is doing a good job of managing the economy").
4. *Regime institutions:* Perceptions of the individual institutions that make up the state (e.g., Parliament, political parties, or the courts).
5. *Political actors:* Feelings toward the individual politicians who hold public office at a given time.

Whereas earlier theorists had idealized a particular "type" of democratic citizen—fully informed and engaged, rational, and devoted to the community—Almond and Verba argued that an entire population of such people would make stable government impossible. For democratic institutions to work properly, most citizens had to be passive and deferential. A disengaged but supportive majority was needed to "limit the individual's commitment to politics and to make that commitment milder"—to "'manage' or keep in place" the activist minority, which might otherwise destabilize the political system.[7]

Advocates of **direct democracy** reject the claim that passivity is preferable to mass public engagement (see Dossier 2.5). Almond and Verba have also been criticized for their pro-American bias and their implicit assumption that political orientations are distributed evenly among the members of a given population (ignoring the clear differences between classes, genders, and ethnic groups).[8] But they must be given credit for drawing attention to a crucial issue: the relationship between political culture and political institutions.

Political cultures may or may not be congruent with the structures of the political system. A congruent political structure would be one appropriate to the culture: in other words, where political cognition in the population would tend to be accurate and where affect and evaluation would tend to be favourable . . . Political systems change, and we are justified in assuming that culture and structure are often incongruent with each other. Particularly in these decades of rapid cultural change, the most numerous political systems may be those that have failed to attain congruence, or are moving from one form of polity to another.[9]

More recent theories of political culture, including Ronald Inglehart's postmaterialist model and Robert Putnam's theory of declining social capital, recognize that there is no single "political culture" in any modern democracy. Instead, national electorates are divided into political subcultures whose members share a distinctive pattern of political orientations. Together, these subcultures account for the overall distribution of political values in a given population.

[E]lites typically have distinctive values and norms (and, invariably, more information about the system), and they often lead the way in large-scale value change. Different ethnic and regional groups within a single country often have different value systems and world-views. In addition, different types of beliefs and norms may prevail in different institutional settings, such as the military, the bureaucracy, and the university. It may even be argued that the differences in basic cultural biases are often greater within nations than between them . . . For these reasons, it is at least somewhat misleading to talk of the political culture of a nation, except as a distinctive mixture or balance of orientations.[10]

Canada's population is divided among dozens of ethnic communities, two official languages, and a variety of ideologies, distinct socioeconomic classes, and diverse regions. If every distinct group produced a politically salient subculture, our national politics would be unmanageable. But as we will see in subsequent chapters, a social **cleavage** does not automatically shape political behaviour. A subculture has to be mobilized into an effective organization that can formulate a coherent set of goals. This is easier said than done, especially in a country with a huge land mass (although electronic communications have partially overcome geographic distance). To take an obvious example: women account for a slight majority of

Canada's adult population, but their political influence is relatively limited. Women are divided by numerous cleavages—including geography, language, culture, religion, socioeconomic status, ideology, and age—which makes it all but impossible to organize them into a coherent political movement. Conversely, a geographically concentrated subculture with a shared political ideology is relatively easy to mobilize; hence the salience of Quebec nationalists (from the 1960s until the 1990s) and Western populists (from the 1980s until the early twenty-first century). The contrast between the relative political strength of over 16 million women, on the one hand, and the much smaller number of Quebec nationalists and Western populists on the other, illustrates the importance of effective organization in politics (see Dossier 2.1).

The emphasis here on these two subcultures does not imply that other groups within the electorate (such as women, postmaterialists, Aboriginal Canadians, or those living in Ontario

DOSSIER 2.1   Two Key Canadian Subcultures

In the twentieth century, Quebec nationalists and Western populists dominated the public debate over Canada's political institutions (see Chapters 4, 5, and 7). Each subculture has a unique political perspective, which inspires discontent with the current political system and demands for reform:

- Quebec nationalists range from hard-core sovereigntists, whose primary goal is to separate from Canada and establish an independent Quebec state, to "soft" nationalists who want to remain in Canada under certain conditions. Those conditions include greater autonomy for the provincial government and the constitutional recognition of Quebec as a "distinct society." Most Quebec nationalists perceive Canada as a compact between two "founding nations," one English and one French. (Recall the discussion of the "Quebec myth" in Dossier 1.2.) The province of Quebec, as the homeland of the French "nation" in North America, merits special status within Confederation. The political impact of Quebec nationalism has been felt most acutely in debates over institutional and constitutional reform. By and large, Quebec nationalists have supported the Bloc Québécois (to the extent that they participate in federal elections) and the Parti Québécois (PQ) provincially. This pattern was broken in the 2006 federal election, when many nationalists voted Conservative. The 2007 Quebec

election brought a surge in support for the Action Démocratique du Québec (ADQ), which takes a moderate position between separatism and federalism. The PQ had its worst showing in almost 40 years; leader André Boisclair was forced out. His successor, Pauline Marois, distanced herself from separatism, the PQ's *raison d'être* since its founding in the 1960s.

- The term "Western populists" is something of a misnomer, insofar as the attitudes and values associated with it are more characteristic of Alberta and British Columbia than Manitoba and Saskatchewan.[11] But it is a convenient shorthand to describe this subculture, which combines regional alienation, faith in direct democracy and "the people," a preference for strong and equal provincial governments, and demands for changes to the federal Parliament (especially Senate reform; see Chapters 3, 5, and 7). In the late 1980s and 1990s, Western populists supported the Reform Party (see Chapter 11). Previously, their votes were divided between regional protest parties—including the Progressives, the United Farmers, and Social Credit—and two of the three major parties (the Progressive Conservatives and New Democrats). The influence of Western populism in national politics started to decline in 2000, with the formation of the Canadian Alliance. When the Alliance merged with the Progressive Conservative Party in 2003, to form the

(continued)

Conservative Party of Canada, the need to appeal to voters from other regions and ideological perspectives trumped adherence to populist principles. At the time of writing, the Conservative Party in government resembled the old PCs, and even the Liberals, more than it did the old Reform Party.

Francophone Quebeckers have constituted a distinct group within Canada, with a common sense of political and social purpose, since at least 1759. In that sense, the Quebec nationalist subculture is nothing new. But it acquired a new form in the 1960s, as a new generation of political leaders strove to modernize the provincial economy and to promote the status of francophones within their own "homeland" (hence the slogan of the Quiet Revolution, "*maîtres chez nous*," which means "masters in our own house"). As successive Quebec governments battled

Ottawa to secure the necessary resources, some nationalists concluded that the only way to ensure the survival of the "distinct society" was to separate from Canada altogether. In contrast, the Western populist subculture has only rarely acquired a separatist tinge. Its primary concern has been the decentralization of power within the federation, coupled with reforms to national institutions that would give the four westernmost provinces—not to mention "the common sense of the common people"—greater influence in the central government.

One final point deserves mention: the mobilization of these subcultures has been greatly assisted by the very institutions that they seek to change. Quebec nationalists have used the resources of the provincial government to promote sovereignty (see Dossier 2.4), while Western populists have repeatedly used the electoral system and the House of Commons as a forum for expressing their grievances.

and the Atlantic region) are unimportant. The point is that these other groups have not been mobilized effectively, or—in the case of Aboriginal Canadians—that their relatively recent mobilization has not yet produced significant changes in national institutions. Nonetheless, Aboriginal groups have made up for lost time in recent years; their demands for institutional change (specifically, self-government) are just starting to bear fruit.

IDEOLOGY

Political ideologies are concerned with power, human nature, and the proper relationship between the citizen and the state. Ideology differs from political culture in at least two ways.[12]

- First, an ideology is narrower and more distinct. "Political culture" refers to the overall distribution of political values within a population, whereas an ideology may be confined to a particular group.
- Second, an ideology is an explicit and often abstract system of ideas, whereas political culture is less well defined. For example, a self-identified socialist may be fully conscious of his or her political beliefs, and may perceive them as a coherent outlook on the world. But most Canadians devote little attention to their political ideas, and do not seem to be troubled by contradictions among them. Ideology is to political culture what opera is to popular music: it attracts a relatively small subculture of (mostly) well-educated people with the information to understand abstractions and the willingness to differentiate themselves from most of their acquaintances.

Dossier 2.2 briefly describes the most influential **ideologies** in Canadian politics.[13] These brief descriptions are only intended to provide a thumbnail sketch of the contending "worldviews" that animate our political debate. For example, the clash between "neoconservative"

- *Conservatism:* The needs of the organic community take priority over those of the individual, where the two conflict. Community, hierarchy, order, and tradition are at least as important as freedom, equality, and individual rights. Conservatives believe that power should rest with those who are best able to exercise it wisely—that hierarchy and inequality are natural and inevitable. Because human nature is flawed, conservatives advocate a strong government to maintain law and order. Often called "right wing"; also known as "toryism." "Neoconservatism," which advocates traditional moral values, smaller government, and freer markets, is more accurately termed "neoliberalism."

- *Liberalism:* Individual rights and freedoms, based on the capacity for reason inherent in every human being, must be respected by those in power. Liberals defend private property and free markets. They prefer a small government with restricted powers, in order to maximize individual liberty. They emphasize equality of opportunity, not equality of condition. Today, liberals are divided over the role of the state: "business liberals" retain the traditional preference for small government and free markets, while "welfare liberals" believe that the state should provide income security and intervene in the market to promote economic justice.[14] Sometimes called "middle of the road."

- *Socialism and social democracy:* As in conservatism, the public good must take priority over individual liberties, where the two conflict. Socialists seek equality of condition, not just equal opportunity to compete in a free market. Social democrats are reformist, not revolutionary; they seek power through elections. They advocate extensive state involvement in the ownership and management of the economy to ensure that everyone benefits from the wealth of society. Usually called "left wing."

- *Nationalism:* The belief that "a people"—a group distinguished from its neighbours by language, ethnicity, religion, history, or some other criterion—has the right to govern itself directly. Alternatively, a sense of pride in one's political community (recall the discussion of the political community in the "Political Culture" section). As noted in Dossier 2.1, Quebec nationalism ranges from separatism to demands for a rebalancing of the federal system.

- *Populism:* "The people" are best qualified to make decisions for themselves, instead of trusting political and economic elites. Often hostile toward existing authorities, who are perceived as unaccountable and corrupt. Populists demand direct democracy and smaller government. Some populists inject explicit moral or religious elements into their political programs. Can be either "left wing" or "right wing." At present, the political salience of populism appears to be waning; the apparent abandonment of populist rhetoric by the Canadian Alliance when it merged with the Progressive Conservatives may have deprived populists of the political vehicle they need in order to stay mobilized.[15]

- *Feminism:* The belief that men and women should have equal opportunities in all spheres of life. Feminists seek to identify and change power structures that oppress women, such as gender stereotyping in the media, the "old boys' network" in party politics, and the "pink-collar ghetto" in the legislative and executive branches of government. Feminism is not a single unified body of ideas; for example, there are liberal, radical, and socialist feminists. Because of their shared emphasis on equal rights and social justice, feminists sometimes cooperate with socialists and postmaterialists in their quest for political influence.

- *Postmaterialism:* "Quality of life" issues—such as the environment; equal rights for women, gays and lesbians, and other marginalized groups; and assistance to

(continued)

developing countries—are at least as important as the more traditional concerns about the creation and distribution of material wealth. Postmaterialists are generally well informed about politics, and they often participate in unconventional political activities (e.g., protest marches). Many reject hierarchical power structures, including political parties and traditional pressure groups; they seek political influence through new social movements.

populists and traditional ("tory") conservatives doomed the first attempt to merge the Reform Party with the Progressive Conservatives (Dossier 11.5). The ideologies are listed in rough chronological order: conservatism and liberalism can be traced at least as far back as the seventeenth century, whereas postmaterialism took root after 1945.

Canada's political institutions embody the liberal and conservative traditions of Britain and France—which helps to explain why people who reject the older ideologies are more likely to clamour for institutional reform. Ironically, ideologues of varying stripes often find themselves on the same side in "megaconstitutional" debates. Both populists and postmaterialists are highly critical of traditional political elites; both neoconservatives and socialists criticize the *Charter of Rights and Freedoms* and its interpretation by the courts. Unfortunately for these advocates of change, they rarely agree on the exact reforms to be adopted; if they did, major institutional reform would be a more realistic possibility.

Although this book is more concerned with political culture than with formal ideologies, we should not overlook the connection between ideologies and institutions. An institution that takes shape during a period when a particular ideology—say, conservatism—dominates the political process will reflect that ideology in its structure and operations. A conservative institution is strictly hierarchical, with a small group of leaders who make and enforce rules for their subordinates to follow. In contrast, a postmaterialist institution (such as the German Green Party in its early years) is egalitarian, without rigid power structures; every member has a chance to participate in making decisions that bind the whole group.

The conservative cast of our legislative institutions, especially the Senate, helps to alienate Canadians who hold different political beliefs. This is not to say that there are no liberal elements in our political system—federalism and judicial review were imported from the United States—but rather to highlight the connection between institutions and ideology. Although ideologies may not play as obvious a role in Canadian politics as they do in other Western democracies, it would be foolish to discount them completely in an analysis of our political institutions.

SOURCES OF CANADIAN POLITICAL CULTURE

Canada has never had a single political culture. Long before Confederation, French and British communities coexisted on Canadian soil with the various Aboriginal peoples. That divided population became even more diverse as immigrants began to arrive from Eastern Europe and then from other parts of the world. The developing Canadian economy produced its own social cleavages, both between socioeconomic classes and among the various regions of the country. We will explore the sources of this complex pattern of political orientations in this section.

■ History

The pattern of political institutions within a given country is decisively shaped by its history. The most influential accounts of the impact of Canadian history on our political culture are Hartz's "fragment theory" and Lipset's "formative events" approach.

The "Fragment Theory"

The fragment theory explains the political cultures of the "new nations"—Canada, the United States, Australia, New Zealand, and South Africa—as the legacy of their unique patterns of European settlement.[16] The settlers from Britain, Ireland, and France brought their political attitudes with them; over the generations, these European "fragments" preserved their distinct political cultures in their new homelands. For example, the *habitants* of New France (later Quebec) were intensely conservative. They accepted the quasi-feudal structure of the colonial economy, and looked to the Catholic Church for instruction and assistance.[17] The English, Scottish, and Irish settlers in North America were more liberal in their outlook. After France ceded New France to Britain in 1763, the two cultures—French conservatives and English-speaking liberals—clashed repeatedly. The *habitants* turned inward, determined to survive as a French Catholic community under the British Crown.

Today, according to the fragment theory, Canada's political culture is still shaped by the original European settlers. Adherents of this approach argue that French-speaking Quebeckers are more collectivist and state-oriented than **anglophones;** they are more deferential to their leaders, and more averse to risk. Conversely, English Canadians are more concerned with individual freedom and less tolerant of state interference in their lives. The fragment theory does not seek to explain every nuance of political culture. Rather, it portrays the culture of the first European settlers as "a kind of *genetic code* that does not determine but sets limits to later cultural developments."[18]

In an influential analysis of the differences between Canadian and American socialist movements, Gad Horowitz argued that the political cultures of English Canada and its southern neighbour are less similar than they appear.[19] Although both cultures are essentially liberal, Canadian liberalism is less "pure." It is influenced by both conservatism (which Horowitz calls "toryism") and socialism, two collectivist ideologies that moderate the radical individualism of the classical liberal world-view. The "tory touch," which was present well before Confederation, opened the door to the socialist ideas introduced by British immigrants in the twentieth century. Because Canada's political culture is not monopolized by a single ideology, unlike American political culture, there is more room for legitimate opposing viewpoints. Although Horowitz's analysis overlooks the important differences between ideology and political culture, which we discussed above, it has made a substantial contribution to the historical analysis of Canadian politics.[20]

The fragment theory may also help to explain the presence of regional subcultures outside Quebec. Each region was disproportionately populated by different European "fragments": English, Scottish, and Irish in the Atlantic region, Ontario, and British Columbia; French in Quebec; and central and Eastern Europeans on the Prairies.[21] Newer subcultures have developed over the past 50 years, as immigration patterns have changed. In effect, Canada's political culture is absorbing new "fragments," mainly from Asia, Latin America, the Caribbean, and the United States. The long-term effect on our politics is not yet clear, although a recent analysis found marked differences in some political orientations between Canadians living in suburban areas—heavily populated by non-European immigrants—and those living in adjacent urban and rural areas. The same study also found that the descendants of British and French settlers hold strikingly divergent views of politics, substantiating the continuing relevance of our founding "fragments."[22]

Allophones (Canadians whose mother tongue is neither English nor French) share most of the key political values of anglophones, which suggests that they have little difficulty adapting to the political culture of their adopted country.[23] Many new Canadians are intensely interested in politics and impatient for entry into our political institutions.[24]

Formative Events

According to Seymour Martin Lipset, national political cultures are shaped by shared historical experiences. He attributed the "conservative" and "deferential" culture of English Canada to a single cataclysmic event: the American Revolution of 1776–83. More specifically, Lipset argued that because Canadians refused to participate in the uprising against the British Crown, and because English Canada absorbed thousands of Loyalist refugees from the new American republic, our political culture is indelibly marked with the conservative and elitist values of eighteenth-century Britain.[25] These values were embodied in Canadian political institutions, which not only preserved but also strengthened them.[26] Subsequent "formative events," particularly the orderly development of the West (in contrast to the lawlessness of the American frontier), reinforced the relatively meek Canadian attitude toward authority figures (in this case, the Mounties).[27]

Lipset's argument is flawed by weak evidence, and by the erroneous assumption that "formative events" affect every person and every group in the same way. In reality, Canada's "formative events" are perceived differently by various subcultures. Take the Battle of the Plains of Abraham in 1759, and the resulting Treaty of Paris, which transferred control of New France to the British Crown in 1763. In English Canada, the British victory is called "the Conquest," whereas Quebeckers bitterly refer to it as "*la cession*" (meaning, roughly, "France abandoned us here with *les anglais*").[28] By ignoring French Canada altogether, Lipset avoided acknowledging the existence of differing interpretations of the same "formative event."

Later milestones in Canadian history—such as Confederation, the National Policy of 1879, and the death of the Meech Lake Accord in 1990—further divided Canada's subcultures. In the process, they created new myths and symbols of power, domination, and rejection. The National Policy was designed to counter the flow of trade across the Canada–U.S. border by creating a national market for the products manufactured in Ontario and Quebec; its effect was to turn Atlantic and Western Canada into "a captive hinterland for central Canadian industrial development,"[29] permanently stunting the economies of the peripheral regions and fuelling regional resentments. The divisive mythologies arising from the Meech Lake Accord have already been discussed (see Dossier 1.2). Whereas American history has usually been interpreted in a unifying way (with obvious exceptions like slavery and the Civil War), Canadian history has left a legacy of division and mistrust that repeatedly flares up into public debate about the very legitimacy of our political system.[30]

However, the core of Lipset's argument is correct: "formative events"—especially those that shape a nation's political institutions—do leave indelible imprints on its political culture. Such events can further unite populations that already share basic political values, but they can also drive wedges between existing subcultures and occasionally create new ones.

▌ Geography

Much has been written about the influence of the land on Canadians' perceptions of ourselves. We are, according to Margaret Atwood and others, a nation fatalistically obsessed with "survival" in a harsh land of rock and snow. The contemporary relevance of such claims is questionable, at least to the majority of Canadians who live in modern cities a stone's throw from the American border. Apart from Progressive Conservative leader John Diefenbaker's successful campaign theme in 1958—"a vision of the North"—it is difficult to detect political echoes of Canada's climate and geology. One possible exception is the high level of environmental concerns among Canadians, relative to people in other countries; this implies an unusually strong connection to our landscape.[31] Another exception is the central place of the land in the rhetoric of Quebec nationalism, which is reflected in Dossier 2.4.

Whether or not our geography has shaped a national political culture, it does help to explain the existence of regional political cultures. The sheer size and diversity of Canada clearly contributes to the sense of "difference" across the regions. As each province developed, from the first European settlement to the present day, "Different environments combined with different technologies and opportunities to produce distinct regional economies."[32] These, in turn, created distinct patterns of political values across the regions. This is not to suggest that geography determines culture; such one-sided explanations are rarely helpful. Rather, it means that the unique terrain and climate in each part of the country can help to shape the social and political values of those who live there, creating the conditions for mobilization into a formal subculture.[33] (See Dossier 2.3.)

Demography

The most obvious demographic influence on Canadian politics is the presence of a large francophone minority. A little over one in five (21.8 percent) of the population claim French as their mother tongue. Anglophones account for 57 percent, and allophones make up less than 20 percent.[34] A majority of francophones live in Quebec, although there are significant francophone populations in New Brunswick and Ontario as well. While the language cleavage has always been a central issue in Canadian politics, its implications have become more serious since the Quiet Revolution remobilized Quebec nationalism into the sovereignty movement. Fears about the future of French in Canada help to fuel the campaign for a separate Quebec. Otherwise, the language cleavage appears to have little impact on political values; francophone and anglophone Canadians hold similar views on most political and social questions, although the former are slightly more permissive on moral issues.[35]

DOSSIER 2.3 Regionalism in Canada

While objective factors such as immigration patterns and geography help to explain the strength of Canadian **regionalism**, they do not tell the whole story. Regionalism is a subjective phenomenon, a social and psychological attachment to a particular place. It has three components: the importance of region in an individual's sense of identity, the degree to which he or she identifies with his or her region, and the strength of his or her commitment to that region.[36] Someone with a strong sense of regional identification and commitment is more likely to vote on the basis of regional interests and to resent perceived mistreatment of his or her region by the national or provincial government than someone who is more concerned

with other aspects of his or her identity (e.g., gender, class, or language).

Despite recent changes in political culture—including the rise of nonterritorial cleavages fostered by postmaterialism, discussed later in this chapter—regionalism remains unusually influential in Canada's national politics. Cross-national comparisons between Canada and other industrialized democracies reveal the relative weakness of social class and church attendance as determinants of voting choice. Canadians are significantly more influenced by territorial cleavages—the rural–urban divide and region of residence—than are Western Europeans.[37] This difference may be partly explained by the incentives set by our national

(continued)

institutions; in particular, Canada's electoral system assumes that MPs represent territory, not ideology, and it exaggerates regional differences among the various party caucuses in the House of Commons. (See Chapter 12.)

Some Canadian scholars emphasize the deliberate fostering of regionalism by provincial governments. They argue that provincial politicians have encouraged affective attachments to their own jurisdictions, often by criticizing Ottawa, in order to strengthen their own support.[38] This claim has recently been called into question. Henderson's analysis of constituency-level data from the 2000 Canadian Election Study found that the distribution of political orientations does not fit neatly within provincial boundaries. People who live in industrial regions—e.g., Windsor, Ontario or Sydney, Nova Scotia—share similar political views. Residents of the "905" suburban belt around Toronto are more likely to agree with their counterparts in the Vancouver suburbs than with their near neighbours in the urban core.[39] Voters in rural Quebec, which Henderson calls "New France," perceive politics rather differently from those in cosmopolitan Montreal. The study concludes that "there is reason to doubt . . . the impact of provincial institutions" on regional political cultures.

Aboriginal Canadians, who accounted for 3.7 percent of the population in the 2006 Census,[40] also seek to reform Canada's political institutions. The distribution of the Aboriginal population varies widely among the provinces and territories, from around 1 percent in Prince Edward Island and Quebec to around 15 percent in Manitoba and Saskatchewan and 85 percent in Nunavut.[41] Status Indians, Métis, and Inuit have become important players in debates over Canada's political future. Recent demands for enhanced political and legal status—ranging from an Aboriginal chamber of Parliament to the constitutional recognition of Aboriginal communities as "a third order of government" with significant sovereignty over their own affairs—pose significant challenges to our existing institutions.

Economics

Marxist thinkers dismiss traditional analyses of political culture as biased, deceptive, and even oppressive. Karl Marx (1818–83) argued that the central dynamic of human history was the struggle between two classes: a small upper class, which owned the means of production (e.g., land, factories), and a much larger working class, which owned nothing except its labour. Over time, as the dominant technology of production evolved from agriculture to industrial manufacturing, European economies shifted from feudalism to capitalism. Their political systems changed dramatically, from absolutist monarchs surrounded by fawning aristocrats to Cabinet governments dependent on elected legislatures. Conservatism gave way to liberalism, and Catholicism (in much of northern Europe) to Protestantism. But the underlying power structure remained intact: the tiny economic elite, through its control of the economy and politics, continued to oppress the workers.[42]

For Marxists, what liberals call "political culture" is an ideological smokescreen. It blinds the working class to its own oppression by glorifying "natural" hierarchies (conservatism) or celebrating the illusion of individual "freedom" (liberalism). This "false consciousness" must be overcome, and the workers made aware of their exploitation, before the class struggle can reach its climax. At some point, according to Marx, the workers will rise up against the elite, seize control of the means of production, and distribute the proceeds among themselves. This final stage of human history is communism: the abolition of private property, or at least the private ownership of the means of production, and the "withering away" of the state.

Whether or not one agrees with Marx, there is little doubt that the material facts of life shape our view of the world. We have already seen that distinct regional economies can produce variations in political culture. But how can we explain the apparent weakness of class as a determinant of Canadian political values and behaviour?[43] Elsewhere in the Western world, the class cleavage has exerted a powerful influence on voter choice (although that influence has diminished in recent years); Canadians are more likely to vote on the basis of region, partisanship, or short-term factors such as party leaders and campaign issues (Chapter 12). From a left-wing viewpoint, we are victims of "false consciousness," duped by our political leaders into believing that class is less important than region or language.[44] Apart from the unfortunate tinge of conspiracy theory in this argument, Marx's central insight remains valid: that despite the growing influence of "postmaterialism," our political orientations are inevitably shaped (though not necessarily determined) by our social and economic status.[45]

RECENT TRENDS IN CANADIAN POLITICAL CULTURE

Before we turn to recent developments, it may be useful to summarize the conventional wisdom about Canadian political culture.[46] Canadians, it is alleged, are more dependent than Americans on the state. We are more deferential to authority, whether that authority is based on democratic processes or on inherited privilege (e.g., the British monarch). We are timid, conservative, and relatively passive in our orientations toward politics.

Whatever merit this stereotype may once have possessed, survey data suggest that it no longer applies.[47] Like their counterparts in other Western democracies, Canadians are increasingly apt to challenge authority, demand direct participation in political decision-making, and criticize the status quo. We are turning away from traditional vehicles of social and political participation—churches, political parties, even voting—and embracing new social movements (e.g., Make Poverty History) along with novel methods of political action (protests and petitions). Whereas previous scholars, including Lipset, argued that Canadians are more deferential to authority than Americans, the reverse now appears to be true—especially among the youngest cohorts.[48]

This new conventional wisdom raises three important questions.

- First, how do we explain the cultural changes just described? To answer this question, we will assess three broad approaches to political culture: legitimacy, social capital, and value change.[49]
- Second, how have Canada's new and old subcultures been mobilized into new forms of political activity? To address this question, we will examine two case studies: Quebec nationalism since the Quiet Revolution, and the impact of the *Canadian Charter of Rights and Freedoms*.
- Third, how will changing political values and mobilized subcultures affect our political institutions? We will address this question at the end of the chapter, and elaborate on the answers throughout the chapters which follow.

EXPLAINING THE CHANGES IN CANADIAN POLITICAL CULTURE

Legitimacy: Declining Support for Canada's Political System?

In a nutshell, "mass support for a given system of governance, and mass confidence in its specific institutions, provide political systems with the legitimacy that they need to govern effectively."[50] In other words, when the citizens of a given country lose faith in some or all of their political institutions, the state is undermined and its ability to govern is eroded. To determine whether the Canadian political system is losing legitimacy, we return to the five elements of the political system identified earlier in this chapter:

1. *The political community:* While support remains high in most democratic states, Canada is a partial exception. Quebec nationalists feel less attachment than other Canadians to "Canada as a whole."[51] Equally worrisome is the relatively low level of attachment among younger Canadians,[52] although it is not clear whether this is the result of disaffection with Canada or an emerging sense of "transnational" or "cosmopolitan" citizenship.[53] Whatever its origin, weaker adherence to the political community is related to lower levels of support for particular national institutions (notably Parliament), for political parties, and for politicians.[54] Generally speaking, however, Canadians' attitudes toward the political community are more positive than their evaluations of the specific elements of the political system.[55]

2. *Regime principles:* Canadians, like people worldwide, overwhelmingly approve of democracy as an abstract concept.[56] This does not mean, however, that they are entirely satisfied with the actual performance of our democratic institutions, as the analysis of the next three elements reveals. Support for the principles of federalism, minority rights, and the rule of law is more difficult to gauge, because the data are either ambiguous or nonexistent. Moreover, support for "democracy" as a broad concept does not necessarily imply support for the particular conception of democracy embodied in existing institutions. To the extent that Canadians wish to see a greater degree of direct democracy in public decision-making, they are likely to become disenchanted with representative institutions.[57]

3. *Regime performance:* Evaluations of the overall performance of Canada's national political institutions have fluctuated in recent years. Citizens' assessments of regime performance are affected by economic conditions,[58] by the perceived fairness of their treatment by the state,[59] and by the overall competence with which governments handle national problems. While a slim majority of Canadians perceive the federal government as both fair and efficient,[60] a perception that sustains overall confidence in regime performance, poor economic conditions in the 1980s and early 1990s produced temporary dips in confidence.[61] Note, too, that changing cultural values can create new and more stringent evaluative criteria. In other words, better-informed and less deferential citizens may hold governments to higher standards of performance than their parents or grandparents did.[62] Over the past few decades, Canadians' sense of personal political efficacy—their confidence in their own ability to evaluate information and make political decisions—has risen,[63] while their belief that politicians listen to their opinions has fallen. In the 2005 World Values Survey, for example, a majority of Canadian respondents said that their country is not "governed by the will of the people."[64] This "efficacy gap" may give Canadians a feeling of alienation from their political institutions, and contribute to declining voter turnout.[65] That same study uncovered a surprising lack of confidence in the electoral process. Two-thirds of Canadian respondents said that our elections are "free and fair"; almost one-third said that they are not. This compares favourably to the world average, which was evenly divided, but it is surprising because Canada is a world leader in electoral administration. This finding could have important implications for the current debate over electoral reform (Chapter 12).

4. *Regime institutions:* If overall evaluations of the Canadian political system are fairly positive, the same cannot be said for individual institutions. Public satisfaction with Parliament and political parties has dropped sharply over the past 30 years. Between 1979 and 1999 the percentage of Canadians who expressed "a great deal of confidence" in political parties fell from 30 percent to 11 percent.[66] From 1965 to 1993, evaluations of the major federal parties declined steadily and partisan attachments weakened.[67] In 1981,

61 percent of Canadians had either "a great deal of confidence" or "some confidence" in national political institutions; by 1991, that figure had fallen to 46 percent, 7 points below the average reported by the Organisation for Economic Co-operation and Development (OECD). While confidence in other institutions, including the police and the military, also declined, public disaffection with Parliament and the political parties accounted for most of the overall drop in public esteem. Given the argument in Chapter 1, that a loss of public confidence threatens the legitimacy of democratic institutions, this "relative lack of popular confidence in [our] democratic institutions"[68] should be cause for concern. But the news is not all bad. First, evaluations of Canada's political institutions— including Parliament and the parties—have remained stable or modestly improved since the early 1990s.[69] Second, Canadians appear to have transferred their confidence to other political institutions, instead of giving up on the political system completely. For example, a substantial majority believe that the courts, not Parliament, should have the final say on the *Charter of Rights*.[70] We will return to the relationship between the judicial and legislative branches in Chapters 6 and 10.

5. *Political actors:* In 1992, after eight years in power, Brian Mulroney was the least popular prime minister in Canadian history. He had launched two unsuccessful rounds of megaconstitutional bargaining that divided the country. (See Chapter 5.) The 1989 Free Trade Agreement with the United States also provoked intense controversy. At the time, some observers feared that the public's anger with the Mulroney Government would inflict severe and permanent damage on support for national political institutions. While there does not appear to be a direct relationship between the popularity of a particular government and the public's evaluation of the political system as a whole,[71] the decline in public confidence levelled off and partially reversed under Jean Chrétien's Liberal Government (1993–2003). By 2005, Canadians were more critical of their political leaders than the world average—although less so than people in countries where political corruption is a routine occurrence.[72]

As in most Western states, Canadians have the most positive feelings toward the broadest level—the political community—and the most negative feelings toward specific institutions and political actors. Table 2.1 reflects this downward trend from the general to the particular elements of the political system.

For legitimacy theorists, the findings just described are disturbing. The relatively low scores for regime performance are particularly significant, given the strong connection between performance evaluations and the perceived legitimacy of the political system as a

TABLE 2.1 CANADIANS' SATISFACTION WITH DEMOCRACY, GOVERNMENT, AND POLITICS, 2000[73]

	DEMOCRACY (%)	GOVERNMENT (%)	POLITICS (%)
Very or fairly satisfied	71	58	53
Not very or not at all satisfied	26	38	43
Not sure/refused	4	4	5
Total	100	100	100
Number of respondents	1278	1278	1278

Note: Columns may not add to 100 due to rounding.

Source: Paul Howe and David Northrup, *Strengthening Canadian Democracy: The Views of Canadians* (Montreal: Institute for Research on Public Policy, 2000), Table 2, p. 7. Reprinted with permission.

whole.[74] On the other hand, Canadians hold their political institutions in fairly high esteem compared to people in many other states. We also have a shared commitment to democratic values, a stable constitution, relatively mild social divisions, and a high level of prosperity. The fate of some other democratic states, which have collapsed into authoritarianism or anarchy, does not await Canada.[75]

Critics of the legitimacy approach argue that declining faith in the political system *per se* has little if any effect on democracy. They point out that some authoritarian states enjoy high levels of regime support, and that positive answers to survey questions about democracy do not necessarily reflect a genuine commitment to freedom and self-government. A wide-ranging statistical analysis using data from dozens of countries found a weak relationship between the standard measures of legitimacy, on the one hand, and the performance of democratic institutions on the other.[76] As we will see, adherents of the value change model are particularly dismissive of the legitimacy approach. They argue that broad attitudes toward freedom and tolerance are more closely related to genuine democracy than narrow beliefs about specific institutions. Defenders of the link between political culture and institutional performance might retort that the value change theorists have put the cart before the horse. Persistently poor regime performance, or repeated misjudgments on the part of political actors, jeopardize the economic and/or physical security of the citizens. The result is a renewed focus on survival, which could reverse the value change that supposedly advances democracy.

▓ Social Capital: A Nation of Couch Potatoes?

Robert Putnam argues that democratic political institutions work most effectively in societies with high levels of social engagement.[77] Volunteer work, attending public meetings on community issues, membership in social clubs, even bowling in a league—all these activities contribute to the stock of "social capital" in the community. Where social capital is high, people tend to trust their neighbours and support their political institutions. They work together to solve common problems, care about the well-being of other people in their communities, and have more respect and tolerance for differing viewpoints.[78] Where social capital is low— where people are more isolated from each other, either by personal choice or because of a lack of opportunities for positive interaction—levels of social trust are correspondingly low and support for political institutions drops.

A lack of civic engagement on the part of the "silent majority" effectively abandons political involvement to extremists, and reduces public understanding of social issues to dangerously low levels.[79] The performance of government suffers, both because of passive noncompliance with the law—refusing to pay taxes, for example—and because political elites know that an uninformed and apathetic electorate will not hold them to account for poor decisions.[80] Putnam concludes that "the health of our public institutions depends, at least in part, on widespread participation in private voluntary groups—those networks of civic engagement that embody social capital."[81] While "the absence of social capital does not eliminate politics,"[82] it reduces public life to a babble of disconnected voices in a social landscape of isolation and mutual distrust.

Putnam's work on social capital is highly regarded and influential, although it has attracted critics. Some argue that he mistook the cause for the effect: we abstain from collective voluntary activities *because* we don't care about our neighbours, not vice versa.[83] Others accuse Putnam of overemphasizing local sources of social capital and underestimating the impact of regional and national political structures on citizen engagement.[84] Moreover, empirical research on individual attitudes has found very weak correlations among voluntary activity, social trust, and evaluations of government institutions.[85] Canadians combine the second-highest level of voluntarism on the planet[86] with higher-than-average cynicism about our governments.

Perhaps most telling, value-change theorists have identified two distinct types of social capital—only one of which promotes democracy. "Bonding" capital characterizes vertical social organizations, like traditional churches or political parties. It cements hierarchical relationships between leaders and their followers. "Bridging" capital connects the members of horizontal organizations, e.g., new social movements connected by the Internet. Because it is weaker than bonding capital, it allows individuals to make up their own minds instead of taking cues from authority figures. Consequently, it is more compatible with democracy.

Inglehart and Welzel argue that Putnam's analysis is overly pessimistic: bonding capital is indeed eroding in **post-industrial** societies, where citizens feel ever-weaker attachments to the social groups into which they were born (socioeconomic class, religious denomination), but bridging capital is growing as people form new social ties (in person or in cyberspace) on the basis of common interests and goals. The shift from bonding to bridging capital "extends the possibilities to initiate public campaigns, [and] to mobilize large numbers of people for collective action."[87] This may indeed be the case, but one might well ask whether a temporary, loosely-knit global campaign with shallow organizational roots (e.g., Make Poverty History) can really deliver tangible change. Moreover, the quality of participation in such movements is open to question. It is one thing to work closely with other human beings over a period of months or years, acquiring new political skills and learning to compromise in pursuit of one's goals; it is quite another to watch a rock concert on television or post one's ideas on a blog.

Before leaving the idea of social capital, we will address the related claim that the mass media—particularly television—have contributed to the recent trends in Canadians' political orientations. This claim has two dimensions. First, Putnam argues that television weakens social capital, by isolating us in our living rooms: "A major commitment to television viewing—such as most of us have come to have—is incompatible with a major commitment to community life."[88] Second, critics of the news media argue that shallow and negative coverage of politics makes voters cynical and undermines their faith in the political system.[89] It may also diminish the capacity of citizens to make informed decisions about candidates and issues,[90] a subject to which we will return in Chapter 14.

Empirical evidence reveals a clear statistical connection between heavy television watching and lack of involvement in the community.[91] However, it is not clear which is the cause and which is the effect: does television isolate people, or do they choose to stay on the couch because they have no interest in mixing with their neighbours? Nor is there a proven causal link between television news and diminishing support for the political system. One study found that regular viewers of news programs display "higher than average levels of political interest, efficacy, knowledge, and social trust."[92] If this finding applies to Canada, it implies that the media have been unjustly blamed for negative attitudes toward politics: "too often we are 'blaming the messenger' for more deep-rooted ills of the body politic."[93] However, it does not appear to apply to Canada. It cannot be entirely coincidental that Canadians' opinions about our institutions and leaders have soured since the 1970s, when our journalists adopted a suspicious, even hostile attitude toward politicians. We will return to the political impact of negative and superficial news coverage in Chapter 14.

◼ Value Change: Postmaterialism and Generational Replacement

Since the baby boomers came of age in the 1960s, political orientations and behaviour in post-industrial democracies have changed significantly. Traditional attachments and hierarchies are losing their power to shape attitudes. Political parties do not attract the young, who are more likely to join new social movements or to opt out of politics altogether (even refusing to vote). The postmaterialist hypothesis, first advanced by Ronald Inglehart, attributes these developments to a profound and irreversible value change arising from worldwide economic conditions. Since 1945, Western publics have enjoyed unprecedented levels of material affluence, physical security, educational opportunity, and access to information. Children who grew up in this environment have different political values from their predecessors. With fewer worries about survival, they are free to concentrate on "quality of life" issues—equal rights, the environment, the developing world. Their extensive formal education and easy access to information give them the cognitive skills to put their issues on the public agenda.[94]

More recently, Inglehart and Welzel have identified a broader set of self-expression values, of which the postmaterialist priorities are only one part. These values include tolerance for homosexuality, acceptance of gender equality, and demands for ever-greater individual participation in politics. They argue that "The degree to which given publics give high priority to self-expression largely shapes the extent to which societies provide democratic rights, the degree to which women are represented in positions of power, and the extent to which elites govern responsively and according to the rule of law."[95] The primary difference between a genuinely democratic state, and one which is democratic in name only, is the incidence of self-expression values among the population. As that incidence rises, political leaders face ever-growing pressure to respond to public priorities and dismantle institutional obstacles to direct participation. More and more citizens turn away from elite-directed organizations and activities (such as political parties and elections) to "elite-challenging" activities like demonstrations, petitions, and boycotts.[96] These trends intensify with each new birth cohort, despite some short-term setbacks arising from economic recessions and isolated threats to physical security.[97]

The value change theory has some impressive strengths. It rests on decades of survey data from dozens of countries. It appears to explain why some of the new democracies that emerged in the 1980s and 1990s have thrived, while others have faltered. It also sheds light on the generational differences in voter turnout and other types of political behaviour around the world (Chapter 12). Finally, it shows why younger generations appear to judge their political systems according to different (and more stringent) criteria than their forebears did.

Like all theories, however, value change has some flaws. One is the failure to appreciate the power of institutions to influence behaviour. For Inglehart and Welzel, values shape institutions: when political and social orientations change, institutions are somehow forced to adapt. They do not explain that process of adaptation, or the directions that it might take in specific countries. Nor do they acknowledge the power of elites to block changes that might threaten their control; they simply assume that the form of government will evolve to suit new public priorities and demands. Yet their own data reveal that this is not necessarily true: Canada ranks at the top of the self-expression scale, but lags on measures of "effective democracy." (We will return to the possible reasons for this lag at the end of the chapter.)

Perhaps the biggest question arising from the value change theory is its endorsement of a particular model of democracy. Inglehart and Welzel's notion of "effective democracy" is characterized by individual autonomy and a rejection of authority. It is difficult to see a place for government in this version of "democracy." We need institutions to make and enforce rules, and to provide public goods that would otherwise be unavailable. If Inglehart and Welzel are correct, Western publics are withdrawing support from hierarchical organizations, abandoning the political parties that link voters to their governments, and expecting to hold leaders to account with a few clicks of the mouse. This vision may be "democratic," but it is hardly "effective." To that extent, the value change hypothesis is less satisfactory than either the legitimacy theory or Putnam's emphasis on preserving older forms of social structure.

Take, for example, Inglehart and Welzel's assertion that "a public that emphasizes self-expression values tends to put its elites under pressure to govern according to the rule of law."[98] It is likely that Canadians reacted more strongly to the Sponsorship Scandal (Dossier 8.2) than they would have in the past, because of post-war value changes. But public anger and disgust at allegations of political corruption would have been meaningless without formal mechanisms of accountability. A commission of inquiry, led by a judge, investigated the failings that produced the scandal. The Royal Canadian Mounted Police and other law-enforcement agencies gathered evidence against the individuals who were eventually charged and prosecuted in the courts. To date, the only punishment meted out to the Liberal Party (both the innocent and the allegedly guilty) was inflicted by the voters, who used the ballot box to reduce the party to a minority in 2004 and to remove it from power altogether in 2006. No amount of protesting, blogging, or petitioning could have held the former government to account for the scandal. If we want our governments to "govern according to the rule of law," citizens must continue to support the institutions that evolved over centuries to hold rulers accountable.

The failure of value change advocates to recognize the importance of institutions explains an otherwise puzzling gap in their argument: they do not tell us how millions of autonomous individuals can pressure political elites to pursue their priorities. The missing piece of the puzzle, as mentioned earlier in this chapter, is the process of mobilization. We will now examine two Canadian cases of political mobilization, to explain how a particular subculture acquires political salience.

■ Mobilizing Canadian Subcultures

Quebec Nationalism and the Quiet Revolution

As Dossier 2.1 explained, French Quebeckers have had a strong attachment to their political community since the eighteenth century. The passive, inward-looking nationalism that emerged after "*la cession*" was mobilized by the Quiet Revolution of the 1960s into an aggressive campaign for greater provincial powers and revenues. The myths and symbols of Quebec nationalism have been used effectively to strengthen the attachment of francophones to the sovereigntist project, as Dossier 2.4 illustrates.

DOSSIER 2.4   Quebec Nationalism

In the fall of 1995, shortly before the province's second sovereignty referendum, the Parti Québécois (PQ) government of Quebec introduced Bill 1, The Sovereignty Bill. The preamble contained a strong and lyrical statement of Quebec nationalism, excerpts of which are reproduced here.

At the dawn of the seventeenth century, the pioneers of what would become a nation and then a people rooted themselves in the soil of Québec. Having come from a *great civilization, they were enriched by that of the First Nations, they forged new alliances, and maintained the heritage of France. The conquest of 1760 did not break the determination of their descendants to remain faithful to a destiny unique in North America. Already in 1774, through the Québec Act, the conqueror recognized the distinct nature of their institutions. Neither attempts at assimilation nor the Act of Union of 1840 could break their endurance. The English community that grew up at their side, the immigrants who have joined them, all have*

(continued)

contributed to forming this people which became in 1867 one of the two founders of the Canadian federation.

We, the men and women of this place,

Because we inhabit the territories delimited by our ancestors, from Abitibi to the Îles-de-la-Madeleine, from Ungava to the American border, because for four hundred years we have cleared, ploughed, paced, surveyed, dug, fished, built, started anew, discussed, protected, and loved this land that is cut across and watered by the St. Lawrence River;

Because the heart of this land beats in French and because that heartbeat is as meaningful as the seasons that hold sway over it, as the winds that bend it, as the men and women who shape it;

Because we have created here a way of being, of believing, of working that is unique;

Because as long ago as 1791 we established here one of the first parliamentary democracies in the world, one we have never ceased to improve;

Because the legacy of the struggles and courage of the past compels us irrevocably to take charge of our own destiny;

Because it is this land alone that represents our pride and the source of our strength, our sole opportunity to express ourselves in the entirety of our individual natures and of our collective heart;

Because this land will be all those men and women who inhabit it, who defend it and define it, and because we are all those people;

We, the people of Québec, declare that we are free to choose our future.

We entered the federation on the faith of a promise of equality in a shared undertaking and of respect for our authority in certain matters that to us are vital. But what was to follow did not live up to those early hopes. The Canadian State contravened the federative pact, by invading in a thousand ways areas in which we are autonomous, and

by serving notice that our secular belief in the equality of the partners was an illusion. We were hoodwinked in 1982 when the governments of Canada and the English-speaking provinces made changes to the Constitution, in depth and to our detriment, in defiance of the categorical opposition of our National Assembly. Twice since then attempts were made to right that wrong. The failure of the Meech Lake Accord in 1990 confirmed a refusal to recognize even our distinct character. And in 1992 the rejection of the Charlottetown Accord by both Canadians and Quebecers confirmed the conclusion that no redress was possible.

Because we have persisted despite the haggling of which we have been the object;

Because Canada, far from taking pride in and proclaiming to the world the alliance between its two founding peoples, has instead consistently trivialized it and decreed the spurious principle of equality between the provinces;

Because we have the deep-seated conviction that continuing within Canada would be tantamount to condemning ourselves to languish and to debasing our very identity;

We, the people of Québec, declare it is our will to be in full possession of all the powers of a State: to vote all our laws, to levy all our taxes, to sign all our treaties and to exercise the highest power of all, conceiving, and controlling, by ourselves, our fundamental law.

We, the people of Québec, through our National Assembly, proclaim: Québec is a sovereign country.

The full text of Bill 1 can be found on the Nelson website for this book at www.parametersofpower5e.nelson.com. Click on "Canadian Politics on the Web," then on "Quebec & National Unity," and then on "The Sovereignty Bill."

Dossier 2.4 reflects at least three central themes in the mythology of Quebec nationalism:
1. The province of Quebec is the homeland of the French people and culture in North America. It is a "distinct society" within Canada. Consequently, the provincial government has a special responsibility to protect and promote that "distinct society," and it requires special powers to carry out that responsibility. If it cannot exercise those powers within the framework of Canadian federalism, it must become an independent state.

2. Confederation is the product of a compact between two "founding nations": the French and the English. (There is little room in this mythology for the Aboriginal peoples of Canada.) It follows that Quebec is not, and never will be, "*une province comme les autres.*" It has the right to negotiate constitutional change directly with the federal government, on a nation-to-nation basis. It also claims a veto over any proposed amendment to the Confederation compact that does not meet the needs of Quebec. In other words, even if the federal government and the other nine provinces agreed to a change in the constitution, Quebec should have the right to block that change.

3. National political institutions cannot thwart the democratic will of Quebeckers. That will is sovereign, and it trumps all other constitutional values (e.g., federalism or the rights of minorities within Quebec).

As we will see in the following chapters, the other senior governments in Canada reject these demands for "special status." The clash between the "two-nations" and "equal-provinces" visions of Canada is yet to be resolved, despite repeated efforts by political leaders (and courts).

The decisive event in generating demands for major constitutional revision was the Quiet Revolution, which transformed Quebec politics in the early 1960s. The decade opened with the defeat of the Union Nationale government of Quebec by the provincial Liberals under the leadership of Jean Lesage. The Lesage Liberals ushered Quebec into the modern era of activist states. Before 1960, the Union Nationale espoused a minimalist, *laissez-faire* approach to the economy and allowed the church to dominate the realms of education and social welfare. In this deeply conservative vision, Quebec francophones were a Catholic, agrarian people for whom modern commercial capitalism was a foreign activity better left to English-speaking Protestants.[99] By 1960, this ideology was at odds with reality: since the beginning of the century, Quebeckers had been leaving their farms in droves and integrating into modern urban, industrial society. The problem was that they had been integrated as workers into enterprises largely controlled and managed by the English community and using English as the language of work, a development that threatened the long-term persistence of French as the primary language in Quebec.

Responding to this reality, the Lesage Liberals embraced the state. If the French language and culture were to survive in Quebec, the government had to intervene in the economy in order to ensure that it was controlled and operated to a much greater extent by francophones. Commerce was no longer to be disdained as a foreign activity; it would be embraced as a form of secular salvation and, wherever possible, conducted in French. By the same token, education and other social services had to be wrested from the church and directed more explicitly to giving French Quebeckers the skills they needed to take control of economic enterprises rather than just supply their labour. In its newfound interventionism, especially in economic matters, Quebec often wanted to go further than the other provinces and occupy realms of activity that had been filled by the federal government. From this perspective, Ottawa could not be trusted to exercise its powers in a manner congenial to Quebec; the federal government would follow the wishes of the English-speaking majority outside the province. In short, the Quiet Revolution sparked demands for a transfer of powers and resources from Ottawa to Quebec City, a demand that has dominated Quebec politics and shaped the national constitutional landscape ever since (Chapters 4 and 5).

The Quiet Revolution is a classic example of political mobilization. The provincial Liberal government began the process, although it quickly lost control of the more extreme elements of the nationalist subculture. In 1968 these united under the umbrella of the separatist Parti Québécois, led by former Lesage Cabinet Minister René Lévesque. The PQ has led the movement for Quebec sovereignty ever since, although it has recently faced competition from the ADQ.[100]

Interestingly, although the ADQ's political nationalism is more moderate than the PQ's outright separatism, its cultural nationalism is more overtly exclusive and **xenophobic**. In the 2007 provincial election campaign, leader Mario Dumont capitalized on some Québécois' fears of "reasonable accommodation" for ethnic and religious minorities. Public anger and resentment against immigrants spilled over in the francophone media. Shortly after winning a narrow re-election, Liberal Premier Jean Charest appointed a commission to study the apparent breakdown of Quebec's social cohesion. The commissioners noted that "*pur laine*" Québécois, the descendants of the original "fragment," were reaping the consequences of their own personal choices. As the province's birthrate fell in the late twentieth century, high rates of immigration became essential to maintain the standard of living. Therefore, Québécois had to come to terms with a more diverse society, instead of lashing out at imagined threats to the French language—still spoken at home by over 80 percent of provincial residents—and the secular society established by the Quiet Revolution. Despite this pro-diversity approach, the commissioners displayed considerable sympathy with the fears of the xenophobes:

> It is important to understand the experience of French-Canadian Quebecers. They are members of a small minority nation in North America and their culture encompasses vivid recollections of humiliation, oppression sustained and overcome, struggles for survival, and battles that they have had to wage singlehandedly, without being able to rely on an external ally. . . . French-speaking Québec must not succumb to fear, the temptation to withdraw and reject, nor don the victim's mantle. In other words, it must reject this scenario of inevitable disappearance.[101]

This passage suggests that the aggressive Quebec nationalism of the late twentieth century grows out of the same fears and insecurities that fuelled the defensive nationalism following *la cession.*

The Rights Revolution

Alan Cairns attributes at least some of the recent changes in Canadian political culture to the influence of the *Canadian Charter of Rights and Freedoms.*[102] He argues that the groups that received particular recognition and protection in the *Constitution Act, 1982*—the so-called "*Charter* Canadians"—have mobilized to defend "their" rights against perceived threats. Women's groups, Aboriginal groups, multicultural groups, and a host of others helped to defeat the Meech Lake and Charlottetown Accords (Chapter 5). One implication is that growing citizen activism, fostered by the *Charter,* is reflected in less deferential political values. Another is that the territorial social cleavages that inspired Canada's federal system, and that in turn have been encouraged by provincial governments, are losing their power to shape political values. In their place are "new cleavages or reinvigorated old cleavages related to sex, ethnicity, the aboriginal communities, the disabled, and others."[103]

While Cairns' argument about the impact of the *Charter* on constitutional politics is plausible, survey evidence contradicts the claim that the entrenchment of rights and freedoms changed our political culture.[104] This does not mean that the *Charter* has had no effect on Canadians' political orientations. The growing prevalence of "rights talk" in Canada's political discourse may fuel popular discontent with the system and erode the legitimacy of traditional political decision-making processes based on compromise and negotiation.[105]

CURRENT DEBATES ABOUT CANADA'S POLITICAL INSTITUTIONS

The existence of multiple subcultures with varying levels of political satisfaction inevitably creates political tensions. These tensions flare into open conflict during public debates over institutional reform. During the 1980s and early 1990s, repeated rounds of "megaconstitutional politics" (see Chapter 1) revealed the depth of subcultural disagreements over the nature and purpose of Canada's political institutions. Although the rejection of the Charlottetown Accord in 1992 marked the end of megaconstitutional politics, debates over institutional reform persist (Chapter 5). We will discuss two of these debates here, and link them to the preceding discussion of political culture.

▓ Representative Democracy versus Direct Democracy

Populists and postmaterialists take a rather dim view of **representative democracy.** They criticize the lack of opportunities for direct citizen involvement in policy-making. They want to reform, or even bypass, Canada's existing political institutions by using direct-democracy devices: referenda (the plural of "referendum"), initiatives, and recall. In referenda and initiatives, voters determine the outcome of a particular policy debate by voting "yes" or "no" on a ballot question. Referenda are sponsored by governments, whereas initiatives are triggered by citizens (more accurately, by advocacy groups). A "recall" is an organized campaign to remove a legislator from office between elections. In both initiative and recall campaigns, the organizers must collect and submit signatures on a petition. If they collect enough verified signatures, the government is required to hold a vote—on a particular policy question, in the former case, or on the legislator's right to remain in office in the latter instance. A successful recall vote will normally trigger a special election to choose a replacement for the ousted official.

Referenda and initiatives can be categorized in at least three different ways: binding/advisory, direct/indirect, and positive/negative:

1. The results of binding referenda and initiatives must be enacted into law by the appropriate government. Advisory results may legally be disregarded by political elites, although this strategy carries obvious political risks. (Advisory votes are often called "plebiscites.")
2. Direct votes bypass representative political institutions altogether, and have the force of law as soon as the results are announced; in indirect votes, the question must be approved by the legislature before it goes to the people.
3. Positive votes create new legislation or determine the direction of future legislation, whereas negative or "abrogative" votes strike down existing legislation.[106]

There has been considerable debate in recent years over the pros and cons of these mechanisms. For populists, direct democracy is the only way to ensure that "the voice of the people" is reflected in public decision-making. Postmaterialists also welcome direct democracy, because it bypasses traditional hierarchies and gives every citizen an equal right to participate. For those who do not share this enthusiasm for individualist and egalitarian politics, direct democracy represents a threat to Canada's system of representative democracy. The controversy is briefly summarized in Dossier 2.5.

The case for referenda and initiatives is straightforward: they allow citizens to govern themselves directly, at least in particular policy areas. As a result, citizens will take a more active interest in, and become more informed about, politics and policy-making.[107] The arguments against referenda and initiatives are more numerous. First, they allow governments to avoid making decisions on difficult issues.[108] Second, they artificially reduce complex issues to "yes" and "no" opposites, and in so doing they divide the electorate without hope of compromise or healing.[109] Third, instead of giving "the people" control over policy-making, they provide an opportunity for wealthy interest groups to "buy" favourable legislation—or, more commonly, to defeat unfavourable legislation.[110] An entire "initiative industry" has sprung up in the United States: "law firms that draft legislation, petition management firms that guarantee ballot access, direct-mail firms, and campaign consultants who specialize in initiative contests across several states."[111]

Fourth, skeptics argue that "the people are not informed or caring enough to vote on complicated public policy issues."[112] Those who do vote may be motivated by irrational prejudices—either against unpopular minorities or against the government leaders sponsoring a given referendum—or they may simply be too confused to understand what's best for them. Although this argument may be somewhat overstated, there is some evidence to substantiate it. The "no" side won the 1992 Charlottetown Accord referendum partly for reasons unrelated to its actual content: the personal unpopularity of Prime Minister Mulroney,[113] and the widespread perception among English Canadians that Quebec would never be satisfied, no matter how much the rest of the country tried to accommodate its demands.[114] These findings are typical of other referenda and initiatives.

Finally, critics allege that referenda and initiatives inflame hostility against minority groups and that initiatives provide bigots with a golden opportunity to persecute their targets. These critics point to several recent American initiatives that asked voters in particular states or municipalities to restrict the rights of gays and lesbians, illegal immigrants, and anyone whose first language was not English.[115] Defenders of direct democracy point out that the success rate of municipal anti-minority initiatives was higher than that of state-wide initiatives,[116] and that policies that violated constitutional rights were subsequently overturned by the courts. Opponents of direct democracy counter that the public debate surrounding a discriminatory initiative question deepens the stigmas attached to the targeted groups and permanently reduces the majority's tolerance for "difference."[117]

Advocates of recall argue that voters should not be forced to "wait until the next election to rid themselves of an incompetent, dishonest, unresponsive, or irresponsible public official."[118] Critics argue that recall campaigns are "divisive, disruptive, polarizing, and subject to a myriad of abuses and unintended consequences."[119] They point to the United States, where some recall petitions have been motivated by opposing political parties, resentful interest groups, or "sore losers" in the previous election. The 2003 election of Arnold Schwarzenegger as governor of California is a case in point.[120] A Republican state legislator spearheaded a recall drive to remove Democratic Governor Gray Davis from office, to capitalize on public anger against tax increases to deal with the state's massive budget deficit. Under California law, a recall vote must be accompanied by a special election to fill the post that would be vacated if the recall succeeded. Unlike a regular gubernatorial election, the candidates are not selected in party primaries; anyone can run against the challenged incumbent. Schwarzenegger, a relatively moderate Republican on social issues, would not have been chosen by his party's strongly conservative primary voters. California voters ejected an experienced governor and replaced him, not with the lieutenant governor or a seasoned

(continued)

legislator, but with a wealthy political amateur. Fortunately, Schwarzenegger proved to be a reasonably able leader; he was re-elected as governor in 2006.

Canada's Royal Commission on Electoral Reform and Party Financing rejected the idea of recalling elected legislators. It did so for three primary reasons: the recall is inconsistent with a parliamentary system, especially one in which voters are more influenced by partisanship than by individual candidates; it makes little sense to require an MP elected by less than a majority of her constituents to win a majority in a subsequent recall vote; and government would be disrupted if a Cabinet minister or the prime minister were targeted by political opponents.[121]

◼ "Old Politics" versus "New Politics"

Whereas the debate over representative versus direct democracy revolves around the need to reform existing political institutions, the conflict between "old" and "new" politics concerns the legitimacy of political institutions themselves. "Old" politics is about resolving common problems through hierarchical structures such as political parties and Parliaments. The key issue is the production and distribution of material wealth. "New" politics rejects traditional institutions in favour of unconventional political activities, challenges established authorities, and emphasizes quality of life issues: equal rights, reproductive freedom, the environment, assistance to developing countries, and global peace. It is the political manifestation of postmaterialism.[122]

In one respect, the phrase "new politics" is inaccurate. Dissatisfied citizens have always resorted to unconventional protest activities. What is new about "new politics" is the growing readiness to resort to such tactics, especially among postmaterialists. Between 1981 and 1990, the proportion of Canadian respondents to the World Values Survey who reported prior engagement in protest activity rose from 23.6 percent to 32.5 percent. Those who expressed unwillingness to protest dwindled from 67.9 to 56.9 percent of respondents.[123] Contrary to the old stereotype of the passive, deferential Canadian, the World Values Survey found that Canadians were more protest-oriented than Europeans or Americans. If the influence of postmaterialism continues to grow, our political institutions may be confronted with ever more frequent public expressions of dissent.

The antiglobalization movement of the late 1990s provides a dramatic illustration of the conflict between "old" and "new" political values. Political leaders and police reacted to protests in some Canadian cities with escalating violence and a disturbing disregard for *Charter* rights (particularly freedom of expression and peaceful assembly). When students at the University of British Columbia expressed their opposition to the human-rights record of former Indonesian President Suharto at the 1997 Asia–Pacific Economic Conference (APEC) summit in Vancouver, some were pepper-sprayed; others were arrested without due process.[124] The April 2001 Summit of the Americas in Quebec City attracted thousands of demonstrators. A small minority engaged in unjustifiable violence against people and property, but most were attracted by the chance to peacefully express their opposition to trade deals that did not ensure protection for the environment and the rights of workers. While violence in the pursuit of political ends is rarely, if ever, justified, the failure of police and other authorities to differentiate between the peaceful majority and the handful of troublemakers was disturbing.

Until our governments, police, and courts find more positive and measured ways to respond to "new" politics, the legitimacy of "old" politics may well continue to decline. Postmaterialist critiques of the political system go well beyond the current prime minister and Cabinet; they challenge the core values that underlie our political institutions.

CONCLUSION: THE FUTURE OF CANADA'S POLITICAL INSTITUTIONS

To assess the significance of the changes in Canada's political culture, we must try to figure out how they will affect our political institutions. To answer this question, it is helpful to summarize what we have learned:

- Canadians—especially younger Canadians—hold a less favourable opinion of their political institutions today than they did in the past.
- Both the legitimacy theory and the value-change theory offer some insight into the reasons for this change. As Canadians become more educated and more independent-minded, they are less likely to accept authority unquestioningly. At the same time, their criteria for evaluating their political system have become more stringent. It is no longer enough for a government to deliver prosperity and security; it must do so in a responsive and transparent way.
- In principle, more Canadians seem to believe that our politics and government would work better if we had more opportunities to participate directly. In practice, fewer of us are taking advantage of the opportunities currently available—joining a political party or casting a ballot. Many younger Canadians are prepared to engage in easy, short-term activities like emailing an MP or donating money online to an environmental group, but few are willing to commit to the hard work of real politics. There are exceptions, of course; someone has to organize the protests and write the petitions. But on the whole, the institutions that link us directly to our political leaders and allow us to hold them accountable are shriveling away for a lack of volunteers.

If we wanted to change our existing institutions to make them more participatory, there are some obvious options:

- electing the Senate;
- making our electoral system more proportional, so that every ballot counts;
- reviving our political parties; and
- opening up our policy-making processes.

As we will see in the rest of this book, however, there are major obstacles to all of these reforms. Real Senate reform would require a constitutional amendment, which is all but impossible under our current procedures. The existing electoral system is fiercely defended by governing parties (both federal and provincial), because it serves their political self-interest. Parties have little or no incentive to reach out to younger voters, partly because generous public subsidies have reduced their dependence on engaged citizens. Finally, the executive branch of government operates behind closed doors, often for legitimate reasons of confidentiality and security. Legislatures do their work in public, albeit in ways that sometimes alienate voters; the norms of strict party discipline and noisy adversarialism serve a purpose in the parliamentary setting, however off-putting they may be to citizens who are unfamiliar with their role in the legislative process.

For the foreseeable future, the mismatch between the political values of many Canadians and the nature of our political institutions will persist. Unless and until we can agree on whether and how to change our political system, reforms will be difficult if not impossible to achieve. As we will see in the next section of the book, our written constitution cannot be amended without a broad consensus. However, there are other tools at the disposal of institutional reformers: non-entrenched laws, court rulings, and unwritten conventions. While these have their limitations, they are currently the best hope for narrowing the gap between the expectations of Canadians and the performance of their institutions.

GLOSSARY OF KEY TERMS

Anglophone: English-speaking. For statistical purposes, the term "anglophone" normally refers to those Canadians who claim English as their mother tongue.

Cleavage: A politically significant distinction among identifiable groups in a given population. Examples: Catholic versus Protestant; religious versus nonobservant; French versus English; working class versus middle class; centre versus periphery; materialist versus postmaterialist. A distinction among groups becomes politically significant when it affects voting behaviour and/or attitudes toward political institutions (see the discussion of mobilization, below). Cleavage structures change over time, as new cleavages emerge (e.g., materialism versus postmaterialism) and as older cleavages either acquire new political significance (e.g., the French–English cleavage) or lose their historic significance (e.g., the Catholic–Protestant cleavage).

Demography: The distribution of certain personal characteristics among a particular population. Key demographic indicators include race, ethnicity, language, religion, age, and gender.

Direct democracy: The citizens govern themselves directly, at least in part, by making decisions about policies or the structure of government through the ballot box.

Francophone: French-speaking. For statistical purposes, the term "francophone" normally refers to those Canadians who claim French as their mother tongue.

Hierarchy: A social system arranged like a pyramid, in which those at the top control a disproportionate share of power (political, social, economic, or religious), while those at the bottom are virtually powerless. The criteria by which the members of the various ranks are chosen vary from culture to culture. In a monarchical society, birth determines one's place in the hierarchy: the king or queen is born to rule, (male) aristocrats are born to wealth and privilege, and the majority of the population is born to serve and to be ruled by their "betters." Other hierarchies are based on money, gender (generally speaking, men are more politically powerful than women), race (e.g., the former apartheid system in South Africa), or military prowess.

Ideology: A partial picture of the world, comprising stories about the past, explanations of the present, and a blueprint for the future. Because each ideology is only a partial picture, it must compete with other ideologies for political influence. It is both *empirical* (a description of the way things are) and *normative* (a prescription for how things should be).

Mobilization: The process by which a distinct group within an electorate is transformed into a politically influential subculture. Typically, a political leader from within the group begins to organize members into a cohesive entity with shared goals and values. In the absence of mobilization, a subculture remains latent; its members do not recognize their potential for collective action, and their common goals (if any) remain unexpressed within the political system. Examples of salient subcultures include Quebec nationalists and Western (especially Alberta) populists; postmaterialists may be a latent subculture, because they have not formed a unified organization with a clear political agenda.

Orientation: The psychological response of a particular individual toward a social object. In political terms, the degree to which a citizen internalizes or adopts prevailing social attitudes toward the political system as a whole, its individual parts, the elites who run it, and the laws that it creates and implements.

Political culture: "The politically relevant values, attitudes, beliefs, and symbols that exert an unseen but crucial influence on the political life of a society. Political culture helps shape the outlook and discourse of both ordinary citizens and political leaders. It affects the way they react and talk to one another, the problems they consider politically significant, the kinds of solutions and government policies deemed legitimate."[125]

Political socialization: The absorption of political knowledge and values by individual citizens. Socialization begins in childhood, with exposure to the political orientations of the parents. It continues in school, peer groups, and adult life. The process is not linear; many adolescents reject their parents' political values, only to return to them later. Orientations often change over time, as the citizen learns more about politics and acquires different life experiences (raising a family, losing a job, retiring). Orientations can also change in response to major political events.

Populism: See Dossier 2.2, page 33.

Post-industrial: The term used to describe advanced capitalist or mixed economies. More people are employed in the public sector or in private-sector service jobs than in factories, resource extraction and processing, and agriculture. Post-industrial states have knowledge-based economies, high levels of female employment, and (usually) declining rates of unionization.

Postmaterialism: See Dossier 2.2, page 33.

Regionalism: A feeling of attachment to a particular part of the country. That part can be a province (e.g., Alberta), a group of provinces (the Atlantic region), or an area within a province (Northern Ontario). Regionalism has both positive and negative aspects. On the positive side, it provides a sense of belonging and community. The negative aspect of regionalism is a sense of grievance against the central government and other regions—a belief that Ottawa discriminates against your region, or that other regions are reaping greater benefits from Confederation. Gibbins defines regionalism as "the intrusion of territorial cleavages into national politics."[126]

Representative democracy: A division of labour between rulers and the ruled. The citizens elect MPs to legislate on their behalf; if they are not satisfied with the results, they can defeat their MP at the next general election.

Subculture: A distinct and relatively stable group within the broader electorate. It may be distinguished by language (e.g., Canadian francophones), by ethnicity, by religion, by ideology (e.g., postmaterialists), or by region (e.g., Manitoba or Newfoundland). To be politically influential, a subculture must be cohesive and mobilized. In other words, its members must share some basic political principles that they are prepared to work hard to defend. Subcultures affect Canadian politics in various ways: they can form pressure groups to influence public policy (see Chapter 13), they can express their views through a political party (see Chapter 11), or they can simply withdraw from political activity altogether if they become alienated from a political system that appears to be unresponsive to their demands.

Xenophobic: Afraid of people who are unfamiliar and different from oneself.

DISCUSSION AND REVIEW QUESTIONS

1. Identify the two most important subcultures in the Canadian electorate. In your own words, describe the principal beliefs and goals of each one.

2. In your own words, summarize and contrast any four of the ideologies described in Dossier 2.2. Which, if any, of the four best describes your own ideas about politics and government?

3. In your own words, explain the concept of political legitimacy. Why is it important?

4. Identify and explain two important changes in Canada's political culture in recent years. What are the implications of those changes for our national political institutions?

5. Explain the concept of mobilization. Why is it crucial to the political influence of a distinct group within the electorate?

6. Identify and explain two of the three central themes in the mythology of Quebec nationalism.

7. Describe two of the direct-democracy devices discussed in Dossier 2.5. In your opinion, should either be used in Canadian federal politics? Why or why not?

SUGGESTED READINGS

Cameron D. Anderson and Elizabeth Goodyear-Grant, "Conceptions of Political Representation in Canada: An Explanation of Public Opinion," *Canadian Journal of Political Science* 38:4 (December 2005), 1029–1958.

David V.J. Bell, *The Roots of Disunity: A Study of Canadian Political Culture,* rev. edition (Toronto: Oxford University Press, 1992).

Robert Bothwell, *Canada and Quebec: One Country, Two Histories,* rev. edition (Vancouver: UBC Press, 1998).

Alan C. Cairns, *Charter versus Federalism: The Dilemmas of Constitutional Reform* (Montreal and Kingston: McGill–Queen's University Press, 1992).

Harold D. Clarke, Allan Kornberg, and Peter Wearing, *A Polity on the Edge: Canada and the Politics of Fragmentation* (Peterborough, ON: Broadview Press, 2000).

Bruce Gilley, "The Determinants of State Legitimacy: Results for 72 Countries," *International Political Science Review,* 27:1 (2006), 47–71.

Ailsa Henderson, "Regional Political Cultures in Canada," *Canadian Journal of Political Science* 37:3 (September 2004), 595–615.

Paul Howe and David Northrup, *Strengthening Canadian Democracy: The Views of Canadians* (Montreal: Institute for Research on Public Policy, 2000).

Ronald Inglehart and Christian Welzel, *Modernization, Cultural Change, and Democracy: The Human Development Sequence* (New York: Cambridge University Press, 2005).

Léger Marketing, *Voice of the People 2006: What the World Thinks on Today's Global Issues* (Montreal: Transcontinental Books, 2006).

John Meisel, Guy Rocher, and Arthur Silver, eds., *As I Recall/Si je me souviens bien: Historical Perspectives* (Montreal: Institute for Research on Public Policy, 1999).

Pippa Norris, ed., *Critical Citizens: Global Support for Democratic Governance* (Oxford: Oxford University Press, 1999).

Susan J. Pharr and Robert D. Putnam, eds., *Disaffected Democracies: What's Troubling the Trilateral Countries?* (Princeton: Princeton University Press, 2000).

Robert D. Putnam, *Bowling Alone: The Collapse and Revival of American Community* (New York: Simon and Schuster, 2000).

David E. Smith, *The Invisible Crown: The First Principle of Canadian Government* (Toronto: University of Toronto Press, 1995).

Lisa Young and Keith Archer, eds., *Regionalism and Party Politics in Canada* (Toronto: Oxford University Press, 2002).

NOTES

1. Donald J. Savoie, *Court Government and the Collapse of Accountability in Canada and the United Kingdom* (Toronto: University of Toronto Press, 2008), 41.

2. Gabriel A. Almond and Sidney Verba, *The Civic Culture: Political Attitudes and Democracy in Five Nations* (Princeton: Princeton University Press, 1963), 5. See also the discussion of congruence between political capacities and political institutions in Chapter 1 of this book.

3. Ibid., 13.

4. Ibid., 15.

5. Pippa Norris, "Introduction: The Growth of Critical Citizens?" in Pippa Norris, ed., *Critical Citizens: Global Support for Democratic Governance* (Oxford: Oxford University Press, 1999), 10–12.

6. Ibid., 10.

7. Almond and Verba, 32.

8. See, for example, Carole Pateman, "The Civic Culture: A Philosophic Critique," in Gabriel A. Almond and Sidney Verba, eds., *The Civic Culture Revisited* (Newbury Park, CA: Sage, 1989 [1980]).

9. Almond and Verba, *The Civic Culture,* 21.

10. Larry Diamond, "Introduction: Political Culture and Democracy," in Larry Diamond, ed., *Political Culture and Democracy in Developing Countries* (Boulder, CO: Lynne Rienner, 1993), 8.]

11. Shawn Henry, "Revisiting Western Alienation: Towards a Better Understanding of Political Alienation and Political Behaviour in Western Canada," in Lisa Young and Keith Archer, eds., *Regionalism and Party Politics in Canada* (Toronto: Oxford University Press, 2002), 85. See also Cameron D. Anderson and Elizabeth Goodyear-Grant, "Conceptions of Political Representation in Canada: An Explanation of Public Opinion," *Canadian Journal of Political Science,* 38:4 (December 2005), 1029–1058, and Ailsa Henderson, "Regional Political Cultures in Canada," *Canadian Journal of Political Science,* 37:3 (September 2004), 595–615.

12. David V.J. Bell, *The Roots of Disunity: A Study of Canadian Political Culture,* rev. edition (Toronto: Oxford University Press, 1992), 11.

13. Although Canada has a Liberal Party and a Conservative Party, these names do not necessarily describe the parties' respective ideologies. The Liberals are a broad political coalition, within which differing ideas are brokered into compromise positions. The Liberal Party has many members who might be described as right wing, and others who are clearly somewhat to the left. We will return to the subject of party ideologies in Chapter 11.

14. Colin Campbell and William Christian, *Parties, Leaders, and Ideologies in Canada* (Toronto: McGraw-Hill Ryerson, 1996), 12–13.

15. Roger Gibbins, "Shifting Sands: Exploring the Political Foundations of SUFA," in Sarah Fortin, Alain Noël, and France St-Hilaire, eds., *Forging the Canadian Social Union: SUFA and Beyond* (Montreal: Institute for Research on Public Policy, 2003), 43.

16. Louis Hartz, "The Fragmentation of European Culture and Ideology," in Louis Hartz, ed., *The Founding of New Societies* (New York: Harcourt Brace, 1964).

17. Hartz, "Fragmentation Patterns: Feudal, Liberal, and Radical" in Hartz, ed., *The Founding of New Societies,* 27; see also Kenneth D. McRae, "The Structure of Canadian History," in the same volume.

18. Bell, 19.

19. Gad Horowitz, "Conservatism, Liberalism, and Socialism in Canada: An Interpretation," in *Canadian Labour in Politics* (Toronto: University of Toronto Press, 1968).

20. Critics of the Horowitz thesis have argued that the "tory touch" is a figment of the imagination. They claim that the most important rival to liberalism in English Canada was not toryism, with its emphasis on hierarchy and deference, but American-inspired republicanism. The latter enshrined the values of popular (i.e., elected) government, rooted in the will of the people. See Janet Ajzenstat and Peter J. Smith, "Liberal–Republicanism: The Revisionist Picture of Canada's Founding," in Janet Ajzenstat and Peter J. Smith, eds., *Canada's Origins: Liberal, Tory, or Republican?* (Ottawa: Carleton University Press, 1995), 1–18; Hamish Telford, "The Reform Party/Canadian Alliance and Canada's Flirtation with Republicanism," in Hamish Telford and Harvey Lazar, eds., *The State of the Federation 2001: Canadian Political Culture(s) in Transition* (Montreal and Kingston: McGill–Queen's University Press/Institute of Intergovernmental Relations, 2002).

21. Bell, 131.

22. Henderson, 603–607.

23. Neil Nevitte, *The Decline of Deference: Canadian Value Change in Cross-National Perspective* (Peterborough, ON: Broadview Press, 1996), Tables 9-3 and 9-5, 296 and 308, respectively.

24. Efforts by particular ethnic communities to enter political parties have provoked a backlash against "bussing in" large numbers of Sikhs, Chinese, Italians, and others to vote for "their" candidates in constituency nomination battles. As we will see in Chapter 11, however, this practice is less common than the media coverage implies.

25. See, for example, S.M. Lipset, *Revolution and Counterrevolution: Change and Persistence in Social Structures,* rev. edition (New Brunswick, NJ: Transaction Books, 1988 [1970]), Chapter 2.

26. Bell, 23.

27. Lipset, 67–71.

28. McRae, "The Structure of Canadian History," 231.

29. Harry H. Hiller, "Region as a Social Construction," in Young and Archer, eds., *Regionalism and Party Politics in Canada,* 26.

30. See, for example, John Meisel, Guy Rocher, and Arthur Silver, eds., *As I Recall/Si je me souviens bien: Historical Perspectives* (Montreal: Institute for Research on Public Policy, 1999); Robert Bothwell, *Canada and Quebec: One Country, Two Histories,* rev. edition (Vancouver: UBC Press, 1998).

31. Nevitte, *The Decline of Deference,* 86. See also Léger Marketing, *Voice of the People 2006: What the World Thinks on Today's Global Issues* (Montreal: Transcontinental Books, 2006), 32 (Table 4).

32. Bell, 123.

33. Munroe Eagles, "Political Geography and the Study of Regionalism," in Young and Archer, eds., *Regionalism and Party Politics in Canada,* 13–14.

34. Statistics Canada, 2006 census data; accessed at www.statcan.gc.ca, May 2008.

35. Nevitte, *The Decline of Deference,* Tables 7-3 and 9-5, 220 and 308, respectively. See also Michael Adams, *Fire and Ice: The United States, Canada and the Myth of Converging Values* (Toronto: Penguin Canada, 2003), 82–83.

36. Ralph Matthews, *The Creation of Regional Dependency* (Toronto: University of Toronto Press, 1983), 22.

37. Russell J. Dalton, "Political Cleavages, Issues, and Electoral Change," in Lawrence LeDuc, Richard G. Niemi, and Pippa Norris, eds., *Comparing Democracies: Elections and Voting in Global Perspective* (Thousand Oaks, CA: Sage, 1996), Table 3.1, 325.

38. Alan C. Cairns, "The Governments and Societies of Canadian Federalism" [1977], in Douglas E. Williams, ed., *Constitution, Government, and Society in Canada: Selected Essays by Alan C. Cairns* (Toronto: McClelland and Stewart, 1988), 145.

39. Henderson, 604-605.

40. The number of respondents who claimed Aboriginal status was 1 172 790. However, the difficulties of administering the census on some reserves may have artificially lowered the true number. Source: Statistics Canada, accessed at www.statcan.gc.ca, May 2008.

41. Statistics Canada, "Number and percentage of population reporting Aboriginal identity, Canada, Provinces and Territories, 2006," accessed at www.statcan.gc.ca, May 2008.

42. For a relatively accessible introduction to Marxist theory, see Karl Marx and Friedrich Engels, *The Communist Manifesto* (Harmondsworth: Penguin, 2002 [1848]), Chapters 1 and 2.

43. See, for example, Dalton, "Political Cleavages, Issues, and Electoral Change," 325.

44. Janine Brodie and Jane Jenson, *Crisis, Challenge and Change: Party and Class in Canada Revisited* (Ottawa: Carleton University Press, 1988).

45. The theory of postmaterialism, despite the name, is actually grounded in a materialist analysis of history. According to Ronald Inglehart, who first formulated the theory, postmaterialist values flourish in a thriving economy and in the absence of direct threats to physical security. Therefore, to argue that Canadians are increasingly attracted to postmaterialist values does not imply that we are no longer influenced by materialism; rather, it means that material scarcity is no longer the only driving force in political conflict. See Ronald Inglehart, *The Silent Revolution: Changing Values and Political Styles* (Princeton: Princeton University Press, 1977); *Culture Shift in Advanced Industrial Society* (Princeton: Princeton University Press, 1990); *Modernization and Postmodernization: Cultural, Economic, and Political Change in 43 Societies* (Princeton: Princeton University Press, 1997).

46. See also Nevitte, *The Decline of Deference*, 32–33, and Bell, Chapter One.

47. Nevitte, *The Decline of Deference*, 311.

48. Adams, 52 and 95.

49. This taxonomy of theories is based on the categorization in Ronald Inglehart and Christian Welzel, *Modernization, Cultural Change, and Democracy: The Human Development Sequence* (New York: Cambridge University Press, 2005), 247.

50. Ibid., 247.

51. Harold D. Clarke, Allan Kornberg, and Peter Wearing, *A Polity on the Edge: Canada and the Politics of Fragmentation* (Peterborough, ON: Broadview Press, 2000), 47 and 163.

52. Neil Nevitte, "Introduction: Value Change and Reorientation in Citizen–State Relations," in Neil Nevitte, ed., *Value Change and Governance in Canada* (Toronto: University of Toronto Press, 2002), 20.

53. On the possible emergence of "transnational" notions of citizenship, especially among immigrants and their children, see Will Kymlicka, "New Forms of Citizenship," in Thomas J. Courchene and Donald J. Savoie, eds., *The Art of the State: Governance in a World Without Frontiers* (Montreal: Institute for Research on Public Policy, 2003), 265–309.

54. Nevitte, "Introduction," 20. See also Richard Nadeau, "Satisfaction with Democracy: The Canadian Paradox," in Nevitte, ed., *Value Change and Governance in Canada*, 37–70.

55. Clarke, Kornberg, and Wearing, 47.

56. Paul Howe and David Northrup, *Strengthening Canadian Democracy: The Views of Canadians* (Montreal: Institute for Research on Public Policy, 2000), 6. In the 2005 World Values Survey, 85 percent of Canadians said that democracy is "the best system of government"; the world average was 79 percent. Léger Marketing, 43 (Table 1).

57. Russell J. Dalton, "Political Support in Advanced Industrial Democracies," in Pippa Norris, ed., *Critical Citizens*, 75.

58. Arthur Miller and Ola Listhaug, "Political Performance and Institutional Trust," in Pippa Norris, ed., *Critical Citizens*, 210.

59. Norris, "Institutional Explanations for Political Support," *Critical Citizens*.

60. Howe and Northrup, 64–65.

61. Miller and Listhaug, 209; Clarke, Kornberg, and Wearing, 74–75. In 1992, in the depths of a recession, 24 percent of Canadians were satisfied with the performance of the federal government, down from 51 percent in 1986. See also Robert D. Putnam, Susan J. Pharr,

and Russell J. Dalton, "Introduction: What's Troubling the Trilateral Democracies?" in Susan J. Pharr and Robert D. Putnam, eds., *Disaffected Democracies: What's Troubling the Trilateral Countries?* (Princeton: Princeton University Press, 2000), 10.

62. Putnam, Pharr and Dalton, 23.

63. Henderson, 600 (Table 1).

64. The figure was 60 percent, compared to 36 percent who said that the country is governed by the will of the people. The world averages were 65 and 30 percent, respectively. Léger Marketing, 49.

65. Nevitte, "Introduction," 21–23.

66. Ibid., 10.

67. Clarke, Kornberg, and Wearing, 127–29.

68. Ian McAllister, "The Economic Performance of Governments," in Pippa Norris, ed., *Critical Citizens*, 195.

69. Howe and Northrup, 9; Mebs Kanji, "Political Discontent, Human Capital, and Representative Governance in Canada," in Neil Nevitte, ed., *Value Change and Governance in Canada*, 79; Gabriela Catterberg and Alejandro Moreno, "The Individual Bases of Political Trust: Trends in New and Established Democracies," *International Journal of Public Opinion Research*, 18:1 (2005), 31–48.

70. Howe and Northrup, 100. See also Darrell Bricker and John Wright, *What Canadians Think (About Almost Everything)* (Toronto: Doubleday Canada, 2005), 13.

71. Norris, "The Growth of Critical Citizens?" *Critical Citizens*, 13.

72. Léger Marketing, *Voice of the People*, 141.

73. Howe and Northrup, Table 2, 7.

74. Bruce Gilley, "The Determinants of State Legitimacy: Results for 72 Countries," *International Political Science Review*, 27:1 (2006), 47–71.

75. Abraham Diskin, Hanna Diskin, and Reuven Hazan, "Why Democracies Collapse: The Reasons for Democratic Failure and Success," *International Political Science Review*, 26:3 (2005), 291–309.

76. Inglehart and Welzel, 250–253 and 263–270.

77. See, for example, Robert D. Putnam, "Bowling Alone: America's Declining Social Capital," in Larry Diamond and Marc F. Plattner, eds., *The Global Resurgence of Democracy*, 2nd edition (Baltimore, MD: Johns Hopkins University Press, 1996); Putnam, *The Decline of Civil Society: How Come? So What?* (Ottawa: Canadian Centre for Management Development, 1996); Putnam, *Bowling Alone: The Collapse and Revival of American Community* (New York: Simon and Schuster, 2000).

78. Putnam, *Bowling Alone*, 288–89.

79. Ibid., 342–43.

80. Ibid., 347.

81. Ibid., 336.

82. Ibid., 341.

83. See, for example, Eric M. Uslaner, "Democracy and Social Capital," in Mark E. Warren, ed., *Democracy and Trust* (Cambridge: Cambridge University Press, 1999).

84. Richard A. Couto with Catherine S. Guthrie, *Making Democracy Work Better: Mediating Structures, Social Capital, and the Democratic Prospect* (Chapel Hill: University of North Carolina Press, 1999), 68.

85. Kenneth Newton, "Social and Political Trust in Established Democracies," in Pippa Norris, ed., *Critical Citizens*, 172–73 and 180.

86. In the 2005 World Values Survey, 57 percent of Canadians reported that they had done volunteer work in the past 12 months. That figure is twice as high as the global average (28 percent), and second only to Norway (67 percent). Léger Marketing, *Voice of the People*, 123.

87. Inglehart and Welzel, 294.

88. Putnam, *Bowling Alone,* 229.

89. Thomas E. Patterson, *Out of Order* (New York: Vintage, 1994); David Taras, *The Newsmakers: The Media's Influence on Canadian Politics* (Toronto: Nelson, 1990).

90. Neil Postman, *Amusing Ourselves to Death: Public Discourse in the Age of Show Business* (Harmondsworth: Penguin, 1985); Benjamin I. Page, *Who Deliberates? Mass Media in Modern Democracy* (Chicago: University of Chicago Press, 1996).

91. Pippa Norris, "The Impact of Television on Civic Malaise," in Pharr and Putnam, eds., *Disaffected Democracies,* Table 10.4, 238.

92. Ibid., 246.

93. Pippa Norris, *A Virtuous Circle: Political Communications in Postindustrial Societies* (Cambridge: Cambridge University Press, 2000), 20.

94. Ronald Inglehart, *The Silent Revolution: Changing Values and Political Styles* (Princeton: Princeton University Press, 1977); *Culture Shift in Advanced Industrial Society* (Princeton: Princeton University Press, 1990); *Modernization and Postmodernization: Cultural, Economic, and Political Change in 43 Societies* (Princeton: Princeton University Press, 1997).

95. Inglehart and Welzel, 4.

96. Ibid., 123.

97. Although Inglehart and Welzel's data do not explicitly reflect the impact of 9/11, those events may have prompted a temporary revival of survival values at the expense of self-expression.

98. Inglehart and Welzel, 299.

99. Kenneth McRoberts, *Quebec: Social Change and Political Crisis,* 3rd edition (Toronto: McClelland and Stewart, 1988), Chapter 4.

100. Significantly, the PQ's surviving electoral base—like that of its federal cousin, the Bloc Québécois—overlaps to a high degree with Henderson's "New France" constituencies. Despite the legacy of this conservative "fragment," Québécois are more likely than other Canadians to espouse "self-expression values," including equality for women and for gays and lesbians. If Inglehart and Welzel are correct, these values may be linked to the unusual frequency of referenda in that province; they might also help to explain why so many francophone Quebeckers support the idea of sovereignty, which promises symbolic recognition for their "nation" at the risk of economic costs.

101. Quebec, Commission de consultation sur les pratiques d'accommodement reliées aux différences culturelles, *Final Report* (abridged version) (Gouvernement du Québec 2008), 94 and 86; accessed at www.accommodements.qc.ca, May 2008.

102. Alan C. Cairns, *Disruptions: Constitutional Struggles, from the Charter to Meech Lake,* edited by Douglas E. Williams (Toronto: McClelland and Stewart, 1991).

103. Alan C. Cairns, *Charter versus Federalism: The Dilemmas of Constitutional Reform* (Montreal and Kingston: McGill–Queen's University Press, 1992), 3.

104. Ian Brodie and Neil Nevitte, "Evaluating the Citizens' Constitution Theory," *Canadian Journal of Political Science,* 26:2 (June 1993), 258.

105. F.L. Morton and Rainer Knopff, *The Charter Revolution and the Court Party* (Peterborough, ON: Broadview Press, 2000). We will return to the *Charter* and its impact on Canadian politics in Chapters 6 and 10.

106. Ian Budge, *The New Challenge of Direct Democracy* (Cambridge: Polity Press, 1996), 101.

107. Todd Donovan and Shaun Bowler, "An Overview of Direct Democracy in the American States," in Shaun Bowler, Todd Donovan, and Caroline J. Tolbert, eds., *Citizens as Legislators: Direct Democracy in the United States* (Columbus: Ohio State University Press, 1998), 2; Thomas E. Cronin, *Direct Democracy: The Politics of Initiative, Referendum, and Recall* (Cambridge, MA: Harvard University Press, 1989), 182–83.

108. Canada, *Royal Commission on Electoral Reform and Party Financing, Reforming Electoral Democracy,* volume 2 (Ottawa: Minister of Supply and Services Canada, 1991), 238.

109. Ibid.

110. Cronin, 109.

111. Donovan and Bowler, 12.

112. Cronin, 61.

113. Lawrence LeDuc and Jon H. Pammett, "Referendum Voting: Attitudes and Behaviour in the 1992 Constitutional Referendum," *Canadian Journal of Political Science,* 28:1 (March 1995), 31.

114. Richard Johnston, André Blais, Elisabeth Gidengil, and Neil Nevitte, *The Challenge of Direct Democracy: The 1992 Canadian Referendum* (Montreal and Kingston: McGill–Queen's University Press, 1996), 177 and 189.

115. Caroline J. Tolbert and Rodney E. Hero, "Race/Ethnicity and Direct Democracy: The Contextual Basis of Support for Anti-Immigrant and Official English Measures," in Bowler, Donovan, and Tolbert, eds., 209–27; Cronin, 94–96.

116. Todd Donovan and Shaun Bowler, "Responsive or Responsible Government?" in Bowler, Donovan, and Tolbert, eds., 270.

117. James Wenzel, Todd Donovan, and Shaun Bowler, "Direct Democracy and Minorities: Changing Attitudes about Minorities Targeted by Initiatives," in Bowler, Donovan, and Tolbert, eds., 245.

118. Cronin, 133.

119. Ibid., 137.

120. See Samuel Issacharoff, "Collateral Damage: The Endangered Center in American Politics," *William and Mary Law Review,* 2005 (accessed at http://ssrn.com/abstract=508384, October 15, 2004); Elizabeth Garrett, "Democracy in the Wake of the California Recall," *University of Pennsylvania Law Review,* volume 152, 2004 (accessed at http://ssrn.com/abstract=487623, October 15, 2004).

121. *Reforming Electoral Democracy,* volume 2, 245–47.

122. Inglehart, *Modernization and Postmodernization,* Chapter 8; Brodie and Nevitte, 239–40.

123. Nevitte, *The Decline of Deference,* Figure 4-2, 80.

124. W. Wesley Pue, ed., *Pepper in Our Eyes: The APEC Affair* (Vancouver: UBC Press, 2000).

125. Bell, 19.

126. Roger Gibbins, *Regionalism: Territorial Politics in Canada and the United States* (Toronto: Butterworths, 1982), 5.

Part II

The Canadian Constitution

3

Constitutions

After you finish reading this chapter, you should be able to:

- *define* a "constitution," and *explain* its role in law and government;
- *identify* and *explain* the four elements of the Canadian *Constitution*, providing at least one *example* to illustrate each one; and
- *describe* and *distinguish* among the major amending formulas in the *Constitution Act, 1982*.

INTRODUCTION

Imagine a group of friends getting together to watch a big international soccer match on television. A few root for one team or the other; the rest don't care who wins—they just enjoy watching the action. After 80 minutes of a scoreless tie, two players from opposing sides confront each other. One head-butts the other, who promptly falls to the ground and appears to be seriously injured (this being soccer, it's hard to tell). The referee's ruling on the head-butt could determine the outcome of the match, if the injured player's side is awarded a penalty kick or the attacker—who happens to be his team's best striker—is thrown out. The spectators in the living room start to argue about the legality of the head-butt and the sanction that should follow.

How should the conflict be resolved? Which rules of the game should apply to this case? What if the referee, instead of holding up a penalty card, asked the crowd to decide by voting? If this particular referee were known (or widely believed) to be biased in favour of the home team, how would that affect the likelihood of his decision being accepted by both sides? The intensely competitive nature of sports inevitably leads to conflict. To prevent matters from getting out of hand, there must be clear and binding rules with clear sanctions for deliberate violations. Some are contained in a rule book; others emerge over years of competition and hundreds of referee rulings. Whether they are written or unwritten, the rules of the game are (or should be) known to every player before he or she takes the field. That way, the athletes, officials, and spectators know what is permissible and what is not.

Politics, like soccer, is an intensely competitive game. The most important rules are set out in the *Constitution*. Recall the Supreme Court's statement (Dossier 1.5, p. 16) that "the exercise of all public power must find its ultimate source in a legal rule." As the "supreme law of Canada," our *Constitution* both grants and limits the legitimate power that our governments may exert over our lives. This chapter explains the general principles of constitutional law, the four key elements of the Canadian *Constitution*, and the procedures for adapting a constitution to changing circumstances. Chapter 4 discusses federalism and the mechanisms of intergovernmental relations through which it operates. Chapter 5 describes two rounds of "megaconstitutional" negotiations in the 1980s and 1990s, and the nonconstitutional methods of institutional change to which our governments have resorted since 1992. Chapter 6 explores the impact of the *Canadian Charter of Rights and Freedoms* on Canada's government and politics.

THE PURPOSE OF A CONSTITUTION

Constitutions do more than set out the rules by which the political game is played. They also define the relationships among the various players. Three such relationships are particularly important:

1. the balance among the executive, legislative, and judicial branches of government;
2. the division of powers and responsibilities between the national government and the **subnational** governments (recall the discussion of federal and unitary states in Chapter 1); and
3. the relationship between the state and the people: the rights and obligations of citizens, the shared values and symbols that legitimate political authority, and the collective aspirations of the political community.

These three relationships are summarized in Table 3.1.

TABLE 3.1 THE THREE RELATIONSHIPS GOVERNED BY THE ENTRENCHED CONSTITUTION

RELATIONSHIP	RELEVANT SECTIONS OF THE ENTRENCHED CONSTITUTION
Balance among the various branches of government: legislature, executive, and judiciary[1]	*Constitution Act, 1867*: Preamble (responsible Cabinet government); Part III (executive power); Part IV (legislative power); Part VII (judicial power); section 132 (treaty-making powers)
	Constitution Act, 1982: Section 24 (judicial remedy for a breach of rights); section 33 (the "notwithstanding clause"); section 52 (the power of the courts to strike down laws that conflict with the *Constitution*)
Division of powers and responsibilities among the federal and provincial governments	*Constitution Act, 1867*: Part V (provincial constitutions); sections 57, 58, and 90 (reservation and disallowance of provincial laws); Part VI (distribution of legislative powers); section 109 (mineral rights and revenues assigned to the provinces)
	Constitution Act, 1982: Part III (equalization and regional disparities); Part V (amending formula)
Relationship between the state and the people	*Constitution Act, 1987*: Sections 37, 40–41, 50–52 (election of members of the House of Commons); section 92(13) (property and civil rights); section 94 (uniformity of laws concerning civil rights)
	Constitution Act, 1982: Part I (*Canadian Charter of Rights and Freedoms*); Part II (Aboriginal rights)

THE FOUR ELEMENTS OF THE CANADIAN *CONSTITUTION*

Although we usually speak of "the *Constitution*" as though it were found in a single document, the supreme law of Canada incorporates both written and unwritten rules of political conduct. The written elements are **entrenched** constitutional laws, **nonentrenched** laws, and judicial rulings on the *Constitution*. The unwritten *Constitution* is made up of **constitutional conventions** that guide the behaviour of politicians and the expectations of voters. Collectively, these four elements strike a balance between two requirements: the need for stability and continuity in the basic rules of politics, and the need to adapt the *Constitution* to changing social and political conditions (see Table 3.2).

■ Entrenched Constitutional Law

The written *Constitution* overrides all other written laws. Unlike ordinary statutes, which can be changed or repealed at any time, entrenched constitutional laws remain in force for decades or even centuries. This permanence reflects the need for stable government: the basic rules of the political game must not be changed on a whim or manipulated to serve the interest of the current government.

Because constitutional text is supposed to remain intact for years at a time, it must be written broadly to allow its interpretation to change as the society evolves. The process of ratifying or amending a written constitution is deliberately made complex and difficult, to deter ill-considered or harmful changes. The term "entrenched" refers to the specific written laws that have been ratified under this special procedure. Canada's constitutional **amendment** process is described in Dossier 3.3.

TABLE 3.2 **THE FOUR ELEMENTS OF THE CANADIAN *CONSTITUTION***

CATEGORY	PARTICULAR ELEMENTS	DEFINITION	EXAMPLES
Written	Entrenched laws	Constitutional documents and formal amendments	*Constitution Act, 1867* *Constitution Act, 1982*
	Nonentrenched laws	Ordinary federal laws that regulate the application of entrenched laws	The *Supreme Court Act*, 1875 The *Indian Act*, 1876 The *Bill of Rights*, 1960 The *Regional Veto Act*, 1996
	Common law	Judicial interpretations of the *Constitution* by the Judicial Committee of the Privy Council (pre-1949) and the Supreme Court of Canada (1875–present)	*Edwards v. A-G Canada, 1929* (the "Persons Case") The *Patriation Reference, 1981* The *Secession Reference, 1998*
Unwritten	Constitutional convention	Unwritten, binding rules that constrain the behaviour of political actors; not enforceable by the courts, but violations may bring political sanctions	Executive power is exercised by the prime minister and Cabinet, not by the governor general

In Canada, the most important entrenched documents are the 1867 and 1982 *Constitution Acts*. The *Constitution Act, 1867*—formerly called the *British North America Act* or "*BNA Act*"—established the new Dominion of Canada. It defines the powers of the national political institutions and divides jurisdiction over policy-making between the federal and provincial governments. However, it says very little about the relationship between states and citizens.[2] The protection of individual rights and freedoms was left to Parliament and the British **common law** (in Quebec, the civil law). The only legitimating symbol is the Crown; there was no attempt to enshrine uniquely Canadian myths and symbols to inspire and unite the new country.

While the *Constitution Act, 1982* defined individual and group rights—in the *Canadian Charter of Rights and Freedoms,* and the subsequent sections on Aboriginal rights—it too was silent about shared values and symbols. Many national constitutions begin with a lyrical preamble about shared beliefs and collective aspirations. The preamble of the 1982 Act simply states that "Canada is founded upon the principles that recognize the supremacy of God and the rule of law."

Although the permanence of entrenched constitutional text helps to preserve political stability, it can cause problems. Over time, political values and social conditions evolve. If the constitution cannot adapt, the widening gap between the values of citizens and the character of their political institutions may undermine the legitimacy of the political system. A proper balance must be struck between permanence and flexibility. Formal amending processes are often inadequate in this respect, because their slowness and complexity are obstacles to change. Fortunately, the other three elements of the constitution provide a degree of flexibility.

◼ Nonentrenched Law

Some laws and documents are considered to have quasi-constitutional status, although they are not formally entrenched.[3] These include:

- the *Supreme Court Act* of 1875, which established Canada's highest court of appeal and gave the executive branch the right to refer constitutional questions directly to the courts (these are called **reference** cases);
- The *Canadian Bill of Rights* (Dossier 6.1);
- The *Canada Elections Act,* which regulates elections to the House of Commons (Chapters 11 and 12);
- The *Clarity Act,* which prescribes the process by which a province can legally separate from Canada (Dossier 5.3); and
- The *Regional Veto Act* of 1996, which prohibits the federal Parliament from ratifying any future constitutional amendment that has not been approved by all five "regions" (Chapter 5).

In form, these are ordinary federal laws that may be amended or repealed by a simple majority of both Houses of Parliament. However, their content belongs within the constitutional realm. The *Constitution* establishes the general rules for the political system; the nonentrenched laws spell out the detailed processes for putting those rules into practice. For example, Section 3 of the *Charter* states that every Canadian citizen has the right to vote, and to run, in elections to the House of Commons (as well as provincial legislatures). The vast and intricate machinery required to elect over 300 MPs in separate constituencies on a single day is set out in the *Canada Elections Act.*

Because these nonentrenched laws can be amended quickly and easily, they provide some flexibility in the application of the rules. On the other hand, "nonconstitutional renewal" suffers from serious limitations—including the difficulty of enforcement. We will return to the question of institutional change via nonentrenched statutes in Chapter 5.

■ Judicial Decisions

The third written element in our constitutional law is the collection of judicial rulings that interpret the meaning of its various provisions. Collectively, court decisions are called "common law" or "case law." As we have seen, written constitutions remain in force for many years. Because the people who write them cannot foresee the future, they deliberately use vague and general language to cover all possible circumstances. The precise meaning of the *Constitution* is left to judges, who must interpret its general principles and apply them to each unique situation. The process of authoritative constitutional interpretation is called **judicial review**.

Dossier 3.1 describes a famous example of judicial review. It shows how judges reinterpret constitutional phrases to keep pace with changing public attitudes.

The doctrine of judicial review is an American invention. It was created by former U.S. Chief Justice John Marshall in the 1803 case *Marbury v. Madison*.[4] Marshall declared that his Supreme Court had the power to strike down laws that violated the *U.S. Constitution*. The claim that a court can overrule an elected legislature is alien to the British tradition of parliamentary supremacy, which gives the legislative branch the final word on public policy. But in a federation that divides the legislative power between two levels of government, there must be some mechanism to settle disputes. A supreme or constitutional court with the power to strike down laws is

DOSSIER 3.1 The "Persons Case"

Section 24 of the *BNA Act* sets out the procedure for appointing senators. It reads, in part: "The Governor General shall from Time to Time . . . summon qualified Persons to the Senate." In 1927 the Supreme Court of Canada was asked to determine whether the word "Persons" included women. Until that time, no woman had ever been "summoned" to the Canadian Senate. Five Alberta women—Irene Parlby, Nellie McClung, Emily Murphy, Louise McKinney, and Henrietta Muir Edwards—took the Government of Canada to court to try to force Prime Minister Mackenzie King to appoint Murphy to the Senate. Each was already a public figure in her own right.[5] Nellie McClung led the fight for female suffrage in Manitoba and later served in the Alberta legislature. Emily Murphy was the first female magistrate in the British Empire. Louise McKinney was the first woman in the British Empire to be sworn in as an elected legislator. Henrietta Muir Edwards and Irene Parlby were the chair and vice chair of the Legal Committee of the National Council of Women; the latter was also the second woman ever appointed to a provincial Cabinet (the first was in British Columbia). With the support of the Alberta government, the "Famous Five" argued that women had already won the

right to vote and to run for elective office; therefore, it made no sense to exclude them from the appointed Senate.

The Supreme Court of Canada disagreed, ruling unanimously that women were not "Persons." They relied on past legal precedents, which had denied women the right to hold public office, and claimed that the Fathers of Confederation could not have intended section 24 to include women. Because women were not legal "Persons" in 1867, they could not be considered as such in 1928.

The case was appealed to the Judicial **Committee of the Privy Council (JCPC)**.[6] On October 18, 1929, the JCPC overturned the Supreme Court decision.[7] Declaring that "the exclusion of women from all public offices is a relic of days more barbarous than ours," the Law Lords refused to restrict the meaning of the *BNA Act* to what it had been in 1867: "The *British North America Act* planted in Canada a living tree capable of growth and expansion within its natural limits. . . . Their Lordships do not conceive it to be the duty of this Board to cut down the provisions of this Act by a narrow and technical construction, but rather to give it a large and liberal interpretation." They noted that sections 41 and

(continued)

84 of the Act referred to the election of "Persons" to Parliament and the provincial legislatures; in that context, the word "Persons" now expressly included women (except in Quebec). Therefore, the meaning of the word "Persons" was clearly adaptable to changing attitudes and circumstances. The JCPC concluded that "the word 'per-sons' in s. 24 includes members both of the male and female sex." The "Persons Case" was a legal triumph for Canadian women, although none of the victorious five was ever appointed to the Senate. On October 18, 2000, a monument to the "Famous Five" was unveiled on Parliament Hill—right next to the Senate Chamber.

| Irene Parlby | Louise McKinney | Nellie McClung | Henrietta Muir Edwards | Emily Murphy |

(Glenbow Archives, NA-273-3, NA-273-1, NA-325-1, NA-15143, NA-2607-1)

the most common such mechanism. Before the proclamation of the *Canadian Charter of Rights and Freedoms* in 1982, judicial review of our *Constitution* was largely confined to the division of powers in the *BNA Act*. Since 1982, the courts have also had the power to declare null and void any federal and provincial laws that infringe protected rights and freedoms.[8]

Constitutional Conventions: The Unwritten *Constitution*

Constitutional conventions are unwritten rules for political conduct. They are based on custom and precedent, although they are more than just practical expedients or habits. Political actors obey a constitutional convention because they feel morally and/or politically obligated to do so. To be accepted as valid, a convention must reflect one or more of the central constitutional values identified in Dossier 1.5.

This unwritten element in Canada's *Constitution* is the third and final source of flexibility. It allows the *Constitution* to adapt to changes in the political environment—such as evolving cultural values or new socioeconomic conditions—without resorting to the difficult process of formal amendment.[9]

> *Constitutional conventions are the means through which constitutional morality is brought into contact with political reality. For their meaning is dependent upon the configuration of power in a society and upon popular assumptions about how that power should be regulated.*[10]

Because they are unwritten, conventions cannot be enforced by the courts. Nonetheless, Canadian governments sometimes ask the courts to resolve disputes about the meaning, even the very existence, of a constitutional convention. The most famous example is the 1981 *Patriation Reference*, in which three provincial governments asked their Courts of Appeal whether the federal government had the power to entrench the *Charter* and an **amending formula** without their consent. (See Chapter 5.) At the time, there were no written rules for amending the *BNA Act*. So the provincial courts, and eventually the Supreme Court of Canada, had to resort to the unwritten rules of constitutional procedure. What were the constitutional conventions governing constitutional amendment? Specifically, was there a constitutional convention requiring either unanimous or substantial provincial consent to a constitutional amendment altering the division of powers between Ottawa and the provinces?

The majority ruling of the Supreme Court defined the purpose of constitutional conventions: "to ensure that the legal framework of the Constitution will be operated in accordance with the prevailing constitutional values or principles of the period."[11] The justices observed that conventions allow our political institutions to adapt to changes in political culture, without the necessity of formally amending the written constitution. After reviewing the historical evidence, the majority concluded that a constitutional convention had been established. No amendment to the division of powers in the *BNA Act* could be ratified without substantial—but not unanimous—provincial consent. So while the Trudeau Government's plan to amend the *Constitution* unilaterally was technically legal (there were no written rules to be broken), it violated the unwritten rules of constitutional procedure.

The *Patriation Reference* ruling "cast a heavy mantle of political illegitimacy"[12] over the Trudeau plan, forcing the federal government to seek provincial consent for its constitutional amendment package. In this instance, the judicial review of a constitutional convention resolved a paralyzing political conflict. At the same time, it provoked a serious and still unresolved conflict over another alleged convention: Quebec's claim to a veto over constitutional amendments. (See Dossier 3.2.)

DOSSIER 3.2   Are Constitutional Conventions in the Eye of the Beholder?

The majority ruling in the *Patriation Reference* sent the 11 senior governments back to the constitutional bargaining table in November 1981. The federal government and nine of the provinces eventually agreed to patriate the *Constitution* and to entrench both the *Charter of Rights* and an amending formula. The government of Quebec, the lone holdout, appealed to the Supreme Court to strike down the *Constitution Act, 1982.* (See Chapter 5 for a more extensive discussion of the 1981 accord.)

The Quebec government argued that proclaiming a constitutional amendment without its consent would violate two conventions. First, it asserted a convention of unanimous provincial consent to amendments that altered the division of powers between the two levels of government. The court had already declared in the *Patriation Reference* that no such convention existed; it upheld that finding in the 1982 *Quebec Veto Reference.* Second, Quebec cited the "two-nations" vision of Canadian federalism—the Quebec nationalist claim that Confederation was a deal between two founding nations, English and French.[13] Because Quebec nationalists

perceive their province as the homeland of the French "nation" in Canada, they claim the right to veto any proposed change to national institutions. The justices dismissed this argument, ruling that the historical evidence did not support the alleged convention of special status. Having rejected Quebec's claim to a unilateral veto over constitutional amendments, the court allowed the proclamation of the *Constitution Act, 1982* to proceed.

Angry Quebec nationalists charged that the Supreme Court was biased in favour of the federal government that appointed its members. Although the court's decision may have been correct as a matter of law, the political fallout was damaging. If constitutional conventions are indeed a reflection of political culture, as argued earlier, it is reasonable to expect that different subcultures will interpret historical precedents in varying ways. So it is no surprise that Quebec nationalists still claim the right to a veto over changes to the original "deal" on which Canada was founded. That claim became a central issue in the megaconstitutional politics of the late 1980s and early 1990s, as we will see in Chapter 5.

Despite the difficulties arising from subjectivity and the need for historical evidence, unwritten conventions are an essential element in our constitutional and political structure. Over time, some parts of a written constitution become obsolete as historical circumstances and political culture change. Possible examples include the federal powers of disallowance and reservation in the *BNA Act* (see Table 4.1) and the "notwithstanding clause" in the *Charter.* Other provisions, which reflected the prevailing political values at the time of their adoption, lose their moral force as the political culture changes. New conventions evolve to take their place, some of which are inconsistent with the wording of the entrenched *Constitution.*

Today, students are often surprised by the difference between the text of the *Constitution Act, 1867* and the day-to-day operation of our political system. For example, the entrenched *Constitution* gives the governor general virtually unlimited executive power: "a dictatorship, the autocratic rule of one central figure, acting in the place of the Sovereign, who governs the Dominion with little reference to, or control by the people. The only popular element is apparently supplied by a House of Commons, which meets when the governor desires, considers financial legislation which he recommends, and can be forced into an election whenever he deems it desirable."[14] In reality, of course, Canada is a parliamentary democracy. Most of the executive powers of the Crown are exercised by the prime minister and his or her Cabinet. While as a matter of law they merely "advise" the governor general, in practice he or she always defers to the "political executive." Any attempt by a governor general to exercise executive power without the consent of the Cabinet and the House of Commons would be an outrageous violation of democratic norms and constitutional conventions, even though it would be technically legal under the terms of the *1867 Constitution.*

In effect, "The critical underpinnings of democratic, responsible government in Canada are to be found not in the 'written' *Constitution* but in the constitutional conventions inherited from the United Kingdom."[15] Those conventions are enshrined in the Preamble to the *BNA Act,* which refers to "a Constitution similar in Principle to that of the United Kingdom." On that seemingly innocuous phrase rests the entire structure of responsible Cabinet government. The power of conventions was demonstrated in November 2005, when the Opposition parties passed a motion declaring that the House of Commons had lost confidence in the minority Liberal Government of Paul Martin. Martin had to resign as prime minister and ask the governor general to dissolve Parliament for a general election. The rule that the Government remains in office only so long as it enjoys the confidence of a majority of MPs does not appear anywhere in the written *Constitution;* it is one of the conventions inherited from Britain and implicitly cited in the 1867 Preamble. Yet it brought down a prime minister and Cabinet after less than two years in power, and ultimately led to the election of a new Government in its place. As if to illustrate the flexibility of unwritten conventions, the Governor General deviated from past precedent in December 2008: she granted Prime Minister Harper's request to prorogue Parliament (see Chapter 7) in order to avoid defeat on a confidence vote. In so doing, she may have irreparably weakened our tradition of responsible government and eroded the power of future Crown representatives in Canada; but we will not know until a future prime minister makes a similar request whether the December 2008 incident was an exception or a permanent change to constitutional convention.

CHANGING CANADA'S ENTRENCHED *CONSTITUTION:* THE 1982 AMENDING FORMULAS

As we explained earlier, entrenched written constitutions are expected to last for decades. Consequently, the process of amending constitutions requires a broader consensus than the procedure for changing an ordinary statute. Whereas a regular federal or provincial law can be changed or repealed by a simple majority vote in one legislature, a proposed constitutional amendment may need the support of two-thirds of the legislators (as in the United States). Some countries also require ratification (i.e., formal approval) by a majority of the voters in a referendum. In most federal states, an amendment that affects the division of powers must be ratified by at least a majority of the subnational governments. In the United States, for example, any amendment to the *Constitution* must be approved by the federal Congress and three-quarters of the state legislatures (Article V).

The *Constitution Act, 1867* did not contain a comprehensive amending formula. It was an ordinary British statute, passed by the Parliament at Westminster. Therefore, it could only be amended by the British Parliament. As Chapter 5 explains, the "patriation" of our *Constitution* and the creation of an amending formula were at least as important to the drafters of the *Constitution Act, 1982* as the entrenchment of the *Charter of Rights*. After decades of conflict between Ottawa and the provinces, Part V of the *Constitution Act, 1982* entrenched a varied menu of amending formulas (see Dossier 3.3 for a brief summary).

DOSSIER 3.3   The 1982 Amending Formulas

Sections 38–40 set out the *general* amending formula. Unless otherwise specified, amendments to the Canadian *Constitution* must be ratified by resolutions of both Houses of the federal Parliament and the legislatures of at least seven provinces containing at least 50 percent of the population; hence the general formula is also called the "seven–50 rule." In practice, this meant that the Atlantic and Prairie provinces cannot pass an amendment over the objections of Ontario, Quebec, and British Columbia. The 1996 *Regional Veto Act* will make the general formula even more rigid.[16]

An amendment under the general formula that reduces provincial powers must be approved by a majority of the members of each legislature, not just a majority of those present at the time of the vote. A provincial legislature that objects to a proposed amendment may formally reject it by a majority vote of its members, which ensures that the amendment will not apply to that province. The seven–50 rule is subject to a three-year time limit. For example, if one legislature starts the ball rolling, approving the amendment on January 1, 2009, the remainder must do so by January 1, 2012, or the amendment dies unratified. Finally, any amendment in this category that transfers powers over education or culture to the federal Parliament must be accompanied by an offer of financial compensation to any province that rejects it.

Section 42 lists the matters subject to the general amending formula. These include "the method of selecting senators" and "the number of members by which a province is entitled to be represented in the Senate." The "seven–50 rule" was used in 1983 to amend sections 25 and 35 of the *Constitution Act, 1982*.[17] These amendments clarified and extended the scope of Aboriginal rights (see sections 25, 35, and 35.1 in the Appendix).

Section 41 lists the subjects that can be amended only with the *unanimous* approval of all 10 provincial legislatures and the two federal Houses. The unanimity rule applies to the powers of the Crown, the composition of the Supreme Court, the two official languages, and section 41 itself. In other words, the extension of the unanimity rule requires unanimous consent. This became a crucial issue in the "mega-constitutional" politics of the 1980s and 1990s, because the only practical way to meet Quebec's demand for a veto over all future amendments was to expand the matters subject to the unanimity rule—in effect, to give *every* province a veto. (The Meech Lake and Charlottetown Accords are discussed in Chapter 5.) To date, section 41 has not been used successfully.

The formulas in sections 43 and 44 have been used more than the others. They are the easiest to employ, because they require the agreement of the fewest parties. Section 43 provides for a constitutional amendment affecting one or more (but not all) provinces, requiring only the consent of the provincial legislature(s) concerned and the federal Parliament. At the time of writing, this section had been used seven times.[18]

Section 44 gives the federal government the power to amend the provisions relating to the national executive and legislative branches of government (Parts III and IV of the *BNA Act*), subject to the exceptions listed in sections 41 and 42.

(continued)

At the time of writing, section 44 had been used twice: to amend the procedure for distributing Commons seats among the provinces (the *Constitution Act, 1985* [Representation]), and to create a Senate seat for the new Territory of Nunavut (the *Constitution Act, 1999* [Nunavut]).[19]

Section 46 allows a legislature that has already ratified a proposed amendment to rescind (i.e., revoke or withdraw) its consent before the amendment takes effect. One of the crucial milestones in the Meech Lake saga was the revocation of Newfoundland's consent to the Accord in April 1990. Finally, section 47 limits the power of the Senate to a suspensory veto. In other words, the Upper House of the federal Parliament can delay a constitutional amendment but it cannot kill it outright. This provision was applied to the 1997 amendment regarding Newfoundland's education system; the Senate refused to approve the amendment, but its refusal was overridden by a second vote of approval in the House of Commons.

The authors of the 1982 amending formulas expected them to make future changes to the written *Constitution* easier. The establishment of clear rules should have allowed the federal and provincial governments to resolve their differences and achieve consensus more quickly than in previous constitutional rounds. Instead, the general and unanimity formulas have made it all but impossible to amend the entrenched *Constitution*. Section 43 has not had this "chilling" effect, because it only requires the consent of two governments. Moreover, all of the amendments made under this formula have been initiated by the provinces involved; once Ottawa's agreement is secured, the process moves quickly.

The impact of section 44 is a little more difficult to determine, at least in relation to one of Prime Minister Harper's pet projects: Senate reform. As noted in Dossier 3.4, two aspects of the Senate—the method of choosing senators and the distribution of seats among the provinces—are explicitly subjected to the general amending formula. The rest fall under section 44, which allows the federal Parliament to amend "the Constitution of Canada in relation to . . . the Senate and House of Commons." It is not always easy to tell which proposed changes to the Senate would require provincial consent, and which would not. Dossier 3.4 describes the difficulties encountered by the Harper Government as it attempted to reform the Senate without amending the entrenched constitution.

DOSSIER 3.4 Step-by-Step Senate Reform?

In May 2006 the Leader of the Government in the Senate tabled Bill S-4, "An Act to amend the *Constitution Act, 1867* (Senate tenure)" and referred it to a Special Senate Committee (SSC). The Bill would limit the tenure of newly appointed senators to eight years, while allowing those appointed before its proclamation to remain until their 75th birthdays.[20] The Bill did not indicate whether a senator could be re-appointed after serving her eight-year term, although Prime Minister Harper told the SSC that renewable terms would be appropriate in the event that future senators were elected.[21]

The Preamble asserted an exclusive federal power to amend the tenure of senators, based on section 44 of the *Constitution Act, 1982.* This assertion was questioned by some experts who appeared before the SSC. They pointed to the 1980 Supreme Court decision in the *Upper House Reference,* which concerned the constitutionality of an attempt by the Trudeau Government to replace the Senate with an upper house chosen by the provincial governments. The court had ruled that the national government could not unilaterally alter the Senate, which was a central feature of the Canadian federal system. Any change to the "essential character" and functions of the Senate—including a reduction in Senate tenure that diminished senators' capacity to

(continued)

provide "sober second thought" in the legislative process—would require provincial consent.[22] In an attempt to immunize the Bill against a challenge arising from the *Upper House Reference,* they declared that "Parliament wishes to maintain the essential characteristics of the Senate within Canada's parliamentary democracy as a chamber of independent, sober second thought."[23]

The SSC concluded that the Government was right: section 44 of the amending formula allowed Parliament to enact Bill S-4 without provincial consent.[24] However, it questioned the constitutionality of a second reform initiative: the idea of electing "senators in waiting" who would then be appointed by the prime minister. Since 1989, in response to the Senate reform provisions in the Meech Lake Accord (Chapter 5), the province of Alberta had held three Senate elections.[25] The 2006 Conservative platform promised to extend this practice to the rest of the country, a pledge that Prime Minister Harper repeated in his September 2006 testimony before the SSC. The Committee decided to canvass expert opinion on the possibility of "advisory elections" for potential senators, without waiting for the Government to table specific legislation. Without reaching a final conclusion, the Committee raised "the possibility that advisory elections would require a constitutional process involving provincial ratification."[26] This was bad news for the prime minister, who had told the SSC that he intended to proceed "without engaging other levels of government in a complex constitutional discussion or amendment process."[27]

In December 2006, two months after the SSC issued its first report, the Government tabled Bill C-43, *An Act to provide for consultations with electors on their preferences for appointments to the Senate.* The Bill provided for province-wide elections to choose a pool of Senate "nominees" for each province. It did not refer to them as elections, but rather as "consultations"—even though the "consultative" process, administered by Elections Canada, in which citizens cast ballots to choose among candidates, looks exactly like an election to any reasonable person. The use of the word "consultation" can only be a deliberate effort to avoid amending the *BNA Act.*[28]

Bill S-4 passed second reading in the Senate in February 2007 and was referred to the Standing Committee on Legal and Constitutional Affairs (SCLCA). Despite strong pressure from the Government to send the Bill to the Commons, the Committee took its time. It called several new witnesses, most of whom warned the SCLCA that the Government could not enact its entire Senate reform package unilaterally. Because a court would likely assess the constitutionality of both Bills as a package, it might well conclude that both required the approval of at least seven provinces.

The SCLCA witnesses also argued that the Government's interpretation of section 44 was too broad: the list of exceptions in section 42 did not imply that the federal Parliament could unilaterally amend every other aspect of the Senate. Most agreed on two points: (1) that eight-year renewable appointments threatened the independence of the Senate, and (2) that the Government risked judicial nullification of its Senate reform package if it proceeded without provincial consent.

In June 2007, the Committee endorsed those two conclusions in its final report. It amended the Bill to provide for 15-year non-renewable terms, and called on the full Senate to refuse to grant third reading to Bill S-4 until after the Government had referred the package to the Supreme Court of Canada and been assured that it could enact both Bills under section 44. The Senate, a majority of whose members were Liberals, agreed. So Bill S-4 was stalled, because the Government refused to refer the constitutionality of its Senate reform proposals to the Supreme Court of Canada.

Unlike Bill S-4, C-43 addressed an aspect of the Senate that was explicitly exempted from section 44. Under section 42, any change to "the method of selecting senators" requires an amendment under the general formula (section 38). As we saw in Dossier 3.1, section 24 of the *BNA Act* empowers the prime minister (technically the governor general) to appoint senators. The SSC concluded that if the prime minister were required by law to appoint only those individuals elected in the "consultations," the "essential character" of the institution would

(continued)

be changed. A formal amendment to section 24 of the *BNA Act*, requiring the consent of at least seven provinces, would be unavoidable.[29]

Presumably in response to this analysis, Bill C-43 did not require the prime minister to appoint the winners of Senate "consultations." It implied that the prime minister would appoint the Senate "nominee" who had received the largest share of the votes in his or her province, but it did not make that requirement explicit.[30] This telling omission, combined with the use of the word "consultation," demonstrates the Government's desire to enact the Bill without having to use the formal amending procedure. A leading expert on second chambers scolded the Harper Government for skirting the issue in this manner:

> *The purpose of the amendment procedure outlined in section 38(1) is to ensure a broad consensus for amendments to the basic features of our constitutional structure. Difficult as this may make amendments, nevertheless this requirement is fundamental to the operation of Canadian federal democracy. The effort to avoid this procedure by reforming the Senate on the sly through the devious use of ordinary legislation constitutes an anti-constitutional process.*[31]

Bill C-43 was stuck at first reading until Parliament was prorogued in August 2007, when both Bills died on the Order Paper.

The Harper Government reintroduced both Bills in November 2007. Bill S-4 was moved to the Commons and renamed C-19; the new version specified that the eight-year Senate terms would not be renewable. Otherwise, the Government showed little willingness to compromise with the critics of its reform package; most notably, there was no reference to the Supreme Court. In February 2008 the re-named Bill C-20—formerly C-43—was sent to a Legislative Committee before second reading.[32] The committee was no more enthusiastic about either Bill than its Senate counterparts had been. In May 2008 the government of Quebec announced that it was planning to refer the question of the Bill's constitutionality to its own Court of Appeal. By then, Saskatchewan and Manitoba had come out in support of Bill C-20; both provinces were preparing to enact legislation similar to the Alberta *Senatorial Selection Act*.[33] Both Bills died for a second time when the House was dissolved for the October 2008 general election. The Conservative platform promised to reintroduce them, but Parliament was prorogued in December 2008 before either could be brought back. In the meantime, Prime Minister Harper announced shortly after the election that he would start to appoint unelected Conservative Senators in order to ensure passage of his reform Bills. Immediately following the December 2008 prorogation, which the Governor General granted without putting limits on the appointment power, Harper declared his intention to fill 18 Senate vacancies before the end of the year. Although some Conservatives accused Harper of breaking his promise to reform the Senate, his defenders argued that there was no other way to overcome the resistance of the Liberal majority in the upper house.

CONCLUSION

The rules of politics, like the rules of soccer or hockey, are not always as clear in practice as they are on paper. To understand how Canada's political game is really played, we can't just read the entrenched documents. We also have to study ordinary (nonentrenched) laws, judicial interpretations of the entrenched texts, and the unwritten rules of government. Only then can we make sense of the institutions and processes that make and enforce the laws.

Despite its basis in an entrenched division of powers, our federal system is no exception. On paper, the rules of the game are clear. But even here, nonentrenched laws, judicial review, and unwritten conventions determine the day-to-day operation of Canadian federalism.

Chapter 4 explains how the black and white provisions of the *BNA Act* have been modified over the decades, by the emergence of various mechanisms of intergovernmental relations and fiscal federalism. At the same time, the very meaning of the division of powers (sections 91–95 of the *BNA Act*) has been transformed by British and Canadian judges. The difficulty of formal amendment has, if anything, been increased by the amending formulas in sections 38 and 41 of the *Constitution Act, 1982*. As a result, provincial demands for a wholesale revision of the written rules of federalism have been stymied. The 11 senior governments have reverted to nonconstitutional tinkering, nonentrenched laws, and renewed assertions that the unwritten rules favour their particular goals.

If the 1982 amending formulas have had less impact than their authors intended, the same cannot be said of the *Charter*. Indeed, its effects on Canadian government and politics have been considerably greater than anyone could have predicted. The primary reason is that the courts have interpreted its provisions broadly, and used their new powers to remedy violations of rights and freedoms aggressively. Most Canadians approve of the *Charter*, both as a legal instrument and as a symbol of Canada's nationhood and values. On the other hand, the unanticipated consequences of its entrenchment should remind us of one central theme of this chapter: amending the supreme law of a country is a significant step that should not be undertaken lightly.

GLOSSARY OF KEY TERMS

Amending formula: The formal process for changing entrenched constitutional provisions. The formula is usually included in the constitution itself. Amending a constitution is a complex and difficult process, requiring a broad consensus among the key players in the political system. Because the constitution sets out the rules of the political game, and it is intended to provide continuity and stability to the political system, the amending formula must protect the written constitution against changes that are purely temporary in nature, or that violate the core principles on which the political system is based (e.g., democracy and federalism).

Amendment: Any proposed or actual alteration in the wording of a written constitution. An amendment can insert one or more new provisions into the constitution, it can delete one or more existing provisions, or it can rewrite part of a constitution to keep it up to date with changing circumstances.

Common law: The collective term for the body of judicial rulings on a particular subject; e.g., the due-process rights of suspected criminals or the division of powers between governments. Also called "case law."

Constitutional convention: An unwritten principle of political practice, which gradually acquires binding force over time. It may evolve to fill a gap in the written constitution, or it may directly contradict the legal text. Conventions provide greater flexibility than the written constitution, allowing national institutions to adapt to changes in political culture. Unlike written constitutional law, conventions cannot be enforced by the courts (although they may be interpreted by judges as a way to resolve disputes). Violations are usually subject to political punishment by the voters, not to prosecution.

Entrenched constitutional law: Written legal provisions that have been ratified through the appropriate amending formula. They take priority over ordinary laws in case of a conflict.

Judicial Committee of the Privy Council (JCPC):   A panel of British Law Lords, appointed by the Crown to act as the final court of appeals for the Empire (later the Commonwealth). Any apparent conflict between a British law (e.g., the *BNA Act*) and a statute adopted by a former colony could be given a definitive resolution only by the JCPC. Canada abolished the right of appeal to Westminster (the common name for the British government) in 1949; since then, the Supreme Court of Canada has been the highest court of appeal in Canadian law.

Judicial review: The process by which courts provide authoritative interpretations of law. Generally speaking, the judicial review of a particular law can be triggered in one of two ways: by a normal court case (criminal or civil), in which a dispute arises over a general issue of law (which must be settled during the appeals process, as described in Chapter 10), or by the reference procedure, in which the executive branch poses a direct question to the courts. In constitutional terms, judicial review is the interpretation of the *Constitution* (usually the written text, although a reference question may focus on a particular constitutional convention) and its application to a specific case. Before the *Charter of Rights* was proclaimed in 1982, most judicial review of the *Constitution Act, 1867* revolved around the division of powers between the federal and provincial governments; since 1982, judicial review has expanded to include questions about the precise meanings of rights and freedoms (see Chapter 10).

Nonentrenched law: An ordinary statute (either federal or provincial, but usually federal) that supplements the entrenched *Constitution* by applying a general principle to specific circumstances. Example: the *Canada Elections Act,* which sets out the rules and procedures by which Canadians exercise their democratic rights. Unlike entrenched constitutional law, nonentrenched laws may be amended through the normal legislative process; they do not take priority over regular statutes.

Reference cases: Court rulings on legal or constitutional issues that do not arise from lower-court appeals. In a reference case, the executive branch of government submits a question to the judicial branch for a definitive resolution. Governments may initiate reference cases in order to prevent future conflict between governments—by clarifying the division of powers in a federation, for example—or in an effort to resolve an issue that has already provoked disagreement. The 1981 *Patriation Reference* and the 1998 *Secession Reference* are the best-known examples, although there have been reference cases concerning the division of powers since the days of the JCPC.

Subnational: Literally, "below national." Used to refer to the provinces or states within a federation, e.g., British Columbia or California.

DISCUSSION AND REVIEW QUESTIONS

1. Briefly describe each of the four elements of the Canadian *Constitution,* and give an example of each one.

2. Could the governor general fire the prime minister just because she didn't like him? Why or why not?

3. Identify and briefly explain at least three of the amending formulas contained in the *Constitution Act, 1982.* Which one has been used most often, and why?

4. Identify and explain two constitutional obstacles to the enactment of the Conservative Government's Senate reform legislation.

SUGGESTED READINGS

Books and Articles

Vernon Bogdanor, ed., *Constitutions in Democratic Politics* (Aldershot, UK: Gower, 1988).

Andrew Heard, *Canadian Constitutional Conventions: The Marriage of Law and Politics* (Toronto: Oxford University Press, 1991).

James Ross Hurley, *Amending Canada's Constitution: History, Processes, Problems and Prospects* (Ottawa: Minister of Supply and Services Canada, 1996).

Senate of Canada, Special Senate Committee on Senate Reform, "Report on the Subject-matter of Bill S-4, An Act to amend the *Constitution Act, 1867* (Senate tenure), October 2006 (accessed at www.parl.gc.ca).

Mark D. Walters, "The Common Law Constitution in Canada: The Return of *Lex Non Scripta* as Fundamental Law," *University of Toronto Law Journal,* 51 (2001), 91–141.

Websites

The website of the Canadian Legal Information Institute (www.canlii.org) provides a vast array of judicial decisions and federal statutes information (including the *Constitution Acts of 1867 and 1982,* which are in the Appendix to this book), as does the federal Department of Justice (www.canada.justice.gc.ca). To find a more comprehensive historical collection of constitutional documents, go to www.solon.org. You can also find useful documents—including helpful historical surveys of Canada's constitutional development—on the website of the Intergovernmental Affairs Secretariat of the Privy Council Office: go to www.pco-bcp.gc.ca, click on "PCO Secretariats," then select "Intergovernmental Affairs," and check the menu on the left-hand side of the screen.

NOTES

1. Unlike most top courts, the Supreme Court of Canada is not entrenched in the *Constitution.* It was founded eight years after Confederation, and its powers are defined in the *Supreme Court Act.* However, the *1867 Constitution* does provide for the appointment of federal judges, the division of judicial responsibilities between the federal and provincial governments, and the eventual establishment of federal courts to meet new legal needs. Therefore, it is broadly correct to say that the *1867 Constitution* divides powers among the three branches of government.

2. See "The Evolution of Rights in Canada" in Chapter 6 of this book.

3. James Ross Hurley, *Amending Canada's Constitution: History, Processes, Problems and Prospects* (Ottawa: Minister of Supply and Services Canada, 1996), 2.

4. *Marbury v. Madison,* 5 U.S. 137 (1803); accessed at www.findlaw.com.

5. Grant MacEwan, *Mighty Women: Stories of Western Canadian Pioneers* (Vancouver: Greystone Books, 1995 [1975]).

6. See Chapter 4 for a description of the JCPC.

7. *Henrietta Muir Edwards and Others v. Attorney General for Canada and Others,* JC 1929, in Richard A. Olmsted, ed., *Decisions of the Judicial Committee of the Privy Council,* volume 2 (Ottawa: Queen's Printer, 1954).

8. The leading division-of-powers cases are summarized in Chapter 4; we will discuss judicial review of the *Charter* in Chapters 6 and 10.

9. For an excellent discussion of the divergence between constitutional text and political practice in Canada, see Jennifer Smith, "The Constitutional Debate and Beyond," in François Rocher and Miriam Smith, eds., *New Trends in Canadian Federalism,* 2nd edition (Peterborough, ON: Broadview Press, 2003).

10. Vernon Bogdanor, "Introduction," in Vernon Bogdanor, ed., *Constitutions in Democratic Politics* (Aldershot, UK: Gower, 1988), 6.

11. *Re: Resolution to Amend the Constitution,* [1981] 1 S.C.R. 753 [the *Patriation Reference*], quoted in Peter H. Russell, Rainer Knopff, Thomas M.J. Bateman, and Janet L. Hiebert, eds. *The Court and the Constitution: Leading Cases* (Toronto: Emond Montgomery, 2008), 495.

12. Peter H. Russell, "The Supreme Court Decision: Bold Statecraft Based on Questionable Jurisprudence," in Peter H. Russell et al., *The Court and the Constitution: Comments on the Supreme Court Reference on Constitutional Amendment* (Kingston: Queen's University Institute of Intergovernmental Relations, 1982), 1.

13. Recall the discussion of Quebec nationalism in Chapter 2.

14. R. MacGregor Dawson, *The Government of Canada,* 5th edition, rev'd Norman Ward (Toronto: University of Toronto Press, 1970), 59.

15. Hurley, 11.

16. Law Professor Patrick Monahan argues that the 1996 *Regional Veto Act* (discussed in Chapter 5, "Nonconstitutional Responses to Quebec Nationalism") effectively raised the population requirement from 50 percent to 92 percent. See Monahan, *Constitutional Law*, 2nd ed. (Irwin Law: Toronto, 2002), 207. This author conducted a comparison of national, provincial, and regional populations according to the 1981 and 2006 Census data, which confirmed Monahan's finding (the actual minimum population figure using the 2006 data is 92.7 percent). Not only has the *Regional Veto Act* nearly doubled the required proportion of the population represented by the provinces in favour of an amendment; it has also reduced the number of possible combinations of provinces required to amend the *Constitution*. One reason is that both British Columbia and Alberta have vetoes under the legislation—BC explicitly, and Alberta because over 60 percent of the "Western" population live in that province—which they would not have had under the original "seven–50" rule.

17. The text of the *Constitution Amendment Proclamation, 1983* and subsequent amendments to the *Constitution* can be found on the Nelson website at www.parametersofpower5e.nelson.com in the "Canadian Politics on the Web" section, under "The Constitution."

18. Section 43 was used three times to change Newfoundland's religion-based education system (1987, 1997, and 1998); once to change the name of that province to Newfoundland and Labrador; once to alter the organizational basis of Quebec's school boards from religion to language (1997); once to entrench equal status for francophones and anglophones in New Brunswick (1993); and once to permit the construction of the fixed link to Prince Edward Island (1994).

19. The Harper Government's proposed redistribution of Commons seats among the provinces, which is discussed in Chapters 7 and 12, would have been a third example. At the time of writing, it had been tabled in the House of Commons twice without being passed.

20. The Bill would have replaced section 29 of the *Constitution Act, 1867*, which requires senators to retire at the age of 75. Before this section was amended in 1965, Senate appointments were for life.

21. Senate of Canada, *Proceedings of the Special Senate Committee on Senate Reform*, September 12, 2006, 2:12 (accessed at www.parl.gc.ca).

22. *Authority of Parliament in relation to the Upper House (Re)*, [1980] 1 S.C.R. 54.

23. Bill S-4, First Session, Thirty-ninth Parliament, 55 Elizabeth II, 2006 (first reading version); accessed at www.parl.gc.ca. Most of the experts who testified about the Bill argued that the subsequent enactment of the constitutional amendment formulas made the *Upper House Reference* irrelevant; their opinions are summarized at Senate of Canada, Special Senate Committee on Senate Reform, "Report on the Subject-matter of Bill S-4, An Act to amend the *Constitution Act, 1867* (Senate tenure), October 2006, 17–19 (accessed at www.parl.gc.ca).

24. Special Senate Committee, 29.

25. See the discussion of recent Senate appointments in Chapter 7.

26. Special Senate Committee, 21.

27. *Proceedings of the Special Senate Committee on Senate Reform*, September 12, 2006, 2:9-2:10.

28. The details of the Bill are discussed further in Chapters 7 and 12.

29. Special Senate Committee, 21–22.

30. The Bill contained at least one potential constitutional landmine: section 16 provides that the "consultation" in a particular province will be cancelled if the number of candidates is equal to or smaller than the number of expected Senate vacancies. In that circumstance, the Prime Minister's discretion would be removed altogether. According to the Special Senate Committee, this would make a formal amendment to section 24 of the *BNA Act* unavoidable.

31. Ronald L. Watts, "Bill C-20: Faulty Procedure and Inadequate Solution (Testimony before the Legislative Committee on Bill C-20, House of Commons, May 7, 2008)", 1; accessed at www.queensu.ca/iigr.ca, May 2008.

32. This procedure, an exception to the usual legislative process, is discussed in detail in Chapter 7.

33. Brian Laghi and Bill Curry, "Manitoba moves on Senate changes," *The Globe and Mail*, May 22, 2008; Joan Bryden, "Quebec prepared to go to court to block Harper's Senate reform," *The Globe and Mail*, May 23, 2008 (both accessed at www.theglobeandmail.com).

4 Federalism and Intergovernmental Relations

LEARNING OBJECTIVES

After you finish reading this chapter, you should be able to:

- *explain* why Canadian federalism evolved from independence to interdependence;
- *identify* and *explain* at least two reasons why Canadian federalism has become less hierarchical since the 1970s;
- *summarize* the evidence for the vertical and horizontal imbalances in fiscal federalism, and *identify* one policy intended to address each imbalance;
- *identify* and *describe* the principal institutions and processes of intergovernmental relations in Canada;
- *describe* and *evaluate* the impacts of "glocalization" on Canadian federalism.

INTRODUCTION

In Dossier 1.4, we distinguished between three types of state: federal, unitary, and quasi-federal. Although Canada has always been a federation, the federal system entrenched in the *BNA Act* was very different from the system we have today. The Fathers of Confederation intended (1) that the two levels of government would operate independently of each other, and (2) that the national government would be supreme over the provincial governments.[1]

1. *Mutual independence:* With a few exceptions—notably the concurrent powers over agriculture and immigration (section 95)[2]—the national and provincial governments were expected to operate independently of each other. Each had its own defined policy fields, over which it exercised both legislative and executive/administrative authority. In other words, the province of Ontario could make laws in relation to primary education within its boundaries, and it could take whatever steps were necessary to put those laws into effect (e.g., establishing local school boards). Each province also had its own tax base. In theory, it could pay for its assigned responsibilities from its own revenues, without assistance from Ottawa. (As we will see, those provincial tax revenues quickly proved inadequate in practice.)

TABLE 4.1 FEDERAL AND QUASI-FEDERAL ELEMENTS IN THE CANADIAN *CONSTITUTION*

FEDERAL ELEMENTS	CANADIAN EQUIVALENT
Division of legislative powers between national and subnational governments, set out in written constitutional law	Part VI of the *Constitution Act, 1867* (especially sections 91 and 92)
Representation of the subnational governments in the institutions of the central government	The Senate of Canada formally represents the provinces in the central government, although there is no rational division of seats among the provinces and the senators are appointed by the prime minister
A court with the authority to settle legal disputes	The Supreme Court of Canada (also appointed by the prime minister, without formal provincial involvement)
Intergovernmental relations	A complex network of contracts and agencies — mostly ad hoc, but increasingly institutionalized — that bring together members of the permanent and political executives in the 11 senior governments to work out conflicts and harmonize different policies
Division of taxing powers between the national and subnational governments	Sections 91(3) and 92(2) of the *BNA Act*
QUASI-FEDERAL ELEMENTS	CANADIAN EQUIVALENT
The national government may veto laws passed by the subnational governments	The reservation and disallowance powers of the lieutenants governor (sections 57, 58, and 90 of the *BNA Act*)
The residual power is vested in the national government	The preamble to section 91 of the *BNA Act*

2. *Hierarchy:* In the rare cases when the two levels of government rubbed up against each other in the management of their exclusive policy fields, the federal government was expected to be paramount. It had the power to delay or veto provincial laws, and the **residual power** to legislate in fields not explicitly controlled by the provinces (see Table 4.1). A clear hierarchy was established, in which Ottawa was expected to prevail over the provinces. Without a strong central government, it was feared, the new Dominion of Canada could not build a strong national economy; in the worst-case scenario, prompted by the recent horrors of the American Civil War, Confederation might collapse altogether.

Canada was only the third modern federation (following Switzerland and the United States), and the first state to combine federalism with parliamentary institutions. The Fathers of Confederation had no precedents from which to learn, which may explain why some features of the federal system have not worked as well as they hoped:

- The *BNA Act* contains no formal dispute-resolution mechanism, and no provision for future alterations to the division of powers. The Supreme Court is not entrenched in the *Constitution*, although it is mentioned in the 1982 amending formulas (see Dossier 3.3).

- The drafters of the *BNA Act* could not foresee how quickly the "watertight compartments" in sections 91 and 92 would collapse. Even before Confederation took effect on July 1, 1867, the new Dominion had agreed to assist the provinces with their financial obligations. This was the origin of **fiscal federalism**. Over time, the **federal spending power** expanded into exclusively provincial jurisdictions—most notably health care, postsecondary education (PSE), and social welfare. The federal spending power has no clear basis in Canada's constitution, unlike the equivalent powers in newer federations.

- By the middle of the twentieth century, the federal and provincial governments recognized that they had to work together to make and implement policy. Consequently, **intergovernmental relations (IGRs)** became a central focus of Canadian government and politics. The absence of any constitutional provision for collaborative policy-making between the two levels of government has resulted in the piecemeal evolution of **ad hoc** arrangements (e.g., the First Ministers' Conference). Newer federations have recognized the inevitability of IGRs, and made constitutional provision for permanent institutions to facilitate and enforce cooperation across jurisdictions.[3] In the absence of such constitutional provisions, Canadian IGRs have fallen to the executive branch by default. They are conducted by first ministers, ministers, and public servants, with little if any involvement by legislators or the wider public.

- The decisions that flow from **executive federalism** are not enforceable by the courts;[4] at best, they may achieve the status of constitutional conventions (which, as we saw in Chapter 3, are only enforceable through the political process). Therefore, participating governments have no real obligation to live up to their agreements. At the same time, executive federalism blurs the lines of accountability to Parliament and provincial legislatures, and to the various electorates represented at the bargaining table.[5] It is therefore incompatible with "the logic of responsible government in a Westminster system."[6]

- The Fathers of Confederation assumed that the existence of a separate Quebec government would satisfy the aspirations of French Canadians. In fact, Quebec's status as one province among four (now 10) has provoked bitter conflict. For most of the twentieth century, Quebec governments pursued two constitutional goals: (1) the recognition of Quebec as "*une province pas comme les autres*" (more recently, "a distinct society") and (2) greater autonomy from Ottawa.[7] Quebec's continuing rejection of the federal spending power in provincial policy fields, and its enduring suspicion of Ottawa, have helped to thwart recent efforts to place intergovernmental cooperation on a firmer legal footing (e.g., by creating binding enforcement and dispute-resolution mechanisms).

- Confederation was an arrangement by and for governments. There was no place for advocacy groups or individual citizens. As Canadian political culture has evolved (Chapter 2), the elite-driven processes of executive federalism have lost whatever legitimacy they may once have possessed. This creates a dilemma: on the one hand, a large majority of Canadians want their governments to stop fighting over money and powers,[8] which implies the creation of binding agreements backed up by a powerful enforcement mechanism. On the other hand, binding intergovernmental agreements—negotiated and enforced by executives—would further restrict the powers of elected legislators and deepen the "democratic deficit."[9]

- In recent decades, Aboriginal organizations have claimed an inherent right to self-government; the federal government accepted this claim in 1995. Since then, many First Nations have achieved unprecedented sovereignty through new treaties and land claims agreements (involving Ottawa and the relevant provinces), while long-established band councils have gained a measure of additional autonomy and responsibility from the federal government. The logical conclusion of these developments is that Aboriginal leaders—band chiefs and/or the leaders of "peak" organizations—should play a formal role in IGRs.[10] Once the leaders of nongovernmental organizations (NGOs) received a place at the table in the 1990–92 constitutional negotiations, the demands of territorial governments to participate in IGRs on an equal footing with the provinces could no longer be resisted. While it may be perfectly reasonable, and even praiseworthy, to include Aboriginal groups and territories in IGRs, the difficulty of reaching consensus increases with every new participant.[11]

- Finally, the federal system was designed for an independent nation–state (although it took a few decades for Canada to gain full sovereignty from Britain). It was not intended to handle the complexities of globalization, which undermines "the tidy distinction between domestic and foreign."[12] As nation–states yield some of their sovereignty to supranational institutions, and as cities become more independent players in international affairs, the two-level model of federalism has become a four-level model (five, if we include regional organizations like the Annual Conference of New England Governors and Eastern Canadian Premiers). This new "multi-tiered" federalism greatly increases the complexity of relations between national and provincial governments,[13] which are now faced with new problems: Should provinces play a direct role in international negotiations that restrict their activities within their own jurisdictions? Can Ottawa fulfill its obligations under international treaties (e.g., the Kyoto Protocol on Climate Change) if one or more provinces refuse to cooperate? Should the federal government deal directly with municipalities, bypassing the provinces (which enjoy exclusive responsibility for municipal governments under the *BNA Act*)?

Over the decades, a multitude of nonconstitutional mechanisms evolved to deal with these unforeseen circumstances and conflicts.[14] Such mechanisms include the First Ministers' Conference, ministerial and official committees, and intergovernmental Accords of various types. While these mechanisms may help to resolve immediate crises in the short term, they do not have the legal or constitutional muscle to ensure genuinely collaborative policy-making and implementation over the long term. Nor can they establish stable and predictable fiscal arrangements. In short, there is no institutional incentive for governments to respect each other's jurisdictions, or to work together productively on common problems. Recognizing the limits of nonconstitutional mechanisms, provincial governments have proposed formal amendments to the *BNA Act* since at least 1887.[15] As we will see in Chapter 5, however, the failure of the Meech Lake and Charlottetown Accords prompted Canada's political leaders to abandon large-scale constitutional reform in favour of "incremental political adaptation"[16]—in other words, nonconstitutional renewal.

Students of federalism have traditionally focused their attention on the two senior levels of government. For example, they asked whether a particular federation had grown more centralized or decentralized over time—i.e., whether the power to make and enforce decisions had moved from the national government to the subnational (provincial) governments, or vice versa. The consensus is that Canada, despite its origins as a "quasi-federal" state, is now, on balance, "one of the most decentralized federations in the world."[17] Although the pendulum has swung back and forth, the general trend is clear: the centralized federation envisaged by Sir John A. Macdonald has been transformed almost beyond recognition.

While these traditional conceptions of federalism are not obsolete, their usefulness is diminishing. To say, for example, that Canada is a "decentralized" federation implies that the provinces have evolved into 10 autonomous fiefdoms, each pursuing its own independent policy agenda. This picture understates the degree of interdependence in the federal system. It also obscures the growing importance of interprovincial, and now provincial–territorial (PT), collaboration, most recently in the establishment of the Council of the Federation. At this point, such collaboration is fairly limited; the chief goal of most PT meetings is to forge a "common front" against the federal government—a clear assertion of parity within the federation—not to make policy.

"Decentralization" also understates the mutual interdependence, not only between the federal, provincial, and territorial (FPT) governments, but also among nation–states, supranational organizations and agreements (e.g., the North American Free Trade Agreement, or NAFTA), municipal governments, Aboriginal governments, and NGOs. While the impact (to date) of these factors should not be overstated,[18] there is little doubt that the old functional boundaries between and within states are breaking down. Their erosion reinforces the preexisting trends away from independence and hierarchy, and toward interdependence and parity; it also magnifies the complexity of making and enforcing public policy, and brings new actors to the table. Hamish Telford cites some recent examples:

> *The various crises that confronted Canada in the summer of 2003—SARS, mad-cow, West Nile Virus, the electricity blackout in Ontario—all illustrate that contemporary political problems spill over multiple jurisdictional boundaries, and require for resolution the collaborative efforts of local, provincial, federal and international agencies.*[19]

To this list, one might add terrorism, trade disputes (e.g., the dispute between Canada and the United States over softwood lumber), and climate change. The point is that, in most policy fields, no single government can craft and implement programs without considering their effects on the agendas of other governments—provincial, national, local, foreign—or the constraints imposed by external factors over which that government has little if any control.

THE EVOLUTION OF CANADIAN FEDERALISM SINCE 1867

Over the years, Canadian federalism has continually adapted to changing conditions. At various times, the balance between independence and interdependence has shifted back and forth, as has the balance of power between Ottawa and the provinces. The period from 1945 to the mid-1970s is often called the era of "cooperative federalism," which was succeeded in the 1980s by "collaborative federalism." In both periods, Ottawa transferred millions of dollars to the provinces to pay for programs in provincial jurisdiction; in other words, there was a high degree of fiscal interdependence. The key difference between the two eras was Ottawa's power to set priorities in provincial fields: "collaborative federalism envisages partnership and equality between orders of government, whereas cooperative federalism involves strong federal government leadership."[20] This shift from hierarchy to relative parity is the direct result of cuts to federal transfer payments, and the gradual replacement of **conditional grants** with block grants since the 1970s.

Before we turn to a more detailed discussion of the economic trends just described, we will consider three additional influences on Canadian federalism: the logic of the federal institutions themselves, judicial review of the division of powers, and changes in Canada's political culture, specifically Western regionalism and Quebec nationalism (Dossier 2.1).

▨ The Institutional Logic of Federalism

The erosion of independence and hierarchy is partially explained by the character of Canada's federal institutions themselves.

- First, federalism—like every political institution—creates incentives for those who operate within it. The very existence of provincial governments provides a focus for local grievances and ambitions. In effect, ambitious provincial politicians have an incentive to "get the best deal" from the federal government, in order to prove their worth to the voters. Over time, the provinces have learned that "ganging up" on Ottawa is more effective than going it alone; one premier cannot credibly claim to be the equal of the prime minister, whereas 10 premiers have a better chance to assert parity within Confederation.

- Second, the numerical balance between Ottawa and the provinces has changed dramatically since 1867. Between 1873 and 1949, six new provinces were added to the original four, each with its own local needs and conditions. As the number of provinces grew, Ottawa's dominance at the bargaining table shrank.[21] The recent entry of the territories and NGOs seems likely to reinforce this trend.

- Third, the division of jurisdictions in the *BNA Act*—which initially favoured the central government—has now tipped the balance of power toward the provinces. By the end of the twentieth century, federal powers over defence and railways were far less important than they had been in 1867, and most Canadians considered the provincial realms of health care and education to be the highest political priorities.[22]

So the federal system itself, combined with the growing number of provinces and the unforeseen effect of the division of powers, doomed "watertight compartments" and federal paramountcy over the long term.

Judicial Review of the *BNA Act*

As we saw in the previous chapter, judicial review is the process by which courts interpret laws in order to resolve a dispute between two parties. When the majority of judges on the highest court agree on a particular interpretation of the entrenched constitution, their decision is binding on all branches and both levels of government. In a federal state, the authoritative resolution of disputes between the national and subnational governments is especially important; recall Table 4.1.

Canada is unusual in at least three respects. First, judicial review of the division of powers was entrusted to a foreign court for more than 80 years after Confederation. Second, the Supreme Court of Canada is both the highest court of appeal and the constitutional court of record; newer federations (such as Germany) often separate these functions. Third, the membership of the Supreme Court is determined solely by the national government. There is no provision for consultation with, or approval by, provincial governments when vacancies arise on the Supreme Court of Canada.[23]

The impact of judicial review on Canadian federalism has diminished in recent years, partly because the Supreme Court treads very cautiously in division-of-powers cases. The increasing reliance on intergovernmental accords instead of entrenched constitutional text has sidelined the judicial branch: courts may agree to interpret political agreements, but they cannot enforce them.[24] Moreover, governments can find ways to get around unfavourable court rulings. In the early years of the federation, however, judicial interpretations of the *Constitution* did much to shape the emerging federal system. These interpretations were issued by British judges whose understanding of the *BNA Act* had little to do with the realities of building a new federal state across an enormous land mass.

The Judicial Committee of the Privy Council, 1867–1949

Britain's **Judicial Committee of the Privy Council (JCPC)** was the final court of appeal for Canada until 1949, when appeals to London were finally abolished.[25] The JCPC was established in 1833 to hear appeals to the Crown against the decisions of colonial governments.[26] Its members were lawyers and judges who sat in the House of Lords. Under the 1865 *Colonial Laws Validity Act,* an "imperial statute" could override a law passed by the

Canadian Parliament or a provincial legislature when the two conflicted. The JCPC, as the highest court in the Empire, had the ultimate responsibility to determine whether or not Canadian laws conflicted with British laws, the most important of which was the *BNA Act*. It had the authority to overturn constitutional rulings of the Canadian Supreme Court, as well as the right to hear constitutional appeals directly from provincial courts. The Supreme Court was bypassed altogether in about half of the JCPC's cases on the *BNA Act*.[27] So judicial review of the Canadian *Constitution* in its crucial early years was primarily a British operation.

While the JCPC's impact on Canadian federalism is the subject of heated debate, one fact is clear: most of the Law Lords who wrote the decisions in Canadian appeals disapproved of the "quasi-federal" elements in the *BNA Act* (Table 4.1). They endorsed the "compact theory" of Confederation: the provinces had been and remained "autonomous kingdoms," which had delegated minor powers to a national government to handle matters that the provincial governments could not (such as currency and national defence).[28]

The JCPC's interpretation of the Canadian *Constitution* is directly contrary to the intent of the Fathers of Confederation. The historical record of the deliberations at Quebec City, Charlottetown, and London shows that the delegates from Ontario and the Maritimes had deliberately subordinated the provincial governments to the national government—partly at the insistence of the British government, and partly as a reaction against what they perceived as the weaknesses in the American federation.[29] Hence the quasi-federal elements listed in Table 4.1. They had also given Ottawa the enumerated powers over "Trade and Commerce" and the criminal law. There can be little doubt that they intended to establish a strong central government with "the capacity, the institutions and the resources to develop and manage a national economy."[30] Giving the provinces jurisdiction over "Property and Civil Rights" (section 92(13)) was not intended to limit the power of the national government; rather, it protected Quebec's unique civil-law system (which had been recognized by the British Crown since 1774) by giving all the provincial governments the power to regulate contracts and other private legal matters. To do otherwise would have doomed the new Union, because Quebec could not have joined under any other condition.[31]

The Law Lords refused to consider the evidence just summarized, arguing that their rulings must be based solely on their interpretation of the *BNA Act*.[32] That interpretation, more often than not, reflected a strong bias against federal paramountcy and in favour of provincial parity and mutual independence. Between 1889 and 1928 the two Lords who had the greatest influence on Canadian federalism, Lord Watson and Viscount Haldane, effectively rewrote the division of powers in sections 91 and 92. Indeed, Haldane boasted that he and Watson had transformed the Canadian *Constitution* by raising the status of the provinces to "equal authority co-ordinate with the Dominion" (i.e., the national government).[33] Haldane and Watson did this in four ways.

- First, they denied that the POGG clause gave broad residual powers to the national government. Instead, they insisted that it only applied during severe national emergencies such as war.

> *In the event of war, when the national life may require for its preservation the employment of very exceptional means, the provision of peace, order and good government for the country as a whole may involve effort on behalf of the whole nation, in which the interests of individuals may have to be subordinated to that of the community in a fashion which required s. 91 as providing for such an emergency. The general control of property and civil rights for normal purposes remains with the Provincial Legislatures. But questions may arise by reason of the special circumstances of the national emergency which concern nothing short of the peace, order and good government of Canada as a whole.*[34]

By restricting the application of the POGG clause to wartime, the JCPC effectively forbade its use during peacetime. In the 1925 *Snider* case, the Lords repeated that only a severe national emergency could trigger the use of the residual powers.[35] When the Great Depression of 1929, combined with a serious Prairie drought, threw millions out of work and created near-famine conditions in Western Canada, the federal government brought in "New Deal" legislation to address the unemployment crisis. In 1937 the JCPC struck down most of the "New Deal" laws. The Law Lords concluded that the programs were ***ultra vires,*** because they dealt with property and civil rights. They dismissed the argument that unemployment was a national crisis severe enough to invoke the POGG clause.[36] Shortly before appeals to the JCPC were abolished, Viscount Simon rejected Haldane's "emergency power" interpretation of the POGG clause and substituted a "national concern" doctrine.

> *In their Lordships' opinion, the true test [of constitutionality] must be found in the real subject matter of the legislation: if it is such that it goes beyond local or provincial concern or interests and must from its inherent nature be the concern of the Dominion as a whole, then it will fall within the competence of the Dominion Parliament as a matter affecting the peace, order and good government of Canada, though it may in another aspect touch on matters specially reserved to the provincial legislatures.*[37]

Simon's colleagues ignored this reformulation of the residual power in the JCPC's remaining Canadian appeals, returning to the "emergency powers" approach favoured by Haldane. The full implications of the "national concern" doctrine were left for the Supreme Court of Canada to determine after 1949—including the question of whether the POGG clause could justify permanent laws, as opposed to temporary emergency measures.

- Second, Haldane treated section 92(13) as though it, and not the POGG clause, were the real source of residual powers in the *BNA Act*. He interpreted the phrase "Property and Civil Rights in the Province" very broadly, and used it to expand the jurisdiction of the provincial governments at the expense of the national government.

- Third, Haldane restricted the scope of the enumerated federal power over "Trade and Commerce," repeatedly ruling that the national government could not regulate business activity if, in so doing, it intruded on "property and civil rights."[38] Consequently, the JCPC deprived the federal government of the legislative tools needed to create and promote a national economy.

- Fourth and finally, Haldane refused to allow the federal Parliament to use its criminal-law power in areas of provincial jurisdiction. He made it clear that "you cannot usurp power under section 92 under the title of criminal law."[39]

Despite the best efforts of Watson and Haldane, the JCPC was not entirely consistent on the issue of Canadian federalism. Unlike most appeal courts, its members did not consider themselves to be bound by ***stare decisis*** (Chapter 10); moreover, the panel usually left the writing of opinions to a single member, which meant that the law shifted with the whims of each author.[40] In two 1932 rulings—the *Aeronautics Reference* and the *Radio Reference*—their Lordships had ruled in favour of the central government. Both cases turned on the federal government's power to implement international treaties. Did Ottawa, by virtue of signing a treaty with other sovereign states, acquire the capacity to legislate in areas of provincial jurisdiction in order to carry out its responsibilities under that treaty? In the *Aeronautics Reference,* Lord Sankey repudiated the Haldane doctrine in favour of a more centralist interpretation of the *BNA Act*:

> *While the Courts should be jealous in upholding the charter of the Provinces as enacted in s. 92 it must no less be borne in mind that the real object of the Act was to give the central Government*

those high functions and almost sovereign powers by which uniformity of legislation might be secured on all questions which were of common concern to all the Provinces as members of a constituent whole.[41]

Sankey also supplemented the emergency powers doctrine by "reading in" to section 132 of the *BNA Act* an entitlement for the federal government to make laws in areas of provincial jurisdiction, where such laws were a necessary consequence of a foreign treaty. He concluded that "substantially the whole field of legislation in regard to aerial navigation belongs to the Dominion." In the *Radio Reference,* Viscount Dunedin agreed that the federal government must have the power to implement treaties. However, he located that power in the POGG clause, not in section 132.[42]

The 1937 *Labour Conventions* case reversed the 1932 rulings, stripping Ottawa of the power to enforce international treaties in fields of provincial jurisdiction and returning to the JCPC's usual pro-province approach. Lord Atkin distinguished between treaty making and treaty implementation, arguing that the former was an executive power and the latter a legislative responsibility.[43] Therefore, while the national executive had the right to negotiate and assent to foreign treaties, it could not endow the national Parliament with unlimited power to enact them into law. Atkin argued that neither of the 1932 cases constituted a binding precedent for "holding that legislation to perform a Canadian treaty is exclusively within the Dominion legislative power."[44] To accept that doctrine, he claimed, would "undermine the constitutional safeguards of Provincial constitutional autonomy." The federal government might negotiate treaties with other countries with the sole intent to override the division of powers in sections 91 and 92, and thus "clothe itself with legislative authority inconsistent with the constitution which gave it birth."[45] Atkin ended with a now-famous metaphor for Canadian federalism: "While the ship of state now sails on larger ventures and into foreign waters she still retains the watertight compartments which are an essential part of her original structure." This ruling remains in effect,[46] forcing Ottawa to involve the provinces in the crafting of international treaties. Without *Labour Conventions,* globalization might well have restored federal paramountcy, as it appears to have done in Australia;[47] with *Labour Conventions,* the impact of Canada's international commitments on provincial jurisdiction is less clear (see "Federalism and 'Glocalization,'" on page 112).

Although the JCPC, and Watson and Haldane in particular, have attracted considerable criticism,[48] their Lordships have powerful defenders as well. Alan Cairns argues that "the provincial bias of the Privy Council was generally harmonious with Canadian developments," and that the JCPC's popularity with Quebec governments—which generally favoured provincial autonomy—may well have saved Canada from breaking up.[49] Contrary to the complaints of centralist lawyers that the committee had reduced the federal government to an empty shell, "Canada was run in a highly centralist fashion" from 1945 until about 1960.[50] As Cairns observes, the federal government was far from helpless in the face of the JCPC's decisions. After the committee struck down the *Employment and Social Insurance Act* in 1937, the *BNA Act* was amended in 1940 to insert "Unemployment Insurance" in section 91. Given the strength of the other influences on Canadian federalism, Cairns concludes that "Judicial review scarcely seems to have been as important a determinant of constitutional evolution as has often been imagined."[51] But while the JCPC did not solely determine the evolution of Canadian federalism, it did set many of the rules under which the provincial and federal governments competed for power and resources.

The Supreme Court of Canada, 1949–present

Appeals to the JCPC were abolished in 1949, establishing the Supreme Court of Canada as the final arbiter in constitutional disputes. The degree to which Canadian judges were bound to follow the JCPC's rulings was debatable (see the discussion of *stare decisis* in Dossier 10.4). Provincial governments feared that a Canadian court appointed by the prime minister would favour Ottawa in jurisdictional disputes. Those fears have persisted, prompting repeated calls for provincial participation in the appointment of Supreme Court justices.[52] On the whole, however, the court has tried to strike a balance between federal and provincial powers in its federalism jurisprudence.[53] We can see the differences between its approach and that of the JCPC by revisiting the themes listed in the previous section.

- First, the Supreme Court has cautiously broadened the interpretation of the POGG clause. In its first definitive ruling on the division of powers, the Supreme Court relied on Viscount Simon's "national concern" doctrine to uphold a national law that affected property and civil rights.[54] The "national concern" approach was reinforced in 1967, when the court determined that control over offshore minerals was not expressly included in the *BNA Act* and thereby awarded it to the federal government under the residual power.[55] The justices have also ruled that POGG can be used to justify permanent federal legislation (thus laying the emergency powers doctrine to rest). The residual powers clause "applies both to new matters which did not exist at Confederation and to matters which, although originally matters of a local or private nature in a province, have, since, in the absence of national emergency, become matters of national concern."[56] In more recent cases, the court has backed away from the "national concern" doctrine because it "inevitably raises profound issues respecting the federal structure of our constitution."[57] By 1988, the court had developed "a 'provincial inability' test that would justify federal legislation if it could be established that a particular problem required national treatment unobtainable through provincial co-operation."[58] However, it remains reluctant to expand federal powers unilaterally.[59]

- Second, the Supreme Court does not treat section 92(13) as an implicit residual-powers clause that can trump Parliament's right to legislate in matters affecting the country as a whole. It will not strike down federal laws that are otherwise valid on the ground that they incidentally affect "property and civil rights." Having said that, the court has made it clear that a federal provision that regulates the subject-matter of section 92(13), and that is not essential to the achievement of a valid federal objective, may be struck down as *ultra vires*.[60]

- Third, the Supreme Court has rejected the JCPC's subordination of the federal trade and commerce power to the provincial property and civil rights power,[61] and reasserted federal paramountcy over interprovincial trade.[62] But that paramountcy is limited: the federal government may not encroach on provincial jurisdiction except as part of a broad regulatory scheme that is beyond the constitutional competence of the provinces (either individually or acting in concert).[63] As we will see in "Federalism and 'Glocalization,'" this tentative expansion of federal power over trade could have significant implications for the provinces in an era of binding trade agreements between national governments.

- Fourth and finally, some observers argue that the Supreme Court has turned federal jurisdiction over the criminal law into an effective residual-powers clause (Dossier 4.1).[64] In policy fields ranging from environmental protection to tobacco advertising,[65] the court has recognized the right of the federal Parliament to define new criminal offences and prescribe sanctions for noncompliance. "When the Court has been faced with the opportunity to choose between criminal law and the POGG power, it has increasingly opted for the former."[66] In 2003, for instance, the Supreme Court rejected a claim that the federal law against marijuana possession is *ultra vires*; although it held that marijuana use might be a matter of "national concern," it ultimately relied on the criminal law power to uphold the law as *intra vires*.[67] However, the court has stated that

Parliament cannot use the criminal-law power to "invade areas of exclusively provincial legislative competence" merely by "legislating in the proper form."[68] For example, it could not invade the provincial field of health-care delivery by making it a criminal offence to keep a patient waiting for a hip replacement for more than a year. The federal government must have a very good reason for creating new criminal offences and sanctions in policy fields that would otherwise be exclusively or concurrently provincial.[69]

In general, we can conclude that the Supreme Court is more sympathetic to the national government than the JCPC had been. But the difference is more modest than provincial-rights advocates had feared. A 1979 study concluded that the justices had "favoured the provincial interest at least as often as they have favoured the federal interest";[70] more recent studies have found that the Court continues to strike an appropriate balance between the two levels of government.[71] However, it is misleading to portray the court's approach to federalism as a zero-sum game between two levels of government. Instead of dividing powers into "watertight compartments," the court has often expanded the scope of shared, or concurrent, jurisdictions.[72] Its preference for concurrency over exclusive powers likely helps to explain the reliance on the criminal law power, rather than the POGG clause, as the basis for a federal role in environmental regulation. Unlike the POGG clause, which grants exclusive power

DOSSIER 4.1   The Reference re the *Firearms Act*

In 1995 the federal government introduced Bill C-68, the *Firearms Act*. The Act requires all gun owners to register their firearms with the federal government and to obtain licences for their legal use. In 1996 the Alberta government asked the province's Court of Appeal to rule on the constitutionality of the law. Under section 92(13) of the *Constitution Act, 1867,* the provinces have jurisdiction over property and civil rights. Alberta argued that the Act was *ultra vires* the federal Parliament, because it regulated the property of gun owners. A majority on the Court of Appeal upheld the law. The Alberta government appealed the ruling to the Supreme Court of Canada.

The Supreme Court agreed with the Court of Appeal.[73] The justices ruled unanimously that the *Firearms Act* was primarily a criminal statute, because it was designed to prevent and punish the harmful use of firearms. As such, it was "a valid exercise of Parliament's jurisdiction over criminal law" (section 91(27)). There was no federal intrusion on provincial powers, because "gun control has been the subject of federal law since Confederation." The justices rejected the provincial argument based on section 92(13):

The Firearms Act does not trench on provincial powers such that upholding it as criminal law will upset the balance of federalism. The provinces have not established that the effects of the Act on provincial jurisdiction over property and civil rights are more than incidental . . . the mere fact that guns are property does not suffice to show that a gun control law is in pith and substance a provincial matter.

The court held that "A federal state depends for its very existence on a just and workable balance between the central and provincial levels of government. . . . The question is not whether such a balance is necessary, but whether the 1995 gun control law upsets that balance." Because gun control was already a matter of federal jurisdiction, the justices concluded that the *Firearms Act* did not affect the division of powers. Despite the court's talk of "balance," the outcome might have been different under the JCPC, inasmuch as the Law Lords tended to favour the provinces in most jurisdictional disputes involving property and civil rights.

to the national government, jurisdiction over the criminal law is shared between Ottawa (which writes the statutes) and the provinces (which administer, enforce, and prosecute).[74] In summary, the court has not deliberately expanded federal powers at the expense of the provinces, or vice versa; rather, it has expanded the power of government generally, and opened up new areas of overlap within which the two levels of government must cooperate. Whereas the JCPC promoted parity and independence, the Supreme Court has cautiously restored some powers to the federal government—where this appears to be consistent with the intentions of the Fathers of Confederation[75]—and fostered interdependence.

Even if the Supreme Court were unfairly biased in favour of Ottawa, as its critics allege, the provinces would still hold the political resources to overcome the effects of judicial review. Provincial "losses" at the Supreme Court have often been followed by "wins" in subsequent political bargaining with Ottawa. In 1978, for example, the Supreme Court struck down a Saskatchewan law imposing royalties on oil wells, on the ground that the royalty was an indirect tax and thus a violation of sections 91(3) and 92(2). Three years later, when Prime Minister Trudeau needed the support of Saskatchewan's NDP government for his plan to patriate the *Constitution*, he agreed to an amendment recognizing provincial rights to levy taxes on natural resources.[76] (This is now section 92A of the *Constitution Act, 1867*.)

The Political Culture of Federalism: Quebec Nationalism and Western Regional Alienation

A third influence on Canadian federalism is political culture (recall Chapter 2). Regionalism has always existed in the Maritime (now Atlantic) provinces and the Western provinces. Since 1960, Western regionalism has been mobilized as a political resource. The inspiration for this "province-building" activity was the Quiet Revolution in Quebec. As regional grievances were mobilized by provincial governments, especially those of Alberta and British Columbia, provincial challenges to central power grew, and the legitimacy of the federal government diminished. The battles between the federal and provincial governments eventually culminated in the 1980–82 constitutional negotiations that produced the *Constitution Act, 1982*.

Quebec's demand for more powers arises, in large measure, from the central myth of Quebec nationalism: the belief that Confederation was a deal between two founding nations, French and English.[77] Quebec is the primary home of the French nation in North America; therefore, the Quebec government is that nation's chief institutional expression. The rest of Canada is the home of an English Canadian nation, which, as a majority in the federal Parliament, naturally controls the federal government. In short, Ottawa is primarily the government of English Canada, just as Quebec is the true government of the French nation. As we saw in Chapter 2, this "two-nations" myth implies that Quebec is not a province like the others; it requires special status and powers to protect it as a founding nation, and it has the right to negotiate changes to the federation one-on-one with the federal government.

This myth, with its attendant symbols of humiliation and sovereignty (see Dossiers 1.2 and 2.4), drives Quebec's demands for independence and parity in the federal system. It also underlies the recurring demand for constitutional recognition as a "distinct society," which was a crucial factor in the failures of the Meech Lake and Charlottetown Accords (Chapter 5). The Quebec nationalist claim to "distinct society" status has three implications:

1. Quebec's uniqueness must be recognized in the entrenched written constitution.
2. The government of Quebec requires special powers to protect its distinct language and culture. These include a veto over constitutional change and the right to socialize immigrants into francophone society. Quebec also demands the right to "opt out" of national

shared-cost programs in provincial jurisdiction, and receive federal money to operate its own separate program (e.g., the separate Canada and Quebec Pension Plans).

3. National political institutions must reflect Quebec's special character and laws. For example, there is a constitutional convention that three members of the Supreme Court of Canada come from the Quebec civil bar; successive Quebec governments sought to entrench that requirement, and to play a role in the selection of those three justices.

In many ways, Canada's *Constitution* already recognizes Quebec as a "distinct society." Britain's *Quebec Act* of 1774 granted the former French colonists the right to practise the Roman Catholic faith and to use civil law (as opposed to English common law) to resolve their private disputes. The *BNA Act* perpetuated these rights. However, successive Quebec governments have argued that these protections are insufficient.

Western Canadians, especially those in Alberta and British Columbia, have long complained about central Canadian dominance in the House of Commons. Those complaints arise from two basic elements of our political system:

1. The two westernmost provinces are under-represented in the House of Commons (Chapters 7 and 12). Together, Ontario and Quebec account for over half of the seats in the House (181 of 308, or 59 percent), while the four Western provinces can claim less than one-third (92 of 308 seats, or 29 percent). While it is mathematically possible to form a majority government with very few Western seats—as the Liberals did in 1980—no national party that seeks to govern can afford to ignore the interests of Central Canada.

2. The numerical disadvantage of the Western provinces is reinforced by the conventions of party discipline and Cabinet solidarity. Even in government, Western MPs cannot openly address regional issues in a way that threatens their party's base in Ontario and Quebec. (These points are discussed in greater detail in Chapter 7.)

To make matters worse, from the Western perspective, the threat of Quebec separatism dominated the national political agenda during the last quarter of the twentieth century. A province that can credibly threaten to break up the country is likely, all other things being equal, to receive more than its fair share of attention and resources from the national government.

Western discontent with the federal system exploded in the 1970s, as the economic interests of Alberta oil producers clashed head-on with those of industrial Ontario and Quebec. When the world price of oil soared in the 1970s, Alberta grew rich while Central Canada stagnated. A new national-unity crisis erupted, which came to a head when the Trudeau Government introduced the National Energy Program (NEP) in the fall of 1980. The NEP was designed to control the increase in oil prices, to give the federal government a larger share of oil and gas revenues, to increase Canadian ownership in the energy industry, and to shift exploration from provincial lands to "Canada lands" in the North and offshore.

The NEP brought Western resentment of Canada's political institutions to a head. It was introduced by a national Liberal Government that held only two seats in Western Canada—both in Manitoba—but that nonetheless commanded a solid national majority. Thus, even to Western Canadians outside Alberta, the NEP demonstrated a serious flaw in parliamentary institutions. Moreover, the outrage that greeted the NEP in the West demonstrated what can happen when the national government lacks elected members to sell its programs in a region.

In 1984, Western Canadians voted massively for the Progressive Conservatives under Brian Mulroney. They hoped that a federal Cabinet with a large Western contingent would be more sensitive to regional concerns. That hope ended in 1986: the Mulroney Government awarded a major contract for the maintenance of CF-18 fighter aircraft to a Montreal firm, despite the fact that a cheaper and technically superior bid had been submitted by a Winnipeg firm. Many Westerners realized that even when their region was solidly represented on the government benches, Ontario and Quebec would always carry greater weight in a chamber based on representation by population; worse, Western members of the government party would be silenced by party discipline and Cabinet solidarity. So powerful was the Western discontent with the CF-18 contract that it became the galvanizing event in the creation of the Reform Party, which entered national politics under the slogan "The West Wants In."[78]

The Quebec nationalist agenda for institutional reform overlaps with the Western regionalist agenda in one key respect: both want to carve out the broadest possible sphere of fiscal and legislative autonomy for provincial governments. However, the two agendas contradict each other in at least three fundamental ways. First, whereas Quebec nationalists claim special status for their province, Westerners—like most "English" Canadians—believe that Canada is composed of 10 equal provinces. Second, Quebec's constitutional agenda is driven by nationalism, while recent Western demands have been fuelled by regional alienation and populist rejection of representative democratic structures. Third, the two subcultures cannot agree over the best way to turn our national institutions into more effective forums for accommodating regional interests. Since the 1970s, would-be reformers have been divided between **interstate federalism** and **intrastate federalism.**

- Interstate federalism resolves regional conflict through negotiations between heads of government (e.g., First Ministers' Conferences or the Council of the Federation). Provincial premiers are not just the heads of regional governments; they are national political figures in their own right, as the designated spokespersons for regional interests in federal politics. Claims to provincial parity are the logical accompaniment to interstate bargaining.
- Intrastate federalism is designed to resolve regional conflicts by reflecting regionalism within the institutions of the central government; regional electorates choose their national representatives, often members of the upper house of the federal Parliament, bypassing their premiers.

In general, Quebec nationalists favour interstate federalism. It is analogous to the intergovernmental negotiations among national leaders, which fits the "two-nations" vision of Confederation. Western regionalists tend to prefer intrastate solutions, which would enhance the representation of the smaller provinces within the national political system. If the two subcultures could agree on a single set of reform proposals, it might be possible to resolve Canada's lingering megaconstitutional debates (Chapter 5); otherwise, there is little chance of fixing our federal machinery. Most of the changes discussed in this chapter, including the fiscal measures explained in the following section, have been achieved without formal constitutional amendment. The limitations of the nonconstitutional approach are explored in the following chapter.

FISCAL FEDERALISM: EXPLAINING INTERDEPENDENCE AND PARITY

Collectively, the financial relationships between the federal and provincial governments are called "fiscal federalism." (The word "fiscal" refers to public finance.) While fiscal federalism is hardly the sexiest topic in political science, it does have a direct and significant impact on the lives of Canadians. For example, postsecondary tuition fees have risen sharply since the introduction of the Canada Health and Social Transfer in 1995. Concern about the future of the health-care system was a central issue in the 2000 and 2004 federal elections. Welfare recipients have seen their benefits slashed by provincial and municipal governments strug-gling to cope with federal transfer cuts. So while fiscal federalism appears abstract, its effects are real and sometimes painful.

■ The Evolution of Fiscal Federalism, 1867–2007

When delegates from the Province of Canada and the Maritime colonies met in Quebec City in 1864, they had to grapple with the fiscal implications of union. In particular, the transfer of customs and tariffs to the new Dominion Government would leave the provinces (espe-cially Nova Scotia and New Brunswick) with little revenue-raising capacity. At the time, cus-toms and tariffs were by far the most lucrative sources of government funding; income and corporate taxes were not introduced until the early twentieth century. To compensate the Maritimes, and to ensure that all four provinces could meet their relatively meagre obligations under section 92, the delegates agreed to four short-term fiscal measures:

- the Dominion would assume responsibility for colonial debts at the time of Confederation;
- each province would receive a grant of $80 per capita (which was subsequently raised for the Maritimes);
- each province would receive federal money "in support of government and legislation" (also more generous to the Maritimes than to Ontario or Quebec); and
- New Brunswick received a special top-up grant for a 10-year period.[79]

The 1864 deal set the tone for future fiscal arrangements in at least four ways.

- First, it introduced the transfer of revenues collected by the national government to the provincial governments so the latter could fulfill their constitutional obligations. Such transfers have been part of Canadian federalism ever since.
- Second, it put the onus on the federal government to impose taxes, while letting the provinces off the hook. The four founding provinces could have opted for a tax-sharing agreement with Ottawa, which would have allowed them to raise their own revenues; instead, they chose to receive cash transfers.[80] Under the *BNA Act*, both levels of govern-ment have broad taxing powers. However, provincial governments understandably prefer the political benefits of spending money to the political costs of raising it.
- Third, there were no conditions attached to the transfers. Although fiscal federalism in the twentieth century was largely based on conditional grants (as we will see), today most of the money transferred to the provincial governments from Ottawa comes with few or no strings attached.
- Fourth and finally, the 1864 fiscal arrangements recognized that some provinces—in this case, Nova Scotia and New Brunswick—were poorer than others, and provided special transfers to equalize their revenues.

In the 1870s and 1880s, the new Dominion struggled with a severe recession. As trade slowed down, customs and excise duties shrank. The federal government could barely afford the cost of building railroads and other essential infrastructure; its efforts to create a truly national economy suffered, along with its paramountcy over the provinces. The very first premiers' con-ference, held in 1887, issued a demand for more federal money to cover provincial costs.[81] Prime Minister Wilfrid Laurier refused. He told the provincial governments that if they needed more money, they should raise it themselves. Although motivated partly by the poor state of the national finances, Laurier's response was also based on a conception of federalism that pre-vailed until the 1930s. He declared that "The principle by which one government collects the revenues and another government spends them is wholly false."[82] In other words, each province had sufficient tax room to sustain its constitutional responsibilities under the division of powers (although this was less true of some provinces than others); the "watertight compartments" had to be preserved intact, and the only way to preserve them was to maintain the link between taxing and spending in each separate jurisdiction. Although the premiers shared Laurier's preference for exclusive provincial control of the policy fields listed in section 92 of the *BNA Act*, they still refused to impose direct taxes on personal and corporate income.[83]

The national economy began to boom in the 1890s. Federal transfers to the provinces grew along with national revenues. As their populations expanded and technology advanced, provincial governments invested heavily in schools, roads, and telephone lines.[84] Most had begun to impose direct taxes on corporations, but they still needed more money from Ottawa. In response, the federal government introduced conditional grants in 1912.[85] The extraordinary circumstances of World War I forced the federal government to impose temporary income and corporate taxes, which soon became permanent. Similar provincial taxes followed, although the rates were considerably lower. After the war ended, federal transfers to the provinces accounted for a dwindling share of provincial revenues; by 1930, less than 10 percent of the money spent by the provinces came from Ottawa.[86]

In October 1929, the bubble of prosperity burst. Stock markets crashed and millions of people lost their jobs. The Great Depression drastically reduced federal and provincial revenues. To make matters worse, a prolonged drought in western North America destroyed crops and led to widespread famine. Provincial governments, particularly those in the Prairies, were overwhelmed by demands for unemployment insurance and welfare. Both levels of government were forced to raise taxes, which seemed likely to prolong the Depression, and to run deficits (which was completely contrary to the conventional wisdom of the day). The provinces also demanded a dramatic increase in financial assistance from Ottawa. By 1938, federal transfers accounted for 36 percent of provincial government spending—a fourfold increase from 1930.[87] A succession of Dominion-provincial conferences failed to reach agreement on solutions to the fiscal crisis, although the provincial governments did concede two important responsibilities to Ottawa: the provision of unemployment insurance[88] and a monopoly over the collection of income taxes.

In 1937 the federal government appointed the Rowell-Sirois Commission on fiscal federalism. By 1940, when it issued its report, Canada was embroiled in World War II. As part of its war effort, the Dominion assumed broad powers to manage the national economy. In addition, the prevailing economic orthodoxy had changed. The fear of deficits had been replaced by the belief (first promoted by British economist Maynard Keynes) that government activity must expand during recessions, in order to keep the economy afloat.[89] One of the Commission's key recommendations—to centralize taxing powers in Ottawa, in order to prevent federal–provincial tax competition and the exhaustion of available revenues—had already been enacted. The 1940 tax-rental agreement gave Ottawa complete control over personal and corporate income tax. Although the provinces initially accepted this as an emergency wartime measure, it persisted until 1957 with the consent of all the provinces except Quebec (and, initially, Ontario).[90]

The Commission also recommended that the ad hoc system of unconditional fiscal transfers be made permanent.[91] It was strongly opposed to conditional grants, which weakened the "watertight compartments" that were still perceived as an essential element of federalism.[92] The combination of World War II and the Rowell-Sirois Report brought significant and lasting changes to the fiscal relationship between the two senior levels of government.[93]

After peace was restored in 1945, the federal government sought to retain its broad wartime powers. It argued that the Keynesian policies adopted in the late 1930s required strong central control over employment, inflation, and public spending. At the same time, Ottawa was planning an unprecedented expansion in the size and activities of the federal public sector. The "welfare state" would provide income security, health care and education to every Canadian who needed them. Together, the Keynesian approach to government and the growth of the welfare state justified the federal government's insistence on keeping the lion's share of tax revenues.

Given the fact that the welfare state was almost entirely within provincial jurisdiction as defined by the *BNA Act*, it was inevitable that the Rowell-Sirois warning against conditional grants would be ignored. The federal spending power ballooned in the post-war years. While public health insurance and other social programs were largely federal initiatives, the provinces were mostly responsible for delivering them. Increased funding for health care, social welfare, and postsecondary education (PSE) prompted rapid growth in provincial public sectors. As their roles and responsibilities expanded, provincial governments became increasingly dependent on federal funds. Thus, the federal government became heavily involved in financing programs within the legislative jurisdiction of provincial governments.

In order to maintain its control of income tax, while ensuring that the 10 provincial governments carried out its wishes, the federal government developed the complex modern system of fiscal federalism. It collected income taxes from every Canadian—except those in Quebec, which has long collected its own income tax[94]—and distributed part of the proceeds to the provincial governments on the condition that their programs met the criteria set by Ottawa. In effect, the federal government used its spending power to determine provincial programs, spending priorities, and standards. By attaching conditions to the receipt of federal funding, Ottawa was able to legislate indirectly in provincial fields of jurisdiction. Thus the era of cooperative federalism witnessed the persistence of hierarchy, even as policy-making became ever more interdependent.

During the heyday of cooperative federalism in the 1950s, the principal form of cost-sharing was the conditional or matching grant. Ottawa would offer money to the provinces to offset the costs of new programs in health care, PSE, and social welfare. For every dollar spent on these programs, Ottawa would reimburse the province 50 cents (in the case of a matching grant). As previously noted, however, the reimbursement was conditional: the provincial program had to meet criteria set by the federal government. In effect, the federal spending power was used to legislate indirectly in provincial jurisdictions. The provinces spent lavishly on new hospitals, universities, and social-assistance programs, thus committing Ottawa to ever-larger reimbursements. While the direct transfer of federal cash gave the national government effective paramountcy, at least in the broad sense of setting policy priorities, controlling the federal budget was virtually impossible because the spending decisions were being made elsewhere.

By the 1970s, the federal government was losing its economic preeminence in the federal system. The provinces had gained autonomy and policy-making capacity as their social programs grew. At the same time, the Keynesian approach to government was discredited by a prolonged economic slump that began with the 1973 oil price shock. As faith in national economic management eroded, so did the basis of Ottawa's claim for "a large enough share of the tax system" to control the economy.[95] Meanwhile, the federal government faced new and growing constraints on its spending power: after almost three decades of annual budget surpluses, it consistently incurred deficits after 1974.[96] Over time,

> *an accumulation of federal government deficits and rising debt-service costs . . . reduced its ability to undertake new spending initiatives and hence to shape and influence provincial spending patterns through the use of federal–provincial matching grants or other cost-sharing programs. The federal government even found it difficult to maintain its commitments for existing joint programs.*[97]

In response to its fiscal crisis, the federal government gradually reduced its cash transfers to the provinces; in the process, it gave up much of its control over provincial policy-making.

The transition from cooperative to collaborative federalism began in 1977, when Ottawa negotiated the Established Programs Financing (EPF) framework with the provinces. Cash grants for health care and PSE were partially replaced by **"tax points."** Instead of collecting income taxes and then sending the money to the provinces, under the extended wartime tax-rental agreement, the federal government agreed to let the provinces collect a fixed share of income tax in their jurisdictions and decide how to spend the revenues. (In practice, most provinces found it easier and more efficient to let Revenue Canada—now the Canada Revenue Agency—process their income taxes.)

By reducing its direct cash transfers, the federal government hoped to regain control over its own expenditures (which would no longer be determined by provincial priorities), and to shift more financial responsibility for health care, PSE, and welfare to the provinces.[98] To the extent that direct transfers were replaced by tax points, EPF was a program of **block funding,** not conditional funding. By reducing its cash subsidies, the federal government effectively gave up control over programs in provincial jurisdiction; at one stroke, it reduced both hierarchy and, to a lesser degree, interdependence.

The other major cost-sharing program was the Canada Assistance Plan (CAP), which was established in 1966 to provide conditional grants to the provinces for their social-assistance programs. Ottawa paid 50 cents for every dollar of eligible provincial welfare expenditures.[99] As the federal purse strings tightened, CAP became an obstacle to budget management. In 1990, at the same time that Ottawa froze the cash portion of its EPF transfers, it set a 5-percent "cap on CAP" for the wealthiest provinces. Alberta, British Columbia, and Ontario would no longer receive an automatic reimbursement of 50 percent of their welfare costs; the federal contribution would increase by a maximum of 5 percent a year, regardless of provincial spending. The "cap on CAP" took effect at the start of a serious recession, which hit Ontario particularly hard and placed unusual demands on its welfare system. As the CAP transfer shrank and the cost of social assistance rose, the federal contribution to welfare costs in Ontario fell from 50 percent to 25 percent.[100]

The trend from conditional to block funding continued into the 1990s. Successive federal governments were forced by fiscal constraints to reduce the cash portion of shared-cost programs and rely more heavily on tax points. The 1995 federal budget replaced EPF and CAP with the Canada Health and Social Transfer (CHST), which represented the culmination of this trend. Then-Finance Minister Paul Martin pledged to "complete the gradual evolution away from cost-sharing to block funding of programs in areas of provincial responsibility."[101] This pledge was motivated, not by the desire to erode federal paramountcy, but by the urgent need to rescue the Canadian economy from impending disaster.[102] At least three features of the CHST merit emphasis:

- First, it was a block grant. The only conditions attached to the funding were the observance of the principles of the *Canada Health Act*—public administration, comprehensiveness, universality, portability, and accessibility—and the prohibition of provincial residency requirements for social assistance. If a province violated either of these conditions, it risked a federal "claw-back" of funds.[103] However, Ottawa gave up any right to dictate the types of programs that the provinces could deliver in these fields.

- Second, each province was free to allocate the CHST among the three components (health care, PSE, and social welfare) as it saw fit. In practice, given the strong political constituency supporting the health-care system, this meant that PSE and welfare were left relatively unprotected. When the federal government introduced the CHST, it predicted that the provinces would spend 43 percent of the total transfer on health care;[104] by 2004, that share had risen to 62 percent. Moreover, the CHST monies went into general provincial revenues, not directly into social programs; if they so chose, provinces could spend their CHST dollars on other policy priorities.

- Third, the amount transferred under the CHST was substantially smaller than the total of the two programs it replaced. Without consulting the provinces, the federal government cut its transfers by one-third over the first two years of the CHST.[105] Over time, under the initial CHST formula, the cash portion of the transfer would shrink relative to the value of the tax points. Within a year, Ottawa had recognized the implications of this trend for its ability to impose national standards, and announced that cash transfers would not fall below a certain percentage of the total CHST package.

The political fallout from the CHST was enormous. Janice MacKinnon, a former Finance minister in Saskatchewan, describes the 1995 federal budget as "a watershed in Canada's history":

Years of wrangling at constitutional tables had not changed federal–provincial fiscal relations as dramatically as this one budget did. While constitutional proposals had been the subject of intense debate, and even of a referendum, the wholesale changes made in 1995 were unilateral decisions, made with no national debate, except in the private discussions of the finance ministers. The Canada of the past, in which a strong federal government funded and set national standards for health and social programs, was swept aside in favour of a more decentralized federation, in which the provinces became the main guardians of the programs most Canadians cherished.[106]

Provincial governments were no longer willing to obey national standards in their own fields of jurisdiction, when these were imposed by a federal government that had unilaterally slashed its cash transfers.

By the time Martin presented the 1999 federal budget, two things had changed: (1) Ottawa's fiscal position had improved dramatically, and (2) health care had become the dominant issue in Canadian politics. Martin announced immediate and substantial increases in cash transfers under the CHST—all of which would be targeted to health care. This marked the beginning of Ottawa's efforts to reassert itself in provincial policy fields: it was the first time since 1977 that the federal government had expressly earmarked funds for health care.[107] (Note that while health care dominated public and intergovernmental discussion, the virtual elimination of federal funding for social assistance was often overlooked.[108])

For the next several years, the 11 senior governments wrangled over health-care funding. The provinces got a boost from the 2002 report of the federally sponsored Romanow Commission on Health Care,[109] which called on Ottawa to underwrite at least 25 percent of provincial health-care expenses through cash transfers—not tax points or a blend of the two.[110] Provincial governments, claiming that federal cash transfers amounted to roughly 15 cents for every dollar of health-care spending, demanded that Ottawa come up with more money to close the "Romanow gap."

In February 2003 the first ministers concluded the Accord on Health Care Renewal, under which the federal government "topped up" health transfers by more than $2 billion in 2003–04. Ottawa also created a new Health Reform Transfer (HRT), which was targeted to primary health care (i.e., family doctors), home care, and "catastrophic drug coverage." The budget for the HRT was $16 billion over five years. The provinces pointed out that this one-time infusion of cash would help them to rebuild their delivery systems, but there was no guarantee that the added operating costs associated with this new infrastructure would be matched by Ottawa in future years.[111] This complaint reveals the long-term impact of the 1995 federal budget on fiscal federalism: a legacy of mistrust. Having suffered through the "deficit wars," provincial governments were no longer willing to accept federal promises of future shared-cost program funding at face value.[112]

Another element of the 2003 Accord was a revamped CHST. On April 1, 2004, the CHST was divided in two: the Canada Health Transfer (CHT), accounting for 62 percent of the former total CHST payment, and the Canada Social Transfer (CST), worth the remaining 38 percent. The stated purpose of dividing the CHST in this manner was to "enhance the transparency and accountability of federal support for health while continuing to provide provinces and territories with the flexibility to allocate funds among social programs according to their respective priorities."[113] Romanow had recommended a targeted CHT, in order to ensure that the provinces actually spent federal money on health care—not on tax cuts, highway maintenance, or other unrelated items.[114]

From Ottawa's perspective, a separate health transfer makes good political sense: it allows the federal government to show the public exactly how much money it spends on health care, instead of giving the provincial governments a block grant for all social programs and letting them decide how to spend it. In effect, Ottawa will now determine exactly how many federal dollars each province can spend on hospitals and other delivery systems. The provinces complained that Ottawa had fixed the 62–38 split between the CHT and CST arbitrarily, without consulting them; this was a direct violation of the 1999 Social Union Framework Agreement (SUFA), which requires the federal government to consult the provinces before making any significant changes to shared-cost programs.[115] (We will discuss the SUFA in Chapter 5.)

In March 2004, after announcing yet another funding increase for health care in its latest budget, the federal government claimed that its direct provincial transfers—under the CHST, the Health Reform Transfer, and other rubrics—amounted to 32 percent of provincial health-care spending in 2003–04. After factoring in **equalization** and direct federal spending on health (e.g., the delivery of services to Aboriginal Canadians on reserves), "the federal government is providing about $34 billion a year, or about 40 percent of all national public spending on health care in Canada."[116] As usual, the provinces begged to differ. At the July 2004 meeting of the Council of the Federation, the premiers argued that the new federal funding was far smaller than the federal government claimed. They echoed Romanow's call to raise the cash transfer portion of the CHT to cover 25 percent of their health-care costs.[117]

This call for more cash, and fewer tax points, is somewhat puzzling, especially coming from the premiers. The cash portion was projected to grow to two-thirds of the CHT in 2007–08, compared to a little over half in 2003–04.[118] More important, a greater reliance on cash transfers could strengthen Ottawa's case for more direct federal involvement in policy-making on health care. As we have seen, more federal cash equals more federal control. After the federal deficit disappeared in the late 1990s, Ottawa steadily increased the number of conditions on transfer payments and took other steps to reassert a degree of federal paramountcy in provincial jurisdictions.[119] The unilateral withdrawal of federal cash from shared-cost programs in the 1995 budget produced an unprecedented degree of parity in the policy fields dearest to Canadians' hearts.[120] Why would the provinces continue to demand greater infusions of money from Ottawa and risk a revival of federal paramountcy? The answer may lie in the SUFA, which recognized the legitimacy of the federal spending power while imposing conditions on its use in provincial jurisdictions.

The SUFA was largely disregarded by the Chrétien and Martin Governments (although it was at least temporarily revived by the Harper Government; see Chapter 5). As federal surpluses grew between 1999 and 2006, much of the new money was invested in provincial policy fields: health care, PSE, and social assistance programs targeted to children. When the funds were provided directly to provincial governments, they were accompanied by new standards for program design and delivery (although these were considerably less onerous than the standards imposed during the era of cooperative federalism). As often as possible, Ottawa bypassed the provincial governments altogether and gave money directly to individual Canadians or institutions. For example, the Chrétien Government chose to provide additional funds to universities by subsidizing academic research and assisting students with their tuition costs, not by increasing the CST at a rate comparable to the CHT.[121]

By the late twentieth century, therefore, a fifth characteristic of Canadian fiscal federalism had become apparent: the degree of federal paramountcy in provincial jurisdictions depends largely on the spending power of the national government. When Ottawa runs a surplus, allowing it to distribute large cash transfers among the provincial governments, it can set priorities in provincial policy fields. The federal spending power makes it the dominant partner in Confederation: when its revenues shrink—because of economic recession or high interest payments on the public debt—so do its cash transfers to the provinces and, consequently, its power to set the agenda in provincial jurisdictions. In the 1990s, the Chrétien Government unilaterally slashed transfers to the provinces and lost much of its ability to intervene in the politically sensitive field of health care; a few years later, it tried to recoup those losses by pouring money into new programs. The shock of the "deficit wars" had long-term implications for Canadian federalism, which are still in evidence. While we can trace the current battles over equalization and the federal spending power back to 1864, their intensity is the product of the 1995 federal budget and its aftermath. We will take a closer look at these conflicts in the next two sections.

Equalization: Redressing the Horizontal Imbalance in the Federation

As previously described, the Confederation bargain recognized the variations in revenue-generating capacity among the provinces. These variations became more pronounced with the addition of six more provinces. By 2000, per-capita income levels in the three "have" provinces—Ontario, British Columbia, and Alberta—were significantly higher than those in the seven "have-not" provinces.[122] Without subsidies from Ottawa, the provincial governments in the Atlantic region, Quebec, Manitoba, and (sometimes) Saskatchewan would be unable to provide services comparable to those available to Canadians in the wealthier parts of the country. Similar disparities exist in all federations, most of which provide "equalization" payments to their poorer subnational governments to redress the "horizontal imbalance."[123] Equalization does not promote federal paramountcy, because there are no conditions attached to the federal money; nor does it affect interdependence, because the recipient provinces are free to spend the funds on whatever they wish.

The importance of Canada's equalization program, which was established in 1957, is reflected in its entrenchment in section 36 of the *Constitution Act, 1982*. Its purpose is "to ensure that provincial governments have sufficient revenues to provide reasonably comparable levels of public services at reasonably comparable levels of taxation."[124] Put simply, the federal government provides annual cash transfers from its general revenues to any province whose per-capita fiscal capacity falls below a certain standard. Since 1982, that standard had been based on the average fiscal capacity of the five "middle-income" provinces (energy-rich Alberta and the four Atlantic provinces were excluded from the calculation). The formula was based on fiscal capacity—the size of the province's potential tax revenue base—not the amount of revenue actually collected. This meant that if a province chose to lower its tax rates, the equalization program would not cover the resulting shortfall. Nor did the formula reflect the actual spending needs of each provincial government. For example, a recipient province with an unusually high proportion of senior citizens (and consequently higher costs for health care and social services) was entitled to exactly the same per-capita equalization as a province with a more favourable demographic mix.[125]

In 2004–05, the last year of the formula, the five-province average for per-capita fiscal capacity was $6217. The averages in the four Atlantic provinces and Manitoba ranged between

$4000 and $5000; equalization payments accounted for between 14 and 21 percent of annual revenues in each of these provinces. The Quebec average was a little over $5500, generating payments worth about 5 percent of the provincial budget. (Although Quebec receives less equalization per capita than most other provinces—$700 in 2006–07, compared to between $1000 and $2000 in the Atlantic and Manitoba[126]—it is the biggest beneficiary of the program because it has by far the largest population of the recipient provinces.) At the other end of the spectrum, Alberta could boast a capacity of more than $10 000.[127]

Given the amount of money involved, political conflicts over equalization are inevitable. Since at least the 1990s, complaints about the formula used to calculate equalization entitlements have been a staple of federal-provincial relations. Provincial criticisms focused on three central issues. First, the five-province average produced unpredictable and often substantial fluctuations in revenue from year to year.[128] Because natural resource revenues were included in the equalization formula, the recipient provinces were affected by volatile world prices for oil and gas. Moreover, unusual economic conditions in one province could skew the formula. For example, the economy of Ontario grew rapidly in the 1990s, raising the five-province standard and entitling the "have-not" provinces to higher payments; after 2001, provincial fiscal capacity grew more evenly and equalization entitlements shrank.[129] So New Brunswick would receive more or less money from Ottawa in a given year, based on events over which it had no control. Moreover, Saskatchewan and British Columbia—whose per-capita fiscal capacities were close to the five-province standard—qualified for equalization payments in some years but not in others. Consequently, it was difficult for Finance ministers in the recipient provinces to make accurate revenue projections when they prepared their annual budgets.

Second, the complexity of the calculations sometimes generated errors in the collection and processing of data. Some provinces were unpleasantly surprised to discover that they had been overpaid, especially when they were ordered to return part of the money that they had already planned to spend.[130] Third, provincial governments always want more money. This provoked repeated calls to enrich the equalization program—if not for everyone, then at least for the province making a particular demand. Because different formulas benefit some provinces more than others, the very basis of the calculations often became a bone of contention among provincial governments. Dossier 4.2 describes recent federal-provincial battles over equalization.

DOSSIER 4.2   The 2007 Equalization Formula and the Atlantic Accords

In 2004, the federal government decided to make the equalization system more predictable. At a first ministers' meeting, then-Prime Minister Paul Martin announced the suspension of the 1982 formula. Over the next 10 years, total annual payments would not exceed a fixed ceiling nor fall below a guaranteed floor. Each province's payment would increase by 3.5 percent every year.[131] Overall, this represented a significant increase in entitlements for all of the recipient provinces: they were guaranteed almost $11 billion in 2005–06, compared to $8.7 billion in 2003–04. But there were winners and losers: Quebec did slightly worse under the 2004 framework than it would have done under the previous formula, whereas the per-capita fiscal capacity of Newfoundland and Labrador actually exceeded that in Ontario (even before the negotiation of the Accord discussed below).[132] The capped payments turned equalization into a zero-sum game: if one province's entitlement grew in a given year, another would lose out by the same

(continued)

amount.[133] Finally, Martin's plan did not address the problem of volatility for the recipient provinces; the size of the pie was predictable, but each province's share would still fluctuate from year to year.[134]

To resolve the long-term issues that bedevilled equalization, Martin appointed an Expert Panel to recommend a new formula. The most contentious issue was whether, and to what extent, non-renewable energy resources should be incorporated into a new formula. Over time, deposits of oil, natural gas, and minerals run out. So for a have-not province, the exploitation of non-renewable resources provides a one-time opportunity to achieve prosperity and build a diversified economic base for the future. To reap the full benefit, those provinces argue that they should not be forced to give up equalization payments to which they would otherwise be entitled under section 36 of the *Constitution Act, 1982*.

For Saskatchewan, the inclusion of these revenues in the equalization formula was a double-edged sword. On the one hand, it raised the five-province standard (though not by much, because Alberta was excluded) and thus entitled all of the have-not provinces to higher payments. On the other hand, Saskatchewan's own oil and gas revenues increased its own fiscal capacity and consequently reduced its per-capita equalization entitlement. In effect, the federal government clawed back the profits from oil and gas. Over the last decade of the 1982 formula, Saskatchewan lost an estimated $4 billion in equalization payments.[135]

The issue was further complicated in the 1980s and 1990s, with the development of oil and gas deposits off the shores of Nova Scotia and Newfoundland. Whereas revenues from the territorial deposits in the Prairies belong exclusively to those provincial governments (section 92A of the *BNA Act*), offshore deposits are the property of the federal government. The two Atlantic provinces argue that they should be permitted to profit from their oil and gas reserves to precisely the same extent as Alberta and Saskatchewan. This position has been accepted by successive federal governments since the early 1980s, when the first Atlantic Accords were nego-

tiated with Nova Scotia and Newfoundland.[136] For example, the 2005 Accord between Ottawa and Nova Scotia contains the following provision: "Nova Scotia already receives and will continue to receive 100 percent of offshore resource revenues as if these resources were on land."[137] However, such arrangements are purely political; they have no constitutional basis, so they cannot be enforced by the courts. At the same time, the two Atlantic provinces secured protection against the equalization clawback. This protection was particularly important to Newfoundland and Labrador, which reaped much higher profits from the offshore than Nova Scotia. (In 2008, as world energy prices hit record highs, Newfoundland and Labrador was so prosperous that it did not qualify for equalization.)

When the federal government suspended the equalization formula in 2004, it also quashed the Atlantic Accords. Premier Danny Williams of Newfoundland and Labrador, and his counterpart John Hamm in Nova Scotia, demanded new Accords. At the time, Prime Minister Martin led a minority government with 22 badly needed seats in the Atlantic provinces. He faced a strong political challenge from Conservative Leader Stephen Harper, who attacked the new equalization framework as a betrayal of Martin's campaign promises to the region. Harper said the following in the House of Commons in November 2004:

> Why should Newfoundland's possibility of achieving levels of prosperity comparable to the rest of Canada be limited to an artificial eight-year period? Remember in particular that these are in any case non-renewable resources that will run out. Why is the government so eager to ensure that Newfoundland and Labrador will always remain below the economic level of Ontario? . . . [the] message to that province, to Nova Scotia and to all of Atlantic Canada is absolutely clear. They can only get what they were promised if they agree to remain have-not provinces forever. That is absolutely unacceptable.[138]

In early 2005, Martin agreed to side deals with Premiers Williams and Hamm. The new Atlantic Accords guaranteed that each province

(continued)

would keep 100 percent of its offshore resource revenues and its full equalization entitlement for an eight-year period.[139] Premier Lorne Calvert of Saskatchewan tried to obtain a similar deal from Ottawa, without success. Meanwhile, the Conservatives' 2006 platform promised to restore formula-based equalization funding. They also pledged to exclude all non-renewable resource revenues from the calculation of fiscal capacity, and to "ensure that no province is adversely affected from changes to the equalization formula."[140]

The Expert Panel finally issued its report in May 2006, a few months after the Harper Government took office. Its lucid summary of the resource revenue dilemma is worth reproducing here:

> In general terms, receiving provinces with significant natural resources but lower than average revenues from other tax bases (e.g., Saskatchewan and British Columbia) receive substantially higher benefits if resource revenues are excluded from Equalization or included only on a limited basis. Receiving provinces with little or no resource revenues (e.g., New Brunswick and Prince Edward Island) benefit the most if 100 percent of resource revenues are included because it means the total pool of Equalization and the allocations they receive are higher. In the case of nonreceiving provinces with no resources (i.e., Ontario), if resource revenues are included, combined with a 10-province standard, then its taxpayers, already hit by higher oil and gas prices, are asked to pay even more to assist receiving provinces. The greater the percentage of resource revenues included in Equalization, the greater the burden could be on Ontario taxpayers. It's clearly a Canadian conundrum.[141]

The Panel endorsed the principle that recipient provinces should be allowed to benefit from their non-renewable resources, but it denied that lower equalization payments amount to a federal "clawback." After all, lowering equalization payments in response to higher provincial revenues is "precisely how Equalization is intended to work."[142] It pointed

out that excluding all resource revenues from the formula would shrink the entire pie, with particularly drastic effects for recipient provinces without such resources (including Quebec). Instead, it recommended that half of the natural resource revenues accruing annually to all 10 provinces be incorporated into a simplified equalization formula. Finally, the Panel argued that the combination of resource revenues and equalization payments should be limited in the interest of fairness:

> Equalization should provide equity among provinces. However, it should not result in less wealthy provinces having a greater fiscal capacity than provinces that do not receive Equalization. The Panel's recommendations for including 50 percent of resource revenues in the Equalization formula will benefit receiving provinces with resource revenues. However, in some scenarios, a receiving province like British Columbia, Newfoundland and Labrador, or Saskatchewan could end up with a higher fiscal capacity after Equalization than a non-receiving province like Ontario. That runs counter to a fundamental principle of equity that should underlie any changes to the Equalization program. Consequently, the Panel recommends that a fiscal capacity cap be implemented. To determine a province's post-Equalization fiscal capacity and whether or not it is entitled to Equalization, the Panel's view is that 100 percent of a province's resource revenues should be included in calculating a province's fiscal capacity for the purposes of the cap. If a province's resulting fiscal capacity is higher than that of the lowest non-receiving province, then its entitlement to Equalization would be capped.[143]

In his 2007 federal budget, Finance Minister Jim Flaherty announced a new equalization formula based on the work of the Expert Panel.
- First, the five-province average was replaced by a 10-province standard. The incorporation of Alberta's fiscal capacity into the formula implied a bigger gap between the average and the fiscal capacity of the "have-not" provinces, hence higher equalization payments in the future.[144]

(continued)

- Second, payments to a province with a relatively large fiscal capacity would be capped to ensure that equalization did not raise its per-capita capacity above that of provinces which did not receive equalization. This provision infuriated Newfoundland and Labrador and Saskatchewan (Nova Scotia was unaffected).
- Third, the formula was simplified. The number of revenue sources used to estimate fiscal capacity was reduced from 33 to five, and the Government promised more predictable and stable payments to provinces.
- Fourth, and most significant in political terms, the new formula incorporated "a new approach to the treatment of natural resource revenues under which resource-producing provinces would retain additional fiscal benefits from their resources through a 50-percent exclusion of those revenues from the calculation of Equalization payments." In other words, the Conservative Government would not—as it had promised in its 2006 platform—exclude non-renewable resource revenues from the calculation of fiscal capacity altogether; it would only exclude half of those revenues.[145] However, it insisted that it had kept its platform promise, arguing that the new formula "provides both a substantial incentive to provinces to develop their natural resources and higher payments to most provinces than one that fully excludes non-renewable resources."[146]

The 2007 formula touched off a political firestorm in Saskatchewan and the Atlantic provinces. The latter should have been placated by the following promise: "To respect the Offshore Accords, Nova Scotia, and Newfoundland and Labrador may continue to operate under the previous Equalization system until their existing offshore agreements expire."[147] However, unlike the 2005 deals with the Martin Government, the Conservative budget did not hold out the possibility of extending the clawback protection for a further 10 years after the 2012 expiration date. All three provinces condemned the Harper Government for breaking its promise to exclude resource revenues from the equalization formula.

Premier Williams was furious. He placed full-page attack advertisements in national newspapers, and urged his voters to spurn the Conservatives in the next federal election (which they did; all of the Conservative candidates in the province lost in the October 2008 election). The new Nova Scotia Premier, Rodney MacDonald, initially adopted a quieter approach: he attempted to negotiate a better deal for his province, without success.[148] The battle between two Progressive Conservative premiers and their national party put fellow Atlantic Conservatives in a difficult spot. In June 2007 Nova Scotia Conservative MP Bill Casey voted against his party's budget (and was immediately expelled from the Government caucus). This act of defiance brought widespread public and media attention to the equalization controversy, and ensured Casey's re-election as an Independent in October 2008.

The biggest beneficiaries of the new equalization formula will be Quebec, Manitoba, Prince Edward Island, and New Brunswick—the recipient provinces without oil and gas. Newfoundland and Labrador and Nova Scotia would have been adversely affected, if the Atlantic Accords had not been grandfathered. The biggest loser is probably Saskatchewan. Perhaps coincidentally, Premier Calvert lost power in a provincial election in 2007.

The Vertical Fiscal Imbalance: Fact or Fiction?

By the 1980s, the federal spending power had become a contentious political issue. Some provinces, notably Quebec, argued that the national government was trying to subvert the division of powers by attaching conditions to cash transfers. In both the Meech Lake and Charlottetown Accords (Chapter 5), the premiers insisted on constitutional provisions to limit the use of federal money in provincial jurisdictions. Since the failure of the second attempt in 1992, the issue has become even more contentious. As previously described, the Chrétien Government unilaterally cut transfers to the provinces (other than equalization) in the 1995 federal budget; as soon as the books were balanced, Ottawa devoted a large chunk of its surpluses to new health-care programs and tried to impose conditions on program delivery. Meanwhile, the provinces banded together to impose nonconstitutional limits on the federal spending power (the SUFA).

In the new century, the principal bone of contention between Ottawa and the provincial governments was the vertical fiscal imbalance. In a nutshell, the provinces argued that they had too little taxing power to support their constitutional obligations to their citizens. On the other hand, the federal government collected tax revenues far in excess of what it needed for its responsibilities under section 91. Although most tax fields in Canada are shared between the two senior levels of government, Ottawa occupies a disproportionately large share of income taxes; since these revenues tend to rise faster than those from other sources, Ottawa can run up huge surpluses in good economic times while the provinces benefit to a far smaller degree.[149] This vertical fiscal gap is one dimension of the alleged imbalance. According to the Quebec government, there are two additional dimensions: the federal government does not transfer enough revenue to the provinces to allow them to meet their obligations, and the transfers that it does make are overly conditional.[150] In other words, Ottawa is using its excessive spending power to subvert the federal system by forcing the provincial governments to pursue national priorities in their own jurisdictions; the inadequate size of its contributions adds insult to injury.

For its part, the federal Liberal Government argued that the vertical fiscal imbalance was a political myth cooked up by the provinces to justify their incessant demands for bigger transfers with fewer strings attached. First, it denied the claim that the national government collected a disproportionate share of tax revenues. Former Intergovernmental Affairs Minister (later Liberal leader) Stéphane Dion pointed out that the Canadian government receives the second-smallest share of tax revenues among federal states, while the provincial share is the biggest in the world.[151] Despite recent provincial tax cuts, the provinces collect significantly more tax revenue than Ottawa. Indeed, Dion pointed to those cuts as proof that the provinces possessed ample fiscal capacity if they chose to exploit it.[152] For example, the provincial governments could have moved further into the income and corporate tax fields after Ottawa started to lower its tax rates in 2000. Instead, they preferred to rely on transfers from the federal government to pay their bills—as they had since 1864.[153]

Second, federal transfers had grown rapidly since 1999; between the CHT, the CST, equalization, and other programs, funding to the provinces had been more than restored after the shock of 1995. Third, Dion refuted the assertion that Canadian fiscal transfers were bound by overly strict conditions. In reality, Canada imposes the least stringent conditions among all federations. Dion summed up the federal case as follows:

> All of this shows that in the world of federations our provinces are leading in all categories in terms of fiscal capacity, from the viewpoint of share of government revenues, access to tax bases, freedom to set their own fiscal policies, proportion of own-source revenues to their total revenues, and the importance of conditions that accompany federal transfers.[154]

As it did with equalization, the Conservative Opposition in the House of Commons seized on the conflict over vertical imbalance to score political points against the Liberals. The 2006 Conservative platform uncritically accepted the provincial claims, and contained a promise to "work with the provinces in order to achieve a long-term agreement which would address the issue of fiscal imbalance in a permanent fashion."[155] The 2006 federal budget called on each level of government to focus on, and where possible to pay for, its own constitutional obligations. Ottawa would invest more in national defence, security, and other explicitly national responsibilities; at the same time, it would reduce the impact of the federal spending power in areas of provincial jurisdiction by replacing some shared-cost programs with subsidies and targeted tax cuts to individuals.[156] The best example is the 2006 child-care policy, which scrapped the shared-cost program negotiated with the provinces by the Martin Government and introduced direct payments to parents together with tax cuts for families with children.

Finance Minister Jim Flaherty also pledged to discuss the vertical imbalance with his provincial counterparts, hoping to reach a long-term solution. He quickly discovered that the provinces could not agree on a basic definition of the problem, let alone its scope. Moreover, his officials appear to have convinced him that the imbalance was a myth—in effect, that the Liberals had been right all along. The 2007 budget documents contain a chart showing that federal revenues are falling, while provincial revenues—including equalization and other transfers from Ottawa—rose quickly even before the Conservatives took power. In short, if there is a vertical fiscal imbalance in the Canadian federation, the provinces are on the top end and not the bottom end.[157]

So the word "imbalance" discreetly disappeared from the 2007 budget, as did any reference to long-term intergovernmental solutions. In their place, Flaherty reverted to the approach of his immediate Liberal predecessors:

- substantially enriched transfer payments across the board;
- written promises of stable and predictable funding for the next several years;
- dividing the CST into separate and fixed grants for social assistance, programs for children, and PSE, which essentially tells each province how much it can spend on each area; and
- the provision of new funds directly to provincial governments to assist in constructing child-care spaces (perhaps a tacit acknowledgment that giving money to parents does not ensure the provision of services).[158]

In most political disputes, there are valid claims on both sides. But in the conflict over the vertical fiscal imbalance, the weight of evidence falls heavily on the federal side:

- In every federation, the national government possesses a larger revenue-raising capacity than the subnational governments. There are good reasons for this unequal allocation. National governments bear responsibilities that state or provincial governments do not. They need the tools to redistribute wealth, manage the national economy, and regulate the economic union. Most federal states reserve a substantially larger share of revenue sources to the national government than Canada does. Unlike the subnational governments in Australia, Germany, and the United States, "Canadian provinces are largely self-financing."[159]
- It is true that fiscal transfers are smaller in Canada than in comparable federations. On average, federal payments account for 13 percent of provincial revenues, compared to 30 and 41 percent for American and Australian states respectively.[160] On the other hand, the unusually broad taxing power allocated to the provinces makes larger transfers unnecessary; moreover, a clear linkage between the raising and spending of public funds makes all governments more accountable to the electorate.[161]
- Finally, as previously noted, there are fewer strings attached to fiscal transfers in Canada than in other federal states. "The spending power is in fact a widely used policy instrument in federations around the world, and its use in Canada is actually more innocuous than elsewhere. The main objections to its use are political rather than legal."[162]

This last point brings us to the real issue that underlies every fiscal controversy in the Canadian federation. In the words of a former advisor to Prime Minister Chrétien, "all provincial premiers will naturally want the federal government to levy taxes and send the revenues to the provinces."[163] When the flow of funds suddenly narrows, as it did in the mid-1990s, insoluble political conflicts erupt. Unlike most newer federations, Canada lacks an independent finance commission to measure fiscal trends and resolve disputes between the two levels of government.[164] This is typical of our ad hoc system of IGRs, in which decisions are made by consensus (as opposed to formal voting rules), and to the refusal of Canadian governments to yield even a modicum of their individual sovereignty to an enforcement body.[165] Compared to other federal states, Canada's IGR mechanisms are undeveloped and ineffective; as a result, "Canada has been less well-equipped to manage the contemporary challenges of interdependence than most federations."[166] We will explore these problems in the next section.

NO MORE WATERTIGHT COMPARTMENTS: INTERGOVERNMENTAL RELATIONS IN CANADA

As the preceding discussion of fiscal federalism makes clear, the two levels of government in the Canadian federation are much more equal and interdependent than the Fathers of Confederation intended. In addition to the fiscal reasons just discussed, the practical overlap between the powers listed in sections 91–95 of the *Constitution* made interdependence inevitable. The scope of modern government was unimaginable in 1867. Today the federal and provincial governments are active in fields that are not explicitly assigned by the *Constitution* to either order of government. Policy issues like genetically modified foods, climate change, and Internet regulation do not fall easily into "watertight compartments." As a result, Canada's 11 senior governments—more specifically, members of their political and permanent executives—work together constantly to develop and implement policies in virtually every field of activity.

Historically, the key intergovernmental relationships have been those (1) between the national government (formerly called "the Dominion") and one or more provincial governments, and (2) among the provinces themselves. Relations in the former category are now labelled "FPT," for "federal, provincial, and territorial"; the shorthand for the latter is "PT." In legal and constitutional terms, the three territories do not enjoy the status of provinces; they are created and controlled by the federal government. Strictly speaking, therefore, Ottawa's relationship to Nunavut or Yukon is not "intergovernmental." Nonetheless, the leaders of their governments are now included in most meetings of the first ministers, and they have been full participants in the Annual Premiers' Conference (now the Council of the Federation) since 1991.[167]

In the Canadian federation, as noted earlier, relationships among the various governments are managed by the executive branch. Members of the political and permanent executives meet regularly to share information, hammer out agreements, and try to resolve disputes. These activities are collectively called "executive federalism." The formal relations among the executives of Canada's senior governments occur at three distinct levels:

1. *Peak:* First ministers' meetings (the leaders of some or all FPT governments), the Council of the Federation, and bilateral meetings between two or more government leaders.
2. *Ministerial:* Some or all of the FPT or PT Cabinet ministers responsible for a particular policy field; for example, the Canadian Council of Ministers of the Environment (FPT) or the Council of Ministers of Education, Canada (PT).
3. *Official:* The FPT or PT public servants who make and enforce policy in a specific field; for example, the Deputy Ministers' Committee, which supports the work of the Canadian Council of Ministers of the Environment.[168]

■ Peak Institutions

The peak institution, at the FPT level, is the First Ministers' Conference (FMC). (After the failure of the intergovernmental bargaining over the Meech Lake and Charlottetown Accords, these events were renamed first ministers' meetings, or FMMs, perhaps to lower public expectations by presenting a more relaxed image.[169]) The first official FMC was the 1906 Dominion–Provincial Conference on fiscal relations; the second was held in 1918, and the third in 1927.[170] The FMC did not become a regular event until after the fiscal crisis of the Great Depression, which prompted a Royal Commission to recommend frequent Dominion–Provincial Conferences, with a permanent secretariat to coordinate IGRs. When the welfare state began to take shape after World War II, FMCs became annual events. While their official purpose was to discuss fiscal relations, and especially the creation of national shared-cost programs in provincial policy fields, they quickly became the most prominent arena for federal–provincial combat. By the 1960s, the Quiet Revolution in Quebec had sparked a more aggressive attitude on the part of several premiers. The agenda now included oil and gas pricing, constitutional amendment, and provincial demands for more powers and greater autonomy from Ottawa (i.e., both independence and parity).

Despite the increasingly hostile dynamic, the first ministers met 21 times between 1971 and 1983. Over time, "Meetings became more structured, with an agenda defined well in advance and greater follow-up."[171] The Canadian Intergovernmental Conference Secretariat (CICS) was created in 1973, to provide logistical support for FMCs and other intergovernmental meetings. Its limited mandate left the responsibility for agenda-setting, compliance, and policy development to the individual governments; there was no genuinely intergovernmental mechanism for dispute resolution and enforcement. During this period, some premiers played to the television cameras; they aggressively challenged the legitimacy of the federal government, and claimed an equal right to speak for Canadians. Although he agreed to a provincial request to entrench FMCs in the *Constitution Act, 1982*—albeit only for a limited time—Prime Minister Trudeau came to loathe them.[172] His successor, Brian Mulroney, promised Canadians a new era of intergovernmental harmony and cooperation. He chaired several FMCs on social and economic issues, Aboriginal concerns, and constitutional reform. The contentious megaconstitutional debates discussed in Chapter 5 ultimately poisoned the relationship between Ottawa and the provinces. Consequently, little was accomplished at the other FMCs.

Under the Chrétien government (1993–2003), formal gatherings of government leaders were infrequent. Prime Minister Chrétien chaired only seven formal gatherings of the FPT first ministers. Unlike the highly charged and media-driven FMCs of the 1970s and 1980s, these were private and relatively low-key FMMs.[173] None was devoted to constitutional change; as we will see in Chapter 5, the defeat of the Charlottetown Accord in 1992 led Canada's governments to pursue nonconstitutional avenues for resolving conflicts within the federation. Therefore, the FMMs of the Chrétien era produced agreements and Accords—on internal trade, the social union, and health-care renewal—which were, at best, morally binding on all governments. Few of these Accords involved the Quebec government, which was controlled during most of this period by the separatist Bloc Québécois.

For the most part, Chrétien preferred to discuss matters of shared concern in less public and formal settings. During the late 1990s, Chrétien led several "Team Canada" trade missions to foreign countries. He would invite premiers and business leaders to accompany him, using his prestige as the prime minister of Canada to entice foreign businesspeople to strike deals with Canadian entrepreneurs. During the lengthy airplane trips to and from the "Team Canada" destinations, Chrétien would hold informal talks with the premiers on board. There are no written records of these conversations, but it is reasonable to assume that the participants found it somewhat easier to reach an understanding in the absence of television cameras and entourages anxious to score political points.

Like his predecessors, former Prime Minister Paul Martin came to office promising a new era of FPT collaboration. The omens were not promising: the premiers remembered Martin as the architect of the notorious 1995 federal budget. The tense dynamic between Ottawa and the provinces persisted, despite the presence of Liberal governments in Ontario, Quebec, and British Columbia. In September 2004, the much-anticipated Health Care Summit of the FPT first ministers nearly broke down over money. At the August meeting of the Council of the Federation, the premiers had demanded that the federal government allocate a total of $13 billion per year to health-care spending. Ottawa countered by offering substantially less money. At the start of the September 2004 Summit, the premiers submitted a revised plan calling for an additional $5.2 billion in annual health-care funding.[174] After the first day of the three-day Summit, no agreement between the governments seemed possible. Finally, in the early hours of the last day, the federal government agreed to spend an additional $18 billion on health care over the following six years, and exempted the province of Quebec from most of the reporting requirements imposed on the other provinces in exchange for the new funding.[175] An attempt to negotiate a similar agreement on equalization in October 2004 failed: Martin announced a unilateral federal cap on payments, and the Conservative premier of Newfoundland and Labrador walked out. (See Dossier 4.2.)

As for the FMC as an institution, it has no more legal or constitutional status today than it had a century ago. It lacks "a set of fixed rules and procedures, an established organization, and a set of distinct incentives, disincentives and constraints that are capable of influencing or shaping the behaviour and strategies of political actors."[176]

Until 2003, the peak institution at the PT level was the Annual Premiers' Conference. Since its inception in 1960, the APC had held annual meetings to discuss issues of common importance. It was chaired, on a rotating basis, by each of the provinces in turn. It lacked a permanent secretariat or staff, relying instead on whatever resources the host government for each year could provide. The turnover of premiers and territorial leaders varied: sometimes there was considerable continuity from one year to the next, while other annual meetings turned into get-acquainted sessions for new members. As a result, the institutional memory of the APC was unreliable and it could not pursue goals that required more than a year or two to accomplish.

The initiative for the new Council of the Federation came from the Quebec Liberal Party, which proposed a more institutionalized forum for interprovincial cooperation in its 2001 report on Quebec's place in Canada.[177] In spring 2003, Quebec elected a federalist government for the first time in almost a decade. The new premier, Liberal Jean Charest, immediately made the Council of the Federation a top priority. Its purpose, according to the December 2003 founding agreement, is to create a formal and stable structure that can exercise effective "leadership on national issues of importance to provinces and territories." The council will meet at least twice a year and will receive and consider reports from PT ministerial and official committees (discussed below). A steering committee, made up of deputy ministers responsible for intergovernmental relations, and a permanent secretariat will carry out the work of the council between the twice-yearly meetings of the PT government leaders.[178] In principle, they will be responsible for monitoring progress on the strategic goals set by the council and for helping to identify shared priorities for future interprovincial collaboration.

In practice, however, the Council of the Federation may amount to little more than "a slightly more formalized APC." If this is the case, "it will likely serve only to reinforce the current tendency of premiers to get together principally to fashion a common position against Ottawa" in the never-ending battle over money and power.[179] Indeed, the Council might be said to have an incentive to justify its existence, by allowing intergovernmental conflict to fester instead of trying to resolve it.[180] This pessimistic assessment overlooks one positive aspect of the council: the full participation of Quebec. After years of sitting on the sidelines or backing out of intergovernmental agreements at the last minute, the new Liberal government in Quebec became a strong advocate of "collaborative federalism." It has backed off in subsequent years, likely because of its growing unpopularity at home (Charest barely eked out a minority in the 2007 provincial election).

In addition to these national peak institutions, the Council of Atlantic Premiers and the Western Premiers' Conference meet at least once a year. (The latter includes the territorial leaders.) These regional PT groups have established working relationships with their counterparts in neighbouring U.S. states (the Western Governors' Association and the New England Governors, respectively[181]). Since 9/11, the primary focus of the annual cross-border meetings has been trade and border security, although the PT leaders and governors also deal with economic development, environmental policy, and energy issues (the latter gaining particular importance after the August 2003 blackout in eastern North America). The Western premiers and territorial leaders have also demanded a seat at the table in international trade negotiations,[182] a request that Ottawa has yet to fully accept.

Ministerial and Official Councils

The peak institutions of executive federalism receive considerable media coverage. However, most of the actual work is accomplished at the ministerial and official levels. The FPT and PT ministers responsible for particular policy sectors meet regularly, as do their deputy ministers and other senior civil servants. Some of these are national councils, others are regional forums. In 2005–06, the CICS reported 47 FPT and PT ministerial meetings, compared to 50 meetings among deputy ministers. These numbers are consistent with the yearly averages since 1974.[183] (Note that the CICS data are incomplete; they do not include all intergovernmental meetings of officials below the deputy minister rank.) There is a growing trend for PT ministers and officials to meet without their federal counterparts, ostensibly to coordinate work on purely provincial matters. In reality, these gatherings—whether peak, ministerial, or official—seem to be less concerned with interprovincial issues and more focused on forging a "common front" against Ottawa.[184] The CICS data are revealing: FPT meetings of ministers and/or officials are often preceded by a gathering of the provincial and territorial participants. This pattern suggests a provincial awareness of the danger of a federal "divide and conquer" strategy, such as the manoeuvre by Prime Minister Trudeau that led to the adoption of the *Constitution Act, 1982* (Chapter 5).

At present, some ministers and officials are abandoning the traditional ad hoc approach to intergovernmental relations. In some sectors, they have established more or less formal and institutionalized procedures for collective decision-making and the sharing of information. At the FPT level, the best example is probably the Canadian Council of Ministers of the Environment (CCME). It is co-chaired by the federal Environment minister and a provincial minister; the latter position rotates annually among the PT governments. The CCME has a permanent secretariat in Winnipeg, with a staff averaging eight full-time positions. The secretariat oversees the work of several committees of deputy ministers and other officials. The council also collaborates with the Council of Energy Ministers on shared files, including air quality and climate change.[185]

Of the purely PT organizations, the Council of Ministers of Education, Canada (CMEC) is the oldest and most well established. It was created in 1967 to provide a forum for interprovincial cooperation and a clearing-house for information about new policy challenges.[186] Although the CMEC has long had a secretariat, its functions have been restricted to administrative tasks. The agenda of the CMEC fluctuated from year to year, in response to emerging issues and crises. At the annual meetings, most of the time was devoted to information-sharing; there was no mechanism to set strategic goals or to follow up on previous agreements. The CMEC reviewed its structure and operations in 2003–04, with one primary goal: to become a partner with Ottawa and the Council of the Federation in policy-making and implementation.

In addition to the formal intergovernmental meetings just described, there are countless informal contacts between ministers and officials. Most of these arise in the day-to-day business of administering policy in shared jurisdictions. Some involve specialists in intergovernmental relations, most of whom work in discrete departments (e.g., the Federal–Provincial Relations Office in Ottawa); others involve policy experts looking for "best practices" and other useful advice, or members of the various intergovernmental committees that do the heavy lifting for the political executives. As the number of FPT and PT councils and forums has grown in recent years, so has the volume of intergovernmental agreements (numbering somewhere between 1500 and 2000 per year[187]).

FEDERALISM AND "GLOCALIZATION"

In the coming years, relations between the federal and provincial governments will be further complicated by the participation of two additional levels of government: supranational and municipal. It is often argued that globalization has shifted policy-making and enforcement authority upward to supranational agencies, and downward to local bodies—hence the new buzzword "glocalization."[188] Any transfer of power to Canadian cities should not be overstated; although some world capitals are becoming semiautonomous "city regions,"[189] our municipalities remain "what they have always been: mechanisms by which local people arrange for public infrastructure and the provision of local public services."[190] Nonetheless, they appear set to become key players in the politics of Canadian federalism. The formal distinctions among levels of government are giving way to the recognition that global events, as much as national and provincial policies, have direct impacts on local communities. For example, international commitments to reduce agricultural subsidies—commitments that the United States, among other key producers, see fit to ignore—magnified the economic damage inflicted on Canadian farmers by poor weather, volatile markets, and the discovery of "mad cow disease" in one Alberta animal in 2003. The effects are felt most acutely at the local level:

> Economic hardship strains marriages, which burdens local social services; it affects the behaviour of children in school; it reinforces rural–urban migration, which erodes the social capacity of cities, while leaving rural localities languishing. . .[191]

Given the severity of these problems, it is both unfair and unrealistic to expect municipal governments to deal with them unassisted. It may be equally unfair to deny local governments an opportunity to participate in provincial, national, and even global decision-making, particularly where environmental and immigration issues are involved. In recognition of this fact, and of the growing political independence of cities, Ontario Premier Dalton McGuinty signed a memorandum of understanding with the Association of Municipalities of Ontario (AMO) in August 2004. It guaranteed a role for AMO representatives in future intergovernmental discussions with possible ramifications for urban governments.[192]

Former Prime Minister Martin put cities at the centre of the federal government's policy agenda, ignoring the fact that municipal institutions fall under provincial jurisdiction (section 92(8)).[193] Canada's largest cities bore the brunt of federal and provincial "downloading" in the 1990s, especially with regard to social assistance. They struggle to maintain their existing infrastructure—e.g., roads, waterworks, and public transit—while their expanding populations demand new facilities. The implications of the fiscal crisis in municipal governance are profound. Most Canadians (a little over 80 percent in the 2006 Census[194]) live in cities or towns. They need safe housing and streets, clean drinking water, and adequate policing. Public transit must be a key element of any meaningful strategy to reduce greenhouse gases. Martin, recognizing the need for federal assistance to cities, promised them millions of dollars in gasoline tax revenue in the 2005 federal budget. The premiers complained about encroachment on their jurisdiction, arguing that federal transfers to cities should "flow through provincial governments so that the latter can ensure that [it] is used in accordance with provincial priorities and policies."[195] The Harper Government reverted to a more traditional approach to municipal affairs: cities are the responsibility of local and provincial governments, and Ottawa has little or no role to play in regulating or funding their activities.[196]

At the supranational level, the NAFTA and other binding treaties between states may alter the balance of power between subnational governments (e.g., American states or Canadian provinces) and national governments. Before the 1980s, international trade agreements usually focused on **tariff** barriers to the import of foreign goods. Under section 91 of the *BNA Act,* the federal government had jurisdiction over tariffs and other import policies. The global push toward open markets forced states to reduce or eliminate tariffs. Recent rounds of trade negotiations, whether at the World Trade Organization (WTO) or within particular regions— such as the European Union (EU) or North America (e.g., NAFTA)—have focused on **nontariff barriers** to trade, many of which fall under provincial jurisdiction. Recall that under the JCPC's *Labour Conventions* ruling, the federal government has the power to make binding treaties but lacks the power to implement them in fields assigned to the provinces under section 92. Consequently, the new emphasis on reducing nontariff barriers has forced the federal government to seek provincial cooperation in the negotiation and implementation of trade deals with other countries.[197] Although the premiers do not enjoy formal standing with the WTO and other bodies, the division of jurisdictions in the *BNA Act* gives them considerable capacity to frustrate the implementation of trade treaties that impinge—as most do—on their policy fields.[198]

To date, the level of intergovernmental conflict in trade matters has been relatively low.[199] This could change, as the PT leaders—nationally, regionally, and individually— become more aggressive in their pursuit of independent relationships with other countries and U.S. states.[200] At its first meeting in July 2004, the Council of the Federation unanimously demanded "full provincial and territorial participation in Canada's international activities that affect their jurisdiction and responsibilities, including development of positions, involvement in negotiations, and management of disputes."[201] This demand makes some sense, given the increasing emphasis in global trade talks on culture, education, and other provincial jurisdictions. Of course, Ottawa does not quite see it this way. The federal government generally denies provincial governments their own seats at the bargaining table, preferring instead to consult with the provinces on national priorities and implementation mechanisms.[202] For a short time, Stephen Harper appeared to be more accommodating: in December 2005 he promised to give Quebec its own delegation at the United Nations Educational, Social and Cultural Organization (UNESCO).[203] That promise helped the Conservatives to win 10 Quebec seats in the 2006 election. After he became prime minister, however, he was only able to deliver a permanent Quebec seat within the Canadian delegation—a rather different thing from the original promise. It turns out that United Nations agencies only permit delegations from sovereign states, not from "sub-national entities like provinces."[204]

Canada's participation in global environmental Accords provoked sharp and highly public disagreements. The 1997 Kyoto Protocol on Climate Change provoked a fierce battle between Ottawa and the provinces, especially Alberta. Before the Kyoto talks, the federal government had promised the provinces that it would agree to reduce Canada's emissions of greenhouse gases to 1990 levels by the year 2010. During the negotiations with other states, Canada agreed to additional cuts in emissions.[205] The provinces were placated by a promise from the federal minister of the Environment that Kyoto would not be ratified if the costs were too high. For the next five years, while the federal government considered whether to ratify the Protocol, the senior governments worked together to develop a plan to implement Canada's commitments on climate change. The collaboration was fairly harmonious, but it produced few results. The main reason for the lack of progress was the opposition of eight provinces (Manitoba and Quebec were the exceptions).[206]

When, in September 2002, former Prime Minister Chrétien suddenly announced that his government would ratify the Kyoto Protocol by the end of the year, the Government of Alberta reacted with fury and defiance. Former Premier Ralph Klein argued that the Kyoto agreement would inflict severe damage on the fossil-fuel industries in his province. Alberta's economy is driven by oil and natural gas; the extraction and refining of these commodities—especially oil from the tar sands—releases tonnes of carbon dioxide into the atmosphere. Meeting the Protocol targets would require Canadians to burn less fossil fuel in their cars, furnaces, and power plants, thus shrinking the domestic market for Alberta oil and gas. After U.S. President George W. Bush had announced in 2001 that his country would not ratify Kyoto, which freed American fossil-fuel producers and consumers from complying with its provisions, Klein's arguments[207] found receptive ears outside Alberta. Why, some Canadians wondered, should they have to pay the high cost of meeting the Kyoto emission targets when their American competitors did not? And what was the point of ratifying Kyoto when the world's largest producer of greenhouse gases refused to make it work?

The opposing provinces demanded that Ottawa pay the full cost of meeting the Kyoto targets; when Ottawa refused, they boycotted a meeting of FPT Energy and Environment ministers. The House of Commons subsequently passed a symbolic resolution in favour of ratification, but only after the prime minister cracked the whip on his Liberal backbenchers. Alberta, British Columbia, and Ontario have initiated their own "Action Plans" on climate change, bypassing the Kyoto process. In any event, enforcing the Kyoto Protocol was a moot point until it was ratified by countries that collectively produce at least 55 percent of the world's greenhouse gases; it finally took effect in February 2005. The following year, the new Harper Conservative Government announced that Canada would not meet its Kyoto commitments and effectively repudiated Canada's signature on the protocol.

The impact of Canada's federal system on our participation in global economic and environmental treaties has received considerable attention. Less obvious, although no less significant, are the potential effects of globalization on the division of powers between Ottawa and the provinces. Those effects will likely vary across policy fields. One study of NAFTA's Chapter 11 rules, which regulate **foreign direct investment (FDI),** suggests that their enforcement will shift some power from the provinces to Ottawa. The FDI provisions require Canadian governments to treat American and Mexican companies as though they were domestically owned. They effectively prohibit the imposition of laws and regulations that put foreign-owned companies at a disadvantage, relative both to locally owned companies and to the jurisdiction in which the company is based. These might include labour standards and benefits, environmental regulations, or local procurement policies. If an individual or corporate investor believes that a Canadian government has violated Chapter 11, that investor can seek a legal ruling from a NAFTA tribunal. If the tribunal rules in favour of the investor, the tribunal can order the national government to pay monetary damages—even if the alleged violation of the NAFTA treaty was committed by a provincial government. In effect, the federal government is liable, as a signatory to NAFTA, for provincial laws over which it has no direct control.[208]

Damage awards ordered by NAFTA tribunals are enforceable in the domestic courts of the host country. The Supreme Court of Canada would have to decide whether the costs of breaching Chapter 11 should be borne by the federal government or by the province that lost the case. In the process, it would surely be asked whether the federal government could legislate in areas of provincial jurisdiction in order to ensure future compliance. As we saw in the earlier discussion of Supreme Court jurisprudence on the trade and commerce clause of section 91 (page 91), the court has recently extended the federal government's power to regulate internal trade. Moreover, the post-1949 revival of the "national concern" doctrine could have an impact on jurisprudence; under NAFTA and other binding trade agreements, "subject matters that would have traditionally fallen into provincial power now take on an importance that transcends provincial boundaries."[209] Therefore, globalization could produce "an expansion of federal powers that could intrude deeply into areas of exclusive provincial jurisdiction," partly as a result of Supreme Court rulings arising from NAFTA appeals.[210] This could signal at least a temporary revival of federal paramountcy. On the other hand, the fact that the national government has to take provincial concerns into account when it negotiates such agreements in the first place implies a greater degree of parity than meets the eye.[211]

Whatever the long-term impact of NAFTA on provincial jurisdictions, one broader point is clear: the territorial logic of federalism is in direct conflict with the nonterritorial logic of globalization. Whereas provincial jurisdiction—e.g., "Property and Civil Rights in the Province"—is territorially bound, NAFTA and other trade treaties transcend political and geographic borders.[212] As the nation–state yields more of its sovereignty to supranational organizations, it also loses some of its authority to actors outside the formal constitution: "the private sector, communities and civil society."[213]

Territorial forms of organization are also under assault from new technologies, including the Internet.[214] The ease and low cost of communication in cyberspace reduce the political salience of territory, and provoke public impatience with the "boundary maintenance" that preoccupies political leaders in federations. They also allow nonstate actors to form networks and share information without regard for geographic distance or administrative demarcations. As Pierre Marc Johnson (a former premier of Quebec) recently observed, "a data transfer that used to cost $150,000 in 1970 only cost 12¢ in 1999."[215] If knowledge is power, as it surely is in the information economy, then the rapid and cheap diffusion of knowledge implies that national and provincial states are losing some of their capacity to resist challenges to their authority. "In short, [new communication technologies] give federalism the dated look of a concept designed for a territorial and segmented political world that is rapidly disappearing."[216]

Paradoxically, another recent global phenomenon—the "war on terror"—has temporarily reversed the erosion of international borders,[217] but it also has the potential to empower the national government at the expense of the provinces. A renewed emphasis on national security "will heighten the relative importance of the federal government in the eyes of citizens," and require or permit the federal government to respond with policies that trench on provincial jurisdictions.[218]

One possible example is the emerging national policy on public health. Whereas the delivery of health care, as we have seen, is an exclusively provincial field, the creation and management of public health programs (education, prevention, coordination) is shared between Ottawa and the provinces. Early in the new century, public health became a matter of urgent national concern. The 9/11 attacks provoked fears of bioterrorism, which were fuelled by subsequent panics over anthrax and other biological weapons. In 2003, Canada suffered an outbreak of SARS (severe acute respiratory syndrome), which killed several people and hurt tourism in Toronto. SARS also highlighted Canada's vulnerability to new global epidemics, and revealed the shortcomings of our public health system—in particular, the lack of coordination among the federal and provincial governments and the effects of sustained underfunding. In October 2003 the National Advisory Committee on SARS and Public Health recommended the creation of a National Agency for Public Health, headed by a new chief public health officer.[219] The committee's chair, Dr. David Naylor, called the lack of intergovernmental collaboration during the SARS crisis "a national embarrassment," a sentiment later endorsed by the Ontario Commission of Inquiry into the outbreak.[220]

In September 2003, before the National Advisory Committee issued its report, the federal, provincial, and territorial (FPT) Health ministers met to discuss public health. They agreed to "clarify roles and responsibilities for preventing and responding to public health threats," while respecting jurisdictional boundaries, and to strengthen intergovernmental coordination in advance of the next epidemic.[221] The language of the agreement did not indicate that Ottawa would take the lead role in public health; the provincial Health ministers appear to have assumed that jurisdiction would remain in their hands. In December 2003, however, incoming Prime Minister Paul Martin created a new Cabinet portfolio, the Ministry of State for Public Health, and appointed Dr. Carolyn Bennett to the position. Her mandate was to create a new Canada Public Health Agency, a centrepiece of the February 2004 Throne Speech.

While the agency will operate under the aegis of Health Canada, its creation appears to be related to the simultaneous announcement of a new federal Department of Public Safety and Emergency Preparedness. Significantly, the discussion paper issued by Bennett in the spring of 2004 begins, "Over the past three years [i.e., since 2001], concerns have grown about the capacity of Canada's public health system to anticipate and respond effectively to public health threats."[222] Although the letter refers to West Nile virus and "mad cow disease" (bovine spongiform encephalopathy, or BSE) as well as SARS, neither was perceived as a significant threat to Canada until 2002 at the earliest. The implicit connection between the new federal assertiveness in the field of public health, and the post-9/11 concern about bioterrorism, is made explicit in the Naylor report:

> Compounding the challenges of dealing with emerging and re-emerging infectious diseases is the threat of the accidental or intentional release of biological agents as highlighted by the intentional release of anthrax spores in the USA in the Fall of 2003.[223]

Naylor also offered some interesting comments about federal jurisdiction:

> From a constitutional perspective, public health is primarily a provincial concern. However, the federal government has authority to legislate aspects of public health owing to its powers over, variously, the criminal law, matters of national concern for the maintenance of "peace, order and good government," quarantine provisions and national borders, and trade and commerce of an interprovincial or international nature.[224]

The references to the criminal law power and the "national concern" branch of POGG indicate a link between national security, on the one hand, and public health on the other.[225] It appears that the federal government wanted to assume the leading role in a policy field that is, at the very least, a shared jurisdiction with the provinces, and found a convenient justification in post-9/11 security concerns. Such a federal role may well be valid, given the problems revealed by SARS and the fact that the national government has the duty to coordinate with the World Health Organization in the event of a severe pandemic.[226] However, there is much to be said for a more open and principled approach to the shift of policy jurisdictions in a federal state.

CONCLUSION

At Confederation, the Dominion government was intended to be independent from, and supreme over, the provinces. Today, our federation is a highly interdependent system in which the provinces and territories claim parity with Ottawa. There seemed, in 1867, to be no need for strong mechanisms to coordinate and collaborate in making policy, or to enforce mutual agreements. The absence of such mechanisms has produced decades of intergovernmental bickering and little effective cooperation (at least at the peak level of IGRs). As we will see in Chapter 5, there has been no shortage of proposed reforms to bring Canada's federal institutions up to date. Since 1992, however, the emphasis has shifted from the high-stakes game of constitutional amendment to the gentler arena of nonconstitutional renewal; some of the developments discussed in this chapter, notably the Council of the Federation, illustrate these incremental and nonbinding processes.

There is little prospect that Ottawa will regain the upper hand. At the time of writing, the Harper Government's tax cuts seemed to have put an end to a decade of federal surpluses. At the same time, Martin's efforts to reassert federal paramountcy—the "new deal" for cities and a larger post-9/11 role for the federal government—were reversed by a Conservative Government that believed that each level of government should "stick to its own knitting."[227] Harper's approach, which he calls "open federalism," emphasizes "the clarification of the respective roles and responsibilities of each order of government, through limiting the use of the federal spending power."[228] This did not mean that Harper planned to abandon federal paramountcy altogether; he intended "to build a strong national government through an emphasis on its constitutional fields of jurisdiction."[229] Nonetheless, restricting the federal spending power is a risky strategy for a prime minister—especially one who promised shorter health-care waiting times and more child-care spaces, neither of which materialized before the 2008 election.

Although Harper's posture of respect for provincial jurisdictions should have produced a lengthy honeymoon in IGRs, conflict over money and powers returned shortly after the new Government took office. A former senior advisor to Prime Minister Chrétien summarized this central truth of Canadian politics:

> *Prime ministers will continue to discover to their shock and horror that when push comes to shove, provincial premiers . . . will always continue to put their own re-election interests ahead of the re-election interests of the prime minister, no matter how nice and understanding that PM—unlike his or her terrible predecessors—may have tried to be with them.*[230]

Given the inevitability of such conflicts, the search for some institutional solution will continue. The next chapter describes the history of that search, and explains why it has yet to produce significant results.

GLOSSARY OF KEY TERMS

Ad hoc: A Latin term meaning "temporary" or "expedient." For example, the prime minister may establish an ad hoc committee of ministers to deal with a short-term issue, and disband it after it reports its recommendations back to the full Cabinet.

Block funding: A fiscal transfer from Ottawa to one or more provinces that imposes few, if any, conditions on the way the money is to be spent. For example, the 1995 CHST provided money for health care, PSE, and social assistance, without specifying the percentages to be spent in each policy field.

Conditional grants: Transfer payments from Ottawa to one or more provinces, which come with strings attached. The recipient provinces must spend the money as directed by the federal government, or risk losing some or all of the transfer.

Equalization: The federal government collects tax revenues from the richer or "have" provinces (usually British Columbia, Alberta, and Ontario) and distributes them among the poorer or "have-not" provinces (the other seven). The purpose of equalization payments is to ensure that every provincial government can provide "reasonably comparable" services to its citizens, without regard to the size of its tax base. Equalization payments may be used for any purpose; they are not conditional. The system was entrenched in the *Constitution Act, 1982* (section 36).

Executive federalism: The collective term for the relations among the political and permanent executives of Canada's senior governments.

Federal spending power: Ottawa's use of fiscal transfers to determine provincial priorities in areas of provincial jurisdiction, particularly health care, postsecondary education, and social assistance. It arises from the federal powers to tax (section 91(3)), to regulate public property (section 91(1A)), and to spend federal funds as it sees fit (section 106).[231] This taxing power provides Ottawa with more money than it needs to carry out its own constitutional responsibilities. The spending power allows Ottawa to transfer those excess revenues for purposes outside its areas of jurisdiction. The federal spending power is not explicitly defined in the *Constitution*.

Fiscal federalism: The term used to refer to the flow of money—both cash and tax points—from Ottawa to the provinces and territories. That money is supposed to redress both the vertical imbalance between the two senior levels of government, and the horizontal imbalance among the "have" and "have-not" provinces.

Foreign direct investment (FDI): Refers to any business or other undertaking that operates in Canada and is owned (in whole or in part) by non-Canadians.

Intergovernmental relations (IGRs): In a federation, frequent conflicts flare up between two or more levels of government. The processes for resolving those conflicts at the political level (as distinct from court rulings on the division of powers) are collectively termed "intergovernmental relations." In Canada, IGRs entail more than the resolution of conflicts over jurisdiction and resources: joint policy-making and implementation are also involved.

Interstate federalism: A political system in which regional and intergovernmental conflicts are resolved by bargaining among the various political units. Interstate federalism is premised on the belief that the premiers are the most effective spokespersons for their respective regions. It is analogous to international diplomacy, in which sovereign states negotiate solutions to their common problems. Literally, "interstate" means "between states."

Intrastate federalism: A political system in which regional and intergovernmental conflicts are resolved within representative national institutions. For example, the upper house of the German federal Parliament (*Bundesrat*) is made up of delegations from the *Länd* (state) governments, a majority of whom must approve all legislation proposed by the national executive. In an intrastate federation, unlike an interstate federation, the premiers are not the sole legitimate representatives of their respective regions. The task of representing the regions in national politics is carried out by national, not provincial, politicians. "Intrastate" means "within the state."

Judicial Committee of the Privy Council (JCPC): A panel of British Law Lords, appointed by the Crown to act as the final court of appeals for the Empire (later the Commonwealth). Any apparent conflict between a British law (e.g., the *BNA Act*) and a statute adopted by a former colony could be given a definitive resolution only by the JCPC. Canada abolished the right of appeal to Westminster (the common name for the British government) in 1949; since then, the Supreme Court of Canada has been the highest court of appeal in Canadian law.

Nontariff barriers: Laws and policies that protect local producers of goods and services from competitors in other provinces or countries. These include government procurement policies that favour local suppliers; licensing regimes for service providers that restrict foreign access to local markets; and regulations that discourage the flow of goods, services, and direct investment across provincial or national borders (e.g., the imposition of stricter labour or environmental standards in one jurisdiction relative to another).

Residual power: In a federal system, the written constitution divides existing policy jurisdictions between the two levels of government. It must also provide for the allocation of jurisdictions that were omitted by the drafters, and of unforeseen policy areas that may emerge long after the constitution takes effect, in order to avoid irresolvable disputes. The mechanism that allocates authority over unspecified policy areas is called the "residual power." It is normally assigned to one level of government or the other. In Canada, the residual power is assigned to the federal government by the preamble to section 91 of the *BNA Act* (the "POGG clause").

Shared-cost programs: The federal government pays part of the cost for provincial programs concerning health care, postsecondary education, and social assistance. When federal money comes with strings attached, requiring provinces to adapt their federally funded programs to standards set by Ottawa, it is called a conditional grant. Conditional grants allow Ottawa to use its spending power to influence policy-making in areas of provincial jurisdiction, usually to ensure that provincial programs follow national standards (e.g., the five principles of the *Canada Health Act*). In recent years, conditional grants have been phased out and replaced with block funding: the federal government contributes to provincial programs without specifying how the money will be spent, or in what specific areas.

Stare decisis: Latin for "the decision stands." In English common law, the doctrine that judges are bound to follow previous interpretations of the law (by higher courts, or by the same court). Over time, judicial precedents build up into a body of case law that shapes the application of the law for decades or even centuries to come.

Tariff: A policy mechanism that protects domestic producers (e.g., farmers and manufacturers) from competition by overseas producers. In essence, a tariff is a tax imposed by the national government on goods imported from other countries. The tariff raises the price of the imported item, so that it becomes more expensive to purchase than the equivalent domestically produced item. The lower purchase price encourages domestic consumers to buy goods produced in their own country, even though the actual production cost may be higher (and the goods of lower quality) than the competing foreign imports.

Tax points: The term used to describe the percentage of income tax revenue that Ottawa allocates to the provinces. One percent of tax revenue equals one tax point. Under tax rental agreements, the federal government sends each province a sum of money equal to the specified percentage of income tax collected in that province each year. Tax collection arrangements allow the provinces to set their own income tax levels, although the Canada Revenue Agency actually collects the taxes and remits the difference to the provincial government (except in Quebec, which collects its own share of income tax). In effect, the transfer of tax points from Ottawa to the provinces is an indirect form of block funding; Ottawa has no say over how a provincial government spends its own tax revenues, even those that the federal government collects on its behalf.

Ultra vires: Latin for "beyond the power of." When a court rules that a particular law does not belong within the constitutional jurisdiction of the government that adopted it (e.g., Ottawa or a province), it declares the law to be *ultra vires*. Once a law has been declared *ultra vires*, it immediately ceases to have any force or effect. Before 1982, a law that was *ultra vires* the federal Parliament might be *intra vires* (within the proper jurisdiction, and therefore constitutional) if enacted by a provincial government, and vice versa.

DISCUSSION AND REVIEW QUESTIONS

1. Identify at least one federal and one quasi-federal element in the *BNA Act*. How do they differ?

2. How have the rulings of the JCPC and the Supreme Court of Canada affected the balance of power between the federal and provincial governments?

3. How has Canada's system of fiscal federalism changed since the 1970s? What is the historical significance of the CHST?

4. Briefly explain the meanings of "interdependence" and "parity" in the context of Canadian federalism.

5. Identify and briefly describe two important peak institutions of Canadian intergovernmental relations.

SUGGESTED READINGS

Books and Articles

Gerald Baier, *Courts and Federalism: Judicial Doctrine in the United States, Australia, and Canada* (Vancouver: UBC Press, 2006).

Herman Bakvis and Grace Skogstad, eds., *Canadian Federalism: Performance, Effectiveness, and Legitimacy* (Toronto: Oxford University Press, 2002).

David Cameron and Richard Simeon, "Intergovernmental Relations in Canada: The Emergence of Collaborative Federalism," *Publius: The Journal of Federalism,* 32:2 (Spring 2002).

Alain-G. Gagnon and Hugh Segal, eds., *The Canadian Social Union Without Quebec: Eight Critical Analyses* (Montreal: Institute for Research in Public Policy, 2000).

Roger Gibbins, *Regionalism: Territorial Politics in Canada and the United States* (Toronto: Butterworths, 1982).

James Ross Hurley, *Amending Canada's Constitution: History, Processes, Problems and Prospects* (Ottawa: Minister of Supply and Services Canada, 1996).

Harvey Lazar, ed., *Canadian Fiscal Arrangements: What Works, What Might Work Better* (Montreal and Kingston: McGill-Queen's University Press, 2005).

Harvey Lazar, ed., *Toward a New Mission Statement for Canadian Fiscal Federalism* (Montreal and Kingston: McGill–Queen's University Press/Queen's University School of Policy Studies, 2000).

Akhtar Majeed, Ronald L. Watts, and Douglas M. Brown, eds., *Distribution of Powers and Responsibilities in Federal Countries* (Montreal and Kingston: McGill-Queen's University Press, 2006).

J. Peter Meekison, Hamish Telford, and Harvey Lazar, eds., *Reconsidering the Institutions of Canadian Federalism* (Montreal and Kingston: Institute of Intergovernmental Relations/McGill–Queen's University Press, 2004).

François Rocher and Miriam Smith, eds., *New Trends in Canadian Federalism*, 2nd edition (Peterborough, ON: Broadview Press, 2003).

John T. Saywell, *The Lawmakers: Judicial Power and the Shaping of Canadian Federalism* (Toronto: University of Toronto Press/Osgoode Society for Canadian Legal History, 2002).

Websites

The Canadian Intergovernmental Conference Secretariat, an agency of the federal government, maintains a website (www.scics.gc.ca) listing all major intergovernmental meetings that took place in recent years. There are links to major documents (statements or agreements) produced by or at these meetings. This website is an excellent resource on fiscal and executive federalism. The federal Department of Finance provides a wealth of information about the fiscal relations between the federal and provincial/territorial governments. Go to www.fin.gc.ca and click on the "Transfer Payments to Provinces" icon. You can also access these pages from the website of the Intergovernmental Affairs Secretariat within the federal Privy Council Office; go to www.pco-bcp.gc.ca and click on "Other PCO Sites: Intergovernmental Affairs." For a different perspective on IGRs, check out some of the provincial sites. Alberta's Department of International and Intergovernmental Relations (www.iir.gov.ab.ca) is an excellent source of information. Most provincial IGR sites are less informative, although the BC site provides useful links to other governments (go to www.portaltest.bc.ca and enter "intergovernmental" in the Search window). See also the Ontario site (www.mia.gov.on.ca) and the Quebec site (www.mce.gouv.qc.ca).

NOTES

1. These dichotomies are taken from J. Peter Meekison, Hamish Telford, and Harvey Lazar, "The Institutions of Executive Federalism: Myths and Realities," in J. Peter Meekison, Hamish Telford, and Harvey Lazar, eds., *Reconsidering the Institutions of Canadian Federalism* (Montreal and Kingston: Institute of Intergovernmental Relations/McGill–Queen's University Press, 2004), 4.

2. Other concurrent powers are less explicit: sections 91 and 92 awarded legislative powers over criminal law and marriage to Ottawa, while the administration of those laws was left to the provinces. See the discussion of Canada's court system in Chapter 10.

3. Perhaps the best known is the upper house of the German national Parliament, the *Bundesrat,* which is made up of delegations from the *Land* (state) governments. A majority in the *Bundesrat* must approve any law that affects the activities of the *Länder.*

4. However, they are subject to judicial review, which implies the possible evolution of full judicial enforcement; see Chapter 5.

5. Donald J. Savoie, *Court Government and the Collapse of Accountability in Canada and the United Kingdom* (Toronto: University of Toronto Press, 2008), 273.

6. David Cameron and Richard Simeon, "Intergovernmental Relations in Canada: The Emergence of Collaborative Federalism," *Publius: The Journal of Federalism,* 32:2 (Spring 2002), 66–67.

7. Alain Noël, *The End of a Model? Quebec and the Council of the Federation* (Kingston and Montreal: Institute for Intergovernmental Relations/Institute for Research on Public Policy, 2003), 2; available at www.irpp.org.

8. In a 2003 survey by the Centre for Research and Information on Canada (CRIC), 70 percent of respondents thought that "improved federal–provincial cooperation" should be a high priority for the new prime minister. The same proportion believed that both levels of government were equally to blame for the persistent conflicts between them; only 42 percent believed that the federal and provincial governments worked well together. See CRIC, "Canadians' Priorities: More Money for Health Care, Education; and Improved Federal/Provincial Cooperation," October 28, 2003; accessed at www.cric.ca.

9. Cameron and Simeon, 66–67.

10. See, for example, Frances Abele and Michael J. Prince, *Counsel for Canadian Federalism: Aboriginal Governments and the Council of the Federation* (Kingston and Montreal: Institute for Intergovernmental Relations/Institute for Research on Public Policy, 2003), 2; available online at www.irpp.org. See also Abele and Prince, "Aboriginal Governance and Canadian Federalism: A To-Do List for Canada," in François Rocher and Miriam Smith, eds., *New Trends in Canadian Federalism,* 2nd edition (Peterborough, ON: Broadview Press, 2003); Abele and Prince, "Alternative Futures: Aboriginal Peoples and Canadian Federalism," in Herman Bakvis and Grace Skogstad, eds., *Canadian Federalism: Performance, Effectiveness, and Legitimacy* (Toronto: Oxford University Press, 2002).

11. Cameron and Simeon, 63.

12. Douglas M. Brown, *Getting Things Done in the Federation: Do We Need New Rules for an Old Game?* (Kingston and Montreal: Institute for Intergovernmental Relations/Institute for Research on Public Policy, 2003), 3; available at www.irpp.org.

13. Ronald L. Watts, *Comparing Federal Systems,* 2nd edition (Montreal and Kingston: Institute of Intergovernmental Relations/McGill–Queen's University Press, 1999), 69–70. See also Ronald L. Watts, *Intergovernmental Councils in Federations* (Kingston and Montreal: Institute for Intergovernmental Relations/Institute for Research on Public Policy, 2003), 3; accessed at www.irpp.org, July 2003.

14. See Jennifer Smith, "The Constitutional Debate and Beyond," in François Rocher and Miriam Smith, eds., *New Trends in Canadian Federalism,* 2nd edition (Peterborough, ON: Broadview Press, 2003), and "Informal Constitutional Development: Change by Other Means," in Bakvis and Skogstad, eds.

15. J. Peter Meekison, "The Annual Premiers' Conference: Forging a Common Front," in Meekison, Telford, and Lazar, eds., 143.

16. Watts, *Comparing Federal Systems,* 123.

17. Ibid., 119.

18. Richard Simeon, "Important? Yes. Transformative? No: North American Integration and Canadian Federalism," in Harvey Lazar, Hamish Telford, and Ronald L. Watts, eds., *The Impact of Global and Regional Integration on Federal Systems* (Montreal and Kingston: Institute for Intergovernmental Relations/McGill–Queen's University Press, 2003).

19. Hamish Telford, *Expanding the Partnership: The Proposed Council of the Federation and the Challenge of Glocalization* (Kingston and Montreal: Institute for Intergovernmental Relations/Institute for Research on Public Policy, 2003), 2; accessed at www.irpp.org, July 2003.

20. Harvey Lazar, "In Search of a New Mission Statement for Canadian Fiscal Federalism," in Harvey Lazar, ed., *The State of the Federation 1999–2000: Toward a New Mission Statement for Canadian Fiscal Federalism* (Montreal and Kingston: Institute for Intergovernmental Relations/McGill–Queen's University Press, 2000), 29.

21. Alan C. Cairns, "The Judicial Committee and its Critics," in Douglas E. Williams, ed., *Constitution, Government, and Society in Canada: Selected Essays by Alan C. Cairns* (Toronto: McClelland and Stewart, 1988), 59–60.

22. Among respondents to the 2003 CRIC poll, greater spending on health care and education were by far the highest policy priorities (named by 73 and 70 percent, respectively).

23. The topic of judicial appointment is discussed in Chapter 10.

24. Gerald Baier, *Courts and Federalism: Judicial Doctrine in the United States, Australia, and Canada* (Vancouver: UBC Press, 2006), 146–151. See also *Reference Re Canada Assistance Plan (B.C.)*, [1991] 2 S.C.R. 525.

25. As early as 1875, when the *Supreme Court Act* was adopted, the Government of Canada tried to put an end to JCPC appeals from Canadian courts. Britain refused, insisting that an impartial arbiter was required to resolve disputes between the political majority in the new Dominion and its various minorities. John T. Saywell, *The Lawmakers: Judicial Power and the Shaping of Canadian Federalism* (Toronto: University of Toronto Press/Osgoode Society for Canadian Legal History, 2002), 57–61.

26. Donald V. Smiley, *The Federal Condition in Canada* (Toronto: McGraw-Hill Ryerson, 1987), 48.

27. Peter H. Russell, Rainer Knopff, and Ted Morton, "Introduction," in Russell, Knopff, and Morton, eds., *Federalism and the Charter* (Ottawa: Carleton University Press, 1989), 6.

28. Haldane used the phrase "autonomous kingdoms" during an oral hearing; he is quoted in Saywell, 161. Lord Watson expressed the belief that Canada was a compact among sovereign provinces in *Liquidators of the Maritime Bank of Canada v. Receiver-General of New Brunswick*, [1892]; quoted in Saywell, 128.

29. Saywell, Chapter One.

30. Ibid., 12.

31. bid., 13–14.

32. Ibid., 74.

33. Viscount Haldane, "The Work for the Empire of the Judicial Committee of the Privy Council," *Cambridge Law Journal*, 1 (1923), 150; quoted in Cairns, "The Judicial Committee and Its Critics," 90.

34. *Fort Frances Pulp and Power Company v. Manitoba Free Press*, JC 1923, in Olmsted, volume 2, 313–14.

35. *Toronto Electric Commissioners v. Snider*, JC 1925, in Olmsted, volume 2, 408–09.

36. *Reference re Employment and Social Insurance Act*, JC 1937, in Olmsted, volume 3, 217.

37. *Attorney General of Canada v. Canada Temperance Federation*, JC 1946, in Russell, Knopff, and Morton, eds., 120.

38. Saywell, 167–168.

39. Quoted in ibid., 167.

40. Ibid., 67–71.

41. In re *The Regulation and Control of Aeronautics in Canada*, JC 1932, in Olmsted, volume 3, 724.

42. In re *Regulation and Control of Radio Communications in Canada*, JC 1932, in Olmsted, volume 3, 25.

43. *Attorney General for Canada v. Attorney General for Ontario* [the Labour Conventions Case], JC 1937, in Olmsted, volume 3, 200.

44. Ibid., 203.

45. Ibid., 204.

46. Whether it will continue to do so is an open question. Some scholars suggest that the Supreme Court has been nibbling away at the *Labour Conventions* doctrine, and may overturn it altogether in the near future. Saywell, 298–301.

47. Harvey Lazar, Hamish Telford, and Ronald L. Watts, "Divergent Trajectories: The Impact of Global and Regional Integration on Federal Systems," in Lazar, Telford, and Watts, eds., 17.

48. See, for example, Frank R. Scott, "The Privy Council and Mr. Bennett's 'New Deal' Legislation," and "Centralization and Decentralization," in Frank R. Scott, *Essays on the Constitution: Aspects of Canadian Law and Politics* (Toronto: University of Toronto Press, 1977), 90–101 and 260–72, respectively.

49. Cairns, "The Judicial Committee and Its Critics," 61–63.

50. Ibid., 80.

51. Ibid., 80–81.

52. The appointment process became an issue in the 2004 federal election. Shortly before the campaign began, the Justice Committee in the House of Commons reviewed the process (discussed in Chapter 10). In the campaign itself, Conservative leader Stephen Harper demanded that the pool of candidates be restricted to nominees put forward by provincial governments. The federal Liberal Government did not follow this practice when it appointed two new justices from Ontario in August 2004; neither did Harper when he appointed Justice Rothstein in 2006. See the discussion of judicial appointments in Chapter 10.

53. Russell, Knopff, and Morton, "Introduction," 9.

54. *Johannesson v. West St. Paul*, S.C.R. 1952, in Russell, Knopff, and Morton, eds., 134–35.

55. *Reference re Offshore Mineral Rights of British Columbia*, S.C.R. 1967, in Russell, Knopff, and Morton, eds., 150.

56. *R. v. Crown Zellerbach Canada Ltd.*, [1988] 1 S.C.R. 401.

57. *R. v. Hydro-Québec*, [1997] 3 S.C.R. 213, paragraph 110.

58. Russell, Knopff, and Morton, "Comment on *The Queen v. Crown Zellerbach Canada Ltd.*, 1988," in Russell, Knopff, and Morton, eds., 273.

59. Baier, *Courts and Federalism*, 135–138.

60. *Reference re Goods and Services Tax*, [1992] 2 S.C.R. 445, paragraph 34, *per* Lamer C.J.

61. Reference re *The Farm Products Marketing Act (Ontario)*, S.C.R. 1957, in Russell, Knopff, and Morton, eds., 142–43.

62. *Attorney General of Manitoba v. Manitoba Egg and Poultry Association* (Chicken and Egg Reference), S.C.R. 1971, in Russell, Knopff, and Morton, eds., 152–61.

63. *General Motors of Canada Ltd. v. City National Leasing*, [1989] 1 S.C.R. 641.

64. Gerald Baier, "Judicial Review and Canadian Federalism," in Bakvis and Skogstad, eds., 27; Gerald Baier, "The Law of Federalism: Judicial Review and the Division of Powers," in Rocher and Smith, eds., 126–27; A. Wayne MacKay, "The Supreme Court of Canada and Federalism: Does/Should Anyone Care Anymore?" *Canadian Bar Review*, 80:1–2 (March–June 2001).

65. *R. v. Hydro-Québec; RJR-MacDonald Inc. v. Canada (Attorney General)*, [1995] 3 S.C.R. 199.

66. Baier, *Courts and Federalism*, 142.

67. *R. v. Malmo-Levine; R. v. Caine*, [2003] 3 S.C.R. 571, paragraphs 69–78, *per* Gonthier and Binnie, JJ.

68. *R. v. Hydro-Québec*, paragraph 121.

69. *R. v. Malmo-Levine*, paragraph 74.

70. Peter W. Hogg, "Is the Supreme Court of Canada Biased in Constitutional Cases?" *Canadian Bar Review*, 57 (1979).

71. Baier, "The Law of Federalism," 127–28.

72. MacKay, 268; Saywell, 254.

73. *Reference re Firearms Act (Can.)*, [2000] 1 S.C.R. 783.

74. MacKay, 274–75; Saywell, 284–87. In 2005 the Supreme Court restricted the doctrine of federal paramountcy, under which a provincial law that conflicts with a federal law in a concurrent jurisdiction is invalid: *Rothmans, Benson & Hedges Inc. v. Saskatchewan*, [2005] 1 S.C.R. 188, paragraphs 11–26, *per* Major J.

75. Saywell, 271.

76. Russell, Knopff, and Morton, "Comment on *Canadian Industrial Gas and Oil Ltd. v. Government of Saskatchewan,* 1978," in Russell, Knopff, and Morton, eds., 188–89.

77. Daniel Johnson, *Égalité ou Indépendance* (Montreal: Les Éditions de L'Homme Ltée, 1965).

78. See Tom Flanagan, *Waiting for the Wave: The Reform Party and Preston Manning* (Toronto: Stoddart, 1996), Chapter 3.

79. Joe Ruggeri, "The Evolution of Provincial Responsibility," in Harvey Lazar, ed., *Canadian Fiscal Arrangements: What Works, What Might Work Better* (Montreal and Kingston: McGill–Queen's University Press, 2005), 87–88.

80. Ibid., 87–88.

81. Meekison, "The Annual Premiers' Conference," 143.

82. Quoted in Ruggeri, 96.

83. Ibid., 97.

84. Ibid., 94.

85. Canada, *Report of the Royal Commission on Dominion-Provincial Relations,* volume 1, abridged by Donald V. Smiley (Ottawa: Carleton University Press, 1963 [1940]), 210.

86. Ruggeri, 97.

87. Ibid., 100.

88. The *Constitution Act, 1940* inserted clause 2A into section 91 of the *BNA Act;* see Appendix.

89. Ruggeri, 101–102.

90. Hamish Telford, "The Federal Spending Power in Canada: Nation-Building or Nation-Destroying?" *Publius: The Journal of Federalism,* 33:1 (Winter 2003), 32–33.

91. Richard Simeon and Ian Robinson, *State, Society, and the Development of Canadian Federalism,* volume 65 of the collected research studies for the Royal Commission on the Economic Union and Development Prospects for Canada (Toronto: University of Toronto Press, 1986), 106.

92. *Report of the Royal Commission on Dominion–Provincial Relations,* 210–14.

93. See Lazar, "In Search of a New Mission Statement for Canadian Fiscal Federalism," 7–10.

94. Telford, "The Federal Spending Power in Canada," 33.

95. Lazar, "In Search of a New Mission Statement for Canadian Fiscal Federalism", 10.

96. Stephen Laurent and François Vaillancourt, *Federal-Provincial Transfers for Social Programs in Canada: Their Status in May 2004* (Montreal: Institute for Research on Public Policy, July 2004), 4; accessed at www.irpp.org, August 2004.

97. Ibid.

98. Hobson and St-Hilaire, 162–63.

99. Ibid., 166.

100. Ibid., 167.

101. Quoted in ibid., 167.

102. Janice MacKinnon, *Minding the Public Purse: The Fiscal Crisis, Political Trade-Offs, and Canada's Future* (Montreal and Kingston: McGill–Queen's University Press, 2003), Chapter 1.

103. In November 1995, for example, the federal government held back over $400,000 of its planned cash payment to Alberta; it claimed that an equal amount had been charged to patients by private clinics in the province, which violated the nonprofit element of the public administration criterion. Andrew C. Tzembelicos, "Chronology of Events July 1995–June 1996," in Patrick C. Fafard and Douglas M. Brown, eds., *Canada: The State of the Federation, 1996* (Kingston: Institute for Intergovernmental Relations, 1997), 258. This should not be taken to suggest that Ottawa is zealous in its enforcement of the *Canada Health Act;* federal clawbacks between 1984 and 2002 totalled $8.3 million, a pittance compared to the tens of billions of dollars spent during that period. Stéphane Dion, "Fiscal Balance in Canada," in Lazar, ed., *Canadian Fiscal Arrangements,* 167.

104. Keith Banting and Robin Boadway, "Defining the Sharing Community: The Federal Role in Health Care," in Harvey Lazar and France St-Hilaire, eds., *Money, Politics and Health Care: Reconstructing the Federal-Provincial Partnership* (Montreal and Kingston: Institute for Research on Public Policy and Institute for Intergovernmental Relations, 2004), 13.

105. Alain-G. Gagnon and Hugh Segal, "Introduction," in Gagnon and Segal, eds., 2.

106. MacKinnon, x.

107. Laurent and Vaillancourt, 10–11.

108. Hobson and St-Hilaire, 175.

109. Roy Romanow is a former NDP premier of Saskatchewan and a passionate defender of publicly funded health care. He is also a savvy veteran of intergovernmental conflict, having played a key role in the 1980–82 constitutional negotiations (discussed in Chapter 5).

110. Roy Romanow is a former NDP premier of Saskatchewan and a passionate defender of publicly funded health care. He is also a savvy veteran of intergovernmental conflict, having played a key role in the 1980–82 constitutional negotiations (discussed in Chapter 5).

111. "Federal/Provincial/Territorial Fiscal Relations in Transition: A Report to Canada's Western Premiers from the Finance Ministers of British Columbia, Alberta, Saskatchewan, Manitoba, Yukon, Northwest Territories and Nunavut," June 2003, 6; available at www.scics.gc.ca.

112. Lazar, "In Search of a New Mission Statement for Canadian Fiscal Federalism," 6; Robin Boadway, "The Vertical Fiscal Gap: Conceptions and Misconceptions," in Lazar, ed., *Canadian Fiscal Arrangements*, 51.

113. Canada, Department of Finance, "Backgrounder: Canada Health Transfer," March 2004; available at www.fin.gc.ca/fedpriov/chte.html.

114. Report of the Commission on the Future of Health Care in Canada, 67; Laurent and Vaillancourt, 11.

115. "Federal/Provincial/Territorial Fiscal Relations in Transition," 11–12.

116. Canada, Department of Finance, "Federal Support for Health Care: The Facts," March 2004; available at www.fin.gc.ca/facts/fshc6_e.html.

117. Council of the Federation, "Premiers' Action Plan for Better Health Care: Resolving Issues in the Spirit of True Federalism," July 30, 2004, 2; available at www.scics.gc.ca.

118. "Backgrounder: Canada Health Transfer," 3.

119. Laurent and Vaillancourt, 16–18.

120. Pierre Marc Johnson with Karel Mayrand, "Citizens, States and International Regimes: International Governance Challenges in a Globalized World," in Thomas J. Courchene and Donald J. Savoie, eds., *The Art of the State: Governance in a World Without Frontiers* (Montreal: Institute for Research on Public Policy, 2003), 376.

121. Canada, Department of Finance, "Turning a New Leaf: Budget 2006" (Ottawa: Her Majesty the Queen in Right of Canada, 2006), 36–40; accessed at www.fin.gc.ca, May 2007.

122. As this chapter was revised in May 2008, Ontario was in danger of being declared a "have-not" province because of job losses in the manufacturing sector. Meanwhile, Newfoundland and Labrador capitalized on record world prices for oil, declaring itself to be a "have" province in its 2008 budget. These developments remind us that there are few constants in Canadian politics.

123. Ronald L. Watts, "Comparative Conclusions," in Akhtar Majeed, Ronald L. Watts, and Douglas M. Brown, eds., *Distribution of Powers and Responsibilities in Federal Countries* (Montreal and Kingston: McGill–Queen's University Press, 2006), 334.

124. Paul A.R. Hobson and France St-Hilaire, "The Evolution of Federal–Provincial Fiscal Arrangements: Putting Humpty Together Again," in Lazar, ed., *Toward a New Mission Statement for Canadian Fiscal Federalism*, 163.

125. The Expert Panel on Equalization considered taking resource needs into account, but decided that this would make the formula too complicated. Canada, Expert Panel on Equalization and Territorial Formula Financing, *Achieving A National Purpose: Putting*

Equalization Back on Track (Ottawa: Department of Finance Canada, May 2006), 45–46 (accessed at www.eqtff-pfft.ca, June 2007).

126. Ibid., 32.

127. Michael Holden, "Equalization: Implications of Recent Changes" (Ottawa: Library of Parliament Research Branch, 2006), 7.

128. Paul Boothe, "The Stabilization Properties of Canada's Equalization Program," in Lazar, ed., *Canadian Fiscal Arrangements*, 175–183.

129. Holden, 3.

130. In 2001–02, the federal government paid an extra $3.4 billion in equalization to four provinces because of an accounting error by Revenue Canada. Prime Minister Chrétien demanded that the provinces repay the money, much of which had already been spent. His then-Finance minister, Paul Martin, argued that the money should be forgiven and directed toward health care. Thus the accounting error caused a major political conflict, not only between governments, but also within the federal Cabinet. Susan Delacourt, *Juggernaut: Paul Martin's Campaign for Chrétien's Crown* (Toronto: McClelland and Stewart, 2003), 232–34.

131. Holden, 5.

132. *Achieving A National Purpose: Putting Equalization Back on Track* (Ottawa: Department of Finance Canada, May 2006), 24–25.

133. Holden, 9.

134. *Achieving A National Purpose*, 25.

135. Holden, 11.

136. The name of the province of Newfoundland was officially changed to Newfoundland and Labrador in 2001.

137. "Arrangement between the Government of Canada and the Government of Nova Scotia on Offshore Revenues" (February 2005), 1; accessed at www.fin.gc.ca/FEDPROV05/OffshoreResAcc/novascotiaarr-e.html.

138. Canada, House of Commons, *Hansard*, November 4, 2004, 1194.

139. Holden, 10.

140. "Conservative Party of Canada Federal Election Platform, 2006", 43 (accessed at www.conservative.ca, January 2006).

141. *Achieving a National Purpose*, 55.

142. Ibid., 55.

143. Ibid., 61.

144. Although the fiscal capacity of the Atlantic provinces is considerably below the Canadian average, it does little to offset the enormous wealth of Alberta in the calculation of a national standard. Thomas J. Courchene, "Resource Revenues and Equalization: Five-Province vs. National-Average Standards, Alternatives to the Representative Tax System, and Revenue-Sharing Pools" (Montreal: Institute for Research on Public Policy Working Papers, September 2005), 8; accessed at www.irpp.org, March 2007.

145. "Restoring Fiscal Balance for a Stronger Federation: Budget Backgrounder 2007," 14 (accessed at www.fin.gc.ca, May 2007).

146. Ibid., 15.

147. Ibid., 16.

148. The differences between the two premiers were more than stylistic. Had the 2007 formula applied to both provinces, it would have lowered the equalization and offshore offset payments to Newfoundland and Labrador by $228 million in 2007–08; conversely, Nova Scotia would have received an additional $90 million. Ibid., 17.

149. Alain Noël, "'A Report That Almost No One Has Discussed': Early Responses to Quebec's Commission on Fiscal Imbalance," in Lazar, ed., *Canadian Fiscal Arrangements*, 134.

150. Ibid., 133.

151. Dion, 163.

152. Ibid., 155 and 159.

153. A classic example occurred in 2007: the Harper Government boosted transfer payments to Quebec in the run-up to an election in that province, hoping to portray incumbent Liberal Premier Jean Charest as the leader who could best advance Quebec's interests in dealings with Ottawa. The money was supposed to be spent on social programs. Instead, Charest announced on the day after the federal budget that he would use the new money to lower taxes in the province. This move appears to have backfired politically, for both Charest and Harper.

154. Dion, 165.

155. "Conservative Party of Canada Federal Election Platform, 2006," 43.

156. "Turning a New Leaf: Budget 2006," Chapter 6.

157. "Restoring Fiscal Balance for a Stronger Federation: Budget Backgrounder 2007," 50 (Chart 9).

158. "Restoring Fiscal Balance for a Stronger Federation: Budget Backgrounder 2007".

159. Richard Simeon and Martin Papillon, "Canada," in Majeed, Watts and Brown, eds., *Distribution of Powers and Responsibilities in Federal Countries*, 103.

160. Ibid., 103; see also Watts, 334.

161. Harvey Lazar, "Trust in Intergovernmental Fiscal Relations," in Lazar, ed., *Canadian Fiscal Arrangements*, 8.

162. Boadway, 55.

163. Eddie Goldenberg, *The Way It Works: Inside Ottawa* (Toronto: McClelland and Stewart, 2006), 389.

164. Lazar, 29; Simeon and Papillon, 106.

165. Brown, *Getting Things Done in the Federation*. In 2002 the first ministers agreed to a dispute-resolution process in the health-care field, to deal with issues like the Alberta–Ottawa fight over private for-profit clinics and the resulting federal "clawback." However, the final decision in any given dispute rests with the federal Health minister, which calls into question the genuinely intergovernmental nature of the process. For details, see Health Canada, *Fact Sheet: CHA Dispute Avoidance and Resolution;* available at www.hcsc.gc.ca/english/media/releases/2002/health_act/cha.htm.

166. Watts, *Intergovernmental Councils in Federations*, 8–9.

167. Meekison, "The Annual Premiers' Conference," 147.

168. For more on the CCME and its operation, see Julie M. Simmons, "Securing the Threads of Co-operation in the Tapestry of Intergovernmental Relations: Does the Institutionalization of Ministerial Conferences Matter?" in Meekison, Telford, and Lazar, eds., 285–311.

169. Martin Papillon and Richard Simeon, "The Weakest Link? First Ministers' Conferences in Canadian Intergovernmental Relations," in Meekison, Telford, and Lazar, eds., 144.

170. Ibid., 116–117.

171. Ibid., 119.

172. The requirement was contained in section 37, which was repealed automatically in 1987. See Appendix, footnote 98.

173. Papillon and Simeon, 123.

174. *Provincial–Territorial Backgrounder,* September 14, 2004; accessed at www.scics.gc.ca/pdf/800042010_e.pdf.

175. Campbell Clark, "Brinksmanship nearly scuttled health deal," *The Globe and Mail,* September 20, 2004.

176. Papillon and Simeon, 125.

177. J. Peter Meekison, *Council of the Federation: An Idea Whose Time Has Come* (Kingston and Montreal: Institute for Intergovernmental Relations/Institute for Research on Public Policy, 2003), 1; available at www.irpp.org.

178. "Council of the Federation: Founding Agreement," December 5, 2003; accessed at www.scics.gc.ca.

179. Gregory P. Marchildon, *The Health Council of Canada Proposal in Light of the Council of the Federation* (Kingston and Montreal: Institute for Intergovernmental Relations/Institute for Research on Public Policy, 2003), 5; available at www.irpp.org.

180. Andrew Teliszewsky and Christopher Stoney, "Addressing the Fiscal Imbalance through Asymmetrical Federalism: Dangerous Times for the Harper Government and for Canada," in G. Bruce Doern, ed., *How Ottawa Spends, 2007–2008: The Harper Conservatives—Climate of Change* (Montreal and Kingston: McGill–Queen's University Press, 2007), 41.

181. The Province of Quebec participates in the Annual Conference of New England Governors and Eastern Canadian Premiers, but not in the Council of Atlantic Premiers meetings.

182. J. Peter Meekison, "The Western Premiers' Conference: Intergovernmental Co-operation at the Regional Level," in Meekison, Telford, and Lazar, eds., 199.

183. The data for 2005–06 are taken from the Secretariat's 2007 annual report to the federal and provincial governments. It is available on the Canadian Intergovernmental Conference Secretariat website (go to www.scisc.gc.ca and click on "Publications"). The historical data are from Simmons, Table 1, 289.

184. Meekison, "The Annual Premiers' Conference," 157; Simmons, 290.

185. For more information, see the Council's website: www.ccme.ca.

186. The history and purpose of the CMEC are described in its December 2003 *Framework for the Future* document, available at www.cmec.ca. Appendix D of the document also contains a very useful analysis of the CCME and other FPT bodies.

187. Johanne Poirier, "Intergovernmental Agreements in Canada: At the Crossroads Between Law and Politics," in Meekison, Telford, and Lazar, eds., 427.

188. Thomas J. Courchene, "Glocalization: The Regional/International Interface," *Canadian Journal of Regional Science,* 18:1 (Spring 1995).

189. Michael Keating, "The Territorial State: Functional Restructuring and Political Change," in Courchene and Savoie, eds., 339–40.

190. Andrew Sancton, "Municipalities, Cities, and Globalization: Implications for Canadian Federalism," in Bakvis and Skogstad, eds., 268.

191. Telford, *Expanding the Partnership,* 4.

192. Toronto's city council was outraged by the agreement, which it interpreted as a denial of the city's special status as the largest urban government in Canada. Its mayor and several councillors argued that Toronto should be able to deal directly with the federal government. McGuinty tried to reassure the city's leaders that the memorandum did not forestall direct relations between Toronto and Ottawa, but the dispute threatened to split the AMO. Simon Tuck and Katherine Harding, "Cities can sit in on Ottawa talks, province promises," *The Globe and Mail,* August 24, 2004 (accessed at www.globeandmail.com); Gillian Livingston, "New deal won't hurt big cities: McGuinty," Canadian Press, August 25, 2004 (accessed at www.canada.com).

193. Some observers argue that provincial jurisdiction over municipalities does not prevent the federal government from intervening in urban affairs, any more than the provincial responsibility for hospitals prohibits Ottawa from putting conditions on transfer payments for health care. The real barrier to federal involvement in cities is a lack of political will and financial wherewithal. See Roger Gibbins, "The Missing Link: Policy Options for Engaging Ottawa in Canada's Urban Centres," in Meekison, Telford, and Lazar, eds., 412.

194. Data retrieved at www.statcan.ca/english/census06/data/popdwell/highlights.cfm, May 2008.

195. Ibid., 264.

196. Teliszewsky and Stoney, 40.

197. Grace Skogstad, "International Trade Policy," in Bakvis and Skogstad, eds., 160.

198. It should be noted that the Council of Ministers of Education Canada (CMEC) has long been the principal Canadian voice in international agreements relating to education policy, despite being a purely PT organization. See the CMEC website for more information: www.cmec.ca.

199. Skogstad, 161–62.

200. One interesting symbol of this aggression is the renaming of Alberta's IGR department: it is now the Department of International and Intergovernmental Relations.

201. "Premiers Announce Progress on Key Initiatives," news release, July 30, 2004, 3; available at www.scics.gc.ca.

202. Skogstad, 162–65.

203. Chantal Hébert, *French Kiss: Stephen Harper's Blind Date with Quebec* (Toronto: Knopf Canada, 2007), 61–62.

204. Paul Wells, *Right Side Up: The Fall of Paul Martin and the Rise of Stephen Harper's New Conservatism* (Toronto: McClelland & Stewart, 2006), 289.

205. Kathryn Harrison, "Passing the Environmental Buck," in Rocher and Smith, eds., 337–38.

206. Harrison, 338. See also Mark S. Winfield, "Environmental Policy and Federalism," in Bakvis and Skogstad, eds., 133.

207. Alberta, "Alberta stands firm on pledge to protect economy against impact of Kyoto Protocol, Klein says," news release; accessed at www.gov.ab.ca/home/index.cfm?Page=350.

208. Mark A. Luz and C. Marc Miller, "Globalization and Canadian Federalism: Implications of the NAFTA's Investment Rules," *McGill Law Journal*, 47 (2001–02), 984.

209. Luz and Millar, 985.

210. Ibid., 988.

211. Simeon, "Important? Yes," 154–56.

212. One recent dispute, which fell outside the purview of NAFTA, illustrates the complexity of "multitiered" federalism under globalization. In 1999, the Ontario government of Mike Harris leased the 407 toll highway to a private consortium controlled by a Spanish company. In 2004 the consortium raised the toll rates, which it claimed it had the right to do under the terms of the lease. The new premier, Dalton McGuinty, argued that the province had the power to veto any rate increases as it saw fit. In retaliation, the Spanish government asked the European Union (EU) to raise the issue with Canadian officials during negotiations over a proposed Canada–EU trade agreement. Concerned that the talks might be derailed by the dispute, Canada's minister of Trade asked McGuinty to reconsider his opposition to the toll increase. At the time of writing, the clash between Ontario and the Spanish consortium had not been resolved. Associated Press and Canadian Press, "Working to end Ontario row over toll road, EU says," *The Globe and Mail*, August 12, 2004; Richard Mackie, "McGuinty shrugs off highway toll spat," *The Globe and Mail*, August 12, 2004 (both accessed at www.globeandmail.com).

213. Johnson and Mayrand, 375.

214. Roger Gibbins, "Federalism in a Digital World," *Canadian Journal of Political Science*, 33:4 (December 2000).

215. Johnson and Mayrand, 374.

216. Gibbins, "Federalism in a Digital World," 674.

217. Peter Andreas and Thomas J. Biersteker, eds., *The Rebordering of North America: Integration and Exclusion in a New Security Context* (New York: Routledge, 2003).

218. Ronald L. Watts, "Managing Interdependence in a Federal Political System," in Courchene and Savoie, eds., 147.

219. *Learning from SARS: Renewal of Public Health in Canada* (Ottawa: Health Canada, October 2003); available at www.hc-sc.gc.ca.

220. Marina Jimenez and Brian Laghi, "Squabbling abetted SARS, panel says," *The Globe and Mail*, October 8, 2003 (accessed at www.globeandmail.com); Hon. Mr. Justice Archie

Campbell, "The SARS Commission Interim Report: SARS and Public Health in Ontario" (Toronto, April 15, 2004); available at www.hc-sc.gc.ca.

221. Annual Conference of Federal–Provincial–Territorial Ministers of Health, news release, September 4, 2003, 1; accessed at www.scics.gc.ca.

222. *Strengthening the Pan-Canadian Public Health System,* discussion paper (Ottawa: Health Canada, 2004); available at www.hc-sc.gc.ca.

223. *Learning from SARS,* 2.

224. Ibid., 2.

225. The reference in the Naylor report to "national concern," as opposed to "emergency," is also intriguing. Because SARS was clearly an "emergency" within the meaning of the POGG jurisprudence from both the JCPC and the Supreme Court, it would serve to justify only a temporary federal intrusion into provincial jurisdiction. "National concern," on the other hand, could underpin a permanent federal role that goes beyond anything envisioned by the provinces in September 2003.

226. Kumanan Wilson and Harvey Lazar, "Planning for the Next Pandemic Threat: Defining the Federal Role in Public Health Emergencies", *IRPP Policy Matters* 6:5 (November 2005), 15.

227. Hébert, 244.

228. Peter Graefe and Rachel Laforest, "La Grande Seduction: Wooing Quebec," in G. Bruce Doern, ed., *How Ottawa Spends, 2007–2008: The Harper Conservatives—Climate of Change* (Montreal and Kingston: McGill–Queen's University Press, 2007), 52.

229. Ibid.

230. Goldenberg, 389.

231. Peter Hogg, *Constitutional Law of Canada,* 3rd edition (supp.) (Toronto: Carswell, 1992), 6–16.

5

From Megaconstitutional Politics to Nonconstitutional Renewal

LEARNING OBJECTIVES

After you finish reading this chapter, you should be able to:
- *describe* and *explain* megaconstitutional politics in Canada;
- *explain* the failures of the Meech Lake and Charlottetown Accords;
- *summarize* the Supreme Court's ruling in the *Secession Reference,* and compare it to the texts of the federal *Clarity Act* and Quebec's Bill 99;
- *explain* the recent emphasis on nonconstitutional renewal of the federation, and *summarize* the most important developments flowing from it;
- *identify* one key element in Prime Minister Harper's megaconstitutional agenda.

INTRODUCTION: REWRITING THE RULES OF THE CANADIAN FEDERATION

Wherever human beings compete—in the soccer match described at the start of Chapter 3, for example—there must be rules to regulate the competition. Often, these rules, which are supposed to resolve conflicts, are themselves a source of conflict. That applies to governments as well as individuals or small groups: when one side believes that the game is rigged against them, they demand that the rules be rewritten in their favour (which would, of course, be "fairer" for everyone in the game).

Almost as soon as the rules of Confederation took effect, they were challenged. Some provinces, particularly Ontario and Quebec, claimed that the division of powers in sections 91 and 92 was too restrictive. As more provinces joined the federation, their divergent perspectives on government and society produced more calls for reform.

Beginning with the first Premiers' Conference in 1886, provincial governments demanded formal **amendments** to the *Constitution.* But before 1982, Canada had no written **amending formula.** The legal power to change the *BNA Act* remained with the British Parliament—although it was clearly understood that no such change would be carried out except in response to a request from the federal government. The tricky question was the degree of provincial consent to such a request. Did it require the unanimous consent of the provinces, a majority of the provinces, or something less? For obvious reasons, the provinces argued for unanimity, or at least a high degree of consensus; the federal government tried to preserve as much flexibility as it could. Although repeated attempts to agree on an amending formula failed, this did not prevent the senior government from amending the *BNA Act* several times between 1867 and 1982.
- Six new provinces were added between 1870 and 1949; each addition required an amendment to the *BNA Act.*

- In 1940 the provinces agreed to transfer responsibility for Unemployment Insurance to the federal government; the resulting amendment is enshrined in clause 2A of section 91.
- Appeals to the Judicial Committee of the Privy Council were abolished in 1949.
- The provinces agreed to transfer pensions to the federal government; the resulting amendments were adopted in 1951 and 1964 (clause 94A).

Every change to the division of powers received unanimous provincial consent before the federal government submitted the amendment to the British Parliament—even while Ottawa refused to formally acknowledge that unanimity was required.[1] So while altering the text of the *BNA Act* was hardly a routine procedure, it was clearly achievable.

The adoption of an amending formula in 1982 should have made future changes easier, by reducing intergovernmental disputes about decision rules and the powers of the various players. Instead, it appears to have produced a constitutional stalemate.[2] The general amending formula (Dossier 3.3) has been successfully invoked only once. Two attempts to use the unanimity formula—the Meech Lake and Charlottetown Accords—ended in spectacular and embittering failure. The rejection of the Charlottetown Accord in a 1992 referendum brought a temporary respite from megaconstitutional politics. No one had any appetite for yet another round of haggling, horse-trading, and public protest. Instead of amending the entrenched *Constitution,* Canada's governments would attempt to make improvements and resolve disputes through nonconstitutional renewal (NCR).

There is nothing new in this resort to NCR. Although the megaconstitutional battles of the 1980s and early 1990s suggested otherwise, most adjustments to our political institutions have occurred without amending the entrenched text. These adjustments were, and are, incremental and often ad hoc. Many began as short-term solutions to immediate practical problems, and have persisted for decades because of institutional inertia. These include the use of the federal spending power in provincial jurisdictions, executive federalism, and the complex structure of intergovernmental relations (Chapter 4). Some incremental adjustments have now been recognized as unwritten constitutional conventions; others have been enshrined in statutes and/or written agreements among governments.[3]

There have always been significant differences between the entrenched *Constitution* and the political practices followed by Canadian governments.[4] In large measure, these arise from the persistence of British constitutional conventions. As explained in Chapter 3, conventions provide a useful degree of flexibility in the operations of government; they allow our institutions to adapt to changing social conditions and attitudes, without requiring the difficult and contentious formal amendment process. The same might be said of written intergovernmental agreements, although few of these have proven effective in practice. Their implementation depends on the political will of the participants, a shaky foundation at best.[5] Unlike amendments to the entrenched *Constitution,* neither conventions nor intergovernmental agreements are subject to enforcement by the courts. As yet, there are no effective mechanisms for decision-making, enforcement, or dispute resolution. Their absence reveals the limitations of the NCR strategy, and suggests that the suspension of megaconstitutional politics cannot persist indefinitely.[6]

This chapter traces recent efforts to reform Confederation in response to political and social change. It begins with an analysis of megaconstitutional politics between 1960 and 1992, focusing on two driving forces for constitutional change: Quebec nationalism and Western regionalism (Dossier 2.1). Following an account of the Charlottetown Accord, whose failure terminated 30 years of megaconstitutional politics, the chapter summarizes the shift to nonconstitutional renewal in the 1990s. It deals with three key issues: (1) the crisis provoked by the 1995 Quebec sovereignty referendum; (2) the desire (partly provoked by globalization) to forge a stronger **economic union;** and (3) the pursuit of a collaborative **social union.** Because the last issue received considerable attention in Chapter 4, the discussion in this chapter is confined to the 1999 Social Union Framework Agreement (SUFA)—an attempt to craft new rules for the management of social policy. The chapter concludes by analyzing the Harper agenda for nonconstitutional renewal, which might (paradoxically) provoke a new round of formal constitutional amendment.

"MEGACONSTITUTIONAL POLITICS": DEBATING CANADA'S POLITICAL INSTITUTIONS

Megaconstitutional Politics before 1980

Since 1960, constitutional politics in Canada has revolved around complex and divisive questions:

- Is Canada a partnership of two founding nations (the Quebec vision) or a Confederation of 10 equal provinces?
- Should constitutional politics revolve around territorial cleavages, such as regionalism, or around nonterritorial cleavages such as language, gender, and Aboriginality?
- Do our rights as citizens belong to each of us as equal individuals, or as members of particular groups?
- How should we make decisions about the nature of the Canadian community? Should we leave the process of constitutional amendment to the political elites (the "governments' constitution" approach), or should citizens have the right to participate in constitution-making in a meaningful way (the "citizens' constitution" approach)?
- Finally, who should bear the rising costs of social programs, how should the money be spent, and who should decide?

For almost a century after Confederation, constitutional politics rarely involved open challenges to the very legitimacy of the *BNA Act*. Amendments to the entrenched *Constitution* were limited in scope, addressing particular, well-focused issues. They were sporadic and individual, not lumped together in packages large enough to raise questions about the legitimacy of the entire constitutional structure. On the whole, pre-1960 constitutional politics was an elite-driven process of improving Canada's existing political institutions, not a public and passionate debate over their very legitimacy.

Quebec's Quiet Revolution signalled the end of this elite-dominated and incremental constitutional politics. The mobilization of Quebec nationalism into an aggressive separatist movement challenged the entire political system. While Quebec's demands received the highest priority, rising Western regionalism also forced the federal government to respond. In addition, the Liberal governments of Lester Pearson (1963–68) and Pierre Elliott Trudeau (1968–79 and 1980–84) had their own constitutional agenda:

- First, the federal government wanted to patriate (literally, "bring home") the Canadian *Constitution*. As we have seen, the 1867 *BNA Act* was an ordinary statute of the British Parliament, not a Canadian law, and it could not be amended by Canadian parliamentarians.
- Second, all parties agreed that Canada needed a written amending formula.
- Third, Trudeau was determined to entrench a *Charter of Rights*,[7] which would not only protect the rights and freedoms of individual Canadians but also counteract the growing force of regionalism. A *Charter* would be a unifying symbol for Canadians in every province, not least for those in Quebec.

Between 1960 and 1971, there were two failed rounds of constitutional bargaining. The 1964–65 round—which produced an amendment to give Ottawa powers over pensions—attempted to create an amending formula, while the 1971 *Victoria Charter* also included a few entrenched rights and some minor changes to the division of powers between Ottawa and the provinces. The *Victoria Charter*'s amending formula required, in addition to the consent of the federal government, the consent of Ontario, Quebec, any two Eastern provinces, and two Western provinces having at least 50 percent of the Western population.[8] Quebec's opposition, based in part on the federal government's refusal to provide financial compensation for provinces that "opted out" of amendments transferring powers to Ottawa, doomed both processes.

The 1976 election of Quebec's first separatist government provoked intense concern outside the province and inspired dozens of proposals for institutional reform. In 1978, as his electoral defeat loomed, Trudeau introduced Bill C-60. The bill contained a *Charter of Rights*, an amending formula, and **intrastate** reforms to national institutions. The most important of the institutional reforms was the replacement of the Senate with a House of the Provinces, which would comprise delegations from the provincial governments. The bill encountered fierce opposition, including a constitutional challenge in the courts. It died when the House of Commons was dissolved for the 1979 election. The Progressive Conservatives formed a minority government, Trudeau announced his retirement from politics, and the constitutional issue was placed on the back burner. When the PC government was defeated in the House of Commons in December 1979 on a budget vote, Trudeau revoked his retirement. He led the Liberals to a majority government in February 1980, shortly before the Parti Québécois government held the first Quebec sovereignty referendum.

The *Constitution Act, 1982*

Trudeau was now in a position to offer Quebec something in return for defeating separation—which the PQ had rebranded as "sovereignty-association," a mix of political independence and economic union—in the 1980 referendum. What he offered was a vague promise to renew Canada's *Constitution*.[9] When 60 percent of Quebeckers voted "no," Trudeau immediately kicked off another round of constitutional negotiations. The first stage culminated in a First Ministers' Conference (FMC) in September 1980.[10]

Many Quebeckers believed that Trudeau had promised to devolve powers to the provinces. Indeed, when federal and provincial officials met in 1978 to set the agenda for constitutional discussions, the reallocation of powers was included as a priority item. But the political situation had changed dramatically in two years, to the detriment of the provinces. By September 1980 Trudeau had been re-elected with a majority; the PQ government had lost the referendum and faced a tough re-election battle of its own. Trudeau revoked the concessions he had made to the provinces in Bill C-60, and re-imposed his preferred centralist view of Confederation. Many Quebeckers felt that Trudeau had broken his promise of constitutional renewal. That sense of betrayal, coupled with the preexisting conflict between Quebec nationalism and the equal-provinces vision of Confederation, doomed the September 1980 FMC to failure.

Shortly thereafter, Trudeau decided to proceed without the consent of the provinces. He argued that, in the absence of a written amending formula, unanimous provincial consent was not required to amend the division of powers. Because it was not entrenched, the principle of unanimous provincial consent lacked the status of constitutional law. If it existed at all, the unanimity rule was a constitutional "convention," and conventions were unenforceable. According to this view, it was perfectly legal for Ottawa to request amendments unilaterally.

The October 1980 federal package was much smaller than the 1978 version. It only contained the agenda items that Trudeau considered essential: patriation; the *Victoria Charter*'s amending formula, plus the option of a national referendum to override the provincial governments; and an entrenched *Charter of Rights*. The referendum proposal was the clearest indication of Trudeau's strategy to undermine the opposing premiers by going over their heads to the Canadian electorate. Although two provinces (Ontario and New Brunswick) supported Ottawa's initiative, the other eight mounted vigorous opposition. Having lost the independence referendum, the PQ government felt compelled to participate in the attempt to reform the Canadian *Constitution;* despite this concession, it never abandoned its long-term sovereigntist inclinations.

The so-called "Gang of Eight" provinces challenged Ottawa's unilateralism in the courts, arguing that (1) there was a convention of provincial consent and (2) it was legally binding. The dissident premiers signed an Accord on April 16, 1981, setting out their counterproposals to the Trudeau package:

- They demanded an amending formula based on provinces, not on regions. Any future changes to the division of powers would require the consent of at least seven provincial legislatures representing at least 50 percent of the national population (the seven–50 rule); up to three provinces could "opt out" of the amendment, which would not apply within their borders. This "Alberta formula" reflected the "governments' constitution," in contrast to the "citizens' constitution" reflected in Trudeau's referendum proposal.
- Quebec had its own condition for joining the "Gang of Eight": full financial compensation for any province that opted out of amendments transferring provincial powers to Ottawa.
- The Gang of Eight also proposed a very limited *Charter of Rights,* whose weak guarantees echoed the 1960 *Bill of Rights.*

Under pressure from the Opposition parties in the House of Commons—whose provincial wings happened to control most of the provincial governments[11]—Trudeau agreed to postpone any unilateral action pending a court ruling. In September 1981 the Supreme Court ruled that while Ottawa was legally entitled to proceed unilaterally, its package would be unconstitutional in political terms unless it received "substantial" provincial consent. (See pp. 70–71)

This ruling sent the 11 first ministers back to the bargaining table in November 1981. They hammered out a deal that led to the *Constitution Act, 1982.*

- The first major compromise was a tradeoff between parliamentary supremacy and entrenched rights. Parliamentary supremacy implies the possibility of policy variation among provinces in matters within their jurisdiction. The imposition of a uniform standard of rights and freedoms could enforce uniformity across provincial jurisdictions. An entrenched *Charter* would also give the Supreme Court the power to strike down provincial laws, which some premiers strongly opposed. In the end, the dissenting provinces grudgingly accepted the *Charter* in exchange for the power to override some of its provisions. Section 33 of the *Constitution Act, 1982* allows a legislature to declare that a particular law will operate "notwithstanding" the fundamental freedoms in section 2, the legal rights in sections 7–14, or the equality rights in section 15. The premiers hoped to use this remnant of parliamentary supremacy to protect their jurisdictions against the *Charter*'s nationalizing standards. In practice, negative public reaction to the "notwithstanding clause" has raised the political cost of a section-33 declaration to unacceptably high levels outside Quebec.
- The second major compromise involved the *Charter* and the amending formula.[12] In essence, the Gang of Eight swapped its preferred amending formula—minus compensation for opting out in most cases—for a stronger version of the *Charter* than they had previously been willing to accept.

Trudeau's proposal to incorporate referenda into the amending process was scrapped at the November 1981 meeting, but not before it drove a wedge into the "Gang of Eight." The prime minister suggested breaking the deadlock by submitting the two contending packages to a national vote. Quebec Premier René Lévesque endorsed that suggestion, which alienated the other seven dissenting premiers. With their common front shattered, each member of the Gang was free to make its own deal with Ottawa. The key was Ottawa's decision to accept both the notwithstanding clause and the general amending formula (Dossier 3.3). Trudeau also sweetened the deal for the Western provinces by inserting section 92A into the *BNA Act*, guaranteeing the provinces a measure of control over the exploitation of their non-renewable natural resources.

The Quebec government refused to sign the November 1981 agreement. When the other seven members of the Gang of Eight reached a deal with Ottawa, Lévesque felt betrayed. Worse yet, the agreement was hammered out at a late-night meeting (known in Quebec as the "night of the long knives") to which the Quebec delegation had not been invited.[13]

Quebec raised several objections to the package, including the fact that the new seven–50 amending formula would deprive the province of what it considered its traditional veto over constitutional change. The formula had been proposed by the Gang of Eight (of which Quebec was a member), but Quebec had only agreed reluctantly. Lévesque had hoped to cement the united front required to derail the constitutional process completely. If its own project were scuttled, Ottawa would certainly not agree to implement the Gang of Eight's alternative project, and Quebec would be off the hook.[14] Lévesque might have accepted the November 1981 package if it had provided full compensation to provinces that opted out of new national programs, but this would have been completely unacceptable to Ottawa. Unwilling to see their compromise deal unravel, the other premiers rejected Lévesque's pleas for full compensation. Lévesque then bitterly announced that his government could not accept the Accord.[15]

Despite Quebec's refusal to sign the November 1981 accord, the British Parliament enacted it into law. Quebec tried to block its proclamation by asking the courts to declare that any change to the entrenched *Constitution* required its consent; the Supreme Court of Canada dismissed that claim (Dossier 3.2). The *Constitution Act, 1982*—incorporating the new *Charter of Rights* in Part I (sections 1–34) and the new amending formula in Part V (sections 38–49)—came into force on April 17, 1982.[16]

Even before the *Charter* was enacted, it weakened the "governments' constitution" and gave new prominence to groups of citizens for whom territorial politics were irrelevant. Women, Aboriginal peoples, ethnic groups, people with disabilities, and seniors all sensed the advantages of constitutional recognition; they lobbied hard, and often successfully, for entrenched group rights. "*Charter* Canadians" (Chapter 2) had no role in the crafting of the 1982 amending formulas, which were the product of horse-trading among governments. Inevitably, those formulas excluded nongovernment actors, most explicitly by rejecting Trudeau's referendum proposals. If the *Charter* entrenched the "citizens' constitution," the amending formulas entrenched the "governments' constitution" and elite accommodation. The tension between these competing visions of Canada doomed subsequent attempts to amend the *Constitution*.

Although the 1982 entrenchment of the *Charter* represented the triumph of Trudeau's vision of Canada—a strong central government representing a national community of equal citizens—it did not end megaconstitutional politics. The Quebec nationalist myth of two nations, which had provoked recurring constitutional crises since 1960, was not reflected in the 1982 reforms. Indeed, both the *Charter* and the new amending formula represented a forceful denial of the two-nations theory. Ever since, Quebec governments have denied the legitimacy of the 1982 *Constitution Act* and demanded further constitutional changes to protect the province's distinct society. Nor did the 1982 constitutional package address the intrastate agenda or devolve powers to the provincial governments. The continuing strength of Quebec nationalism and Western regionalism would provoke subsequent rounds of constitutional negotiation, but they would no longer have the playing field to themselves. The new "*Charter* groups" would mobilize against any perceived threat to their entrenched status, while

Queen Elizabeth II signs the *Constitution Act, 1982*, as Prime Minister Pierre Elliott Trudeau looks on. (CP/Ron Poling)

the long-standing grievances of Aboriginal groups would ultimately force federal and provincial governments to respond.

Megaconstitutional Politics, 1982–92: From Meech Lake to Charlottetown

Having explored the relationship between political institutions and political values (Chapter 1), recent changes in Canadian political values (Chapter 2), and the strains inherent in Canada's federal system (Chapter 4), we are now ready to understand the megaconstitutional politics of the 1980s and 1990s. While territorial cleavages remained important, they were no longer the only considerations. The value changes discussed in Chapter 2 brought new interests to the table, which cut across territorial divisions. These conflicting political values, and the proposed institutional reforms arising from them, are briefly summarized in Table 5.1.

There are at least three striking features of the demands listed in this table.

- First, the decentralizing demands arising from Quebec nationalism overlap with those inspired by Western regionalism; others do not. For example, the constitutional recognition of Quebec as a "distinct society" flies in the face of the demand to treat all 10 provinces equally.
- Second, the proposed nonterritorial reforms conflict with the territorial demands. Intrastate federalism is based on relations between heads of governments, whereas direct democracy seeks to bypass "backroom deals" by vesting power directly in the people. Aboriginal self-government contradicts the territorial integrity of provinces, and may threaten the rights of other groups.
- Third and finally, populist demands for direct democracy based on majority opinion can undermine special legal protections for minority groups.

SPECIFIC DEMAND	ORIGIN	CATEGORY	EXAMPLES
Constitutional recognition of Quebec as a distinct society	Quebec nationalism	Territorial	Meech Lake: "distinct-society" clause; Charlottetown Accord "distinct-society" clause
Decentralization of powers over culture, immigration, and economic development	Quebec nationalism, regionalism	Territorial	Meech Lake: provincial opt-out of constitutional amendments with full compensation; entrenchment of existing Ottawa—Quebec agreements over immigration Charlottetown: withdrawal of the federal government from labour market training
Restrictions on federal spending power in provincial jurisdictions	Quebec nationalism, regionalism	Territorial	Meech Lake: provincial opt out of new shared-cost programs with full compensation
Intrastate federalism	Quebec nationalism, regionalism	Territorial	Meech Lake: provincial role in selection of Supreme Court judges and senators; entrenchment of the Supreme Court
Quebec veto over future constitutional amendments	Quebec nationalism	Territorial	Meech Lake: extension of the unanimity formula
Triple-E Senate	Regionalism	Territorial	Charlottetown: Triple-E Senate
Constitutional recognition of provincial equality	Regionalism	Territorial	Meech Lake: extension of Quebec's demands to all 10 provinces (except the distinct-society demand)
Aboriginal self-government	Aboriginal rights	Nonterritorial	Charlottetown: Aboriginal self-government
Direct democracy	Value change (postmaterialism and populism)	Nonterritorial	Charlottetown: referendum on Accord
Group rights	Value change	Nonterritorial	*Charter of Rights and Freedoms* Charlottetown: *Social Charter*

Bringing Quebec Back In

Although the Quebec government has never formally approved the *Constitution Act, 1982*, its provisions apply as fully in that province as they do in the rest of Canada. Ten days after the Supreme Court of Canada rejected Quebec's claim to veto the November 1981 deal (Dossier 3.2), Quebec's National Assembly passed a resolution setting out the conditions for its acceptance of the new entrenched provisions:

1. It must be recognized that the two founding peoples of Canada are fundamentally equal and that Québec, by virtue of its language, culture and institutions, forms a distinct society within the Canadian federal system and has all the attributes of a distinct national community;

2. *The constitutional amending formula*

   (a) *must either maintain Québec's right of veto or*

   (b) *be in keeping with the Constitutional Accord signed by Québec on April 16, 1981 [the Gang of Eight Accord] whereby Québec would not be subject to any amendment which would diminish its powers or rights, and would be entitled, where necessary, to reasonable and obligatory compensation.*[17]

This resolution established Quebec's bargaining position in future constitutional negotiations. After the separatist Parti Québécois government was defeated in December 1985, the Liberal government of Premier Robert Bourassa set out five conditions under which the Quebec government would agree to sign the *Constitution Act, 1982*. If the federal government and the other nine provinces would agree to Quebec's proposed amendments, the province's symbolic exclusion from the new *Constitution* would end. (See Dossier 5.1.) The five demands were as follows:

1. constitutional recognition of Quebec's "distinct society";
2. restoration of Quebec's constitutional veto;
3. greater control over immigration;
4. a role in selecting future senators and Supreme Court justices from the province (together with the entrenchment of the Supreme Court); and
5. restrictions on the federal spending power in areas of provincial jurisdiction.

DOSSIER 5.1   Key Dates in the Quebec and Canada Rounds of Constitutional Negotiation[18]

- *August 1984:* Progressive Conservative leader Brian Mulroney promises to bring Quebec "back into the Canadian constitutional family."
- *September 1984:* Mulroney becomes prime minister.
- *December 1985:* The PQ Government is defeated and a federalist Liberal Government takes power in Quebec.
- *May 1986:* The Quebec government sets out five conditions for its acceptance of the *Constitution Act, 1982;* the federal government accepts the five conditions and sets out to sell them to the other provincial governments.
- *August 1986:* The premiers agree to negotiate on the basis of Quebec's demands.
- *April 1987:* The first ministers hammer out a deal at Meech Lake, Quebec.
- *June 1987:* The first ministers approve a legal text of the Meech Lake deal; Quebec ratifies the legal text, setting the three-year clock in motion.
- *September 1987:* Saskatchewan ratifies the Accord.

- *October 1987:* New Brunswick election won by Frank McKenna, who opposes the Accord; House of Commons ratifies the Accord.
- *December 1987:* Alberta ratifies the Accord.
- *April 1988:* Manitoba election produces a minority Progressive Conservative Government, with the Liberals led by Meech opponent Sharon Carstairs holding the balance of power in the legislature.
- *May–July 1988:* Prince Edward Island, Nova Scotia, British Columbia, Ontario, and Newfoundland ratify the Accord.
- *December 1988:* Quebec government announces that it will use section 33 (p. 190) to override a Supreme Court decision striking down a ban on English-only commercial signs; outraged reaction in English Canada.
- *April 1989:* Newfoundland election won by Clyde Wells, who refuses to accept the "distinct-society" clause.
- *March 1990:* New Brunswick proposes, and Ottawa accepts, a "parallel Accord" to

(continued)

- address the concerns of Meech critics while preserving the 1987 deal intact.
- *April 1990:* Quebec rejects a parallel Accord that could weaken Meech's protection of its distinct society; Newfoundland rescinds its approval of the Accord.
- *May 1990:* Parliamentary Committee recommends a "parallel Accord"; federal Cabinet Minister Lucien Bouchard quits in protest, and later forms the Bloc Québécois.
- *June 1990:* After six days of heated negotiations, the first ministers work out a "parallel Accord" without the full approval of Wells; Manitoba legislator Elijah Harper refuses to allow the legislature to vote on the ratification motion; the Accord is ratified in New Brunswick, but Wells adjourns the Newfoundland legislature without a vote, and the Accord dies on June 23; Quebec erupts in anger, and federalist Premier Robert Bourassa announces that he will hold a referendum on sovereignty unless Quebec's demands are addressed in another round of constitutional talks.
- *November 1990:* Ottawa establishes the Spicer Commission to investigate the constitutional priorities of the ROC ("rest of Canada").
- *January 1991:* Publication of the Allaire Report, calling for a massive decentralization of powers to the provinces.
- *March 1991:* Publication of the Bélanger–Campeau Report, recommending a Quebec sovereignty referendum by October 1992 unless the ROC makes an acceptable offer of constitutional change.

- *September 1991:* Ottawa releases its proposed constitutional package, entitled *Shaping Canada's Future Together.*
- *October 1991:* Special joint committee begins ill-fated public hearings on the federal proposals; after weeks of disarray, it finally gets back on track.
- *March 1992:* Release of special joint committee report, which is quickly rejected by Quebec; talks begin among the ROC first ministers and Aboriginal leaders.
- *May 1992:* Federal government introduces referendum legislation; talks nearly break down over Triple-E Senate.
- *July 1992:* ROC first ministers announce a deal; Quebec agrees to discuss it, but not to formal negotiations.
- *August 1992:* Quebec formally returns to the bargaining table; accepts Triple-E Senate in exchange for a perpetual guarantee of 25 percent of the Commons; at final meeting in Charlottetown, all first ministers sign the Accord and kick off referendum campaign.
- *September 1992:* "Yes" campaign runs into trouble, as the unpopularity of Prime Minister Mulroney rubs off on the Accord.
- *October 1992:* Quebec voters decide that the Accord does not go far enough, while ROC voters conclude that the Accord gave Quebec too much; the Accord is rejected by voters in Nova Scotia, Quebec, the four Western provinces, and Yukon.

The first two demands reflect only the Quebec nationalist agenda; others echo the demands of other provincial governments for greater autonomy from Ottawa. Both the Meech Lake and Charlottetown Accords gave the Quebec government what it wanted. The "two-nations" vision had little appeal outside Quebec, where the "equal-provinces" vision shaped public expectations of federalism. The "distinct-society" clause in Meech, and a special provision in Charlottetown to offset Quebec's objections to a "Triple-E" Senate, led directly to the defeat of both Accords.

When Meech died, the Quebec government refused to participate in any future constitutional negotiations as one province among 10 equals. Instead, the province would pursue a two-nations strategy. Quebec would wait until the rest of Canada came up with its own constitutional proposal, and then negotiate on a nation-to-nation basis. In the meantime, Quebec would conduct public consultations on the *Constitution* and develop its own positions. The resulting "two-track" process—one track in Quebec and the other in the ROC—began in the fall of 1990 and culminated with the announcement of the Charlottetown Accord in August 1992.

The "Quebec track" revolved around two public consultations on future constitutional options: the constitutional committee of the provincial Liberal Party, chaired by Jean Allaire, and the Bélanger–Campeau Commission. The latter was a broad-based task force with members from all parties in the Quebec National Assembly as well as the private sector. The Allaire Committee was more highly nationalistic and decentralist than the Bélanger–Campeau Commission, but both bodies proceeded on classic Quebec nationalist assumptions.

For its part, the federal government established the Citizens Forum on Canada's Future (popularly known as the Spicer Commission, after its chairman) and a joint committee of the Senate and House of Commons on constitutional amendment, chaired by Gérald Beaudoin and Jim Edwards. The Spicer Commission found considerable discontent with the political process, particularly the secretive and unaccountable backroom deals of first ministers. This finding reflected both the increasing influence of postmaterialist and populist sentiments, and the declining public satisfaction with representative political institutions. Concerns about the legitimacy of the constitutional process were shared by the Beaudoin–Edwards Committee, which recommended that any future constitutional deal be submitted to the public in a referendum. The Spicer Report also found that most Canadians outside Quebec preferred a strong central government, contrary to the assumptions of both Quebec nationalists and regionalists.

Matters came to a head in May 1991 when Quebec's National Assembly, in response to the Bélanger–Campeau recommendations, passed a law requiring a provincial referendum on sovereignty no later than October 28, 1992. The federal government responded in the fall of 1991 with a new set of constitutional proposals, *Shaping Canada's Future Together*.[19] While the federal proposals were primarily a response to Quebec's ultimatum, their substance was shaped by the fallout from Meech Lake. Political leaders in the ROC sought to avoid the perception of a reform package driven mainly by Quebec's concerns, emanating from private negotiations of First Ministers, and presented for legislative approval as a seamless and unalterable web. To have any chance of success, the outcome of the "Canada Round" had to reflect both the "citizens' constitution" and the "governments' constitution," while satisfying populist demands for direct democracy and the equal-provinces vision of the ROC.

The ROC package, particularly the Triple-E Senate, directly contradicted the Quebec nationalist agenda—even though the whole purpose of the ROC process was to devise a package that would satisfy Quebec. Predictably, it failed. Despite his reservations about certain parts of the deal, particularly the Triple-E Senate, Premier Robert Bourassa eventually agreed to sign what became the Charlottetown Accord. He accepted the Triple-E Senate in exchange for a guarantee that Quebec would hold 25 percent of the seats in the House of Commons in perpetuity (i.e., even if its share of the national population fell well below that figure).

Regionalism: Provincial Equality and Intrastate Federalism

As we have seen, the Meech Lake Accord was intended to meet Quebec's five conditions for signing the *Constitution Act, 1982*. But the process by which it was created and the resulting content were shaped by the principle of provincial equality. Quebec's demands, apart from the distinct-society clause, were extended to the other provinces on an equal basis. Thus, Quebec's demand for a say in Supreme Court appointments became a general right of provinces to submit lists of potential justices from which the prime minister would choose.

Similarly, Quebec's desire for a constitutional role in immigration policy became the right of all provincial governments to negotiate constitutionally entrenched agreements "relating to immigration" with the federal government. Quebec's proposal to restrict federal spending power gave rise to a general provincial right to opt out of national shared-cost programs with "reasonable compensation" from Ottawa. Finally, Quebec's demand for a veto over future constitutional amendments resulted in a proposal to expand the list of subjects that could be amended only with unanimous provincial consent, effectively extending a veto to every province. This strategy not only respected the equality of the provinces; it also encouraged other premiers to accept Quebec's demands, by guaranteeing that every player (with the possible exception of the federal government) would win.

Had the Accord been entrenched, it would have decentralized powers to all of the provinces. Indeed, it has been aptly described as a "provincialist revenge against the nationalizing thrust of [the *Charter*]."[20] It was an attempt by proponents of the "governments' constitution" to regain some of the ground they had lost in 1982.[21] The Accord's architects simply assumed that the 1982 amending procedures would be implemented in the old way—by interstate negotiations among the first ministers. Thus, the Accord was worked out behind closed doors by the prime minister and the premiers and presented to the public as an unalterable *fait accompli*.

By 1987, when the Meech Lake negotiations opened, interstate proposals had to compete with those inspired by intrastate federalism. The idea was to reform national institutions—particularly the Senate and the Supreme Court—in order to make the federal government more sensitive to provincial concerns, thereby forestalling further demands for decentralization. While the intrastate approach had great appeal in the West, it was regarded with suspicion in Quebec, which wanted a role in appointing Supreme Court justices, but rejected a Triple-E Senate that would entrench the equal-provinces principle. Under the current *Constitution,* Quebec controls nearly one-quarter of the seats in the upper house (24 of 105). A Triple-E Senate would reduce the Quebec contingent to just under one-tenth of the total. This reduction in the province's parliamentary representation was unacceptable to the Quebec government. In this respect, as in others, the constitutional aspirations of Quebec nationalism were directly opposed to those of the other nine provinces. This contradiction proved fatal to both Accords.

The "Citizens' Constitution": Direct Democracy, Group Rights, and "New Politics"

"*Charter* Canadians" were strongly opposed to any constitutional amendment that appeared to threaten their protected rights. As postmaterialist values and populist demands for direct democracy grew, the *Constitution* was redefined. It was no longer the exclusive property of governments, a matter of interest only to politicians, lawyers, and academics; it was now a powerful symbol for hundreds of thousands of Canadians. The clash between citizens and governments helped to defeat Meech and prompted the referendum on Charlottetown that rejected the first ministers' handiwork.

Both the content and the process of Meech jeopardized the newly won constitutional status of the "*Charter* groups." The Accord favoured territorial over nonterritorial interests. Feminists worried that Quebec might use the "distinct-society" clause to infringe on women's rights—in effect, that a more restrictive approach to gender equality could prove to be part of Quebec's distinctiveness.[22] Aboriginal peoples wondered why only Quebec deserved constitutional recognition as a distinct society within Canada. "*Charter* groups" believed that the Meech Lake process treated the *Constitution* as the property of political elites, to amend as they saw fit. They argued that the *Constitution* belonged not to governments but to citizens, and citizens had to be directly involved in its amendment. These groups had been major players in the amendments of 1982 and they resented being shut out of the process now.

In their battle against Meech, "*Charter* groups" were assisted by two features of the 1982 amending formulas:

1. Amendments to some elements of the *Constitution* require the unanimous consent of the federal and provincial governments, while others required the consent only of Ottawa and seven provinces having 50 percent of the Canadian population (Dossier 3.3). The Meech Lake Accord contained both types of amendment. For example, entrenching the right to opt out of shared-cost programs with financial compensation fell under the seven–50 formula, while amendment of the amending formulas themselves—in order to meet Quebec's demand for a veto—required unanimous consent. Instead of dividing the Accord into two packages corresponding to the two different amending formulas, it was presented as a "seamless web" that had to be passed as a whole or not at all. This meant simultaneously meeting the requirements of the unanimity and seven–50 amending formulas. There is no time limit on amendments requiring unanimous consent, but there is a three-year deadline for ratification under the seven–50 rule. Consequently, the Accord had to be ratified by all 10 provincial legislatures and the federal Parliament within three years. The three-year clock starts running when the first legislature passes a proposed amendment. Canada's first ministers had signed the Meech Lake Accord on June 3, 1987, and Quebec's legislature approved it on June 23. Thus, the Accord would die if a single province failed to ratify it before midnight, June 23, 1990.

2. Constitutional deals struck by first ministers had to be ratified by federal and provincial legislators. First ministers with disciplined legislative majorities can usually pass whatever they like in the legislature in a very short time. But the ratification process was delayed by legislative hearings in some provinces, and two of the first ministers lost power before they could ratify the Accord. A third, Newfoundland's Brian Peckford, steered the Accord through the legislature before losing an election. That approval was later rescinded by the new premier, Clyde Wells. These developments gave the "*Charter* groups" opposed to Meech the time they needed to mobilize public opinion against the Accord. The longer they could delay final approval, the more likely it was that some province would refuse to ratify it before the deadline.[23] In the end, two provincial legislatures were denied the opportunity to vote on the Accord before the June 23, 1990, deadline.

Canada's political leaders learned a lesson from the failure of Meech. The "Canada Round," at least in the early stages, reflected the logic of the citizens' constitution in several respects:

- First, the federal government sought public feedback for its constitutional proposals; it tried to prevent the rejection of a potential deal as the product of closed-door intergovernmental negotiations.
- Second, a special joint committee of the Senate and House of Commons (the Beaudoin–Dobbie Committee) held extensive public hearings on the federal package.
- Third, when the special committee ran into logistical problems and an indifferent public response, the federal government organized five conferences across the country in early 1992, to invite discussion of various parts of the package.

All of this delayed the onset of traditional intergovernmental negotiation by first ministers and emphasized public participation and consultation. The citizens' constitution prevailed, at least temporarily, over the governments' constitution.

However, intergovernmental negotiation could only be delayed; it could not be avoided indefinitely. The amending formula expressly requires the consent of federal and provincial legislatures. While political executives could no longer ratify constitutional amendments without the consent of their legislatures, the first ministers would still be the key players in the actual negotiations. Those negotiations began shortly after the Beaudoin–Dobbie Committee reported at the end of February 1992, and continued throughout the summer.

Although the interstate bargaining went on behind closed doors, the federal minister for Constitutional Affairs worked hard to keep the media and public informed. The 10 first ministers (the prime minister and the premiers of the ROC provinces) were joined at the table by teams from the territories and four national Aboriginal organizations. Aboriginal peoples had played a leading role in the death of the Meech Lake Accord. This time, they would participate in the bargaining process. These features of the negotiations reflected efforts to graft the "citizens' constitution" onto an amending procedure formally based on the "governments' constitution." Despite these efforts, some "*Charter* groups" (particularly women's groups) complained of their exclusion from the negotiations. In a particularly dramatic objection of this kind, Aboriginal women's groups, alleging that their interests were not adequately represented by the male-dominated Aboriginal organizations admitted to the negotiations, asked the courts to force the federal government to fund their participation in the Charlottetown process. The federal government refused to grant this request; this refusal was later approved by the Supreme Court of Canada.[24]

The tension between direct democracy and executive federalism was evident in both the content and the process of the Accord. Under the proposed revisions of the 1982 amending procedures, some matters, such as reform of the Senate, were to be shifted from the seven–50 category to the unanimity rule. However, the actual process of amendment would remain in the hands of political elites. Although the text of the Charlottetown Accord reflected the governments' constitution, its ratification would recognize the citizens' constitution. The Accord would be submitted to the electorate in a referendum. There was no provision for a referendum in the 1982 amending formula; its results would not be legally binding on the politicians, but would certainly carry political weight. Recall that Quebec was already committed to holding a referendum on sovereignty in October 1992. The provincial government changed the question: instead of asking Quebeckers to approve sovereignty, they would ask them to accept the Charlottetown Accord. British Columbia and Alberta had also committed themselves to consulting their populations through referenda, and Ottawa had passed legislation enabling a national referendum. Ottawa and Quebec arranged separate referenda, held under Quebec's law in that province and the federal law in the rest of Canada. Both were held on October 26, 1992. Most observers agree that these referenda established a new constitutional convention.[25] In future, major amendments of the megaconstitutional scope and significance of the Charlottetown Accord will likely be ratified—if at all—by the voters, and not just by the legislative and executive branches of the two senior levels of government.

The Accord was rejected by a majority of the voters in a majority of provinces, including Quebec. There were many reasons for its failure, but the bottom line was that voters were less willing than political leaders to compromise their political values and aspirations. As Peter Russell puts it, "The Charlottetown Accord was defeated because, outside Quebec, it was perceived as giving Quebec too much, while inside Quebec it was perceived as not giving Quebec enough."[26] In other words, the conflict between the two-nations vision of Canada and the equal-provinces principle was unresolved. It might have worked, if the electorate had been willing to leave constitutional matters in the hands of the politicians. As Canada's political culture becomes less deferential and more participatory, resolving disputes over core political values becomes increasingly difficult, if not impossible.[27]

Aboriginal Rights

The Meech Lake Accord was finally ratified in New Brunswick, after the adoption of the "parallel Accord," but it failed to pass in Newfoundland and Manitoba. In the latter province, Aboriginal discontent with the Meech process sealed the fate of the Accord. At the eleventh hour, the difficulties of minority government had been overcome and the leaders of all parties agreed to ratification. By then there was not enough time to pass the necessary motion while respecting all the procedures of the Manitoba legislature. Those procedures could be suspended and passage expedited, but only with the unanimous consent of all members of the legislature. Aboriginal MLA Elijah Harper, reflecting his community's opposition to Meech, repeatedly refused to give his consent. Aboriginal peoples were upset by the exclusion of their leaders from the Meech Lake process, and by the possibility that the distinct-society clause would infringe Aboriginal rights. The fact that the Accord did not pass in Newfoundland was at least partly due to the perception in that province's legislature that Harper's resistance had already killed it in Manitoba. That a single legislator could effectively derail a major constitutional amendment is surely one of the more dramatic illustrations of the power of institutional rules.

By the summer of 1990, when the Meech Lake Accord died unratified, Aboriginal issues had risen to the top of the political agenda. A confrontation between Aboriginal activists and Quebec Provincial Police at Oka, Quebec, turned into a lengthy standoff between Mohawk warriors and the Canadian Armed Forces. The "Oka crisis" forced non-Aboriginal leaders to recognize the depth of Aboriginal discontent with the legal and constitutional status quo, as did Elijah Harper's role in the death of Meech, with the result that Aboriginal groups became key players in the negotiation of the Charlottetown Accord. Their leaders sat at the bargaining table with the First Ministers, and they won the agreement of all 11 governments to a plan for Aboriginal self-government.

Elijah Harper blocking the Meech Lake Accord in the Manitoba Legislature
(CP/WFP/Wayne Glowacki)

The participation of Aboriginal leaders reflected a general acceptance of the claim that Aboriginal peoples, like Quebeckers, constituted distinct societies within Canada. The Charlottetown Accord recognized Aboriginal peoples as "the first peoples to govern this land," with "the right to promote their languages, cultures and traditions and to ensure the integrity of their societies." Moreover, Aboriginal peoples would express their distinctiveness through their own governments, governments to which they had an inherent right and that were said to be "one of the three orders of government in Canada" and thus of equal status with the government of Quebec. That government could not accept equal constitutional status for Aboriginal "nations," which contradicted the "two-nations" myth of Quebec nationalism. Nonetheless, by leaving the details of self-government to be worked out after the Accord was ratified, the federal government succeeded in obtaining Quebec's approval for the package. Although the outcome of the October 1992 referendum was widely perceived as a rejection of Aboriginal aspirations by the majority, the truth is rather different: a significant majority of Aboriginal Canadians themselves voted against Charlottetown, because the proposed changes did not go far enough.[28] The parallel with the Accord's rejection in Quebec is unmistakable.

"NONCONSTITUTIONAL RENEWAL": MEGACONSTITUTIONAL POLITICS BY OTHER MEANS

The public rejection of the Charlottetown Accord left Canadians with a profound sense of constitutional weariness and a marked distaste for megaconstitutional politics.[29] However, it did nothing to address the demands for institutional change that had driven the two previous rounds of bargaining. Quebec still wanted Ottawa to vacate shared policy fields, including labour market training. At the same time, most provincial governments agreed that the use of the federal spending power in provincial jurisdictions should be restricted in some way, so that Ottawa could no longer impose its own priorities in health care, postsecondary education (PSE), and social welfare. Business groups demanded freer domestic markets for goods, services, and labour, which meant eliminating or reducing provincial barriers to trade and mobility.

These forces for change gained added impetus in 1995, when two events shook the federation to its core.

- First, the Quebec sovereignty referendum came within a whisker of breaking up the country. The Chrétien government was determined to prove that Canadian federalism could work, even without large-scale constitutional change.
- Second, the federal budget ended the existing system of transfer payments to the provinces and replaced it with the Canadian Health and Social Transfer (CHST). As we saw in Chapter 4, the unilateral decision to slash transfers and rewrite the rules of fiscal federalism infuriated the provinces. They banded together in self-defence, and demanded a more formalized and collaborative process for decision-making on social policy.

Before 1992, these pressures for change would likely have triggered constitutional talks. After the failure of Charlottetown, they had to be resolved in some other way. Prime Minister Chrétien, an instinctively cautious politician, responded with a variety of proposals for nonconstitutional renewal (NCR).[30] As we will see in the next section, the federal government's "Plan A" strategy for dealing with Quebec sovereignty included legislated promises to respect Quebec's distinct society and its claim to a veto. Other items on the Meech Lake and Charlottetown agendas were partly addressed by formal intergovernmental agreements. By the end of the twentieth century, Ottawa and the provinces had negotiated agreements on shared management of the economic and social union. These developments are summarized in Table 5.2, which also includes the more recent reform proposals of the Harper Government (presented in bold).

Table 5.2 demonstrates the lack of progress on some key megaconstitutional issues since the suspension of constitutional negotiations in 1992. The primary difference between high-priority and low-priority items appears to be the receptiveness of the federal government to particular demands. When Ottawa perceives an opportunity to gain political ground by passing a law or participating in an FPT agreement, it does so. For instance, the Agreement on Internal Trade was popular among business groups frustrated by internal barriers to trade and labour mobility. The *Regional Veto Act* was a key part of the "Plan A" strategy to minimize the political damage from the 1995 Quebec referendum. However, federal concessions are strictly limited in scope and likely to be ignored when they become politically inconvenient (like the SUFA restrictions on the federal spending power, at least until 2006).

Throughout this period, the government of Quebec was, at best, an intermittent participant in the federation. While it often sent observers to intergovernmental meetings, and it endorsed the agreement on the economic union, Quebec did not sign the 1999 SUFA. This points up one of the key differences between megaconstitutional politics and the more recent NCR strategy:[31]

> *In earlier periods, Ottawa and at least some of the provinces would have gone to great lengths to avoid "isolating Quebec." Today, governments appear to have reluctantly accepted that they must get on with business even if Quebec absents itself or assumes observer status only.*[32]

TABLE 5.2 NONCONSTITUTIONAL RESPONSES TO MEGACONSTITUTIONAL DEMANDS, 1992–2007

SPECIFIC DEMAND	NONCONSTITUTIONAL RESPONSE
Constitutional recognition of Quebec as a distinct society	1995 resolution in the House of Commons, recognizing Quebec's distinctiveness **2006 motion in the House of Commons, recognizing the Québécois as a nation within a united Canada**
Decentralization of powers over culture, immigration, and economic development	Beginning in 1996, Ottawa negotiated specific arrangements with each province for labour market training; more collaborative approach to policy-making; under the Agreement on Internal Trade (AIT), provinces and Ottawa share responsibility for managing the economic union[33]
Restrictions on federal spending power in provincial jurisdictions	Social Union Framework Agreement (SUFA); has done nothing to prevent unilateral federal spending and policy-making in provincial jurisdictions
Intrastate federalism	No progress; continuing provincial demands for a role in appointing Supreme Court justices and senators denied
Quebec veto over future constitutional amendments	1996 *Regional Veto Act*
Triple-E Senate	**Two Senate reform Bills (Dossier 3.4)**
Constitutional recognition of provincial Equality	No progress; the SUFA violates the equal-provinces principle[34]
Aboriginal self-government	Completion of several land claims and treaty negotiations; recognition of "inherent right to self-government" by federal government; some efforts to include Aboriginal "peak" organizations in PT and FPT processes
Direct democracy	No progress; populism seems to be a waning force in Canadian politics[35]
Group rights	No progress

The NCR strategy differs from the megaconstitutional approach in at least two important ways.

- First, entrenched amendments are subject to judicial enforcement. Intergovernmental agreements are not, unless they are enshrined in federal or provincial legislation.[36] The Supreme Court of Canada has twice ruled against plaintiffs who sought to challenge government decisions made under the Canada Assistance Plan (CAP).[37] In both cases, the court refused to interpret the terms of intergovernmental agreements in a way that would require it to intervene directly. This reluctance arises, in part, from the federal principle; the justices have consistently recognized the legitimacy of divergent provincial policies to meet local needs, and allowed considerable flexibility to provincial policymakers.[38] It is also grounded in the principle of parliamentary supremacy: agreements flowing from the process of executive federalism are not binding on the legislatures of the participating governments, unless they are subsequently ratified by legislators or enshrined in enabling statutes.[39] But the court rulings may also reflect the uncertain legal status of intergovernmental deals that are not enacted into constitutional amendments. Unless they contain effective mechanisms for enforcement and dispute resolution, agreements and Accords have little (if any) power to constrain the decisions of governments.

- Second, constitutional amendments establish permanent rules for political conduct; nonconstitutional measures establish temporary rules that can be revoked (or ignored) when political circumstances change. On the positive side, nonconstitutional change allows flexibility in the resolution of intergovernmental conflict; a short-term crisis, such as the 1995 CHST, can be resolved by negotiating new rules for both orders of government. If the crisis passes, the temporary arrangements, which may or may not be useful for other purposes, can be allowed to lapse. The potential downside of NCR is the political uncertainty generated by impermanent arrangements. A long-standing political problem, like Quebec separatism, may require a permanent constitutional solution; anything less could be perceived as an inadequate stopgap.

Nonconstitutional Responses to Quebec Nationalism

The renewed focus on Quebec's constitutional aspirations began with the 1994 Quebec election. The Parti Québécois returned to power under the leadership of hard-line separatist Jacques Parizeau. The Parizeau Government announced that it would hold a referendum on independence in the first year of its mandate. This referendum, which took place on October 30, 1995, plunged Canada into the deepest of its modern megaconstitutional crises.

Parizeau initially wanted to hold a referendum on outright independence. However, the polls showed that Quebeckers were not prepared to vote for sovereignty without some form of continuing association with Canada.[40] Although many francophones were convinced that their "nation" could not reach its full potential within Canada, their fears about the economic costs of complete separation outweighed their nationalism.[41] As in 1980, therefore, a compromise position was worked out. Ultimately, Parizeau's Parti Québécois agreed with the federal Bloc Québécois and the provincial Action Démocratique du Québec (the third party in the Quebec legislature) that Quebeckers should be asked whether the province "should become sovereign, after having made a formal offer to Canada for a new economic and political partnership." (Dossier 5.2) Note that sovereignty was conditional only on an "offer" of partnership, not on Canada's acceptance of that offer. If partnership negotiations broke down, Quebec could unilaterally declare its independence. The compromise among the three parties was enshrined in Bill 1 (Dossier 2.4), which would become law after a successful referendum on sovereignty.

Even with an ambiguous question, campaign polls in the early fall of 1995 showed the sovereigntists trailing. In desperation, Parizeau effectively turned the leadership of the "yes" campaign over to the more charismatic Lucien Bouchard, leader of the Bloc Québécois. Officially, Bouchard was appointed Quebec's chief negotiator in the anticipated post-referendum partnership negotiations with Canada, but everyone understood that he was now in charge of the referendum campaign itself. An effective campaigner, capable of rousing public emotions, Bouchard soon turned the tide and recaptured momentum for the "yes" side. Sensing disaster, Prime Minister Jean Chrétien, who had been content to lie low for much of the campaign, stepped into the fray in its latter stages.[42] Despite his staunch opposition to the constitutional recognition of Quebec as a distinct society, Chrétien now committed his government to pursuing a distinct-society provision. He also agreed to promote a Quebec veto over constitutional amendments.

DOSSIER 5.2 The Quebec Referendum Questions in 1980 and 1995

In the 1980 and 1995 referenda on sovereignty, PQ governments posed questions that were carefully crafted to maximize the "yes" vote. Instead of asking outright "Do you want Quebec to separate from Canada?"—a question that, according to polling data, would produce a strong "no"—both questions fudged the issue by referring to "economic association" and "partnership." The 1980 question also requested not outright sovereignty, but merely a "mandate to negotiate." Soft nationalists who wanted a renewed federalism, not a complete separation, could still vote "yes" in the hope that this would strengthen Quebec's bargaining position vis-à-vis the federal government. Unlike the previous question, the 1995 version did not hold out the promise of a second referendum before separation could take place.

Although the PQ has always argued that the questions were perfectly clear to the voters, federalists accuse the separatists of trying to trick or confuse Québécois voters into voting "yes." Such an outcome, they argue, could not be regarded as a genuine expression of political will and would not have to be respected by the ROC. Judge for yourself.

Question asked at the 1980 referendum:

The Government of Québec has made public its proposal to negotiate a new agreement with the rest of Canada, based on the equality of nations; this agreement would enable Québec to acquire the exclusive power to make its laws, administer its taxes, and establish relations abroad—in other words, sovereignty—and at the same time, to maintain with Canada an economic association including a common currency; any change in political status resulting from these negotiations will be submitted to the people through a referendum; on these terms, do you agree to give the Government of Québec the mandate to negotiate the proposed agreement between Québec and Canada?

Question asked at the 1995 referendum:

Do you agree that Québec should become sovereign, after having made a formal offer to Canada for a new Economic and Political Partnership, within the scope of the Bill respecting the future of Québec and of the agreement signed on June 12, 1995?[43]

At its August 2004 convention, held while the PQ was in Opposition, the party voted to adopt a new strategy. Whenever it returned to power in the province, the PQ would hold a third referendum on sovereignty. This time, the question would be absolutely clear, along the lines of "Do you want Quebec to become a separate country?"[44] Although the PQ refuses to accord any legitimacy to the *Clarity Act,* it is unlikely that the party would have abandoned its cautious *étapiste* (step-by-step) approach to separation if it had not been forced to do so.

In any event, the separatists lost the referendum—but only by a whisker. Whereas about 60 percent of Quebeckers had voted "no" in the 1980 referendum, the result in 1995 was 50.6 percent "no" and 49.4 percent "yes" (with a voter turnout of over 90 percent). The difference between the vote totals was just over 50 000. Francophones voted 60 percent "yes" (up from 50 percent in 1980) while anglophones and allophones voted over 90 percent "no," provoking an embittered Jacques Parizeau to declare on referendum night that the sovereignty option had been defeated by "money and the ethnic vote." Shortly thereafter, Parizeau resigned as premier and Lucien Bouchard left federal politics to become the new PQ premier of Quebec. Disappointed by the referendum loss but buoyed by the close result, the Parti Québécois promised to hold yet another independence referendum when the "winning conditions" were in place.

The close call of 1995 forced Canadians outside Quebec to confront the reality of a possible separation.[45] On one hand, this led to renewed efforts to win the "hearts and minds" of Quebec nationalists (Plan A); on the other, it required realistic planning for a potential secession (Plan B). The Chrétien Government's immediate post-referendum strategy was based on Plan A. In particular, the government soon made good on its promise to do something about "distinct society" and the Quebec veto. On the distinct-society front, the House of Commons quickly passed a resolution recognizing Quebec as a "distinct society within Canada." The resolution declared that the House itself would "be guided" by the reality of Quebec's distinct society and "encourag[ed] all components of the legislative and executive branches of government to take note of this recognition and be guided in their conduct accordingly."[46] In other words, Quebec's distinctiveness would be a guiding principle not only for parliamentarians but also for all federal government bureaucrats. Although this commitment was not entrenched, it could be seen as the first step toward constitutional recognition of the "two-nations" vision.

In early 1996, the federal government also gave Quebec a veto over constitutional amendments by "lending" its veto to Quebec. Under the *Regional Veto Act,*[47] Ottawa would pass a constitutional resolution only if it had first been approved by Quebec, Ontario, British Columbia, two of the Prairie provinces having 50 percent of the Prairie population, and two of the Atlantic provinces having 50 percent of that region's population. As so often in the past, a proposal designed for Quebec was extended to other provinces in order to ensure its acceptance in the ROC, although this particular proposal reflected the regionalist vision of Canada rather than the equal-provinces approach. (The *Regional Veto Act* is discussed in Chapter 3.)

In addition to the distinct-society resolution and the veto legislation, Ottawa's Plan A strategy gave the provinces more autonomy. Ottawa withdrew from the field of labour market training and gave the funds for that purpose to the provinces.[48] It also gave up most of its regulatory powers over forestry, mining, and tourism[49]—apart from environmental issues and other related matters of national importance. The federal government also committed itself to negotiate a new intergovernmental agreement on Canada's social union, which would give the provinces more influence over the federal spending power (see "The 1999 Social Union Framework Agreement" on page 158).

While the Plan A strategy played out, some federal strategists confronted the previously unthinkable question: what would happen if Quebec actually decided to leave Confederation? If Ottawa did nothing to plan for that eventuality, Quebec might unilaterally set the rules for its own departure by default. So the Government of Canada decided to set clear and stringent rules and conditions under which secession could take place. By demonstrating the difficulties and costs involved in separation, such rules might cause Quebeckers to think twice before voting "yes" in the next independence referendum. This was the Plan B strategy, which had three main elements:

1. Although Quebec was entitled to separate, a unilateral declaration of independence (UDI) would be illegal under both Canadian constitutional law and international law. If Quebec wished to respect the rule of law, and to ensure its global recognition as a sovereign state, separation could be achieved only through an amendment to the existing

Canadian *Constitution.* Because such a fundamental change would require the consent of all the other Canadian legislatures, including the Parliament of Canada, the details of disengagement—e.g., the division of the debt—would have to be negotiated while Quebec was still part of Canada.[50] As part of this dimension of its Plan B strategy, the Chrétien Government referred the question of the legality of a UDI to the Supreme Court of Canada (see Dossier 1.5).

2. Federal Intergovernmental Affairs Minister Stéphane Dion rejected Quebec's argument that a 50-percent plus one "yes" vote in an independence referendum would be sufficient to trigger even a legal secession process. He argued that "Secession, the act of choosing between one's fellow citizens, is one of the most consequence-laden choices a society can ever make." It is one of those "virtually irreversible changes that deeply affect not only our own lives but also those of future generations," and should thus be subject to more than an ordinary majority decision rule. "It would be too dangerous," he continued, "to attempt such an operation in an atmosphere of division, on the basis of a narrow, 'soft' majority . . . which could evaporate in the face of difficulties." A more substantial consensus would have to be shown.[51]

3. Dion raised the contentious issue of dividing Quebec itself. If Quebec could separate from Canada, he suggested, parts of the province were entitled to secede from Quebec and remain in Canada.[52] Dion highlighted the right of Quebec's Aboriginal peoples to remain in Canada. This example was no doubt strategically chosen; immediately before the 1995 referendum, three Aboriginal nations held their own votes on whether to stay in an independent Quebec. "The Cree voted 96% No; the Inuit voted 95% No; and the French-speaking Montagnais voted an astonishing 99% No."[53] Clearly, there would be pressure for the partition of Quebec, and Dion asserted that no one could "predict that the borders of an independent Quebec would be those now guaranteed by the Canadian *Constitution.*"[54]

The ROC provinces also played a role in the evolving and shifting balance between the Plan A and Plan B responses to the separatist threat. In September 1997, a meeting of PT leaders (except the Quebec premier) issued the "Calgary Declaration" in response to the federal strategies. The ROC leaders recognized the "unique character" of Quebec society, reformulating the distinct-society principle. At the same time, it asserted the primacy of provincial equality: "if any future constitutional amendment confers powers on one province, these powers must be available to all provinces." Within a short time, all of the ROC legislatures passed resolutions supporting it. Even the Reform Party, the only federalist party to oppose the Charlottetown Accord, endorsed the "Calgary Declaration"; indeed, it introduced the Commons resolution.[55] This broad agreement was possible because the declaration comprised a set of principles for discussion, not a set of formal constitutional proposals. Any attempt to incorporate the "Calgary Declaration" into the entrenched *Constitution* would have met the same fate as the Meech and Charlottetown Accords. Public opinion in the ROC was strongly opposed to constitutional recognition of "distinct-society" status or a special Quebec veto. "At the end of 1995, only 22 percent of people in the ROC regarded Canada as a 'pact between two founding groups,' while 75 percent agreed that it is 'a relationship between ten equal provinces.'"[56]

By the fall of 1998, all attention was focused on the Supreme Court's pending judgment in the *Secession Reference.* Nearing the end of its mandate, the Quebec government was considering the timing of an election; many observers speculated that Premier Bouchard was anxious to use a pro-Ottawa judgment by the court as the pretext for an election call. Quebec had portrayed the reference as an illegitimate tactic by Ottawa to impose its will in a matter that only Quebeckers could decide, and had thus refused to participate in the case. (Ottawa had to appoint an *amicus curiae,* or "friend of the court," to present Quebec's side of the argument.) The PQ government was waiting to pounce on a predictably anti-secessionist judgment by "Ottawa's Court."

The court did not oblige Bouchard. As in the 1981 *Patriation Reference,* it gave enough to both sides to prevent a simple rejection by either. The court ruled that Quebec had no legal right to secede unilaterally: a legal separation would require a negotiated constitutional amendment, as Ottawa had insisted. On the other hand, if a "clear" referendum question yielded a "clear" result in favour of secession, the rest of Canada had a constitutional obligation to negotiate in good faith with Quebec. The court also implied that such negotiations should be open to compromise options—"sovereignty association," perhaps, or a "new partnership." This was too good for Quebec nationalists to pass up. No longer could the federal government argue that Canada was indivisible. No longer could it refuse to negotiate a new "partnership" with Quebec, on the basis that separation was a simple in-or-out proposition. So instead of rejecting the decision, the Quebec government tried to turn it to its advantage, emphasizing the parts it liked and ignoring others.

The court left several key questions to be answered by politicians. What exactly was a "clear" referendum question? Did it have to be simpler and more direct than the 1980 and 1995 questions, as Ottawa maintained, or were those questions perfectly acceptable, as the PQ government argued? And what percentage of the voters would constitute a "clear" majority in a secession referendum? Would 50 percent plus one suffice, as Quebec had always insisted, or would a more substantial majority be required to break up the country, as Stéphane Dion argued? A clear result on a clear question was necessary to trigger the constitutional "obligation to negotiate," said the court, but whether either the question or the result was sufficiently clear was a matter for political, not legal, judgment. In effect, the judges asked the questions; political leaders would supply the answers. In 2000, the House of Commons did just that (Dossier 5.3).

DOSSIER 5.3 Ottawa's *Clarity Act* versus Quebec's Bill 99

In December 1999 federal Intergovernmental Affairs Minister Stéphane Dion introduced Bill C-20 in the House of Commons. The *"Clarity Act,"* as it was quickly dubbed, provided some of the answers to the political questions posed by the court. In particular, it addressed the issues of a "clear majority" and a "clear question." It gave the House of Commons the power to determine whether a provincial referendum question on secession was sufficiently clear to provide "a clear expression of the will of the population of a province on whether the province should cease to be part of Canada and become an independent state."[57] In a pointed rebuke to the PQ, the *Clarity Act* condemned the 1980 and 1995 referendum questions (Dossier 5.2): "a clear expression of the will of the population of a province that the province ceases to be part of Canada could not result from

(a) a referendum question that merely focuses on a mandate to negotiate without soliciting a

direct expression of the will of the population of that province on whether the province should cease to be part of Canada; or

(b) a referendum question that envisages other possibilities in addition to the secession of the province from Canada, such as economic or political arrangements with Canada, that obscure a direct expression of the will of the population of that province on whether the province should cease to be part of Canada."[58]

If the House of Commons determined, after consultations with Opposition parties, Aboriginal groups, and other interested parties, that the question was not sufficiently clear, the federal government would not enter into negotiations on secession following a "yes" majority. Nor would Ottawa be obliged to negotiate if the "yes" majority was too small, or if it did not represent a majority of the entire electorate. The Bill does not define "a clear majority" precisely,

(continued)

although Dion repeatedly declared that 50 percent plus one is an insufficient basis to break up the country. Finally, the Bill set out the mandatory subjects to be negotiated: "the division of assets and liabilities, any changes to the borders of the province, the rights, interests and territorial claims of the Aboriginal peoples of Canada, and the protection of minority rights."[59] In effect, the federal government warned Quebec voters that they could not take the existing provincial borders for granted; if anglophone or Aboriginal communities wanted to remain in Canada, they could count on Ottawa's support.

The Quebec government reacted angrily to the *Clarity Act*, and quickly tabled a legislative response. Bill 99 effectively declared the *Secession Reference* inapplicable to Quebec, and proclaimed "the right of the Québec people to self-determination."[60] Section 4 defined a "clear majority" as "a majority of the valid votes cast, namely 50 percent of the valid votes cast plus one." There was no reference to the percentage of the overall electorate. Bill 99 concluded with the defiant assertion that "No other parliament or government may reduce the powers, authority, sovereignty or legitimacy of the National Assembly, or impose constraint on the democratic will of the Québec people to determine its own future." This refusal to accept the Supreme Court ruling in its entirety was hardly surprising. One month before the tabling of the *Clarity Act*, Quebec's Intergovernmental Affairs minister had publicly condemned the *Secession Reference* as "a federally orchestrated strategy which sought to use the highest court of the land to obtain the answers that the federal government was looking for in response to questions of its own devising."[61] Nor is it surprising that a separatist government would respond with hostility to the Plan B strategy, the centrepiece of which was the Supreme Court reference. As a matter of law, however, it seems clear that Quebec is bound by the *Clarity Act* in the event of a future "yes" vote in a referendum on sovereignty.

◼ Strengthening the Economic Union: The 1994 Agreement on Internal Trade

In every federation, a balance must be struck between the legitimate diversity of provincial priorities, including the promotion of local economic interests, and the maintenance of a strong national economy. Reconciling these competing goals is often a difficult process. In political terms, the immediate benefits of enacting policies that benefit local farmers, industries, and professionals are usually irresistible. The same cannot be said for collaborating with other governments to harmonize policies and eliminate barriers to commerce and labour mobility.

As far back as 1940, the Rowell-Sirois Commission identified provincial nontariff barriers as a potential threat to Canada's economic growth. By the 1980s, as the Canadian and American economies became more integrated, Ontarians were discovering that it was easier to do business in Michigan than in Quebec. Business leaders pressured the federal and provincial governments to dismantle the complex network of internal-trade barriers that had grown incrementally over the past century. Broadly speaking, these barriers took two forms:

1. discriminatory policies that deliberately excluded out-of-province competition (e.g., laws that restricted construction work to provincial unions, or forbade the sale of beer brewed in another province); and
2. otherwise legitimate regulations that differed from those in other provinces, thereby making it more difficult for workers and industries to set up shop across provincial borders.

Many barriers in the second category were imposed, not by provincial governments themselves, but by self-regulating professional bodies whose standards for accreditation were too narrowly drawn; for example, requiring an occupational therapist to hold a particular postsecondary qualification that was offered only at an institution in that province. Some of these variations among provincial standards—those pertaining to lawyers—had been eliminated by court rulings under the mobility rights clause of the *Charter* (section 6);[62] most were unaffected.

Both the "Quebec Round" and the "Canada Round" of negotiations featured discussions of the economic union, although these received less attention than Quebec's specific demands. The search for a binding intergovernmental solution to internal-trade barriers received added urgency from the failure of the Charlottetown Accord. The Mulroney and Chrétien Governments were anxious to show the provinces, especially Quebec, that federalism could be improved without the cumbersome process of constitutional amendment.[63] In late 1992 the Progressive Conservative Industry minister initiated the process by tabling a proposed *Statement of Principles* for collaborative management of the economic union. Negotiations among the FPT trade ministers began shortly thereafter and proceeded without interruption when the federal government changed hands. In July 1994 Prime Minister Chrétien signed the Agreement on Internal Trade (AIT), along with the 10 premiers. The AIT took effect on July 1, 1995.[64] By 2007, it had been amended seven times.[65]

The agreement requires the federal and provincial governments to do certain things, and to refrain from doing others.

- First, governments are expected to eliminate existing trade barriers. For example, they must not restrict their purchases of goods and services to local companies. When a provincial government needs to upgrade its computers, it has to accept and consider bids from companies outside the province on the same footing as a supplier inside the province. The senior governments also have to work together to establish uniform standards (e.g., labour qualifications and environmental regulations). In many cases, this requires them to work closely with private-sector groups. Doctors, lawyers, and other professionals are regulated by their own provincial associations (e.g., the Law Society of Nova Scotia or the Ontario College of Physicians and Surgeons). Those associations are required by the AIT to ensure that a professional licensed to practice in one province can pursue the same profession in another province without having to submit to a lengthy recertification process.

- Second, governments cannot adopt new practices that may be perceived by other provinces as unfair or discriminatory. However, governments can still pursue development initiatives for their poorest regions (e.g., subsidizing new businesses in depressed communities). This gives provinces an incentive to circumvent the AIT: unemployed workers can vote, whereas intergovernmental agreements cannot.

- Third, the AIT established a Committee on Internal Trade (CIT), made up of ministers from the 11 senior governments. The CIT monitors the implementation of the agreement and conducts an annual review to determine priorities for future improvement. Unfortunately for advocates of a stronger economic union, the committee has been hampered by two institutional problems. The first is that it makes decisions by consensus, which means that an individual province can block a particular decision that it perceives as contrary to its interests.[66] Second, the participating ministers do not control all of the policies that affect the agreement. There are separate intergovernmental committees with responsibility for labour, communications, transport, and many other policy fields directly related to the mandate of the CIT. This diffusion of decision-making power reduces the impact of the Agreement.[67] However, it appears that all departments within the senior governments have begun to take their agreement seriously when they review proposed policies.[68] If this is true, it suggests a more coordinated approach to internal trade within each government, which would give members of the CIT the confidence that their governments will honour their commitments.

- Fourth and finally, the signatory governments established an Internal Trade Secretariat (ITS) based in Winnipeg. The ITS is not a part of any individual government; it reports to all of the FP governments.[69] Although it is a genuinely intergovernmental institution, it lacks the power to enforce the AIT effectively. Instead, the AIT established a quasi-judicial dispute-resolution system. Take the example of a 2002 complaint by accountants in New Brunswick against the Government of Quebec. The Certified General Accountants of New Brunswick (CGA-NB) argued that Quebec was shutting out some of their members. In 2005, a panel convened under the AIT ruled in favour of the CGA-NB and recommended that the Quebec government amend its laws and regulations to bring them into line with the Agreement. In 2006, the Quebec government complied with the ruling.[70] This example is not entirely typical, in two respects. First, the parties pursued the dispute all the way to a panel; the majority of AIT disputes are either resolved between the parties or allowed to lapse.[71] Second, governments do not always comply with adverse rulings. Panel decisions are nonbinding, so a government that is found to have violated the AIT is not required to abide by the ruling.[72] A government in that position might have an incentive to abide by the panel's decision, if only to ensure smooth trading relations with other governments in the future.[73] On the other hand, it could face a stronger political incentive to ignore panel rulings that, if followed, could jeopardize local jobs and votes. To offset these protectionist forces would require a very powerful intergovernmental agency with a binding dispute-resolution mechanism or, alternatively, a ministerial committee in which decisions could be made by a majority, rather than a consensus. Given the realities of Canadian federalism, especially the equal-provinces principle, neither seems likely.

For some observers, "progress in implementing the AIT has been disappointing, at best. Most of the targets and goals included at its signing have not been met."[74] The Internal Trade Secretariat claims that the participating governments are meeting their reporting obligations under the agreement.[75] But compliance with the more difficult requirements—those which require actual change in policy—is spotty.[76] Most of the original deadlines for specific actions have been missed or extended; where no clear deadline was set, little appears to have been achieved.[77] Moreover, the dispute-resolution mechanism proved unsatisfactory: some panel members had no experience with the applicable areas of law and policy; there was no mechanism for the enforcement of rulings; and the rules of procedure did not meet the normal standards for quasi-judicial proceedings.[78] These problems were addressed in the 2007 amendments to the AIT; however, enforcement remains a weakness of the AIT process—as is so often the case in Canadian IGRs.[79]

Overall, however, the economic union is stronger today than it was in 1995. For example, government procurement is increasingly open to competition from other provinces.[80] When the interests of business "stakeholders" are served by freer internal trade, the AIT provides a framework for ensuring that their goals are met. Elsewhere, businesses, unions, and professional organizations have resisted changing a status quo that suits their own interests.[81] Consequently, the impact of the agreement varies from sector to sector. For example, FPT governments had worked to harmonize highway and transport policies for over two decades before the AIT was signed; as a result, the interprovincial trucking sector is highly integrated across Canada.[82] In this instance, the removal of internal-trade barriers was clearly a priority of both the governments and the businesses involved in the trucking industry. Under those circumstances, policy harmonization in this sector would likely have occurred without the AIT.

In the long run, the symbolism of the AIT may be at least as important as its tangible effects on internal trade. The negotiation of the agreement, and its unanimous acceptance, placed the 11 senior governments on an equal footing in the management of Canada's economic union. Instead of invoking its powers under section 91 of the *Constitution Act,*

1982—the responsibility to regulate trade and commerce, or the "national concern" branch of the residual power—the federal government agreed to share the governance of internal trade with the provinces.[83] So while the AIT shares the failings of other nonconstitutional mechanisms, its mere existence seems to reflect a shared determination to make the federation work better.

The 1999 Social Union Framework Agreement: Institutionalizing Intergovernmental Relations?

In February 1999, shortly before the federal budget that began to restore CHST transfers for health care, the federal government and nine of the 10 provinces signed the Social Union Framework Agreement (SUFA). The SUFA initiative originated with the provinces, which had been outraged by the unilateral federal announcement of the CHST in February 1995 (Chapter 4). In self-defence, the provincial governments banded together to devise "new ground rules to govern federal–provincial negotiations in the social policy arena."[84]

At the Annual Premiers' Conference in August 1995, the provincial governments agreed to establish the Ministerial Council on Social Policy Reform and Renewal. The council developed a set of proposals to "constrain the federal spending power [and] clarify the jurisdictions of each order of government."[85] In June 1996 the federal government agreed to work with the council to develop a national strategy to strengthen Canada's social union. The term "social union" is difficult to define. In this context, it appears to refer to a nationwide system of social programs delivered by both levels of government, with primary program responsibility at the provincial level. In December 1997 the 11 first ministers agreed to negotiate a Social Union Framework Agreement (SUFA). While it would not be entrenched in the *Constitution,* a SUFA would impose political pressure on the federal and provincial governments to cooperate and consult on future changes to social programs.

To secure Quebec's participation in the SUFA process, the other provinces agreed in 1998 that all provinces would have "the ability to opt out of any new or modified Canada-wide social program in areas of provincial/territorial jurisdiction with full compensation, provided that the province/territory carries on a program or initiative that addresses the priority areas of the Canada-wide program."[86] Since the 1960s, Quebec governments had insisted that they be given the chance to opt out of new national shared-cost programs, with full compensation from Ottawa for the benefits that they would have received had they agreed to the program. (As noted earlier, this demand played a key role in the constitutional bargaining of the 1980s and 1990s.)

The 1998 "Saskatoon Consensus" among the provinces and territories was translated into a formal SUFA proposal in January 1999. This "Victoria Proposal" declared that "Under the Constitution, provinces and territories are primarily responsible for social policy and the delivery of social programs." It called for:

- "full federal restoration of the funding cut from the Canada Health and Social Transfer";
- full escalation of federal transfer payments to cover rising program costs;
- consent of a majority of provinces to "any new or modified Canada-wide program in areas of provincial jurisdiction";
- "joint agreement of objectives and principles for new or modified Canada-wide programs"; and
- full compensation to any province that opted out of a new or modified program, as long as it provided similar services under its own responsibility.[87]

The proposal also included mechanisms for resolving disputes between governments and for seeking "public input in developing priorities and objectives for social programs." No new federal shared-cost program would be introduced without the agreement of a majority of the provincial governments. There was no requirement that these governments represent a majority of the Canadian population; in principle, an agreement under this provision could exclude Ontario, British Columbia, Alberta, and (perhaps inevitably) Quebec. In political terms, however, this is surely a far-fetched scenario.[88] Finally, the Victoria Proposal recognized the close connection between the economic union and the social union; it contained explicit provisions to enhance social mobility, paralleling the AIT provisions on labour mobility.

On February 4, 1999, the federal government and all of the provinces except Quebec agreed to the final SUFA text.[89] The agreement differed from the Victoria Proposal in at least three key respects.[90]

- First, it contained an explicit declaration that "The use of the federal spending power under the Constitution has been essential to the development of Canada's social union," as the basis for both intergovernmental transfers and direct transfers to individuals. No such declaration was included in the provincial proposal.
- Second, the reference to provincial supremacy over social policy was deleted.
- Third, Ottawa refused to accept the opting-out provision in the Victoria Proposal. The SUFA simply states that "All provincial and territorial governments that meet or commit to meet the agreed Canada-wide objectives and agree to respect the accountability framework will receive their share of available funding." Without the opt-out provision, Quebec refused to sign the agreement.

The differences between the PT agreement and the final FPT version can be explained quite simply: when the federal government joined the SUFA process, it brought a large pot of money to the table. It used the promise of substantial increases to the CHST to win over nine of the premiers, persuading them to modify their opposition to the federal spending power in exchange for its more lavish employment.[91] So "what had begun in large part as a provincial and territorial initiative to bell the federal spending power ended up as a framework to facilitate federal government involvement in provincial programs."[92] On the other hand, if the federal government respected the SUFA, its power would be exercised in "a more cooperative and consensual manner through a Council of Ministers,"[93] rather than unilaterally.

Reaction to the SUFA was mixed. Critics in Quebec condemned the other premiers for "selling out." Instead of keeping faith with Quebec, they jumped at Ottawa's promise of restored health-care funding.[94] Observers outside Quebec were more favourable, suggesting that "the provinces 'won' to the extent that Ottawa agreed to put into an intergovernmental agreement a set of decision rules that gives the provinces a formal if modest role in the exercise of [the federal spending] power that they had not previously had."[95]

The SUFA is a political accord, not entrenched constitutional law. So while its advocates heralded "a new era of collaboration, mutual respect among orders of government and a more coherent and systematic approach to social policy-making,"[96] it was more likely a collection of hollow promises. Less than two weeks after the SUFA was signed, the 1999 federal budget introduced a new formula for calculating CHST transfers, which had not been crafted in consultation with the provinces. This unilateral federal announcement suggests that the agreement, despite its language about cooperation and joint decision-making, "offers no guarantee of stability or predictability in federal spending"[97]—a guarantee that had been one of the chief provincial goals in the SUFA process. The Chrétien Government continued to make unilateral changes to transfers and policies, flouting the express terms of the agreement.

Unlike the AIT, the SUFA did not establish a dedicated intergovernmental secretariat to monitor implementation. Instead, its implementation was entrusted to ad hoc PT and FPT councils, whose annual reports reflected considerable frustration with Chrétien's refusal to recognize a lead role for the PT governments in the design of social policy, adopt an effective dispute-resolution mechanism, or consult the provinces before altering transfer payments and creating new programs (e.g., the 2000 homelessness initiative).[98]

Between 1999 and 2006, the 10 participating governments made modest progress on some policy fronts, including social mobility, child poverty, early childhood development, and disability.[99] However, the highest-profile social policy field—health care—was relatively unaffected by SUFA. Ottawa and the nine ROC provinces signed three health-care Accords, none of which made any reference to the agreement.[100] One might well question the value of a supposedly binding agreement on social policy that seems to be irrelevant to the overriding social-policy issue in Canada. The SUFA was also invisible in the 2000 FPT Accord on Early Childhood Development. All in all, the SUFA appeared to be a dead letter within a few years of its adoption; it was not reflected in either the process of social policy-making or the text of the resulting agreements.[101]

As part of its strategy to win support from provincial governments, the Conservative Party promised to revive the SUFA. Although its 2006 platform did not explicitly refer to the agreement, it pledged to "Ensure that any new shared-cost programs in areas of provincial/territorial responsibility have the consent of the majority of provinces to proceed, and that provinces should be given the right to opt out of the federal program with compensation, so long as the province offers a similar program with similar accountability structures."[102] The 2006 federal budget repeated that promise, "In keeping with the Social Union Framework Agreement (SUFA) signed by the federal government and all provinces other than Quebec in 1999."[103] No new shared-cost programs had been initiated at the time of writing, so the Harper Government's actual commitment to that promise is impossible to assess. Interestingly, the 2007 federal budget contained no reference to the SUFA; however, it reiterated the platform promises and reported on consultations with the provinces. The jury is still out about the practical impact of the SUFA.

THE HARPER AGENDA: TESTING THE LIMITS OF NONCONSTITUTIONAL RENEWAL

Given its precarious minority status, the Conservative Government elected in 2006 was in no position to advance an ambitious constitutional agenda. Nonetheless, it tried to implement some of its promised reforms to Canada's national institutions. In particular, it pursued an incremental strategy to move the Senate closer to the Triple-E model. First, it introduced legislation to limit the terms of senators. Second, it tabled a Bill to extend the Alberta system of Senate elections to the rest of Canada. (These initiatives are described in detail in Dossier 3.4.) In both instances, the Harper Government insisted that it could proceed without provincial consent; the amendments to the *BNA Act* fell under the exclusive federal power in section 44 of the *Constitution Act, 1982*.

In his testimony before the Special Senate Committee on Senate Reform, Prime Minister Harper said the following:

The government has proceeded with this proposed legislation [Bill S-4] first because it believes Parliament can act, without engaging other levels of government in a complex constitutional discussion or amendment process. . . . There are three general paths we could go down. The two alternatives to step-by-step reform are, first, maintain the status quo; and, second, an attempt at comprehensive reform through, in a sense, megaconstitutional negotiations. On the first alternative, the people of Canada believe that the status quo is not acceptable and, perhaps more pertinently, it is not compatible with the commitments that this government made to the people of Canada in its election campaign. My observations over the last 20 years of federal-provincial politics, despite my relatively young age, are such that I do not see comprehensive Senate reform achievable today, except, perhaps, one kind of comprehensive reform—abolition. For that reason, I would urge all senators on this committee to conclude that step-by-step reform is the preferable way to proceed.[104]

Notwithstanding the prime minister's assurances, the Senate rejected the step-by-step approach (Dossier 3.4).[105]

The Harper Government had more success on another front: responding to Quebec's demand for special recognition. In November 2006 the Bloc Québécois announced that it would ask the Commons to recognize Quebec as a nation. Prime Minister Harper caught everyone off-guard by pre-empting the Bloc motion—perhaps because some of his own Quebec ministers would have voted in favour of it. He introduced his own motion: "That this House recognize that the Québécois form a nation within a united Canada." In this context, Harper argued that the difference between "Quebec" and "the Québécois" is significant. Recognizing Quebec as a nation could foster separatist ambitions, by implying that the province should or does enjoy political sovereignty. On the other hand, the Québécois "nation" is a sociological rather than a political entity. Its recognition by the federal Parliament is merely a statement of the obvious, rather than an implicit (or explicit) change in the province's political status. Harper concluded his opening remarks on the motion as follows:

> *Once again, the leader of the Bloc and his separatist friends are not concerned with defining who Quebeckers are but rather what they want them to become, a separate country. The separatists do not need the Parliament of Canada to define what is meant by the sociological term "nation". My preference has been well known. I believe this is not the job of the federal Parliament. It is the job of the legislature of Quebec. However, the Bloc Québécois has asked us to define this and perhaps that is a good thing because it reminds us that all Canadians have a say in the future of this country. . . . Having been asked by the Bloc to define the Québécois, we must take a position. Our position is clear. Do the Québécois form a nation within Canada? The answer is yes. Do the Québécois form an independent nation? The answer is no, and the answer will always be no. . . .*[106]

Predictably, the BQ expressed outrage at the prime minister's manoeuvre. They were not alone: Intergovernmental Affairs Minister Michael Chong resigned, citing his opposition to ethnic nationalism.[107] When he announced his resignation, Chong told reporters that he had not been consulted about the motion before the prime minister announced it in the House; instead, the PMO had sought advice from former Liberal Minister Stéphane Dion.[108] In the end, the vast majority of MPs voted in favour of the Government motion—including BQ MPs, despite their criticism of the phrase "within a united Canada."

To date, the motion has had little impact on the Canadian constitutional debate. However, the failure to define "nation" in the text of the motion could cause problems in the future. BQ leader Gilles Duceppe told the Commons that "Now that the issue of Quebeckers' status has been symbolically addressed by the unanimous recognition of the parties in this House, we can move on to the next step"—i.e., full sovereignty based on political nationhood. In June 2007, Dion publicly called on Harper to clarify the motion in order to avert "the next step."[109] Perhaps he feared that Duceppe's prediction during the Commons debate would come true:

> *From today on, the relationship that Quebeckers may have with Canada will be a nation-to-nation relationship. We will demand, as representatives of Quebec here in the House of Commons, that the rights of the Quebec nation, that has now been recognized, be respected. . . . We are now in a much better position not only to claim those rights after being recognized for the nation that we are, but also to interact with all other nations in the world that know what that recognition means. The day*

we decide to become a country, it will be a lot easier for these nations to say that they recognize this new nation that has formed a country because the House of Commons will have recognized, some time ago, that the Quebec nation in fact exists.[110]

Indeed, in spring 2008 the BQ issued a series of demands to transfer policy and taxing powers from Ottawa to Quebec City, arguing that these demands "flowed from" the November 2006 motion. The party did not get what it wanted, but neither did the Conservatives. Despite granting Quebec nationalists the recognition they sought, Harper managed to elect only 10 candidates in the province in October 2008 (the same number elected in 2006).

CONCLUSION

The reforms and reform proposals discussed in this chapter, both constitutional and non-constitutional, reflect the lack of consensus about the character of Canada's political community. Two strongly mobilized subcultures—Quebec nationalism and Western regionalism—have been joined by new, latent cleavages fostered by value change and the *Charter of Rights*. While these latter groups have not produced fully formed subcultures, they mobilized effectively around the perceived threat to the "citizens' constitution" from the Meech Lake and Charlottetown Accords. As the old territorial issues remained unresolved, the addition of new nonterritorial claims for constitutional recognition and the populist critique of executive federalism fatally complicated the process of megaconstitutional politics. The substitution of referenda for elite accommodation as the decisive decision-making device made it more difficult than ever to satisfy the rapidly multiplying demands for institutional reform.

At present, populism appears to be losing some of its political force. The new Conservative Party seems to lack the populist enthusiasm of its predecessors, the Reform Party and the Canadian Alliance—although it understood the need to promise Senate reform, to appease the old Reform base in Alberta. But the other pressures for change will persist. In times of crisis, they may escalate until Canada's political elites have no choice but to confront them. There is no guarantee, however, that a successful return to constitutional bargaining would have the desired effects. The *Constitution Act, 1982,* the only successful product of megaconstitutional politics to date, has had significant and largely unanticipated effects on our government and politics. We turn to the *Charter* in the next chapter.

GLOSSARY OF KEY TERMS

Amending formula: See Chapter 3.

Amendments: See Chapter 3.

Economic union: The goal of creating a single national economy, without internal barriers to trade or mobility, transcending provincial jurisdictions. In Canada, this goal is manifested most prominently in the 1994 Agreement on Internal Trade (AIT).

Intrastate: See Chapter 4.

Social union: The goal of creating a cohesive national network of social programs (e.g., health care), so that Canadians in every province and territory receive a similar package of services. The opposite of "checkerboard federalism," in which Canadians in one province receive fewer, lesser, or entirely different social programs from those available in a neighbouring province.

DISCUSSION AND REVIEW QUESTIONS

1. Identify and briefly summarize *two* key elements in Trudeau's 1980 constitutional package.

2. Name and briefly analyze *two* of Quebec's long-standing demands for reform of the Canadian *Constitution*. How, if at all, have these demands been met?

3. Why did the Meech Lake and Charlottetown Accords fail? In your opinion, would Canadian politics be different if either Accord had been ratified? Why or why not?

4. Can the competing constitutional (and nonconstitutional) agendas of Canada's major subcultures ever be reconciled? If so, how?

5. Are nonconstitutional reforms effective responses to megaconstitutional demands? Why or why not? Answer with specific reference to at least one recent nonconstitutional initiative.

SUGGESTED READINGS

Books and Articles

Stéphane Dion, *Straight Talk: Speeches and Writings on Canadian Unity*, Peter H. Russell, ed. (Montreal and Kingston: McGill–Queen's University Press, 1999).

Alain-G. Gagnon and Hugh Segal, eds., *The Canadian Social Union Without Quebec: Eight Critical Analyses* (Montreal: Institute for Research in Public Policy, 2000).

Sarah Fortin, Alain Noël, and France St-Hilaire, eds., *Forging the Canadian Social Union: SUFA and Beyond* (Montreal: Institute for Research on Public Policy, 2003).

James Ross Hurley, *Amending Canada's Constitution: History, Processes, Problems and Prospects* (Ottawa: Minister of Supply and Services Canada, 1996).

Harvey Lazar, "Non-Constitutional Renewal: Toward a New Equilibrium in the Federation," in Harvey Lazar, ed., *The State of the Federation 1997: Non-Constitutional Renewal* (Kingston, ON: Institute of Intergovernmental Relations, 1998).

Peter H. Russell, *Constitutional Odyssey: Can Canadians Become a Sovereign People?* 3rd ed. (Toronto: University of Toronto Press, 2004).

Robert A. Young, *The Struggle for Quebec: From Referendum to Referendum?* (Montreal and Kingston: McGill–Queen's University Press, 1999).

Websites

The most useful website for this chapter is maintained by the Canadian Intergovernmental Conference Secretariat (www.scics.gc.ca), which provides a full list of PT and FPT ministerial meetings and many of the countless gatherings of officials that have taken place since 1996. Go to the website, click on "Conference Information," and then select the month and year of a particular conference (e.g., the September 2004 FPT Health Care Summit). For the major meetings, you will often find links to official documents—the final communiqués as well as the working papers.

Another helpful source of information is the Intergovernmental Affairs page of the Privy Council Office website (www.pco-bcp.gc.ca). Click on "Intergovernmental Relations by Sector" to find a wealth of documents on the cooperation (and conflicts) among Canada's senior governments.

Finally, there are two outstanding sources of academic commentary on Canadian intergovernmental relations: the Institute for Research on Public Policy (www.irpp.org) and the Queen's University Institute of Intergovernmental Relations (www.iigr.ca). At the IRPP site, click "Publication Search" and select "Canadian federalism" or "Council of the Federation" from the pull-down menu of public policy subjects. Select "Research" from the menu at the top of the screen, and then "Browse Publications" or "Current Research" from the pull-down menu. The "Working Papers" page provides up-to-date analysis of trends in Canadian federalism and nonconstitutional renewal. The Queen's IIGR site also provides a wide range of information that is readily available.

NOTES

1. James Ross Hurley, *Amending Canada's Constitution: History, Processes, Problems and Prospects* (Ottawa: Minister of Supply and Services Canada, 1996), 19–20.

2. There have been several amendments affecting the federal government, including changes to the representation formula used to allocate seats in the House of Commons and the creation of Nunavut as a separate territory. Amendments affecting only one province have also been successfully enacted, including changes to school boards in Quebec and Newfoundland and Labrador. However, these did not employ either the general amending formula or the unanimity rule. For more details, see Dossier 3.3.

3. Jennifer Smith, "Informal Constitutional Development: Change by Other Means," in Herman Bakvis and Grace Skogstad, eds., *Canadian Federalism: Performance, Effectiveness, and Legitimacy* (Toronto: Oxford University Press, 2002), 40.

4. Jennifer Smith, "The Constitutional Debate and Beyond," in François Rocher and Miriam Smith, eds., *New Trends in Canadian Federalism,* 2nd edition (Peterborough, ON: Broadview Press, 2003).

5. Roger Gibbins, "Shifting Sands: Exploring the Political Foundations of SUFA," in Sarah Fortin, Alain Noël, and France St-Hilaire, eds., *Forging the Canadian Social Union: SUFA and Beyond* (Montreal: Institute for Research on Public Policy, 2003).

6. Smith, "The Constitutional Debate and Beyond," 63.

7. Pierre Elliott Trudeau, "A Constitutional Declaration of Rights," in Pierre Elliott Trudeau, *Federalism and the French Canadians* (Toronto: Macmillan, 1968), 52–60.

8. Garth Stevenson, *Unfulfilled Union: Canadian Federalism and National Unity,* rev. edition (Toronto: Gage, 1982), 76–77.

9. Peter H. Russell, *Constitutional Odyssey: Can Canadians Become a Sovereign People?* 2nd edition (Toronto: University of Toronto Press, 1993), 109.

10. Roy Romanow, John Whyte, and Howard Leeson, *Canada Notwithstanding: The Making of the Constitution 1976–1982* (Toronto: Carswell/Methuen, 1984), 60–61.

11. There were Progressive Conservative governments in Manitoba, Newfoundland, Nova Scotia, Alberta, New Brunswick and Ontario; the last two broke with their federal party to support Trudeau's package, which caused some strains within the PC Party. The NDP controlled the Saskatchewan Government, while PEI was ruled by the Liberals. To round out the list of 10 provinces, there was a Social Credit Government in British Columbia, and the PQ Government in Quebec.

12. Alan C. Cairns, "Citizens (Outsiders) and Governments (Insiders) in Constitution-Making: The Case of Meech Lake," in Alan C. Cairns, *Disruptions: Constitutional Struggles, from the Charter to Meech Lake,* ed. Douglas E. Williams (Toronto: McClelland and Stewart, 1991), 110.

13. Romanow et al., 210–11. The historical truth, as always, is more complicated than the political myth. Whereas the other provincial delegations stayed at the Chateau Laurier hotel in Ottawa, the Quebec representatives stayed across the Ottawa River in Hull. The symbolism of this decision may have been irresistible, but it caused serious logistical problems—worsened by Lévesque's insistence on turning off his telephone so he could get a good

night's sleep. When the Justice Ministers of Canada, Ontario, and Saskatchewan met in the wee hours to hammer out the final agreement, they could not get hold of Lévesque to seek his opinion. He and his entourage arrived at the Government Conference Centre the next morning, unaware of any overnight developments, only to find the text of a draft deal sitting on the conference table. So if Lévesque and his team were out of the loop, it was their own fault.

14. Romanow et al., 130–31.

15. Ibid., 210–11.

16. Section 15 of the *Charter* was delayed for three years; see Chapter 6.

17. Resolution of the National Assembly, December 16, 1982. Reproduced in Hurley, Appendix 15, 255.

18. The Meech Lake time line is adapted from Andrew Cohen, *A Deal Undone: The Making and Breaking of the Meech Lake Accord* (Vancouver: Douglas and McIntyre, 1991), 285–89; the Charlottetown Accord time line is adapted from Susan Delacourt, *United We Fall: The Crisis of Democracy in Canada* (Toronto: Viking, 1993).

19. *Shaping Canada's Future Together* (Ottawa: Minister of Supply and Services Canada, 1991).

20. Richard Simeon, "Meech Lake and Shifting Conceptions of Federalism," *Canadian Public Policy 14* (supp.) (1988), 10.

21. Cairns, "Citizens (Outsiders)," 135.

22. This is highly unlikely. With regard to gender equality, Quebec is probably the most progressive jurisdiction in the country.

23. Patrick J. Monahan, *Meech Lake: The Inside Story* (Toronto: University of Toronto Press, 1991), 144–45.

24. *Native Women's Association of Canada v. Canada,* [1994] 3 S.C.R. 627.

25. Smith, "The Constitutional Debate and Beyond," 59.

26. Russell, *Constitutional Odyssey,* 2nd ed., 226.

27. Michael Lusztig, "Constitutional Paralysis: Why Canadian Constitutional Initiatives Are Doomed to Fail," *Canadian Journal of Political Science,* XXVII:4 (December 1994), 747–71.

28. Ken S. Coates, *The Marshall Decision and Native Rights* (Montreal and Kingston: McGill–Queen's University Press, 2000), 78.

29. Peter H. Russell, *Constitutional Odyssey: Can Canadians Become a Sovereign People?* 3rd ed. (Toronto: University of Toronto Press, 2004), 228.

30. Harvey Lazar, "Non-Constitutional Renewal: Toward a New Equilibrium in the Federation," in Harvey Lazar, ed., *The State of the Federation 1997: Non-Constitutional Renewal* (Kingston, ON: Institute of Intergovernmental Relations, 1998).

31. Of course, the isolation of Quebec could be described as an instance of continuity rather than change, given the entrenchment of the *Constitution Act, 1982* without the province's consent.

32. Lazar, "Non-Constitutional Renewal," 26.

33. Rodney Haddow, "Canadian Federalism and Active Labour Market Policy," in Rocher and Smith, eds.; Herman Bakvis, "Checkerboard Federalism? Labour Market Development Policy in Canada," in Bakvis and Skogstad, eds.

34. Decision-making under the SUFA is based on a majority of governments, so that no single government has a veto.

35. Gibbins, "Shifting Sands," 43.

36. Even then, the courts are unlikely to accept challenges to their constitutionality. Law Professor Lorne Sossin suggested in 1998 that the CHST—specifically, the removal of the conditions under the CAP, which it replaced—might be open to a court challenge under the *Charter of Rights* (sections 7 and 15). Subsequently, the Supreme Court of Canada has rejected the claim that either section protects welfare recipients from the unilateral reduction of their benefits. See Sossin, "Salvaging the Welfare State? The Prospects for Judicial Review of the Canada Health and Social Transfer," *Dalhousie Law Journal,* 21:1 (Spring 1998); *Gosselin v. Quebec (Attorney General),* [2002] 4 S.C.R. 429.

37. In the 1991 *Reference Re Canada Assistance Plan (B.C.),* the court considered the legality of the 1990 "cap on CAP" (Chapter 4). A unanimous court agreed that a cost-sharing agreement was justiciable—that is, open to judicial review—but it determined that the British Columbia government could not expect judicial relief for the federal government's unilateral decision to limit transfer payments. *Reference Re Canada Assistance Plan (B.C.),* [1991] 2 S.C.R. 525. The 1993 *Finlay* case dealt with a challenge by a Manitoba welfare recipient. He argued that the provincial government had violated the terms of the CAP agreement when it deducted money from his welfare cheques to recover an earlier overpayment. The majority on the court disagreed, holding that "the conditions attached to the federal government's contribution are not designed to dictate the precise terms of the provincial legislation, but rather to promote legislation which achieves substantial compliance with the objectives of CAP." *Finlay v. Canada (Minister of Finance),* [1993] 1 S.C.R. 1080, head notes.

38. See Heather MacIvor, *Canadian Politics and Government in the Charter Era* (Toronto: Nelson Thomson, 2005), Chapter 7.

39. Johanne Poirier, "Intergovernmental Agreements in Canada: At the Crossroads Between Law and Politics," in J. Peter Meekison, Hamish Telford, and Harvey Lazar, eds., *Reconsidering the Institutions of Canadian Federalism* (Montreal and Kingston: Institute of Intergovernmental Relations/McGill–Queen's University Press, 2004), 435.

40. Robert A. Young, *The Struggle for Quebec: From Referendum to Referendum?* (Montreal and Kingston: McGill–Queen's University Press, 1999), 18.

41. Ibid., 40–41.

42. Ironically, Chrétien's refusal to consider a return to megaconstitutional negotiations may have hampered his efforts in the 1995 referendum campaign. Unlike Trudeau in 1980, he could not or would not promise formal constitutional amendments in order to sway undecided voters toward the "No" side. Russell, 234.

43. The premier of Quebec at the time of the 1995 referendum, Jacques Parizeau, actually wanted a clear question. However, his hard-line approach was overruled by Lucien Bouchard, the Bloc Québécois leader (and Parizeau's eventual successor as premier). Russell, 230–232.

44. Rhéal Séguin, "Landry stays as PQ leader—for now," *The Globe and Mail,* August 30, 2004 (accessed at www.globeandmail.com); "Sovereigntists design new referendum rules," August 29, 2004 (accessed at www.cbc.ca).

45. Alan C. Cairns, "The Legacy of the Referendum: Who Are We Now?" *Constitutional Forum 7,* nos. 2 and 3 (Winter and Spring 1996), 101.

46. Young, 95 and 175 (note 53).

47. *An Act Respecting Constitutional Amendments,* Royal Assent, February 2, 1996; formerly Bill C-110, 35th Parliament, 1st Session.

48. "Speech from the Throne to Open the Second Session of the Thirty-Fifth Parliament of Canada," February 27, 1996, 4–5; accessed at www.pco-bcp.gc.ca, June 2007.

49. Russell, 2nd ed., 253.

50. Stéphane Dion, "Letter to Mr. Lucien Bouchard," August 25, 1998; reprinted in Stéphane Dion, *Straight Talk: Speeches and Writings on Canadian Unity,* Peter H. Russell, ed. (Montreal and Kingston: McGill–Queen's University Press, 1999), 246.

51. Stéphane Dion, "Letter to Mr. Lucien Bouchard," August 14, 1997; reprinted in *Straight Talk,* 191.

52. Stéphane Dion, "Letter to Mr. Bernard Landry," August 26, 1997, reprinted in *Straight Talk,* 195; "Letter to Mr. Jacques Brassard," November 19, 1997, reprinted in *Straight Talk,* 209 and 211.

53. Cairns, "The Legacy of the Referendum," 36.

54. Dion, "Letter to Mr. Lucien Bouchard," August 14, 1997; reprinted in *Straight Talk,* 191.

55. The Reform Party subsequently became the Canadian Alliance, and then merged with the Progressive Conservatives to form the Conservative Party of Canada; see Chapter 11.

56. Young, 76.

57. House of Commons of Canada, 2nd Session, 36th Parliament, 48–49 Elizabeth II, 1999–2000, Bill C-20: *An Act to give effect to the requirement for clarity as set out in the opinion of*

the Supreme Court of Canada in the Quebec Secession Reference (as adopted in June 2000), section 1(3).

58. Ibid., section 3(2).

59. Ibid., section 1(4).

60. Québec, National Assembly, 2000, Bill 99: *An Act respecting the exercise of the fundamental rights and prerogatives of the Québec people and the Québec State,* section 1.

61. Joseph Facal, "Quebec Sovereignty and the Rule of Law," November 17, 1999; available on the Nelson website: www.parametersofpower5e.nelson.com. Click on "Quebec & National Unity" and then scroll down to "Quebec Sovereignty and the Rule of Law."

62. *Law Society of Upper Canada v. Skapinker,* [1984] 1 S.C.R. 357; *Black v. Law Society of Alberta,* [1989] 1 S.C.R. 591.

63. Mark R. MacDonald, "The Agreement on Internal Trade: Trade-offs for Economic Union and Federalism," in Bakvis and Skogstad, eds., 142.

64. On the creation of the AIT, see Robert H. Knox, "Economic Integration in Canada through the Agreement on Internal Trade," in Harvey Lazar, ed., *The State of the Federation 1997: Non-Constitutional Renewal* (Kingston, ON: Institute of Intergovernmental Relations, 1998), 139–43, and MacDonald, 140–41.

65. Internal Trade Secretariat, *Agreement on Internal Trade: Consolidated Version* (Winnipeg, May 2007), vi (accessed at www.ait-aci.ca/, July 2007).

66. Knox, 158–59.

67. Ibid., 157–58.

68. Donald G. Lenihan with David Hume, "Governance in the Agreement on Internal Trade" (Ottawa: KTA Centre for Collaborative Government, 2004), 16.

69. MacDonald, 145.

70. This summary of the CGA dispute is based on information from three sources: Internal Trade Secretariat, "Annual Report 2005–2006", 15; Internal Trade Secretariat, "Annual Report 2006-2007", 17; and Internal Trade Secretariat; "Status of AIT Disputes by Chapter, July 2007", 1 (all accessed at www.ait-aci.ca/, July 2007).

71. This claim is based on the data reported in "Status of AIT Disputes by Chapter, July 2007."

72. MacDonald, 145–46.

73. Ibid., 147.

74. Lenihan and Hume, 3.

75. Internal Trade Secretariat, "Status of Obligations by Party, June 2007" (accessed at www.ait-aci.ca/, July 2007).

76. By 2004, 65 percent of provincially regulated Canadian workers who moved from one province to another had their credentials recognized in their new locations. That figure dropped to just over half for foreign-born workers. Forum of Labour Market Ministers, "Report of Survey Results: Inter-provincial Labour Market Mobility in Canada, 2004–2005," 2 (accessed at www.ait-aci.ca/, July 2007).

77. Internal Trade Secretariat, "Outstanding Obligations by Chapter, September 2006" (accessed at www.ait-aci.ca/, July 2007).

78. Internal Trade Secretariat, "Annual Report 2005–2006," 13–14 (accessed at www.ait-aci.ca/, July 2007).

79. *Agreement on Internal Trade: Consolidated Version,* annexes 1704.1 and 1705.1.

80. Russell, 2nd ed., 251.

81. Lenihan and Hume, 3.

82. Lenihan and Hume, 8.

83. MacDonald, 143.

84. Alain-G. Gagnon and Hugh Segal, "Introduction," in Gagnon and Segal, eds., *The Canadian Social Union Without Quebec: Eight Critical Analyses* (Montreal: Institute for Research in Public Policy, 2000) 1.

85. Ibid., 2.

86. The "Saskatoon Consensus," reproduced in Gagnon and Segal, Appendix 1, 228.

87. The "Victoria Proposal," reproduced in Gagnon and Segal, Appendix 2, 231.

88. Linda A. White, "The Child Care Agenda and the Social Union," in Bakvis and Skogstad, eds., 114.

89. The full text of the SUFA is available at www.socialunion.ca or at the website of the Canadian Intergovernmental Conference Secretariat: www.scics.gc.ca; click on "Conference Information," select "1999," and scroll down to "February."

90. "A Framework to Improve the Social Union for Canadians," reproduced in Gagnon and Segal, Appendix 3.

91. John Richards, "Backgrounder: The Paradox of the Social Union Framework Agreement" (Toronto: C.D. Howe Institute, March 2002), 4; available at www.cdhowe.org.

92. Gibbins, "Shifting Sands," 33.

93. Russell, 2nd ed., 254.

94. Alain-G. Gagnon, "Working in Partnership for Canadians," in Gagnon and Segal, 139.

95. Harvey Lazar, "The Social Union Framework Agreement and the Future of Fiscal Federalism," in Lazar, ed., *Toward a New Mission Statement for Canadian Fiscal Federalism,* 115.

96. Ibid., 100.

97. Noël, 24; see also Hobson and St-Hilaire, 177.

98. *Progress Report to Premiers No. 5,* 5.

99. Michael J. Prince, "SUFA: Sea Change or Mere Ripple for Canadian Social Policy?" in Fortin, Noël, and St-Hilaire, eds.

100. Alain Noël, France St-Hilaire, and Sarah Fortin, "Learning from the SUFA Experience," in Fortin, Noël, and St-Hilaire, eds., 3. The three Accords mentioned are the 2000 First Ministers' Agreement on Health; the 2003 First Ministers' Accord on Health Care Renewal; and the 2004 agreement between Prime Minister Martin and the nine ROC Premiers, with a side deal for Quebec. All three are available at www.scics.gc.ca.

101. Harvey Lazar, "Managing Interdependencies in the Canadian Federation: Lessons from the Social Union Framework Agreement" (Kingston and Montreal: Institute for Intergovernmental Relations/Institute for Research on Public Policy, 2003), 2; available at www.irpp.org.

102. "Conservative Party of Canada Federal Election Platform, 2006," 43.

103. Senate of Canada, *Proceedings of the Special Senate Committee on Senate Reform,* September 7, 2006, 2:9–11 (accessed at www.parl.gc.ca). "Focusing on Priorities," 56.

104. Senate of Canada, *Thirteenth Report of the Standing Committee on Legal and Constitutional Affairs,* June 12, 2007 (accessed at www.parl.gc.ca).

105. Ibid.

106. Canada, House of Commons, *Hansard,* November 22, 2006, 5198 (accessed at www.parl.gc.ca).

107. Bea Vongdouangchanh, "Québécois form a nation," *The Hill Times,* December 4, 2006, 4. The meaning of the term "Québécois" turned out to be a potential problem: Harper's Quebec lieutenant (Transportation Minister Lawrence Cannon) suggested that it was restricted to "*pur laine*" Quebeckers—descendants of the original French settlers—whereas other Cabinet ministers insisted that everyone who identifies with Quebec culture (whether they live inside or outside the province) is a Québécois.

108. Editorial, "Government Communications Strategy," *The Hill Times,* December 4, 2006, 8.

109. Brian Laghi, "Clarify Quebec stand, Dion urges PM," *The Globe and Mail,* June 25, 2007, A4.

110. Canada, House of Commons, *Hansard,* November 24, 2006, 5305.

6

The *Canadian Charter of Rights and Freedoms*

LEARNING OBJECTIVES

After you finish reading this chapter, you should be able to:

*   *identify* and *explain* three key differences between the 1960 *Bill of Rights* and the 1982 *Charter of Rights and Freedoms;*
*   *define* "first-order" and "second-order" *Charter* duties;
*   *explain* the three-stage process of *Charter* application by the courts, and the relationship between section 1 and other *Charter* sections;
*   *summarize* the legal and political debate over same-sex marriage; and
*   *identify* and *explain* the implications of the "war on terror" for *Charter* rights and freedoms.

INTRODUCTION: DEMOCRACY AND THE *CHARTER*

In April 1982 the *Canadian Charter of Rights and Freedoms* took effect. This was by far the most significant change in the entrenched written *Constitution* since 1867. In the years since 1982, the *Charter* has had far-reaching effects on the courts, Parliament, and the policy-making process. However, these effects cannot be attributed entirely to the *Charter* itself, which is, after all, only a piece of paper. They have been magnified by changes in the behaviour of other institutions and groups, especially courts and advocacy groups.

Canadian judges, especially those working in appellate courts (Chapter 10), modified their traditional attitude of **judicial deference** to Parliament and became more assertive under the *Charter*. In this respect, they mirrored a change in Canada's political culture; since 1945, the influence of American conceptions of rights and freedoms has grown at the expense of the British tradition of parliamentary supremacy. Advocacy groups added **public-interest litigation** to their toolkit for policy change (discussed in Chapter 13). As policymakers in the legislative and executive branches of government realized that their decisions would be challenged on *Charter* grounds, and that judges would sometimes rule in favour of the **plaintiffs,** they began to incorporate the protected rights and freedoms into their own analyses and "outputs." After more than 25 years under the *Charter*, the courts, Parliament, or the executive cannot claim a monopoly over the interpretation and protection of rights and freedoms. Each has its own distinct and important role to play.

Before the *Charter* took effect,[1] it was rare for Canadian policymakers (including judges) to resolve controversial issues on the basis of rights. Today, while some policy questions are unaffected by the *Charter*, many of the most contentious issues revolve around protected rights and freedoms:

- Under what circumstances can a doctor perform a legal abortion?[2]
- Can a terminally ill person seek a doctor's assistance to commit suicide?[3]
- Should public funds be spent on sign-language interpreters for deaf patients in hospitals?[4]
- Who is entitled to Canadian citizenship? How differently should the state treat Canadian citizens from residents who are not citizens?[5]
- Should entitlements such as pensions and parental benefits be distributed without regard to marital status, sexual orientation, age, or gender?[6]
- Does a police officer have the right to search your home without a warrant, and, if so, under what conditions?[7]
- Can a police officer obtain your DNA without your consent?[8]
- Is a confession or plea bargain valid if you made it without consulting a lawyer?[9]
- What does "guilty beyond a reasonable doubt" mean in practice? Does it apply if you were drunk when you committed a crime?[10] Does it apply to a battered woman who killed her abuser?[11] Does it apply to a man who unsuccessfully tried to prevent his partner in crime from shooting a robbery victim, or who accidentally injected an overdose of cocaine into a woman's arm?[12]
- How can the state protect its citizens from the threat of terrorism without excessive infringements on rights and freedoms?[13]

Because these and other issues have been addressed in high-profile and controversial Supreme Court judgments, some critics argue that judges have taken too much power away from Parliament. They question the legitimacy of judicial policy-making.[14] Should unelected judges have the power to overrule Parliament when the two institutions disagree? Has the Supreme Court of Canada been taken captive by "special interests" whose policy priorities are rejected by the majority of Canadians?

Critics of "undemocratic" judicial power cite two reasons for its growth in the *Charter* era. First, the vague and general provisions of the *Charter* give judges *carte blanche* to rewrite and strike down laws; they "neither restrain nor guide the judges."[15] Second, the shift of policy-making power from legislatures to courts has empowered "national unity advocates, civil libertarians, equality-seekers, social engineers, and postmaterialists."[16] These "Court Party" groups, together with law professors, court clerks, and constitutional lawyers, allegedly work together to foist "the intensely held policy priorities of [left-wing] minorities"[17] on an unsuspecting majority.

A closer look at the cases listed above suggests that these concerns are overstated:

- In the cases dealing with abortion, the distribution of state entitlements, medical services for the hearing-impaired, and the imprisonment of suspected (but not convicted) terrorists, the Supreme Court declared an existing policy unconstitutional; however, it left the details of any replacement policy to be determined by legislators or executives.
- After the rulings on warrantless searches, DNA, and intoxication, Parliament amended the *Criminal Code* to modify (or undo) the effects of the Supreme Court's decisions.
- The ruling on physician-assisted suicide upheld the existing law, and left any adjustments to be made by Parliament.

So it is inaccurate to suggest that the *Charter* transferred all policy-making power to unelected judges. While **judicial activism** should raise some concerns in a democratic political system—principally because judges lack the expertise to craft and enforce good public policy

(Chapter 10)—the *Charter* does not spell the end of Canadian democracy. In this sense, the arguments of some *Charter* critics are exaggerated. Nonetheless, those arguments have exerted considerable influence on Canadian politics, especially under the Harper Government.[18]

Charter opponents also tend to overstate its independent impact on Canadian government and politics. Both rights-based **litigation** and judicial policy-making existed in Canada before 1982. It is certainly true that the *Charter* has inspired many groups and individuals to seek a remedy in the courts for alleged violations of their rights and freedoms. However, it is equally true that the conditions for such lawsuits—a Supreme Court that controlled its own caseload, policy-oriented lawyers, and a rights-influenced political culture—were already in place before 1982, and that these heightened the impact of the *Charter* on Canadian politics and government.[19]

Moreover, any group or individual who seeks to challenge the constitutionality of a law faces long odds of success. There are daunting procedural and financial barriers to litigation.[20] Once the case reaches the courts, the plaintiff must confront the vast resources and privileged status of the government that passed the law—or whose official allegedly breached the *Charter*—and now wishes to defend its actions.[21] Two-thirds of *Charter* claims are dismissed by the courts,[22] a point overlooked by critics who focus selectively on controversial cases like the 1988 *Morgentaler* ruling (Dossier 6.2).

If *Charter* critics focus on the process of law-making by unelected judges, some of its defenders are more concerned with the substance of laws. Under section 1 of the *Charter*, judges are required to determine whether or not infringements of the guaranteed rights and freedoms are justified in "a free and democratic society." Laws that violate protected rights without justification have no place in a democratic society, even when they are made by elected officials.[23]

Charter advocates argue that accusations of excessive judicial power are misplaced. When the Supreme Court strikes down an unconstitutional law, it is not arrogantly usurping the rightful place of Parliament; it is simply doing what the constitution requires it to do (see the discussion of *Charter* remedies in "The Three-Stage Process of *Charter* Review" on page 181). When the Supreme Court defers to the legislative branch, upholding laws without stringent constitutional analysis, it fails in its duty to enforce the "supreme law of Canada."[24]

Moreover, judges are sometimes forced to confront moral issues like abortion and euthanasia because politicians avoid them like the plague. When judges strike down laws, or reinterpret them to conform to the *Charter*, they are not usurping the power of the legislature; rather, they are forcing legislators and the justice system to take rights seriously. This brings us to the two central themes of this chapter:

- First, the *Charter* imposes two types of duties on governing institutions: a "first-order" duty to ensure their own compliance with the guarantees of rights and freedoms, and a "second-order" duty to review the decisions of other institutions.[25] Primary "first-order" duties lie with the executive branch that drafts and implements laws, and the Parliament that ratifies them. The courts have a "second-order" duty to examine those laws. If judges find that a particular law or government action violates the *Charter*, and the violation cannot be justified by the responsible government, they are required by the remedial provisions to grant a remedy. When the legislative and executive branches take their first-order duties seriously, the courts properly defer to their decisions; when they do not, the courts are required to perform their second-order duties.

- Second, judges do not have a completely free hand when they interpret the *Charter*. They are constrained by strict rules, including long-standing principles of common law and "tests" for applying specific *Charter* provisions. The most famous of the latter, the "*Oakes* test," requires the executive and legislative branches of government to justify laws that infringe protected rights and freedoms. At the same time, it requires judges to defer to the elected branches whenever possible. So it is exaggerated to claim that the courts have exploited the *Charter* to seize power that properly belongs elsewhere.

In the *Charter*'s first decade, the Supreme Court of Canada exercised its second-order duties with vigour and assertiveness. Since then, the justices have gradually adopted a more deferential approach to the other two branches, particularly at the justification and remedy stages of *Charter* analysis. When the courts find in favour of a rights claimant, they usually spell out the precise nature of the *Charter* violation and allow the relevant legislature or the executive branch to determine the proper solution. In some policy fields, notably criminal law, the three branches of government have engaged in a constructive "dialogue" about the practical difficulties of balancing individual rights against competing social values.[26] In others, including the controversial issue of same-sex marriage, judges have set the policy agenda (partly by default; see Dossier 6.4).

Over the past quarter-century, Canada's political institutions have gradually adjusted to the *Charter*. Although conflict between judges and politicians will likely persist, a constructive balance among the three branches of government is being restored. Unfortunately, this does not mean that Canadians can take their freedoms for granted. Defenders of parliamentary supremacy often overlook a key historical fact: in times of crisis, it is all too tempting for legislators, Cabinet ministers, and law enforcement officers to ignore the rights of particular minorities. This temptation was clearly evident in the aftermath of the 9/11 terrorist attacks. The executive branch of the federal government—in Canada, the United States, the United Kingdom, and elsewhere—invoked its powers over national security to justify new laws and administrative procedures that violated individual rights. Initially, judges deferred to the executive and refused to perform their "second-order" *Charter* duties in terrorism-related cases. More recently, in light of clear evidence that the human rights of innocent Muslims have been abused,[27] courts have reasserted their proper role in the enforcement of constitutional values.[28] So despite some legitimate concerns about the impact of entrenched rights and freedoms on democracy, "judicial activism" is not always a bad thing. After all, if we could always trust elected officials to protect unpopular minorities against the fear and vengeance of the majority, there would be no need for a *Charter*.

ENTRENCHED RIGHTS VERSUS PARLIAMENTARY SUPREMACY

Since 1867, and especially since the end of World War II, the influence of British political and legal traditions has diminished in Canada.[29] As we saw in Chapters 3 and 4, the *Constitution Act, 1867* enshrined "a Constitution similar in Principle to that of the United Kingdom." Parliamentary supremacy is at the core of that inherited constitution: the legislative branch makes the laws, subject to the financial control of the Crown, and only the legislative branch can change or abolish a law. The courts have no discretion over the content of laws; they cannot declare a particular statute invalid because it treats a particular group unfairly.

Apart from a few key documents—such as the 1215 *Magna Carta* and the 1689 *Bill of Rights*—the British constitution is essentially unwritten. It is based on conventions, not on entrenched written rules.[30] Canada, as a federal state, required the greater certainty of a written constitution. However, the *BNA Act* was virtually silent on the subject of rights. Under the doctrine of parliamentary supremacy, the courts generally upheld any law that was enacted by the proper level of government. The power to legislate was divided, but it was not restrained by any higher standard of right or morality. Therefore, the courts almost always deferred to the legislative branch. Judges were reluctant to criticize the choices of legislators, even when those choices were clearly distasteful.

The American tradition of judicial review is very different from the British convention of parliamentary supremacy. It is founded on the assumption that the courts, and not the legislative branch, should provide the authoritative definition of law. As Britain's influence in Canadian society declined, it was replaced to a degree by the influence of American law and politics. People who watched American cop shows assumed that they could "plead the Fifth" (i.e., invoke a constitutional right against self-incrimination); they also expected to be read their "Miranda rights" by a police officer. The absence of comparable rights in Canada eventually attracted public criticism.

THE EVOLUTION OF RIGHTS IN CANADA, 1867–1982

■ The *BNA Act*, 1867–1960

Parliamentary supremacy means, among other things, that the legislative branch is the principal guardian of the rights and freedoms of citizens. As previously noted, the unwritten rights embodied in British common law (e.g., the presumption of innocence or the civil rights of unpopular minorities) are sometimes disregarded by the legislative and executive branches of government. Between the 1930s and the 1960s, Alberta law required the forcible sterilization of "mental defectives." In 1942, shortly after Japan attacked the United States, the Canadian and American governments arrested and interned thousands of innocent people of Japanese descent. Until 1947, Canadians of Asian descent—both naturalized immigrants and citizens who were born in Canada—were barred from voting. During the 1950s the Quebec government persecuted communists (actual or suspected) and Jehovah's Witnesses. During the 1970 "October Crisis" in Quebec,[31] the Trudeau Government suspended civil rights in the province of Quebec by imposing the *War Measures Act*. Almost 500 innocent Quebeckers were rounded up by the police and thrown into jail, without being charged with any offence or allowed to speak to lawyers.

When legislators and executives refused to respect rights and freedoms, judges were either unwilling or unable to do anything about it. The JCPC (Chapter 4) upheld federal and provincial laws that violated human rights, as long as they were *intra vires*. In the 1903 *Tomey Homma* case, the JCPC upheld a British Columbia law that denied voting rights to persons of Asian descent. Because the law did not conflict with the federal power over "Naturalization of Aliens," it was *intra vires* the provincial government and therefore valid. The injustice of racial disqualification from the franchise, said the JCPC, "is not a topic which their Lordships are entitled to consider."[32] Similarly, the Law Lords accepted the internment, dispossession, and deportation of Japanese Canadians because the *War Measures Act* overrode provincial control on "Property and Civil Rights."[33]

The Supreme Court of Canada was slightly more willing to protect freedoms, particularly freedom of speech. In 1938, then-Chief Justice Sir Lyman Poore Duff argued that two elements of the *BNA Act*—the Preamble and the provision for a parliamentary system of government—contained an "implied bill of rights" inherited from Britain. The court struck down an Alberta censorship law, on the grounds that "free public discussion of public affairs . . . is the breath of life for parliamentary institutions." It established that any common-law right that was required to preserve "a constitution similar in Principle to that of the United Kingdom" was worthy of judicial protection.[34] However, that precedent never commanded the support of a majority on the court.

After the abolition of Privy Council appeals in 1949, the Canadian Supreme Court became somewhat more vigilant in the protection of rights. It was particularly concerned about Quebec laws that targeted religious and political minorities. Justice Ivan Rand, sometimes with the support of one or two colleagues, argued that such laws violated the "implied bill of rights" and should be nullified on that basis. Other justices preferred to use the division of powers to invalidate these laws; they argued that the Quebec government could not usurp Ottawa's criminal-law power in order to persecute minorities. But because of parliamentary supremacy, a majority of justices deferred to the other two branches of government. "The failure of the Supreme Court to establish clear, majority support for the jurisprudence of an implied bill of rights in the *BNA Act* was an important contributing factor in the movement to establish a formal bill of rights in Canada."[35] (Ironically, Duff's notion of an "implied bill of rights" has enjoyed a renaissance under the *Charter*; the Supreme Court has repeatedly referred to the Preamble to the *Constitution Act, 1867* as the foundation of Canada's system of government.[36])

The establishment of the United Nations in 1948 inspired calls for an entrenched *Charter of Rights* in Canada. The *UN Charter* and the *Universal Declaration on Human Rights* influenced Canadian lawyers and academics and "provided domestic groups with a powerful rights rhetoric."[37] While the idea of entrenched rights still provoked unease, especially among those who feared the erosion of parliamentary supremacy, by the late 1950s "a Bill of Rights [had become] an almost essential attribute of contemporary statehood."[38]

DOSSIER 6.1   Excerpts from the 1960 *Bill of Rights*

1. It is hereby recognized and declared that in Canada there have existed and shall continue to exist without discrimination by reason of race, national origin, colour, religion or sex, the following human rights and fundamental freedoms, namely,
   (a) the right of the individual to life, liberty, security of the person and enjoyment of property, and the right not to be deprived thereof except by due process of law;
   (b) the right of the individual to equality before the law and the protection of the law;
   (c) freedom of religion;
   (d) freedom of speech;
   (e) freedom of assembly and association; and
   (f) freedom of the press.
2. Every law of Canada shall, unless it is expressly declared by an Act of the Parliament of Canada that it shall operate notwithstanding the Canadian *Bill of Rights*, be so construed and applied as not to abrogate, abridge or infringe or to authorize the abrogation, abridgment or infringement of any of the rights or freedoms herein recognized and declared, and in particular, no law of Canada shall be construed or applied so as to

(a) authorize or effect the arbitrary detention, imprisonment or exile of any person;
(b) impose or authorize the imposition of cruel and unusual treatment or punishment;
(c) deprive a person who has been arrested or detained
   (i) of the right to be informed promptly of the reason for his arrest or detention,
   (ii) of the right to retain and instruct counsel without delay, or
   (iii) of the remedy by way of habeas corpus for the determination of the validity of his detention and for his release if the detention is not lawful;
(d) authorize a court, tribunal, commission, board or other authority to compel a person to give evidence if he is denied counsel, protection against self-incrimination or other constitutional safeguards;
(e) deprive a person of the right to a fair hearing in accordance with the principles of fundamental justice for the determination of his rights and obligations;

(continued)

(f) deprive a person charged with a criminal offence of the right to be presumed innocent until proved guilty according to law in a fair and public hearing by an independent and impartial tribunal, or of the right to reasonable bail without just cause; or

(g) deprive a person of the right to the assistance of an interpreter in any proceedings in which he is involved or in which he is a party or a witness, before a court, commission, board or other tribunal, if he does not understand or speak the language in which such proceedings are conducted.

Source: The Nelson website for this book: www.parametersofpower5e.nelson.com; click on "Canadian Politics on the Web," then "The *Constitution*," and then scroll down to "1960 Canadian *Bill of Rights*."

■ The 1960 *Bill of Rights*

In the late 1950s, in response to the growing global emphasis on human rights, the federal government decided to codify existing common-law rights in statute law. An amendment to the BNA Act, which would have required provincial assent, was impossible; all of the provinces, except Saskatchewan, were opposed to what they perceived as a direct attack on both parliamentary supremacy and provincial autonomy. Prime Minister Diefenbaker eventually adopted the Canadian *Bill of Rights* in 1960. (See Dossier 6.1.)

Although its advocates hoped that it would provide effective protection for individual rights and freedoms, the Bill suffered from four serious limitations:

* The Bill was not entrenched in the *Constitution*; it was an ordinary federal statute, or at best quasiconstitutional (see Chapter 3). Therefore, it did not override other federal laws with which it conflicted.
* The Bill did not apply to the provincial governments or to their areas of jurisdiction as defined by the *BNA Act*. Therefore, discriminatory provincial laws (e.g., in the fields of education and welfare) were not subject to the provisions of the Bill.
* The Bill contained no explicit judicial remedies for violations of rights. At most, it instructed courts in the proper interpretation of laws. Judges were required to interpret a statute in such a way that it did not conflict with the Bill. If they could not find a way to do this, they lacked a clear mandate to strike down the offending law or to grant another appropriate remedy to a person whose rights had been infringed.
* The language of the Bill—particularly the phrase "there have existed and shall continue to exist" in clause 1—implied that the protected rights were "frozen" at the moment when the Bill came into effect. In effect, the scope of each right was defined by the statutory and common-law limits in place in 1960. So judges could not use the Bill to expand rights beyond the restrictions that had been imposed in previous decades, even if those restrictions were out of step with an evolving society.[39]

Although the preamble promised to "ensure the protection of these rights and freedoms in Canada," the *Bill of Rights* had little impact on Canadian law. Apart from its own inherent weaknesses, its potential influence was greatly reduced by judicial deference to parliamentary supremacy. Between 1960 and 1982, the justices invalidated only one law on the ground that it conflicted with the *Bill of Rights*. In the 1970 *Drybones* case, the Supreme Court struck down a section of the *Indian Act*. The **impugned** section made it illegal for an Indian to be intoxicated anywhere off-reserve. Justice Roland Almon Ritchie, writing for the majority, rejected the conservative approach to the Bill:

> This proposition [i.e., that the impugned law was valid despite its violation of the Bill] appears to me to strike at the very foundations of the Bill of Rights and to convert it from its apparent character as a statutory declaration of the fundamental human rights and freedoms which it recognizes, into being little more than a rule for the construction of federal statutes. . . .[40]

Ritchie added that if a particular law could not be interpreted to make it consistent with the *Bill of Rights*, then it should be "declared inoperative" by the courts. In the case at hand, the *Indian Act* made it illegal for one group of Canadians to get drunk under circumstances that would be entirely legal for everyone else:

> I think that s. 1(b) [of the Bill] means at least that no individual or group of individuals is to be treated more harshly than another under that law, and I am therefore of the opinion that an individual is denied equality before the law if it is made an offence punishable at law, on account of his race, for him to do something which his fellow Canadians are free to do without having committed any offence or having been made subject to any penalty.[41]

In every other *Bill of Rights* case, the justices deferred to Parliament. Whereas *Drybones* struck down a racist law, even though there was no evidence that it was being applied unfairly, the court reversed itself in subsequent cases and upheld discriminatory laws on the grounds that they were administered equally.[42] Parliamentary supremacy was still a cardinal principle of the *Constitution*, and only Parliament could pass judgment on the substance of a law. The courts' reluctance to apply the *Bill of Rights* sparked demands for entrenched protection of rights and freedoms. Advocates of an entrenched *Charter* argued that if judges had a "supreme law" to work with, instead of an ordinary statute, they would take a more aggressive approach to violations of rights and freedoms. In this respect, at least, their hopes have been fulfilled.

Dossier 6.2 illustrates the major differences between pre- and post-*Charter* judicial review. After 1982, a majority of Supreme Court justices were willing to strike down laws that, in their view, infringed a protected right or freedom. They were authorized by the explicit judicial remedies prescribed by the *Charter* to order the legislative and executive branches to respect the rights and freedoms of Canadians (for a detailed discussion of *Charter* remedies, see "The Three-Stage Process of *Charter* Review" on page 181). Although the rulings discussed in Dossier 6.2 concerned a federal law (the *Criminal Code*), the same remedies also apply to provincial laws.

DOSSIER 6.2   The Transformation of Judicial Review: Pre-1982 and Post-1982

The *Charter*'s impact on judicial review can best be understood by comparing the Supreme Court's approach to the same law before and after 1982. The two *Morgentaler* rulings serve the purpose well, because the justices themselves used the second ruling to clarify the *Charter*'s impact on their interpretation of the abortion law. In 1975 the court upheld section 251 of the *Criminal Code*, which prohibited abortion. The only exceptions to the law were "therapeutic abortions": those performed in a hospital with the approval of a Therapeutic Abortion Committee (TAC) made

up of three doctors (not including the doctor who would perform the actual procedure).

In the mid-1970s, one-quarter of Canadian hospitals had fewer than four doctors on staff and were therefore unable to establish TACs. In larger hospitals, political pressure forced administrators either to forbid the creation of TACs or to disband existing committees. By 1982, only one in five Canadian hospitals had functioning TACs. Under the law, a TAC could authorize an abortion only if the continuation of the pregnancy "would or would be likely to

(continued)

endanger [the] life or health" of the woman. Some doctors interpreted the word "health" broadly, to include mental and emotional well-being, while others would not permit abortions except in grave medical emergencies. Collectively, these provisions created two serious problems. First, access to legal abortion varied widely across Canada. Second, the bureaucratic and arbitrary TAC system delayed abortion procedures—often by eight weeks or more. The result was a significant risk to the life and health of women seeking abortions.

Dr. Henry Morgentaler fought to change the law, largely through a one-man civil disobedience campaign. In 1973 he was charged with performing an illegal abortion in his Montreal clinic. The procedure violated section 251 because it did not take place in a hospital, and there was no TAC approval. He was acquitted by a jury, even though he had clearly broken the law; the Quebec Court of Appeal overturned the verdict and imposed a conviction. That decision was appealed to the Supreme Court in 1975.

The justices refused to consider Morgentaler's argument that the flawed TAC system violated the "due process" guarantee in the *Bill of Rights*. Chief Justice Bora Laskin did address the *Bill of Rights* arguments, but only for the purpose of debunking them. In the first place, he rejected Morgentaler's request for an American-style judicial review of the abortion law: "any interference by a court with the substantive content of legislation" would be "foreign to our constitutional traditions, to our constitutional law and to our conceptions of judicial review."[43] Canada, unlike the United States, did not have a "constitutionally entrenched *Bill of Rights*";[44] as a federal statute, the 1960 Bill did not give the courts the power to strike down other federal laws. Second, Laskin insisted that the courts could not second-guess Parliament, or usurp its power to make and amend laws:

I do not regard s. 1 (b) of the Canadian Bill of Rights as charging the courts with supervising the administrative efficiency of legislation or with evaluating the regional or national organization of its administration . . . Parliament has

made a judgement which does not admit of any interference by the court. . . . Any unevenness in the administration of the relieving provisions is for Parliament to correct and not for the courts to monitor as being a denial of equality before the law and the protection of the law.[45]

Morgentaler's conviction was upheld and he went to prison.

After his release, Morgentaler continued to challenge the abortion law. In 1984 he was arrested in Toronto; once again a jury acquitted him and an Appeals Court convicted him. In 1986 he returned to the Supreme Court, hoping that the entrenched *Charter* would embolden the justices to strike down the law. He argued that because the delays imposed by the TACs threatened "life" and "security of the person," the abortion law violated the rights guaranteed in section 7 of the *Charter*. The late Chief Justice Brian Dickson, who had participated in the 1975 ruling, made it clear from the outset that the court would treat the *Charter* very differently from the *Bill of Rights*:

[S]ince 1975, and the first Morgentaler decision, the Court has been given added responsibilities. . . . Although no doubt it is still fair to say that courts are not the appropriate forum for articulating complex and controversial programmes of public policy, Canadian courts are now charged with the crucial obligation of ensuring that the legislative initiatives pursued by our Parliament and legislatures conform to the democratic values expressed in the Canadian Charter of Rights and Freedoms. . . . It is in this latter sense that the current Morgentaler appeal differs from the one we heard a decade ago.[46]

Former Justice McIntyre, the most conservative member of the Dickson court, shared the Chief Justice's view of the *Charter*'s impact—although he warned against an overly broad interpretation of its provisions:

Before the adoption of the Charter, there was little question of the limits of judicial review of the criminal law. For all practical purposes it

(continued)

was limited to a determination of whether the impugned enactment dealt with a subject which could fall within the criminal law power in s. 91(27) of the Constitution Act, 1867. . . . The adoption of the Charter brought a significant change. The power of judicial review of legislation acquired greater scope but, in my view, that scope is not unlimited and should be carefully confined to that which is ordained by the Charter. I am well aware that there will be disagreement about what was ordained by the Charter and, of course, a measure of interpretation of the Charter will be required in order to give substance and reality to its provisions. But the courts must not, in the guise of interpretation, postulate rights and freedoms which do not have a firm and a reasonably identifiable base in the Charter.[47]

Five of the seven justices on the panel voted to strike down the abortion law, although for varying reasons. The four male justices in the majority agreed with Morgentaler that the TACs violated section 7 of the *Charter*, because they threatened both the physical and psychological well-being of women seeking abortions. The law did not operate "in accordance with the principles of fundamental justice." Justice Bertha Wilson, then the only woman on the court, found that the law violated the right to liberty, as well as the other rights in section 7: "the right to liberty contained in s. 7 guarantees to every individual a degree of personal autonomy over important decisions intimately affecting their private lives."[48] She also found that the law violated section 2(a) of the *Charter*: "I believe that the decision whether or not to terminate a pregnancy is essentially a moral decision, a matter of conscience."[49]

Finally, the court repudiated the previous *Morgentaler* ruling by assuming the power to judge the application of a law:

Although the mandate given to the courts under the Charter does not, generally speaking, enable the judiciary to provide remedies for administrative inefficiencies, when denial of a right as basic as security of the person is infringed by the procedure and administrative structures created by the law itself, the courts are empowered to act. . . . If section 251 of the Criminal Code does indeed breach s. 7 of the Charter through its general effects, that can be sufficient to invalidate the legislation under s. 52.[50]

The 1960 *Bill of Rights* remains in force, despite the proclamation of the *Charter* in 1982. In a 1985 case concerning the rights of refugee claimants, half of the Supreme Court relied on the Bill's guarantee of a fair hearing (clause 2(e)); the other justices based their ruling on section 7 of the *Charter*.[51] The Bill has recently been used, with some success, in litigation touching on property rights; these are not enshrined in the *Charter*, but they are protected by clause 1(a) of the Bill. A class-action suit on behalf of mentally ill World War II veterans, whose pay and benefits were allegedly mismanaged by the federal government, succeeded in the Ontario courts. Unfortunately for the veterans, the Supreme Court of Canada unanimously overturned the earlier rulings. It held that in 1960, when the Bill took effect, the federal government had the power to take away the property of individuals; therefore, the Bill offered no relief to the veterans for the millions of dollars they had lost because of the government's mismanagement.[52] This revival of the "frozen rights" doctrine does not bode well for future attempts to use the Bill to plug gaps in the *Charter*'s protections.

■ Creating the *Charter*, 1980–82

The draft *Charter* that Prime Minister Trudeau submitted for public debate in October 1980 was very different from the version that took effect in April 1982. (If necessary, refer back to the discussion of the 1980–82 constitutional round in Chapter 5.) A special joint committee of the House of Commons and Senate held public hearings on the federal package. Most witnesses demanded stronger entrenched protection for individual and group rights.[53] Some, including women, Aboriginal peoples, and people with disabilities, were successful; sections 15, 25, 28, and 35 were either added or reinforced during the committee process (see the text of the *Charter*, which starts on page 600 in the Appendix). Others, such as gays and lesbians and anti-abortion activists, failed to achieve constitutional recognition for their rights claims. The overall effect of the public hearings was to create strong public support for the *Charter* and its guaranteed rights and freedoms.

The evolution of two particular guarantees merits some comment. Section 1, the "reasonable limitations" clause, had been broadened as part of Trudeau's strategy to win over the premiers. Because the Supreme Court sits at the top of Canada's judicial hierarchy, its interpretations of the *Charter* would bind both levels of government. Therefore, judicial review of the *Charter* would limit the discretion of provincial governments and legislatures. Not surprisingly, most of the provincial governments opposed any restrictions on their powers, and they refused to support the Trudeau *Charter* without the inclusion of a broad limitation clause. An early draft of that clause read as follows:

> *The Canadian Charter of Rights and Freedoms recognizes the following rights and freedoms subject only to such reasonable limits as are generally accepted in a free and democratic society with a parliamentary system of government.*[54]

Members of the Liberal Cabinet stand and applaud Prime Minister Pierre Trudeau in the House of Commons on November 5, 1981, after he signed an historic agreement with nine provinces that would lead to a new Canadian *Constitution*. (CP/Andy Clark)

Several of the witnesses who appeared before the committee demanded that this clause be removed, arguing that it would allow governments to violate rights and freedoms at will. Others wanted to clarify and strengthen the wording by eliminating the phrases "generally accepted" and "parliamentary system of government." Faced with a barrage of criticism, and now determined to proceed without provincial consent, the federal government amended the section "to narrow the scope of limits that could be applied to the rights and freedoms."[55] The final wording of section 1 does not require judges to defer to the legislative branch. Moreover, it explicitly requires a federal or provincial government to justify any law that infringes a protected right or freedom.

Section 15 was also transformed during the public hearings. The original wording of the equality clause essentially reproduced the language of the 1960 *Bill of Rights:* it guaranteed "equality before the law and the equal protection of the law." Women's groups and others pointed out that the interpretation of those phrases by the Supreme Court had been less than satisfactory, and demanded stronger guarantees. The first part of section 15 now protects equality under the law and "equal benefit of the law," to ensure that both the substance and the effects of legislation are taken into consideration by the courts. At the same time, the set of personal characteristics that could not be made subject to legislated discrimination—sex, race, religion, and so forth—was changed from a closed list to a series of illustrations. We will see the results of this alteration in Dossier 6.4, when we examine the concept of "analogous grounds." Finally, the federal government inserted a second clause into section 15, to address concerns that entrenched equality rights would prevent future affirmative action policies. All in all, the guarantee of equality rights in today's *Charter* is much broader than the original version tabled in October 1980.

THE SCOPE AND APPLICATION OF THE *CHARTER*

Many Canadians are confused about the *Charter*'s impact on their daily lives. They assume that it applies to disputes between landlords and tenants, divorcing spouses, or employers and workers. In fact, the scope of the *Charter* is considerably narrower. It only applies to agents of the state—police officers, judges, public servants, and so forth—acting in their official capacities. Under section 32, the guarantees apply with equal force to the federal and provincial governments. Therefore, the *Charter* is engaged in any dispute between a Canadian senior government and an individual or group. Examples of such disputes include criminal trials, civil suits against a particular government (such as the litigation over same-sex marriage), and deportation proceedings. It does not have any role to play in disputes between private individuals or agencies. In the words of former Justice McIntyre, the state "owes a constitutional duty" to its citizens, which private individuals do not owe to one another.[56] There is one exception: if the conduct at issue is regulated by law, that law itself may be subject to challenge.[57] The case of *Miron v. Trudel* (Dossier 6.4) is an example; the dispute was between an individual and a insurance company, but the *Charter* issue concerned the constitutionality of N Ontario law which excluded common-law couples from particular benefits.

Some institutions, including most universities and hospitals, fall somewhere in-between the public and private sectors. They are private corporations that receive public funds to carry out their functions in accordance with the law (usually provincial laws). The Supreme Court has ruled that the *Charter* does not apply to the internal affairs of such institutions (e.g., labour relations), but it does apply to the ways in which they provide public services.[58]

The territorial reach of the *Charter*—specifically, whether it applies to the actions of state officials outside Canada—became a significant issue after 9/11. In general, laws (including entrenched laws) apply only within the territory governed by the state that passed them.

However, the Supreme Court of Canada has carved out an exception in cases where the actions of government agents overseas are not justified by international law. In 2002, Canadian citizen Omar Khadr was arrested in Afghanistan and transported to the American base at Guantanamo Bay, Cuba. He was subsequently charged with the murder of an American medic in a firefight, which allegedly occurred when Khadr was only 15. Unlike the governments of Britain, Australia, and other Western nations with citizens detained at Guantanamo, the Canadian government made no apparent effort to secure Khadr's release or extradition. Instead, it dispatched CSIS agents to Cuba in 2003 to interrogate the boy. In May 2008 the Supreme Court of Canada ruled that the transcripts of those interrogations must be turned over to Khadr's defence lawyers to allow them to prepare for his upcoming trial before a U.S. military commission. The unanimous ruling held that the *Charter* applied to the CSIS interrogation because Khadr's incarceration at Guantanamo, and the military commission process that was scheduled to try him, had already been declared by the United States Supreme Court to be contrary to both domestic and international law. The court wrote that "at the time Canada handed over the fruits of the interviews to U.S. officials, it was bound by the *Charter*, because at that point it became a participant in a process that violated Canada's international obligations."[59]

THE THREE-STAGE PROCESS OF *CHARTER* REVIEW

Since 1982, the Supreme Court has developed several principles to guide *Charter* interpretation. These are binding on lower courts and, to a lesser extent, on policymakers in the executive and legislative branches of government. As we saw in Chapter 3, the written constitution cannot be understood simply by reading the text. One must also consider the ways in which that text has been interpreted and applied by the courts—the common law of constitutional jurisprudence. This is particularly true for the *Charter*, given the broad language in which its provisions are phrased and the huge volume of *Charter* rulings over a quarter-century. To explain the judicial interpretation of the entrenched guarantees, we will describe the process that a judge follows when he or she rules on a *Charter* challenge to a law (as distinct from a challenge to the action of a public official). That process unfolds in three stages, each of which is guided by specific legal principles:

1. infringement;
2. justification; and
3. remedy.

The Infringement Stage of *Charter* Analysis

At this first stage, the judge must answer a central question: "Does the impugned law infringe one or more *Charter* guarantees?" The burden of proof, also called the onus, is on the person or group seeking to challenge the government that sponsored the law. In the *Egan* case (Dossier 6.4), for example, the two men who wanted to extend spousal pension benefits to same-sex couples had to prove that the law violated section 15(1) of the *Charter*. The standard of proof is "a balance of probabilities," not the criminal standard "beyond a reasonable doubt." This means that the claimant must show that the infringement is more likely than not—a relatively low hurdle, but hardly a slam-dunk. To determine whether or not the claimant has met that standard, a judge must determine (1) the purpose of the *Charter* guarantee; (2) the purpose of the impugned law; and (3) the effect of the law on the exercise of the right or freedom at issue. This "purposive approach" was established by the late Chief Justice Brian Dickson in two of the first Supreme Court rulings on the *Charter*. Judges must begin by identifying "the nature of the interests [that the relevant *Charter* provision] is meant to protect."[60]

Protesters lobby for their *Charter* rights and freedoms in front of the constituency office of Justice Minister Anne McLellan on December 8, 2001. About 20 protesters spent the previous night in the office on an anti-terrorism bill sit-in. (CP/Edmonton Sun/Darryl Dyck)

In my view this analysis is to be undertaken, and the purpose of the right or freedom in question is to be sought by reference to the character and the larger objects of the Charter itself, to the language chosen to articulate the specific right or freedom, to the historical origins of the concepts enshrined, and where applicable, to the meaning and purpose of the other specific rights and freedoms with which it is associated within the text of the Charter. The interpretation should be . . . a generous rather than a legalistic one, aimed at fulfilling the purpose of the guarantee and securing for individuals the full benefit of the Charter's protection. At the same time it is important not to overshoot the actual purpose of the right or freedom in question, but to recall that the Charter was not enacted in a vacuum, and must therefore . . . be placed in its proper linguistic, philosophic and historical contexts.[61]

Dossier 6.3 explains how the determination of purpose works, focusing on the right to vote as guaranteed by section 3 of the *Charter*.

Today, after more than 25 years, judges can usually rely on precedents to decide the purpose of the guarantee. (See the discussion of *stare decisis* in Dossier 10.4.) The same is true for the determination of the law's effects. Both issues should be addressed in light of the facts of the case at bar. Instead of interpreting *Charter* guarantees abstractly, in a factual vacuum, the court is required to interpret them in relation to the specific dispute that it is called upon to resolve. Former Justice Bertha Wilson pointed out that "a right or freedom may have different meanings in different contexts. Security of the person, for example, might mean one thing when addressed to the issue of over-crowding in prisons and something quite different when addressed to the issue of noxious fumes from industrial smoke-stacks."[62] She also argued that the task of balancing rights against competing social values, which is required under section 1 of the *Charter*, can be performed more effectively when both are defined with specific reference to the dispute at bar.

DOSSIER 6.3   The Purpose of the Right to Vote

Section 3 of the *Charter* guarantees to every Canadian citizen the right to vote in federal and provincial elections, and the right to run for election to the federal and provincial legislatures. The Supreme Court has ruled that the right to vote protects two distinct interests. First, it guarantees "effective representation" in government to every citizen. "Representation comprehends the idea of having a voice in the deliberations of government as well as the idea of the right to bring one's grievances and concerns to the attention of one's government representative."[63] "Effective representation" also implies "relative parity of voting power" among citizens. This means that the population in one constituency may not grossly exceed the population in another, although some variation in constituency size may be justified for geographic or other reasons. Where the variance is too great,

the voting rights of citizens in large constituencies are diluted relative to those in less-populated ridings. In other words, a ballot cast in a constituency with 250 000 voters has less impact on the election of an MP than a ballot cast in a constituency with 100 000 voters.

The second interest protected by the right to vote is "the right to play a meaningful role in the selection of elected representatives."[64] The content of that "meaningful role" was spelled out in the 2003 *Figueroa* ruling, which struck down the law requiring political parties to run at least 50 candidates in a general election to qualify for state benefits (see the discussion of party registration in Chapter 11). At a minimum, each citizen must have the opportunity to vote and, if desired, to seek election to a federal or provincial legislature. He or she must be able to choose among a wide range of

(continued)

competing political parties or candidates, so that his or her own political views are reflected in public debate and, perhaps, in government. Any law that erects barriers to free and fair competition among political parties and candidates restricts the range of political options and makes it more difficult for some citizens to play a "meaningful role" in elections.

Whereas the first "purpose" of section 3 emphasizes the outcome of an election, the second focuses on the electoral process. The identification of two distinct purposes for a single *Charter* guarantee caused some legal confusion. The trial judge who heard the *Figueroa* case ruled that the party-registration law violated section 3, and struck down or modified several sections of the *Canada Elections Act*. She followed the "meaningful role" interpretation of the guarantee. The federal government appealed parts of her ruling to the Ontario Court of Appeal, which relied on the "effective representation" purpose; it overturned most of the trial ruling and restored the impugned sections of the Act. The Supreme Court of Canada finally resolved the issue when it declared that the true purpose of section 3, in relation to electoral participation, was the "meaningful role." Consequently, it restored much of the original ruling of the trial judge. The fluctuating and uncertain status of Canada's election law might have been avoided if the Supreme Court had identified a single purpose for section 3 in the first place.

■ The Justification Stage: Section 1

If the judge finds that the impugned law infringes one or more *Charter* guarantees, she moves on to the second stage of analysis. She must decide whether or not the infringement is justified under section 1. The onus shifts to the government that passed the impugned law. Its lawyers must prove, on a balance of probabilities, that (1) the law constitutes "a reasonable limit" on the infringed *Charter* right and (2) this limit is "demonstrably justifiable in a free and democratic society." If the government succeeds, the law is upheld. If it fails, the law will be found unconstitutional and the court will impose a remedy (discussed in the next section).

Section 1 serves two purposes: to limit the application of the enumerated rights and freedoms, and to balance *Charter* guarantees against competing social interests. In practice, no right or freedom can be exercised without restraint. For example, freedom of speech (section 2(b)) is a prerequisite for a healthy democracy; the liberty to express unpopular opinions must be protected against the annoyance of the majority. But hate propaganda against scapegoated minorities undermines the social tolerance on which democracy depends and threatens the safety of the targeted groups. Similarly, anyone who has been charged with a criminal offence is entitled to the full protection of the due-process legal rights in sections 7–14. At the same time, Canadians must be protected against the devastating effects of crime. Section 1 allows the three branches of government to strike appropriate balances between conflicting rights and freedoms, while safeguarding interests that are not explicitly protected in the *Charter*.

The first major ruling on section 1 was *R. v. Oakes* (1986), a criminal appeal challenging the constitutionality of the federal *Narcotics Act*. Writing for the majority, the late Chief Justice Dickson offered a sweeping definition of the phrase "free and democratic society":

Inclusion of these words as the final standard of justification for limits on rights and freedoms refers the Court to the very purpose for which the Charter was originally entrenched in the Constitution: Canadian society is to be free and democratic. The Court must be guided by the values and principles essential to a free and democratic society which I believe embody, to name but a few, respect for the inherent dignity of the human person, commitment to social justice and equality, accommodation of a wide variety of beliefs, respect for cultural and group identity, and faith in social and political institutions which enhance the participation of individuals and groups in society.[65]

In applying the "*Oakes* test," a judge must answer a series of questions:[66]

1. Is the objective of the impugned law "pressing and substantial" in "a free and democratic society"? In other words, does it serve a purpose that is sufficiently important to justify infringing one or more *Charter* guarantees? If the answer is yes, the judge moves on to the proportionality stage of the "test."

2. Is the law "rationally connected" to its objective? This question asks whether or not the specific policy mechanism chosen by the sponsoring government actually achieves its purpose. Because most judges are poorly equipped to analyze the real-world impact of public policy, they usually accept the government's claim of a "rational connection."

3. Is the law "minimally impairing" of the *Charter* guarantee at issue? The answer to this question may depend on the existence of an alternative means to achieve the objective which does not infringe the guarantee as severely as the impugned law. (See Dossier 6.5.) It may also depend on the government's ability to prove that it considered other policy mechanisms, and determined that none of them would achieve the law's objective as effectively as the one enshrined in the law. This is the most difficult part of the "*Oakes* test" for the sponsoring government; most of the laws which are struck down on *Charter* grounds fail the "minimal impairment" standard.[67]

4. Finally, do the positive effects of the impugned law outweigh the harm caused by the *Charter* infringement? This question is only addressed when a law has already passed the "rational connection" and "minimal impairment" stages. With a few exceptions, courts generally answer this question in the affirmative.

As governments become increasingly skilled in "*Charter*-proofing" their laws (see the discussion of policy-making, pp. 189–190), their laws are more likely to pass the "*Oakes* test." Older laws, adopted before the *Charter* took effect, are the most vulnerable. Newer laws are only struck down when the legislative and executive branches have paid insufficient attention to their "first-order" duties; the security certificate provisions discussed in Dossier 6.5 provide an example.

◼ The Remedy Stage

If the claimants prove that the law infringes the *Charter*, and the government fails to prove that the infringement is justified under section 1, the judge moves on to the third stage: to determine the appropriate remedy for the party or parties whose rights have been infringed by the impugned law. As we saw earlier in this chapter, the 1960 *Bill of Rights* did not include explicit judicial remedies for violations of rights and freedoms. When the *Charter* was drafted, most of the rights and freedoms contained in its guarantees already existed in Canadian statutes and common-law precedents. Therefore, it can be argued that the remedial provisions are the only real innovations in the *Charter*. Moreover, in policy terms, they are by far the most important sections: if courts did not have the power to remedy violations of rights and freedoms as part of the "second-order" duties, there would be much less incentive for the other two branches of government to take their "first-order" duties seriously (despite the popularity of the *Charter*).

- Section 24(1) allows any individual or group whose *Charter* rights have been infringed to ask the courts for "such remedy as the court considers appropriate and just in the circumstances." For example, a person convicted of a criminal offence after an unfair trial can appeal his conviction; if his appeal succeeds, he will be granted a new trial.

- Section 24(2) requires trial judges to exclude evidence obtained in violation of the rights guaranteed in sections 7–14. Police officers know that if they search a private home without a warrant, or interrogate a suspect without allowing him or her to call a lawyer, any evidence or confessions obtained may be thrown out before the trial. Alternatively, a conviction based on improperly admitted evidence can be overturned on appeal.
- Section 52(1) of the *Constitution Act, 1982* gives judges the power to strike down any law, federal or provincial, that is found to be inconsistent with the *Charter*, "to the extent of the inconsistency." This means that a particular section of the *Criminal Code* may be struck down (nullified") as an infringement on a *Charter* right, but the rest of the Code will remain in force. Instead of striking down a law immediately, it can suspend the **nullification** for a specified period. This gives the legislature a chance to replace the offending law before it expires. In addition, the court may provide guidelines to legislators for amending or reenacting the impugned law.

When a law is struck down, the sponsoring legislature has three options: it can pass an amended version of the law that is more consistent with the *Charter* (e.g., more "minimally impairing"); it can invoke the "notwithstanding clause" (discussed below); or it can give up on using law to achieve that particular objective. As mentioned earlier, some experts argue that the *Charter* has provoked a policy "dialogue" among the three branches of government. They note that legislators usually respond to nullification by amending the law, often in a way which reflects the court's preferences. Critics of the "dialogue" metaphor point out, correctly, that "legislative sequels" which simply parrot court rulings, are akin to "*Charter* ventriloquism";[68] instead of performing their own "first-order" duties, legislators concede policy-making supremacy to the courts by default. (The same can be said of "*Charter*-proofing" within the executive branch, as we will see below.) Apart from the implications for democracy, excessive deference to the courts by the legislative and executive branches of government is problematic because judges lack the skills to make good public policy (Chapter10).

If a judge decides that a law violates the *Charter*, but he or she does not consider striking it down to be the appropriate remedy, he or she can effectively amend the law by either **"reading in"** or **"reading down"** the offending provision(s).

- "Reading in" widens the application of the law by adding one or more groups that were previously excluded from the wording of the provision.[69] The actual wording of the law does not change, but the Supreme Court's interpretation requires all lower courts and lawyers to treat the provision as though it had.
- "Reading down" narrows the application of the law, to eliminate a conflict with the *Charter* (either in general or in a particular case). According to the late Justice John Sopinka, "reading down" allows a court to protect guaranteed rights while respecting the authority of the legislature.[70]

When the Supreme Court "reads in" to an ordinary law, and the sponsoring legislature does not approve of the result, it can amend the law in order to undo the court's work.[71] However, it is all but impossible to undo judicial decisions that change the meaning of the *Charter* itself. The Supreme Court has "read in" several groups that were originally excluded from section 15(1) of the *Charter*: residents of Canada who are not legal citizens,[72] gays and lesbians,[73] and common-law spouses.[74] (See the discussion of "analogous grounds" in Dossier 6.4.) In theory, legislators or Cabinet ministers who disagree with these additions could use the amending formula to remove them. In practice, such an amendment would require the unanimous consent of all 11 senior governments, which (as we saw in Chapters 3 and 5) is very difficult to achieve.

To understand the *Charter*'s general effects on policy-making and politics, we will look at the impact of court rulings (and remedies) on one particular policy. Dossier 6.4 describes the extension of civil marriage to same-sex couples.

The Supreme Court of Canada issued its first major ruling on equality rights in 1989. One of the key principles in that ruling is that the list of prohibited grounds for discrimination is not exhaustive. Through the process of "reading in," section 15(1) can be expanded to include personal characteristics "analogous" to those already enumerated.

The burden of proof for a new claim of "analogous grounds" rests with the party challenging the law. The plaintiff must demonstrate unequal treatment arising from a genuine disability[75] or from "the stereotypical application of presumed group or personal characteristics".[76] Those characteristics must be directly relevant to the impugned law.[77] To trigger a judicial remedy under section 15(1), they must also be directly related to "the essential dignity and worth of the individual,"[78] and they must be either permanent or difficult to change.

Of all the analogous grounds read in to section 15(1), sexual orientation is by far the most controversial. The 1995 *Egan* ruling established that this section protects gays and lesbians from discrimination. Two men who had lived together in a committed relationship for decades had been denied pension benefits that would automatically have been provided to married or common-law heterosexual spouses. Although the appellants lost their case, they scored a major legal victory when a majority of the Supreme Court declared sexual orientation to be an "analogous ground." Once a personal characteristic has been granted this recognition, it cannot be taken away in a subsequent ruling (see the discussion of *stare decisis* in Dossier 10.4). On the same day as *Egan*, the court declared that it was unconstitutional to discriminate against heterosexual common-law couples by denying them benefits to which married couples were entitled.[79] It amended Ontario's *Insurance Act* by "reading in" common-law couples to the definition of "spouses." The stage was set for the next battle: the designation of cohabiting same-sex couples as "common-law."

Advocates for same-sex rights won that battle in 1999, when the Supreme Court struck down an Ontario law that defined common-law "spouses" as two persons of the opposite sex.[80] This meant that two men or two women who lived together as romantic partners for a specified period of time would be considered "common-law spouses," with all the attendant rights and responsibilities attaching to opposite-sex couples in the same situation. For many gays and lesbians, this was enough; the social and legal stigma of homosexuality was fading, and they saw no reason to go further. Others wanted to challenge the last remaining barrier: the definition of civil marriage as an exclusively heterosexual institution. (Whereas common-law marriage does not require a marriage licence or a legally prescribed ceremony, civil marriage requires both.)

Same-sex couples in several provinces launched *Charter* challenges by attempting to procure marriage licences; when they were turned away, they went to court. The first victories came in 2002, when trial courts in both Ontario and Quebec ruled that the exclusively heterosexual definition of marriage violated section 15(1) by discriminating on the basis of sexual orientation.[81] The federal government, which has jurisdiction over marriage and divorce, appealed both rulings. In the meantime, the BC Court of Appeal endorsed the Ontario and Quebec rulings. It ordered that same-sex couples be permitted to marry, and suspended the effect of this order for two years to give Parliament a chance to amend the law. In June 2003 the Ontario Court of Appeal upheld the lower-court ruling in that province; the Quebec Court of Appeal followed suit in March 2004. The Ontario Court of Appeal ordered the province to issue marriage licences to same-sex couples immediately, prompting the BC Court of Appeal to lift the suspension of its own remedial order a few weeks later. Within hours of the Ontario appellate ruling, same-sex couples in the province flocked to registry offices to obtain marriage licences. In the following weeks and months, hundreds of same-sex

(continued)

couples travelled from across Canada and other countries to get married in Ontario or British Columbia.[82] There was no guarantee that the marriages would receive legal recognition in other jurisdictions; but for many couples who had waited years for the chance to marry legally, the opportunity was too good to pass up.

The federal government decided not to appeal the Ontario and British Columbia rulings. Instead, in July 2003 it announced an amendment to the marriage law. The new law would define civil marriage as "the lawful union of two persons to the exclusion of all others." It would also exempt religious clergy and denominations from having to perform same-sex weddings if these were contrary to their beliefs.[83] Before the law was submitted to a vote in Parliament, the Government referred it to the Supreme Court to determine its constitutionality. The Government asked three questions: (1) which level of government had jurisdiction over the issue; (2) whether the law was consistent with the equality rights in section 15; and (3) whether the proposed law violated the *Charter* guarantee of religious freedom (despite an explicit exemption for denominations that rejected same-sex marriage).[84] After Paul Martin became prime minister in late 2003, he referred a fourth question to the court: whether a separate category of "civil unions" for same-sex couples—as distinct from full civil "marriage"—would violate section 15(1).[85]

The federal government's decision upset opponents of same-sex marriage, who perceived it as an attack on their values and beliefs. Critics of judicial power argued that Parliament, not the Supreme Court, should have the final say on the issue. During the 2004 federal election campaign, both the Liberals and the new Conservative Party under Stephen Harper tried to use the issue to their own political advantage. Harper promised to withdraw the Supreme Court reference and allow Parliament to decide; he predicted (probably incorrectly) that if elected MPs refused to legalize same-sex marriage, the courts would respect that decision.[86] Harper also claimed that the *Charter* did not prohibit discrimination on the grounds of sexual orientation. This is inaccurate: while sexual orientation is not listed among the enumerated grounds, it is firmly established as an "analogous ground."

Paul Martin countered by accusing Harper of trying to weaken minority rights—a charge that gained some credibility when a videotaped interview with Conservative MP Randy White was leaked just before the election. In the interview, White said "To heck with the courts, eh?" and promised that a Conservative Government would use the "notwithstanding clause" to overturn *Charter* rulings with which it disagreed.[87] After the Conservatives' disappointing election result, some party strategists blamed White and other indiscreet Conservative MPs for reinforcing Liberal charges of a "hidden agenda" and alienating Ontario voters.[88]

In December 2004, the Supreme Court issued its reference ruling on same-sex marriage. The nine justices answered the first three questions unanimously: (1) the definition of marriage is a matter falling exclusively within federal jurisdiction, (2) the extension of civil marriage to same-sex couples does not violate the *Charter*—indeed, it "flows from" the equality rights in section 15(1), and (3) the provision in the law that exempted religious officials from performing same-sex marriages if this contravened their particular faiths was consistent with the guarantee of religious freedom.[89] However, the court refused to answer the fourth question that had been added by the Martin Government. It observed that the federal government had refused to appeal the earlier rulings from the provincial courts, deciding instead to accept the constitutionality of same-sex marriage and amend the law accordingly. Had the Cabinet entertained doubts about the provincial rulings that altered the definition of marriage, it should have let the appeals proceed. In addition, since June 2003, thousands of same-sex couples had relied in good faith on the government's acceptance of the earlier rulings and entered into legal marriages. For these reasons, the court gave no answer to the fourth question. It sent the issue of same-sex marriage back to Parliament.

(continued)

The Supreme Court refused to say in so many words that the denial of marriage to same-sex couples violated the *Charter*, which might have made it easier for Prime Minister Martin to pass the legislation through a divided Parliament. However, it was clear to most observers that MPs had only two options: (1) to pass the Bill, or (2) to invoke the "notwith-standing clause" in defence of "traditional marriage."[90] The Parliamentary debate on Bill C-38 divided the Liberal, Conservative, and New Democratic caucuses. The Bill passed narrowly, and received royal assent in July 2005.

THE IMPACT OF THE *CHARTER* ON CANADIAN POLITICS AND POLICY-MAKING

As we have seen, the *Charter* imposes two types of duty on Canada's political institutions: the "first-order" duty to comply with the *Charter*, and the "second-order" duty to monitor the compliance of others. Although the "second-order" activities of the courts attract most of the public and media attention, the "first-order" activities of the legislative and executive branches have more impact on the daily lives of Canadians. This is because judicial rulings affect few people directly (see Chapter 10), and because relatively few laws and executive decisions are challenged in the courts. If the legislative and executive branches of government neglect their "first-order" obligation to balance *Charter* guarantees against other policy considerations—such as cost, administrative convenience, or political popularity—the judicial branch cannot protect rights and freedoms all by itself.

Perhaps the best example of a "first-order" duty is the "*Charter*-proofing" process conducted by the federal Department of Justice (DOJ). James Kelly argues that the *Charter* has transformed the DOJ into a new central agency within the federal government (see Dossier 9.2), because its legal experts are responsible for ensuring *Charter* compliance within the executive branch.[91] At the same time, the DOJ's monopoly of "first-order" review may have reinforced the dominance of the executive branch over Parliament.[92]

From the earliest developmental stages, new federal policies are scrutinized for their conformity to the *Charter*. The DOJ lawyers try to determine the risk of nullification (or an alternative remedy) in the event that a law is challenged in court.[93] The "risk assessment" focuses on the justification stage (section 1), and especially the "minimal impairment" prong of the *Oakes* "test." If the lawyers identify a potentially unconstitutional element in the proposed legislation, the legislative and executive branches must either amend the draft law or risk its eventual nullification.

As suggested previously, the DOJ has a very good track record of "*Charter*-proofing." Few federal laws passed since 1988, when the "risk assessment" procedure was introduced, have failed the "*Oakes* test." But there is a problem with the DOJ's approach to its "first-order" duties: its over-reliance on Supreme Court rulings as the criterion of constitutionality. If legislators can be accused of "*Charter* ventriloquism" when they enact court rulings into law, the same charge can be laid against the executive branch when it "*Charter*-proofs" in an overly deferential (and defensive) way. The permanent executive, unlike the courts, has the resources to make and enforce good policy.

In addition to its effects on the policy-making process, the *Charter* has had important political consequences. Some of these are described elsewhere in this book (Chapters 2 and 10).

Two others are illustrated in Dossier 6.4, above. First, the court rulings on same-sex marriage appear to have influenced many Canadians' opinions about the issue. "Framing" it as a question of equal rights, rather than morality, legitimized a policy goal that would otherwise have been widely unpopular.[94] However, this does not mean that every *Charter* decision has the power to change minds. Some rulings, particularly those which favour the due-process rights of criminal suspects, provoke public outrage (or at least a lot of angry rhetoric from particular advocacy groups and politicians).[95] Nonetheless, the popularity of the *Charter* itself seems to rub off on some policies, especially those relating to equality rights.

Second, the squabble between the Liberal and Conservative parties over the "notwithstanding clause" exposed a longstanding controversy over the balance between rights and freedoms and competing policy goals—and, by extension, over the relationship between judges and legislators.[96] Section 33 of the *Charter* allows a federal or provincial legislature to pass a law that infringes fundamental freedoms, legal rights, and/or equality rights. The law must contain an explicit declaration that it operates "notwithstanding" a particular *Charter* guarantee. Once passed, the law expires after five years; however, it can be re-enacted if the legislature so chooses.

Section 33 was inserted into the *Charter* in November 1981, to secure provincial consent for the *Constitution Act, 1982*. It is rarely used, because politicians fear the public backlash against any deliberate violation of rights and freedoms. Some observers have even argued that the "notwithstanding clause" has become a dead letter, like the federal power in the *BNA Act* to veto or delay provincial laws. As suggested in Dossier 6.4, some Conservatives may have made a serious political mistake in 2004 by promising to revive section 33. While few Canadians know what the *Charter* means or how it works, a majority believe that its entrenchment has changed Canada for the better.[97] Under those circumstances, a politician who vows to override its provisions is taking a political risk.

As a result, Cabinet ministers and legislators sometimes look for other ways to get around the *Charter*—in effect, to evade their "first-order" duties. Under difficult conditions, and especially in the wake of a severe public trauma, the courts may be unwilling to carry out their "second-order" duties. In other words, the courts let the other two branches off the hook.

THE *CHARTER* AFTER 9/11

The willingness of judges to challenge the other two branches of government determines the *Charter*'s practical effect on the lives of Canadians. When judges defer to legislators or executives, their policy-making power shrinks; when *Charter* rights and freedoms yield to other priorities, their influence wanes. This relationship between judicial attitudes and *Charter* enforcement became particularly apparent after 9/11. In the wake of the terrorist attacks in the United States, heightened national security concerns partially eclipsed *Charter* rights and freedoms.

A month after the attacks on New York and Washington, the federal government tabled Bill C-36—(the *Anti-Terrorism Act* (ATA)—in the House of Commons. The Bill contained numerous amendments to the *Criminal Code*, the *Official Secrets Act*, and other federal legislation. Among other things, the ATA made it a criminal offence to participate in a terrorist organization (whether or not the accused individual knew of any planned terrorist activity); permitted the preventive arrest of a person suspected of planning to commit a terrorist act; provided for secret investigative hearings at which any individual may be compelled to testify, whether or not a terrorist act has taken place; and defined terrorism as any criminal offence committed "in whole or in part for a political, religious or ideological purpose, objective or cause."[98] The ATA appeared to infringe several of the protected rights and freedoms in the *Charter*, including some legal rights and the fundamental freedoms in section 2.[99]

To the surprise of some observers, the Supreme Court of Canada upheld the investigative hearing provisions in June 2004.[100] The majority found that there was no infringement of the *Charter*, and so no need even to justify the law. The justices had previously signalled their willingness to accept anti-terrorism laws as "reasonable limitations" on the *Charter* in the

Suresh case, which was decided shortly after the attacks on Washington and New York.[101] When national security concerns become paramount, courts usually defer to the executive branch, which is ultimately responsible for protecting life and property within a particular state.[102] In *Suresh*, the court unanimously endorsed the following statement made by a British Law Lord a month after the 9/11 attacks:

> [T]he recent events in New York and Washington . . . are a reminder that in matters of national security, the cost of failure can be high. This seems to me to underline the need for the judicial arm of government to respect the decisions of ministers of the Crown on the question of whether support for terrorist activities in a foreign country constitutes a threat to national security . . . the executive has access to special information and expertise in these matters.[103]

On the other side of the coin, the *Suresh* ruling prohibited the Canadian government from deporting a foreign citizen to face a credible risk of torture or execution in his native country. As Dossier 6.5 shows, that part of the ruling had more impact than appeared likely at the time of its publication.

The 1988 *Emergencies Act*, which replaced the old *War Measures Act*, was carefully crafted to conform to the requirements of the *Charter*. It explicitly referred to "those fundamental rights that are not to be limited or abridged even in a national emergency," limited the exercise of emergency powers to strict time periods, and forbade "the detention, imprisonment or internment of Canadian citizens or permanent residents as defined in the *Immigration Act* on the basis of race, national or ethnic origin, colour, religion, sex, age or mental or physical disability."[104] There are no such protections in the ATA. Muslim, Arab, and South Asian Canadians have complained that the police are using their powers under the ATA to harass and "profile" them. Both the Commission of Inquiry into the Maher Arar case, and the Special Senate Committee on the *Anti-Terrorism Act*, found evidence to substantiate these allegations.[105]

For those who fear the impact of national security crises on rights and freedoms, especially those of individuals and groups who seem to pose a threat to the majority, the lessons of history are worrisome (p. 173). However, history also tells a more positive story: over time, an acceptable balance between civil liberties and public safety is usually restored. This happens, in part, because the anger and fear provoked by an event such as 9/11 eventually fade. Additionally, there is often a public backlash against the excesses of an executive branch that unnecessarily violates human rights in pursuit of national security. When the pendulum swings too far in one direction, it must eventually swing back again.

DOSSIER 6.5 The *Charkaoui* Ruling

In February 2007, the Supreme Court of Canada released its long-awaited ruling on the constitutionality of the security certificate provisions in the *Immigration and Refugee Protection Act* (IRPA). These provisions, which have been in effect since 1988, were not explicitly intended to deal with suspected terrorists. Since 9/11, however, they have been used almost exclusively to detain Muslim men who were alleged to have contact with terrorist organizations.[106]

In a nutshell, the law permits the indefinite detention of any landed immigrant, permanent resident, or refugee if that person is believed by the Canadian Security and Intelligence Service (CSIS) to pose a threat to Canadian security. Upon receipt of a report from CSIS, the federal ministers of Citizenship and Immigration and Public Safety may issue a certificate authorizing the immediate arrest of the person named therein. The original purpose of that detention was to ensure speedy deportation to his country of origin. However, as previously described, the *Suresh* ruling from the Supreme Court of Canada forbade the deportation of any

(continued)

individual who faced a credible threat of torture or death. Most of the Muslim men detained under security certificates between 2001 and 2007 came from states whose governments were known to use torture and other inhumane methods on suspects. Consequently, they found themselves in legal limbo: they could not be deported, and they were unlikely to be released from detention as long as the federal government perceived them as threats to the security of Canada. None were formally charged with any criminal offence, so they had no opportunity to clear their names and win their release.

By the fall of 2006, three of the men had unsuccessfully challenged their detentions at the Federal Court of Appeal (see Chapter 10). The Supreme Court of Canada agreed to hear their appeals, which were consolidated into a single case under the name of appellant Adil Charkaoui. The key legal issues concerned the process for judicial review of the certificates. The government insisted that the evidence against the alleged terrorists would imperil national security if the accused were allowed to see it. Therefore, it was not disclosed to the individuals named on the certificates or to their lawyers. Without access to this evidence, the individuals could not defend themselves against false accusations of terrorist activity. Their lawyers could not cross-examine witnesses, or determine the reliability of the evidence provided to the hearing judge by CSIS and other agencies. In effect, the security certificate provisions in the IRPA condemned individuals who had never been proven guilty of any crime to spend years in jail with little prospect of due process. The three appellants argued that the provisions violated section 7 of the *Charter*, which forbids the state to deprive anyone of his or her liberty unless the deprivation is consistent with the principles of fundamental justice.[107]

The unanimous Supreme Court ruling in *Charkaoui*, written by Chief Justice McLachlin, explicitly restored the balance between the *Charter* and national security in the post-9/11 era. It also, albeit implicitly, acknowledged that the court had been too deferential to the executive branch in the immediate aftermath of the terrorist attacks in the United States. First, McLachlin made it clear that national security concerns would no longer override the *Charter*.

> *[S]ecurity concerns cannot be used to excuse procedures that do not conform to fundamental justice at the s. 7 stage of the analysis. . . . The procedures required to conform to the principles of fundamental justice must reflect the exigencies of the security context. Yet they cannot be permitted to erode the essence of s. 7. The principles of fundamental justice cannot be reduced to the point where they cease to provide the protection of due process that lies at the heart of s. 7 of the Charter. The protection may not be as complete as in a case where national security constraints do not operate. But to satisfy s. 7, meaningful and substantial protection there must be.*[108]

Because the IRPA did not provide "meaningful and substantial protection" to the individuals named on security certificates, the law violated the *Charter*.

Second, McLachlin held that the violations of section 7 were not justified under section 1. She found that the objective of the provisions—the protection of Canada's national security—was "pressing and substantial," and that they were "rationally connected" to that objective. However, the complete denial of access to government evidence was not "minimally impairing" of the rights guaranteed in section 7. Other countries had struck a better balance between individual rights and public safety, such as Britain's appointment of special advocates with security clearances to assist detainees at judicial hearings. The existence of a less impairing alternative generally leads to a finding that the *Charter* infringement is unjustified. The court declared the judicial hearing provisions in the IRPA invalid, and suspended the effect of the declaration for 12 months to allow Parliament to create an alternative mechanism. At the time of writing, the new provisions, which differed relatively little from those struck down in *Charkaoui*,[109] had not yet been passed into law.

CONCLUSION

The *Charkaoui* ruling illustrates some of the central themes in Canadian politics since 1982. After their initial burst of enthusiasm, judges have tried to balance their second-order *Charter* duties with a proper degree of respect for the legislative and executive branches of government. When lawmakers fail to take their first-order duties seriously enough, the courts are left with no option but to impose remedies for *Charter* violations. At the same time, courts have acknowledged that they cannot make good policies (Chapter 10). Therefore, they suspend the effect of the most drastic remedy—the nullification of a law—to give the sponsoring legislature a chance to respond.

There are at least four reasons for the revival of judicial deference in the past 15 years.

- The first is the nature of judicial review itself. When judges are presented with a new constitutional document, they must create an entirely new set of doctrines and principles for its interpretation. Once those doctrines have taken shape, the impetus for judicial activism weakens, and the court becomes more deferential to the legislature.[110]

- Second, the Supreme Court was confronted with a backlog of pre-*Charter* legislation in the 1980s. After nearly two decades, legislative drafters have become more careful to avoid remedial action by the courts. In effect, the "large and liberal" approach of the early years forced the other branches of government to take their first-order *Charter* duties more seriously than they might otherwise have done;[111] consequently, fewer laws require "fixing" to conform to the *Charter* (as interpreted by the courts).

- A third possible reason for greater judicial deference is the Supreme Court's unwillingness to impose a national conception of rights on diverse provincial communities.[112]

- Fourth and finally, judges have likely been stung by public criticism, and have tried to keep their heads down. They were particularly reluctant to run afoul of public opinion after 9/11, although this reluctance has faded as the years passed without further terrorist attacks in North America.

Whatever the outcome of a particular dispute, every *Charter* case makes a contribution to the constitutional common law of Canada. As we saw in Chapter 3, entrenched laws are written in broad and general language. The precise application of words like "equality," and phrases such as "a free and democratic society," is left for the courts to determine. Although the *Charter* has existed for a relatively short time, its meaning has already been shaped (some would say distorted) by judicial rulings. It will continue to evolve as Canadian society changes, a "living tree" which grows in new and unexpected directions.

GLOSSARY OF KEY TERMS

Impugned: When a court is asked to rule on the constitutionality of a particular law, that legal provision is said to be "impugned." In a *Charter* case, one or more parties before the court seeks to prove that the law is unconstitutional on the grounds that it conflicts with a *Charter* right or freedom. The challenged law, or the specific sections of the law on which the appeal turns, are impugned by the plaintiff. The term applies whether or not the court agrees that the law is unconstitutional.

Judicial activism: Activist judges use their policy-making power to overturn or effectively rewrite ordinary statutes and constitutional texts. Activist judges are less likely to defer to the legislative or executive branches of government and more likely to put their own stamp on the law through judicial review.

Judicial deference: Also called "judicial conservatism." An institutional norm among appeal court judges that restrains them in their legal interpretations. Judges defer to Parliament, upholding most or all of the laws passed by the legislative branch and taking a narrow approach to constitutional law.

Litigation: Seeking the resolution of a dispute in the courts. Examples include constitutional challenges, private lawsuits, and criminal appeals.

Nullification: When a court finds an impugned law to be unconstitutional, it can declare that law to be null and void (section 52 of the *Constitution* Act, 1982). This power to nullify laws is also referred to as "striking down."

Plaintiff: In the context of this chapter, an individual or group that challenges the constitutionality of a particular law or administrative act under the *Charter*. The plaintiff must demonstrate that his or her *Charter* rights or freedoms, or those of the represented group, have been infringed. If the plaintiff succeeds in proving that an impugned law infringes the *Charter*, the court proceeds to consider whether that law should be upheld as a "reasonable limit" under section 1. In the case of an administrative act—e.g., a police investigation or an adverse ruling on a refugee claim—there is no section 1 analysis; a proven *Charter* infringement will usually trigger a remedy from the court.

Public-interest litigation: The effort to change laws and other government policies through the courts. In the *Charter* context, this involves a legal challenge to the constitutionality of a particular law or program, or a claim that a specific government official violated the rights or freedoms of the plaintiff.

"Reading down": When a court finds that an impugned law violates the *Charter* under a certain set of circumstances, it can set out a narrow interpretation of that law that prevents such a violation in the future. The application of the law is restricted, but it is not struck down altogether.

"Reading in": When a court finds that a particular group has been unfairly excluded from constitutional protection, it can use the remedial power under section 52 to "read in" that group. In effect, the court rewrites the *Charter*—usually section 15—to broaden the rights guaranteed therein. The actual wording of the *Constitution* does not change, but lawyers and judges know that they are bound to interpret its provisions as though they had been formally amended.

DISCUSSION AND REVIEW QUESTIONS

1. Identify and briefly explain TWO important differences between the 1960 *Bill of Rights* and the *Charter*.

2. Identify and briefly explain both categories of remedy for *Charter* violations provided by the *Constitution Act, 1982*.

3. In your own words, explain the three stages of *Charter* review by a judge.

4. Identify and briefly define the first-order and second-order duties imposed on Canada's political institutions by the *Charter*. Give ONE example of each type of duty.

5. Why did the federal government amend the laws to extend civil marriage to same-sex couples? What alternatives did it have, and why did it refuse to take them?

SUGGESTED READINGS

Books and Articles

W.A. Bogart, *Courts and Country: The Limits of Litigation and the Social and Political Life of Canada* (Toronto: Oxford University Press, 1994).

Ronald J. Daniels, Patrick Macklem, and Kent Roach, eds., *The Security of Freedom: Essays on Canada's Anti-Terrorism Bill* (Toronto: University of Toronto Press, 2002).

Charles R. Epp, *The Rights Revolution: Lawyers, Activists, and Supreme Courts in Comparative Perspective* (Chicago: University of Chicago Press, 1998).

Janet L. Hiebert, *Charter Conflicts: What Is Parliament's Role?* (Montreal and Kingston: McGill– Queen's University Press, 2002).

Janet L. Hiebert, *Limiting Rights: The Dilemma of Judicial Review* (Montreal and Kingston: McGill–Queen's University Press, 1996).

Paul Howe and Peter H. Russell, eds., *Judicial Power and Canadian Democracy* (Montreal and Kingston: McGill–Queen's University Press/Institute for Research on Public Policy, 2001).

James B. Kelly, "Bureaucratic Activism and the Charter of Rights and Freedoms: The Department of Justice and Its Entry Into the Centre of Government," *Canadian Public Administration,* 42:4 (Winter 1999).

James B. Kelly, *Governing with the Charter: Legislative and Judicial Activism and Framers' Intent* (Vancouver: UBC Press, 2005).

James B. Kelly, "The Charter of Rights and Freedoms and the Rebalancing of Liberal Constitutionalism in Canada, 1982–1997," *Osgoode Hall Law Journal,* volume 37 (Fall 1999).

Heather MacIvor, *Canadian Government and Politics in the Charter Era* (Toronto: Thomson Nelson, 2005).

Christopher P. Manfredi, *Judicial Power and the Charter: Canada and the Paradox of Liberal Constitutionalism,* 2nd edition (Toronto: Oxford University Press, 2001).

F.L. Morton and Rainer Knopff, *The Charter Revolution and the Court Party* (Peterborough, ON: Broadview Press, 2000).

Kent Roach, *September 11: Consequences for Canada* (Montreal and Kingston: McGill–Queen's University Press, 2003).

Kent Roach, *The Supreme Court on Trial: Judicial Activism or Democratic Dialogue?* (Toronto: Irwin Law, 2001).

Peter H. Russell, *Constitutional Odyssey: Can Canadians Become a Sovereign People?* 2nd edition (Toronto: University of Toronto Press, 1993).

Peter H. Russell, Rainer Knopff, and Ted Morton, eds., *Leading Constitutional Decisions: Federalism and the Charter* (Ottawa: Carleton University Press, 1989).

F. Leslie Seidle, ed., *Equity and Community: The Charter, Interest Advocacy and Representation* (Montreal: Institute for Research on Public Policy, 1993).

Robert J. Sharpe, Katherine E. Swinton, and Kent Roach, *The Charter of Rights and Freedoms*, 2nd edition (Toronto: Irwin Law, 2002).

Brian Slattery, "A Theory of the Charter," *Osgoode Hall Law Journal*, volume 25 (1987), 701 747.

Websites

All of the *Charter* rulings by the Supreme Court of Canada are available at the LexUM website (www.lexum.umontreal.ca; click on "Supreme Court of Canada"), which offers a searchable database of rulings issued back to 1985 and the ability to download these rulings in WordPerfect. An option is to go to the Supreme Court of Canada website (www.scc-csc.gc.ca) and click on "Judgments" at the top of the screen. Follow the links to LexUM.

Another source of Supreme Court rulings is the Canadian Legal Information Institute website (www.canlii.org); under "Canada," click on "Supreme Court of Canada." The CanLII site also offers a useful digest of *Charter* rulings by a senior official at the federal Department of Justice (under "Canada," in the "Commentary" section, click on "Decisions Digest") and a searchable database of federal and provincial laws and court rulings.

NOTES

1. The *Charter* was proclaimed into law on April 17, 1982. However, the implementation of section 15 (equality rights) was delayed for three years to allow governments to bring their laws into conformity with its provisions.
2. *R. v. Morgentaler,* [1988] 1 S.C.R. 30.
3. *Rodriguez v. British Columbia (Attorney General),* [1993] 3 S.C.R. 519.
4. *Eldridge v. British Columbia (Attorney General),* [1997] 3 S.C.R. 624.
5. *Singh v. Minister of Employment and Immigration,* [1985] 1 S.C.R. 177; *Andrews v. Law Society of British Columbia,* [1989] 1 S.C.R. 143; *Benner v. Canada (Secretary of State),* [1997] 1 S.C.R. 358.
6. *Vriend v. Alberta,* [1998] 1 S.C.R. 493; *McKinney v. University of Guelph,* [1990] 3 S.C.R. 229; *Egan v. Canada,* [1995] 2 S.C.R. 513; *Law v. Canada (Minister of Employment and Immigration),* [1999] 1 S.C.R. 497; *Schachter v. Canada,* [1992] 2 S.C.R. 679; *Thibaudeau v. Canada,* [1995] 2 S.C.R. 627.
7. *R. v. Feeney,* [1997] 2 S.C.R. 13.
8. *R. v. Stillman,* [1997] 1 S.C.R. 607.
9. *R. v. Manninen,* [1987] 1 S.C.R. 1233; *R. v. Burlingham,* [1995] 2 S.C.R. 206.
10. *R. v. Daviault,* [1994] 3 S.C.R. 63.
11. *R. v. Lavallée,* [1990] 1 S.C.R. 852; *R. v. Malott,* [1998] 1 S.C.R. 123.
12. *R. v. Vaillancourt,* [1987] 2 S.C.R. 636; *R. v. Creighton,* [1993] 3 S.C.R. 3.
13. *Charkaoui v. Canada (Minister of Citizenship and Immigration),* [2007] 1 S.C.R. 350.
14. See, e.g., Christopher P. Manfredi, *Judicial Power and the Charter: Canada and the Paradox of Liberal Constitutionalism,* 2nd edition (Toronto: Oxford University Press, 2001); Michael Mandel, *The Charter of Rights and the Legalization of Politics in Canada,* rev. edition (Toronto: Thomson, 1994).
15. Mandel, 43.
16. F. L. Morton and Rainer Knopff, *The Charter Revolution and the Court Party* (Peterborough, ON: Broadview Press, 2000), 31.
17. Ibid., 166. In reality, right-wing groups and corporations use the *Charter* at least as often as the "Court Party" groups identified by Morton and Knopff, with considerable success. See, for example, *Lavigne v. Ontario Public Service Employees Union,* [1991] 2 S.C.R.

211, an anti-union challenge funded by the right-wing National Citizens' Coalition (NCC), and the NCC's own challenges to the *Canada Elections Act: Somerville v. Canada (Attorney General)* (1996), 136 D.L.R. (4th) 205 and *Harper v. Attorney General for Canada*, [2000]. Note, however, that the NCC eventually lost the *Harper* case—a challenge to the laws restricting interest-group advertising during election campaigns—in a May 2004 ruling from the Supreme Court of Canada. See *Harper v. Canada (Attorney General)*, [2004] 1 S.C.R. 827.

18. Harper's former Chief of Staff, Ian Brodie, was a political scientist before he went to work for the new Canadian Alliance leader in 2002. Most of his scholarly writings criticized the courts and their interpretation of the *Charter*. See Ian Brodie, *Friends of the Court: The Privileging of Interest-Group Litigants in Canada* (Albany: State University of New York Press, 2002); Ian Brodie, "Interest Group Litigation and the Embedded State: Canada's Court Challenges Program," *Canadian Journal of Political Science*, 34:2 (June 2001), 357–76. Brodie was particularly opposed to the Court Challenges Program, which funded *Charter* cases based on equality and language rights. The Program was cancelled in the Harper Government's first budget. (See the discussion of judicial appointments and salaries in Chapter 10.)

19. See Charles R. Epp, "Do Bills of Rights Matter? The Canadian *Charter* of Rights and Freedoms," *American Political Science Review*, 90:4 (December 1996); Charles R. Epp, *The Rights Revolution: Lawyers, Activists, and Supreme Courts in Comparative Perspective* (Chicago: University of Chicago Press, 1998), Chapter One.

20. Kent Roach, "The Role of Litigation and the *Charter* in Interest Advocacy," in F. Leslie Seidle, ed., *Equity and Community: The Charter, Interest Advocacy and Representation* (Montreal: Institute for Research on Public Policy, 1993), 173–74.

21. Ibid., 174–75.

22. A survey of *Charter* rulings from 1984 to 1997 found that roughly one-third of plaintiffs succeeded at the Supreme Court. James B. Kelly, "The *Charter of Rights and Freedoms* and the Rebalancing of Liberal Constitutionalism in Canada, 1982–1997," *Osgoode Hall Law Journal*, volume 37 (Fall 1999), Table 2, 641.

23. Janet L. Hiebert, *Limiting Rights: The Dilemma of Judicial Review* (Montreal and Kingston: McGill–Queen's University Press, 1996), 118.

24. David Beatty, *Constitutional Law in Theory and Practice* (Toronto: University of Toronto Press, 1995), 91 and 95.

25. Brian Slattery, "A Theory of the *Charter*," *Osgoode Hall Law Journal*, volume 25 (1987), 701–747.

26. Peter W. Hogg and Allison A. Bushell, "The *Charter* Dialogue Between Courts and Legislatures (Or Perhaps The *Charter* of Rights Isn't Such a Bad Thing After All)," *Osgoode Hall Law Journal*, volume 35 (Spring 1997), 75. See also Kent Roach, *The Supreme Court on Trial: Judicial Activism or Democratic Dialogue?* (Toronto: Irwin Law, 2001); Janet L. Hiebert, *Charter Conflicts: What Is Parliament's Role?* (Montreal and Kingston: McGill–Queen's University Press, 2002). The role of lower courts in the "dialogue" is described in Matthew Hennigar, "Expanding the 'Dialogue' Debate: Canadian Federal Government Responses to Lower Court *Charter* Decisions," *Canadian Journal of Political Science*, 37:1 (March 2004), 3–21. For critiques of the "dialogue" metaphor, see Christopher P. Manfredi and James B. Kelly, "Six Degrees of Dialogue: A Response to Hogg and Bushell," *Osgoode Hall Law Journal*, volume 37, (Fall 1999), 513, and F.L. Morton, "Dialogue or Monologue?" in Paul Howe and Peter H. Russell, eds., *Judicial Power and Canadian Democracy* (Montreal and Kingston: McGill–Queen's University Press/Institute for Research on Public Policy, 2001). See also Heather MacIvor, *Canadian Politics and Government in the Charter Era* (Toronto: Thomson Nelson, 2005), Chapter 4.

27. Canada, Commission of Inquiry into the Actions of Canadian Officials in Relation to Maher Arar, *Analysis and Recommendations* (Ottawa: Minister of Public Works and Government Services, 2006), particularly 356; Senate of Canada, "Fundamental Justice in Extraordinary Times: Main Report of the Special Senate Committee on the *Anti-Terrorism Act*" (Ottawa, February 2007), 20–24.

28. See Dossier 6.5. See also the June 2006 ruling of the United States Supreme Court in *Hamdan v. Rumsfeld.*

29. Alan C. Cairns, *Charter versus Federalism: The Dilemmas of Constitutional Reform* (Montreal and Kingston: McGill–Queen's University Press, 1992), 17–18.

30. That historic structure was modified in 1998, by the adoption of the *Human Rights Act.* Today, the *European Convention on Human Rights* is binding on British judges. Although they still lack the power to strike down laws passed by the Westminster Parliament, their rulings on rights and freedoms carry significant political weight. See, for example, the 2004 ruling of the Law Lords (the highest court of appeal in Britain) on the indefinite detention of suspected terrorists: *A (FC) and others v. Secretary of State for the Home Department.*

31. In Montreal in October 1970, a small group of radical separatists, the Front de Libération du Québec (FLQ), first kidnapped British Trade Commissioner James Cross and, five days later, provincial Labour Minister Pierre Laporte. The Quebec government asked Prime Minister Trudeau to invoke the *War Measures Act,* which gave police and soldiers the power to arrest and detain potential suspects without charge. The Act remained in force for several weeks, during which time almost 500 people were rounded up and thrown into jail. Only five were ever convicted of a criminal offence relating to the crisis. Most of the FLQ members involved were given safe passage to Cuba in return for releasing the trade commissioner, although a few served relatively short jail sentences after returning to Canada. Shortly after the Act was imposed, Laporte was murdered by his kidnappers. See Denis Smith, *Bleeding Hearts . . . Bleeding Country* (Edmonton: Hurtig, 1971), and Walter Surma Tarnopolsky, *The Canadian Bill of Rights*, 2nd rev. edition (Toronto: McClelland and Stewart, 1975).

32. *Attorney General for British Columbia v. Tomey Homma*, JCPC 1903, in Richard A. Olmsted, ed., *Decisions of the Judicial Committee of the Privy Council*, volume 1 (Ottawa: Queen's Printer, 1954), 484.

33. *Co-operative Committee on Japanese Canadians v. Attorney General for Canada*, JCPC 1947, in Olmsted, volume 3, 472–73.

34. *Reference re Alberta Statutes*, S.C.R. 1938, in Peter H. Russell, Rainer Knopff, and Ted Morton, eds., *Leading Constitutional Decisions: Federalism and the Charter* (Ottawa: Carleton University Press, 1989), 293–98.

35. Russell, Knopff, and Morton, "Comment on *Switzman v. Elbling*," in *Leading Constitutional Decisions*, 318.

36. *Ontario (Attorney General) v. OPSEU*, [1987] 2 S.C.R. 2; *New Brunswick Broadcasting Co. v. Nova Scotia (Speaker of the House of Assembly)*, [1993] 1 S.C.R. 319; *Reference re Remuneration of Judges of the Provincial Court (P.E.I.)*, [1997] 3 S.C.R. 3; *Reference re Secession of Quebec*, [1998] 2 S.C.R. 217.

37. Cairns, 29.

38. Ibid.

39. MacIvor, *Canadian Politics and Government in the Charter Era*, 60–67.

40. *R. v. Drybones*, [1970] S.C.R. 282.

41. Ibid.

42. *Attorney General of Canada v. Lavell; Isaac v. Bedard*, [1974] S.C.R. 1349.

43. *Morgentaler v. the Queen*, [1976] S.C.R. 632.

44. Ibid., 633.

45. Ibid., 636.

46. *R. v. Morgentaler*, [1988] 1 S.C.R. 30, paragraph 3, *per* Dickson C.J.

47. Ibid., paragraph 185, *per* McIntyre J.

48. Ibid., paragraph 237, *per* Wilson J.

49. Ibid., paragraph 246.

50. Ibid., paragraphs 31 and 32, *per* Dickson C.J.

51. *Singh v. Minister of Employment and Immigration*, [1985] 1 S.C.R. 177.

52. *Authorson v. Canada (Attorney General)*, [2003] 2 S.C.R. 40.

53. Peter H. Russell, *Constitutional Odyssey: Can Canadians Become a Sovereign People?* 2nd edition (Toronto: University of Toronto Press, 1993), 114.

54. MacIvor, 73.

55. Hiebert, *Limiting Rights*, 24.

56. *RWDSU v. Dolphin Delivery Ltd.*, [1986] 2 S.C.R. 573, paragraph 39.

57. *Vriend v. Alberta*, [1998] 1 S.C.R. 493, paragraph 66.

58. *McKinney v. University of Guelph*, [1990] 3 S.C.R. 229; *Eldridge v. British Columbia (Attorney General)*, [1997] 3 S.C.R. 624.

59. *Canada (Justice) v. Khadr*, 2008 SCC 28, paragraph 27, *per curiam.*

60. *Hunter v. Southam Inc.*, [1984] 2 S.C.R.

61. *R. v. Big M Drug Mart Ltd.*, paragraph 117.

62. *Edmonton Journal v. Alberta (Attorney General)*, [1989] 2 S.C.R. 1326, paragraph 52.

63. *Reference re Prov. Electoral Boundaries (Sask.)*, [1991] 2 S.C.R. 158, paragraph 49.

64. *Haig v. Canada; Haig v. Canada (Chief Electoral Officer)*, [1993] 2 S.C.R. 995, paragraph 61.

65. *R. v. Oakes*, paragraph 64.

66. See MacIvor, 27–29.

67. Leon Trakman, William Cole-Hamilton, and Sean Gatien, "*R. v. Oakes* 1986–1997: Back To the Drawing Board," *Osgoode Hall Law Journal*, volume 36 (Spring 1998), 100.

68. Manfredi and Kelly, 521.

69. *Schachter v. Canada*, [1992] 2 S.C.R. 679.

70. *Osborne v. Canada (Treasury Board)*, [1991] 2 S.C.R. 69.

71. However, Hennigar argues that legislatures have greater difficulty in reacting to a judicial amendment than a judicial nullification. See Hennigar, 14.

72. *Andrews v. Law Society of British Columbia*, [1989] 1 S.C.R. 143; *Benner v. Canada (Secretary of State)*, [1997] 1 S.C.R. 358.

73. *Egan v. Canada*, [1995] 2 S.C.R. 513; *Vriend v. Alberta*, [1998] 1 S.C.R. 493; *M. v. H.*, [1999] 2 S.C.R. 3.

74. *Miron v. Trudel*, [1995] 2 S.C.R. 418.

75. *Eaton v. Brant County Board of Education*, [1997] 1 S.C.R. 241, paragraph 67.

76. *Miron v. Trudel*, paragraph 131.

77. *Eldridge v. British Columbia (Attorney General)*, paragraph 56.

78. *Miron v. Trudel*, paragraph 151.

79. Ibid.

80. *M. v. H.*, [1999] 2 S.C.R. 3.

81. *Halpern v. Canada (Attorney General)*, [2002] O.J. No. 2714 (2002) 215 D.L.R. (4th) 223; *Hendricks v. Québec (Attorney General)*, [2002] J.Q. No. 3816.

82. Kathleen A. Lahey and Kevin Alderson, *Same-Sex Marriage: The Personal and the Political* (Toronto: Insomniac Press, 2004), 91–92.

83. The text of the July 2003 draft law was accessed at the Department of Justice website: www.canada.justice.gc.ca.

84. Department of Justice website: www.canada.justice.gc.ca.

85. The Department of Justice claimed that the new question would address public concerns that the government had prejudged the issue in its original reference questions, and that it would "allow individuals and groups who disagree with the Government's approach to put their case before the Supreme Court." The revised reference, which was filed on January 28, 2004, was accessed at www.canada.justice.gc.ca/en/news.

86. Brian Laghi, "Top court wouldn't block same-sex law, Harper says," *The Globe and Mail*, June 3, 2004; accessed at www.globeandmail.com.

87. Rod Mickleburgh and Mark Hume, "White harsh critic of justice, immigration systems," *The Globe and Mail*, June 26, 2004 (accessed at www.globeandmail.com); Canadian Press, "We'd use notwithstanding clause: Tory MP," *Toronto Star*, June 25, 2004 (accessed at www.thestar.com).

88. Robert Benzie, "Tories pin blame on fear, rogue candidates," *Toronto Star*, June 30, 2004 (accessed at www.thestar.com).

89. *Reference re Same-Sex Marriage*, [2004] 3 S.C.R. 698.

90. Jeffrey Simpson, "Stephen Harper just doesn't get it," *The Globe and Mail*, December 15, 2004; Peter Hogg, "So, where do we go from here?" *The Globe and Mail*, December 15, 2004.

91. For an excellent description of "*Charter*-proofing" by the Human Rights Law Section in the federal Department of Justice, see James B. Kelly, "Bureaucratic Activism and the *Charter* of Rights and Freedoms: The Department of Justice and its entry into the centre of government," *Canadian Public Administration*, 42:4 (Winter 1999). See also Hiebert, *Charter Conflicts*, 7–13.

92. James B. Kelly, *Governing with the Charter: Legislative and Judicial Activism and Framers' Intent* (Vancouver: UBC Press, 2005), 223

93. MacIvor, *Canadian Politics and Government in the Charter Era*, Chapter 5.

94. J. Scott Matthews, "The Political Foundations of Support for Same-Sex Marriage in Canada," *Canadian Journal of Political Science*, 38:4 (December 2005), 841–866.

95. Kent Roach, *Due Process and Victims' Rights: The New Law and Politics of Criminal Justice* (Toronto: University of Toronto Press, 1999). See also Joseph F. Fletcher and Paul Howe, "Supreme Court Cases and Court Support: The State of Canadian Public Opinion," *Choices* 6:3 (May 2000), 30–56.

96. MacIvor, 379–383.

97. Fletcher and Howe, "Canadian Attitudes toward the *Charter* and the Courts in Comparative Perspective," *Choices*, 6:3 (May 2000), 4–29; "Supreme Court Cases," 53; Kirk Makin, "Two-thirds back electing judges: Twenty-five years later, poll shows strong support for *Charter*," *The Globe and Mail*, April 9, 2007 (accessed at www.theglobeandmail.com, April 9, 2007).

98. *Anti-Terrorism Act*, S.C. 2001, c. 41, sections 83.18, 83.3, 83.28, and 83.01(b)(i)(A).

99. See Ronald J. Daniels, Patrick Macklem, and Kent Roach, eds., *The Security of Freedom: Essays on Canada's Anti-Terrorism Bill* (Toronto: University of Toronto Press, 2002), and Kent Roach, *September 11: Consequences for Canada* (Montreal and Kingston: McGill–Queen's University Press, 2003), Chapters 2–4. In October 2004 a judge of the Ontario Superior Court struck down part of the definition of "terrorist activity." This was the "motive clause," which distinguished terrorism from other violent crimes on the basis of a "political, religious or ideological objective or cause." *R. v. Khawaja*, [2006] O.J. No. 4245 (Ont. S.C.J.), accessed at www.theglobeandmail.com/special/audio/Rutherford.pdf, April 19, 2007. The trial ruling was subsequently overturned and the law upheld. Khawaja's trial began in Ottawa in June 2008.

100. *Application under s. 83.28 of the Criminal Code (Re)*, [2004] SCC 42; *Vancouver Sun (Re)*, [2004] SCC 43.

101. *Suresh v. Canada (Minister of Citizenship and Immigration)*, [2002] 1 S.C.R. 3.

102. See David Dyzenhaus, "The Permanence of the Temporary: Can Emergency Powers be Normalized?"; Oren Gross, "Cutting Down Trees: Law-Making Under the Shadow of Great Calamities"; and David Schneiderman, "Terrorism and the Risk Society," all in Daniels, Macklem, and Roach, eds.

103. *Secretary of State for the Home Department v. Rehman*, [2001] 3 W.L.R. 877, paragraph 62. This passage was cited with approval in the *Suresh* ruling from the Supreme Court of Canada, at paragraph 33.

104. *Emergencies Act*, 1988, c. 29.

105. Canada, Commission of Inquiry into the Actions of Canadian Officials in Relation to Maher Arar, *Analysis and Recommendations* (Ottawa: Minister of Public Works and Government Services, 2006), particularly 356; Senate of Canada, "Fundamental Justice in Extraordinary Times: Main Report of the Special Senate Committee on the *Anti-Terrorism Act*" (Ottawa, February 2007), 20–24.

106. Senate of Canada, "Fundamental Justice in Extraordinary Times," 100; Colleen Bell, "Subject to Exception: Security Certificates, National Security and Canada's Role in the 'War on Terror,'" *Canadian Journal of Law and Society*, 21:1 (2006), 76–77.

107. The appellants also referred to several other sections of the *Charter*, but the Supreme Court ruling focused primarily on section 7.

108. *Charkaoui*, paragraphs 23 and 27.

109. Laura Barnett, "Legislative Summary, Bill S-3: An Act to Amend the Criminal Code (Investigative Hearing and Recognizance with Conditions)" (Ottawa: Library of Parliament Research Branch, March 2008).

110. Beatty, 11–12.

111. Kelly, "Bureaucratic Activism and the *Charter of Rights and Freedoms*."

112. Jeremy A. Clarke, "Beyond the Democratic Dialogue, and Towards a Federalist One: Provincial Arguments and Supreme Court Responses in *Charter* Litigation," *Canadian Journal of Political Science*, 39:2 (June 2006), 293–314.

Part III

The Three Branches of Canada's Federal Government

7 Parliamentary Democracy and the Legislative Process

LEARNING OBJECTIVES

After you finish reading this chapter, you should be able to:

- *identify* the reasons for Cabinet dominance, strict party discipline, and adversarial politics in the Canadian House of Commons, and *explain* why they persist;
- *explain* how a Bill becomes law in Canada;
- *explain* the functions of the House of Commons and the Senate, and *evaluate* the performance of our national legislative institutions;
- *explain* the differences between a majority Parliament and a minority Parliament;
- *explain* and *evaluate* some of the proposed reforms to Canada's Parliament.

INTRODUCTION

If the design of the buildings is any indication, the Canadian Parliament is supposed to be a place of dignity and stirring oratory. Unfortunately, this is rarely the case. If you watch the daily Question Period, either on television or in the visitors' gallery above the chamber, you will probably see Canada's MPs behaving like rowdy schoolchildren or brawling hockey players. The spectacle is often embarrassing to the spectators and occasionally—as Dossier 7.1 reveals—to MPs themselves.

How can we explain the chasm between the dignity of parliamentary tradition and procedure, on the one hand, and the reality of heckling, booing, and partisan attacks on the other? The answer lies in the incentives imposed by the House of Commons (and, to a lesser degree, the Senate) on their members. Ideally, our parliamentary institutions would focus their members on their proper legislative functions (although only the Commons is expected to perform the last three):[1]

1. debating, improving, and ratifying the laws proposed by the Cabinet;
2. representing the electorate in the national government;
3. monitoring and controlling government expenditure (the **power of the purse**);
4. holding individual Cabinet ministers accountable for the operation of their departments; and
5. holding the entire Cabinet accountable for the conduct of the executive branch.

On October 20, 2000, shortly before the House was dissolved for the November general election, MP Lee Morrison bade farewell to the Commons. Morrison had been a member of the Reform caucus elected in 1993, whose hopes for a more open legislative process were dashed by their experiences on Parliament Hill. He had decided not to seek a third term, for reasons that are abundantly clear in his remarks:

Mr. Lee Morrison (Cypress Hills–Grasslands, Canadian Alliance): Mr. Speaker, this will probably be my last day in the House.

I will not regret leaving what has become, under Liberal management, a totally dysfunctional institution. I will not miss the thrill of

making well-researched speeches in a virtually empty room. I will not miss working long hours on irrelevant ministerially-guided committees. I will not miss the posturing. I will not miss the emasculated government members howling because they do not understand the difference between intelligent heckling and boorish noise. Perhaps it is their subconscious recognition of their own political impotence that drives them to act like hyperactive children.

I do not know what I will be doing for the next few years, but whatever it is I expect that I will be dealing with grown-ups. I am sure that it will be more useful than this past seven years that I have spent in this rubber-stamp Parliament.

I shall not look back.

While our MPs participate in the legislative process, and they work hard to represent their constituents, they do a poor job (individually and collectively) of financial monitoring and accountability. They lack the resources and the expertise to hold Cabinet ministers and public servants to account for their spending and policy decisions. They have few incentives to devote their time to the hard and often private work of executive scrutiny. Instead, they are encouraged to focus on short-term political advantage and partisan combat. Three institutional characteristics of the House of Commons (and, to a lesser extent, the Senate) exert a particularly strong influence on the behaviour of Canadian legislators:

- Cabinet dominance;
- strict party discipline; and
- adversarial politics.

In the past half-century, Canadians have lost respect for our parliamentary institutions (Chapter 2). That drop in public esteem, and the discontent expressed by many MPs and senators themselves, have provoked repeated efforts to reform our national legislative branch. Most such proposals were intended to redress the vast imbalance of power between the legislative and executive branches of government. Few have had any effect, because they left the fundamental characteristics of the institution intact. The mismatch between the ideal functions of a legislative chamber, and the institutional incentives operating on our MPs and senators, cannot be fixed by tinkering with the Standing Orders.

At the time of writing, MPs and senators enjoyed greater freedom and influence than they had since the late 1970s. But that was not the result of deliberate reforms; it was the unintended consequence of Canada's third consecutive **minority government.** In a minority Parliament, the largest party has less than half of the membership of the House of Commons. The Liberal Government elected in 2004 held 43.8 percent of the seats (135 of 308). It was defeated less than 18 months later, triggering the 2006 election that brought the Conservatives to power with 40.3 percent of the Commons (124 of 308 seats).[3] The Harper Government elected in October 2008 held 46.4 percent of the Commons. Minority governments differ from majorities—the norm in Canadian politics since 1980—in three important ways:

- First, the party in Government must win the support of at least some Opposition MPs in order to pass its legislation and fiscal measures; alternatively, a large number of

Opposition MPs must abstain from voting against the Government on confidence measures (as the Liberal caucus did during the second session of the 39th Parliament).

- Second, the Opposition parties collectively hold a majority of the seats on each parliamentary committee. If they work together, they can amend **Bills** (proposed laws) over the objections of the Government.
- Third, a Government that loses a vote on a matter of confidence must resign. This "**confidence convention**" brought down the former Liberal Government in November 2005, when a majority of MPs voted in favour of the motion that "This House has lost confidence in the Government."[4] Minority governments, unlike majorities, are vulnerable to defeat in the House; they last an average of about a year and a half, whereas majorities typically govern for roughly four years between elections. (The 2006 Harper Government lasted for two years and eight months, one of the longest minority governments in Canadian history.)

Minority governments face daily challenges, especially under the current rules of parliamentary procedure. As we will see, changes to the committee system since the 1980s have slowed the passage of legislation and occasionally paralyzed the process altogether. Constant speculation about an early election raises the political temperature in the Commons (and, to a lesser degree, in the Senate). The already partisan and adversarial behaviour of parliamentarians grows more intense. In the 39th Parliament (elected in 2006), the legislative process occasionally broke down altogether. However, this does not mean that minority Parliaments are inherently bad: the 38th Parliament, elected in 2004, performed its legislative functions well and held the executive to account more effectively than its immediate predecessors had done.

THE HISTORY AND EVOLUTION OF PARLIAMENTARY INSTITUTIONS[5]

Britain's parliamentary institutions, which Canada inherited in the nineteenth century, evolved through a long series of power struggles among the Crown, the people, and the legislature that links the two sides. The powers of the Crown are now exercised by the executive branch—both political (the Cabinet) and permanent (the federal public service)—and the judiciary. Under the *Constitution Act, 1867*, law-making powers are divided between the Crown, the House of Commons, and the Senate. A government Bill is sponsored by the Crown, represented in this case by a particular Cabinet minister, and it must be given royal assent after its adoption by both Houses of Parliament.

Like its British model, Canada's federal Parliament has two chambers. The "lower house," elected by the citizens on the basis of "representation by population," controls the public purse and holds the Cabinet to account. In Canada, as in Britain, the lower house is called the House of Commons. Most Cabinet ministers are members of the lower house. The unelected upper house is intended to serve two legislative purposes: to check the power of the Cabinet, and to give "sober second thought" to proposed laws that may have been rushed through the lower house without adequate examination.[6] Canada's upper house, the Senate, is appointed by the prime minister. Its members serve until the age of 75.[7]

King Edward I summoned the first British Parliament in 1295. The word "Parliament" is an anglicized version of the French "parlement," or "talking place." Edward invited the peers of the realm, together with representatives of the "commoners" and the Church, to the Palace of Westminster to discuss (and, he hoped, to solve) his cash-flow problem. After King John signed the *Magna Carta* ("great charter") in 1215, the Crown had to receive the consent of the leading men of the realm before imposing taxes.

England's tax base was primarily agricultural, although the towns gained economic clout as manufacture and trade grew. The economy of rural England was controlled by landed aristocrats, while the towns were run by guilds. The Church was also an economic force in its own right: its vast landholdings, and the revenues from its parishioners, made it a tempting target for a cash-strapped king. Instead of asking each individual landowner, guildmaster, and bishop for money, it was more efficient to gather them all in one place. In exchange, those assembled presented petitions to the king, asking him to address local grievances and settle disputes. The petitions were the forerunner of today's parliamentary Bills. Resolving disputes was part of the Crown's judicial power; the king, as the font of justice, moved his court around the kingdom to hear local cases. We still refer to the institution that dispenses justice as a "court."

The crowd that descended on the Palace of Westminster was too large to sit in the Great Hall, so it was divided into two separate groups: the Lords (including the bishops) and the Commons. The latter met in the chapel, where the benches were arranged in rows down the length of the building, each side facing the centre aisle. To this day, "Westminster" Parliaments use the same seating plan (see Figure 7.1).

FIGURE 7.1   FLOOR PLAN OF THE CANADIAN HOUSE OF COMMONS

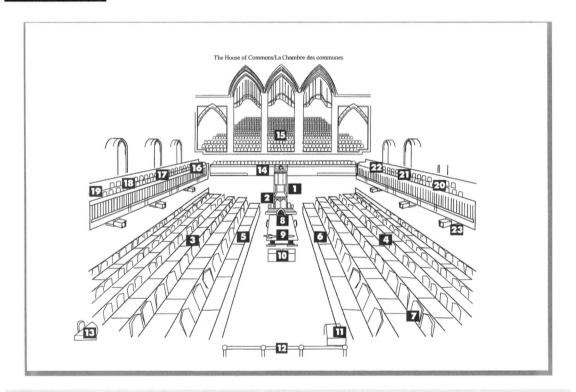

The House of Commons/La Chambre des communes

1. Speaker	**8.** Clerk and Table Officers	**16.** Official Gallery
2. Pages	**9.** Mace	**17.** Leader of the Opposition's Gallery
3. Government Members	**10.** *Hansard* Reporters	**18.** MPs' Gallery
4. Opposition Members	**11.** Sergeant-at-Arms	**19.** MPs' Gallery
5. Prime Minister	**12.** The Bar	**20.** MPs' Gallery
6. Leader of the Opposition	**13.** Interpreters	**21.** Speaker's Gallery
7. Leader of the second-largest party in opposition	**14.** Press Gallery	**22.** Senate Gallery
	15. Public Gallery	**23.** T.V. Camera

Source: © Library of Parliament/Bibliotheque du Parlement.

King Edward's first Parliament was a great success. It was repeated whenever the Crown needed money (which was quite often, especially during wartime). By 1320, the separation of the two chambers had become a permanent arrangement. By 1340, the Crown had formally conceded the "power of the purse" to the Commons. This remained the crucial bargaining chip in struggles between the Crown and the legislature. In 1376 the Commons refused to grant supply (tax revenues) to King Edward III, and it elected a Speaker to deliver the bad news.[8] Over time, the Speaker became the liaison between the Commons and the Crown. He chaired parliamentary debates, and reported their results to the king. Members of the Commons addressed their remarks to the Speaker (and not to each other), a practice that survives today. Parliamentary procedure prohibits members of the Commons (who are commonly referred to as members of Parliament, or MPs for short) to speak to each other directly; they must refer to each other in the third person, as "the Honourable Member" from a particular constituency.

By 1500, the consent of both Houses of Parliament was required for a law to take effect. Informal rules for the election of MPs had taken shape, although these were a far cry from today's **universal suffrage**—only a few wealthy men could vote, and they often chose corrupt members who took bribes in exchange for supporting particular Bills. There were no political parties in the modern sense of the word, merely loose parliamentary factions dominated by particular nobles. In the exercise of its executive functions, the monarch relied on his Privy Council. This small group of aristocrats and churchmen was not accountable to Parliament.

The kings of the Stuart dynasty (1603–1714) believed that their "divine right" to rule entitled them to govern as absolute monarchs. Unlike their Tudor predecessors (1485–1603), they treated Parliament with overt disdain. Charles I and II avoided summoning Parliament whenever possible, relying instead on other methods to raise money (some of dubious legality). When they were forced to call the MPs and Lords to Westminster, they were confronted by a Protestant majority deeply suspicious of the Catholic Stuarts. The tension boiled over in 1642, when King Charles I burst into the Commons chamber with a group of armed henchmen. They came to arrest a group of MPs who publicly opposed the King. The rebels had been tipped off, and the chamber was empty. To this day, representatives of the Crown are still forbidden to enter the Commons; Canada's governor general reads the Speech from the Throne, which opens each session of the Canadian Parliament, in the Senate Chamber. After this incident, Parliament declared war on the king. The English Civil War ended in 1649 with the execution of Charles I and the establishment of a republic.

After Charles II was restored to the throne in 1660, the Stuarts managed to avoid further bloodshed. But in 1688, Charles' brother and successor James II was forced to abdicate. Parliament and the nobility invited his daughter Mary and her husband, Prince William of Orange (the ruler of the Netherlands), to rule England and Scotland in his place. In 1689 the new monarchs accepted the *Bill of Rights,* which formally established a limited, or constitutional, monarchy and recognized Parliament as the chief law-making body in the realm. The Crown was no longer above the law; both the monarch and the Privy Council were subject to the laws made by Parliament. Privy councillors would require the support of Parliament, although there was as yet no formal mechanism to hold them accountable. Over time, the Privy Council evolved into the Cabinet: a subcommittee of the Commons and Lords that exercised the Crown's executive powers on behalf of the monarch. By the turn of the eighteenth century, constitutional convention required the monarch to give royal assent to any law passed by Parliament. (Another legacy of William and Mary, the 1701 *Act of Settlement*, is discussed in Chapter 10.)

In 1714, after the death of the last Stuart monarch, an obscure German prince inherited the British throne. Because George I spoke little English, he could not chair Privy Council meetings. In his place, the Council appointed a prime minister. Although officially *primus inter pares* (first among equals), the prime minister gradually became the dominant figure in the political executive. He chose the other members of the Cabinet (who were then formally appointed by the king or queen), he ensured that the Commons would support his Cabinet and grant supply to pay for its policies, and he advised the monarch on the exercise of the Crown's prerogative powers.

During the nineteenth century, the British House of Commons was transformed in two important ways. First, the electorate was expanded from a few wealthy magnates to most of the adult male population. Second, and resulting from the first, disciplined political parties appeared. There had been two contending factions in the Commons, the Whigs and the Tories; the former opposed arbitrary monarchical power, while the latter supported Crown prerogatives. With the expansion of the franchise, these parliamentary factions were forced to seek political support across the country. The United Kingdom was already divided into electoral districts (called **constituencies** or ridings), each of which returned one MP to Westminster. Now the two parties, renamed the Liberals and the Conservatives, had to establish political organizations in each riding, to win the support of the newly enfranchised voters. As the party organizations outside Parliament became stronger, so did **party discipline** inside Parliament—to the detriment of the institution: "the heyday for the parliamentary system was in the nineteenth century before the advent of disciplined political parties."[9]

By the late nineteenth century, Britain's Parliament had assumed its modern form. The prime minister was the leader of the party that held the most seats in the Commons. He hand-picked members of his caucus to serve in Cabinet, and kept his **backbenchers** in line with bribes and threats. The government sat at the Speaker's right side. The other party or parties in the Commons, known collectively as the Opposition, sat on the opposite side of the House, facing the government caucus. The largest party on the Speaker's left was the official Opposition, responsible for keeping the government accountable and providing a constructive alternative to the party in power. The Speaker chaired the debates and kept order in the House. The king or queen was a figurehead, with no active role in politics. The Crown's prerogative powers of appointment, legislation, and royal assent remained, but the monarch had lost the discretion to use them as he or she saw fit. The Cabinet reigned supreme.

Canada inherited this system of parliamentary government in 1867. Within 30 years a disciplined two-party system had emerged.[10] The prime minister was an even more commanding figure in Canada than in Britain, partly because the Liberal and Conservative parties were quite similar ideologically; the leaders, not party principles, became the focus of electoral campaigning. In the twentieth century the power of the political executive vis-à-vis Parliament was further strengthened by the explosive growth of the federal government and the ever-increasing complexity of public policy. Nowadays, the prime minister of Canada is as powerful domestically as any head of government in the world. Some observers argue that the very nature of our political system has been transformed: instead of parliamentary government, we now have prime-ministerial government. We will return to the question of prime-ministerial power in Chapter 8. For now, we will examine the incentives that constrain the legislative branch of government and limit its effectiveness. Then we will return to the list of functions presented at the start of the chapter, and evaluate how well the House of Commons and Senate perform each one.

THE INSTITUTIONAL INCENTIVES FOR PARLIAMENTARIANS

It was the rise of political parties that transformed parliamentary politics into party politics. Political parties were the vehicle by which political power was secured, and as these parties grew, the party leader and professional party officials began to exert considerable influence on them. The House of Commons divided and remains divided between the government party and opposition parties or between 'them' and 'us', making the institution partisan and adversarial. . . . Before parties came to dominate the House of Commons, the prime minister and ministers were accountable to Parliament but could not yet control it. Now, though they remain accountable to Parliament, they can and do control it whenever they have a majority mandate.[11]

As we saw in Dossier 1.1, institutions exert a powerful influence on the behaviour of those who operate within them. They set incentives for ambitious people who seek to advance their careers. An individual MP, no matter how determined, cannot resist those incentives for long. He or she must either give in and follow the institutional norms of behaviour, or leave Parliament. The experience of the Reform MPs elected in 1993 is instructive. Most were critical of the parliamentary system and determined to represent their ridings instead of toeing the party line. Formal critic positions were abolished, leader Preston Manning was symbolically relegated to the second row (even though the leader traditionally sits on the "front bench"), and the MPs repeatedly vowed to change the rules of Parliament. Within three years, the reverse had happened: they changed, while the rules remained intact. The unconventional caucus structure reduced Reform's effectiveness as an Opposition party, forcing them to acknowledge that "some parliamentary rules serve legitimate purposes."[12] While Reform's pledge to transform the House of Commons played a role in its electoral success, that pledge was based on a naive and simplistic approach to the institutional norms of parliamentary government.

As just mentioned, the most important of those norms are Cabinet dominance, strict party discipline, and adversarial politics. Although the three phenomena are closely related, we will discuss them separately.

Cabinet Dominance

The House of Commons is controlled by the political executive, at least when one party holds a majority of the seats. The Senate has considerably more autonomy, because it is not a confidence chamber. The Cabinet can force Government MPs to support its legislation by invoking the "confidence convention." While a lost vote rarely spells the end of a majority Government, it is a political embarrassment and damages the credibility of the party in power. As a result, prime ministers sometimes designate controversial Bills as "confidence votes," even though their defeat would not normally trigger a resignation under the constitutional conventions of parliamentary government.

Some degree of Cabinet control over the lower house is an essential feature of parliamentary systems. If the Government could not count on the support of a majority for its key measures, the business of government would grind to a halt. But that control goes further in Canada than in any other Westminster democracy.[13] In a majority government, Government Bills usually pass with few (if any) amendments and little meaningful debate. Moreover, the Cabinet has the power to issue delegated laws (such as Orders in Council and Regulations) without ratification by Parliament.[14]

Most MPs lack the independence, experience, and expertise to hold the Cabinet accountable, either individually or collectively. The high turnover of MPs from election to election weakens the Commons as an institution. Members are also overwhelmed by conflicting demands on their time and attention, which leaves little opportunity to challenge the executive. The power of the purse, traditionally an important bargaining chip for disgruntled legislators, has been reduced to empty ritual (with a few exceptions; the Harper Government's November 2008 fiscal update was condemned by all three Opposition parties, prompting them to strike a coalition agreement that would have toppled the Conservatives if Harper had not persuaded the Governor General to prorogue Parliament).

Despite its poor public image, the Senate is a more effective legislative chamber than the Commons. Because senators do not have the power to bring down a government, and they are not (yet) subject to election or re-election, they are more independent of the political executive and less constrained by party discipline. Unlike most MPs, many senators remain in Parliament for long periods of time (although this could change, as Dossier 3.4 explains); this allows them to master parliamentary procedure and the details of policy. Some new senators have years of experience in government and policy-making, whereas most MPs are policy amateurs when they first arrive on the Hill.[15]

■ Party Discipline

The term "party discipline" suggests—incorrectly—that MPs are forcibly prevented from breaking ranks, under threat of punishment. It is true that an MP, especially a government MP, who votes against his or her party on an important issue pays a high price. Any chance of a Cabinet appointment may be lost and access to key decision-makers curtailed. Prized committee assignments are taken away. When committee chairs were appointed by the prime minister (pre-2002), they risked being fired for insubordination. Projects and programs of interest to a dissident MP's constituency may be threatened. Thus, the incentive structures of Parliament reinforce party discipline in a variety of ways. It is also true that votes in the House are orchestrated by the party "whips," a term that reinforces the negative connotations of party discipline.[16]

In most cases, however, parliamentarians willingly vote with their parties.[17] There are at least five reasons why MPs generally choose to follow the party line, even if they don't fully agree with it:

1. Political parties nominate candidates, campaign to elect MPs, and help to structure the voting patterns of the electorate (Chapters 11 and 12). Consequently, most MPs are committed partisans who owe a great political debt to their local constituency associations. This enhances the "team spirit" within caucuses, while making it harder for MPs to work with members from other parties.
2. Many MPs believe that they are morally obliged to keep their campaign promises. Where a particular Bill relates directly to their party's platform, or to its core principles, they feel duty-bound to express the views of their party.[18]
3. Party discipline shields MPs from vocal and aggressive minority interests.[19] In such cases, an MP may believe that his or her party's position is a more faithful reflection of majority opinion, or he or she may simply wish to deflect the blame for offending voters on one (or all) sides of a contentious issue.[20]
4. If every member of a caucus votes with the party leadership, all of them are protected from constituency reprisals. When one or more MPs defy the whip and vote against their party, their teammates are left exposed to public criticism.[21] Therefore, backbenchers often pressure each other to toe the party line, instead of relying on caucus officers to twist arms.
5. Reporters are eager to pounce on any hint of dissension within a party caucus. Journalists' enthusiasm for reporting conflict distorts what should be a normal part of parliamentary life: the exercise of individual conscience, or constituency representation, by an individual MP. The appearance of party disunity can hurt the chances of winning the next election; no one wants to carry the blame for an avoidable defeat at the polls.

So MPs have good and positive reasons to follow the party line, despite the fact that a growing percentage of voters seem to want more independence from their elected representatives. Between 1990 and 2000, the percentage of Canadians who believed that MPs should not always vote along party lines rose from 72 to 77 percent.[22] Having said that, reactions to recent floor-crossings in the House of Commons suggests that we prefer the idea of party disloyalty to the reality (Dossier 7.2). On occasion, party leaders do resort to overt discipline. Former Prime Minister Chrétien, who led three majority governments, used to keep rebellious backbenchers under control by threatening an early election in which they might lose their seats.[23] The result was "a compromise of ministerial accountability, a lack of significant parliamentary input into developing legislation, and a perception that government was far less open than it could, or should, have been."[24] (A less direct result was the introduction of fixed elected dates; see Dossier 12.1.)

When party discipline becomes excessive, it prevents government MPs from openly challenging the Cabinet. Under a majority government, it also denies Opposition MPs a meaningful opportunity to propose or amend Bills. Party discipline constrains the autonomy of MPs at all stages of the legislative process. There is one exception: government MPs can sometimes express dissenting views in the weekly **caucus** meeting. Although these confrontations between ministers and backbenchers go on behind closed doors and their influence is difficult to measure, ministers may be forced to delay, amend, or withdraw proposed legislation by concerted opposition from their MPs. The overwhelming majority of Liberal MPs surveyed in 1999 reported that caucus was an effective forum for internal policy debate.[25] However, the influence of caucus should not be overstated. Although one former minister claimed that "strong caucus opposition to any government proposal imposes an absolute veto on that proposal,"[26] recent changes to House and Cabinet timetabling have reduced the power of government backbenchers. Whereas caucuses used to meet on the day before Cabinet, so that caucus feedback could be incorporated into Cabinet discussions of proposed legislation, Cabinet now meets on Tuesday mornings and the caucuses on Wednesdays.[27] In addition, anecdotal evidence suggests that Prime Minister Harper and his Office imposed tight controls on the Conservative caucus; current Government MPs have fewer opportunities to speak freely than their predecessors enjoyed.[28]

Although past prime ministers reminded their Cabinets to pay attention to the views of government MPs,[29] ministers have little incentive to do so. Staying in Cabinet requires the goodwill of the prime minister, not the Government caucus. As noted earlier, senators are less subject to party discipline; consequently, they normally operate in a less adversarial way. This helps to explain why Senate committees often produce better amendments and policy analyses than their counterparts in the Commons.[30]

DOSSIER 7.2 Crossing the Floor

In Parliamentary parlance, "crossing the floor" refers to an MP (or senator) who leaves the party that he or she was elected or appointed to represent. Despite the power of party discipline, floor-crossing is not uncommon. Between 1921 and 2005, an average of two or three MPs left their caucuses every year (a total of 229). Some were expelled from caucus for political or personal reasons; most of these eventually joined another caucus, while the rest sat as Independent MPs until the next election.[31] The most attention-getting cases involve MPs who jump from one party to another without being pushed. For example, Nova Scotia MP Scott Brison—who had run for

the leadership of the federal Progressive Conservative Party in May 2003—crossed to the Liberals in December 2003 because he opposed the PC merger with the Canadian Alliance (Chapter 11). Brison was appointed a Parliamentary Secretary by Prime Minister Martin.

Since 2000, the amount of movement in the Commons has increased markedly. Whereas there were an average of 27 switches per decade between 1921 and 2000, there were 50 defections between January 2001 and June 2007. The most controversial cases involved two MPs who jumped from the Official Opposition straight

(continued)

into the federal Cabinet. In May 2005, Conservative MP Belinda Stronach shocked Ottawa when she joined the Liberal Cabinet. Stronach was one of the best-known MPs in the House, largely because of her personal wealth and celebrity. In 2003 she played a minor role in the merger negotiations between the Progressive Conservatives and the Canadian Alliance. Once the new party was launched, Stronach ran for the leadership despite a complete lack of political experience. She hired the best strategists and organizers that money could buy, and placed a surprisingly strong second to Stephen Harper. She ran for the party in her home riding of Newmarket-Aurora in 2004 and narrowly beat Liberal candidate Martha Hall Findlay (see Dossier 11.2).

Stronach seemed uncomfortable in the Conservative caucus. She was an outspoken critic of the party's policies on social issues, including same-sex marriage. Less than a year after her leadership bid, Stronach told friends in the Liberal Party that she could no longer work with Harper. They seized the opportunity to lure her across the floor, knowing that the minority Liberal Government was at risk of losing a vote on its budget. They also recognized that the defection of the party's best-known female MP would raise doubts about Harper's claim that the new Conservative Party was more moderate than the Canadian Alliance. On May 17, two days before the scheduled vote on the budget, Stronach walked into a press conference with Prime Minister Martin. She announced that she had joined the Liberal Party, and he announced that Stronach would be his new minister of Human Resources Development. When both denied that the Cabinet position was a reward for saving the minority government from a likely defeat in the House, the assembled reporters burst into derisive laughter—an unusual event at a prime ministerial press conference.

Stronach became the target of ridicule and personal attacks, including some offensively sexist remarks from former Conservative colleagues.[32] Forty Conservative MPs publicly endorsed a Private Member's Motion to ban floor-crossing in exchange for a Cabinet post, a position that was consistent with public opinion on the issue.[33] Stronach's switch also raised an important legal question: does crossing the floor in exchange for a Cabinet position violate conflict of interest rules? According to the "Conflict of Interest Code for Members of the House of Commons," MPs may not derive financial benefits from their public service.[34] Because an appointment to Cabinet brings a substantial increase in pay and benefits, some observers have questioned whether an MP who crosses the floor in exchange for a ministerial position should be found in breach of the code.

The issue flared up again in February 2006, when the brand new Harper Cabinet was sworn in. Among the MPs arriving at Rideau Hall for the ceremony was David Emerson, a Liberal MP and former minister in the Martin Government. Emerson was one of Paul Martin's "star" candidates in the 2004 election. He had been the CEO of a forestry company. His business background, and his expertise in forestry, made him the obvious candidate to work on the softwood lumber dispute with the United States. He ran for re-election in 2006 as a Liberal, boasting on election night that he would be "Harper's worst nightmare." A few weeks later, he accepted the International Trade portfolio in the Conservative Cabinet. Emerson became Foreign Affairs minister in May 2008.[35] Liberals howled with outrage, as did many voters in Emerson's riding of Vancouver-Kingsway. They had voted for a Liberal candidate in 2006, just as Stronach's constituents in Newmarket-Aurora had voted for a Conservative in 2004, only to see their MP defect to the opposing team.

The Ethics Commissioner investigated the Emerson case, at the request of three Opposition MPs. He found that neither the prime minister nor Mr. Emerson had violated the conflict of interest rules appended to the Standing Orders of Parliament. This conclusion was partly based on a technicality: Parliament was not sitting at the time when the Conservative Cabinet was sworn in, so there was no improper influence on Mr. Emerson's performance of his legislative duties.[36] It also reflected the fact that a PM is acting in his or her executive capacity

(continued)

when he or she appoints his or her Cabinet, not in a legislative capacity. To that extent, the Members' Code did not apply.

Despite his finding that the Code had not been breached, Mr. Shapiro expressed concern about the impact of Emerson's actions on public perceptions of politics: "Fairly or unfairly, this particular instance seems to have given many citizens a 'sense' that their vote—the cornerstone of our democratic system—was somehow devalued, if not betrayed."[37] He also implied that, had he been asked to review the Stronach case, he might have reached a different conclusion: "Clearly, if the Prime Minister were to approach a member with an offer of a Cabinet position with the sole intent and specific purpose of acquiring that member's vote directly linked to a parliamentary proceeding existing at that time, such conduct would be inappropriate and unacceptable."[38] While it appears that Stronach's Liberal friends approached Prime Minister Martin on her behalf, and not vice versa, she was certainly appointed to Cabinet 48 hours before a critical vote on the budget—i.e., "a parliamentary proceeding existing at that time."

Shapiro's findings, while controversial, were correct: the Standing Orders do not prohibit floor-crossing. Neither does the *Parliament of Canada Act*, which expressly exempts sitting MPs who take up Cabinet portfolios from its own conflict of interest provisions. Some critics of Stronach and Emerson argued that they should have resigned from Parliament to run in

by-elections under their new party colours before being sworn in to Cabinet. Their refusal to do so was perfectly legal, because the *Parliament of Canada Act* is silent on the issue. But it was not always thus. Between 1867 and 1931, the *Senate and House of Commons Act* required every MP who accepted a Cabinet post to resign his or her seat and win a by-election before taking up his or her new office. In practice, Government MPs often ignored this rule; but it was strictly applied to Opposition MPs who crossed the floor in exchange for a seat at the Cabinet table.[39]

The by-election requirement was repealed in 1931, over the objections of some Opposition MPs. One, Liberal Ernest Lapointe, made the following observation: "If a government goes to another group in the house and invites to the cabinet a member who has been elected by his constituents to oppose the government, and that gentleman is willing to accept the invitation, I object to his transferring his electors with him to the government side."[40] Given that all major-party candidates are identified by party label on the ballot, one could argue that they have made a bargain with their voters: vote for me as a member of Party X, and I will sit in the House of Commons with the other MPs from that party.[41] Breaking that bargain carries serious political risks. Brison and Stronach were re-elected as Liberals, but few other floor-crossers have been as fortunate.[42] (Neither Emerson nor Stronach sought re-election in 2008.)

Adversarial Politics

In the House of Commons, political debate often reduces complex issues to two polar opposites. Like the soccer players depicted in Chapter 3, MPs are driven by team spirit. Each side firmly believes that it deserves to win. The contending teams bicker and belittle each other, instead of working together on constructive solutions. Adversarial politics is also encouraged by the confidence convention, which pits the governing "team" against an Opposition determined to bring it down; by the constant clash between the government's desire for speedy passage of its Bills and the constitutional prerogative of Parliament to review legislation and financial measures;[43] and by the prospect of the next election.

The very architecture of Parliament encourages mutual hostility. Government and Opposition MPs confront each other across a centre aisle, their physical disposition signalling

Prime Minister Harper stands during Question Period as other members look on in the House of Commons. (CP/Tom Hanson)

that there are two opposing sides to the issue at hand and little if any common ground. The most basic rules and procedures of parliamentary debate encourage this clash of opposing teams. The objective of parliamentary debate is not to reach a compromise solution, but to present diametrically opposed points of view. The adversarial character of the House shapes its most basic operating rules and procedures.

It would be wrong to attribute the public conflict among parliamentary caucuses entirely to the rules of Parliament. While institutional norms and structures do have a powerful influence on individual and group behaviour, there are other reasons for the adversarial nature of the Commons. As we have seen, most MPs are loyal partisans. They genuinely believe that their team has the best answers to the public questions of the day, and they wish to support and assist their teammates. In a high-pressure situation such as Question Period (QP), these emotions come to the fore in boisterous and sometimes undignified ways. Perhaps because the overwhelming majority of Canadians—84 percent, according to a 2000 survey[44]—have never belonged to political parties, they find these noisy partisan displays puzzling and distasteful. In a 1997 survey, fully 90 percent of respondents agreed with the statement that "Canadian parties bicker too much"; 59 percent accused the parties of dividing the country, instead of bringing people together.[45]

The public perception of MPs as brawling combatants is somewhat exaggerated. In private, many parliamentarians from different parties like and respect each other.[46] Because the television cameras in the Commons chamber focus on the member who is speaking at a given moment, viewers rarely witness the off-camera chats between members of differing partisan stripes. News reporters prefer to cover conflict, not cooperation; consequently, Canadians receive a distorted picture of the Commons. Journalists emphasize the fireworks provided by

Question Period (QP),[47] which is held every day when the House is in session (Dossier 7.3). Members of the Cabinet, including the prime minister, are grilled by Opposition MPs about the public issues of the day—in particular, those that make the Government appear to be incompetent or corrupt (which are rarely the most important in the long term).[48] Symbolically, at least, QP gives the Opposition a chance to hold the government accountable to the House and to the electorate. Indeed, a recent document from the Treasury Board Secretariat (TBS) described QP as "arguably [Parliament's] most powerful instrument of accountability."[49]

Question Period is valued by Opposition MPs and journalists because it forces ministers, day in and day out, to respond to their critics. It is the best opportunity for Opposition parties to mobilize the public and draw media attention to problems in government policy and performance.[50] As we will see in Chapters 8 and 9, the top levels of the executive branch—both political and permanent—spend much of their time protecting the prime minister from embarrassing questions by Opposition MPs. Chapter 14 describes the close working relationship between the Opposition and the news media, who share and exploit juicy revelations about government mistakes. A Cabinet minister or senior public servant who exposes the prime minister to embarrassment in QP risks his or her career.

However, there are good reasons to question the claim that QP is an effective tool of accountability. As a former public official pointed out, "There are few instances where sustained opposition attacks have severely damaged a government or caused it to change its policy."[51] Experienced ministers can evade questions by ridiculing the Opposition, a skill at which former Prime Minister Chrétien excelled. Central agencies often refuse to share detailed information about policy and administration with Opposition MPs,[52] although they may be forced to comply with Access to Information requests filed by parliamentarians or journalists.[53] Over the long term, the entire House of Commons pays a price for short-term victories in QP: while journalists love to see ministers squirm, the media coverage of Question Period captures MPs in their most adversarial and abrasive temper and further erodes public support for parliamentary institutions.

DOSSIER 7.3 Question Period

At 2:15 p.m., four times each week, 11:15 on Fridays, the Speaker of the House of Commons calls for oral questions. The leader of the official Opposition rises in his or her place, is recognized by the Speaker, and begins the day's grilling of the government. Nowhere else in the world, even in the "Mother of Parliaments" in the United Kingdom, is the entire government held to daily account in such a fashion, being subjected to questions about virtually any of its programs and policies.

Amid applause and shouts of encouragement from his or her caucus colleagues, and catcalls and heckling from those opposite, the Opposition Leader calls on a member of the Cabinet to respond to some matter of urgent and pressing need, some great calamity that has befallen Canada since the day before, a question about which the Government has received no official notice.

Usually to similar noise and action, that Cabinet minister, or the prime minister, will rise and respond, stating that whatever has exercised the member opposite has been solved already, will be taken under advisement, or, more often, is not really of any consequence or importance to any except those who have been less favoured by the voters. The rhetorical barbs fly in both directions, reminding us why the benches of the House are set two sword-lengths apart. The process of question and answer, supplementary and reply, is repeated 10 to 12 times, in this apparent free-for-all that is the pinnacle of government accountability in Canada—the daily Question Period.

According to the rules and to tradition, the Speaker of the House controls Question Period; this is known as QP to the gaggle of insiders who seemingly make it the central concern of their life. The Speaker will see a member rising in his

(continued)

or her place and call on the MP to direct a question to the government. Any Member can be called on, in any order, from any party. To those watching the live broadcasts at home this appears to be what is occurring.

But for those on the floor of the House, or in its galleries, there is another reality. While many Members may indeed be rising in their places, the Speaker is calling them not as he sees them, but from lists supplied by the House Leaders of the two opposition parties. These lists are often amended as QP progresses, changes called to the Speaker from House Leaders—who sometimes appear more like baseball managers signalling their on-deck batters and runners to bunt, steal, or run—by waving arms, pointing, nodding, and stepping into the fray as the moment dictates. . . .

So, even though it may appear to be mayhem to the uninitiated, the degree of management that goes into the planning of Question Period is considerable. The effort to get the right "spin" onto an issue, to attract the attention of the media and of the government, consumes a great deal of time for a large number of people every day the House is in session, an effort that goes unnoticed, perhaps intentionally so, by those who watch from the outside.

Source: Reprinted with permission from Michael Kalnay, "Managed Mayhem: Question Period in the House of Commons," *Parliamentary Government*, 8, no. 4 (Summer 1989), 3–6.

Summary: The Institutional Incentives for MPs

Collectively, these three norms of behaviour create a clear set of incentives for anyone who wants to become an MP, and for MPs who wish to secure leadership positions in their caucuses or Cabinet:

- To become a candidate, you must first become a member of a political party and demonstrate your attachment to its principles and goals. Your contacts with other party members, and your own experiences within the party organization, usually generate a strong sense of "team spirit" that shapes your behaviour and priorities. There are exceptions, mostly "star" candidates recruited from outside the active party membership because of their prominence in some other field of endeavour.

- Once elected, your chances of re-election rest on the fortunes of your party, not on your own individual efforts.[54] Similarly, your odds of either remaining in government or becoming part of a future government depend on the effectiveness of your leader and the popularity of your party as a whole. The fate of the "team" largely determines the political longevity of each individual member.

- A government MP who wishes to become a Cabinet minister—which most do[55]—must be a "team player," supporting the Cabinet and following the dictates of the prime minister with loyalty and enthusiasm. To publicly defy the prime minister is to risk immediate punishment and the loss of a promising political future. The turmoil in the Liberal caucus that followed the 2000 federal election can be attributed to the clash between two competing incentives: to stay loyal to incumbent Prime Minister Jean Chrétien, in the hope of an immediate promotion to Cabinet, or to support aspiring Prime Minister Paul Martin and wait for a Cabinet appointment in his future government.

- An Opposition MP who seeks a higher position in his or her caucus must be a vigorous critic of the government and a loyal supporter of the party leadership (at least in public). However, the enforcement of party discipline is less powerful on the Opposition benches. Without the carrot of immediate appointment, or the stick of the confidence convention, an Opposition leader must rely on team spirit and personal persuasion to win over rebellious MPs. Historically, Opposition leaders have been more vulnerable to revolts from their caucuses and extraparliamentary organizations than prime ministers.

The institutional incentives for MPs do not reward independence of spirit, serious legislative work, policy innovation,[56] or service to the constituency. Nonetheless, the latter is a high priority for most MPs: even if it does not guarantee re-election[57] or promotion, constituency work is often the most satisfying part of the job. No matter how dedicated their pursuit of a particular policy or how well informed their arguments, backbench MPs (both government and Opposition) have little if any power to shape legislation. Even Private Members' Bills (PMBs), which should give backbenchers direct law-making power, are usually given a low priority in House proceedings, although the Parliament elected in 2006 was an exception to this rule (Dossier 7.5). While government MPs exercise some influence in the secrecy of the caucus room, they pay a high price for criticizing Cabinet decisions in public. Most MPs serve only one or two terms before leaving the Commons, either voluntarily or through electoral defeat. Just as they start to figure out the arcane rules of parliamentary procedure, and master one or two policy fields, they return to private life.

Having examined the incentives for Canada's parliamentarians, we will now return to the five functions listed at the start of the chapter:

1. debating, improving, and ratifying the laws proposed by the Cabinet;
2. representing the electorate in the national government;
3. monitoring and controlling government expenditure (the power of the purse);
4. holding individual Cabinet ministers accountable for the operation of their departments; and
5. holding the entire Cabinet accountable for the conduct of the executive branch.

We will discuss each function in turn.

THE LEGISLATIVE PROCESS

Law-Making in the House of Commons

Before a Bill can become law, it must pass a series of parliamentary votes and reviews. The process is described in Dossier 7.4.

DOSSIER 7.4   How a Bill Becomes Law in Canada

The standard procedure for adopting a government Bill—let's call our hypothetical Bill C-x—is as follows:

- *First reading:* The sponsoring minister asks leave of the House to present Bill C-x, "An Act Respecting Y." The prefix C- before the number (e.g., C-68) means that the Bill originated in the Commons. A few government Bills are introduced in the Senate; they are designated by the prefix S- (e.g., S-2). Any Bill that requires the expenditure

of public funds must originate in the Commons. The motion for first reading is a formality; there is no debate, and the House almost always assents. After first reading, the Bill is printed in both official languages and distributed to all MPs. The newly numbered Bill is placed on the Order Paper for future debate. An Order Paper lists all the items of business that could be considered by the House according to an established order.

(continued)

- *Second reading:* On a day determined by the House leaders of the official parties (those with 12 or more MPs), Bill C-x is debated for the first time. Only the principle of the Bill may be debated at second reading; the details are left to later stages of the process. The sponsoring minister makes a speech defending the Bill, explaining its provisions and outlining the problem or problems the Bill is designed to address. The Speaker then recognizes the Official Opposition critic assigned to the minister's department. He or she presents his or her party's response to the Bill, followed by the critics for the other Opposition parties. Other MPs may take part in the debate if they so choose. That choice usually depends on the relevance of the issue to their particular party or constituency, or the extent of their personal expertise on the subject matter of the Bill. After all of the MPs who wish to speak have had an opportunity to do so, the Speaker recognizes the sponsoring minister to respond to the critics and close the debate. Then the House votes on Bill C-x. When the government controls a majority of the seats in the Commons, its Bills are approved as a matter of routine. Once the House has voted in favour of a Bill at second reading, the principle of the Bill may not be changed at subsequent stages of the legislative process.
- *Committee stage:* The Bill is automatically sent to the appropriate standing committee of the House of Commons. Every department of the federal government is mirrored by a standing committee. If Bill C-x were sponsored by the minister of Justice, for example, it would be assigned to the Standing Committee on Justice, Human Rights, Public Safety and Emergency Preparedness. On occasion, Bills are sent to special legislative committees. The committee may hold public hearings on the Bill, summoning witnesses to testify about its possible effects. Typically, witnesses include officials from the responsible department, policy experts, and representatives of advocacy groups affected by the Bill. After the hearings end, the committee examines the Bill clause by clause. It considers amendments proposed by its members, or by witnesses, relying on advice from officials of the sponsoring department.[58] When the committee finishes its deliberations, it prepares a report to the House, including any amendments that were approved by a majority of the membership. While they have the power to amend Bills, committees in a majority Parliament rarely adopt amendments that the sponsoring minister does not approve.[59] In a minority Parliament, where the governing party holds fewer than half of the seats on each committee, some amendments conflict with the Government's preferences. These amendments may not change the principle of the Bill, as adopted by the House at second reading, nor can they increase the total cost of implementing the Bill.[60] Ideally, the committee submits a consensus report with the agreement of all four parties; in practice, one or more Opposition parties often submit dissenting reports that reject the views of the government majority on the committee.[61]
- *Report stage:* The House debates the Bill as amended by the committee. Other amendments may be proposed from the floor by MPs who are not committee members. If the sponsoring minister considers a proposed amendment to be "friendly"—if, in other words, he believes that it would improve the legislation—he can accept the amendment without further ado. "Unfriendly" amendments are put to a vote of the House. Under a majority government, the House rarely accepts a change that does not meet with the Cabinet's approval; in a minority situation, a united Opposition can prevail over the objections of the minister (or initiate a bargaining process to reach a compromise).[62] If amendments are made to Bill C-x at report stage, either by the minister or by the House, the Bill is revised and reprinted.

(continued)

- *Third reading:* The revised Bill is put to the House for a final debate and vote. As soon as it passes at third reading, the Bill leaves the Commons and goes to the Senate.
- *Senate:* The upper house follows a similar procedure to the Commons, with one major exception: because MPs cannot speak on the floor of the Senate (and vice versa), government Bills are sponsored by the government leader in the Senate. The Senate has the power to veto most Bills.[63] This power is rarely used—only five times between 1945 and 1999[64]—but its existence requires the government to take proposed Senate amendments seriously.[65] Because a Bill must be passed in the identical form by both Houses, Senate amendments must be either accepted by the Commons or withdrawn. If the Senate amends Bill C-x and the Government refuses to accept those amendments,[66] the leadership of the two Houses must hammer out a compromise before the Bill can proceed. Such showdowns have become more frequent since the 1980s.[67] After the Bill is passed by the Senate at third reading, it goes to the governor general for royal assent.
- *Royal assent:* The Crown's representative signs the Bill into law. The new law may take effect immediately or at a later date specified in its text.

As we will see in Dossier 7.5, some elements of this procedure may be varied with the consent of the Cabinet and a majority of the House. Since an amendment to the Standing Orders in 1994, the government may refer a Bill to the appropriate standing committee before second reading.

The Purpose of Parliamentary Debate

The vast majority of legislation originates in the executive branch. At first reading, the government serves notice to the House, and through the House to the country, that the Bill has been placed on the legislative agenda. Substantive debate begins with second reading, at which time the Bill is discussed in principle. The government also signals the importance it attaches to the Bill, and how strictly party discipline will apply to its MPs in the voting process.

Even in a minority Parliament, debate is not intended to change the minds of MPs.[68] (According to one former MP, "the purpose of most debates in the House of Commons is not to enlighten but to beat one's opponents to death by dullness."[69]) The real audience is outside the House. Government and Opposition MPs try to persuade the public that the Bill should be passed or defeated and that it resolves—or fails to resolve—a problem of pressing importance to the national community. The debate is therefore symbolically important, even though votes in the House may not change as a consequence.

The Committee System

A great deal of the work of Parliament is carried out in committees. Indeed, one of the reasons that there are often so few members in the Chamber is that many of them are attending committee meetings. It is not uncommon for there to be 50 or even 60 meetings during the course of a week, and 20 to 25 meetings on a particular day.[70]

After (occasionally before) second reading, Bills are sent to committee for detailed, clause-by-clause examination. Whereas the whole House debates each government Bill for an average of eight hours, a committee can spend "many dozens of hours examining a Bill, hearing from witnesses and considering amendments."[71] Committees perform two important functions in the legislative process:

- Within the limitations mentioned in Dossier 7.4, they can amend the text of a Bill. If the Government disagrees with an amendment, it can attempt to restore the original wording at Report Stage. The amending power is particularly significant in a minority Parliament, a fact that caused the Harper Government considerable frustration.
- By holding public hearings, either in Ottawa or across the country, committees give advocacy groups and others who may be affected by the proposed legislation direct access to the policy process.[72] In so doing, they help to legitimize the legislative process and the laws that it produces.

There are five types of Parliamentary committee:

1. *Committee of the Whole:* The entire House becomes a committee. The strict rules of parliamentary debate are relaxed, and members may discuss issues in a freer and less formal way. "Members are not required to be in their assigned seats, but can congregate around the Table . . . this facilitates intimacy and an exchange of views by participants."[73] The Commons usually goes into Committee of the Whole during the examination of supply Bills (see "Parliament and the Public Purse").

2. *Standing Committees:* Specialist committees are established at the beginning of a Parliament (i.e., as soon as the Commons and Senate reconvene after a general election) and remain in place until Parliament is dissolved for a general election. Each department of the federal government is monitored by a Commons standing committee (see Table 7.1). Because the Senate is roughly one-third the size of the Commons, its standing committees are few in number and their mandates are broader. Each standing committee has extensive formal powers and responsibilities: to examine matters referred to it by the House, including Order-in-Council appointments, Bills, and pressing policy issues; to report its findings and recommendations back to the House; to hold public hearings, summon witnesses, and "send for" all necessary documents; and to delegate these tasks to any subcommittee that it sees fit to establish.[74] In the 38th Parliament there were 20 standing committees; that number rose to 25 after the 2006 election.

3. *Legislative Committees:* These are temporary Commons committees, established for the sole purpose of examining a particular Bill. They are struck immediately after second reading and dissolved as soon as they have reported the Bill back to the House with or without amendments. Legislative committees were first created in 1985, on the recommendation of the Special Committee on House of Commons Reform (the McGrath Committee). In practice, the membership of legislative committees overlapped considerably with that of the standing committees in the same policy field, and the difficulty of scheduling meetings for dozens of standing and legislative committees created delays in the legislative process. Since the early 1990s, legislative committees have been rare. One notable exception is the Legislative Committee on Bill C-30, which is discussed in Dossier 7.5.

4. *Joint Committees:* Standing or special committees with members from both Houses of Parliament. They include the Committees on the Scrutiny of Regulations and Official Languages.

5. *Special Committees:* These committees are established to study and report on a particular issue, and then dissolved. Some are composed entirely of MPs or senators; special joint committees include members of both Houses. There was only one Special Committee of the Commons in 2008, which was devoted to the Canadian mission in Afghanistan.

The partisan composition of each Commons (and Senate) committee is roughly proportional to the distribution of seats in the House as a whole. Under a majority government, each committee has a majority of members from the government party, with representation from

HOUSE OF COMMONS STANDING COMMITTEES, JUNE 2008*

NAME OF COMMITTEE

Aboriginal Affairs and Northern Development

Access to Information, Privacy and Ethics

Agriculture and Agri-Food

Canadian Heritage

Citizenship and Immigration

Environment and Sustainable Development

Finance

Fisheries and Oceans

Foreign Affairs and International Development

Government Operations and Estimates

Health

Human Resources, Social Development and the Status of Persons with Disabilities

Industry, Science and Technology

International Trade

Justice and Human Rights

Liaison

National Defence

Natural Resources

Official Languages

Procedure and House Affairs

Public Accounts

Public Safety and National Security

Status of Women

Transport, Infrastructure and Communities

Veterans Affairs

*Source: House of Commons Standing Committees. From: http://cmte.parl.gc.ca/cmte/CommitteeList.aspx?Lang=1&PARLSES=391&JNT=0&SELID=e2_. Reprinted with permission from the House of Commons. Retrieved May 2008.

the Opposition parties roughly in proportion to the size of their caucuses. In a minority Parliament, the Opposition parties collectively control a majority of the seats, although the governing party retains the largest single share. In the Parliament elected in 2006, each Commons committee had 12 permanent members: five Conservatives, four Liberals, two from the BQ, and one from the NDP. Before 2002, committee chairs were appointed by the prime minister. Under the new rules, each committee elects a chair and two vice chairs at the beginning of each session of a new Parliament. Most, but not all, committee chairs belong to the governing party, while at least one vice chair is drawn from the Opposition parties.[75]

Under majority governments, Canadian parliamentary committees are among the weakest in any Westminster system.[76] As we saw at the beginning of this chapter, backbench MPs have repeatedly demanded a more independent and meaningful role for standing committees. In response, successive governments have agreed to changes in the Standing Orders to give committees more powers. None of these reforms worked as well as its creators hoped, because they did not address the real constraints on committees: Cabinet dominance, party discipline, and most MPs' lack of policy expertise. Adversarial politics can be less pronounced on committees than in the House as a whole—but not always. In 2007 and 2008 several committees were paralyzed (or shut down altogether) as tensions between the Government and the three Opposition parties boiled over. The crisis was triggered, in part, by a leaked Conservative manual for committee chairs. The manual explained how to manipulate witness lists, circumvent Opposition motions, and prevent the use of committee hearings as a forum for Opposition MPs to criticize the Government.[77]

The 2007–08 committee breakdown was unprecedented in its scale, but even the normal adversarial tensions on committees can weaken their impact. For example, Justice Gomery's report on the Sponsorship Scandal found that the Public Accounts Committee is an effective tool of accountability—but only when its members refrain from indulging in "partisan hyperbole."[78] To make matters worse, the membership of Commons committees is often rotated; this prevents them from developing an *esprit de corps* and an institutional memory.[79]

A final constraint on standing committees is the inclusion of Parliamentary Secretaries among the Government members. As discussed in Chapter 8, Parliamentary Secretaries are Government MPs who assist specific Cabinet ministers with their duties. At committee, the Parliamentary Secretary is responsible for "sharing departmental information . . . representing the Minister's views and addressing political issues which may arise."[80] Allowing MPs with quasi-executive functions to sit as voting members of supposedly independent committees is highly unusual in a parliamentary democracy.[81] It has been an irritant for Opposition MPs since at least the 1980s—especially under former Prime Minister Martin.[82]

When the various reforms to the Commons committee system were adopted in the 1980s and 1990s, no one seems to have anticipated their potential impact on a minority Parliament. As it turns out, that impact has been highly significant. Perhaps the best example is the 1994 change to the standing orders, which allows the House to refer a Bill to committee before second reading. This opportunity is important for two reasons. First, the committee can amend the principle of the Bill, not just the technical details by which that principle will be achieved. Second, the various parties have not yet committed themselves to a particular position on the Bill during House debate. The full potential of this amendment was not realized until after the 2006 election, when the Opposition parties found themselves in a position to determine which Bills would go to committee after first reading. However, as Dossier 7.5 explains, the Cabinet can let the amended Bill die if it disagrees with the committee's work.

DOSSIER 7.5 The *Clean Air Act* (Bill C-30), 2006–07

In October 2006, then-Environment Minister Rona Ambrose introduced the Harper Government's long-awaited legislation on climate change and air pollution. Well before Bill C-30 was tabled, the Government had attracted widespread criticism for its handling of the environment issue. Ambrose had announced that Canada could not and would not meet its CO_2 reduction targets under the Kyoto Protocol. She, and other members of the Cabinet, had also made statements about climate change that

some critics took to mean that they rejected the scientific consensus on the issue.[83] The delayed introduction of C-30 gave the Opposition an opportunity to pre-empt the Government: in May 2006, Liberal MP Pablo Rodriguez introduced a Private Members' Bill, C-288, "An Act to ensure Canada meets its global climate change obligations under the Kyoto Protocol." By the fall of 2006, the environment was an important policy concern for Canadians—especially in Quebec, where the Conservatives needed to

(continued)

consolidate their 2006 gains. The stage was set for a parliamentary showdown.

Predictably, the unveiling of Bill C-30 prompted howls of outrage from interest groups and the Opposition. All three Opposition parties vowed to vote against the Bill at second reading. If this happened, C-30 would be dead. The Government had several options, none of which was particularly attractive: stall the Bill on the Order Paper, hoping for a more cooperative attitude in a few months' time; push ahead with Second Reading and hope that the Opposition would take the blame for killing the *Clean Air Act*; or designate C-30 as a confidence matter and call an election immediately following its defeat. The latter option would conflict with the principle of fixed election dates (Dossier 12.1) and pose serious political risks, given the unpopularity of the Government's approach to the environment in Ontario and Quebec.

In November, NDP Leader Jack Layton offered the Government a way out of its political trap: his party would support a motion to refer the Bill to a Commons committee before second reading. The committee's members, representing all parties in the House, would be free to re-write the Bill in its entirety. This strategy had its own risks, principally the likelihood that the rewritten Bill would be unacceptable to the Government. But since it was the only hope for passing any kind of Government legislation on the most pressing issue of the day, the Government agreed and the Bill was referred to committee in early December. (The Government had already announced plans to issue regulations under existing legislation that would have the same effect as several provisions in Bill C-30; the use of delegated legislation would have cut Parliament out of the process altogether, as explained on p. 331.)

Because the Standing Committee on the Environment was already preoccupied with Bill C-288, a special legislative committee on Bill C-30 was created. It had 13 members: six Conservative MPs (one of whom was the chair), four Liberal MPs, two BQ MPs, and one NDP MP. The committee proceeded to rewrite the Bill.[84] In effect, the Opposition parties formed a separate sub-committee, meeting with environmental groups to canvass their suggestions for amendments. Midway through this process, the prime minister replaced Ambrose with John Baird in the January 2007 Cabinet shuffle.[85]

Before the committee finished its work, Bill C-288 passed third reading in the Commons—a rare feat for a Private Member's Bill. If adopted by the Senate, the Bill would force the Government to publish a strict emission-reduction plan no later than August 2007. If the Government failed to comply with the Kyoto targets, it would face lawsuits from environmental groups. Conservative suggestions that C-288 was a purely symbolic gesture, meant to distract voters from the Liberals' failure to implement Kyoto when they were in power,[86] were belied by the Government's vitriolic attacks on the Private Member's Bill. In April 2007, Environment Minister Baird told a Senate committee that complying with C-288 would plunge the Canadian economy into recession—a claim that was dismissed as "fear-mongering" by Opposition politicians.[87] Despite these tactics, Bill C-288 received Royal Assent and became law on June 22. Two months later the Government issued the plan required by the Bill, even while insisting that Kyoto compliance would inflict severe damage on the Canadian economy.[88] One advocacy group, Friends of the Earth, launched a lawsuit against the Government in 2008, trying to force compliance with the law; at the time of writing, no ruling had been issued.[89]

Meanwhile, the Legislative Committee on Bill C-30 submitted its report in late March. It had adopted more than 100 amendments to C-30, most of which the Government rejected.[90] Some amendments were relatively minor—e.g., changing the title to the *Clean Air and Climate Change Act*—while others directly contradicted the Government's policy on the environment. Among the latter were provisions to implement the greenhouse gas emissions and carbon credit trading systems in the Kyoto Protocol; the replacement of the "Clean Air" section with a new "Climate Change Action" section

(continued)

containing mandatory greenhouse gas reduction targets with specific dates; and strong measures to control "large industrial emitters," including oil-sands extraction facilities in northern Alberta.

By declaring the revised Bill unacceptable, the Government found itself in an unusual situation. On the one hand, the new version could have helped it to shore up its popularity by addressing the most important issue of the day in a manner that appealed to many voters. On the other hand, the Government had already ruled out those very measures that had the greatest resonance with voters, especially in Quebec. Some observers speculated that the Government was more afraid of upsetting the oil and gas industry in Alberta, where all of the seats were held by Conservatives, than of further alienating environmentally minded voters in central Canada. Whatever its motives, the Government made it clear that it would take no further action on the revised Bill C-30. The *Clean Air and Climate Change Act* would be allowed to die on the Order Paper whenever Parliament was **prorogued** or dissolved.[91]

Opposition MPs pressed the Government to bring the Bill back to the House for debate. In May 2007, the NDP introduced a motion to force the Government to bring the Bill back to the House; the motion passed by a vote of 155 to 121, but the Government ignored it.[92] The Bill duly died in August 2007 when the prime minister prorogued Parliament, ending the First Session. To no one's surprise, it was not reintroduced in the Second Session.

The saga of Bill C-30 illustrates both the potential and the limitations of referring Bills to Committee before Second Reading. On the one hand, it gives backbench MPs a real opportunity to craft legislation—including Opposition MPs, at least in a minority Parliament. The Liberal, BQ, and NDP members of Parliament on the legislative committee worked together fairly harmoniously, at least until the Liberals tabled dozens of amendments at the last minute. On the other hand, the Government's refusal to move the revised Bill forward demonstrates that a change in the Standing Orders cannot reduce the Cabinet's control of the legislative process.

As Dossier 7.5 illustrates, a minority Cabinet has relatively little control over Commons committees. That is particularly true when the committee is chaired by a Government MP, because the chair only votes in the event of a tie. The heightened adversarialism arising from constant pre-election jockeying often paralyzed the legislative process altogether during the 39th Parliament. The minority Conservative Government was determined to enact its campaign platform into legislation, over the objections of the three Opposition parties. Prime Minister Harper was reluctant to compromise on controversial Bills, such as his "law and order" amendments to the *Criminal Code*. The Justice committee held up these Bills for months, and eventually deleted numerous provisions with which the Opposition parties disagreed.[93]

The Harper Government's frustration with Opposition tactics shows how the transition from Opposition to Government can alter one's perceptions. The 2006 Conservative platform contained a promise—identical to previous Liberal pledges—to "Make all votes in Parliament, except the budget and main estimates, 'free votes' for ordinary Members of Parliament" and "Increase the power of Parliament and parliamentary committees to review the spending estimates of departments and hold ministers to account."[94] At the time of writing, only part of the second promise had been kept. As a final note, the Opposition MP who initiated the change to the Standing Orders allowing committees to elect their own chairs was none other than Stephen Harper.

Private Members' Business

Although the government has the sole right to introduce **money Bills**, backbenchers may propose legislation that does not require significant new expenditures. MPs and senators can introduce Private Members' Bills (PMBs) and motions, thereby initiating policy debate separately from the Cabinet. Many backbenchers take their legislative projects seriously, despite the rarity of their enactment into law. In the 37th and 38th Parliaments, 221 PMBs were debated for at least one hour apiece at second reading. Only 16 (or 9 percent) passed through the entire legislative process and received royal assent.[95] Partly in response to this waste of time and effort, the Standing Orders for Private Members' Business were amended in 2005. Whereas the rules had previously limited the number of "votable" PMBs to a handful, the current Standing Orders designate all such Bills as "votable" unless the Standing Committee on Procedure and House Affairs decides otherwise. This change is significant: a "votable" item receives three hours of debate in the House at second reading; if a majority of MPs vote in favour, it will proceed through the normal legislative process. If adopted by the Senate, it will become law.

Votable items are debated at second reading for up to three hours, after which they must be put to the House for a decision. The three hours of debate are not scheduled on consecutive days; votable PMBs bounce around the Order Paper in an arbitrary and often unpredictable way. A PMB that passes at second reading is referred to a committee, which must report back to the House within 60 sitting days. (The committee may request a 30-day extension, but if it fails to report within that time the Bill is deemed to have been reported without amendment.) Report stage is limited to one and three-quarter hours (also on random days) and must be immediately followed by third reading. If the PMB is adopted at third reading, it goes to the Senate.

In the 39th Parliament, Opposition MPs put the PMB process to new uses. Liberal MP Pablo Rodriguez and NDP Leader Jack Layton tabled PMBs to force the Government to implement the Kyoto Protocol (Bills C-288 and C-377, respectively; Bill C-288 is discussed in Dossier 7.5).[96] Former Prime Minister Paul Martin, who retained his seat in the Commons after resigning the Liberal leadership, sponsored a PMB (C-292) to implement the Kelowna Accord, a deal he had negotiated with the provinces, territories, and Aboriginal groups in 2005. That Bill passed and received Royal Assent in June 2008. These PMBs appear to have been designed to embarrass the Conservatives into honouring commitments made by the previous Liberal Government. Other PMBs were intended to provoke debate on policy issues other than the Cabinet's five priorities, or perhaps to forestall Government legislation by placing another Bill on the Order Paper first.[97] (Only one Bill on a given subject can be considered by the House in a given session of Parliament.)

▪ Sober Second Thought: The Legislative Role of the Senate

The Senate was created to perform a legislative role similar to that performed by the House of Lords in Britain, though the two institutions have different social and political foundations. The appointed Senate was intended to be a chamber of "sober second thought," whose experienced members—free from the political constraints and short-term perspective imposed by the need for re-election—could improve the details of legislation after it was passed by the Commons. It was also intended to ensure that minority interests—regional, linguistic, or political—were adequately protected in the legislative process.[98] For example, its committees are required by Senate rules to seek the views of provincial and/or territorial governments on Bills that directly affect their particular region.[99]

The Senate is held in low esteem by most Canadians, and it has been the target of frequent criticism by the Conservative Government. In all the rhetoric about "undemocratic" **patronage** appointments and lazy senators, one fact is usually overlooked: the Senate and its committees play a valuable role in the legislative process. Senators review and amend legislation, using their own expertise and their excellent committee work to improve flawed Bills. Their relative independence from the Cabinet, and their freedom from constituency work and electoral considerations, allows them to operate in a more consensual and deliberative way than MPs. Without attracting much public attention, the Senate has quietly taken on several important tasks that the Commons cannot or will not do. These include scrutinizing regulations, examining Bills for potential conflicts with the *Charter of Rights,* and hearing from witnesses who might not have had an opportunity to appear before the more rushed Commons committees.[100]

Senators are well aware that legislation originating in the House already carries the stamp of democratic approval. As a result, they rarely challenge decisions made by their elected colleagues in "the other place." Although the Senate's lack of public legitimacy has made it the less powerful of the two chambers, its formal powers are almost identical to those of the House of Commons. It has an absolute veto on ordinary legislation and a suspensive veto on constitutional amendments.[101] While money Bills cannot be introduced in the Senate, the upper house can defeat money Bills initiated in the Commons. For the reasons just explained, however, the Senate rarely vetoes legislation passed by the Commons.

The upper house is more willing to amend Government Bills, although it amends fewer than 10 percent of them.[102] Both Houses must agree on the version of a Bill to be passed at third reading; where a discrepancy arises, as when the Senate amends a Bill after passage by the Commons, it must be resolved. When the government accepts a Senate amendment, it asks the Commons to vote for a motion to amend the law as the Senate sees fit. If the government rejects the amendment and the written reasons for it that the Senate appends to the changed Bill, it rarely if ever resorts to the formal dispute-resolution mechanism: a conference of the two houses (in practice, the MPs and senators on the committees that reviewed the Bill). Instead, the Leader of the Government in the Senate usually holds informal discussions with his or her opposite number in the Commons, and perhaps with the sponsoring minister, to try to work out a compromise. If no compromise can be reached, the Senate usually—but not always—defers to the Commons. (See the discussion of Bill C-16 in Dossier 12.1.)

In some cases, the Senate can stall the progress of Government legislation for several months. The *Federal Accountability Act,* the centrepiece of the Harper Government's legislative agenda, passed all of the stages in the Commons in 10 weeks. It received first and second reading in the Senate within one week. Then a Senate committee studied the Bill for months, finally submitting its report in late October. The Bill was reported back to the House of Commons with several amendments in early November. Two weeks later, the Commons sent it back with several of the Senate amendments deleted. The Senate initially refused to accept the deletions; it finally gave in on December 8, and the Bill received Royal Assent on the December 12. In total, the Senate spent about three times as long on Bill C-2 as the Commons—although part of that time overlapped with the summer recess, when neither House was sitting.

The dispute over Bill C-2 reflects a broader pattern in relations between the two legislative chambers. When governments change, opposing majorities in the House and Senate are almost guaranteed by the length of Senate tenure. Because senators currently serve until they reach the age of 75, a new governing majority in the House usually faces an opposition majority in the Senate. Such was the case after the 1984 and 1993 elections, when the caucuses of the former governing parties were suddenly dominated by senators. Partly for partisan reasons, these senators refused to defer to the Commons in the usual manner. Instead, they flexed their legislative muscles to block (but not defeat) controversial government legislation.[103] The

| TABLE 7.2 | SENATE STANDINGS, OCTOBER 2008 |

PARTY/OTHER DESIGNATION	NUMBER
Liberal	58
Conservative	21
Progressive Conservative	3
Independent New Democrat	1
Independent	4
Undesignated*	1
Vacancies	17
TOTAL	105

*Senator Anne Cools had been appointed as a Liberal; she subsequently crossed to the Progressive Conservatives. By 2008 she was no longer a member of the Conservative caucus, although she refused to designate herself officially as an Independent.

Source: The Parliamentary Website (www.parl.gc.ca), accessed online May 2008. Reproduced with the permission of the Minister of Public Works and Government Services, 2008, and courtesy of the Law Clerk & Parliamentary Counsel of the Canadian Senate.

problem took care of itself over time, as Opposition senators retired and the prime minister appointed members of his own party to replace them.

The partisan standoff was renewed after the 2006 election, which pitted a fragile Conservative minority government against a Liberal Senate majority. Table 7.2 displays the party standings in the upper house in October 2008.

Unlike previous prime ministers, Harper did not rush to fill Senate vacancies with supporters of his party. During his first two years in office, he only appointed two Conservative senators.[104] Otherwise, he left a rapidly growing number of vacancies unfilled. Harper was constrained by a promise in the Conservative platform to "creat[e] a national process for choosing elected Senators from each province and territory."[105] (See Dossier 3.4.) Shortly after the 2008 election, Harper signalled that he had rethought this approach and would start appointing Conservative senators in order to speed the passage of his legislation.

As mentioned previously, the Senate's principal contribution to the legislative process occurs in its committees. These are typically "more knowledgeable and more familiar with the subjects and the potential impact of legislation" than their Commons counterparts.[106]

> Membership on committees in the Upper House is stable, thus allowing members to develop expertise and experience in their areas of responsibility. Free of the constraints imposed by constituency duties, Senators are able to devote more time to committee work. Partisanship on Senate Committees is less pronounced and their actions and recommendations less threatening to government. Collectively, these attributes allow committees of the Senate to offer useful insights into problems facing Canadian society and to suggest creative ideas for their solution. Even some of the Senate's harshest detractors readily acknowledge the useful role performed by the Upper Chamber's committees.[107]

Three standing committees merit particular attention here. The first is the Standing Joint Committee for the Scrutiny of Regulations (SJCSR), which reviews the detailed regulations made by public officials in the process of implementing the laws passed by Parliament. It is composed of 10 MPs and five senators, and co-chaired by a government member and an Opposition member. The senators tend to be the most active members of the committee, because they are not preoccupied with more politically sensitive matters (such as constituency work). Although the SJCSR can examine only about one-quarter of the thousand or so regulations issued each year, its analyses carry considerable weight because it has the power to recommend that a particular regulation be revoked. Under the Standing Orders, a recommendation to revoke a regulation is deemed to have been adopted by Parliament unless a minister files a formal objection within 15 sitting days after the report has been tabled.[108] The SJCSR has used this power sparingly, usually in relation to potential violations of the *Charter of Rights*. However, the threat of revocation can often persuade the executive branch to amend regulations where necessary.[109]

The Standing Committee on National Finance often does a more thorough job of reviewing the annual Main Spending Estimates than the Commons committees—despite the fact that the Commons, and not the Senate, holds the "power of the purse."[110] The Standing Committee on Human Rights was established in May 2001.[111] Its mandate is to ensure that federal legislation conforms to the *Charter*—a task that it shares with the Standing Committee on Legal and Constitutional Affairs—and to the international human rights instruments that Canada has signed since 1945.[112]

Several of its members also belonged to the Special Senate Committee on Bill C-36, the *Anti-Terrorism Act*. That special committee heard from a multitude of witnesses and produced a thoughtful and thorough report on the issues raised by the new police powers. Although the government had used its majority in the Commons to push the Bill through, despite serious concerns about its impact on rights (particularly those of particular minorities), the all-party report of the Special Senate Committee forced the minister of Justice to accept some (though not all) of its amendments.[113] Other special committees have tackled difficult and complex policy issues ranging from post-secondary education to the legalization of marijuana.[114] Although the government of the day is under no obligation to enact their recommendations into law, the high quality of these reports often exerts a long-term influence on public policy. Unlike the members of Royal Commissions and other formal inquiries, senators remain directly engaged in the legislative process after their reports are issued. They can call upon ministers and public servants to follow up on their recommendations, and use their leverage to ensure that their proposals are at least considered.[115]

Most Canadians are unaware of the contributions made by Senate committees. The upper house rarely attracts the attention of the news media and the public. The exceptions to this neglect are usually unflattering; most news stories about the Senate concern conflicts between the two Houses of Parliament (which should be treated as a normal part of the legislative process), or scandals over the conduct of individual senators (e.g., persistent absenteeism). The fact that many senators can claim an expertise in public policy unmatched by most MPs, and the diligence with which they carry out their legislative and investigative work, are rarely mentioned.

In a recent analysis of the upper house, C.E.S. Franks suggested that Canada has not one but three upper houses: the real Senate, which makes important but little-known contributions to the legislative process; the Senate portrayed by its critics, a failed institution that serves no useful purpose (especially in the area of regional representation); and a hypothetical reformed Senate, which changes its shape with the fashion of the moment.[116] The current vogue, as noted earlier, is for a Triple-E Senate. We will discuss the pros and cons of this proposal at the end of this chapter.

REPRESENTING THE ELECTORATE IN THE NATIONAL GOVERNMENT

Conflicting Notions of Representation

Public evaluations of MPs' representativeness focus on two separate issues: Who are they, and what do they do? The answers to these questions are important, notwithstanding the earlier comments about the relative powerlessness of MPs in the legislative process. When MPs are perceived as effective representatives, the House has the legitimacy to support and to challenge the executive branch. If they are perceived as unrepresentative and out of touch with important subcultures, the legitimacy of Parliament suffers.

The debate over the meaning and purpose of parliamentary representation reflects the conflicting political values discussed elsewhere in this book. Three specific conflicts may be identified:

1. Should MPs speak for the national political community as a whole, or for their particular regions? In the trustee model of parliamentary representation, members of the Commons are elected to give voice to the collective will of the nation. They have more information and experience about national issues than their constituents do, and they should exercise their own judgment instead of taking orders from the voters. The opposing view, which has particular appeal for Western populists, treats MPs as delegates from their ridings, whose speeches and votes should reflect the majority opinion of their electors.[117]

    Neither model reflects the reality of the Canadian House of Commons. MPs generally vote according to party, not their own judgment or the will of their constituents. On occasion, conflicting duties to the party and the region place an MP in an intolerable situation. When a Government MP votes against his or her party on a motion that could force the resignation of the prime minister, constitutional convention requires that he or she be removed from the caucus. In June 2007, for example, Nova Scotia Conservative MP Bill Casey voted against his Government's budget because it contained an equalization formula that was less favourable to his province than the Atlantic Accord negotiated with the previous Liberal Government (Chapter 4). Having voted against the Cabinet on a matter of confidence, Casey was promptly expelled from the Conservative caucus. The delegate model is both impractical and unconstitutional, in the sense that it undermines the disciplined parties on which effective Cabinet government ultimately depends.

    In any case, the division of legislative responsibility between two Houses of Parliament assigns different representational tasks to the Commons and the Senate. The former represents the national electorate. It is elected, at least in theory, on the basis of representation by population ("rep by pop," for short). Although each MP serves a defined geographic area—or, more precisely, the people who live within it—he or she is expected to be more than simply a mouthpiece for local concerns. Collectively, members of the Commons make binding decisions in the national interest. Meanwhile, the Senate was intended to represent the various regional populations—as distinct from provincial governments—in the national legislative process. As we have seen, few Canadians believe that the upper house has been effective in this regard. In reality, the Senate has often used its legislative powers to amend proposed laws in order to make them more sensitive to the particular needs of one or more regions.[118]

2. Do parliamentarians represent only the territorial interests of their constituency, or do they also represent personal (i.e., non-territorial) characteristics? Whom does a Liberal Jamaican-Canadian female MP from Toronto really represent in Parliament: Visible minorities? Women? The Liberal Party? The Government? Her particular constituency? The entire Toronto area? The province of Ontario? Any or all of the above? The claim that she represents women or visible minorities reflects the **numerical** or **pictorial** approach to political representation. From this perspective, parliamentary institutions should be microcosms of the Canadian electorate, with the same balance of demographic characteristics found in the broader population. The claim that she represents the Liberal Party, and the government that it controls, reflects the partisan model of representation. Most candidates for the House of Commons are long-time members of their

respective parties who are wholeheartedly committed to the goals and principles of their political "teams." Responsible Cabinet government requires that the political executive maintain the support of the House, which means in practice that government back-benchers must vote in favour of the initiatives put forth by their party leaders. While partisan representation is the strongest institutional norm faced by most MPs, its legitimacy among voters has diminished in recent decades.

The claim that the female MP from Toronto represents her region—in this case, the City of Toronto or the Province of Ontario—reflects the territorial approach to representation. She is expected to promote the interests of her region, by lobbying for increased government spending in that area and by expressing local concerns about proposed legislation. Finally, the claim that she represents her constituency reflects both a territorial and a functional understanding of representation. She must speak on behalf of her entire riding within Parliament, while working hard for individual constituents who request her assistance.

In practice, every MP has to juggle at least three conflicting representational tasks: partisan, territorial, and functional. Female MPs, and those who belong to particular demographic minorities, face additional demands for representation. In recent years, the Senate has become the more "representative" House in the pictorial sense. Prime Ministers Chrétien and Martin used their appointment power to increase the numbers of female, visible-minority, and Aboriginal senators.[119] Whereas the proportion of women in the House of Commons has been stuck at around 20 percent since 1997, no such "glass ceiling" is apparent in the Senate; recent prime ministers have increased the percentage of women in the upper house to a little over one-third of the active membership.[120] In a similar vein, members of visible minorities and Aboriginal Canadians make up a considerably higher proportion of the Senate than the Commons.[121]

3. Is the whole idea of representative democracy outdated? In other words, should we continue to elect MPs to speak and vote on our behalf, or should we take advantage of new technologies to make public decisions for ourselves through referenda and initiatives? As we saw in Chapter 2, some Canadians advocate direct democracy as the solution to a parliamentary system that fails to meet the expectations of many Canadians. The success of the Reform Party in the 1990s was based, in large measure, on its critique of party discipline and Cabinet dominance. Many Reform voters favoured the delegate model of representation, condemning MPs who follow the party line as traitors to the people who elected them. At the very least, direct democracy advocates argue that voters should have the power to recall MPs who do not represent their interests effectively (see Dossier 2.4). However, the political force of arguments for populist reform (or bypass) of Canada's legislative institutions has diminished in the past few years, as the Reform Party morphed into the Canadian Alliance and then the Conservative Party; the latter's statement of principles makes no mention of plebiscitary democracy or recall votes.

■ The House of Commons: Rep by Pop?

The allocation of seats in the House of Commons is supposedly based on the principle of representation by population ("rep by pop"). This means that every MP should represent roughly the same number of constituents. In practice, there are significant deviations from the principle of "rep by pop" (see "Drawing the Electoral Map" in Chapter 12). Some MPs represent huge and sparsely populated rural ridings, while others struggle to serve rapidly growing suburban populations. The 10-year period between redistributions puts MPs from British Columbia,

TABLE 7.3 **AVERAGE CONSTITUENCY POPULATION SIZE AND SHARE, PROVINCES AND TERRITORIES, 2006**

PROVINCE/TERRITORY	AVERAGE CONSTITUENCY SIZE	SHARE OF CANADA'S POPULATION (%)	SHARE OF COMMONS SEATS
Newfoundland/Labrador	72 210	1.6	2.3
PEI	33 963	0.4	1.3
Nova Scotia	83 042	2.9	3.6
New Brunswick	73 000	2.3	3.2
Quebec	100 615	23.8	24.4
Ontario	114 720	38.5	34.4
Manitoba	82 029	3.6	4.5
Saskatchewan	69 154	3.1	4.5
Alberta	117 513	10.4	9.1
BC	114 263	13.0	12.0
Yukon	30 372	0.1	0.3
NWT	41 464	0.1	0.3
Nunavut	29 474	0.1	0.3
CANADA	102 639	100.0	100.0

The numbers in this table were calculated by the author, using the 2006 Census figures for provincial and territorial populations and the number of Commons seats for each jurisdiction.

Alberta, and Ontario at a disadvantage relative to their colleagues from provinces with stable or shrinking populations. They must deal with ever-increasing requests for assistance, without additional resources for constituency work. Table 7.3 compares the average population per constituency across the provinces and territories, and compares each jurisdiction's share of the House of Commons to its share of the national population.

The Conservative Government took steps in 2007 to create additional seats in the three fastest-growing provinces. By introducing a Bill to add seats in some provinces, it sparked protests from provinces whose Commons representation would shrink in relative terms. Table 7.4 compares each province's share of Commons seats under the 2004 redistribution to its share under the projected 2014 formula. It shows that most of the proposed changes are modest, with the important exception of Quebec. Nonetheless, the implications of a relative loss of Commons seats are significant because most Cabinet ministers are drawn from the ranks of MPs (Chapter 8).[122]

Regional Representation in the Senate

The need for sober second thought was not enough to justify a second legislative chamber in Canada. (Nor was it important enough to sustain provincial second chambers, which have now disappeared from the central and eastern provinces and were never constituted in the West.) For the Fathers of Confederation, the Senate was the product of a political compromise without which the country might never have come into being.[123] The Maritime colonies wanted assurances that their perspectives would not be drowned out by the larger Commons

	SEATS, 2004 (%)	SEATS, 2014 (%)	DIFFERENCE (PERCENTAGE POINTS)
Newfoundland/ Labrador	2.3	2.1	−0.2
PEI	1.3	1.2	−0.1
Nova Scotia	3.6	3.3	−0.3
New Brunswick	3.2	3.0	−0.2
Quebec	24.4	22.7	−1.7
Ontario	34.4	35.2	+0.8
Manitoba	4.5	4.2	−0.3
Saskatchewan	4.5	4.2	−0.3
Alberta	9.1	10.0	+0.9
BC	12.0	13.0	+1
Yukon	0.3	0.3	0
NWT	0.3	0.3	0
Nunavut	0.3	0.3	0
CANADA	100.0	100.0	

delegations from Ontario and Quebec; the latter insisted that it must be over-represented in the upper house, to protect the francophone population against the ever-growing English majority. The Fathers of Confederation looked to the American Senate for inspiration.[124] The Senate, unlike the British House of Lords, was a federal chamber within which each state, regardless of its population, had two representatives. At first, American senators were indirectly elected by their state legislatures. Since 1911, American senators have been directly elected by the voters in their respective states.

Yet the Canadian Senate, while it was meant to reflect the same federal principles as its American counterpart, differs in important ways from the American model. First, Canadian senators are not selected by provincial legislatures or governments; they are appointed by the prime minister, without consulting the provincial governments.[125] Second, Canadians opted for equal representation by region rather than equal representation by province. Thus, in 1867, Ontario, Quebec, and the Maritimes were each given 24 Senate seats. When a 1915 constitutional amendment recognized Western Canada as a senatorial region, it too was assigned 24 seats, divided equally among the four western provinces. Representation for Newfoundland in 1949 and for the two northern territories in 1975 was added to the initial regional allocation of seats. In 1999 the new Territory of Nunavut also received a Senate seat; this brought the total number of senators to 105.

Table 7.5 displays the idiosyncratic distribution of Senate seats among the provinces. British Columbia, Alberta, and Ontario are the most under-represented provinces in the existing Senate. These provincial inequities are defended on the ground that the Senate provides for equal regional representation, but even regional equality in the Senate takes some strange twists. The West, for example, is under-represented in the Senate relative to its share of the national population; the region has 30 percent of the national population (according

TABLE 7.5 | DISTRIBUTION OF SENATE SEATS, 2007

PROVINCE	NO. OF SENATE SEATS	POPULATION PER SENATOR*
Newfoundland/Labrador	6	84 200
Prince Edward Island	4	34 000
Nova Scotia	10	91 300
New Brunswick	10	73 000
Quebec	24	314 400
Ontario	24	506 700
Manitoba	6	191 400
Saskatchewan	6	161 400
Alberta	6	548 400
British Columbia	6	685 600
Yukon	1	30 400
Northwest Territories	1	41 500
Nunavut	1	29 500

*Population figures based on 2006 Census; rounded up or down to the nearest hundred for clarity.

to the 2001 Census) but only 23 percent of the Senate seats. Atlantic Canada, with less than 8 percent of the national population and almost 29 percent of the Senate seats, is the primary beneficiary of Senate representation based on regional equality, a principle that was jettisoned in any event when Newfoundland's Senate seats were added to rather than drawn from the preexisting Maritime allotment.

In June 2006, Senator Lowell Murray tabled a proposed amendment to the *Constitution Act, 1867,* which would have added 12 seats to the Senate—all from the West, and all but two from British Columbia and Alberta. The proposal was referred to the Special Senate Committee on Senate Reform, which issued its report in October 2006. The majority of Committee members disagreed with the proposal to recognize British Columbia as a separate "region" for the purpose of Senate membership, but they endorsed the idea that the rapid population growth in the two westernmost provinces justified greater representation for British Columbia and Alberta in the Senate.[126]

The Senate's perceived failure to represent the regions is not solely the result of its unequal composition. Its lack of democratic legitimacy, combined with partisanship—which, although weaker than partisanship in the House of Commons, is still an important institutional norm—have prevented the upper house from expressing the distinct concerns of Canada's regions. Behind closed doors, government senators join their Commons colleagues in lobbying for the interests of their provinces or territories. But this representative role, like their legislative role, goes unnoticed by most voters.

The Representation of Nonterritorial Groups

Historically, most MPs have been white males from professional and business backgrounds. Although the demographic composition of the national and provincial legislatures is changing, it does not fully reflect the diversity of Canada's population. The under-representation of women in the Commons has been a matter of concern since the 1970s (see Chapter 12). More recently, there have been complaints about the scarcity of visible-minority and Aboriginal MPs, and MPs with disabilities.[127]

The proportion of women and visible minorities in Parliament is not just an issue of abstract fairness or "political correctness." While there are no guarantees, it is sometimes argued that a "critical mass" of female legislators (15 percent or higher) can raise the level of debate and produce better legislation.[128] At 22 and 34 percent respectively, women in the Commons and Senate surpass this threshold. But those who wish to represent Canadian women in more than a numerical way face a number of obstacles. They are divided along party lines, constricted by party discipline, and disproportionately concentrated in "touchy-feely" Cabinet portfolios and standing committees (the "pink-collar ghetto" of public policy).[129]

Some women have brought a strong feminist sensibility to Canadian politics. Others reject feminism and refuse to identify themselves as spokespersons for Canadian women in general. The situation of women in the House of Commons illustrates a central flaw in the numerical or pictorial approach to representation: unless the designated "representatives" actively seek to promote the interests of "their" groups, however they define those interests, they are little more than "tokens." It can be argued that some male MPs, such as the NDP's Svend Robinson (former MP for Burnaby–Douglas),[130] have been more effective advocates of gender equality than the nonfeminist women in the House.

■ Casework: The MP as Constituency Representative

While there is some conflict among the various understandings of parliamentary representation, few MPs have any doubt about their importance as constituency representatives. Constituency service has two dimensions:

1. The MP is an ombudsman[131] for individual constituents who become entangled in disputes about pensions, Employment Insurance, passports, agricultural subsidies, and a myriad of other program areas in which the federal government plays a role. This is the **"casework"** aspect of parliamentary service.
2. MPs lobby the government for program spending and public services that will benefit their constituencies as a whole. Examples include public works, job-creation funds, and the location of federal government offices outside Ottawa.

Most parliamentary candidates have extensive backgrounds in volunteer community service, in addition to their partisan activities.[132] Many are inspired to run for public office as a result of their community involvement. At least half of all MPs cite constituency service as the most important factor in their initial decision to seek election.[133]

On average, most MPs devote significantly more time to constituency service than to any other aspect of their jobs, including legislative work and policy development.[134] Even those who were motivated to run because of other factors, such as partisanship or policy interest, quickly become active ombudsmen. There are at least three reasons for the emphasis on constituency work:

- First, MPs fear the electoral consequences of neglecting their constituents. There is some evidence that dedicated service boosts the odds of re-election,[135] although this "personal vote" does not become an important factor until after the first two terms in office.[136] Nonetheless, most MPs believe that "a failure to engage in district work can kill members politically."[137]
- Second, MPs whose Cabinet ambitions or policy proposals are thwarted can still find job satisfaction in helping their constituents. Changing government policy is a slow process with no guarantee of success, but cutting through red tape on behalf of a voter brings instant gratification to both parties.

- Third, constituency service is not constrained by party discipline. It is true that government MPs have more frequent access to ministers, which can make it easier to resolve particular cases. But in general, Cabinet ministers and public servants assist all MPs without discrimination on the basis of party.

PARLIAMENT AND THE PUBLIC PURSE

The established procedures for handling supply in the House of Commons are based on two fundamental principles. If it is to continue with its activities, Government must have some assurance that its requests for funds be answered by certain fixed dates. Parliament, on the other hand, must be assured reasonable opportunity to examine these requests before they are granted. The first principle recognizes the need for an efficient, smoothly functioning government, the second the importance of accountability, a central tenet of parliamentary democracy.[138]

As we have seen, the lower house in a Westminster Parliament has the constitutional right to control the public purse. However, the Crown retains the power to initiate spending and revenue measures. Under sections 53 and 54 of the *Constitution Act, 1867*, money Bills and taxes must be *proposed* by a member of Cabinet, *recommended* by the governor general, and *approved* by the House of Commons. The process by which Parliament approves the Cabinet's tax and spending plans is divided into two parts: Ways and Means motions, which authorize the Crown to collect revenues; and Supply motions, which authorize spending on the hundreds of different programs and services provided by the federal government.[139] The spending approved by Parliament takes two forms: the annual Main Estimates, which must be approved by May 31 of each year, and two subsequent sets of Supplementary Estimates, which allow the government to alter its original spending plans (within limits) in response to unforeseen events. The first set of Supplementary Estimates must be passed before December 10, and the second before March 26.[140]

Because public finance is crucial to the operations of government, majority Governments carefully control the Business of Supply—the process by which the Government asks Parliament to appropriate (or authorize) the funds required to meet its financial obligations. This control takes two forms. First, the deadlines are strictly enforced in the Chamber (under the normal rules of debate, and in Committee of the Whole) and in standing committees. Second, the government ensures that its proposed allocation of funds among particular priorities remains unchanged.[141] While the current procedures give the executive branch greater stability and predictability in its financial arrangements, they have deprived the House of Commons of one of its key constitutional functions.[142] The situation is quite different under a minority government, which does not control the House or its Committees.

Ideally, the Business of Supply allows MPs to develop expertise about the machinery of government. It also provides an opportunity to hold the political and permanent executives accountable to the electorate for their policies, their spending plans, and the overall expenditure of tax dollars. Because MPs have the final word on public spending, their advice should be sought early in the budget process; that advice should be based on full and complete information, to which the parliamentarians apply their own experience and expertise in public policy.[143] None of these ideal conditions exists in Canada. The first principle described in the above quotation has triumphed over the second: the quest for administrative efficiency has all but eliminated Parliament's power to hold the executive accountable for its use of public funds.

- Every year, on or before March 1, the Main Estimates are tabled in the Commons and referred to the appropriate standing committees. Each committee must report back to the House no later than May 31. If committee members miss the deadline, or even if they ignore the Estimates altogether, they are deemed to have approved the Estimates without amendment. As a result, there is little incentive for committee members to devote scarce time and energy to reviewing the government's spending plans.[144] Committees may not increase the amount allocated to any item; only the Crown can propose new expenditures. Nor can committees reallocate funds from one vote to another.[145] Because of these restrictions, and the competing demands on their time, few committees devote serious effort to the Estimates.[146]

- The fiscal year is divided into three "supply periods," ending on December 10, March 26, and June 30. For each period, the government tables an *Appropriation Act* authorizing its overall expenditure. These general spending measures, unlike the detailed Estimates, are handled in Committee of the Whole (see "The Committee System" on page 221), which usually disposes of them within a few hours.[147] This process may be admirably efficient, but it does not permit meaningful deliberation or accountability.

- In recent years, committees have been given more opportunity to participate in the formulation of future spending plans. The pre-budget consultations conducted by the Standing Committee on Finance are the most important part of this process; other standing committees also propose new spending initiatives in their policy reviews, which may be taken into consideration by the government as it crafts the next year's budget. The pre-budget work of committees is an important opportunity for interest groups and individual Canadians to express their views and lobby for their spending priorities; in 2001, for example, the Finance Committee heard from almost 250 witnesses.[148]

However, the actual influence of the committee reports seems to be limited, especially in a majority Parliament. Few MPs understand the technical details of public finance,[149] whereas public servants have years of experience, an intimate knowledge of past and present policy, and extensive control over the flow of information. They may also have a vested interest in particular spending priorities and the means to defend them against the most determined opposition. In short, they have no incentive to provide clear information to Parliament.[150]

Widespread dissatisfaction with the current Estimates process has provoked repeated calls for greater Parliamentary control over public spending. Whenever a particularly troubling instance of fiscal mismanagement comes to light—such as the enormous cost overruns in the federal long gun registry, or the Sponsorship Scandal (Dossier 8.2)—MPs wonder whether, "had they seriously reviewed Estimates, they could have identified the problem earlier and pressed for cost controls."[151] (See Dossier 7.6.) In his recommendations to improve government accountability, Justice Gomery called on the government to level the playing field by giving committees more time and resources to carry out their scrutiny of public spending. The 2006 *Federal Accountability Act* created the position of Parliamentary Budget officer. Part of the mandate of this position is to assist committees in their examination of the Estimates.[152]

DOSSIER 7.6 Justice Gomery on the Estimates Process[153]

The Estimates have two functions. First, they are major policy documents. The Government's spending plans and annual Budget documentation express the Government's priorities, the emphasis it has chosen to place on different programs, and how it has decided to respond to the needs and challenges facing Canada and the Canadian people. Second, the Estimates are essential documents for control of the public purse. Since parliamentary votes of funds define the amounts and purposes that constrain government spending, Parliament, for effective control of the public purse, must assure itself that the Government respects the constraints

(continued)

on spending authorized by the appropriation acts. Assurance that the Government has complied with the statutes and other authorities governing each parliamentary vote of funds is the first step in the audit process by the Auditor General and in accountability to Parliament for financial administration.

Members have limited time to fulfill their unlimited obligations to constituency and party, their roles in debate and in Question Period in the House, and their duties as committee members. If MPs who are part of the executive or who hold special responsibilities (e.g., Leader of the Opposition or party Whip) are removed, only about 210 MPs are available to hold the Government accountable in the Estimates process. Each backbench member sits on at least one parliamentary committee. Some sit on two or three (there are 20 parliamentary standing committees). In addition, members must attend functions and deal with all kinds of responsibilities in their constituencies and on Parliament Hill, and, in comparison, committee work does not attract much attention in the media. It is not surprising that, given the frustration they find in committee examination of Estimates and programs, many members do not devote much time to it.

The research and other resources provided by Parliament to committees are not generous.

Committee membership and committee chairs change much too frequently, giving the committees little sense of common purpose or corporate identity. Consideration of the Estimates comes well down on the list of priorities of both members and committees.

The Commission's *Fact Finding Report* found that the Sponsorship Program was not identified in the Estimates as a separate activity and that the statutory authority for the program was far from clear. Indeed, concerns about both the ability of the Estimates to serve as a control document over government financial administration and the adequacy of the review of the Estimates by Parliament and parliamentary committees appear to be shared by experts and parliamentarians alike.

When faced with the almost unlimited resources the Government can marshal when defending its administration of a program that has come under attack before a parliamentary committee, members of the committee in question should be able to engage whatever expert assistance they need to assist them in their inquiries. Having access to such assistance would probably stimulate committee members to conduct their inquiries with more diligence and in a less partisan fashion.

Although Parliament's scrutiny of the public purse is generally inadequate, there is at least one partial exception. The Public Accounts Committee (PAC) is specifically empowered to "ensure that the Government has used public money only for the purposes authorized by Parliament, that extravagance and waste are minimized, and that sound practices are encouraged in financial administration."[154] So unlike other standing committees, which review Estimates for the next fiscal year, the PAC focuses on past government spending.

Despite its status as the parliamentary spending "watchdog," the PAC lacks the resources to monitor a huge and complex executive branch. Its members are just as busy as other MPs, and they rotate on and off the PAC as they would any committee. "Many of its members do not seem to value, much less covet, the assignment; nor do they necessarily have appropriate backgrounds or experience to investigate issues of government administration."[155] With little expert assistance, they are supposed to extract information from "long-serving officials who are well versed in the ways of government and who have ready access to expertise and the elaborate interdepartmental consultative process."[156] Moreover, since "the primary loyalty of civil servants is to the government of the day," they understandably treat questions from Opposition MPs with great caution.[157] Finally, as we will see in Chapters 8 and 9, ministers and officials usually point the finger at each other for problems arising in a given department; a culture of "plausible deniability" within the executive branch thwarts MPs' efforts to hold either the political or the permanent executive to account.[158]

On a more positive note, the PAC works closely with the experts in the Office of the Auditor General; they provide detailed information about the activities of the permanent executive.[159] The Auditor General is an officer of Parliament (Dossier 7.7), whose reports usually set the agenda for the work of the PAC.[160] Indeed, "the massive profile and esteem enjoyed by the Auditor General may mean that PAC members find little political visibility or reward in their roles."[161] Nonetheless, those MPs who do take their work on the PAC seriously can make an important contribution to Parliamentary control of the public purse. They can question witnesses (including ministers and public servants) in a public forum, which the Auditor General cannot.[162] The degree to which those witnesses can provide the answers that the MPs seek is a matter of considerable dispute between the legislative and executive branches; we will discuss the differences between accountability and "answerability" in Chapter 8.

DOSSIER 7.7   Officers of Parliament

Since the 1970s, the task of holding the executive branch to account has gradually shifted away from Parliament itself to an expanding roster of officials who report to Parliament. Their powers are grounded in statute, not the whims of Cabinet ministers. They are appointed by the prime minister (subject to ratification by the Commons and Senate, which is usually a formality) and most hold office during good behaviour until the age of 65.[163] In short, their appointment process and security of tenure are directly comparable to those of judges, and for similar reasons.[164] To carry out their particular mandates, these officials must be completely independent from the government of the day.[165] The budget for each agency is submitted to Parliament via the Speaker (to keep Cabinet ministers out of the loop) and the agency staff are selected by the officer without interference by the Crown. Although each officer has a unique mandate, most are tasked with monitoring a particular activity carried out by the executive branch.

By the turn of this century, Canada had five officers of Parliament: "the Auditor General, Chief Electoral Officer, Commissioner of Official Languages, Privacy Commissioner, and Information Commissioner."[166] When the Office of the Auditor General (OAG) was established in 1878, the only employee was the Auditor General himself. Today, Sheila Fraser

leads an agency with almost 600 full-time employees.[167] The official mission of the OAG is to scrutinize government spending and to report regularly to Parliament. The OAG also works closely with the Public Accounts Committee, providing the auditing expertise that few MPs possess. Whereas past Auditors General were self-effacing accountants, Ms. Fraser is a media star (at least by Ottawa standards). After she issued her first report on the Sponsorship Scandal (Dossier 8.2), telling a press conference that public servants "broke every rule in the book," some callers to open-line radio programs expressed the hope that she would run for prime minister.[168]

The Office of the Chief Electoral officer, later renamed Elections Canada, was established in 1920. As described in Chapter 12, the mandate of Elections Canada is different from the other officers of Parliament. Whereas they are expected to hold the government to account, Elections Canada is responsible for organizing federal elections and referenda.

The next three officers of Parliament were created by Prime Minister Trudeau: the Commissioner of Official Languages in 1969, the Privacy Commissioner in 1977, and the Information Commissioner in 1983.[169] All three commissioners are responsible for overseeing the implementation of a particular statute (the *Official Languages*, *Privacy*, and *Access to*

(continued)

Information Acts, respectively). Each has the power to investigate complaints from the public and to report the results of those investigations to Parliament. Previous occupants of these positions have complained about a lack of attention from MPs, who are only interested in the scandal of the moment. Consequently, officers of Parliament have sometimes yielded to the temptation to overstate their findings in an effort to attract media attention: "as officers of Parliament, they can only 'bark,' not bite, [so] they have to make sure their bark is heard."[170]

Since 2000 the number of parliamentary officers has grown further. The *Federal Accountability Act* created a host of new positions, including a Conflict of Interest and Ethics commissioner, a commissioner of Lobbying, a Parliamentary Budget officer, and a Public Sector Integrity commissioner (informally called the "'whistle-blower' commissioner").[171] Like their forerunners, these new officers occupy an unusual position within government. They do not belong to any of the three branches of government. They are supposed to hold the execu-

tive branch accountable to Parliament (and potentially, through media coverage of their reports, to the electorate as a whole), despite being unelected themselves. At the time of writing, only one of these officials had ever come close to being fired: former Privacy Commissioner George Radwanski was forced out in 2003 over allegations of mismanagement and extravagance.[172] A leading scholar of Canadian government interpreted the Radwanski episode as proof that "accountability is even more difficult with officers of Parliament than with government departments and agencies."[173]

On a more positive note, officers of Parliament help to redress the disparity in expertise between the permanent executive and the legislature. The trained auditors and investigators on their staffs are a valuable resource for MPs and senators who want to scrutinize the implementation of laws.[174] Unfortunately, as we have seen throughout this chapter, such parliamentarians are few in number—largely because the incentives of Parliament do not reward sustained, intensive investigatory work.

HOLDING THE EXECUTIVE TO ACCOUNT

In a parliamentary democracy, the legislative branch is supposed to hold the executive branch accountable to the electorate. While the Commons has little direct control over the permanent executive—apart from committee scrutiny of Order-in-Council appointments, including deputy ministers and ambassadors—it does have the constitutional right to remove the political executive from office. If a majority of MPs vote against a money Bill, or votes for a motion of no confidence in the government, the government is deemed to have lost the support of the House. Recall that executive power in Canada is still vested in the Crown, which delegates that power to a Cabinet with the support of the Commons. If that support is lost, constitutional convention requires the prime minister to relinquish executive power and seek a new mandate from the electorate. In practice, however, a prime minister who loses a vote on a money Bill has two options:

1. He or she can resign immediately and ask the governor general to dissolve the House for a general election. Technically, the governor general has the right to refuse the request and ask another party leader to form a government. This has not happened since 1926;[175] as a matter of constitutional convention, its revival is extremely unlikely. Most recently, the minority Conservative Government of Joe Clark lost a budget vote in the House in December 1979. Clark promptly resigned and called an election, which resulted in a Liberal majority.

2. He or she can clarify the intention of the House by moving an immediate motion of confidence. If the motion fails, then he or she has no choice but to resign. If it carries, however, the prime minister can claim that the defeat of the money Bill was unintentional and remain in office. The minority Liberal Government of Lester Pearson lost a budget vote in early 1968, while most of his Cabinet ministers were absent from the House. The Liberals were in the midst of a leadership race, and several of the ministers were campaigning across the country. Pearson accused the Conservatives of deliberately engineering the vote to take advantage of his party's disarray and refused to resign.[176] He won a nonconfidence motion nine days later.

While the "confidence convention" is the Achilles' heel of a minority Cabinet, it used to be an effective weapon for prime ministers in majority governments. A Cabinet that controlled a majority in the Commons could invoke the "confidence convention" to keep its MPs in line, even though defeat in the House was rarely a realistic threat. By treating every vote as a question of confidence in the government—a practice that is neither required nor sanctioned by parliamentary tradition[177]—the Cabinet could bludgeon reluctant MPs into supporting controversial legislation. A notorious recent case was the 1998 debate over the government's compensation package for hepatitis C victims. It was well known that some Liberal MPs wanted to compensate all of the people who contracted the virus through tainted blood transfusions; instead, the Cabinet limited eligibility to those who had been infected during a specific period of time. The Reform Party introduced an amendment that was explicitly not framed as a confidence test; the government insisted that it was, thereby taking advantage of an opportunity to snuff out revolt within its own ranks. This painful episode "seemed to mark a turning point in the relationship between Chrétien and his backbench."[178]

Despite the insistence of previous prime ministers to the contrary, failure to pass an ordinary Bill does not signal a loss of confidence in the government. Indeed, the Conservative administration of Sir John A. Macdonald lost a total of nine votes in the Commons between 1867 and 1873, two of which were money Bills. It did not feel bound to resign, and there was no organized Opposition to force it to do so.[179] This reveals that, despite the claims of successive prime ministers in the twentieth century, the "historic tradition" of total confidence is at least as much a political fiction as a constitutional requirement. So does the fact that when a parliamentary session ends before final reading and royal assent (by prorogation or dissolution), the Bill simply dies. There are no consequences beyond the fact that the proposed legislation is not put into place, and the legislation can be reintroduced in the next session of Parliament. If it is a Private Members' Bill, or if it is subjected to a free vote in which MPs and senators are not constrained by party discipline, the same conclusion applies.

By the 1990s, the "confidence convention" had been turned on its head. What was once a powerful tool for Parliament in its efforts to hold the political executive to account became an effective shield against dissent within the governing party. The situation changed again in 2004, with the election of the first minority government in 25 years. As described previously, the Martin Government was defeated in the House in November 2005. In 2007, Parliament adopted a Conservative Bill that set fixed dates for future elections (Dossier 12.1). In principle, fixed election dates make it politically impossible for a prime minister with a majority of MPs to "pull the plug" early when his or her party's political fortunes are especially promising. However, it does not prevent the Opposition from bringing down a minority government—with or without the connivance of the prime minister.

In summary, the Cabinet cannot be held to account by the House of Commons except when it has a minority of the seats and the Opposition parties are prepared to fight an election. Regardless of the number of MPs in the Government caucus, the House has also lost the power to force the resignation of an individual Cabinet minister. As we will see in Chapter 8, each minister is theoretically responsible to the House for the operation of his or her department. This supposedly means that the exposure of corruption, widespread incompetence, or a single catastrophic error on the minister's watch triggers his or her resignation from the government.

In practice, this constitutional convention is honoured more in the breach than in the observance. Cabinet ministers do resign from time to time; but these resignations are almost always triggered by revelations of personal misconduct or foolishness, not by problems within their departments. The confidence of the prime minister, as opposed to Parliament or the voters, is the most powerful determinant of a Cabinet minister's longevity. A minister whose personal ineptitude embarrasses the Government casts doubt on the judgment of the prime minister who appointed him or her. In May 2008, for example, Foreign Affairs Minister Maxime Bernier resigned his portfolio after a series of public gaffes. Among other things, he had called publicly for the replacement of a senior official in Afghanistan (a no-no in international diplomacy) and promised to lend a Canadian transport plane to a relief effort without checking to see if one was available (it wasn't). Bernier finally resigned, in a letter to Prime Minister Harper, just a few hours before his ex-girlfriend—who also happened to be the ex-partner of three men with alleged ties to criminal activity—gave a television interview about their relationship. She revealed that Bernier had left secret documents at her house a few weeks earlier, which is a violation of the Cabinet oath of confidentiality (discussed in Chapter 8). When Harper announced the sudden resignation, he insisted that this breach was the only reason; few who understood the ways of government believed him.[180]

The fact that Bernier's resignation was made to the PM, and not to the Commons, highlights the failure of the Commons to hold the political executive directly accountable (and the permanent executive indirectly accountable) to Canadians. There are several possible reasons for these shortcomings.

- First, the prime minister has every incentive to protect the executive branch from parliamentary criticism. (We will return to this topic in Chapter 8.)
- Second, the Canadian House of Commons has an unusually high turnover rate. Most backbenchers serve only one or two terms before they quit or are defeated. Consequently, "a strong, solidly entrenched Prime Minister faces an insecure and transient House of Commons."[181] Few parliamentarians stick around long enough to master the details of policy and public administration, which greatly reduces their effectiveness as watchdogs.
- Third, government MPs face powerful pressures to support the Cabinet. While they can, and do, express reservations about particular policies and ministers in the privacy of caucus, they are unlikely to issue public demands for accountability.
- Fourth, apart from their opportunities to embarrass Cabinet ministers (in QP, for example), Opposition MPs are powerless against a majority government. Even in a minority situation, they must work together across party lines to exert real power. Moreover, the government controls the flow of information from the permanent executive to the House of Commons. If they so choose, Cabinet ministers (and especially the prime minister) can deny MPs access to the documents they need to hold the political executive accountable.
- Fifth, Canada's parliamentary institutions have changed relatively little since 1867, whereas the executive branch has been transformed beyond recognition. "In Canada, in 1867, there were about ten civil servants for every member of Parliament. Today, there are about 1,000, and this figure does not include crown corporations."[182] The proliferation of departments, agencies, and programs makes it extremely difficult to hold anyone accountable. While the permanent executive has become larger and more complex, it has also become increasingly impervious to parliamentary control.[183] As we will see in Chapters 8 and 9, the growing power of the prime minister and his central agencies raise serious questions about democratic accountability in the federal government.

THE QUEST FOR PARLIAMENTARY REFORM

As we saw in Chapter 2, conflicting and evolving political values pose challenges for Canada's political institutions. This is particularly true for Parliament, both because of its recent loss of legitimacy and because the Commons is at the heart of Canadian representative democracy. The Senate has attracted criticism on several fronts from the moment of its creation. Fads in Senate reform come and go, but one theme remains constant: the Senate as currently constituted has few defenders. The debate over reforming the Commons is both more recent and more consistent. The goals of reformers are summarized in a June 2001 report:

> There is a general desire to re-assert the pre-eminence of the House of Commons, and increase its effectiveness and efficiency. Members want to increase the accountability of individual Ministers and the Government as a whole, and increase the opportunities for parliamentary influence in the legislative process. There is a feeling that individual Members of the House of Commons need to be empowered, and the role of the Speaker, as the servant of the House and its spokesperson, enhanced. A balance needs to be achieved between the Government's interests in implementing its legislative agenda, and the Opposition's interests in questioning and criticizing the Government. Similarly, other competing interests need to be reconciled, such as the inevitable tensions between individual Members and their parties, and between the chamber and its committees, to name but two. Parliamentary debate should be enhanced, by creating opportunities for more meaningful dialogue and increasing the relevance of the parliamentary processes.[184]

Both Houses of Parliament should be reformed to enhance their effectiveness as legislative bodies, as watchdogs over the executive, and as representative institutions. However, the precise nature of those reforms, and how they are to be accomplished, are matters of intense debate.

▨ Reforming the House of Commons

As previously noted, the House of Commons is often criticized by the public and by MPs themselves.[185] Here the primary concern, one that goes to the core of parliamentary democracy, has been the pervasive impact of Cabinet dominance, party discipline, and adversarialism on the procedures of the House and its capacity to represent the electorate.

Public discontent with party discipline is not a new phenomenon, especially in Western Canada. Ever since the Progressives swept into Parliament in 1921, Western protest parties—including the CCF, Social Credit, and the Reform/Alliance—have targeted party discipline as a priority for institutional reform. The problems that any significant reduction in party discipline might pose for responsible government, and indeed for electoral empowerment, are largely ignored. As we have seen throughout this chapter, some degree of party discipline and adversarialism are inherent in responsible parliamentary government. Both arise from the very architecture of British legislative institutions, and are reinforced by the incentive structures of representative democracy and party politics. To eliminate these institutional characteristics altogether, assuming that such a thing were possible, would undermine the authority of the political executive and make it difficult for voters to determine which group of politicians should be rewarded or punished for its conduct in government. So despite the problems caused by the excesses of Cabinet dominance, the reality is that sweeping reform of the legislative branch is neither practical nor, in some respects, desirable.

Despite these obstacles to reform, the internal procedures of the House of Commons have evolved considerably over time and will continue to evolve. Parliamentary government is a remarkably flexible institution that can evolve to meet new challenges and unique social conditions.[186] Unfortunately, most of the reforms discussed in this chapter have been noticed only by MPs and aficionados of Parliament Hill. They have done little to address public dissatisfaction with the House and the behaviour of MPs, or the more general discontent with the responsiveness and representativeness of parliamentary democracy. The most effective way to enhance the legitimacy of the Commons and the Senate may not be to destroy a system of responsible government that has evolved over centuries. Rather, the answer could lie in a better-educated electorate, which understands the conflicting institutional incentives for their elected officials and appreciates the less publicized contributions of MPs and senators. But given the anti-institutional bias of some journalists, well-informed and sympathetic reporting of elected legislators may be too much to ask (see Chapter 14).

▉ Senate Reform

As we saw in Chapter 5, Senate reform is perceived (especially in Western Canada) as the solution to a variety of political and institutional problems. The movement for Senate reform has focused on enhancing regional representation, with little attention to the legislative and investigative aspects of the Senate's work. Most of the recent proposals have sought to make the Senate a more effective vehicle for intrastate federalism. In the late 1970s and early 1980s, the prevailing model was a House of the Provinces (modelled on the German *Bundesrat*). Provincial governments would send delegations that would vote as a bloc on instructions from their government. Such a chamber would allow provincial governments to review the legislative activities of the House of Commons, particularly the use of the federal spending power in areas of exclusive provincial jurisdiction. The emphasis was on the representation of provincial *governments,* as opposed to provincial *electorates,* within the national legislative process.

By the mid-1980s, the fashion had changed. The House of the Provinces model was replaced by the Triple-E Senate. Advocates argued that an elected Senate would remedy the democratic failings of the existing upper house, while a Senate with equal representation from all provinces would enshrine the "equal provinces" vision of Canada. They claimed that the role of provincial governments and premiers on the national stage would be diminished, and regional alienation would be addressed in a number of ways:

- The election of senators would strengthen ties between citizens and their national government.
- An equal number of seats for all provinces would give "outer Canada" sufficient legislative clout to counterbalance central Canadian domination of the House of Commons.
- An effective Senate would ensure that regional representatives would in fact be heard in Ottawa.

Support for an elected Senate, although not necessarily for an equal or effective Senate, gained additional momentum from public discontent with parliamentary institutions and executive federalism. Public opinion is divided between those who support the direct election of senators and those who support the Senate's abolition. What is clear, however, is that few Canadians support the status quo. The controversy over former Senator Andrew Thompson, who attended less than 5 percent of the Senate sittings in the 1990s while maintaining a full-time residence in Mexico, fuelled public anger.[187] Nonetheless, the status quo continues, with little sign of governmental enthusiasm for even modest reform. The Senate is still appointed, not elected. The Senate still has formal legislative powers virtually equal to those of the House. It is still based on an antiquated formula of regional representation that makes little sense to most contemporary Canadians. It is still an institution that attracts unrelenting public criticism and no discernible public support.

This should not lead automatically to the suggestion that the existing Senate is worthless or that senators do not provide reasonable value in return for their salaries and perks. As discussed in previous sections of this chapter, the Senate plays a valuable role in the legislative process; more recently, it has taken on a more active role in the investigation of public policy issues and the oversight of the executive. Its strengths lie in its differences from the House of Commons. Because the Senate does not hold the fate of the government in its hands, and its members are not subject to election or re-election, the chamber is more independent and less adversarial than the "other place."

The more consensual and unhurried style of the Senate has enhanced its effectiveness as a legislative chamber. The primary obstacle to even greater effectiveness is the appointment process, which diminishes its legitimacy as a legislative institution and creates a public perception of senators as time-serving party hacks. Paradoxically, however, the fact that senators are appointed and not elected can be viewed as an important asset. As we have seen, the composition of the Senate more closely approximates Canadian society than does that of the Commons. The prime minister can, if he or she chooses, appoint distinguished public servants, former Cabinet ministers, community activists, and others with a wealth of expertise. When the appointment power is used sensibly, the result is a legislative chamber whose collective knowledge and experience far exceeds that of the elected MPs.

In all likelihood, the Triple-E proposal would fail to secure its chief goal—the promotion of regional perspectives in the national Parliament—while reducing the Senate's value as a legislative body. If senators were elected for fixed, renewable terms, the reformed Senate would impose the same institutional incentives that handicap the Commons: strong partisanship, high turnover, and amateurism. There is little evidence to support the claim that regional representation in national politics should be performed exclusively by the upper house of Parliament.[188] Indeed, as we saw in Chapter 4, intergovernmental relations are becoming increasingly institutionalized, although there is still no effective mechanism for holding executives to account for the deals struck among themselves.

On the other side of the debate, the New Democratic Party and other left-wing critics have long argued that the Senate should be abolished altogether. As we have seen, however, the dominance of the Commons by the federal Cabinet points up the need for a chamber of "sober second thought" to prevent hasty or ill-conceived Bills from becoming law. Moreover, abolishing the Senate shares at least one failing with the Triple-E proposal: it would require a unanimous amendment to the *Constitution*. For political reasons, the province of Quebec is unlikely to agree to any change that would diminish its representation in the national Parliament.[189]

More promising and practical suggestions for reform have been advanced by proponents of nonconstitutional change. The independence of senators from the government of the day could be enhanced by excluding government senators from the weekly caucus meeting. A new Senate committee could be established to review the details of proposed treaties between Canada and other states. In the era of globalization and internationalization, a legislative body with the time and the expertise to examine the implications of treaties for Canadian law and policy makes considerable sense.[190] An independent and nonpartisan appointment commission, similar to the one adopted in the United Kingdom, could ensure the continuing quality of Senate appointments while removing the taint of partisan patronage.[191] Perhaps most important, the Senate should make every effort to explain to the public, the government, and the media what it does and how well it does it. Given the near-certainty that the institution will persist in its current form for at least the foreseeable future, there is much to be said for educating the public about its strengths and contributions.

CONCLUSION

Canada's national legislature does not adequately perform the five functions listed at the beginning of this chapter. The House of Commons is dominated by the Cabinet, which it is supposed to hold accountable to the electorate. Instead of *making* laws, the best that MPs and senators can to is to *improve* or *delay* laws. While MPs devote much of their time and energy to serving their constituents, they do not represent the public in a demographic sense. Collectively, they lack the experience and the expertise to monitor the implementation of public policy. The incentives for parliamentarians reward obedience and adversarialism, not policy initiative or independent action. In the words of Canada's leading scholar of public administration, our parliamentarians "have contracted out their accountability responsibilities to commissions of inquiries, to officers of Parliament, and to the media."[192]

The institutional norms of Cabinet dominance, party discipline, and adversarialism evolved over centuries. In moderation, they make responsible government possible; in excess, they damage the reputation of both Houses of Parliament—notwithstanding the fact that each norm is considerably weaker in the Senate than in the Commons. Without a clear public consensus about the meaning of political representation and a better understanding of the institutional incentives that shape the behaviour of our elected officials, the mismatch between MPs' behaviour and the expectations of voters will likely continue.

GLOSSARY OF KEY TERMS

Backbenchers: Members of the House of Commons who do not belong to the Cabinet of the day. Backbenchers make up almost 80 percent of the Commons. All Opposition MPs are backbenchers, as are roughly half of government MPs.

Bill: A draft law introduced into Parliament by a minister of the Crown (i.e., a Cabinet minister), or by a private member (a backbench MP). After the Bill has received royal assent, it becomes a statute (another word for "law").

Casework: The services provided to individual constituents by an MP and his or her staff. Anyone in Canada who encounters a problem with the federal government—e.g., citizenship, Employment Insurance, or the Canada Pension Plan—can seek assistance from the local office of his or her representative in the House of Commons. Casework is the most time-consuming, and often the most satisfying, of the many tasks assigned to MPs.

Caucus: The parliamentary contingent representing each of the various parties in Parliament. For the Liberals and Conservatives, caucus includes both MPs and senators. The NDP and the Bloc Québécois have no Senate representation. The caucuses meet separately on Wednesday mornings when the House of Commons is in session. The Liberal caucus is divided into regional caucuses, which often meet just before the full caucus. Within the secrecy of the caucus meeting, MPs and senators can speak freely about political and policy issues. Once the meeting ends, all members of caucus are expected to keep the discussions confidential.

Confidence convention: In a British parliamentary system, the Cabinet can remain in office only as long as it enjoys the support of the House of Commons for its policies and money Bills. If the Cabinet loses a vote on a money Bill or a key piece of legislation, constitutional convention requires the prime minister to tender the resignation of his or her government to the Crown (in Canada, the governor general). In practice, there are no legal sanctions for violating a convention (see Chapter 8); therefore, a prime minister may choose to stay in office and try to pass a vote of confidence in the House instead of resigning immediately. Prime ministers sometimes rely on a misinterpretation of the confidence convention to persuade their backbench MPs to support government legislation.

Constituency: An electoral district that sends one or more members to the national or provincial legislature. In Canada, also called a "riding." The word "constituency" may also be used to refer to an informal group within the electorate that expects a particular MP to speak on its behalf. Therefore, we might say that a female MP from Halifax has three constituencies: her particular riding, women, and the Atlantic region as a whole.

Minority government: One party holds a plurality of the seats in the House of Commons (i.e., more than any other party), but not an absolute majority. Because the Commons works on the principle of majority voting, a minority government cannot pass legislation or financial measures without the support of some Opposition MPs. It may secure this support by striking a bargain with one or more Opposition parties, or it can try to win over individual MPs on a case-by-case basis. If it cannot do either, it risks defeat in the House (e.g., by losing a budget vote); in that circumstance, constitutional convention normally requires the prime minister to submit his or her resignation to the governor general. Moreover, a government with a minority in the House cannot dominate Commons committees, where seats are allocated according to the parties' respective shares of the House.

Money Bill: A formal authorization by the House of Commons to the Cabinet (technically, the Crown) to raise or spend public revenues. Ways and Means Bills authorize the Crown to raise money; appropriations Bills authorize the spending of public funds.

Numerical/pictorial representation: The idea that the demographic characteristics of a particular political body (such as a legislature) should mirror those in the population at large. For example, women make up slightly over half of the Canadian electorate; therefore, a numerically representative House of Commons would also be 51 percent female.

Party discipline: The requirement that individual legislators vote according to the wishes of their leaders (or of the party caucus as a whole). Party discipline is strongest on the government side of the House, partly because of the confidence convention, but it affects MPs and senators from all parties. While discipline is somewhat weaker in the Senate, which is not a confidence chamber, few senators are willing to break ranks in public. Party discipline affects the behaviour of MPs on parliamentary committees, not just on the floor of the Commons or the Senate.

Patronage: The appointment of party supporters to public office, resting on the exercise of the Crown prerogative by the head of government.

Power of the purse: The right of the House of Commons to approve or reject money Bills proposed by the Cabinet. That right is grounded in British constitutional convention. It was entrenched in section 53 of the *Constitution Act, 1867.*

Prorogation: A temporary suspension of Parliament between elections. The Governor General prorogues Parliament by issuing a writ on the advice of the Prime Minister. In December 2008 Governor General Michaelle Jean granted a prorogation to Prime Minister Harper without limits or conditions, despite the fact that he requested the suspension of Parliament because his Government had lost the confidence of the Commons.

Universal suffrage: Every citizen has the right to vote in parliamentary elections, without regard to wealth, gender, or social status.

DISCUSSION AND REVIEW QUESTIONS

1. Briefly define three of the conceptions of political representation discussed in this chapter. Which do you consider the most important, and why?
2. Briefly explain the stages through which a Bill becomes law.
3. Explain the roles and functions of House of Commons standing committees. Identify two ways in which their effectiveness could be enhanced.

4. In your own words, explain the phenomena of adversarialism and party discipline in the Canadian parliament. How do they affect the operation of our legislative branch of government?

5. Explain the procedures which govern Private Members' Business. How were these used by the Opposition in the 39th Parliament?

6. In your own words, explain the confidence convention.

7. What would you think if your MP crossed the floor to join a different party (Dossier 7.2)? Would you want the chance to vote for or against that MP in a by-election? Why or why not?

SUGGESTED READINGS

Books and Articles

David C. Docherty, *Mr. Smith Goes to Ottawa: Life in the House of Commons* (Vancouver: UBC Press, 1997).

C.E.S. Franks, *The Parliament of Canada* (Toronto: University of Toronto Press, 1987).

David A. Good, *The Politics of Public Management: The HRDC Audit of Grants and Contributions* (Toronto: University of Toronto Press/The Institute of Public Administration of Canada, 2003).

Serge Joyal, ed., *Protecting Canadian Democracy: The Senate You Never Knew* (Montreal and Kingston: McGill–Queen's University Press/Canadian Centre for Management Development, 2003).

David McInnes, *Taking It to the Hill: The Complete Guide to Appearing Before Parliamentary Committees,* 2nd ed. (Ottawa: University of Ottawa Press, 2005).

Donald J. Savoie, *Court Government and the Collapse of Accountability in Canada and the United Kingdom* (Toronto: University of Toronto Press, 2008).

Donald J. Savoie, *Governing from the Centre: The Concentration of Power in Canadian Politics* (Toronto: University of Toronto Press, 1999).

F. Leslie Seidle and David C. Docherty, eds., *Reforming Parliamentary Democracy* (Montreal and Kingston: McGill–Queen's University Press, 2003).

Websites

The Parliament of Canada website (www.parl.gc.ca) is a gold mine of information about the last five parliaments (numbers 36–40, at the time of writing). It provides the full text of government and Private Members' Bills, the Standing Orders, *Legislative Summaries* prepared by the Library of Parliament, and committee minutes and reports.

NOTES

1. As we saw in Chapter 1, every government is divided into three branches: legislative, executive, and judicial. The legislative branch makes the laws that are implemented by the executive and interpreted by the judiciary. Strictly speaking, Canada's Parliament does not *make* laws, nor can it *propose* public expenditures. Government legislation, which comprises the vast majority of laws passed by Parliament, originates with the executive branch. Money Bills—formal authorizations to raise or spend public revenues—must be formulated by the Cabinet, and approved by the governor general, before they are introduced into the House of Commons.

2. 36th Parliament, 2nd Session, *Hansard,* Number 133, Friday, October 20, 2000, 1105–10; accessed at www.parl.gc.ca, March 2001.

3. The Conservatives had 143 MPs as of June 2008. See the discussion of floor-crossing in Dossier 7.2.

4. See Andrew Heard, "Just What Is a Vote of Confidence? The Curious Case of May 10, 2005," *Canadian Journal of Political Science*, 40:2 (June 2007), 395–416.

5. The primary source for this section is Colin Pilkington, *Representative Democracy in Britain Today* (Manchester: Manchester University Press, 1997), Chapter 1. See also David C. Docherty and F. Leslie Seidle, "Introduction," in F. Leslie Seidle and David C. Docherty, eds., *Reforming Parliamentary Democracy* (Montreal and Kingston: McGill–Queen's University Press, 2003), 5–7.

6. Janet Ajzenstat, "Bicameralism and Canada's Founders: The Origins of the Canadian Senate," in Serge Joyal, ed., *Protecting Canadian Democracy: The Senate You Never Knew* (Montreal and Kingston: McGill–Queen's University Press/Canadian Centre for Management Development, 2003), 3–8.

7. This information was accurate at the time of writing; a Bill to change the length of Senate tenure (Bill C-19, discussed in Dossier 3.4) had not yet passed both Houses. Until the mid-twentieth century, the members of Britain's House of Lords were hereditary peers. The eldest son of an aristocrat inherited his father's lands, his title, and his seat in the Lords. After the 1950s the proportion of hereditary peers shrank, as prime ministers appointed growing numbers of "life peers": lords with honorary titles that could not be passed down to their descendants. In 1999, Britain's government began to phase out hereditary seats in the upper house. As of June 2008, its efforts to replace prime ministerial appointment with a more democratic selection method had failed.

8. In tribute to the courage of past Speakers, who sometimes risked their necks when they had to tell the king that the Commons refused his requests for money, modern Speakers traditionally put on a show of reluctance when they are sworn in to office.

9. Donald J. Savoie, *Court Government and the Collapse of Accountability in Canada and the United Kingdom* (Toronto: University of Toronto Press, 2008), 9.

10. See the history of the Canadian party system in Chapter 11.

11. Savoie, *Court Government and the Collapse of Accountability*, 48–49.

12. David C. Docherty, *Mr. Smith Goes to Ottawa: Life in the House of Commons* (Vancouver: UBC Press, 1997), 157.

13. Peter Dobell, "Reforming Parliamentary Practice: The Views of MPs," *Policy Matters*, 1:9 (Montreal: Institute for Research on Public Policy, December 2000), 8; accessed at www.irpp.org.

14. Most laws passed by Parliament authorize the Crown to make any regulations necessary for their implementation. For example, a Bill that establishes a Crown corporation will contain provisions empowering the Cabinet to appoint directors to its board. Although regulations, as a matter of constitutional convention, should not usurp the power of Parliament (for example, by imposing new taxes or expenditures, or creating new criminal offences), there is little Parliament can do when the Cabinet decides to interpret its delegated legislative powers very broadly. Source: Privy Council Office, *Cabinet Directive on Law-Making* (Ottawa, March 1999), section 2; to access this document, go to www.pco-bcp.gc.ca and enter "Cabinet Directive on Law-Making" in the Search window. (Regulations are discussed in greater detail on pp. 311–312 of this book.)

15. Lowell Murray, "Which Criticisms Are Founded?" 139; Franks, "The Canadian Senate in Modern Times," 164–65 and 169–73; Thomas, "Comparing the Lawmaking Roles of the Senate and House of Commons," 201–06; all in Joyal, ed., *Protecting Canadian Democracy*.

16. The whip is an MP or senator appointed by his or her party leader to ensure that members turn up to vote, committees are staffed, and legislative procedures run as smoothly as partisan debate allows.

17. The incidence of public dissension in government ranks was unusually high during the 37th Parliament (2000–04). The most obvious explanation is the nasty battle over the Liberal leadership between Paul Martin's supporters and those of then-Prime Minister Chrétien. A less obvious, but intriguing, explanation is that the turnover at the 2000 general election

was much lower than the average; a "critical mass" of MPs with one or two terms in Parliament under their belts may have felt emboldened to challenge the Cabinet in a way that less experienced members may not. This explanation also applies to the Opposition, particularly the Canadian Alliance. Dobell, "Reforming Parliamentary Practice," 4. A recent comparative study of British and Canadian Government MPs found that "every additional term spent in office increases the level of dissenting behaviour by almost 4 per cent." Garner and Letki, 474.

18. Docherty, *Mr. Smith Goes to Ottawa*, 148.

19. Ibid., 150.

20. Ibid., 160.

21. Ibid., 169–170.

22. Paul Howe and David Northrup, *Strengthening Canadian Democracy: The Views of Canadians* (Montreal: Institute for Research on Public Policy, July 2000), 31, Table 19; accessed at www.irpp.org, June 2001.

23. David C. Docherty, "Conclusion: Can Canada Learn Some Lessons?" in Seidle and Docherty, eds., *Reforming Parliamentary Democracy*, 231; David C. Docherty, "Could the Rebels Find a Cause? House of Commons Reform in the Chrétien Era," in Lois Harder and Steve Patten, eds., *The Chrétien Legacy: Politics and Public Policy in Canada* (Montreal and Kingston: McGill–Queen's University Press, 2006), 300–320.

24. David C. Docherty and Stephen White, "Parliamentary Democracy in Canada," *Parliamentary Affairs*, 57:3 (2004), 622.

25. Christopher Garner and Natalia Letki, "Party Structure and Backbench Dissent in the Canadian and British Parliaments," *Canadian Journal of Political Science*, 38:2 (June 2005), 471.

26. Mark MacGuigan, quoted in Robert J. Jackson and Doreen Jackson, *Politics in Canada*, 3rd edition (Scarborough, ON: Prentice Hall, 1994), 347.

27. Donald J. Savoie, *Governing from the Centre: The Concentration of Power in Canadian Politics* (Toronto: University of Toronto Press, 1999), 93.

28. Garth Turner, "MP paid big price for speaking out in Harper's Ottawa," *The Toronto Star*, May 27, 2008 (accessed at www.thestar.com). Turner, a former Progressive Conservative MP (and briefly a Cabinet minister under Kim Campbell), was elected as the Conservative MP for Halton in the 2006 federal election. After his expulsion from the Conservative caucus for publicly criticizing Government policy, he joined the Liberal caucus in 2007.

29. Savoie, *Governing from the Centre*, 262.

30. Thomas, "Comparing the Lawmaking Roles," 212–225.

31. Desmond Morton, "A Note on Party Switchers," *Canadian Parliamentary Review*, Summer 2006, 5–7. Recent examples of MPs who were expelled from caucus include Garth Turner, who was suspended from the Conservative caucus in October 2006 for allegedly leaking caucus secrets on his blog (he joined the Liberals in February 2007); and Wajid Khan, who was partially suspended from the Liberal caucus in August 2006 when he took a position as special advisor to Prime Minister Harper on the Middle East, and who formally joined the Conservative caucus in January 2007.

32. Throughout her political career, Stronach's personal life eclipsed her political abilities. Her decision to cross the floor marked the end of her romance with fellow Conservative MP Peter MacKay. The breakup turned into a soap opera: MacKay gave an emotional television interview, standing in his father's garden next to his faithful border collie. More than a year after the breakup, MacKay got into trouble in the Commons for allegedly referring to Stronach as "a dog." By then, Stronach had been named as the "other woman" in a divorce case involving a former NHL player. She announced her retirement from politics in 2007.

33. Abbas Rana, "Morale low in Conservative caucus after shaky start for government," *The Hill Times*, February 13, 2006, 30.

34. Canada, House of Commons, "Conflict of Interest Code For Members of the House of Commons" (Ottawa, March 2007), section 3; accessed at www.parl.gc.ca.

35. Emerson became acting Foreign Affairs minister in May 2008, upon the resignation of Maxime Bernier. He was formally appointed to the portfolio in June 2008.

36. Office of the Ethics Commissioner, "The Harper-Emerson Inquiry" (Ottawa, 2006, 11 (accessed at www.parl.gc.ca/oec-bce, May 2007). This finding refers to the wording of the Members' Code as it existed at the time of the Ethics Commissioner's investigation; it has since been amended.

37. Ibid., 14.

38. Ibid., 11.

39. David Gussow, "Crossing the Floor, Conflict of Interest and the *Parliament of Canada Act*," *Canadian Parliamentary Review*, Summer 2006, 9–11

40. Quoted in Gussow, 10.

41. Morton, 8.

42. Ibid.

43. Dobell, "Reforming Parliamentary Practice," 9–10.

44. Howe and Northrup, Table 19, 31.

45. Harold D. Clarke, Allan Kornberg, and Peter Wearing, *A Polity on the Edge: Canada and the Politics of Fragmentation* (Peterborough, ON: Broadview Press, 2000), 189.

46. This observation may not apply to the most recent Parliaments. Former NDP leader Ed Broadbent, who had been an MP in the 1970s and 1980s, returned to the Commons in the 2004 election. He was appalled by the increase in adversarialism and bad behaviour during his absence. Other veteran MPs have made similar comparisons. In May 2007, a Conservative MP was accused of (but not charged with) assault for grabbing the shoulder of a Liberal MP during a debate in the Commons; such behaviour is extremely rare, but it has increased somewhat since the early 1990s. Bea Vongdouangchanh, "Fifth week of five-week House sitting creates a very testy House, say MPs," *The Hill Times*, May 21, 2007, 14.

47. Canada, House of Commons Standing Committee on Organization and Procedure, *Minutes*, November 20, 1975, 9–10.

48. Peter Aucoin and Mark D. Jarvis, *Modernizing Government Accountability: A Framework for Reform* (Ottawa: Canada School of Public Service, 2005), 24 (accessed at www.myschool-monecole.gc.ca/Research/publications/html/p131/1_e.html, March 2007).

49. Treasury Board of Canada Secretariat, *Meeting the Expectations of Canadians: Review of the Responsibilities and Accountabilities of Ministers and Senior Officials* (Ottawa: President of the Treasury Board, 2005), 15 (accessed at www.tbs-sct.gc.ca/report/rev-exa/ar-er_e.asp, March 2007).

50. Commission of Inquiry into the Sponsorship Program and Advertising Activities [the Gomery Commission], *Restoring Accountability: Recommendations* (Ottawa: Minister of Public Works and Government Services, 2006), 73.

51. David A. Good, *The Politics of Public Management: The HRDC Audit of Grants and Contributions* (Toronto: University of Toronto Press/Institute of Public Administration of Canada, 2003), 161.

52. Savoie, *Governing from the Centre*, 340.

53. Ibid., 289–90. See also Good, *The Politics of Public Management*, 58–59.

54. There is some evidence of a "personal vote" for veteran MPs. However, this does not develop until after an MP has won two consecutive elections—which many fail to do. See Docherty, *Mr. Smith Goes to Ottawa*, 212.

55. Docherty, *Mr. Smith Goes to Ottawa*, 101.

56. Note, however, that some government backbenchers regard policy expertise as a prerequisite for Cabinet appointment. Therefore, they perceive a strong incentive to demonstrate a thorough grasp of at least one field of public policy. See Docherty, *Mr. Smith Goes to Ottawa*, 128.

57. Docherty, *Mr. Smith Goes to Ottawa*, 173.

58. David McInnes, *Taking It to the Hill: The Complete Guide to Appearing Before (and Surviving) Parliamentary Committees* (Ottawa: University of Ottawa Press, 1999), 71.

59. Peter Dobell, "What Could Canadians Expect From a Minority Government?" *Policy Matters,* 1:6 (Montreal: Institute for Research on Public Policy, November 2000), 12; accessed at www.irpp.org.

60. McInnes, 70.

61. The growing incidence of minority reports in recent years is a bad sign for committees. A lack of consensus weakens the political impact of committee recommendations, and makes it easier for the government of the day to ignore proposals with which it does not agree. See Dobell, "Reforming Parliamentary Practice," 26–27.

62. Dobell, "What Could Canadians Expect from a Minority Government?" 12–13.

63. The exceptions are proposed constitutional amendments, over which the Senate has a suspensive veto; it can delay their passage for up to 180 sitting days, but it cannot block them altogether.

64. Mark Audcent, "The Senate Veto: Opinion of the Law Clerk and Parliamentary Counsel" (Ottawa: Senate of Canada, 1999), 63, quoted in David E. Smith, "The Improvement of the Senate by Nonconstitutional Means" in Joyal, ed., *Protecting Canadian Democracy*, 244.

65. Paul G. Thomas, "Comparing the Lawmaking Roles of the Senate and House of Commons," in Joyal, ed., *Protecting Canadian Democracy,* 198.

66. Most Senate amendments are technical in nature. They reflect the policy expertise of individual senators, and the higher quality of most Senate committee reviews. The majority of amendments are accepted by the government. See C.E.S. Franks, "The Canadian Senate in Modern Times," in Joyal, ed., *Protecting Canadian Democracy,* 151–88.

67. *The Hill Times,* June 18, 2007, 4.

68. C.E.S. Franks, "The 'Problem' of Debate and Question Period," in John C. Courtney, ed., *The Canadian House of Commons: Essays in Honor of Norman Ward* (Calgary: University of Calgary Press, 1985).

69. Ibid., 9.

70. Standing Committee on Procedure and House Affairs, *Nineteenth Report,* 37th Parliament, 1st Session (April 2001), 2.

71. McInnes, xv.

72. Leslie A. Pal, "Advocacy Organizations and Legislative Politics: The Effect of the Charter of Rights and Freedoms on Interest Lobbying of Federal Legislation, 1989–91," in F. Leslie Seidle, ed., *Equity and Community: The Charter, Interest Advocacy and Representation* (Montreal: Institute for Research on Public Policy, 1993), 121.

73. *Report of the Special Committee on the Modernization and Improvement of the Procedures of the House of Commons,* June 1, 2001, paragraph 29.

74. House of Commons, *Précis of Procedure,* section 14(b); accessed at www.parl.gc.ca, July 2000.

75. Standing Orders of the House of Commons (accessed September 2004), section 106(2).

76. Geoff Dubrow, "Systems of Governance and Parliamentary Accountability," in *Parliamentary Accountability and Good Governance: A Parliamentarian's Handbook* (Ottawa: Parliamentary Centre and World Bank Institute, undated), 26 (accessed at http://parlcent.parl.gc.ca).

77. The manual was not released to the public, despite repeated demands by the Opposition. Leaked excerpts appeared in *The Hill Times,* May 28, 2007, 5.

78. *Restoring Accountability: Recommendations,* 72–73 and 79.

79. Jonathan Malloy, "The Standing Committee on Public Accounts," in Donald Savoie, ed., *Restoring Accountability: Parliament, Ministers and Deputy Ministers,* volume 1 of the collected research studies for the Commission of Inquiry Into the Sponsorship Program and Advertising Activities [the Gomery Commission] (Ottawa: Minister of Public Works and Government Services, 2006), 71–75.

80. Canada, Privy Council Office, *Accountable Government: A Guide for Ministers* (Ottawa: Privy Council Office, 2006), 8–9 (accessed at www.pco-bcp.gc.ca, March 2007).

81. National Democratic Institute for International Affairs, *Toward the Development of International Standards For Democratic Legislatures: A Discussion Document for Review by Interested Legislatures, Donors and International Organizations* (Washington: NDI, January 2007), 30 (accessed at www.ndi.org).

82. See the discussion of Parliamentary Secretaries in Chapter 8.

83. Simon Doyle, "Ambrose not yet briefed on science of climate change: critics," *The Hill Times*, October 16, 2006, 1 and 5.

84. Ibid.

85. Simon Doyle, "Clean Air Act to be 'unrecognizable' after emerging from House legislative committee," *The Hill Times*, January 8, 2007, 14.

86. Bea Vongdouangchanh, "PM Harper, Hill, Kenney say Kyoto private member's bill won't sway Conservative plans," *The Hill Times*, February 19, 2007, 4.

87. Bea Vongdouangchanh, "Government quiet on overhauled Clean Air," *The Hill Times*, April 23, 2007, 22 and 25.

88. Environment Canada, "A Climate Change Plan for the Purposes of the *Kyoto Protocol Implementation Act 2007*"; accessed at www.ec.gc.ca, August 2007.

89. Bill Curry, "Tories say they won't be bound by NDP climate bill," *The Globe and Mail*, June 4, 2008 (accessed at www.globeandmail.com, June 4, 2008).

90. Bea Vongdouangchanh, "Will PM stay put, or, pull Parliamentary election plug?" *The Hill Times*, April 2, 2007, 13.

91. Bea Vongdouangchanh, "Tories have 'no intention' of passing Clean Air Act: Van Loan," *The Hill Times*, April 30, 2007, 1.

92. Bea Vongdouangchanh, "Legislation," *The Hill Times*, June 4, 2007, 4.

93. Bill C-10, a package of amendments concerning gun-related crimes, is a case in point. The version tabled by the Justice minister in May 2006 was 19 pages long and contained 31 clauses. The amended version reported by the Standing Committee on Justice in February 2007 was only five pages long and contained nine clauses; all of the others had been deleted by the Opposition MPs. Both versions were accessed at www.parl.gc.ca, March 2007.

94. Conservative Party of Canada, "Stand Up for Canada: the 2006 Conservative Platform" (accessed at www.conservative.ca, December 2005), 44.

95. Paul E. J. Thomas, "Measuring the Effectiveness of a Minority Parliament," *Canadian Parliamentary Review* (Spring 2007), Table 6, 24.

96. Layton's Bill was passed by the Commons in June 2008.

97. Bea Vongdouangchanh, "Private members' bills important to minority parliament: opposition," *The Hill Times*, June 18, 2007, 4 and 31.

98. Ajzenstat, "Bicameralism and Canada's Founders," 6–7.

99. David McInnes, *Taking It to the Hill: The Complete Guide to Appearing Before Parliamentary Committees*, 2nd ed. (Ottawa: University of Ottawa Press, 2005), 49.

100. Murray, "Which Criticisms Are Founded?" 138–39.

101. See section 47(1) of the *Constitution Act, 1982*. Because the Senate has only a suspensory veto, not an absolute veto, over constitutional amendments, it cannot block its own reform. In recent years, some government Bills have explicitly weakened the Senate's power to block or suspend legislation adopted by the Commons. See Serge Joyal, "Introduction," in Joyal, ed., *Protecting Canadian Democracy*, xx.

102. Franks, "The Canadian Senate in Modern Times," 172; Thomas, "Comparing the Lawmaking Roles," 202–03.

103. Murray, "Which Criticisms Are Founded?" 134–35; Franks, "The Canadian Senate in Modern Times," 155–68. In 1988, Liberal senators delayed the Conservative government's free trade deal with the United States and forced the prime minister to call an election on the issue; after the Conservatives won a second majority, the senators capitulated and passed the enabling Bill. Conservative senators repeatedly challenged Liberal legislation between

1993 and 1997, at a time when there were only two Conservative MPs and the party was in danger of disappearing altogether.

104. Michael Fortier was appointed to the Senate in early 2006, on the same day when he was sworn into Cabinet (see Chapter 8). Harper appointed Bert Brown to the Senate in 2007. Brown had led a grassroots campaign for a "triple-E Senate" since the 1980s, and he had twice been elected as a "Senate nominee" in Alberta (see Dossier 3.4).

105. Conservative Party of Canada, "Stand Up for Canada" (accessed at www.conservative.ca/media/20060113-Platform.pdf, May 2007), 44.

106. C.E.S. Franks, *The Parliament of Canada* (Toronto: University of Toronto Press, 1987) 169.

107. Brian O'Neal, *Senate Committees: Role and Effectiveness* (Ottawa: Library of Parliament Research Branch, June 1994), 2 (accessed at www.parl.gc.ca/information/library/PRBpubs/bp361-e.htm, May 2007); endnotes omitted.

108. Sections 123–128 of the Standing Orders. See also Michael Dewing, "Parliamentary Committee Review of Regulations" (Ottawa: Library of Parliament Research Branch, January 2006), 11–12.

109. Thomas, "Comparing the Lawmaking Roles," 212–14.

110. Ibid., 222–23.

111. Rémillard and Turner, "Senate Reform," 123–24.

112. The committee's mission, and its rationale for taking international human rights instruments into account, are contained in its December 2001 report. The report, entitled "Promises to Keep: Implementing Canada's Human Rights Obligations," is available at www.parl.gc.ca. Go to "Committee Business," click on "Senate Committee List," and follow the links to the Standing Senate Committee on Human Rights. The second report was issued during the first session of the 37th Parliament.

113. Kent Roach, *September 11: Consequences for Canada* (Montreal and Kingston: McGill–Queen's University Press, 2003), 66–69.

114. The report of the Special Committee on Illegal Drugs, issued in September 2002, recommended that the simple possession of cannabis (marijuana) be decriminalized. The report is available on the Senate Committees website; go to www.parl.gc.ca and follow the links (the report was listed in the Committee Archives under the second session of the 37th Parliament).

115. Thomas, "Comparing the Lawmaking Roles," 220.

116. Franks, "The Canadian Senate in Modern Times," 152.

117. Docherty, *Mr. Smith Goes to Ottawa,* 143–44; John C. Courtney, *Elections* (Vancouver: UBC Press, 2004), 129–133.

118. Thomas, "Comparing the Lawmaking Roles," 206–09.

119. Murray, "Which Criticisms Are Founded?" 147.

120. As of October 2008, there were 30 female senators; there were 88 senators in total, taking vacancies into account. Membership lists for the Senate, showing the number of women, can be found at www.parl.gc.ca.

121. In late 2000, visible minorities and Aboriginals accounted for roughly 7 percent of MPs and 10 percent of senators. See Jonathan Nagle, "Appendix: Database and Charts on the Composition of the Senate and House of Commons," in Joyal, ed., *Protecting Canadian Democracy,* Chart C-1, 326.

122. Courtney, *Elections,* 53.

123. Ajzenstat, "Bicameralism and Canada's Founders," 15.

124. See Jennifer Smith, "Canadian Confederation and the Influence of American Federalism," *Canadian Journal of Political Science,* 21:3 (September 1988), 443–64.

125. The brief exception to this rule came during the three years between the initial signing of the Meech Lake Accord in 1987 and its collapse in June 1990. During this interregnum, Prime Minister Mulroney agreed to make Senate appointments from lists submitted by provincial governments.

126. Senate of Canada, Special Senate Committee on Senate Reform, "Report on The Motion to Amend the Constitution of Canada (western regional representation in the Senate)" (Ottawa, October 2006); accessed at www.parl.gc.ca.

127. For a discussion of this issue, see Howe and Northrup, 10–22.

128. See, for example, Louise Carbert, "Governing on 'The Correct, the Compassionate, the Saskatchewan Side of the Border,'" in Jane Arscott and Linda Trimble, eds., *In the Presence of Women: Representation in Canadian Governments* (Toronto: Harcourt Brace, 1997), 161–64.

129. Heather MacIvor, *Women and Politics in Canada: An Introductory Text* (Peterborough, ON: Broadview Press, 1996), Chapters 8 and 9. See also Lisa Young, "Fulfilling the Mandate of Difference: Women in the Canadian House of Commons," in Arscott and Trimble, eds., *In the Presence of Women*, 82–103.

130. Robinson represented a British Columbia constituency in the Commons for a quarter-century. He resigned for personal reasons in early 2004. He ran in a different constituency in 2006 and lost to a Liberal candidate.

131. An ombudsman is a public official empowered to investigate citizen complaints about treatment received from, and within, the bureaucracy. While not authorized to investigate complaints about the general nature of public policy, an ombudsman has a wide range of investigative powers relating to the administration of public policy.

132. Docherty, *Mr. Smith Goes to Ottawa*, 251.

133. Ibid., 121.

134. Ibid., 129.

135. John Ferejohn and Brian Gaines, "The Personal Vote in Canada," in Bakvis, ed., *Representation, Integration and Political Parties in Canada*, 295–96.

136. Docherty, *Mr. Smith Goes to Ottawa*, 212–13.

137. Ibid., 194.

138. *The Business of Supply: Completing the Circle of Control*, 51st Report from the Standing Committee on Procedure and House Affairs, House of Commons, October 1998, 1.

139. House of Commons, *Précis of Procedure*, section 13.

140. Canada, House of Commons, Standing Committee on Government Operations and Estimates, *Meaningful Scrutiny: Practical Improvements to the Estimates Process* (Ottawa, September 2003), 29.

141. Dobell, "What Could Canadians Expect from a Minority Government?" 14.

142. *The Business of Supply: Completing the Circle of Control*, 1.

143. Ibid., 3.

144. Ibid., 3.

145. House of Commons, *Précis of Procedure*, section 13, (a)(i).

146. In 1990, for example, the 20 standing committees held fewer than 50 meetings on the Estimates, and none reported back to the House. *The Business of Supply: Completing the Circle of Control*, 17.

147. The first *Appropriation Act* for the 2000–01 fiscal year is a typical case. In a few hours on a single day, the Act was introduced and read the first time; read the second time and referred to a Committee of the Whole; considered in Committee of the Whole; reported without amendment; concurred in at report stage; read the third time and passed. Status of House Business: Sunday, October 22, 2000," *Government Bills*, Commons, Bill C-30 (R). The "R" designates a money Bill that has been "recommended" by the governor general.

148. Peter Dobell and Martin Ulrich, "Parliament's Performance in the Budget Process: A Case Study," *Policy Matters*, 3:5 (Montreal: Institute for Research on Public Policy, June 2002), 9.

149. Peter Dobell and Martin Ulrich, "Parliament and Financial Accountability," in Savoie, ed., *Restoring Accountability: Parliament, Ministers and Deputy Ministers*, 29. After repeated demands from committees, public servants in the Treasury Board Secretariat (TBS) have made some effort to clarify and explain the Estimates and related documents. But these efforts have not

gone far enough, in the opinion of the Standing Committee on Government Operations and Estimates. In some cases, TBS officials have invoked Cabinet confidentiality (Chapter 8) as a reason for withholding information from Parliament; elsewhere, experts have argued that the Royal Recommendation process prevents the TBS from sharing details with MPs. *Meaningful Scrutiny*, 13, 19–27, and 33–34.

150. Good, *The Politics of Public Management*, 196.

151. Dobell and Ulrich, "Parliament and Financial Accountability," 25.

152. The relevant provisions are contained in section 116 of the Act.

153. *Restoring Accountability: Recommendations*, 55–61 [excerpts]. Commission of Inquiry into the Sponsorship Program and Advertising Activities [the Gomery Commission], *Volume 2: Restoring Accountability*, 2006, 55–61. Notes omitted. Reproduced with the permission of the Minister of Public Works and Government Services, 2008, and courtesy of the Privy Council Office.

154. Ibid., 75.

155. Malloy, "The Standing Committee on Public Accounts," 64.

156. Savoie, *Court Government*, 277.

157. Ibid., 281.

158. Ibid., 92 and 259.

159. Ibid., 277.

160. *Restoring Accountability: Recommendations*, 29.

161. Malloy, "The Standing Committee on Public Accounts," 65.

162. Ibid., 83.

163. Note, however, that in 2006 the Harper Government provided for a maximum 10-year term for future Auditors General, and gave the Cabinet the power to remove officers of Parliament for cause. Library of Parliament, Parliamentary Information and Research Service, *Legislative Summary: Bill C-2, The Federal Accountability Act* (Ottawa, December 2006), 36.

164. See the discussion of individual judicial independence in Chapter 10.

165. There is one possible exception to their independence: some officers of Parliament have recently complained that their offices are underfunded, and argued that they should have guaranteed multi-year funding to insulate their work from political pressure (from either the Crown or the Commons). Kristen Douglas and Nancy Holmes, "Funding Officers of Parliament," *Canadian Parliamentary Review* (Autumn 2005), 13–17.

166. Jeffrey Graham Bell, "Agents of Parliament: A New Branch of Government?" *Canadian Parliamentary Review* (Spring 2006), 15.

167. Ibid.

168. Savoie, *Court Government and the Collapse of Accountability*, 168.

169. Bell, 16.

170. Savoie, *Court Government*, 168.

171. Ibid.

172. Radwanski was not fired by a joint resolution of the two Houses, as required by the law at that time. He resigned after it became clear that his position was politically untenable because of public revelations of lavish spending, and allegations that he had mistreated some employees and misled a parliamentary committee.

173. Savoie, *Court Government*, 167.

174. Paul G. Thomas, "The past, present and future of officers of Parliament," *Canadian Public Administration* 46:3 (Autumn 2003), accessed at http://find.galegroup.com, June 2008.

175. In 1925, Liberal Prime Minister Mackenzie King dissolved Parliament for a general election. The voters returned fewer Liberals than Conservatives (104 to 115). According to constitutional convention, King should have resigned immediately and allowed the governor

general, Lord Byng, to call upon Conservative leader Arthur Meighen to form a government. Instead, King stayed in office and delayed the return of Parliament for as long as he could. Finally, in 1926, he had to summon the Commons so that his government could secure the funds it needed to operate. Within a short time, his government was defeated in the House. Instead of resigning, King went to Lord Byng and asked him to dissolve Parliament for another election. Byng refused, accepted King's resignation, and called on Meighen to form a government. Meighen's government lasted only a few days; after it too was defeated, Byng dissolved Parliament. In the ensuing election, King turned the governor general's actions into the central campaign issue. He was re-elected with a majority. The "King-Byng crisis" may have established a new constitutional convention in Canada: that the governor general must accept the advice of a prime minister to dissolve Parliament for an election, even when there is an alternative government available.

176. John C. Courtney, *The Selection of National Party Leaders in Canada* (Toronto: Macmillan, 1973), 222.

177. *Report of the Special Committee on Reform of the House of Commons* (the McGrath Report) (Ottawa: Minister of Supply and Services, 1985), 7.

178. Docherty, "Could the Rebels Find a Cause?" 311.

179. Courtney, *Elections*, 111.

180. "Editorial: Maxime Bernier: The wrong man for the job," *The Globe and Mail*, May 27, 2008 (accessed at www.theglobeandmail.com); Les Whittington, "Lightweight MP appointed in a bid for Quebec votes," *The Toronto Star*, May 27, 2008 (accessed at www.thestar.com).

181. Franks, *The Parliament of Canada*, 24; see also 74–75.

182. Savoie, *Court Government*, 38.

183. Ibid.

184. *Report of the Special Committee on the Modernization and Improvement of the Procedures of the House of Commons,* June 1, 2001, paragraph 6.

185. See, for example, Jennifer Smith, "Debating the Reform of Canada's Parliament," 150–67; Howe and Northrup, 22–24; Dobell, "Reforming Parliamentary Practice."

186. Docherty and Seidle, "Introduction," 3–17.

187. Under pressure from his colleagues, who voted to suspend him without pay, Thompson resigned his Senate seat in 1997. See Joyal, "Introduction," xviii.

188. Stilborn, "Forty Years," 55–59.

189. As discussed in Chapter 5, the late Quebec premier Robert Bourassa did accept a Triple-E Senate as part of the Charlottetown Accord. However, he insisted that Quebec be compensated for its loss of Senate seats by receiving a permanent 25 percent share of the Commons. This tradeoff angered English Canadians, who felt that Quebec was getting too much, while some Quebeckers feared that they would lose too much power in national politics.

190. Rémillard and Turner, "Senate Reform," 128.

191. Smith, "The Improvement of the Senate by Nonconstitutional Means," 258–59.

192. Savoie, *Court Government*, 289.

8

The Cabinet

LEARNING OBJECTIVES

After you finish reading this chapter, you should be able to:

- *identify* and *define* the three main elements of Canada's national executive branch;
- *identify* and *explain* at least six sources of the prime minister's power;
- *summarize* and *evaluate* the claim that Canada is now governed by the prime minister's "court," rather than the Cabinet;
- *list* and briefly *explain* three criteria that the prime minister uses to select Cabinet ministers;
- *describe* the work of the Cabinet committee system, and *contrast* it to the activities of the full Cabinet;
- *summarize* the central elements of the Sponsorship Scandal.

INTRODUCTION

At the start of Chapter 2, you were asked to imagine that your entire class had been stranded on a desert island and forced to create governing institutions from scratch. It is possible, but unlikely, that you would give most of the decision-making power to one person, who would be chosen (and ultimately removed) by a tiny elite group—not elected by all the inhabitants. It is even less likely that you would empower him or her to reshape the government whenever and however he or she wants; to appoint the people who will enforce and interpret the rules; or to fire the enforcers whenever he felt like it. Entrusting one human being with that much power is unwise, especially in the absence of a clear mechanism to take that power away.

If you think that such a potent head of government would be impossible in a modern democracy, brace yourself: the above paragraph describes the prime minister of Canada. Because he[1] is never mentioned in the constitution, he exercises his broad powers with few explicit entrenched constraints. He is selected to lead his party by a few thousand people; if that party holds more seats in the House of Commons than any other, he becomes the head of government. Only the voters who live in his constituency vote directly for him. The PM hires and fires Cabinet ministers, appoints the top judges, and rearranges the structure of the executive branch as he sees fit. He is the dominant figure in the Canadian executive, which is by far the largest and most powerful of the three branches of government. Indeed, when we refer casually to "the federal government," we usually mean the executive branch alone.

Whereas the judicial branch consists of one type of institution (the courts), and the legislative branch comprises the Crown, House of Commons, and Senate, the executive comprises a complex and sprawling array of institutions and programs. In its simplest terms, Canada's national executive can be divided into three major elements:

1. The **Crown** is represented by the governor general (except when the monarch is in Canada). The governor general is appointed for a five-year term by the prime minister. Over the centuries, her role in the executive branch has diminished from broad discretionary powers to a largely ceremonial function; however, she retains the reserve and emergency powers of the Crown to be used in case of constitutional emergency.[2] The **prerogative** powers of the Crown are normally exercised by the second and third elements of the executive branch.

2. The **political executive** includes the prime minister of the day and his Cabinet. The term "Cabinet" refers to the MPs (and one or more senators) from the governing party who hold ministerial portfolios at the pleasure of the prime minister, while they collectively enjoy the confidence of the House of Commons. Canada, unlike most European countries, has little experience of **coalition** governments; with the sole exception of the wartime Union cabinet, all of our national Cabinets have been composed of MPs and Senators from a single party.

3. The **permanent executive** (the **federal public service**) consists of career public servants who work in **central agencies, line departments, Crown corporations,** and other components of the federal government. (It is described in Chapter 9.)

Collectively, the three elements of the executive branch perform key government functions:

- Drafting, approving, enacting, and enforcing regulations made under the law-making authority delegated by Parliament.
- Initiating, drafting, sponsoring, and implementing the laws passed by Parliament.
- Making and executing agreements with other governments—provincial as well as foreign—often without the approval of Parliament.
- Raising, allocating, and spending public funds, nominally with the consent of Parliament, and monitoring that spending to ensure that it remains within the approved limits and has the desired effect.

Most of the activity in the executive branch is guided by written laws and policies that have been in effect for decades, and by the unwritten constitutional conventions inherited from Britain. Although new legislation and changes in policy attract most of the attention from the media and the public, these innovations are only a small part of what Canada's executive actually does.

In theory, the Cabinet is a collegial decision-making body. The prime minister is *primus inter pares* (Latin for "first among equals"), but he does not run the show. Cabinet ministers are collectively responsible to the House of Commons for the direction of public policy and the operation of the federal government. Each individual minister is responsible to Parliament for the administration of her department. Within that department, the minister is the political master; the public servants act only on her direction. There is a strict separation between politics and administration.

If the above was ever an accurate portrayal of Canada's political executive, it is no longer.

- As previously explained, the prime minister dominates both legislative and executive branches of government. The Cabinet has been reduced to a focus group for the PM. Power now resides with the PM's inner circle, which one leading expert on Canadian government—hearkening back to the Middle Ages—has dubbed the "court."

By court government I do not mean the rise of judicial power. Rather, I mean that effective political power now rests with the prime minister and a small group of carefully selected courtiers. I also mean a shift from formal decision-making processes in cabinet and, as a consequence, in the civil service, to informal processes involving only a handful of key actors.[3]

- Second, as we saw in Chapter 7, Parliament cannot hold the Cabinet collectively accountable when the governing party has a majority in the House of Commons. Even in a minority Parliament, MPs lack the expertise to monitor the details of executive activity. In practice, Cabinet ministers are accountable only to the prime minister, because he has the sole power to hire and fire them. Consequently, ministers have a powerful incentive to do his bidding.
- Third, ministers are no longer willing to accept responsibility for administrative problems in their departments. This change in attitudes has weakened the traditional distinction between politics and administration. As we will see in Chapter 9, deputy ministers—the public servants who run government departments—are no longer shielded from Parliamentary and media scrutiny by their political masters. At the same time, the boundary between political decisions and administrative decisions has become fuzzy. The elite members of the permanent executive owe their jobs to the favour of the prime minister, which gives them an incentive to shield the Government of the day from political embarrassment.

All members of the political executive are supposed to follow the constitutional convention of collective responsibility. Given the current confusion about the precise meaning of "responsibility" in this context, it is useful to compare it to the related concepts of "accountability" and "answerability" as defined by Justice Gomery (Dossier 8.1).

The gap between the theory of responsible Cabinet government and the reality of our executive branch was starkly revealed by the Sponsorship Scandal in the Department of Public Works and Government Services (Dossier 8.2). The public servant in charge, acting on the

DOSSIER 8.1 Justice Gomery on Ministerial Responsibility

Responsible government in Canada is based on the individual and collective responsibilities of Ministers to Parliament. Ministers of the Crown are responsible for the conduct of government. They are accountable to Parliament.

Three words are used to designate the duties of Ministers: responsibility, accountability and answerability. . . . A Minister is *responsible* for the department of which he or she has the overall direction and management. . . . A Minister is *accountable* in that he or she must render an account to Parliament of how his or her ministerial responsibilities have been carried out. The Minister must take corrective action should problems have occurred, must

correct any problems that have been identified, and must accept the consequences if the problem is attributable to the Minister's own actions or inactions. Answerability refers to a duty to inform and explain to Parliament what has occurred in a department of the Government. A Minister is *answerable* to Parliament for the department under his or her jurisdiction, even if the subject of the questions refers to the administration under a previous Minister. Accordingly, answerability is narrower in scope than accountability in that it entails neither responsibility to take action nor the personal consequences associated with accountability.[4]

direction of the Prime Minister's Office, steered government contracts for advertising and event planning to firms that had donated money to the Liberal Party. According to Justice Gomery's report, the normal controls on the contracting-out process were circumvented, or perhaps ignored altogether, by the members of the political and permanent executives involved. As Justice Gomery put it, blurring the lines between politics and public administration made it possible for the Department of Public Works to provide "arbitrary handouts to the governing party's present or potential friends and supporters, for partisan considerations."[5]

DOSSIER 8.2 The Sponsorship Scandal

Shortly after the 1995 sovereignty referendum in Quebec, the federal Cabinet decided that the federal government and its symbols (especially the Canadian flag) should be more visible in that province. Then-Prime Minister Chrétien and his Chief of Staff, Jean Pelletier, decided to establish a new Sponsorship Program to raise the profile of the federal government. The Program would subsidize community events throughout Quebec, ranging from the Montreal Indy race to fishing shows in far-flung towns; in return, the organizers would display the logo and symbols of the Canadian government in prominent places.

Although the Program was initially funded from the Unity Reserve—a special fund administered by the prime minister, without parliamentary oversight—it would be administered by a government advertising agency housed in the Department of Public Works and Government Services Canada (PWGSC). More precisely, it would be run by a mid-level public servant personally selected by Pelletier: Charles (Chuck) Guité, a man with a reputation for "cutting red tape" to get things done quickly.[6] Guité took his orders directly from the Prime Minister's Office (PMO), including lists of events to be sponsored. The deputy minister of Public Works was completely cut out of the loop. When Alfonso Gagliano (a key Liberal organizer in Montreal) was appointed minister of Public Works in 1997, he too worked directly with Guité.[7]

In a nutshell, Guité gave contracts to Montreal advertising agencies to work with event organizers and produce the display materials containing federal government logos. These contracts were awarded at Guité's per-

sonal discretion and without competition, in direct violation of the rules set by the Treasury Board Secretariat. Each firm was paid a 15-percent commission on top of the actual work performed under contract. In addition, the production costs were billed separately from the contract amount—which raises questions about what exactly the contracts themselves were for.[8] In some cases, advertising agencies were paid thousands of dollars for little or no actual work. When work was done, some agencies charged inflated fees that were never questioned by Guité or his staff. In summary, "the owners of the agencies that handled most sponsorship contracts became very wealthy very rapidly."[9]

A second element of the Cabinet's post-referendum strategy was "a substantial strengthening of the organization of the Liberal Party of Canada in Quebec [LPCQ]." This required headquarters to hire several new full-time employees—an expensive proposition at a time when the LPCQ was in desperate financial straits.[10] It had two options: find a way to raise a lot of money very quickly, or persuade someone else to pay the salaries of its new employees. At some point between 1995 and 1997, someone—allegedly Jacques Corriveau, a close friend of Prime Minister Chrétien—realized that the Sponsorship Program could be used to serve both objectives.

The combination of a poorly administered funding program and the pressing need to raise money for the LPCQ produced the Sponsorship Scandal. Former Prime Minister Chrétien testified that the only ad agencies who were considered for contracts were "federalist friendly." In Justice Gomery's words, "One of the ways an

(continued)

agency could demonstrate that it was 'federalist friendly' was by making contributions to the party in power [i.e., the LPCQ]. Certainly the agencies concerned believed that the political contributions they were making were one of the most important reasons why they were awarded sponsorship contracts."[11] Between 1997 and 2003, the Sponsorship Program contributed roughly $250 million to almost two thousand events; of that amount, more than $100 million was spent on production fees and commissions to communications and advertising firms. Most of these firms were linked to the LPCQ in some way.[12]

The most notorious firm, Groupaction, was owned by Jean Brault. At the Gomery hearings, Brault acknowledged (in Justice Gomery's words) that "the payment by Groupaction of sums of money to officers and representatives of the LPCQ, or the furnishing of employment to certain persons at its request, had as its objective the securing of additional sponsorship contracts from PWGSC."[13] In the mid-1990s, Brault had started to make substantial (and entirely legal) donations to the Liberal Party; he also attended fundraising events where he hoped to make contacts that would help his business. In 1996 he met both Guité and Jean Carle, Pelletier's assistant in the PMO. Mr. Brault was told by various persons connected to the Liberals that if he wanted to profit from sponsorship contracts, he would have to contribute more money to the LPCQ. Unlike his previous donations, these would be illegal and unreported contributions through unofficial channels.[14] He was also pressured to put two LPCQ strategists—who worked full-time for the party, and did no work for the ad agency—on the Groupaction payroll, and to cover some fundraising expenses incurred by the party. Starting in 1997, Groupaction received sponsorship contracts worth millions of dollars. The firm became the target of intense public scrutiny in 2002, when it was revealed that Groupaction had been paid over a million dollars for two reports; the second report was simply a copy of the first, and both were worthless to the government.

Parliament was not told about the Sponsorship Program until 1999, when its funding was shifted from the Unity Reserve to the budget of PWGSC and it first appeared in the departmental Estimates.[15] In October 2000, a scathing internal audit of the Sponsorship Program appeared on the PWGSC website.[16] Opposition MPs began to ask questions in Parliament about the Program, and especially about the enrichment of ad firms that also worked for the Liberal Party. This was the first time that most Cabinet ministers heard about the Program and its activities, according to their later testimony before Justice Gomery.[17] After months of hectoring from Opposition MPs, Gagliano was shuffled out of the Cabinet and appointed ambassador to Denmark. His replacement, Don Boudria, could not put out the political fire. In May 2002 Chrétien's favourite "fixer," Ralph Goodale, was appointed minister of Public Works. Within a short time, Goodale imposed proper management controls on government advertising and sponsorships.

Shortly after Goodale's appointment, Auditor General Sheila Fraser issued a special report on the Sponsorship Program and three of the contracts that it had awarded to Groupaction. The report showed that there was no documentation to demonstrate why any of the examined expenditures had been necessary, or why Groupaction had received contracts at Guité's discretion that should have been subject to public competition.[18] At a news conference, Fraser declared that "Senior public servants broke just about every rule in the book," and announced that she had asked the RCMP to investigate possible criminal wrongdoing.[19]

Following the release of the May 2002 report, the Office of the Auditor General undertook a wide-ranging review of federal sponsorship and advertising programs. The final report was due for tabling in Parliament in November 2003. In the same month, former Finance Minister Paul Martin won the leadership of the Liberal Party of Canada. Perhaps partly in revenge for the coup that had forced him from office (Chapter 11), outgoing Prime Minister Chrétien prorogued Parliament before the OAG could table its report.[20] This meant that any new revelations about the Sponsorship

(continued)

Program would hit the headlines as soon as the new prime minister called the House back to work—so Martin, not Chrétien, would have to answer publicly for the findings. Within 48 hours of the report's release in February 2004, the Liberals fell almost 20 points in national polls. Panicked, Martin made two crucial political mistakes. First, he launched a judicial inquiry into the Sponsorship Scandal. This might have been the right decision from a moral perspective, but it ensured two more years of damaging revelations about the Liberal Party. Second, Martin embarked on a cross-country "mad as hell" tour in which he strove desperately to deflect blame. The tour backfired badly: instead of convincing Canadians that he was kept in the dark about the corrupt use of public money—which was almost certainly true—Martin's denials persuaded many that he was either incompetent or dishonest.[21]

The Commission of Inquiry into the scandal, headed by Justice John Gomery, started public hearings in Ottawa in September 2004. The testimony of former senior public servants about the poor administration of the Sponsorship Program, which often focused on boring details, received relatively little media coverage. The public really started to pay attention in the spring of 2005, after the hearings moved to Montreal. Testimony from some LPCQ members and advertising executives painted a vivid picture of political corruption; Brault's story of leaving thousands of dollars in cash on the table in an Italian restaurant during a dinner with LPCQ fundraisers was particularly memorable. In the hullabaloo about cash-stuffed envelopes, more important issues were overlooked: the breakdown of accountability in the federal executive branch; the failure to distinguish between politics and public administration; and the ease with which the prime minister and his staff could override the normal operation of a government department.

This chapter focuses on the prime minister and Cabinet; the next chapter describes the public service and its relationship to the Cabinet. We begin with a brief overview of the executive branch of government.

THE CROWN AND GOVERNOR GENERAL

Section 9 of the *Constitution Act, 1867* vests the executive power in the Crown. That power is formally exercised by "the Governor in Council"—i.e., the governor general acting on the advice of the **Privy Council** (section 12). At the provincial level, the lieutenant governor holds many of the same formal executive powers, plays the same ceremonial roles, and occupies the same position in the legislative process as does the governor general in Ottawa. While the Crown's executive powers are vast, they are exercised only on the advice of the prime minister. The political executive makes the decisions, which are then formally ratified by the Crown's representative. Every Cabinet minister, past and present, has been sworn in to the Privy Council, and they retain that status after they leave the political executive. However, the only Privy councillors who really matter are the small group (between 30 and 40) who belong to the Cabinet of the day.

The division between the prime minister as the political head of government, and the formal executive authority of the state vested in the Crown, ensures that the executive branch exists separately from the Government of the day, ensuring continuity and stability. The distinction between the head of state and the head of government also has important practical consequences for the operation of government. By carrying much of the ceremonial load that would otherwise fall on the shoulders of the prime minister, the governor general frees the PM to get on with the business of running the country.

The most important of these ceremonial duties are as follows:

- appointing the prime minister and swearing in the Cabinet (in both cases, the governor general merely ratifies the appointments);
- delivering the Speech from the Throne, which sets out the government's legislative agenda at the beginning of each session of Parliament;
- dissolving Parliament and issuing a proclamation for a general election (on the advice of the prime minister);
- bestowing Royal Recommendations on bills that authorize the raising or spending of public money (section 54 of the *Constitution Act, 1867*); and
- giving royal assent to legislation that has been adopted by both Houses of Parliament (in practice, the Chief Justice of the Supreme Court often performs this task).[22]

The Crown's representative in Canada has lost the executive discretion which was routinely exercised by British officials before Confederation. Nonetheless, the institution of the governor general provides a potential check on the power of the political executive. She retains the reserve power to reject the advice of the Cabinet and the emergency power to keep the government running in a severe national crisis (for example, the sudden death or resignation of a prime minister). While there are alternative models for a head of state—such as the elected presidents of the United States and France—the Crown possesses the advantage of political neutrality. The Crown's representative must act in the best interests of the country, not of a particular political party. None of the foregoing implies that the Governor General should exercise her reserve or emergency powers lightly; the principle of democracy would be offended by a Crown representative who refused the Prime Minister's advice.

In the United States, the ceremonial burden of a head of state is shared by the vice president. Vice presidential nominees are usually chosen to "balance the ticket" by representing a region (and perhaps an ideological faction) different from that represented by the presidential candidate. Ideally, however, a presidential nominee chooses a partisan running mate with the experience and the competence to replace him in case of death, incapacity, or impeachment. Because Canada's governor general has no partisan, electoral, or administrative role to play, the selection criteria are rather different. He or she is a symbolic bridge between the major linguistic and cultural communities in Canada; consequently, the office alternates between anglophone and francophone appointees, and the governor general must be fluent in both official languages. More recently, the selection of governors general and lieutenant governors has reflected new criteria for political representation, particularly gender and ethnicity. Adrienne Clarkson's 1999 appointment as governor general was symbolically important in two ways: she was the second woman to hold the post, and the first Chinese-Canadian. She was succeeded in 2005 by Michaëlle Jean, a Haitian-Canadian who had immigrated to Canada as a child refugee.

Beginning in the 1970s, Rideau Hall (the official residence of the governor general) was occupied by a series of former politicians. However qualified these individuals might have been, their appointment raised doubts about their impartiality in a possible political crisis. The appointment of former journalist Adrienne Clarkson signalled a return to political neutrality—even though her imperious style and lavish spending eventually triggered controversy in the House of Commons.[23] Although Michaëlle Jean is also a former journalist, her political neutrality was called into question shortly after her appointment. Some BQ MPs alleged that she and her husband supported the Quebec sovereignty movement, triggering Conservative demands for Prime Minister Martin to rescind her appointment.[24] Jean's dignified response to the outcry eventually quieted the storm, and she became a popular head of state within months after taking office. This ugly incident shows that the officially nonpolitical status of the governor general cannot protect the incumbent against the partisan machinations on Parliament Hill. However, Jean's decision to grant Prime Minister Harper an unconditional prorogation in December 2008 does raise questions about her independence from the Government of the day.

Governor General Michaëlle Jean arriving for the Canada Day celebrations on Parliament Hill, July 1, 2008. (CP/Sean Kilpatrick)

Suspending Parliament before it had a chance to express its lack of confidence in the Prime Minister seems to run counter to her central duty: to ensure that the political executive is held accountable to the citizens.

THE POLITICAL EXECUTIVE

When Britain granted responsible government to its North American colonies in the 1840s, the exercise of executive power shifted from the Crown to an appointed council whose members commanded the support of a majority in the legislature.[25] In 1867, responsible government was entrenched in the preamble to the *Constitution Act, 1867* (recall the discussion of constitutional conventions in Chapter 3). In principle, responsible government means four things:

1. The Cabinet is collectively responsible to the House of Commons, and the prime minister must resign as soon as his government loses the confidence of Parliament.
2. Individual ministers are responsible to Parliament for the conduct of their departments.
3. Ministers are responsible to the Crown, on whose behalf they exercise authority.
4. Ministers are responsible to one another, in the sense that all must adhere to collective decisions.

In practice, as noted at the beginning of this chapter, Canadian ministers are no longer individually responsible to the House of Commons. (The entire Cabinet remains collectively accountable to the House of Commons, at least in a minority Parliament; the Martin Government was defeated on a motion of non-confidence in November 2005.) Instead, ministers are directly responsible to the prime minister. Indirectly, they are also responsible to their Cabinet colleagues. The principle of Cabinet solidarity means that deliberations are held in secret, documents are confidential, and ministers who cannot publicly support the government's policy are expected to resign. The constraints of Cabinet solidarity on ministerial behaviour reinforce the constraints of party discipline to which all MPs are subject.

Because these rules are unwritten, they allow PMs to reshape the political and permanent executives to suit their own preferences and priorities. When a new PM takes office, he usually rearranges the executive branch of government to better serve his political and policy goals. Over time, some of these innovations are adopted by succeeding PMs. On occasion, an established PM will tinker with the executive branch to respond to new challenges; such alterations are usually less drastic than those imposed by brand-new PMs with a self-declared mandate for "change." While the transition from one party to another following an election loss receives most of the attention—perhaps because it is relatively rare in Canada (Chapters 11 and 12)—other changes in government are also important.[26] For example, Paul Martin overhauled the executive branch in important ways when he succeeded fellow Liberal Jean Chrétien. In either case, the mechanics of "transition" leave a deep mark on the subsequent operations of government (Dossier 8.3).

DOSSIER 8.3 Transitions in Government

Governing is an enormously complicated task. It takes time for a new prime minister to learn the ropes, and for his Cabinet ministers to master their portfolios. Because the business of government never stops, a new political executive has to get down to work as soon as it takes office. Therefore, the installation of a new government is usually preceded by a period of "transition planning."

For an Opposition leader, the question of when to appoint a transition team can be a delicate political issue. Jean Chrétien appointed his transition team more than a year before the 1993 election, as the governing Progressive Conservatives plumbed new depths in the polls, without suffering political consequences.[27] But Stephen Harper ran into trouble toward the end of the 2004 election campaign, when his decision to appoint a transition team was leaked to the media. Preparing to govern was a prudent move on Harper's part, given that his party had a slight lead in the polls, but it alarmed some voters who were not quite ready for a Conservative Government.[28] To avoid repeating this mistake, Harper's chief of staff Ian Brodie waited until the final week of the 2006 campaign before contacting the Clerk of the Privy Council to start transition planning.[29]

That short notice might have caused serious problems for the new PM. Fortunately the permanent executive had already spent two months preparing for a possible change of government (as it always does during an election campaign). Their task was made easier by the clarity and

(continued)

concreteness of the Conservative platform; most of the 400-plus promises translated easily into specific policies.[30] The public service does not work for a particular political party. Its job is to keep the machinery of government working smoothly, regardless of changes in the political executive. The senior public servants who are authorized to brief the Opposition (the Clerk of the Privy Council and his or her staff, not Departmental officials[31]) must seek the permission of the current PM before providing information to his possible successor, and they only disclose that information which has been approved by the PMO.[32] The briefer must strike a balance between the legitimate demands of Cabinet confidentiality, on the one hand, and the requirements of successful transition planning on the other. Before he can appoint qualified ministers, restructure the executive branch, and "learn the ropes," a new PM needs detailed information about the operations of government and the fiscal and policy constraints within which he must operate; only the senior members of the permanent executive can provide that information.

Once a new prime minister has been chosen—whether by the party in power or the electorate—he meets with the outgoing PM and the Clerk to discuss the details of the transition. Some details are routine: setting the date to swear in the new Cabinet, moving into the PMO, and taking possession of 24 Sussex Drive (the PM's official residence). Other pressing matters require more time and attention from the incoming PM: the size of the Cabinet, the selection and portfolio assignments of ministers, and the hiring of **exempt staff**. Although the outgoing ministers remain in place until their replacements are sworn in, they cannot make important decisions that will bind their successors. If a crucial decision must be made during this period, the soon-to-be-ex-minister or her staff will consult with the new prime minister's advisors.[33]

The transition period normally lasts for about two weeks. It is an extremely busy time for the new PM, crammed with meetings and difficult decisions. He must work closely with the Clerk to master the mechanics of government, prepare to implement any changes to the structure of the

executive branch, meet with prospective ministers to assess their fitness for particular portfolios, and set the broad policy outlines for his new Government (see the discussion of mandate letters, pp. 272–272). To assist with this overwhelming workload, recent PMs have appointed individuals with extensive experience in government to their transition teams. Ideally, the members have no personal axe to grind, because they do not expect to play important roles in the new government. The team should also include at least one person with deep knowledge of the party who can recommend qualified people to serve in ministerial offices. Otherwise, the process of hiring hundreds of exempt staff can drag on for weeks or months and produce mixed results.[34]

In addition to the nuts and bolts of establishing a new government, the transition phase should also forge good working relationships between the permanent executive and its new political masters. Government cannot work properly without trust and confidence between the Cabinet and the public service. Too often, a party (like the Conservatives) that is usually in Opposition regards the permanent executive as a nest of traitors–or, at the very least, as an extension of the governing party. Conservative suspicion of the public service was sharpened in recent years by the neoliberal suspicion of government in general.[35] The omens for the Harper Government were not promising: shortly before the 2006 election, Stephen Harper described the permanent executive as "a Liberal civil service," which would block the implementation of Conservative policies.[36] At his first meeting with Harper following the election, the then-Clerk of the Privy Council reportedly reassured the new PM that "the civil service is not only prepared to help you with the transition— we *welcome* the transition of government."[37] This statement does not reflect a particular partisan affiliation; rather, it signals both the professionalism of Canada's public service and its preference for a focused government with a few clear policy priorities. To judge from appearances, the Harper Government quickly settled down to work with the permanent executive. In this respect, the 2006 transition was a success.[38]

The Prime Minister

As noted in Chapter 7, the origins of the prime ministership were relatively modest: Britain's Privy Council needed an English-speaking chairman. Over time, as party politics evolved, the British prime minister became the leader of a disciplined parliamentary majority and acquired the use of the Crown's prerogative to select Cabinet ministers. Today, Canada's

TABLE 8.1 PRIME MINISTERS OF CANADA, 1867–2008

NAME	POLITICAL PARTY	TERM OF OFFICE
Macdonald, Sir John Alexander	Conservative	July 1, 1867–November 5, 1873
		October 17, 1878–June 6, 1891 (died in office)
MacKenzie, Sir Alexander	Liberal	November 7, 1873–October 8, 1878
Abbott, Sir John	Conservative	June 16, 1891–November 24, 1892
Thompson, Sir John	Conservative	December 5, 1892–December 12, 1894 (died in office)
Bowell, Sir Mackenzie	Conservative	December 21, 1894–April 27, 1896
Tupper, Sir Charles	Conservative	May 1, 1896–July 8, 1896
Laurier, Sir Wilfrid	Liberal	July 11, 1896–October 6, 1911
Borden, Sir Robert	Conservative	October 10, 1911–October 11, 1917
Borden, Sir Robert	Unionist*	October 12, 1917–July 9, 1920
Meighen, Arthur	Conservative	July 10, 1920–December 28, 1921 June 29, 1926–September 24, 1926
King, William Lyon Mackenzie	Liberal	December 29, 1921–June 28, 1926 September 25, 1926–August 6, 1930 October 23, 1935–November 14, 1948
Bennett, Richard	Conservative	August 7, 1930–October 22, 1935
Saint-Laurent, Louis	Liberal	November 15, 1948–June 20, 1957
Diefenbaker, John	Conservative	June 21, 1957–April 21, 1963
Pearson, Lester	Liberal	April 22, 1963–April 19, 1968
Trudeau, Pierre	Liberal	April 20, 1968–June 3, 1979 March 3, 1980–June 29, 1984
Clark, Joe	Conservative	June 4, 1979–March 2, 1980
Turner, John	Liberal	June 30, 1984–September 16, 1984
Mulroney, Brian	Conservative	September 17, 1984–June 24, 1993
Campbell, Kim	Conservative	June 25, 1993–November 3, 1993
Chrétien, Jean	Liberal	November 4, 1993–December 11, 2003
Martin, Paul	Liberal	December 12, 2003–February 6, 2006
Harper, Stephen	Conservative	February 6, 2006–

*During World War I, the country was deeply divided over the question of whether or not Canadian men should be conscripted (i.e., drafted against their will) to fight overseas. The Conservative Cabinet was joined by English-speaking Liberals in the Union Government and was able to impose conscription after the 1917 federal election.

prime minister is among the most powerful heads of government in the world (at least inside the country). Because the PM's power is based on constitutional convention rather than entrenched written law, and because the scope of the Crown prerogatives that he exercises is so vast, he "has no outer limits defining his political authority within the Government."[39] His control of Parliament, at least in a majority government, ensures legislative approval for his priorities. His control of the transition process (Dossier 8.3) puts him in the driver's seat even before the new government takes office.[40]

We have already seen that the prime minister has broad powers; these are summarized in the following list:

1. The PM can reshape the executive branch as he sees fit. He can create, merge, or abolish departments; establish new agencies and programs; and change the size and structure of the Cabinet whenever he wishes.[41]

2. The PM chooses Cabinet ministers, senators, and Supreme Court justices.[42] While the PM normally consults knowledgeable advisers about each appointment, the final decision is his alone. There are conventional constraints on the appointment of Cabinet ministers—most important, they must be members of the government caucus[43]—but within those constraints the prime minister has complete discretion.

3. Unlike senators and judges, whose tenure is protected by law, Cabinet ministers can be fired by the prime minister at any time. While individual firings are rare, PMs usually "shuffle" their Cabinets every year or two. Weak ministers whose ineptitude has embarrassed the government may be "shuffled out." In January 2002, for example, Prime Minister Chrétien fired Alfonso Gagliano from the Cabinet in response to public criticism of the Sponsorship Scandal (Dossier 8.2). A more wholesale housecleaning usually accompanies the swearing-in of a new prime minister from the incumbent governing party. Of the 39 ministers in Martin's first Cabinet in December 2003, only 17 had served in the previous Chrétien Cabinet. (Some of those survivors were later defeated in the June 2004 election, or left out of the second Cabinet when it took office in July 2004.) The two primary reasons for the December purge were Martin's desire to project the image of a new government, and the need to reward supporters of his leadership (while getting rid of stalwart Chrétien supporters).[44]

4. The PM also appoints Parliamentary Secretaries. These are Government MPs who assist Cabinet ministers in the performance of their duties. Parliamentary Secretaries sit on the Commons committees that monitor their departments, and report any political problems back to the minister. They may also stand in for their ministers in the House of Commons and at public events. The position of Parliamentary Secretary has existed for almost a century, but it lacks a clear definition. On the one hand, the Secretary is a backbench MP with most of the privileges attaching to that position (except the ability to ask questions or introduce Private Members' Bills).[45] On the other, Parliamentary Secretaries receive their own mandate letters from the prime minister, and they may be given specific departmental responsibilities by their ministers;[46] however, they cannot attend meetings of the Cabinet or Cabinet committees, because they do not take the Privy Council Oath.[47] The job of Parliamentary Secretary is widely seen as a stepping stone to Cabinet, and it is coveted by ambitious government backbenchers. The PM's appointment prerogative helps to ensure that most of his MPs follow the party line (Chapter 7).

5. The PM, as the leader of the party with the most seats in the Commons, has a democratic legitimacy denied to the rest of the Cabinet. His public profile is by far the highest of any minister. The news media focus on the activities of the PM, which can be a mixed blessing in difficult times. A PM who can manipulate the media effectively enjoys a political resource denied to other Cabinet members; he and his office can exploit news coverage to "strengthen the prime minister's institutional prerogatives by

setting the government's agenda and so further circumvent the very real collegial constraints of parliamentary government."[48] Today, it is rare for an important announcement to be made by anyone other than the PM. The minister whose portfolio is directly involved usually attends, but he is relegated a supporting role. At best, he will "provide background information to the media after the announcement. Harper's PMO explains that leaving announcements to the responsible minister will 'not draw television cameras to the show.'"[49] Having said as much, an unhelpful and iron-fisted approach to reporters can backfire.[50]

6. Until recently, the PM in a majority government could call an election at any time within the five-year life of a Parliament. This power has now been limited by statute (Dossier 12.1). However, it may still be possible for a PM with a minority in the Commons to engineer his Government's defeat at a politically beneficial time. In September 2008, all that PM Harper had to do was to advise the governor general that the current Parliament was unworkable; she granted his request for a dissolution immediately. The voters were not quite so obliging, denying Harper the majority that he sought.

7. When his party wins (and especially when it wins a majority), the PM takes the credit. He can silence dissent in Cabinet and caucus by reminding ministers and MPs that many of them were elected on his coattails. Even in the face of electoral setbacks, such as the 2004 Liberal minority, the PM rarely faces reprisals from his party.[51] Although he may be subject to a leadership-review vote at a party convention, there is no formal mechanism in Canada for the caucus or Cabinet to fire an ineffective leader. This is in stark contrast to former British PM Margaret Thatcher, whose caucus threw her out of office in 1990.[52]

8. The most powerful central agency in the Canadian government, the Privy Council Office, reports directly to the PM. The Clerk of the Privy Council is the top official in the permanent executive. His or her appointment is entirely subject to the discretion of the prime minister of the day.[53] Therefore, the PM is the only member of the Cabinet who chooses his own deputy minister. (See Chapter 9 for a discussion of the Clerk's role.) In turn, the Clerk recommends the hiring, transfer, and firing of deputy ministers and other senior public servants. He or she also monitors the entire permanent executive, through frequent meetings with deputy ministers, as well as the political executive, through the PCO note-takers who attend all Cabinet and Cabinet committee meetings. Every morning the Clerk briefs the PM on current developments in the executive branch. The close working relationship between the PM and the Clerk has at least two advantages for the PM:

   • it ensures that he—and he alone—has access to information about all departments and agencies; and
   • the individual to whom every senior public servant is directly accountable has a powerful incentive to keep the PM happy.

   In addition, the PCO handles all the paperwork for the Cabinet and its committees. It sets meeting agendas, takes and distributes the minutes, and prepares briefing materials on the issues to be resolved. The Clerk provides all these materials to the PM and submits proposed agendas for his approval. The PM can add or delete agenda items as he wishes, which gives him an absolute veto over the policy direction of the government.

9. The PM chairs Cabinet meetings and summarizes the discussions. No formal votes are taken in Cabinet; the PM's summary is the only official record of the deliberations. As such, it sets out the overall policy of the government and directs the operations of the executive branch. A PM usually "goes with the flow" on low-priority issues, but he can sometimes ignore an opposing majority and declare a consensus in support of his own position on a high-priority issue.[54]

10. The PM issues a mandate letter to each minister, deputy minister, and Parliamentary Secretary at the beginning of his or her tenure.[55] The mandate letters for Cabinet ministers

explain the responsibilities of Cabinet office, describe the major issues relating to the specific portfolio, and set out the PM's priorities in that policy field.[56] Some portfolios are not expected to be politically sensitive or to generate much policy innovation during a given mandate; their ministers may be instructed to manage existing programs, not to rock the boat.[57] The letters are drafted by the PCO, but each is revised and approved by the PM. He can change a department's mandate and priority if and when he sees fit.[58]

11. The PM has his own central agency, the Prime Minister's Office, which straddles the line between the political and permanent executives. Whereas the PCO provides non-partisan policy and operational advice, the PMO serves as the "political antennae" of the PM. It enhances the PM's authority over the Cabinet, the government caucus, and the party organization outside Parliament. (See "The Prime Minister's Office" in Chapter 9.)

12. Although the PM does not have a specific portfolio, he is traditionally responsible for three policy fields: foreign affairs and security, national unity, and federal–provincial relations. Indeed, former Prime Minister Chrétien testified before Justice Gomery that "the maintenance of Canadian unity was his duty and his first priority as Prime Minister."[59] On these issues, the Cabinet usually defers to the PM. He can participate in constitutional negotiations, trade talks, and informal meetings with premiers, without any interference from the Cabinet. As Justice Gomery put it, "There are no established limits to restrict the involvement of the Prime Minister and his or her senior staff in whatever issue they decide to take over and manage."[60]

13. As globalization shifts decision-making power from national governments to supranational agencies, the PM's position as the head of Canada's government acquires even greater importance. He meets with other world leaders, collectively or individually, striking agreements that bind the federal government without the necessity of Cabinet or parliamentary approval. Examples include World Summits, the Organization of American States, and the World Trade Organization.[61] The PM's independent role on the world stage is increasingly mirrored at home in Ottawa: when he decided to reject the Bush Administration's request for military intervention in Iraq, former Prime Minister Chrétien "did not even bother to secure cabinet's approval."[62]

14. Finally, the PM can intervene in any issue that particularly interests him, or that threatens to become a problem for his government. As soon as a particular issue is identified as a prime ministerial priority, the machinery of government mobilizes to serve his will:

> [W]hen Canadian or British prime ministers and their courts wish to approve a new initiative, they move everything out of the reach of ministers, departments, and career officials and simply get it done. This approach can be described as policy making by announcements. That is, prime ministers simply deliver a major speech to unveil a new policy and then let the government decision-making process pick up the pieces as best it can. Given that the prime minister has a direct say in the career prospects of ministers, aspiring ministers, heads of departments, and aspiring heads of departments, everyone has an interest in seeing the prime minister's initiative come to a successful conclusion.[63]

No Cabinet minister can enact a policy without the PM's support; conversely, prime ministers can—and sometimes do—override ministers whose preferences clash with their own. The PM is also the final umpire in conflicts between ministers.

The exact degree of power exercised by any particular PM is impossible to quantify. It depends on intangible traits like charisma, focus, competence, and media skill.[64] However, in general, the lack of formal constraints make Canada's prime minister more powerful than his counterparts in other democratic states—especially when he has a majority in the Commons.[65]

Having said as much, the formal powers of a Canadian PM do have some limits:

1. The PM cannot act unconstitutionally. While the scope of executive power at the federal level is poorly defined, it is limited by the division of powers and by judicial review of the *Charter.* In particular, sections 4 and 5 of the *Charter* require prime ministers to seek a new mandate from the electorate at least once every five years[66] and to submit annually to the scrutiny of Parliament.

2. A PM usually seeks to avoid controversy and embarrassment. The Opposition in the Commons, together with the media, can grill the PM over real or apparent errors in policy and administration. Preventing or "managing" such errors consumes much of the PM's scarce time and attention—and that of his senior officials in the supposedly "apolitical" PCO.

3. A wise PM will recognize the limits of his political capital and use it sparingly. For example, the power to summarize Cabinet discussions in a way that conflicts with the views of the majority should be exercised sparingly. Otherwise, the PM risks a public revolt against his leadership and ultimately the collapse of the government.[67]

4. Because of the scarcity of time, a PM can pursue only a few priorities. All other issues must be either delegated to the Cabinet, or ignored. Pierre Trudeau's priorities included the *Constitution,* the threat of Quebec sovereignty, inflation, and foreign affairs. Brian Mulroney also focused on constitutional and national-unity issues, as well as free trade with the United States.[68] Jean Chrétien was forced to respond to the national-unity crisis provoked by the 1995 Quebec referendum (see Chapter 5). In fact, his focus on Quebec sowed the seeds of the Sponsorship Scandal.[69] His other priorities included international trade—both multilateral negotiations through summit meetings and informal contacts with foreign buyers on Team Canada missions and deficit and debt reduction. Toward the end of his decade as prime minister, Chrétien focused on his "legacy" projects. These included a new campaign-finance law[70] and stronger ethics rules for government officials. Paul Martin's inability to focus on a few key priorities likely shortened his tenure as prime minister, and limited his effectiveness in the job.[71] At the very least, it may have made Stephen Harper's 2006 campaign, with its clear list of five policy priorities, more attractive to voters. Martin appears to have overlooked the single greatest constraint on a PM's power: his limited time and energy.[72] Ironically, his successor may have missed that lesson; some observers have described Prime Minister Harper as a "control freak" who tries to run the entire government with the assistance of a small inner circle.[73] But even Harper has to respond to unexpected events:

> A prime minister's focus, even on a handful of priorities, can never be taken for granted. It only takes a crisis to shift his or her attention elsewhere. One can only imagine what it was like in Harper's PMO when national newspapers took his government to task for being asleep at the switch in the summer of 2006 when Canadians citizens were left stranded in Beirut while citizens of other countries were being evacuated. . . .[74]

In summary, the prime minister is not just the "first among equals," except perhaps when he or she attends meetings of first ministers.[75] Even then, the federal spending power in areas of provincial jurisdiction ensures that the PM's goals sometimes take priority over the demands of the premiers (Chapter 4). Among his Cabinet colleagues, the PM's preeminence is unquestioned. He sets the agenda, has the final say on high-priority issues, and enjoys a broad overview of government activities that is denied to other ministers. (The minister of Finance is a partial exception to this last point, because of his responsibility for the budget process.)

The prime minister is always designated "The Right Honourable." All other Cabinet ministers are styled "Honourable." Those titles have been omitted here to save space. The order of precedence is determined by two factors: (1) the date on which the individual became a member of the House of Commons—or the Senate, in the case of LeBreton; and (2) where two or more ministers were first sworn in on the same day, by alphabetical order. The only portfolio that determines precedence is that of the prime minister, who always appears at the top of the list.

NAME	PORTFOLIO
SENIOR MINISTERS	
Stephen Joseph Harper	Prime Minister of Canada
Robert Douglas Nicholson	Minister of Justice and Attorney General of Canada
Jean-Pierre Blackburn	Minister of National Revenue and Minister of State (Agriculture)
Gregory Francis Thompson	Minister of Veterans Affairs
Marjory LeBreton	Leader of the Government in the Senate and Minister of State (Seniors)
Chuck Strahl	Minister of Indian Affairs and Northern Development and Federal Interlocutor for Métis and Non-Status Indians
Peter Gordon MacKay	Minister of National Defence and Minister for the Atlantic Gateway
Stockwell Day	Minister of International Trade and Minister for the Asia-Pacific Gateway
Vic Toews	President of the Treasury Board
Rona Ambrose	Minister of Labour
Diane Finley	Minister of Human Resources and Skills Development
Beverley J. Oda	Minister of International Cooperation
Jim Prentice	Minister of the Environment
John Baird	Minister of Transport, Infrastructure and Communities
Lawrence Cannon	Minister of Foreign Affairs
Tony Clement	Minister of Industry
James Michael Flaherty	Minister of Finance
Josée Verner	Minister of Intergovernmental Affairs, President of the Queen's Privy Council for Canada and Minister for La Francophonie
Jay D. Hill	Leader of the Government in the House of Commons
Peter Van Loan	Minister of Public Safety
Gerry Ritz	Minister of Agriculture and Agri-Food and Minister for the Canadian Wheat Board
Jason Kenney	Minister of Citizenship, Immigration and Multiculturalism
Christian Paradis	Minister of Public Works and Government Services
James Moore	Minister of Canadian Heritage and Official Languages
Leona Aglukkaq	Minister of Health
Lisa Raitt	Minister of Natural Resources
Gail Shea	Minister of Fisheries and Oceans

Gary Lunn	Minister of State (Sport)
Gordon O'Connor	Minister of State and Chief Government Whip
Helena Guergis	Minister of State (Status of Women)
Diane Ablonczy	Minister of State (Small Business and Tourism)
Rob Merrifield	Minister of State (Transport)
Lynne Yelich	Minister of State (Western Economic Diversification)
Steven John Fletcher	Minister of State (Democratic Reform)
Gary Goodyear	Minister of State (Science and Technology)
Denis Lebel	Minister of State (Economic Development Agency of Canada for the Regions of Quebec)
Keith Ashfield	Minister of State (Atlantic Canada Opportunities Agency)
Peter Kent	Minister of State of Foreign Affairs (Americas)

Source: The Cabinet in order of precedence: http://www.pm.gc.ca/eng/cabinet.asp? Retrieved October 30, 2008. Reproduced with the permission of the Minister of Public Works and Government Services, 2008, and courtesy of the Privy Council Office.

■ The Rest of the Cabinet

When a PM takes office, or decides to reshape the political executive, he must first decide how large the Cabinet will be and whether to appoint one or more categories of minister. These considerations are directly related. For example, the last Chrétien Cabinet had only 28 members, whereas the ministry as a whole included almost 40 people. The reason is that Chrétien distinguished between senior ministers and junior Secretaries of State. The latter were not formally designated as members of the Cabinet, but they were entitled to most of the perks of office (including salaries, benefits, and government drivers). Chrétien's insistence on presenting the appearance of a small Cabinet likely arose from the standard set by his predecessor, PC Kim Campbell; she shrank the Cabinet from 35 to 23 ministers, to signal her determination to run a cost-effective government.

Chrétien's successor, Paul Martin, erased the distinction between junior and senior ministers.[76] He expanded the Cabinet to 39 members, because he had to repay political debts to dozens of Liberal MPs.[77] Initially, Stephen Harper tried to have it both ways: he appointed a 27-member Cabinet, all of them designated as full ministers.[78] When he shuffled his Cabinet in January 2007, Harper reverted to the Chrétien model: he added five Secretaries of State. He insisted, however, that the Cabinet was as small as before, because the junior ministers were part of the ministry but not part of the Cabinet.[79]

Junior ministers (now known as Ministers of State) are often relegated to ceremonial tasks: announcing new policies, visiting government-funded projects in Canada and overseas, and substituting for senior ministers when necessary. Under Prime Minister Martin, each received a mandate letter outlining their specific responsibilities.[80] Prime Minister Harper appears to have ended this practice, leaving the specific tasks of Ministers of State to be determined by their respective senior ministers.[81] Regardless of their formal role in government, the real purpose of appointing junior ministers is to give the PM greater scope for regional and demographic representation and rewarding loyal supporters. (See Table 8.2 on page 279.)

Each minister is responsible for a particular policy field, or **portfolio,** within the executive branch. Although that responsibility may be shared with one or more Ministers of State, the senior minister must answer to Parliament "for all aspects of his or her portfolio."[82] In most cases, a senior minister is the political head of a line department; two are responsible for central agencies (the minister of Finance and the president of the Treasury Board) and one, the minister for Intergovernmental Affairs, has no separate department or agency. (The differences between central agencies and line departments are explained in Dossier 9.2.) The leaders in the House and Senate coordinate the legislative activities of the government, and are not responsible for particular policy fields (although the government leader in the House normally sponsors amendments to the *Canada Elections Act*).[83]

Few members of the Cabinet are appointed because of their expertise in a particular field of policy. There are some exceptions: the minister of Finance requires experience and connections within the business community, and the Justice minister must be licensed to practice law. Ideally, the portfolios that are central to the priorities of that particular PM are filled by the most competent and experienced people available, to ensure that the Government fulfills its key promises.[84] But in general, Cabinet ministers are appointed for reasons unrelated to their professional backgrounds or abilities. Every Cabinet contains at least one minister who is clearly in over his or her head, but whose appointment satisfies one or more of the criteria discussed below. For example, former Foreign Affairs Minister Maxime Bernier knew little or nothing about international issues before he was appointed to the sensitive portfolio in August 2007; he was chosen because Prime Minister Harper needed another high-profile francophone minister, and because he hoped that Bernier could "sell" the Afghanistan mission to hostile Quebeckers.[85] In contrast, the American president must look outside Congress for his Cabinet secretaries; the separation of powers in the American *Constitution* forbids legislators to serve in the executive branch. This gives the president a huge pool of potential Cabinet appointees, whereas the Canadian PM is restricted to his or her party caucus (both the Commons and the Senate).

The criteria for inclusion in Canada's political executive are based on four primary principles:
1. constitutional convention;
2. regional and demographic representation;
3. seniority; and
4. the minister's political and personal relationship to the prime minister.

Constitutional Conventions

A Cabinet minister must be either an MP or a senator from the prime minister's party. On rare occasions, the PM will appoint a Cabinet minister from outside Parliament; in that case, the minister must win a seat in the Commons at the earliest opportunity, usually through a by-election (a special election held to fill a single seat in the Commons). After the shock of the 1995 Quebec referendum, Prime Minister Chrétien appointed Stéphane Dion and Pierre Pettigrew to his Cabinet to strengthen his Quebec contingent. Both easily won by-elections shortly thereafter. Had either man lost, constitutional convention would have required him to resign from the Cabinet.[86]

The principles of responsible government limit the number of senators who can sit in the Cabinet. Although the government leader in the Senate is always a member of the Cabinet, senators cannot appear on the floor of the Commons; hence, ministers drawn from the Senate weaken the Cabinet's daily accountability to the House. In special circumstances, however, additional senators have held Cabinet posts.[87] Prime Minister Harper appointed Michael Fortier, a Montreal-based Conservative strategist (and 1998 PC leadership contender) to the

Senate on February 6, 2006, and gave him the portfolio of Public Works and Government Services on the same day. Fortier's appointment sparked controversy, for at least four reasons:

- First, Harper had promised a new, more democratic method for choosing senators; his appointment of Fortier was at odds with his campaign rhetoric.[88]
- Second, the Conservatives had condemned the practice of awarding Cabinet seats to senators, partly because they are not elected and partly because they cannot be held to account in the Commons.
- Third, several long-serving Reform/Alliance MPs had been excluded from Cabinet. They resented Fortier's inclusion, especially after he stated publicly that he hadn't run as a candidate in the 2006 election because he simply didn't want to.[89]
- Fourth and finally, the Public Works portfolio was particularly sensitive in the wake of the Sponsorship Scandal (Dossier 8.2); appointing a minister who could not answer questions in the Commons seemed to contradict the Conservatives' promise to increase government accountability.

Harper defended Fortier's appointment—and the even more controversial inclusion of Liberal MP David Emerson (Dossier 7.2)—by arguing that Montreal and Vancouver needed Cabinet representation, even though the Conservatives had failed to elect a single MP in either city. Ironically, Emerson proved to be a far more effective minister than most of the Conservative MPs who surrounded him. His inclusion in Harper's "court" was confirmed in June 2008, when he was officially appointed to the crucial Foreign Affairs portfolio. As for Fortier, he was moved to International Trade in the June 2008 shuffle; his place at Public Works was taken by a Quebec MP. (As noted in Dossier 7.2, Emerson did not run in the 2008 election. Fortier resigned his Senate seat to run as an MP, but he was defeated in a Montreal-area riding.)

Regional and Demographic Representation

Regionalism has shaped Canadian Cabinets since Confederation. There are two distinct principles at work:

1. The Cabinet must include at least one minister from each region, and preferably one from each province. This poses problems for a PM whose party is weak in particular areas of the country. Ontario and Quebec usually dominate federal Cabinets; the smaller provinces provide fewer ministers, although this does not necessarily imply a lack of influence within the political executive. Powerful regional ministers from provinces such as Nova Scotia (Peter MacKay) or British Columbia (Chuck Strahl) can become political "patrons" within their regions, securing program spending and infrastructure projects through close ties to the PM. A province that elects only one or two government MPs may find itself with a lacklustre minister, but this is not always the case.
2. Certain portfolios are traditionally awarded to particular regions. Fisheries and Oceans is reserved for ministers from the East and West coasts. Finance and Industry are often associated with Ontario,[90] while Justice and Public Works are disproportionately awarded to Quebeckers.

The practice of awarding portfolios on the basis of region, rather than personal competence or expertise, is usually defended on three grounds:

- First, the Cabinet is the supreme body where competing regional claims are brokered. In effect, the Cabinet is the highest intrastate institution within the Canadian federal state (see the Glossary to Chapter 4).
- Second, regional ministers have historically played a key role in linking the provincial political communities with the national executive.[91]
- Third, the national government must reflect the two national linguistic communities. This means in practice that Quebec ministers must be sufficiently numerous to reflect the "two nations" vision of the political community.

Prime Minister Stephen Harper, Governor General Michaëlle Jean, and the federal Cabinet at Rideau Hall in Ottawa, 2006. (CP/Tom Hanson).

Table 8.2 provides a regional breakdown of the federal Cabinet as of October 2008.

While the major language and religious groups have been represented in Cabinet since Confederation, gender and ethnicity are more recent considerations. The first woman was appointed to Cabinet in 1957 (Ellen Fairclough), and the first nonwhite minister was appointed in 1979 (Lincoln Alexander). Since the 1970s, prime ministers have tried to include at least one woman and one member of a visible minority group in each Cabinet. In short, the federal Cabinet has come to be seen as a mirror, if an imperfect one, of Canadian society. Partly because citizens expected to find their reflection in the composition of the Cabinet, the Cabinet grew in the 1970s and 1980s as Canadian society became more complex. By the early 1990s, there were 40 ministers in the Mulroney Cabinet.

Seniority

The seniority criterion receives less public attention than the representational issues just discussed, but it has greater practical significance for the operation of the political executive. Generally speaking, the prime minister prefers to appoint experienced MPs rather than newcomers. Where he has no choice—because he leads a new government with a high proportion of rookies, or he has only a few MPs from a particular region or demographic group—the prime minister may be forced to appoint an unknown quantity. But where he has a choice, he will naturally prefer to elevate people who have proven themselves to be politically skilled.

| | TABLE 8.2 | GEOGRAPHIC REPRESENTATION IN THE FEDERAL CABINET, OCTOBER 2008 |

PROVINCE/TERRITORY	NUMBER OF MINISTERS	CABINET PERCENTAGE
Newfoundland/Labrador	0S	0
Prince Edward Island	1S	3.7
New Brunswick	1S, 1J	3.7
Nova Scotia	1S	3.7
Quebec	4S/1J	14.8
Ontario	9S/4J	33.3
Manitoba	1S, 1J	3.7
Saskatchewan	1S, 1J	3.7
Alberta	4S/2J	14.8
British Columbia	4S/1J	14.8
Territories	1S	3.7
CANADA	27S/11J	

Note: "S" refers to a full Cabinet minister; "J" refers to a junior minister (Minister of State). Only the full Cabinet ministers are counted in Column 3.

Source: Prime Minister of Canada website: www.pm.gc.ca

While some rookie MPs have excelled in Cabinet, inexperienced ministers are more accident-prone than their more seasoned colleagues.[92] Cabinets normally include the most experienced MPs in the Commons; the backbenchers on both sides lack that experience and are therefore less effective in holding the Cabinet to account.[93]

Relationship to the Prime Minister

The political criteria for Cabinet appointments are the most difficult to define, but they are often the most important:

- Caucus members who played key roles in the prime minister's successful campaign for the party leadership are often rewarded with Cabinet posts. Prime ministers like to surround themselves with trusted allies.
- The candidate who finished second in the most recent leadership contest, if she remains in politics, is usually guaranteed a senior portfolio.[94] However, her caucus supporters may be shut out of Cabinet unless they are entitled to portfolios for other reasons (e.g., regional representation or seniority in the party).
- Prominent caucus members from different ideological perspectives may be included in the Cabinet, in order to avoid alienating factions within the party organization. However, their experience in Cabinet is often frustrating, especially when they find themselves on the opposite side of an issue from the PM and his advisers. Lloyd Axworthy, a powerful regional (Western) minister under Pierre Trudeau, lost several key battles with Paul Martin when both served in the first Chrétien Cabinet. Although he was a leading member of the Liberal left wing, he could not protect his Human Resources Development portfolio against the 1995 cutbacks.[95] After scoring some notable successes as minister of Foreign Affairs in the second Chrétien Government, he retired from politics in 2000.

- MPs assume that "loyalty to the party leader matters more than expertise or merit in deciding who makes it to cabinet."[96] This perception explains the power of the incentives discussed in Chapter 7. Once appointed, the influence of a given minister may depend more on her relationship to the PM than the importance of her portfolio.[97] The PM's "court" will include a few "carefully selected ministers"; the others are left out in the political wilderness.[98]

To summarize: the criteria governing the selection of Cabinet ministers favour the appointment of men and women who enjoy the trust of the PM, but most of whom have little or no expertise in the details of their portfolios. This tends to reduce the power of the Cabinet vis-à-vis both the PM and the permanent executive. Those few ministers who enter the Cabinet with a solid grasp of their portfolios, extensive political experience, a clear set of priorities, and the support of the PM can bend their departments to their will. Most end up, if not the captives of their public servants, highly dependent on them for expert advice about policy and governance.[99]

THE OPERATION OF CABINET GOVERNMENT

Individual Cabinet Ministers

A Cabinet minister is expected to play several roles, some political and some administrative. A Cabinet minister:
- Is a member of Parliament (in rare cases, a senator) and, like any MP, must keep in touch with the constituency and serve its needs. Even ministers with safe seats know that they cannot afford to neglect their ridings. Ministers with perilous seats may have difficulty balancing their Cabinet duties with their assiduous re-election efforts between campaigns.
- Is a member of the government caucus. The caucus meets weekly when Parliament is in session, and Cabinet ministers are expected to attend.[100]
- Sits on at least one Cabinet committee. Although these smaller groups are more efficient than the full Cabinet, their meetings still consume a great deal of time and energy.
- Must attend the weekly meeting of the full Cabinet.
- Is the political head of a line department. While the day-to-day administrative and policy tasks are handled by the deputy minister and other public servants, the minister must stay abreast of all major developments in the portfolio. Failure to do so can result in an embarrassing public slip-up at Question Period or in a media scrum.
- Is expected to maintain good relations with the important "client groups" associated with the department. For example, the minister of Justice needs to pay attention to the Canadian Bar Association; if the minister neglects to appear at its annual convention or to consult its members about pending legislation, loss of the association's cooperation and goodwill could result.
- Sponsors all legislation that originates in the department. In addition to making speeches in the House, the minister must appear before the parliamentary committee that examines each minister's Bills and evaluates proposed amendments.
- Is a prominent member of a national political party. At the very least, ministers are expected to make speeches at fundraising dinners and other party events across the country, and to participate in party conventions.

- Until recently, ministers devoted considerable time and effort to media appearances: public announcements of new policies, daily scrums after Question Period, interviews, and "photo ops." Initially, Ministers in the Harper Cabinet were much less visible (and audible) in the media. Harper appeared to trust only a select few ministers to appear before reporters. He also relied on a few Parliamentary Secretaries to field questions (both in scrums and at Question Period), bypassing the senior members of the political executive. These were unusual practices for a Canadian prime minister.[101]

Given these multiple and conflicting demands, individual ministers are too busy to give much time and attention to any one role. As a result, they play little if any part in the administration of their departments, which is left to the deputy ministers.[102] We will return to the relationship between ministers and public servants in Chapter 9.

▨ Cabinet Committees

Much of the work of Cabinet takes place in Cabinet committees. Apart from the Treasury Board, which dates back to Confederation, Cabinet committees are a relatively recent invention. In the nineteenth century, federal Cabinets were small and informal; they had little administrative support. By the early twentieth century, as the permanent executive began to grow, individual Cabinet ministers acquired more autonomy in the running of their departments. The 1960s brought a massive expansion in the executive branch, which made it difficult to coordinate government policy. One result was the "institutionalized" Cabinet, with several standing committees and increasingly powerful central agencies (Chapter 9). Today, the political executive is dominated by the prime minister.[103] As described previously, the Privy Council Office works directly for him, not for the Cabinet as a whole. The standing committees of Cabinet have lost some of the power they enjoyed from the 1960s until the 1990s; in particular, they are no longer entrusted with the allocation of funds among competing priorities. That task now belongs to the PM and his minister of Finance, and the senior officials in the central agencies.[104]

These days, the primary purpose of Cabinet committees is to ease the burden on the full Cabinet. There are three types of committee:
- standing executive committees, which set the broad outlines of activity for the entire federal government;
- standing policy committees, which review proposed legislation and program changes within a particular area of policy; and
- ad hoc committees, established for brief periods to handle a specific problem or issue.

The number of committees has fluctuated over the years, as prime ministers experimented with different models of Cabinet decision-making. During the second Mulroney Government (1988–93) there were 11 standing committees. Most had little influence. The two executive committees—Priorities and Planning, and Operations—were essentially "inner Cabinets": small groups of senior ministers who controlled the overall direction of government policy. The sheer number of committees placed huge demands on ministers, and left them little choice but to accept the recommendations of officials from the central agencies and the line departments.

When he took power in 1993, Jean Chrétien tried to revive the more personalized, less bureaucratic decision-making style of the 1960s. His preference for smaller Cabinets allowed him to dispense with an "inner Cabinet," at least during his first mandate. He relented in June 1997, as part of a general reorganization of Cabinet decision-making following the government's disappointing performance in the federal election of that year. The Special Committee of Council was responsible for "the Government's overall legislative planning and for specific legislative issues requiring decisions by Cabinet."[105] At the same time, Chrétien set up an ad hoc Government Communications Committee that "look[ed] at Government-wide communications issues, and work[ed] to ensure consistency in how all parts of the Government reach out to better inform and listen to Canadians."[106] By the end of Chrétien's term as prime minister, his Cabinet had only five standing committees. In contrast, his successor created eight standing committees and one subcommittee (see Dossier 8.5).

Until recently, the decisions of Cabinet committees were reported to the full Cabinet for final approval. In the Chrétien and Martin Cabinets, the fourth item on the agenda of the weekly Cabinet meeting was an appendix containing committee reports. Although ministers had the right to challenge committee decisions, PMs frowned on anyone who actually did so.[107] In the Harper Cabinet, the Priorities and Planning Committee (P&P) appears to be solely responsible for handling committee decisions. This is a potentially significant change, for two reasons. First, all of the committee chairs sit on P&P; this makes it even less likely that committee decisions will be challenged, and concentrates power within the political executive in a very small group. Second, P&P has only 13 members—including the PM, who chairs the committee. A small group makes it easier for the PM to control the outcome, while making it more difficult to ensure adequate representation from all of the regions.[108]

The committees are supported by PCO officials, who report directly to the Clerk of the Privy Council. The Clerk, in turn, informs the PM of any problems on a committee. If there is reason to suspect that a committee report will divide the Cabinet, the PM can simply delete that item from the Cabinet agenda.[109]

DOSSIER 8.5 Standing Committees of Cabinet, October 2008

The Chrétien Cabinet had two policy committees—Economic Union and Social Union—and three executive committees: Treasury Board, the Special Committee of Council (SCC), and Government Communications. The Chrétien Cabinets were relatively small, although the size of the ministry as a whole was swollen by the appointment of several junior ministers. Paul Martin divided his large Cabinet among four executive committees and five policy committees. Unusually, Martin himself chaired two of the latter. This complicated structure produced serious problems: it overtaxed the prime minister, prevented him from focusing on a few core issues, and slowed the decision-making process to a crawl.[110]

Stephen Harper shrank the Cabinet and reduced the number of committees to six. He retained three executive committees:

• Priorities and Planning, which "provides strategic direction on government priorities and expenditure management, ratifies committee recommendations and approves appointments";

• Operations, which "provides the day-to-day coordination of the government's agenda, including issues management, legislation and house planning, and communications"; and

• Treasury Board, which is responsible for "accountability and ethics, financial, personnel and administrative management, comptrollership, approving regulations and most orders-in-council."[111]

The first two committees, commonly called "P&P" and "Ops" respectively, are "inner Cabinets." They coordinate the policy agenda across the entire federal government, both in the long term (P&P) and the short term (Ops). The P&P Committee, like the full Cabinet, is chaired by the prime minister. It has 13 members, including the chairs of all the other Cabinet committees. The Ops Committee is chaired by the Hon. Jim Prentice, one of only two ministers to serve on both Committees. It has eight full members, and two non-voting members (both Ministers of State).

The Treasury Board is the only Cabinet Committee to be defined in statute law (section 5 of the *Financial Administration Act*); it cannot be altered or abolished by the prime minister. It is chaired by the president of the Treasury Board. Normally, Treasury Board is co-chaired by the minister of Finance,[112] although this was not the case in 2008. Unlike the other committees, which rely on individual line departments and the Privy Council Office for assistance, the Treasury Board is supported by its own central agency, the Treasury Board Secretariat (Chapter 9).

When he took office in February 2006, Harper created three policy committees:

- The Social Affairs Committee is responsible for "health care, justice, Aboriginal, training and skills development, culture, and immigration policy issues." It was originally chaired by Health Minister Tony Clement; he was replaced by Chuck Strahl in 2008, and then by Chuck Strahl following the 2008 election.

- The Economic Affairs Committee, now renamed "Economic Growth and Long-term Prosperity," is responsible for "international trade, sustainable development, natural resources, fisheries, agriculture, transport, infrastructure and communities, and regional development," along with "longer-term matters concerning Canada's economic growth and prosperity." It was originally chaired by Finance Minister Jim Flaherty; after August 2007 it was chaired by Foreign Affairs Minister (formerly International Trade Minister) David Emerson. In 2008, it is chaired by Tony Clement.

- The Foreign Affairs and Security Committee "considers foreign affairs, international development, public and national security, and defence policy issues."[113] Traditionally, this committee is chaired by the Foreign Affairs minister. From January to August 2007, however, it was chaired by Justice Minister Rob Nicholson. Since the August 2007 Cabinet shuffle, the committee has been chaired by Defence Minister Peter MacKay.

Harper added a fourth policy committee in January 2007, in response to widespread public perceptions that his Government was doing too little about climate change and related issues. The new Environment and Energy Security Committee was chaired by Indian Affairs Minister Jim Prentice, not—as might be expected—by Environment Minister John Baird or Natural Resources Minister Gary Lunn. After the 2008 election, Baird finally took the chair; however, he did so as Transport Minister rather than Environment Minister (the latter portfolio had been awarded to Jim Prentice). A fifth and final policy committee, dealing with the Canadian mission in Afghanistan, was established in February 2008. Like the Economic Affairs Committee, it was chaired by David Emerson. Following Emerson's retirement in 2008, the Afghanistan committee was chaired by Stockwell Day (who had just been moved from Public Safety to International Trade).

In addition to these standing committees, the first Harper Cabinet featured at least one ad hoc committee.[114] The PM chaired an informal committee on security and intelligence issues, whose other core members included the ministers of Foreign Affairs, Defence, and National Security. Other ministers attended when their portfolios were relevant to a particular intelligence briefing. It is not clear why the PM would establish a separate, secret body to deal with issues that would normally be addressed by the Standing Committee on Foreign Affairs and National Security, particularly since the membership of the two groups overlapped considerably.[115]

The membership of Harper's Cabinet committees suggests that the prime minister depended on a few trusted ministers to manage the political executive, especially Prentice (and Emerson, before his retirement).[116] The choice of committee chairs is one of the most important decisions a prime minister can make, because it allows him to control the agenda of the real decision-making agencies within the political executive. Consequently, prime ministers favour ministers with an instinct for avoiding trouble and resolving disputes in private.

The Full Cabinet

Cabinet is not where decisions are made. Rather, it is where briefings are presented, information is shared, and where the prime minister and certain ministers provide a general tour d'horizon. The issues that keep surfacing at regular Cabinet meetings include the Government's fiscal position, national unity, the Government's political standing, and foreign affairs. These issues do not lend themselves to Cabinet decisions.[117]

Cabinet ministers rarely engage in detailed policy debates during their weekly meetings. Any such debates are supposed to take place, and to be resolved, before that particular issue arrives on the Cabinet agenda.[118] Instead, Cabinet discusses political issues raised by the PM. The ministers may watch PowerPoint® presentations from ministers about particular areas of concern (e.g., a slide show from the minister and deputy minister of Finance about the current state of the economy). PowerPoint® has become increasingly popular in recent years, as an alternative to recording policy proposals on paper (and risking their potentially embarrassing release to the public under the *Access to Information Act*).[119] In previous governments, the third and fourth items on the agenda were the ratification of Order-in-Council appointments[120] and Cabinet committee decisions; Prime Minister Harper reassigned both powers to the P&P Committee (Dossier 8.5). Harper's preference for handling political issues within the "inner Cabinet" (an unusual choice, given the small size of the full Cabinet) makes the political executive as a whole even less important than it was under Chrétien and Martin. According to a former Chrétien minister, the Cabinet of his day had been reduced from "a decision-making body" to "a kind of focus group for the prime minister";[121] this appears to be even more the case under Harper.

As noted earlier, there are no formal votes in Cabinet. Voting only makes sense as a decision-making technique if all participants are considered equal. But on a given issue, different ministers will have more or less say over the outcome (assuming that the issue in question is not a high priority for the PM, in which case Cabinet will have little if any say in the matter). For example, the ministers of Defence and Foreign Affairs will carry more weight in a decision about defence procurement than the ministers of Justice or Natural Resources. A minister from Saskatchewan would contribute less to a discussion of fishing policy than his or her colleagues from Atlantic Canada. In the Harper Cabinet, as previously noted, the PM's assessment of a minister's political instincts appears to determine his or her power more than the status of his or her portfolio.[122] Prime Minister Harper appears to rely heavily on a few key ministers.[123] His hand-picked committee chairs ensure that the PM's priorities are reflected in committee decisions. Like him, they have the power to summarize the "consensus" at the end of a discussion; that summary appears in the official record of the meeting, whereas any dissenting views expressed by Cabinet colleagues do not.

Records of Cabinet and committee discussions, like all Cabinet documents, are held in strict secrecy.[124] To some degree, this secrecy is required by the nature of the issues being discussed. Public disclosure of some Cabinet documents might undermine national security, or unfairly benefit private interests. More important, secrecy is supposed to permit frank discussion within Cabinet and committees while still retaining Cabinet unity before the Commons, the media, and the electorate. In practice, given the unprecedented control that Prime Minister Harper appears to exercise, open disagreements within the political executive appear unlikely.

The downside of Cabinet secrecy is that regional and group representation takes place behind closed doors. The institutional barriers to public representation of regional and demographic interests allow provincial premiers and pressure groups to claim this role as their own. We will return to the issue of advocacy-group involvement in policy-making in Chapter 13.

CONCLUSION

As we have seen throughout this chapter, the prime minister dominates Canada's political executive. He enjoys more power and discretion than his counterparts in other parliamentary systems. One aspect of that discretion is his ability to reshape and reshuffle the Cabinet whenever he sees fit. Another is the power to determine his ministers' job descriptions, priorities, even staffing decisions (Chapter 9). Although he complained about the centralization of power in the PMO as Opposition Leader, Stephen Harper seems to have changed his mind during the transition to power. To all appearances, his PMO exerts unprecedented control over the political executive.

As we will see in the next chapter, the PM also dominates the permanent executive. His "court" includes the most senior public servants as well as the handpicked Cabinet heavyweights. The blurring distinction between politics and administration at the very top of Canada's government is reflected further down the hierarchy, as we will see in the next chapter. One consequence is the growing difficulty of holding anyone to account when things go wrong. Members of the political and permanent executives blame each other, ensuring "plausible deniability" for both sides.[125]

GLOSSARY OF KEY TERMS

Central agencies: Those departments within the federal government whose primary responsibility is to monitor and coordinate policy-making and implementation across the entire executive branch. The four primary central agencies are the Privy Council Office (PCO), the Prime Minister's Office (PMO), the Treasury Board Secretariat (TBS), and the Department of Finance.

Coalition: A Cabinet comprising Ministers from two or more political parties.

Crown: The source and symbol of executive power in Canada. As a former British colony, Canada inherited "a *Constitution* similar in Principle to that of the United Kingdom." Although most of the Crown's powers are now delegated to the political executive, and particularly to the prime minister, the residual and emergency powers of the Crown are vested in the governor general, who must approve all spending measures before they are submitted to the House of Commons. In addition, the Crown's representative formally appoints the political executive and signs Bills passed by the legislative branch into law.

Crown corporations: Public agencies that provide goods and services to a particular clientele. Examples include the CBC, VIA Rail, and—at one time—Air Canada. Crown corporations are ultimately responsible to the federal government, but they are normally operated at arm's length from the political executive. Canada's Crown corporations were originally established to provide goods and services that were too costly for the private sector, such as national railways and coast-to-coast broadcasting. In recent years, many have been privatized (sold to the private sector), partly because of complaints about unfair competition and partly to raise money.

Exempt staff: The political staff who work in the offices of the prime minister, individual Cabinet ministers, and the Leader of the Official Opposition. They are called "exempt staff" because they are expressly exempted from the hiring rules in the *Public Service Employment Act*. Most are hired through "political and personal connections" to the party in power, the minister, or the prime minister.[126] In theory, their jobs are limited to purely political tasks such as speech-writing and correspondence; in practice, exempt staff often "exert a substantial degree of influence on the development, and in some cases, administration, of public policy in Canada."[127] Exempt staff are discussed further in Dossier 9.3.

Federal public service: Another name for the permanent executive. The federal public service includes the line and staff employees of all federal government departments, both inside and outside Ottawa.

Line departments: Departments within the federal government that make and implement policy in particular fields, such as agriculture, transport, and foreign affairs. Line departments deliver services to the public, whereas central agencies normally serve other government organizations.

Permanent executive: The federal public service. In principle, the permanent executive is politically neutral; as the name suggests, it remains in place when the governing party changes. It is organized hierarchically, with the Clerk of the Privy Council at the top. Within each department, the permanent executive is headed by the deputy minister.

Political executive: The Cabinet of the day. Often referred to, in colloquial terms, as "the government."

Portfolio: The traditional term for the policy assignment given to a particular Cabinet minister or secretary of state. For example, Finance Minister Jim Flaherty is said to hold the "Finance portfolio."

Prerogative powers: "The residue of discretionary or arbitrary authority which at any given time is legally left in the hands of the Crown."[128] Over the past millennium, the virtually unlimited power enjoyed by British monarchs has been reduced to a tiny sphere of "reserve powers," to be employed only in emergencies. Most of the executive, legislative, and judicial powers of the Crown are now exercised by the Cabinet, Parliament, and the courts, respectively. The prerogative remains an important source of executive authority, especially over appointments—e.g., senators, ambassadors, and federal judges—and is, therefore, the ultimate source of political patronage.

Privy Council: The historic term for the political executive. The *Constitution Act, 1867* refers to the executive branch of government as "the Governor in Council; the Crown's representative, the governor general, exercises supreme executive power on the advice of the Government of the day." In reality, as we have seen repeatedly, the governor general is an essentially ceremonial figure. The power of the Crown is exercised by the political executive: the prime minister and his or her Cabinet. The Privy Council does not exist, for all practical purposes, even though the central agency that serves the Cabinet is still called the Privy Council Office. The Privy Council is a constitutional fiction; the Privy Council Office is not.

DISCUSSION AND REVIEW QUESTIONS

1. What is "court government"? How does it differ from Cabinet government?

2. Why is Canada's prime minister an unusually powerful head of government? What is his relationship to the rest of the Cabinet?

3. When the prime minister chooses his Cabinet, what criteria does he use to decide which MPs will become ministers and which will not? In your opinion, do these criteria make sense? Why or why not?

4. What do Cabinet committees do?

5. What is the role of the Crown in the Canadian executive branch?

SUGGESTED READINGS

Books and Articles

Herman Bakvis, *Regional Ministers: Power and Influence in the Canadian Cabinet* (Toronto: University of Toronto Press, 1991).

Luc Bernier, Keith Brownsey and Michael Howlett, eds., *Executive Styles in Canada: Cabinet Structure and Leadership Practices in Canadian Government* (Toronto: University of Toronto Press, 2005).

Commission of Inquiry Into the Sponsorship Program and Advertising Activities [the Gomery Commission], *Volume 1: Who Is Responsible?* (Ottawa: Minister of Public Works and Government Services, 2005).

Commission of Inquiry Into the Sponsorship Program and Advertising Activities [the Gomery Commission], *Volume 2: Restoring Accountability* (Ottawa: Minister of Public Works and Government Services, 2006).

David A. Good, *The Politics of Public Management: The HRDC Audit of Grants and Contributions* (Toronto: University of Toronto Press, 2003).

Edward Greenspon and Anthony Wilson-Smith, *Double Vision: The Inside Story of the Liberals in Power* (Toronto: Doubleday Canada, 1996).

Richard Heffernan, "The Prime Minister and the News Media: Political Communication as a Leadership Resource," *Parliamentary Affairs,* 59:4 (2006).

Eoin O'Malley, "The Power of Prime Ministers: Results of an Expert Survey," *International Political Science Review,* 28:1 (2007), 7–27.

Donald J. Savoie, *Breaking the Bargain: Public Servants, Ministers, and Parliament* (Toronto: University of Toronto Press, 2003).

Donald J. Savoie, *Governing from the Centre: The Concentration of Power in Canadian Politics* (Toronto: University of Toronto Press, 1999).

Donald J. Savoie, ed., *Restoring Accountability: Parliament, Ministers and Deputy Ministers,* volume 1 of the collected research studies for the Commission of Inquiry Into the Sponsorship Program and Advertising Activities [the Gomery Commission] (Ottawa: Minister of Public Works and Government Services, 2006).

David E. Smith, *The Invisible Crown: The First Principle of Canadian Government* (Toronto: University of Toronto Press, 1995).

Websites

Information about the Privy Council Office is available in the "Publications" section of its website: www.pco-bcp.gc.ca.

The prime minister has his own website, which also lists the Cabinet and its committees; go to www.pm.gc.ca.

Individual departments and agencies of the federal government have their own websites; to find them, go to the main government site (www.gc.ca) and click on "About Government" and then "Departments and Agencies" for an alphabetical listing of all departments and agencies and direct links to their sites.

NOTES

1. To date, Canada has had one female prime minister (see Table 8.1). Because current PM Stephen Harper is male, we will use the pronoun "he" to refer to prime ministers in this chapter.

2. David E. Smith, *The Invisible Crown: The First Principle of Canadian Government* (Toronto: University of Toronto Press, 1995), 59.

3. Donald J. Savoie, *Court Government and the Collapse of Accountability in Canada and the United Kingdom* (Toronto: University of Toronto Press, 2008), 16.

4. Commission of Inquiry Into the Sponsorship Program and Advertising Activities [the Gomery Commission], *Volume 1: Who Is Responsible? : Fact Finding Report*, 2005, 30. Reproduced with the permission of the Minister of Public Works and Government Services, 2008, and courtesy of the Privy Council Office. (emphasis added, notes omitted).

5. Ibid., 427.

6. Ibid., 60 and 138. At page 162, Gomery observed that "cutting red tape" is "not necessarily a desirable attribute of a public servant responsible for allocating discretionary funds with little or no supervision."

7. Guité was well accustomed to working directly with a minister, instead of taking direction from his deputy minister. Under the Progressive Conservative Government of Brian Mulroney, Guité ran an advertising program in collaboration with Intergovernmental Affairs Minister Lowell Murray. Ibid., 105.

8. Ibid., 172.

9. Ibid., 123.

10. Ibid., 69.

11. Ibid., 246.

12. Since the 1960s, both the Liberal and Progressive Conservative parties had relied heavily on professional advertising firms in their election campaigns. The winning party awarded government advertising contracts to the firms that had helped to put it in office. In this respect, there was nothing new about the Sponsorship Program. Ibid., 105–106.

13. Ibid., 248.

14. Ibid., 251.

15. Ibid., 98.

16. This timeline relies, in part, on the time line prepared by CBC staff and posted on the corporation's website in fall 2004: www.cbc.ca/news/background/groupaction/timeline_origin.html.

17. *Who Is Responsible?* 143.

18. Office of the Auditor General, *Report to the Minister of Public Works and Government Services on Three Contracts Awarded to Groupaction* (Ottawa: Office of the Auditor General, May 2002); accessed at www.oag-bvg.gc.ca/domino/reports.nsf/html/02sprepe.html.

19. Office of the Auditor General, *Report to the Minister of Public Works and Government Services on Three Contracts Awarded to Groupaction*, news release (Ottawa, May 8, 2002); accessed at www.oag-bvg.gc.ca/domino/media.nsf/html/02prsp_e.html.

20. As an officer of Parliament, the Auditor General cannot publicize a report when the Commons is not in session. See Dossier 7.7 for more information on Officers of Parliament.

21. Chantal Hébert, *French Kiss: Stephen Harper's Blind Date with Quebec* (Toronto: Knopf Canada, 2007), 30–32; Paul Wells, *Right Side Up: The Fall of Paul Martin and the Rise of Stephen Harper's New Conservatism* (Toronto: McClelland & Stewart, 2006), 94-100. The political fallout of the scandal is discussed further in Chapters 11 and 12 of this book.

22. Smith, *The Invisible Crown*, 114 and 124–25.

23. In 2003, Clarkson and her husband (author John Ralston Saul) became the targets of public criticism for their spending habits. The House of Commons Standing Committee on

Government Operations and Estimates questioned the substantial increase in spending by Rideau Hall since Clarkson's appointment. The MPs were particularly incensed by a three-week trip to Russia and Scandinavia, with a planned budget of over $1 million. Clarkson and Saul had invited nearly three dozen artists, writers, and businesspeople to accompany them on their travels. The governor general's staff defended the trip, pointing out that the initiative had come from the Department of Foreign Affairs and International Trade, which was also footing the bill. In the end, the committee backed down and did not formally criticize her spending—even when it was revealed that the trip cost more than $5 million. Steven Chase, "MPs query Clarkson's costly tour," *The Globe and Mail*, September 19, 2003; accessed at www.globeandmail.com; Kathleen Harris, "Clarkson's polar jaunt cost $5.3M," *London Free Press*, February 14, 2004; accessed at www.canoe.ca.

24. Hébert, 58–60.

25. David E. Smith, "Clarifying the Doctrine of Ministerial Responsibility As It Applies To the Government and Parliament of Canada," in Donald Savoie, ed., *Restoring Accountability: Parliament, Ministers and Deputy Ministers*, volume 1 of the collected research studies for the Commission of Inquiry Into the Sponsorship Program and Advertising Activities [the Gomery Commission] (Ottawa: Minister of Public Works and Government Services, 2006), 101–144.

26. Bill Neville, "The 6 "P's" of Effective Transitions," in Peter E. Larson, ed., *Effective Management of Transitions in Government* (Ottawa: Public Policy Forum, January 2001), 11 (accessed at www.ppforum.ca, April 2007).

27. Peter E. Larson, "Introduction," in Larson, ed., 7.

28. Bob Plamondon, *Full Circle: Death and Resurrection in Canadian Conservative Politics* (Toronto: Key Porter, 2006), 367.

29. Wells, 244–245.

30. Ibid., 245–246.

31. Nicholas d'Ombrain, "Managing Transitions at the Federal Level," in Larson, ed., 34.

32. Larson, 8.

33. d'Ombrain, 36.

34. There were no such people on the Harper transition team, which led to serious staffing problems for ministers; these persisted for months after the Conservatives took over the federal government. Wells, 248.

35. See Dossier 2.2 for an explanation of "neoliberalism."

36. Wells, 231; Faron Ellis and Peter Woolstencroft, "A Change of Government, Not a Change of Country: The Conservatives and the 2006 Election," in Jon H. Pammett and Christopher Dornan, eds., *The Canadian Federal Election of 2006* (Toronto: Dundurn Press, 2006), 85.

37. Wells, 247 (emphasis in original).

38. Bea Vongdouangchanh, "Harper's transition is 'the best I've seen,' says Arthur Kroeger," *The Hill Times*, August 14, 2006, 17–18.

39. Donald J. Savoie, *Governing from the Centre: The Concentration of Power in Canadian Politics* (Toronto: University of Toronto Press, 1999), 108.

40. Donald Savoie, "The Federal Government: Revisiting Court Government in Canada," in Luc Bernier, Keith Brownsey and Michael Howlett, eds., *Executive Styles in Canada: Cabinet Structure and Leadership Practices in Canadian Government* (Toronto: University of Toronto Press, 2005), 33.

41. When she became prime minister in 1993, Kim Campbell reduced the size of the Cabinet from 36 to 25 ministers and merged several departments into so-called "superministries." The new Department of Human Resources Development Canada (HRDC) included the former Department of Labour, the Employment section of Employment and Immigration, the Student Loans program from the defunct Secretary of State Department, and other related agencies and activities. In December 2003, one of Paul Martin's first acts as prime minister was to divide it into two separate departments: Human Resources and Skills

Development, and Social Development. When Stephen Harper became prime minister in February 2006, he reunited the two entities to create the Department of Human Resources and Social Development.

42. This information was accurate at the time of writing, despite the introduction of Bill C-20 (Senate "consultations," discussed in Dossier 3.4) and several proposals to give Parliament a role in the choice of Supreme Court justices. See the discussion of appointments to the Supreme Court in Chapter 10. At the time of writing, Bill C-20 has not yet been enacted.

43. There are occasional exceptions to this rule. Two members of the 2006 Harper Cabinet, David Emerson and Michael Fortier, only became members of the Conservative caucus on the day of their swearing in. Their appointments are discussed later in the chapter.

44. *The Globe and Mail* staff, "Cabinet prepares for purge," *The Globe and Mail*, December 11, 2003; accessed at www.globeandmail.com.

45. Michael Dewing, "The Role of Parliamentary Secretaries" (Ottawa: Library of Parliament Research Branch, April 2006), 2–3 (accessed at www.parl.gc.ca).

46. Canada, Privy Council Office, *Accountable Government: A Guide for Ministers* (Ottawa: Privy Council Office, 2006), 9 (accessed at www.pco-bcp.gc.ca, March 2007).

47. Former Prime Minister Martin increased the executive powers of Parliamentary Secretaries: he had them sworn in to the Privy Council, enabling them to attend meetings of Cabinet and its committees. Prime Minister Harper discontinued this practice, as part of his plan "to streamline and simplify the executive"; see *Accountable Government*, iii.

48. Richard Heffernan, "The Prime Minister and the News Media: Political Communication as a Leadership Resource," *Parliamentary Affairs*, 59:4 (2006), 590.

49. Savoie, *Court Government*, 236.

50. See the discussion of Harper's relationship with the Parliamentary Press Gallery in Chapter 14.

51. In September 2004, newspapers began to report rumours that two former Cabinet ministers, Martin Cauchon and Maurizio Bevilacqua, had launched unofficial leadership campaigns. Martin quickly denied the reports, and insisted that he had the full support of all members of the Liberal caucus.

52. See the discussion of party leadership selection and review in Chapter 11.

53. There had been a few calls for the replacement of the incumbent Clerk, Alex Himelfarb, prior to the swearing-in of the Martin Government in December 2003; however, Martin made it clear that he valued Himelfarb's advice and would not consider replacing him.

54. Savoie, *Governing from the Centre*, 86.

55. For a useful "generic" example of a mandate letter, see d'Ombrain, 45–46.

56. Savoie, *Governing from the Centre*, 137–39.

57. Savoie, "The Federal Government: Revisiting Court Government in Canada," 34–35.

58. Savoie, *Governing from the Centre*, 138.

59. Paraphrase by Justice Gomery in *Who Is Responsible?* 67.

60. *Who Is Responsible?* 31.

61. Savoie, "The Federal Government," 30.

62. Savoie, *Court Government*, 293.

63. Ibid., 150–151.

64. Heffernan, 589 and 598.

65. Eoin O'Malley, "The Power of Prime Ministers: Results of an Expert Survey," *International Political Science Review*, 28:1 (2007), 7–27.

66. The adoption of fixed election dates in 2007 has modified this constitutional rule; see Dossier 12.1.

67. For example, a Cabinet revolt destroyed the Diefenbaker Government in 1963. Although Diefenbaker led a minority government, which increased the danger of a split in Cabinet, he refused to heed the advice of those ministers who opposed his stand on American

nuclear weapons. The result was catastrophic: the government fell and Diefenbaker lost the ensuing general election. See Denis Smith, *Rogue Tory: The Life and Legend of John G. Diefenbaker* (Toronto: Macfarlane Walter and Ross, 1995), Chapter 12.

68. Savoie, *Governing from the Centre,* 318.

69. *Who Is Responsible?* 67 and 425.

70. Bill C-24, discussed in Chapters 11 and 12.

71. Hébert, 35–37 and 133; Wells, 210–211.

72. Savoie, *Governing from the Centre,* 108.

73. See, e.g., G. Bruce Doern, "The Harper Conservatives in Power: Emissions Impossible," in G. Bruce Doern, ed., *How Ottawa Spends, 2007–2008: The Harper Conservatives—Climate of Change* (Montreal and Kingston: McGill–Queen's University Press, 2007), 3: "[Harper] was de facto from the outset his own environment minister in a super centralized government which he controlled in a very detailed way."

74. Savoie, *Court Government,* 233.

75. Savoie, *Governing from the Centre,* 348.

76. The Martin Government's guidebook for Cabinet members was explicit on this point: "While a Minister of State does not have a portfolio independent of the Minister he or she assists, the Minister of State is Cabinet colleague and peer, not a subordinate, of that Minister." Privy Council Office, *Governing Responsibly: A Guide For Ministers* (Ottawa: Privy Council Office, 2003), 8.

77. Wells, 88–89.

78. Canada, Privy Council Office, *Governing Accountably: A Guide for Ministers* (Ottawa, 2006), 8 (accessed at www.pco-bcp.gc.ca, March 2007).

79. In defending his change of heart, Harper said that "I don't believe that it's necessary [to appoint junior ministers], but I believe that it's a benefit for the long-term to give experience to some new Cabinet members." Quoted in Simon Doyle, "PM Harper's New Expanded Ministry A Political Move, Say Experts," *The Hill Times,* January 8, 2007, 5.

80. Privy Council Office, *Governing Responsibly,* 8.

81. Canada, Privy Council Office, *Accountable Government: A Guide for Ministers and Secretaries of State* (Ottawa: Privy Council Office, 2007), 16–17.

82. Ibid., 6.

83. One of Martin's innovations in December 2003 was to appoint the government whip and deputy House leader to Cabinet; previously, this individual had no Cabinet rank. The elevation of the government whip to ministerial rank was proclaimed as part of Martin's plan to close the distance between the Cabinet and the Liberal backbench; it may also have reflected his need to promote as many of his supporters to the political executive as he possibly could.

84. Neville, 17–18. Recent examples include the appointment of former Ontario Cabinet Minister John Baird as president of the Treasury Board in February 2006. Baird was the minister responsible for the Harper Government's top priority, the *Federal Accountability Act.* His lengthy experience as a provincial minister helped him to stickhandle the complex and controversial legislation through a minority Commons and an Opposition-dominated Senate, tasks which might have exceeded the ability of a less seasoned minister.

85. Les Whittington, "Lightweight MP appointed in a bid for Quebec votes," *The Toronto Star,* May 27, 2008 (accessed at www.thestar.com). Bernier's resignation is discussed in Chapter 7.

86. Former Prime Minister Trudeau appointed a past president of the CBC to the Communications portfolio in 1978. Pierre Juneau subsequently ran in a by-election, and lost. He resigned his Cabinet seat immediately.

87. For example, the Progressive Conservative Government elected in 1979 included only one MP from Quebec. Prime Minister Joe Clark appointed two Quebec senators to his Cabinet, to boost that province's representation. Similarly, Prime Minister Pierre Trudeau used Western Canadian senators to provide regional representation in the Cabinet after the 1980

election, which returned two Liberal MPs from Manitoba and none from the other Western provinces.

88. See the discussions of Senate reform in chapters 3 and 7.

89. Abbas Rana, "Morale low in Conservative caucus after shaky start for government," *The Hill Times*, February 13, 2006, 30.

90. At the time of writing (October 2008), Harper's Finance minister is from Ontario; the Public Works minister is from Quebec.

91. Herman Bakvis, *Regional Ministers: Power and Influence in the Canadian Cabinet* (Toronto: University of Toronto Press, 1991), 297.

92. Sharon L. Sutherland, "The Consequences of Electoral Volatility: Inexperienced Ministers 1949–90," in Herman Bakvis, ed., *Representation, Integration and Political Parties in Canada*, volume 14 of the collected research studies for the Royal Commission on Electoral Reform and Party Financing (Toronto: Dundurn Press, 1991), 336–37.

93. David C. Docherty, *Mr. Smith Goes to Ottawa: Life in the House of Commons* (Vancouver: UBC Press, 1997), 55.

94. Usually, but not always. Long-time MP and Cabinet Minister Sheila Copps was the only candidate willing to take on the Paul Martin "juggernaut" in 2003. She was excluded from Martin's first Cabinet. Then her riding boundaries were re-drawn, forcing her into a renomination battle with Martin loyalist Tony Valeri. Valeri won; Copps flirted with the idea of running for the NDP, but eventually decided to leave politics altogether.

95. Edward Greenspon and Anthony Wilson-Smith, *Double Vision: The Inside Story of the Liberals in Power* (Toronto: Doubleday Canada, 1996), Chapters 9 and 13–15.

96. Savoie, *Court Government*, 35.

97. Ibid., 233.

98. Ibid., 229.

99. Donald J. Savoie, *Breaking the Bargain: Public Servants, Ministers, and Parliament* (Toronto: University of Toronto Press, 2003), 165.

100. But recall from Chapter 7 that the caucus meets the day after the weekly Cabinet meeting, which reduces its potential influence on ministerial deliberations.

101. In early 2008, Parliamentary Secretaries James Moore and Pierre Poilievre were tapped to deal with the Chuck Cadman scandal and the Conservative "in-and-out" scheme respectively (these scandals are described elsewhere in the book). Harper's media strategy is discussed in Chapter 14. Moore's performance must have pleased the PM: he was promoted to Secretary of State in June 2008.

102. Savoie, *Governing from the Centre*, 245.

103. The evolution of the Canadian Cabinet is summarized in Michael Howlett, et al., "Modern Canadian Governance: Political-Administrative Styles and Executive Organization in Canada," in Bernier, Brownsey and Howlett, eds., 3–13.

104. Savoie, "The Federal Government," 36–37.

105. Privy Council Office, *Cabinet Directive on Law-Making*, Section 3, accessed at www.pco-bcp.gc.ca/legislation/directive_e.htm, June 2000.

106. Prime minister of Canada's website: *The Cabinet:* www.pm.gc.ca; accessed June 2001.

107. Savoie, *Governing from the Centre*, 128.

108. In June 2008, the 13 members of P&P included four ministers from Ontario (30.7 percent); three from Quebec (23 percent); two each from Alberta and British Columbia (15.4 percent per province); and one apiece from Nova Scotia and Manitoba (7.7 percent each). Alberta and BC were significantly under-represented, and Ontario over-represented, relative to the provincial distribution in the Conservative caucus.

109. Savoie, *Governing from the Centre*, 265.

110. Wells, 89–91. Wells implies that the unwieldy Cabinet structure allowed Martin's inner circle (the "Board," discussed in Chapters 11 and 12) to run the government behind the scenes.

111. "Cabinet Committee Mandates and Membership, January 2007," accessed at www.pm.gc.ca.

112. In his testimony before the Gomery Commission, Paul Martin stated that he rarely attended meetings of the Treasury Board—despite having been its co-chair for nearly a decade. This appears to be the standard arrangement for federal Finance ministers. *Who Is Responsible?* 48.

113. "Cabinet Committee Mandates and Membership, June 25, 2008"; accessed at www.pm.gc.ca, June 2008.

114. Former PM Chrétien often established temporary Cabinet committees to deal with a particular short-term issue. Unlike Chrétien's ad hoc committees, Harper's seems to have been in place for a long period of time; its ad hoc status may have been intended simply to shield its existence from the public, perhaps for reasons of confidentiality.

115. Simon Doyle, "PM chairs ad hoc 'intelligence committee' [which] meets at Harper's call," *The Hill Times*, April 2, 2007, 21.

116. Simon Doyle, "A move from 'Cabinet government' to 'court government:' who's in Prime Minister's court?" *The Hill Times*, January 15, 2007, 7.

117. Savoie, *Governing from the Centre,* 127.

118. "Accountable Government," 42.

119. When he informed his Cabinet that he wanted to send troops to the war in Iraq, former British PM Tony Blair relied entirely on a PowerPoint presentation. Savoie, *Court Government,* 287.

120. Savoie, *Governing from the Centre,* 262–63.

121. Quoted in Savoie, "The Federal Government," 31.

122. Simon Doyle, "A move from 'Cabinet government' to 'court government:' who's in Prime Minister's court?" *The Hill Times*, January 15, 2007, 7.

123. Savoie, "The Federal Government."

124. Since taking power in 2001, the Liberal Government in British Columbia has opened Cabinet meetings to the media and the public. Video of the meetings is available on the BC government's website: www.prov.gov.bc.ca/prem/popt/cabinet. To date, no other Canadian government has taken such a significant step away from the British convention of Cabinet secrecy.

125. Savoie, *Court Government,* 92.

126. Alex Smith, "Ministerial Staff: Issues of Accountability and Ethics" (Ottawa: Library of Parliament Research Branch, April 2006), 2 (accessed at www.parl.gc.ca).

127. Liane E. Benoit, "Ministerial Staff: The Life and Times of Parliament's Statutory Orphans," in Donald Savoie, ed., *Restoring Accountability: Parliament, Ministers and Deputy Ministers,* volume 1 of the collected research studies for the Commission of Inquiry Into the Sponsorship Program and Advertising Activities [the Gomery Commission] (Ottawa: Minister of Public Works and Government Services, 2006), 146.

128. David E. Smith, *The Invisible Crown: The First Principle of Canadian Government* (Toronto: University of Toronto Press, 1995), 32.

9 The Permanent Executive

LEARNING OBJECTIVES

After you finish reading this chapter, you should be able to:
* *describe* and *evaluate* at least two recent changes to Canada's permanent executive;
* *explain* the differences between a central agency and a line department;
* *identify* and briefly *describe* two of the four main central agencies in Ottawa, and explain their roles in the policy process;
* *describe* and *evaluate* the power of exempt political staff in ministers' offices and the PMO;
* *evaluate* the degree of accountability by the executive branch to the legislative branch.

INTRODUCTION

In the previous chapter, we looked at the prime minister and Cabinet. This chapter describes the work of the thousands of public servants who implement the decisions taken by the political executive. It sketches the outlines of a large and complex organization:

> *250,000 Canadians work in what is known as the core federal Public Service—these are the people employed in the 20 departments and 180 regulatory and administrative agencies of the federal government. Beyond this are the 220,000 Canadians who are members of the Canadian Forces, the RCMP (some 20,000 regular and civilian members) and Crown corporations (for example, employees of CBC, VIA Rail and Canada Post).*[1]

We will focus on four main themes:
1. the relationship between the **permanent executive** and the **political executive**;
2. the impact of "court government" on that relationship;
3. the lessons learned from Justice Gomery's inquiry into the operation of the permanent executive; and
4. recent efforts to enhance the accountability of the permanent executive. These fall into two main categories: Gomery's recommendations for reform, and the measures contained in the Harper Government's *Federal Accountability Act*. There is some overlap between the two, although not quite as much as Justice Gomery seems to have wished.[2]

THE RELATIONSHIP BETWEEN THE POLITICAL AND PERMANENT EXECUTIVES

In the ideal model of responsible Cabinet government, there is a clear division of responsibility between the political executive and the permanent executive. Ministers, individually and collectively, make policy. They are driven by partisan political incentives—particularly the desire for re-election—to choose policies that benefit the electorate (or at least their particular constituency). The menu of choices is prepared by public servants, the experts in policy and governance. Once the Cabinet makes a decision, the permanent executive puts it into effect. In the jargon of the 1990s, the ministers steer the ship of state; they leave the rowing to the public servants within their departments.[3] The Cabinet is collectively responsible to Parliament, and ultimately to the public, for the broad outlines of policy. The public servants are ultimately responsible to the minister, and through him or her to Parliament, for the administrative operation of government. They cannot be held to account directly, either by legislators or by the electorate. They are anonymous, nonpolitical, and loyal to the **Crown** rather than to the party in power.[4] They adapt to the changing ideologies of successive governments, developing and implementing policies targeted to different political constituencies.[5] In exchange, ministers are supposed to respect the neutrality and expertise of the public service and to resist the temptation to blame their officials when things go wrong.

In practice, the traditional distinction between politics and administration is increasingly difficult to sustain. To succeed in their jobs, senior public servants (e.g., deputy ministers and the staff of **central agencies**) must be aware of, and sensitive to, the political incentives under which Cabinet members operate—especially the need to protect the prime minister from criticism and scandal. The top public servants are courtiers to the prime minister, participants in an informal and secretive policy process rather than the leaders of a formal process defined by constitutional and statute law.[6] At the same time, the "bargain" between the political and permanent executives has broken down.

- Members of the political executive surround themselves with a growing cadre of political aides, who sometimes breach the barriers between politics and public administration. "Exempt staff" sometimes exploit their relationships with their ministers (and prime ministers) by ordering public servants to engage in politically sensitive tasks. (See the discussion of the Sponsorship Scandal in Dossier 8.2, and the discussion of exempt staff in Dossier 9.3.)

- The appointment of deputy ministers by the prime minister, on the advice of the Clerk of the **Privy Council,** gives senior public servants a strong incentive to serve the PM, rather than the government and people of Canada.[7] A leading Canadian scholar of public administration worries that public servants are expected to be "advocates, even cheerleaders, for the government's agenda in order to demonstrate their loyalty."[8]

- Ministers who encounter problems with their **portfolios** no longer accept personal responsibility for them. Instead, they point the finger at their senior officials. To some degree, this makes sense; as pointed out in the previous chapter, it is the deputy minister—not the minister—who actually runs the department. Nonetheless, it is a central principle of Canadian government that the minister alone is directly accountable to Parliament. That principle properly insulates officials from public scrutiny and punishment as long as they act within the law. But it can also ensure "plausible deniability" for both minister and deputy.[9] (See Dossier 9.1.) Recent efforts to hold deputy ministers personally accountable threaten to undermine the confidentiality and mutual trust between the two elements of the executive branch.[10] The introduction of the British "accounting officer" model by the *Federal Accountability Act*, which requires deputies to appear in person before Parliamentary committees, has sparked considerable controversy between the political and permanent executives, and between the executive and legislative branches of government (Dossier 9.4).

Mohamed Al-Mashat had been Iraq's ambassador to the United States, and his country's primary spokesman in the West, during the 1990–91 Gulf War.[11] A few months after the war ended, the media revealed that Al-Mashat had been granted landed immigrant status in Canada. The Opposition demanded the resignations of Joe Clark and Barbara McDougall, respectively the ministers of External Affairs (now Foreign Affairs) and Immigration. Clark and McDougall refused to take responsibility for the incident, pinning the blame instead on an associate deputy minister of External Affairs (and an exempt staffer in Clark's office, as explained in Dossier 9.3). That ADM happened to be Raymond Chrétien, the nephew of then-Opposition leader Jean Chrétien. The Clerk of the PCO forced him to apologize publicly for his department's political error in accepting Al-Mashat's application to enter Canada.[12] Raymond Chrétien's treatment by his minister and by the Clerk sent a chill through the entire permanent executive:

> Senior executives now heard a mixed message from the Government: We want you to take risks, we expect you to make mistakes sometimes; but if you screw up, we may hang you out to dry publicly. The refusal of ministers Joe Clark and Barbara McDougall to take responsibility in the traditional manner for departmental errors reinforced public service caution and scepticism about taking risks.[13]

The Sponsorship Scandal in the Department of Public Works and Government Services shows what can happen when the permanent executive becomes overly politicized (Dossier 8.2). Note, however, that the problems in the Sponsorship Program were atypical. Justice Gomery made this clear in his report:

> The vast majority of public servants try, in good faith, to do their jobs properly and effectively, and the Canadian government system consists of solid political institutions with a long and distinguished history of public service. The Sponsorship Program involved only a tiny proportion of the annual expenditures of the Government. Its mishandling was an aberration. The majority of the expenditures of the federal government are well handled, and citizens usually get value for money from them.[14]

These words should be borne in mind as we examine the permanent executive.

THE FEDERAL PUBLIC SERVICE

■ The Structure of the Permanent Executive

There are several types of organization within Canada's **federal public service,** including:

1. central agencies;
2. **line departments**; and
3. an array of **Crown corporations,** service-delivery agencies, and regulatory tribunals.

Each organization falls under a particular portfolio. It is (in principle) accountable to Parliament via a particular minister. Central agencies and line departments have a more direct relationship to their respective ministers, compared to Crown corporations and agencies; the latter are intended to operate at arm's length from the Government of the day. We will discuss each type of organization in turn, beginning with an explanation of the differences between central agencies and line departments (Dossier 9.2).

Broadly speaking, line departments are responsible for a functional area of government policy such as agriculture, health, or transportation. Each is headed by a Cabinet minister. Despite their nominal supremacy, ministers do not have the time or the expertise to actually run their departments; the deputy minister oversees day-to-day operations. The deputy is a senior public servant, who is responsible for the policy and administrative activities of the department. Each line department is divided into several branches, each of which reports to an assistant deputy minister. Typical branches include Audit and Evaluation, Corporate Management, Communications, and the appropriate Policy, Programs and Services units for that particular portfolio.

Most public servants who work within a department occupy either line positions or staff positions. Line employees are linked directly to the rest of the permanent executive by the Privy Council Office (PCO), to which they report. Staff employees deliver programs and services to the public and manage the internal operations of the department. In effect, line employees participate in making the policies implemented by the staff employees. A list of line departments can be found in the right-hand column of Dossier 8.4.

Central agencies are smaller in size but more powerful in policy terms. Their responsibilities cut across the functional areas of government; they focus on making policy, not delivering services. The staff of central agencies are less likely than those in line departments to be career public servants; many have considerable experience outside the bureaucracy (e.g., in business or academia). The four key central agencies are the PCO, the Prime Minister's Office (PMO), the Department of Finance, and the Treasury Board Secretariat (TBS).

■ Central Agencies

The Privy Council Office (PCO)

The senior officials of the PCO are at the heart of the federal decision-making process. They work closely with the prime minister and, to a lesser degree, with the rest of the Cabinet. Their position at the centre of government gives them unparalleled knowledge of policy developments across the entire executive branch. According to official PCO documents,

> The Privy Council Office plays a key role in the elaboration of Government policy, supporting the Prime Minister in providing leadership and direction to the Government. This role also involves coordination. The Privy Council Office must work closely with line departments, as well as with the Prime Minister's Office, the Treasury Board Secretariat and the Department of Finance to ensure that new proposals are consistent with the Government's overall objectives and policies, and that all affected interests have been consulted. Once a decision is reached by Cabinet, the Privy Council Office ensures that it is communicated to the affected departments and oversees its effective implementation.[15]

By 2006 the PCO housed more than a dozen secretariats. Each standing committee of Cabinet has its own PCO secretariat to handle paperwork, provide policy advice, and coordinate departmental activities (apart from the Treasury Board, which is served by the TBS). Other units are responsible for the machinery of government; these include Orders in Council, Legislation and House Planning, and Intergovernmental Affairs.[16] Like the other central agencies, the PCO grew in size and influence after Pierre Trudeau became prime minister in 1968. Between 1969 and 2006, the full-time staff at the PCO grew almost sixfold (from 200 to 1100).

What had been a small group of senior officials housed in the Langevin Block (across the street from Parliament Hill) had overflowed into three office buildings.[17]

This expansion is only partly explained by the larger Cabinets and complex committee systems of recent years. Over time, as successive PMs re-engineered the agency to pursue their own priorities, the number of PCO secretariats multiplied. The fact that the PM is also the minister responsible for the Privy Council Office[18] gives him or her a particular incentive to increase the amount of expertise and control available to him or her. While it is difficult to hold any minister accountable for the management of his or her own department, it is all but impossible to challenge the PM's performance in that role. In his second report on the Sponsorship Scandal, Justice Gomery questioned "whether the increase in the number of central agency officials and the growth in their policy advisory role have served to dilute accountability in government."[19]

Shortly after he took office in 2006, Prime Minister Harper reversed the trend. Five PCO secretariats were transferred to line departments, and another two were moved to the Treasury Board Secretariat.[20] The move eliminated much of the duplication that Paul Martin had created in December 2003, when he effectively turned the PCO into a microcosm of the federal government.[21] It also reflected Harper's focus on a short list of priorities.[22] Some observers interpreted the "downsizing" of the PCO as part of a broader strategy to concentrate power in the Prime Minister's Office, which is largely staffed by political operatives rather than public servants.[23] But Harper's new Clerk of the Privy Council, Kevin Lynch, and his senior officials defended the streamlining of the agency, trumpeting the return to its core mission of supporting the Cabinet and the restoration of decision-making to the more accountable line departments.[24] By January 2007, the PCO staff had shrunk from over 1000 to around 750.[25]

The Clerk of the Privy Council is the head of the agency. He or she (currently he) is the most senior public servant in the federal government. His responsibilities are threefold:

1. The Clerk is the PM's deputy minister. He informs and advises the prime minister on emerging political and administrative problems, and provides an overview of activity in the entire federal executive branch. He also assists the PM in his capacity as the political head of government.

2. The Clerk is the Secretary to the Cabinet. He and his senior officials support the work of the ministry and its committees.

3. The Clerk is the head of the federal public service. He recommends candidates for promotion to deputy minister rank and oversees the transfer of deputies between departments. He meets frequently with other deputy ministers and assistant deputy ministers, and chairs the key committees of senior officials.[26] The Clerk is ultimately responsible for maintaining the Canadian tradition of an expert, professional, and nonpartisan public service.[27]

The importance of the Clerk's position is reflected in the rule that official Cabinet business cannot be transacted—either in the full Cabinet or a committee—in the absence of the Clerk or his representative.[28] In recent years, critics of prime ministerial power have focused on the need to reform the position. They argue that allowing the PM to hire and fire the most senior official in the permanent executive, and vesting sole discretion over deputy minister appointments in those two individuals, gives the PM too much control over senior public servants. In effect, they become accountable only to him and his Clerk, not to their own ministers. At the same time, the close working relationship between the PM and the Cabinet Secretary allows the PM to control the Cabinet agenda to an unhealthy degree. The PM and his Chief of Staff meet with the Clerk every day when the PM is in Ottawa, and the Clerk enjoys a great deal of influence over the policy agenda and the administration of government. In turn, the Clerk's job is to make sure that the PM's priorities are carried out.

The broad powers assigned to the Clerk, and the potential for conflicts among his various roles, led Justice Gomery to recommend important changes.[29] First, he argued that the Clerk should not have the sole discretion to advise the PM on deputy ministerial appointments; instead, deputy ministers should be hired on merit, following an open competition. Second, the titles of "deputy minister to the prime minister" and "Clerk of the Privy Council" should be abolished, and replaced with the single designation of "Cabinet Secretary." This change would re-emphasize the traditional role of the Clerk as a servant of the entire ministry, not just of the PM. Finally, Gomery pointed out that the TBS—not the PCO—is responsible for the public service; consequently, the formal title of "Head of the Public Service" should be transferred to the Secretary to the Treasury Board (the top public servant in the TBS).[30] At the time of writing, none of these recommendations had been put into effect.[31]

DOSSIER 9.3 The Twilight World of Exempt Staff

Prime ministers and members of the ministry (including Secretaries of State) are entitled to hire partisan political staff from outside the federal public service. These are called "exempt staff," because they are explicitly exempted from the laws governing public service appointments. Since the 1960s, the number of political staffers in the PMO and ministers' offices has ballooned. Today, the average ministerial office houses between 12 and 20 full-time employees.[32] Some of these are seconded from the public service, but the majority are "exempt." These include a Chief of Staff (formerly called the "Executive Assistant"), a director of Communications (and at least one assistant), two or three policy advisors, one or two legislative assistants, and a variety of "Special Assistants."

Exempt staff are supposed to give ministers politically sensitive policy and logistical support that the permanent executive cannot provide.[33] Their hiring serves additional purposes, which are rarely acknowledged in public: ensuring a "soft landing" for defeated candidates from the governing party, rewarding campaign workers, and ensuring that the minister follows the PMO line in his or her decisions and public pronouncements.[34] Personal loyalty to the PM is an important criterion, for staff as well as ministers: Prime Minister Harper reportedly "directed his minister of foreign affairs not to hire . . . a well-known supporter of the Conservative Party and a highly regarded political analyst, as his chief of staff because he had been publicly critical of Harper's leadership in the past. Loyalty to the leader has become more important than loyalty to the party."[35]

Finding qualified people to fill these positions can be a challenge. Many exempt staffers are recruited directly from campus political clubs and party youth wings; "daughters, sons, nieces, nephews and cousins of members of Parliament, their friends or their financial supporters" also account for a substantial proportion.[36] While their youth and energy can be an important asset to the minister, their lack of knowledge and experience frustrates career public servants and puts them at risk of unknowingly violating ethical standards.[37]

Communications staff are the exception: in recent years, several ministers (and prime ministers) have hired experienced journalists for these positions. Although these individuals may be regarded with suspicion by their former press gallery colleagues, they are greeted with enthusiasm by senior public officials fed up with the "little darlings" fresh out of University. A study for the Gomery Commission quotes a deputy minister: "Finally, we'll have someone who won't lose the Minister's papers, who will be competent, who will have sufficient experience, who will be more intelligent, and with whom we can finally speak as adults. . . ."[38] It is telling that policy aides are less likely to have relevant experience and expertise than their colleagues in the communications unit.

Public servants and former ministerial aides interviewed for the Gomery study estimated the proportion of competent exempt staff at between 50 and 60 percent.[39] The uneven quality of exempt staff is a serious issue for at least two reasons. First, they often wield considerable power, which is neither recognized

(continued)

nor regulated within the official structure of the federal government. According to the PCO, "Exempt staff do not have the authority to give direction to public servants, but they can ask for information or transmit the Minister's instructions, normally through the deputy minister."[40] This description does not always accord with reality. At least since the 1960s, some ministers have allowed their young partisan aides to boss around public servants.[41] A former political aide interviewed for the Gomery study "admitted that he and his colleagues were pretty loose with the term, 'the Minister wants,' when it came to their dealings with the department and that, in many cases, only the broad strokes behind such instruction had been issued by the Minister."[42] These episodes are inconsistent with TBS policy, which states that the Chief of Staff is responsible for "developing and implementing strategic plans in order to assist in delivering the Department's and Minister's mandate" and "on behalf of the Minister, for liaising with Senior Departmental Officials in order to ensure a positive working relationship between the Minister and the public service."[43] Both functions require exempt staff to provide direction to senior public servants. Consequently, the fact that so many exempt staff lack governmental experience is worrisome.

Second, exempt staff have long enjoyed privileged access to senior positions in the public service. The *Public Service Employment Act* entitled former exempt staffers "to be appointed without competition to any position in the Public Service for which they are qualified, in priority to all other persons."[44] For example, a Chief of Staff position is ranked by the Public Service Commission as equivalent to an assistant deputy minister; so a former Chief of Staff who had served at that rank for at least three years was automatically entitled to apply for an ADM position. Allowing political staff to bypass the normal process of internal competition and assessment—in effect, to enter the top levels of the permanent executive "through the back door"—further eroded the distinction between politics and the public service.[45] Given the apparently low quality of exempt staffers, it also raised serious questions about the impact on

the permanent executive. Two of the public servants found to be partially responsible for the Sponsorship Scandal had previously served as political aides to Public Works Minister Alfonso Gagliano.[46] Justice Gomery pointed to their shift from the political side to the public service within that particular department as both a reflection of and a contributor to the breakdown of ethical standards.[47]

The scope of this particular problem should not be overstated. Relatively few exempt staff took advantage of the opportunity to secure public service positions without having to compete for them. The majority of former political aides prefer to pursue lobbying careers, where they can continue to serve their parties openly.[48] (As we will see in Chapter 13, the *Federal Accountability Act* imposed new constraints on the movement between ministers' offices and lobbying firms.) Moreover, "Many former exempt staff members have gone on to become topflight public servants, including some who are currently Deputy Ministers."[49] Nonetheless, Gomery recommended that the law be amended to require all former exempt staff to compete for public service positions in the same manner as any other applicants.[50] Prime Minister Harper accepted that recommendation, perhaps hoping to mend fences with the public service after criticizing "Liberal civil servants" during the 2006 election campaign (Chapter 8).[51] The *Federal Accountability Act* repealed the relevant sections of the *Public Service Employment Act*.[52] Today, the law allows former exempt staffers with at least three years' experience to enter—but not to bypass—internal competitions for public service positions. As Justice Gomery pointed out, "the skills and knowledge gained in a Minister's office should serve such persons well in a merit-based competition. Entering through the front door would remove any notion of entitlement and potential politicization of the public service."[53]

Justice Gomery also reminded ministers that they are "they are accountable, responsible and answerable for all the actions of their exempt staff"[54]—although this principle does not seem to carry much weight with ministers. In the 1991

(continued)

"Al-Mashat Affair" (Dossier 9.1), then-Foreign Affairs Minister Joe Clark blamed his Chief of Staff for failing to warn him that a former official in the Iraqi regime had immigrated to Canada.[55] However, it is possible that Clark's Chief of Staff—himself a former Progressive Conservative MP—withheld that information in order to insulate his boss from political damage. The Commission of Inquiry into the Maher Arar case (Chapter 1) wanted to know whether the minister of Foreign Affairs at the time of Mr. Arar's detention in Syria, Liberal Bill Graham, knew that Mr. Arar was being tortured. Mr. Graham insisted that he had not been given that information, despite efforts by senior officials in his department to make him aware of it.[56] It appears that some of the exempt staff in Mr. Graham's office decided to withhold the information from their boss, to ensure "plausible deniability" in the event that the torture was publicly disclosed (and to prevent the minister from publicly defending a person whom CSIS regarded as a terrorist).[57]

This ability of Ministers to deny responsibility or accountability in matters where their staff either choose not to inform them as a strategically political protective measure, or where their advisors, through ignorance, incompetence or lack of judgement, fail to inform them because they did not recognize the significance of the information, raises important and serious questions about the current integrity of our system of accountability. If Ministers cannot be held responsible or accountable for the actions (or inactions) of their staff, then who can be?[58]

The Prime Minister's Office (PMO)

Unlike the PCO, which is staffed by public servants, the PMO is primarily a political and partisan body. Most of the people who work in its Langevin Block offices are exempt staff (Dossier 9.3). Its size and structure are entirely at the discretion of the incumbent prime minister. Pierre Trudeau, who served as PM from 1968 until 1984, inherited a small administrative and correspondence unit. He expanded the PMO to include policy analysts, regional desks, and political advisers. Trudeau envisioned his office as a "counterweight" to the policy advice of the PCO and the line departments, and a centre for planning and coordination within the federal government.[59] Although its success in meeting these goals was mixed, no subsequent PM has reversed Trudeau's expansion of the PMO. The creation of a central agency to provide independent partisan and political advice reduced the influence of the government caucus, while reinforcing the PM's already considerable power over the operations of the executive branch.

The PMO is headed by the Chief of Staff, who works more closely with the PM than anyone other than the Clerk of the Privy Council. While the precise responsibilities of the Chief vary with the expectations of his PM, there are some consistent features.

- First, the Chief of Staff runs the PMO. He or she ensures that the key positions are staffed with competent people, and oversees the operation of the various departments.
- Second, he or she controls access to the prime minister. There are constant demands on a PM's time and attention, most of which must be screened out so he can focus on a few key tasks.
- Third, the Chief of Staff is "a political problem solver for the prime minister."[60] He or she attends Cabinet meetings, taking note of any problems or disputes and working to resolve them.
- Fourth and finally, the Chief is the PM's "enforcer." He or she has to make sure that the PM's decisions are followed by Cabinet ministers, MPs, and public servants—whether they agree with those decisions or not.

One of Prime Minister Harper's first acts following the 2006 election was to appoint Ian Brodie as Chief of Staff. Brodie, a political scientist by training, had been a senior manager in the 2004 and 2006 Conservative campaigns, and served at various times as executive director of the party and Chief of Staff in the Opposition Leader's Office (OLO).[61] Like most members of the Harper team, Brodie had no experience in government. This is unusual: other recent Chiefs of Staff have held senior positions in ministerial offices before their elevation to the PMO. Derek Burney, a career public servant, was seconded to Brian Mulroney's team in 1986 "in order to rescue the Prime Minister's Office from its obvious disarray."[62] Jean Pelletier, Chief of Staff to Prime Minister Chrétien, had been mayor of Quebec City and president of the Canadian Federation of Municipalities.[63] However, Brodie brought at least three important strengths to the position. First, he had spent years working closely with Stephen Harper. To be effective, a Chief of Staff must have the full trust of the PM; that was certainly the case for Brodie. Second, Brodie was a willing and able enforcer. He had a proven ability to eliminate political problems quickly and ruthlessly.[64] This was a particular asset to a PM determined to control his Government with an iron hand. Third, Brodie knew how to control access to the PM, which kept Harper focused on the five priorities set out in the 2006 campaign. Brodie stepped down in May 2008, shortly before the release of a report which found that he had probably leaked confidential information to a journalist.[65] He was replaced by Guy Giorno, who had been Chief of Staff to former Ontario Premier Mike Harris.

As of February 2007, there were almost 100 full-time exempt staff in the PMO.[66] The Communications unit was the largest, reflecting Prime Minister Harper's efforts to control his government's media relations from the centre (see Chapter 14). The PMO also included a Strategic Planning unit, led by Conservative strategist Patrick Muttart (Dossier 12.3), a Policy and Research unit, the Tour and Advance Office, and an Appointments secretariat. The latter produces lists of "politically acceptable nominees" for the Order-in-Council appointments made by the prime minister. It does so after consulting "with the line and regional ministers with an interest in a specific appointment and perhaps also with groups like the caucus and the political party's hierarchy."[67] Its presence in the Harper PMO contradicts the Conservatives' campaign pledge to prohibit party patronage in Order-in-Council positions and establish a Public Appointments Commission to screen potential candidates.[68] Other important PMO staffers include the Legislative Assistant, who prepares the PM for the daily Question Period in the Commons; the Correspondence unit; and the official photographer. Finally, as noted in Dossier 9.3, the PMO oversees the selection of exempt staff in ministers' Offices—yet another means to exert control over the activities of individual ministers.[69]

The senior PMO staff work closely with their counterparts in the PCO. The latter controls the information on which the PM's effectiveness as head of government depends, while the former is responsible for advising the PM on "priorities, political strategy and tactics, and political dimensions of policy initiatives."[70] Justice Gomery described the relationship as follows:

> [T]he Prime Minister's Office (PMO) links the Prime Minister to the world of politics, and thus to Cabinet Ministers, caucus members, the party and the media. The PCO, meanwhile, links the Prime Minister to the world of administration and government departments. Accordingly, the Prime Minister receives streams of information from two sources, the PMO and the PCO. The two worlds overlap from time to time, and there is close cooperation between the two offices. But both recognize or, at least, should recognize where the world of purely partisan politics begins, one that PCO intuitively tries to avoid. . . . It is in their mutual interest to collaborate, and, on the great majority of files, there is, indeed, close cooperation.[71]

The distinction between political decision-making and administration is not always clear in practice, as the close working relationship between the PMO and PCO illustrates. A PCO official who lacks political sensitivity will find his or her policy advice ignored, however sound his or her grasp of the issues and the machinery. The Cabinet papers system introduced in early 2004 appears to reflect this reality: Ministerial recommendations approved by the PCO must now include "political perspectives, risks and strategies to address them . . . and communications considerations."[72] These are not the traditional tasks of the permanent executive; in theory, the responsibility for providing political analyses of proposed policies rests with the PMO and the ministers' political staffers.[73] On the other side, a PMO official who does not understand how the federal government works is of little value to his or her boss.

In 1971, a former Clerk observed that each office had a unique mandate:

> The Prime Minister's Office is partisan, politically oriented, yet operationally sensitive. The Privy Council Office is non-partisan, operationally oriented yet politically sensitive. . . . What is known in each office is provided freely and openly to the other if it is relevant or needed for its work, but each acts from a perspective and in a role quite different from the other.[74]

Today, this functional distinction between the PCO and the PMO appears to be eroding. Neither side, political nor administrative, seems willing to take responsibility for its own decisions when things go wrong. Justice Gomery made the following observation about the Sponsorship Scandal:

> Ministers pointed their fingers at public servants, as did the exempt political staff in both the Prime Minister's Office (PMO) and the ministerial offices. Public servants, in turn, pointed their fingers at politicians and their staff, and sometimes at each other. On the face of it, it is tempting to conclude that the doctrine of ministerial responsibility has become a process of mutual deniability.[75]

Justice Gomery attributed many of the problems to "the unprecedented decision to direct the Sponsorship Program from the PMO," instead of placing the deputy minister of Public Works in charge.[76]

> As shown by the evidence, if a proposal or program is perceived as being supported by the PMO, politicians, and public servants alike, mindful of the effect that opposition might have upon their careers, hesitate to object to it in any fashion, no matter how ill-conceived or poorly administered it may be. This undermines the whole concept of a professional and non-partisan public service, fearlessly giving objective advice to its political masters.[77]

Gomery became convinced that "The concentration of power in the PMO makes it progressively more difficult for counter-balancing forces in Cabinet, in the public service and in Parliament to modify or to oppose measures advocated by the Prime Minister."[78] Despite this warning, Gomery made no recommendations to address the issue.

The Harper Government does not appear to share Justice Gomery's concern about the excessive centralization of power in the PMO. Within a year of taking office, some observers described Harper's PMO as the most powerful in Canadian history. Examples of centralized control, bypassing line departments and their ministers, abounded. During her brief and troubled tenure as Environment minister, Rona Ambrose had considerably less influence on the file than the PMO staff assigned to the issue of climate change. The motion to recognize the Québécois as a nation (Chapter 5) originated in the PMO, not the Intergovernmental Affairs Secretariat of the PCO. As we saw in Chapter 5, the responsible minister was not even consulted before Prime Minister Harper made the announcement.[79]

The Department of Finance

Finance occupies a unique position among the departments of the federal government. On the one hand, it is a line department with responsibility for a particular portfolio. Its policy experts monitor developments in the Canadian and global economies and advise the government on appropriate responses to current economic trends. Finance also manages particular programs and services; for example, its Federal–Provincial Relations and Social Policy branch delivers the Canada Health Transfer, Canada Social Transfer, and equalization payments to the provinces (see Chapter 4). In this sense, it resembles Agriculture and Agri-Food Canada or Health Canada.

On the other hand, Finance is a central agency: it coordinates fiscal policy and prepares the annual federal budget. The Chrétien Government's emphasis on budget-cutting in the mid-1990s elevated the status of Finance even further, because it required the department to sign off on any new spending proposals (which gave it effective veto power over other departments). The annual budget became "the government's major policy statement," restricting the program activities of all departments and forcing reluctant public servants to implement the priorities of the PM and the minister of Finance.[80] Even after several successive budget surpluses, Finance retained its key position within the federal executive branch. Its minister was usually the most powerful member of Cabinet, after the prime minister. The two worked together to determine the spending priorities of the Government and allocate funds among the various departments and programs.[81]

The work of the Economic and Fiscal Policy Branch is dominated by the annual budget process. Every year, usually in February or March, the Finance minister presents the federal budget to the House of Commons. The Budget Speech is the culmination of months of effort, beginning in October when Finance releases budget consultation papers to the public and the minister makes an "Economic Statement" to the Standing Commons Committee on Finance. The committee holds public hearings to consult with interest groups and individuals, while the minister seeks input from the business and financial communities. Traditionally, the budget process was wrapped in a thick blanket of secrecy. Leaks that might provide an economic advantage to certain groups—for example, the banking sector—were avoided at all costs. As Finance minister, Paul Martin ended this tradition, preferring instead to consult widely and to build up political support for the budget before its formal introduction in the House.

As the budget takes shape, the Cabinet and its committees evaluate the proposed spending and revenue targets. Under the new Cabinet structure, this task would likely be carried out by Priorities and Planning and the Treasury Board. Finance officials and the PCO's Liaison Secretariat for Macroeconomic Policy advise ministers about the strategic and economic implications of the draft budget and its spending targets for each department. After extensive economic and political analysis, the minister delivers the speech. His or her officials keep a close eye on its fiscal impact, and prepare to make any necessary adjustments to their overall revenue and spending plans.

The Treasury Board Secretariat (TBS)

The TBS supports the work of the Treasury Board, a standing committee of the federal Cabinet whose mandate is set out in the *Financial Administration Act* (Dossier 8.5). The Department of Finance sets the broad outlines of economic and fiscal policy; the TBS oversees the detailed spending estimates tabled in the House shortly after the Budget Speech. It works closely with Finance during the budget process, advising on expenditure targets and possible funding reallocations. (The TBS was part of the Department of Finance until the 1930s, and the two agencies still share personnel and administrative resources.) The TBS estimates the likely cost of new policy or program initiatives. In setting expenditure targets for individual departments and programs, the TBS relies on the business plans submitted by deputy ministers.[82] Once the budget and the detailed Estimates have been submitted to the House, the TBS monitors departmental spending and keeps the PCO informed of any problems.

Finally, the TBS is "the employer and general manager of the public service."[83] It works with the Public Service Commission (PSC)—an arm's-length agency that reports to Parliament—to ensure that public servants are properly recruited and trained.[84] The TBS and the PSC establish broad policy guidelines for the public service, which are implemented by the administrative branches within the various departments and agencies of the federal government.

The TBS was a key player in the 1990s, when the Chrétien Government focused on cutting the federal deficit. Its power appears to have diminished since the nation's finances improved at the turn of this century. In 2006, the Auditor General reported that the TBS routinely approved billions of dollars in annual spending on established programs without any meaningful input into the decision-making process. It lacked the information necessary to assess these programs, in order to determine whether their continued funding was appropriate.[85] At the same time, new program spending and unplanned expenditures (such as emergency assistance to countries stricken by the 2004 tsunami) were rushed through Cabinet without proper TBS review.[86] The Auditor General concluded that the concentration of power in the Cabinet—and especially in the hands of the prime minister and Finance minister—made it impossible for the TBS to oversee public spending effectively.[87] This finding reinforces Justice Gomery's concerns about the power of the PM and his Office, and raises serious questions about the accountability of the executive branch to Parliament (see "Parliament and the Public Purse" in Chapter 7).

Line Departments

As we saw in Dossier 9.2, each line department is responsible for programs and service delivery in a particular policy field (e.g., transport or agriculture). It used to be the case that policy originated within the line departments, but today the policy-making process is more diffuse and complex:

> [A]ny proposed policy not co-opted by the prime minister, and perhaps the minister of finance, invariably brings together several federal departments or agencies, provincial departments, interest groups, consultants, lobbyists, think-tanks, and pollsters. . . . as issues became more complex and interconnected, it became apparent that no single department had all the necessary policy tools and program instruments to deal with them. The result is that each department now comes to the table with only part of the answer in hand, unable on its own to impose comprehensive solutions. The great majority of policy issues no longer respect organizational boundaries; as a result, policy making has now become horizontal, consultative, and porous.[88]

Within each department, the deputy minister is responsible for the implementation of departmental policy and the administration of its programs. In the conduct of his or her duties, he or she is bound by a variety of laws. Each department is governed by its own separate statute, which spells out the authority granted to it by Parliament. Deputies are also required to abide by laws that apply to the entire executive branch, including the *Financial Administration Act* and the *Interpretation Act*.[89] As the preceding quotation suggests, deputy ministers also work together across portfolios to coordinate the work of the federal executive branch. When appropriate, they consult regularly with officials in the provincial governments (see the discussion of intergovernmental relations in Chapter 4).

Finally, deputy ministers are answerable to Parliament for the administration of their portfolios. They can be compelled to provide information, within the limits imposed by legislation (e.g., the *Privacy Act*) and by the traditional distinction between politics and administration. Until recently, MPs could not question deputies about allegations of incompetence or wrongdoing (Dossier 9.4); only the minister could be compelled to appear before a committee. The reason, as we saw at the beginning of this chapter, was the "bargain" between the political and permanent executives.

When Canadian Cabinet ministers refuse to take responsibility for errors or wrongdoing in their portfolios, they often argue that the deputies actually run the department; therefore, the minister could not have been expected to know about or to correct any problems. It might seem logical to close this accountability gap by requiring deputies to answer to Parliament instead. This is done in Britain, where the administrative heads of departments are designated as "Accounting Officers" and required to account for their use of public money before the Public Accounts Committee (PAC). (See the discussion of the Canadian PAC in Chapter 7.) There have been calls for the adoption of a similar provision in Canada since the 1980s. Attempting to impose greater accountability on deputies is a tempting response to this breakdown in constitutional convention, but it carries two risks: further eroding the traditional distinction between politics and administration, and undermining the trust between ministers and deputies without which the executive branch cannot function.

In his investigation of the Sponsorship Scandal, Justice Gomery criticized the former deputy minister of Public Works for turning a blind eye to the spending irregularities in the Sponsorship Program. Gomery characterized the deputy's attitude as "an abdication of his responsibility to control, direct and oversee the actions of officials in his department."[90] He recommended that deputies be held accountable to Parliament for the financial management of their departments. In Gomery's view, this measure would close the accountability gap that plagued the executive branch. In practical terms, it would give deputies a strong incentive to pay closer attention to the day-to-day affairs of their departments:

> The administrative culture that permitted the Sponsorship abuses will be improved only if there are strong motivations for Deputy Ministers, senior officials, and heads of agencies and Crown Corporations to put more emphasis on efficiency and probity in financial

administration and on the willingness to accept responsibility. To make that happen, an environment must be created in which heads of the Government's administrative apparatus take seriously the responsibility they hold for management. They must know that they will be held accountable for any deficiency in their stewardship of the public purse. An enhanced role for Parliament and parliamentary committees in supervising and enforcing accountability for financial administration, including the accountability of senior bureaucrats, must be affirmed if this environment is to become a reality.[91]

> The Commission is not satisfied that the present procedures for the accountability of Deputy Ministers ensure that they place sufficient emphasis on their obligations and duties, apart from their loyalty to their Ministers and the Government of the day. The accountability of Deputy Ministers before the Public Accounts Committee would not only encourage but demand that they pay more attention, in the public interest, to their duties, to the law and to Parliament.[92]

The 2006 Conservative platform promised to "Designate the deputy minister of each government department or agency as the Accounting Officer for that department. The deputy will be responsible to Parliament for the departmental spending and administrative practices of his or her department."[93] Once in power, Harper "watered down his proposal on the accounting officer concept," probably under pressure from a reluctant PCO.[94] The Harper Government's *Federal Accountability Act* does designate deputies as "Accounting Officers" for their departments, within the meaning of the *Financial Administration Act*. This makes them *answerable* to the Public Accounts Committee (PAC) concerning the use of public funds by their departments. However, it does not make them either *responsible* or *accountable* (see Dossier 8.1). So the new arrangement preserves the constitutional convention that only Ministers are accountable to Parliament,

(continued)

whereas deputies are accountable to their ministers (as well as the prime minister and the Clerk of the Privy Council).[95]

Given the intense partisanship of Canada's PAC, some experts feared that the British system would not work well here; Opposition MPs would be tempted to try to embarrass or punish deputies, instead of restricting themselves to seeking information.[96] In other words, they would ignore the distinction between answerability and responsibility. Whether for partisan advantage or some other reason, the Opposition majority on the PAC was dissatisfied with the watered-down version of Harper's promise. In March 2007 the committee (or at least the Opposition members) adopted a protocol for the appearance of Accounting Officers. The protocol gives the PAC the power to summon deputies separately from their ministers, to question them on all matters pertaining to their statutory responsibilities, and to probe problems which arose during their service in a prior portfolio.[97] In contrast, the PCO policy states that Accounting Officers may only appear before committees with the permission of, and on behalf of, their current minister and department (not previous ministers or portfolios).[98] The PAC protocol asserts the power to hold deputies accountable in their own right, whereas the PCO insists—as does the president of the Treasury Board[99]—that they have no authority independent of their ministers and, consequently, that they cannot be held personally to account.

The result is that accounting officers in Canada will have to deal with two competing sets of rules governing their role and accountability, one established by Parliament and the other by the Privy Council Office. It is unfortunate that, while the accounting officer concept was designed to eliminate confusion over responsibility and accountability, it now appears to have made matters worse. Parliament has the constitutional right to dictate how it conducts its business, including the terms and conditions for the attendance of witnesses before its committees. The Privy Council Office, in its enthusiasm for the status quo and the doctrine of ministerial responsibility, appears to have forgotten this other fundamental constitutional principle.[100]

Both protocols agree that neither Parliament nor its committees can punish deputies for questionable uses of public money, and that MPs must always respect the political neutrality of the public service. Deputy ministers, in their capacity as Accounting Officers, are "accountable *before*" the PAC—a term that seems to correspond to Gomery's definition of "answerability" (Dossier 8.1)—but not "accountable *to*" any legislative body.[101] In May 2007 the House of Commons adopted the PAC protocol—"against the desires of the minority Conservative Harper government, most of whose members voted against this implementation of their own election platform commitment"[102]—and extended it to all standing committees.

Most deputy ministers reach that position after decades in the public service,[103] including a stint in the PCO,[104] although a growing number are recruited at mid-career from academia and the private sector. Most experts argue that a deputy minister should remain in the same portfolio for at least three years. It takes time to master the details of policy and administration within a particular department, while juggling the competing demands of government-wide coordination. Yet the average length of a deputy's assignment is one-quarter of the average tenure a century ago (three years versus 12 years).[105] This means that the average deputy minister is shuffled into a new portfolio at just about the time when he or she is fully prepared for the challenges of his or her old portfolio.[106] When a new government takes office, the pace of movement usually accelerates. In his first 10 months in power, Prime Minister Harper shuffled 41 deputy-level officials among the central agencies and line departments; over the preceding 18 months, fewer than a dozen deputies had been moved.[107]

The rapid turnover of deputies raises two problems. The first, as just mentioned, is the steep learning curve for the administrative head of a new portfolio. Expertise in policy cannot be acquired overnight. Second, the "revolving door" for deputies strengthens the control of the prime minister and Clerk over the senior ranks of the permanent executive.[108] Indeed, this appears to be the primary reason for the frequent movement of deputies: reinforcing the power of the PM and PCO over the line departments: "As a rule, the deputy minister owes his loyalty first to his minister. Where there are conflicts with government priorities, however, the loyalty of the deputy minister will go to the Prime Minister since he represents the government for the minister."[109] As part of his proposals to curb the power of the PMO, Justice Gomery recommended that deputies be appointed for five-year terms and spend a minimum of three years in each portfolio.[110] The Harper Government does not appear to have adopted this measure.

Ministers cannot be blamed for the turnover, because they rarely have any say in the choice of deputies—despite the crucial importance of the working relationship between the political and administrative heads of each department. When conflicts erupt, the deputy can seek the Clerk's assistance to resolve them; in severe cases, the Clerk may involve the prime minister. Victory in a power struggle between the minister and the deputy depends on the perceived effectiveness of the former: "a veteran deputy minister is sure to win over a new, erratic minister with little support, while a pillar of the party may get his deputy head transferred."[111]

Below the deputy minister in the departmental hierarchy are a handful of assistant deputy ministers, responsible for the various units within the portfolio. In turn, they oversee the work of hundreds or thousands of people spread across the country. In general, the recruitment and promotion of public servants are based on demonstrated qualifications. The major exception to the merit principle, until recently, was the hiring of former political aides (Dossier 9.3).

Crown Corporations and Service-Delivery Agencies

Crown corporations are "distinct legal entities established by government to pursue public policy and commercial objectives."[112] The word "commercial" is the key: Crown corporations, like private businesses, sell goods and services in order to make a profit. Unlike most private businesses, the prices which Crown corporations can charge are strictly regulated, as part of their Parliamentary mandate to fulfill certain policy goals. As of 2006, there were 43 federal Crown corporations (along with dozens of subsidiaries and shared-governance corporations), employing 73 000 workers in a variety of economic sectors.[113] The best-known are VIA Rail, Canada Post, and the CBC/Radio-Canada. Some Crown corporations are established to provide services that the private sector cannot or will not provide because of high costs (e.g., affordable train travel across Canada's huge land mass);[114] others compete with private-sector rivals (e.g., the courier division of Canada Post), which raises some questions about their legitimacy in the marketplace.

As mentioned previously, each Crown corporation is affiliated with a particular line department. It is run by a board of directors, whose members are appointed by the Governor in Council. The minister responsible for a particular Crown corporation may not interfere directly with its operations; the most he or she can do is to issue a directive to the board. (All such directives must be in writing, and tabled in Parliament.[115]) However, he or she is accountable to Parliament for its overall performance.[116] When necessary, the minister sponsors proposed amendments to the statute that establishes and governs the corporation. The president or chief executive officer of the corporation reports annually to Parliament, both in writing and by appearing before the parliamentary committee that oversees its portfolio. The Auditor General is empowered to review the books of most Crown corporations; if he or she finds any irregularities or errors in its accounts, he or she reports them to Parliament; the Public Accounts Committee may, if it chooses, dig deeper into the problems.

Service-delivery agencies resemble Crown corporations in several respects:

- First, they operate at arm's length from the government of the day. They are run by boards or commissions, appointed by Order in Council, instead of being managed directly by public servants and ultimately by the minister.
- Second, each agency belongs to a particular ministerial portfolio. For example, the Canada Border Services Agency reports to the minister of Public Safety, while the minister of National Revenue is accountable to Parliament for the work of the Canada Revenue Agency.
- Third, each agency has a unique role and mandate, which is set out in an enabling statute passed by Parliament.
- Fourth and finally, ministers and their exempt staff are expected to refrain from direct interference in the work of these arm's-length organizations. In particular, they must not attempt to procure benefits for any person associated with the minister, including a constituent, from a corporation or agency within the minister's portfolio.[117]

There are two principal differences between corporations and agencies. First, the agencies do not sell goods and services in the marketplace; they perform standard government activities, such as collecting taxes and safeguarding public health. Second, whereas federal Crown corporations have existed since 1922,[118] the agencies discussed in this section are a relatively recent innovation. They are a product of the New Public Management trend of the 1980s and 1990s, which sought to separate policy-making from policy implementation and delivery. The goal was "to have managers responsible for operations focus their attention first and foremost on continuously improving management and achieving economy, efficiency and effectiveness."[119]

PROGRAMS AND SERVICES

As discussed in Chapter 4, many high-profile and costly government programs—health care, social assistance, and education—are delivered by the provinces, with financial assistance from Ottawa. But the federal government also delivers a wide range of programs and services to Canadians:

- Public Safety and Emergency Preparedness Canada is responsible, among other things, for Corrections Canada (which operates the federal prison system) and the RCMP.
- Agriculture and Agri-Food Canada provides financial assistance to farmers who suffer poor yields or declining prices for their harvests.
- Health Canada tests new drugs and medical devices before they reach the market.
- Social Development Canada provides funding for local job-creation projects and community training initiatives. It also manages the Employment Insurance and Canada Student Loans programs.
- International Trade Canada assists Canadian exporters in reaching foreign markets.
- Foreign Affairs Canada issues passports to citizens who wish to travel outside Canada.

Many of these programs and services are delivered by regional offices, some—such as the Summer Career Placements Program—by temporary employees, and others by full-time public servants. Still other programs are delivered by private-sector companies and managed by public servants; for example, Canada Student Loans are obtained from chartered banks, subject to the guidelines and regulations set by the federal government.

REGULATIONS

Regulations are a form of law, often referred to as delegated or subordinate legislation. Like Acts, they have the same binding legal effect and usually state rules that apply generally, rather than to specific persons or things. However, regulations are not made by Parliament. Rather, they are made by persons or bodies to whom Parliament has delegated the authority to make them, such as the Governor in Council, a minister or an administrative agency. Authority to make regulations must be expressly delegated by an Act. Acts that authorize the making of regulations are called enabling Acts.[120]

When Parliament approves a government Bill, it delegates to the executive the power to make any regulations necessary for its implementation. This delegated law-making authority should not be overly broad, and it should not usurp Parliament's right to amend the details of legislation.[121] Most regulations are made by public servants in the line departments and central agencies, subject to the approval of the Governor in Council (i.e., the Cabinet). New legislation should contain the text of the regulations that will be required to put it into effect; regulations made under existing legislation cannot exceed the authority granted by the relevant law. All new regulations must be examined by legal counsel in the Justice department and the PCO; they must be registered with the Orders in Council Secretariat of the PCO for review by the Treasury Board; and, once adopted, they must be published in the weekly *Canada Gazette*. The criteria for approving or rejecting draft regulations are set out in the regulatory policy of the Government of Canada:

- Regulatory authorities must demonstrate both that a problem or risk exists and that federal intervention is justified.
- All possible alternative means—whether regulatory or nonregulatory—of addressing the problem or risk have been considered.
- Stakeholders—industry, labour, consumer groups, professional organizations, other governments, and interested individuals—have been consulted on all phases of the identification of problems and the development of the regulatory solution.
- Intergovernmental agreements must be respected and opportunities for intergovernmental coordination exploited.
- Benefits and costs of the regulatory interventions under consideration have been assessed, the benefits justify the costs, and limited government resources are used where they will do the most good.
- Adverse impacts on the economy must be minimized.
- Systems are in place to manage regulatory resources effectively.
- Compliance and, when appropriate, enforcement policies must be implemented.
- The regulators have the resources for monitoring compliance and enforcing the regulations.[122]

Once a regulation has been published in the *Canada Gazette,* it is tabled with the Standing Joint Committee on Statutory Instruments. While this group of MPs and senators has the formal power to review any and all Orders in Council, its limited resources prevent it from undertaking a detailed examination of more than a quarter of them. In a sense, therefore, Parliament colludes in the shift of law-making power from the legislative branch to the executive.

Although the purpose of the regulatory policy is to minimize government interference in economic and social activity, Canada remains a highly regulated society. In addition to the regulations enforced by government departments, there are several regulatory agencies—statutory bodies "charged with responsibility to administer, to fix, to establish, to control, or to regulate an economic, cultural, environmental, or social activity by regularized and established means in the public interest and in accordance with general policy guidelines specified by the government."[123] What we watch on Canadian television is determined by broadcast regulations established by the Canadian Radio-television and Telecommunications Commission (CRTC). Marketing boards set the prices and production quantities of chickens, eggs, turkeys, milk, and a host of other farm and agricultural products. The medicines we take, the vehicles we drive, even our food and water are subject to government standards and regulations.

By the 1980s, there was a widespread perception that government had grown too big and intrusive. Technological changes, globalization, and the election of more ideologically conservative governments in the 1980s have led to deregulation in some policy sectors. Transport Canada, the federal department responsible for aviation, railways, and marine traffic, houses a Programs and Divestiture Branch whose mandate includes "the transfer of ports, harbours, and airports to communities and other interests."[124] The federal government set up a non-profit corporation, NAV CANADA, to take over its air-traffic control services. Similarly, the Economic Development and Corporate Finance branch of the Finance department houses a Privatization, Crown Corporations, and Defence unit, the responsibilities of which include "the disposition of the Government's Crown commercial holdings."[125]

However, the reduction of direct regulation by the federal government does not imply the end of regulation altogether. Some federal regulatory activities have been shifted upward to international agreements such as NAFTA and international agencies such as the World Trade Organization; others have moved downward, to the provincial governments (e.g., the devolution of labour market training in the late 1990s). In other cases, regulatory activities that once were undertaken by government departments have been shifted to private, non-commercial agencies. Government is not out of the regulatory game; it is simply changing the rules and its strategies.

THE POLITICAL AND PERMANENT EXECUTIVES IN THE POLICY-MAKING PROCESS

According to Donald Savoie, there are now "two distinct policy processes" in Ottawa: "one for the prime minister and his or her court of advisers, usually pitched to the media, and another for everybody else."[126] The first, as described in Chapter 8, is rapid and secretive; only the PM's inner circle (the "courtiers") are consulted. The second, described in this section, applies to the vast majority of matters that are not prime ministerial priorities. It can take years for a policy to emerge from the complex consultations with dozens of "stakeholders" inside and outside government. Once there is sufficient "buy-in," the established process resumes. Because a Bill must be sponsored by a minister of the Crown, a particular line department will be responsible for seeing it through the legislative process.

Immediately after the Speech from the Throne, which kicks off a new session of Parliament, the assistant secretary to the Cabinet for Legislation and House Planning sends a letter to all deputy ministers requesting a list of Bill proposals. The first stage is the preparation of a two-page Issue Brief for review by the Operations Committee of Cabinet. In a single sentence, this document must describe the policy issue to be addressed. It also identifies "Strategic Considerations," including possible environmental, intergovernmental, regional, or international implications of accepting or rejecting the proposed policy; summarizes the views of the government caucus and Parliament as a whole; describes the funding implications, the way in which the minister expects to proceed, and expected outcomes; and suggests "Communications Considerations" (e.g., the timing of the proposal in relation to future federal–provincial or international meetings).[127] The required format for the Issue Brief demonstrates the heightened importance of international and provincial governments in national policy-making, as well as the close connection between policy and politics.

The Operations Committee determines whether the proposed policy will go ahead. Together with the Priorities and Planning Committee, it decides which of the approved Issue Briefs should be turned into proposed legislation during the upcoming or current parliamentary session. The House of Commons operates on a tight schedule. Relatively few Bills can be debated, scrutinized, and passed within a given session of Parliament (which normally lasts for about two years). Therefore, Cabinet must be careful not to overload Parliament; it must decide which Bills to introduce early in the session, when the chances of passage are greatest. In general, high-priority items are those that implement key policy promises in the Throne Speech, the annual budget, or the party platform;[128] those required by international or federal–provincial agreements; or those that address pressing public issues, such as the economic and financial crisis which erupted in 2008.

When a department is notified that the Cabinet has given priority to its Issue Brief, the experts in its policy branch prepare a Memorandum to Cabinet (MC). The MC is designed to secure "policy approval and an authorization for the Legislation Section of the Department of Justice to draft the bill."[129] Ideally, a department should follow four steps in preparing an MC:

1. Analyze the policy issue to be addressed, and compare alternative solutions to the one proposed in the Bill.
2. Consult its client groups, other departments, and other governments that may be affected by the Bill.
3. Determine and justify the impact of the proposed Bill.
4. Calculate the resources required to implement the Bill.[130]

The draft MC is submitted by the sponsoring department to the PCO for review. If it meets with the approval of the PCO, it goes to both the Operations Committee and the appropriate policy committee of Cabinet (Dossier 8.5). As explained in Chapter 8, the decisions of Cabinet committees are almost always accepted by the full Cabinet. After the MC has been accepted by Cabinet, it is sent to the Justice department for drafting in proper legislative form.

The Legislation section at Justice must follow several guidelines when drafting Bills for Parliament:

- The draft Bill must be constitutional.
- It must be consistent with both the civil law of Quebec and the common-law system in the other provinces.
- It must be drafted simultaneously in both English and French; because both official-language versions are equally authoritative, "it is not acceptable for one version to be a mere translation of the other."[131]

Most government Bills include three main elements:

1. the preamble sets out the purpose of the Bill (these sections are not enforceable);
2. the substance of the legislation, consisting of new legislative provisions and/or amendments to existing laws; and
3. the schedules, which contain draft regulations and any other provisions required to put the substance of the Bill into effect.

When the drafting is complete, the Bill is sent to the Legislation and House Planning Secretariat of the PCO. This secretariat distributes the Bill to the Government Leader in the House of Commons and to the other members of the Operations Committee. If it meets with their approval, the Bill returns to the relevant policy committee of Cabinet where the government leader "seeks delegated authority to arrange for the introduction of the bill in either the House of Commons or the Senate."[132] Once this authority has been granted, the Government Leader and the sponsoring minister sign off on the Bill and prepare to introduce it in Parliament. The assistant secretary to the Cabinet for Legislation and House Planning notifies the Clerk of the House (occasionally the Senate) that the Bill will be introduced; the Government Leader meets with the other parties' House Leaders to work out the legislative timetable. Then it proceeds through the legislative stages described in Dossier 7.4. When it has been adopted in the same form by both Houses of Parliament, the Bill comes full circle: it must receive royal assent from the governor general before it becomes law.

CONCLUSION

In the past three chapters, we have explored the relationship between the legislative and executive branches of Canada's national government. Laws are sponsored by the political executive, move through the ratification process in Parliament, and return to the permanent executive for implementation. The Crown authorizes the raising and spending of public money, subject to approval by the House of Commons. In principle, the political executive is directly accountable to MPs; the permanent executive is accountable to the prime minister and the Clerk of the PCO, and answerable to Parliament. Partisan politics is the most powerful norm of behaviour in the Commons and the Cabinet; it has no place in the permanent executive, which is supposed to carry out its responsibilities in a neutral and anonymous fashion.

As we have seen, however, there are some flaws in this picture. The Commons no longer holds individual Cabinet ministers accountable for problems in their departments. Collective Cabinet responsibility to Parliament is still a reality, but only when the Government holds a minority in the Commons. Instead of taking responsibility, ministers blame their deputies and other officials (even if the exempt staff are to blame). In their turn, public servants hide behind the fiction that ministers and their political aides run the departments. The Sponsorship Scandal revealed the gaps in our scheme of accountability, and provided the occasion for a searching review of our legislative and executive branches.

The scandal also helped to bring a new government to power, with a self-proclaimed mandate to restore accountability and integrity in Canadian government. Its top priority, the *Federal Accountability Act*, introduced a variety of rules and regulators and made dozens of amendments to existing statutes. Although these sweeping changes are beyond the scope of this chapter, a few comments are in order. The FAA imposed a host of new legal and regulatory constraints on Parliamentarians, ministers, and public servants. In addition to the measures previously discussed, they include stricter conflict-of-interest provisions; the establishment of a Director of Public Prosecutions; stronger protection for public servants who "blow the whistle" on alleged wrongdoing within their portfolios; and wider investigatory powers for the Auditor General.

These are "horizontal" accountability measures: new checks and balances within the institutions of government that are supposed to make its workings more honest and transparent.[133] In reality, they almost always fail to change the behaviour of those who are subjected to them.[134] They are either unrealistically strict, or too costly to justify their limited results.[135] Such measures also obscure the internal activities of the executive branch, which further reduces transparency instead of enhancing it. Even worse, they can grind the business of government to a halt. The Martin Government had already overhauled procedures in an attempt to distance the new prime minister from the Sponsorship mess. "A dizzying array of new guidelines were drafted, and even tighter controls were put in place, often stalling the operation of an already slow government, but often also failing to ensure a more transparent system."[136]

Justice Gomery made it clear that further "horizontal" measures would serve no useful purpose: "more regulations and oversight agencies will not provide solutions to these problems."[137] Instead, he called for greater "vertical" accountability: elected parliamentarians must have the tools to monitor public spending and to hold the members of the political and permanent executives responsible for their wrongdoing. For Gomery, the underlying cause of the scandal was a culture of governance that tolerated deviations from the formal rules: "within the Government, the system of incentives and disincentives is dysfunctional and ineffective in promoting good conduct. Appropriate sanctions seem to be disconnected from the actions of both elected and non-elected public officials."[138] The best way to prevent future scandals is to change the culture within the legislative and executive branches:

> *The administrative culture that permitted the Sponsorship abuses will be improved only if there are strong motivations for Deputy Ministers, senior officials, and heads of agencies and Crown Corporations to put more emphasis on efficiency and probity in financial administration and on the willingness to accept responsibility. To make that happen, an environment must be created in which heads of the Government's administrative apparatus take seriously the responsibility they hold for management. They must know that they will be held accountable for any deficiency in their stewardship of the public purse. An enhanced role for Parliament and parliamentary committees in supervising and enforcing accountability for financial administration, including the accountability of senior bureaucrats, must be affirmed if this environment is to become a reality.[139]*

At the time of writing, the effects of the FAA on Canada's culture of governance were not yet clear. But if Gomery's analysis is correct, stronger incentives for compliance with existing laws and guidelines would have been a more effective solution to the accountability problems revealed by the Sponsorship Scandal—albeit less politically advantageous. As we saw in Chapter 2, many Canadians have lost faith in our political institutions and those who work within them. Tougher laws can provide short-term reassurance, but in the absence of enforcement they produce little or no long-term change. We turn to the chief mechanism of enforcement in the next chapter.

GLOSSARY OF KEY TERMS

Central agencies: Those departments within the federal government whose primary responsibility is to monitor and coordinate policy-making and implementation across the entire executive branch. The four primary central agencies are the Privy Council Office (PCO), the Prime Minister's Office (PMO), the Treasury Board Secretariat (TBS), and the Department of Finance.

Crown: The source and symbol of executive power in Canada. As a former British colony, Canada inherited "a *Constitution* similar in Principle to that of the United Kingdom." Although most of the Crown's powers are now delegated to the political executive, and particularly to the prime minister, the residual and emergency powers of the Crown are vested in the governor general, who must approve all spending measures before they are submitted to the House of Commons. In addition, the Crown's representative formally appoints the political executive and signs Bills passed by the legislative branch into law.

Crown corporations: Public agencies that provide goods and services to a particular clientele. Examples include the CBC, VIA Rail, and—at one time—Air Canada. Crown corporations are ultimately responsible to the federal government, but they are normally operated at arm's length from the political executive. Canada's Crown corporations were originally established to provide goods and services that were too costly for the private sector, such as national railways and coast-to-coast broadcasting. In recent years, many have been privatized (sold to the private sector), partly because of complaints about unfair competition and partly to raise money.

Federal public service: Another name for the permanent executive. The federal public service includes the line and staff employees of all federal government departments, both inside and outside Ottawa.

Line departments: Departments within the federal government that make and implement policy in particular fields, such as agriculture, transport, and foreign affairs. Line departments deliver services to the public, whereas central agencies normally serve other government organizations.

Permanent executive: The federal public service. In principle, the permanent executive is politically neutral; as the name suggests, it remains in place when the governing party changes. It is organized hierarchically, with the Clerk of the Privy Council at the top. Within each department, the permanent executive is headed by the deputy minister.

Political executive: The Cabinet of the day. Often referred to, in colloquial terms, as "the government."

Portfolio: The traditional term for the policy assignment given to a particular Cabinet minister or secretary of state. For example, the Finance minister is said to hold the "Finance portfolio."

Privy Council: The historic term for the political executive. The *Constitution Act, 1867* refers to the executive branch of government as "the Governor in Council; the Crown's representative, the governor general, exercises supreme executive power on the advice of the Government of the day." In reality, as we have seen repeatedly, the governor general is an essentially ceremonial figure. The power of the Crown is exercised by the political executive: the prime minister and his or her Cabinet. The Privy Council does not exist, for all practical purposes, even though the central agency that serves the Cabinet is still called the Privy Council Office. The Privy Council is a constitutional fiction; the Privy Council Office is not.

DISCUSSION AND REVIEW QUESTIONS

1. Distinguish between the political executive and the permanent executive, and briefly describe the relationship between them. What roles do they play in the creation of public policy? How has the relationship changed in recent years?

2. Briefly explain the roles and responsibilities of the four primary central agencies. In your opinion, are they too powerful? Why or why not?

3. In your opinion, should deputy ministers be held directly accountable to Parliament for their administration of their departments? Why or why not?

SUGGESTED READINGS

Books and Articles

Herman Bakvis, *Regional Ministers: Power and Influence in the Canadian Cabinet* (Toronto: University of Toronto Press, 1991).

Commission of Inquiry Into the Sponsorship Program and Advertising Activities [the Gomery Commission], *Volume 1: Who Is Responsible?* (Ottawa: Minister of Public Works and Government Services, 2005).

Commission of Inquiry Into the Sponsorship Program and Advertising Activities [the Gomery Commission], *Volume 2: Restoring Accountability* (Ottawa: Minister of Public Works and Government Services, 2006).

David A. Good, *The Politics of Public Management: The HRDC Audit of Grants and Contributions* (Toronto: University of Toronto Press, 2003).

Edward Greenspon and Anthony Wilson-Smith, *Double Vision: The Inside Story of the Liberals in Power* (Toronto: Doubleday Canada, 1996).

Donald J. Savoie, *Breaking the Bargain: Public Servants, Ministers, and Parliament* (Toronto: University of Toronto Press, 2003).

Donald J. Savoie, *Governing from the Centre: The Concentration of Power in Canadian Politics* (Toronto: University of Toronto Press, 1999).

Donald J. Savoie, ed., *Restoring Accountability: Parliament, Ministers and Deputy Ministers,* volume 1 of the collected research studies for the Commission of Inquiry Into the Sponsorship Program and Advertising Activities [the Gomery Commission] (Ottawa: Minister of Public Works and Government Services, 2006).

David E. Smith, *The Invisible Crown: The First Principle of Canadian Government* (Toronto: University of Toronto Press, 1995).

Websites

Information about the Privy Council Office is available in the "Publications" section of its website: www.pco-bcp.gc.ca.

Individual departments and agencies of the federal government have their own websites; to find them, go to the main government site (www.gc.ca) and click on "About Government" and then "Departments and Agencies" for an alphabetical listing of all departments and agencies and direct links to their sites.

NOTES

1. Clerk of the Privy Council and Secretary to the Cabinet, "Fourteenth Annual Report to the Prime Minister on the Public Service of Canada" (Ottawa: Privy Council Office, 2007), 38 (accessed at www.pco-bcp.gc.ca, June 2007).

2. In March 2008, more than two years after submitting his recommendations, Justice Gomery complained to a House of Commons Committee that the Harper Government had ignored his report. Although he acknowledged that there was some similarity between his prescriptions for restoring accountability and the contents of the *Federal Accountability Act*, he argued that the latter had been drafted before he submitted the second volume of his report. He also claimed that his recommendations would have done more to address the central problem in Canada's political institutions: the growing power of the prime minister at the expense of Parliament and the rest of the political executive. Canada, House of Commons, *Minutes of Proceedings and Evidence of the Standing Committee on Government Operations and Estimates,* March 13, 2008 (accessed at www.parl.gc.ca, April 2008).

3. The metaphor of "steering" and "rowing" comes from David Osborne and Ted Gaebler, *Reinventing Government* (New York: Addison-Wesley, 1992); quoted in Donald J. Savoie, *Breaking the Bargain: Public Servants, Ministers, and Parliament* (Toronto: University of Toronto Press, 2003), 11.

4. Savoie, *Breaking the Bargain,* Chapter 3.

5. Peter Aucoin, "The Staffing and Evaluation of Canadian Deputy Ministers in Comparative Westminster Perspective: A Proposal for Reform," Donald Savoie, ed., *Restoring Accountability:*

Parliament, Ministers and Deputy Ministers, volume 1 of the collected research studies for the Commission of Inquiry Into the Sponsorship Program and Advertising Activities [the Gomery Commission] (Ottawa: Minister of Public Works and Government Services, 2006), 307.

6. Donald J. Savoie, *Court Government and the Collapse of Accountability in Canada and the United Kingdom* (Toronto: University of Toronto Press, 2008), 16.

7. Aucoin, 309.

8. Ibid., 327.

9. Savoie, *Court Government*, 92.

10. Jonathan Malloy and Scott Millar, "Why Ministerial Accountability Can Still Work," in G. Bruce Doern, ed., *How Ottawa Spends, 2007–2008: The Harper Conservatives—Climate of Change* (Montreal and Kingston: McGill–Queen's University Press, 2007), 105–122, particularly 119.

11. Savoie, *Governing From the Centre*, 212.

12. Ibid., 303–04.

13. Gene Swimmer et al., "Public Service 2000: Dead or Alive?" in Susan Phillips, ed., *How Ottawa Spends 1994–95* (Ottawa: Carleton University Press, 1994), 172; quoted in Savoie, *Governing From the Centre*, 212.

14. Commission of Inquiry into the Sponsorship Program and Advertising Activities [the Gomery Commission], *Volume 2: Restoring Accountability*, 2006, 10. Reproduced with the permission of the Minister of Public Works and Government Services, 2008, and courtesy of the Privy Council Office.

15. Privy Council Office, *Decision-Making Processes and Central Agencies in Canada: Federal, Provincial and Territorial Practices* (Ottawa: PCO, 1998), Section 3; available at www.pco-bcp.gc.ca/Decision/canada-e.htm; accessed June 2001.

16. Canada, Privy Council Office, "The Role and Structure of the Privy Council Office" (Ottawa: Her Majesty the Queen in Right of Canada, May 2007); accessed at www.pco-bcp.gc.ca, June 2007.

17. Mike de Souza, "Transition period is full of possibilities, potential gaffes, government warned," *The Hill Times*, February 20, 2006. 21.

18. Sharon Sutherland, "The Role of the Clerk of the Privy Council," in Donald J. Savoie, ed., Linkages: Responsibilities and Accountabilities, volume 3 of the collected research studies for the Commission of Inquiry Into the Sponsorship Program and Advertising Activities [the Gomery Commission] (Ottawa: Minister of Public Works and Government Services, 2006), 23.

19. *Restoring Accountability*, 146.

20. Simon Doyle, "Moving 140 staff from PCO to slay 'two-headed monster': LeBreton," *The Hill Times*, May 22, 2006, 1 and 22.

21. See Paul Wells, *Right Side Up: The Fall of Paul Martin and the Rise of Stephen Harper's New Conservatism* (Toronto: McClelland & Stewart, 2006), 89.

22. Doyle, "Moving 140 staff," 22.

23. Ibid., 22.

24. Simon Doyle, "New, streamlined PCO better serves 'the Centre' and 'bread and butter' of Cabinet: Borbey," *The Hill Times*, November 27, 2006, 1 and 42.

25. Simon Doyle, "At election time, policymaking tightly controlled in PMO," *The Hill Times*, January 29, 2007, 33.

26. The Coordinating Committee of Deputy Ministers brings together the most influential public servants in the federal government for weekly discussions of emerging issues that cut across the functions of line departments. The Committee of Senior Officials advises the Clerk on matters relating to the administration of the public service. The Clerk also holds a weekly breakfast meeting with all deputy ministers and other senior officials with equivalent rank, such as agency presidents. Sutherland, 36; Simon Doyle, "Government's 'very big' DM committee structure," *The Hill Times*, May 28, 2007, 27–28.

27. "The Role and Structure of the Privy Council Office," 1.

28. Sutherland, 27.

29. The PCO bears no responsibility for the Sponsorship Scandal; indeed, Justice Gomery praised former Clerk Jocelyne Bourgon for trying to persuade Prime Minister Chrétien to impose proper oversight and control on the Sponsorship Program from the very beginning. *Who Is Responsible?* Chapter Four and 428–429.

30. *Restoring Accountability*, 151–152.

31. The May 2007 version of the PCO's official self-portrait referred to the "Clerk of the Privy Council and Secretary to the Cabinet"; his job description was essentially the same as it has been for the past several years. See Canada, "The Role and Structure of the Privy Council Office," May 2007 (accessed at www.pco-bcp.gc.ca, June 2007). According to Justice Gomery, this recommendation was publicly rejected by the prime minister as soon as it was issued; see Canada, House of Commons, *Minutes of Proceedings and Evidence of the Standing Committee on Government Operations and Estimates*, March 13, 2008, 2 (accessed at www.parl.gc.ca, April 2008).

32. This claim is based on the list of PMO and ministerial staff published in *The Hill Times*, February 26, 2007, 30–31 and 35.

33. *Accountable Government*, 37.

34. Liane E. Benoit, "Ministerial Staff: The Life and Times of Parliament's Statutory Orphans," in Donald Savoie, ed., *Restoring Accountability: Parliament, Ministers and Deputy Ministers*, volume 1 of the collected research studies for the Commission of Inquiry Into the Sponsorship Program and Advertising Activities [the Gomery Commission] (Ottawa: Minister of Public Works and Government Services, 2006), 166–168 and 172–174. Savoie reports that exempt staff were recently turned into spies for the prime minister: "Harper's PMO went so far as to ask exempt staff working for cabinet ministers to 'secretly provide' an assessment of their bosses' communication skills." *Court Government*, 238.

35. Savoie, *Court Government*, 175.

36. Ibid., 166–167.

37. Ibid., 181.

38. Ibid., 169.

39. Ibid., 248.

40. *Accountable Government*, 37.

41. Aucoin, "The Staffing and Evaluation of Canadian Deputy Ministers in Comparative Westminster Perspective," 306–307.

42. Benoit, 192.

43. Treasury Board Secretariat, *Guidelines for Ministers' Offices*, (2003), Appendix A, "Exempt Staff Position Structure," quoted in Benoit, 177.

44. Treasury Board of Canada Secretariat, *Guidelines for Ministers' Offices*, (2003), Appendix E—Information on the Minister's Staff Priority—The Public Service Commission of Canada; quoted in Benoit, 213.

45. *Restoring Accountability*, 138.

46. Benoit, 223–232.

47. *Who Is Responsible?* 163; *Restoring Accountability*, 138.

48. Benoit, 219–220.

49. *Restoring Accountability*, 138.

50. Ibid., 138.

51. Bea Vongdouangchanh, "Ministerial exempt political staffers no longer exempt: Prime Minister Harper," *The Hill Times*, March 27, 2006, 31.

52. Parliament of Canada, 39th Parliament, Bill C-2, *The Federal Accountability Act*, sections 100–107.

53. *Restoring Accountability*, 138.

54. Ibid., 139.

55. Benoit, 202–204.

56. Commission of Inquiry into the Actions of Canadian Officials in Relation to Maher Arar, *Analysis and Recommendations* (Ottawa: Minister of Public Works and Government Services, 2006), 44 and 191–194; accessed at www.pco-bcp.gc.ca, March 2007.

57. Benoit, 200–202.

58. Ibid., 201–202.

59. Savoie, *Governing from the Centre*, 99.

60. Eddie Goldenberg, *The Way It Works: Inside Ottawa* (Toronto: McClelland and Stewart, 2006), 77.

61. Wells, 140 and 154.

62. Aucoin, 308.

63. Goldenberg, 35–36.

64. Wells, 175–176.

65. Bruce Campion-Smith, "PM's top aide stepping down," *The Toronto Star*, May 21, 2008 (accessed at www.thestar.com). The report, written by PCO Clerk Kevin Lynch, found that Brodie was partially responsible for the so-called "NAFTAgate affair" of February–March 2008. During the campaign for the Democratic primary in Ohio, both Senator Barack Obama and Senator Hillary Clinton blamed the North American Free Trade Accord for the loss of manufacturing jobs in the state; each promised to renegotiate the deal if elected to the U.S. presidency. In early February a representative of the Obama campaign allegedly informed officials in the Canadian consulate in Chicago that the Illinois Senator did not really intend to withdraw the U.S. from the trade deal. In late February, at the budget lock-up for reporters, Brodie apparently told a CTV reporter not to take the Clinton and Obama threats too literally. A few days later someone leaked the minutes of the Chicago meeting to the Associated Press, which ran stories alleging that Obama was being less than truthful in his comments on NAFTA. The Lynch report found that Brodie had been indiscreet, but that he had not leaked classified information: Government of Canada, Privy Council Office, "Report on the Investigation into Unauthorized Disclosure of Sensitive Diplomatic Information," Ottawa, May 22, 2008; accessed at www.thestar.com, May 28, 2008. Shortly after the report was issued, a *Toronto Star* columnist alleged that the findings were a whitewash, and that someone in the PMO had provided the minutes of the Chicago meeting to a Republican operative with close ties to the Conservative Party of Canada. James Travers, "Signs point to PMO in NAFTA leak," *The Toronto Star*, May 27, 2008 (accessed at www.thestar.com).

66. This description is based on the list of PMO and ministerial exempt staff published in *The Hill Times*, February 26, 2007, 30.

67. Bill Neville, "The 6 'P's' of Effective Transitions," in Peter E. Larson, ed., *Effective Management of Transitions in Government* (Ottawa: Public Policy Forum, January 2001), 20 (accessed at www.ppforum.ca, April 2007).

68. The pledge was contained in the 2006 Conservative platform, and enshrined in the *Federal Accountability Act*. While the Act was still before Parliament, the prime minister nominated former mining executive Gwyn Morgan to serve as the commissioner. Morgan's appointment was rejected by the Government Operations and Estimates in May 2006; the Opposition majority on the committee was skeptical about the choice of a former Canadian Alliance fundraiser to head a supposedly non-partisan commission. An angry Stephen Harper immediately declared that he would not implement the commission until he had a majority government to ensure the ratification of his nominees. He also stated that "the government will proceed with nominations in the traditional manner"; hence the retention of the partisan Appointments unit in the PMO. Bea Vongdouangchanh, "Conservatives, NDP 'bulldoze' FAA through House committee," *The Hill Times*, May 22, 2006, 26. Despite the supposed shutdown of the commission, it managed to spend over $1 million during the 2006 fiscal year: Bea Vongdouangchanh, "Opposition parties want to know what million-dollar Public Appointments Commission has been up to without a commissioner,"

The Hill Times, March 5, 2007, 4 and 7. The 2008 Conservative Platform implicitly acknowledged that the Prime Minister's fit of pique had not been helpful; it pledged to "appoint members to the Public Appointments Commission" and to get the body "up and running" at last. Conservative Party of Canada, "The True North Strong and Free: Stephen Harper's Plan for Canadians" (accessed at www.conservative.ca, October 2008), 25.

69. Benoit, 172–173.

70. Privy Council Office, *Decision-Making Processes and Central Agencies in Canada,* Section 2; accessed at www.pco-bcp.gc.ca, June 2001.

71. *Restoring Accountability*, 142. Reproduced with the permission of the Minister of Public Works and Government Services, 2008, and courtesy of the Privy Council Office.

72. Privy Council Office, *Memoranda to Cabinet* (January 2004), 3; accessed at www.pco-bcp.gc.ca, January 2004.

73. According to Savoie, "the majority of cabinet documents in Canada are now produced by consultants rather than by career civil servants" (*Court Government*, 241–242). If this is the case, it may help to explain the new emphasis on communications and spin rather than policy.

74. R.G. Robertson, "The Changing Role of the Privy Council Office," a paper presented to the 23rd Annual Meeting of the Institute of Public Administration of Canada on September 8, 1971 and published in *Canadian Public Administration*, XIV:4 (1971), 506.

75. *Restoring Accountability*, 6. Reproduced with the permission of the Minister of Public Works and Government Services, 2008, and courtesy of the Privy Council Office.

76. *Who Is Responsible?* 425.

77. Ibid., 434. Reproduced with the permission of the Minister of Public Works and Government Services, 2008, and courtesy of the Privy Council Office.

78. Ibid., 128.

79. Doyle, "At election time," 33.

80. Savoie, *Governing from the Centre*, 189.

81. The close working relationship between former Prime Minister Chrétien and his Finance minister, Paul Martin, is described in detail in Goldenberg, Chapter Eight.

82. Privy Council Office, *A Guide Book for Heads of Agencies,* Section VII; accessed at www.pco-bcp.gc.ca, June 2001.

83. Privy Council Office, *Decision-Making Processes and Central Agencies in Canada,* Section 3.

84. Savoie, *Governing from the Centre*, 223.

85. Office of the Auditor General, *Report of the Auditor General of Canada to the House of Commons: Matters of Special Importance—2006* (Ottawa, November 2006), 39–42 (accessed at www. oag-bvg.gc.ca, June 2007).

86. Ibid., 44–46.

87. Ibid., 12.

88. Savoie, *Court Government*, 151–152.

89. James Ross Hurley, "Responsibility, Accountability and the Role of Deputy Ministers in the Government of Canada," in Donald J. Savoie, ed., *Linkages: Responsibilities and Accountabilities*, volume 3 of the collected research studies for the Commission of Inquiry Into the Sponsorship Program and Advertising Activities [the Gomery Commission] (Ottawa: Minister of Public Works and Government Services, 2006), 132–133.

90. *Restoring Accountability*, 432.

91. Ibid., 11. Reproduced with the permission of the Minister of Public Works and Government Services, 2008, and courtesy of the Privy Council Office.

92. Ibid., 116. Reproduced with the permission of the Minister of Public Works and Government Services, 2008, and courtesy of the Privy Council Office.

93. Conservative Party of Canada, "Stand Up for Canada," 13; accessed at www.conservative.ca, January 2006.

94. Savoie, *Court Government*, 56.

95. Library of Parliament Research Branch, *Bill C-2: The Federal Accountability Act* (Ottawa, 2006), 62–63 (accessed at www.parl.gc.ca); Peter Aucoin and Mark D. Jarvis, *Modernizing Government Accountability: A Framework for Reform* (Ottawa: Canada School of Public Service, 2005), 47–55 (accessed at www.myschool-monecole.gc.ca/Research/publications/html/p131/1_e.html); Treasury Board of Canada Secretariat, *Review of the Responsibilities and Accountabilities of Ministers and Senior Officials*, 14–15; Hurley, 133–137; Privy Council Office, "Accounting Officers: Guidance on Roles, Responsibilities and Appearances Before Parliamentary Committees" (Ottawa, 2007); accessed at www.pco-bcp.gc.ca.

96. Hurley, 147–148.

97. House of Commons Standing Committee on Public Accounts, "Protocol For the Appearance of Accounting Officers As Witnesses Before the Standing Committee on Public Accounts" (Ottawa, March 2007), 11–12; accessed at www.parl.gc.ca.

98. "Accounting Officers: Guidance on Roles, Responsibilities and Appearances Before Parliamentary Committees," 15.

99. Simon Doyle, "No debate over accounting officer model in U.K., says former British accounting officer," *The Hill Times*, June 11, 2007, 22.

100. Savoie, *Court Government*, 58.

101. Privy Council Office, "Accounting Officers," 8 and 11.

102. Savoie, *Court Government*, 57.

103. Jacques Bourgault, "The Deputy Minister's Role in the Government of Canada: His Responsibility and His Accountability," in Donald Savoie, ed., *Restoring Accountability: Parliament, Ministers and Deputy Ministers*, volume 1 of the collected research studies for the Commission of Inquiry Into the Sponsorship Program and Advertising Activities [the Gomery Commission] (Ottawa: Minister of Public Works and Government Services, 2006), 256.

104. Ibid., 264.

105. Ibid., 265–266.

106. Bea Vongdouangchanh, "Experts say DMs being shuffled too often," *The Hill Times*, October 30, 2006, 30.

107. Ibid, 30; Bea Vongdouangchanh, "Deputy ministerial shuffles since Feb. 6, 2006," *The Hill Times*, August 14, 17; Bea Vongdouangchanh, "Deputy minister shuffles, December 2004 to April 2006," *The Hill Times*, May 8, 2006, 35.

108. Aucoin, 333. Savoie claims that Pierre Trudeau started the rapid turnover of deputies for precisely this reason: to "place ministers and senior bureaucrats on a more equal footing." *Court Government*, 224–225.

109. Bourgault, 277 (citation omitted).

110. *Restoring Accountability*, 109.

111. Ibid., 279.

112. Tara Gray, "Crown Corporation Governance and Accountability Framework: A Review of Recently Proposed Reforms" (Ottawa: Library of Parliament Research Branch, March 2006), 1.

113. Ibid., 2.

114. Canada, President of the Treasury Board, *Annual Report to Parliament: Crown Corporations and Other Corporate Interests of Canada, 2004* (Ottawa: President of the Treasury Board, 2004), 9 (accessed at www.tbs-sct.gc.ca, June 2007).

115. Treasury Board of Canada Secretariat, *Review of the Governance Framework for Canada's Crown Corporations* (Ottawa: President of the Treasury Board, 2005), 11; accessed at www.tbs-sct.gc.ca, June 2007.

116. *Accountable Government*, 14.

117. Ibid., 65–66.

118. *Review of the Governance Framework for Canada's Crown Corporations*, 9.

119. Aucoin, 313.

120. Privy Council Office, Regulatory Affairs and Order in Council Secretariat, "What are regulations and where do they come from?" accessed at www.pco-bcp.ca, June 2007.

121. Privy Council Office, "Cabinet Directive on Law-Making," in *Guide to Making Federal Acts and Regulations*, 2nd edition (Ottawa, 2001), 8–9; accessed June 2007.

122. Privy Council Office, "Cabinet Directive on Law-Making," in *Guide to Making Federal Acts and Regulations*, 2nd edition (Ottawa, 2001), 8–9; accessed June 2007.

123. Kenneth Kernaghan and David Siegel, *Public Administration in Canada*, 3rd edition (Scarborough: ITP Nelson, 1995), 226.

124. See the Transport Canada website: www.tc.gc.ca.

125. Department of Finance, *Structure and Role* (Ottawa, December 1999), 12.

126. Savoie, *Court Government*, 150.

127. Canada, Privy Council Office, *Memoranda to Cabinet* (January 2004), 6; accessed at www.pco-bcp.gc.ca.

128. Privy Council Office, *Decision-Making Processes and Central Agencies in Canada*, Section 1.

129. Ibid.

130. "Cabinet Directive on Law-making," Section 2. As of December 2003, each MC must be accompanied by the written approval of the Departmental Comptroller and the Comptroller-General of Canada. These positions were established by the Martin Government as a step toward "effective control, oversight and monitoring systems on public expenditure." Treasury Board Secretariat, *Strengthening Public Sector Management*, 7.

131. Ibid., 10.

132. Ibid., 14.

133. Philippe C. Schmitter, "The Ambiguous Virtues of Accountability," *Journal of Democracy*, 15:4 (October 2004), 53.

134. Michael M. Atkinson and Gerald Bierling, "Politicians, the Public and Political Ethics: Worlds Apart," *Canadian Journal of Political Science*, 38:4 (December 2005), 1003–1028.

135. Months after the FAA received royal assent, many of its key provisions had not yet been implemented; this suggests that they were either too difficult to put into effect, or more expensive than the Government had anticipated.

136. Chantal Hébert, *French Kiss: Stephen Harper's Blind Date with Quebec* (Toronto: Knopf Canada, 2007), 74.

137. *Who Is Responsible?* 10.

138. *Restoring Accountability*, 41.

139. *Who Is Responsible?* 11. Reproduced with the permission of the Minister of Public Works and Government Services, 2008, and courtesy of the Privy Council Office.

10 The Courts

LEARNING OBJECTIVES

After you finish reading this chapter, you should be able to:

- *summarize* and *explain* the core functions of Canadian courts;
- *describe* and *explain* the structure of the judicial branch;
- *describe* and *evaluate* the processes for appointing judges to section 92 and section 96 courts, and to the Supreme Court of Canada;
- *identify* and *evaluate* two recent changes to the processes for appointing federal judges;
- *describe* and briefly *explain* the work of a trial judge and an appellate judge, and *identify* one key difference between the two;
- *identify* the three pillars of judicial independence, and *explain* why judicial independence is important.

INTRODUCTION

In the three preceding chapters, we examined the two "political" branches of Canada's national government. This chapter examines the third branch: Canada's courts and the judges who sit on them. Unlike MPs, who must be re-elected periodically, judges are appointed to office; they usually serve until they retire at the age of 75. Unlike Cabinet ministers, judges cannot be held accountable by any other institution (except in extreme cases). And unlike civil servants, judges are not supposed to follow the orders of the Government when they perform their official duties. Independence and impartiality—as opposed to accountability and partisanship—are the key institutional characteristics of the judicial branch. These qualities are especially important in high-stakes or politically sensitive cases, as the soccer game described in Chapter 3 suggests.

As we saw in Dossier 1.5, the Supreme Court of Canada has identified four central principles that underpin our constitution: "federalism; democracy; constitutionalism and the rule of law; and respect for minorities."[1] The judicial branch plays a role, sometimes the key role, in protecting all four principles:

- Most obviously, judges uphold the *Constitution* and the rule of law. Every day, trial and appellate judges are asked to measure individual conduct against the standards set by written laws (statutes) and common law (previous judicial rulings). Less often, they are asked to decide whether a particular law or administrative decision conforms to the *Constitution*.

- In a federal system, the courts (especially the highest court) referee disputes between the two senior levels of government.[2] They must decide whether a particular government has exceeded its jurisdictions under the *BNA Act*—for example, a provincial government passing a law to regulate national defence.

- The *Canadian Charter of Rights and Freedoms* gave judges the responsibility to protect minority rights (or majority rights, in the case of laws that discriminate against women). When the other two branches take their *Charter* duties seriously (see Chapter 6), the courts have no role to play; when political or financial considerations take priority over rights or freedoms, the courts have a duty to impose remedies—including the nullification of laws. These remedies have prompted charges of "judicial activism." Although these allegations are generally overstated,[3] they raise an important issue: whether or not judges are competent to devise new laws to replace those which failed constitutional muster. We will examine that issue in this chapter.

- Since the *Charter* took effect, some Canadian judges have claimed a new role: "preservation of the democratic process."[4] This assertion might seem odd, considering that judges are neither elected by nor accountable to the citizens. On the other hand, the growing legal regulation of political parties and elections (Chapters 11 and 12), and the guarantee of democratic rights in the *Charter* (Dossier 6.3), means that political disputes are increasingly settled in the courts. When one or both of the "political branches" seeks to exclude a particular group from the franchise, or manipulates the statute law to improve the electoral chances of one or more parties, the courts may be asked to level the playing field. In so doing, they generally tread carefully; but they cannot ignore the potential dangers posed to democracy and rule of law by the political incentives operating on elected legislators and Cabinet ministers.

The core function of a court is to apply the law to the facts of a particular case in order to resolve a dispute between two parties. Legal disputes can be divided into three categories, depending on the parties involved:

1. two governments battling over policy jurisdiction (e.g., the federalism cases discussed in Chapter 4, or the constitutional reference rulings summarized in Chapters 3 and 5);
2. the Crown versus a private individual or corporation (e.g., a criminal trial); or
3. two private parties embroiled in a civil suit (a divorce, a broken contract, or a **tort**).

When two parties bring a dispute to court, the judge(s) must impose a binding resolution according to the law. (Strictly speaking, there is only one party in a reference case: the government that posed the question to the court.) A judge is required to identify the applicable law—statutory, common-law, conventional, or entrenched—and to interpret it in the context of that particular dispute. The legitimacy of the court's decision depends on the independence and impartiality of the judge(s) involved. More generally, judges cannot defend the *Constitution* and the rule of law if they are punished for ruling against the Crown or nullifying a law passed by Parliament. In particular, judges cannot favour (or be seen to favour) the interests of the government over those of private individuals or groups. Nor can they deliberately advance the policy agenda of one political party over another.

The next section of the chapter describes the structure of Canada's courts, which are divided between the federal and provincial governments. Then we will turn to judicial appointments, and assess some recent changes to the process for choosing federal and Supreme Court judges. The following section describes the work of the courts, and the mechanisms that are supposed to safeguard their independence from the other two branches of government. We will conclude with an evaluation of the Harper Government's treatment of the courts.

THE STRUCTURE OF THE CANADIAN JUDICIAL BRANCH

Because Canada is a federation, the power to make and execute laws is divided between the national government and the provincial governments (sections 91–94 of the *Constitution Act, 1867*). The power to apply and interpret laws is similarly divided between provincial courts and federal (superior) courts. But unlike the legislative and executive branches, Canada's judicial branch is explicitly structured as a hierarchy: the provincial courts are at the bottom of the pyramid, while the Supreme Court of Canada is at the top (see Figure 10.1).

The relevant provisions of the *Constitution Act, 1867* are as follows:

- Section 91(26) empowers the federal Parliament to make laws concerning marriage and divorce. However, the criteria for granting marriage licenses are left for the provinces to determine under section 92(12).

FIGURE 10.1   THE STRUCTURE OF CANADA'S COURT SYSTEM

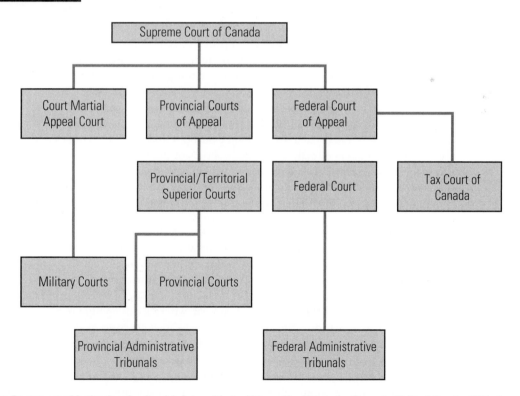

Source: Department of Justice Canada, *Canada's System of Justice* (Ottawa: Her Majesty the Queen in Right of Canada, 2005). Accessed at www.justice.gc.ca/eng/dept-min/pub/ccs-ajc/page3.html, Department of Justice Canada, 2005. Reproduced with the permission of the Minister of Public Works and Government Services Canada, 2008.

- Section 91(27) assigns the content of the criminal law to the federal Parliament. Most criminal offences, and the corresponding punishments, are set out in the *Criminal Code* of Canada. However, section 92(15) permits the provinces to define and punish provincial offences (e.g., violations of highway safety laws).

- Parliament determines the procedures for trying criminal cases and appeals (s. 91(27)), whereas the provinces set the rules of procedure in civil trials (e.g., contract disputes). Assigning the civil law to the provinces was an essential part of the Confederation bargain: it permitted Quebec to retain its unique civil code, while preserving the English common-law tradition in the nine English-speaking provinces.

- Section 92(14) provides for provincial courts—sometimes called "lower" or "inferior" courts—to handle civil and criminal trials. "Provincial courts try most criminal offences and, in some provinces, civil cases involving small amounts of money. Provincial courts may also include specialized courts, such as youth courts, family courts and small claims court."[5] Provincial judges are appointed by the Lieutenant Governor in Council of the relevant province (in practice, the provincial Attorney General). There are roughly 1000 provincial judges in Canada.[6]

- In each province, there are two distinct superior courts: one for trials and the other for appeals. The names vary across jurisdictions: Alberta's superior trial court is styled the Court of Queen's Bench, while its counterpart in Nova Scotia is called the Supreme Court (Trial Division). The provincial government provides the budget and facilities for the superior courts within its jurisdiction, apart from judicial salaries (which are paid by the federal government). The superior trial courts deal with the more serious criminal and civil matters. They also review lower-court decisions, if asked to do so. Appeal courts review the decisions of the superior trial courts. Under section 96 of the *BNA Act,* superior-court judges are appointed by the federal Governor-in-Council. Hence, these are called "section 96 courts." Canada has approximately 1000 federally appointed judges.[7] Each level of the superior court in a given province is headed by a Chief Justice; the Chief of the appellate court is the highest-ranking judge in that jurisdiction.

- Section 101 of the *BNA Act* empowers the federal government to establish "a General Court of Appeal for Canada" and "any additional Courts for the better Administration of the Laws of Canada." The Supreme Court of Canada was created in 1875, to serve as the highest court of appeal in all legal matters.[8] Three additional section 101 courts have subsequently been established: the Federal Court of Canada, which handles administrative law and other matters directly within the purview of the federal government; the Federal Court of Appeal, which reviews the decisions of the Federal Court; and the Tax Court of Canada. The members of the federal courts are appointed by the minister of Justice; the prime minister is also involved in appointments to the Supreme Court of Canada.

The complexity of the court system can be daunting. It provides several levels of judicial review, which permits the eventual correction of legal errors, but at a high cost. To illustrate, imagine that a person has been convicted of a criminal offence in an Ontario provincial court. She (more precisely, her lawyer) asks the Superior Court (trial division) to review the case. The Superior Court judge confirms the conviction. She seeks and is granted a review of the second decision by the Ontario Court of Appeal, where a three-judge panel upholds the conviction by a 2 to 1 margin. The division on the appellate court permits an automatic appeal to the Supreme Court of Canada, which finally overturns the conviction. Along the way, the original conviction in provincial court has been reviewed by three additional courts, a process that can take years and cost hundreds of thousands of dollars in legal fees.[9] There is some public funding for criminal defendants, but little or no support for civil litigation and appeals. The stress of waiting for a case to grind its way through the process is often worse than the financial strain.

Supreme Court justices pose during 2006 swearing in ceremony.
Back Row: The Honourable Madam Justice Louise Charron, the Honourable Mr. Justice Morris J. Fish, the Honourable Madam Justice Rosalie Silberman Abella, and the Honourable Mr. Justice Marshall Rothstein.
Front Row: The Honourable Mr. Justice Louis LeBel, the Honourable Mr. Justice Michel Bastarache (now retired), the Right Honourable Beverley McLachlin, P.C. Chief Justice of Canada, the Honourable William Ian Corneil Binnie, and the Honourable Madam Justice Marie Deschamps.
(CP/Fred Chartrand)

JUDICIAL APPOINTMENTS: THE INCENTIVE STRUCTURE FOR AMBITIOUS JURISTS

All Canadian judges are appointed. In contrast, most lower-court judges in the United States are elected (a highly unusual practice even in democratic states).[10] The power to appoint Canadian judges is a Crown prerogative, exercised by the Government of the day in each jurisdiction. As we saw in the previous section, the provincial Attorneys-General appoint section 92 judges. The federal minister of Justice (who is also the Attorney General for Canada) chooses section 96 judges and the members of the federal courts. The Supreme Court of Canada is the exception: reflecting the unique importance of the highest court in the land, its members are selected by the prime minister. (The PM also appoints the Chief Justices of the superior courts.) His or her choice is constrained by the *Supreme Court Act*, which requires that three of the nine justices must be appointed from the civil bar of Quebec. This ensures that the court has the necessary expertise to handle cases arising from the Quebec civil code. By convention, another three justices must come from Ontario, two from the Western provinces, and one from the Atlantic region. Most justices serve on appellate courts (e.g., the

Ontario Court of Appeal or the Federal Court of Appeal) before their elevation to the Supreme Court of Canada, although a few practising lawyers have been appointed in recent years (including current Justice Ian Binnie).

The *Constitution* says nothing about the criteria for choosing judges, or the process of elevating a judge within the court hierarchy. For more than a century after Confederation, many (if not most) provincial and federal judges were chosen on the basis of party patronage.[11] The federal or provincial government of the day rewarded its supporters in the legal profession by giving them well-paid, secure positions on the bench. Not even the Supreme Court of Canada was immune. Former Prime Minister Mackenzie King paid little heed to judicial experience; instead, he favoured appointees with "service to the Liberal Party, some minimum level of ability, and influential friends."[12] Since Pierre Trudeau became prime minister in 1968, Supreme Court appointments have been based solely on merit—subject to the representational criteria previously mentioned.[13] Apart from the 1979 Progressive Conservative Government of Joe Clark,[14] Trudeau's successors in the PMO have avoided partisanship in Supreme Court appointments—partly because of increasing public and media scrutiny of the court since the *Charter* took effect in 1982.[15]

Another post-*Charter* development may be less positive. Some advocacy groups have lobbied for the appointment of individuals who share their policy goals, or who possess particular demographic characteristics (e.g., gender or ethnicity).[16] The long-standing convention of regional representation on the Supreme Court of Canada, which pits provinces against each other when a Western or Atlantic vacancy occurs, has now been complicated by expectations of gender and linguistic representation. In 1999, following the untimely death of Justice Sopinka, "supporters of John Laskin and Rosie Abella, both members of the Ontario Court of Appeal . . . actively lobbied for their favoured candidate" to replace him. Chief Justice Antonio Lamer "publicly rebuked both factions for engaging in conduct that, in his view, was bound to tarnish the Court's good image in the public eye."[17]

The broad Crown discretion over judicial appointment and promotion raises three serious issues:

- The first issue is the merit of the men (and increasingly women) who preside over our courtrooms. At a minimum, a judge must have a thorough knowledge of the laws and procedures that apply to the cases before him or her. He or she has to understand the relevant common-law precedents, the requirements of the *Constitution,* and the basic principles of our justice system. He or she should also possess certain personal characteristics: strong communication skills, an ability to make fair decisions quickly, and the stamina to endure long and sometimes tedious legal proceedings. The higher his or her rank in the court hierarchy, the more profoundly a judge can shape the law through his or her rulings and interpretations. But regardless of rank, the competence of judges affects all Canadians to one degree or another. This is not to suggest that a judge who happens to belong to a particular political party (or any other group) is necessarily incompetent, but rather to emphasize that merit should always be the overriding criterion for judicial appointments.

- The second issue is the degree of independence that might reasonably be expected of a judge who owes his or her position to the Government of the day. As we have seen, judicial independence is a cornerstone of our constitutional and political structure. It would be highly improper for a member of the executive or legislative branch to try to influence a judge directly. Such contacts are extremely rare, at least since 1976; in that year, former Prime Minister Trudeau publicly prohibited Cabinet members (apart from the minister of Justice) from talking directly to judges in their professional capacity. The most recent case at the federal level occurred in 1990: Amateur Sports Minister Jean Charest (now premier of Quebec) was fired from the Cabinet of former Prime Minister Brian Mulroney for calling a judge who was about to rule on the firing of a track and field coach.[18] However, influence can take more subtle forms. Consider a minister who enjoys a social relationship with a judge, dating back to their days as members of their party's youth wing. Their private conversations might affect that judge's opinions, deliberately or otherwise. The problem of undue influence is not confined to partisanship; it is inherent in the incentives for an ambitious judge hoping to rise in the hierarchy. For example, a superior court trial judge who aspires to a seat on the Court of Appeal might tailor her rulings to please the federal minister of Justice, in hopes that he will exercise his section 96 power in her favour.[19] That minister is the political head of the federal Department of Justice (DOJ), which houses the federal government's litigation unit. DOJ lawyers defend federal statutes against *Charter* challenges, and federal jurisdiction against division-of-powers claims by the provinces. In the absence of binding criteria, the minister might be tempted to appoint or promote judges solely because they favour the Crown and/or the national government.

- Third and finally, a government can stack the bench with judges who share its particular ideology—which may or may not be in tune with the needs of the justice system or the perspective of a subsequent Government. That risk is especially acute in jurisdictions where a particular party governs for long periods of time. By 1971, the Progressive Conservative Party of Ontario had been in office for a quarter-century. Consequently, "most 'section 92' provincial court magistrates were past or present supporters of the Progressive Conservative Party."[20] When the PC reign ended in 1985, a bench dominated by PC members confronted an executive branch controlled by Liberals and a legislature in which the NDP propped up the Government. In 1990 the NDP formed a majority government in the province. Although the process for appointing provincial judges had been reformed by then (see below), the long tenure of judges ensured that many of the PC appointees were still in place. The PCs returned to power in Ontario in 1995, under Premier Mike Harris. Harris believed that the new appointments process was biased toward left-leaning candidates, so he took steps to widen the pool (thus expanding his own discretion to appoint like-minded judges).[21] He eventually backed down.[22] In February 2007, Prime Minister Harper sparked controversy when he told the House of Commons that he wanted to appoint judges who shared his government's determination to toughen the criminal law. Harper's comments seemed to confirm suspicions that he would try to remake the courts in his own ideological image.[23] (The Harper Government's changes to the appointment process are discussed in detail in Dossier 10.1.)

Since the 1980s, these three issues have prompted reforms to the judicial selection process at both levels. Broadly speaking, these reforms were designed to restrict Crown discretion in the selection of judges; to ensure that all judges are well-qualified for their positions; and to make the judicial branch more demographically representative (i.e., increasing the number of women and non-white men appointed to the bench). We will take a brief look at the current appointments process for section 92 judges, section 96 judges, and justices of the Supreme Court.

Appointments to Provincial Courts

The process for appointing section 92 judges varies from province to province. Every province has a judicial council, including laypeople as well as lawyers, to advise the Attorney General on nominees for provincial judgeships. There are two types of judicial council: those that evaluate nominees which have already been selected by the minister, and those that do the actual selecting.[24] The latter assess the merits of applicants for judicial positions and compile a short list of candidates for each vacancy on the provincial bench. Although the Attorney General is not required to appoint the top person on the list, he or she cannot go outside the list to appoint someone who has not been recommended by the council. In provinces with strong judicial councils, the restriction of Crown discretion has reduced the importance of party patronage as a criterion for appointment.[25] Elsewhere, the Attorney General retains wide latitude in appointments; that latitude can be used to reward party supporters or like-minded lawyers, with or without due regard to merit. The persistence of Crown discretion raises questions about the independence of provincial judges from the executive branch of government.

◼ Appointments to Superior and Federal Courts

In 1989, the Mulroney Government established a uniform national process for selecting section 96 judges and members of the Federal and Tax Courts. Each province and territory has its own Judicial Advisory Committee (JAC).[26] The size, composition, and functions of the JACs are not defined by statute; they can be, and have been, altered by successive ministers of Justice without the consent of Parliament. Originally, there were five members on each JAC, representing the Canadian Bar Association, the provincial bar, the provincial and federal Attorneys General, and the Chief Justice of the province or territory. The JACs grew to seven members in 1994, with the addition of two more representatives of the federal Attorney General. The three members chosen by the federal government are laypeople, not practising lawyers.

To become a section 96 judge, a qualified candidate—either a lawyer with at least 10 years' experience, or a section 92 judge—must apply to the commissioner for Federal Judicial Affairs.[27] The JAC evaluates the qualifications of lawyers who apply for judicial positions within its jurisdiction, and reports its evaluations to the minister of Justice. Unlike the strong provincial councils, a JAC cannot compile a short-list of the best candidates and thus narrow the minister's discretion. Originally, the JACs designated each applicant as either "qualified" or "not qualified." In 1991 the government introduced a new ranking system: each applicant would be "highly recommended," "recommended," or "unable to recommend." This change did not enhance the power of the committees, because the minister was not required by law to restrict his or her choices to "highly recommended" or even "recommended" candidates (although at least one former Justice minister did so voluntarily[28]).

There is one final, and crucial, limitation on the power of the JACs: they do not assess applications by sitting judges for promotion to a higher court. There are no limits on the Justice minister's discretion to promote a superior court judge from the trial division to the court of appeal, or to a federal court. This is a serious concern, because a majority of appeal court judges reach that position after serving on the superior courts within their provinces.[29] A 1995 report commissioned by the Canadian Judicial Council recommended that advisory committees review proposed elevations; no action was ever taken on that proposal.[30] The federal government argues that the lawyers on a JAC should not be asked to evaluate the performance of sitting judges, presumably because they might find themselves appearing before those judges.[31]

The JAC system has reduced party patronage as a criterion for appointing section 96 judges, but not by much. A 1991 study investigated section 96 appointments (including promotions) during the first Mulroney Government (1984–88), immediately before the introduction of the JACs. Almost half of the Government's judicial appointees were known to have some connection to the Progressive Conservative (PC) Party. The proportions were higher in the Maritime and Prairie provinces, and considerably lower in Ontario, Alberta, and British Columbia. In all provinces, individuals with PC connections were much more likely to receive judicial appointments than those with Liberal connections. (Under the previous Liberal Government, in all likelihood, the proportions were reversed.) Affiliation with the governing party in Ottawa also played a role in promotions from one level of the judicial hierarchy to another, although not to the same extent as in initial appointments.[32] On the whole, the judges appointed by the first Mulroney Government were qualified for their positions; but among the minority who were not, partisan considerations appeared to play the decisive role in their selection.[33]

Since 1991, the appointment of judges with connections to the governing party of the day has continued more or less unabated. Although there are no comprehensive data, a 2003 study of section 96 appointments in Alberta found that almost half of the judges were affiliated in some way with the Liberal Party.[34] This finding is particularly striking, given the relative scarcity of Liberals and the dominance of the PC Party in that province. Other studies have examined individual donations to federal political parties, which are publicly disclosed on the Elections Canada website.[35] They found that a significant proportion of judicial appointees had previously donated money to the party whose government subsequently appointed them to the bench; there was no difference in this regard between the Liberal and PC Parties.[36] In sum, the available data suggest that the relatively weak JAC system has not substantially reduced the importance of partisanship as a criterion for section 96 appointments—assuming that it was actually intended to do so in the first place.

In 2006, the Harper Government announced three potentially significant changes to the JACs. These are discussed in Dossier 10.1.

DOSSIER 10.1   Politicizing the Judicial Advisory Committees?

In November 2006, then-Justice Minister Vic Toews announced[37] that he was revising the process for appointing judges to superior and appellate courts:

- First, he increased the size of each JAC from seven members to eight. The new member, to be appointed by the federal Justice minister, would represent the police. Each committee now includes four non-lawyers appointed by the federal minister of Justice, three lawyers, and one representative of the judiciary.

- Second, each JAC would be chaired by the judicial member. Previously, the members of each JAC elected their own chair; any of the members could serve in that position. Because the chair does not vote except to break a tie among the other members—which is mathematically impossible if all seven are in attendance—this means that the only judge on a Judicial Appointment Committee has no formal role in the final decisions.

- Third, Toews abolished the "highly recommended" designation for judicial applicants. A JAC could rate a potential judge as "recommended" or "unable to recommend," but it could not distinguish between adequate and outstanding candidates.[38]

Unlike his predecessors, Toews did not consult the Canadian Bar Association before announcing these changes—although he did consult the Canadian Police Association.[39]

Toews' announcement sparked public criticism, including an unprecedented protest from the Chief Justice of the Supreme Court (in her capacity as chair of the Canadian Judicial Council).[40] In February 2007, responding to a question about the revised JACs, Prime Minister Harper told the Commons: "we are bringing forward laws to make sure we crack down on crime and make our streets and communities safer. We want to make sure that our selection of judges is in correspondence with those objectives."[41]

The perception of bias arising from Harper's remark prompted a review of the JAC changes by the House of Commons Justice Committee. Opposition MPs, along with most of the witnesses, charged that the Harper Government was trying to manipulate the process in order to appoint judges who shared their particular ideology. Professor Peter Russell, an expert on the Canadian judiciary and the founding chair of Ontario's section 92 committee, was especially blunt. He argued that the abolition of the "highly recommended" category would make it even easier for the Justice minister to make political appointments.

. . . in terms of patronage appointments to the judiciary, there's nothing to choose between the Mulroney Conservative governments and the Martin and Chrétien Liberal governments. They all gave undue influence to political considerations in making judicial appointments. The political considerations of those three governments had more to do with party and personal connections than with ideology. . . .

(continued)

Very often those who were simply recommended, who weren't as good in terms of the assessment committees—five people and then seven people assessed them as not as good as others on the minister's list—got appointed. A number of us studied this process very carefully. They went over the highly recommended down to the recommended in order to appoint their political friends, playing politics with who gets to be a judge in the federal system of Canada, the superior courts of the provinces and territories and the federal courts. I think that's just shameful. I'm ashamed of it as a Canadian.[42]

Most of the criticism was directed to the mandatory inclusion of police officers on the JACs, which was allegedly flawed at least two ways. First, it created a risk of bias, real or perceived, in the appointment of section 96 judges:

[T]he addition to the committee of persons with police backgrounds, restructuring the committee so that four federal government appointees form the majority, and the Prime Minister's statements that he wants judges who will be "tougher on crime" all point in the direction of transforming the committees into ideological certifying bodies rather than bodies responsible for identifying the most qualified candidates for the judiciary. This shift to ideological assessment is particularly threatening to judicial independence in considering the promotion of judges who might well come to believe that their chances for promotion in the federal judiciary are diminished if they do not apply criminal law in the tough way that the majority on the advisory committees are looking for.[43]

Second, the committee concluded that it made no sense to require law-enforcement input into the selection of judges, because "the vast majority of cases heard by the superior courts do not involve the police."[44]

Most of the work of the superior courts involves civil trials requiring high levels of competence in such matters as torts, contracts, intellectual property, taxation, and administrative law. Statistics provided to the Committee indicate that less than 5% of criminal cases are tried in the superior courts. It is not clear what expertise in non-criminal matters the police bring to the judicial advisory committees.[45]

Conservative MPs on the Justice Committee vigorously defended the new JACs. They issued a dissenting report, arguing that the critics themselves were ideologically motivated, and insisting that the Harper Government's actions were driven solely by a desire to improve the process. They accused the Opposition critics of prejudice against the police, "a community no less implicated in the administration of justice than lawyers and judges."[46]

Partly because of the controversial nature of Toews' changes to the JACs, and partly because of the apparently secretive manner of their adoption, several witnesses before the committee called on the Government to enact the process for choosing section 96 judges into legislation. If the process were regulated by law, instead of being left to the discretion of the Justice minister, any future amendments would require the consent of Parliament.[47] Some also proposed that the JACs be given powers similar to the section 92 committee in Ontario: the JAC would submit a short-list to the minister, who would be required to make his or her selection from among those few candidates. The new Justice minister, Rob Nicholson, rejected those suggestions—despite the fact that Toews and other Conservative MPs had endorsed the second proposal when they sat on the Justice Committee in 2005.[48]

Appointments to the Supreme Court of Canada

One might expect the appointment of members of the highest court to be subject to at least as much scrutiny as the choice of superior-court judges. But until recently, the process was remarkably informal and secretive. It was generally known that the prime minister made the final decision, and that he usually consulted the sitting Chief Justice and the Canadian Bar

Association; but the role played by the federal Justice minister and other interested parties was obscure. Finally, in March 2004, then-Justice Minister Irwin Cotler described the appointment process to the House of Commons Justice Committee. At the first stage, the minister of Justice identified possible candidates. The pool of potential justices includes the members of provincial Courts of Appeal, "senior members of the Bar," and prominent legal academics. The minister consulted with the Chief Justice of the Supreme Court, the Chief Justices of the provincial courts in the region, provincial Attorneys General, the Canadian Bar Association, and the local law societies. The input of the Chief Justice is particularly important: as the senior administrator of the court, she knows the needs of the institution at a particular time—for example, if the court lacks expertise in a particular field of law, she can request a new justice with a strong background in that area. This informal process yielded a short-list of candidates.

At the second stage, the minister and prime minister assessed the candidates according to three broad criteria: "professional capacity, personal characteristics, and diversity." The minister relied on his informal contacts within the legal community, and written profiles prepared by the Department of Justice, to determine which candidate best met these criteria. The prime minister was consulted throughout the process, and participated in the final decision. His preferred candidate was recommended to Cabinet, and appointed by an Order-in-Council.[49]

By the late 1990s, the process for appointing Supreme Court justices was widely condemned as secretive and undemocratic,[50] especially given the court's policy-making power under the *Charter* (Chapter 6). The Martin Government yielded to the pressure for change in 2004 (Dossier 10.2).

DOSSIER 10.2   The 2004 Ad Hoc Reform to Supreme Court Appointments

In the spring of 2004 the House of Commons Standing Committee on Justice, Human Rights, Public Safety and Emergency Preparedness recommended reforms to the appointment process for Supreme Court justices.[51] All four parties in the House agreed that the pool of candidates should be evaluated by an advisory committee of lawyers, judges, and laypeople, which would submit a short-list to the Justice minister (similar to the strong provincial councils). They also agreed that Parliament should play some role in the nomination of justices, although they differed over how much power MPs should have. The Liberal majority called for the minister to appear before the Justice Committee after the selection had been made, to explain why that particular person had been chosen. The Conservatives argued that the nominee should be required to appear in person, preferably before the final decision had been made, and that the Commons should have the power to veto proposed appointments. The NDP proposed that the minister appear before the final decision was made, to give MPs meaningful input into the process; it also dealt with the

problems that could arise if an appointment had to be made during a Parliamentary recess, by proposing an ad hoc committee of MPs. Finally, the BQ demanded that potential justices be recommended by the provincial government(s) representing the region that would be represented by the new justice.[52]

The MPs' demand for parliamentary involvement provoked concerns among legal insiders. The Canadian Bar Association warned that the best-qualified candidates for the top court might be dissuaded from accepting a nomination, for fear of a nasty public grilling like those inflicted on some recent U.S. Supreme Court nominees.[53] Retired Justice Claire L'Heureux-Dubé warned more explicitly against "Americanizing" the process:

> *My worry would be that what has never been done in Canada, and what is done in the United States constantly, is that you would go into ideology and partisanship. That would be the end of the independence of the judiciary; that would be the end of the Supreme Court*

(continued)

serving the public, as it has done for so many years, from 1875 onward.[54]

By the time the Justice Committee issued its report, two members of the Supreme Court (both from Ontario) had unexpectedly resigned.[55] Shortly thereafter, Parliament was dissolved for a general election. Because of the impending hearings on the federal government's same-sex marriage law, Chief Justice McLachlin was anxious to fill the two vacancies as soon as possible. However, Parliament was not scheduled to resume until October. So the Liberal minority government cobbled together an ad hoc response to the committee's call for more input. In late August 2004, Justice Minister Cotler announced the nomination of Justices Louise Charron and Rosalie Silberman Abella. The following day, he appeared before an Interim Ad Hoc Committee on the Appointment of Supreme Court Judges to answer questions about the two nominees. The committee was made up of two Liberal MPs (one of whom was the chair), two Conservatives, one New Democrat, and one BQ MP; they were joined by a representative from the Law Society of Upper Canada, who speaks for the Ontario legal community, and one from the Canadian Judicial Council.[56]

The hearing degenerated into a predictable partisan battle: the Conservative and NDP members argued that the two nominees should have appeared in person, instead of being represented by the Justice minister. In the end, the committee paid relatively little attention to the qualifications of the two candidates, preferring instead to argue about the process. Two days later the nominated justices were formally appointed, doubling the number of women on the Supreme Court to four.

Once Parliament had been granted a role in the appointment of Supreme Court justices, there was no going back to the old process. In November 2005, just before the Martin Government was defeated in the Commons, it announced the creation of an Advisory Committee to recommend candidates for the Western vacancy arising from the impending retirement of Justice John Major. That committee included MPs, representatives of the judicial and legal communities in the Western provinces, and two non-lawyers.[57] It was empowered to narrow a pool of eight candidates—all proposed by the minister of Justice—to a short-list of three, one of whom would be appointed by the prime minister.[58]

In February 2006, shortly after taking office, Prime Minister Harper announced that he had chosen former Marshall Rothstein from the short-list. Rothstein, a former Winnipegger, had served on the Federal Court since 1992 and the Federal Court of Appeal since 1999. One expert on judicial appointments suggests that the prime minister chose Rothstein for ideological reasons: "Justice Rothstein's well-known conservative legal philosophy nicely mirrored Harper's conception of the Supreme Court as an interpreter of the law and not as a social reformer."[59] Be that as it may, Rothstein was eminently qualified for the position (apart from his weak French). As the Conservative Opposition had demanded in 2004, Rothstein was questioned by a parliamentary committee before his appointment was made official. Parliament was not yet in session, so the Justice Committee did not formally exist. Instead, Rothstein appeared before an ad hoc committee of MPs. His appearance was carefully stage-managed by the DOJ. It began with formal statements from then-Justice Minister Vic Toews and distinguished constitutional expert Peter Hogg, both of whom exhorted the MPs to refrain from asking unsuitable questions. Hogg's remarks were especially pointed:

> *The critics argue that an open process will tend to politicize the judiciary, and publicly embarrass the distinguished people who are nominated for appointment. This Committee, today, has the opportunity to show the critics that they are wrong. . . . When you think about the role that Mr. Justice Rothstein will be called upon to play if his nomination is confirmed, it becomes obvious*

that there are some questions that he cannot be expected to answer. He cannot express views on cases or issues that could come before the Court. He cannot tell you how he would decide a hypothetical case. He might eventually be faced with that case. For the same reason, he cannot tell you what his views are on controversial issues, such as abortion, same-sex marriage or secession. These issues could come to the Court for decision in some factual context or other. Any public statements about the issues might give the false impression that he had a settled view on how to decide those cases— without knowing what the facts were, without reviewing all the legal material, and without listening to and weighing the arguments on both sides.[60]

For the most part, the MPs heeded Hogg's warnings. The hearing was conducted in a reasonably non-partisan and respectful manner, and Rothstein acquitted himself with dignity and humour. (Part of his opening statement is reproduced in Dossier 10.3.) The committee endorsed his nomination, and he was sworn in shortly thereafter.

On the whole, the men and women who serve in Canada's judicial branch are well qualified for their positions. In some provinces, merit is the dominant criterion for appointment. It is also important at the section 96 level, although party patronage remains a concern (especially in appointments to superior trial courts).[61] In February 2007, the former chair of the Ontario advisory committee told the Commons Justice Committee that "Some people who didn't make the cut in our provincial system were appointed federally because of their political ties to government."[62] The source of the problem is the persistence of broad Crown discretion in the choice of judges. The Conservatives argue that section 96 of the *BNA Act* confers complete discretion on the Crown, so it would be unconstitutional to pass a law restricting that discretion (e.g., by enshrining the JAC process in statute, or requiring the federal Justice minister to choose an appointee from a short-list).[63] This argument is weakened by the fact that the *Judges Act* restricts the pool of judicial candidates to lawyers with at least 10 years' experience[64]—a clear limit on the minister's discretion.

As long as the federal Justice minister and Attorney General enjoys unfettered discretion, the influence of partisanship and/or ideology on judicial appointment will cast doubt on the independence and impartiality of Canadian judges. This is a potentially serious problem, as we will see in the rest of the chapter.

THE WORK OF JUDGES

In this section, we will briefly examine what judges do once they have been appointed (or, in the case of most appellate judges, promoted). Before we begin, it may be useful to look at a judge's perspective on his or her professional role. As just mentioned, Justice Marshall Rothstein appeared before a committee of MPs in February 2006 before he was sworn in as a justice of the Supreme Court. In his opening statement, Rothstein gave the parliamentarians an insight into his duties (Dossier 10.3).

DOSSIER 10.3   Justice Marshall Rothstein on the Judicial Role

It goes without saying that judges must be neutral arbitrators in disputes that come before them. They can have no personal agenda and they must be independent.

We know that judicial independence in some parts of the world is not something people can rely upon, but a cornerstone of a free and democratic society is an independent judiciary. Nowhere is that independence more important than in cases between the government and the individual.

As neutral arbitrators, we are to interpret and apply the law to the facts of each case. Canada is a federation in which Parliament and

(continued)

the provincial legislatures make the laws. When Parliament or the legislatures have conferred a discretionary power on judges, that discretion must be exercised within the bounds established by the legislatures or Parliament, and judges are required to conduct court proceedings in accordance with well-established rules of procedural fairness.

Our judicial system operates on the basis of precedent. We follow the interpretations that our predecessors have developed. We don't follow them slavishly; if it can be demonstrated that a prior decision was clearly in error or that intervening cases have attenuated the validity of a prior decision, we may depart from it. But the obligation of judges is to maintain the consistency, stability, and predictability of the law. Therefore, we abide by precedent.

Lower court decisions may be appealed to higher courts. Our hierarchical system ensures a review mechanism for important legal questions. . . . [A]ppeal courts and the Supreme Court of Canada operate on a collegial basis. Three judges sit in a court of appeal. Five, seven, or nine judges sit in cases in the Supreme Court. So individual judges must be open to the views of their colleagues.

All of this is to say that the role of the judge is subject to constraints, and judges must have the modesty and the humility to understand that.

From the beginning, in 1867, Canada has had a written *Constitution*. Originally it was the *British North America Act*. The laws enacted by Parliament or the legislatures were subject to the *Constitution*. When I went to law school, constitutional law was all about sections 91 and 92

of the *BNA Act* and the division of powers between the federal and provincial governments, and when laws were found to be *ultra vires*, they were struck down. Since the advent of the *Charter* in 1982, laws enacted by Parliament and the legislatures have been struck down by the courts where [they] were found to violate a provision in the *Charter*.

So judges have a role to play in a constitutional democracy. When the issue is raised in litigation before them, judges must decide whether the laws enacted by Parliament or the legislatures conform to the *Constitution* and the *Charter*. If the laws do not, the courts have been given the jurisdiction to strike them down. This doesn't mean that judges have some kind of upper hand over Parliament or the legislatures. They are not a law unto themselves. Constitutional or *Charter* cases must still be decided having regard to legal principles, and because these cases are important and have widespread effect, the Supreme Court hears some of them. So they are reviewed usually by three courts before any final decision is made.

The courts must be mindful that they are being asked to strike down a law that has been enacted by a democratically elected majority of legislators. When laws are struck down, the courts must preserve the intent of the legislature or Parliament to the extent possible. The least intrusive approach must be adopted.

As a judge, I know we have an obligation to work to maintain public confidence in our courts by protecting the integrity and independence of our courts. I will work hard to contribute to those objectives.

Source: Rothstein's statement from Committee minutes; Excerpted from Justice Marshall Rothstein, "Opening Remarks to Ad Hoc Committee to Review a Nominee for the Supreme Court of Canada", February 27, 2006 (accessed at www.justice.gc.ca/en/news/sp/2006/doc_31794.html, July 2007). Department of Justice Canada, 2006. Reproduced with the permission of the Minister of Public Works and Government Services Canada, 2008.

The Trial Courts

Most members of Canada's judicial branch (more than 90 percent) are trial judges.[65] The purpose of a trial, whether civil or criminal, is to provide an authoritative resolution to a dispute between two parties. In a criminal trial, the parties are the Crown and the accused.[66] The issues are relatively narrow: Should the accused be found guilty or innocent? Should the accused go to jail, and, if so, for how long? In most civil cases, both parties are private actors (individuals or corporations). Which of two divorcing parents gets custody of the children, or is custody to be shared? Has there been a breach of contract between the seller and the buyer, and, if so, what is the remedy?

These are the kinds of day-to-day conflicts that trial judges must decide. They focus on the facts admitted into evidence. Was the gun fired in anger, with cool deliberation, or in self-defence? Did the employer violate the employee's contract (or the provincial labour code) when she fired him for making a mistake? The judge applies the law to the facts, which occasionally requires him or her to interpret the law in a new way.[67] At trial, however, such interpretive judicial law-making rarely exceeds what is required to resolve the immediate dispute. The judge's job is to adjudicate—to resolve the dispute at bar—not to make new law or policy.

In some cases, the judge is asked to strike down (nullify) a statute passed by Parliament or a provincial legislature on the ground that it is inconsistent with the *Constitution*. If the **impugned** law infringes the division of powers between the federal and provincial governments, it is declared *ultra vires* and nullified on that ground (see "Judicial Review of the *BNA Act*" in Chapter 4). Today, most constitutional challenges to legislation involve the *Charter*; the majority arise in the context of criminal trials. Because "no one can be convicted under an unconstitutional law," a person accused of a crime can seek to have the law nullified (and the charges consequently dropped) under section 52 of the *Constitution Act, 1982*.[68] In these instances, the trial judge is required to assess the merits of the law on both legal and policy grounds. The policy considerations become particularly important if the judge finds that the law violates one or more *Charter* guarantees; he or she must then determine whether the violation is justified under section 1 and, if not, he or she must impose a remedy (see "The Three-Stage Process of *Charter* Review" in Chapter 6).

Appellate Judging

As previously noted, any legal decision made by a trial judge can be appealed to a higher court. The party seeking to overturn the trial result is called the "appellant"; the other party is called the "respondent." For example, a person convicted of a crime who asks a higher court to overturn the conviction will be designated the appellant. However, if the trial judge struck down a law on *Charter* grounds, the federal government (the Crown) may seek a reversal at a higher court; in this instance, the Crown is the appellant. Findings of fact are not subject to appeal, unless they are so obviously mistaken that they produced an unjust result. According to the Supreme Court of Canada, "a court of appeal should not interfere with a trial judge's reasons unless there is a palpable and overriding error."[69]

Relatively few cases are appealed, partly because of cost and partly because appellate courts have considerable discretion about which cases to revisit. But those few cases can affect all Canadians (not just the two parties directly involved). When the Saskatchewan Court of Appeal issues a ruling, its interpretation of the law immediately becomes the standard for all lawyers and judges in that province. If that ruling is appealed to the Supreme Court of Canada, and the top court overturns it, the new interpretation is binding on all lawyers and judges across the country. The principle that future courts are bound by previous rulings is called *stare decisis* (Latin for "the decision stands"); the significance of this common-law rule is explained in Dossier 10.4.

DOSSIER 10.4 *Stare Decisis*

The rule of *stare decisis* has two principal advantages. First, it imposes a degree of consistency and predictability on what might otherwise become a chaotic and contradictory mass of jurisprudence. Policymakers and lower-court judges need clear guidelines to follow when they apply existing laws or make new ones. This is especially true in constitutional cases, whose outcomes can affect the basic rules for the operation of the political system. (See Chapters 3, 4,

(continued)

and 6.) Second, *stare decisis* requires higher courts to make principled decisions. Instead of following their own personal preferences, judges are expected to develop the common law within the parameters set by established precedents.

In practice, the *stare decisis* rule is more flexible than one might expect. Although their interpretive freedom is restricted by existing precedents, judges have some freedom to decide which precedents apply to a particular case and to modify established legal principles to suit changing social needs. A judge who disagrees with a Supreme Court precedent can "distinguish" it from the case at bar, by ruling that the facts of the two cases are sufficiently different to preclude the application of the earlier ruling.

At the Supreme Court itself, the justices have demonstrated considerable ingenuity in evading their own prior decisions without explicitly overturning them (which they very rarely do).[70] For example, the court unanimously ruled in 2001 that the minister of Justice could not extradite a murder suspect to a jurisdiction that practised capital punishment without first securing a written assurance that the suspect, if convicted, would not be executed. This was a clear reversal of a 1991 ruling, in which seven justices held that the risk of capital punishment should not be a factor in extradition proceedings.[71] The court refused to acknowledge the reversal in the second ruling; it simply stated that the factors to be weighed by the minister remained the same, but the balance among them had shifted over the preceding decade.

Appellate judges focus less on adjudication, and more on law-making, than their colleagues in the lower courts. A Court of Appeal is expected to issue rulings that will serve the cause of justice, not just in the case at bar, but in all similar disputes that arise within its territory. On occasion, a Court of Appeal can exert influence outside its borders—even though its rulings are not legally binding there.[72] Few Court of Appeal rulings are appealed to the Supreme Court of Canada. In practical terms, therefore, the provincial courts of appeal often have the final word on legal and constitutional questions, and their influence can stretch well beyond their official jurisdictions.

The party that loses its case in the Court of Appeal can try to appeal yet again, to the Supreme Court of Canada. As the highest court in the land, Supreme Court rulings are authoritative and binding on the entire country. (For this reason, most of the rulings discussed in this book come from the Supreme Court.) The judicial hierarchy does more than provide an avenue of appeal for disgruntled litigants in the immediate case; it also ensures that laws are applied consistently across Canada. Consequently, the facts of the immediate case are even less central at the Supreme Court than they are in the provincial appellate courts. The adjudication of the case at bar is often secondary to the creation of new common-law rules.

Since 1975, the Supreme Court has had the power to choose which appeals it will hear. The task of sorting through thousands of appellate petitions is left to three-judge panels, which rely heavily on the work of court clerks (recent law school graduates who spend a year working for particular justices). Appeals that raise important legal issues are the most likely to survive the winnowing process. The court's freedom to control its own docket clearly indicates that policy-making, not adjudication, is its primary function.

▮ Judicial Policy-Making: Problems of Institutional Capacity

Whether or not one believes that judicial policy-making is inherently undemocratic, the more practical problem is the mismatch between policy-making and adjudication. The Supreme Court, like all adjudicative bodies, is made up of experts in law. They possess neither the expertise nor the institutional resources to evaluate public policy effectively, or to craft new laws to replace those that they have nullified.[73] This problem arises in every appellate court, but especially the Supreme Court of Canada.

Since the *Charter* took effect, courts have been asked to assess the effectiveness of laws and government programs. As explained in Chapter 6, the "*Oakes* test" for applying section 1 requires the judge to determine whether a law that infringes the *Charter* is "rationally connected" to its objective, and whether it does more harm than good. These questions cannot be answered on the basis of traditional adjudicative facts—i.e., the facts of the specific case at bar.[74] The judge must rely on social science evidence about the seriousness of particular problems, the effects of the impugned law, and possible alternative policies.

The Supreme Court's reliance on social science evidence raises three important issues. First, the justices cannot cross-examine the "expert witnesses" who write affidavits concerning **extrinsic evidence**; in most cases, they can only assume that the factual claims presented by the parties to the appeal are accurate.[75] In effect, the Supreme Court disregards the standards for expert testimony that it imposed on lower-court judges and trial juries. In *R. v. Mohan*, the justices expressed concern about the misleading effect of spurious or unsubstantiated "expert" testimony on impressionable jurors. They required trial judges or jurors to evaluate potential factual evidence "in light of its potential to distort the fact-finding process."[76] No such constraint applies to the Supreme Court's own deliberations.

Second, courts may make broad policy decisions based on insufficient or misinterpreted social science data, with potentially harmful results. One notable example was the 1990 ruling in *Askov v. The Queen*, in which the majority ruled that forcing defendants to wait more than eight months for their trials violated section 11(b) of the *Charter*.[77] This judicially imposed "deadline" was based, in part, on social science data that were misinterpreted by the justice who wrote for the majority.[78] The ruling also appears to have been motivated by the court's disapproval of provincial underfunding for court services, which it blamed for the backlog in the justice system. In response to the eight-month "deadline," Ontario prosecutors dismissed tens of thousands of pending charges.[79] The Supreme Court should not bear all of the blame for this outcome; the Ontario Attorney General used the large-scale dismissal to score political points against the judicial branch, perhaps because he resented the criticism of his inability to secure adequate resources for his portfolio.[80] As we will see in the discussion of institutional independence, the judicial and executive branches are increasingly at odds over court funding.

Third, judicial principles are not the most effective tools for evaluating legislative decisions. In effect, the courts have been granted the power to intervene in the policy-making process, without simultaneously acquiring the expertise to do it properly.

The complexity of policy development makes it difficult for those external to the process to know whether the policy scheme represents the best arrangement possible in terms of reconciling conflicting rights and values. The process of conceptualizing and drafting policy may have to address multiple objectives, and, when considering who will benefit or be affected, distinctions have to be made according to calculations that may not be based on objective principles of empirical certainties. . . . In short, much of policy development is, of necessity, subject to discretionary judgement based on a combination of relevant expertise, comparative experience and informed best estimates.[81]

The justices themselves are aware of their limited policy-making skills, especially in the field of social policy. Former Justice La Forest put it this way:

Although courts are specialists in the protection of liberty and the interpretation of legislation and are, accordingly, well placed to subject criminal justice legislation to careful scrutiny—that is not so in the sphere of policy-making. Policy-making is a role properly assigned to elected parliamentarians who have the necessary institutional resources to enable them to compile and assess social science evidence, to mediate between competing social interests and to reach out and protect vulnerable groups. In according a greater degree of deference to social legislation than to ordinary criminal justice legislation, the courts recognize these important institutional differences.[82]

Despite this admission, the Supreme Court's own interpretation of section 1 has opened the floodgates to extrinsic evidence in many areas of public policy. However, it has not changed the fact that judges and lawyers are not experts in public policy, nor are they trained to assess the credibility of social-science evidence. The difficulties arising from this change in evidentiary rules illustrates a basic problem of institutional adaptation: when an institution acquires new responsibilities for which its existing procedures are inadequate, it may not always discharge those responsibilities as well as we might wish.

Nor do courts have the power to enforce their own rulings.[83] Canada's legislators usually respect the Supreme Court's rulings, particularly those concerning the *Charter.* If a law has been struck down, they either let it go or replace it with a new version that is more consistent with the entrenched rights and freedoms.[84] However, other groups and individuals who may be negatively affected by a particular ruling can blunt its impact in a variety of ways. The practical effect of court decisions depends on the willingness of other government agencies—police, legislatures, public officials—to follow judge-made rules of conduct.[85] This willingness cannot be taken for granted. For example, the 1991 *Stinchcombe* ruling required Crown prosecutors to disclose all relevant evidence in a criminal trial to the defence in a timely manner.[86] Subsequent rulings, and anecdotal evidence from defence lawyers, reveal the resistance of some Crown prosecutors to their new obligations under *Stinchcombe.*[87]

JUDICIAL INDEPENDENCE AND IMPARTIALITY: PRESERVING THE RULE OF LAW

While the legislative and executive branches of the Canadian government are closely linked (see Chapters 7–9), the judicial branch is expected to exercise its powers independently of the other two. Judges cannot be subjected to direct pressure—whether political, financial, or personal—from Cabinet ministers or legislators. The principle of judicial independence, like so much of Canada's *Constitution,* originated in Britain. Dossier 10.5 describes the historical evolution of English courts, and the struggle for judicial independence from the Crown.

DOSSIER 10.5   The Origins of Independent Courts

The ordering of modern governmental powers, in the classical form of the executive, legislative and judiciary, is the outcome of a very lengthy process of refinement of institutions. Initially, the sovereignty of the King took judicial form. The King was thus primarily the great dispenser of justice. His lawyers did their utmost to place this royal authority on a firm footing, by inserting into public discourse such maxims as "The King is the source of all justice" or "All justice comes from the King," and so on. In dis-

pensing justice, the King was assisted by his court, the *Curia Regis.* This phrase has two meanings: "(i) the place where the king resided attended by the chief officials of his court and household; and (ii) the supreme central court where the business of government in all its branches was transacted."

The *Curia Regis* brought together the greatest figures in the kingdom, but increasingly it also included royal officials, often lawyers trained in Bologna and Paris, whose

(continued)

function was the day-to-day running of the kingdom. Some of these royal officers took the name of "justices in the *Curia Regis*." The word "justice" is thus a generic expression for such officers, since they exercised a broad range of functions. . . .

From then on, the emergence of a purely judicial body becomes apparent. However, the officers responsible for the daily management of the kingdom's affairs also performed tasks of a legislative, administrative, and judicial nature at their meetings. The burden of work quickly became too large for a diffuse body such as the *Curia Regis*.

Thus, in the twelfth century, the *Curia Regis* began to break up into separate departments and distinct courts of law. This process was initiated with finance and judicial affairs, two matters of critical importance to the Norman and Angevin kings, for whom good financial management was essential to a strong government, and control over judicial affairs the best way of avoiding internal disorder. More formal courts were established in the Middle Ages, such as the Court of Common Pleas and, later, the Court of King's Bench. Of course, these courts were still not completely autonomous.

It was during the fourteenth and fifteenth centuries that the courts really took shape and became more autonomous, constituting the common law courts. At the same time as these courts were developing, another offshoot of the *Curia Regis* grew in importance: the Council in Parliament, which also performed functions of a judicial nature. In the fourteenth and fifteenth centuries, Parliament broke up into two separate houses: the House of Lords and the House of Commons. The splitting up of the *Curia Regis* into several entities—the judges of the central courts of common law, the House of Lords and the House of Commons—was an indication of the form modern government would take. This process underwent a tumultuous acceleration in the sixteenth and seventeenth centuries, which ended in the Restoration. The reign of James II saw major constitutional disputes between Parliament and the Monarch, which were finally resolved in Parliament's favour and led to the adoption of the *Bill of Rights* in 1689 and, in 1701, the *Act of Settlement*. . . .

The appearance of a modern judiciary is thus the outcome of a lengthy process of refinement and formalization of institutions and functions: the judicial institution gradually differentiating itself from other institutions with which it shared powers, and the judicial function gradually becoming exclusive and retaining few areas in common with the executive and legislative powers.

Source: Canadian Judicial Council on the Origins of Independent Courts, Canadian Judicial Council, *Alternative Models of Court Administration* (Ottawa, September 2006). Accessed at www.cjc-ccm.gc.ca, July 2007, pp. 30–32, footnotes omitted. Reproduced with the permission of the Minister of Public Works and Government Services, 2009.

Among its other purposes, the 1701 *Act of Settlement* insulated the judicial branch from interference by the Crown or Parliament.[88] It established the three core protections for judicial independence:

- First, it gave judges security of tenure. A judge, once appointed, could not be removed from office at the King's pleasure; he "could be removed only for cause, and only by a difficult and unusual process—specifically, joint address by both houses of Parliament, which constituted a form of impeachment."[89] This meant that a judge had no particular incentive to please the King. For example, he could rule against the Crown in a criminal trial without fear of losing his position.
- Second, it provided that judicial salaries would be determined by Parliament, and that all judges in a given category would receive the same pay. This ensured that the King (or Parliament) could not punish judges by cutting (off) their salaries.
- Third and finally, "the Act established that judges were not directly accountable to, or directly supervised by, either politicians or bureaucrats."[90]

In sum, the 1701 Act guaranteed the individual, financial, and institutional/administrative independence of judges. In so doing, it allowed English courts to adjudicate impartially. When a judge resolved a dispute between two parties—even when one of those parties was the King—he could base his decision on the facts and the law, not on the preferences of the political majority or the will of the Crown. By the time of Confederation, the first element of judicial independence was well-established in British North America. Judges held office "during good behaviour," not "at the pleasure of the King"—or, in this instance, the royal governor. In 1997, the Supreme Court of Canada declared that the Preamble to the *BNA Act* had enshrined the *Act of Settlement* in Canadian law: "Judicial independence is an unwritten norm, recognized and affirmed by the preamble to the *Constitution Act, 1867*. In fact, it is in that preamble, which serves as the grand entrance hall to the castle of the Constitution, that the true source of our commitment to this foundational principle is located."[91]

In addition to the preamble, specific sections of the *BNA Act* afford explicit protections to federally appointed judges. Under section 99, judges remain in office until the age of 75. If a judge violates the norms of "good behaviour," he or she can be removed by a joint resolution of the two Houses of the federal Parliament—which, at the time of writing, had never happened, because judges who ran into trouble resigned rather than face impeachment.[92] Section 100 provides that the salaries and pensions of federal judges "shall be fixed and provided by the Parliament of Canada"; these provisions are now contained in the *Judges Act*.

Provincially appointed (section 92) judges had no such constitutional guarantees of independence until 1982, when section 11(d) of the *Charter* took effect. That section guarantees all criminal suspects (most of whom, as we have seen, are tried in provincial courts) the right to "a fair and public hearing by an independent and impartial tribunal." Questions remained about the independence of provincial courts in civil matters, prompting former Chief Justice Lamer to locate the source of judicial independence in the Preamble to the *BNA Act*.

Today, all three elements of the *Act of Settlement* are enshrined in various federal and provincial policies. There are, however, significant gaps in the mechanisms that ensure the individual, financial, and institutional or administrative independence of judges from the legislative and executive branches of government. Consequently, questions remain about the impartiality of the judicial branch. We will look at each of the three elements of independence in turn.

▨ The Independence of Individual Judges

As previously noted, section 96 judges (and, increasingly, section 92 judges) are entitled to security of tenure until they reach the statutory retirement age. They may not be directly influenced by any member of the legislative or executive branch. The code of ethics for federal judges is explicit: "Judges must, of course, reject improper attempts by litigants, politicians, officials or others to influence their decisions. They must also take care that communications with such persons that judges may initiate could not raise reasonable concerns about their independence."[93]

The safeguards for individual independence are incomplete. As we discussed earlier in this chapter, the process for appointing and promoting judges may subject individual jurists to undesirable incentives. The recent changes to the process for appointing section 96 judges (Dossier 10.1) have raised concerns in some quarters about the individual independence—not to mention the impartiality—of future federal judges. The Canadian Judicial Council made clear its opinion of the expanded Judicial Advisory Committees in February 2007, shortly after Prime Minister Harper explicitly linked the new process to his "tough on crime" policy agenda:

> *Because the majority of voting members are now appointed by the Minister, the advisory committees may neither be, nor be seen to be, fully independent of the government. . . . Judicial independence is not the private right of judges but the foundation of judicial impartiality and a constitutional right of all Canadians. As the Supreme Court of Canada has stated, "Litigants who engage our judicial system should be in no doubt that they are before a judge who is demonstrably independent and is motivated only by a search for a just and principled result."*[94]

Moreover, a growing number of disputes are settled out of court, often by adjudicators or Justices of the Peace who are appointed by provincial Attorneys General for fixed terms. This means that Canadians are increasingly dependent on adjudicators, some of whom are unqualified for their jobs, whose appointment (and reappointment) are usually based on party patronage.[95] The implications for the independence and impartiality of these officials are worrisome.

None of this should be taken to mean that our judges ignore their obligation to resolve disputes impartially. As the Supreme Court has observed, individual independence involves more than the institutional characteristics of the judicial branch. It is essentially "a state of mind or attitude in the actual exercise of judicial functions,"[96] which does not depend on salary levels or administrative structures. The Canadian judiciary is among the finest in the world, despite our history of patronage appointments and promotions. Nonetheless, the legitimacy of a judicial ruling depends on the fairness and impartiality with which the court applies the law to the facts of the dispute. Consequently, any undue influence from the Crown or Parliament—whether real or perceived—undermines public confidence in the judicial branch of government.

Although judges cannot, and should not, be held accountable to the other two branches of government or the electorate, this does not mean that individual judges who perform poorly are immune from sanctions. A judge who demonstrated a clear bias for or against one party to a dispute, or who accepted a bribe in return for a particular outcome, would be subject to discipline by a body of his peers. The definition of judicial misconduct is not limited to the courtroom; if a judge makes public statements that cast doubt on his or her objectivity, he or she risks a formal reprimand or—in extreme cases—removal from the bench.[97] The standard for removal, on which the Canadian Judicial Council and other decision-makers rely, is as follows:

> *Is the conduct alleged so manifestly and profoundly destructive of the concept of the impartiality, integrity and independence of the judicial role, that public confidence would be sufficiently undermined to render the judge incapable of executing the judicial office?*[98]

Note that a judge can be disciplined for poor conduct, but not for incompetence in applying the law; legal errors are left to appeal courts to remedy.[99]

Complaints against federally appointed judges are reviewed by the Canadian Judicial Council. This group includes the Chief Justices of the federal and superior courts, along with other senior jurists. It is chaired by the Chief Justice of the Supreme Court of Canada, the country's highest-ranking judge. The council receives between 150 and 200 complaints per year from the public. The vast majority are dismissed at a preliminary stage of inquiry; the more serious and apparently well-founded complaints are referred to a panel of judges for investigation.[100] If the panel finds that the allegations have merit, it recommends the establishment of an Inquiry Committee.[101] Such Inquiry Committees are automatically established to hear complaints originating from a provincial or federal Attorney General.[102] An Inquiry Committee has three options: to dismiss the complaint, to "express disapproval" of the judge's conduct, or to ask the federal Justice minister to initiate the process for removing a judge from office. This would require a resolution of both Houses of the federal Parliament (see the preceding discussion of section 99 of the *BNA Act*)—unless the judge resigns first, which has always happened to date.

Section 92 judges are subject to varying disciplinary procedures, depending on the province in which they work. Before the Supreme Court handed down the *Valente* ruling in 1985, provincial judges could be fired without cause[103]—for example, when a new government took office and decided to appoint its own supporters to the bench. Today, a judge can only be removed from office if a judicial council finds that he or she has committed a serious breach of judicial ethics. For example, a Quebec judge was fired by the provincial legislature after he was found to have concealed a criminal conviction (for which he was subsequently pardoned) when he applied for a seat on the bench.[104] A judge in British Columbia resigned, rather than face impeachment, in 2004 after being convicted of sexual offences against young girls.[105] In the 1990s, a Quebec youth court judge known for her outspoken public advocacy of children's rights challenged a complaint by the province's Chief Judge, who alleged that she had violated the provincial code of ethics for judges by compromising the public perception of impartiality. The Supreme Court of Canada upheld the Quebec law that regulated the inquiry process. The majority found that the Chief Judge's complaint did not unduly interfere with his colleague's independence.[106] If a provincial judge is found to have violated his or her code of ethics, most provinces permit a wider range of sanctions than that available to the Canadian Judicial Council; these may include fines, suspensions, or mandatory sensitivity training.[107]

In general, the disciplinary procedures for Canadian judges permit some degree of accountability—at least to their judicial peers—while preserving individual judicial independence. Indeed, the Supreme Court of Canada held (in a case involving a lawyer who was disciplined by his provincial law society) that "It is entirely appropriate that an individual whose conduct is to be judged should be assessed by a group of his or her peers who are themselves subject to the rules and standards that are being enforced."[108] However, some critics have suggested that allowing judges to judge each other results in a lack of effective discipline. Members of the bench may "circle the wagons" to protect each other from outside criticism. One possible solution is to add laypersons to judicial councils, to bring a more objective viewpoint to bear on allegations of misconduct.[109] To date, this has not been done.

◼ Financial Independence

To remove any taint of political interference, real or perceived, control over judicial salaries and benefits has been shifted from legislators to arm's-length commissions. The federal Judicial Compensation and Benefits Commission is empowered by the *Judges Act* to review the salaries, pensions, and ancillary benefits provided to federally appointed judges every four years. In the 1997 *Remuneration Reference* ruling, the Supreme Court of Canada ordered the provinces and territories to establish independent bodies to regulate judicial payment, in order to safeguard the financial and institutional independence of the judicial branch.

> *What judicial independence requires is an independent body, along the lines of the bodies that exist in many provinces and at the federal level to set or recommend the levels of judicial remuneration. Those bodies are often referred to as commissions. . . . Governments are constitutionally bound to go through the commission process. The recommendations of the commission would not be binding on the executive or the legislature. Nevertheless, though those recommendations are non-binding, they should not be set aside lightly, and, if the executive or the legislature chooses to depart from them, it has to justify its decision—if need be, in a court of law.[110]*

As the preceding quotation indicates, the commissions' recommendations are not binding on the executive and legislative branches. The Government of the day must issue a formal response to a commission report, and it must take the recommendations seriously.

In the end, however, the final decisions about judicial compensation still rest with politicians. The Supreme Court made this clear when it revisited the issue in 2005:

> *The government can reject or vary the commission's recommendations, provided that legitimate reasons are given. Reasons that are complete and that deal with the commission's recommendations in a meaningful way will meet the standard of rationality. Legitimate reasons must be compatible with the common law and the Constitution. The government must deal with the issues at stake in good faith. Bald expressions of rejection or disapproval are inadequate. Instead, the reasons must show that the commission's recommendations have been taken into account and must be based on facts and sound reasoning. They must state in what respect and to what extent they depart from the recommendations, articulating the grounds for rejection or variation. The reasons should reveal a consideration of the judicial office and an intention to deal with it appropriately. They must preclude any suggestion of attempting to manipulate the judiciary. The reasons must reflect the underlying public interest in having a commission process, being the depoliticization of the remuneration process and the need to preserve judicial independence.*[111]

The 2005 ruling arose from a plethora of lawsuits between provincial judges and their governments. Although the provincial (and territorial) governments had complied with the *Remuneration Reference* by establishing independent salary commissions for section 92 judges, they often disagreed with what they perceived as overly generous recommendations. When a provincial government lowered the salary levels devised by the arm's-length body, or froze judicial salaries in response to fiscal constraints, its judges went to superior court to force compliance with the commission report or to contest the pay freeze. "The result has been an unprecedented degree of adversarial contact between provincial governments and provincial judiciaries."[112]

While the 2005 Supreme Court ruling was intended to resolve these disputes, it disappointed section 92 judges, who regarded it as a climb down from the 1997 ruling. Some provincial judges may have been especially embittered by comparing their own salaries to those of the section 96 judges in their jurisdictions, whose salaries and benefits were considerably more generous.[113] Because the federal government generally accepted the recommendations of its own arm's-length commission, such conflicts with section 96 judges did not arise. That situation changed in 2006, as Dossier 10.6 explains.

DOSSIER 10.6   Bill C-17

The *Judges Act* provides for the appointment of a Judicial Compensation and Benefits Commission every four years. (The commission disbands as soon as it has issued its report, and new members are appointed for the next review.) The commission, composed of three senior members of the legal profession, is required by law to take the following considerations into account when it formulates its salary recommendations:

- "prevailing economic conditions," including "the overall economic and financial position of the federal government";

- the need to ensure the financial independence of federally appointed judges; and
- the salary level that may be required to "attract outstanding candidates to the judiciary."[114]

In effect, the commission is required to strike a balance between the fiscal capacity of the federal government and the need to compensate judges appropriately.

In 2003, the federal government appointed a commission to recommend federal judicial salaries for the next four years. The McLennan Commission (named after its chairman)

(continued)

reported in early 2004. It called for a salary increase of 10.8 percent for all section 96 and federal judges, starting April 1, 2004.[115] The Liberal Government accepted the recommendation,[116] although it was prevented from enacting it into law (as required by section 100 of the *BNA Act*) by the dissolution of Parliament shortly thereafter. The resulting Bill was finally introduced in May 2005, but it did not pass before the minority government fell in November of that year. By the time of the 2006 election, the proposed salary increase was almost two years overdue.

Shortly after he was sworn into office, then-Justice Minister Vic Toews reviewed the McLennan Commission report and decided that the salary recommendation was too high.[117] In May 2006 he tabled Bill C-17, which set the salary increase for federally appointed judges at 7.25 percent. The Harper Government also issued a formal written response to the commission, as required by the 1997 *Remuneration Reference*. It focused on the first and third of the considerations listed above (while saying little about judicial independence). According to the Government, the commission had interpreted the first consideration too narrowly. Given the size of the federal surplus, the 10.8-percent increase was affordable in the abstract. However, the commission should also have taken into account "the other economic and social priorities of the Government"[118]—which apparently did not include a pay hike for judges. After listing the five priorities set out in the 2006 Conservative platform, the document concluded that the Government could not afford to comply with the McLennan Commission's report and still keep its promises to Canadians. (Federal judicial salaries set the standard for other senior public officials, so the fiscal implications of the commission recommendations are greater than they might appear.[119]) As for the need to attract qualified candidates, the Government argued that the commission had used the wrong comparator; it should have looked at the average annual income of all Canadian lawyers, instead of focusing on the most highly paid members of the profession.[120]

Before the Commons Standing Committee on Justice, Toews argued that Bill C-17 and the written response were entirely consistent with the 2005 Supreme Court ruling. The Government was not obliged to enact the McLennan report into law, as long as it provided rational written arguments to support the lower salary figure. Having said as much, Toews emphasized the need to respect the integrity of the commission process by enacting the Bill into law as soon as possible after three years of delay.[121] The committee accepted the latter argument; it passed the Bill quickly and without amendment. However, some Opposition MPs were clearly troubled by the testimony of the 2003 commissioners and the Canadian Bar Association. Commissioner Roderick McLennan accused the Government of politicizing the process, and questioned its reasons for lowering the salary figure: "it's inappropriate, in my submission, to focus on a 2006 budget to consider a report that we had to file in May 2004."[122] His colleague Earl Cherniak made the following observations:

[T]he government of the day [in 2004] accepted every one of the recommendations we made. There is no provision in that constitutionally mandated process for what transpired after that. There's no provision for a second report after a new government comes in a year and a half or two years later. In my view, that politicizes the process, and it's extremely dangerous because it causes disrespect for the process among the judiciary, among the public. . . . If a future commission's recommendations can be treated in the way that the process has transpired here, there will be a great deal of difficulty finding the kind of commissioners that this country needs to conduct this process every four years.[123]

Despite sharing these concerns, the Canadian Bar Association encouraged the Justice committee to pass the Bill, because the section 96 judges had waited almost three years for a raise in pay. Nonetheless, its representatives argued that the Government response did

(continued)

not meet the standards set by the Supreme Court: "Although the government identifies key priorities and refers to other budgetary objectives, there is no explanation of how or why the implementation of the recommendations of the commission would impair or affect the ability of the government to pursue these goals or objectives."[124] More broadly, they emphasized—as the Government had not—the implications of Bill C-17 for the financial element of judicial independence.

> Our mandate includes a commitment to an impartial and independent judiciary, without which there is no rule of law. That is the lens through which we have analyzed Bill C-17, and it governs our comments today. While this bill looks to be about money, the underlying issue is that Canadians have a right to have disputes heard by impartial judges who can act freely and without interference. Judicial compensation commissions are established to provide a non-partisan method of reviewing and setting judicial compensation. . . . Judges cannot and should not be drawn into the political fray through the setting of judicial salaries, nor should this process be used to gain political points.
>
> Canadians should not be left with the impression either that judges are beholden to their boss, who decides their salary, or that judges are predisposed against government because of a salary dispute. Depoliticizing judicial compensation isn't simply an ideal; it is a constitutional requirement. Every person in Canada involved in the justice system must receive a hearing by a judge who is fair and impartial, and as importantly, who is seen to be so. This principle is a cornerstone of our democracy.[125]

Bill C-17 became law in December 2006. Given the Conservatives' long-standing and publicly expressed hostility toward judges and courts, the Government's response to the McLennan Commission raises questions about its commitment to judicial independence—especially since this key principle received short shrift in its response to the commission's report.

In 2008 a new commission recommended another large increase in judicial salaries, well above the level that the Harper Government was prepared to pay. In an effort to justify its pending rejection of the commission report, the DOJ asked the Canada Revenue Agency to provide salary information for hundreds of federal judges prior to their appointments; the purpose, apparently, was to show that "salaries for federal judges are generally higher than the income they earned as lawyers."[126] At the time of writing, the Government had neither apologized for the breach of confidentiality nor officially responded to the salary recommendation.

Institutional/Administrative Independence

To this point, we have focused on the job security and financial remuneration of individual judges. The third pillar of judicial independence applies to a court as a whole, as an institution separate from the legislative and executive branches of government. As the Supreme Court observed in 1985, "an individual judge may enjoy the essential conditions of judicial independence but if the court or tribunal over which he or she presides is not independent of the other branches of government, in what is essential to its function, he or she cannot be said to be an independent tribunal."[127]

The Supreme Court has defined this third pillar as "the institutional independence of the tribunal with respect to matters of administration bearing directly on the exercise of its judicial function."

> Judicial control over . . . assignment of judges, sittings of the court, and court lists [,] as well as the related matters of allocation of court rooms and direction of the administrative staff engaged in carrying out these functions, has generally been considered the essential or minimum requirement

for institutional or "collective" independence. . . . [T]he claim for greater administrative autonomy or independence for the courts goes considerably beyond these matters. The insistence is chiefly on a stronger or more independent role in the financial aspects of court administration—budgetary preparation and presentation and allocation of expenditure—and in the personnel aspects of administration—the recruitment, classification, promotion, remuneration, and supervision of the necessary support staff.[128]

To understand this demand for greater autonomy, we must first understand the current administrative structure of Canadian courts. As previously explained, the provincial governments are responsible for the administration of justice within their respective boundaries (section 92(14) of the *BNA Act*). This means that (1) the annual budgets for the provincial and superior courts are proposed by the provincial Attorney General and approved by the legislature; (2) those courts are treated for administrative purposes as "a division of the Attorney General's ministry, rather than as a separate branch or even a separate department of government";[129] and (3) the minister responsible for prosecuting crimes and defending the provincial Crown against civil litigation also controls the resources available to the provincial and superior courts in his or her jurisdiction. Taken together, these features of the "executive model" of court administration permit the legislative and executive branches of government in the provinces to exert unwarranted pressure on judges (both provincial and superior) by cutting their budgets or shutting down courtrooms.

In most instances, the withdrawal of resources from the judicial branch has occurred as a result of broader budget cutbacks. For example, in 2002 the British Columbia government announced the impending closure of one-quarter of the courthouses in the province without prior consultation with the judiciary. The Cabinet reversed the decision after an unprecedented public protest by the provincial Chief Judge, supported by the local law society.[130] As a consequence of this episode, BC's Attorney General signed a written agreement with the Chief Judge that gives the latter unusually wide discretion to allocate the annual budget for the courts in that province.[131] So it is safe to say that when a provincial government provides insufficient resources to the justice system—which they all do, according to the Chief Judges[132]—this is usually an unintended by-product of fiscal constraints and competing priorities, not a deliberate punishment for (or an attempt to avert) unwelcome judicial rulings. "With governments working hard to contain or reduce expenditures and taxes, there is increased competition within government for adequate shares of a constrained budget. . . . The courts are not particularly good at this infighting, and not very effective as vote-getters compared with big-ticket items like medicare and public education, but they have become expensive enough to be a target."[133]

Having said as much, the Canadian Judicial Council has expressed concern about deliberate political interference with court budgets in the current climate of tension between the executive and judicial branches. That tension has two primary sources: the strife arising from the 1997 *Remuneration Reference* (previously discussed), and the impact of some *Charter* rulings on public budgets.[134]

The ever-widening impact of court judgments on the government's budget cannot fail to have an effect on the perception of relations between the judiciary and the executive when the time comes for the latter to prepare and approve the courts' budget. Nor can there be any doubt that chief justices today are increasingly embroiled in ongoing negotiations with governments on court needs and budgets. Under these circumstances, is there not a risk that the judiciary's independence is being compromised in the eyes of an informed observer? Some may reasonably believe that the judiciary might be tempted to defer a decision or limit its scope in order to avoid seeing its budget or human resources shrink. There is cause for concern even if this has never happened. For in these matters it is appearances that count, not reality.[135]

Under these conditions, the council argues, the "executive model" of court administration is outdated. To preserve judicial independence and ensure the proper allocation of limited resources, the courts within each province should be given more autonomy over their budgets and staffing. This approach has already been adopted at the federal level. The Federal Court and the Supreme Court operate independently of the DOJ; their budgets are allocated separately, and each is staffed by administrators who report to the Chief Justice.[136] The success of this model at the federal level suggests that the provinces should follow suit. To date, however, they have refused to give judges more than an informal advisory role in their own administrative affairs. Although this is consistent with the separation of powers among the three branches, insofar as the legislature controls the public purse and the executive administers public services, it is likely to perpetuate tensions between the executive and judicial branches. On occasion, these tensions could boil over into crises, such as the chaos that followed the *Askov* ruling. Institutional or administrative independence will likely remain the weakest of the three pillars for the foreseeable future.

CONCLUSION

This chapter has explained the structure of Canada's judicial branch, its role in our system of government, and its relationships with the other two branches. It has also raised questions about the impact of the Harper Government on the independence of our judiciary, in light of the hostility toward the courts expressed by Harper and some of his supporters. Toward the end of the 2006 election campaign, for example, Harper predicted that his government's policies would be thwarted by "Liberal-appointed judges."[137] As we have seen, Harper had a point about party patronage; but his remarks were inappropriate, insofar as judges refrain from political activity while in office.[138]

Harper's first Justice minister, Vic Toews, had made numerous disparaging remarks about judges while in Opposition. For example, he characterized the 2001 Supreme Court ruling in *Burns and Rafay*, which prevented the federal Justice minister from extraditing suspected criminals to the United States without assurances that they would not be put to death, as "a political decision," adding that "the Supreme Court by its decision today demonstrated that the rule of law was secondary to a political agenda."[139] In 2004 he stated that "this Liberal government has allowed judges to become the most powerful force in setting social policy in Canada. Whether it is by allowing convicted murders to vote or by changing fundamental institutions like marriage, this government has substituted the supremacy of an elected Parliament with unelected judges."[140]

Toews regularly lambasted the Liberals for being soft on criminals, for depriving police officers of the powers and resources they needed to fight crime, and for appointing their friends to judicial office. There may have been some factual basis for his allegations of patronage appointments—a pattern which appears to have continued under the Conservatives—and his assertions about judicial power, although (as discussed in Chapter 6) the courts have hardly overthrown Parliament in a *coup*. The point is that Toews' disdain toward the courts, and his belief that criminal suspects should be treated more harshly, appear to have coloured his actions as Justice minister. His successor in the portfolio, Rob Nicholson, was considerably more measured in his approach to the justice system. Nonetheless, given Prime Minister Harper's statement in the Commons about his intention to appoint hard-line judges, there are reasons to wonder about the security of Canadian judicial independence under a Conservative Government.

If any damage has been (or will be) done, it will likely be limited by the constitutional guarantees discussed in this chapter. It will also be contained by the conventions of judicial impartiality (Dossier 10.3), which require judges to adhere to unwritten norms of conduct (not to mention the written norms contained in their ethics codes).[141] However, the prospect of further conflict between the executive and judicial branches of government is worrisome. Future showdowns over resources and administrative autonomy are likely to occur, especially when Canadians elect parties to power who explicitly campaign against an independent judiciary. It is important to remember that Canadian judges, especially those who serve on appellate and federal courts, are among the most highly regarded in the world. While there is room for improvement, we are fortunate to have a strong and reasonably independent judicial branch. The core principles of our *Constitution* are in safe hands.

GLOSSARY OF KEY TERMS

Adjudication: The process by which the courts resolve disputes.

Extrinsic evidence: Facts placed before a court that do not arise directly from the case at bar. Two types of extrinsic evidence are discussed in this chapter: social science evidence relating to the policy impact of a particular law (used to weigh infringed rights against competing social purposes under section 1 of the *Charter*), and evidence of legislative intent in the drafting of the impugned law.

Impugned: A legal provision that is alleged to conflict with the *Constitution*.

Tort: An injury inflicted by one party on another, either deliberately or through negligence. The injured party can take the wrongdoer to court to try to recover civil damages. Some torts can also lead to separate criminal proceedings.

DISCUSSION AND REVIEW QUESTIONS

1. Do you believe that judges should have the power to strike down or amend laws passed by elected legislators? Why or why not?

2. How are federal judges chosen? Should the voters have a role in selecting judges? Why or why not?

3. In your own words, explain TWO of the three pillars of judicial independence. Why is it so important to insulate judges from political influence?

4. Imagine that you were a trial judge or a member of a provincial court of appeal. In your own words, describe your responsibilities on the bench.

SUGGESTED READINGS

Books and Articles

W.A. Bogart, *Courts and Country: The Limits of Litigation and the Social and Political Life of Canada* (Toronto: Oxford University Press, 1994).

Canada, Department of Justice, *Canada's System of Justice* (Ottawa, 2005).

Canadian Judicial Council, *Alternative Models of Court Administration* (Ottawa, September 2006); accessed at www.cjc-ccm.gc.ca.

Bradley C. Canon and Charles A. Johnson, *Judicial Policies: Implementation and Impact,* 2nd edition (Washington: CQ Press, 1999).

Ian Greene, *The Courts* (Vancouver: UBC Press, 2006).

Kate Malleson and Peter H. Russell, eds., *Appointing Judges in an Age of Judicial Power: Critical Perspectives From Around the World* (Toronto: University of Toronto Press, 2006).

Peter McCormick, "New Questions about an Old Concept: The Supreme Court of Canada's Judicial Independence Decisions," *Canadian Journal of Political Science,* 37:4 (December 2004), 839–862.

Gerald N. Rosenberg, *The Hollow Hope: Can Courts Bring About Social Change?* (Chicago: University of Chicago Press, 1991).

Jacob S. Ziegel, "Merit Selection and Democratization of Appointments to the Supreme Court of Canada," *Choices,* 5:2 (Montreal: IRPP, June 1999).

Websites

All of Canada's federal and provincial courts have their own websites, which provide access to important rulings issued in the past several years. These sites can be accessed quickly and easily from the Canadian Legal Information Institute website: www.canlii.org. The CanLii site also provides full-text versions of federal and provincial statutes, as well as a useful digest of major court rulings on the *Canadian Charter of Rights and Freedoms.*

The Canadian Judicial Council's mandate and publications are posted at www.cjc-ccm.gc.ca. Its site also offers an excellent Resource Centre if you want to find more information about our courts and judges.

NOTES

1. *Reference re Secession of Quebec,* [1998], 2 S.C.R. 217, paragraph 32, *per curiam* [the entire court signed the ruling, instead of identifying one or two justices as the authors].
2. The role of judicial review in federalism is discussed in Chapters 3 and 4 of this book.
3. Recall the discussion of "judicial activism" in Chapter 6.
4. *The Queen v. Beauregard,* [1986] 2 S.C.R. 56, paragraph 28, *per* Dickson C.J.
5. Canada, Department of Justice, *Canada's System of Justice* (Ottawa, 2005); accessed at www.canada.justice.gc.ca, July 2007, 17.
6. Ian Greene, *The Courts* (Vancouver: UBC Press, 2006), 58–59.
7. Ibid.
8. As explained in Chapter 4, the Judicial Committee of the Privy Council (JCPC) in London was the highest court of appeal for Canada until 1949.
9. Legal aid may be available for some criminal appeals, depending on the province; but these payments fall far short of the actual cost of mounting an appeal to the Supreme Court of Canada. Many lawyers work for free (*pro bono*) on a few cases per year, although the supply of *pro bono* time barely scratches the surface of the demand.
10. More than 80 percent of judges on American state courts, from 39 of the 50 states, are elected. Adam Liptak, "Rendering Justice, With One Eye on Re-election," *The New York Times,* May 25, 2008 (accessed at www.nytimes.com).
11. See, e.g., Peter H. Russell and Jacob S. Ziegel, "Federal Judicial Appointments: An Appraisal of the First Mulroney Government's Appointments and the New Judicial Advisory Committees," 41 *University of Toronto Law Journal* (1991), 5–6.
12. James G. Snell and Frederick Vaughan, *The Supreme Court of Canada: History of the Institution* (Toronto: University of Toronto Press/Osgoode Society, 1985), 154.
13. Ibid., 231; Greene, *The Courts,* 23.

14. Julien Chouinard, a Quebec judge, had been a Progressive Conservative candidate in the 1968 federal election. Clark asked him to serve in his Cabinet before appointing him to the Supreme Court. Peter McCormick, *Supreme at Last: The Evolution of the Supreme Court of Canada* (Toronto: Lorimer, 2000), 85.

15. Some observers questioned the 1997 appointment of Justice Michel Bastarache to fill the Atlantic slot on the Supreme Court. Bastarache was a former law partner of then-Prime Minister Chrétien; he had also advised the Liberal Party in 1993. F.L. Morton, "Judicial Appointments in Post-Charter Canada: A System in Transition," in Kate Malleson and Peter H. Russell, eds., *Appointing Judges in an Age of Judicial Power: Critical Perspectives From Around the World* (Toronto: University of Toronto Press, 2006), 62–63.

16. Morton, "Judicial Appointments in Post-Charter Canada," 61–63.

17. Jacob S. Ziegel, "Merit Selection and Democratization of Appointments to the Supreme Court of Canada," *Choices*, 5:2 (Montreal: IRPP, June 1999), 3; accessed at www.irpp.org. In the event, the vacant Ontario seat was filled by lawyer Ian Binnie. Justice Abella was appointed to the Supreme Court in 2004 (her appointment is discussed later in the chapter); Justice Laskin, the son of former Chief Justice Bora Laskin, remains on the Ontario Court of Appeal.

18. André Pratte, *Charest: His Life and Politics* (Toronto: Stoddart, 1998), 96–110.

19. Russell and Ziegel, 22–24.

20. Morton, "Judicial Appointments in Post-Charter Canada," 68.

21. Ibid., 70.

22. Greene, *The Courts*, 15.

23. Gloria Galloway, "Tory Leader warns of activist judges," *The Globe and Mail*, January 19, 2006; "Harper eager to politicize top court, Martin warns," *The Globe and Mail*, January 20, 2006; Richard Blackwell, "Getting tough may jeopardize rights of defendants," *The Globe and Mail* January 6, 2006; all accessed at www.theglobeandmail.com, July 2007.

24. Morton, "Judicial Appointments in Post-Charter Canada," 69.

25. Greene, *The Courts*, 59.

26. Because of their size, Quebec and Ontario are divided into two and three regions, respectively, each with its own JAC.

27. The commissioner operates at arm's length from the federal government, including the DOJ; his office "safeguard[s] the independence of the judiciary" and provides services for active and retired judges. Mr. Marc Giroux, Acting Commissioner, Office of the Commissioner for Federal Judicial Affairs, *Minutes of Proceedings and Evidence of the House of Commons Standing Committee on Justice and Human Rights*, March 20, 2007, 1 (accessed at www.parl.gc.ca, July 2007).

28. Ibid., 1. The minister in question was Liberal Allan Rock, a former Treasurer of the Ontario Bar Society. In his subsequent testimony before the committee, former Chief Justice Antonio Lamer claimed that other Justice ministers had appointed candidates who were not recommended by the applicable JACs, but provided no details; see *Minutes of Proceedings and Evidence of the House of Commons Standing Committee on Justice and Human Rights*, April 17, 2007, 5.

29. Ian Greene, et al., *Final Appeal: Decision-Making in Canadian Courts of Appeal* (Toronto: Lorimer, 1998), 37.

30. Greene, *The Courts*, 23.

31. Russell and Ziegel, 28.

32. Russell and Ziegel, 21–22. The authors point out that, after years of Liberal Governments in Ottawa, the pool of judges from which promotions were drawn would have contained relatively few Progressive Conservatives; this suggests that the Mulroney Government made a concerted effort to favour PCs when it filled vacancies at the higher courts.

33. Ibid., 25.

34. Morton, "Judicial Appointments in Post-Charter Canada," 68.

35. See the discussion of party finance in Chapters 11 and 12.

36. Jacob Ziegel, *Minutes of Proceedings and Evidence of the Standing Committee on Justice and Human Rights*, April 17, 2007, 3.

37. Canada, Department of Justice, "Minister Toews pleased to announce changes to Judicial Advisory Committees," November 10, 2006; accessed at www.canada.justice.gc.ca, July 2007.

38. This summary is based on the May 2007 Report of the House of Commons Standing Committee on Justice and Human Rights, entitled "Preserving Independence in the Judicial Appointment System"; accessed at www.parl.gc.ca, July 2007.

39. J. Parker McCarthy, president of the Canadian Bar Association; *Minutes of Proceedings and Evidence of the House of Commons Standing Committee on Justice and Human Rights*, March 20, 2007, 7. According to the president of the Canadian Police Association, the minister did consult with his organization before announcing the alterations; Tony Cannavino, *Minutes of Proceedings and Evidence of the House of Commons Standing Committee on Justice and Human Rights*, March 28, 2007, 4.

40. Kirk Makin, "Judges' group slams changes to judiciary," *The Globe and Mail*, February 21, 2007; accessed at www.theglobeandmail.com, July 2007.

41. House of Commons, *Hansard*, February 14, 2007, 6809.

42. Peter H, Russell, *Minutes of Proceedings and Evidence of the House of Commons Standing Committee on Justice and Human Rights*, March 20, 2007, 5.

43. Ibid., 6.

44. "Preserving Independence in the Judicial Appointment System," 1.

45. Ibid., 10.

46. Ibid., 27.

47. Prof. Sébastien Grammond, *Minutes of Proceedings and Evidence of the House of Commons Standing Committee on Justice and Human Rights*, March 20, 2007, 4.

48. House of Commons, Standing Committee on Justice, Human Rights, Public Safety and Emergency Preparedness, Sub-Committee on the Judicial Appointments Process, "Interim Report on the Process For Appointment to the Federal Judiciary" (Ottawa, November 2005); accessed at www.parl.gc.ca.

49. *Minutes of Proceedings and Evidence of the House of Commons Standing Committee on Justice, Human Rights, Public Safety and Emergency Preparedness*, March 30, 2004 (accessed at www.parl.gc.ca, April 2004).

50. See, e.g., Ziegel, "Merit Selection"; Peter Russell, *Minutes of Proceedings and Evidence of the House of Commons Standing Committee on Justice, Human Rights, Public Safety and Emergency Preparedness*, March 23, 2004, 15 (accessed at www.parl.gc.ca, April 2004).

51. House of Commons, Standing Committee on Justice, Human Rights, Public Safety and Emergency Preparedness, *Improving the Supreme Court of Canada Appointments Process* (May 2004); accessed at www.parl.gc.ca, May 2004.

52. This attempt to revive the Meech Lake process went nowhere. The history of provincial demands for a role in Supreme Court appointments is described in Chapter 5.

53. House of Commons, *Minutes of Proceedings and Evidence of the Standing Committee on Justice, Human Rights, Public Safety and Emergency Preparedness*, March 25, 2004 (accessed at www.parl.gc.ca, April 2004).

54. House of Commons, *Minutes of Proceedings and Evidence of the Standing Committee on Justice, Human Rights, Public Safety and Emergency Preparedness*, March 30, 2004 (accessed at www.parl.gc.ca, April 2004).

55. In early 2004, Justice Louise Arbour was appointed to lead the United Nations Human Rights Commission. Shortly thereafter, Justice Frank Iacobucci announced his early retirement from the court. Both represented Ontario.

56. Kim Lunman and Brian Laghi, "Commons panel to accept judges," *The Globe and Mail*, August 26, 2004 (accessed at www.globeandmail.com); Tonda MacCharles and Mary Gordon, "MPs to vet top judge picks," *Toronto Star*, August 24, 2004 (accessed at www.thestar.com).

57. Greene, *The Courts*, 26–27.

58. Peter W. Hogg, "Appointment of Justice Marshall Rothstein to the Supreme Court of Canada," 44 *Osgoode Hall Law Journal* (2006), 529; Peter McCormick, "The Serendipitous Solution to the Problem of Supreme Court Appointments," 44 *Osgoode Hall Law Journal* (2006), 543–544.

59. Jacob Ziegel, "A New Era in the Selection of Supreme Court Judges?," 44 *Osgoode Hall Law Journal* (2006), 548.

60. Peter W. Hogg, "Judicial Interview Process: Opening Remarks to Ad Hoc Committee on Supreme Court Appointment," February 27, 2006; accessed at www.justice.gc.ca/en/dept/pub/scc/jud_interview.html, July 2007.

61. In June 2007, for example, the federal government announced the appointment of a new judge to the Superior Court of Newfoundland and Labrador. The judge in question is the daughter-in-law of former Progressive Conservative Cabinet Minister John Crosbie. Kirk Makin, "Winkler appointed chief justice of Ontario," *The Globe and Mail*, June 2, 2007 (accessed at www.theglobeandmail.com).

62. Peter H. Russell, *Minutes of Proceedings and Evidence of the Standing Committee on Justice and Human Rights*, March 20, 2007, 6.

63. This point was made by the Conservative members of the Commons Standing Committee on Justice and Human Rights in their dissenting report on the federal appointments process (May 2007).

64. Sébastien Grammond, *Minutes of Proceedings and Evidence of the Standing Committee on Justice and Human Rights*, March 20, 2007, 4.

65. Greene, *The Courts*, 59.

66. This is why every criminal case is called "*R. v.*" the name of the accused. The *R* stands for "Regina" (Latin for "Queen") or "Rex" (King), depending on the sex of the British monarch at the time of the trial.

67. In a jury trial, 12 citizens are responsible for determining the facts and applying the law under the guidance of the judge. Jury trials are very rare in Canada, accounting for only 2 percent of criminal charges. One reason is that jury trials are only available in superior courts, whereas the vast majority of charges are dealt with in provincial court. Another reason is the high incidence of plea bargains in the Canadian criminal justice system. Finally, anyone accused of a serious offence can opt for a trial by judge alone, which is an attractive option for those who want to speed up the process or who believe that a jury would treat them harshly. Greene, *The Courts*, 37.

68. *R. v. Big M Drug Mart Ltd.*, [1985] 1 S.C.R. 295.

69. *Housen v. Nikolaisen*, [2002] 2 S.C.R. 235, paragraph 1, *per* Iacobucci and Major JJ.

70. One rare exception to this rule occurred in June 2007, when the Supreme Court issued a ruling on a BC law that significantly interfered with the collective bargaining rights of health-care workers in the province. The majority, led by Chief Justice McLachlin and Justice LeBel, explicitly rejected a 20-year-old ruling on section 2(d) of the *Charter* (freedom of association). The earlier ruling had excluded collective bargaining from the scope of the *Charter*. McLachlin and LeBel wrote that "the grounds advanced in the earlier decisions for the exclusion of collective bargaining from the *Charter*'s protection of freedom of association do not withstand principled scrutiny and should be rejected." *Health Services and Support—Facilities Subsector Bargaining Assn. v. British Columbia*, [2007] 2 S.C.R. 391, paragraph 2.

71. *Kindler v. Canada (Minister of Justice)*, [1991] 2 S.C.R. 779; *United States v. Burns* [2001] 1 S.C.R. 283.

72. For example, the June 2003 *Halpern* ruling from the Ontario Court of Appeal made it legal for same-sex couples to marry in that province. The court refused to suspend the legality of same-sex marriage so that Parliament could amend the relevant laws. Instead, it declared that same-sex couples in Ontario could get married as soon as the ruling was issued. Shortly thereafter, as discussed in Dossier 6.4, the BC Court of Appeal amended its earlier ruling on the issue, in which it had suspended the remedy of permitting same-sex marriage for two years; it ordered the province to grant marriage licences to gay and lesbian couples immediately.

73. Heather MacIvor, *Canadian Politics and Government in the Charter Era* (Toronto: Thomson Nelson, 2006), 108–122.

74. Manfredi, *Judicial Power and the Charter*, 157.

75. There is a partial exception: the *Rules of the Supreme Court of Canada* permit a lawyer appointed by the court to conduct a cross-examination of an expert witness on the written evidence that he or she has submitted on behalf of one of the parties. The cross-examination does not take place before the justices; instead, a transcript must be provided within a specified time.

76. *R. v. Mohan,* [1994] 2 S.C.R. 9.

77. *R. v. Askov,* [1990] 2 S.C.R. 1199.

78. MacIvor, 120–121; Greene, *The Courts*, 43–44.

79. More than 60 000 charges were dropped, although the actual number of cases was considerably smaller because many accused faced multiple charges. Most of the stayed charges were relatively minor. Some 90 percent of the criminal charges pending in Ontario when *Askov* was released were unaffected by the stays, and proceeded normally through the justice system. Kent Roach, *Due Process and Victims' Rights*, 92.

80. MacIvor, 120–121.

81. Hiebert, "Debating Policy," 55.

82. *RJR-MacDonald Inc. v. Canada (Attorney General),* [1995] 3 S.C.R. 199, paragraph 68, *per* La Forest J.

83. MacIvor, 126–128.

84. However, this is not always the case. In 2002 the Supreme Court narrowly struck down a section of the *Canada Elections Act* that prohibited federal prisoners (those serving sentences of two or more years) from voting in federal elections. That section still appears in subsequent versions of the Act (section 4(c)).

85. See Bradley C. Canon and Charles A. Johnson, *Judicial Policies: Implementation and Impact,* 2nd edition (Washington: CQ Press, 1999); Gerald N. Rosenberg, *The Hollow Hope: Can Courts Bring About Social Change?* (Chicago: University of Chicago Press, 1991); and W.A. Bogart, *Courts and Country: The Limits of Litigation and the Social and Political Life of Canada* (Toronto: Oxford University Press, 1994).

86. *R. v. Stinchcombe,* [1991] 3 S.C.R. 326.

87. In *R. v. O'Connor,* [1995] 4 S.C.R. 411, the Supreme Court stayed sexual abuse charges against a former Catholic bishop because the Crown had refused to disclose evidence in a timely manner. See also Gerald Owen, "Disclosure after *Stinchcombe*," in Anthony A. Peacock, ed., *Rethinking the Constitution: Perspectives on Canadian Constitutional Reform, Interpretation, and Theory* (Toronto: Oxford University Press, 1996).

88. *Reference re Remuneration of Judges of the Provincial Court of Prince Edward Island,* [1997] 3 S.C.R. 3, paragraph 306, *per* La Forest J. (dissenting, but not on this point).

89. Peter McCormick, "New Questions about an Old Concept: The Supreme Court of Canada's Judicial Independence Decisions," *Canadian Journal of Political Science,* 37:4 (December 2004), 842.

90. Ibid.

91. *Reference re Remuneration of Judges of the Provincial Court of Prince Edward Island,* paragraphs 83 and 109, *per* Lamer C.J. (for the majority).

92. "Preserving Independence in the Judicial Appointment System," 2; Canadian Judicial Council, *The Conduct of Judges and the Role of the Canadian Judicial Council* (Ottawa, n.d.), 8; accessed at www.cjc-ccm.gc.ca, July 2007.

93. Canadian Judicial Council, *Ethical Principles for Judges* (Ottawa, 1989), 9; accessed at www.cjc-ccm.gc.ca, July 2007.

94. Canadian Judicial Council, "Judicial Appointments: Perspective from the Canadian Judicial Council," February 20, 2007; accessed at www.cjc-ccm.gc.ca, July 2007. The quotation from the Supreme Court is taken from *Bodner v, Alberta,* paragraph 1, *per curiam.*

95. Greene, *The Courts*, 82–83.

96. *Valente v. The Queen*, [1985] 2 S.C.R. 673, paragraph 22, *per* Le Dain J.

97. In 1996, the majority of members of an Inquiry Committee recommended the removal from office of Justice Jean Bienvenue, a member of the Quebec Superior Court (trial division). Bienvenue had presided over the trial of a woman charged with murdering her husband. During the proceeding, he made several questionable comments about women and racial minorities (the defendant was of mixed race), although not from the bench. After the jury convicted the accused of second degree murder, despite his instruction to convict her of first-degree murder, the judge chastised the jury in private. Some jurors later told reporters what he had said. The following day, the judge made inflammatory and sexist remarks during the sentencing hearing. Among other things, he claimed that the Nazis killed Jews at Auschwitz "without suffering," in contrast to what he characterized as the cruelty of the convicted woman. The Inquiry Committee, with one dissent, determined that the judge had damaged "public confidence in the justice system" and could no longer exercise the functions of a judge. "Report to the Canadian Judicial Council by the Inquiry Committee Appointed Under Section 63(1) of the *Judges Act* to Conduct a Public Inquiry Into the Conduct of Mr. Justice Paul Bienvenue of the Superior Court of Quebec in *R. v. T. Théberge*" (June 1996), 61; accessed at www.cjc-ccm.gc.ca, July 2007. Before the minister of Justice could make a recommendation to Parliament, Bienvenue resigned.

98. "Report to the Canadian Judicial Council of the Inquiry Committee Established Pursuant to Subsection 63(1) of the *Judges Act* At the Request of the Attorney General of Nova Scotia" (August 1990), 27; accessed at www.cjc-ccm.gc.ca, July 2007.

99. Canadian Judicial Council, *The Conduct of Judges*, 3.

100. Greene, *The Courts*, 95.

101. In 2007, the Federal Court of Appeal ruled that the automatic convening of an Inquiry Committee in response to a complaint from an Attorney General does not violate the independence of judges. The case arose from a 2004 complaint by Ontario's Attorney General to the Canadian Judicial Council against Superior Court Judge Paul Cosgrove (who happened to be a former federal Liberal Cabinet minister). Specifically, Attorney General Michael Bryant alleged that Cosgrove had made numerous errors of law in a 1999 criminal trial. Given that the legal errors had already been reviewed and corrected by the Ontario Court of Appeal, Bryant's complaint might not have made it through the normal screening process if it had been made by an ordinary citizen. However, the Court of Appeal did find "the appearance of a failure by the trial judge to conduct the proceedings impartiality and fairly," as well as evidence that he might be biased against the police. See *R. v. Elliott*, December 4, 2003, paragraphs 125 and 144 (accessed at www.canlii.org). In 2005 the Federal Court accepted Cosgrove's argument that the provision in the *Judges Act* allowing an Attorney General to bypass the council's screening process violated judicial independence, and struck it down. The Federal Court of Appeal overturned that ruling, on the ground that the council had previously refused to convene an Inquiry Committee in a case where the substance of a Crown complaint was relatively trivial; it also pointed out that the federal Justice minister had the discretion to refuse a request for impeachment. See *Canada (Attorney General) v. The Honourable Mr. Justice Paul Cosgrove*, Federal Court of Appeal, March 12, 2007 (accessed at www.canlii.org).

102. Canadian Judicial Council, *The Conduct of Judges*, 5.

103. Greene, *The Courts*, 100.

104. He challenged the recommendation for his removal through the courts; in 2001, the Supreme Court of Canada ruled that the process did not violate judicial independence. *Therrien (Re)*, [2001] 2 S.C.R. 3.

105. Greene, *The Courts*, 101.

106. *Ruffo v. Conseil de la magistrature*, [1995] 4 S.C.R. 267.

107. Greene, *The Courts*, 95.

108. *Pearlman v. Manitoba Law Society Judicial Committee*, [1991] 2 S.C.R. 869, paragraph 44, *per* Iacobucci J. See also *Moreau-Bérubé v. New Brunswick (Judicial Council)*, [2002] 1 S.C.R. 249, 2002 SCC 11: "A council composed primarily of judges, alive to the delicate balance between judicial independence and judicial integrity, is eminently qualified to render a collegial decision regarding the conduct of a judge" (head notes).

109. Greene, *The Courts*, 102.

110. *Reference re Remuneration of Judges of the Provincial Court of Prince Edward Island*, paragraph 133, *per* Lamer C.J.

111. *Bodner v. Alberta*, [2005] 2 S.C.R. 286, paragraph 25, *per curiam*.

112. Canadian Judicial Council, *Alternative Models of Court Administration*, 17.

113. Nancy Holmes, "Legislative Summary of Bill C-17: An Act to Amend the Judges Act and Certain Other Acts in Relation to Courts" (Ottawa: Library of Parliament, May 2007), 15; accessed at www.parl.gc.ca, July 2007.

114. "Response of the Government of Canada to the Report of the 2003 Judicial Compensation and Benefits Commission" (Ottawa, May 26, 2006), 3; accessed at www.justice-canada.net/en/dept/pub/jcbc/table.html, August 2007.

115. Canada, *Report of the Second Judicial Compensation and Benefits Commission* (Ottawa, May 2004); accessed at www.quadcom.gc.ca, July 2007.

116. "Government Response to the 2003 Judicial Benefits and Compensation Commission," May 31, 2004 (accessed at www.justice.gc.ca/en/dept/pub/jcbrj/, July 2007).

117. Toews appears to have reached this conclusion before taking office. In December 2004 he characterized the Liberal Government's acceptance of the 10.8-percent recommendation as "an outrageous abuse of the public trust," and asked then-Justice Minister Irwin Cotler "why he believes judges deserve pay raises so far beyond that of other hard-working Canadians." *Hansard*, December 1, 2004, 2132 (accessed at www.parl.gc.ca, July 2007).

118. "Government Response to the 2003 Judicial Benefits and Compensation Commission," 6.

119. Holmes, 7.

120. "Government Response," 8.

121. House of Commons, *Minutes of Proceedings and Evidence of the Standing Committee on Justice and Human Rights*, October 24, 2006, 1–3.

122. Ibid., 9.

123. Ibid., 14–15.

124. Robert Leurer, Judicial Compensation and Benefits Committee, Canadian Bar Association; reported in House of Commons, *Minutes of Proceedings and Evidence of the Standing Committee on Justice and Human Rights*, October 25, 2006, 2.

125. Tamra Thomson, director, Legislation and Law Reform, Canadian Bar Association, ibid., 1.

126. Tim Naumetz, "Ottawa mined judges' personal tax information," *The Globe and Mail*, June 22, 2008; accessed at www.globeandmail.com.

127. *Valente*, paragraph 20, *per* Le Dain J.

128. *Valente*, paragraphs 47 and 49–50, *per* Le Dain J.

129. Canadian Judicial Council, *Alternative Models of Court Administration*, 2.

130. Greene, *The Courts*, 86–87; *Alternative Models of Court Administration*, 107.

131. *Alternative Models of Court Administration*, 13.

132. Ibid., 19.

133. McCormick, "New Questions about an Old Concept," 855.

134. *Alternative Models of Court Administration*, 17.

135. Ibid., 48–49.

136. "About the Court: The Administration of the Court," www.scc-csc.gc.ca.

137. *The Globe and Mail,* "Harper says courts bear marks of Liberal rule," *The Globe and Mail,* January 18, 2006 (accessed at www.theglobeandmail.com, July 2007).

138. In 1991, for example, a Nova Scotia provincial judge was reprimanded for donating money to the political campaigns of his relatives, among other contributions to the same party. Canadian Judicial Council, *Ethical Principles for Judges,* 41.

139. *Hansard,* February 15, 2001, 774.

140. *Hansard,* February 23, 2004, 929. See also May 8, 2003, 5953: "By the court substituting its political opinion, and I emphasize it is a political decision on the part of the court, this is not a legal decision, for that of elected parliamentarians, Canadians have no reason to believe in the legitimacy of democratic government and the rule of law."

141. These are encapsulated in the Canadian Judicial Council's *Ethical Principles for Judges,* available on the Council's website.

Part IV

Linking Canadians to Their Political Institutions

Political Parties and the Canadian Party System

LEARNING OBJECTIVES

After you finish reading this chapter, you should be able to:
- *explain* the differences between a catch-all party and a programmatic party;
- *identify* and *describe* the three structural elements of party organizations;
- *identify* and *describe* the institutional incentives for party members;
- *identify* and *explain* TWO phases of Canada's national party system since Confederation.

INTRODUCTION

Recall the vignette of the soccer match at the start of Chapter 3. The players on the field are engaged in a vigorous contest, cheered on by thousands of spectators at the stadium and millions watching on television. In some ways, political parties resemble professional sports teams. First, they compete in public battles that only one side can win. Second, the handful of professionals on the field, the ice, or the hardwood rely on a much larger group of people behind the scenes, without whose hard work the games could not happen. Third, a pro franchise has to pull in millions of dollars a year to stay in business, as does a major national party. Fourth, dozens of reporters and commentators make careers out of covering and speculating about the fates of the teams. Finally, none of this high-profile activity could happen without the fans—hundreds of thousands of ordinary people who spend a little of their time and money watching and cheering for "their" team.

There is, of course, one huge difference between sports teams and political parties: the latter are essential ingredients in democratic politics and government. Nearly every member of Canada's legislative branch is either elected or appointed on the basis of party affiliation.[1] The job of prime minister, the key figure in both the legislative and executive branches of government, goes to the leader of the largest party in the House of Commons. The other members of the political executive also belong to that party (there is no tradition of coalition government in Canada; see p. 464). When the House is sitting, the leaders of the various official parties are the stars of the daily Question Period drama. Even outside the House, party leaders are the most prominent players in media coverage of Canadian politics. Party organizations bridge the gap between national political institutions and local issues; to some extent, they express the various ideologies and values within the electorate. In sum, Canadian politics as we know it cannot function without political parties.

Despite their importance, Canada's major parties are losing their supporters. Whereas a successful pro sports franchise can generally sustain its fan base over the years (even a not-so-successful one, like the Toronto Maple Leafs), it seems that parties cannot. Across the Western world, citizens are turning away from the organizations that dominated politics in previous generations. This disaffection with political parties is particularly marked among young people, in Canada as elsewhere.[2] With fewer members in the constituencies, Canada's major parties are losing their ability to mobilize voters, engage citizens in the political process, and link the institutions of government to the people. Those who want to make a difference are increasingly drawn to advocacy groups and single-issue movements, which cannot perform the functions that parties do. The views of some senior Canadian party officials were summarized in a recent paper:

> While [parties] retain some capacity to bring people into the democratic system and—by and large—do elections well, their capacity to be more than electoral machines has severely declined . . . they have constructed a 'potemkin village' of sorts in the theatre of the nation's capital but . . . outside Ottawa, the presence of parties is illusory. While they may project an image of national organizations with reach into every community and a capacity to generate ideas, prepare candidates for office, and run elections, in reality, most parties have little capacity to sustain their organizations much beyond the central office. In the words of one participant, "parties today are weak, hollow shells—unable to discharge their democratic obligation to their supporters or the electorate."[3]

One possible reason for this decline is that parties are no longer providing the incentives necessary to attract and retain active members (which we will examine in this chapter), or that those incentives are less appealing to a postmaterialist generation. Alternatively, Canadian parties may not perceive the need to recruit as many members as they once did, because they have become purely electoralist organizations (Dossier 11.2). If the latter is the case, then our party officials are sadly short-sighted. Vibrant party organizations offer important long-term benefits, not just to the leaders and candidates seeking office, but to the political community as a whole. If Canadians are really as concerned about accountability as they claim, they should flock to the only organizations that can give them any control over the political executive and the legislative branch.

> Citizens may wish to see strong political parties capable of competing with public opinion surveys and focus groups in shaping new initiatives and policy positions for party leaders, but they are not prepared to make the effort to help this process. Fewer and fewer of them want to be involved with political parties, and volunteer political activity is no longer regarded as a civic virtue or something to be valued by society. In fact, it is quite the opposite.[4]

Before we examine the causes of Canada's party malaise, we will take a brief look at recent developments in our national **party system** (Dossier 11.1). Then we will examine the structures, members, and functions of political parties, followed by a description of Canada's past and present party systems.

Canada's national party system has been in flux since the 1993 federal election. The major changes are summarized here, to provide context for the rest of the chapter:

- The number of official parties in the House of Commons rose from three in the 1980s to five in the 1990s.[5] The Progressive Conservative (PC) Party of Canada, which had governed since 1984, fell apart in 1993. Two of the key groups in its electoral coalition defected to new parties: Quebec nationalists flocked to the Bloc Québécois (BQ), while Western populists and social conservatives switched to the Reform Party of Canada.

- What remained of the PC Party spent the next decade struggling to survive. In 2003, it merged with the Canadian Alliance (the successor to the Reform Party of Canada[6]) to create the Conservative Party of Canada. (See Dossier 11.5.) After the 2006 election, there were four official parties in the House: the Conservatives, the Liberal Party of Canada, the New Democratic Party (NDP) of Canada, and the BQ.

- The brand new Conservative Party suffered from growing pains in the 2004 election campaign. Its lack of policy allowed the Liberals to paint the party as too right-wing, too pro-American, and a threat to cherished Canadian values (notably medicare). Its leader (Stephen Harper, the former head of the Canadian Alliance) was perceived by many voters as aloof and ideologically extreme. The new party had hoped to do better than its two founding parties had done in 2000; it did win a few more seats in 2004, but its vote share was several percentage points lower than the combined Alliance and PC vote shares had been. The party's future, and that of its disappointed leader, looked bleak. Conservative fortunes turned around in 2006, partly because the party ran on a relatively moderate (yet detailed) platform and partly because of growing public anger at the

Liberals. In the 2006 election, the Conservative Party managed to win 21 more seats than the Liberals and form a minority government. Its share of the vote was still slightly less than the combined total of its founding parties (see Table 11.4), but the Liberals lost enough support to give the Conservatives a chance to govern. In the 2008 election the Conservatives managed to equal the 38 percent of the vote won by the PC and Alliance parties in 2000. However, this improvement is an illusion caused by a sharp drop in voter turnout: the Conservatives actually won fewer votes in 2008 than they had in 2006. They took 66 more seats than the Liberals.

- The Liberals' 2006 defeat followed four consecutive victories (1993, 1997, 2000, and 2004). Between 1993 and 2004, the party held a majority of the seats in the Commons. Following the 2000 election, former Prime Minister Jean Chrétien was forced to step down; supporters of his long-time Finance minister, Paul Martin, had seized control of the party on the ground and most of the party in public office. When Martin won the leadership in 2003, he replaced the staff at the central office with his own team—a group of loyal strategists nicknamed "the Board." Lingering bitterness between the Chrétien and Martin camps, and the perceived incompetence of Martin and his staff, worsened the political damage inflicted by the Sponsorship Scandal. The Conservative merger deprived the Liberals of their greatest political advantage: a divided opposition. The Liberals were reduced to a minority in 2004, and lost power altogether in 2006. In the 2008 election, the Liberals received their lowest share of the national vote in Canadian history (26 percent) and only one-quarter of the seats in Parliament (77/308).

- Like the PCs, the federal NDP flirted with extinction after the 1993 election. Both parties were sustained by their provincial wings and by financial support from loyal

(continued)

donors (corporations and labour unions, respectively). The NDP made a comeback in 1997, and has since returned to its pre-1993 levels of voting support. Although it remains the smallest **caucus** in the House of Commons, the party managed to punch above its electoral weight in the 2004–2006 Martin Government.

- The BQ, founded in 1990, formed the official Opposition with 54 seats after the 1993 election. The Reform Party of Canada took 52 seats. The two parties switched places in 1997, with Reform moving past the BQ into second place behind the Liberals. The Reform Party disappeared in 2000 (becoming the Canadian Alliance). The BQ is still in Parliament, although its vote share in Quebec—the only province where it runs candidates—has fluctuated considerably. The party's worst performances, in terms of votes, occurred in 2006 and 2008; in the latter election, it took only 38 percent of the provincial vote. However, it won a considerable share of seats in the Commons, largely because of our single-member plurality electoral system (Chapter 12).

WHAT IS A POLITICAL PARTY?

The way in which we choose to define the phrase "political party" reveals much about our attitudes toward politics. For the framers of the American *Constitution*, "party" was synonymous with "faction": a divisive and self-seeking body of men whose pursuit of power threatened the unity of the emerging state.[7] This definition implies a negative view of partisanship. More recent definitions of parties generally reflect a more positive attitude, emphasizing the centrality of political parties to representative democracy. According to one leading Canadian scholar:

> *Parties are, first and foremost, organizations which hinge a society to its institutions of government. In democracies they are the channels which structure and deliver the ideas and leaders thrown up by the social order, and the vehicles which organize the political face of the government. National party systems inevitably reflect the society that has spawned them and the institutions within which they live and work.*[8]

Most such definitions are incomplete. They focus on one or two aspects of parties—in the above quotation, their role as intermediaries between the electorate and the state—while omitting others. Parties are not just creatures of their political systems; they are also organizations in their own right, whose leaders and members are motivated by considerations other than "reflecting their society."

The following definition emphasizes these motivations, linking them to the incentives set by our political institutions: *A **political party** is an organization of members who work together to achieve one or more common goals, one of which is the election of candidates to public office.* If we break down this definition into its component parts, we can gain a clearer understanding of what parties are, what they do, and why they do it:

- *An organization:* Parties are more or less stable institutions with their own formal constitutions and bylaws, and their own informal rules of behaviour. They operate at two distinct levels: national (the parliamentary party, central office, and the party executive) and local (the constituency associations). Although this implies that the local constituency parties are the "lower" level in the party hierarchy, it does not mean that they are unimportant. In fact, "the constituency association remains at the core of Canadian parties."[9]
- *of members:* Canadian parties have fewer members than parties in most other Western democracies.[10] Roughly 2 percent of Canadian voters belong to a party at any given time;[11] approximately 16 percent have held a party membership at some point in their lives.[12] Of those who have never belonged to a political party, 89 percent claim that they have never considered doing so.[13] Party members are more likely to be white, male, middle-aged,

prosperous, and highly educated than the average Canadian voter.[14] They are also more interested in politics than most people, and more likely to have clear ideological principles.[15] However, this interest does not always translate into active involvement. More than three-quarters of respondents to a recent survey of Canadian party members reported that they had spent three hours or less on party activity in the preceding month, while more than a third had not attended a single party meeting or function in the previous year.[16]

- *who work together:* At the grassroots level, parties are essentially social organizations that bring people together in a common cause. Team spirit, friendship, and the adrenaline of competition drive political parties, more than ideology or the fruits of power.
- *to achieve one or more common goals, one of which is the election of candidates to public office:* All political parties pursue two overriding goals: to win votes and to maintain their organizational health. Beyond this generalization, the goals of parties vary (Dossier 11.2).[17]

DOSSIER 11.2 Catch-all and Programmatic Parties

Until recently, most scholars divided Canadian parties into two types: brokerage or cadre, and missionary or ideological. The federal Liberal and Progressive Conservative parties were considered to be brokerage parties; the New Democratic Party (NDP), Bloc Québécois (BQ) and Reform Party were missionary parties. Each type of party supposedly had a distinct structure, membership, funding base, and primary goal:

- Brokerage/cadre parties were described as dominated by the party in public office; they had small and inactive memberships, at least between elections, and they relied on corporations for much of their revenue. Their overriding goal was to win power by appealing to a broad spectrum of the electorate, fudging any ideological or policy principles that could alienate potential voters.
- Missionary/ideological parties were believed to be more internally democratic, placing the ultimate authority over policy in the hands of their members. Those members were more numerous and more continuously active than those in brokerage/cadre parties, and they provided most of the party's funding. They targeted a relatively narrow segment of the electorate.

These categories are no longer valid, for at least four reasons. First, a survey of party members found that the NDP and Reform grassroots were *less* active in party affairs than their PC and Liberal counterparts, at least between elections.[18] This directly contradicts the assumptions underlying the brokerage/missionary distinction. Second, the structures of our national parties are more similar than the old model implies, because all Canadian parties are shaped by the same institutional incentives.

Third, as we will see in the "Party Financing" section of this chapter, Bill C-24 has largely eliminated the differences in funding sources among Canada's major parties. Before the law took effect in 2004, the parties did conform to the classic model: the NDP received most of its donations from unions; the BQ and Reform (and, to a lesser extent, the Canadian Alliance) relied on individual donors; and the old brokerage parties benefited from corporate generosity, especially when they were in power. The 2004 prohibition on corporate and union donations, and the introduction of public subsidies to registered parties, all but eliminated the differences in the parties' funding sources (assuming that the parties' financial disclosures are complete and accurate).

Fourth and finally, the conventional categories have been rendered obsolete by a growing diversity of party types in the past two decades. The old models, based on the experience of Western Europe and the Anglo-American states, do not always fit the new democracies in Eastern Europe, Africa, Asia, and Latin America. When viewed in a global context, the differences among Canadian parties appear less significant than they did in the 1960s and 1970s.

(continued)

All of our major parties belong in the same category: the modern electoralist party.[19]

Parties belonging to this genus are organizationally thin, maintaining a relatively skeletal existence (the offices and staffs supporting their parliamentary groups notwithstanding). At election time, however, these parties spring into action to perform what is unequivocally their primary function, the conduct of the campaign. They utilize "modern" campaign techniques (stressing television and the mass-communications media over the mobilization of party members and affiliated organizations), and they rely heavily on professionals who can skilfully carry out such campaigns. The personal attractiveness of the party's candidates is an important criterion for nomination at the expense of other considerations, such as length of service to, or formal organizational position within, the party.[20]

The electoralist "genus" includes two distinct party "species": **catch-all** and **programmatic.**[21] The catch-all party strongly resembles the classic "brokerage" model:

The overriding (if not sole) purpose of catch-all parties is to maximize votes, win elections and govern. To do so, they seek to aggregate as wide a variety of social interests as possible. . . . catch-all parties will seek to maximize votes by positioning themselves toward the centre of the spectrum, appearing moderate in their policy preferences and behaviour. In an effort to expand their electoral appeal to a wide variety of groups, their policy orientations are eclectic and shift with the public mood. Lacking an explicit ideology, catch-all parties tend to emphasize the attractive personal attributes of their candidates, and nominations are largely determined by the electoral resources of the candidates rather than by such organizational criteria as years of experience in, or service to, the party, or position within key factions within the party.[22]

This passage captures the main features of the Liberal Party of Canada and its former rival, the PC Party.

Until the 2006 election campaign, the Conservative Party of Canada struggled to complete the transition from programmatic to electoralist. A programmatic party—like the old Reform Party—"has much more of a distinct, consistent and coherent programmatic or ideological agenda than does the ideal-type catch-all party, and it clearly incorporates those ideological or programmatic appeals in its electoral campaigns and its legislative and government agenda."[23] Although the Conservatives are trying to win a majority government, which requires them to construct a broad electoral coalition, their electoral strategy is more divisive than catch-all (Dossier 12.3). The NDP and the BQ are also programmatic parties, although neither has had the chance to enact a "legislative and government agenda" (except, to a limited degree, in the post-2004 minority Parliaments).

The old brokerage/missionary distinction is still accurate in one respect: each type of party pursues a different mix of goals. For catch-all parties, the primary goal is to form a government by electing more MPs than any other party. Programmatic parties, especially those which have no realistic hope of power, may focus instead on promoting their distinct principles and policy priorities. The Reform Party originally spoke for Western protest, populism and social conservatism; the New Democratic Party (like its predecessor, the Co-operative Commonwealth Federation or CCF) promotes a social-democratic approach to government. (The NDP has never come close to forming a national government, although it has held power in four provinces at various times.) As we will see later in this chapter, there is no such thing as a party with a single goal; every party organization is divided among members with differing priorities. Our focus here is the primary goal of the party elites in the caucus and central office. In this respect, the Conservative Party of Canada is clearly a catch-all party—despite the persistence of a strongly programmatic sect within the membership.[24]

PARTY STRUCTURES IN CANADA

The structures of Canada's major national parties are summarized in Table 11.1.

While the three elements of party organization (the far left column of Table 11.1) exist in every democratic state, their specific forms and the relationships among them vary with the unique constitutional and political arrangements in each country. Like all political organizations, Canadian political parties are shaped by institutional incentives:

TABLE 11.1   THE THREE STRUCTURAL ELEMENTS OF CANADIAN PARTIES[25]

PARTY ORGANIZATION ELEMENTS	COMPONENTS	DESCRIPTION	PRIMARY TASKS
Extraparliamentary party (also called the party on the ground, or the "grassroots")	Biennial national convention	Officially the highest authority in the party organization	Meets every two years to pass policy resolutions and elect the national executive
	Leader	Elected by party members either directly (OMOV)* or via delegates to a leadership convention	Fundraises, spearheads election campaigns, maintains volunteer morale
	National executive	Elected by delegates to the national convention; includes representatives from the various sections of the party (e.g., provincial wings, women's and youth clubs, caucus)	Meets at least once a year to manage the business of the party between conventions; delegates most decision-making to committees, party headquarters, and other small groups
	Constituency associations	Operate in every constituency where the party wishes to run a candidate for the House of Commons; run by an executive elected by the membership	Recruit and nominate candidates for the House of Commons, raise funds, organize the "ground war"
Parliamentary party (the party in public office)	Leader	Elected by the party members, either directly (OMOV) or via delegates to a leadership convention	In government, defends the ruling party in Question Period as prime minister; in Opposition, leads the charge against the government
	Caucus leaders	House leaders (Commons and Senate), whips, caucus chair	Maintain cohesion and discipline within the caucus, keep the leader informed about the mood of the MPs and senators
	Leader's office and parliamentary staff	Usually party members, often recruited from the youth wing or campus clubs	Communicate with the constituency, organize events, coordinate political activities within the caucus

(continued)

PARTY ORGANIZATION ELEMENTS	COMPONENTS	DESCRIPTION	PRIMARY TASKS
Central office	National headquarters	Run by a national director, usually appointed by and accountable to the leader; normally a small permanent staff that expands before and during general elections and shrinks afterward	Clerical staff keep track of party memberships and other paperwork; organizers prepare for conventions and other major events; technical experts in communications, polling, and political strategy plan and execute national election campaigns (the leader's tour and "air war")
	Official agency	A volunteer board of directors with a small permanent staff; usually located at national headquarters	Records all financial transactions of the national party and discloses them to Elections Canada, submits an annual report for each fiscal year and a separate report after a general election, ensures compliance with the *Canada Elections Act*

*OMOV: One member, one vote

- Canada's parliamentary institutions reward parties that can elect large numbers of MPs and organize them into stable, cohesive caucuses. The party with the most seats forms the government and its leader becomes prime minister, but only as long as its MPs are prepared to support the party's policies and leader. The incentive to stay in power, or to gain power, usually produces a powerful sense of unity and "team spirit" within a parliamentary party.

- Within the government caucus, the Cabinet system concentrates power in the hands of the prime minister. Although leader dominance is less pronounced in the Opposition parties, other factors—including the regulatory requirements of the *Canada Elections Act*, the news media's focus on individual personalities, and the influence of party leaders on voting behaviour—reinforce the authority of Opposition leaders within their respective parties.

- Federalism has shaped the **extraparliamentary** structures of our older parties.[26] There are provincial Liberal and New Democratic parties across Canada, which compete to form provincial governments. There are also Progressive Conservative parties in several provinces. The 2005 Conservative constitution states that "The Party shall promote and maintain relationships with existing provincial conservative parties."[27] Conflicts between the national and provincial wings are common, especially when both are in government. In April 2007, for example, PC Premier Danny Williams of Newfoundland and Labrador launched an advertising campaign attacking Conservative Prime Minister Harper for allegedly breaking a promise on equalization payments to his province.[28] (See Chapter 4.) In general, the sometimes testy relationships between the federal and provincial governments have strained the internal structures of Canadian parties.

- Canada's **electoral system** divides the country into 308 separate constituencies, each of which elects one MP to the House of Commons. Consequently, our extraparliamentary parties are divided into as many as 308 local organizations, one for each constituency where they wish to run candidates. The strong tradition of localism, which predated Confederation, is thus preserved by the structure imposed by the electoral system—and perhaps reinforced by the "franchise" structure discussed on the next page, which allows Canadian parties to manage the conflict between the demands of national cohesion and the realities of local decentralization.[29]

- Finally, the *Canada Elections Act* (CEA) affects the relationships among the various elements of the party structure. The Act regulates party financing, including the flows of money between the national and local parties. It also gives party leaders the power to veto candidates, if they choose. Most recently, relations between the national party office and the local associations have been affected by Bill C-24, *An Act to Amend the* Canada Elections Act *and the* Income Tax Act (*Political Financing*). The Bill, which took effect at the beginning of 2004, is discussed later in this chapter in the "Party Financing" section. As described later in this chapter, Bill C-24 recognized and regulated constituency associations, altered the financial balance between the national and local elements of party organization, and introduced legal rules for nomination and leadership contests.[30]

These institutional incentives have produced nearly identical structures in Canada's major parties. There are some minor differences in the composition of the parties' national conventions (the regular policy and organizational meetings, not leadership conventions discussed later in the chapter.) The NDP sets aside 20 to 25 percent of delegate positions for representatives of its affiliated trade union locals. It also awards delegate spots to constituency associations on a sliding scale relative to the size of the local membership, as does the BQ (and the former Canadian Alliance). The larger the association, the more delegates it can send. In the Liberal Party, each constituency association sends the same number of delegates, regardless of membership. At the same time, the Liberals, BQ, and New Democrats (like the former PCs) encourage women and young people (under age 30) to attend their conventions. As a result, delegates to those national conventions are, on average, younger and less overwhelmingly male than those who attended Reform and Alliance conventions, where no such accommodations were made.[31]

In theory, political parties are hierarchical organizations: there is a clear chain of command, with the leader and his or her inner circle at the top and the grassroots members somewhere near the bottom. This model of party structure, called the "Iron Law of Oligarchy,"[32] is somewhat overstated (at least in Canada). It is certainly true that the leader stands at the top of the pecking order: he or she has the final word on the candidates, platform, and campaign strategy; he or she hires and fires the staff in his or her office and party headquarters; and he or she leads the Commons caucus in Parliament. When his or her party is in government, the leader's power is at its height. As we saw in Part III, a prime minister has powerful tools to impose and enforce discipline within the parliamentary party. The Prime Minister's Office keeps tabs on government MPs, and makes sure they toe the line. The prime minister alone has the power to make or break political careers. Until recently, he or she could threaten to dissolve Parliament for a "snap" election, which was usually sufficient to quell serious rebellions; the introduction of "fixed" election dates in 2007 reduced this power significantly (Dossier 12.1).

However, a prime minister who is perceived as a bully will eventually alienate the grassroots of the party. Jean Chrétien ran the Liberal Party with an iron fist, tightly controlling the caucus and the central office.[33] Eventually this leadership style generated a backlash, which was cleverly exploited by rival Paul Martin and his supporters. They gradually took over the party on the ground and built support in the caucus. In 2002, they forced Chrétien to announce that he would retire in 2004 (he actually left in late 2003). This is an extreme version of a universal problem for governing parties: the Cabinet is responsible, not to the party membership, but to the population as a whole. In consequence, the policy preferences of the grassroots membership are, at best, a minor consideration. Over time, the perception that the party in public office is ignoring the party on the ground erodes the organizational base, and leaves the governing party vulnerable to electoral defeat. This phenomenon reminds us of one enduring truth about Canadian political parties: the importance of committed and active members on the ground.

Notwithstanding the power of Canadian party leaders, the various components of the party structure are more autonomous than those in smaller, unitary states. The decentralizing effects of federalism and the electoral system, combined with the sheer size and diversity of the country, require flexible party structures.[34] The central party elite—the leader, the party in public office, and the national headquarters—make decisions for the party as a whole, while the constituency associations implement those decisions in ways which fit their local conditions. This "franchise"[35] model of party organization combines a national "brand name," advertising strategy, and "product line" (policy and leadership) with local "product delivery" (candidate nomination and campaigning) attuned to the regional "market."[36] Constituency associations choose the party's candidates for the House of Commons (subject to some central control, as we will see) and provide the necessary services to secure their election. All candidates are expected to use the party logo on their campaign signs and literature, and to "sell" the party **platform.** In exchange, they benefit from the expertise of the headquarters staff, well-researched policies, and (ideally) a popular national leader. Coordinating the national and local campaigns—often called the "air war" and the "ground war," respectively—is always a challenge for party strategists (Chapter 12). There is a persistent tension between local autonomy and the need for "message discipline" in the era of 24-hour news coverage of election campaigns. This is only one of the fault lines within Canadian parties, as we will see in the following section.

PARTY MEMBERSHIP IN CANADA: INCENTIVES AND NETWORKS

If political parties are shaped by the incentives set by Canada's political institutions, they also provide incentives for their own members. Despite the growing presence of paid staff at national headquarters, Canadian parties are essentially volunteer organizations. They cannot force their members to behave in particular ways. They must find other ways to attract and reward hard-working activists, while discouraging them from damaging the party through divisive or self-seeking actions.

The organizational health of a party depends on the willingness of talented individuals to donate their time and money over a period of years or decades. What motivates people to join and remain in political parties?

Incentives for Party Members

Successful parties offer four types of incentive to attract and retain members:
1. **Material incentives:** tangible rewards for loyal service (e.g., a seat in the Senate);
2. **Specific solidary incentives:** intangible benefits that are awarded to a few select individuals (e.g., a high-ranking volunteer position in the party);
3. **Collective solidary/social incentives:** intangible rewards available to all party members (the joy of victory, the satisfaction of working together for a shared goal, and the social value of meeting like-minded people), combined with the motivation to impress friends or family members who support the party; and
4. **Purposive/altruistic incentives:** the sense that one is contributing to the greater good by working to elect one's party of choice.[37]

In Canada, the material incentives for party membership—which are usually lumped together, with a sneer, as **"patronage"**—are less important than many people realize. In the first place, they are available only to members of the governing party. Many Canadians join parties that have little hope of ever forming a government, either national or provincial. In the second place, there are relatively few patronage positions available, and most are awarded to individuals with professional qualifications (for example, only lawyers can become judges). At the local level, some volunteers used to receive short-term contracts to enumerate voters at the start of election campaigns; that reward for loyal service was abolished when the National Register of Electors was established in 2000.[38] So material incentives, which were once the glue that held our national parties together,[39] are now relatively unimportant for most partisans. Liberal party members are the exception;[40] they are more likely than members of other parties to seek tangible rewards for party service.

Specific solidary incentives exist in every party, regardless of size or electoral success. As we saw in Dossier 1.4, political institutions are most effective when they can channel the ambition of individuals into constructive activity. Political parties harness ambition by creating opportunities for prestige and influence. At the local level, a party member can aspire to—or, in less active organizations, be forced to accept—the presidency of his or her constituency association or a nomination for public office. At the higher reaches of the party organization, a member can pursue a place on the national executive or a seat on the board of the fundraising agency. Informal selective incentives, such as the attention of the leader, are also important. When the leader pays a visit and greets a local member by name, that member feels important and valued. Wise party leaders, especially those in Opposition who can offer few other incentives, tour the country as often as possible to strengthen the links between the "franchise holders" and the centre. Those who neglect the local activists may become especially vulnerable to hostile factions.

Collective solidary incentives are particularly important for many new recruits. Successful constituency associations organize as many social events as possible, partly to keep their existing members involved and partly to attract newcomers (the "bring a friend" approach).[41] Most new members are recruited during leadership contests and local nomination battles, although it appears that few of these **"instant" members** become committed party activists.[42] Personal ties are an important draw for some new members. Aspiring nominees for Parliament often sell memberships to friends and relatives from outside the party in an effort to boost their share of the vote.[43] Contrary to conventional wisdom, however, most Canadian partisans—especially members of programmatic parties—take the initiative to join a party without being asked.[44] Moreover, members who join for purposive/altruistic reasons are more likely to remain active in the party than those who take out membership cards because a friend or relative asked them to do so.

■ Categories of Party Members

In broad terms, party members can be divided into the inactive majority and the active minority. Within the latter category, there are two primary groups: **"believers" and "careerists."**[45] Believers are motivated by commitment to the party's principles and policies, emotional identification with the party as an organization, or admiration for its leader. They respond to the collective solidary/social and purposive/altruistic incentives just described. Careerists are more self-seeking. Their chief motivations are material (patronage positions) and specific solidary (status within the party hierarchy, business contacts, and the respect of their fellow partisans). In practice, most active party members pursue a mix of these goals. Members may be drawn to join the party by its policies and ideology, and later come to enjoy the personal rewards of status or networking. Nonetheless, it is possible to distinguish the two types by observing parties at work. Some members devote endless hours to "the cause" without seeking recognition for their efforts, while others are driven by personal ambition.

A successful party must attract and retain both types of members, and give each the rewards they seek. Unfortunately for party leaders, conflict between them is a fact of life. For example, the NDP suffers from persistent tensions between believers who want to take the party further to the left, and careerists—many of them veterans of NDP provincial governments, who have experienced the pleasures of power—who want the party to move closer to the political centre.

A different problem arises when the balance between believers and careerists is incompatible with the goals of the party elite, as the federal PC Party discovered in the 1970s and 1980s. The Liberals dominated Canada's federal politics in the twentieth century (see Table 11.4). Their main rivals, the Progressive Conservatives, were usually relegated to the Opposition benches. Over time, ambitious people who were motivated primarily by power and patronage gravitated to the Liberals. (Recall that Liberals are more susceptible to material incentives than other partisans.) The PCs tended to attract members who adhered to particular principles, or who simply felt more comfortable criticizing the government for its failings than building constructive alternatives. By the early 1980s, this **"minority party syndrome"** had seriously weakened the internal unity of the Progressive Conservative Party and diminished the pool of talented people willing to serve as candidates and party officers.[46] The party was caught in a vicious circle: recurring outbreaks of internal conflict reduced its electoral appeal, thwarting the catch-all ambitions of the leadership and perpetuating its Opposition status.

On the Liberal side, the high proportion of careerists is a blessing when the party is in power and a curse following an election defeat. Careerists are more likely to desert their party when the rewards of power are unavailable, taking their talents elsewhere. Shortly after the 1984 federal election, in which the Liberals were humiliated by the Progressive Conservatives, the Ontario Liberal Party formed a minority government with the support of the provincial NDP. Senior Liberal advisers, fundraisers, and organizers left Ottawa for Toronto, as the national party struggled to rebuild its organization and finances. Without a clear set of principles, the catch-all Liberals had few incentives to offer. Meanwhile, the proportion of careerists in the PC party grew during the party's nine years in power.[47] Many of the remaining "believers" defected to the new Reform Party and the BQ, leaving the PCs vulnerable to catastrophe in the 1993 election.

A successful party needs a "critical mass" of both believers and careerists—the former to sustain the party during the lean times and preserve its ideals, and the latter to inject a note of pragmatism and discipline—and it must harness the conflicting motivations of the two groups. Therefore, parties need to offer different incentives to different types of members. Finding the right mix is a constant challenge for party elites.

■ Party Networks

The formal divisions within party structures, summarized in Table 11.1, are complicated by informal divisions among **party networks.**[48] These cliques form in a particular region, or coalesce around particular leaders, interests, or ideologies. They vary in size, in their degree of organization, and in their longevity.

- Every national party is divided into regional networks, some more hostile to central control than others. As we have seen, tensions between Ottawa and the provinces can translate into conflict between a party's national organization and one or more of its provincial organizations. Even in the absence of such external influences, regional or provincial party networks often disagree on questions of policy and organizational structure. These disagreements arise from the varying political cultures of Canada's provincial electorates, as well as the differences in economic structure and resources.

- Leadership contests create new networks and reinvigorate old ones. When a candidate loses, his or her network can survive for years, waiting hopefully for a second chance. The patience of the candidate and his or her supporters eventually runs out, causing the leaders of the network to undermine the unity of the party as a whole. These disruptive networks are often called "factions."[49]
- The caucus constitutes a distinct network within the party, as do the paid staff at party headquarters and the various consultants who work for the party on contract. While they do not agree on everything, they do have their own shared interests arising from their respective positions vis-à-vis the leader, and they work hard to defend those interests.
- The leader's entourage is yet another network, although its membership usually overlaps with other groups (e.g., MPs, party staff, and strategists).[50]
- Networks based on a shared ideology are called "sects."[51] The members of a sect believe that "the party should redefine its basic objectives, perhaps by revising an existing doctrine or reviving a neglected tradition or even by adopting new ideas more suited to the party's circumstances."[52]

An individual party member may belong to two or more networks at the same time. As long as the various networks cut across each other, factional strife is generally manageable. Indeed, networks can actually strengthen a party organization, because they often bring people together from different structural elements.[53] The insurgent campaign that toppled Chrétien and brought Paul Martin to the Liberal leadership began with a few parliamentary staffers, Young Liberals, and a handful of MPs. It eventually grew to encompass members of the national executive, consultants, riding association presidents, and a majority of the caucus. The bitter contest between the Martin and Chrétien forces divided the party in some respects, while uniting each camp internally. But had the split between the two networks reinforced the structural division between two distinct elements of the party structure—e.g., pitting the entire caucus against the constituency activists—it could have threatened the long-term integrity of the party organization.

Conflict among the various networks within a party is usually managed internally; when it bursts into the open, the impact on voter perceptions is invariably negative.[54] A party that appears unable to govern itself will have difficulty persuading voters to trust it to govern them. Public disunity also makes potential donors reluctant to open their wallets and drives away the local activists whose volunteer labour makes election campaigns possible. (See the discussion of the informal rules of Canadian elections in Chapter 12.)

FUNCTIONS OF CANADIAN PARTIES

Nominating Candidates

Every institution provides a structure of opportunities for those who aspire to join its ranks and to achieve a higher status within it (Dossier 1.1). The opportunity structure for a Canadian who aspires to national political office begins in a local party constituency association. To become an MP, one must first be nominated as a candidate in a federal election. Except in rare cases, that means securing the support of a major political party. In the 2008 federal election, a total of 1601 candidates representing 19 parties, together with 68 independents and four candidates with no party affiliation,[55] contested the 308 seats in the House of Commons. Eighty percent of the party candidates, and all but two of the independent and unaffiliated candidates, were defeated. So while winning a party's nomination does not guarantee victory—except in the dwindling number of "safe" party seats[56]—candidates who lack the endorsement of a major party have almost no chance of winning.[57]

Given the importance of nomination in the political opportunity structure, one might expect the process of candidate selection to be highly competitive and well regulated. In many Western democracies, this is indeed the case. But in Canada, there are surprisingly few formal rules for constituency associations.[58] The broad outlines of the process are simple: the constituency association holds a nomination meeting before every general election (and before a by-election, if that seat happens to be vacant).[59] All party members in the constituency are entitled to attend the meeting and vote for their preferred contestant. The parties themselves are left to determine who can become a member, and which members are entitled to vote at the meeting.[60] Once the date of the meeting has been set, there are few formal rules to deter nomination contestants or their supporters from engaging in "dirty tricks." Examples include giving an opponent's supporters incorrect information about the time and place of the meeting, or bussing in hundreds of people with no prior party involvement to vote for "their" contestant.

The parties (national or local) are also free to decide who is qualified to become a candidate, subject to the requirement of Canadian citizenship. All of the major parties pre-screen potential nomination contestants, requiring them to complete detailed questionnaires about their personal and employment histories. The purpose of this exercise is not to determine who is best qualified to become an MP, but to weed out aspirants with potentially embarrassing skeletons in the closet.[61] The completed questionnaires are reviewed by nominating committees; these can be located at the national headquarters, in provincial wings, in the local constituency, or a combination.[62] Any potential candidate who does not meet with the committee's approval can be prohibited from running for the nomination.

Likewise, the conduct of the voting is left for the parties to determine. Some associations use preferential (ordinal) ballots. Others use the method employed at a leadership convention: successive rounds of balloting, with the last-place finisher eliminated each time, until one contestant receives a majority (50 percent plus 1) of the votes.[63] These provisions are rarely used: between two-thirds and three-quarters of nomination meetings feature a single candidate, who wins by acclamation.[64] Sitting MPs enjoy an especially easy road to renomination: almost 90 percent are acclaimed.[65] These figures contradict the public impression, arising from media coverage of hard-fought nomination contests, that Canadian party nominations are subject to intense competition.[66] Given that a constituency nomination meeting is the first step on the political ladder, the shortage of aspirants is surprising. (It might become easier to attract potential candidates in future elections with fixed dates; see Dossier 12.1.)

In recent years, the leader and the party in central office have exerted increasing control over the process. This is partly to avoid embarrassment (the questionnaires previously mentioned), and partly to make it more difficult for single-issue and ethnic groups to flood constituency associations and impose their own candidates. The typical Canadian constituency association has slightly more than 500 members. Only about one-third of the association's membership typically attends a nomination meeting, making these meetings susceptible to takeover by "instant" members.[67]

Since 1970, when party labels were added to the ballots in federal elections, the CEA requires the party leader to endorse the nomination papers of his or her candidates. The ability to veto candidates gave party leaders a powerful tool to ensure the nomination of their preferred candidates. The Liberal Party of Canada enhanced this power in 1992, by giving its leader the prerogative to appoint candidates over the heads of their constituency associations. Former Prime Minister Chrétien appointed several "star" candidates in 1993 and 1997, including several women; despite some local resistance, most of his hand-picked nominees won their seats. Paul Martin revived this practice in the 2004 election, appointing "star" candidates in several Ontario and British Columbia ridings. His choice of hockey legend Ken Dryden in York Centre was widely applauded,[68] but the "parachute" candidates in British Columbia were greeted with dismay by local Liberals.[69]

When Bill C-24 took effect at the start of 2004, it subjected local nomination contests to state regulation for the first time. The new law did not apply to the definition of party membership, the qualifications of candidates, or the conduct of nomination meetings; it merely extended certain elements of the party finance regime (spending limits, disclosure, and agency) to nomination contests. We might conclude that the parties in Parliament are reluctant to impose legally binding rules on their own internal procedures.

Although the refusal to regulate most aspects of candidate nomination is consistent with the Canadian tradition of constituency autonomy,[70] it overlooks the importance of candidate nomination in the electoral process. In the first place, we rely on parties to choose qualified candidates for public office; if they fail to do so, there is no other mechanism of "quality control." In the second place, candidate nomination is a core function of political parties. If it can be easily usurped by outside groups, we might well ask why parties should receive large public subsidies and other state benefits. Finally, "The methods by which the candidates are selected influence their behaviour as parliamentarians."[71] For example, once elected to Parliament, a candidate who owes his nomination to "instant" members from a particular group may find it difficult to work with his constituency association and his caucus colleagues.

Selecting Leaders

The process of choosing party leaders demonstrates the importance of incentives and opportunity structures in political institutions. Different selection methods tend to favour different types of candidate. For the first half-century following Confederation, national party leaders were chosen by the caucus. Leaders headed the parliamentary wing of the party; it seemed natural that they would be chosen from among the MPs who supported their policies. "Leaders chosen by a parliamentary caucus are more likely to be recruited from within those circles, and will often have served long legislative apprenticeships."[72] Allowing MPs (and senators) to choose the party leader rewarded long-serving parliamentarians and Cabinet ministers, which gave aspiring leaders a strong incentive to channel their ambitions into public service.

In the early twentieth century caucus selection gave way to **leadership conventions.** A leadership convention is a gathering of delegates, chosen in the same way as delegates to regular national conventions (recall the discussion of delegate categories in "Party Structures in Canada").[73] The delegates meet the candidates, listen to speeches, and finally mark their ballots. Only those with delegate status may vote; other party members have no role in the process, apart from electing their representatives to the convention.

The Liberals held the first national leadership convention in 1919, shortly after the death of Sir Wilfrid Laurier, while the party was still recovering from the disastrous French–English split over conscription.[74] Had the choice of a leader to replace Laurier been left to the Liberal caucus, most of whose members were francophone Quebeckers, the party's efforts to reconstruct its electoral alliance between French and English would have been seriously jeopardized. After the winner, Mackenzie King, led the Liberals to victory in the 1921 federal election, the Conservative Party decided that leadership conventions were politically advantageous. The 1927 Conservative convention chose R.B. Bennett, who became prime minister three years later. CCF–NDP leaders were chosen at convention from the party's founding in 1933 until the early twenty-first century.[75]

Early conventions (1919–58) were small, elite-dominated, and rarely competitive. Beginning in 1967, leadership conventions were transformed into huge events with as many as a dozen candidates. As the number of constituency delegates mushroomed, the means by which they were chosen became increasingly controversial. Organizers for the various leadership candidates would invade each constituency, sign up as many "instant members" as they could, and bus them to the delegate selection meeting to vote for their candidate's "slate" of delegates. The outcome of a convention was decided long before the delegates arrived at the meeting hall, in the bitterly divisive "trench warfare" at the constituency level.[76] The news media focused on abuses of the process, including the mass recruitment of recent immigrants and allegations of beer parties for minors.

Since 1985, Canadian parties have gradually abandoned the leadership convention in favour of **one member, one vote (OMOV)** methods of leadership selection. In an OMOV system, every party member can vote directly for the leadership candidate of his or her choice. There are at least four reasons for this trend:[77]

1. Giving every member of the party the right to vote for the leader appears to be more "democratic" than a delegated convention.[78] It also satisfies grassroots demands for greater influence,[79] at least on the surface. (In reality, dispersing decision-making among thousands of grassroots members enhances the power of the party elite, by making it more difficult to hold the leader accountable.[80])
2. Advances in communication technology permit party members to vote from their homes, instead of travelling long distances to cast ballots at a convention.
3. The cost of attending a leadership convention—delegate registration, travel, accommodation, meals, and other expenses—have risen sharply in recent years. Under OMOV, a party member can vote inexpensively at home or in a local polling place.
4. The scandals surrounding "trench warfare" forced parties to find a less damaging way to choose their leaders. Most OMOV systems do not require delegate-selection meetings.

Among the major parties, only the Liberals continue to elect their leaders at national conventions. The Conservatives, NDP, and BQ allow all of their members to vote directly for the leadership candidates of their choice. Leadership selection was the most contentious issue in the 2003 merger negotiations between the PCs and the Canadian Alliance. Whereas the Alliance had used a straight OMOV procedure, the PCs weighted the votes to prevent a few large urban centres from determining the outcome. Instead of awarding the leadership to the candidate with the largest number of votes across the country, the party assigned 100 points to each constituency. These points were distributed among the leadership candidates in proportion to their share of the vote in that riding. Thus, a leadership candidate receiving 40 percent of the vote in a constituency would receive 40 points, a candidate receiving 30 percent of the vote would receive 30 points, and so on. The candidate who received a majority of the points was declared the winner.[81] After stiff resistance, the Canadian Alliance finally agreed to use the PC system to elect Conservative leaders; despite an attempt at the 2005 convention to go back to the Alliance system, the Conservatives have retained the weighted constituencies.[82]

The NDP was reluctant to move away from conventions, because OMOV conflicts with the unique relationship between the party and its affiliated unions. Under the old convention model, unions were guaranteed a specific percentage of the delegates. It is impossible to guarantee a specific percentage of the vote to a particular group when all members are empowered to cast ballots. Consequently, the NDP used a "hybrid" system in 1995. All party members were allowed to vote in "primaries" for the leader of their choice (one of which was restricted to union voters); the last-place finisher was dropped from the convention ballot, and the delegates were expected to reflect the primary results in their own decision-making. In the event, they ignored the membership at large.[83] The federal NDP subsequently decided to follow several of its provincial wings, adopting a straight OMOV system for its next leadership contest. Toronto city councillor Jack Layton won the 2003 contest by a convincing margin over longtime MP Bill Blaikie.

The federal Liberals have retained a hybrid system, combining a convention with an element of membership choice. When members gather to elect delegates to a leadership convention, they vote twice: once for their delegates, and once for the leadership candidate of their choice. The delegate spots from each riding are allocated among the candidates in rough proportion to their shares of the local vote. The Liberals' recent decision to retain the leadership convention[84] reminds us that the old "undemocratic" system of party leadership selection provides important benefits. Delegate positions are important specific solidary incentives for local party members. Conventions provide an opportunity for activists from across the country to network with one another and rub elbows with party celebrities. By bringing activists together from across the country, conventions strengthen the national party organization[85] and help to bridge the gap between partisans in different regions.

Perhaps most important, leadership conventions attract the attention of the media and the public. The suspense builds through each successive round of voting, as the last-place candidates are dropped from the ballot and the front-runner approaches a majority. There is high drama as the eliminated candidates announce whom they would support, and everyone waits to see how many of their voters will follow them. There are exceptions, notably the dull 2003 convention which anointed Paul Martin as Liberal leader; his first-ballot victory was such a foregone conclusion that the party seriously considered cancelling the vote altogether.[86] To generate excitement and media coverage—and to entice more delegates to show up[87]—the Liberals invited Bono (leader of the Irish rock band U2) to address the convention. The November 2006 convention marked a return to the good old days of drama (Dossier 11.3).

DOSSIER 11.3 The 2006 Liberal Leadership Convention

The race to succeed Paul Martin as Liberal leader was the most wide-open, unpredictable leadership contest the party had held since 1968. Eleven candidates registered with Elections Canada, although three dropped out before the convention.[88] From the very beginning of the race, in spring 2006, rookie Liberal MP Michael Ignatieff was perceived as the front-runner (although not to the same extent as Paul Martin in 2003). "Iggy" had the support of key Liberal organizers and power-brokers, who hailed the former Harvard professor and international human rights expert as an agent of party renewal and a possible throwback to Pierre Trudeau. Ignatieff had numerous other advantages: he is telegenic, articulate in both official languages, and well known in political and academic circles. He also suffered from two serious liabilities arising from his political inexperience: a penchant for making controversial comments (which he had difficulty "clarifying" afterward), and shallow roots in the Liberal Party. Finally, the fact that Ignatieff had spent most of his adult life in Britain and the United States raised serious questions about his commitment to and understanding of Canadian politics.

Ignatieff's main rival was former Ontario Premier Bob Rae. He, too, was a recent convert to the Liberal Party, having spent his entire political career in the NDP. In fact, the two men, who had been friends since university, had a lot in common: both were articulate, bilingual, and backed by prominent members of the party establishment (including numerous Liberal MPs and senators). The major difference was Rae's extensive political experience—although this proved to be a mixed blessing: his government was not fondly remembered in Canada's largest province (a crucial battleground for the federal Liberals), and his past attacks on the Liberal Party were also vivid in the minds of some delegates.

The high-profile battle between "Iggy" and "Bobby" dominated the media coverage of the race. The other candidates quietly toured the country, meeting Liberals and setting out their ideas on policy and party reform. No one really

(continued)

knew how the candidates stacked up until the end of September, when all of the delegate-selection meetings were held on one "Super Weekend." As expected, Ignatieff won more delegates than any other candidate, although his total of 30 percent fell below expectations. Rae finished 10 percentage points behind, a wider gap than his supporters had predicted. The third and fourth places went to Ontario MPP (and former provincial Cabinet minister) Gerard Kennedy and long-time federal Minister Stéphane Dion. The four remaining candidates—MP and former NHL goalie Ken Dryden, longtime MP Joe Volpe, MP and former PC leadership candidate Scott Brison, and lawyer Martha Hall Findlay—collectively received less than 15 percent of the delegates.

The delegate-selection meetings kicked off a final, feverish campaign. Although most of the delegates were committed to "their" candidate on the first ballot, there were up to 900 uncommitted *ex officio* delegates to be won over. Delegates for the four "second-tier" candidates, who would be eliminated from the ballot early in the convention voting, were also up for grabs. Finally, some Liberals were determined to prevent the election of Ignatieff (because of his gaffes) and/or Rae (because of his record and his NDP ties). The "Anybody But Iggy" and "Anybody But Rae" efforts did not bode well for the front-runners, either of whom would have to pick up the lion's share of *ex officio* and second-choice support to win 50 percent plus one of the convention vote. The fourth-place candidate, Stéphane Dion, had the most growth potential on the second and subsequent ballots;[89] but if he continued to lag behind Kennedy, he would be eliminated before he could capitalize on that support. A further element of uncertainty arose from the expense of attending the convention: a steep registration fee of $995, on top of accommodation and travel costs, could deter delegates from going to Montreal and casting their ballots.[90] In the end, almost 5000 of the 6000 eligible delegates went to the convention.

The results of the first ballot were an unpleasant surprise to the front-runners. Dion had picked up significant support among *ex officio* delegates; Ignatieff and Rae had not. Dion placed third,

just two votes ahead of Kennedy. Ken Dryden stayed on the second ballot, while the other "second-tier" candidates either withdrew or were eliminated. Rae made the biggest gains over the first ballot, but remained in second place; Dion also picked up considerably more votes than Ignatieff, whose support remained at around 30 percent. Ignatieff's fate was sealed when Kennedy withdrew from the third ballot, at the last possible moment, and made a dramatic walk across the convention floor to join the Dion camp. Now there were three men left in the race: Ignatieff, Rae, and Dion.[91]

The outcome of the convention would depend on the loyalty of Kennedy's supporters: how many would follow him to Dion? Kennedy was believed to have the most personally devoted delegates, so it was widely predicted that a majority would go with him; in that case, Dion would move into second place behind Ignatieff, and Rae would be eliminated from the final ballot. The third-ballot results shocked almost everyone: 90 percent of Kennedy's delegates had gone over to Dion, putting him in first place by more than a hundred votes. Rae did not take his elimination well. He openly rebuffed desperate overtures from his old friend Ignatieff, and refused to support either of the remaining candidates. Most members of the party elite who had backed Rae switched to Ignatieff, whom they regarded as a more electable leader than Dion. But a slim majority of Rae's rank-and-file delegates—perhaps influenced by the animosity between the Rae and Ignatieff camps, or the "Anybody But Iggy" campaign—voted for Dion on the final ballot. He won with 55 percent of the vote.

The outcome of the convention was widely interpreted as a repudiation of the Liberal power-brokers who had long controlled party affairs. Dion and Kennedy, the insurgent candidates with little money, had teamed up to beat the "establishment" candidates. To some degree, Dion's victory represented a rebellion of Liberal "believers" against the "careerists" who had backed two men with little history in the party because they perceived them as their ticket back to power.[92] In October 2008, shortly after leading his party to one of its worst election results, Dion resigned as leader.

The widespread adoption of OMOV leadership selection systems has had at least two unintended consequences. First, "In seeking to open their internal processes of leadership selection to wider participation by the electorate, political parties create opportunities for internal factions to contest nominations. Such reforms can also open the door to groups or individuals from outside the party entirely, who may wish to use these institutions as an arena in which to promote a particular issue, candidate or cause."[93] The federal PCs learned this lesson the hard way in 1998, when a party outsider named David Orchard used the party's OMOV leadership race as a platform for his crusade against free trade with the United States. Orchard wound up as one of the two candidates on the final ballot; he was convincingly defeated by former leader Joe Clark, but he had embarrassed the party establishment.[94] The PCs abandoned OMOV in favour of a hybrid convention system, but this did not deter Orchard. He tried again in 2003, and did well enough to force Peter MacKay to sign a deal in exchange for his support (Dossier 11.5).[95]

Second, the move from caucus selection to conventions and finally to OMOV has changed both the incentives for would-be party leaders and the qualifications of successful candidates. As the **selectorate** has expanded from MPs and senators to party delegates and finally to the membership at large, the importance of political and parliamentary experience has declined. This does not mean that a track record is unimportant; as Dossier 11.3 demonstrates, a candidate with proven competence in Parliament and government can still beat a political rookie. But it is difficult to imagine a newcomer like Brian Mulroney, who had never been elected to Parliament, becoming leader of the Progressive Conservative Party if the selectorate had been confined to the caucus. Similarly, Paul Martin Sr. might well have beaten Pierre Trudeau in the 1968 Liberal contest had there been a higher premium on government experience; Martin had served in Cabinet for decades, whereas Trudeau had first entered the Commons only three years earlier.

The point is that larger selectorates weaken the incentive for ambitious politicians to devote themselves to public service in Parliament. Instead, they can spend years in the private sector, often amassing personal fortunes and building networks with other wealthy businesspeople. It was widely alleged that Mulroney used his own money and that of his rich friends to fund his lavish 1976 campaign for the PC leadership; these rumours cannot be proved or disproved, because Mulroney never filed the financial report required by the party. Similarly, there were allegations that Paul Martin's 2003 leadership bid was generously funded by some of the same businesses with whom he had worked closely as Finance minister. Unlike leadership rivals John Manley, Allan Rock, and Sheila Copps, Martin was not a Cabinet minister during the last several months of the race; only members of the government were required by the party to publicly disclose their campaign donors.[96]

Under these circumstances, it may not be entirely coincidental that Martin's bitter rival, Jean Chrétien, introduced new financing rules for party leadership contests in 2003. The 2006 Liberal contest was the first major-party leadership battle waged under the new financing rules in Bill C-24. The $5400 cap on donations[97] made it very difficult for the candidates to raise money; most had to rely on loans from (or guaranteed by) family and friends.[98] Bob Rae borrowed a total of $845 000, mostly from his brother John (a high-ranking Liberal strategist and senior executive at one of Canada's largest companies). The switch from donations to loans has worrisome implications. At the time of writing, there are no limits on the amount of money that a candidate can borrow to finance a campaign, and the repayment rules in the CEA are ambiguous.[99] This is just one of the loopholes in Canada's party finance laws, to which we now turn.[100]

Raising and Spending Money

The relationship between parties and the state is complex. On the one hand, parties are voluntary, private organizations of citizens. This implies that they should be subject to little, if any, state regulation. On the other hand, because parties perform functions that are essential to the health of the political system, they are also public institutions. This latter perspective suggests that parties should be both funded and regulated by the state. The tension between the public and private aspects of party organizations—like the conflict between their national and local characteristics—has grown more acute in recent years. For the first century after Confederation, Canadian parties were subject to relatively little regulation. Since 1970, as the public has become increasingly suspicious of parties, their internal operations have been subject to growing scrutiny and regulation.[101] At the same time, the legal recognition of parties as "public utilities" has vastly expanded their financial support from the state.[102]

Money is the "mother's milk of politics." Election campaigns in the television age are hugely expensive, running into millions of dollars for the major national parties (Table 11.2). Maintaining a national organization between elections is also a costly undertaking. In order to survive, major national parties must raise substantial amounts every year. Before the *Election Expenses Act* took effect in 1974, reliable information on parties' financial affairs was difficult to find. The law required every registered party to disclose its annual revenues and expenditures, and to file a separate report after each election campaign. It also imposed limits on campaign spending and guaranteed public subsidies for party activity. (The law is described in more detail in Chapter 12.)

The 1974 amendments brought the campaign-related activities of political parties (except for candidate nomination) under legal regulation. Between elections, and in their internal affairs, Canada's national parties were still "private clubs." Bill C-24 changed that. Its key provisions are as follows:

- Constituency associations (called "electoral district associations," or EDAs, in the Bill) are now required to register with Elections Canada (section 403). Once registered, they must file annual financial reports. Failure to comply prohibits an association from nominating a candidate in the next election.[103]

- Nomination contests, which were formerly left entirely to the control of the parties, are now partly governed by the *Canada Elections Act* (section 478). Anyone who wishes to seek the nomination of a registered party for election to the House of Commons must appoint a financial agent; those who raise or spend $1000 or more are required to file a report with Elections Canada after the nomination meeting. No nomination contestant may spend more than 20 percent of the maximum spending limit for that particular constituency in the previous federal election. In most ridings, that means a cap of roughly $16 000.[104] While few aspiring candidates can afford to spend that much, the limits are intended to ensure that the wealthy do not squeeze out women and members of visible minority groups. In the past, many such aspirants have been hampered by lack of funds, especially in constituencies where their party is expected to win.[105]

- Leadership contests are also subject to some state regulation. A registered political party (see below for a discussion of registration) must inform Elections Canada as soon as a leadership race begins. All leadership candidates must register with the agency, and each must begin to report any campaign donations and expenditures as soon as his or her registration has been certified by the Chief Electoral Officer and the party leader. The candidate (more precisely, his or her official agent) is required to file a financial report in each of the four weeks immediately preceding the leadership vote, and submit a complete report within six months after the race ends. Note, however, that the law does not impose spending limits on leadership contests; the establishment and enforcement of such limits is still left to the discretion of the party itself.

The amendments in Bill C-24 radically altered the finance regime established in 1974. For the first time, contributions to political parties and candidates are limited by law. Corporations and unions, once the most significant sources of funding for particular parties, were severely restricted in their capacity to support political activity. Both monetary donations and gifts "in kind"—e.g., skilled volunteer labour—are now subject to stringent rules. To make up for the shortfall in donations, Bill C-24 introduced a new system of annual allowances for registered parties[106] and raised the reimbursements for election spending by both parties and candidates. Electoral activity is now primarily funded by the state, not by private interests or individual voters.

The figures in Table 11.2 demonstrate the changes in the major parties' funding bases since C-24 took effect. In 2004, for every dollar given by a private donor, the Liberals received four dollars in reimbursements and allowances from the public purse. The BQ did even better, receiving more than six dollars. The Conservatives and the NDP were less dependent on public funding; both had well-established systems for raising money from individual

TABLE 11.2 PUBLIC AND NON-PUBLIC FUNDING OF FEDERAL POLITICAL PARTIES, 2000 AND 2004

POLITICAL PARTY	TOTAL NON-PUBLIC CONTRIBUTIONS ($)	ELECTIONS EXPENSES ($)	POST-ELECTION REIMBURSEMENT	ANNUAL TOTAL ALLOWANCE ($)	DIRECT PUBLIC FUNDING ($)	PUBLIC FUNDING AS PROPORTION OF NON-PUBLIC CONTRIBU-TIONS (%)
2004						
Liberal	4 719 388	16 604 528	9 962 717	9 141 408	19 104 125	405
Cons	10 910 320	17 284 257	10 370 554	7 913 242	18 283 796	168
NDP	5 194 170	12 018 931	7 211 359	2 883 919	10 095 278	194
BQ	858 746	4 507 531	2 704 519	2 733 868	5 438 387	633
Green	351 031	498 179	298 908	523 694	822 602	234
2000						
Liberal	20 067 820	12 525 174	2 809 219	N/A	2 809 219	14
Alliance	19 641 006	9 669 648	2 167 520	N/A	2 167 520	11
NDP	8 978 136	6 334 585	1 423 516	N/A	1 423 516	16
PC	5 621 694	3 983 301	875 701	N/A	875 701	16
BQ	2 259 752	1 968 693	404 402	N/A	404 402	18
Green	137 171	17 747	N/A	N/A	N/A	0

Source: Data compiled from the Elections Canada website by Kate Malloy in "Public funding too high, political parties becoming 'empty shells'", *The Hill Times,* October 2, 2006, p. 14.

CHAPTER 11: POLITICAL PARTIES AND THE CANADIAN PARTY SYSTEM

members and donors, so they were not as drastically affected by the prohibition of corporate donations (the NDP did suffer somewhat from the abolition of union funding).

Table 11.2 actually understates the parties' dependence on the public purse, in two respects. First, it excludes indirect funding, such as the political tax credits to encourage individual donations or the market value of the free air time provided by broadcasters during election campaigns (Chapter 12). Second, the parties' ability to raise money from private donors was further restricted in late 2006 by the *Federal Accountability Act*. Whereas Bill C-24 capped annual donations from individuals at $5000, the FAA lowered the limit to $1000. It also eliminated the few exceptions to the 2004 ban on corporate and union donations. These changes have hit the constituency associations hardest, because they do not benefit directly from the annual allowances. They also tipped the balance of power within party organizations even further toward the party in central office, which will control the only significant and reliable source of funds: the annual allowance from the government.

The growing reliance of Canada's major parties on public funding could have negative consequences. Comparative studies of political finance suggest that when parties lose the incentive to solicit funds directly from citizens, they become increasingly alienated from the electorate.[107] Consequently, the massive expansion of public funding may undermine the very justification for state subsidies: that parties are "the key intermediary institutions of contemporary democracy," and thus indispensable for a functioning representative polity.[108] The opposing argument is that public disengagement from political parties was well underway before Bill C-24, and that the major parties themselves—those with seats in Parliament, and the capacity to manipulate the laws governing political finance—responded to their dwindling supply of volunteer labour and private revenues by replacing them with state subsidies.[109]

THE CANADIAN PARTY SYSTEM

There are almost as many definitions of "party system" as there are of "political party." Some experts include every official party, while others restrict their focus to the parties in Parliament. For the sake of brevity, this chapter takes the latter approach; for the most part, we have restricted the discussion of Canada's party system to the five parties currently represented in the House of Commons. This does not mean that the smaller parties are irrelevant. As Table 11.3 shows, there were 16 parties on the Official Register in May 2008. Collectively, the eleven smallest parties received just over 7 percent of the vote in the 2008 election; none was able to win a seat. The vast majority of these votes (93 percent) went to the Greens, who succeeded in qualifying for the annual allowance in 2004, 2006 and 2008.

To some extent, Elections Canada treats all registered parties equally. Each must meet the same criteria for registration. Since 1970, the Chief Electoral Officer has maintained a *Registry of Parties* for the purpose of administering the Act. Only registered parties are eligible for financial and broadcasting benefits; in return, they are required by law to submit annual and post-election financial reports. Until 2004, a party had to run at least 50 candidates in a federal general election in order to qualify for registration. This criterion was deleted in May 2004, in response to the *Figueroa* ruling from the Supreme Court of Canada (Dossier 6.3). Today, a party seeking to register must do the following:

- nominate at least one candidate before the nomination deadline at each general election, or in a by-election;
- submit an annual fiscal report by the party's designated official agent, as approved by its official auditor; and
- file an application for registration with the Chief Electoral Officer, including the endorsement by signature of 250 party members (with full names and addresses), an official party name and logo, and the names of the party's leader and three other officers.[110]

TABLE 11.3 NATIONAL REGISTER OF PARTIES, OCTOBER 2008

NAME OF PARTY	PARTY LEADER	NUMBER OF CANDIDATES IN 2008 ELECTION
Animal Alliance Environment Voters Party of Canada	Liz White	4
Bloc Québécois	Gilles Duceppe	75
Canadian Action Party	Constance Fogal	20
Christian Heritage Party of Canada	Ronald Gray	59
Communist Party of Canada	Miguel Figueroa	24
Conservative Party of Canada	Stephen Harper	307
First Peoples National Party of Canada	Barbara Wardlaw	6
Green Party of Canada	Elizabeth May	303
Liberal Party of Canada	Stéphane Dion*	307
Libertarian Party of Canada	Dennis Young	26
Marijuana Party	Blair Longley	8
Marxist–Leninist Party of Canada	Anna Di Carlo	59
neorhino.ca	François Yo Gourd	7
New Democratic Party	Jack Layton	303
Newfoundland and Labrador First Party	Thomas Hickey	3
People's Political Power Party of Canada	Roger F. Poisson	2
Progressive Canadian Party	Hon. Sinclair Stevens	10
Western Block Party	Douglas Christie	1
Work Less Party	Conrad Schmidt	1

Source: Data compiled and used to create the above chart was taken from the website of Elections Canada: www.elections.ca. It is used with the permission of the Chief Electoral Officer but extrapolations and analysis rest with the author. Retrieved October 2008.

*Dion announced his resignation in October 2008, but decided to stay on as interim leader until his replacement could be chosen. In December 2008 Dion was chosen to lead a Liberal-NDP coalition in the event of the Harper Government's defeat in the Commons over its fiscal update. Shortly thereafter, Parliament was prorogued and Dion was forced to step down ahead of schedule. He was replaced as interim leader by deputy leader Michael Ignatieff, after the other two leadership contenders (Bob Rae and New Brunswick MP Dominic Leblanc) withdrew from the contest.

To stay registered, the party must periodically submit written proof that its primary purpose is to participate in the political process by running candidates in elections. The safeguards in the Bill are intended to prevent the formation of fraudulent "parties" for the purpose of abusing the political tax credits. Those credits, which were established in 1974 and revised in 2000 and 2004, allow a contributor to deduct a percentage of each political donation from his or her income tax for that year. Their purpose is to encourage individuals to donate money to political parties, thus reducing the latter's dependence on corporate funding. Since the new party-registration rules took effect, the number of registered parties has risen from nine to 15;[111] none of the new parties that ran in 2004 and/or 2006 received more than a handful of votes.

In addition to the financial provisions discussed above, each registered party also has the right to list its party affiliation on the ballot. In addition, all registered parties belong to the Elections Canada Advisory Committee, which meets regularly with the Chief Electoral Officer to discuss regulatory issues and suggest improvements to the election regime. So excluding 11 of the 15 registered parties may strike readers as arbitrary or unfair, especially the exclusion of the Green Party. Nonetheless, given the impossibility of discussing each of these parties in a brief chapter, we define the Canadian party system as follows: *The sum total of the parties represented in the House of Commons at a given time.* Therefore, with the exception of Table 11.3, this chapter only discusses the parties that have won seats in the House of Commons since 1993.

Most of the literature on party systems focuses on the number of parties. For much of the twentieth century, Canada had a two-and-a-half-party system at the national level. The "half" was the NDP, which won enough seats to play a role in Parliament (especially during Liberal minority governments) but never had a real chance to form a government. The other two parties were the Liberals and the PCs, which alternated in power (albeit fairly infrequently) from 1867 until 1993. The PC collapse in the early 1990s left the Liberals as the only national party capable of winning an election; for a decade, Canada had "a one-party predominant system."[112]

Numbers provide relatively little information. They do not explain why there are more parties in some countries than in others. Nor do they tell us much about the relationships between the party system and the political system as a whole—or, indeed, about the relationships among the various networks within each party. Carty and his co-authors[113] provide a richer and more comprehensive account of party systems. As the following variables change over time, so does the party system:

- the relationships among the various elements and networks within each party (e.g., the caucus, the leader and his or her entourage, and the local members in the constituencies);
- the impact on the party system of changes in other national institutions (e.g., the shift of power from the legislative to the executive branch, the operation of the federal system, changes in electoral laws, and the entrenchment of the *Charter*);
- the methods of choosing party leaders;
- the relationships between national parties and particular subcultures (regional, linguistic, economic, and ideological);
- the sources and regulation of party finance; and
- evolving technologies of mass communication.

However we define a party system, one core idea remains constant: in democratic states with two or more parties, none operates in isolation. Each affects, and is affected by, the other members of the system. Parties compete with each other for money, votes, and other scarce resources. When one party in a system innovates—e.g., adopting an OMOV system for selecting its leaders—the others feel pressured to imitate it. In the electoral context, a strategic choice by one party often provokes a response from rival parties and may even inspire the creation of one or more new parties (recall the discussion of the collapse of the PCs at the start of the chapter). On the other hand, if one party is too dominant, two or more smaller parties may merge in order to provide a more effective challenge (as the Canadian Alliance and the PCs did in 2003).

◼ Explaining the Number of Parties in the System

Political parties do not simply appear out of the blue. They arise at particular points in time in response to a variety of opportunities and constraints, with the purpose of achieving particular representational or governing objectives. The three major theories of party development emphasize social, mobilizational, and institutional explanations, respectively.[114]

Social Cleavages: Political Culture and Class

Societal approaches to the development of the party system emphasize the role played by changes in the economy, social relations, or political culture of a society. From this perspective, a party system is largely determined by and reflective of social relations and/or attitudes of individuals. To understand the development of a particular party system, one must examine the evolution of the underlying social relations. By implication, a party system would change only if the underlying social forces also changed.

Although there are many variants of the social approach to party development, two have been particularly popular in Canada: the political culture model and the class politics model. As we saw in Chapter 2, the "political culture" of a given country is the overall pattern of political orientations within its population. Canada does not have a single political culture, but rather a set of subcultures, including Quebec nationalism and Western populism. The political culture model suggests that the number and ideological diversity of parties in a given party system reflect the different subcultures in the electorate. When we talk about the effect of social divisions on voting behaviour, we refer to them as **cleavages** (see the discussion of Canadian voting behaviour in Chapter 12). In general, social cleavages are based on long-term demographic characteristics such as religion and class. Ideological cleavages also influence the party system, as do partisan attachments (see the discussions of values and party identification in Chapter 12).

The mere presence of a particular cleavage does not automatically translate into a new political party. To understand why some subcultures spawn parties and others do not, we need to consider two factors: the institutional incentives and constraints that affect the creation of political parties, and the organization and strategies that are required to transform a societal cleavage into a political party. Political parties cannot survive unless they attract substantial support—both electoral and financial—from the subculture(s) that they purport to represent. The missing link between political culture and the party system is **mobilization.**

Mobilization

Politics is about establishing priorities, setting goals, and implementing strategies that enable one to pursue objectives. Parties are not passive victims of their environments. They are active agents with the power to define the issues of importance in political conflict and to mobilize voters behind their issue positions. A new party is established when a **political entrepreneur** identifies an unmet need in the political marketplace. He or she mobilizes the members of a particular subculture and constructs a party organization.[115] To succeed, a political entrepreneur requires at least three things:

1. a preexisting base in the electorate, among one or more groups of voters whose political needs are not met by existing parties;
2. an opportunity to exploit that dissatisfaction with the existing party system; and
3. the resources—money, volunteers, media attention—to establish and market a new alternative.

The mobilization of targeted groups of voters is not solely the responsibility of entrepreneurs seeking to create new parties. The leaders of existing parties also make strategic choices when they decide which subcultures in the electorate they wish to attract or retain. Such choices can reshape voting patterns, although not always in the intended direction.[116] The most basic choice is whether to retain and reinforce the party's existing base—its "heartland" within the electorate—or to reach out to subcultures that have not previously been included in the party's electoral coalition. Either option carries risks and opportunities. Maintaining the traditional base is the safest strategy in the short term. But if that base shrinks, or its ties to the party weaken, the party can fade away.[117] On the other hand, trying to add new subcultures to the existing electoral coalition can backfire. It might pay off handsomely in the short term but erode the party's traditional base in the long term. The collapse of the federal Progressive Conservative Party in 1993 provides a classic example.

Compared to the leaders of established parties, political entrepreneurs have more freedom to concentrate on one particular subculture and to mobilize it in the most effective way: by refusing to compromise the needs and goals of that specific group of voters. Dossier 11.4 identifies five long-term subcultures in the Canadian electorate, the last two of which have repeatedly shifted between parties in response to the strategic decisions of party leaders. From this perspective, the five-party system that emerged in 1993 represents not a transformation of Canadian politics, but simply the latest reflection of a stable pattern of subcultures within the electorate. The subcultures themselves are not new; the novelty lies in their successful mobilization into separate party organizations by entrepreneurial political leaders.

The article excerpted in Dossier 11.4 turned out to be the harbinger of an important change in Canada's national party system.[118] Although they could not have known it at the time, the two co-authors would prove to be capable entrepreneurs. In 2003, Harper reunited two of the subcultures—the PCs and Western populists—in the Conservative Party of Canada. During the 2006 election campaign, he reached out to Quebec nationalist voters and brought many of them back into the Conservative fold. In the process, he rebuilt the Mulroney coalition whose 1993 collapse had given the Liberals a monopoly of federal power for over a

---

DOSSIER 11.4 Five Long-Term Subcultures in the Canadian Electorate

Ever since 1921, Canada has had a **multiparty system.** Parties have come and gone, but not these five components of the system:

1. A Liberal party with a national coalition capable of governing. At times in the 1970s and 1980s, the Liberals were virtually shut out of the West, as they are today in francophone Quebec, but they have usually maintained appreciable strength in all parts of the country. . . .

2. A Conservative or Progressive Conservative party claiming a national base, but in fact coming to power only in exceptional circumstances and then governing only for short periods of time. . . .

3. A social-democratic party claiming to be national but with real strength only in Western Canada and Ontario. This element became visible as early as the mid-1920s, when a group of left-wing MPs emerged amid the wreckage of the disintegrating Progressive party. These MPs went on to help found the Co-operative Commonwealth Federation in 1932. The CCF regrouped in 1961 as the New Democratic Party. . . .

4. A right-wing populist party based in Western Canada. Social Credit, the first modern example, entered the House of Commons in 1935. Despite a long history of ups and downs, it continued to elect western members through 1965. Provincial Social Credit parties governed Alberta until 1971 and British Columbia until 1992. The Reform party inherits the conservative populist tradition. Its first leader was Preston Manning, himself a federal Socred candidate in 1965 and the son of Ernest Manning, the long-serving Social Credit premier of Alberta.

5. A francophone nationalist party in Quebec, such as the Bloc Populaire in 1945, the Union des Électeurs in 1949, the Ralliement Créditiste in 1962 through 1979, and the Bloc Québécois in 1993. Plus nationalist parties that ran for office at the provincial level—Maurice Duplessis's Union Nationale, which replaced the Conservatives and dominated provincial politics from the 1930s until 1960; the Parti Québécois, which has governed on and off since 1976; and, most recently, Mario Dumont's Action Démocratique. Interestingly, these nationalist parties have spanned almost the entire ideological spectrum, from socialist left to monetary-reform right.

Source: From Stephen Harper and Tom Flanagan, "Our Benign Dictatorship," *The Next City*, Winter 1996–97, 38. Reprinted with permission.

decade.[119] Flanagan managed Harper's 2002 and 2004 leadership campaigns, and looked after advertising in the 2004 election campaign. They led the team that mobilized three apparently incompatible subcultures into a new electoral coalition, which was smaller than the 1984 PC base but large enough to win a narrow minority government. Although the Conservatives failed to consolidate their gains among Quebec nationalists in the 2008 election, they managed to win a larger plurality of seats (Table 11.4).

Technological Change and the Canadian Party System

As the channels of mass communication evolve, so do the parties that rely on them to persuade voters. Before the widespread use of radio in the 1930s, political communication was restricted to newspapers, magazines, books, and pamphlets. The spread of television in the 1950s transformed Canadian politics, allowing voters to see their aspiring prime ministers, close up, in their living rooms. It also created new advertising techniques based on emotions and images instead of reason and information. As we will see in Chapter 14, television tends to "personalize" abstract issues; consequently, party leaders became even more prominent in election campaigns. The cost of campaigning soared as parties turned to professional advertisers and **"spin doctors."**

At the same time, the rapid evolution of computer and telephone technologies created a new breed of political professional: the pollster. Public-opinion data, gathered and interpreted at great expense, were turned into integrated campaign strategies by teams of experts. In the process, the role of the backbench MP was reduced; he or she was no longer the primary source of political intelligence from the far-flung regions of the country. His or her constituency association also found itself enmeshed in a newly centralized campaign organization, using the same "talking points" and images featured in the national campaign.

In recent election campaigns, the major parties have worked hard to take advantage of the Internet. They have tried to use their websites as campaign tools, initially with limited success. Web pages with sophisticated applications such as video streaming and interactivity alienated users with incompatible hardware or software.[120] Smaller parties lacked the resources needed to maintain and update an information-rich site during the chaos of a campaign.[121] By 2006, the parties' use of the Internet had matured. The Liberal leadership candidates pointed the way: they used blogs, YouTube, and social networking sites like FaceBook and MySpace to reach party members.[122] Politicians embraced these tools as low-cost, effective means of communication. Uploading an attack ad to YouTube is much cheaper than buying airtime on conventional broadcast networks, and the ad is more likely to reach younger voters.[123]

On the other side of the coin, some strategists expressed concern about the impossibility of controlling the message. "Viral videos," often crafted by amateurs with cellphone cameras, had an impact on the 2006 U.S. midterm elections (see the discussion of YouTube on page 543). Canadian party strategists braced themselves for similar "viral" outbreaks in the next federal campaign.[124] YouTube also became the outlet of choice for 2008 U.S. presidential aspirants seeking to generate buzz for their primary campaigns. They posted increasingly expensive and sophisticated videos, hoping to win over undecided voters. Parodies of these ads often appeared within a short time, demonstrating the power of an individual with strong political views and the ability to use software.

Another recent technological advance, wireless hand-held devices (like Canada's BlackBerry) and text messaging on cellphones, altered communication within parties and between parties and the media. Instant messaging allows political strategists to keep in close touch, no matter where they happen to be. It also makes it easier for the "war room" staff—those responsible for "rapid response" during an election campaign—to "spin" a particular story to reporters within minutes. The "CrackBerry" has become an essential accessory for Canadian politicos. Paul Martin's supporters gave their devices a workout during their fight to depose former Prime Minister Chrétien, messaging each other frequently to report new developments in the party's civil war.[125] There are anecdotal reports of Cabinet ministers thumb-typing memos to their staffers during meetings.[126] A cellphone conversation in the midst of a Cabinet meeting would doubtless attract the ire of the prime minister, and its contents would be anything but confidential; text messaging is both quieter and more secure. It would be an overstatement to say that the BlackBerry has transformed Canadian parties, but it has certainly contributed to campaign efforts to "stay on message."

In summary, party systems are shaped by several long-term factors, among which social cleavages and political institutions are the most important. They continue to evolve over time, as short-term variables—such as communication technology and mobilization strategies—change. To understand the patterns of continuity and change in Canada's national party system, we must consider all of these variables.

The History of the Canadian Party System

Table 11.4 presents the results of national elections from 1867 to 2006.

According to R. Kenneth Carty and his co-authors, Canada has had four distinct party systems since Confederation:

1. patronage politics and caucus parties (1867–1911);
2. brokerage politics and ministerialist parties (1921–57);
3. electronic politics and personal parties (1963–84); and
4. postmaterialist politics and targeted parties (1993–).[127]

There have also been three periods of transition between party systems: 1911–21, 1957–63, and 1984–93. In every case, the beginning and end of each system are marked by general elections. While we can observe changes in Canadian politics between elections, the extent of those changes is measurable only when the votes are counted. The transitional periods are marked by flux, uncertainty, and electoral volatility. We cannot be certain whether a new party system has taken shape until it has remained essentially intact for at least two electoral cycles. An election that appears to herald a new alignment of subcultures, such as the 1984 PC breakthrough, may turn out to have been the beginning of a transitional period—not the start of a new and stable party system.

While most Canadian scholars agree with Carty's analysis of the first three party systems, there is considerable debate about the fourth party system.[128] For the moment, let us assume that the third party system ended in 1984, and that the fourth system took shape in 1993. On that basis, we will briefly describe Canada's four party systems.

First Period: 1867–1917

At Confederation, there was little party discipline in Parliament or the provincial legislatures. Sir John A. Macdonald had to knit MPs from two language groups and four provinces into a unified caucus. In the 1880s and 1890s, parliamentary caucuses became increasingly cohesive and leader-dominated. Both the Liberal and Conservative parties hugged the centre of the political spectrum.[129] The Conservatives were considerably more successful than the Liberals during the first three decades after Confederation; the latter remained a loosely knit group of parliamentary factions until well into the 1870s.

TABLE 11.4 PARTY SEATS AND VOTES IN FEDERAL ELECTIONS, 1867–2006

In this table, the seat total of the party that formed the government is shown in boldface. In each cell, the first number is the percentage of the national vote received by that party; the percentage of seats is shown in parentheses.

YEAR	LPC	CONS.	CCF/NDP	SC	BQ	PROG./RPC/CA/CP	OTHER
1867	49 (40)	**50 (60)**	—	—	—	—	1 (0)
1872	49 (48)	**50 (52)**	—	—	—	—	1 (0)
1874	**54 (67)**	45 (33)	—	—	—	—	1 (0.5)
1878	46 (31)	**53 (69)**	—	—	—	—	1.2 (0)
1882	47 (34)	**50 (66)**	—	—	—	—	2.5 (0.5)
1887	49 (41)	**50 (59)**	—	—	—	—	1 (0)
1891	47 (44)	**51 (56)**	—	—	—	—	2 (0)
1896	**45 (55)**	46 (41)	—	—	—	—	9 (3)
1900	**51 (62)**	47 (38)	—	—	—	—	1 (0)
1904	**52 (65)**	46 (35)	—	—	—	—	1.5 (0.5)
1908	**50 (61)**	47 (39)	—	—	—	—	2.7 (0.4)
1911	48 (39)	**51 (61)**	—	—	—	—	1.4 (0)
1917*	40 (35)	**57 (65)**	—	—	—	—	3 (0)
1921	**41 (49)**	30 (21)	—	—	—	23 (27)	6 (2)
1925†	**40 (40)**	47 (47)	—	—	—	9 (10)	5 (2)
1926	**46 (52)**	45 (37)	—	—	—	5 (8)	3 (2)
1930	45 (37)	**49 (56)**	—	—	—	3 (5)	3 (2)
1935	**45 (71)**	30 (16)	9 (3)	4 (7)	—	—	13 (3)
1940	**52 (74)**	31 (16)	9 (4)	3 (4)	—	—	7 (2)
1945	**41 (51)**	27 (27)	16 (11)	4 (5)	—	—	12 (5)
1949	**50 (74)**	30 (16)	13 (5)	2 (4)	—	—	5 (2)
1953	**49 (65)**	31 (19)	22 (9)	5 (6)	—	—	4 (2)
1957	41 (40)	**39 (42)**	11 (9)	7 (7)	—	—	3 (1.5)
1958	**34 (19)**	54 (79)	10 (3)	3 (0)	—	—	1 (0)
1962	37 (38)	**37 (44)**	14 (7)	12 (11)	—	—	0.4 (0)
1963	**42 (49)**	33 (36)	13 (6)	12 (9)	—	—	0.4 (0)
1965	**40 (49)**	32 (37)	18 (8)	8 (5)	—	—	1 (1)
1968	**49 (59)**	31 (27)	17 (8)	5 (5)	—	—	1 (0.4)
1972	**39 (41)**	35 (41)	18 (12)	8 (6)	—	—	1 (1)
1974	**43 (53)**	35 (36)	15 (6)`	5 (4)	—	—	2 (0.4)
1979	40 (40)	**36 (48)**	18 (9)	5 (2)	—	—	1 (0)
1980	**44 (52)**	33 (37)	20 (11)	2 (0)	—	—	1 (0)
1984	28 (14)	**50 (75)**	18 (11)	1 (0)	—	—	3 (0.3)
1988	32 (28)	**43 (57)**	20 (15)	—	—	2 (0)	3 (0)
1993	**41 (60)**	16 (1)	7 (3)	—	14 (18)	19 (18)	4 (0.3)

(continued)

YEAR	LPC	CONS.	CCF/NDP	SC	BQ	PROG./RPC/CA/CP	OTHER
1997	**38 (52)**	19 (7)	11 (7)	—	11 (15)	19 (20)	2 (0.3)
2000	**41 (57)**	12 (4)	9 (4)	—	11 (13)	26 (22)	2 (0)
2004	**37 (44)**	30 (32)	16 (6)	—	12 (18)	—	6 (0.3)[‡]
2006	**30 (33)**	36 (40)	17 (9)	—	10 (17)	—	6 (0.3)[‡]
2008	**26 (25)**	38 (46)	18 (12)	—	10 (16)	—	8 (0.7)

Key to Party Names:

LPC = Liberal Party of Canada

Cons. = Progressive Conservative Party of Canada (1942–2003)

CCF/NDP = Co-operative Commonwealth Federation (1933–61) and New Democratic Party of Canada (1961–)

SC = Social Credit (includes the Ralliement des Créditistes)

BQ = Bloc Québécois (1993–)

Prog./RPC/CA/CP = Progressives (1921–35); Reform Party of Canada (1987–2000); Canadian Alliance (2000–03); Conservative Party of Canada (2003–)

[*]As explained in the text of this chapter, the 1917 election was highly unusual. Instead of a contest between the Liberals and the Conservatives, it pitted the Union Government of Sir Robert Borden—Conservatives and English-speaking Liberals—against the francophone Liberals opposed to conscription.

[†]After the 1925 election, in which the Conservatives won the plurality of seats, Liberal Prime Minister Mackenzie King refused either to resign or to call Parliament. He was afraid that the Commons would pass a vote of nonconfidence and push him out of office. After several months, he was finally forced to call Parliament; his government was indeed defeated, and the governor general refused King's request to dissolve Parliament and call a new election. Instead, Lord Byng called on Conservative leader Arthur Meighen to form a government. Meighen's government was also short-lived, and after he lost the confidence of the Commons, Lord Byng granted a dissolution. The conflict between the Liberal prime minister and the governor general has gone down in Canadian history as the "King-Byng Affair."

[‡]The one seat assigned to "Other" in both the 2004 and 2006 elections, and the two in 2008, were won by Independents. None of the smaller parties won seats in those elections.

As classic cadre parties,[130] the Liberals and Conservatives were slow to develop extraparliamentary organizations. In the first 50 years after Confederation, the Liberal Party held only one national convention and the Conservatives none. Both parties limited political debate to the parliamentary forum and wooed supporters through the widespread use of patronage.

The first party system was also characterized by dominant leaders, secretive and sometimes corrupt party finance, and a partisan press. Because the two parties were so similar in ideological terms, the personalities and rhetoric of their leaders became the main focus of electoral competition. As the French writer André Siegfried wrote of Canadian parties in 1906:

> It is of the first importance to the success of a party that it should be led by someone who inspires confidence, and whose mere name is a programme in itself. As long as the Conservatives had Macdonald for their leader, they voted for him rather than for the party. So it is with Laurier and the Liberals of today. If Laurier disappeared, the Liberals would perhaps find that they had lost the real secret of their victories. . . . They vote as much for the man who symbolizes the policy as for the policy itself.[131]

The leader was also his party's chief fundraiser. The burden of soliciting donations added considerably to Sir John A. Macdonald's workload as prime minister. He was forced to seek party funds from industrialists and financiers who worked with the government—an apparent, if not actual, conflict of interest.[132] Macdonald's begging letters to the head of the

Grand Trunk Railroad provoked the 1873 Pacific Scandal, which brought down the Conservative government. While there were some tentative efforts to clean up party patronage and fundraising in the 1870s, these had little effect until after World War I.

As if raising money, creating a disciplined caucus, and symbolizing the party were not enough, party leaders also spent considerable time managing the press. This task was made somewhat easier by the open partisanship of most newspapers. Macdonald knew that he could count on sympathetic treatment from Conservative papers, while his Liberal opponents expected the same from the Liberal press.

> *A great majority of the weekly and daily newspapers, which existed in far greater numbers than they do today, were little more than partisan instruments. Even as late as 1900, the circulation of the party papers exceeded that of the growing independent press. Politicians wanted and expected subservience, not objectivity, from the media.*[133]

Second Period: 1921–57

During the first two decades of the twentieth century, Canadian society underwent important changes that placed considerable strain on the party system. The continual movement toward urbanization and industrialization (especially in Ontario and Quebec), the rapid agrarian settlement of the Prairie provinces, and the continued support by both political parties of the National Policy—which was perceived (correctly) as favouring the industrializing centre at the expense of the agrarian periphery—led many in the outlying regions to question the degree to which their interests were, or could be, adequately represented in either existing party.[134] While the settlement of the Prairies was facilitated by the Liberal Government of Sir Wilfrid Laurier (1896–1911), neither the Liberals nor the Conservatives fully mobilized this expanding pool of voters. The stage was set for an expansion of the party system, and for the emergence of a new subculture: Western populism.

The conscription crisis during World War I (1914–18) blurred the distinction between the two political parties. The creation of the Union Government inflamed French-English tensions, and reinforced the attachment of the Quebec nationalist subculture to the Liberal Party.[135] In 1917 the Liberals won 62 of the 65 seats in Quebec; in 1921, they won all 65.

A significant institutional change also affected party development during this era. The *Civil Service Commission Act, 1918,* placed the authority for recruitment into the civil service squarely in the hands of a nonpartisan agency, thus eliminating the lion's share of party patronage. This institutional change drastically reduced the material incentives for party activity and could have seriously weakened the party system. However, because disciplined national parties were (and are) essential ingredients in a system of responsible Cabinet government, the parties survived and adapted to the changing political system. As the number of cleavages in the electorate multiplied—with the addition and growth of new provinces, immigration, the enfranchisement of women, and rising nationalism in Quebec—the parties in the second party system had to knit the diverse groups into a national political community. From local patronage machines, they became regional brokers.[136]

The brokerage strategy of the Liberals and Conservatives was based on the premise that conflict could best be mediated within the extraparliamentary parties, rather than between parties inside Parliament. One key element in that strategy was the development of **ministerialism:** individual Cabinet ministers represented particular regional, cultural, or economic groups within the party decision-making process. At the same time, the ministers were required to explain and communicate those decisions to the members of their designated interest group.

If one measures the success of the brokerage strategy by the level of electoral support obtained by the parties, the Liberal Party was without question the better broker of competing interests. It won eight of the nine elections held from 1921 to 1957 and governed for 31 of those 36 years. Its only defeat during this period occurred shortly after the onset of the Great Depression, when the Conservative Party under R.B. Bennett captured 137 of 245 Commons seats, only to plummet to 40 seats five years later. The Liberals were led throughout this period by William Lyon Mackenzie King and Louis St. Laurent, both of whom were noted conciliators.

However, the electoral record also illustrates the limitations inherent in the brokerage model. Groups that perceived the Liberal and Conservative parties as either unwilling or unable to effectively represent their interests had an incentive to establish "third" parties to speak on their behalf. Highly mobilized subcultures that were concentrated in a particular region—notably, Western populists—were more successful in electoral terms than latent subcultures and those scattered across the country (the working-class voters courted by left-wing parties). Both types of party emerged during the second party system, although none was able to challenge the dominance of the Liberals and Conservatives.

The two-party system was shattered in the 1921 election, when the Progressives elected 65 MPs—14 more than the Conservatives. The Progressives won all but a handful of Prairie seats and almost one-third of the Ontario seats (most in northern or rural Ontario). As the second-place party, the Progressives were entitled to form the official Opposition in the House of Commons. However, the Progressive caucus was dominated by populist members. They were hostile to the existing system of disciplined party combat in the legislature, which put too much power in the hands of party leaders. (For a definition of "populism," see Dossier 2.1.) Thus, instead of using their Western regional base as a platform from which to challenge the Central Canadian orientation of the major parties, the Progressives refused the mantle of official Opposition and supported the minority Liberal government instead. Progressive leader T.A. Crerar was even co-opted into the Cabinet. This cooperation with the governing party cost the Progressives much of their populist support over the next decade, and the party had disappeared as a national force by the 1935 federal election.[137]

The Progressives inaugurated a new era of regionally based third parties, including a new party of the left. The 1921 election witnessed the election not only of 65 Progressives but also of two independent labour candidates, J.S. Woodsworth and William Irvine. By the late 1920s, there had emerged in Parliament a loose association of labour MPs and some of the more radical Progressive MPs; they were known as the Ginger Group, for the spice they added to parliamentary debate. At the instigation of the Ginger Group and the League for Social Reconstruction (LSR)—a university-based group of socialists modelled on the British Fabian Society—a meeting of the Western Labour Conference in 1932 voted to create a new socialist political party.[138] The party held its founding convention in Regina the next year, calling itself the "Co-operative Commonwealth Federation—Farmer, Labour, Socialist." As its subtitle suggested, the CCF tried to appeal to regionally (Western) based farmers, the working class, and intellectual socialists.

The farmer–labour alliance within the CCF was an uneasy one. The tendency of farmer votes to be tightly clustered geographically (particularly in the Prairies) and of labour votes to be more dispersed resulted in the CCF's winning more contests in rural Western constituencies than in urban constituencies. Thus the parliamentary wing of the CCF had a distinctly Western-farmer character, which made it more difficult for the party to appeal to the urban working class. That difficulty was compounded by divisions within the union movement, regarding both its organizational structure and its approach to political action. For most of the second party system, the major central union organization, the Trades and

Labour Congress (TLC), was dominated by American-based multinational unions that chose to remain politically independent. In the mid-1930s, a more militant and politically active group of industrial unions was expelled from the TLC and formed the Canadian Congress of Labour (CCL).

Beginning in 1942, the CCL declared at each convention that the CCF was the "political arm of labour" and (unsuccessfully) urged its member unions to affiliate with the party.[139] Organized labour was not able to take a more unified and politically active position until the merger of the TLC and CCL into the Canadian Labour Congress (CLC) in 1956. As we shall see, that merger provided the impetus for the transformation of the CCF into the NDP in the early 1960s. Along with the Liberal and Conservative parties, the CCF–NDP is one of the five relatively stable components of the party system identified in Dossier 11.4.

In addition to contributing members to the Ginger Group and thus influencing the creation of the CCF–NDP, the Progressive Party also demonstrated the tendency of the electoral system to generate regional third parties. Whereas some forms of regional discontent found voice in the leftist CCF, others were more at home in a populist party of the ideological right: Social Credit. Following the political ideas developed by British engineer Major Clifford Douglas and articulated in the Canadian West by fundamentalist minister and radio preacher William ("Bible Bill") Aberhart, the Social Credit Party emerged during the 1935 election, in the middle of the Great Depression, as an important voice for Western farmers.[140]

Social Credit's support (measured by the party's seats rather than votes) came almost exclusively from Alberta during this third period of party development, and from 1935 to 1957 it captured all but a handful of the Commons seats from that province. The party collapsed in 1958 when the Western populist and Quebec nationalist subcultures switched to the Progressive Conservative Party, led by the fiery Westerner John Diefenbaker, contributing to a landslide PC victory.

By the beginning of the second party system in 1921, leadership conventions had already become the preferred method for choosing party leaders. This development reflected another important change: the establishment of extraparliamentary wings by all the major parties. National party offices, staffed by permanent employees, began to appear.[141] As the caucus lost the power to choose the leader, and the representational functions of government backbenchers shifted to regional ministers, power within party structures became more decentralized. Successive fundraising scandals, particularly the Liberal Beauharnois scandal of 1930, convinced party leaders to delegate their fundraising chores to party "bagmen." These individuals, many of them senators, met privately with corporate and individual donors to solicit funds for the new party organization and the special demands of national campaigns. Meanwhile, the partisan press had disappeared, a victim of advertising, public demand for independent papers, and the new medium of radio.[142] Broadcasters were regulated by the federal government, which required them to present balanced news coverage as a condition of licence renewal.

The second party system came to an end with the election of 1957, which brought the Progressive Conservatives to power for the first time since 1935. Although PC leader John Diefenbaker managed to win only a minority, the period of unchallenged Liberal dominance appeared to be over. The 1958 election gave Diefenbaker a massive majority, nearly wiping out the CCF and prompting the formation of the NDP. The New Party (its original name) was launched in 1961, the product of a marriage between the Canadian Labour Congress and the remnants of the CCF. At the same time, the Liberals spent their time in opposition rebuilding their organization from the ground up. By the time the second transitional period ended in 1963, Canada's national party system and the environment in which it operated had changed dramatically.

Third Period: 1963–84

The electoral realignment brought about by Diefenbaker's Conservatives integrated Westerners once again into one of the two major parties and temporarily ended the Liberals' stranglehold under the brokerage model. Thereafter, the representation of third parties in Parliament gradually declined until only the NDP was left.

By 1963, most Canadians had access to television news. The new medium focused on the party leaders, relegating the once-powerful regional ministers to the background. All three parties sought to appeal to voters across the country, using "pan-Canadian"[143] rhetoric and symbolism to overcome subcultural divisions. Instead of brokering among competing interests, the parties used television and other new technologies—public-opinion polling and sophisticated advertising techniques—in an attempt to overcome them. The availability of public-opinion polling enabled the party leadership to bypass traditional sources of information and measure the attitudes and preferences of Canadians directly. No longer was it necessary to have a regional spokesperson represent the views of a section of the country. Such information could now be obtained more directly, and perhaps more accurately, through public-opinion polling.

The CCF–NDP provides a good example of the nationalized or "pan-Canadian"[144] approach that characterized the third party system. Whereas the CCF had attempted to unite the disparate groups that were opposed to the economic powers of Central Canada—namely, farmers, industrial workers, and socialists—the NDP was created to advance the interests of the predominantly urban working class. The strategy was for the NDP to form stronger ties with organized labour and for unions and their members to play a more active role by supporting the party directly.[145] Despite the electoral system's tendency to reward regional voting strength, the NDP adopted an explicitly national approach to political competition and downplayed the regional character of its appeal.[146]

Although the NDP survived this period of declining third parties, the regionally based Social Credit/Ralliement des créditistes party did not. In his landslide election of 1958, Diefenbaker won a majority of seats in each region of the country, not only capturing the traditional Liberal bastion of Quebec but also displacing third parties from the Prairies. Although the Progressive Conservatives were unable to hold Quebec, which briefly drifted to the Créditistes before throwing its support behind the Trudeau Liberals in 1968, they were able to retain the West. The Social Credit caucus, an uneasy mix of Western populists and Quebec nationalists, held the balance of power in the Commons after the 1962 and 1963 elections. It split into separate Western and Quebec caucuses in 1963 and gradually faded away.

Party development in this third system was influenced by profound social and cultural changes. Canadian society was far more urbanized and industrialized in the 1960s and 1970s than it had been at the end of World War II. Thus, Canada's regions became less socially and economically differentiated. Similarly, there was a shift of economic power westward. The economic centre of the country moved from Montreal to Toronto and there was substantial growth in the economic clout of Vancouver and Calgary.

Parties that thrived in the 1960s, 1970s, and 1980s—the Liberals and Progressive Conservatives, and, to a lesser extent, the New Democrats—were forced to adapt themselves to electronic politics. Perhaps the most profound consequence of the third party system was the increased importance of political leadership. With the personalization of electoral politics, a premium was placed on choosing a party leader who could appeal to a broad spectrum of the electorate. The party leader had to sell the party's platform and principles in both official languages, a requirement that met with considerable resistance in the PC Party. When the PCs finally chose a telegenic, fluently bilingual leader from Quebec—Brian Mulroney—in 1983, they were rewarded with a huge majority surpassing even the Diefenbaker landslide of 1958. Once again, the temporary end of Liberal dominance signalled the end of a party system. And once again, the PCs paid a heavy price for this victory; as we saw earlier,

Mulroney's failure to keep the Western populists and Quebec nationalists together in his electoral coalition led to the collapse of his party in 1993. The creation of two new regional parties initiated the fourth party system, in which explicitly regional politics has once again taken the place of nationalizing political appeals (though not for the Liberals).[147]

The institutional environment for political parties changed in important ways between 1963 and 1984. The shift from cooperative to executive federalism (see Chapter 4) increased the prominence of provincial premiers in national politics, which further reduced the brokerage role of the national parties and effectively ended the ministerialist approach to regional representation in the federal government. But regionalism remained a central theme of public discussion, and no amount of nationalistic rhetoric could change the regional reality of partisan politics. Despite their attempts to appeal to the national electorate, the three major parties were often regionally fragmented in the House of Commons. For most of this period, the electoral system gave the Liberal Party a disproportionate share of Quebec seats and shut out both the PCs and the NDP in the province. Likewise, the Progressive Conservatives (and to a lesser extent the NDP) were strong in the West, while the Liberals were also-rans in the region. Even the Liberal majority produced by the so-called Trudeaumania election in 1968—the biggest Liberal majority of this period—was based largely in Ontario and Quebec (120 of the Liberals' 155 seats came from those two provinces); Trudeau at his most popular was unable to improve his party's performance much in the Prairie West or Atlantic Canada.

A second major institutional change was the fundamental shift in the registration and financing of political parties brought about by the 1974 *Election Expenses Act*. As noted earlier in this chapter, the Act introduced direct and indirect public financing of parties and candidates. That Act also created a more open and accountable funding system in which parties were required to publicly declare their revenue and expenditures. Finally, it set limits on the amount of money parties and candidates could spend in election campaigns and on the amount of television exposure parties could purchase. The net effect of these changes was a substantial improvement in the financial stability of each of the major parties (albeit with significant fluctuations, depending on the party's electoral performance) and a consequent expansion in their national headquarters. Parties responded to the new institutional environment by developing direct-mail campaigns and appealing for funds beyond their small memberships.

As party organizations became stronger, more stable, and more financially secure, they were increasingly dominated by the party leader and his entourage. As we have seen, parties relied increasingly on professional consultants to craft their campaigns. The costs of campaigning soared. (As we will see in Chapter 12, this was one of the main reasons for the 1974 election finance law.) As campaigning became more "capital-intensive,"[148] local party members in the constituencies felt increasingly neglected. Parties tried to create new incentives for their members, including a vast increase in constituency-delegate positions at leadership conventions. But throughout the third party system, Canadians who wanted to participate in politics began to drift away from the parties toward pressure groups. Changing political values and intractable economic problems undermined the credibility of party politics, and opened the door for "anti-party" appeals. The "content-free" political rhetoric of the major parties eroded their ties to the electorate,[149] while alienating potential party members who sought more meaningful politics. By 1984, the stage was set for a fourth party system.

Fourth Period: 1993–?

Brian Mulroney's success in attracting the Quebec nationalist subculture into the Progressive Conservative electoral coalition ultimately destroyed his party. The Western populist subculture defected to the Reform Party after 1987, while the establishment of the Bloc Québécois in 1990 provided a political home for the Quebec nationalists. Although the 1988 election produced little overall change, the results of the 1992 Charlottetown Accord revealed deep voter frustration with the three "old-line" parties. Two unsuccessful rounds of constitutional negotiation, together with the divisive trade policy of the Mulroney Government, alienated voters from the PCs. The Spicer Commission found a deep sense of betrayal and alienation among Canadians, as well as a belief that political parties were unresponsive to and unconcerned about their needs. The cultural changes described in Chapter 2 were about to be felt in the national party system.

According to Carty, Cross, and Young, "there are substantial continuities between the third party system and the system that is currently taking shape."[150] Nevertheless, they have identified five distinct characteristics of the fourth party system:

1. "the entry of two new parties [the BQ and Reform/Alliance], which have eclipsed both the Conservatives and NDP in Parliament";
2. a regionally fragmented pattern of party competition;
3. the increasing tendency of party strategists to target particular groups of voters, instead of appealing to a national electorate [see Dossier 12.3];
4. greater ideological diversity among the major parties; and
5. more internal party democracy, as the parties respond to "the participatory demands of an assertive citizenry."[151]

We might add a sixth characteristic: the seemingly invincible dominance of the Liberal Party.[152] Between 1993 and 2000, the party formed three consecutive majority governments. By late 2003, the apparent popularity of new Liberal leader Paul Martin seemed certain to produce an even bigger majority in the next election. Fear of the Martin "juggernaut" helped to push the two leading right-wing parties to merge into one, producing the biggest change in the fourth party system (Dossier 11.5).

The results of the 2006 and 2008 elections raise questions about this picture of the current party system. The Reform Party has vanished, the ideological spectrum has narrowed, and the Liberals are in Opposition. Regionalism has always been an important influence on Canadian voters, although our electoral system exaggerates its impact (see Chapter 12). Table 11.5 displays the regional bases of three parliamentary parties in the fourth party system (the

DOSSIER 11.5 The Creation of the Conservative Party of Canada

After the Western-based Reform Party failed to win seats in Ontario in 1997, leader Preston Manning asked his membership to approve a plan to found a new party: a coalition of groups that might include former Conservatives, Quebec nationalists, and others opposed to the Liberal government. At the 1998 Reform Assembly, 91.3 percent of delegates voted to hold a United Alternative (UA) convention to initiate the process.[153] At the February 1999 UA Conference, participants were given four options: launch an entirely new party; pursue local initiatives with other parties, such as joint nomination meetings; unite behind an existing party (which, given that 80 percent of those in attendance were Reform members, presumably meant a Reform takeover); or merge two or more parties.[154] Creating a new party was the most popular of the four options at the convention, but when it was submitted to the Reform membership in a May 1999 referendum, it was supported by only 60.5 percent of those who voted (less than half of those eligible). Despite Manning's efforts to persuade Reformers that the status quo was not an option, there was little enthusiasm for change among the "believers" in his party. The UA appears to have had its greatest appeal with the "careerists" who wanted to displace the Liberals as the party of government.

(continued)

For their part, the federal PCs wanted nothing to do with the UA[155]—although it did attract some high-profile members of Ontario's PC party, which had been taken further to the right under former Premier Mike Harris than most PCs. In January 2000, the Canadian Reform Conservative Alliance was launched. Two months later, Reform was officially absorbed into the Canadian Alliance by an overwhelming vote (92 percent) in a second party referendum. Shortly thereafter, Manning lost the leadership of the new party to Alberta PC Treasurer Stockwell Day. Day became a controversial figure almost immediately, despite his easy victory in a British Columbia by-election in September 2000. When Prime Minister Chrétien called an early election in October, the Alliance had not had time to jell as a party organization.[156] The scars from the UA debate and the leadership contest were still fresh. To make matters worse, Day did not live up to the expectations of his supporters. Not only did he fail to lead the Alliance to a breakthrough in Ontario—the party won only two seats, largely because of local factors—but his poor performance in the campaign damaged his reputation and that of his fledgling party.[157]

By the summer of 2001, 13 MPs had quit the Alliance caucus in protest against Day's leadership. Five later returned, while the remaining eight dissidents formed the Democratic Representative Caucus (DRC) and announced that they would work with the Progressive Conservatives in Parliament.[158] Day was forced to resign. Stephen Harper, a former Reform MP who had left politics in 1997, won the leadership in March 2002. All but one of the DRC members returned to the Alliance caucus. In the interim, they had formed good working relationships with most of the PC members of Parliament. They shared Harper's view that a merger of the two parties should be a top priority, but PC leader Joe Clark feared that his smaller party would be steamrolled by the Alliance.[159] He refused even to consider the idea, especially after his party won a May 2002 by-election in rural Ontario; the Alliance candidate placed third, despite a massive investment of financial and human resources in a riding that looked winnable.[160]

Clark stepped down in August 2002. Nova Scotia MP Peter MacKay won the leadership in 2003, in unusual and rather damaging circumstances. He needed the support of second-place candidate David Orchard to beat third-place candidate Jim Prentice. He signed a written deal with Orchard, promising that he would not merge the PC party with the Alliance.[161] Shortly thereafter, MacKay entered secret negotiations with Harper.[162] Each leader appointed three "emissaries" to hammer out a deal that members of both parties could accept. The talks appeared stalled by late summer, although the two leaders promised that their caucuses would cooperate in the House of Commons when Parliament resumed in September.[163]

In the fall of 2003, the popularity of aspiring Prime Minister Paul Martin seemed certain to produce a smashing Liberal victory in an anticipated spring 2004 election. Many senior figures in both parties regarded a merger as the only way to survive the onslaught.[164] However, if such a merger were to happen, it would have to be accomplished quickly. The ban on corporate donations in Bill C-24 was set to take effect at the end of the year. For years, Canada's business elite had been withholding donations from the two parties until they got together to defeat the Liberals. Advocates of a PC-Alliance deal wanted to take full advantage of corporate generosity, which meant that a merger had to happen no later than mid-October.[165]

News of the merger talks leaked to the public in late September, forcing Harper and MacKay—especially the latter—to quell dissent within their respective parties. The deal was announced shortly after Thanksgiving. To counter PC fears of an Alliance takeover, Harper had made significant concessions on policy and organization. In addition to adopting the 1998 PC leadership-selection system, the Alliance agreed to endorse several PC principles, including:

- "A balance between fiscal accountability, progressive social policy, and individual rights and responsibilities";
- "the supremacy of democratic parliamentary institutions and the rule of law";

(continued)

- "a belief in the equality of all Canadians"; and
- "a belief that all Canadians should have reasonable access to quality health care regardless of their ability to pay."[166]

There was no reference to direct democracy, social conservatism, or private medical clinics. Indeed, the references to "the rule of law" and "equality" seemed to contradict the deeply held view of many Alliance members that the *Charter of Rights* should be weakened, judges put on a political leash, and same-sex marriage outlawed.

The backlash began immediately. While there were some dissenters in Alliance ranks, the loudest opponents were PCs. David Orchard charged MacKay with breaking the written agreement the two men had signed at the June 2003 PC leadership convention, and later filed a lawsuit in an unsuccessful attempt to prevent the merger.[167] Joe Clark left the party, along with other prominent PC members of Parliament. The deal required the members of both parties

to ratify the merger by mid-December.[168] Almost 96 percent of the Alliance members who voted in their party's referendum—60 percent of the total membership—opted to merge with the PCs.[169] The day after this result was announced, 90 percent of the participants in the PC ratification process did the same.[170] On December 8, the new Conservative Party of Canada was officially registered with Elections Canada. In the meantime, the unofficial merger had produced the desired financial result: whereas the two founding parties had been mired in debt, the prospect of a united Conservative Party inspired an outburst of corporate generosity.[171] As it turned out, the new party did not manage to capture as many votes in the 2004 election as its two founding parties had won in 2000 (see Chapter 4). But this was a temporary setback: just over two years after the merger took effect, the Conservative Party of Canada replaced the Liberals in power.

Peter MacKay and Stephen Harper announce the merger of their two parties, October 15, 2003. (CP/Tom Hanson)

TABLE 11.5 THE REGIONAL DISTRIBUTION OF PARTY SEATS IN THE COMMONS, MAJOR NATIONAL PARTIES 1993–2008

1993

PARTY	ONTARIO	WEST*	QUEBEC	ATLANTIC
Liberal	55.4	16.4	10.7	17.5
Reform	1.9	98.1	—	—
PC	0	0.0	50	50
NDP	0	100	0	0.0
% of seats in the Commons for each region				

1997

PARTY	ONTARIO	WEST*	QUEBEC	ATLANTIC
Liberal	65.2	11	16.8	7.1
Reform	0	100	0	0
PC	5	5	25	65
NDP	0.0	61.9	0.0	38.1
% of seats in the Commons for each region	34.2	29.2	24.9	10.6

2000

PARTY	ONTARIO	WEST*	QUEBEC	ATLANTIC
Liberal	58.1	9.9	20.9	11
Canadian Alliance	3	97	0	0
PC	0.0	16.7	8.3	75
NDP	7.7	61.5	0	30.8
% of seats in the Commons for each region	34.2	29.2	24.9	10.6

2004

PARTY	ONTARIO	WEST*	QUEBEC	ATLANTIC
Liberal	55.6	12.6	15.6	16.3
Conservative	24.2	68.7	0.0	7.1
NDP	36.8	47.4	0.0	15.8
% of seats in the Commons for each region	34.4	31.2	24.4	10.4

2008

PARTY	ONTARIO	WEST*	QUEBEC	ATLANTIC
Liberal	43.4	10.4	18.7	22.1
Conservative	35.7	50.3	7.0	7.0
NDP	45.9	40.5	2.7	10.8
% of seats in the Commons for each region	34.4	31.2	24.4	10.4

*"West" includes Manitoba, Saskatchewan, Alberta, British Columbia, and the Territories. The BQ is excluded from this table because all of its seats are in Quebec.

BQ, which runs candidates only in Quebec, is excluded). The number in each cell is the percentage of each party's caucus elected from a particular region.

We are left with two characteristics of the fourth party system: targeted electoral appeals, and internal party democracy. Targeting is certainly an important feature of modern campaigns, as Dossier 12.3 demonstrates. In some respects, however, the "plebiscitarian" wave in Canadian parties appears to have peaked (see the discussion of ebbing populism in Chapter 2). As we have seen, the Liberals have decided to retain leadership conventions instead of adopting straight OMOV. Local nomination races are subject to increasing control from party headquarters. Constituency associations face ever-tighter restrictions on fundraising, which reduces their power vis-à-vis the party in central office. These developments suggest that our parties are becoming less, not more, democratic in their internal processes.

CONCLUSION

Whatever form Canada's party system takes in the near future, the health of our democratic politics will continue to suffer unless the parties find a way to recapture the trust and engagement of Canadians. Savoie attributes the emergence of "court government," in part, to the erosion of political parties. He argues that "When we move away from political parties to pursue more narrow interests, the connection between citizens and their government is further fragmented."[172]

> There is a much better chance that the concerns of the average citizen will be heard when political parties and their members prepare broad policy preferences, rather than when this responsibility is concentrated in the hands of party leaders and their advisers. Similarly, the concerns of the average citizen in shaping policies are less likely to be taken into account when political power is concentrated in the hands of party leaders and their courtiers.[173]

As we will see in the next chapter, falling voter turnout can be blamed, in part, on electoralist strategies that provide few if any opportunities for direct personal engagement between parties and citizens. But as Chapter 12 also points out, our political franchises no longer rely on their "fan bases" for the resources they need to stay in business. Government subsidies have taken the place of membership fees and most categories of donation. Under those circumstances, there is little incentive for Canadian parties to "rediscover their vitality and regain their relevance."[174]

GLOSSARY OF KEY TERMS

"Believers" and "careerists": Two categories of party members, distinguished on the basis of their primary motivations for party activity. "Believers" are motivated by their faith in the party's principles or its leader; "careerists" are more interested in their own status within the party hierarchy.

Catch-all party: A political party whose primary goal is to win a majority of seats in Parliament and form a government. Because it seeks to appeal to as many voters as possible, it tends to downplay potentially divisive ideologies and principles. Usually a small membership, dominated by the leader and the caucus.

Caucus: The parliamentary wing of a political party. Includes all the MPs (and senators, if any) who represent that party in Parliament.

Cleavage: A stable and long-term division between groups of voters. Examples include religion (Catholic versus Protestant, observant versus nonobservant), language (English versus French), region (West versus East, Quebec versus Alberta), gender, and class.

Collective solidary/social incentives: Intangible rewards for party effort, available to all party members (the joy of victory, the satisfaction of working together for a shared goal, and the social value of meeting like-minded people).

Electoral system: The rules and procedures by which legislators are elected in a given country. Canada's electoral system is called single-member plurality (SMP), because each constituency elects one MP and the candidate with more votes than any other wins the seat. See Chapter 12.

Extraparliamentary: The party organization outside Parliament. Includes the national headquarters, the national executive, and the local constituency associations.

"Instant" party members: Individuals and groups recruited to join a local constituency association en masse, for the purpose of electing a slate of convention delegates committed to a particular leadership candidate (or, under OMOV, to vote directly for the candidate). Also used by organizers for aspiring constituency candidates to "swamp" the nomination meeting. While leadership contests and nomination battles are important opportunities to attract new members to the party, "instant" members rarely stick around for the long term. Increasingly controversial, especially the wholesale importation of people who are not eligible to vote in Canadian elections (e.g., recent immigrants, minors). All parties except the Conservative Party allow ineligible voters to participate, in the name of openness and for recruitment of future citizens.

Leadership convention: A gathering of party delegates to choose a new leader. Thousands of delegates—most elected by constituency associations, campus clubs, women's and youth organizations, and other party branches—cast ballots in successive rounds of voting, until one candidate receives a majority of the valid votes.

Material incentives: Tangible rewards for loyal party service (e.g., a seat in the Senate).

Ministerialism: The practice of treating Cabinet ministers as representatives from their regions. During the second party system (1921–57), the federal Liberals used regional ministers as both conduits of political intelligence and dispensers of patronage. Ministerialism was a key ingredient in the Liberals' successful strategy of regional brokering.

Minority party syndrome: An imbalance between "believers" and "careerists" within a party's membership, caused by prolonged periods of electoral defeat. The internal culture of the party becomes adversarial (instead of constructive), fractious (rather than united), and oriented to criticism instead of governing.

Mobilization: The process of organizing a particular subculture to support a new or existing political party. Examples include Brian Mulroney's attempt to bring Quebec nationalists into the Progressive Conservative Party of Canada in 1984 and Preston Manning's appeal to Western populists to join his fledgling Reform Party in the late 1980s.

Multiparty system: A party system in which three or more parties compete for inclusion in a governing coalition. Usually associated with proportional representation electoral systems.

One member, one vote (OMOV): A system of party leadership selection in which every party member can vote directly for the candidate of his or her choice, instead of electing delegates to vote on his or her behalf.

Party networks: Distinct groups within a party organization. Include factions (formed around leadership aspirants), regional networks, the caucus, the leader's entourage, and ideological sects.

Party system: The sum total of the parties represented in the House of Commons at a given time, reflecting the social cleavages and subcultures in the electorate and the structure of party competition.

Patronage: The practice of appointing party supporters to fill public offices, such as the Order-in-Council appointments awarded at the discretion of the prime minister. Less common today than in the nineteenth century. Often regarded as corrupt and harmful, but this perception is not always correct; material incentives for party members may help to attract and retain the volunteers needed for a vibrant representative democracy.

Platform: The statement of policies and principles issued by a party during an election campaign (e.g., the Liberal *Red Book* of 1993, 1997, and 2000). In theory, a platform provides the foundation for both the party's electoral appeal and its activities if elected to government; in practice, as we will see in Chapter 4, platforms do not necessarily bind parties in office.

Political entrepreneur: An individual who perceives an unmet need in the political marketplace and creates a new political party to fill that need. Examples include Preston Manning's establishment of the Reform Party of Canada to express the views of the Western populist subculture in federal politics and Lucien Bouchard's creation of the Bloc Québécois to give Quebec nationalists a distinct voice in Parliament.

Political party: An organization of members who work together to achieve one or more common goals.

Programmatic party: A party whose primary goal is to promote a particular ideology or policy; while it would welcome the chance to implement its proposals in government, it is less focused on electoral victory than a catch-all party. More internally democratic, less leader-dominated, and places a greater emphasis on attracting a large membership.

Purposive/altruistic incentives: The sense that one is contributing to the greater good by campaigning for a candidate or advocating a particular policy or ideology.

Selectorate: The group of people with the power to choose a candidate or party leader.

Specific solidary incentives: Intangible benefits that are awarded to a few select individuals (e.g., status, a nomination for Parliament, or a high-ranking office in the party).

"Spin doctors": Professional consultants who advise political parties about using the news media effectively. May also include party staffers and volunteers who make themselves available to reporters seeking the party's "spin" on a particular issue or event.

DISCUSSION AND REVIEW QUESTIONS

1. Do you support a particular political party? If so, why? If not, why not?

2. Identify the four parties represented in the House of Commons after the 2006 election. In your own words, briefly describe each party.

3. Identify and explain TWO of the four types of incentive for party membership.

4. Identify and briefly explain ONE difference between a catch-all party and a programmatic party, and give ONE Canadian example of each type.

5. Voter turnout has declined significantly over five of the past six federal elections. Young Canadians are particularly reluctant to cast ballots. In your opinion, are the major parties to blame for this trend? Why or why not?

6. How do Canadian parties nominate candidates for the House of Commons? How do they choose their leaders? In your opinion, are these processes satisfactory? Why or why not?

SUGGESTED READINGS

Books and Articles

Keith Archer and Alan Whitehorn, *Political Activists: The NDP in Convention* (Toronto: Oxford University Press, 1997).

Reginald Austin and Maja Tjernström, eds., *IDEA Handbook: Funding of Political Parties and Election Campaigns* (Stockholm: International Institute for Democracy and Electoral Assistance, 2003).

Herman Bakvis, ed., *Canadian Political Parties: Leaders, Candidates, and Organization,* volume 13 of the collected research studies for the Royal Commission on Electoral Reform and Party Financing (Toronto: Dundurn, 1991).

James Bickerton, Alain-G. Gagnon, and Patrick J. Smith, *Ties that Bind: Parties and Voters in Canada* (Toronto: Oxford University Press, 1999).

André Blais, Elisabeth Gidengil, Richard Nadeau, and Neil Nevitte, *Anatomy of a Liberal Victory: Making Sense of the Vote in the 2000 Canadian Election* (Peterborough, ON: Broadview Press, 2002).

Canada, Royal Commission on Electoral Reform and Party Financing, *Reforming Electoral Democracy,* volume 1 (Canada: Minister of Supply and Services, 1991).

R. Kenneth Carty, *Canadian Political Parties in the Constituencies,* volume 23 of the collected research studies for the Royal Commission on Electoral Reform and Party Financing (Toronto: Dundurn, 1991).

R. Kenneth Carty, "Parties as Franchise Systems: The Stratarchical Organizational Imperative," *Party Politics,* 10:1 (2004).

R. Kenneth Carty, "The Shifting Place of Political Parties in Canadian Public Life," *Choices,* 12:4 (Montreal; IRPP, 2006).

R. Kenneth Carty, William Cross, and Lisa Young, *Rebuilding Canadian Party Politics* (Vancouver: UBC Press, 2000).

R. Kenneth Carty and Munroe Eagles, *Politics is Local: National Politics at the Grassroots* (Toronto: Oxford University Press, 2005).

R. Kenneth Carty, Lynda Erickson, and Donald E. Blake, eds., *Leaders and Parties in Canadian Politics: Experiences of the Provinces* (Toronto: HBJ Canada, 1992).

Stephen Clarkson, *The Big Red Machine: How The Liberal Party Dominates Canadian Politics* (Vancouver: UBC Press, 2005).

John C. Courtney, *Do Conventions Matter? Choosing National Party Leaders in Canada* (Montreal and Kingston: McGill–Queen's University Press, 1995).

John C. Courtney, *Elections* (Vancouver: UBC Press, 2004).

William Cross, *Political Parties* (Vancouver: UBC Press, 2004).

William Cross, ed., *Political Parties, Representation, and Electoral Democracy in Canada* (Toronto: Oxford University Press, 2002).

William Cross and Lisa Young, 2006. "Are Canadian Political Parties Empty Vessels? Membership, Engagement and Policy Capacity," *Choices*, 12:4 (Montreal; IRPP, 2006).

Maurice Duverger, *Political Parties: Their Organization and Activity in the Modern State,* translated by Barbara and Robert North (London: Methuen, 1964 [1954]).

Richard Gunther and Larry Diamond, "Species of Political Parties: A New Topology," *Party Politics,* 9:2 (2003), 167–199.

Lois Harder and Steve Patten, eds., *The Chrétien Legacy: Politics and Public Policy in Canada* (Montreal and Kingston: McGill–Queen's University Press, 2006).

Chantal Hébert, *French Kiss: Stephen Harper's Blind Date with Quebec* (Toronto: Knopf Canada, 2007).

Lawrence LeDuc, "Democratizing Party Leadership Selection," *Party Politics,* 7:3 (2001), 323–341.

Jon H. Pammett and Christopher Dornan, eds., *The Canadian Federal Election of 2006* (Toronto: Dundurn Press, 2006).

Bob Plamondon, *Full Circle: Death and Resurrection in Canadian Conservative Politics* (Toronto: Key Porter, 2006).

Paul Wells, *Right Side Up: The Fall of Paul Martin and the Rise of Stephen Harper's New Conservatism* (Toronto: McClelland & Stewart, 2006).

Websites

Most of the registered parties in national politics have their own websites. Go to the Nelson website for this book (www.parametersofpower5e.nelson.com), click on "Canadian Politics on the Web," and scroll down to "Political Parties."

Alternatively, go to the Elections Canada website (www.elections.ca) and click on "Political Parties, Candidates and Third Parties," where you will find a complete list of registered parties, with links to their Web pages. Elections Canada also provides Acrobat files containing the *Canada Elections Act* and other documents relating to the regulation of national parties (go to "Election Law and Policy" and "Election Financing").

NOTES

1. If the Harper Government's proposal to elect senators goes ahead, parties will nominate and campaign for Senate nominees as well. See Dossier 3.4.
2. Ronald Inglehart and Christian Welzel, *Modernization, Cultural Change, and Democracy: The Human Development Sequence* (New York: Cambridge University Press, 2005), 44 and 117–118.
3. Graham Fox, "Discussion Paper: Rethinking Political Parties" (Ottawa: Public Policy Forum, November 2005), 3; accessed at www.ppforum.ca, August 2007. The phrase "potemkin village" refers to a propaganda technique employed by the chief minister to a Russian Empress in the

nineteenth century. When the Empress toured the countryside, he would order the construction of fake villages along the road before she passed by. That way, she would be impressed by the excellent quality of the housing provided to the Russian peasantry.

4. Donald J. Savoie, *Court Government and the Collapse of Accountability in Canada and the United Kingdom* (Toronto: University of Toronto Press, 2008), 304.

5. An official party, under the rules of the House of Commons, must have at least 12 MPs. Smaller caucuses, such as the nine-member NDP caucus from 1993 to 1997, are not entitled to the privileges of official status (extra funding, committee seats, inclusion on the Speaker's List at Question Period).

6. Reform's founding leader, Preston Manning, decided after the 1997 election that his party could not provide a national alternative to the governing Liberals unless it broadened its appeal to voters in Ontario. To that end, he initiated the United Alternative campaign to bring Reformers and PCs together in one party. The result was the Canadian Alliance, which was officially launched in 2000 under Stockwell Day. (Manning tried, but failed, to become leader of the new party.) Day's performance in the 2000 election campaign was a severe disappointment to his supporters; the Liberals won their third consecutive majority, partly because of fears that the new party and leader were too "extreme." Day was forced out by a caucus revolt in 2001. Stephen Harper became the leader of the Canadian Alliance in 2002. The merger of the Alliance and the PCs is discussed later in the chapter.

7. James Madison, "Federalist No. 10," in Alexander Hamilton, James Madison, and John Jay, *The Federalist Papers*, edited by Clinton Rossiter (New York: New American Library, 1961 [1788]).

8. R. Kenneth Carty, "For the Third Asking: Is There a Future for National Political Parties in Canada?" in Tom Kent, ed., *In Pursuit of the Public Good: Essays in Honour of Allan J. MacEachen* (Montreal and Kingston: McGill–Queen's University Press, 1997), 147.

9. Carty, *Canadian Political Parties in the Constituencies*, volume 23 of the collected research studies for the Royal Commission on Electoral Reform and Party Financing (Toronto: Dundurn, 1991), 12.

10. Steven Weldon, "Downsize My Polity? The Impact of Size on Party Membership and Member Activism," *Party Politics*, 12:4 (2006), 476.

11. Carty, *Canadian Political Parties in the Constituencies*, 28–29; William Cross and Lisa Young, "The Contours of Political Party Membership in Canada," *Party Politics*, 10:4 (2004), 430.

12. Paul Howe and David Northrup, *Strengthening Canadian Democracy: The Views of Canadians* (Montreal: Institute for Research on Public Policy, 2000), 89.

13. Ibid., 91.

14. Cross and Young, "The Contours of Political Party Membership in Canada," 430–38.

15. See the discussion of political ideology in Chapter 2.

16. Cross and Young, "The Contours of Political Party Membership," Tables 10 and 11, 439. Note, however, that the survey was conducted at a time when there was no federal election, and no leadership contest in any of the parties surveyed; both the number of members and their level of activity are generally low during these periods.

17. For a sophisticated analysis of party goals, see Robert Harmel and Kenneth Janda, "An Integrated Theory of Party Goals and Party Change," *Journal of Theoretical Politics*, VI:3 (July 1994), 259–87.

18. Cross and Young, "The Contours of Political Party Membership," Tables 10 and 11, 439.

19. Courtney attributes the dominance of electoralist parties in Canada to the incentives set by the single-member plurality electoral system, which is discussed in Chapter 12. John C. Courtney, *Elections* (Vancouver: UBC Press, 2004), 138.

20. Richard Gunther and Larry Diamond, "Species of Political Parties: A New Typology," *Party Politics*, 9:2 (2003), 185 (citation omitted).

21. Gunther and Diamond identify a third type, the "personalistic" party. This is simply an organizational vehicle for the ambitions of a single person (e.g., Forza Italia, created by billionaire Silvio Berlusconi). There has not yet been a personalistic party in Canada, although there have certainly been personalistic networks within parties—such as the Paul Martin

"juggernaut" in the Liberal Party of Canada, and David Orchard's team, which twice tried unsuccessfully to capture the PC Party.

22. Gunther and Diamond, 185–186.

23. Ibid., 187.

24. In May 2007, former Reform Party members launched an effort to re-establish the party as a separate entity. They perceived the catch-all party led by Prime Minister Harper as a betrayal of Reform principles. Gloria Galloway, "Disgruntled Tories consider rebuilding Reform Party," *The Globe and Mail*, May 12, 2007, A4. See the discussion of party networks later in this chapter.

25. This categorization is based on Peter Mair's "three faces" of party organization: the party on the ground, the party in public office, and the party in central office. Peter Mair, "Party Organizations: From Civil Society to the State," in Richard S. Katz and Peter Mair, eds., *How Parties Organize: Change and Adaptation in Party Organizations in Western Democracies* (Thousand Oaks, Calif.: Sage, 1994), 4.

26. Courtney points out that the administration of federal elections, which has become increasingly centralized since 1867, is an important exception to the apparent decentralization of the Canadian federation. Courtney, *Elections*, 13.

27. "Conservative Party of Canada Constitution," section 15.1 (accessed at www.conservative.ca, May 9, 2007).

28. Brian Laghi, "Tory feud erupts over 'broken promises,'" *The Globe and Mail*, March 29, 2007 (accessed at www.theglobeandmail.com). Williams urged voters not to re-elect the three Conservative MPs from Newfoundland and Labrador. In response, at least one aspiring Conservative candidate withdrew from her nomination contest. There were similar (but quieter) tensions between the federal party and the PC government in Nova Scotia, which prompted Foreign Affairs Minister (and Nova Scotia MP) Peter MacKay to intervene in hopes of a better equalization deal for the Atlantic region. Brian Laghi, "Harper–Williams feud creates doubt in some candidates," *The Globe and Mail*, April 4, 2007 (accessed at www.theglobeandmail.com); Brian Laghi, "MacKay lobbies for the folks back home," *The Globe and Mail*, May 12, 2007, A16. See also Dossier 4.2.

29. Carty, "For the Third Asking: Is There a Future for National Political Parties in Canada?" 148–49.

30. One recent example of the law's impact occurred at the 2006 Liberal convention, where the delegates voted to centralize the party's membership system. The Liberal Party of Canada was always the most decentralized of the major parties. The national headquarters could not claw back money from the constituency associations. This became a major problem in the 1980s, when the national party was broke and some of its associations had brimming bank accounts. Nor could it request donations from party members, who were regulated by the provincial and territorial wings. "Grassroots party fundraising became critical [under] the post C-24 campaign financing laws that banned corporate and union donations. With the new structural change, the Liberal Party would be able to communicate directly with the party members." Abbas Rana and Bea Vongdouangchanh, "Liberals vote to centralize party, shorten campaigns," *The Hill Times*, December 11, 2006, 1.

31. The Conservative constitution requires at least one delegate from each constituency association to "reflect youth participation"; it does not define the term "youth," leaving age qualifications to be determined in party by-laws. The constitution provides for the establishment of "affiliated organizations," including youth and campus clubs, but these are not empowered to send voting delegates to national conventions.

32. The phrase was coined by Robert Michels in his book *Political Parties: A Sociological Study of the Oligarchical Tendencies of Modern Democracy* (New York: Free Press, 1962 [1911]).

33. David Docherty, "Could the Rebels Find a Cause? House of Commons Reform in the Chrétien Era" in Lois Harder and Steve Patten, eds., *The Chrétien Legacy: Politics and Public Policy in Canada* (Montreal and Kingston: McGill–Queen's University Press, 2006), 300–320; Steve Patten, "Jean Chrétien and a Decade of Party System Change," in Harder and Patten, eds., 321–341.

34. R. Kenneth Carty, "Parties as Franchise Systems: The Stratarchical Organizational Imperative," *Party Politics,* 10:1 (2004), 7–9.

35. In this context, the word "franchise" denotes a structural similarity to companies like McDonald's, in which local businesspeople purchase the right to use the company name, menu, and graphic design in their home markets. It should not be confused with the political meaning of "franchise," which refers to the right to vote in elections.

36. Carty, "Parties as Franchise Systems," 11.

37. The first two categories are taken from James Q. Wilson, *Political Organizations* (Princeton: Princeton University Press, 1995 [1974]), 33–34. The third and fourth combine categories used by Wilson ("collective solidary" and "purposive") with two from Lisa Young and William Cross, "Incentives to Membership in Canadian Political Parties," *Political Research Quarterly,* 55:3 (September 2002), 550 ("social norms" and "altruistic").

38. Courtney, *Elections,* 81–82.

39. See Gordon T. Stewart, *The Origins of Canadian Politics: A Comparative Approach* (Vancouver: UBC Press, 1986), Chapters 3 and 4.

40. Young and Cross, "Incentives to Membership in Canadian Political Parties," 558.

41. Carty, *Canadian Political Parties in the Constituencies,* Table 3.17, 60.

42. Cross and Young ("The Contours of Political Party Membership," 436) found that the major parties (except the governing Liberals) had attracted few new members in the decade prior to their survey. They speculate, with good reason, that many (if not most) "instant" members allow their new memberships to lapse shortly after the nomination or leadership contest ends.

43. Carty, *Canadian Political Parties in the Constituencies,* 173–76.

44. Young and Cross, "Incentives to Membership in Canadian Political Parties," Table 1, 556.

45. These terms are taken from Angelo Panebianco, *Political Parties: Organization and Power* (Cambridge: Cambridge University Press, 1988), 26.

46. George C. Perlin, *The Tory Syndrome: Leadership Politics in the Progressive Conservative Party* (Montreal and Kingston: McGill–Queen's University Press, 1980), 198–200.

47. This conclusion is supported by Young and Cross, "Incentives to Membership in Canadian Political Parties." Figure 2 (564) shows that for PCs who joined the party in the 1980s and 1990s, material and other self-seeking incentives were considerably more important than for those who joined during the party's "wilderness years" of the 1960s and 1970s.

48. S.J.R. Noel, "Patronage and Entourages, Action-Sets, Networks," in A. Brian Tanguay and Alain-G. Gagnon, eds., *Canadian Parties in Transition,* second ed. (Scarborough: Nelson Canada, 1996), 247–48; Mildred A. Schwartz, *The Party Network: The Robust Organization of Illinois Republicans* (Madison: University of Wisconsin Press, 1990).

49. B.D. Graham, *Representation and Party Politics: A Comparative Perspective* (Oxford: Blackwell, 1993), 156.

50. See Noel for a discussion of the leader's entourage.

51. Graham, 154.

52. Ibid.

53. Carty, "Parties as Franchise Systems," 15.

54. Between April and July 2001, the Canadian Alliance caucus ruptured. The exodus began with the resignations of the House leader and deputy leader/caucus chair from their caucus positions, in protest against the leadership of Stockwell Day. Over the next three months, 13 MPs left the Alliance caucus to sit as independents. In late July, after Day had promised to resign at some unspecified future date, one of the dissidents returned to the Alliance; the other 12 decided to form a separate parliamentary group, the Democratic Representative (DR) Caucus. Although four of the dissidents soon returned to the Canadian Alliance, the remaining eight agreed to a coalition arrangement with the Progressive Conservatives. The resulting "PC–DR Coalition" did not receive official party status from the Speaker of the House, but its 20 members were allowed to sit together and to carry out their parliamentary

tasks as a single unit. During this period of turmoil, Alliance support in the polls plunged into the single digits.

55. Independent candidates are those who have not been nominated by a political party. Candidates with no party affiliation were nominated by a party, but the party failed to fulfill the requirements for registered party status.

56. A "safe" seat is defined by the long-term dominance of one party in that particular district. In a party stronghold, "it is the candidate-selection procedure—and not the general election—that determines who will become a member of parliament." Gideon Rahat, "Candidate Selection: The Choice before the Choice," *Journal of Democracy*, 18:1 (January 2007), 159. Since 1984, the proportion of "safe" Commons seats has shrunk.

57. On average, one independent candidate wins in each federal general election. In 2004, the late Chuck Cadman held his riding of Surrey North despite having lost the Conservative nomination. In 2006, former radio-show host André Arthur won a seat in Quebec as an independent candidate; he was re-elected as an Independent in 2008, along with former Conservative MP Bill Casey in Nova Scotia. As Chapter 7 explains, an independent can play an important role in a minority Parliament; otherwise, they enjoy few of the benefits that come with membership in an official caucus.

58. William Cross, "Candidate Nomination in Canada's Political Parties," in Jon H. Pammett and Christopher Dornan, eds., *The Canadian Federal Election of 2006* (Toronto: Dundurn Press, 2006), 171–172.

59. The 2006 election was an exception: both the Liberal and Conservative parties protected their incumbent MPs, and there were no nomination (or renomination) meetings in constituencies where Liberals and Conservatives were running for re-election. Cross, 176.

60. In most cases, a person wishing to vote at a nomination or delegate-selection meeting must have held a party membership for a specified period of time before the meeting is held. The purpose of an early cut-off date is to prevent the association from being flooded by "instant" members with no real tie to the party—or, in some cases, to protect incumbent MPs from being denied renomination. Later "cut-off" dates are intended to facilitate membership recruitment at a time of heightened political interest and activity.

61. Cross, 179–180.

62. The Conservative Party requires each of its constituency associations to establish its own Candidate Nomination Committee, whose decisions are reviewed (and can be overturned) by the National Candidate Selection Committee. The national committee has the power to disallow the candidate chosen by the nomination meeting; the local committee does not. Conservative Party of Canada, "Candidate Nomination Rules and Procedures," October 2006 (accessed at www.conservative.ca). The Liberal Party of Canada does not explicitly require local nomination committees, nor does it establish a separate national committee; all decisions concerning candidate nomination are to be made by the National Election Readiness Committee, which is responsible for all campaign-related activities. Liberal Party of Canada Constitution (as amended in 2006), accessed at www.liberal.ca.

63. The Conservative Party permits the use of either electoral system; the other parties leave specific voting procedures to be determined by the various constituency associations.

64. Carty and Erickson, 120; Cross, 181.

65. In 2006, both the Liberals and the Conservatives decided to protect their incumbent MPs from challenge by prohibiting renomination meetings.

66. In the run-up to the 2004 election, constituency boundaries were redrawn to reflect the results of the 2001 census. The new constituency of Hamilton East–Stoney Creek overlapped two old ridings, both held by Liberal MPs. The two sitting members, Sheila Copps and Tony Valeri, squared off in a pitched battle for the new riding. Copps, who had been an MP since 1984 and a Cabinet minister since 1993, had recently lost the Liberal leadership to Prime Minister Paul Martin by a wide margin. Although her defeat was clearly inevitable, Copps insisted that the November 2003 leadership convention should not be turned into a coronation. Her persistence apparently earned her the enmity of the Martin forces; she was fired from Cabinet in December 2003, on the same day that Valeri (a prominent Martin loyalist)

received his first ministerial portfolio. Even though Copps controlled the new riding associa-tion executive and canvassed hard for the nomination, Valeri won the battle. Copps claimed that the vote was rigged, and appealed to the national executive. They rejected her appeal. Eventually, after flirting with the possibility of running either for the NDP or as an inde-pendent, Copps left politics. Oliver Moore, "Copps wants nomination battle restaged," *The Globe and Mail,* March 10, 2004; Jane Taber, "Copps alleges tampering by Valeri campaign," *The Globe and Mail,* March 10, 2004 (both accessed at www.globeandmail.com).

67. R. Kenneth Carty and Lynda Erickson, "Candidate Nomination in Canada's National Political Parties," in Bakvis, ed., *Canadian Political Parties,* 114.

68. Gloria Galloway, "Dryden makes his candidacy official," *The Globe and Mail,* May 18, 2004; accessed at www.globeandmail.com.

69. One aspiring candidate in Burnaby–Douglas held a tearful news conference, begging Martin for a fair and open nomination meeting. His pleas did not deter the leader from appointing the president of the provincial wing of the party—Martin organizer Bill Cunningham—who lost the election after the entire Liberal riding association executive quit in protest.

70. Lynda Erickson, "Canada," in Pippa Norris, ed., *Passages to Power: Legislative recruitment in advanced democracies* (Cambridge: Cambridge University Press, 1997), 38–39.

71. Rahat, 159.

72. Lawrence LeDuc, "Democratizing Party Leadership Selection," *Party Politics* 7:3 (2001), 326.

73. Unlike the other major parties, the NDP permits leadership votes at its policy conventions. If a candidate steps forward to challenge the incumbent, the meeting is transformed into a leadership convention. To date, no national NDP leader has faced a serious challenge in this manner.

74. In 1917, the British government asked Canada to send more troops to Europe to support the Allies. Because the pool of willing volunteers was more or less exhausted, the Canadian government had to consider imposing conscription (mandatory military duty). The idea was bitterly opposed by French Canadians, who saw no reason to send their sons to die for the British cause. The Liberal caucus split, with the anglophones joining the ruling Conservative caucus (thus creating the Union government) under Prime Minister Sir Robert Borden; the Union government won a federal election in 1917, and promptly imposed conscription. Francophone Liberals were left as a rump caucus in Opposition.

75. For a comprehensive history of national leadership conventions in Canada, see John C. Courtney, *The Selection of National Party Leaders in Canada* (Toronto: Macmillan, 1973) and *Do Conventions Matter? Choosing National Party Leaders in Canada* (Montreal and Kingston: McGill–Queen's University Press, 1995).

76. See R. Kenneth Carty, "Campaigning in the Trenches: The Transformation of Constituency Politics," in George C. Perlin, ed., *Party Democracy in Canada: The Politics of National Party Conventions* (Scarborough: Prentice-Hall Canada, 1988), 84–96.

77. See Heather MacIvor, "From Emergence to Electronics: Explaining the Changes in Canadian Party Leadership Selection, 1919–1995," *National History,* I:2 (Spring 1997).

78. This claim is open to question, because OMOV leadership contests generally suffer from low turnout. In the 2004 Conservative contest, for example, fewer than 10 000 (37 percent) of the 250 000 people on the membership list bothered to vote for the first leader of the new party. Steven Chase, "Voters in West and Ontario delivered win to Harper," *The Globe and Mail,* March 22, 2004; accessed at www.theglobeandmail.com. This is a little lower than the average turnout for OMOV contests: R.K. Carty and Donald E. Blake, "The Adoption of Membership Votes for Choosing Party Leaders: The Experience of Canadian Parties," *Party Politics,* 5:2 (1999), 219–220.

79. Young and Cross, "The Rise of Plebiscitary Democracy," 678.

80. Mair, "Party Organizations: From Civil Society to the State," 16–17.

81. David K. Stewart and R. Kenneth Carty, "Leadership Politics as Party Building: The Conservatives in 1998," in William Cross, ed., *Political Parties, Representation, and Electoral Democracy in Canada* (Toronto: Oxford University Press, 2002), 55–67.

82. Bob Plamondon, *Full Circle: Death and Resurrection in Canadian Conservative Politics* (Toronto: Key Porter, 2006), 310–318 and 379–381.

83. Former MP Lorne Nystrom, who had won the primaries, placed third (and last) on the first ballot at the convention; former Nova Scotia NDP leader Alexa McDonough, who had run a fairly distant third in the primaries, ended up winning the leadership after second-place finisher Svend Robinson pulled out before a second ballot could be held.

84. At its November 2006 convention, the Liberal Party rejected a proposal to adopt a straight OMOV system. Abbas Rana, "Liberal delegates reject one-member, one-vote system," *The Hill Times*, December 4, 2006, 6.

85. Daniel Latouche, "Universal Democracy and Effective Leadership: Lessons from the Parti Québécois Experience," in R. Kenneth Carty, Lynda Erickson, and Donald E. Blake, eds., *Leaders and Parties in Canadian Politics: Experiences of the Provinces* (Toronto: HBJ Canada, 1992), 174–202.

86. Allison Dunfield, "Liberal executive may ask Copps to bow out," *The Globe and Mail*, September 24, 2003; accessed at www.globeandmail.com.

87. Campbell Clark and Stephanie Nolen, "Liberals get impressive warm-up act," *The Globe and Mail*, November 5, 2004; Gloria Galloway, "Chrétien goodbye an exercise in logistics," *The Globe and Mail*, November 13, 2004 (both accessed at www.globeandmail.com).

88. All three were Liberal MPs: Carolyn Bennett, Maurizio Bevilacqua, and Hedy Fry.

89. Kate Malloy and Abbas Rana, "Late-night Liberal backroom machinations to begin in Montreal," *The Hill Times*, November 27, 2006, 28–29.

90. Abbas Rana, "Liberal leadership candidates woo crucial ex-officios," *The Hill Times*, October 9, 2006, 16. In the past, leadership candidates had used some of their funds to subsidize travel costs or "their" delegates. Bill C-24 ruled this out, both by directly prohibiting such payments and by imposing new donation limits that made it extremely difficult for the contestants to raise money.

91. Dryden came last on the second ballot and was automatically eliminated; he went to Rae, but he did not try to take his delegates with him.

92. Derek Raymaker, "The melée at the Palais: Stéphane Dion's win is also a victory for gut instinct over careerist ambition," *The Hill Times*, December 11, 2006, 17.

93. LeDuc, 326.

94. Ibid., 335–336.

95. When MacKay reneged on his promise not to merge the PC Party with the Canadian Alliance, Orchard filed suit to try to block the merger. His suit was rejected by the Ontario courts. However, he did enjoy a measure of revenge: the controversy over the broken promise damaged MacKay's political career, and prevented him from running for the leadership of the new Conservative Party.

96. In July 2002 the three Cabinet ministers in the running (Allan Rock, Sheila Copps, and John Manley) publicly disclosed the amounts and sources of donations to their leadership campaigns. Martin considered making a similar disclosure, to avoid the appearance of excessive secrecy (and possible conflict-of-interest allegations), but decided against it. He argued that people and businesses had given money to his campaign without being aware that their names would be made public. He also alleged that donors who depended on the federal government for their livelihoods might be subject to retribution from the Chrétien government (e.g., cancellation of contracts). Susan Delacourt, *Juggernaut: Paul Martin's Campaign for Chrétien's Crown* (Toronto: McClelland and Stewart, 2003), 255–56.

97. The original limit of $5000 per year had been adjusted upward for inflation by 2006.

98. The financial disclosure reports for the Liberal leadership candidates are available at www.elections.ca. See also Abbas Rana, "Lib leadership candidates can take longer than 18 months to pay back loans: Liberal Party," *The Hill Times*, January 8, 2007, 7.

99. If an outstanding campaign debt is not paid within 18 months, it is automatically converted into a contribution for the purposes of the law. Therefore, an unpaid loan greater than $5400 would violate the contribution limit, at least retroactively. However, loans are exempted from this rule; each is governed by the repayment schedule negotiated at the time when the loan was secured, which can be longer than 18 months. The Liberal Party of Canada has stated publicly that its former leadership candidates can take as long as they want to repay their collective $2 million in campaign loans; Elections Canada insists that "all leadership contestants are required to pay back loans within 18 months after the convention." Rana, "Lib leadership candidates." When Dion announced his resignation from the leadership in October 2008, media reports suggested that he still carried a substantial personal debt from his leadership run almost two years earlier.

100. In April 2007, the Harper Government tabled amendments to the CEA to clarify the rules for political loans. At the time of writing, the Bill had not been enacted into law.

101. John C. Courtney, "Recognition of Canadian Political Parties in Parliament and in Law," *Canadian Journal of Political Science,* XI:1 (March 1978), 33–60.

102. Leon D. Epstein, *Political Parties in the American Mold* (Madison: University of Wisconsin Press, 1986), 155–58; Ingrid van Biezen, "Political Parties As Public Utilities," *Party Politics* 10:6 (2004), 701–722.

103. Abbas Rana, "Elections Canada 'deregisters' five federal riding associations, Liberals and NDP working to 'reregister' for next election," *The Hill Times*, January 22, 2007, 15.

104. The spending limits for candidates in the most recent general election, issued by Elections Canada on January 16, 2006, range from a little over $60 000 (in Prince Edward Island) to a little over $100 000 in large northern ridings. The limit for each electoral district depends on its geographical size and the number of registered voters living within its boundaries. The 2006 candidate spending limits were accessed at www.elections.ca/pas/39ge/can/lim_final.pdf.

105. In the original version of Bill C-24, the limit was 50 percent of the previous constituency maximum. The Standing Committee on Procedure and House Affairs, which reviewed the Bill, lowered the percentage at the urging of female MPs.

106. Each registered party is entitled to an annual allowance of $1.75 (adjusted for inflation) per valid vote received in the previous general election. To qualify for the allowance, a party had to earn at least 2 percent of the national vote or 5 percent of the total votes in the constituencies where it ran candidates. This vote threshold was struck down by the Ontario Superior Court of Justice in October 2006. The judge ruled that it violated section 3 of the *Charter,* as defined in the 2003 *Figueroa* ruling (Dossier 6.3). The decision was overturned by the Ontario Court of Appeal in 2007. The Supreme Court of Canada refused to hear the case.

107. Karl-Heinz Nassmacher, "Introduction: Political Parties, Funding and Democracy," in Reginald Austin and Maja Tjernström, eds., *IDEA Handbook: Funding of Political Parties and Election Campaigns* (Stockholm: International Institute for Democracy and Electoral Assistance, 2003), 7.

108. van Biezen, 704.

109. Richard S. Katz and Peter Mair, "Changing Models of Party Organization and Party Democracy: The Emergence of the Cartel Party," *Party Politics,* 1:1 (1995), 15.

110. All listed party members and officers must be registered voters. The *Register of Electors* is discussed in Chapter 12.

111. The Christian Heritage Party, which failed to nominate 50 candidates in the 2000 election and thus lost its registered status, had contested federal elections since 1988. The Libertarian Party and the Progressive Canadian Party (a rump of former Progressive Conservatives opposed to the merger with the Canadian Alliance) were new to politics.

112. Alan Siaroff, "Two-and-a-Half Party Systems and the Comparative Role of the 'Half,'" *Party Politics,* 9:3 (2003), 273.

113. R. Kenneth Carty, William Cross, and Lisa Young, *Rebuilding Canadian Party Politics* (Vancouver: UBC Press, 2000) 3–4.

114. For a further discussion on these factors, see Herbert Kitschelt, *The Logics of Party Formation: Ecological Politics in Belgium and West Germany* (Ithaca, NY: Cornell University Press, 1989); and Keith Archer and Faron Ellis, "Opinion Structure of Party Activists: The Reform Party of Canada," *Canadian Journal of Political Science*, XXVII (1994), 277–308.

115. See the discussion of mobilization and subcultures in Chapter 2.

116. Peter Mair, "Party Systems and Structures of Competition," in Lawrence LeDuc, Richard G. Niemi, and Pippa Norris, eds., *Comparing Democracies: Elections and Voting in Global Perspective* (Thousand Oaks, Calif.: Sage, 1996).

117. The troubled relationship between the NDP and organized labour illustrates the point. The private-sector unions that provide the lion's share of NDP resources are losing members, as plants close and manufacturers contract out to nonunionized suppliers. While public-sector unions grew rapidly after World War II (until the downsizing of the 1980s and 1990s), they are constrained in their ability to support a particular party by laws and norms that require public servants to remain politically neutral. They are also affected by the new contribution rules in Bill C-24, which limit the amount of money and volunteer labour that unions can donate. Even in the heyday of the union movement, the NDP failed to capture even a plurality of the labour vote. Relations between the party and its key labour supporters—both private-sector unions such as the Canadian Auto Workers and public-sector unions such as the Canadian Union of Public Employees—became tense and sometimes antagonistic in the 1990s.

118. Paul Wells, *Right Side Up: The Fall of Paul Martin and the Rise of Stephen Harper's New Conservatism* (Toronto: McClelland & Stewart, 2006), 49–49.

119. Chantal Hébert, *French Kiss: Stephen Harper's Blind Date with Quebec* (Toronto: Knopf Canada, 2007), 211 and 263.

120. Carty, Cross, and Young, 207.

121. This was a particular problem for the Progressive Conservatives in the 2000 federal election campaign. See Paul Attallah and Angela Burton, "Television, the Internet, and the Canadian Federal Election of 2000," in Pammett and Dornan, eds., *The Canadian General Election of 2000*, 229.

122. One expert slammed the Liberal candidates' websites, although some of the problems that he identified likely arose from the novelty of some communication tools and the shortage of money that plagued most of the contestants. Allan Bonner, "It's a big mystery why Liberal candidates' web pages are generally so poor," *The Hill Times*, October 9, 2006, 20.

123. Abbas Rana and Bea Vongdouangchanh, "YouTube 'road warriors' could define the next election campaign," *The Hill Times*, April 2, 2007, 4.

124. Rana and Vongdouangchanh, "YouTube 'road warriors,'" 1 and 4–5.

125. Delacourt, *Jugggernaut*, 265.

126. Ibid., 196.

127. The descriptions of the first three party systems are taken from R. Kenneth Carty, "Three Canadian Party Systems: An Interpretation of the Development of National Politics," in Perlin, ed., *Party Democracy in Canada*, 15–30. See also Carty, Cross, and Young. The description of the fourth party system is original to this volume, although based on the analysis of Carty, Cross, and Young. Note that some of the dates have been changed, to reflect the argument of this chapter.

128. For example, Clarkson argues that the distinction between the third and fourth systems is exaggerated: "there is much less evidence of change than [Carty, Cross, and Young] maintain—whether this be change in the party system, change in the nature of the parties themselves, or change in the manner in which they wage their campaigns." Stephen Clarkson, "The Liberal Threepeat: The Multi-System Party in the Multi-Party System," in Pammett and Dornan, eds., *The Canadian General Election of 2000*, 15.

129. André Siegfried, *The Race Question in Canada* (Toronto: McClelland and Stewart, 1966 [1906]), 114.

130. See Duverger.

131. Siegfried, 136.

132. William T. Stanbury, *Money in Politics: Financing Federal Parties and Candidates in Canada,* volume 1 of the collected research studies for the Royal Commission on Electoral Reform and Party Financing (Toronto: Dundurn Press, 1991), 27–28.

133. Carty, "Three Canadian Party Systems," 19.

134. Brodie and Jenson, *Crisis, Challenge and Change.*

135. Carty, "Three Canadian Party Systems," 20.

136. Ibid., 19–21.

137. In 1943 John Bracken, premier of Manitoba from 1922 to 1943, was persuaded to move to federal politics and lead the Conservative Party. Bracken had led the Manitoba Progressives, and his anti-party views had contributed to the formation of a "Liberal–Progressive" coalition, which won three successive provincial elections in the 1930s. In 1941 Bracken invited all parties in the Manitoba legislature to join in a coalition government, and all but a handful of members did so. In 1943 the same anti-party sentiment led Bracken to demand the addition of "Progressive" to the name of the Conservative Party as the price of agreeing to lead that party at the national level. Bracken never led his renamed party to victory, so he was unable to duplicate his provincial success at the national level.

138. Michiel Horn, "The LSR, the CCF, and the Regina Manifesto," in William J. Brennan, ed., *Building the Co-operative Commonwealth: Essays on the Democratic Socialist Tradition in Canada* (Regina: Canadian Plains Research Centre, 1984), 25–41.

139. God Horowitz, *Canadian Labour in Politics* (Toronto: University of Toronto Press, 1968).

140. C.B. MacPherson, *Democracy in Alberta: Social Credit and the Party System,* second ed. (Toronto: University of Toronto Press, 1962); Alvin Finkel, *The Social Credit Phenomenon in Alberta* (Toronto: University of Toronto Press, 1989).

141. On the establishment of the Dominion Conservative Association and the first party headquarters in Ottawa, see Larry A. Glassford, *Reaction and Reform: The Politics of the Conservative Party under R.B. Bennett, 1927–1938* (Toronto: University of Toronto Press, 1992), Chapter 3; the history of the extraparliamentary Liberal party is described in Reginald Whitaker, *The Government Party: Organizing and Financing the Liberal Party of Canada, 1930–58* (Toronto: University of Toronto Press, 1977), Chapter 1.

142. Carty, "Three Canadian Party Systems," 23.

143. David E. Smith, "Party Government, Representation and National Integration in Canada," in Peter Aucoin, ed., *Party Government and Regional Representation in Canada,* volume 36 of the collected research studies for the Royal Commission on the Economic Union and Development prospects for Canada (Toronto: University of Toronto Press, 1985), 1–68.

144. Smith, 25.

145. Desmond Morton, *The New Democrats 1961–1986: The Politics of Change* (Toronto: Copp Clark Pitman, 1986).

146. The NDP's strategy has not been entirely successful, for a number of reasons. First, unions did not provide the level of financial support that was anticipated at the time of the party's founding. Second, the Canadian workforce is not highly unionized. Less than 40 percent of those who are employed belong to a union. Of those who do, many belong to public-sector unions, which are prevented by law or convention from directly supporting a particular party. Third, many union members ignore the suggestions of their union leadership in political matters. There are countless reasons for voting for one party or another, and the wishes of one's union leadership do not always prevail. Finally, in many constituencies, the NDP is not electorally competitive, and it has never formed the government nationally. For many voters, supporting a third party is viewed as a wasted vote. See Keith Archer, *Political Choices and Electoral Consequences: A Study of Organized Labour and the New Democratic Party* (Montreal and Kingston: McGill–Queens University Press, 1990).

147. Clarkson, "The Liberal Threepeat," 31.

148. David M. Farrell, "Campaign Strategies and Tactics," in Lawrence LeDuc, Richard G, Niemi, and Pippa Norris, eds., *Comparing Democracies: Elections and Voting in Global Perspective* (Thousand Oaks, CA: Sage, 1996), 176.

149. See Harold D. Clarke, Jane Jenson, Lawrence LeDuc, and Jon H. Pammett, *Absent Mandate: Interpreting Change in Canadian Elections,* 2nd edition (Toronto: Gage, 1991), especially Chapter 3.

150. Carty, Cross and Young, 218.

151. Ibid., 219.

152. Stephen Clarkson, *The Big Red Machine: How The Liberal Party Dominates Canadian Politics* (Vancouver: UBC Press, 2005), especially 266.

153. Faron Ellis, "The More Things Change . . . The Alliance Campaign," in Jon H. Pammett and Christopher Dornan, eds., *The Canadian General Election of 2000* (Ottawa: Carleton University Press, 2001), 62.

154. Ellis, 64–65.

155. Ibid., 68.

156. Ibid., 83–84.

157. André Turcotte, "Fallen Heroes: Leaders and Voters in the 2000 Canadian General Election," in Pammett and Dornan, eds., *The Canadian General Election of 2000,* 285.

158. Wells, 50–51; Plamondon, 215–219 and 223–226.

159. Plamondon, 224–227.

160. Wells, 60–62.

161. The text of the agreement is reproduced in Plamondon, 264.

162. Plamondon, 289–320.

163. Allison Dunfield, "Alliance, Tories head back in co-operative mood," *The Globe and Mail,* September 15, 2003; accessed at www.globeandmail.com.

164. Drew Fagan, "The motivating force? Fear of Paul Martin," *The Globe and Mail,* October 16, 2003; Drew Fagan, "Burden of bridge-building fell on leaders," *The Globe and Mail,* October 17, 2003 (both accessed at www.globeandmail.com).

165. Brian Laghi and Drew Fagan, "Let's pick leader by February, Alliance tells Conservatives," *The Globe and Mail,* September 19, 2003 (accessed at www.globeandmail.com); Sean Gordon, "'Swords will point at Liberals,'" *Ottawa Citizen,* October 17, 2003 (accessed at www.canada.com).

166. Excerpted from Stephen Harper and Peter MacKay, "Agreement-in-principle on the establishment of the Conservative Party of Canada," October 15, 2003; accessed at www.pcparty.ca (the site no longer exists), 1–3.

167. In December 2003 an Ontario Superior Court judge dismissed the suit. He ruled that the PC merger process conformed to the requirements in the *Canada Elections Act* for two registered parties to become one. See *Ahenakew v. MacKay,* December 5, 2003 (available at www.canlii.org).

168. This was an easier proposition for the Alliance, whose constitution could be amended by a simple majority vote of the members, than for the PCs. Their constitution stipulated amendment by a two-thirds vote at a national convention. Because of the tight time frame, the PC Management Committee decided to hold a "virtual" convention on December 6. Party members in the constituencies would elect delegates to regional meetings, which would be linked electronically (Plamondon, 322–323). If two-thirds of the delegates voted in favour of the merger, the party would disappear. The cutoff for new members to join the PC Party was set for November, infuriating merger opponents who argued that this would allow Alliance members to flood into the party in order to vote for the deal. There were some anecdotal reports of "crossover" members, although it is not clear whether they made much difference to the outcome. Jeff Sallot, "Orchard vows to stop new memberships," *The Globe and Mail,* October 20, 2003; accessed at www.globe andmail.com.

169. Allison Dunfield, "95.9% of Alliance voters agree to merger," *The Globe and Mail*, December 5, 2003; accessed at www.globeandmail.com.

170. Luma Muhtadie, "Tories vote to unite the right," *The Globe and Mail*, December 6, 2003; accessed at www.globeandmail.com.

171. Andrew Willis, "United right wins Street's hearts, wallets," *The Globe and Mail*, October 17, 2003; Brian Laghi, "Tories push corporations for cash," *The Globe and Mail*, December 2, 2004 (both accessed at www.globeandmail.com).

172. Savoie, *Court Government*, 304.

173. Ibid., 307.

174. Fox, 16.

12 Elections and Voting

LEARNING OBJECTIVES

After you finish reading this chapter, you should be able to:

- *explain* the differences among the major categories of electoral systems;
- *analyze* and *evaluate* the arguments in favour of a more proportional electoral system for Canada;
- *describe* and *evaluate* the current election-finance regime;
- *identify* and *describe* at least TWO long-term and TWO short-term influences on Canadian voting behaviour;
- *identify* and *explain* two reasons why fewer Canadians, especially younger Canadians, are voting in elections.

INTRODUCTION

If political parties are like sports teams, as we suggested in the previous chapter, then a federal general election is bigger than the Super Bowl and the Stanley Cup put together. Whereas the team that lost this year's Super Bowl will have another chance next year, Canadians only go to the polls every three to four years (on average). The captain of the winning hockey team gets to hoist the Stanley Cup (and eventually to see his name on it); the captain of the winning political team becomes the prime minister of Canada.

This chapter explains the role of elections in our national politics, describes and evaluates the operation of Canada's electoral system, and examines the patterns in Canadian voting behaviour. It touches on three of the central themes in this book:

1. the importance of regionalism as a motivating force in Canadian politics;
2. the influence of institutions on political behaviour, specifically the incentives for parties and voters that are imposed by our current electoral system; and
3. the ongoing debate about the nature and reform of our political institutions.

THE ROLE OF ELECTIONS IN CANADIAN POLITICS

Our system of government is an "indirect" democracy. Citizens do not govern themselves directly; instead, they elect representatives to govern them. In this way, the consent of citizens is secured, however indirectly and imperfectly.[1] Periodic competitive elections based on universal adult **suffrage,** administered by an impartial agency according to fixed and fair rules, are the crucial distinction between democratic and nondemocratic governments.[2] But although every democratic state holds elections, the ways in which those elections are conducted vary widely. Different electoral systems can have varying effects on the composition of the legislature and the political executive, the number of parties in the party system, the incentives for parties seeking to win seats, and the behaviour of voters.

In a **general election,** the entire House of Commons is dissolved and all 308 seats are filled simultaneously. A **by-election** occurs when a single seat becomes vacant between elections, and the voters in that constituency choose a new MP. In either case, the prime minister asks the governor general to issue a writ of election, which sets the date on which ballots will be cast. (This is the origin of the phrase "dropping the writ" to describe the official start of an election campaign.) If his or her party wins more seats than any other, he or she will remain in office; if not, he or she must go back to the governor general to resign as prime minister.

In the British tradition, the PM decides when to dissolve Parliament for a general election. The only exception is the defeat of a minority government in the House of Commons. When, for example, the Liberal Government lost a non-confidence vote in November 2005, Prime Minister Martin submitted his resignation to the governor general; she dissolved the Commons for an early election. However, this particular defeat was unusual because it was initiated by the Opposition; most defeats in the House are actually engineered by the governing party, to take advantage of political circumstances that could produce a majority election victory.[3]

The PM's control of election timing enhanced the prime minister's control of his caucus, his Cabinet, and the House of Commons as a whole. It also infuriated Opposition parties, which often found themselves at a disadvantage on the first day of a campaign; the governing party was able to plan ahead, whereas they could only guess at the prime minister's intentions. During the 2006 election campaign, Stephen Harper promised to give up that part of his prerogative powers. (See Dossier 12.1).

Every general election, is preceded by weeks or months of anticipation and speculation. By the time the prime minister meets the governor general at Rideau Hall and obtains his or her signature on the writ of dissolution, campaign preparations are well under way. The major parties have nominated candidates in at least some of Canada's 308 constituencies, raised money to fight the campaign, and planned their electoral strategies on the basis of survey data gathered by their pollsters. Each of the major parties starts the election campaign with a base of electoral support, although the Liberals can usually count on a larger base than their rivals.

From the perspective of a party strategist, the goals of the campaign are straightforward:
- to persuade "soft" supporters to remain loyal;
- to convert supporters of other parties; and
- to attract undecided voters.

From a less partisan perspective, election campaigns are supposed to benefit the political system in two ways:
- giving voters a choice between competing platforms, which allows them to set the broad outlines of government policy; and
- engaging citizens in the political process.

Since Confederation, prime ministers and premiers have been able to dissolve Parliament whenever an election would serve the political interests of their particular parties. This power is based on the unwritten constitutional conventions inherited from Britain (see Chapter 3). Although the *Constitution Act, 1867* gives the governor general or lieutenant governor the prerogative to dissolve the legislature for an election, in practice the Crown representative does so only on the advice of the elected head of government.[4]

Under section 50 of the *Constitution Act, 1867* and section 4 of the *Canadian Charter of Rights and Freedoms*, the maximum term of a Parliament or provincial legislature is five years. Traditionally, majority governments have lasted roughly four years. This pattern has established public expectations of a four-year electoral cycle, and perhaps a constitutional convention to that effect, despite the five-year term provided in the written *Constitution*.

The conventional four-year cycle imposes political constraints. If an unpopular prime minister or premier tries to hang on for more than four and a half years, hoping for a political miracle, voters seem to punish the Government for overstaying its welcome. There was no resurrection for the federal Liberals in 1979, the federal Progressive Conservatives in 1993, or the Ontario New Democrats in 1995.

At the other end of the spectrum, former Prime Minister Chrétien called two successive elections (in 1997 and 2000) approximately three and a half years after the prior elections. On both occasions, he was accused of crass political opportunism: the Official Opposition (the Bloc Québécois and the Canadian Alliance, respectively) had just elected a new and untried leader, leaving its party organization divided and unprepared for the organizational demands of an election campaign. In 1997, Chrétien failed to justify the early election call. The false start damaged the Liberals' campaign, and contributed to a significant loss of seats.[5] The Liberals learned from that mistake: on the first day of the 2000 campaign, Chrétien

delivered a prepared speech portraying the Alliance as a threat to Canadian values. Implicitly, the prime minister was telling Canadians that their country was at risk and he had to act quickly to defend it.[6]

The Cabinet in a parliamentary system of government is responsible to the lower House. When the Government of the day loses the confidence of the legislature, it must resign. Contrary to conventional wisdom, however, this does not mean that prime ministers must be free to call elections whenever they wish.

[U]nlike Canada, the majority of countries with parliamentary or mixed regimes set a fixed date for their legislative elections, which is known and, as a rule, respected. In concrete terms, what distinguishes fixed-date countries is not whether they make premature elections possible, but whether they have a law that sets out clear rules for the date on which (or the specific period within which) the subsequent regular election will take place after any such premature election, such that it is known to all.[7]

Partly because of perceived abuses of the prime minister's prerogative, the idea of fixed election dates became increasingly popular in Canada. A 2000 survey found that 54 percent of respondents (nearly three-quarters of those who had an opinion on the issue) supported the proposal.[8] In 2001, British Columbia adopted the first fixed election date law in Canadian history. It provided that future elections would be held at four-year intervals, on the second Tuesday in May. The first fixed-date election was held on May 17, 2005. According to the provincial election agency, the predictability of the vote offered numerous benefits:

- Elections BC was completely prepared for the election, including the rental of office space and voting locations, well ahead of voting day. This led to a more efficient electoral process, although the cost savings were smaller than anticipated.

(continued)

- The agency had more time to recruit and train returning officers and other key workers.
- The permanent voters' list was updated shortly before the election, in an effort to ensure the greatest possible accuracy.
- Finally, the turnout rate rose by 3 percent after several years of steady decline.[9]

Contrary to expectations, the fixed date did not lead to an American-style permanent campaign in the year leading up to the vote; nor did it paralyze the legislature and reduce the Government to "lame duck" status. The success of BC's experiment with fixed election dates impressed other provinces. Ontario and Newfoundland and Labrador scheduled their next provincial elections in October 2007, to be followed by elections every four years thereafter. By 2008, most of the remaining provinces had either adopted or were considering fixed dates.

In May 2006, the Harper Government introduced a fixed-date amendment to the *Canada Elections Act (CEA)*. Bill C-16 copied the "fixed flexible" model adopted in BC and Ontario. Future federal general elections would be held every four years, on the Monday after Thanksgiving, starting in October 2009. However, in the event that a Government lost the confidence of the House of Commons, the prime minister could still ask the governor general to dissolve Parliament early and the statutory electoral cycle would be adjusted accordingly. As just noted, Bill C-16 requires that federal general elections be held in October 2009, October 2013, and October 2017. But if the Government fell in January 2008, and an election followed in March, the next two scheduled elections would be held in October 2011 (the fourth year of the mandate) and October 2015.

Most MPs supported Bill C-16, as did the Chief Electoral Officer. They identified several possible benefits, in addition to those experienced in BC. These included:
- a higher calibre of parliamentary candidates, because more people would be willing to commit themselves to running if they could plan ahead;
- a level playing field between the parties, since all—not just the governing party—would know when to prepare for the next election;
- more successful recruitment of female and visible-minority candidates;
- more efficient legislative planning (especially for committees engaged in lengthy studies);
- more collaboration between minority Governments and Opposition parties, to avoid triggering unnecessary elections;
- more effective campaigns to encourage young voters to cast ballots; and
- a reduction in the powers of the prime minister.

Opponents of the Bill argued that it conflicted with Canadian constitutional conventions, particularly the governor general's prerogative. They also pointed out that a four-year parliamentary term was at odds with the five-year term specified in section 4 of the *Canadian Charter of Rights and Freedoms*. The Government insisted that the Bill did not violate either the written or the unwritten *Constitution*; if anything, it merely enacted the established convention of the four-year electoral cycle into law.

Bill C-16 passed third reading in the Commons in November 2006 and was referred to the Senate. Then-Chief Electoral Officer (CEO) Jean-Pierre Kingsley told the Standing Senate Committee on Legal and Constitutional Affairs that he was concerned about the clause which permitted the CEO to alter the election date in case of a conflict with "a day of cultural or religious significance or a provincial or municipal election." He asked the senators to clarify the meaning of the phrase "cultural or religious significance," and to specify the degree of importance that a holy day or cultural festival must have in order to postpone a general election. Some senators expressed concern about possible conflicts with the Muslim religious festival of Ramadan, which occurs at varying times

(continued)

of the year, and about the possible difficulties raised by the term "cultural." For example, would German Canadians be offended if an election were held during Oktoberfest?[10]

Although the committee decided not to amend the Bill, Liberal Senator Serge Joyal moved an amendment to the controversial clause at third reading. He proposed that the words "or cultural" be deleted, and added a provision to avoid conflict with federal, provincial, or municipal referenda. The Senate adopted the amendment. The amended Bill was referred back to the Commons in late March. Despite the technical nature of the amendment, the Conservative Government refused to accept it. (As explained in Chapter 7, a Bill must be passed in the identical form by both Houses of Parliament before it receives royal assent and becomes law.) Some Liberals depicted the refusal as a stalling tactic, designed to delay the adoption of a 2009 election date so the Government could engineer its own defeat and try to win a majority in the spring of 2007.[11]

At the time, Ottawa was gripped by intense speculation about an early election. The minority Conservative Government was at loggerheads with the Opposition over key Bills, including its environmental legislation and its "law and order" package. Some national polls put the Conservatives within striking distance of a majority government. The party had millions of dollars in the bank and a strong organization—unlike the struggling Liberals and NDP. The BQ was in disarray following the third-place finish of the Parti Québécois in the March 2007 Quebec election. All the Government had to do was declare one of its controversial Bills to be a matter of confidence, and engineer its own defeat in the Commons. Most of Prime Minister Harper's predecessors would have seized the opportunity to trigger a snap election.

However, Harper faced an unprecedented political obstacle. As the minister who sponsored Bill C-16 told the Commons Standing Committee on Procedure and House Affairs, "a Prime Minister who has indicated a certain date to the public would be very hard pressed to unilaterally pull the plug for no other reason than that he or she felt there was an electoral advantage."[12] Having introduced Bill C-16, the prime minister had greatly increased the political risk of an early election: not only would he have sent Canadians back to the voting booth for the third time in three years, but he would have broken his promise on fixed election dates.

Liberal senators finally backed down in late April, agreeing to withdraw their amendment to the Bill. Coincidentally, Bill C-16 received royal assent on May 3, 2007—just as the Government's popularity started to drop because of its perceived poor performance on climate change and the Canadian mission in Afghanistan.[13] For the moment, speculation about an early election was over. This left the prime minister to deal with the unanticipated consequences of the Bill: he had to find something for his Government to do in the remaining two years of his mandate, having done as much as he could to complete the agenda on which he ran in 2006.[14] In September 2008, Harper decided to disregard his own law: he advised the Governor General that Parliament was unworkable, and secured a dissolution.

As we will see in this chapter, Canadian elections do not fully achieve these goals. While campaign promises have some influence on public policy, other factors often force governments to abandon their platforms. If falling turnout rates are any indication, citizens in all Western democracies are losing interest in elections. To some extent, this disengagement is the result of the mismatch between campaign promises and government policies. As we will see, however, there are a variety of reasons for voters to opt out of the electoral process. Fortunately, a majority of Canadians still vote in general elections. The choices they make, and the reasons for those choices, are explored in later sections of this chapter.

ELECTIONS AND PUBLIC POLICY

Chapter 2 described rising public interest in **referenda** and other direct-democracy devices. This can be explained, in part, by the weak connection between parties' election promises and the policies that they subsequently adopt in government. Some "U-turns" are entirely understandable. Governments must operate within the limits set by the rule of law and the *Constitution*, not to mention fiscal constraints and the need to respond to unforeseen events. Today, their policy choices are increasingly constrained by global economic conditions and supranational agreements and institutions. On the other hand, governments still enjoy considerable latitude in some policy fields, such as criminal law[15] and social policy. Consequently, it is an overstatement to suggest that elections are irrelevant in the era of globalization.[16] When power changes hands in an election, the new governing party can impose its distinct priorities in some policy fields. The question is the degree to which those priorities match its promises to the voters.

The connection between a party's pre-election platform and its post-election priorities can be understood in either of two ways: the agenda model and the mandate model.[17] The agenda model predicts that a party in government will seek to enact the specific policies that it promised during the most recent campaign. For example, the 2006 Conservative campaign focused on five priorities:

- enhancing integrity and accountability in the federal government;
- toughening criminal laws, particularly those against violent crime;
- cutting taxes, starting with a reduction in the Goods and Services Tax (GST);
- replacing the Liberal child-care plan with a direct payment to families with children; and
- improving the delivery of health care by the provinces.[18]

By the end of 2006 the Harper Government had passed the *Federal Accountability Act,* tabled several amendments to the *Criminal Code,* cut the GST, and implemented its "choice in child-care" payment. Its determination to enact its platform into policy seems to support the agenda model of elections. (If so, it is somewhat unusual: comparative studies of Western democracies have found that the agenda effect is weaker in Canada than elsewhere.[19]) As we will see shortly, however, the agenda model does not provide a completely accurate account of the relationship between elections and public policy.

The mandate model takes a broader view of the link between parties and policies. It has three primary elements:

1. "the belief that elections carry messages about problems, policies, and programs—messages plain to all and specific enough to be directive";
2. the claim that "certain of these messages must be treated as authoritative commands" to the party that wins an election; and
3. the assumption that "governments should not undertake major innovation in policy or procedure, except in emergencies, unless the electorate has had an opportunity to consider them in an election and thus to express its views."[20]

It is customary for newly elected governments, particularly new governments with large majorities in Parliament, to claim a mandate from the people to implement their platforms. The belief that the governing party has the legitimate authority to enact the will of the people is a powerful political tool. But it is usually a false belief. Neither the agenda model nor the mandate model provides a satisfactory account of the relationship between policy and elections.

There are at least four reasons why Canadian general elections do not determine the policy agenda, or create specific policy mandates for governments:

1. The claim that voters use their ballots to express specific policy preferences is not supported by the evidence about Canadian voting behaviour. While the parties' varying

approaches to critical issues do affect election outcomes, that effect is usually too small and too diffuse to constitute a clear and specific command. As we will see in later sections of this chapter, Canadian voters are influenced by a host of factors—party loyalty, social cleavages, impressions of the various leaders—and they are as likely to interpret party platforms through these lenses as they are to make up their minds about parties on the basis of their policy pledges.[21] In any case, elections are not referenda. They are designed to elect the people who will sit in Parliament, not to resolve particular policy disputes.[22] Therefore, the relationship between elections and public policy is indirect at best.

2. With some exceptions, including the Harper Government, Canada's major parties usually avoid making specific promises that might alienate potential voters.[23] (See the discussion of brokerage parties in Chapter 11.) They rely instead on vague, leader-centred campaigns that build broad electoral coalitions and leave the winning party with the maximum flexibility in government.[24] Without a clear and consistent choice among party principles, voters cannot express their preferences by casting ballots for party candidates.[25]

3. Canadian governments rarely seek a new mandate from the voters before undertaking significant changes in policy. While a government may pay a political price for a blatant "U-turn," there is no written or unwritten rule to deter it from breaking its promises.[26] In October 2006 Conservative Finance Minister Jim Flaherty announced new taxes on companies that converted themselves into income trusts. Income trusts pay lower taxes than regular corporations; they share their profits directly with investors, instead of merely paying dividends on shares.[27] This was a direct reversal of the party's platform promise not to impose new taxes on income trusts. The promise had been popular with investors, especially those who had built their retirement planning around cash distributions from income trusts. The Toronto Stock Exchange suffered serious losses on the day after Flaherty's announcement, as did individual investors who had taken the Conservatives at their word and put more money in the trusts. Anger at the broken promise, fanned by a lobby group called the Canadian Association of Income Trusts, threatened to erode the Conservatives' support in Alberta (income trusts were particularly common in the energy sector) and among older voters. The investors who had lost money had no other recourse: because campaign pledges have no legal status, they cannot be enforced by the courts.[28]

4. Finally, both models overlook the practical difficulties that prevent a party in government from keeping its promises. As LeDuc points out, "Even politicians who are determined to carry through on their commitments may encounter difficulty in discerning a specific electoral message and translating it into effective public policy."[29] Shortly after winning the 1993 election, Prime Minister Chrétien told his new Cabinet that they would spend the first half of their mandate fulfilling their *Red Book* promises.[30] Unfortunately for the Liberals, the country's fiscal situation forced them to cut program spending, slash transfers to the provinces, and scale back Employment Insurance benefits—policies not anticipated in the *Red Book*. At least in that instance, the Liberals wrote the *Red Book* in the expectation that they would win the election; the policies were crafted with an eye to practicality. The same could not be said of the Ontario New Democrats, who were astounded when they won a majority in the 1990 provincial election. Their campaign platform, the "Agenda for People," had promised billions of dollars worth of new spending on social programs, environmental protection, and infrastructure. Almost immediately after the election, Premier-elect Bob Rae began to distance himself from his party's promises. The "Agenda for People" was an effective tool for motivating NDP activists and supporters, but it was not a practical "blueprint for governing."[31] As one member of the NDP caucus put it, "We . . . had no notion that we would ever have to implement it."[32] When parties accustomed to the freedom of opposition run up against the reality of governing, the policies

they adopted so enthusiastically may be revealed as impractical and potentially damaging. Under those circumstances, there is something to be said in favour of broken campaign promises.

If we conclude that elections do not determine the direction of public policy, then what exactly do they do?

- Free, competitive elections allow citizens to remove a government that has failed to live up to expectations and to replace it with an alternative government. In this way, citizens hold their rulers to account for their use of power. The prospect of losing the next election can act as a brake on a government that might otherwise abuse its power. (On the other hand, the scramble to raise campaign funds in order to stay in office can have the opposite effect; see the discussion of the Sponsorship Scandal in Chapters 8 and 11.)
- Elections are almost always used to select the members of the legislative branch.[33] In some countries, including the United States, selected executive and judicial offices are also filled by election. Popular election legitimates the exercise of state power by signifying the consent of the governed.
- Elections may allow voters to express their broad political preferences, even if they do not produce specific policies.
- Finally, elections permit voters to engage directly with their political institutions. They use the electoral system to elect MPs, some of whom will sit in the Cabinet and one of whom will become (or remain) the prime minister.

THE FORMAL AND INFORMAL RULES FOR THE CONDUCT OF CANADIAN ELECTIONS

To ensure fairness, and encourage orderly transfers of power between governments,[34] elections must be organized and administered by a nonpartisan agency. Elections Canada, like its provincial counterparts, operates at arm's length from the government of the day. It is led by the Chief Electoral Officer (CEO), an Officer of Parliament who cannot be removed from office for partisan reasons (Dossier 7.7). He or she reports directly to Parliament (in practice, to the Standing Committee on Procedure and House Affairs), not to the government of the day. The CEO is forbidden to vote in federal elections and referenda, to preserve an aura of impartiality. While the governing party can amend the laws that regulate elections, it cannot be seen to manipulate the law to serve its own political goals.[35]

In addition to the formal rules in the *Canada Elections Act*, there are informal (and often unwritten) rules for the parties and candidates who participate in campaigns. Together, the formal and informal rules provide a complete picture of Canadian elections.

■ The Formal Rules

Drawing the Electoral Map

The primary purpose of an election is to choose the members of a legislature. Each MP represents a particular district, which is called a constituency or riding in Canada.[36] This requires the division of the country or province into geographical units, each of which elects one or more MPs. Constituency boundaries can be manipulated by the party in power, to ensure the most favourable result; this practice is called **"gerrymandering."**

For nearly a century after Confederation, Canada's federal and provincial constituencies were often gerrymandered by the incumbent governments. Beginning in the 1950s, all of the senior governments yielded the power to draw constituency boundaries to independent commissions.[37] A federal boundary commission is appointed for each province following the decennial census (the official count of the population held at 10-year intervals). Both the number of ridings and the boundaries of existing ridings are adjusted to reflect changes in the size and distribution of the electorate, according to a formula established in 1985 (section 51(1) of the *Constitution Act, 1867*).

In principle, there should be a rough proportionality between the number of Commons seats from each province and its share of the national population. By the 1980s, there were considerable deviations from "rep by pop." The three provinces with rapidly growing populations—Alberta, British Columbia, and Ontario[38]—were under-represented in the Commons, and the other provinces were over-represented. (See Table 7.3.) This under-representation was a political sore point. MPs from those three provinces were overwhelmed by burgeoning populations, without any additional resources to assist constituents.[39] On average, MPs from Ontario, British Columbia and Alberta represented 21 000 more voters than their colleagues from other provinces.[40] Moreover, immigration was the primary source of this growth; the under-representation of areas with expanding visible-minority populations deprives new Canadians of political influence and might infringe the *Charter* guarantees of voting rights and equality.[41]

The 1985 formula was designed to adjust for changes in population, without expanding the Commons to an unmanageable size. As a first step, the combined population of the provinces was divided by 279 (the number of provincial seats in the House in 1985); the result was called the National Quotient.[42] This number was then divided into the population of each province to determine the number of seats to which it was entitled. If the process had ended there, the formula might have allocated seats in rough proportion to population.[43] However, there was a second step: the minimum seat guarantees in sections 51(1) and 51A were factored in, which raised the shares of the smaller provinces well above their proportions of the national population. Every province is entitled to keep the seats that it had in the previous redistribution (which protects Quebec, Manitoba, Saskatchewan, Nova Scotia, and Newfoundland and Labrador), and no province may have fewer seats in the Commons than it has in the Senate (which protects Prince Edward Island and New Brunswick).[44]

In effect, the 1985 formula limited the growth of the Commons at the expense of provinces whose share of the national electorate had grown disproportionately since it took effect. After the 2001 Census, for example, the number of ridings increased from 301 to 308; Ontario received three new seats, while British Columbia and Alberta received two additional seats apiece. This allocation did not reflect the actual rate of population growth in those provinces. Table 12.1 compares the number of seats to which each province would be entitled under a strict "rep by pop" formula to its actual number after the 2004 redistribution.

In May 2007, the Harper Government proposed a complicated new distribution formula to address these deviations.[45] It would have increased the seat totals for Alberta and British Columbia more rapidly than the 1985 formula, bringing them into line with the population shares of those provinces. Ontario would also have benefited, but not by quite as much. The allocations for the other provinces would remain unchanged. According to the sponsoring minister, there would be 330 seats in the Commons by 2014—an increase of 22 from the 2004 redistribution. Predictably, the Ontario and Quebec governments opposed the new formula. The premier of Ontario condemned what he perceived as preferential treatment for the two westernmost provinces, while the Quebec National Assembly protested against the reduction in its share of Commons seats. Two Ontario Liberal MPs accused the Conservatives of "gerrymandering," because they proposed to give extra seats to their Alberta stronghold.[46] This is not quite fair, because the new formula would have given Alberta exactly the number of seats to which it was mathematically entitled.[47] Table 12.2 compares the mathematically correct seat totals from Table 12.1 to the projected seat totals under the proposed Conservative

TABLE 12.1 DEVIATIONS FROM "REP BY POP," CANADIAN HOUSE OF COMMONS, 2008

PROVINCE/TERRITORY	ACCURATE NUMBER OF CONSTITUENCIES	ACTUAL NUMBER OF CONSTITUENCIES	DIFFERENCE
Newfoundland/Labrador	5	7	+2
PEI	1	4	+3
Nova Scotia	8	11	+3
New Brunswick	7	10	+3
Quebec	73	75	+2
Ontario	118	106	−12
Manitoba	11	14	+3
Saskatchewan	9	14	+5
Alberta	32	28	−4
BC	40	36	−4

Notes: The numbers in Column 2 were calculated by dividing the total population of the 10 provinces by the number of seats allocated to the provinces in 2004 (305). The resulting number (103 317) was then divided into the population of each province as reported by the 2006 Census. The territorial population was excluded, because it is the subject of a separate formula.

TABLE 12.2 COMPARING THE PROPOSED 2007 FORMULA TO THE 2004 SEAT ALLOCATIONS

PROVINCE/TERRITORY	ACCURATE NUMBER OF CONSTITUENCIES	PROJECTED NUMBER OF CONSTITUENCIES, 2014	DIFFERENCE
Newfoundland/Labrador	5	7	+2
PEI	1	4	+3
Nova Scotia	8	11	+3
New Brunswick	7	10	+3
Quebec	73	75	+2
Ontario	118	116	−2
Manitoba	11	14	+3
Saskatchewan	9	14	+5
Alberta	32	33	+1
BC	40	43	+3
TOTALS	305*	330	+25

*The numbers in the column add up to only 304, because the figures were rounded off for clarity.

formula. (At the time of writing, the Bill had not been passed by either House of the federal Parliament.)

Once the seats have been allocated among the provinces, the commissions start to work on the constituency boundaries. The *Electoral Boundaries Readjustment Act* imposes two restrictions on their work. First, the population within each federal constituency should not deviate by more than 25 percent from the electoral quota (the population of the province divided by the number of its MPs in the previous Parliament). Exceptions are made for thinly populated areas; the commissioners try to ensure that the territory of each constituency is not unrealistically large, although there are several Canadian ridings (mostly in the North) where candidates must campaign by airplane. Second, riding boundaries should coincide with "communities of identity"[48] wherever possible. In other words, a long-established town should not be divided across two or more districts unless its population size requires that it be split up. In practice, these rules produce electoral maps which over-represent rural and small-town voters relative to urban and suburban voters.

The *Canada Elections Act* (CEA)

The CEA is a wide-ranging and detailed piece of legislation. It sets out the rules for Elections Canada and its staff to follow. It defines the qualifications of voters, and regulates their behaviour in polling places (for example, the rule that each person may vote only once). It lays down the ground rules for broadcasters, interest groups, and other indirect participants in campaigns. Finally, it establishes the legal rules for political parties and candidates. (Some of these are discussed in Chapter 11.) The latter have received the most public attention—especially in the wake of the Gomery Commission, which uncovered some serious violations of the law. (At the time of writing, no one affiliated with a political party had been prosecuted.[49])

Until recently, Canadian parties were subject to comparatively little formal regulation. There were a few rules for candidates, but the law did not even acknowledge the existence of political parties until 1970. When the *Election Expenses Act* took effect in 1974, the formal rules for election campaigns were transformed. Despite subsequent amendments (discussed in Chapter 11), the central principles of the 1974 legislation remain intact:

- *Agency:* The registered party must, as a condition of registration, appoint an official agent (e.g., the Federal Liberal Agency of Canada), which is responsible for issuing tax receipts to donors and keeping complete records of revenues and expenditures;[50]
- *Disclosure:* The party's official agent must submit an annual fiscal report to Elections Canada, including the source and amount of each donation,[51] as well as a special report on each election campaign that details the revenues and expenditures of the national party organization[52] (candidates do not have to submit an annual report);
- *Spending limits:* The amount that a registered party can legally spend on its national campaign is determined by the number of candidates who run under its banner, and by the number of voters in the constituencies where those candidates are nominated;[53]
- *Public reimbursement of election expenses:* A registered party that receives at least 2 percent of the valid national vote, or at least 5 percent of the valid vote in the constituencies where it ran candidates, is eligible for a reimbursement of 50 percent of its allowable election expenses if it complies with the reporting requirements of the Act (the figure for the 2004 general election was 60 percent);[54] and
- *Tax credits for political donations:* A donation of $25 or more to a registered party, a registered constituency association, or an official candidate is eligible for a tax credit, which reduces the amount of income tax owing to the federal government (e.g., a donation of $400 to the official agent of a candidate entitles the donor to deduct $300 from his or her income tax).[55]

In addition, registered parties are subject to the broadcasting provisions of the *Canada Elections Act:*

- During the campaign period, every Canadian broadcaster—independent radio stations and radio and TV networks—must make 61.5 hours of prime time available for purchase by the registered parties for their election advertising. That time is divided among the registered parties on the basis of their seat percentages in the Commons, their share of the vote in the previous general election, and the number of candidates each party nominated during the last campaign period. The allocation of time among the parties is determined by the Broadcasting Arbitrator, an official appointed by the Chief Electoral Officer before each election. No single party may receive more than 50 percent of the total broadcasting time.[56]

- Every radio and television network must provide free airtime to the registered parties in proportion to the allocation of paid airtime just described.
- Broadcasters and publishers may not charge inflated rates for campaign advertising.

Before 1974, when the *Election Expenses Act* took effect, parties and candidates were not required to disclose the amounts and sources of their revenues or to restrict their campaign spending. It may seem strange that parties would deliberately impose such laws on themselves, but they had good practical and political reasons to do so.

- The cost of campaigning had soared in previous years, as electoral politics became increasingly capital-intensive and elections more frequent. Party volunteers on the ground, who gave their time and effort freely to the cause, were being replaced by professional consultants, television advertising, public-opinion polling, and other costly innovations. A comparison between the 1972 and 1974 campaigns is instructive. The 1972 campaign produced a minority Liberal government, the fourth minority in 10 years (the others were elected in 1962, 1963, and 1965); it fell after two years in office, during which time it had been supported by the NDP. In the 1974 federal election, the last one held before the new regulations took effect, the Liberals spent 7 percent more than they had in 1972; PC spending rose by 20 percent, while NDP spending rose by more than one-third.[57] Overall, candidates for the three major parties reported expenditures of over $10.4 million in the 1974 campaign.[58] (Note, however, that almost 20 percent of major-party candidates in 1974 did not file fiscal returns, so these figures are incomplete.)
- The NDP exacted several policy concessions from the Liberals in exchange for supporting the 1972–74 minority, one of which was the *Election Expenses Act*. Rising campaign costs, and the frequency of general elections, were especially onerous for the NDP, which did not have access to the generous corporate contributors who supported the Liberals and PCs. Whereas Liberal candidates reported nearly $5 million in total spending in 1974, and PC candidates over $4.2 million, NDP candidates reported a total expenditure of less than $1.3 million.[59] The New Democrats were at a competitive disadvantage, which worsened as campaign costs escalated. Without spending limits, direct public reimbursements, and incentives for individual donors, the gap between the NDP and the wealthier parties would likely have widened over time, despite the loyal support of several labour unions. Beyond the immediate self-interest of the party, the NDP was ideologically committed to democratic reform. All in all, "The passage of the new act was part of the price it elicited in return for its support of the government."[60]
- Repeated election-expense scandals in Canada and elsewhere increased public cynicism and created a political climate conducive to reform. The Watergate scandal in the United States, which destroyed the presidency of Richard Nixon in 1974, revolved around the illegal use of campaign funds by the Committee to Re-Elect the President (also known as "CREEP"). Politicians throughout the Western democracies scrambled to avoid Nixon's fate by enacting (apparently) tough new laws concerning campaign finance.
- Finally, there had been a general trend toward reform of campaign finance in Canada since the early 1960s. The Quebec government cleaned up its election finance laws in 1963,[61] prompting the creation of a federal Advisory Committee on Election Expenses (the Barbeau Committee) in 1964. Its 1966 report, which laid the foundations for the 1974 Act, sat on a shelf until political circumstances forced the Trudeau government to adopt its recommendations.

In practice, some of the restrictions imposed by the 1974 Act and its subsequent amendments were more apparent than real. The most important loophole was the exclusion of the parties' local constituency associations. Constituency associations are the bedrock of party organizations, especially during election campaigns. The spending limits and other rules in the CEA applied to official candidates, not to their local party organizations or to the nomination contests that selected them. Transfers of money between registered parties and their local associations, or between candidates and local party officials, could not be traced. One expert described constituency associations as the "'black hole' in the regulatory regime."[62]

In 2003, former Prime Minister Chrétien introduced a large package of amendments to the CEA. The far-reaching reforms in Bill C-24 were surprising, because governments rarely impose stringent new rules on themselves unless forced to do so by a severe political crisis (recall the earlier discussion of the Watergate scandal). The impetus for change was the determination of former Prime Minister Jean Chrétien to leave a political legacy when he retired in 2003. The amendments to the *Canada Elections Act* were a key part of that legacy.[63]

Bill C-24 closed some of the loopholes in the *Canada Elections Act*. Since the amendments took effect at the beginning of 2004, constituency associations, leadership races, and nomination contests have been regulated by law. (Leadership and nomination contests are discussed on pp. 375–381.) Every constituency association of a registered party has to register with Elections Canada. Only registered associations can accept donations and spend money.[64] In principle, this means that a constituency association that does not register cannot run an election campaign. The **agency** and **disclosure** provisions that used to apply only to national party organizations now apply at the local level. A registered constituency association must appoint an official agent, who is responsible for receiving donations and submitting an audited annual report of financial transactions to Elections Canada.[65]

Whereas the rules for parties and constituency associations are always in effect, those that apply to candidates only operate during (and shortly after) the campaign period. Any candidate who received at least 10 percent of the valid votes cast in his or her constituency is eligible for reimbursement of up to 60 percent of the electoral and personal expenses incurred by his or her campaign.[66] To qualify for the reimbursement, the candidate's official agent must submit a report to Elections Canada detailing the revenues received by the campaign, election expenditures, and personal expenses incurred by the candidate.[67]

Once the campaign ends, the candidate's electoral bank account is wound up. Any surplus funds, including the reimbursement, are supposed to be transferred to the bank account of his or her constituency association. Most of these amounts are fairly small, although one candidate in the 2000 election reported a transfer of well over $100 000.[68] Over time, in well-organized constituency associations with popular incumbent MPs, those transfers can build up into very substantial amounts. Disclosure reports reveal that a few associations hold assets totalling tens of thousands of dollars, although most appear to be struggling financially.

Despite the requirement to give surplus funds to the party, some candidates may have transferred surplus campaign funds to trust accounts instead. The evidence of this practice is anecdotal, because trust funds are not covered by the disclosure provisions in the CEA. The *Federal Accountability Act* (Chapters 7–9) requires sitting MPs to wind up any existing political trusts; however, it does not provide penalties for those who fail to report the existence of such accounts. Trusts associated with former MPs and defeated candidates are not regulated by law.

Hence, despite the recent amendments to the CEA, numerous loopholes remain. One is the definition of "election expenses." Recall that the election expenses of both parties and candidates are limited by law; they must be disclosed after voting day, and they are subject to partial reimbursement. The problem is that "election expenses" do not exist until the day the writ drops, and they cease to exist on the day the ballots are cast. In other words, there are no restrictions on spending by parties and candidates outside the official campaign period. Disclosure reports reveal that the "operating expenses" of the major parties—especially the governing party—often rise dramatically in the months before an election, as organizers "bank" the resources they intend to use during the upcoming campaign.

In 2003, for example, the federal Liberal Party reported "operating and administrative" expenditures that were nearly double those reported in 2002. Additionally, they reported over 10 times as much pre-election spending, and $1.5 million more in fundraising costs, compared to a year earlier.[69] These figures suggest that the Liberals planned their 2004 campaign well ahead of time, and may have circumvented the spending limits by incurring expenses before the campaign period officially began. Such practices are quite common, at least for governing parties with plenty of money in the bank. In April 2007, for example, the Conservative Party opened a huge, costly campaign headquarters filled with state-of-the-art media equipment.[70] This followed a barrage of television ads attacking new Liberal leader Stéphane Dion, which likely cost millions of dollars.[71] The Conservative Party was well ahead of the others in fundraising, and it also benefited from the largest share of the annual allowance paid to registered parties (Chapter 11). When he resigned as Liberal leader shortly after the October 2008 general election, Dion acknowledged that his image had never recovered from the Conservative onslaught. He called on his party to modernize its fundraising practices, to ensure that it would never again be overwhelmed by unregulated negative ad spending between elections. This call became even more urgent in November 2008, when the Harper Government pledged to abolish the allowances—ostensibly as a gesture of fiscal restraint during an economic crisis. The three Opposition parties, fearing for their very survival, threatened to bring down the Conservative minority Cabinet. The Government quickly withdrew the proposal, but this did not assuage the anger of the Liberals, New Democrats and

Conservative party leader Stephen Harper delivers a speech at an election campaign rally in Oshawa, Ontario, January 20, 2006. (CP/Tom Hanson)

Bloc. As mentioned in previous chapters, Harper was forced to obtain a prorogation from the Governor General to save his brand new Government from defeat in the House.

Given the precariousness of their minority government, and the unpredictability of the next election date, it made sense for the Conservatives to spend some of their surplus wealth before the spending limits could take effect. Then again, the greater predictability of future election dates (Dossier 12.1) could encourage more pre-writ spending by all parties (or at least those which can afford it). If everyone knows when the next election will be held—as they would in a majority government—they can set up their "war rooms," start paying staff, buy goods and services, and generally evade the spending limits as much as possible. Under those circumstances, it may be necessary to push back the spending limits to six months or a year ahead of the fixed voting date.

A second loophole in the CEA is the ability to move money from one political entity—say, the party in central office—to another (a constituency association) in order to get around spending limits at one level or the other. A third loophole is the absence of any independent auditing or verification of political finance disclosures. Because Elections Canada has no way to check that the information submitted is complete and accurate, it is possible for parties, candidates, and agents to conceal transactions if they so desire.[72]

■ The Informal Rules: Getting Out the Vote

A Canadian general election is really 308 separate elections held on the same day. Each constituency elects one MP from among the various candidates. Most are nominated by party constituency organizations; others are independent (or "nonaffiliated") candidates. Every constituency campaign must do at least three things, and do them well, if it hopes to succeed:
1. It must identify its committed supporters.
2. It must win over undecided voters and those who are weakly committed to other parties or candidates.
3. It must "pull" its voters out to the polls on election day.

There are two traditional ways of identifying real and potential supporters: the door-to-door **canvass** and the telephone canvass. Volunteers used to spend long hours contacting voters in person or by phone. The Internet is an increasingly important tool for this purpose, although it has not completely replaced the traditional methods. The old-fashioned methods are labour-intensive; they require large numbers of dedicated foot soldiers to contact the voters and clerical volunteers to collect and process the information they provide.

Elections Canada divides every constituency into small territorial units called "polls," which determine where a given elector will cast his or her ballot. The polling divisions are also used by the parties to target and keep track of their canvassing efforts. If a particular poll voted heavily for the Liberals in the previous election, the Liberal campaign manager and the canvass chair may send fewer volunteers to that neighbourhood; that way, they can concentrate their scarce resources in a neighbouring poll where the vote was more evenly split last time. A poll that has always voted NDP by a wide margin may receive only a token canvass, because it will be perceived by the Liberals as a lost cause. Each poll is assigned to a "poll captain," who organizes the volunteers and collects their canvass reports. As the volunteers go from door to door or work down their phone lists, they sort the voters on their lists into categories. They often use different-coloured highlighters to indicate which voters are strongly committed, which are wavering, which are undecided, and which cannot be persuaded to support their candidate.

When election day rolls around, the Get Out the Vote (GOTV) organization swings into action. The volunteers at the candidate's headquarters have colour-coded voters' lists, which contain all the information collected during the canvass. They keep track of their committed and potential supporters: Which ones have voted? Which ones haven't? This information is provided by the "inside workers," who represent their party at the polling stations and report back to headquarters as they cross the names off their own lists. Supporters who have not yet voted receive phone calls from headquarters. Have they forgotten to vote? Do they need a lift to the polling place, a baby-sitter for their children, or some other type of assistance? In a close contest, where every vote counts, a well-organized and well-staffed GOTV effort can make the difference between winning and losing.[73]

ELECTORAL SYSTEMS

Table 11.4 in the previous chapter raised several important questions about the fairness of Canada's electoral process:

- Why did the Liberal Party form three successive majority governments with 38–43 percent of the popular vote between 1993 and 2000? And why did it form a majority government (155/301 seats) with 38 percent in 1997, but only a minority (135/108 seats) with 36.7 percent in 2004?

- Why did the Canadian Alliance win only two seats in Ontario in 2000, despite winning almost one-quarter of the votes in that province, and almost all the seats in Alberta with just under 60 percent of the vote?

- How can a party with only 14 percent of the national vote form the Official Opposition with 54 seats—as the BQ did in 1993—while the Progressive Conservative Party, with 16 percent of the vote, won only two seats?

- Why, despite shifting partisan allegiances among a majority of voters, did the Liberals govern Canada for most of the twentieth century?

Many of the answers to these questions lie in the workings of Canada's electoral system: the set of rules and procedures which translate the preferences of citizens, as expressed on ballots, into the distribution of legislative seats among the various political parties. There are a wide variety of electoral systems in use around the world, which can be distinguished according to three major dimensions:

1. ballot structure: the way in which voters express their preferences (e.g., choosing among parties, or voting for an individual candidate);
2. district magnitude: the number of legislators elected in each constituency; and
3. **electoral formula** (the method by which votes are cast, counted, and translated into results).[74]

Table 12.3 compares some of the major electoral systems in use today. The choice of ballot structure, district magnitude, and electoral formula can affect electoral outcomes, sometimes profoundly. The incentives set by these three dimensions of the electoral system shape the behaviour of political parties, elected officials, and voters.

◼ Ballot Structure: Expressing Your Preference

Voting is only one way for citizens to express their opinions about candidates in an election. Citizens can also campaign actively for a favourite candidate, contribute money to the campaign, place campaign signs on their lawns, or attend meetings to demonstrate political support. However, these activities do not determine who wins or loses. The winner is not the candidate with the most money, or the most volunteers, or the most lawn signs. The preferences expressed when votes are cast are the only ones that count, the only ones that are counted. Suppose, then, that a voter likes candidate A, dislikes candidate B, and is indifferent to candidate C. To what extent can that voter express these feelings on the ballot?

The simplest and crudest way of expressing preferences on an electoral ballot is through a **categorical** choice. A categorical ballot allows the voter to choose one, and only one, of the

TABLE 12.3 CATEGORIZING ELECTORAL SYSTEMS

SYSTEM	BALLOT STRUCTURE	DISTRICT MAGNITUDE	ELECTORAL FORMULA
Single-Member Plurality (SMP)	Categorical	one	Plurality: the candidate with the most votes wins
Alternative Vote (AV)	Ordinal	one	Majority
Two-Round System	Categorical	one	Majority: if no candidate receives 50 percent plus one in the first round; the top two finishers compete in a run-off election
Single Transferable Vote (STV)	Ordinal	three or more	Proportional: a quota is calculated
List-Proportional Representation (List-PR)	Categorical (both open and closed lists)	three or more	Proportional: each party is awarded seats in proportion to its share of the vote
Mixed Member Proportional (MMP)	Two categorical votes, one for an SMP candidate and one for a party list (the list vote determines the number of seats to which each party is entitled)	one in the SMP districts and more than one on the lists	Plurality in the SMP seats, proportional in the lists; the overall outcome is proportional
Additional Member System (AMS) (also called Parallel)	Two categorical votes, one for an SMP candidate and one for a party list (the two sets of MPs are elected separately)	one in the SMP districts and more than one on the lists	Plurality in the SMP seats, proportional in the lists; the overall outcome is somewhat proportional

candidates listed (see Figure 12.1). Given a choice between candidates A, B, and C, the voter may put an "X" beside one of them or beside none of them (thereby spoiling the ballot). Note that with this method the voter is able to express a preference for Green over both Doe and Smith, but is unable to express a second preference for either Doe or Smith. If the voter dislikes Doe more intensely than he likes Green, a categorical ballot may encourage strategic voting—that is, voting for Green in order to defeat Doe. Under this condition, the voter has made a complex calculation, little of which is communicated through the ballot. Categorical ballots are used in federal and provincial elections in Canada.

Ordinal ballots allow (or require) voters to rank-order some or all of the candidates from most preferred to least preferred. In Figure 12.2, the voter has rank-ordered all of the candidates listed on the ballot. In this way, the voter expresses a wide range of preferences by positioning each candidate relative to all the others. Whereas the categorical ballot has the virtue of simplicity, an ordinal ballot can take a long time to fill out and demand much greater

FIGURE 12.1 THE CATEGORICAL BALLOT

DOE, John	( )
GREEN, Elizabeth	(X)
SMITH, Frederick	( )

FIGURE 12.2   THE ORDINAL BALLOT

CHAN, Dorothy	(1)
DOE, John	(4)
GREEN, Elizabeth	(2)
SINGH, Gurbinder	(5)
SMITH, Frederick	(6)
ZEFFIRELLI, Giovanna	(3)

information and sophistication from the voter. Counting ordinal ballots is considerably more complex and time-consuming than counting categorical votes, as our later discussion of electoral formulas demonstrates.

District Magnitude: The Number of MPs per Constituency

Canada has a single-member system: every constituency elects one MP to the House of Commons. Therefore, the district magnitude is one. Most democracies use proportional or semi-proportional systems, in which the district magnitude is greater than one; the larger the district magnitude, the more accurate the distribution of legislative seats among the various parties. In other words, large multi-member districts produce more proportional results than small or single-member districts. In fact, a district magnitude of one cannot produce a proportional result; it turns an election into zero-sum game, in which one candidate or party wins and all the others lose. For the same reason, single-member constituencies make it more difficult for non-traditional candidates (i.e., those who are not white and male) to win seats in the legislature.

Electoral Formula: Translating Votes into Seats

An electoral formula is the rule or set of rules used to determine which candidate or candidates have been elected. Each electoral formula answers two questions:

1. How many votes are required to win a legislative seat?
2. Is a party's share of seats in proportion to its share of the vote?

The answer to the first question depends, in part, on the district magnitude. In single-member districts, there are two main alternatives: plurality and majority. In a **single-member plurality (SMP) system,** sometimes called "first past the post" (FPTP), the winner is the candidate who receives more votes than any other. The candidate need not (and often does not) obtain the support of a majority of the voters in the electoral district. The SMP system is used in all Canadian federal and provincial elections.

Under a majority formula, the winner must receive at least 50 percent plus one of all valid votes cast. Because a single round of voting often fails to produce a majority winner, majority systems are somewhat more complex than plurality systems. There are two principal methods for ensuring that one candidate receives a majority of the vote:

1. run-off systems, which require a second round of voting (usually restricted to the top two candidates from the first ballot); and
2. ordinal systems, in which the voter rank-orders the candidates as described above. In an ordinal majority system, such as alternative vote (AV), the valid ballots are counted and a quota—in this case, 50 percent plus one of the total number of valid ballots—is calculated. When the preferences are recorded, the candidate with the fewest first-preference

votes is eliminated and that candidate's second-preference votes are redistributed among the remaining candidates according to the distribution of references by the voters. The counting continues until one candidate reaches the quota.

In multi-member districts, which elect two or more MPs, the electoral formulas are very different. One way of electing members for such districts is **"list-proportional representation,"** (list-PR). Citizens vote for party lists, not for individual candidates; the parties are then awarded parliamentary seats in proportion to their shares of the vote. In a 100-seat district, for example, a party would draw up a ranked list of 100 candidates. If that party received 30 percent of the vote, it would receive 30 percent of the seats, which it would fill with the top 30 candidates on its list.

When citizens vote directly for individual candidates in a multi-member district—as they do in a single transferable vote, or STV, system—each winning candidate must receive a predetermined quota of the valid votes cast. Most such quotas are slightly higher than the proportion of the district's seats represented by the one seat the candidate hopes to fill. In other words, one seat would represent 12.5 percent of the votes cast in an eight-member district, and the quota of votes required to fill that seat would be set at just over 12.5 percent. Voters rank the candidates on an ordinal ballot, and if the distribution of first preferences does not fill all of the seats, unused lower preferences are successively counted until all the seats are filled.

As to the second question concerning electoral formulas—whether a party's share of legislative seats will be proportional to its share of the vote—the answer depends on the type of electoral system in use. List-PR translates the vote share for each party list into a proportional share of seats in the legislature, although the degree of proportionality varies with the district magnitude. Similarly, STV produces more or less proportionality depending on the number of seats per constituency. Canada's SMP system does not produce **proportional representation.** Indeed, all single-member systems distort the translation of votes into seats to a greater or lesser degree. Suppose, for example, that the same three parties contest every district in an election based on the single-member plurality system. In order to win a seat, a party's candidate need only garner more votes than his or her competitors. If those opponents split the opposition vote evenly, a candidate can win with just over one-third of the vote. If the same party wins in this manner in every district, it could win 100 percent of the seats with only 35 to 40 percent of the vote. This hypothetical example, though extreme and improbable, illustrates the distorting effect of SMP.

Mixed Systems: The Best of Both Worlds?

List-PR and SMP have both defenders and critics.[75] Proportional representation has the obvious merit of ensuring that a party's strength in the legislature is roughly equivalent to its popularity among the electorate. On the other hand, list-PR and STV can encourage political parties to split into smaller factions. In particular, STV requires candidates from the same party to compete against each other, which weakens local constituency associations (see Chapter 11); this was one reason why Manitoba replaced STV with SMP in the 1950s.[76] Proportional systems also make it impossible for any one party to win a majority of legislative seats, except in the rare instances when a single party wins more than 50 percent of the popular vote. As explained in Chapters 7 and 8, the political executive must be able to rely on the support of a majority of members in the lower house of Parliament in order to carry out its responsibilities. Because list-PR does not manufacture artificial majority governments, unlike SMP, it increases the likelihood of **coalition** governments: Cabinets made up of ministers from two or more parties. Critics of list-PR argue that it promotes political instability and leads to the formation of weak and fragile governments. There may be some truth in this charge, but only in divided societies like Italy and Israel; peaceful societies like Sweden and Norway have enjoyed long periods of stable coalition government under list-PR.

A growing number of electoral systems combine two different electoral formulas. Countries with **mixed electoral systems** have two types of MP in their national legislatures: some represent single-member constituencies, while the rest are elected from national or regional party lists. The voter casts two ballots on voting day, one for a constituency MP and the other for a party list. The proportionality of a mixed system depends on two factors: (1) whether each party's share of the seats in Parliament is based solely on the list vote, and (2) the ratio of list MPs to constituency MPs. A system in which the list votes determine seat shares is called "mixed-member proportional," or MMP. Conversely, in an additional member system (AMS), also called a "parallel" system, the two types of MP are elected separately, The seat total for each party is the sum of the constituency seats plus the list seats. The disproportional results of the SMP votes are only partly offset by the proportional distribution of list seats among the parties. In an AMS system, therefore, a larger percentage of list seats produces a more proportional result overall.

THE UNREFORMED CANADIAN ELECTORAL SYSTEM

Since Confederation, with a few exceptions,[77] Canadians have used the single-member plurality system to elect their MPs and provincial legislators. There was no debate about the choice; SMP had been used to elect the members of colonial assemblies, and it was the system used in the "mother country" of Great Britain.[78] In a federal election, a registered party is entitled to nominate a single candidate in each constituency (section 68(1) of the CEA). Voters mark a single "X" on a categorical ballot, which is counted together with the others cast in that polling division. The candidate who wins more votes than any other, regardless of the actual proportion received, is declared elected (section 313(1) of the CEA).

According to its defenders, SMP has five principal advantages:[79]
1. the simplicity of casting and counting the votes;
2. the clear line of accountability in a single-party majority government;
3. the stability of single-party majority governments;
4. the incentive for parties that hope to form governments to bridge cleavages among regions, linguistic groups, and ethnicities;[80] and
5. the direct relationship between an MP and the voters who live in his or her constituency.

The alleged disadvantages of SMP include the following:
1. it produces disproportional results, often awarding an artificial majority of seats to the largest party while depriving smaller and regionally dispersed parties of representation in the legislature (see Table 12.3);
2. it encourages regional divisions, both by over-representing parties with strong territorial bases (like the Bloc Québécois) and by creating a false impression of one-party dominance in particular provinces (e.g., the Liberals in Quebec prior to 1984, or the Conservatives in Alberta today);
3. it deters voters from "wasting" their support on candidates who have little chance of winning in their particular constituencies, which eventually destroys parties that do not have distinct regional bases of support;
4. it encourages strategic voting, rather than the expression of genuine political preferences;
5. it reduces voter turnout, because the ballots cast for losing candidates and the surplus ballots cast for the winner are "wasted" (i.e., they do not count toward the result); and
6. it reduces the proportion of female and/or visible-minority legislators.[81]

▣ Does Every Vote Count?

Table 12.4 demonstrates the disproportionality between the parties' vote shares and seat shares under SMP. For each federal election between 1945 and 2008, it displays the ratio of

TABLE 12.4 RATIO OF POLITICAL PARTIES' VOTE SHARES AND SEAT SHARES, 1945–2006

YEAR	1	2	3	4	5
1945	Lib 1.24	PC 1.00	CCF 0.73	SC 1.29	–
1949	Lib 1.49	PC 0.53	CCF 0.37	SC 1.03	–
1953	Lib 1.32	PC 0.62	CCF 0.77	SC 1.06	–
1957	Lib 0.97	PC 1.09	CCF 0.88	SC 1.09	–
1958	PC 1.45	Lib 0.55	CCF 0.32	–	–
1962	PC 1.17	Lib 1.01	NDP 0.53	SC 0.97	–
1963	Lib 1.17	PC 1.09	NDP 0.49	SC 0.76	–
1965	Lib 1.23	PC 1.13	NDP 0.44	Cdt 0.72	–
1968	Lib 1.29	PC 0.87	NDP 0.49	SC 1.21	–
1972	Lib 0.93	PC 1.16	NDP 0.66	SC 0.75	–
1974	Lib 1.24	PC 1.02	NDP 0.39	SC 0.82	–
1979	Lib 1.01	PC 1.34	NDP 0.52	SC 0.46	–
1980	Lib 1.18	PC 1.13	NDP 0.57	–	–
1984	PC 1.51	Lib 0.51	NDP 0.57	–	–
1988	PC 1.33	Lib 0.88	NDP 0.72	–	–
1993	Lib 1.46	BQ 1.37	Ref 0.94	NDP 0.39	PC 0.04
1997	Lib 1.34	Ref 1.03	BQ 1.36	NDP 0.64	PC 0.35
2000	Lib 1.40	CA 0.86	BQ 1.18	NDP 0.51	PC 0.33
2004	Lib 1.19	CP 1.08	BQ 1.41	NDP 0.39	–
2006	CP 1.11	Lib 1.11	BQ 1.58	NDP 0.52	–
2008	CP 1.23	Lib 0.95	BQ 1.59	NDP 0.66	–

Legend:

Lib:	Liberal Party	SC:	Social Credit Party
PC:	Progressive Conservative Party	Cdt:	Créditiste
CCF:	Co-operative Commonwealth Federation	BQ:	Bloc Québécois
NDP:	New Democratic Party	Ref:	Reform
CA:	Canadian Alliance	CP	Conservative Party of Canada

Note: Very small parties and independents are excluded.

Sources: F. Leslie Seidle, "The Canadian Electoral System and Proposals for Its Reform," in Alain-G. Gagnon and A. Brian Tanguay, eds., *Canadian Parties in Transition: Discourse, Organization, Representation* (Scarborough: ITP Nelson, 1989), 251. Reprinted with permission; calculated from data from Chief Electoral Officer of Canada, *Thirty-Fourth General Election, Report of the Chief Electoral Officer,* 1988; Appendices (Revised), (Ottawa, 1988), 20–21. Reprinted with permission of the Minister of Supply and Services Canada, 1994. Data from 1993, 1997, 2004, 2006 and 2008 elections taken from the website of Elections Canada: www.elections.ca. Data for the 2000 election taken from Jon H. Pammett and Christopher Dornan, eds., *The Canadian General Election of 2000* (Ottawa: Carleton University Press, 2001), Appendix.

each party's vote share to its share of seats in the Commons. A ratio of 1.0 indicates that a party's seat percentage equalled its vote percentage (e.g., 30 percent of all seats and 30 percent of all votes). A ratio greater than 1.0 indicates that the party received a higher percentage of seats than votes—in effect, that it received an unfair advantage from SMP—whereas a ratio less than 1.0 indicates that it was penalized by our electoral system. Column 1 displays the vote and seat shares for the party that "won" each election, column 2 displays the results for the second-place party, and so forth.

With some exceptions, both the Liberals and the Conservatives have been fairly well served by the electoral system. In 15 of the 20 elections since 1945, the Liberal Party's share of seats was greater than its share of the popular vote. Likewise, the Progressive Conservative Party's share of seats exceeded its popular vote in 11 of the 14 elections held between 1949 and 1993, and the Conservative Party has received a boost from SMP in the three elections which it has contested (2004–2008). Conversely, the NDP regularly received less than two-thirds of the seats it would have won had the same votes been cast under a proportional system. One of the more striking features of the table is the "bonus" given to parties with between 38 and 50 percent of the national vote. Another is the discrepancy between the large ratios for regionally concentrated parties (like the BQ), and the penalty inflicted on smaller parties with dispersed support (such as the NDP).

Magnifying the size of election victories is one thing; awarding the election to the losing party is something else altogether. In 1957 and 1979, the Liberal Party received more votes than any other party—but the Conservatives won more seats. In both elections, the Conservatives translated votes into seats more effectively than the Liberals. Consequently, the governor general invited the Conservatives to form a minority government.

In the 1993 federal election, the Canadian electoral system created one of the least proportional results ever recorded in a Western democracy. The Liberal Party received 60 percent of the Commons seats based on 41.1 percent of the vote—an abnormally high ratio of 1.46. At the other extreme was the Progressive Conservative (PC) Party, which won two Commons seats (0.67 percent) on the basis of 16 percent of the votes, for a representation ratio of 0.04. In other words, the PC Party received 4 percent of the seats to which it would have been entitled in a system of proportional representation.

In the 2006 election, both the Liberals and the Conservatives benefited from SMP. To explain why, Table 12.4 displays the provincial ratios for both parties. The Liberals won "extra" seats in the Atlantic Provinces and Ontario, but were denied a proportionate share of seats in Quebec and the Western provinces; they were completely shut out in Alberta. The Conservatives also did disproportionately well in Ontario, and received significant bonuses in the four Western provinces; these more than offset the SMP penalty in the Atlantic and Quebec. Table 12.5 also

TABLE 12.5 PROVINCIAL SEAT/VOTE RATIOS FOR THE LIBERAL AND CONSERVATIVE PARTIES, 2006 GENERAL ELECTION

PROVINCE	CONSERVATIVE RATIO			LIBERAL RATIO		
	% seats	% votes	Ratio	% seats	% votes	Ratio
Newfoundland and Labrador	42.9	42.7	1.00	57.1	42.8	1.34
Prince Edward Island	0	33.4	0	100	52.5	1.90
Nova Scotia	27.3	29.7	0.92	54.5	37.2	1.47
New Brunswick	30	35.8	0.84	60	39.2	1.53
Quebec	13.3	24.6	0.54	17.3	20.7	0.84
Ontario	37.7	35.1	1.08	50.9	39.9	1.28
Manitoba	57.1	42.8	1.34	21.4	26	0.82
Saskatchewan	85.7	48.9	1.75	14.2	22.4	0.64
Alberta	100	65	1.54	0	15.3	0
British Columbia	45.9	37.3	1.23	24.3	27.6	0.88
CANADA	40.3	36.3	1.11	33.4	30.2	1.11

Source: The data in the table are taken from the Elections Canada website: www.elections.ca.

TABLE 12.6 THE NUMBER OF VOTES CAST PER MP ELECTED, CANADA'S MAJOR NATIONAL PARTIES, 1993 AND 2006

PARTY	1993	2006
Liberal	31 601	43 489
BQ	33 838	30 455
Reform/Conservative*	49 578	43 339
NDP	103 869	89 296
PC	1 088 706	–

*The Canadian Alliance and Progressive Conservative parties merged to form the Conservative Party of Canada shortly before the 2004 federal election. See Chapter 11.

illustrates one of the disadvantages of SMP listed above: the creation of phony provincial "fiefdoms" (in this instance, Prince Edward Island and Alberta).

The distorted translation of votes into seats is more than a violation of abstract or mathematical rules of fairness; it may also be a violation of voting rights. While the Supreme Court stated in 1991 that section 3 of the *Charter* does not guarantee absolute parity of voting power, the majority added that "A system which dilutes one citizen's vote unduly as compared with another citizen's vote runs the risk of providing inadequate representation to the citizen whose vote is diluted."[82] There can be little question that votes cast for smaller parties, and for parties that are less competitive in a particular region, are diluted relative to those of voters who support the winning party (either nationally or regionally). Table 12.6 displays the number of votes required to elect an MP for each of the major parties in the 1993 and 2006 general elections.

If we take the chance of electing an MP as a reflection of the value of an individual vote, we find that in 1993 a Liberal vote was worth 34 times as much as a PC vote. Even in the 2006 election, which produced a relatively fair result, two NDP votes counted for approximately as much as one Liberal or Conservative vote; three NDP votes equalled the power of one BQ vote.

Our single-member constituencies and plurality electoral formula, together with the way in which party votes are distributed across the country, can affect the outcome of national (and provincial) elections. Table 12.7 compares the actual outcome of the 1993 election under SMP to the hypothetical outcome under a purely proportional system. The numbers in the bottom row were calculated by multiplying the number of seats in the Commons by the percentage of the national vote received by each of the five major parties. (Note that such hypothetical outcomes are inherently flawed by the assumption that each party would have received the same number of votes under an alternative electoral system; as noted earlier, SMP tends to reduce support for smaller parties.) Instead of forming a majority government (more than 148 of the 295 seats in the House at that time), the Liberals would have held a

TABLE 12.7 THE OUTCOME OF THE 1993 GENERAL ELECTION UNDER SMP AND PR (NUMBER OF SEATS PER PARTY OUT OF 295)

	LIBERAL	REFORM	BQ	NDP	PC
Actual	177	52	54	9	2
Proportional	121	56	40	21	47

minority of the seats. A moderately proportional system, such as a mixed system, might have produced a slim majority with a more regionally balanced government caucus and a stronger Opposition.

■ The Electoral System and the Party System

The relationship between electoral systems and party systems is a perennial theme in political science. The classic description of that relationship is Duverger's Law: single-member constituencies favour two-party systems, while list-PR favours multi-party systems (four or more parties in Parliament).[83] Proportional representation systems erect few barriers to smaller parties seeking election to Parliament; the **threshold of election** (the percentage of votes required to win a seat) is typically low (between 3 and 5 percent), and the accurate translation of vote shares into seat shares ensures that most parties will secure at least some parliamentary representation. In contrast, electoral systems based on single-member constituencies tend to reduce the number of parties in Parliament and eventually in the party system as a whole.[84]

Given the connection between SMP and two-party systems, how do we explain the fact that Canada has not had a two-party system since 1921? The answer lies in the tendency of SMP to award a disproportionately large number of seats to parties whose support is regionally concentrated. Even smaller parties like the NDP, which run national campaigns, win most of their seats in their strongest regions (in this case, the Prairies and British Columbia). The same is true for India and the United Kingdom, which also use SMP. Therefore, the impact of SMP on the number of parties depends on an intervening variable: the size and mobilization of regional subcultures within the electorate.

■ Does Our Electoral System Encourage Regional Discord?

The SMP system distorts the regional composition of party caucuses in the House of Commons. It over-rewards the party with the most votes in a given province, while denying other parties their rightful share of parliamentary representation. By artificially relegating entire regions to the Opposition benches, SMP has reinforced regional alienation in Canada. In the 1970s and early 1980s, the governing Liberals were all but shut out of the West, while the Progressive Conservatives were nearly invisible in Quebec, despite significant electoral support in each case. As a consequence, Western Canadians lacked significant elected representation in the government caucus and the Cabinet when the National Energy Program was introduced in 1980. Not only was the legislation less sensitive to regional concerns than it might have been, but the Liberal government lacked elected members to sell the package in the West. Distortions in the electoral system thus reinforced long-standing sentiments of regional alienation and further eroded the legitimacy of parliamentary institutions within the region. Similarly, in Quebec the electoral system contributed significantly to the "Tory syndrome"[85] or minority-party syndrome: it bedevilled Conservative efforts to build the party within Quebec and to convince Canadian voters at large that the Progressive Conservatives were indeed a national party that could span linguistic divisions within the country.

For advocates of intrastate federalism (see Chapter 4), who wanted Canada's national political institutions to bridge our regional divisions, SMP became an obvious target. In addition to (or as an alternative to) promoting intrastate reforms to the Canadian Senate, it was often suggested that proportional representation would create truly national parliamentary caucuses—parties whose seats in various parts of the country would reflect the votes cast for them there, rather than the unnecessarily regionalized parties produced by the current electoral system.

Electoral reform to dampen the fires of regionalism seemed less necessary by 1984, when Brian Mulroney finally overcame the "Tory syndrome" to lead a Conservative government with strong representation from all parts of the country. Mulroney managed this feat largely by knitting together a national alliance that encompassed Quebec nationalists and alienated Westerners. But in 1993, as we saw in Chapter 11, this alliance fell apart: Quebec nationalists left the Progressive Conservative Party for the Bloc Québécois, while Westerners migrated to the Reform Party. The impact of this regionalized system of party competition was exaggerated by the electoral system.

Does Our Electoral System Discriminate Against Non-Traditional Candidates?

Whereas the electoral systems used in most Western countries are designed to provide proportional representation for different parties—as surrogates for the various social and ideological groupings in the electorate—SMP evolved in Britain as a way to represent defined geographic territories. It gives every Canadian voter an elected representative in Parliament who is responsible for protecting the various interests of his or her constituents. (See the discussion of constituency "casework" in Chapter 7.) One of the chief complaints about SMP is that it exaggerates regional cleavages at the expense of effective national integration[86] (see "Does the Electoral System Encourage Regional Discord?" on the previous page 442). But while territorial representation is still the guiding principle of Canada's political institutions—especially federalism and parliamentary government—it is increasingly challenged by nonterritorial concepts of representation based on gender, ethnicity, and ideology (see Chapter 2). Table 12.8 compares the proportion of female legislators in several Western democracies, to illustrate the impact that different electoral systems may have on nonterritorial representation.

As Table 12.8 shows, women account for only 22 percent of the Canadian House of Commons—slightly above the world average for female representation, but far less than the proportion of women in the electorate (51 percent). If we decide to reform the electoral system to increase the number of women in Parliament, should we do this through separate (though geographically overlapping) constituencies for men and women, with each gender electing its own member? Or should there be two members, one a woman and one a man, elected by both genders in each constituency? Or—as some advocates of electoral reform argue[87]—would the adoption of a more proportional electoral system encourage Canadian parties to nominate more women in winnable seats, thus improving female representation without special quotas?

The Political Barriers to Electoral Reform

Some of these criticisms of SMP are new, but the calls for reform are not. During and after World War I, the federal Parliament seriously considered adopting a new electoral system. In 1924, two Western provinces adopted a mix of STV for urban ridings and AV for rural constituencies.[88] Today, most Canadian advocates of electoral reform favour some type of mixed system. (The BC Citizens Assembly is the major exception; see Dossier 12.2.) They contend that a mixed system would preserve some of the benefits of SMP—including local representation in the legislature, a direct relationship between MPs and their constituents, and simplicity—while ensuring greater proportionality, increasing voter choice, and making it easier for non-traditional candidates to win seats.[89] The sticking point, for most defenders of SMP, is the fear of unstable minority or coalition governments paralyzed by fragmented legislatures. In response, proponents of reform have proposed mixed systems with relatively low ratios of SMP to list seats. For example, in April 2004 the Law Commission of Canada recommended the adoption of an MMP system in which one-third of MPs would be elected from

TABLE 12.8 **THE REPRESENTATION OF WOMEN IN NATIONAL PARLIAMENTS, SELECTED COUNTRIES, 2008**

COUNTRY	% OF WOMEN IN LOWER HOUSE OF PARLIAMENT	TYPE OF ELECTORAL SYSTEM
Rwanda	48.8	List-PR
Sweden	47.0	List-PR
Cuba	43.2	SMM
Finland	41.5	List-PR
Argentina	40.0	List-PR
Netherlands	39.3	List-PR
Denmark	38.0	List-PR
Costa Rica	36.8	List-PR
Spain	36.3	List-PR
Norway	36.1	List-PR
Belgium	35.3	List-PR
Mozambique	34.8	List-PR
Iceland	33.3	List-PR
New Zealand	33.1	MMP
South Africa	33.0	List-PR
Austria	32.8	List-PR
Germany	31.6	MMP
Uganda	30.7	SMP
Switzerland	28.5	List-PR
Portugal	28.3	List-PR
Afghanistan	27.7	SNTV
Australia	26.7	AV
Iraq	25.5	List-PR
Luxembourg	23.3	List-PR
Canada	22.1	SMP
United Kingdom	19.7	SMP
France	18.2	SMM
World Average	**18.0**	
Italy	17.3	List-PR
United States	16.8	SMP
Greece	14.7	List-PR
Israel	14.2	List-PR
Ireland	13.3	STV
Japan	9.4	MMP

Source: The Representation of Women in National Parliaments, Selected Countries, June 2008. Inter-Parliamentary Union: www.ipu.org/wmn-e/classif.htm; accessed June 2008. Reprinted with permission from Interparliamentary Union.

provincial lists (plus three seats from the territories).[90] Because the parties' seat shares would be determined by the list votes, this would be a highly proportional system.

One potential problem arising from the adoption of a mixed system is the presence of two different categories of MP in the legislature.[91] We might expect the MPs elected on SMP ballots to feel a stronger incentive to perform constituency "casework" (discussed in Chapter 7), whereas their colleagues chosen from party lists would have more time to spend on committees and policy work.[92] This expectation of a division of labour is refuted by the evidence from New Zealand, Germany, Scotland, and Wales (all of which use some type of mixed system). The constituency members do a little more constituency work, and the list members spend a little more time on policy work, but the differences are slight.[93] Instead of complementing each other, the two groups compete for local visibility and support. This rivalry appears to be encouraged by systems that allow a candidate to run for an SMP seat and a list seat on the same ballot. Where list MPs are regarded as "second-class" legislators, as they seem to be in New Zealand and Britain,[94] they aspire to win constituency seats in the next election; this leads them to raise their political profiles in their regional districts, and to "poach" popular constituency issues.[95] Tensions among MPs are also heightened when one or two parties monopolize the constituency seats, and their rivals dominate the lists.[96] Given that one of the goals of adopting a more proportional electoral system is to increase the representation of smaller parties, this pattern of results is all but inevitable.

The Law Commission report provoked some discussion of electoral reform at the federal level, but no real action. The NDP favours a more proportional system, for obvious reasons (recall Table 12.3). So do the Greens, whose leader Elizabeth May said in April 2007 that "The thing that Greens care about more fundamentally than anything—perhaps for some Greens it matters more than climate—is that we fix the voting system."[97] The election of two minority governments in a row gave the NDP some bargaining power, which leader Jack Layton used to extract a promise in the 2004 Throne Speech to study electoral reform. Most Liberal MPs are opposed to the creation of a more proportional system, while their Conservative counterparts are lukewarm at best. Consequently, the Standing Committee could not reach a consensus; its June 2005 report was ignored in the hullabaloo over the Sponsorship Scandal.[98]

The NDP tried again after the 2006 election, pressuring the new Conservative Government (whose platform made no mention of electoral reform) to include the following commitment in its first Throne Speech: "Building on the work begun in the last Parliament, this Government will seek to involve parliamentarians and citizens in examining the challenges facing Canada's electoral system and democratic institutions."[99] In January 2007, Government House Leader Peter Van Loan announced a series of public consultations on a variety of institutions, including Parliament and the electoral system. The press release stated that 12 "citizens' forums" would be held across the country, without providing any details about the number and selection of participants.[100] The forums were held, but no further action had been taken at the time of writing. Liberal leader Stéphane Dion struck a deal with the Greens in early 2007, promising to consider electoral reform in exchange for political support in the next election. Neither party appeared to benefit from that deal in the October 2008 election, and neither was in a position to implement electoral reform.

In his public comments on the Green deal, Dion expressed some support for a mixed electoral system like those considered in several provinces.[101] Despite the lack of serious action on electoral reform in Ottawa, five provincial governments had taken various steps toward changing the electoral systems in their jurisdictions. These are described in Dossier 12.2. To date, none of these efforts has borne fruit. By definition, an elected legislator—especially a first minister or Cabinet minister in an artificial majority government—owes a debt of gratitude to SMP. He or she is therefore likely to regard the prospect of proportionality (and especially the increased possibility of minority or coalition government) with distaste. Opposition parties with a realistic chance of forming a majority government in the near future often share this fear of reform. Responding to public rejection of the current electoral system, they may promise to improve matters if elected to office; but they usually change their minds once they taste power.[102] Smaller parties, which are placed at a serious disadvantage by SMP, tend to favour a switch to proportionality.

Although politicians' public comments about electoral systems are generally expressed in terms of core political values—"stable government" on the one side, "democracy" or "fairness" on the other—they are really based on calculations of political advantage.[103] In an effort to circumvent the self-interest of politicians, reformers often argue that decisions about electoral systems should be made by "ordinary citizens": either the entire electorate in a referendum, or a small sample of voters in a constituent assembly (sometimes both). The problem, as Dossier 12.2 explains, is that politicians cannot be completely excluded from the process. As long as they control the laws governing referenda, they will use that control to block possible changes to the electoral system.[104]

DOSSIER 12.2   Electoral Reform in the Provinces

In 2004, the British Columbia Government appointed a Citizens' Assembly to consider electoral reform. Two citizens, one male and one female, were randomly chosen from each provincial constituency. Their mandate was twofold: to decide whether or not BC needed a new voting system; and if so, to design an alternative method for electing the provincial legislature. That alternative would be subjected to a referendum held concurrently with the May 2005 provincial election.[105] The BC Government set a high threshold for the referendum: 60 percent of the valid vote province-wide, plus a majority of the vote in at least 60 percent of the constituencies. The Assembly decided to reject SMP, and chose STV to replace it.[106] This decision surprised most experts on electoral systems, who favoured some type of mixed system; it appears to have been motivated, in large measure, by a desire to reduce the power of political parties in BC's electoral politics.[107] The number of MLAs per district would vary from two in sparsely populated northern regions to seven in dense urban areas.[108] Despite the complexity of STV, which may have deterred some voters, the 2005 referendum almost passed: 57 percent of voters overall, and a majority of voters in 77 of 79 constituencies, opted for BC-STV.[109] The close

result forced the Government to schedule a second referendum to coincide with the May 2009 provincial election.[110]

In December 2003, a judge in Prince Edward Island issued a report recommending the replacement of SMP with some form of MMP.[111] In May 2004 the Conservative premier appointed a commission to design a new electoral system and conduct a public-education campaign. He also promised to hold a referendum in November 2005. Less than six weeks before the vote, the Cabinet fixed the "Yes" threshold at 60 percent. Unlike the BC referendum, the PEI vote was not held in conjunction with a provincial election; only one-quarter of the usual number of polling places were set up. Unsurprisingly, the official turnout rate was less than one-third (although the failure to update the voters' list before the referendum casts some doubt on that figure), despite the fact that PEI boasts the highest voter turnout in Canada. Finally, the provincial government did not deliver the intensive public education campaign that it had promised. In the end, the MMP proposal was soundly defeated: only 36.4 percent of those who participated in the referendum chose the new system.[112]

In December 2004 the Quebec Government tabled a draft Bill to reform the

(continued)

provincial *Elections Act*. It proposed a mixed electoral system, in which 60 percent of the MNAs would represent single-member ridings and the remaining 40 percent would represent "compensatory" regional districts. Each district would cover three single-member ridings, and send two MNAs to the legislature. When a voter went to the polls, he or she would cast a single ballot to elect an MNA in his or her riding. That vote would be pooled with the others cast in the same district to determine which parties would fill the two "compensatory" seats.[113] Critics argued that the one-ballot system would distort the preferences of voters, and it would do little to offset the disadvantages of SMP.[114] In 2005 the Government appointed a Special Committee of MNAs to examine the proposal, in conjunction with a group of eight citizens. In 2006 the combined committees rejected the one-vote proposal, and called for a two-vote system of MMP similar to that used in Germany.[115] Unlike the panels in the other provinces, it did not recommend a referendum; this was partly because of the history of divisive and costly referendum campaigns in Quebec. At the time of writing, the Government had taken no action on the report.

The Government of Ontario established a Democratic Reform Secretariat shortly after it took office in late 2003. One of the stated goals of the secretariat was to foster "an open debate on our electoral process, leading to a referendum on electoral reform."[116] In 2004 the Government announced that it would follow the BC example and establish a Citizens' Assembly on Electoral Reform. By the fall of 2006, the Assembly—106 voters, one from each provincial riding—had begun its work. The members studied SMP and alternative electoral systems, and held public meetings across the province. In May 2007 the Assembly issued its final report, calling for an MMP system. Seventy percent of provincial legislators would be chosen from SMP districts, and the other 30 percent would be elected from closed province-wide lists. The list votes would determine each party's share of seats in the legislature.

Each voter would cast two votes: one for an SMP candidate, and one for a party list.

The Ontario Government was committed to holding a referendum on the Assembly's recommendations, in tandem with the October 2007 provincial election. Like its counterparts in BC and PEI, the Ontario Cabinet set the threshold at 60 percent instead of the usual 50 percent plus one threshold for a referendum. The consistency of this government tactic to block electoral reform—characterized by the architect of the BC Citizens' assembly as "prima facie evidence of an intent to strangle reform at birth"[117]—demonstrates the reluctance of those who have benefited from SMP to permit any change to the status quo (despite their rhetoric about "democratic renewal"). Perhaps predictably, the Ontario referendum failed.

In late 2003 the Government of New Brunswick set up a Commission on Legislative Democracy. Among other issues, the commission was mandated to "examine and make recommendations on implementing a proportional representation electoral system for the New Brunswick Legislative Assembly."[118] In early 2005, it recommended a mixed system: 64 percent of MLAs would be elected from single-member ridings, and the rest would represent four regional districts superimposed on the ridings. Unlike the district model proposed by the Quebec Government in 2004, the New Brunswick system would use two ballots. Unlike the Ontario system, the party list vote in each region would not determine the number of seats awarded to each party; instead, the SMP and list ballots would be counted separately.[119] The commission also called on the provincial government to hold a binding referendum on its recommendations, preferably in conjunction with the next provincial election. In June 2006, then-Premier Bernard Lord finally promised to hold the referendum in May 2008. But his Progressive Conservative Government was defeated in September 2006, and replaced by a Liberal Government that refused to hold a referendum on electoral reform.[120]

VOTING AND NONVOTING

Since the mid-1960s, voter turnout has declined worldwide. In both established and new democracies, the percentage of citizens who cast ballots fell from 79 to 67 percent between 1965 and 2006.[121] Voter turnout in Canada is below average, relative to other Western democracies and to the emerging democracies in Africa, Asia, and Latin America.[122] In 2004, only 60.5 percent of eligible voters cast ballots—the lowest official turnout rate ever recorded in a Canadian national election. Turnout rose significantly in the 2006 election, to 64.9 percent of the voters listed in the Permanent Register of Electors.[123] It was not clear whether this was a blip or the start of a sustained recovery.[124] However, the fact that turnout fell to a historic low in the 2008 election—only 59.1 percent of registered voters—suggests that the 2006 election was an anomaly.

Political scientists have not identified the exact causes of falling turnout, but most agree that three sets of variables are involved: socio-economic, institutional, and political.[125] The first two sets include such long-term factors as the percentage of highly educated voters, the presence or absence of compulsory-voting laws, and the degree of proportionality in the electoral system. Conversely, the political conditions vary from election to election; the most important are the closeness of the contest between the two leading parties, the amount of campaign spending, and the perceived impact of casting a vote.

In the past, scholars believed that the likelihood of voting was determined by the individual characteristics of voters. Both age and education are positively correlated with voting: in other words, older people are much more likely to vote than those in their 20s, and people with university degrees are somewhat more likely to vote than those who did not finish high school.[126] When we look at the entire electorate, however, the correlations seems to disappear. Education levels have risen sharply in Western democracies since 1965, the very period during which voter turnout fell.[127] Recent studies suggest that older people are more frequent voters, not because of age per se, but because they acquired the habit of voting in their younger days; if their children and grandchildren do not get into the habit early, they may never become active voters.[128] The only socio-economic variable that seems to affect turnout is population size: people are more likely to vote when there are fewer of them, perhaps because they believe that their ballot will have a real impact on the result.[129]

Among the institutional variables, the most important are compulsory voting laws, the relative difficulty of registering to vote, and the proportionality of the electoral system.[130] The first is self-explanatory: if the law requires them to vote or pay a fine, most people will cast ballots (although more of those ballots will be spoiled than in countries where voting is voluntary).[131] Second, a registration system that requires the voter to take the initiative may exclude many citizens from the **franchise,** as does a system that inadvertently excludes some people who should be entitled to vote.[132] For most of the twentieth century, Canadian voters were enumerated (counted) at the start of every general election campaign. Two-person teams of enumerators, chosen from the ranks of activists in the two parties that polled the most votes in the constituency in the previous election, went door to door. They did more than compile the voters' list; by contacting them directly, they made citizens aware of the election campaign and may have encouraged them to turn out to the polls.[133]

We suggested earlier in this chapter that SMP discourages voting by "wasting" a large number of votes. One major cross-national study found that "turnout is 5 or 6 percentage points higher in countries in which the voting system is proportional or mixed,"[134] which suggests that the type of electoral system exerts an independent effect. However, a more recent study found that the impact of proportionality on turnout was less direct. The key is a short-term political variable: the perceived closeness of the electoral contest, both at the national level and in the individual constituency. More citizens will make the effort to cast a ballot when they believe that it will affect the outcome of the election. "In districts where the race is a foregone conclusion, many potential voters will not see the point of voting and turnout will be lower," regardless of ballot structure, district magnitude, or electoral formula.[135]

The 2006 federal election supports the claim that competitiveness affects turnout. For the first time since 1993, a change of government appeared to be a real possibility. In 1997 and 2000 the Liberals, confronted with a divided Opposition and riding high in the polls, won easily. There was little incentive for marginal voters (those who were not strongly committed to the act of voting) to invest time and effort in going to the polls. The situation started to change in 2004, when the newly merged Conservative Party offered a united alternative to voters (see Chapter 11), but the full impact of the change in the party system was not felt until the 2006 campaign. The number of close three- and even four-way races increased substantially, especially in BC, Ontario, Quebec, and Manitoba. Turnout rose slightly in BC, and significantly in the remaining three provinces, compared to 2004. (Turnout in Ontario had already gone up in 2004, largely because of increased competition between the Liberals and the merged Conservatives.[136]) The emergence of a real alternative to the "Natural Governing Party" likely gave voters, who might otherwise have stayed home, a reason to cast their ballots on election day. But this does not fully explain why turnout fell sharply in 2008; although most observers expected the Conservatives to win, there was some suspense about the size of their victory (a majority or a minority). Some journalists attributed the drop to disaffected Liberal supporters who could not bring themselves to vote for leader Stephane Dion and his "Green Shift" platform.

Despite the influence of short-term factors, much of the long-term decline in voter participation remains unexplained. The claim that shrinking social capital has depressed turnout (Chapter 2) is not supported by the evidence. While feelings of alienation and apathy toward the political system seem to be increasing, there is no direct proof that these are deterring people from voting. On the other hand, there is some evidence of a reverse effect. Attitudes that encourage voting, including a sense of civic engagement and party identification, appear to have reduced what would otherwise have been a steeper decline in turnout; if that is correct, it suggests that what really needs to be explained is why so many people continue to vote.[137]

To the extent that discontent with political institutions reduces voter turnout, this effect is most pronounced among the youngest citizens. Once an individual has cast a ballot in three or more elections, the habit of voting becomes ingrained.[138] He or she is relatively immune to either the long-term or the short-term variables that discourage voting. Before that time, he or she may be dissuaded from casting a ballot by registration problems, bad weather, or some other obstacle; alternatively, he or she may decide not to vote because he or she simply can't be bothered. If that attitude persists, he or she may never acquire the habit of voting; he or she might vote every now and then, when a particular campaign engages his or her interest, but otherwise he or she will remain disengaged from the electoral process.

Fortunately, a majority of Canadians (albeit perhaps a bare majority) do acquire the voting habit. Before they mark their ballots, they have to make a choice—which, as we saw in the discussion of electoral systems, is a choice to vote for one candidate in that particular constituency. The factors that affect that choice are explained in the next section.

THE CANADIAN VOTER

We know that persistent and well-mobilized subcultures within the electorate shape our national party system by influencing voting behaviour. But Canadian voters are not solely motivated by long-term factors such as class, region, partisanship, or ideology. Many, perhaps most, are swayed by short-term factors: current economic conditions, the parties' stands on key issues, or their perceptions of the party leaders. While the act of expressing a preference may be simple, at least in Canada, determining one's electoral preference can be a complicated process. In this section we will examine the major short-term and long-term determinants of Canadian voting behaviour.

Long-Term Influences on Voter Choice

Social Cleavages

As we saw in Chapter 2, Western electorates are divided along lines of social cleavage: class, religion, language, ethnicity, region, and gender. These demographic characteristics are relatively stable and persistent, underlying long-term patterns of voting behaviour. This is not to say that every member of the Canadian Auto Workers votes for the NDP, or that every woman votes for female candidates; nothing in voting behaviour is that simple. For a particular social cleavage to influence the way in which a person votes, certain conditions must be present:

- There must be a political party that reflects the interests and values of that particular group, either exclusively or as part of a broader electoral coalition (see Chapter 11).
- The cleavage must be politically salient—in other words, voters' identity as members of a particular group must be important enough to override other potential factors in voting choice, such as short-term issues and party leaders.
- The voters within the group must interpret political events and issues through the filter of the particular values associated with that subculture (e.g., Catholicism or feminism); in effect, they must be mobilized to see the world through the same lens.

The politically salient demographic characteristics of a given voter shape that voter's perceptions of political parties, issues, and leaders. These characteristics do not necessarily determine his or her vote, but they do influence his or her judgments about the other long-term and short-term factors that affect voting choice. The impact of five specific characteristics will be summarized here: class, region, religion, ethnicity, and gender.

- Compared to voters in Western Europe, Canadians are relatively indifferent to class.[139] Despite the presence of economic disparities in Canada, the class cleavage does not exert a significant influence on voting behaviour. Advocates of class voting consider this unusual cleavage pattern to be a sign of immaturity on the part of Canadian voters. They argue that the division between socioeconomic classes should take priority over all others. In reality, although a market economy may produce a fundamental conflict between the interests of those who own or control businesses and those who do not, the range of conflicting interests in a complex post-industrial society extends far beyond simple class conflict. Differences among various ethnic, linguistic, or religious groups; between those on the ideological left and right; among regions; between young and old, men and women, farmers and industrial workers, and many other groups occur in all modern societies— and all of these differences may be reflected in the party system.
- The regional cleavage is unusually powerful in Canada.[140] This should come as no surprise, given the discussions of regionalism in previous chapters.
- The strength of the religious cleavage in Canada is surprising. In a country like the Netherlands, with a strong tradition of Catholic and Protestant parties, the persistence of the denominational cleavage is easier to understand. But during the twentieth century, the salience of religious issues in Canadian politics declined rapidly. There is no explicitly Catholic party, dedicated to promoting the specific interests of that faith. Nonetheless, there are clear and consistent differences in voting behaviour among Canada's largest religious denominations. In every election held from 1965 to 2004, "the propensity to vote Liberal in Ontario and Atlantic Canada increase[d] by 18 points when the person is Catholic."[141] For their part, Protestants are more likely to vote for the Conservatives (as they did for the Progressive Conservative, Reform, and Canadian Alliance parties), while voters without a religious affiliation disproportionately support the NDP.[142]

- As Canada's population becomes more diverse, ethnic cleavages become more numerous and potentially more influential in voting decisions. The Liberals have long been the most popular party among Canadians of non-European origin—a fact that helps to explain their dominance in Toronto and Montreal, which have large populations of first- and second-generation citizens. "Everything else being equal, the probability of voting Liberal is 23 points higher when one comes from Asia, Latin America or Africa than when one is of British origin. . . . The Liberals also do quite well among South Europeans and those of French origin."[143] After the 2004 election the Conservatives, whose ethnic base has long been restricted to Canadians of northern European origin,[144] began assiduously wooing other ethnic communities.[145] The urgency of this effort arose from the party's failure to win a single seat in Vancouver, Toronto, or Montreal, which have high concentrations of Asian, Latin American, and African immigrants.[146] The Conservatives were shut out of the urban cores of Canada's major cities in 2006 and 2008. However, in the latter election they made important gains in the Toronto suburbs, which are heavily populated by new Canadians.
- Finally, gender cuts across the four cleavages previously discussed. Female voters disproportionately support parties on the left, and male voters are more attracted to parties on the right. From 1974 to 1993, the Liberals enjoyed the disproportionate support of women; today, the "gender gap" benefits the NDP.[147] In English Canada, Conservative support among female voters is 10 points lower than among male voters. Women are more likely than men to reject socially conservative attitudes (e.g., opposition to same-sex marriage), to favour gun control, and to express reservations about closer ties to the United States; the Conservatives' opposing stands on these issues likely explain most of the gender gap in their support. Although it managed to win the 2006 election, "the fact that it could not attract as many votes from women as it did from men may well have prevented the Conservative Party from achieving majority status."[148]

Voting patterns in Quebec are somewhat less complex than those in English Canada. The two dominant cleavages are language—anglophone/allophone versus francophone—and age. Nonfrancophones overwhelmingly favour the Liberals, while younger French-speaking voters support the BQ.[149] The evidence is clear: Canadian voters are strongly, although not exclusively, influenced by the long-term cleavage patterns in the electorate.

Values

The relationship between social cleavages and political values is complex. On the one hand, values can be shaped by membership in a particular subculture. For example, we have seen that Western populists and Quebec nationalists have differing attitudes toward federalism. On the other hand, a particular set of values cannot automatically be attributed to every member of a given group—not all Catholics are pro-life, for example—nor can it be reduced to a set of subcultural biases. Finally, political values change over time (see Chapter 2), even when the makeup of the electorate remains fairly constant. They shift in response to historical events, institutional innovations, and long-term economic and social trends. While values are often related to social cleavages, therefore, these two factors may affect voting behaviour in different ways.

Before political values can affect voting behaviour, they must be mobilized by a political party or some other agency. Latent values—those that remain unexpressed or outside the public realm—do not play a role in politics. The core strategy of the Liberal campaign in 2000 was to mobilize latent fears about the Canadian Alliance and its new leader, Stockwell Day. To solidify the Liberal vote, party strategists crafted a campaign that pitted "Liberal values" against the socially conservative values of the Alliance.[150] The strategy succeeded, in part because Day's mixed messages about issues such as abortion and homosexuality made Liberal allegations of a "hidden agenda" more credible to many voters.[151]

A Suffragette rally, 1913 (AP)

According to Blais et al., the four core values in the Canadian electorate are "attitudes about free enterprise, moral traditionalism, and sympathy/antipathy towards racial minorities and feminism." In addition, voters are influenced by two "fundamental beliefs": "general disaffection with political parties and a sense of regional alienation."[152] Overall, these values and beliefs explained approximately 10 percent of voting choice in the 2000 election.[153] Voters who believed strongly in the value of free markets were more likely to support the Canadian Alliance or the Progressive Conservatives; the Alliance also benefited from the support of moral traditionalists—e.g., people opposed to same-sex marriage—and those with negative feelings toward minorities and feminists. Conversely, the Liberals and New Democrats had a stronger appeal to voters who were ambivalent about free enterprise, who held less traditional views on morality, and who were sympathetic toward minorities and feminists. As the incumbent government, the Liberals suffered a loss in support among voters who were particularly cynical toward politics; they also bore the brunt of anger from voters who believed that their particular regions were shortchanged in Confederation.[154]

The Sponsorship Scandal that broke in early 2004 reinforced the anger and cynicism of many voters (see Dossier 8.2). During the first few weeks of the 2004 election campaign, it appeared that the scandal would cost the Liberals enough seats to relegate them to Opposition. In the end, other factors—likely including partisan attachment to the Liberals and concerns about a Conservative "hidden agenda"—gave them a plurality of seats in the Commons.

Also in 2004, Stephen Harper's efforts to position his new Conservative Party as a moderate political force were undermined by a handful of "freelancing" MPs. Two caucus members made statements indicating that the party might attempt to restrict access to abortion if it formed a government; a third promised that his party would use the "notwithstanding clause" in the *Charter of Rights* to ban same-sex marriage. Harper tried to defuse the situation by disclaiming any intention of legislating on abortion, although he muddied the waters by speculating about allowing free votes on Private Members' Bills (see Chapter 7).[155] The Liberals seized on the "hidden agenda" supposedly revealed by the Conservative candidates' remarks, painting the Conservatives as extremists opposed to basic human rights.

Shortly after their disappointing performance in the 2004 election, some Conservative strategists argued that Liberal "fear-mongering" had scared Ontario voters away from the new party.[156] If this is true, it suggests that the Conservatives (or at least those who spoke out of turn) misread the values of a majority of Canadians. Another possible reason for the party's poor showing was the poor fit between the two parties that merged to form the Conservatives in late 2003. Supporters of the Canadian Alliance and the Progressive Conservatives held similar views on economic issues (i.e., the free market), but markedly different opinions on moral traditionalism, minorities, and feminism.[157] Despite optimistic predictions by party founders that "one plus one equals two"—i.e., that supporters of both founding parties would automatically vote for the new merged party—the Conservatives wound up with 29.6 percent of the vote, a full eight points lower than the two parties' combined share of 37.7 percent in 2000. The apparent defection of some former Progressive Conservative voters to other parties was no surprise; pre-merger surveys showed that most would pick the Liberals, not the Canadian Alliance, as their second choice.[158] Simplistic talk of "uniting the right" (Dossier 11.4) overlooked the obvious value differences between supporters of the two conservative parties. The 2006 Conservative platform all but ignored "values" in favour of specific and concrete policies, which seem to have trumped the more abstract appeals of their main rivals.[159]

The preceding discussion of values applies to English Canada. Quebec is a unique case. The most salient value cleavage in that province divides sovereigntists from federalists: the former vote overwhelmingly for the Bloc, while the latter support the Liberals. Other value cleavages are present, but they have little impact on voting choice.[160] There are two possible reasons for their lack of influence: either they are not fully mobilized, or they are less salient than other influences on voting choice. By late 2003, it appeared that this particular cleavage had lost much of its power. The BQ was trailing badly in the polls. A federalist government was in power in Quebec City. Separation seemed to have fallen off the political agenda. The BQ's comeback in the 2004 election (Dossier 11.5) does not necessarily signal a resurgence of sovereigntist sentiment. In the 2006 and 2008 elections, especially the latter, the BQ downplayed the sovereigntist elements of its platform; although it won fewer votes than it did in its heyday, the party held on to roughly two-thirds of the seats in Quebec.

Party Identification

On the surface, the Canadian electorate appears to be fairly stable and consistent. With the exception of infrequent electoral "earthquakes," as in 1958 and 1984, most elections produce little change in the relative vote shares of the major parties. Only the Liberal and Progressive Conservative parties have ever formed the government at the national level and in four of the 10 provinces. In addition, there have been prolonged periods of one-party government both federally and provincially. The PCs governed continuously from 1867 to 1896, except for a brief stint in Opposition from 1873 to 1878; in the twentieth century, as we saw in Chapter 3, the Liberals spent far more time in government than in Opposition. This trend has been repeated, with variations, at the provincial level. The Union Nationale governed Quebec from 1936 to 1960, with the exception of the four years the party spent in Opposition during World War II. The Social Credit Party governed continuously in Alberta from 1935 to 1971 and in British Columbia from 1953 to 1991 (with the exception of three years of NDP government, from 1972 to 1975). The record for longevity in office belongs to Ontario's PC Party, which governed without interruption from 1943 to 1985.

However, this aggregate level of stability in Canadian voting behaviour is deceptive. First, it obscures the fact that the electoral system tends to over-reward parties with the greatest support and penalize others. Thus, majority governments may be based on population minorities, and shifting minorities at that. Second, the existence of aggregate stability in governing parties may hide considerable changes in the government's position relative to the legislature. In 13 of the 17 federal elections from 1957 to 2006, either the government changed hands or the same party stayed in power but shifted between minority and majority status.

Third, and perhaps most important, one should not infer that the aggregate stability in Canadian election outcomes reflects consistency in the voting behaviour of individual Canadians. Indeed, the appearance of aggregate stability masks a relatively high level of volatility among individual voters. This volatility is illustrated by the experience of the former Progressive Conservative Party. When the PCs under Brian Mulroney won a landslide victory in 1984, their success did not represent a historic realignment of the electorate. Such realignments rarely happen in Canada. Instead, Mulroney benefited from high levels of short-term support on policy and leadership issues. Specifically, the Trudeau Liberals had alienated Quebec voters by imposing the *Constitution Act, 1982* over the objections of the provincial government; they had angered the West with the National Energy Program; and they had acquired a reputation for arrogance and aloofness since taking power in 1968. The new PC government's precarious hold on its newfound supporters was illustrated by its dive in the public-opinion polls in 1987,[161] and by its fluctuating levels of support throughout the 1988 election campaign.[162] Although the party was re-elected in 1988, its victory owed more to the vagaries of the electoral system and the popularity of Mulroney's Canada–U.S. Free Trade Agreement in Ontario and Quebec, than to a long-term realignment from the Liberals to the PCs. The volatility of Canadian partisanship was evident in the 1993 election, when the PCs plummeted to 16 percent of the vote and two seats in the House of Commons. The 1993 election dispelled any doubts about a Progressive Conservative realignment in 1984.

Nonetheless, it would be wrong to assume that long-term attachments to a particular party play no part in Canadian voting behaviour. To explain long-term voting patterns, political scientists use the American concept of **party identification:** a long-term emotional attachment to a particular party, acquired early in life, which shapes the individual's perceptions of political issues and personalities. Party identification may be related to demographic characteristics, but it is a distinct concept. Take the example of an African-American woman who consistently votes for the Democrats. The cleavage model of voting, discussed earlier, would explain this choice as the product of ethnicity and/or gender. Women, and African-Americans of both sexes, are more likely to vote Democrat than Republican. However, the party identification model offers a different explanation: our hypothetical voter feels an emotional affinity to the Democrats, as a result of socialization by her parents and peers. She shares their distrust of Republican candidates and policies, and she expresses her political identity by voting for their opponents. On rare occasions, she may vote for a Republican candidate if she feels betrayed by the Democrats; but she will probably return to her "default setting" in the next election.

The party identification model is more difficult to apply in Canada. Many U.S. states require voters to register as supporters of one of the political parties, so that they can participate in the state's primary elections to choose a presidential nominee for their party. There is no counterpart to this public declaration of partisanship in Canada; the Register of Electors (see above) does not record partisan affiliations. Moreover, general elections in the United States, both in presidential election years and in off-year congressional elections, usually feature a large and complex ballot. In addition to voting for candidates for the presidency, one may also participate in elections for the U.S. Senate, House of Representatives, governor, state legislatures, and a host of county and municipal offices. Party identification provides an efficient and effective way of managing a complex election process. It also provides a way to choose among the candidates running for less important offices (such as county sheriff) without having to depend on detailed information about these individuals (gathering and assessing such information can be relatively costly).

Elections in Canada are markedly different from their American counterparts. The typical Canadian ballot in a federal election has a short list of three to seven contestants for a single seat in the House of Commons. Most provincial election ballots are equally simple. In voting for a single office, there is a less pressing need for a party label to simplify electoral choice. There is also less of an institutional requirement to retain one's party identification if, in the current election, it proves inconsistent with candidate preferences.

As a result, Canadian scholars have found it difficult to measure party identification. There is considerable disagreement over the level of partisanship in Canada: how many of us are strongly identified with a particular party, and how does this affect our voting choices? Some scholars argue that fewer than 40 percent of Canadians have enduring ties to "their" parties, while others put the figure at between 50 and 60 percent.[163] However large the proportion of party identifiers in the Canadian electorate may be, one fact is clear: more of them identify with the Liberals than with any other party. Roughly 30 percent of Canadian voters feel a durable attachment to the Liberal Party of Canada, a figure that has remained constant for more than a decade.[164] Over the same period, the Conservative base in the electorate has grown. In 1997, fewer than 18 percent of voters felt at home in the Reform and Progressive Conservative parties (combined);[165] by 2006, the merged party was "home" to a little over one-quarter of voters.[166] The small increase in Conservative partisans, together with a slight increase in NDP partisans, probably accounts for a five-point drop in the number of respondents to the Canadian Election Study who claimed no partisan attachment (from 27 percent in 2004 to 22 percent in 2006).[167]

Despite their different outcomes, the 2004 and 2006 federal elections suggest that long-term party identifications play an important role in Canadian election outcomes. In 2004, at least three-quarters of voters with a strong attachment to a particular party reported voting for a candidate from that party. Seventy-three percent of Liberal partisans stayed loyal, as did 76 percent of NDP supporters, 85 percent for Conservative partisans, and 92 percent of BQ voters.[168] These are impressive indicators of party identification. Compared to the results of the previous election, however, they paint a different picture. In 2000 some 86 percent of Liberal identifiers voted for "their" party, compared to 99 percent of Alliance supporters, over 90 percent of Bloc supporters, and almost 80 percent of NDP supporters.[169] The 2004 trend intensified in 2006, when only 62 percent of those who identified themselves as Liberal partisans actually voted for Liberal candidates. In contrast, 92 percent of Conservative partisans stayed loyal.[170] These numbers go a long way toward explaining why the Conservatives were able to win the 2006 election, having lost to the Liberals less than two years earlier.

The change in voting intentions between 2004 and 2006 does not disprove the party identification model. Instead, it suggests that partisans are "predisposed," not "predetermined," to vote for their favourite party.[171] A partisan will usually mark his or her ballot next to the name of his or her party's candidate, but not always. Every now and then, he or she will perceive a compelling reason to vote for a different party. Perhaps he or she believes that his or her party has been in power too long, and it (or the country) needs a break. He or she may feel that the party has erred in adopting a particular policy, which he or she strongly opposes. He or she might be disappointed in the party leader, or disillusioned by a scandal. Under such conditions, he or she has three options: to hold his or her nose and vote for the party's candidate anyway, to vote for a candidate from another party, or to abstain from voting altogether. If he or she chooses the second or third option, he or she will probably (but not inevitably) return to "his or her" party in the next election—assuming that the reason for vote-switching no longer exists.

In summary, the concept of party identification helps us to understand what happened in the 2004 and 2006 Canadian elections. It shows that a substantial proportion of Liberal partisans drifted away in 2004—reducing the Liberals from a majority government to a minority—and that more followed in 2006. In the latter election, more switched to the Conservatives than the NDP (reversing the situation in 2004), allowing the Conservatives to win some tight three-way races in Ontario. Perhaps most important, enduring attachments to the Liberal Party explain the narrowness of the Conservative win. Despite strongly unfavourable short-term factors—the unpopularity of Paul Martin, public anger at the Sponsorship Scandal, and a strong campaign by Stephen Harper—the margin of victory was only six percentage points of the national vote. The Liberals won considerably more seats than most observers predicted, partly because thousands of their voters returned to the fold at the last minute.[172] This pattern was not repeated in 2008. Although there were no confirmed data available as this book went to press, some observers attributed much of the drop in voter turnout to a decision by Liberal supporters to stay home rather than vote for a leader and/or a platform which they disliked.

■ Short-Term Influences on Voter Choice

It's the Economy, Stupid[173]

The way in which voters perceive the national economy influences their opinion of the incumbent governing party. It is generally believed that the fortunes of the governing party rise and fall with the economic health of Canadians. Comparative studies have found that "for every percentage point that real GDP [gross domestic product] grows in the election year, the major incumbent party stands to gain roughly 1.5 percent of the vote above its normal share."[174] In Canada, "everything else being equal, the vote for the incumbent party typically decreases by two points when the relative unemployment rate increases by one point."[175]

However, the relationship between economics and voting behaviour is neither straightforward nor inevitable. The governing party benefits from a strong economy only under two conditions:

1. The voters are willing to give it the credit for their current prosperity.
2. That prosperity has been achieved, at least in the public mind, through policies that are consistent with the values of a majority of voters (i.e., the social costs of an economic boom are not unacceptably high).[176]

Parties that have acquired a reputation for sound economic management are more likely to receive credit in good times and to ride out bad times. In Canada, the Liberals historically benefited from such a reputation, while the NDP has suffered from a lack of credibility on fiscal issues. The Conservatives have been stigmatized by their past failures in government; ever since the Bennett Government struggled to cope with the Great Depression of the 1930s, some voters have equated "Tory times" with hard times. Many Canadians remember that the Chrétien Liberals had to take strong action in the 1990s to eliminate the huge deficit left by the Mulroney Conservatives. It is ironic that Paul Martin, the Finance minister credited with restoring the nation's finances, squandered his reputation for fiscal competence during his brief time as prime minister.[177] This might help to explain why the incumbent government was defeated despite a booming economy and historically low rates of unemployment. The global economic and financial crisis which erupted in 2008, and worsened during the October general election campaign, may have encouraged some voters to stick with the incumbent Conservatives instead of risking a change; but there was no solid evidence of its impact on voting choice as this book went to press.

Issues

Voters' perceptions of specific issues—as distinct from their views about the economy in general—can change dramatically from election to election, as can the relative importance of a given issue. As Table 12.9 demonstrates, the issue that dominates one campaign—most

TABLE 12.9 **MOST IMPORTANT ELECTION ISSUES, SELECTED ELECTIONS, 1988–2006**

ISSUE	1988	1993	2000	2004	2006
Economy in general	2	8	3	3	3
Taxes	4	–	7	3	4
Government spending, deficit, budget	7	18	6	4	3
Unemployment, jobs	2	44	2	1	1
Free trade	88	2	–	–	–
National unity, regionalism, Quebec separatism	6	3	3	1	2
Resources, environment	9	1	2	2	2
Social issues (including health care)	14	5	35	33	21
Government, trust, parties, accountability, leaders	7	10	8	18	14
Sponsorship scandal	–	–	–	4	6
All other issues	3	4	5	12	4
None, no important issues, don't know	5	10	29	19	34

Note: The number in each cell represents the percentage of respondents who named that particular issue as the most important in the campaign.

Sources: For 1988: Harold D. Clarke, Jane Jenson, Lawrence LeDuc, and Jon Pammett, *Absent Mandate: Canadian Electoral Politics in an Era of Restructuring*, 3rd ed. (Toronto: Gage, 1996), 29. For 1993 and 2000: Jon H. Pammett, "The People's Verdict," in Christopher Dornan and Jon H. Pammett, eds., *The Canadian General Election of 2000* (Ottawa: Carleton University Press, 2001), 300. For 2004 and 2006: André Turcotte, "After Fifty-Six Days . . . The Verdict," in Jon H. Pammett and Christopher Dornan, eds., *The Canadian Federal Election of 2006* (Toronto: Dundurn Press, 2006), 286.

obviously, free trade in 1988—can vanish before the next election call. The table illustrates at least three important facts about issue voting in recent Canadian elections:

- First, the salience of a given issue in a particular campaign is determined by short-term events, not just by its intrinsic long-term importance. For example, the salience of the unemployment issue rose in 1993, during a severe economic recession. The Sponsorship Scandal in particular and government trust in general, were fairly important in the 2004 and 2006 elections. When new issues capture the public's attention, they seem to crowd out the old ones.

- Second, the salience of an issue is determined both by preexisting public perceptions and by the parties' campaign strategies. By focusing on patronage, Mulroney elevated the importance of the issue in a way that benefited his party. Similarly, the Liberals focused on health care in 2000, not because their own record on the issue was particularly glowing (see the discussion of the Canadian Health and Social Transfer in Chapter 4), but because their pre-election polling found that the Canadian Alliance was vulnerable on the issue of "two-tier" medicine.[178] While voters were already concerned about the future of medicare, the Liberals heightened their anxiety in order to drive a wedge between the Alliance and the electorate. The new Conservative Party tried to capitalize on Liberal scandals in 2004, with limited success. By 2006, after months of shocking revelations at the televised hearings of the Gomery Commission, perceived Liberal corruption had become sufficiently salient (especially in Quebec) to persuade some voters to give the Conservatives a chance.[179] The salience of the issue was reinforced in mid-campaign, when the RCMP announced that it was investigating a possible leak of confidential tax information to Liberal insiders. Before that announcement, the Conservatives were trailing the Liberals; immediately afterward, the Conservatives moved into the lead and never looked back.[180]

- Third, Canadian elections are rarely fought over a single issue. (The 1988 "free-trade" election was an obvious exception.) In general, the government of the day will try to avoid calling an election when the voters are deeply preoccupied with one or two burning issues. In 2000 and 2006, substantial minorities of voters could not name a single major issue; this seems to have helped the Liberals in the former election, but in the latter it may have left more space for voters to express a desire for change in government.

It is rare for one political party to "win" the issue debate decisively. In most cases, the voters are divided over which party has the best approach to a particular problem. Nonetheless, issues can make an important difference in the outcome of an election. For this to happen, three conditions must be met:

1. The issue must be salient. In other words, large numbers of voters will think about that issue when deciding how to vote.

2. The issue must be linked to the parties. No matter how salient an issue may be to some voters, it will not structure the vote unless the parties stake out distinctive positions on it. Even when parties do take relatively clear and distinctive positions on issues, the linkage may not be clear to all voters. For example, although research on the 1988 federal election has shown that one of the major effects of the campaign was to establish and solidify the connection between an individual's position on the Free Trade Agreement and that person's partisan support, a significant number of Canadians nonetheless voted for the party that opposed their own position on this key issue.[181]

3. The voters' opinions about the issue must be skewed. "Skewness" refers to the distribution of support on an issue. Opinion is skewed when significantly more people are on one side of an issue than the other. Alternatively, as was the case with the Free Trade Agreement issue in 1988, opinion is skewed if there are similar proportions of the electorate on either side of an issue but with one side linked to one party and the other side divided between two or more parties.[182]

The 2006 campaign was fairly typical of recent Canadian elections. There were a few issues that appealed strongly to very small segments of the electorate, such as same-sex marriage and gun crime; they attracted considerable attention from journalists and politicians, but none played a significant role in the outcome. The Conservatives dominated the issue agenda with their early morning policy announcements, and they may have won over some voters with their promises to cut the GST and give money for child care directly to parents. On the whole, however, their promises were more likely to have appealed to voters who were already planning to vote Conservative—at least in English Canada. The picture is somewhat different in Quebec, which Harper wooed with a pledge to redress the fiscal imbalance (Chapter 4) and the prospect of a separate seat at international meetings.[183] Suddenly, voting Conservative seemed like a respectable option in Quebec for the first time since 1988. Nationalist Quebeckers switched from the BQ to the Conservatives in substantial numbers, joining federalists who had been looking for an alternative to the discredited Liberals. Harper won 10 seats in the province, allowing him to claim national support and opening a decisive margin over the Liberals.

Party Leaders

As their parties' chief spokespersons, particularly in an age of televised campaigns, we would expect party leaders to exert a powerful influence on the voting behaviour of Canadians. The evidence suggests that leader evaluations do affect voting choice, but they are rarely decisive.[184] In the first place, the influence of party leaders on electoral behaviour is relatively small and getting smaller. It increased in the 1993 election, when the popularity of Jean Chrétien may have contributed significantly to the Liberal victory; but in general, the leader does not determine the fate of his or her party. Second, a given leader may have a small net effect on voter choice; in other words, the voters who are attracted to his or her party by the leader's personality or policies may be offset by those whom he or she alienates. Third, no leader—however attractive or charismatic—can overcome the disadvantages posed by weak party organization and public hostility.[185] Fourth and finally, popular evaluations of political leaders are increasingly unflattering. As captured and presented through the jaundiced eye of the media, party leaders usually become less popular the longer they remain in the public arena.

Canadian voters evaluate party leaders on two separate dimensions: competence and character.[186] Assessments of competence depend on perceptions of the leader as intelligent, knowledgeable, and able to provide strong leadership and a vision of Canada. The character perception is based on their ability to portray themselves as moral, trustworthy, and compassionate. If a leader scores high on the competence index but falls short on perceived character, as Brian Mulroney did in 1988, his net effect may still be positive; after all, voters want a prime minister they can trust to do the job, even if they don't particularly want to invite him over for dinner. But over time, a serious deficit on the character dimension undermines public trust and can overcome even the most positive assessments of competence. Simply put, voters get tired of seeing someone on their television screens whom they dislike.

On the other side of the coin, a likeable leader who does not appear to have the "right stuff" to lead the country may inspire affection, but will not draw many votes. Paul Martin had been a remarkably popular Finance minister in the Chrétien Government, but he was unable to sustain his image of competence as prime minister. When he became Liberal leader in 2003, his party expected him to carry it to a smashing victory. Instead, he quickly became a liability: "all those Liberal candidates and incumbents who once looked to Martin as their main electoral asset managed to win their seats in 2006 despite him."[187]

For voter evaluations of a leader to benefit his or her party, three conditions must be met:

1. The leader must be significantly more popular or respected than the other leaders (otherwise the net benefit will be too small to matter).
2. The leader's positive evaluations must be backed up by a strong party organization.
3. The other short-term factors that affect voting choice (the economy, issues) must be less salient than normal. In effect, opinions about party leaders may fill the vacuum left by a lack of issues.[188]

In the 2004 election, three of the four major parties had new leaders: Paul Martin of the Liberals, Stephen Harper of the Conservative Party (which was itself a new entity in national politics), and Jack Layton of the NDP. BQ leader Gilles Duceppe was the veteran, having led his party in the 1997 and 2000 campaigns. In general, new leaders are more popular than familiar faces;[189] they also attract more attention, as voters seek to take their measure. In 2004, therefore, party leaders collectively had more influence on voter choice than they had since 1984 (25 percent). The 2006 campaign featured the same cast of leaders; consequently, the reported impact of the leaders on voter decisions shrank.[190] Despite efforts to portray himself as warmer and more approachable, Stephen Harper still struck many voters as cold and aloof. Fortunately for Harper, his skilful campaign conveyed an impression of competence and readiness to govern. He was also lucky in his choice of opponent: Martin's indecisive and unfocused leadership, captured in the nickname "Mr. Dithers,"[191] made Harper's "five priorities" look even more attractive to many voters. On television, Martin's spluttering speech and excitable manner contrasted poorly with Harper's low-key and deliberate delivery. Harper had his own liabilities, most notably a tendency to lash out verbally when under stress.[192] In general, he did poorly on evaluations of likeability. On balance, however, he performed well enough to overcome some lingering concerns about a hidden social conservative agenda—partly because, unlike in 2004, he was able to keep some of the more extreme Conservative MPs and candidates under wraps throughout the campaign period.[193] As previously mentioned, the Liberals' poor showing in 2008 was widely attributed to leader Stephane Dion, whose struggles with English made it difficult for him to explain his policies to voters. To make matters worse, Dion's image had been shaped by Conservative attack ads which portrayed him as weak and indecisive.

Campaign Effects

Seasoned election watchers—journalists, party strategists, and political scientists alike—are convinced that a party that runs a sloppy, chaotic campaign quickly loses public support. At the very least, it raises doubts about the competence of the leader and his or her inner circle; if they can't convey a clear message, or stage a successful public event, how can they be trusted to run the country? Until recently, there was little statistical evidence to substantiate this connection.[194] Voters are rarely asked whether a leader's gaffe or an organizational miscue raised doubts in their minds about the party's fitness to govern and convinced them to vote for someone else. So we must look for indirect proof that campaigns affect voting decisions.

A recent comparative study of campaign effects concluded that "(1) campaigns do matter, but (2) how they matter can vary in a number of respects, and (3) is contingent on circumstances."[195] In particular, the impact of a campaign depends on the number of voters who are open to persuasion. Voters who decide which party to support before the election call, or within the first two or three days of the campaign, are strongly influenced by long-term factors. They do not need to wait to see how the campaign turns out; they are already predisposed to vote for "their" party, and they see no particular reason to consider the alternatives. Those who wait until the middle or the end of the campaign to decide which party to support are more likely to be influenced by short-term factors, including the campaigns. Table 12.10 compares the data on the time of voting choice for three recent federal elections.

Table 12.10 reinforces a point that has already been made: under normal circumstances, the Liberals have an advantage over their rivals even before the campaign begins. Among those voters who decide which party to support either before or at the start of the electoral period, the Liberals usually hold a commanding lead. The 2006 election is an anomaly because the Conservatives were slightly ahead of the Liberals before the campaign started. This shows how much the Gomery Commission and the perception of incompetent leadership had hurt the Liberals. It also suggests a widespread desire for a change of government, which vindicated Harper's decision to bring down the Martin Government in November 2005.

Having said as much, the data in Table 12.10 show that an unusually high percentage of voters were open to persuasion in the 2006 campaign. This implies that the parties' efforts to attract voters were especially important in that election, an assumption which is supported by the available anecdotal and survey evidence. The Conservatives ran a tightly scripted, targeted campaign that focused on a few clear and practical policy promises. Their events were well organized, they catered to the needs of reporters, and they stayed "on message." The Liberals did not fare as well. The campaign period was unusually long (56 days, instead of the usual 36), because the Government fell in late November. To avoid holding the vote over the Christmas holidays, election day was pushed back to January 23. So the campaign had three phases: pre-Christmas, followed by a holiday break, and then the final push. In the first phase, the Liberals took it easy; they assumed that the public wouldn't pay attention until after New Year's Day. This allowed the Conservatives to seize the agenda, albeit with no visible impact in the polls. The first leaders' debates were held in December, with equally little effect.

TABLE 12.10 **TIMING OF VOTE DECISION IN 1997, 2000, AND 2006**

PARTY/ELECTION	BEFORE ELECTION CALLED (%)	WHEN ELECTION CALLED (%)	DURING CAMPAIGN (%)	FINAL DAYS (%)
1997				
Liberal	44	45	28	41
PC	12	18	20	25
NDP	11	12	15	11
Reform	21	18	27	15
BQ	12	8	11	7
Total	54	10	13	23
2000				
Liberal	40	39	30	35
PC	8	9	21	18
NDP	9	11	12	12
Reform	28	30	31	22
BQ	14	10	3	8
Total	47	13	16	24
2006				
Liberal	45	10	23	22
Conservative	47	10	22	21
NDP	30	5	26	39
BQ	51	3	27	19
Total	40	9	26	24

Note: In each cell, the number represents the percentage of respondents voting for each of the major parties who claimed to have made their voting decision at a particular stage of the campaign.

Sources: Jon H. Pammett, "The Voters Decide," in Alan Frizzell and Jon H. Pammett, eds., *The Canadian General Election of 1997* (Ottawa: Carleton University Press, 1998), 242; Jon H. Pammett, "The People's Verdict," in Jon H. Pammett and Christopher Dornan, eds., *The Canadian General Election of 2000* (Ottawa: Carleton University Press, 2001), 306; André Turcotte, "After Fifty-Six Days . . . The Verdict," in Jon H. Pammett and Christopher Dornan, eds., *The Canadian Federal Election of 2006* (Toronto: Dundurn Press, 2006), 294–295.

Ironically, the turning point came during the week between Christmas Day and New Year's Day, when most politicians and reporters were taking a break (recall the previous discussion of the RCMP announcement). By the time campaigning resumed on January 2, the momentum had swung to the Conservatives. The Liberals scrambled to play catch-up, airing a series of attack ads that portrayed Harper and his party as a severe threat to Canada's values, its prosperity, and even its sovereignty. This time, unlike 2004, the ads failed to resonate with the electorate. Worse, they backfired: the slogan "We're not making this up" became a national joke.[196] The ridicule directed at the Liberal campaign exemplifies an interesting phenomenon: the unintentional campaign effect that can damage a party's efforts to win over voters (and can even alienate its supporters).[197] (See Dossier 12.3.)

In the summer of 2005, the Conservative Party of Canada appointed consultant Patrick Muttart to craft a strategic plan for the next federal election. Muttart studied past elections won by right-wing parties, looking for a formula that would allow the Conservatives to build a winning coalition in the electorate. The goal was to retain voters who had opted for the party in 2004, while winning new support from former Liberal voters and to draw disengaged Canadians to the polls.

Muttart found his template in the 1996 Australian election that brought John Howard to power after years of Labor government. Like Harper, Howard had been widely regarded as too conservative to win a general election. Yet he formed a majority government in 1996, and remained in power for more than a decade. He did it by moderating his policies, and by targeting his message to "middle-class voters whose obligations seemed forever just a little bigger than their wallets."[198]

Inspired by Howard's success, Muttart devised a tightly focused plan to appeal to identifiable pockets of the electorate. These pockets added up to around 45 percent of the voting population, which was dubbed the Conservative "universe."[199] Other groups, which would be unlikely to support the Conservatives under any imaginable circumstance, were simply ignored; there was no point wasting time and effort in trying to attract them.[200] Under SMP, 45 percent is more than enough to elect a comfortable majority in the Commons.

Muttart's work became the basis for the 2006 Conservative platform, entitled *Stand Up For Canada*. Unlike some previous platforms, this one contained few references to abstract "values."[201] It did contain more than 400 specific promises, each designed to appeal to a particular type of voter. These were summed up in archetypes, based on sophisticated survey data, which were given nicknames.[202]

- Zoë was a young single urban woman; she was not part of the Conservative "universe" and never would be.[203]

- Marcus and Fiona were a double-income couple without children, living close to their professional jobs in a city core. They were written off as Liberal sympathizers.[204]

- Dougie was a manual worker, living in rural Canada, who liked hunting but didn't like politicians. To induce him to vote—and, of course, to vote Conservative—the platform promised a $500-annual tax deduction on the purchase of tools and equipment required by tradesmen.[205] Dougie would also appreciate the pledge to eliminate the long-gun registry. His neighbours who worked in resource industries would be impressed by the measures to assist the forestry, mining, and fisheries sectors.[206]

- Mike and Theresa were a single-income couple with two children, living in the suburbs in a mortgaged house. Theresa stayed home to look after the kids, and the couple struggled to make the payments on their home and minivan.[207] The Conservatives showered promises on Mike and Theresa: replacing the Liberals' child-care program with an annual payment of $1200 per child; cutting the GST on all purchases from 7 to 6 percent; creating a tax credit to offset the cost of children's sporting activities; and, in the longer term, measures to help post-secondary students and their families to meet the costs of higher education.

- Eunice was an elderly widow living on pension and investment income. She would approve of the pledge not to tax income trusts (although, presumably, not the reversal discussed at the beginning of this chapter), and the commitment to maintain and strengthen the Canada Pension Plan.[208]

These archetypes overlap with some of the long-term factors previously discussed. However, the platform appeals were based, not on permanent characteristics like language or religion, but on the more fluid concept of "lifestyle."[209] To some degree, they were defined by class; but this was a rather different approach to socioeconomic status than the one posited in the tradi-

(continued)

tional model of "class voting." The point was to appeal to the short-term financial self-interest of particular voters, not to make a symbolic statement about the relative positions of workers and owners. It worked pretty well: if the estimates of the Conservative "universe" are correct, the party managed to win 80 percent of its target electorate (36 percent compared to 45 percent), in 2006. However, the Conservatives were unable to build on that success in the 2008 election: they won slightly fewer votes overall, despite significant seat gains (especially in the "905" suburbs around Toronto).

Both of the largest parties tried to appeal to entire regions—for example, the Conservatives promised to retain regional development agencies and to address the fiscal imbalance between Ottawa and the provinces—but the Liberals paid less attention to characteristics that cut across regional boundaries.[210] "Mike and Theresa" lived in a suburb of Toronto, but they could just as easily have come from the outskirts of Vancouver, Calgary, Montreal, or Halifax. "Dougie" the rural Nova Scotian tradesman had his counterparts in every province and territory. There are seniors like "Eunice" in every community across Canada. In this respect, the 2006 Conservative platform represents a departure from recent election campaigns: it focused on non-territorial characteristics, and on the immediate personal self-interest of voters, more than broad geographic and "pocketbook" appeals.

The strategy was unusual in at least one additional respect: it distinguished clearly between the voters whom the Conservatives considered worthy of attention, and those who were not. Targeting unique groups of voters is nothing new; indeed, it is a defining characteristic of Canada's fourth party system (Chapter 11). What is new is the deliberate decision to ignore a majority of the electorate. Even after the 2006 election, as the Conservatives tried to leverage their victory into a majority government, the Conservatives seem to have maintained their focus on "Mike," "Theresa," and "Dougie."[211] In the process, however, they may have reinforced the ceiling on their own future growth. By distinguishing so overtly between "us" and "them," the Conservatives risk alienating voters who might otherwise have given them a chance to govern with a majority of MPs.[212]

CONCLUSION

Elections are central to representative democracy. They provide the only opportunity for the citizens, en masse, to engage directly with their political institutions. Those institutions are the electoral system, which determines the expression of their preferences and sets incentives for voters to follow, and the House of Commons, whose members are elected in their separate constituencies. The outcome of a Canadian general election—the partisan makeup of the Commons—is the product of the interaction between the long-term and short-term factors that govern voting behaviour, and their translation by the electoral system. Nowhere else is the relationship between society and the state as clear and direct as it is on election day.

The conduct of Canada's general elections is subject to the same pressures for reform as those that affect all of our national political institutions. Citizens are turning away from electoral politics. Some are frustrated with an electoral system that "wastes" their votes and distorts their preferences. Others believe that their vote doesn't matter, largely because they perceive little difference among the parties. Many have given up on voting because they think politics is corrupt, distant, or simply irrelevant. Demands for greater direct participation in decision-making, together with the growing salience of nonterritorial forms of representation, have given new impetus to the campaign for reform of the electoral system and other national institutions.

The prospects for electoral reform depend on the willingness of other political institutions—specifically, the political executive whose power often rests on artificial majorities created by SMP—to accept changes that threaten their security. As we have seen repeatedly throughout this book, each of our national political institutions is affected by, and sometimes preserved by, the others. If our electoral system is to keep pace with changing democratic values, it must be reformed by the very political actors whose self-interest is served by the status quo. The same is true for some of the other possible reforms discussed in this book, including a reduction in party discipline and the introduction of a greater degree of direct democracy. Such reforms, in turn, would have far-reaching effects on the House of Commons, the political executive, and the incentives for voters. If institutional reform is blocked, the gap between the political values of some Canadian citizens and those reflected in our political system may widen.

The recent decline in voter turnout merits particular attention from would-be institutional reformers—despite the temporary upturn in 2006. Unfortunately, there are few institutional avenues for improvement. Few Canadians appear to make the connection between their electoral malaise and the flaws in SMP. The real barriers to participation are attitudinal, not institutional. Perhaps young people would find politics more engaging if they were given more opportunities to vote directly on the issues of the day, or if the parties used their websites in more creative ways. Reducing party discipline in the House of Commons might shorten the perceived distance between voters and their elected representatives. On the other hand, institutional reform may not be the most promising approach. A more concerted effort to educate young people about politics might inspire a sense of civic duty and involvement. The parties could make a stronger effort to contact young voters, and recruit more Canadians under 30 to run for office. There is no guarantee that any of these speculative suggestions would reverse the trend, but this much is clear: if younger Canadians continue to avoid the polling booth, the long-term implications for our democracy are worrisome.

GLOSSARY OF KEY TERMS

Agency: The legal requirement for registered parties and candidates to appoint an official agent, who is responsible for ensuring compliance with the election-expense rules in the *Canada Elections Act*.

By-election: A special election held to fill one seat in the Commons (e.g., after the death or retirement of the incumbent MP).

Canvass: The process by which party volunteers identify potential supporters during an election campaign; can be done face to face (knocking on doors) or over the telephone.

Categorical: A ballot structure that forces the voter to indicate a single preference among the available candidates.

Coalition: A Cabinet made up of ministers from two or more parties; the usual way of ensuring that the political executive is supported by a parliamentary majority in legislatures elected by proportional representation, where one party rarely wins more than half of the seats.

Disclosure: The legal requirement for registered parties to publicly disclose the amount and the source of all contributions.

Electoral formula: The method by which votes are cast, counted, and translated into the distribution of parliamentary seats.

Franchise: The right to vote in elections.

General election: The House of Commons is dissolved by the governor general on the advice of the prime minister, and every seat is filled by election on the same day.

Gerrymandering: Deliberately drawing constituency boundaries in a way that increases the electoral chances of a particular party or candidate.

List-proportional representation (list-PR): Proportional representation based on party lists; the voter marks a preference for one of the lists of candidates on the ballot, and the seats in Parliament are distributed among the parties on the basis of their vote shares (e.g., 30 percent of the vote in a 10-seat constituency entitles the party to three seats).

Mixed electoral system: A system that combines two or more electoral formulas in a single election (e.g., the New Zealand system, which uses SMP to elect some MPs and party lists to choose the rest).

Ordinal: A ballot structure that allows (or requires) the voter to rank-order some or all of the candidates listed.

Party identification: A long-term emotional attachment to a particular party, its policies, and its leader(s). Voters may form this attachment in childhood, through the absorption of their parents' political values. Throughout adult life, the voter perceives and interprets political events through the lens of party identification.

Proportional representation: The general name for electoral systems based on multi-member constituencies, which are designed to translate the parties' vote shares into their seat shares in Parliament with as little distortion as possible.

Referenda: The plural of "referendum." See the discussion of direct democracy in Chapter 2.

Single-member plurality (SMP) system: The country is divided into territorial constituencies, each of which elects one MP; the winning candidate needs only a simple plurality of the votes; 50 percent plus one of the valid votes cast is not required.

Suffrage: The right to vote in elections, and to run for office.

Threshold of election: The percentage of votes required to win a seat under a given electoral system.

DISCUSSION AND REVIEW QUESTIONS

1. What are the three variables which distinguish different types of electoral system? Give TWO examples of each variable.

2. In your view, should the internal activities of Canadian parties be regulated by law? Should political parties and candidates receive public subsidies, either direct (reimbursement of election expenses) or indirect (tax credits)? Why or why not?

3. What are the key short- and long-term factors that affect voting choice in Canada? If you have voted in a previous federal or provincial election, which of those factors was foremost in your mind when you marked your ballot?

4. If you were eligible to vote in the last federal or provincial election but decided not to cast a ballot, what were the primary reasons for your decision not to vote?

5. If you had to choose one reform to the Canadian electoral process, which would you pick: compulsory voting or a more proportional electoral system? Justify your answer.

SUGGESTED READINGS

Books and Articles

André Blais, Elisabeth Gidengil, Richard Nadeau, and Neil Nevitte, *Anatomy of a Liberal Victory: Making Sense of the Vote in the 2000 Canadian Election* (Peterborough, ON: Broadview Press, 2002).

Canada, Royal Commission on Electoral Reform and Party Financing, *Reforming Electoral Democracy* (Ottawa: Minister of Supply and Services, 1991).

John C. Courtney, *Elections* (Vancouver: UBC Press, 2004).

Andrew Ellis et al., *Engaging the Electorate: Initiatives to Promote Voter Turnout From Around the World* (Stockholm: International Institute for Democracy and Electoral Assistance, 2006).

David M. Farrell and Rüdiger Schmitt-Beck, eds., *Do Political Campaigns Matter? Campaign Effects in Elections and Referendums* (New York: Routledge, 2002).

Mark N. Franklin, *Voter Turnout and the Dynamics of Electoral Competition in Established Democracies Since 1945* (Cambridge: Cambridge University Press, 2004).

Law Commission of Canada, *Voting Counts: Electoral Reform for Canada* (Ottawa: Minister of Public Works and Government Services, 2004).

Lawrence LeDuc, Richard G. Niemi, and Pippa Norris, eds., *Comparing Democracies: Elections and Voting in Global Perspective* (Thousand Oaks, Calif.: Sage, 1996).

Henry Milner, "Fixing Canada's Unfixed Election Dates: A Political Season to Reduce the Democratic Deficit," *Choices,* 6:6 (Montreal: IRPP, December 2005).

Henry Milner, ed., *Making Every Vote Count: Reassessing Canada's Electoral System* (Peterborough, Ont.: Broadview Press, 1999).

Pippa Norris, *Electoral Engineering: Voting Rules and Political Behaviour* (Cambridge: Cambridge University Press, 2004).

Jon H. Pammett and Christopher Dornan, eds., *The Canadian Federal Election of 2006* (Toronto: Dundurn Press, 2006). Bob Plamondon, *Full Circle: Death and Resurrection in Canadian Conservative Politics* (Toronto: Key Porter, 2006).

Andrew Reynolds et al., *Electoral System Design: The New International IDEA Handbook* (Stockholm: International Institute for Democracy and Electoral Assistance, 2005).

William T. Stanbury, *Money in Politics: Financing Federal Parties and Candidates in Canada,* volume 1 of the collected research studies for the Royal Commission on Electoral Reform and Party Financing (Toronto: Dundurn Press, 1991).

Paul Wells, *Right Side Up: The Fall of Paul Martin and the Rise of Stephen Harper's New Conservatism* (Toronto: McClelland & Stewart, 2006).

Websites

The website of Canada's federal electoral agency, Elections Canada (www.elections.ca), provides a wealth of information. Click on "Electoral Law and Policy" to find the *Canada Elections Act* and background papers about recent amendments. Under "Election Financing," you can access the annual disclosure reports from Canada's registered parties, as well as their election-expense reports (and those of individual candidates). Updates to watch for: the disclosure of the parties' and candidates' election expenses; financial statements from electoral district associations, which should reveal the size of their "war chests"; and the number of registered parties.

For more information on electoral systems around the world, check the websites of the Inter-Parliamentary Union (www.ipu.org) and the International Federation for Electoral Systems (www.ifes.org).

The Institute for Democratic Education and Assistance (www.idea.int) studies electoral systems and the conduct of elections around the world. Its publications are available for free on its website.

NOTES

1. Canada, Royal Commission on Electoral Reform and Party Financing, *Reforming Electoral Democracy,* volume 1 (Ottawa: Minister of Supply and Services, 1991), 26.

2. John C. Courtney, *Elections* (Vancouver: UBC Press, 2004), 5.

3. Peter Dobell, "What Could Canadians Expect From a Minority Government?" *Policy Matters,* 1:6 (Montreal: Institute for Research on Public Policy, November 2000), 9.

4. The 1926 "King-Byng" affair is the only exception; see the endnotes to Chapter 7.

5. Edward Greenspon, "Following the Trail of Campaign '97," in Alan Frizzell and Jon H. Pammett, eds., *The Canadian General Election of 1997* (Ottawa: Carleton University Press, 1997), p. 23.

6. Stephen Clarkson, "The Liberal Threepeat: The Multi-System Party in the Multi-Party System," in Jon H. Pammett and Christopher Dornan, eds., *The Canadian General Election of 2000* (Ottawa: Carleton University Press, 2001), 33–34.

7. Henry Milner, "Fixing Canada's Unfixed Election Dates: A Political Season to Reduce the Democratic Deficit," *Choices,* 6:6 (Montreal: IRPP, December 2005), 14–15.

8. Paul Howe and David Northrup, "Strengthening Canadian Democracy: The Views of Canadians," *Choices,* 1:5 (Montreal: IRPP, July 2000), 12.

9. Linda Johnson, Deputy Chief Electoral Officer, Elections BC, in House of Commons Standing Committee on Procedure and House Affairs, *Minutes of Proceedings and Evidence,* September 28, 2006; accessed at www.parl.gc.ca.

10. Senate of Canada, *Proceedings of the Standing Senate Committee on Legal and Constitutional Affairs,* February 1, 2007; accessed at www.parl.gc.ca.

11. Bea Vongdouangchanh, "Will PM stay put, or pull Parliamentary election plug?" *The Hill Times,* April 2, 2007, 1.

12. Hon. Rob Nicholson, Government House Leader and Minister Responsible for Democratic Renewal, House of Commons Standing Committee on Procedure and House Affairs, *Minutes of Proceedings and Evidence,* September 26, 2006, 5.

13. Canadian Press, "Senators seen backing down on election-date bill," *The Globe and Mail,* April 26, 2007; Brian Laghi, "Tory support slips to 2006 vote level," *The Globe and Mail,* April 26, 2007 (both accessed at www.theglobeandmail.com).

14. Brian Laghi, "Harper's staying power: No one expected the Conservative government to last this long," *The Globe and Mail,* June 16, 2007, A4.

15. This does not mean that criminal law is unaffected by external pressures. Western countries rushed to adopt new anti-terrorism laws after 9/11, partly to reassure nervous citizens and partly in response to UN Conventions and other international obligations. In Canada's case, the federal government strengthened criminal sanctions against alleged terrorists and illegal immigrants as part of an overall strategy to keep the Canada–U.S. border open for trade.

16. For example, Keith Banting argues that Canadian social programs have been affected less by "convergence" with the United States and other trading partners than by the fiscal crisis of the mid-1990s (and, as we will see in Chapter 8, by the politics of federalism). Keith Banting, "Social Policy," in G. Bruce Doern, Leslie A. Pal, and Brian W. Tomlin, eds., *Border Crossings: The Internationalization of Canadian Public Policy* (Toronto: Oxford University Press, 1996), especially 50–52.

17. Lawrence LeDuc, "Elections and Democratic Governance," in Lawrence LeDuc, Richard G. Niemi, and Pippa Norris, eds., *Comparing Democracies: Elections and Voting in Global Perspective* (Thousand Oaks, CA: Sage, 1996), 349.

18. Faron Ellis and Peter Woolstencroft, "A Change of Government, Not a Change of Country: The Conservatives and the 2006 Election," in Jon H. Pammett and Christopher Dornan, eds., *The Canadian Federal Election of 2006* (Toronto: Dundurn Press, 2006), 77. The five priorities are spelled out in greater detail in the 2006 Conservative platform, and in the February 2006 Speech from the Throne (the latter was accessed at www.pm.gc.ca).

19. G. Bingham Powell Jr., *Elections as Instruments of Democracy: Majoritarian and Proportional Visions* (New Haven: Yale University Press, 2000). See also LeDuc, "Elections and Democratic Governance," 351.

20. Stanley Kelley Jr., *Interpreting Elections* (Princeton: Princeton University Press, 1983), 126–28.

21. Harold D. Clarke, Jane Jenson, Lawrence LeDuc, and Jon H. Pammett, *Absent Mandate: Interpreting Change in Canadian Elections,* 2nd edition (Toronto: Gage, 1991), 154; André Blais, Elisabeth Gidengil, Neil Nevitte, and Richard Nadeau, "Making Sense of the Vote in the 2000 General Election," paper delivered at the 2001 Annual Meeting of the Canadian Political Science Association, Quebec City; available at www.fax.umontreal.ca/pol/ces-eec.

22. Anthony King, "What Do Elections Decide?" in David Butler, Howard R. Penniman, and Austin Ranney, eds., *Democracy at the Polls: A Comparative Study of Competitive National Elections* (Washington: American Enterprise Institute for Public Policy Research, 1981), 200.

23. In a study of parties' campaign platforms across several established democracies, Canadian parties were found to offer little real choice compared to parties in Western Europe. Ian Budge and Michael D. McDonald, "Choices Parties Define: Policy Alternatives in Representative Elections, 17 Countries 1945–1998," *Party Politics,* 12:4 (2006), 451–466.

24. Clarke et al., 9–10.

25. The 1988 and 1993 elections were unusual, in the sense that the Liberals and PCs staked out clear and distinct positions on one or more crucial issues. In 1988 the PCs were forced to call an election on their free trade deal with the United States (the FTA), when the Liberal majority in the Senate refused to ratify the deal without consulting the electorate. Even in that campaign, which was dominated by a single issue to an extraordinary degree, the PC victory did not produce a clear-cut mandate for the FTA. See Clarke et al., 147–48.

26. In 1974 Pierre Trudeau campaigned against a legislated "freeze" on wages and prices; in 1993 Jean Chrétien campaigned against the North American Free Trade Agreement (NAFTA) with the United States and Mexico. Both subsequently reversed themselves: Trudeau imposed wage and price controls, and Chrétien signed the NAFTA deal without the significant improvements in labour and environmental protection he had demanded during the campaign.

27. Paul Wells, *Right Side Up: The Fall of Paul Martin and the Rise of Stephen Harper's New Conservatism* (Toronto: McClelland & Stewart, 2006), 205.

28. See *Canadian Taxpayers Federation v. Ontario (Minister of Finance)* (2004), 73 O.R. (3d) 621(accessed at www.canlii.org).

29. LeDuc, 351.

30. Greenspon and Wilson-Smith, 7.

31. Patrick J. Monahan, *Storming the Pink Palace: The NDP In Power, A Cautionary Tale* (Toronto: Lester, 1995), 16.

32. David Reville, quoted in George Ehring and Wayne Roberts, *Giving Away a Miracle: Lost Dreams, Broken Promises, and the Ontario NDP* (Oakville, ON: Mosaic Press, 1993), 277.

33. Canada's appointed Senate is an obvious exception, although that could change; see Dossier 3.4 and the discussion of Senate reform in Chapter 7.

34. Courtney, *Elections*, 14.

35. This may explain why Bills containing amendments to the *Canada Elections Act* are sometimes referred to the House of Commons Standing Committee on Procedure and House Affairs before second reading. This allows MPs from all parties to review and amend the legislation more thoroughly than usual. See the discussion of standing committees in Chapter 7.

36. A few countries with list-PR systems, including The Netherlands and Israel, do not have separate districts; the entire country is one district for the purpose of electing members of the national Parliament.

37. Courtney, *Elections*, 47–50 and 55–58. You can find maps of every federal constituency on the Elections Canada website: www.elections.ca. The site also provides information about the process of drawing electoral district boundaries. Click on "Electoral Districts" and follow the links to the "Federal Representation 2004" icon. It will take you to a Backgrounder entitled "Readjustment of Electoral Boundaries and Representation in the House of Commons."

38. Between 2001 and 2006, the population of Alberta grew by 10.6 percent, compared to 6.6 percent for Ontario and 5.3 percent for BC. The national growth rate was 5.4 percent. Statistics Canada, "Population and dwelling counts, for Canadian provinces and territories, 2006 and 2001 Censuses" (accessed at www.statcan.ca, May 2007).

39. For example, the 2006 Census found that the population of Brampton West (near Toronto) had increased by 50 percent since 2001; by 2011, when the next boundary adjustment was scheduled to take place, it might well double. Christopher Guly, "Census out, MPs wait until 2011," *The Hill Times*, March 19, 2007, 1.

40. Brian Laghi, "Ottawa wants to increase Commons seats to 330," *The Globe and Mail*, May 12, 2007, A13.

41. Michael Pal and Sujit Choudhry, "Is Every Ballot Equal? Visible-Minority Vote Dilution in Canada," *IRPP Choices*, 13:1 (January 2007).

42. The three territories are excluded from the formula; each is entitled to one seat (section 51(2) of the *Constitution Act, 1867*).

43. Or not. The supporting documentation for Bill C-56, tabled in May 2007, pointed out that "provinces with fast-growing populations only get a proportionate share of 279 seats rather than of the total number of House seats." Hence, the 1985 formula put Ontario, Alberta, and BC at a disadvantage even before the rest of the allocation formula was applied. Government of Canada, Office of the Leader of the Government in the House of Commons, "Canada's New Government Moves to Restore the Principle of Representation by Population," May 11, 2007 (accessed at www.pco-bcp.gc.ca, May 2007).

44. The "Senate floor rule" was adopted in 1915. It is entrenched in section 51A of the *Constitution Act, 1867*. Under the 1982 amending formula (section 41(b), it cannot be amended without the consent of all of the provinces.

45. Canada, First Session, Thirty-ninth Parliament, 55–56 Elizabeth II, 2006–2007, Bill C-56, *An Act to amend the Constitution Act, 1867 (Democratic representation)*

46. Bill Curry, Karen Howlett and Katherine Harding, "B.C. and Alberta break ranks with Ontario," *The Globe and Mail*, May 19, 2007, A6. Note that BC's share of the national population did not change between 2001 and 2006, while Ontario's share increased slightly. So in mathematical terms, it is difficult to justify giving BC more seats under the new formula than Ontario.

47. In fact, if the population trends from 2001 to 2006 continue between 2006 and 2011, Alberta could be under-represented. It would have roughly 11 percent of the national population by the time of the next redistribution; under the Harper Government's proposed formula, the province would have 10 percent of Commons seats. The current provincial shares of the national population are displayed in Table 7.3.

48. *Electoral Boundaries Readjustment Act*, section 15.

49. Heather MacIvor, "Shining a Harsh Light on Political Financing," *Policy Options* (June 2005), 34–40.

50. *Canada Elections Act,* sections 415–16.

51. *Canada Elections Act,* sections 424–27.

52. *Canada Elections Act,* sections 429–34.

53. *Canada Elections Act,* sections 422–23.

54. *Canada Elections Act,* section 435.

55. Bill C-24, section 73.

56. The broadcasting rules are set out in the *Canada Elections Act,* sections 332–48. The allocations of airtime among the parties are available on the Elections Canada website: www.elections.ca.

57. Khayyam Zev Paltiel, "Campaign Financing in Canada and its Reform," in Howard R. Penniman, ed., *Canada at the Polls: The General Election of 1974* (Washington: American Enterprise Institute for Public Policy Research, 1975), 188.

58. Paltiel, Table 7-1, 186.

59. Ibid.

60. Ibid., 201.

61. Louis Massicotte, "Party Financing in Quebec: An Analysis of the Financial Reports of Parties 1977–89," in F. Leslie Seidle, ed., *Provincial Party and Election Finance in Canada,* volume 3 of the collected research studies for the Royal Commission on Electoral Reform and Party Financing (Toronto: Dundurn Press, 1991), 4.

62. William T. Stanbury, *Money in Politics: Financing Federal Parties and Candidates in Canada,* volume 1 of the collected research studies for the Royal Commission on Electoral Reform and Party Financing (Toronto: Dundurn Press, 1991), 9.

63. Eddie Goldenberg, *The Way It Works: Inside Ottawa* (Toronto: McClelland and Stewart, 2006), 381–385.

64. *Canada Elections Act,* as amended January 1, 2004, section 403.01.

65. The constituency associations are also affected by the new rules for nomination contests, which are discussed in Chapter 11.

66. *Canada Elections Act,* as amended January 1, 2004, sections 464–65.

67. *Canada Elections Act,* sections 451–56.

68. Former Liberal MP and Deputy Prime Minister John Manley transferred $131 483 to the Ottawa South constituency association in 2001. Five years later, the association disclosed assets of only $20 732.24—an oddly low figure, given that Liberal David McGuinty held the seat in 2004 and 2006. Sources: Elections Canada, "Disposition of Surplus, 37th General Election," 11; Elections Canada, "Registered Electoral District Associations–Statements of Assets and Liabilities (as of April 27, 2007)" (both accessed at www.elections.ca, May 2007).

69. Federal Liberal Agency of Canada, *Financial Statements,* December 31, 2003; available at www.elections.ca/fin/rep/2003/liberal_2003.pdf.

70. Simon Doyle and Abbas Rana, "Tories unveil war room to demonstrate winning, slick campaign," *The Hill Times,* April 9, 2007, 1 and 4–5.

71. Abbas Rana, "Conservatives say Dion's image in 'free-fall,' TV ads helped target his credibility: Hill," *The Hill Times,* February 26, 2007, 1 and 20.

72. For a detailed discussion of loopholes in the CEA, see Heather MacIvor, "A Missed Opportunity: Political Finance and the *Federal Accountability Act,*" *Journal of Parliamentary and Political Law,* I:1 (Autumn 2008), 95–143.

73. On the importance of local campaigns to the success of national parties, see: R. Kenneth Carty, William Cross, and Lisa Young, *Rebuilding Canadian Party Politics* (Vancouver: UBC Press, 2000), 171–72; David M. Farrell, "Campaign Strategies and Tactics," in Lawrence LeDuc, Richard G, Niemi, and Pippa Norris, eds., *Comparing Democracies: Elections and Voting in Global Perspective* (Thousand Oaks, CA: Sage, 1996), 179–80.

74. Douglas Rae, *The Political Consequences of Electoral Laws,* rev. edition (New Haven: Yale University Press, 1971), 16.

75. For an excellent overview of this debate, see Law Commission of Canada, *Voting Counts: Electoral Reform for Canada* (Ottawa: Minister of Public Works and Government Services, 2004).

76. Courtney, *Elections,* 56–57.

77. Both Alberta and Manitoba experimented with STV between 1924 and the mid-1950s. Dennis Pilon, "The History of Voting System Reform in Canada," in Henry Milner, ed., *Making Every Vote Count: Reassessing Canada's Electoral System* (Peterborough: Broadview Press, 1999), 121.

78. Courtney, *Elections,* 114.

79. Andrew Reynolds et al., *Electoral System Design: The New International IDEA Handbook* (Stockholm: International Institute for Democracy and Electoral Assistance, 2005), 36–37. See also Pippa Norris, *Electoral Engineering: Voting Rules and Political Behaviour* (Cambridge: Cambridge University Press, 2004), 68–73.

80. Norris, 121.

81. Reynolds, 37 and 43–44; Benny Geys, "Explaining voter turnout: A review of aggregate-level research," *Electoral Studies,* 25 (2006), 651.

82. *Reference re Provincial Electoral Boundaries (Sask.),* [1991] 2 S.C.R. 158.

83. Maurice Duverger, *Political Parties: Their Organization and Activity in the Modern State,* translated by Barbara and Robert North (London: Methuen, 1964 [1954]), Book II, Chapter 1.

84. Norris, Chapter 4.

85. George C. Perlin, *The Tory Syndrome: Leadership Politics in the Progressive Conservative Party* (Montreal and Kingston: McGill–Queen's University Press, 1980).

86. The definitive article is Alan C. Cairns, "The Electoral System and the Party System in Canada, 1921–1965," in Douglas E. Williams, ed., *Constitution, Government, and Society in Canada* (Toronto: McClelland and Stewart, 1988).

87. See Heather MacIvor, "Women and the Electoral System," in Manon Tremblay and Linda Trimble, eds., *Women and Electoral Politics in Canada* (Toronto: Oxford University Press, 2003); Donley Studlar, "Will Canada Seriously Consider Electoral Reform? Women and Aboriginals Should," and Thérèse Arseneau, "Electing Proportional Legislatures: Lessons from New Zealand," both in Henry Milner, ed., *Making Every Vote Count: Reassessing Canada's Electoral System* (Peterborough, ON: Broadview Press, 1999).

88. F. Leslie Seidle, "Electoral System Reform in Canada: Objectives, Advocacy and Implications for Governance" (Canadian Policy Research Networks, 2002), 2.

89. See, e.g., the Final Report of the Ontario Citizens' Assembly, *One Ballot, Two Votes: A New Way to Vote in Ontario* (May 15, 2007); accessed at www.citizensassembly.gov.on.ca/en/default.asp, May 2007.

90. The Commission recommended that the list seats be allocated according to the formula used to elect the Scottish Assembly. The complex calculations are very well explained in the Law Commission Report, 97–99.

91. Reynolds *et al.,* 95; Law Commission, 145.

92. United Kingdom, Independent Commission to Review Britain's Experience of PR Voting Systems, *Changed Voting, Changed Politics: Lessons of Britain's Experience of PR since 1997* (London: The Constitution Unit, University College London, 2003), 85 (accessed at www.ucl.ac.uk/constitution-unit/).

93. Ibid., 85–89.

94. New Zealand Election Study, "Electoral System Opinion and the Evolution of MMP: A Report to the Electoral Commission" (Auckland, 2000), 20 (accessed at www.nzes.org); *Changed Voting, Changed Politics,* 89–93.

95. Peter Lynch, "Making Every Vote Count in Scotland: Devolution and Electoral Reform," in Henry Milner, eds., *Steps Toward Making Every Vote Count: Electoral System Reform in Canada and its Provinces* (Peterborough: Broadview, 2004), 155.

96. Ibid., 154–155.

97. Canadian Press, "Dion willing to study electoral reform as apart of deal with May," *The Globe and Mail,* April 22, 2007; accessed at www.globeandmail.com.

98. Louis Massicotte, "Electoral Legislation Since 1997: Parliament Regains the Initiative," in Pammett and Dornan, eds., *The Canadian Federal Election of 2006,* 212.

99. Louis Massicotte, "Electoral Legislation Since 1997: Parliament Regains the Initiative," in Pammett and Dornan, eds., *The Canadian Federal Election of 2006,* 212.

100. Canada, Privy Council Office, "Press Release: Canada's New Government Consults Canadians on Democratic Reform," January 9, 2007; accessed at www.pco-bcp.gc.ca, April 2007.

101. In a recent publication, Dion (a former political scientist) expressed serious concerns about the possible consequences of adopting a mixed system. Stéphane Dion, "Institutional Reform: The Grass Isn't Always Greener on the Other Side," in Hans J. Michelmann, Donald C. Story, and Jeffrey S. Steeves, eds., *Political Leadership and Representation in Canada: Essays in Honour of John C. Courtney* (Toronto: University of Toronto Press, 2007), 176–193.

102. Matthew Mendelsohn and Andrew Parkin, with Alex Van Kralingen, "Getting From Here to There: A Process for Electoral Reform in Canada," *Policy Options* July August 2001, 55. There are two exceptions to this rule. First, in the wake of a serious scandal or political crisis, politicians may decide to wipe the slate clean by adopting a new electoral system. Second, when political parties fragment, and none can realistically hope to form a majority government under SMP, political elites can be more receptive to public demands for reform. See Dunleavy and Margetts; see also André Blais, Agnieszka Dobrzynska, and Indridi H. Indridason, "To Adopt or Not to Adopt Proportional Representation: The Politics of Institutional Choice," *British Journal of Political Science,* 35 (2004), 182–190.

103. See, e.g., Patrick Dunleavy and Helen Margetts, "Understanding the Dynamics of Electoral Reform," *International Political Science Review* 16:1 (1995), 9–29; Reynolds *et al.,* 21.

104. There is one partial exception: Bill C-43, which provided for "consultations" with voters to choose potential senators. (See Dossier 3.4 and Chapter 7.) Sections 52–56 set out the details of an STV system for selecting "nominees." This differs from Alberta's *Senatorial Selection Act,* under which voters cast a categorical ballot; the candidate with the highest vote total (or candidates, where two or more vacancies are to be filled) is declared elected. Perhaps the Harper Government felt that it was safe to use a semi-proportional electoral system for choosing senators, because the Senate—unlike the House of Commons—is not a confidence chamber. In other words, the survival of the Cabinet does not depend on a majority in the Upper House (see Chapters 7 and 8).

105. Information on the Citizens' Assembly, and useful learning resources, can be found at www.citizensassembly.bc.ca.

106. According to one former Assembly member, STV was preferred over MMP because it reduced the power of political parties, gave voters more choice, and encouraged strong constituency representation by MLAs. Jack MacDonald, *Randomocracy: A Citizen's Guide to Electoral Reform in British Columbia* (Vancouver: FCG Publications, 2005), 49 (accessed at www.bcelectoralreform.ca, March 2005).

107. Amy Lang, "But Is It For Real? The British Columbia Citizens' Assembly as a Model of State-Sponsored Citizen Empowerment," *Politics & Society,* 35:1 (March 2007), 60–61.

108. BC Citizens Assembly, *Making Every Vote Count: The Case for Electoral Reform in British Columbia (Technical Report)* (Vancouver, December 2004), 17 (accessed at www.citizensassembly.bc.ca, January 2005).

109. James R. Robertson and Michael Rowland, "Electoral Reform Initiatives in Canadian Provinces" (Ottawa: Library of Parliament Research Branch, June 2006), 2.

110. Patrick Thomson and James Maunder, "Electoral Reform in BC: So Near and Yet So Far," *Policy Options,* (October 2005), 72–76.

111. The Carruthers report and related documents are available at www.gov.pe.ca/electoralreform. The May 2004 announcement by Premier Binns was accessed at www.pei.cbc.ca from a link on the B.C. Citizens' Assembly website.

112. *Report of the Chief Electoral Officer of Prince Edward Island: Plebiscite for the Proposed Mixed-Member Proportional System,* November 28, 2005 (Charlottetown: Elections PEI, December 2005), accessed at www.electionspei.ca; CBC News, "P.E.I. votes on new way to elect government" and "P.E.I. voters say 'no' to electoral reform," November 28, 2005; accessed at www.cbc.ca; and F. Leslie Seidle, "Lessons from PEI's plebiscite on electoral reform," *Opinion Canada,* 7:40 (Ottawa: Centre for Research and Information on Canada, December 2005); accessed at www.cric.ca.

113. Quebec National Assembly, Select Committee on the Election Act, "Information Booklet: Our Electoral System" (Quebec City, 2005), 20; accessed at www.assnat.qc.ca/eng, March 2006).

114. Henry Milner, "First Past the Post? Progress Report on Electoral Reform Initiatives in Canadian Provinces," *Policy Matters,* 5, no. 9 (Montreal: Institute for Research on Public Policy, September 2004), 25–27 (accessed at www.irpp.org, March 2006).

115. Robertson and Rowland, 10–11. See also the Report of the Select Committee on the Election Act, Chapter 3 (accessed at www.assnat.qc.ca/eng/37legislature2/commissions/csle/index.shtml).

116. The website of the Democratic Renewal Secretariat can be accessed directly from the Ontario Government site (www.gov.on.ca) or via the Ministry of the Attorney General.

117. Gordon Gibson, "BC Electoral Reform: Voters to Decide, Again," *Policy Options* (October 2005), 79; accessed at www.irpp.org.

118. The Commission's mandate, and other useful materials, can be found at www.gnb.ca (select the keyword "Democracy" in the Search database).

119. New Brunswick Commission on Legislative Democracy, *Final Report and Recommendations* (Fredericton, December 2004), Chapter 3; accessed at www.gnb.ca, January 2005.

120. New Brunswick, "Improving the Way Government Works: Government Response to the Final Report of the Commission on Legislative Democracy" (Fredericton, June 2006); accessed at www.gnb.ca/cnb/Promos/Leg-Dem/response-e.asp. The new Liberal Government's response was issued in June 2007: "An Accountable and Responsible Government," 6 (accessed at www.gnb.ca/0100/PDF/ResponseFinalReport-CLD-June2007-e.pdf, June 2008).

121. Andrew Ellis et al., *Engaging the Electorate: Initiatives to Promote Voter Turnout From Around the World* (Stockholm: International Institute for Democracy and Electoral Assistance, 2006), 11.

122. Mark N. Franklin, *Voter Turnout and the Dynamics of Electoral Competition in Established Democracies Since 1945* (Cambridge: Cambridge University Press, 2004), 11.

123. These figures are probably inflated, because the number of voting-age citizens is greater than the number of people on the Permanent Register of Electors; in 1997, for example, the official turnout rate was 67.8 percent; but the number of ballots cast represented only 56.2 percent of those eligible to vote. André Blais, Louis Massicotte, and Agnieszka Dobrzynska, *Why Is Turnout Higher in Some Countries Than in Others?* (Ottawa: Elections Canada, March 2003), 22; accessed at www.elections.ca/loi/tur/tuh/TurnoutHigher.pdf.

124. Lawrence LeDuc and Jon H. Pammett, "Voter Turnout in 2006: More Than Just the Weather," in Pammett and Dornan, eds., 321–322.

125. Geys, 641; Blais, Massicotte and Dobrzynska, 2.

126. Jon H. Pammett and Lawrence LeDuc, "Explaining the Turnout Decline in Canadian Federal Elections: A New Survey of Non-Voters" (Ottawa: Elections Canada, 2003), 19–28 (accessed at www.elections.ca).

127. Franklin, 19.

128. Ibid., Chapter 3. It has recently been suggested that lower turnout among young voters affects election outcomes. Martinez and Gill argue that the Liberals were helped in Quebec in the 1997 election by the fact that so many young voters—who tend to support the BQ—stayed home. This benefit was partly offset by Liberal losses outside Quebec, where older voters were more likely to support Reform and young Liberals sat out the election. Michael D. Martinez and Jeff Gill, "Does Turnout Decline Matter? Electoral Turnout and Partisan Choice in the 1997 Canadian Federal Election," *Canadian Journal of Political Science,* 39:2 (June 2006), 343–362.

129. Geys, 642. The fact that turnout in Prince Edward Island is roughly 10 points higher than the Canadian average seems to confirm this correlation, although it is contradicted by the very low turnout (around 50 percent) in three of the other four smallest jurisdictions in Canada (Newfoundland and Labrador, the Northwest Territories, and Nunavut). See Elections Canada, *Report of the Chief Electoral Officer of Canada on the 39th general election of January 23, 2006* (Ottawa: Chief Electoral Officer of Canada, 2006), 121; accessed at www.elections.ca, October 2006. It might appear that the density of population is as important as size; inhabitants of PEI are less dispersed than those in Newfoundland and Labrador or the Territories, which results in more community pressure to vote and makes it easier to get to a polling place. However, comparative studies find no correlation between population density and turnout; Geys, 643.

130. One aspect of the electoral system that does not seem to affect turnout is the introduction of annual allowances for registered parties (see the discussion of Bill C-24 in this chapter). Despite speculation that parties would try harder to get their supporters to the polls, because each vote would be worth $1.75 per year regardless of the outcome, the evidence does not show any such effect. Peter John Loewen and André Blais, "Did Bill C-24 Affect Voter Turnout? Evidence from the 2000 and 2004 Elections," *Canadian Journal of Political Science* 39:4 (December 2006), 935–943. Another factor that has little or no effect on turnout is the day of the week on which voting takes place: Blais, Massicotte, and Dobrzynska, 11. In May 2007, the Harper Government introduced a bill to permit voting at advance polls on the two Sundays immediately before election day; its claim that Bill C-55 would "increase voter participation" is not supported by scholarly evidence. Canada, Privy Council Office, "Canada's New Government Introduces the Expanded Voting Opportunities Bill," May 9, 2007 (accessed at http://news.gc.ca).

131. Courtney, *Elections*, 165.

132. Ibid., Chapter Four. In 1997, Canada replaced the old system of door-to-door enumeration with a computerized database of voters. Courtney reports that there were three times as many election-day corrections to the voters' list in 2000 (the first general election after the creation of the National Register of Electors) as there had been in the 1997 election. Moreover, Elections Canada mistakenly informed voters that they could not vote unless their names were on the list before election day; in reality, anyone who is legally entitled to vote in a Canadian election can add his or name to the Register just before casting a ballot.

133. Courtney, *Elections*, 97–98.

134. Blais, Massicotte and Dobrzynska, 8.

135. Franklin, 143.

136. LeDuc and Pammett, 314–320.

137. Franklin, 166–167.

138. Ibid., 79.

139. Russell J. Dalton, "Political Cleavages, Issues, and Electoral Change," in Lawrence LeDuc, Richard G. Niemi, and Pippa Norris, eds., *Comparing Democracies 2: New Challenges in the Study of Elections and Voting* (Thousand Oaks, CA: Sage, 2002), 193–94.

140. André Blais, Elisabeth Gidengil, Richard Nadeau, and Neil Nevitte, *Anatomy of a Liberal Victory: Making Sense of the Vote in the 2000 Canadian Election* (Peterborough, ON: Broadview Press, 2002), 91.

141. André Blais, "Accounting for the Electoral Success of the Liberal Party in Canada," *Canadian Journal of Political Science,* 38:4 (December 2005), 823.

142. Blais et al., *Anatomy of a Liberal Victory,* 93.

143. Blais, "Accounting," 823.

144. Blais et al., *Anatomy of a Liberal Victory,* 94.

145. Abbas Rana, "Conservatives to target urban, ethnic ridings in next election," *The Hill Times,* January 22, 2007, 1 and 4.

146. This effort reached the Cabinet level in January 2007, when Calgary MP Jason Kenney was appointed Secretary of State for Multiculturalism and Canadian Identity. His real job was to

build Conservative support in ethnic communities, by attending cultural events and networking with community leaders. Abbas Rana, "'Secretary of State of Curry in a Hurry,'" *The Hill Times*, April 30, 2007, 6.

147. Peter Wearing and Joseph Wearing, "Does Gender Make a Difference in Voting Behaviour?" in Joseph Wearing, ed., *The Ballot and Its Message: Voting in Canada* (Toronto: Copp Clark Pitman, 1991), 343; Elisabeth Gidengil *et al.*, "Women to the Left/Men to the Right" (accessed at www.ces-eec.umontreal.ca/ces.html, April 2007), 1.

148. Gidengil *et al.*, 3.

149. Blais et al., *Anatomy of a Liberal Victory*, 94–95.

150. Michael Marzolini, "The Politics of Values: Designing the 2000 Liberal Campaign," in Dornan and Pammett, eds., *The Canadian General Election of 2000*, 263–76.

151. Ibid.

152. Blais et al., "Making Sense of the Vote in the 2000 Canadian Election," 7.

153. Blais et al., *Anatomy of a Liberal Victory,* 109.

154. Ibid.

155. Allison Dunfield, "Tories wouldn't outlaw abortion, Harper says," *The Globe and Mail,* June 1, 2004 (accessed at www.globeandmail.com); Canadian Press, "We'd use notwithstanding clause: Tory MP," *Toronto Star,* June 25, 2004: accessed at www.thestar.com.

156. Robert Benzie, "Tories pin blame on fear, rogue candidates," *Toronto Star,* June 30, 2004: accessed at www.thestar.com.

157. Blais et al., *Anatomy of a Liberal Victory,* 203.

158. See, e.g., ibid., 77, Table 4.3.

159. Graham Fox and Nik Nanos, "Trading Places: The Story of the 2006 General Election" (Ottawa: Public Policy Forum, February 2006), 8 (accessed at www.ppforum.ca, April 2007).

160. Blais et al., "Making Sense of the Vote in the 2000 Canadian Election," 11. However, the results of the 2007 provincial election suggest the emergence of a more complex voting pattern, as the nationalist vote split between the left (the Parti Québécois) and the right (the Action Democratique du Québec). See G. Bruce Doern, "The Harper Conservatives in Power: Emissions Impossible," in G. Bruce Doern, ed., *How Ottawa Spends, 2007–2008: The Harper Conservatives—Climate of Change* (Montreal and Kingston: McGill–Queen's University Press, 2007), 20.

161. Clarke et al., *Absent Mandate: Interpreting Change in Canadian Elections.*

162. Alan Frizzell, "The Perils of Polling," in Alan Frizzell, Jon H. Pammett, and Anthony Westell, eds., *The Canadian General Election of 1988* (Ottawa: Carleton University Press, 1989).

163. The lower figure comes from Clarke et al., *Absent Mandate: Interpreting Change in Canadian Elections,* 48–49; Harold D. Clarke, Jane Jenson, Lawrence LeDuc, and Jon H. Pammett, "Voting Behaviour and the Outcome of the 1979 Federal Election: The Impact of Leaders and Issues," *Canadian Journal of Political Science,* XV:3 (1982), 517–52. The higher figure is taken from the 2000 Canadian Election Study: Blais et al., "Making Sense of the Vote in the 2000 Canadian Election," 12–13.

164. Blais et al., "Making Sense of the Vote in the 2000 Canadian Election," 13; Elisabeth Gidengil *et al.*, "Is the Concept of Party Identification Applicable in Canada? A Panel-Based Analysis," paper presented to the European Consortium on Political Research, Nicosia, April 2006, Table 1 (accessed at www.ces-eec.umontreal.ca/ces.html).

165. Neil Nevitte, André Blais, Elisabeth Gidengil, and Richard Nadeau, *Unsteady State: The 1997 Canadian Federal Election* (Toronto: Oxford University Press, 2000),70.

166. Gidengil *et al.*, "Is the Concept of Party Identification Applicable in Canada?" Table 1.

167. Ibid., Table 1.

168. Ibid., Table 4.

169. Blais et al., *Anatomy of a Liberal Victory,* 121, Figure 8.3.

170. Gidengil *et al.*, "Is the Concept of Party Identification Applicable in Canada?" Table 4.

171. Blais et al., *Anatomy of a Liberal Victory*, 117.

172. Fox and Nanos, 3; Turcotte, "After Fifty-Six Days," Tables 4 and 5.

173. A reference to the famous sign in the Clinton "war room" during the 1992 American presidential campaign.

174. Helmut Norpoth, "The Economy," in LeDuc, Niemi, and Norris, eds., *Comparing Democracies*, 303.

175. Richard Nadeau and André Blais, "Explaining Election Outcomes in Canada," *Canadian Journal of Political Science*, 26, 775–90; summarized in Blais et al., *Anatomy of a Liberal Victory*, 129.

176. Norpoth, 299–318.

177. Stephen Clarkson, "How the Big Red Machine Became the Little Red Machine," in Pammett and Dornan, eds., 24–57.

178. Marzolini, 268.

179. André Blais et al., "Election 2006: How Big Were the Changes . . . Really?" 2 (accessed at www.ces-eec.umontreal.ca/ces.html, April 2007).

180. Fox and Nanos, 3–4.

181. Richard Johnston, André Blais, Henry E. Brady, and Jean Crête, "Free Trade and the Dynamics of the 1988 Canadian Election," in Wearing, ed., *The Ballot and Its Message*, 321.

182. In that instance, the PC government had negotiated the Free Trade Agreement with the Americans, and the party defended the deal vigorously. Voters who did not share this enthusiasm were split between the Liberals—whose credibility as crusaders against free enterprise was relatively weak—and the NDP, which had better ideological credentials for the anti-FTA fight but lacked credibility in other issue areas. In the end, the PCs were re-elected with a reduced majority.

183. Chantal Hébert, *French Kiss: Stephen Harper's Blind Date with Quebec* (Toronto: Knopf Canada, 2007), 61–62.

184. Elisabeth Gidengil and André Blais, "Are Party Leaders Becoming More Important to Vote Choice in Canada?" in Michelmann, Story, and Steeves, eds., *Political Leadership and Representation in Canada*, 39–59.

185. The fate of former PC leader (later Quebec Liberal Premier) Jean Charest in 1997 is a good example. Charest performed well in the two leaders' debates and ended the campaign as the most popular party leader in Quebec. But his party performed poorly on election day, partly because two-thirds of Quebec voters considered Charest to be "a one-man show." (Nevitte et al., *Unsteady State*, 87.) There was no strong team of PC candidates and little party organization on the ground to capitalize on the leader's popularity. As Charest himself said after the campaign ended, "There were people knocking on our door, but there was nobody home to let them in." (Jean Charest, remarks to the National Council of the Progressive Conservative Party of Canada, February 1998.)

186. Richard Johnston, André Blais, Henry E. Brady, and Jean Crête, *Letting the People Decide: Dynamics of a Canadian Election* (Montreal and Kingston: McGill–Queen's University Press, 1992), 169–96.

187. Turcotte, "After Fifty-Six Days," 299.

188. Gidengil and Blais, "Party Leaders," 48.

189. Ibid., 46.

190. Turcotte, 292.

191. He was dubbed "Mr. Dithers" by *The Economist*, a leading global newsmagazine based in Britain. See Clarkson, "Big Red Machine," 27.

192. Wells, 120–122.

193. Bob Plamondon, *Full Circle: Death and Resurrection in Canadian Conservative Politics* (Toronto: Key Porter, 2006), 364 and 401–402; Ellis and Woolstencroft, "A Change of Government," 59–62 and 73.

194. See Nevitte et al., *Unsteady State,* 132; Farrell, 179–82.

195. Rüdiger Schmitt-Beck and David M. Farrell, "Do Political Campaigns Matter? Yes, But It Depends," in David M. Farrell and Rüdiger Schmitt-Beck, eds., *Do Political Campaigns Matter? Campaign Effects in Elections and Referendums* (New York: Routledge, 2002), 183.

196. Clarkson, "Big Red Machine," 50.

197. Rüdiger Schmitt-Beck and David M. Farrell, "Studying Political Campaigns and Their Effects," in Farrell and Schmitt-Beck, eds., 13–14.

198. Wells, 156.

199. Ibid., 233.

200. Ibid., 213.

201. Fox and Nanos, 8.

202. Wells, 214; Plamondon, 413–414.

203. Wells, 214; Plamondon, 413.

204. Plamondon, 413.

205. Conservative Party of Canada, "Stand Up For Canada: Federal Election Platform 2006" (Ottawa, 2006), 17 (accessed at www.conservative.ca, February 2006).

206. Wells, 214; Plamondon, 413.

207. Wells, 214; Plamondon, 413.

208. Plamondon, 413.

209. Wells, 213.

210. Ibid., 213–215.

211. It is noteworthy, for example, that the 2007 federal budget slapped tax penalties on the purchase of gas-guzzling vehicles. It targeted SUVs and Hummers, but not pickup trucks (Dougie's wheels of choice) or minivans (the suburban family vehicle *par excellence*).

212. Simon Doyle, "Tories Run 'Narrowcast' Government: Says Pollster," *The Hill Times*, October 23, 2006, 1 and 24.

13 Advocacy Groups and the Canadian Political System

LEARNING OBJECTIVES

After you finish reading this chapter, you should be able to:

*   *distinguish* an interest group from an advocacy group;
*   *define* the term "policy community" and explain its importance in the policy-making process;
*   *distinguish* between the **subgovernment** and the discourse community;
*   *explain* why some advocacy groups have more policy influence than others;
*   *explain* why advocacy groups are increasingly opting for supporters instead of active memberships.

INTRODUCTION

The preceding chapters describe governmental institutions and processes, and the quasi-public organizations (political parties) that link citizens directly to those institutions. The three branches of government are regulated by laws, both entrenched and nonentrenched. Their leaders can be held accountable to the Canadian public, to a greater or lesser degree, either by their members or by other agencies of government. Their structures and activities are generally well understood and extensively studied.

Advocacy groups, despite their public role, are private organizations. Their internal structures and operations are generally closed to public view. While we can describe their efforts to influence public policy, the extent of that influence is impossible to measure. The scholarly literature on advocacy groups is relatively thin and the quality is uneven: some studies draw general conclusions from anecdotal evidence,[1] while others overstate group influence by overlooking alternative explanations for particular policy changes.[2]

The deficiencies in the literature, and the impossibility of drawing firm conclusions about advocacy groups, are necessarily reflected in this chapter. Apart from their public contacts with the legislative and judicial branches, and their mandatory disclosures about lobbying activities and election campaign advertising, our knowledge of advocacy groups is sketchy. At best, we can assume that organized interests enjoy some success in achieving their policy goals; otherwise, they would go out of business. Of their internal life, their memberships, even their numbers, we can say relatively little with any confidence.

With these caveats in mind, we turn to a discussion of advocacy groups and their participation in the policy process. We will begin by defining the various interests that seek to influence public policy, and summarizing the available information about their structures, activities, and resources. Then we will discuss the relationships between advocacy groups and the three branches of the Canadian government, followed by a consideration of their attempts to sway voters during election campaigns. We will conclude by describing the growing international cooperation among advocacy groups. The central theme of this chapter is that advocacy groups (like political parties) do not effectively perform the most important function attributed to them: linking Canadians to their governing institutions. More and more groups that purport to speak for thousands of "ordinary citizens" have dispensed with members altogether. Under these circumstances, we should question the claim of some advocacy-group leaders to speak on behalf of anyone other than themselves.

WHAT IS AN ADVOCACY GROUP?

▇ Interest Groups versus Advocacy Groups

We must begin by clarifying the terminology used to describe organized interests in politics. A variety of terms appear in the academic and political discourse about these groups, which often leads to confusion. We will use the term **interest group** to describe an organization of people who seek to promote a common goal. It may be local—e.g., a group of homeowners who protest against a proposed trash incinerator in their neighbourhood—provincial, national, or global (e.g., Amnesty International). The scope of interest-group organizing has widened significantly with the introduction of the Internet, which allows far-flung groups to form worldwide alliances and to mobilize like-minded individuals around the world very cheaply.

Most interest groups are founded for nonpolitical purposes, although some are drawn into the policy-making process to protect the interests of their members. For example, people who enjoy hiking in the Rockies might establish an organization to allow them to communicate with like-minded individuals, to pool resources, or to achieve ends that they might not be able to achieve singly. It is easy to go hiking by yourself, but by joining a club you meet others with the same interest and perhaps find out about new trails. As a group, the hikers might be able to get discounts on transportation or equipment. None of this requires political action. It is certainly **collective action,** in the sense that individuals are trying to act in concert, but it is not political.

However, it is easy to imagine how this group's activities might become political. Hiking requires wilderness, and wilderness areas depend on government protection. Since it is in the interest of hikers to have a place to hike, it is also in their interest to persuade government to protect wilderness areas. This is the rationale behind the extensive political activities of groups such as the Sierra Club. Their members may not be interested in politics per se, but their shared interests (e.g., wilderness recreation) often require them to engage directly with political institutions.

So we will distinguish between two types of organized group, based on the degree to which its leaders and members focus on public policy. The first type, the interest group, is essentially non-political. It may be drawn into the policy process intermittently, but its primary goals and activities are directed elsewhere. Examples include churches, service clubs, and sports leagues. The second type is oriented exclusively (or nearly so) toward the goal of influencing government decisions that affect its members. We will describe an organization that devotes most or all of its resources to influencing public policy as an **advocacy group.** Admittedly, this distinction is clearer on paper than it is in practice. The primary purpose of a labour union, for example, is to negotiate contracts with the employer on behalf of its members; from the very beginnings of the modern labour movement, however, union leaders have been active participants in politics. Nonetheless, we need to draw a distinction between advocacy groups and other organized interests, and the relative importance of public policy vis-à-vis other collective goals is the most promising criterion available.

The above definition is incomplete, because it does not fully explain how advocacy groups differ from other policy-oriented organizations—most notably, political parties. For our purposes, Young and Everitt's definition of advocacy groups is the most suitable: "any organization that seeks to influence government policy, but not to govern."[3] Unlike parties, advocacy groups do not run candidates for election to public office (although some groups participate in the electoral process by advertising for or against particular policies or candidates). Another difference is the narrow scope of advocacy groups: whereas catch-all parties must appeal to as many sections of the electorate as possible (especially under our plurality electoral system), advocacy groups focus on advancing the interests and goals of one segment of the population.

Characteristics of Canadian Advocacy Groups

Because they are private organizations, advocacy groups are notoriously difficult to describe with any precision. Moreover, their sizes and structures vary widely; it is impossible to generalize about advocacy groups with any precision. Despite these difficulties, there are a few established facts about the universe of advocacy groups that operate in Canada.

First, Canadians hold a largely favourable opinion of advocacy groups. When asked whether they would join a political party or an interest group in order to advance a particular policy goal, 60 percent of respondents to a 1999 survey opted for the group—three times more than the figure for political parties.[4] This preference is reflected in actual participation rates: Canadians are more likely to belong to advocacy groups than to parties, and we have higher rates of group membership than our counterparts in other Western democracies.[5] At the same time, some Canadians express concern about the pernicious influence of "special interests" in national politics. This suggests that we favour the influence of groups whose goals we happen to share, but fear those dedicated to causes with which we disagree. Note that membership in political parties and advocacy groups is not mutually exclusive; indeed, group members are three times more likely to participate in party activities as Canadians who do not belong to an advocacy group.[6]

Second, the number of advocacy groups appears to have grown significantly over the past 50 years—although there is no comprehensive catalogue of groups, so one must be careful about putting too much faith in the data. At Confederation, there were relatively few organized groups. National and provincial governments had close ties to business interests, but these did not begin to form advocacy groups until the 1870s.[7] By the early twentieth century, women and manual labourers were forming organizations to pressure governments for policy change; this was likely a response to their exclusion from the formal institutions of government. At the turn of the twenty-first century, the range of interests represented by one or more groups was much broader. Table 13.1 lists some of those interests, with their corresponding groups.

Third, those who belong to advocacy groups are quite different from the Canadian population as a whole. Like party members, they are disproportionately white, male, affluent, and well-educated; however, environmental and women's groups are more reflective of the population than unions or professional associations. Younger Canadians are somewhat more numerous in advocacy groups than in parties, although they are still under-represented relative to their numbers in the population as a whole.[8] The leaders of advocacy groups are especially unrepresentative. Although some claim to represent the disadvantaged, group leaders

TABLE 13.1 A SAMPLE OF CANADIAN ADVOCACY GROUPS

TYPE OF INTEREST	ADVOCACY GROUP(S)	KEY ISSUE(S)
Business/Corporate	Canadian Council of Chief Executives Canadian Federation of Independent Business Canadian Chamber of Commerce Canadian Manufacturers' Association Conseil du Patronat du Québec	Trade Taxation Subsidies
Labour	Canadian Labour Congress Canadian Union of Public Employees Fédération des Travailleurs et Travailleuses du Québec	Labour laws
Women	Canadian Research Institute for the Advancement of Women Women's Legal Education and Action Fund (LEAF)	Gender discrimination Child care Reproductive choice
Environment	Greenpeace Pollution Probe Sierra Club Canada Ducks Unlimited	Climate change Habitat protection Air quality
Ethnic Minorities	Canadian Ethno-Cultural Council B'nai Brith Canada	Equal rights Religious and cultural freedom
Aboriginal Peoples	Assembly of First Nations Inuit Tapirisat	Living conditions on-reserve Land claims
Poverty	National Anti-Poverty Organization Canadian Council on Social Development	Social assistance Social justice
Sexual Orientation	Equality for Gays and Lesbians Everywhere (EGALE) Equal Marriage	Discrimination Same-sex marriage

Source: www.hillwatch.com; © Hillwatch Inc., 2003, accessed June 2008.

themselves are generally among the best educated and often the best paid members of society. However, there are good reasons to choose such leaders, as we will see in our discussion of the factors that make advocacy groups influential in the policy process.

Fourth, most members are relatively detached from the day-to-day activity of their groups, including—perhaps especially—their efforts to influence public policy. On average, "group members are much less active than members of political parties" (whom, as we saw in Chapter 11, are hardly paragons of involvement).[9] This finding raises two important issues. First, it casts doubt on the widespread belief that joining an advocacy group is a more effective way for an individual to achieve his or her policy goals than joining a political party. Second, the stated purpose of these organizations is to pressure governments on behalf of their members. But if the members themselves rarely turn out to meetings or participate in internal decision-making, how can group leaders claim to speak on their behalf? As we will see, however, there are good reasons for advocacy group leaders to downplay the role of the membership in their organizations; indeed, an active membership can be an obstacle to the leadership's efforts to achieve its policy goals.

THE ORGANIZATION AND STRUCTURE OF ADVOCACY GROUPS

It is impossible to generalize about the formal structures of advocacy groups. One reason is the scarcity of reliable data. Unlike political parties, such groups are not required to disclose financial and organizational information to the public. Another reason is the sheer diversity of group structures. They range from a few dozen neighbours trying to prevent the construction of a highway through their neighbourhood to a national umbrella organization claiming to represent tens of thousands of auto workers, students, or taxpayers. The difficulty is compounded by the informality and the short-term existence of some groups, which take shape quickly and then dissipate within a few months or years.

Despite these obstacles, we can identify two factors that shape the structures of Canadian advocacy groups: the relationship between a group's grassroots and its leadership; and the impact of federalism, which divides policy jurisdictions between two levels of government.

Relationships between Group Leaders and Members

In organizational terms, advocacy groups fall into two broad categories.
- Membership-based groups are internally democratic (at least in principle). They provide opportunities for their members to participate in decision-making, including decisions about who will lead the group. For practical reasons, smaller and locally based groups can involve individual members more directly and more frequently than larger national organizations—although the Internet has made communication among thousands of members spread across large distances much quicker and cheaper than it used to be. When members are empowered to make decisions collectively, they expect the group's leadership to implement those decisions in their policy activities; this can pose problems, as we will see below. Among the groups that engage directly with the federal government "membership-based organizations appear to be the exception rather than the rule."[10]
- Staff-led groups have few members, often by choice. Some dispense with membership altogether, relying instead on financial donations from "supporters" to fund the professionals who work at the group's headquarters. This "member-free" model is increasingly common in Western democracies.[11] It liberates the full-time staff or executive of the organization from the need to build an internal consensus among a large group, while protecting the organization from invasion by its opponents.[12]

From a democratic perspective, the growing number of staff-led groups is a disturbing trend. Anyone can claim to represent a particular interest, and demand a role in policy-making on that basis. But when that claim is based solely on a list of donors who play no meaningful role in the internal life of the group, why should governments give in to their demands? In principle, the policy influence of a group's leaders should depend on the size of the membership and their commitment to the goals of their members. A former Royal Commissioner put it this way: "We had people saying that they represented a certain group with over 3000 members. Then [when] we asked how they consulted all these members, it became clear they didn't. . . . We couldn't presume that just because they were the presidents of these groups that they had actually consulted their members in a systematic way."[13]

From a policy perspective, an active membership can actually hinder a group's efforts to influence government decisions. Freed from the pressure to consult members and build a consensus, "group leaders are able to respond quickly to government requests for consultations, or to government announcements of policy."[14] The experience of the National Action Committee on the Status of Women (NAC) illustrates the problem. In the 1980s, the federal government was caught off guard by an explosion of new reproductive technologies (NRTs); it eventually decided to regulate their use, and established a Royal Commission to explore the issues. As the largest national women's organization in Canada, NAC should have played a leading role in the Commission's deliberations and the development of public policy following its report. Instead, NAC was relegated to the sidelines by its internal ethos of membership consultation and consensus. Its complex structure, based on hundreds of local grassroots groups, was incompatible with the deadlines imposed by policymakers. The complexity of the subject demanded a high level of technical expertise, which pitted elite members of NAC's leadership against the grassroots organizations that were supposed to legitimate their policy prescriptions. NAC's official leadership opposed NRTs, contradicting the positions of some member organizations. In summary, "NAC's capacity to influence and participate in the formulation of policy was challenged by its inability to resolve the demand of institutional politics for professional advocacy with internal demands for deliberation and participation emanating from its 'non-expert' member groups."[15]

NAC's difficulties illustrate a broader issue: the link between the characteristics of an advocacy group's membership and its political influence (or lack thereof). Groups that refuse to cooperate with the government, or whose members fear co-optation into political institutions, will exercise less influence than those whose members are willing to accept the norms of the subgovernment. (See the discussion of policy communities, below.) The leaders and staff of an advocacy group must have sufficient autonomy to participate in the policy process without constant accusations of selling out, or demands for consultation, from their members.

Pross describes the "vertical information problem" that can arise when an advocacy group becomes more institutionalized, with leaders and staff taking on distinct roles and values from the people whose interests they are expected to express. The leaders, who interact directly with other members of the policy community, "become knowledgeable about the policy process, come to feel more effective in it, and consequently tend to move away from their followers."[16] At this point, the emerging political salience of the advocacy group may be undermined by a perception among public officials that its constituency does not support the goals and tactics of the leaders. When this happens, officials wonder whether they can rely on the group's members to support the policies approved by their leaders, or to participate effectively in their implementation.

In sum, the leaders of advocacy groups are caught in a dilemma. On the one hand, the demands of participation in the subgovernment cannot be met without the financial and moral support of their members. Nor will they be admitted to the subgovernment without a firm mandate from the grassroots of their organizations—"the express assignment of representative capacity to a group's leadership by its membership."[17] On the other hand, advocacy-group leaders cannot respond quickly to requests for information and advice if they are required to seek the formal approval of their members for every policy pronouncement. While it may be desirable in theory for leaders to be fully accountable to those in whose name they speak, it is clear that advocacy-group leaders are most effective when they achieve the autonomy and the experience to participate in detailed policy-making.

Such leaders may also acquire the polish and the communications skills that allow them to use the news media to raise the profile of their group and its issues. "Studies have repeatedly cited media coverage as critical to the success or failure of social movements and interest group efforts."[18] There are advantages and disadvantages to close working relationships between journalists and advocacy-group leaders. On the plus side, frequent media appearances by a group leader or spokesperson "may help to keep the movement's concerns before the public, and enhance its status in the eyes of policy makers."[19] The downside, particularly for advocacy groups with "radical" agendas, is that sustained media attention "may alienate policy makers, if the latter perceive the movement's tactics as illegitimate or embarrassing."[20] Furthermore, "the transformation of activists into media celebrities can foster internal envy and resentment."[21] The leader of a membership-based group may incur hostility, and perhaps outright revolt, if he or she appears to be co-opted into the elite stratum of society. In this respect, as in others previously discussed, the absence of committed members affords useful flexibility to a staff-led group.

Overall, the institutional incentives for membership-based advocacy groups—at least those who seek admission to the subgovernment—can pull their leaders and their members in opposite directions. The former must adapt to the requirements of policy-making and media relations, while the latter resist allowing their leaders to lose touch with the grassroots. This tension likely explains why staff-led groups are more influential within Canada's policy communities than their more internally democratic counterparts.

■ Federalism

Canada's federal system directly affects the internal organization of advocacy groups, or at least those that seek to operate over a wide geographic area. Most obviously, it requires many of them to divide their resources between Ottawa and the provincial governments. Some are primarily focused on the provincial level; the national umbrella organization is secondary. For example, advocacy groups involved in primary and secondary education target provincial governments. Those with a particular focus on foreign aid confine themselves to the federal government.

Chapter 4 describes the growing autonomy and parity of Canada's provincial governments. As policy capacity shifts from Ottawa to the provinces, the institutional incentives for advocacy groups change. The federal government effectively eliminated conditions on transfer payments in 1995, when it introduced the Canadian Health and Social Transfer (CHST). The impact on advocacy groups in health care and other affected fields was immediate:

> Previously, the social services policy community was strongly oriented to the federal level, since Ottawa not only spent money in the field but was seen to be a leader. Now, as the core responsibility shifts to the provincial level, the corresponding policy communities will fragment and focus more on local/provincial dynamics.[22]

As we saw in Chapter 11, conflicts between the federal government and one or more provinces can strain relations within the major parties; the same is probably true for advocacy groups. At the same time, different provinces or regions have different needs. For example, a national organization that represents the interests of manufacturers would have difficulty forging a consensus on energy pricing. High prices benefit its Alberta-based members, which supply goods and services to the oil and gas sector; meanwhile, auto-parts plants in Ontario and Quebec go out of business as consumers switch to fuel-efficient Japanese cars.

A second characteristic of Canadian federalism is the presence of Quebec. While the presence of provincial governments requires national interest groups to organize themselves on a regional basis, the special circumstances in Quebec pose unique challenges for coordination. The practical difficulties created by two official languages are compounded by different social traditions. In the field of human rights, for example, Quebec has a rich tradition of Catholic overseas missionary work and social action that differs significantly from the English Canadian pattern. Consequently, many human rights organizations are split between Quebec and "Canadian" offices. Amnesty International, for example, whose "Canadian section" was established in 1973 as one organization, now has two branches, one in Montreal (francophone) and one in Ottawa (mostly anglophone). This "two-nations" approach to interest-group organization can threaten the unity of a national group, particularly when constitutional issues are on the table. The National Action Committee on the Status of Women (NAC) came close to a serious rupture during the public debate over the Meech Lake Accord, when Quebec feminist groups accused their "sisters" in English Canada of bigotry over their concerns about the implications of the distinct-society clause for gender rights.[23]

Third, the division of policy-making power may afford groups more opportunities to influence decision-making than they would have in a unitary state. In practice, however, the growing reliance on executive federalism since the 1960s has effectively excluded most non-governmental actors from the policy process. Aboriginal "peak" organizations (those that represent a wide spectrum of Aboriginal Canadians, such as the Assembly of First Nations) are often invited to participate in discussions among federal, provincial, and territorial leaders, but other groups are rarely consulted in an official way.

THE UNEVEN PLAYING FIELD: ADVOCACY-GROUP RESOURCES

In the early twentieth century, American political scientists coined the term "pluralism" to describe the relationships between interest groups and the state. Pluralists assumed that groups competed with each other for resources and influence, under "rules of the game" that were fair to all players. The state was a neutral referee, enforcing the rules without systematically favouring any of the contending teams. Since the 1960s, pluralism has been largely disproved by evidence of bias on the part of government agencies. In other words, the rules of the advocacy-group game are far from neutral. Certain interests, and certain types of advocacy groups, enjoy significantly more influence than others. It makes sense that groups whose interests dovetail with those of state actors exercise greater influence than those that are perceived, fairly or otherwise, as "fringe" movements. What is less obvious, at least initially, is the organizational and resource base that distinguishes subgovernment groups from their marginalized rivals.

To achieve and retain a privileged place in the subgovernment, an advocacy group must have both political salience and **policy capacity.** The political salience of a particular group is determined by several factors,[24] some of which have already been discussed:

- the size, cohesion, socioeconomic status, and political leverage of its membership;
- its willingness and ability to build coalitions with like-minded groups;
- its tangible and intangible resources;
- its ability to represent its membership effectively and to mobilize that membership in support of its political activities (e.g., letter-writing campaigns to politicians); and
- its effectiveness as a channel of communication between the government and its membership.

The policy capacity of a particular group depends on its ability to use its political salience to advance its goals. A group with a large and wealthy membership will not automatically secure entry into the subgovernment on that basis. It must repeatedly demonstrate its value as a participant in the making and implementation of public policy. The key ingredients in policy capacity are:

- tangible resources: money, expert staff (in-house or contract lobbyists and policy specialists), and a stable, continuous organizational presence (e.g., a large national office in Ottawa); and
- intangible resources: expertise in both the substance of policy and the process of policy-making (not only the formal flow charts of political science textbooks but also the informal hierarchy of status and influence within the relevant departments and agencies); a reputation with ministers, senior officials, and other groups within the subgovernment;

a track record of competent and reliable service to the subgovernment (providing reliable information, building support for new measures among the membership, assisting in the implementation of policy). The bottom line: policy capacity costs a lot of time and money.

When governments and their agencies decide that specific groups speak for a significant part of the population and that their views are legitimate, they turn to them frequently, inviting them to sit on advisory committees and consulting them on issues far afield from the immediate concerns of the groups themselves. Responding to these overtures takes considerable effort. Membership opinions may have to be elicited, or specialized knowledge tapped. More frequently, the organization may have to dedicate the time of its research staff to the government's question, diverting it from tasks more important to the group and its members. Even participation on advisory boards can siphon off valuable executive time. . . . The cost of participation is the price the group pays for acceptance as a full-fledged member of the policy community.[25]

Groups that can afford to acquire the necessary expertise in the technical details of policy and the art of governance, while simultaneously providing the permanent and political executives with the necessary information, support, and regulatory assistance, may become and remain core members of the subgovernment. Indeed, a leading expert on Canadian government suggests that certain advocacy groups are more influential than political parties, precisely because of their "research capacity," networking skills, and media savvy.[26] Less fortunate groups usually enjoy less influence, regardless of the intrinsic merits of their policy recommendations.

Business groups and associations are often the target of concern about the influence of groups on public policy.

- Given the capitalist nature of the Canadian economy, prosperity and jobs depend on private-sector decisions about investment and development. If business is unhappy with taxes or social policies, the argument runs, it will invest elsewhere. This assumption alone ensures a more attentive hearing for groups like the Canadian Bankers' Association, the Council of Chief Executives, and the Canadian Chamber of Commerce.

- Business groups command far greater financial resources than others. They can establish well-funded advocacy offices, hire lobbyists, and go to court in hopes of striking down unfavourable laws. The disparity between business groups and those claiming to represent the disadvantaged has only grown in recent years (Dossier 13.1).

- Many politicians are either drawn from the business community or have extensive social connections with members of that community. This gives the latter privileged access and a sympathetic hearing.

DOSSIER 13.1 Government Support for Advocacy Groups

In the late 1960s and 1970s, Canada's federal government deliberately mobilized latent interests in the electorate. It identified particular groups—official language minorities, women, ethnic minorities, and Aboriginal communities—and encouraged them to create their own advocacy groups. State support for these embryonic organizations took two primary forms: positional and financial.[27]

Positional support means access for some groups and not others to information or to decision-makers or to a formal or quasi-formal role in decision-making. . . . . Usually, the

(continued)

organization will have to establish its credibility before it is granted this positional support, but once such support is granted, its position vis-à-vis its competitors in the policy field is considerably enhanced.[28]

State financial support for advocacy groups included annual core funding, which covered the daily overhead costs of running an organization, and grants for individual projects. The process of applying for public funding consumed a substantial amount of the scarce time and energy that may be available to a volunteer organization or a nonprofit agency. More seriously, in the view of some advocacy groups, government funding might compromise their freedom to criticize state policy.[29] They feared **co-optation** into the policy agenda of the ruling party. Alternatively, they worried that an over-reliance on granting programs could distort their organizational priorities—a realistic fear, according to studies of Canadian women's groups and Aboriginal organizations.[30] Nonetheless, most eligible groups did apply for public funding. Unlike the United States, which has a well-developed network of private charitable foundations, Canadian advocacy groups have few opportunities to secure funding from non-state sources. "Groups clearly recognize the possibility of co-optation but prefer being vigilant recipients to pristine paupers."[31]

While it is easy to understand why an interest group would seek available funding from the state, it may be less easy to understand why a government would wish to subsidize groups that might be inclined to criticize its activities. According to Pal, there are at least two reasons for state funding of interest groups. First, a particular agency might seek to create a well-organized political constituency for its programs and services. Should the agency face a challenge to its autonomy or its finances, whether from inside or outside the federal government, such an external constituency may become a crucial resource in its self-defence campaign.[32] Second, from the perspective of the government as a whole, giving money to groups that will, in turn, demand even more public resources makes long-term strategic sense. Advocacy organizations whose primary purpose is to secure programs for disadvantaged social groups—women, people with disabilities, Aboriginal peoples, and others—provide arguments to justify the continual expansion of the state.[33]

Such arguments serve the interests of the state during periods of prosperity, which helps to explain the boom in advocacy funding during the late 1960s and early 1970s, but they tend to fall on deaf ears during periods of fiscal constraint. The spending cuts that began to affect the federal government in the 1980s go a long way to explain declining state support for advocacy groups since that time—not just directly, in the sense that government had less money to spend on core and project funding, but indirectly, because advocacy groups became more of a nuisance than a political resource.

By the turn of the century, "core" funding for the ongoing activities of advocacy groups had all but disappeared. Instead, groups who relied on federal funding had to apply for grants for separate projects.[34] Grant applications are very time-consuming, and their outcomes are uncertain. Some groups were forced to shut down their operations. Others shifted from lobbying the legislative and executive branches to *Charter* litigation, to take advantage of funding from the Court Challenges Program.[35] (This program was shut down in 2006.) The scarcity and unpredictability of government funding helps to explain the growing number of "staff-led" groups that rely on direct-mail fundraising to sustain their professional operations, as opposed to membership-based groups dependent on volunteers.

HOW DO ADVOCACY GROUPS PURSUE THEIR POLICY GOALS?

The Rules of Engagement

Broadly speaking, advocacy groups engage in the policy process in three distinct ways: lobbying, representation, and consultation.[36]

- The term **"lobbying"** refers to one-way communication from an advocacy group to the state actors in the relevant policy field. In other words, it describes the effort by a particular group to convince government decision-makers to incorporate its goals into public policy. Lobbying occurs at the initiative of the advocacy group, not the government. Today, lobbying is a major industry in Ottawa (and, to a lesser degree, in provincial capitals). Most lobbying activity is directed toward the executive branch; consequently, it occurs behind closed doors.

- **Representation** refers to advocacy-group participation in formal policy-making activities at the invitation of the government. For example, Canadian governments sometimes appoint Royal Commissions to investigate complex policy issues. Most commissions hold public hearings, where advocacy-group spokespersons try to set the policy agenda and attract media coverage. Whereas commissions are relatively infrequent, Standing Committees of the House of Commons and the Senate conduct public hearings whenever Parliament is in session (Chapter 7). Each committee has the power to invite or exclude particular advocacy groups. Every year, an average of approximately 5000 witnesses appear in front of House of Commons and Senate committees;[37] others submit written briefs setting out their members' position on proposed laws or broader policy issues. Many, if not most, of the witnesses represent organized interests.

- Whereas lobbying and representation can be intermittent activities, **consultation** refers to a continual two-way flow of communication. In consultative processes, members of the executive branch work with group representatives to resolve common problems. Like representation, consultation is initiated by the government; unlike representation, consultation normally implies "an ongoing process, not a one-off exchange of views."[38] Since the 1980s, consultations with "stakeholders" have become an increasingly important part of Canadian policy-making and program implementation. The downsizing of the federal public service forced the government to rely more heavily on the specialized knowledge of its "client groups," knowledge that can be "bought" only in exchange for a seat at the policy table.

Advocacy groups that participate in regular consultations are more likely to achieve their policy goals than those which are restricted to lobbying from the outside. The effectiveness of representation likely falls somewhere in the middle: a strong presentation to a Parliamentary Committee can produce minor amendments to a particular law, but it does nothing to ensure that future policies will reflect the group's priorities. In reality, of course, an effective advocacy group will engage in as many of these activities as its resources permit; for instance, a particular lobbying campaign or committee appearance might be directed, not to a specific policy change, but to securing a place in future consultations.

The Policy Community

Collectively, the government officials and advocacy groups who work together in a given policy field are called the **policy community**. Much public policy-making in Canada occurs within policy communities: loosely defined groups, made up primarily of state actors and representatives of organized interests, which interact to shape public policy in a given sector over time. Within a given policy community, we can distinguish between the subgovernment (the inner circle) and the **discourse community** (the outer circle).

- The subgovernment makes the actual policy decisions. It includes the relevant minister or ministers, along with some of their exempt staff; the senior policy officials in their departments or agencies; provincial officials, where appropriate; and "representatives of the few [advocacy] groups whose opinions and support are essential."[39] These groups possess the resources and the political clout to "meet the demands of subgovernment work":

  > *day-to-day communication between agency officials and representatives of companies or groups; automatic group inclusion on advisory committees and panels of experts; invitations to comment on draft policy; participation on committees or commissions charged with long-range policy review; and continual formal and informal access to agency officials.*[40]

  To be included in the subgovernment, an advocacy group must participate in regular consultations; some may also participate in the design and implementation of regulatory policies.

- The discourse community includes those groups and individuals that are excluded from the subgovernment. They include academic specialists (in universities, think tanks, and private consulting firms); journalists with a particular interest in the policy field; and groups that lack the resources or the political legitimacy to secure a place at the table where policy choices are made.

There are five key differences between the advocacy groups that are included in the subgovernment and those that are excluded.

1. As previously discussed, some advocacy groups possess the structure and the resources to meet the demands of subgovernment participation; others do not.

2. The members of some advocacy groups are prepared to make compromises in exchange for securing some of their policy goals. Others are reluctant to play the political game, because they fear being "co-opted" or they question the legitimacy of the power structure as a whole. The former are more likely to gain access to the subgovernment than the latter.

3. In general, a group that espouses mainstream policy positions is more likely to gain access to the subgovernment than one that speaks for a "fringe" element in society.[41] The distinction between "legitimate" and "fringe" positions can shift, depending on political circumstances.[42] For example, in the 1990s the Reform Party successfully refocused the discourse on criminal justice away from the rights of suspects to the rights of victims. As the **political salience** of violent crime increased, victims' rights groups—which had been absent from the drafting of the legal rights in the *Charter*—became increasingly prominent in legislative battles over amendments to the *Criminal Code*.[43] Similarly, women's groups were generally excluded from the policy process until the 1970s; when representatives of women did appear before a Parliamentary Committee or a Royal Commission, they were patronized and their submissions were dismissed.[44]

4. A group leader or spokesperson with expertise in the policy field and the processes of government will enjoy considerably more influence than a political neophyte.[45] Fluency in the arcane language of policy-making allows the leader to fit in with the public servants; intimate knowledge of the process permits the leader to make valued contributions to the work of the subgovernment.

5. Finally, an advocacy group that forges long-term coalitions with other subgovernment groups will be more effective than one that isolates itself from potential allies. When groups form coalitions, they maximize their collective resources and demonstrate a long-term commitment to the subgovernment.[46] In contrast, dissension among the non-government organizations allows public servants to divide and conquer—which

makes it easier for them to withhold resources and reject demands on behalf of the members.

Once an advocacy group has gained access to the subgovernment, it must secure its position by following unwritten rules of policy-making.[47] In particular, the leadership must observe the usual norms of bureaucratic behaviour: discretion, cooperation (as opposed to confrontation), decision-making based on solid factual information and rational debate, and a clear understanding of the division of responsibilities within the political and permanent executives. A subgovernment advocacy group that provides reliable information and advice to policymakers, and represents its membership according to the norms and values of the permanent executive, can exercise significant and continuing influence within the policy process. On the other hand, a group that publicly criticizes a minister or the Government as a whole risks forfeiting the goodwill of the executive branch and losing its place in the subgovernment.

ADVOCACY GROUPS AND CANADIAN POLITICAL INSTITUTIONS

■ The Executive Branch

From a dead start thirty-five years ago in Canada, there are now some fifty lobbying firms listed in the Ottawa directory. . . . By one count, there are now about 2,000 lobbyists in Ottawa. A number of these are highly paid and politically partisan; they could not easily survive a change of political power in Ottawa. However, because they are politically partisan, they have access to ministers and to the prime minister and his or her court.[48]

In the past quarter-century, Ottawa and the provincial capitals have blossomed with companies and individuals promising to influence the executive branch of government on behalf of their clients. For reasons of ideology and personal contacts, specific firms tend to be in favour with specific governments at any given time. For example, questions were raised about Prime Minister Martin's relationship with Ottawa-based Earnscliffe Research and Communications. Earnscliffe had two separate departments: "one did more traditional lobbying and consulting work with industries and private-sector interests; the other, the research arm, worked primarily with government departments and ministers' offices."[49] Several senior members of the firm's research department, and at least one of its lobbyists, played key roles in Paul Martin's campaign to replace Jean Chrétien as Liberal leader and prime minister between 2000 and 2003. The nasty and high-profile power struggle within the governing party drew public and media attention to Earnscliffe, and raised questions about potential conflicts of interest. One parliamentary reporter put it this way: "You could go to Earnscliffe to lobby for an item in the budget, fully aware that the other side was deeply involved in preparing that budget."[50]

These questions grew more pointed after Martin became prime minister. Some former Earnscliffe staffers joined his transition team, and subsequently took positions in the Prime Minister's Office (PMO). To date, no allegations of conflict have been proven. Earnscliffe's senior partners insisted that there was no improper communication between the two halves of the business, which were formally separated into two distinct companies during Martin's term as prime minister. However, it is unlikely that the "government relations" side is as active or as powerful today as it was before the 2006 election: when governments change, so do their favoured lobbying firms.[51]

In 1989, long-standing concerns about the influence of cronyism and high-priced "consultants" finally led to the adoption of the *Lobbyists Registration Act* (LRA). The LRA was subsequently amended four times between 1995 and 2004.[52] The preamble states that "lobbying public office holders is a legitimate activity," which should not be unduly restricted; at the same time, "it is desirable that public office holders and the public be able to know who is engaged in lobbying activities."[53] The text of the law suggests that its authors were more concerned about facilitating lobbying than about making information public.

The law defines a lobbyist as a person who arranges a meeting between a client and a public official to discuss matters related to public policy or government funding, or who communicates directly with a public official on behalf of a client, in exchange for payment. The registration requirements in the 1989 law were minimal at best. Professional lobbyists—the "hired guns" whose activities had inspired the law—only had to disclose the names of their clients and the subject-matter of their contacts with public officials to the Registrar. In-house lobbyists, employed full-time by corporations and advocacy groups, "were not required to report their lobbying activities; interest groups were not required to file even minimal information concerning their objectives and supporters."[54]

Section 14 of the LRA required periodic parliamentary reviews to improve its effectiveness, which helps to explain the frequent amendments. By 2004 the law was somewhat stronger, but still unsatisfactory. It applies to three separate categories of lobbyists, all of whom must register and file public reports of their lobbying activities:

1. A consultant lobbyist is an individual who seeks to influence a public office holder on behalf of a client, in exchange for monetary payment. These are the professional, full-time "government relations" personnel employed by companies like Earnscliffe.

2. An in-house corporate lobbyist is a person who works for a commercial company (other than a lobbying firm), and who spends a certain percentage of his or her working time on lobbying the federal government.

3. An in-house organizational lobbyist is similar to a corporate lobbyist, except that he or she works for an entity other than a for-profit corporation—including an advocacy group.[55]

The amended LRA did not require the disclosure of payments to consultant lobbyists, or of the costs incurred in pursuit of policy influence. The 1996 amendments did require the disclosure of the specific departments targeted by lobbying efforts, the general subject-matter of each contact, and the methods used to communicate with officials and with the public (including "grassroots" media campaigns).[56] No steps were taken to ensure compliance with the registration and disclosure requirements. In practice, lobbyists and their clients or employers could evade the law easily if they wished to do so (for example, to conceal trade secrets from competing government relations firms).[57] A more common problem was a simple lack of awareness of the LRA. The relatively small circle of Ottawa-based consultant lobbyists was keenly aware of the registration and disclosure requirements. "Outside this community, the *Lobbyists Registration Act* is largely unknown, even though many businesses, universities, hospitals, social service organizations and other non-profit organizations have regular dealings with the federal government, often employing legal advisors and consultants who undertake activities that the Act describes as lobbying."[58] Partly as a result, "there is no way of knowing how many individuals are, at any one time, communicating with government with a view to influencing public decisions."[59]

In addition to the LRA, Canadian lobbyists are expected to comply with a Code of Conduct that took effect in 1997. The Code is a brief document that contains few specifics. For example, it requires lobbyists to "observe the highest professional and ethical standards," without spelling out what those might be.[60] The Code is not legally binding, and there are no formal penalties for lobbyists who are found to have violated one or more of the rules. The Registrar was responsible for investigating alleged breaches of the Code, and reporting any substantiated breaches to Parliament. Only one such report appeared on the Registrar's website in August 2007 (it subsequently disappeared from the website); that report exonerated the lobbyist involved.

By 2004, despite the numerous amendments, the LRA was little more effective than it had been in 1989. In particular, the law did not regulate the activities of lobbyists; nor did it provide for the meaningful investigation and punishment of infractions. As Dossier 13.2 explains, the Sponsorship Scandal finally provided the political impetus to tighten the regulatory regime for lobbyists, although lobbying played a fairly minor role in the scandal.

Despite its limitations, the LRA has generated a large (though incomplete) volume of data about the activities of registered lobbyists in Ottawa. The number of registered lobbyists has risen dramatically in recent years, at least in the in-house categories. Table 13.2 displays the number of lobbyists in each category in 2000–01 and 2007. It also displays the number of active registrations reported in August 2007. The discrepancy between the two sets of numbers for 2007 is particularly interesting: it shows that the average professional (consultant) lobbyist had reported 3.4 separate communication campaigns, whereas only a small fraction of the in-house lobbyists had disclosed even one.

DOSSIER 13.2 The Impact of the Sponsorship Scandal on Canadian Lobbyists

The Gomery Inquiry into the Sponsorship Scandal (Dossier 8.2) drew public attention to the loopholes in the regulatory regime for lobbyists. Justice Gomery found that several individuals had lobbied the Department of Government Works and Public Services on behalf of advertising firms looking to profit from federal sponsorship and advertising contracts. None of these individuals had complied with the *Lobbyists Registration Act*. Recall that anyone who contacted a public official on behalf of a client, and who received money for doing so, was required by law to register as a lobbyist. One of those who failed to register was Chuck Guité, the public servant in charge of the Sponsorship Program. When Guité retired from the federal government in 1999, "he immediately offered his services as a consultant, lobbyist or intermediary to the persons and corporations in the private sector with whom he had been contracting on behalf of Public Works and Government Services Canada. This gave rise to obvious suspicions that there may have been a connection between the benefits accruing to Mr. Guité from his post-retirement activities and the contracts that he dispensed while he was working for the Government."[61] Guité's lobbying activities also violated the Government of Canada post-employment code, which prohibited former public servants from lobbying their prior departments for a full year after their retirement or resignation.[62]

Although Gomery believed that lobbying was a legitimate activity, he expressed concern about the apparently widespread failure to comply with the applicable laws and policies.[63] He identified two reasons for this failure: a lack of political will to enforce the LRA, and a refusal to allocate sufficient resources to the Registrar of Lobbyists.[64] Gomery recommended that the Office of the Registrar be removed from the Department of Industry and given a direct reporting relationship to Parliament. He also called on future governments to increase funding for public education about the LRA and enforcement of its provisions.

Gomery's recommendations were echoed in the *Federal Accountability Act,* along with additional measures to strengthen the regulatory regime.
- First, the Registrar of Lobbying was replaced by a new Officer of Parliament, styled the Commissioner of Lobbying.
- Second, the investigatory powers of the commissioner are significantly stronger than those that were available to the

(continued)

Registrar. However, he or she does not have the power to penalize or prosecute anyone on the basis of his or her investigations; that power remains with the RCMP, which did not lay a single charge under the LRA between 1989 and 2007.

- Third, the FAA banned lobbyists from charging or accepting contingency fees for their services. Under a contingency arrangement, the lobbyist defers payment until the client's goals have been achieved— for example, arranging a meeting between the client and a Cabinet minister. This gives the lobbyist a powerful incentive to promote the client's interest by any means necessary, possibly including corruption or manipulation of public officials.
- Fourth, the FAA prohibited ministers, parliamentarians, exempt staff, senior public servants, and other designated office holders from engaging in paid lobbying for a full five years after leaving government service.[65]
- Finally, the disclosure provisions were broadened: lobbyists must now disclose, on a monthly basis, the name of every public office holder whom they have contacted on behalf of a client, as well as the purpose of each contact. A lobbyist who is convicted of a serious violation under the renamed

Lobbyists Act is liable to a stiff fine, and may be barred from lobbying for up to two years.[66]

Like several key provisions in the FAA, the amendments to the LRA were not implemented until well after the law received royal assent in December 2006. They were set to take effect in July 2008.[67] At the time of writing, the potential impact of the changes was unknown. At least one loophole remains: lobbyists are required to disclose any prior positions they may have held in government (a change made in 2003), but not their connections to a political party. This information gap is partially addressed by the provisions applying to exempt staff and the transition team of an incoming prime minister; but other party members can fly under the radar. When a lobbyist can call in a political debt from a Cabinet minister on behalf of his or her clients, "the person or firm that can afford to buy the lobbyist's time [receives] preferential access to public office holders."[68] Well-connected lobbyists can charge their clients higher fees, on the assumption that they are more likely to get results. To the extent that lobbying actually works (which, as we have seen, is impossible to measure), this gives the wealthiest interests a better chance to influence policymakers than their poorer rivals.

TABLE 13.2 NUMBER OF ACTIVE LOBBYISTS IN THE THREE CATEGORIES, 2000–07

CATEGORY	NUMBER OF ACTIVE LOBBYISTS, 2000–01	NUMBER OF ACTIVE LOBBYISTS, AUGUST 2007	NUMBER OF ACTIVE REGISTRATIONS, AUGUST 2007
Consultants	788	852	2913
In-house (corporate)	299	1736	287
In-house (other organizations)	356	2396	426
TOTAL	1443	4984	3626

Sources: From "Lobbyists' Registration Act Annual Report for the Year Ended March 31, 2002" and "Active Lobbyists by Type, 2007/08/21," Office of the Commissioner of Lobbying of Canada (ocl-cal.gc.ca). Reproduced with the permission of the Minister of Public Works and Government Services Canada, 2008.

One limitation of the LRA data is that they do not distinguish between the three activities identified at the beginning of this chapter. Every contact between an in-house representative of an advocacy group (the third category) and a public official is categorized as "lobbying," regardless of its nature. In all likelihood, many if not most of the individuals in the third category engage in continuing subgovernment consultations rather than one-off "lobbying" campaigns. (Note that many instances of representation, such as an appearance before a parliamentary committee, are expressly exempted from the reporting requirements.) Therefore, the data do not allow us to measure the true extent of advocacy groups' policy-related activities.

However, they do tell us which policy areas and government departments attract the greatest attention from advocacy groups. Table 13.3 shows the top 20 subjects of lobbying at the federal level. The top three categories are business-related, highlighting concerns about the influence and resources of corporate interests. Table 13.4 lists the federal departments and agencies that were the most frequent targets of lobbying in 2000–01 and 2007, according to the information filed by registered lobbyists in those years. It is no coincidence that three of the top five departments—Industry, Finance, and Foreign Affairs and International Trade—are particularly important to the business sector.

TABLE 13.3 TOP SUBJECTS OF LOBBYING, BY NUMBER OF ACTIVE REGISTRATIONS, 2000–01 AND 2007

SUBJECT OF LOBBYING	2000–01 RANKING	2007 RANKING
Industry	1	1
International Trade	2	3
Taxation and Finance	3	2
Environment	4	4
Science and Technology	5	6
Health	6	5
Consumer Issues	7	11
Transportation	8	7
Employment and Training	9	8
Internal Trade	10	19
International Relations	11	14
Energy	12	9
Regional Development	13	10
Intellectual Property	14	18
Government Procurement	15	12
Agriculture	16	16
Small Business	17	–
Infrastructure	18	13
Labour	19	–
Telecommunications	20	–
Aboriginal Affairs	–	15
Defence	–	17
Financial Institutions	–	20

Sources: From "Lobbyists' Registration Act Annual Report for the Year Ended March 31, 2002" and "Active Lobbyists by Type, 2007/08/21," Office of the Commissioner of Lobbying of Canada (ocl-cal.gc.ca). Reproduced with the permission of the Minister of Public Works and Government Services Canada, 2008.

TABLE 13.4 FEDERAL GOVERNMENTS AND AGENCIES, RANKED BY NUMBER OF ACTIVE REGISTRATIONS, 2000–01 AND 2007

DEPARTMENT OR AGENCY	2000–01 RANKING	2007 RANKING
Industry Canada	1	1
Finance Canada	2	2
Foreign Affairs and International Trade	3	5
Members of the House of Commons	—	4
Environment Canada	5	6
Transport Canada	7	8
Health Canada	6	7
Revenue Canada	4	12
Prime Minister's Office	—	10
Privy Council Office	8	3
Natural Resources Canada	10	11
Human Resources Development Canada	11	14
Public Works and Government Services Canada	9	13
Canadian Heritage	13	18
Agriculture and Agri-Food Canada	14	15
Treasury Board of Canada	12	9
Fisheries and Oceans Canada	15	21
National Defence	16	17
Justice Canada	17	19
Western Economic Diversification Canada	19	20
Indian and Northern Affairs Canada*	—	16
Canadian International Development Agency	18	22

*This department was not in the top 20 identified by lobbyists in their registrations for the 2000–01 period.

Sources: From "Lobbyists' Registration Act Annual Report for the Year Ended March 31, 2002" and "Active Lobbyists by Type, 2007/08/21," Office of the Commissioner of Lobbying of Canada (ocl-cal.gc.ca). Reproduced with the permission of the Minister of Public Works and Government Services Canada, 2008.

Table 13.4 reveals that lobbyists have altered their targets in recent years. The most interesting changes concern the two key central agencies (Chapter 9). Between 2001 and 2007, the Privy Council Office attracted a much greater volume of lobbying and the Prime Minister's Office became a significant target of lobbyists for the first time. The government relations industry has clearly recognized the concentration of power at the centre of the executive branch, and refocused its efforts accordingly. Moreover, lobbying central agencies illustrates a key problem: the secretive and unaccountable nature of contacts between the representatives of organized interests and the executive branch of government.

▓ The Legislative Branch

Cabinet ministers and senior officials are more frequent targets of lobbying than backbench MPs and senators. For a few years, former Prime Minister Martin's pledge to give backbench

MPs more influence prompted some lobbyists to change their strategies.[69] In general, however, lobbyists recognize that individual MPs are minor players in the policy process (not without reason, as Chapter 7 explains) so they direct their persuasive efforts elsewhere.[70]

As we saw in Chapter 7, there have been repeated attempts to reform the House of Commons in order to provide greater autonomy to backbench MPs. Recent reforms to the standing committee system have encouraged advocacy groups to divert some of their attention from the subgovernment to the parliamentary arena. As a result, the scope of parliamentary consultations over major pieces of legislation has expanded dramatically. This is true of foreign and trade policy, where, for example, there are now annual consultations on broad policy and on human rights.[71] It also applies to the annual federal budget, which has been shaped since 1994 by consultations with the Standing Committee on Finance.[72] Thousands of Canadians appear before the committees of the House of Commons and Senate every year. For advocacy groups that are excluded from the subgovernment, such an opportunity for representation may be their best chance to influence public policy. But as we saw in Chapters 7 and 8, a Cabinet that controls a majority of the seats in the Commons can disregard committee recommendations that do not conform to the priorities of the political executive and the central agencies.

◼ The Judicial Branch

Since 1982, the *Charter of Rights and Freedoms* has expanded the policy role of the courts (Chapters 6 and 10). Previously, groups disgruntled with a particular law or policy could only lobby the legislative and executive branches of government. Now, if they have the resources, they can pursue *Charter*-based litigation in the hope of changing public policy. For example, the October 2004 Supreme Court hearings into the constitutionality of same-sex marriage attracted more than two dozen interventions—many from interest groups on both sides of the issue.[73] The day before the hearings began, two separate news conferences were held in Ottawa: one sponsored by groups favouring same-sex marriage and the other by opponents. Because the issue concerns section 15 of the *Charter*, the guarantee of equality rights, many of these groups would have been eligible for support from the federally funded Court Challenges Program (CCP). The CCP was established in 1985, shut down in 1992, and revived in 1993; the Harper Government cancelled the program for a second time in 2006 (see Chapter 6).[74] The CCP supported **public-interest litigation** based on either the equality rights or the official-language minority rights (sections 16–23) in the *Charter*. As the example of the same-sex marriage hearings demonstrates, there are no guarantees of success in *Charter* litigation; the groups opposed to same-sex marriage failed in their efforts to sway the Supreme Court. Moreover, public-interest litigation is enormously expensive, which makes it a risky strategy for advocacy groups with limited resources.[75]

ADVOCACY GROUPS AND GLOBALIZATION

As policy-making shifts from the nation–state to supranational bodies, advocacy groups are forming international, sometimes worldwide, coalitions with other state-based groups and with older transnational organizations. For example, Canada's Aboriginal organizations have forged strong links with similar groups in other countries, and with environmentalists. These alliances succeeded in forcing Canadian governments to change certain policies. The James Bay Cree recruited American environmental activist Robert Kennedy Jr. to pressure U.S. states not to buy hydroelectric power from Quebec as a protest against provincial efforts to expand its power-generating facilities on Cree land.[76]

Rows of makeshift tombstones representing job losses at Canadian manufacturing facilities are lined up on the front lawn of Parliament Hill as part of a protest organized by labour unions, May 30, 2007. (CP/Fred Chartrand)

There is nothing new about international networks of activists; decades before the term "globalization" was coined, **nongovernmental organizations (NGOs)** took shape across borders to combat the slave trade and the oppression of women. "What *is* new is the recent explosion in numbers, activity, and visibility of international initiatives by civil society actors on a variety of issues, at least in part linked to the rapid expansion of globalization of communications, transportation, and production."[77] The attraction of global networks for domestic advocacy groups is obvious: they "enable citizens who have only limited political voice within national political institutions to amplify their voice, and to highlight harms and injustices that might otherwise be neglected."[78] It must be noted, however, that transnational advocacy groups direct most of their lobbying efforts toward national and provincial states; supranational bodies are increasingly important, but they have not yet supplanted nation-states as the prime target of policy campaigns.

CONCLUSION

This chapter has argued that advocacy groups, despite their relative success in achieving their policy goals, do not provide an effective link between Canadian citizens and their political institutions. Group leaders claim to speak on behalf of others, but those claims should not be taken at face value without some proof that they represent an active and engaged membership. Notwithstanding their flaws, advocacy groups will continue to play an important role in the policy-making process. Unlike politicians and political parties, whose legitimacy has

Police keep watch as several thousand protesters march towards the U.S. embassy in Ottawa, August 2007. The march was to protest Prime Minister Stephen Harper's two-day meeting with U.S. President George W. Bush and Mexico's President Felipe Calderon. (CP/Jonathan Hayward)

declined in recent decades, advocacy groups are generally held in high regard by most Canadians. The elimination of the CCP has made it more difficult for less wealthy groups to initiate *Charter* litigation, but some of the better-established groups will continue to pursue their policy goals in the courts.

At the same time, the executive branches at both the federal and provincial levels of government are increasingly dependent on NGOs for policy expertise and program delivery—despite deep cuts to funding and support for advocacy groups since the 1980s. While much of the responsibility for delivering social services has been downloaded to the "third sector" (voluntary and charitable organizations), the financial and logistical support needed to make program delivery work effectively have diminished. Finally, as mentioned above, advocacy groups are using new information technologies to build their capacity to mobilize and to build coalitions; these developments may give them greater influence in policy-making, although dispersed networks of activists lack the tools to hold governments accountable for their promises or to participate in the delivery of the programs that they seek to promote.

GLOSSARY OF KEY TERMS

Advocacy groups: Movements or interest groups that try to influence public policy, to alter conventional perceptions of the political and social status quo, and/or to mobilize support for projects for political and social change. Examples include the women's movement, the Aboriginal rights movement, and the environmental movement.

Collective action: The organized pursuit of a shared goal by a group of people; can be formal and structured (a military unit in combat) or informal and loosely structured (neighbours gathering to protest a zoning change).

Consultation: A state-sponsored process of cooperation between one or more government agencies and select advocacy groups. May include the development of public policy, the shared implementation of new programs, or alternative service-delivery arrangements.

Co-optation: The process by which an advocacy group, which opposes certain elements of state policy, is induced to accept the ideology or the policy priorities of the government. The most powerful tool of co-optation is public funding, although some groups fear that a close working relationship with state agencies could have the same effect. Groups that oppose the status quo on principle fear that the exercise of power might erode their independence and even corrupt their leaders.

Discourse community: See the definition of policy community below.

Interest group: An organization of people who seek to promote a common goal.

Lobbying: The effort to influence public policy directly, by persuading decision-makers in the political and permanent executives to adopt the goals of a particular group or individual. May be public (media events, appearing before a Commons committee) or private (meeting with the assistant deputy minister responsible for that policy file).

Nongovernmental organization (NGO): A group that operates outside the formal structure of government, as defined in the *Constitution,* and that seeks to participate in the policy process (from agenda-setting to policy formulation, and, ultimately, implementation).

Policy capacity: The tangible and intangible resources that an advocacy group can devote to its participation in the policy community. If it has sufficient policy capacity—e.g., expert knowledge and the resources to mobilize its members to implement a new program—it can become a member of the subgovernment.

Policy community: The mix of groups and individuals with a particular interest in a specific policy field. Divided into the subgovernment (inner circle) and the discourse community, a broader universe of groups and individuals "who have some knowledge of the policy issue in question and who collectively construct a policy discourse"[79] (outer circle). Usually contains one or more distinct policy networks. The structure and influence of the policy community in a given policy sector depends on three factors: the autonomy and policy capacity of the state agency or agencies, the strength of the advocacy groups in that sector, and the relationship among the members of the subgovernment.

Policy network: The term used to describe the web of relationships among the members of a particular policy community.

Political salience: (1) The perceived legitimacy of a particular advocacy group; the congruence between its goals and those of the government. (2) The importance accorded to a particular policy issue at a given time by the news media, advocacy groups, respondents to opinion surveys, and/or politicians. The political salience of a particular issue at a given time is reflected in its position on the policy agenda: the most salient issues (e.g., health care) receive the greatest amount of government attention, whereas those with less salience may be ignored. The salience of an issue is not a function of its intrinsic importance. For example, environmental issues had relatively little salience in the early twenty-first century, despite the obvious dangers posed by climate change and expanding human population. They were eclipsed by fears of terrorism, the wars in Afghanistan and Iraq, and concerns about the apparent shrinkage of world oil supply, among other issues.

Public-interest litigation: The effort to change laws and other government policies through the courts. In the *Charter* context, this involves a legal challenge to the constitutionality of a particular law or program, or a claim that a specific government official violated the rights or freedoms of the plaintiff.

Representation: In the context of the policy community, representation is the midpoint between lobbying from the outside and consultations on the inside. Representation entails speaking on behalf of a particular interest, usually at the invitation of the state, but unlike consultation, it may not reflect a continuing and close working relationship between the advocacy group and the government agencies in a particular policy field.

Subgovernment: The inner circle of the policy community. Includes the key advocacy groups and members of the political and permanent executives, who work together to formulate and implement public policy in a specific area (e.g., health care or agriculture).

DISCUSSION AND REVIEW QUESTIONS

1. Why are Canadians increasingly turning to advocacy groups, rather than political parties, to represent their interests in federal politics? In your opinion, is this the right choice? Why or why not?

2. Have you ever belonged to an advocacy group? If so, did you participate in efforts to influence political decision-makers? What were those efforts? In your view, did they succeed?

3. Identify and briefly describe TWO important differences between the groups that are admitted to the subgovernment, and those that are excluded.

4. Should a staff-led advocacy group be admitted to the subgovernment? Why or why not?

SUGGESTED READINGS

Books and Articles

Robert M. Campbell and Leslie A. Pal, *The Real Worlds of Canadian Politics: Cases in Process and Policy,* 3rd edition (Peterborough, ON: Broadview Press, 1994).

William D. Coleman and Grace Skogstad, eds., *Policy Communities and Public Policy in Canada: A Structural Approach* (Toronto: Copp Clark Pitman, 1990).

Michael Howlett, "Do Networks Matter? Linking Policy Network Structure to Policy Outcomes: Evidence from Four Canadian Policy Sectors 1990–2000," *Canadian Journal of Political Science,* 35:2 (June 2002), 235–67.

Leslie A. Pal, *Interests of State: The Politics of Language, Multiculturalism, and Feminism in Canada* (Montreal and Kingston: McGill–Queen's University Press, 1993).

A. Paul Pross, *Group Politics and Public Policy,* 2nd edition (Toronto: Oxford University Press, 1992).

Francesca Scala, Éric Montpetit and Isabelle Fortier, "The NAC's Organizational Practices and the Politics of Assisted Reproductive Technologies in Canada," *Canadian Journal of Political Science,* 38:3 (September 2005), 581–604.

Miriam Smith, *A Civil Society? Collective Actors in Canadian Political Life* (Peterborough: Broadview Press, 2005).

A. Trevor Thrall, "The Myth of the Outside Strategy: Mass Media News Coverage of Interest Groups," *Political Communication,* 23 (2006), 407–420.

Lisa Young and Joanna Everitt, *Advocacy Groups* (Vancouver: UBC Press, 2004).

Websites

Most of the major advocacy groups in Canada and elsewhere have set up websites, either for themselves alone or shared with related organizations. Examples include the Child Care Advocacy Association of Canada (www.childcareadvocacy.ca); Greenpeace International (www.greenpeace.org), which is linked to national Greenpeace sites; and the Canadian Council of Chief Executives, formerly the Business Council on National Issues (www.bcni.com). Industry Canada's Strategis website (www.strategis.gc.ca), devoted to Canadian business and consumer matters, provides information about the Lobbyists Registration System.

NOTES

1. Kennith G. Hunter, "An Application of Herd Theory to Interest Group Behavior," *Administration and Society,* 34:4 (September 2002), 390.

2. For example, a recent—and generally excellent—study of policy networks in Canada implicitly attributes recent changes in federal funding for postsecondary education (PSE) to the relationship between government and nongovernment actors in that policy field. See Michael Howlett, "Do Networks Matter? Linking Policy Network Structure to Policy Outcomes: Evidence from Four Canadian Policy Sectors 1990–2000," *Canadian Journal of Political Science,* 35:2 (June 2002), 235–67. But among the policy changes listed in the study are the 1995 CHST and the subsequent increases in the amount of federal cash given to the provinces for health care and PSE. As explained in Chapter 4 of this book, the CHST was inspired by the federal Cabinet's determination to eliminate the national deficit, not by

extraneous lobbying from the PSE sector. Moreover, the later increases in cash payments to the provinces were driven, not by the demands of universities, colleges, and students, but by growing public concern over the delivery of health care.

3. Lisa Young and Joanna Everitt, *Advocacy Groups* (Vancouver: UBC Press, 2004), 5.

4. Paul Howe and David Northrup, "Strengthening Canadian Democracy: The Views of Canadians," *Policy Matters*, 1:5 (Montreal: Institute for Research on Public Policy, July 2000), 33; accessed at www.irpp.org.

5. Young and Everitt, 27–29.

6. Howe and Northrup, 34.

7. Miriam Smith, *A Civil Society? Collective Actors in Canadian Political Life* (Peterborough: Broadview Press, 2005), 52–53.

8. Young and Everitt, 30–34.

9. Ibid., 34–35.

10. Ibid., 53.

11. Ibid., 55.

12. Young and Everitt (54) cite the example of membership-based environmental groups that have been invaded by forestry unions, in an effort to silence their opposition to logging.

13. Bartha Knoppers, member of the Royal Commission on New Reproductive Technologies, quoted in Francesca Scala, Éric Montpetit, and Isabelle Fortier, "The NAC's Organizational Practices and the Politics of Assisted Reproductive Technologies in Canada," *Canadian Journal of Political Science*, 38:3 (September 2005), 593 (square brackets in original).

14. Young and Everitt, 56.

15. Scala, Montpetit and Fortier, 581–582.

16. A. Paul Pross, *Group Politics and Public Policy*, 2nd edition (Toronto: Oxford University Press, 1992), 199.

17. Ibid., 200.

18. A. Trevor Thrall, "The Myth of the Outside Strategy: Mass Media News Coverage of Interest Groups," *Political Communication*, 23 (2006), 408.

19. Robert A. Hackett, *News and Dissent: The Press and the Politics of Peace in Canada* (Norwood, N.J.: Ablex Publishing Corporation, 1991), 23.

20. Ibid., 22.

21. Ibid., 22.

22. Leslie A. Pal, *Beyond Policy Analysis: Public Issue Management in Turbulent Times*, 1st edition (Scarborough, Ont.: ITP Nelson, 1997), 212.

23. Patrick J. Monahan, *Meech Lake: The Inside Story* (Toronto: University of Toronto Press, 1991), 141–42.

24. Pross, *Group Politics*, 101.

25. Ibid., 155.

26. Donald J. Savoie, *Breaking the Bargain: Public Servants, Ministers, and Parliament* (Toronto: University of Toronto Press, 2003), 106.

27. Leslie A. Pal, *Interests of State: The Politics of Language, Multiculturalism, and Feminism in Canada* (Montreal and Kingston: McGill–Queen's University Press, 1993), 42.

28. Ibid., 42.

29. Ibid., 43.

30. Ibid., 48–51.

31. Ibid., 277.

32. Ibid., 43.

33. Ibid., 44–45.

34. Young and Everitt, 78.

35. Ibid., 79.

36. Pal, *Beyond Policy Analysis,* 213.

37. David McInnes, *Taking It to the Hill: The Complete Guide to Appearing Before (and Surviving) Parliamentary Committees* (Ottawa: University of Ottawa Press, 1999), 1.

38. Pal, *Beyond Policy Analysis,* 218.

39. Pross, *Group Politics,* 121.

40. Ibid., 121.

41. Ibid., 96.

42. Howlett found that the number of groups involved in trade and transportation policy shrank between 1990 and 2000, although the membership of the policy community remained relatively stable. In contrast, the number of groups with an interest in PSE and banking policy expanded over the same period, and the membership of the policy community was far less stable. See Howlett, "Do Networks Matter?" 254–59.

43. See Kent Roach, *Due Process and Victims' Rights: The New Law and Politics of Criminal Justice* (Toronto: University of Toronto Press, 1999), especially 48–50, 79–81, and 278–312.

44. Matt James, *Misrecognized Materialists: Social Movements in Canadian Constitutional Politics* (Vancouver: UBC Press, 2006), 17–22 and 35–37.

45. A classic illustration of this difference occurred during the 1943 hearings of the House of Commons Special Committee on Reconstruction. One of Canada's two largest labour organizations, the Trades and Labour Congress of Canada, was represented by acting president Percy Bengough. His inflammatory statements and his lack of formal credentials provoked hostility and condescension from the committee members; he failed to present his organization's policy demands effectively. The other, the Canadian Congress of Labour, sent its director of Research to speak to the Committee. Dr. Eugene Forsey "received an almost deferential response" from the MPs, despite offering a critique of capitalism that strongly resembled Bengough's. "Forsey's academic credentials, intellectual skills, and professional polish garnered his presentation the respectful attention that Bengough's was denied." James, 32–35. Forsey enjoyed a lengthy and influential career as a political expert and gadfly; he was appointed to the Senate by Prime Minister Trudeau in 1970.

46. Pross, *Group Politics,* 156.

47. Ibid., 147–54.

48. Donald J. Savoie, *Court Government and the Collapse of Accountability in Canada and the United Kingdom* (Toronto: University of Toronto Press, 2008), 156.

49. Susan Delacourt, *Juggernaut: Paul Martin's Campaign for Chrétien's Crown* (Toronto: McClelland and Stewart, 2003), 87.

50. Ibid., 87.

51. John Sawatsky, *The Insiders: Government, Business, and the Lobbyists* (Toronto: McClelland and Stewart, 1987).

52. A. Paul Pross, "The *Lobbyists Registration Act:* Its Application and Effectiveness," in Donald Savoie, ed., *The Public Service and Transparency,* volume 2 of the collected research studies for the Commission of Inquiry into the Sponsorship Program and Advertising Activities [the Gomery Inquiry] (Ottawa: Minister of Public Works and Government Services, 2006), 163.

53. *Lobbyists Registration Act,* R.S. 1985, c. 44; accessed at www.canlii.org, August 2007.

54. Pross, "The Lobbyists Registration Act," 166.

55. *Lobbyists Registration Act,* sections 5–7.

56. Ibid., section 5(2)(j).

57. Pross, "The Lobbyists Registration Act," 188.

58. Ibid., 186.

59. Ibid., 187.

60. Canada, Office of the Registrar of Lobbyists, "Lobbyists' Code of Conduct"; accessed at http://www.ocl-cal.gc.ca/epic/site/lobbyist-lobbyiste1.nsf/en/h_nx00269e.html, August 2007. Please note that the changes to the *Lobbying Act* and the Code, as well as the regulations arising from the *Federal Accountability Act,* had not yet taken effect as of June 2008.

61. Commission of Inquiry Into the Sponsorship Program and Advertising Activities, *What Went Wrong?* (Ottawa: Minister of Public Works and Government Services, 2005), 402.

62. Ibid., 414.

63. Commission of Inquiry into the Sponsorship Program and Advertising Activities [the Gomery Commission], *Restoring Accountability: Recommendations* (Ottawa: Minister of Public Works and Government Services, 2006), 171–172.

64. Ibid., 173.

65. This provision has allegedly made it more difficult for ministers to recruit top-quality exempt staff. As explained in Dossier 9.3, political staffers often move into the "government relations" business after a few years. By closing the "revolving door" between government and lobbying, the FAA made exempt positions less attractive to ambitious young politicos. Kady O'Malley, "FAA makes it tough to recruit top talent in ministerial offices," *The Hill Times,* February 13, 2006, 1. See also Savoie, *Court Government,* 239.

66. Bill C-2, 39th Parliament, 1st Session, sections 65–98; Library of Parliament Research Branch, "Legislative Summary: Bill C-2, The *Federal Accountability Act*" (Ottawa, December 2006), 26–34; both accessed at www.parl.gc.ca, April 2007.

67. Jenefer Curtis, "New FAA regulations still a mystery to some consultant lobbyists," *The Hill Times,* March 5, 2007, 12.

68. Pross, "The Lobbyists Registration Act," 195.

69. Campbell Clark, "Power corridor extends to Q Street," *The Globe and Mail,* January 5, 2004; accessed at www.globeandmail.com.

70. Public Policy Forum, "Members of Parliament and Government Relations Representatives—Defining a New Relationship" (Ottawa, n.d.), 5–6; accessed at www.ppforum.ca, August 2007.

71. Robert M. Campbell and Leslie Pal, *The Real Worlds of Canadian Politics: Cases in Process and Policy,* 3rd edition (Peterborough, ON: Broadview Press, 1994), Chapter 4.

72. Evert A. Lindquist, "Citizens, Experts and Budgets: Evaluating Ottawa's Emerging Budget Process," in Susan D. Phillips, ed., *How Ottawa Spends, 1994–95: Making Change* (Ottawa: Carleton University Press, 1994), 91–128.

73. Luma Muhtadie, "Groups spar over same-sex marriage," *The Globe and Mail,* October 6, 2004; accessed at www.globeandmail.com.

74. On the history of the CCP, see Ian Brodie, "Interest Group Litigation and the Embedded State: Canada's Court Challenges Program," *Canadian Journal of Political Science,* 34:2 (June 2001), 357–76. Brodie became Chief of Staff to Prime Minister Harper in 2006 (Chapter 9).

75. For a more extensive discussion of advocacy groups and the *Charter,* see Heather MacIvor, *Canadian Politics and Government in the Charter Era* (Toronto: Thomson Nelson, 2005), Chapter 6.

76. Will Kymlicka, "New Forms of Citizenship," in Thomas J. Courchene and Donald J. Savoie, eds., *The Art of the State: Governance in a World Without Frontiers* (Montreal: Institute for Research on Public Policy, 2003), 290.

77. L. David Brown, Sanjeev Khagram, Mark H. Moore, and Peter Frumkin, "Globalization, NGOs, and Multisectoral Relations," in Joseph S. Nye and John D. Donahue, eds., *Governance in a Globalizing World* (Washington, D.C.: Brookings Institution Press, 2000), 272.

78. Kymlicka, 291.

79. Howlett, "Do Networks Matter," 248.

Chapter

14

The News Media

LEARNING OBJECTIVES

After you finish reading this chapter, you should be able to:

- *summarize* the political role of the news media in a democracy;
- *identify* and *explain* two ways in which ownership patterns in the Canadian media affect news coverage;
- *define* "news framing," and *analyze* its impact on news coverage of election campaigns;
- *define* "agenda-setting," and *explain* how it influences citizens and political institutions;
- *evaluate* the claim that the Internet undermines the "mainstream media."

INTRODUCTION

Millions of us watch global sporting events like the final game of the World Cup of soccer on television. Tens of thousands pack the stadium. A couple of dozen people are directly involved (the players, officials, and coaches). Their experience of the game is intense but partial and often chaotic; they won't know everything that happened until they watch the tape afterward. The spectators in the stadium see the whole picture, but their perception is indistinct because of the distance from their seats to the pitch. Meanwhile, the TV viewers see only what the camera operators cover, from the angles selected by the producers in the control room. If there was no camera coverage on the spot where a fight started (see p. 65), you may not know who was to blame; you have to rely on the commentators and soccer pundits. A "talking head" who used to be a player may assume that the officials are always wrong, whereas his colleague the retired referee believes that the officials usually get it right. In the end, the only people who really know for certain may be the players directly involved, although their personal stake in the outcome makes them less than reliable witnesses.

Just as relatively few people will ever compete for, or attend, a world championship in any sport, few Canadians have any personal experience of national politics. You may have shaken the hand of an MP or cast a ballot in an election but in all likelihood, you have never attended a party convention or sat in the Commons gallery during Question Period. By reporting on the activities of the Cabinet, the Parliament and the courts, journalists link us to our political institutions. They also provide essential information to politicians—both about their constituents and about each other. Journalists help to set the agenda of political debate. We see political events through the frames that they choose. Because we depend so heavily on the news media for information about politics, that information should be as accurate and comprehensive as possible. Unfortunately, that is not always the case, for reasons which we will explore in this chapter.

Strictly speaking, the news media do not constitute a single, unified institution like the House of Commons or the Supreme Court. Nonetheless, the thousands of professionals who write, record, edit, broadcast, and publish information and opinion about Canadian politics collectively constitute an entity with many of the characteristics of a formal institution:[1]

- shared norms and values;
- a hierarchy of power and status;
- clear incentives for ambitious participants; and
- a distinct role in the political system.

The news media both influence and are influenced by the environment within which they operate. In particular, Canadian media organizations are affected by the powerful American media market, whose products hold great appeal for their English-speaking (and many of their French-speaking) customers. Today's economic and technological environment is changing the structure and operations of media companies around the world, and nowhere more so than in Canada. Despite all the changes, at least one thing remains constant: the crucial role of news coverage in self-government:

> *News matters. Journalism matters. No real democracy can function without healthy, diverse and independent news media to inform people about the way their society works, what is going well and, perhaps most important, what is not going well or needs to be improved. The news of the day is always a rough and ready thing, produced in a rush to deadline and inevitably based on imperfect understanding of complex realities, but it is the first guide citizens have to understanding their own community, and often the only such guide that can plausibly claim not to be self-interested.*[2]

In this chapter, we will focus on four topics:
1. the institutional characteristics of the major news organizations in Canada;
2. the relationship between the media and Canadian citizens;
3. media influence on the three branches of our national government; and
4. the growing political importance of "new media," especially the Internet.

THE CANADIAN NEWS MEDIA: INSTITUTIONAL CHARACTERISTICS

Ownership of Canadian Media Companies

Apart from the Canadian Broadcasting Corporation (which produces the CBC website, Société Radio-Canada, CBC *Newsworld,* and Radio Canada International), Canadian media companies are privately owned. (Most of the owners are Canadian, because of legal restrictions on foreign direct investment in our media industries.) Even the CBC, a Crown corporation subsidized by parliamentary appropriations, has become increasingly dependent on advertising revenues over two decades of spending cuts.

Private ownership affects the ways in which media companies discharge their primary public service: the collection and dissemination of political information. In recent years, Canadian policymakers and journalists have expressed serious concerns about four specific aspects of media ownership:
- the emphasis on profitability over public service;
- the concentration of media ownership in a few hands;

- the absorption of news companies into conglomerates that own other types of media (cross-ownership), or which control a variety of other industries; and
- the real or perceived control of news content by some owners.

The Profit Motive

Like any privately owned company, newspapers and broadcast stations are expected to make money for their owners and shareholders. To do this, they must keep their costs down while boosting their revenues. Both of these economic imperatives conflict with the duty to provide comprehensive political information to citizens. Over the past two decades, the profit motive appears to have become increasingly important to media owners. Today, on average, the profit margin of a Canadian newspaper is between 20 and 30 percent. This is higher than the average for most industries.[3] Conventional television stations and networks are more profitable than specialty cable channels, and radio is more profitable than either, although the news divisions do not contribute much (if any) revenue to the bottom line.[4] For television stations, networks, and channels, it is cheaper to buy American entertainment series than to produce quality news and public affairs programming.[5]

In practice, "cost-cutting" means firing reporters. Maintaining a separate bureau in each region of the country, and permanent offices in foreign capitals, represents a major investment. Serious investigative journalism costs money. Long-term coverage of complex policy issues demands intensive resources and generates few catchy headlines. So the hunt for profit leads private media owners to sacrifice the quantity and quality of news coverage. Dossier 14.1

DOSSIER 14.1 From Family Ownership to Chain Ownership

I am a reporter and editor at the *London Free Press*. . . . We have been sold twice. First, we were sold to Sun Media and then to Quebecor, which now owns Sun Media. If you had looked at our operation 10 to 15 years ago, you would have seen that we had 152 people in the editorial department. Today, the number is 77.

When the *London Free Press* was owned by the Blackburn family, it had twice as many reporters as it does now. It had many more beats. Today, we no longer have reporters assigned to cover agriculture, consumer affairs, environment, labour, religion, social services, and other areas of interest as we once did. The days when the *Free Press* would routinely send beat reporters to national conventions and conferences to cover their beat areas are gone.

We also had bureaus. Our paper had a bureau in Ottawa and in Queen's Park. The bureaus are gone. Those beats are gone. The days when our paper would send reporters to Italy, China, Russia, or even Northern Ontario in pursuit of stories with local angles are all largely gone.

We do not have the space. We do not have the person-power that we once did. There is not the same commitment on the part of employers to do that kind of work on a local basis. There is much more chain content in the papers. There is a reduction in local voices. At my place of employment one of the people who I admired most greatly edited our weekend commentaries section for six years before these takeovers occurred. He tried to continue in his job for one year after we were purchased. He told me he just could not because he had spent six years really beefing up local voices in the paper and, suddenly, we were using Sun Media columnists, many of whom seemed to come out of the same sausage machine.

About 10 years ago, I was told by a manager that I was too thorough, and they did not want that. The manager actually apologized to me. He said, "I hate to say this, but we want quantity, not quality. We want more stories, not fewer good ones." Look at your papers, and look at how many stories are what I would describe as the

(continued)

two-interview story. That is the way it is today. My employer would rather have reporters doing three or four short stories in a day, say, 10 inches, than one or two longer, more informative, more probative stories. We do a lot of the two-interview stories, which is basically get two sides of a question and you have it covered. Anyone who has been a reporter for a long time and worked under the old methods can tell you that sometimes you do not know the story until you have talked to 10, 15, even 20 people and then finally you realize what the story is really all about.

This is the fallout of mergers and chain ownership. The Blackburn family was happy to make a 10-percent return on their investment because they put a lot into the local product. They lived in the community; they were proud of it; they were responsible for it; and they had to account to the people in their own community where they lived and worked. The owners today live afar, they do not have that relationship and they are making vastly greater profits. In the case of the *London Free Press* . . . we are told by recent Sun Media reports that the return was 26 percent in 2002 and 2003. That money goes outside the community to make other media purchases, to finance other mergers and acquisitions. The money does not remain in the community to create better media where it could be better. These changes hit us every day and in every way. It is not that the people who work at regional papers do not care. They still care. People work hard. They are committed. However, the whole nature of the beast has changed.

Source: Joe Matyas, Testimony before the Senate Standing Committee on Transport and Communications, November 24, 2004; *Minutes of Proceedings and Evidence*, 2:40–2:42 (accessed at the Parliamentary Website www.parl.gc.ca, July 2007). Reproduced with the permission of the Minister of Public Works and Government Services, 2008, and courtesy of the Law Clerk & Parliamentary Counsel of the Canadian Senate. [The excerpts in the Dossier were edited and rearranged slightly.]

presents the testimony of one newspaper reporter, whose experience is typical of Canadian news organizations over the past quarter-century.[6]

As their investment in bureaus and local coverage declines, local newspapers rely increasingly on wire services, press releases, and prepackaged news. Wire services make stories available to print and broadcast companies that do not have their own reporters in a particular region. Canada has two national wire services: Canadian Press/Broadcast News, which operates in both official languages, and the CanWest News Service. Canadian Press (CP) is a co-operative agency that distributes wire copy from its own journalists and circulates stories submitted by the 100 newspapers that subscribe to its services.[7] The CanWest service provides an alternative source of copy to the newspapers owned by the CanWest Company. Unlike Canadian Press, the CanWest wire service is expected to turn a profit. When the Southam chain (the former owner of several CanWest papers) threatened to pull out of CP in 1996, the co-operative was forced to lower its subscription fees in order to survive. As a result, CP laid off reporters and closed bureaus in Canada and elsewhere. The Ottawa bureau, which supplies coverage of national politics to most of Canada's news outlets, shrank by almost half.[8] In addition to the domestic wire services, Canadian media companies rely on American and British services (Associated Press, United Press International, Thomson Reuters) for foreign stories. Currently, "about one-third to one-half of news and editorial content found in Canadian newspapers comes from news agencies, wire services or press associations."[9]

As of November 2005, Canadian media companies maintained 39 foreign bureaus. (Note that this figure might be inflated: CTV and the *Globe and Mail* are owned by the same company.) Almost one-third (12) belonged to the CBC/Radio-Canada. CTV had nine, the *Globe and Mail* seven, Torstar (the publisher of the *Toronto Star*) six, Gesca three, and CanWest two.[10] The low CanWest figure is particularly striking. In the first place, the company dominates the English-language news media in much of Canada (discussed below). Second, CanWest inherited 11 foreign bureaus when it acquired the Southam chain as part of its acquisition of

CONTINENT	CITY/COUNTRY	NUMBER	COMPANY NAME(S)
Americas (outside Canada)	Washington, D.C.	6	All
	New York	3	CBC, CTV, *Globe and Mail*
	Los Angeles	1	CTV
	Mexico City	2	CBC, TorStar
	Rio de Janeiro	1	CBC
	TOTAL	13	
Europe	London	6	All
	Paris	2	CBC, Gesca
	Moscow	3	CBC, CTV, *Globe and Mail*
	TOTAL	11	
Asia	Hong Kong	1	TorStar
	Beijing	3	CBC, Torstar, *Globe and Mail*
	Shanghai	1	CBC
	New Delhi	2	CTV, TorStar
	Bangkok	1	CBC
	TOTAL	8	
Middle East	Jerusalem/Israel	4	CBC, CTV, *Globe and Mail*, TorStar
	TOTAL	4	
Africa	Johannesburg	1	*Globe and Mail*
	Dakar	1	CBC
	Kampala	1	CTV
	TOTAL	3	

Hollinger in 2000. The decision to close all but the Washington and London offices says much about the priorities of the new owners.

Table 14.1 displays the locations of the 39 bureaus. One-third are located in the Americas, 10 of which are in the United States. The next most-covered continent is Europe, followed by Asia (where the majority of bureaus are in China). The Middle East hosts four bureaus, compared to three for the entire continent of Africa. Some of these bureaus are staffed by full-time reporters who work in one small area; others are staging posts for far-flung travels across a huge region. For example, CBC's Bangkok correspondent covers most of Asia; one Dakar-based reporter was responsible for all of Africa. While this is better than nothing, it forces journalists to hopscotch from crisis to crisis instead of providing in-depth analysis of a single country or issue.

Toronto Star columnist Chantal Hébert laments the fact that "at a time when what takes place outside our borders has rarely had more importance, and despite Canada's increasingly diverse population, news organizations are cutting back on foreign-based international reporting."[11] A former deputy minister of Foreign Affairs echoed this concern:

> *Canadian media outlets—news chains, television networks, etc.—are less and less global in their coverage. Yet Canada has the most at stake in terms of the impact that globalization is having on us. Forty-two per cent of our GDP is trade-based. We're more dependent on the outside world than just about any other country for our capital, for investment, for economic growth. And the international literacy of our journalists falls far short of reflecting that dependence.*[12]

Another *Toronto Star* columnist, James Travers, made the following observations to a Senate committee in 2003:

Internationally, correspondents see the world through Canadian and different eyes. Anyone who doubts that need only compare domestic and U.S. coverage of the Iraq invasion. One struggled for balance and understanding while the other tilted to jingoism, and occasionally tumbled into propaganda. Maintaining foreign bureaus also ensures momentous events will not take readers by surprise. That has never been more important and the importance will continue to grow as world events accelerate and this country tries to find its place in them. More practically, keeping Canadian journalists in the field ensures that the government and its agencies do not operate overseas with an immunity that taxpayers would never tolerate at home. If we are to understand ourselves and be full citizens of the world and if we are to grasp the importance of evolving patterns, then newspapers must have the resources to play a meaningful part. Without those resources, readers, newsrooms and the quality of public debate suffer irreparable harm.[13]

The lack of attention to Africa is a particular concern to some observers, given the magnitude of the AIDS crisis, the massacres in Darfur, brutal civil wars in Ivory Coast and elsewhere, and the near-collapse of the Zimbabwean economy and civil society. With the possible exception of AIDS, none has received adequate media coverage in the wealthy countries whose governments could have intervened if their voters demanded that they do so. A former Canadian journalist has suggested that media neglect of Africa helped to create the conditions for the horrific 1994 genocide in Rwanda:

At the height of the killing in Rwanda, many television viewers in the West were transfixed by O.J. Simpson. . . . There is some debate whether or not more informed and comprehensive coverage of the Rwanda genocide might have mitigated or even halted the killing by sparking an international outcry. Some have asked: Did the western media's failure to report adequately on the genocide in Rwanda possibly contribute to the international indifference and inaction and hence contribute to the crime itself? . . . I think it is fair to say that we missed the story in Rwanda, in large measure because we do not care and we were not there. We could be making the same mistake right now in Ivory Coast and Darfur, or some other location that is well off the news radar.[14]

Both at home and abroad, the loss of specialized beat reporters translates into a lower quantity and quality of news reporting. At one time, a large urban newspaper would have assigned at least one full-time reporter to city hall, another to the criminal courts, and still others to issue beats of particular concern to the local community. Although there is still some degree of specialization (if only to assign breaking stories more quickly), very few reporters have the luxury of focusing on one particular institution or policy field. As a former CBC Ottawa bureau chief put it, "They may cover same-sex marriages at the Supreme Court one day, the government's plans for the Kyoto Protocol the next day and the federal-provincial health negotiations the day after that. In that world there is never enough time to develop any expertise."

With barely enough people to file every day, the only option is to turn your reporters into general assignment reporters. That means they match newspaper stories, cover Question Period and attend staged events—the release of reports and news conferences organized by interest groups. The result is that more and more reporters know less and less about what they are covering. . . . There is a lack of context and perspective in how stories are reported and played in the media, and there are plenty of examples of that. . . . No matter how little you might know about a subject area, there are always two things you can cover: personality and conflict. Is it any surprise that media coverage of politics and public policy is increasingly centred on personality and conflict? . . . I suspect the result is that we have a public that knows less and less about the issues and is, therefore, less and less engaged in the debate that is essential to shaping public policy and future directions for the country.[15]

Cutting costs is one side of the profit equation; raising revenues is the other. In the media business, including the news side, most of the revenues come from advertising. As a senior Canadian television producer put it, "The product of commercial television is not the program. The product that is being bought and sold is the viewer. . . . The advertiser is buying 'eyeballs' by the hundreds of thousands and by the millions from the network."[16] The same is true for newspapers, on a smaller scale. There are two primary types of advertising. Classified ads are a reliable source of revenue for newspapers, especially ads for real estate, jobs, and vehicles. Print media also depend on sales of commercial advertising space. Broadcast stations, both radio and television, depend almost exclusively on commercial advertising revenue. The money comes from the sale of space (print media) or time (broadcast) to companies seeking to promote their goods or services. These days, most of the actual purchases are made by advertising agencies that produce the ads and "place" them in appropriate publications or programs.

There are two basic strategies to maximize advertising revenue: (1) increase the space or time available for sale, and (2) increase the size of your readership or audience so you can charge higher rates to advertisers. Increased ad space in publications usually means cutting back on content—although this is not inevitable, since more pages (paper or virtual) can be added if necessary. Because time is finite, there is a more direct, and inverse, relationship between ads and content in the broadcast media. More time for advertising necessarily means less time for news and other programming.

The second strategy requires the media company to attract new readers, listeners or viewers (depending on the medium). So privately owned news organizations have an incentive to downplay costly political coverage in favour of attention-grabbing scandal, conflict, and "news you can use."[17] Competition among media companies translates into a battle for readers and ratings, a battle in which celebrity gossip and hyped-up crime stories often take priority over in-depth coverage and analysis of government and policy-making. Journalists who operate in a free market "give the people what they want," not necessarily what they need. "For the most part, modern media organizations have tipped the balance toward treating their audience as consumers rather than citizens."[18] While this trend is fuelled, in part, by the perception on the part of news editors and producers that "the public is not interested in the complex issues that make up routine coverage of public bodies and the bureaucracy,"[19] we cannot blame shallow and superficial coverage of political events on the media alone.[20] In a culture where *American Idol* and "Brangelina" attract greater public interest than electoral corruption or the process by which political leaders make the laws that directly affect our lives, it is hardly surprising that market-driven news producers focus on personalities at the expense of complicated issues.

The Concentration of Media Ownership

In recent decades, ownership in the newspaper business has been concentrated in fewer and fewer hands: "Of all the capitalist countries in the world today, Canada has the highest concentration of media ownership."[21] Table 14.2 illustrates recent trends in Canadian newspaper ownership. It shows that concentration grew in the 1990s, peaking toward the end of the decade, and then modestly declining (although remaining a little above 1994 levels). The table also shows how rapidly some papers have changed hands in the past 15 years, as older companies like Thomson and Southam disappeared and new ones (CanWest) moved in to take their places.

Private radio stations are also owned by a relatively small group of companies, which has shrunk rapidly in recent years. In 2000, the top 10 radio companies owned 51 percent of the 493 private radio stations in Canada; two years later, they owned 63 percent of 525 stations.

TABLE 14.2 **TOP FIVE CANADIAN NEWSPAPER COMPANIES, BY CIRCULATION; 1994, 1999, AND 2003**

	1994		1999		2003	
NAME	% OF NATIONAL CIRCULATION	NAME	% OF NATIONAL CIRCULATION	NAME	% OF NATIONAL CIRCULATION	
Southam	27	Hollinger/ Southam	42	CanWest	28.5	
Thomson	20.6	Quebecor	21.3	Quebecor	21	
Toronto Sun	11	Torstar	13.7	Torstar	13.8	
Quebecor	8.8	Thomson	10.5	Gesca	9.2	
Gesca	6	Gesca	5.7	Bell Globemedia	6.4	
TOTAL	73.4	TOTAL	93.2	TOTAL	78.9	

Notes: The *Globe and Mail* was owned by Thomson until it was bought by Bell Canada Enterprises (BCE) in 2001. Bell Globemedia changed its name to CTV Globemedia in January 2007. Torstar, the parent company of the *Toronto Star*, was considered an Independent until 1999. The *Toronto Sun* is now part of Quebecor. Hollinger, the company formerly controlled by Conrad (Lord) Black, sold most of its holdings—including the *National Post*—to CanWest in 2000. Before it purchased the Hollinger holdings, CanWest was not in the newspaper business. Gesca owns La Presse, the largest francophone daily in the country.

Source: A portion of "Table 1: Canadian Newspaper Ownership as a Percentage of Total Circulation Selected Years, 1994–2003," found in the Senate Standing Committee on Transport & Communications, *Interim Report on the Canadian News Media* (Ottawa, April 2004). Accessed at the Parliamentary Website www.parl.gc.ca, July 2007. Reproduced with the permission of the Minister of Public Works and Government Services, 2008, and courtesy of the Law Clerk & Parliamentary Counsel of the Canadian Senate.

The number of stations owned by Rogers Broadcasting, the second-largest company, rose from 29 to 49 over that period, while third-place Standard Broadcasting and fourth-place Astral Radio also expanded their station holdings substantially (from 12 to 50 and 12 to 38, respectively.)[22] In February 2007, Astral announced its intention to purchase Standard–another quantum leap in radio concentration.[23] Shortly after the purchase was completed, Astral expressed an interest in acquiring Corus Broadcasting, which had been the largest owner of Canadian radio stations only five years previously.[24]

Measuring concentration in the private television industry is more difficult, because of the expanding range of specialty channels and the division of viewing time between Canadian and American channels.[25] In the nine English-speaking provinces and three territories, three companies accounted for 42 percent of audience share in 2002: BellGlobemedia, CanWest, and CHUM (which owned CityTV, along with MuchMusic and other specialty channels). In Quebec, three companies drew a combined 60-percent share of the television market; the biggest player was Quebecor, followed by Radio-Canada (which draws a bigger audience among francophones than CBC does among anglophones).[26]

Since 2002, ownership concentration has accelerated. In May 2007 the Canadian Radio-television and Telecommunications Commission (CRTC)—the federal regulatory agency for broadcasters—allowed CanWest to purchase a controlling share of Alliance Atlantis, which operates a number of specialty television channels. The following month, the CRTC approved CTV Globemedia's purchase of CHUM, on the condition that the new company sell CHUM's CityTV stations in Toronto and western Canada (but not its extensive radio holdings).[27] Two commissioners dissented, arguing that CTV Globemedia should not have been required to divest itself of local television stations in the same markets as existing CTV stations.[28] These two decisions, and especially the dissent concerning the divestiture, renewed concerns about Canada's existing policies on media concentration.

National ownership figures do not tell the whole story, because the concentration of media holdings varies from one market to the next. In Vancouver, for example, both of the daily newspapers (the *Sun* and the *Province*) are owned by CanWest, as is the only daily in the provincial capital (the Victoria *Times-Colonist*). CanWest closed down the Vancouver papers' bureaus at the British Columbia legislature, so Vancouverites now get their provincial political coverage from the Victoria paper.[29] There are three English-language daily newspapers in New Brunswick (located in Moncton, Fredericton, and Saint John), all of which are owned by the Irving family. These are just the most extreme examples of a national phenomenon.

Critics argue that the concentration of media ownership has had negative consequences for Canadian news reporting. First, the purchase of multiple newspapers and/or broadcast stations has saddled their new owners (especially CanWest) with large debt loads, which helps to explain the single-minded emphasis on profit.[30] Second, as the example of the Vancouver and Victoria papers suggests, a company that owns several newspapers can save money by shutting down bureaus and establishing one central source for news coverage. Indeed, this is precisely the business model that CanWest has followed across Canada. When it bought the assets of the old Southam chain, CanWest inherited the Southam News Service. The Asper family treated the CanWest News Service as a mandatory source for its papers rather than a useful supplement to local coverage. In 2001, shortly after it took over 11 of Canada's largest daily newspapers, CanWest announced that the Winnipeg head office would issue three national editorials per week. Those editorials had to appear in every CanWest paper, and dissenting views would not be published.[31] There was an outcry from journalists, including some who worked for CanWest. The Aspers backed down shortly thereafter, but they still require their papers to print material from the CanWest News Service (instead of CP). Apart from the threat to editorial freedom, this centralized production of news content also reduces the availability of local news. As one critic of the Irving monopoly in New Brunswick observed, "If I decide that I do not necessarily want to have the Irving papers, I cannot just necessarily go and get a Nova Scotia paper, go on the Internet, or go to the national papers . . . no one else is going to have that local information."[32] More broadly, the dominance of the media business by a handful of companies results in a "loss of diversity in analysis and opinion."[33]

A third problem arising from media concentration was most evident in the wake of the CanWest editorial incident just described. Few of the reporters and columnists who protested the Aspers' interference with editorial freedom still work for CanWest. Although many found new jobs, their range of options was considerably narrower than it would have been 50 years earlier. Russell Mills, the former publisher of the *Ottawa Citizen*, was fired by CanWest for protesting the Aspers' incursions on his editorial independence. A few years later, having left the profession of journalism, he testified before a Senate committee investigating the Canadian news media. In response to a senator's comment that "If a journalist finds him or herself working for an owner that places restrictions on the ability to do the job as he or she sees fit, then the commercial reality is that you leave and move on to another place," Mills replied that "there are not many places to move to because there are so few owners in Canada."[34]

Shrinking newsrooms affect not just journalists looking to change jobs, but younger people trying to break in to the field. Once employed, reporters have a strong incentive to avoid stories that could anger the owners. Of course, they might just be too busy to do any investigative journalism: "At times, we have been left with a severe shortage of reporters to cover important local news events. Some editors are now responsible for more than one section, while our copy editors have been left severely stretched."[35]

Mixed Ownership

The third issue is the growing phenomenon of mixed ownership, which takes two forms. The first, cross-ownership, occurs when a company that already owns one or more media outlets of one type acquires outlets of a different type—for example, a newspaper company buying a television network. Whereas Canada's large media companies once specialized in either print or broadcast, "convergence" has been the buzzword in recent years. As of July 2003, there were several notable examples of cross-ownership in Canadian media industries:

- CanWest (the Aspers) owned Global Television and several major newspapers (including the *National Post*), along with radio stations.
- BCE owned CTV and the *Globe and Mail*, as well as specialty channels and a satellite distribution business.
- Quebecor owned several newspapers and the TVA network, as well as a cable distribution company.
- The Irving family owned radio stations in New Brunswick, in addition to its near-monopoly of English-language newspapers in the province.
- Rogers owned television stations and channels, several dozen radio stations, and a cable television business.[36]

As we have seen, ownership patterns vary from one market to another. In Vancouver, CanWest controls 100 percent of daily newspaper circulation and 70.6 percent of the audience for local television news. In Quebec City, Quebecor has a majority of the daily newspaper circulation and a near-majority of local television news viewership.

Cross-ownership raises many of the same issues as concentration. It reduces the diversity of news and opinion available to citizens, and makes it even more tempting for owners to cut back on reportorial staff. Along the way, the quality of news coverage suffers: "if you have five different people for five different organizations chasing the same story, the likelihood is that some of them will come up with more information than others. Some of them will be more entrepreneurial than others, and you will get four or five versions of the story, some better and some worse. One of them may turn up something no one else does. If you have one person doing that, you have less opportunity for that to happen. . . ."[37]

There are also problems unique to cross-ownership. One is the fact that broadcast enterprises are regulated by the federal government, through the CRTC, whereas print media are not. This raises some questions about journalistic independence in "converged" companies:

> *Broadcasters require licences from government in order to operate their businesses. A broadcast licence is an extremely valuable asset for a company and this may give the company a powerful interest in remaining on good terms with the government. This has the potential to affect the objectivity of journalism. Broadcast journalists, of course, have no choice but to operate in this environment but there is a public interest in not having print journalists compromised by the ties of their owners to government. . . . The Globe and Mail, for example, would not permit one of its reporters to accept a free airline ticket from government in order to cover a story because of concern that this might influence content. However, BCE, the owner of The Globe and Mail, receives a broadcast licence from the government to operate the CTV network, which enables the company to make millions of dollars in profits each year. Owners should be subject to the same ethical standards as they impose on their employees; they should accept no benefits.*[38]

Another problem arising from cross-ownership is the growing prevalence of "cross-promotion." For example, when the owner of a television station buys an expensive American program, he naturally wants to promote it to the potential audience. If he also happens to own the local newspaper, he need not spend money on advertising; he can simply ensure that the program is covered as a "news" story in the pages of the paper.

I am not sure how much "Canadian Idol" was a real phenomenon independent of being driven by television stations and newspapers that have the same owner. Another example is "Survivor," which the CanWest papers seem to play up fairly regularly as a news story. Could that be related to the fact that CanWest also broadcasts "Survivor"? The question that comes out of that is whether that coverage replaces news that might be considered of more value to people.[39]

A similar situation arose in Quebec, where the francophone version of *Canadian Idol* aired on TVA and received extensive "news" coverage from Quebecor's newspapers. One journalism expert in the province described the "news items" about *Star Académie* as "almost more important than the war in Iraq or elections in Quebec."[40]

The second type of mixed ownership is called conglomeration. It occurs when a company that owns one or more businesses outside the media industries acquires a newspaper or broadcast station (or vice versa). As we have seen, the Irving family dominates the anglophone media in New Brunswick. It also owns a range of other businesses, all of which receive positive coverage from the Irving newspapers and radio stations.

The Irving empire, which includes over 300 companies, has an estimated net worth of approximately $4 billion, and employs 8 percent of the New Brunswick labour force in operations that span forestry, transportation, and construction, is not exposed to investigative journalistic inquiry in the province's daily papers. Instead, critical observers of the media can easily identify the self-serving nature of the Irvings' media coverage on any issue that concerns themselves. . . . The history of the Irvings' ownership of the media is peppered with stories of journalists forbidden to name the Irvings as the ones responsible for oil spills, of Irving executives prohibited from speaking to the press, and a case where the editor of the Saint John paper was denied permission to report that an Irving-owned tugboat had run aground for fear that it would result in an insurance hike for the company.[41]

Conglomeration can also pose problems for smaller papers. The only major newspaper in New Brunswick that is not owned by the Irvings, *L'Acadie Nouvelle*, has to buy its newsprint from an Irving-owned paper mill. *Le Devoir*, the sole independent francophone paper in Quebec, relied on Quebecor—the biggest printer in the province until recently—to produce and distribute its daily editions.[42] This makes smaller companies vulnerable to predatory tactics by the conglomerates, if they should choose to run competitors for their media outlets out of business. That vulnerability likely explains why most industrialized countries prohibit this kind of ownership structure (as we will see).

Owner Interference In News Coverage

A fourth and final issue with private media ownership (already mentioned in passing) is the risk of direct managerial interference with news content. It is an old joke in the newspaper business that the freedom of the press belongs to the man who owns it. Nevertheless, by the twentieth century most Canadian media companies strove for political objectivity in their news coverage. For the broadcast outlets, that objectivity was (and is) imposed upon them by the conditions of their licences. In the print media, it was a self-imposed principle of good journalistic practice—as well as a pragmatic business tactic to avoid alienating potential readers and advertisers. Opinions were expressed on the editorial page, which was deliberately set apart from the news coverage.

All of that changed in the 1990s, when Conrad Black bought the Southam newspaper chain. By 1999, Black's Hollinger Corporation controlled by far the largest share of circulation in the country (Table 14.2). His various companies also owned newspapers in Britain, the United States, and Israel. Black perceived himself as an old-fashioned newspaper proprietor: he deliberately fashioned the opinions expressed in his papers to reflect his own conservative ideology, instead of hewing to a neutral political line. His efforts to exert political influence peaked in 1998, when he launched the *National Post*. Black hired editors and reporters who shared his pro-free-market, anti-Liberal views.[43] He also spearheaded the *Post*'s campaign against "judicial activism" (see Chapters 6 and 10).[44]

The *Post*'s lively prose and Black's determination to outdo the *Globe and Mail* (the established national English-language newspaper) unleashed a more aggressive style in Canadian political coverage. According to a former Southam reporter, the fierce competition between the two papers affected the Liberal leadership battle between Prime Minister Chrétien and Finance Minister Paul Martin: "there was a rush to publish any or all tips or leaked information. It became far easier for strategists to plant their stories in the national press, sometimes just for mischief, sometimes to send messages to their rivals."[45] The newspaper wars also heightened the conflicts between the Liberals and the Reform Opposition in the House of Commons in the late 1990s. Some *Post* reporters worked with Reform MPs to expose scandals in the management of public funds, to such an extent that "journalists became part of the story and were making their own news."[46] However, the *National Post* failed to turn a profit; its losses contributed to Hollinger Southam's financial woes, which eventually forced Black to sell his Canadian newspapers to CanWest in 2000–01.[47]

When the Asper family, the owners of CanWest, took control of the Hollinger/Southam newspapers, they slashed costs and drastically reduced political coverage (see above). Whereas Black had been willing to pay generously for good writing, the Aspers were not. There might have been some compensation for the newsroom survivors if the new owners had refrained from interfering with the editorial pages. Instead, the Aspers have intervened at least as actively as Black, albeit they do not share all of his opinions. The former publisher of a CanWest paper described the Aspers' approach in blunt terms:

> The principals of the company have been quite open about their desire to use their newspapers to promote their interests and views. Staffs of the newspapers have learned which issues are sensitive and when to censor themselves. For example, you are unlikely to find much that is favourable about the CBC or about Palestinians in CanWest newspapers. Managers of the papers have learned that Canadian broadcasting and the conflict in the Middle East are highly sensitive matters with the proprietors.[48]

Closer to home, there have been allegations that CanWest reporters were instructed to treat the Liberals gently in the 2004 election campaign because "a Liberal defeat would mean the end of federal investment in the Aspers' pet human rights museum for Winnipeg."[49] In a similar vein, the Irvings publicly contradicted their papers' endorsement of the Progressive Conservatives in the 1997 federal election campaign, perhaps because one of them happened to have an incumbent New Brunswick Liberal MP as a son-in-law.[50] This was not unusual: a former editor of the Irvings' Saint John paper "told reporters that the paper's owner, J.K. Irving, called him every day telling him what he liked, and did not like in the paper."[51]

In other media organizations, such direct interventions appear to be rare. However, it may not be necessary for an owner with a well-known ideological position to keep his or her journalists on a short leash. Consciously or otherwise, the biases of those at the top of the hierarchy—newspaper publishers and editors, and news producers on radio and TV—can influence the reporters who cover politics. They know that a story that conflicts with the beliefs of their superiors could be rewritten or "spiked" (killed outright). In order to survive in "an organizational culture where promotions, higher salaries, and top assignments require a certain amount of team play,"[52] a reporter may decide not to cover a particular story or to cover it in a way that pleases management.

Can the Ownership Problems be Fixed?

The growing incidence of concentration and cross-ownership in the Canadian media has provoked numerous investigations and recommendations over the past 30 years.[53] In 2006 the Senate Standing Committee on Transport and Communications issued a report that expressed serious concern about ownership patterns and called on the government to take action. The committee noted that most comparable countries have laws in place to restrict ownership concentration, both nationally and in local media markets.[54] Cross-ownership and conglomeration are less strictly regulated, although Australia is an exception: the *Trade Practices Act* provides that "A person must not control (have more than a 15-percent interest in) more than one of the three basic media (television, radio, newspaper) in the same licence area."[55]

Currently, regulatory powers over media ownership in Canada are divided between the CRTC (broadcasting and telecommunications) and the Competition Bureau (most other businesses, including newspapers). Neither has been willing or able to address the problems described in this section, perhaps partly because the statute that it applies (the *Broadcasting Act* and the *Competition Act*, respectively) does not explicitly restrict concentration or cross-ownership. The Senate Committee recommended that both acts be strengthened, to require the regulators to review (and, where appropriate, to reject) future media mergers. [56] In November 2006, the Harper Government refused to act on the recommendations, asserting that "the balance contained in the current legislative, regulatory, and policy frameworks, supported by various government programs, has served Canadians well."[57] However, the CRTC took the Committee's concerns and recommendations more seriously. In April 2007 it announced that, "in light of the current wave of consolidation in the Canadian broadcasting industry," it would undertake a public review of media ownership. Specifically, the CRTC proposed to evaluate concentration, cross-ownership, conglomeration, and its "relationship with the Competition Bureau" in the regulation of media mergers.[58]

In January 2008, the commission issued a revised statement on regulatory policy. Although it expressed concern about the impact of concentrated ownership on the "diversity of voices" in Canadian media, especially in particular local markets, the commission did not adopt effective measures to stem the tide. Instead, it decided to continue its case-by-case approach to takeovers and licence renewals.[59] At the same time, the CRTC announced that the Canadian Broadcast Standards Council (CBSC) would implement a new Journalistic Independence Code: coverage and production decisions in affiliated newspaper and broadcast newsrooms would be made separately, to ensure that different media owned by the same company did not air or publish identical content.[60] In the absence of sanctions for violating the Code, its effectiveness is doubtful.

▨ The Institutional Characteristics of Journalism

Regardless of ownership—public or private, concentrated or dispersed–journalists are subject to their own institutional incentives and pressures. These include:
- the values and practices of the profession;
- news values;
- deadlines and competition;
- reliance on official sources; and
- the requirements of technology (especially in television).

Self-Regulation and the Journalists' "Creed"

In the past few decades, journalism schools and programs have sprung up across the country to train and socialize aspiring reporters. The core values of professional journalists include accuracy, the rapid transmission of information to the public, the investigation of public institutions, and the analysis of complex issues.[61] Although these ideals are not always followed in practice, to disregard them completely would ruin a reporter's career. At the very least, a political story must be balanced between opposing viewpoints; a quotation or a video clip from one side of an issue must be followed by a similar contribution from the other side. However, as Dossier 14.1 makes clear, reporters usually lack the time and resources to go beyond this simple "he-said-she-said" formula; the range and nuance of opinion is too narrow for Canadians who rely on the media for political information.

A 1996 survey of Canadian journalists found that most subscribed to a professional "creed." They identified five central tasks as extremely important: "accurately reporting the views of public figures, getting information to the public quickly, giving ordinary people a chance to express their views, investigating the activities of government and public institutions, and providing analysis and interpretation of complex problems."[62] In practice, these goals contradict each other. Speed is the enemy of both accuracy (Dossier 14.3) and analysis. Reporters rarely have enough time or space to present the views of both "public figures" and "ordinary people." Moreover, as we have seen, the growing emphasis on profitability makes it impossible to investigate "the activities of government and public institutions" or to interpret "complex problems" in any sustained way. Nonetheless, the fact that most Canadian journalists identified these goals as guiding principles of their profession was encouraging.

A follow-up survey conducted in 2003 painted a less rosy picture. Many of the same journalists were re-interviewed to see whether their professional values had remained constant in the wake of media mergers and technological change. Although the respondents still considered the five tasks just listed to be the most important, their emphasis on accuracy, analysis, and giving a voice to ordinary citizens had diminished since 1996.[63] Anglophone journalists accounted for most of the decline, with a particularly steep drop in the importance that they attached to accurately transmitting the views of politicians and business leaders. The authors of the study speculated that reporters working for English-language news outlets were more strongly affected by scandals in the federal government and North American businesses (such as Enron) than their francophone counterparts, who devote considerably less attention to events outside the province of Quebec. They also suggested that "the distinct professional culture of francophone journalism may play a role in making the professional values of French-language journalists somewhat resistant to the kind of rapid change we have documented among journalists at English-language media."[64] Unlike their counterparts in the rest of Canada, Quebec journalists have a cohesive professional identity that likely reinforces the standards and traditions of their craft.

Some critics argue that an overt sympathy for Quebec sovereignty is part of the "distinct professional culture" in the francophone media. Federalist politicians have long alleged that francophone Quebec journalists (including those at Radio-Canada) are overly sympathetic to the separatist cause.[65] Reciprocal accusations of bias were levelled at the anglophone media during the 1995 Quebec referendum campaign. One telling indicator of the gulf between the perceptions of the two "media solitudes" is the coverage of the pro-Canada rally in Montreal shortly before the referendum vote: "CBC *Newsworld* estimated the crowd at 150,000, while RDI [the francophone equivalent of *Newsworld*] reported that only 30 or 40 thousand people had attended the rally."[66]

While most or all journalists subscribe to the "creed" previously discussed, they differ in their interpretation of their public duties. One reason for such differences is the varying life experience of individual reporters, editors, and producers. Judgments about which stories to cover, and how to cover them, are influenced by the perspectives of those in charge.[67] A recent survey of Canadian news directors found a preponderance of middle-class, well-educated white men with no religious affiliation. On the whole, the respondents' political views were in line with the population at large; however, CBC personnel were more sympathetic to the NDP (and less favourable to conservative parties) than the rest of the electorate.[68]

Partly in response to the under-representation of visible minorities in the mainstream news media, ethnic community newspapers have sprung up in major cities across the country. As of 2006, "there are over 250 ethnic newspapers and about 14 full-service radio stations. These ethnic media, which are predominant in larger urban areas such as Toronto, Vancouver and Montreal, represent over 50 cultures and over five million Canadians whose cultural heritages are neither French nor Anglo-Saxon."[69] The ethnic papers serve their specific communities in at least three ways. First, they print positive stories about members of their communities, publicizing achievements that are overlooked by the major media outlets (see the discussion of stereotyping, below). Second, they can educate recent immigrants about Canadian politics, helping them to become good citizens of their adopted country.[70] Third, they provide an inexpensive advertising vehicle for community-owned businesses. However, their utility to their readers (and advertisers) appears to be fairly limited. For example, Montreal's *Community Contact,* a newspaper for black residents of that city, reaches less than 10 percent of its target audience.[71] The lack of penetration can be explained, in part, by heavy Internet use among Canadians who immigrated from other countries—especially those whose first language is neither English nor French.[72] Although many ethnic newspapers publish in the native language of their intended readers, they cannot offer the same coverage of events "back home" as the websites of foreign newspapers and broadcasters.

News Values and News Frames

As mentioned on the previous page, the 1995 pro-Canada rally in Montreal received extensive coverage in the national news media. For news editors and broadcast producers, this was an obvious choice: Canadians were gripped by the closeness of the referendum battle, prominent politicians made passionate speeches from which good clips could be extracted, the visual images of thousands of people in the streets were irresistible (especially the overhead shots of an enormous Canadian flag), and there was a ready-made narrative—the tension between Quebec and the rest of Canada—to help put the story in perspective. Other events, which could be more important in the long run, may or may not be covered, depending on the choices made by editors, producers, and the reporters who work for them.

All institutions are required to create order out of chaos—to impose coherence on a welter of competing ideas, interests, priorities, and viewpoints. For the news media, the "chaos" is the infinite number of events that happen every day. Only a few can be made to fit in the pages of a newspaper or the brief period of a newscast. The criteria editors and producers use to select which stories to cover are called **"news values."** These are politically significant, because the decision to cover one type of story entails a decision not to report other events that may be intrinsically important for citizens, but not as appealing to consumers. To paraphrase an old philosophical question: if a tree falls in the forest, and there are no cameras or microphones to record it, did it really happen? In political terms, if the prime minister announces a new policy and the press gallery stays away, does it really matter?

The prevailing news values include "proximity, timeliness, impact, prominence and conflict."[73] To illustrate, take the example of a murder in a medium-sized Ontario city. The act of killing another human being is inherently conflictual (hence the rule in local television news: "if it bleeds, it leads"). The discovery of the victim provokes an initial flurry of coverage in the local newspaper and news broadcasts. If the victim is particularly vulnerable—a child or an elderly person—the coverage will be more intense and longer-lasting, and it may be picked up by media outlets further away. Otherwise, the story will stay local and fade away after a few days (especially if an arrest follows quickly). If the victim is a prominent person (e.g., a high-ranking politician), or the crime itself has an unusual twist, the event might "go national."

Once an editor or producer decides to cover a particular story, he or she must decide *how* to cover it. (This assumes that he or she has chosen to run an original item, as opposed to simply printing or airing a story from a wire service or an affiliated outlet.) These decisions, which are almost as significant as the preliminary choice to cover or not to cover, are not made in a vacuum. Reporters work within a relatively narrow range of **"news frames,"** or preset narratives. News frames are "those rhetorical and stylistic choices . . . that alter the interpretations of the topics treated and are a consistent part of the news environment."[74]

> *They simplify, prioritize, and structure the narrative flow of events. News frames bundle key concepts, stock phrases, and stereotyped images to reinforce certain common ways of interpreting developments. The essence of framing is selection to prioritize some facts, events, and developments over others, thereby promoting a particular interpretation. Reporters can "tell it like it is" within sixty seconds, rapidly sorting key events from surrounding trivia, by drawing on reservoirs of familiar stories to cue readers. New developments are understood within regular patterns. . . . Dominant frames are so widespread within journalistic culture that they come to be seen as natural and inevitable, with contradictory information discounted as failing to fit preexisting views.[75]*

Any given event can be presented and explained in a number of different ways. For example, a general election may be "framed" by journalists as a horserace among the party leaders, as a contest among ideologies and principles, as the supreme expression of Canadian democracy, or as a turning point in our national history. Each of these "frames" is based on a set of assumptions about politics, about the preexisting knowledge and beliefs of the audience, and about the motivations of the actors who "star" in the nightly newscast. The hypothetical murder discussed above can also be portrayed in a variety of ways, depending on which preexisting narrative it seems to fit. Depending on the circumstances and the preferences of the reporter, the killing of a child might be framed as the sacrifice of an innocent (harking back to the Biblical story of Isaac), as another in a string of failures by child-protection agencies, or as the unintended consequence of rampant gang violence.

In both Canada and the United States, elections are usually "framed" as strategic battles between self-interested and perhaps dishonest politicians.[76] Sports and military metaphors abound, creating a macho narrative that marginalizes female politicians.[77] Journalists seem to prefer the "game frame" because it lends itself to television's need for arresting visual images and juicy "revelations" about underhanded political tactics. Moreover, as we saw earlier in this chapter, reporters who lack expertise in politics or government may substitute conflict for context. Whatever the reasons for their popularity, contest narratives "encourage a trivialization of politics, and contribute to a general decline in political discourse and the quality of political life."[78]

The Sponsorship Scandal offers another example of media "framing." As Dossier 8.2 explains, the scandal had two primary sources: the failure to impose proper financial controls on the Sponsorship Program, and the "kickback scheme" allegedly orchestrated by a few members of the federal Liberal Party in Quebec. Fiscal administration within the permanent executive is a complex issue that does not lend itself to snappy news coverage. So is the regulation of political finance under the *Canada Elections Act*. Consequently, reporters focused on more peripheral elements of the story: overblown Opposition accusations of Liberal "theft," the personalities involved (especially the colourful Chuck Guité), and a few juicy snippets of testimony before the Gomery Commission. Although Justice Gomery himself became a media star, especially in francophone Quebec,[79] the trenchant analyses contained in his two reports were ignored. To date, no one affiliated with the Liberal Party has been charged with a criminal offence arising from the scandal. Nonetheless, the public perception of Liberal corruption lingers.[80]

The scandal "frame" was also applied to an earlier event: the alleged "billion-dollar boondoggle" in the former Human Resources Development Department. In 1999, an internal audit revealed that the Transitional Jobs Fund (a $100-million program to provide grants to local job-training programs) was poorly managed. The news media, led by the *National Post*, leaped to the conclusion that the entire HRDC Grants and Contributions program was rife with incompetence and political corruption. The annual cost of all HRDC grants and contributions totalled roughly $1 billion. The Reform Opposition in the House of Commons assailed the Liberal Government daily in Question Period, reaping headlines with their allegations of a billion-dollar slush fund for Liberal ridings. After several months, a follow-up audit found no evidence of corruption or political favouritism. The department had simply lost track of some grants because of sloppy paperwork. The total amount of missing money, which was eventually recovered, was $65 000. "This information was downplayed and largely ignored because it was significantly different from the original storyline that $1 billion had been lost."[81] As often happens in political coverage, "The media reported new and unexpected negative events that reinforced the original storyline, and ignored those that did not."[82]

The choice of news frame can have repercussions well beyond the ranks of politicians. Faced with a complex issue and a limited space or time in which to cover it, reporters often resort to stereotypes of particular social groups. These simplified images fit within a preexisting narrative about that group's place in Canadian society.[83] Some stereotypes are innocuous or even flattering—for example, the conventional assumption that the opinions of highly educated "experts" should be taken seriously. Others are negative and sometimes damaging, especially those that are applied to certain racial and religious minorities. News coverage of election contests between candidates of different races often focuses on those racial differences, whereas race is never mentioned when two white candidates go head-to-head.[84] Crime reporters routinely identify the race of non-white suspects, but not of white suspects.[85] Entire ethnic communities—Jamaicans and Vietnamese in Toronto, Sikhs in Vancouver, and Aboriginal peoples—are portrayed as a threat.[86] Since 9/11, Muslim Canadians have often been tarred with the brush of terrorism or terrorist sympathies. According to the Canadian wing of the Council on American-Islamic Relations, the "Muslim terrorist" frame is particularly common in the CanWest newspapers.[87]

Such stereotypes hurt every member of the affected group. By reinforcing and legitimizing prejudice, they contribute to racial profiling by the police and other social institutions. When individuals who belong to "problem" communities find it harder to obtain education, employment, housing, or other necessities as a result, a stereotype can turn into a self-fulfilling prophecy. Significantly, a crime committed (or allegedly committed) by a white person does not lead to widespread news coverage of the "white community" as a hotbed of illegal activity.[88] Conrad Black's 2007 conviction on charges of fraud and obstruction of justice did not trigger journalistic speculation about the threat posed by Canadians of British descent or holders of graduate degrees from prestigious universities. Those groups are not generally considered to be dangerous to society; there is no preexisting narrative to inspire negative stereotyping. Yet the mere allegation that a black or Muslim individual committed a violent offence—for example, the 2005 Boxing Day shooting on Yonge Street in Toronto, or the alleged "terrorist cell" rounded up in July 2006[89]—is immediately accepted as reality by most journalists (and presumably their audiences), despite the constitutional guarantee that everyone will be presumed innocent until proven guilty in a court of law.

Packs and Deadlines: Competitive Pressures on Reporters

As previously noted, "convergence" and concentration in Canada's news business are reducing the number of journalists. Particularly in local politics, many events unfold in the presence of a single reporter (or none at all). At the other extreme, dozens of reporters, editors and producers work in the parliamentary press gallery in Ottawa. In that setting, journalists are subject to the competitive pressures of gathering and reporting news to a tight deadline. They cannot afford to miss out on a "hot" story. When a senior politician steps on a political land mine, or a minority Government appears to be headed for defeat in the Commons, the gallery resembles a pack of hungry wolves (Dossier 14.2).[90]

DOSSIER 14.2 Pack Journalism in Ottawa[91]

The dynamic of Ottawa's pack-journalism culture is not easy to dissect. Reporters don't conspire to pursue the same story or personality. There are no head-office directives distributed to members of the parliamentary press gallery, as conspiracy theorists might imagine. Rather, the media will be seized with a single idea simultaneously and spontaneously, and then collectively pursue it to death. Media competition exaggerates this tendency, as rival reporters scramble to outdo each other. One story begets a follow-up story. One question in a scrum leads to another along the same lines. The morning chitchat on the Sparks Street Mall [a pedestrian thoroughfare a block south of Parliament Hill] turns into an item by lunch and an issue by pre-dinner drinks. Soon, the theme seeps into the wider culture.

Once the "pack" seizes on its target, reporters pursue the unfortunate politician relentlessly (and often physically). Every day, their editors and producers expect them to come up with a new angle to keep the story alive. This is particularly crucial for reporters who work for all-news channels, who are expected to provide live "updates" several times a day. These "feeding frenzies" are also motivated by the fear of missing an important development, and being "scooped" by their rivals. Reporters know that if they drop the ball on the big story of the day, they will face criticism from their colleagues and competitors as well as their bosses.[92]

The process of political news-gathering also fosters the "pack" mentality. Journalists spend hours or days crammed together in hallways, buses, planes, and other confined spaces with little to do except wait for their prey and exchange the latest gossip and speculation. In the process, "They end up playing off each other, consulting to get an agreed interpretation of what's going on. It doesn't leave much room for originality of insights and drums out any suggestions that stray from the agreed analysis."[93]

While a political scandal in Ottawa may generate little interest in the rest of the country, it immediately becomes the only topic of conversation in the nation's capital. Members of the press gallery live for such stories, just as their counterparts in Washington live in hopes of the next sex scandal involving a politician, however much this obsessive focus on wrongdoing and foolishness by political leaders may damage public support for politics (and journalism).

Even for reporters who face little (or no) competition for the scoop of the day, deadlines are a constant and growing pressure. In the past, a newspaper reporter might face one deadline per day: a single story for tomorrow's print edition. Today, that same reporter may also be expected to file a series of updates or breaking-news bulletins on his or her paper's website. The pace of reporting has accelerated at least as much in television newsrooms. Thirty years ago, a reporter and producer would be required to prepare one pre-taped story for a supper-hour newscast; the same item would be repeated, with a few updates, at 11 p.m. The introduction of round-the-clock live news channels in the 1980s changed all that. Today, a reporter might be on-call for an entire day, feeding live "hits" to the anchor desk. He or she may also be required to prepare a taped report for the supper-hour news, or a package of clips to be aired in-between live exchanges with the anchor. At all hours of the day (and night, in the case of big breaking stories), there is a premium on "live" exchanges, often called "double-enders," between an anchor and a reporter on-location.

All of these short-term demands consume a great deal of time and energy, which could be better spent on fact-checking and gathering additional sources. A political reporter for *La Presse* made the following comments in June 2005:

> *In today's world of fast communication, newspapers try to compete with the Internet and 24-hour news channels, so they think what is most important is to produce stories fast. Speed is the big thing. Now you've got the BlackBerry. If there had been an election called in May, my boss wanted me to*

carry one in case there were breaking stories for our Internet site. There are always requests for a few paragraphs on what came out of the scrum when cabinet breaks up. So we all get caught up behaving as though we're working for a wire service, and we're all writing the same thing. Filing all the time takes up a lot of time that could be spent investigating some aspect of the story that everybody else isn't writing as well. We're investing far too much in speed and far too little in investigative reporting. It can take one month, two months, three months to fully investigate a story. That takes up a lot of resources.[94]

The insistence on live "updates" and two-way conversations—as opposed to carefully supervised and packaged stories—carries real risks. First, it puts reporters at the mercy of politicians and their **"spin doctors."** Imagine a television reporter sitting in the audience at a staged event where the prime minister announces a new Government policy. She has to provide a live "update" to the anchor desk as soon as the event concludes. All that she, her producer, and her camera operator can do is throw together a handful of video clips and come up with a few comments for the "two-way." There is little, if any, time to solicit comments from the Opposition or other interested parties. There is no opportunity to research the issue that the policy addresses and put the announcement into a broader context for the audience. Next to her, a newspaper reporter scribbles notes, scans the press release for usable quotes, and tries to put together a quick posting for the website. The Government can be certain that its message will be conveyed more or less directly to the public, at least initially. In effect, the news media have been turned into mouthpieces for the prime minister. While there is nothing new about political "spin," the ever-shrinking time frame for news coverage makes the spin doctors' lives considerably easier.

Second, reporters can make mistakes when they are forced to go live on-air without time for confirmation or reflection. For citizens, accuracy and context are more important characteristics of political news than speed or "scoops." Even if a journalist has the facts right, a slip of the tongue or an ill-judged answer to an anchor's spontaneous question can cause serious trouble—and not just for the news organization involved. Dossier 14.3 tells the story of a live "two-way" that went horribly wrong. While the "Kelly affair" was an extreme case, it illustrates the broader problems arising from the "need for speed."

DOSSIER 14.3 The Death of a Confidential Source

In May 2003, the British Broadcasting Corporation (BBC) was investigating rumours that the British Government had been less than straightforward when it made the case for participating in the American-led invasion of Iraq. Back in September 2002, then-Prime Minister Tony Blair had released an intelligence dossier describing Saddam Hussein's inventory of weapons of mass destruction (WMD). One passage in the dossier read as follows: "Iraq's military forces are able to use chemical and biological weapons, with command, control and logistical arrangements in place. The Iraqi military are able to deploy these weapons within forty-five minutes of a decision to do so."[95] This assertion was refuted by chief United Nations weapons inspector Hans Blix, who repeatedly asserted that Saddam did not possess significant chemical or biological weapons. Two months after the March 2003 invasion, intensive searches for Saddam's alleged WMD stockpiles had proven Blix right.

At 6:07 a.m. on May 29, 2003, BBC Defence correspondent Andrew Gilligan went live on BBC Radio 4 with a hot scoop. Speaking on the telephone from his home, Gilligan told the program's anchor that "one of the senior officials in charge of drawing up that dossier" had told him that top intelligence officials "probably knew that that forty-five-minute figure was wrong." Nonetheless, they put it in the dossier because "Downing Street, our source says . . .

(continued)

ordered it [the dossier] to be sexed up, to be made more exciting."[96] In summary, Gilligan claimed that Blair or someone working at his direction had deliberately lied to the British people in order to build support for the Iraq war. Later that day, Gilligan tried to make it clear that he was accusing the Government, not of deliberate lying, but of the normal practice of "spinning" content to make it more persuasive. By then, the damage was already done.

Everyone wanted to know the identity of Gilligan's anonymous source. The House of Commons Foreign Affairs Committee launched an investigation into the Government's alleged manipulation of intelligence data to justify the Iraq invasion, while the Ministry of Defence (MoD) tried to uncover the whistleblower. In the meantime, Gilligan milked his scoop in a variety of print and broadcast stories, including a newspaper article in which he named the person allegedly responsible for "sexing up" the dossier: Alastair Campbell, Blair's director of communications and head "spin doctor." Before the Foreign Affairs Committee, Campbell accused the BBC of false and biased journalism. Gilligan himself appeared before the committee in June 2003; while he refused to name his source,[97] he described the MoD whistleblower in a way that allowed insiders to make an educated guess. They inferred that the source was Dr. David Kelly, an MoD expert on biological weapons. Kelly, a world-renowned scientist and former international weapons inspector, was expected to brief journalists—but only with prior authorization from his superiors. He had not sought or received permission to discuss the preparation of the Iraq dossier, either on or off the record. Nor had he been "one of the senior officials in charge of drawing up that dossier," as Gilligan had claimed.

When he became aware of the rumours, Kelly wrote to his supervisors admitting that he had spoken to Gilligan. He insisted that he never accused the Government of deliberate dishonesty and had never identified Campbell by name. On July 7 the Foreign Affairs Committee (most of whose members were Government MPs) exonerated Campbell of any wrongdoing in the preparation of the dossier, while calling for further investigations into Gilligan's contacts with MoD officials. By then, Blair and his Cabinet knew Kelly's identity. Two days later, a persistent reporter received confirmation from the MoD.

Kelly and his wife fled to the west of England as a media siege descended on their home. Both were very upset by the public attention, although Dr. Kelly told friends that he was looking forward to a trip to Iraq on MoD business a week later. At around 3 p.m. on the 17th, shortly after taking a call from the MoD inquiring about another conversation with a BBC reporter (which he had not disclosed to his superiors), he told his wife that he was going for a walk. When he did not return, his family called the police. Dr. Kelly's body was found the next morning. He had committed suicide.

When the death was made public, the BBC publicly confirmed that Kelly was Gilligan's main source and expressed deep regret about the outcome of the story. Blair quickly appointed a senior judge, Lord Hutton, to investigate the suicide. Hutton concluded that Kelly's sense of public disgrace and exposure arising from his involvement with the British news media, exacerbated by his fear of losing his position, drove a respected scientist to take his own life.

Hutton also investigated the accuracy of Gilligan's initial "two-way" on the Iraq dossier and the specific allegation that the Government knowingly lied about the 45-minute issue. He concluded that Gilligan's claim of deliberate lying was wrong and should not have been aired. (Gilligan himself had acknowledged his errors in cross-examination before the Inquiry.[98]) Although Downing Street, and Campbell in particular, had "wanted the dossier to be worded to make as strong a case as possible in relation to the threat posed by Saddam Hussein's WMD,"[99] Hutton did not hold the Government responsible for the misleading statements in the report; nor did he blame anyone associated with the MoD for leaking Dr. Kelly's name to reporters (although he criticized their failure to warn Kelly ahead of time).

(continued)

Instead, he focused on the consequences of the BBC's rush to "scoop" other news organizations and the risks of a live, unscripted[100] "two-way" about a politically sensitive story:

> *The allegations that Mr Gilligan was intending to broadcast in respect of the Government and the preparation of the dossier were very grave allegations in relation to a subject of great importance and I consider that the editorial system which the BBC permitted was defective in that Mr Gilligan was allowed to broadcast his report at 6:07 am without editors having seen a script of what he was going to say and having considered whether it should be approved.*[101]

Predictably, BBC management were unhappy with the Hutton Report. They were not alone: British news outlets uniformly dismissed the Inquiry's conclusions as a "whitewash."[102] BBC Chairman Gavyn Davies had always maintained that Government attacks on Gilligan's story were politically motivated, and defended the BBC's right to air the allegations on the grounds of journalistic independence. (Ironically, Davies had been appointed to the top job at Britain's public broadcaster by Prime Minister Blair, an old friend and political ally.[103]) Davies was forced to resign in the wake of the Hutton Report, and the BBC conducted an internal review of its journalistic practices. The review panel acknowledged that "When the BBC is breaking stories containing *serious or potentially defamatory allegations*, live two-ways are normally inappropriate."[104] The panel also implicitly criticized the circumstances of Gilligan's early morning conversation with the radio anchor: "While two-ways from home are acceptable . . . they should not be the natural transmission source for contentious stories or stories involving serious allegations where preparation in the production office with the editorial team is essential."[105] One can infer from this statement that the BBC's journalistic ethics, not to mention simple common sense, had been compromised in the rush to put a "scoop" on the airwaves.

Official Sources Say . . .

Most political reporters rely heavily on official "sources," including Cabinet ministers and senior public officials.[106] As previously discussed, the daily "news cycle" is unforgiving, especially in an era of 24-hour news channels. A journalist must have immediate and secure access to informed sources, either to generate stories or to confirm information received elsewhere. The need to maintain cordial working relationships with powerful people places the reporter in a dilemma: if she "burns" a source, she loses her access and other political actors may never trust her again; if she accepts a source's version of events uncritically, she becomes a mouthpiece for that individual or group and loses her credibility as a journalist.[107]

Today, reporters seem to be increasingly dependent on press releases, "photo ops," and other pre-packaged sources of content. There are at least four reasons.

- First, as discussed in the previous section, tight deadlines make it impossible to verify or question the work of the "spin doctors."
- Second, the communication directors who work for politicians understand the technical requirements of television and provide irresistible "visuals" whenever they can.
- Third, news budgets are shrinking while the demand for news content is growing. Reporters and news editors have to find something to fill the "news hole": 24 hours of daily live news, a constantly updated website, or a few dozen pages of newsprint. Sometimes they have no choice but to print or air prepackaged content. A newspaper reporter facing a deadline may be given a "strategic leak" from a minister's office, on condition that he or she run it "clean"—in other words, without critical analysis or

Opposition reaction.[108] Or a news director with too little money and too much empty airtime might decide to air a "video news release" (VNR) from a politician or a pharmaceutical company, with or without telling the audience that they are watching an advertisement and not an objective news story. The following passage describes a typical VNR, which was produced by U.S. Department of Health and Human Services in 2004:

> Two "reporters" named Karen Ryan and Alberto Garcia had appeared in TV spots distributed to local news stations around the country to promote the administration's new Medicare prescription-drug benefit as the best thing to happen to America's elderly since Social Security. . . . Replete with tag lines like "In Washington, I'm Karen Ryan reporting," the elaborate fictional skits were broadcast whole or in part as actual news by more than fifty stations in forty markets. The departmental budget devoted to this PR campaign, some $124 million, dwarfed that of most actual American news organizations.[109]

- Fourth and finally, fewer and fewer reporters are equipped with the expert knowledge to question politicians' claims or put them in a broader context. As we have seen, most journalists are assigned to cover a wide range of stories instead of specializing in a particular institution or policy field. The disappearance of "beat" reporters puts news organizations, and the citizens who rely on them for political information, at the mercy of spin doctors.

Another recent development is the ability of politicians to bypass the news media entirely and communicate directly with the public. Today, most elected officials have their own websites. The quantity and quality of the content on these sites varies widely. A survey of the Web pages devoted to individual members of the U.S. Congress found that some consisted of little more than a photo and contact information, while others (mostly belonging to senators) provided state-of-the-art multimedia content and interactivity. However, as we will see in our discussion of new media (at the end of this chapter), the ability of the Internet to displace the older forms of news coverage should not be overstated. The study just mentioned found that most Congressional Web pages were designed to attract journalists, not constituents. Three-quarters of the sites contained a "News Room" feature, providing the text of speeches and press releases and (less commonly) streaming video of the politician's public appearances. The study's authors concluded that the main purpose of these "new media" outlets was to attract favourable coverage from members of the "old media," who rely on the Internet to obtain information quickly.[110]

The Power of Technology

All journalists are affected by the constraints and incentives previously described. Those who work in television face additional pressures arising from the technical requirements of the medium. A story with good "visuals" is more attractive to news producers than one without. Political developments that take place behind closed doors, in the absence of cameras, or that lack eye-catching visual symbolism or settings are difficult to convey on TV. Because television is primarily a visual medium, events that require extensive verbal explanation and context are given short shrift—whatever their intrinsic importance. "Talking heads" are considered boring; action and confrontation are not.

When a politician gives a speech or is interviewed on camera, the preferred length of the "clip" included in an individual story is 10 to 12 seconds. Clips have become shorter in recent years—an average of 7.8 seconds in the 2000 U.S. presidential race[111]—largely because of "the perceived attention span of viewers and the need to grab and hold the audience with sharp, fast-paced, action-oriented stories."[112] Most political and administrative issues are too complex for an audience to understand without explanation. Consequently, they are unsuited to the demands of television news. Small wonder, then, that TV coverage of G8 summits and World Trade Organization meetings focuses on dramatic footage of protests in the streets around the conference sites, not on the substance of the discussions inside. Riots, tear gas and street theatre are perfect for TV; lengthy debates over trade policy and Third World debt are not.

Since the 1970s, television news has been reshaped by improvements in broadcast technology. In particular, near-instantaneous satellite transmission of sound and images has made it possible to cover "live" and "breaking" stories around the corner or around the world. As we have seen, live (or apparently live) "two-ways" between a reporter on the ground and an anchor in the studio have become a staple of news programming. While this is especially true of 24-hour cable channels such as CNN and CBC *Newsworld,* "stand-ups" are also an important element in pre-packaged supper-hour and prime-time news programs like the *NBC Nightly News* and CBC's *The National.* The "two-ways" follow a consistent format, illustrated here by a typical Ottawa story on *The National.* Anchor Peter Mansbridge sets up the story, and then says, "Our Chief Political correspondent Keith Boag is in Ottawa tonight. Keith?" The screen is split vertically, with Mansbridge on the left and Boag—standing outside, with the illuminated Parliament Buildings visible in the background—on the right. Boag begins his "stand-up" by saying, "Peter," and then delivers a brief script picking up on the key elements of the story as identified by Mansbridge. The packaged story follows, combining carefully selected clips with Boag's recorded voice-over. When the package ends, Boag reappears in front of the Parliament Buildings to deliver a scripted wrap-up. When he says, "Peter?" the story is over. Sometimes Mansbridge follows up with a question to the reporter; otherwise, he thanks Boag and moves on to the next story in the line-up.

These live chats between the reporter and the anchor are supposed to make the news more immediate and relevant for the audience. (When the reporter is working in a far-flung country, such as Afghanistan, the disparity in time zones often requires the chats to be as pre-packaged as the stories that they surround.) For local stations, acquiring the technology to cover stories "at the scene" resulted in a competition-driven emphasis on "eyewitness" and "action news." This emphasis has arguably distorted producers' news judgments. "Rather than report on government and political activities with the aim of informing citizens, local news merely entertained and scared them with stories of scandal, crime, and violence"[113]—stories told live by a reporter exuding excitement or empathy as the occasion requires. In addition, the "eyewitness" frame makes the visuals even more crucial in the selection of stories, at the expense of other news values (notably the intrinsic importance of the stories themselves). It is one thing to send a reporter and camera crew to a breaking story, to capture the immediate aftermath of a storm or a terrorist attack. It is quite another to dispatch the crew and the satellite truck to the location of a story that ended several hours previously. A reporter "standing in front of fluttering yellow police tape when no one else is there" adds little or nothing to the audience's understanding of the events.[114]

In theory, live coverage on the ground is supposed to reduce journalists' dependence on "officials in highly managed institutional settings" and the news frames that governments try to impose on events.[115] In practice, reporters still seek out official sources whenever possible. The initial coverage of a breaking story, such as Hurricane Katrina, may focus on the actual event, the people directly affected, and the impact on the surrounding area. But within a short time, public officials (the mayor of New Orleans, the director of the Federal Emergency Management Agency) rush to appear on camera, expressing concern and sympathy and promising assistance. They become the focus of the story, while the victims gradually fade into the background. A recent study of foreign "live" coverage by American news organizations concluded that "When an unpredicted, conscripted, spontaneous event is covered in the news, the one predictable component of coverage is the presence of official sources."[116]

THE RELATIONSHIPS BETWEEN THE NEWS MEDIA AND CITIZENS

If the news media are supposed to link citizens to the institutions that govern us, they must do certain things. Recall the earlier quotation from the Senate Committee report on Canada's news media: "No real democracy can function without healthy, diverse and independent news media to inform people about the way their society works, what is going well and, perhaps most important, what is not going well or needs to be improved." In this section and the next, we measure the performance of Canada's news media against this standard. We have already raised questions about the health, diversity, and independence of news organizations in an era of cross-ownership and concentration. Now we will ask whether they really (a) inform us about political issues and processes and (b) distinguish clearly between "what is going well" and what is not. We will also consider the ways in which the news media, as an institution, can set the political agenda for both rulers and ruled.

■ Do the News Media Inform Canadian Citizens Effectively?

As we have seen, news values emphasize conflict, drama, novelty, and "human interest" over detailed policy analysis or descriptions of the political process.[117] For both technological and financial reasons, this is particularly true of television—by far the most popular news medium in Canada. In 2005, eighty-nine percent of Canadians reportedly followed the news frequently (every day or two).[118] The most avid news junkies were older Canadians, francophones, and those with higher education and incomes. Most (91 percent) watched television news, although TV was the sole source for only 17 percent; almost three-quarters relied on two or more additional news sources, of which newspapers were the most frequent (70 percent). (Radio and the Internet were used by 53 and 30 percent of news consumers, respectively; seniors were more likely to use the former and younger Canadians the latter.)

Comparative studies suggest that Canadians are less likely to read newspapers, and more likely to obtain their news from television, than people in many other developed countries.[119] This is worrisome for two reasons. First, people for whom television is the only or principal source of news are less politically active than those who read newspapers.[120] This may help to explain why younger Canadians, who are the most likely to depend on TV news, are less politically engaged than their elders (see Chapters 2 and 12). Second, both the quantity and quality of political information depend in part on the medium used to obtain it. At best, television coverage of politics increases the audience's knowledge about personalities; it has little if any positive effect on their knowledge of issues or their understanding of the political system or context. In contrast, newspapers improve the reader's mastery of political facts.[121] The relationship between Internet use and political information is variable: reading the online edition of a newspaper enhances political learning, even more effectively than reading the hard copy of the same newspaper,[122] whereas the informational effect of reading other types of Web content is as yet undetermined. Some observers argue that Canadians' relatively high dependence on television for political information contributes to our relatively low levels of "civic literacy," compared to countries whose citizens rely more on newspapers for their political information.[123]

On the other hand, it may be that Canadians are relatively less informed about politics because of the limitations of the news media themselves. Shrinking news budgets, declining expertise, and the rush to be "first" with a story have reduced the quality and quantity of political information available to even the most dedicated news junkie.

◼ Setting the Political Agenda

The concept of **agenda-setting** refers to the alleged power of the news media to influence public perceptions of the relative importance of a given event. Studies of media effects have consistently found "a correlation between the frequency of a topic covered by the news media and its ranking in public opinion polls."[124] The long-term effect on the population at large may be even more significant in light of our dependence on the media for "secondhand" information about politics and government: "By directing audience attention towards some aspects of reality and away from others, the news media help to define reality for their audiences and to structure the public's perceptions of the political world."[125] However, the power of news directors to set the agenda should not be overstated. The degree to which media coverage shapes public perceptions varies with the type of issue involved. Perceptions of a problem like unemployment, which directly affects millions of Canadians, are less likely to be affected by media coverage than abstract issues beyond the daily experience of the average voter.[126]

When news coverage does heighten public concern about a problem, it often becomes a higher priority than it would otherwise have been. Climate change is a likely example. Whereas catastrophic storms like Katrina were once presented as human interest stories, they are now framed as the consequence of human impacts on the environment. In 2006, climate change was widely perceived as the most serious problem facing the country. The Harper Government was forced to abandon its dismissive attitude toward the problem and take steps to control greenhouse gas emissions. Similarly, the collapse of a highway bridge in Quebec is no longer an isolated event; it is evidence of a widespread deterioration of Canada's infrastructure, which was neglected by all levels of government during the budget cuts of the 1990s. Politicians have to act quickly to reassure the public, although they may not follow through on costly promises to remedy the problem if reporters' attention quickly shifts to the next "crisis."

Given that editorial choices—the news frame and the quantity of coverage—can influence the political response to events, journalists have a responsibility to choose wisely. This does not always happen. Political leaders sometimes react to a media-generated perception of a problem, rather than the objective reality. For example, news values favour stories about crime, rather than in-depth investigations of the social conditions that may foster criminality. By devoting disproportionate time to acts of violence, especially in local television news, the media convince us that crime is a constant and growing problem. Politicians try to capitalize on public concern by "cracking down" on criminals. The fact that violent crime rates have decreased significantly over the past decade is lost in the media frame and the political rhetoric. In particular, "the media spotlight on 'youth gangs' and violent crimes involving young people helped place revisions to the *Young Offenders Act* on the Parliamentary agenda."[127] This does not mean that politicians necessarily jump on every media bandwagon; the situation is more complex than that. When MPs and ministers monitor news coverage, they are not just looking for cues. They want to identify the prevailing news frames, so they can take advantage of them.[128] The "agenda-setting game"[129] between reporters and politicians can distort the policy-making process, as we will see in the next section.

THE EFFECT OF NEWS COVERAGE ON CANADIAN POLITICAL INSTITUTIONS

Generally, it can be said that there are two types of reporters: those who see themselves as part of the institutions they cover, and those who believe that it's the media's job to crusade against the institutions where they work. . . . Now, it is fair to say that for every one institutionally minded reporter in Ottawa, there is at least one reporter with an anti-institutional bent.[130]

For many observers, the role of the news media in Canadian politics has changed in recent years. Whereas the parliamentary press gallery was once "a narrator or an independent observer reporting and commenting on political events," today it is "a major political actor in its own right."[131] Its political role takes three forms:

- First, the news media provide the most important channel of communication between the state and the citizens. Today, governments have the capacity to communicate directly via the Internet; but the print and broadcast media remain the most important source of information for most Canadians, especially those who lack the resources required for Internet access.[132] As we have seen, news coverage of political events is not neutral; it is shaped by the institutional constraints on media workers and by the conventions of news coverage itself—agenda-setting, framing, and priming.

- Second, reporters act as conduits of information and opinion *between* government actors.[133] During political crises, when politicians may not be in direct contact with each other, they communicate through the media. An ill-judged public statement by one participant may provoke another to respond with equal defiance, leading to a showdown that may have undesirable results. The near-collapse of the minority Liberal Government in October 2004 demonstrated the risks of indirect communication via the press gallery. The leaders of the Conservative Party and the Bloc Québécois (Stephen Harper and Gilles Duceppe, respectively) told reporters that they would vote for a BQ sub-amendment to the Speech from the Throne; the Liberals responded, also via the media, that they would interpret such a result as a vote of no confidence and ask the governor general to call an election immediately.[134] As the hours ticked away, both sides dug in their heels. They could not retreat from the hard-line positions they had taken publicly, without risking embarrassment and the loss of support from their MPs. The defeat of the government after four days in the Commons—a result that no rational person could have wanted— seemed increasingly possible. Finally, Prime Minister Martin invited Harper and Duceppe to his office for a face-to-face discussion. Shortly afterward, the BQ changed the wording of its sub-amendment to remove the offending passages. It passed unanimously, and a crisis was averted.[135] If the three men had met earlier, instead of indulging in macho posturing before the television cameras, it is unlikely that a crisis would have erupted so soon in the life of the 38th Parliament.

- Third, the media's more aggressive coverage of politics and government has forced politicians and public servants to change the ways in which they work. They have adapted to the needs and values of the news media: the demand for instant answers, the tendency to put a negative "spin" on relatively innocuous events, and Cabinet ministers' fear of being perceived as either corrupt or incompetent. A more specific adaptation arises from reporters' use of access-to-information requests to obtain internal documents from government departments. A former policy adviser in the federal government recalls the "chilling" effect on policy-making: "I saw myself that officials are extremely leery of putting things on paper that they wouldn't like to see made public or find their way to the media, several months later, that could be embarrassing to the minister."[136] That caution now extends to emails as well as paper documents produced by public servants.

As suggested at the beginning of the previous section, journalists should help citizens to distinguish between the successes and failures of their political leaders and institutions. Some observers, including reporters themselves, perceive Canadian political coverage as overly negative—an "anti-political approach to covering politics."[137] A journalism professor recently described Canadian newspapers as "one big catalogue of complaint—a daily digest of everything that went wrong the day before." He added, "If you had to live in a house with a partner or roommate whose standard mode of address was a harping, carping litany of complaint about everything under the sun, you'd eventually have to quit the premises or blow your brains out. But that's what most Canadian journalism comes across as."[138] To see whether these descriptions are merited, we will look at the broader patterns in news coverage of the three branches of Canada's national government.

◼ The Legislative Branch

Much of the coverage of the House of Commons is focused on question period. This is only part—and, arguably, a distorted view—of the work of the House, and involves only a handful of Members. It is important that Canadians get a fuller picture. They need to be given an opportunity to see other MPs at work, and to see what committees are doing.[139]

Neither the House of Commons nor the Senate attracts much serious attention from the news media, despite the crucial role of legislative institutions as a forum for the discussion of national issues.[140] The daily Question Period in the Commons is the sole exception, not because of its intrinsic importance in the legislative process, but because "it has everything required for a good story":

There is no shortage of ten-second clips containing the needed quotient of personal vitriol and conflict. Personalities are magnified and issues condensed. . . . For the prime minister and opposition party leaders, the daily dramatics of Question Period can have a corrosive effect. Instead of being shown in a dignified setting where their authority is respected, they are seen hurling accusations at each other and in shouting matches.[141]

Regular debates and committee hearings, despite their greater potential importance and (sometimes) content, are generally ignored by the media.[142] This is despite the fact that television cameras have been allowed into committee rooms since 2001, and CPAC (the cable parliamentary channel) often broadcasts gavel-to-gavel coverage of House debates and particularly important meetings.[143] As one reporter told MPs, "By and large, once the lead-off speaker [of] each party has spoken, you know what every other speaker is going to say and, let us face it, you do not even go to hear them yourselves."[144] Reporters pay attention to debate or committees only when the system breaks down: an Opposition party tries to block legislation through procedural shenanigans, a government backbencher breaks with his or her party, or a committee hearing dissolves into chaos. This distorted focus "encourages the worst aspects of parliamentary behaviour"[145] and likely contributes to the decline in public support for Parliament (Chapters 2 and 7).[146] It appears that Question Period and other highly adversarial encounters receive disproportionate media attention because they suit the requirements of television: conflict, good visuals, and short, emphatic statements. The fact that they present the legislative branch in the worst possible light is overlooked. "Parliament itself, inasmuch as it seems to have the atmosphere of a prize-fight—at least as presented on television—has dropped considerably in public esteem in recent years."[147]

Three additional aspects of the media's relationship to Parliament deserve mention.

- First, reporters rarely give the Senate positive coverage, despite its valuable role in the legislative process (see "Sober Second Thought: The Legislative Role of the Senate" in Chapter 7). If more Canadians understood and appreciated the work done by senators, the institution might enjoy greater public legitimacy.

- Second, journalists hostile to political authority have effectively usurped the role of the official Opposition in the Commons.[148] The function of an official Opposition is not just to criticize the government of the day; it is to provide an alternative government, one that can be held accountable to the voters. Journalists cannot perform this function. All they can do is undermine public faith in the wisdom and integrity of elected officials, by emphasizing undignified partisan name-calling at the expense of valuable legislative work.

- Third, the media and the Opposition parties often work together to get the most mileage out of Question Period. Opposition MPs attend morning tactics meetings, armed with piles of newspaper clippings and primed by watching videotapes of last night's newscasts. They use the headlines and the top stories to determine the content and order of their questions for that day. Don Newman, the host of "Politics" on CBC *Newsworld* and formerly a reporter for the *Globe and Mail*, once remarked that "When you were writing your story you knew that you were writing Question Period the next day."[149] To the extent that reporters and Opposition MPs uncover genuinely important information about problems in the executive branch, their cooperation can provide the most effective guarantee of government accountability to the people. On the downside, a close working relationship between journalists and Opposition MPs who share an ideological agenda and an antipathy to the government can produce distorted news coverage and turn Question Period into a pointless witch-hunt.

Much of the cooperation between the media and the Opposition produces nothing but sound and fury: phony outrage, manufactured or exaggerated scandals, and questionable reporting. But on occasion, media cooperation with the auditor general and other parliamentary watchdogs can force the government to fix real problems in policy or management that would otherwise have gone unaddressed. The Sponsorship Scandal is the best recent example. Had it not been for the investigative work of the *Globe and Mail's* parliamentary bureau, the lack of proper oversight in the Sponsorship Program might never have come to light.[150] When the auditor general announced in early 2004 that a few public servants in the Department of Public Works and Government Services "broke every rule in the book," the Government of the day was engulfed in a political crisis that ultimately destroyed it (Dossier 8.2).

◼ The Executive Branch

Prime ministers and those who work for them devote enormous time and effort to "managing" problems. Members of both the political and permanent executives measure their success not only by their accomplishments but also by their ability to "manage" media crises.

> *The work of the media by all accounts dominates the agenda of morning meetings between the prime minister and the Clerk of the Privy Council. What the evening news on national television reported the night before and what the headlines in morning newspapers say have a profound impact on question period, and by extension, on government operations.*[151]

In other words, they try to keep potentially embarrassing mistakes and conflicts from reaching the media; if that fails, they want to "spin" the story in order to minimize the political damage. Since the 1980s, the ranks of "spin doctors" in the PMO and ministers' offices have grown significantly. Spin doctors are former journalists, who use their inside knowledge of the news-gathering process to present their political bosses in the most flattering light (Dossier 9.3).[152]

On occasion, the "spin" staff themselves become part of the story—usually in unflattering ways. Scott Reid, then director of Communications for Prime Minister Paul Martin, appeared on a CBC news panel during the 2006 election campaign. In the course of attacking the Conservatives' promise to replace the Liberals' child-care program with direct payments to parents, Reid sneered that some recipients would "blow" the money on "beer and popcorn." The Conservatives pounced on Reid's gaffe, characterizing it as an illustration of Liberal arrogance.[153] The clip was replayed over and over, and the gaffe became a major news story during a slow period in the campaign.[154] Although it probably had little impact on the election result, Reid's slip of the tongue damaged the Liberals' re-election effort in the short term. The Conservatives have not been immune to such gaffes; Prime Minister Harper lost his Chief of Staff in summer 2008 following a leak of confidential information that may have influenced the outcome of an American presidential primary (see Chapter 9).

Until recently, relations between the executive branch and the news media were generally smooth. Each side acknowledged and (sometimes grudgingly) respected the other's power to help or hinder its work. That changed when Prime Minister Harper took office in early 2006, determined to control his Government's message and "to manage issues so that the media will not be able to obtain information that might place the government in a bad light."[155] To an unprecedented degree, he and his staff restricted ministers' and MPs' contacts with reporters. As soon as his Government took office, Harper ended the long-standing practice of post-Cabinet "scrums." He banned reporters from the area outside the Cabinet room, and refused to announce meeting times to the media.[156] He even went so far as to enter the Centre Block (which houses the prime minister's parliamentary office) through a side door, instead of the front entrance where reporters congregate. Individual ministers are kept on a tight leash: before a minister can make an announcement, deliver a speech, or grant an interview, he or she must receive permission from the PMO.[157] Draft speeches, written by the minister's staff and senior public servants, may be revised by the prime minister's team before delivery. Relations between the ministers' press staff and the PMO deteriorated rapidly. Some Communication directors, angered by central interference with their work, quit their jobs; others leaked damaging details of the PMO's control strategy to reporters.[158] Such leaks were extremely rare in the tightly managed Harper Government; most ministers and exempt staff quickly fell into line, fearful of the prime minister's wrath.

Harper himself disdained the established rules of the parliamentary press gallery, which he perceives as a cabal of anti-Conservative ideologues. Shortly after being sworn in, he declared that "if we can break that [the Gallery] up in any way, that is helpful for democracy."[159] With rare exceptions, Harper refuses to make announcements in the press gallery theatre in Ottawa, where a gallery official decides which reporters will ask questions.[160] Instead, he prefers to meet the press (at lengthy intervals) in settings where he and his staff can control the questioning. Former Communications Director Sandra Buckler made it clear that Harper would answer very few questions. Worse yet, he would take questions from some reporters but not from others (presumably those whom he considered hostile to his Government). When gallery reporters protested by walking out of a Harper press event in May 2006, the PM promptly stopped holding media events in Ottawa.[161] Instead, he usually makes announcements outside the capital. For example, he and several Cabinet ministers flew to Vancouver in fall 2006 to announce that the Government would introduce its *Clean Air Act* at some point in the future. The purpose of this event was obscure, but at least it kept Harper away from the gallery. Local reporters, lacking an in-depth knowledge of national political institutions and processes, generally ask softer questions and treat the prime minister with more deference than their Ottawa-based colleagues.

The extraordinary cocoon of secrecy surrounding the Harper Government could signal a new relationship between the Canadian executive branch and the news media. Future prime ministers, aware of their power to impose "message discipline" on the executive branch, will be tempted to follow Harper's example. Then again, if Harper pays a political price for his feud with the press gallery, his tight control could serve as a cautionary tale for his successors.

Within a year of taking office, the war between the Government and the news media was damaging public perceptions of Harper and his Cabinet.[162] The appearance of excessive secrecy is bound to raise concerns about any Government's activities, and questions about what it might be hiding. Paradoxically, poor relations with the media also make it more difficult for the Government to convey a positive message to the voters. As senior Ottawa reporter James Travers put it in October 2006, "I'm quite stunned by the fact that this government, or this Prime Minister, doesn't see that it's to his advantage to meet regularly with the national gallery because it's an opportunity for them to broadcast their message in a relatively controlled environment."[163] It may be that the short-term advantages of "message discipline," especially for a brand-new government with inexperienced ministers and staff, are outweighed in the long run by the refusal to work constructively with reporters.[164]

The Judicial Branch

Until the 1980s, neither journalists nor their audiences paid much attention to the Supreme Court of Canada or the provincial Courts of Appeal. An individual judge might acquire some notoriety during a high-profile criminal trial, or (like John Gomery) while presiding over a public inquiry. Apart from these rare cases, the judicial branch operated beyond the reach of the media spotlight. That obscurity was compromised in 1981, when television cameras were admitted into the Supreme Court chamber to cover the justices' ruling on the *Patriation Reference*. As the top court in the country, and one of the most powerful of Canada's national political institutions, the court was bound to attract growing media interest—especially after the *Charter of Rights* took effect in 1982.

Shortly after the *Patriation Reference*, Brian Dickson took over as chief justice. He set out to create a new working relationship between the court and the media.[165] Dickson appointed the first Executive Legal Officer (ELO), responsible for briefing reporters on important rulings and ensuring that the court's decisions are reported accurately.[166] He also broke precedent by granting interviews and permitting cameras within the private precincts of the Supreme Court building.[167] Since 1997, CPAC has provided gavel-to-gavel coverage of court hearings on high-profile appeals and constitutional references.[168] These broadcasts may hold little appeal for nonexperts; the legal arguments are often difficult for the layperson to understand. Nonetheless, they offer a unique glimpse into the judicial policy-making process.

Despite the relatively harmonious working relationship between the court and the press (fostered by the Media Relations Committee, which brings together justices and reporters to resolve disputes), the Supreme Court has incurred considerable media criticism for its interpretations of the *Charter of Rights*. That criticism peaked between 1998 and 2000, when Conrad Black owned the *National Post*; he appointed a full-time reporter to cover the Supreme Court (the only one in recent years), and turned the paper into a forum for attacks on "judicial activism."[169] According to one of the paper's columnists, Andrew Coyne, "The *Post* is against any attempt on the part of unelected judges to impose their will on a democratically elected legislature."[170] While the justice reporter for the *Globe and Mail*, Kirk Makin, agreed that the *Post* was "leading the charge" against the Supreme Court, he argues that the roots of journalistic hostility lie deeper: "Having demystified and demythologized every other institution in society, I see the media now turning a great deal of attention to judges, judicial behaviour, and actual judgments."[171]

Former Chief Justice Antonio Lamer acknowledged that fear of widespread public and media criticism affected the court: "Judges are human beings. I would be remiss if I were to say that we are superhuman or that we are not influenced sometimes."[172] A survey of appellate judges in the early 1990s found that some were concerned about "the impact of media criticism that they could not respond to without themselves violating judicial independence." Others worried that "the inaccurate or sensationalist handling of judicial decisions by the media was in a sense putting pressure on them to make decisions that would result in a 'good press.'" [173] While there are legitimate concerns about the accountability of the Supreme Court in the *Charter* era, shallow and sensationalistic news coverage is not a constructive solution to the problem.

Court rulings that appear to protect the due-process rights of the accused against the rights of actual or potential victims have been particularly controversial. The court's reluctance to allow the introduction of improperly obtained evidence in criminal trials is sometimes portrayed as a callous disregard for public safety and an assault on the legitimate investigative powers of the police.[174] The fact that section 24(2) of the *Constitution Act, 1982* not only permits, but actually requires, judges to exclude tainted evidence is rarely mentioned. A handful of judicial rulings on the right to a fair trial (such as *Askov*, discussed in Chapter 10) have provoked widespread media and pressure-group criticism of the court. Note, however, that when a *Charter* ruling attracts severe and sustained criticism from the media and from pressure groups, Parliament usually responds by amending or reintroducing the impugned law. So the media can play an important role, both in the "dialogue" between legislators and judges and in the improvement of our laws. For that reason, it is essential that they provide accurate coverage—which is not always the case.

Perhaps the most hostile media response to a *Charter* decision (apart from the 1988 *Morgentaler* ruling) concerned the court's 1994 ruling in *Daviault*. It quashed a conviction for sexual assault on the ground that the accused was too drunk at the time of the offence to form the requisite criminal intent. In other words, he could not be found guilty because the Crown could not prove that he knew what he was doing when he committed the crime.[175] The court's ruling hit the front pages, amid howls of outrage from women's groups and victims' rights groups. The news coverage implied that the court had not only set the man free—when, in reality, it had ordered him to stand trial a second time—but had declared open season on women for any man who was physically capable of sexual assault while he was drunk enough to meet the standard of "extreme intoxication." Daviault's 65-year-old victim was confined to a wheelchair, a fact that sharpened accusations of callousness on the part of the justices (whereas, in law, the relative vulnerability of an adult victim generally plays little if any role in determining guilt). When the worst fears of the court's critics were confirmed, and five men were acquitted of sexual-assault charges under the *Daviault* doctrine within a year of the ruling, the media played up the theme that victims' rights were being ignored. Notably, however, "The six unsuccessful uses of the defence and the reversal on appeal of two of the five acquittals received less attention."[176] In this highly charged political and journalistic climate, it was hardly surprising that Parliament closed the *Daviault* loophole a year after the ruling.

The fallout from *Daviault* illustrates some broader trends in media coverage of the Supreme Court. First, reporters tend to focus on cases that fit within preexisting cultural narratives or "news frames," regardless of their intrinsic legal importance. Whenever the justices rule on a case that engages public or political attention, reporters flock to the lobby of the Supreme Court building. All the ingredients of a good news story are right there: conflict, emotion, eager pundits, and articulate pressure-group leaders who can personalize abstract issues. Criminal cases may also provide sympathetic victims and "villainous" crooks, colourful characters right out of a prime-time drama. On occasion, public sympathy is divided between the accused and the victim; such controversial cases are especially high-profile. In a recent study of the Supreme Court and its treatment by the news media, the authors found that the *Latimer* ruling received significantly more coverage than any other decision handed down during the 2000–01 term.[177] The case of a Saskatchewan farmer who confessed to killing his disabled daughter provoked a public debate about "mercy killing," the rights of the disabled, and the adequacy of government support for parents and caregivers.[178] In the end, the Supreme Court of Canada upheld Latimer's conviction and life sentence (with parole eligibility after 10 years).[179] From a legal standpoint, the *Latimer* ruling was less important than some others handed down in the same year; but the human drama ensured intense media attention.

Second, reporters apply their customary political news frames to court rulings. This produces distorted and often inaccurate coverage of the decisions themselves. Print and broadcast stories focus on the "winners" and "losers," ignoring the justices' reasons for their decision.[180] The "contest" frame is problematic because the institutional legitimacy of the Supreme Court is jeopardized when Canadians do not understand how justices do their jobs or why they take the decisions they do.[181] As Justice Ian Binnie put it, ""They [the media] should therefore exercise their power of explanation with a sense of responsibility."[182]

Moreover, the stark contrast between victors and vanquished misrepresents the careful balancing act that the court undertakes when it interprets and applies the law.[183] The 2002 *Sauvé* ruling, in which a divided Court narrowly voted to strike down a legislated ban on voting by federal prisoners, was portrayed by most media outlets as a victory for murderers at the expense of law-abiding citizens. The justices were pilloried by reporters and Opposition MPs for giving the "morally unworthy" the right to vote. The reality was very different. Lawyers for the federal government had conceded that the law violated section 3 of the *Charter,* which gives every Canadian citizen the right to vote in federal elections. The majority ruling turned on two key issues: whether the deliberate infringement of a core democratic right could be justified under section 1; and the degree to which the court should defer when the other two branches of government refused to take the *Charter* seriously.[184] The government failed to prove that the voting ban was necessary to safeguard the integrity of the electoral process, or that the right to vote should be denied to those who were morally blameworthy. So the issue, from the perspective of the five justices in the majority, was not whether convicted murderer Paul Bernardo should be allowed to mark a ballot; it was their second-order duty to uphold the *Charter* when elected politicians failed in their first-order duties. (See Chapters 6 and 10.)

Why do reporters assigned to cover court rulings rely on familiar narratives and news frames? Because they lack the expertise to properly interpret legal documents. If the scarcity of specialized beat reporters weakens coverage of policy issues, as previously argued, the problem is especially acute when journalists confront complex constitutional arguments. An untrained layperson cannot be expected to digest and accurately summarize the key points in a lengthy legal decision. Most court decisions are shaped by precedents (see the discussion of *stare decisis* in Chapter 10), which are well understood by lawyers but not by laypeople. The concrete facts of the case, as presented at trial, are easy to report; the abstract legal principles in an appellate decision are not.

To make matters worse, as previously discussed, a reporter assigned to a "breaking" story may be called upon to do a live "two-way" with the anchor desk (or post a brief synopsis to a website) within minutes of the decision's release. Since 2003, the ELO has provided "lock-ups" for reporters immediately before the publication of the court's reasons for judgment in especially newsworthy cases.[185] A lock-up is a briefing session, usually off-the-record, in which a government official guides journalists and other interested observers through a complicated document that is about to be released to the public (e.g., the annual federal budget). While a lock-up can help a reporter to identify the key points in a judgment, it cannot make up for a lack of background knowledge and context. The 2003 Supreme Court ruling in *Figueroa* (Dossier 6.3) is a typical example. The ruling was issued at 9:45 a.m. Less than half an hour later, a CBC reporter who had been inside the lock-up went live in the lobby of the court building. She appeared flustered as she flipped through the lengthy ruling, misidentified the key points in the decision, and repeatedly characterized the nullification of a section of the *Canada Elections Act* as a "loss" for the federal government. When the anchor asked her to predict how the Government might respond to the ruling, the reporter suggested that it might invoke the "notwithstanding clause" (p. 190). She was apparently unaware that the clause does not apply to section 3 of the *Charter,* which was infringed by the nullified law. This example suggests that, despite the best efforts of the ELO, the systemic problems in news coverage of court rulings persist.

For all of the reasons just discussed, media stories about the courts are rife with inaccuracies and misinterpretations. Reporters' synopses of judgments often bear only a passing resemblance to the judgments themselves. Judges are "sometimes frustrated when their judgments come off the news assembly line looking far different from what they thought had gone in."[186] Journalists focus on the human drama of the parties or which side scores the "win," not on the legal rules that the court establishes for future cases. Unless and until news organizations invest more resources in legal reporting, perhaps by hiring lawyers and training them in journalistic techniques,[187] few Canadians will have the opportunity to understand the work of the courts. In the *Charter* era, when judges are often called on to resolve controversial political and moral issues, this is an unacceptable situation.

"NEW MEDIA" VERSUS THE "MAINSTREAM MEDIA": HOW BIG ARE THE DIFFERENCES?

We have seen that new communication and information technologies are changing the ways in which journalists work. For the rest of us, those technologies provide access to an unprecedented range of news and opinion. A few decades ago, citizens looking for political information and analysis had four options: newspapers, magazines, radio, and the nightly network newscasts. Stories that made it through the filter of "news values" were published or broadcast; those which did not were known only to the people directly involved. Anyone who was not a journalist or an "expert" had few opportunities to share his or her opinions with other citizens beyond his or her immediate social circle.

The picture is very different today. The proliferation of 24-hour cable news channels and the explosive growth of the Internet provide an astonishing array of stories and opinion. As the Web became more interactive, blogs and YouTube broke the monopoly of politicians and pundits and allowed anyone with an Internet connection to disseminate their own stories and perspectives. As search engines evolved, the journalistic monopoly over the selection and arrangement of information was broken.

> *Technology is transforming citizens from passive consumers of news produced by professionals into active participants who can assemble their own journalism from disparate elements. As people Google for information, graze across a seemingly infinite array of outlets, and read blogs or write them, they are becoming their own editors, researchers, and even correspondents.*[188]

The "new media" are changing politics and public discourse, largely (but not entirely) for the better. At the same time, they raise important questions about the continued survival of traditional journalism (often called the **"mainstream media,"** or MSM for short).

- At one time, everyone watched the same networks and read the same newspapers. Today the audience is fragmented among a host of various cable channels and websites. This is a worrisome trend for commercial television networks, and newspapers, whose economic survival depends on assembling the largest possible audience to "sell" to advertisers. The quality of our public discourse could be further reduced as the electorate is divided into isolated pockets of opinion and analysis—especially given the prevalence of misleading and biased "information" available on the Web, and the overt political agendas of some cable news programs.
- The Web is drawing advertisers away from the print and broadcast media. Newspapers are particularly hard hit by the migration of classified ads for jobs, cars, and real estate to specialized websites like Craigslist.[189] If this trend continues, newspapers will go out of business; even the *New York Times* was forced to lay off reporters and production employees in early 2008.
- The immediacy of cable and Web-based news coverage puts the networks and print media at a disadvantage. When a breaking story happens without warning, such as the 9/11 attacks, news consumers will not wait for the nightly newscast or the next morning's paper; they will

immediately turn on CNN or go online to find out what's happening right now. Under those circumstances, the continued relevance of the "old" news media is in some doubt.

- Finally, young Canadians (like their peers around the world) appear to reject the top-down structure of the MSM. According to a 2006 study of American media consumption, "Newspapers, news magazines, and television news are losing young consumers and are building business models that do not include them. . . . Only 18 percent of eighteen to twenty-nine-year-old adults watch the nightly network news, and only 23 percent of them have read a newspaper within the past day."[190] Why waste time turning the pages of a newspaper, hoping to find a story that engages your interest, when you can Google it online? When the prime minister makes an announcement, why would you take a reporter's "spin" at face value when you can watch the video and read the text of the speech on the prime minister's website? Finally, why pay attention to pundits when you can post your own written and video content on your blog, YouTube, or a message board? Despite the potential benefits of interactivity and direct access to political information, there is widespread concern about the patterns of media use among young people. Dossier 14.4 examines one recent controversy related to this broader concern.

DOSSIER 14.4 Laughing or Learning?

Since 2000, annual surveys of media use by the Pew Research Centre have found that a growing proportion of young Americans (aged 18–34 years) get their political news from comedians—especially Jon Stewart, host of *The Daily Show*—even as their consumption of "serious" network or cable news programming shrinks.[191] These findings disturb some media scholars and traditional journalists. The former argue that comedy shows do not really educate viewers; at best, they fool their young audience into thinking that they know something about politics and government.[192] The journalists claim that the crucial distinction between news and entertainment has all but disappeared. (Stewart himself has no problem distinguishing the two: when then-Senator John Edwards announced his candidacy for the 2004 Democratic presidential nomination on *The Daily Show,* the host "promptly reminded Edwards that his is a fake news show, and that he might have to make the announcement again somewhere."[193]) Some journalists also fret about the future of American democracy, bemoaning the political illiteracy of the younger generation.

Amidst the hand-wringing, two facts are generally overlooked. First, as Stewart points out, his viewers have to know something about politics before they watch the show; otherwise, "it wouldn't make any sense to them."[194] (The same could be said about Canadian satire programs like the *Rick Mercer Report* and *This Hour Has 22 Minutes.*) Stewart's claim is substantiated by two recent studies of *Daily Show* viewers, which found that most are heavy consumers of political news from a variety of sources. They watch political satire in addition to, not instead of, "real" news.[195] Second, those who dismiss *The Daily Show* as fluff are missing the point. The program won important journalism awards, including a Peabody—the highest honour in the news business—for its coverage of the 2000 U.S. presidential election.[196] Stewart and his coworkers often focus on stories that are ignored or downplayed by the MSM; in so doing, they force the "serious" reporters to pay closer attention to those events.

On balance, the popularity of *The Daily Show* (which attracts an average of 1 million viewers per episode[197]) is good news for the news business—although the celebrity journalists who are routinely lampooned on the program might disagree. Because it assumes a certain degree of political knowledge in its audience, the program is "encouraging young viewers to tune into traditional forms of news so that they have the context necessary to appreciate [its] topical humour." In the process, "*The Daily Show* promotes interest in news and politics."[198] This is a positive outcome, not just for the MSM but for the future of democratic participation.

These developments have led to gloomy predictions about the future of the traditional news media. "From newspaper executives at the *New York Times* who have asked whether there will be a print version of their paper in 10 years, to television news executives who openly speculate on whether there will be network nightly news,"[199] doomsday scenarios have been rife in recent years. Before we jump to conclusions, we should recognize that the MSM are trying to adapt to—even profit from—the new technologies.

- The fragmentation of the news audience is more apparent than real, for two reasons. First, as previously discussed, ownership of media companies is concentrated in fewer and fewer hands. Second, newspaper readers are turning to the Internet to supplement, not to replace, the older medium. A little over 10 percent of Americans surveyed in 2006 had completely substituted online for "offline" news sources, whereas a sizable majority reporting using both.[200] Similarly, Canadians follow Internet news in addition to, not instead of, print and broadcast media.[201] Moreover the most popular news websites are the online versions of mainstream newspapers, magazines, and broadcasters: "people who go online for their news tend to use media brands online that they know and trust from the offline world."[202] Apart from brand-name loyalty, the reliance on established sources for online news can be attributed to doubts about the credibility of other websites. "It will take time for online media sources to establish levels of credibility similar to traditional media sources."[203] For media companies that have embraced the new technology, the Web has become a powerful asset both domestically and overseas. By 2006, 15 million people visited the *New York Times* website every month—more than 10 million of whom did not (or could not) buy the print edition.[204] The *Guardian*, a leading British newspaper, also attracts millions of readers from around the world.[205] Broadcast-based sites, like CNN.com, BBC.co.uk, and cbc.ca, also draw a lot of traffic. Over time, these sites have supplemented their original print-based content with a growing volume of video and audio clips—including entire programs, in live-streaming video and podcast formats. In the words of a senior CBC executive, "the moment the bandwidth becomes acceptable, everything goes to the Internet. That is where your new channels will come from."[206]

- Concentrated ownership and Web dominance by established media companies have also mitigated the impact of Internet advertising. Less than 15 percent of advertising has shifted from traditional outlets to the Internet. The owners of multi-media conglomerates are recouping much of the lost revenue from their newspapers and broadcast stations by attracting more ads online.[207] The profitability of online advertising will continue to grow, as ownership concentration spreads from the MSM to the Internet. Rupert Murdoch, one of the world's leading newspaper and television moguls, bought MySpace in 2005. The following year, Google paid almost $2 billion to acquire YouTube.[208]

- The immediacy of the new technologies will not make newspapers and nightly newscasts obsolete. Instead, it is changing the role and position of the older news outlets, although the direction of that change is not yet clear. "The conventional response of the so-called serious press to the new media culture has been that its place is to add more context and interpretation to the news."[209] In other words, we will surf the Web for breaking news until we become overwhelmed by the mass of disconnected information; then we will turn to newspapers and evening newscasts to figure out how everything fits together. Alternatively, traditional journalists will focus more on verifying information that has already become available—for example, digging for the facts behind political "spin"—and less on conveying the information itself. They will distinguish between reliable and unreliable sources; they will "[s]ift out the rumour, the innuendo, the insignificant, and the spin, and concentrate on what is true and important about a story."[210]

User-generated Web content—discussion boards, blogs, YouTube, and Facebook—has attracted a great deal of attention over the past few years. Advocates predicted that "bottom-up" news and opinion sites would challenge the elitism of the MSM and enrich the political discourse by fostering online deliberation among citizens. Critics feared the proliferation of ideological "echo chambers," where like-minded people would reinforce each other's prejudices and irresponsible posturing would mislead the unwary.[211] In all likelihood, "we media"[212] (also called "Web 2.0"[213]) will not have the cataclysmic political effects predicted by both its advocates and its detractors.

Discussion Boards

In recent years, Government agencies, MSM companies, political parties, and advocacy groups have set up discussion boards on their websites. These are forums for public comment and debate, often on topics chosen by the users themselves (discussion "threads"). Advocates of discussion boards believe that they will provide a space for meaningful public deliberation, level the playing field between pundits and "ordinary" citizens, and give decision-makers a better sense of public opinion. Critics point to the tendency for a few dedicated users to dominate the discussion, often by "flaming" users who do not share their particular ideology.

A recent study of two political message boards substantiated the claims of the critics, but not entirely.[214] The authors compared the 2001 BC Votes message board, a temporary election-related site sponsored by a consortium of British Columbia media companies, to a permanent national website for political news and messages. They found that the BC Votes board attracted relatively few users, most of whom posted only one or two messages. A handful of users (one in particular) dominated the discussion: they set the daily agenda by starting new threads, and then posted most of the contributions. The quality of the postings did not meet the standard of genuine deliberation: fewer than 2 percent provided evidence to support the opinions expressed, and the large majority lacked substance. Most users copied the MSM by emphasizing the election horse-race; they indulged in "amateur punditry" instead of substantive debate about policies and issues. The tone of the messages was overwhelmingly negative, confirming the perception of the Internet as "a haven for complainers." On a happier note, "flaming" was a rare occurrence. The Bourque NewsWatch board showed similar patterns, which suggests that these findings may be typical of political message boards in Canada.

Blogs

Instead of providing an alternative to the MSM, the most widely read political blogs "rely heavily on professional news sites and stories by journalists associated with professional media organizations."[215] The number and political impact of blogs grew rapidly in the early 2000s; by 2004, a few American political bloggers had been anointed as celebrities by the "old" media, and received accreditation to cover the Republican and Democratic National Conventions. During the 2004 U.S. presidential race, "both commentary and investigative reporting by blogs were credited with setting the news agenda at points in the campaign"[216]— despite the fact that only 5 percent of Americans with Internet access read blogs regularly.[217]

Some bloggers set out to monitor news coverage by the MSM and to expose its flaws (real or perceived). When CBS News aired a report alleging that President Bush had received preferential treatment during his stint in the Texas National Guard (a favoured alternative to the Vietnam draft for privileged young men), a blogger in Georgia questioned the authenticity of the documents used to substantiate the allegation. Almost immediately, the "blogosphere" became a hotbed of analysis and speculation. It soon emerged that the documents could not be verified, and that the person who had given them to CBS had lied about where he obtained them. Anchorman Dan Rather was pressured into early retirement, the producer of the story was fired, and the head of CBS News stepped down.[218]

The bloggers' political influence peaked in the weeks before election day. The downhill slide started on the day itself, when many political blogs posted exit polls that erroneously predicted a victory for Democrat John Kerry. Mainstream reporters (who had ignored the exit polls, having been embarrassed by them in 2000) gloated as their upstart rivals seemed to confirm their reputation for irresponsibility and unreliability—ignoring the bloggers' explicit warnings not to put too much faith in the data.[219] Bloggers were less visible in the 2006 midterm elections; the attention had shifted to YouTube (see below).

By 2007, the mushrooming growth of blogs had slowed and the fad seemed to be passing. Warren Kinsella, a Liberal strategist in Ottawa, admitted that he and his fellow bloggers were losing their audience to social networking sites and the MSM.[220] This does not mean the end of online political posturing: in their efforts to compete with bloggers, mainstream news sites now invite readers to post their reactions to stories. Unlike grassroots blogs, however, these discussions are moderated and often edited by mainstream journalists. This filtering process is necessary because some postings contain obscene language and/or vicious attacks on particular individuals.[221]

YouTube and Facebook

At the time of writing, YouTube and Facebook were too new to permit an assessment of their impact on politics. There is anecdotal evidence that YouTube helped to determine the outcome of the 2006 U.S. midterm elections. Republican Senator George Allen lost his Virginia seat in that midterm election, largely because his racist slur during a campaign speech was captured on video and posted to his opponent's website; shortly afterward, it appeared on YouTube and got nearly half a million hits. Had Allen held his seat, his party would have had a majority of seats in the U.S. Senate.[222] As the 2008 presidential primary campaigns kicked off in early 2007, YouTube became the advertising venue of choice for the leading Democratic candidates.

As usual, Canadian politicians quickly copied the campaign tactics of their American counterparts. Since the 1960s, party leaders and candidates have assigned workers, called "road warriors," to monitor their opponents' public appearances.[223] In the past, any attempt to videotape a gaffe or a poorly received speech would have been too obvious; the "road warrior" would have been spotted and ejected from the event. Today, cell phone cameras make it possible to surreptitiously record embarrassing moments and post them on YouTube for the whole world to see. The Conservatives were caught in the act in 2007 when one of their Parliament Hill researchers was filmed while videotaping a speech by Liberal leader Stéphane Dion. Critics questioned the use of taxpayer-funded staff for an explicitly political purpose.[224] Of course, YouTube is more than a repository of surreptitious "gotcha" clips; Canadian parties post their own glossy ads on the site, which provides a cost-effective way to reach younger voters. This tactic first gained prominence during the 2006 Liberal leadership race.

So did the use of Facebook as a campaign tool—by early 2007 a handful of Canadian politicians, including the leaders of the three major parties outside Quebec, were using the networking site to communicate with their supporters and organize political events.[225] The site's popularity among young exempt staffers caused some embarrassment for the Harper Government in early 2007, when the CBC aired comments from the Facebook page belonging to a Cabinet minister's assistant.[226] The Prime Minister's Office ordered all exempt staff to shut down their Facebook accounts and stay off social networking sites. This episode illustrates the risks of user-generated content, especially for a Government that is determined to control its messaging from the centre.

CONCLUSION

Collectively, the men and women who report and analyze the news possess considerable power to shape political events. Unlike the prime minister or the Chief Justice of the Supreme Court, reporters are not constrained by the *Constitution* in their exercise of that power. Broadcast organizations can be held to account by the CRTC, in extreme cases; print journalists are accountable to no one except their bosses and (in the private sector) the owners of the company, although the latter may be willing to tolerate irresponsible journalism as long as it draws in readers.

Shortly after the "reasonable accommodation" of ethnic and religious minorities became a political issue in the 2007 Quebec election, Premier Jean Charest appointed a commission to study the issue and make recommendations. The commission's public hearings around the province attracted dozens of disgruntled Quebeckers, whose bigoted verbal attacks on Muslims and other "newcomers" embarrassed the government and alienated minority groups. In its 2008 report, the Bouchard-Taylor Commission blamed the news media for distorting the facts and creating a false impression that minorities were demanding and receiving excessive privileges.[227] The commissioners commented that "we can only ask ourselves what form debate would have taken if the public had obtained complete, objective information. The most likely hypothesis is that an accommodation crisis would not have arisen."[228] In other words, a full-blown social and political crisis arose, not because of an actual problem, but because of sensational and sometimes falsified news coverage.

This "crisis" fixation in the news media, exacerbated by 24-hour news, superficial coverage, and an antipathy toward politicians, has forced Western governments to adopt a "'perpetual election campaign' mode."[229] According to Savoie, "court government" is the direct result of the siege mentality in Ottawa:

> Court government provides quick and unencumbered access to the levels of power to make things happen and to pick and choose those political, policy, and administrative issues that appeal to prime ministers or that need resolution because the media are demanding immediate answers. Only the prime minister is in a position to provide quick answers to the media on virtually any issue confronting the government. . . . Court government suits prime ministers and their courtiers because it enables them to get things done, to see results, and to manage the news and the media better than they can when formal cabinet processes are respected. . . . News management is made easier when only a handful of individuals is involved, rather than full cabinet and many elements of the bureaucracy.[230]

It would be nonsensical to lay all the blame on the media for the problems identified in previous chapters—the declining legitimacy of our political institutions, falling voter turnout, shrinking political parties, and the accountability gap in the executive branch—but there can be little doubt that hostile news coverage has played a role in all of them. It is easier to jump to negative conclusions about the individual motives of politicians than to examine the institutional incentives that shape their behaviour (especially for reporters with little background in political science). If more Canadian journalists were willing to give MPs credit for their hard work and sacrifices, or to recognize the skill and dedication of public servants, fewer Canadians would express negative feelings about their political system.

GLOSSARY OF KEY TERMS

Agenda-setting: The process of determining which public issues will be given high priority by government actors.

Mainstream media (MSM): Newspapers, mass-market magazines, and the long-established radio and television networks. For the most part, the MSM are one-way channels of communication; their content is strongly influenced by the advertisers and sponsors who pay the bills. In contrast, the Internet offers interactivity, easy outlets for user-generated content, and niches for every specialized interest.

News frames: Consistent perspectives on news events, which put a particular event in a single context and tell the audience how they should interpret it. Example: framing a general election as a horse race, rather than a contest of ideologies or policy proposals.

News values: The criteria used by journalists to determine which events to cover and the "spin" they will apply to that coverage.

"Spin doctor":   A political staffer responsible for working with the media. His or her job is "not only to sell a message but also to contain the political fallout from negative developments or news stories."[231]

DISCUSSION AND REVIEW QUESTIONS

1. How often do you watch a television newscast? How many times a week do you read the front section of a newspaper? If you are a regular consumer of Canadian political news, what is your opinion of the information and analysis available from our media companies?

2. Try the following experiment: The next time a big political story breaks, make a point of watching three different newscasts (e.g., CBC *Newsworld,* CTV *Newsnet,* CPAC, or Global) AND reading the coverage in three different newspapers (e.g., the *Globe and Mail,* the *National Post,* and the *Toronto Star*). Can you identify different "spins" or "frames" in the coverage? Do the news values of each media organization differ? How might a habitual reader or viewer or listener of one paper or broadcast perceive politics differently from someone who chooses a different source for his or her daily news? How much information did you receive from the television reporting compared to the newspaper coverage?

3. Identify and briefly explain THREE ways in which the private ownership of media companies affects news coverage of politics and public affairs. Should we be concerned about these effects? If so, what should we do?

4. Do you watch Canadian and/or American political satire shows (e.g., *The Daily Show* or *The Mercer Report*)? If so, do these programs inspire you to learn more about politics?

SUGGESTED READINGS

Books and Articles

W. Lance Bennett and Robert M. Entman, eds., *Mediated Politics: Communication in the Future of Democracy* (Cambridge, UK: Cambridge University Press, 2001).

Robert M. Campbell and Leslie A. Pal, *The Real Worlds of Canadian Politics: Cases in Process and Policy,* 3rd edition (Peterborough, ON: Broadview Press, 1994).

Joseph N. Cappella and Kathleen Hall Jamieson, *Spiral of Cynicism: The Press and the Public Good* (New York: Oxford University Press, 1997).

Susan Delacourt, *Juggernaut: Paul Martin's Campaign for Chrétien's Crown* (Toronto: McClelland and Stewart, 2003).

Paul Nesbitt-Larking, *Politics, Society and the Media: Canadian Perspectives* (Peterborough, ON: Broadview Press, 2001).

Stuart N. Soroka, *Agenda-Setting Dynamics in Canada* (Vancouver: University of British Columbia Press, 2002).

David Taras, *The Newsmakers: The Media's Influence on Canadian Politics* (Scarborough, ON: Nelson Canada, 1990).

David Taras, *Power and Betrayal in the Canadian Media* (Peterborough, ON: Broadview Press, 1999).

Websites

While most media companies have their own websites, there is a growing trend away from free access in favour of paid or unpaid registration. As of October 2004, both the *Globe and Mail* (www.globeandmail.com) and the *National Post* (www.nationalpost.com) required paid subscriptions from anyone wishing to read their full news content online. Canadian Press (www.canoe.ca) and the Canadian Broadcasting Corporation (www.cbc.ca) still allowed free access to their news content.

Many American news outlets, such as Microsoft's online *Slate* magazine (www.slate.com) and the Cable News Network (CNN) (www.cnn.com) were still free, as were some leading British newspapers, such as the *Guardian* (www.guardian.co.uk) and *The Independent* (www.independent.co.uk). Slate.com provides a daily summary of what has been covered by major U.S. newspapers.

NOTES

1. Timothy E. Cook, "The Future of the Institutional Media," in W. Lance Bennett and Robert M. Entman, eds., *Mediated Politics: Communication in the Future of Democracy* (Cambridge, UK: Cambridge University Press, 2001), 182–200. See also Cook, "The News Media as a Political Institution: Looking Backward and Looking Forward," *Political Communication*, 23 (2006), 159–171; David Michael Ryfe, "The Nature of News Rules," *Political Communication*, 23 (2006), 203–214; and Richard L. Kaplan, "The News About New Institutionalism: Journalism's Ethic of Objectivity and Its Political Origins," *Political Communication*, 23 (2006), 173–185.

2. Senate of Canada, Standing Committee on Transport and Communications, *Interim Report on the Canadian News Media* (Ottawa, April 2004), 1; accessed at www.parl.gc.ca.

3. Ibid., 39–40.

4. Ibid., 39.

5. Ibid., 39.

6. On the universality of the trends described in the Dossier, see ibid.; see also Dan Turner, "Canadian Journalism" (Ottawa: Public Policy Forum, 2005) (accessed at www.ppforum.ca, July 2007).

7. *Interim Report*, 27.

8. Scott Edmonds, Vice-President, Canadian Press Branch, Canadian Media Guild, testimony before the Senate Standing Committee on Transport and Communications; *Minutes of Proceedings and Evidence*, March 9, 2004, 2:9.

9. *Final Report*, 53.

10. Ibid., 10.

11. Quoted in Turner, "Canadian Journalism," 7.

12. Quoted in Turner, "Canadian Journalism," 9.

13. Testimony before the Senate Standing Committee on Transport and Communications; *Minutes of Proceedings and Evidence*, June 19, 2003, 12:71.

14. Allan Thompson, Carleton University School of Journalism, testimony before the Senate Standing Committee on Transport and Communications; *Minutes of Proceedings and Evidence*, December 1, 2004, 3:7.

15. Christopher Waddell, testimony before the Senate Standing Committee on Transport and Communications; *Minutes of Proceedings and Evidence*, November 24, 2004, 2:56.

16. Mark Starowicz, testimony before the Senate Standing Committee on Transport and Communications; *Minutes of Proceedings and Evidence*, April 29, 2003, 7:20.

17. Doug Underwood, "Reporting and the Push for Market-Oriented Journalism: Media Organizations as Businesses," in Bennett and Entman, eds., *Mediated Politics*, 99–116.

18. Ibid., 113.

19. Ibid., 101.

20. Robert M. Entman, *Democracy Without Citizens: Media and the Decay of American Politics* (New York: Oxford University Press, 1989), 10.

21. Paul Nesbitt-Larking, *Politics, Society and the Media: Canadian Perspectives* (Peterborough, ON: Broadview Press, 2001), 110.

22. *Interim Report*, Table 8, 14.

23. Grant Robertson, "Aussie rules eyed for media mergers," *The Globe and Mail*, August 6, 2007; accessed at www.globeandmail.com, August 2007.

24. Grant Robertson, "Affluent Astral open to new media deals," *The Globe and Mail*, July 13, 2007 (accessed at www.globeandmail.com, August 2007).

25. According to the CRTC, anglophone Canadians devoted about 56 percent of their viewing time to Canadian broadcasters in 2006 (evenly divided between conventional and pay/specialty channels). The corresponding figure for Quebec francophones was close to 100 percent. Canadian Radio-television and Telecommunications Commission, "Broadcasting Policy Monitoring Report, 2007" (Ottawa: CRTC, July 2007), 48 (accessed at www.crtc.gc.ca, August 2007).

26. Ibid., 19.

27. Information about the 2007 mergers was obtained from the CRTC's website: www.crtc.gc.ca. The documents were downloaded in August 2007.

28. CRTC, "Broadcasting Decision CRTC 2007-165" (Ottawa, June 8, 2007); accessed at www.crtc.gc.ca, August 2007.

29. *Final Report*, 12.

30. Russell Mills, Nieman Fellow at Harvard University and former publisher of the Ottawa Citizen, testimony before the Senate Standing Committee on Transport and Communications; *Minutes of Proceedings and Evidence*, May 1, 2003, 7:49–7:50.

31. *Final Report*, 13.

32. Dr. Erin Steuter, Department of Sociology, Mount Allison University, testimony before the Senate Standing Committee on Transport and Communications; *Minutes of Proceedings and Evidence*, April 21, 2005, 17:15.

33. *Final Report*, 13.

34. Mills, 7:55.

35. Lois Kirkup, President, Ottawa Newspaper Guild, testimony before the Senate Standing Committee on Transport and Communications; *Minutes of Proceedings and Evidence*, March 11, 2004, 2:39.

36. *Interim Report*, Table 24, 36.

37. Waddell, 2:72.

38. Mills, 7:50.

39. Waddell, 2:72.

40. Florian Sauvageau, testimony before the Senate Standing Committee on Transport and Communications; *Minutes of Proceedings and Evidence*, May 1, 2003, 7:60.

41. Steuter, 17:7 and 17:9–10.

42. Bernard Descoteaux, Director and Editor, *Le Devoir*, testimony before the Senate Standing Committee on Transport and Communications; *Minutes of Proceedings and Evidence*, April 27, 2004, 7:19 and 7:22.

43. David Taras, *Power and Betrayal in the Canadian Media* (Peterborough, ON: Broadview Press, 1999), 19 and 213; Nesbitt-Larking, 180; David A. Good, *The Politics of Public Management: The HRDC Audit of Grants and Contributions* (Toronto: University of Toronto Press, 2003), 60.

44. Florian Sauvageau, David Schneiderman, and David Taras, *The Last Word: Media Coverage of the Supreme Court of Canada* (Vancouver: UBC Press, 2006), 15–17 and 220.

45. Susan Delacourt, *Juggernaut: Paul Martin's Campaign for Chrétien's Crown* (Toronto: McClelland and Stewart, 2003), 127.

46. Good, 70–71.

47. The full extent of Black's financial troubles became public shortly after the sale to CanWest. In July 2007 he was convicted in Chicago of fraud and obstruction of justice.

48. Mills, 7:48.

49. Neil MacDonald, quoted in Turner, "Canadian Journalism," 21.

50. Steuter, 17:10.

51. Ibid.

52. David Taras, *The Newsmakers: The Media's Influence on Canadian Politics* (Scarborough, ON: Nelson Canada, 1990), 14.

53. *Interim Report*, 2.

54. Ibid., 32.

55. Ibid., 33.

56. *Final Report*, volume 1, 88.

57. Canada, Department of Canadian Heritage, "Government Response to the Report of the Standing Senate Committee on Transport and Communications: Final Report on the Canadian News Media" (Ottawa, November 2006), 14; accessed at www.pch.gc.ca/progs/ac-ca/progs/ri-bpi/pubs/bacon/lettre_e.cfm, July 2007.

58. CRTC, "Broadcasting Policy Monitoring Report, 2007," 6.

59. Canadian Radio-television and Telecommunications Commission, "Broadcasting Public Notice CRTC 2008-4" (Ottawa, January 2008); accessed at www.crtc.gc.ca, May 2008.

60. Canadian Radio-television and Telecommunications Commission, "Broadcasting Public Notice CRTC 2008-5" (Ottawa, January 2008); accessed at www.crtc.gc.ca, May 2008.

61. David Pritchard and Florian Sauvageau, "English and French and Generation X: The Professional Values of Canadian Journalists," in Harvey Lazar and Tom McIntosh, eds., *Canada, The State of the Federation 1998/99: How Canadians Connect* (Montreal and Kingston: McGill–Queen's University Press, 1999), 287.

62. David Pritchard, Paul R. Brewer, and Florian Sauvageau, "Changes in Canadian Journalists' Views about the Social and Political Roles of the News Media: A Panel Study, 1996–2003," *Canadian Journal of Political Science*, 38:2 (June 2005), 290.

63. Ibid., 294–295.

64. Ibid., 302.

65. Taras, *Power and Betrayal*, 142.

66. Ibid., 157.

67. Marsha Barber and Ann Rauhala, "The Canadian News Directors Study: Demographics and Political Leanings of Television Decision-Makers," *Canadian Journal of Communication*, 30 (2005), 284–285.

68. Ibid.

69. Tokunbo Ojo, "Ethnic print media in the multicultural nation of Canada: A case study of the black newspaper in Montreal," *Journalism*, 7:3 (2006), 343.

70. Thomas S. Saras, President, National Ethnic Press and Media Council of Canada, testimony before the Senate Standing Committee on Transport and Communications; *Minutes of Proceedings and Evidence*, November 17, 2004, 1:24–1:25.

71. Ojo, 356.

72. Leslie-Anne Keown, "Keeping up with the times: Canadians and their news media diet," *Canadian Social Trends*, 83 (Summer 2007) (Ottawa: Statistics Canada, 2007), 14.

73. C.A. Tuggle, Suzanne Huffman, and Dana Scott Rosengard, "Reporting Live From the Scene: Enough to Attract the 18–24 Audience?" *Journal of Broadcasting and Electronic Media* 51:1 (March 2007), 58.

74. Taras, *The Newsmakers*, 40.

75. Pippa Norris, "News of the World," in Pippa Norris, ed., *Politics and the Press: The News Media and Their Influences* (Boulder: Lynne Rienner, 1997), 275–276.

76. Ibid., 39; Matthew Mendelsohn, "Television News Frames in the 1993 Canadian Election," in Helen Holmes and David Taras, eds., *Seeing Ourselves: Media Power and Policy in Canada,* 2nd edition (Toronto: Harcourt Brace, 1996).

77. Linda Trimble and Shannon Sampert, "Who's in the Game? The Framing of the Canadian Election 2000 by *The Globe and Mail* and *The National Post,*" *Canadian Journal of Political Science,* 37:1 (March 2004), 53 and 60.

78. Mendelsohn, 17.

79. Unlike most national political events, which occur mostly or exclusively in English, the commission conducted much of its televised work in French. Throughout the spring and summer of 2005, Quebeckers could watch the live coverage directly, without having to rely on translators. This broadened the daily audience for the hearings, and heightened their political impact, which in turn, may have helped to seal the Liberals' fate in the province in the 2006 election. Chantal Hébert, *French Kiss: Stephen Harper's Blind Date with Quebec* (Toronto: Knopf Canada, 2007), 44.

80. A November 2006 poll by SES Research asked respondents to name what they disliked about the Liberal Party. One-third, by far the largest group, said either "corruption" or "scandal." SES Research, "What Canadians Like and Dislike about the Liberal Party of Canada," 3; accessed at www.sesresearch.com, April 2007.

81. Good, 74.

82. Ibid., 83.

83. Augie Fleras and Jean Lock Kunz, *Media and Minorities: Representing Diversity in a Multicultural Canada* (Toronto: Thompson Educational Publishing, 2001), 79.

84. Stephen M. Caliendo and Charlton D. McIlwain, "Minority Candidates, Media Framing, and Racial Cues in the 2004 Election," *The Harvard International Journal of Press/Politics,* 11:4 (2006), 45–69.

85. Frances Henry and Carol Tator, *Discourses of Domination: Racial Bias in the English-Language Press* (Toronto: University of Toronto Press, 2002), 164–165.

86. Ibid., 45 and 168; Fleras and Kunz, 136 and 145.

87. Sheena Khan, Chair of the Council on American-Islamic Relations Canada, and Riad Saloojee, Executive Director, testimony before the Senate Standing Committee on Transport and Communications; *Minutes of Proceedings and Evidence,* February 26, 2004, 1:33–1:34.

88. Henry and Tator, 28.

89. As of June 2008, charges against seven of the alleged "terrorists" had been dropped. None had been convicted of a criminal offence in court, despite the sensationalistic news coverage that portrayed the suspects as guilty.

90. See, for example, George Bain, *Gotcha!: How the Media Distort the News* (Toronto: Key Porter, 1994); Larry Sabato, *Feeding Frenzy: How Attack Journalism Has Transformed American Politics* (New York: Free Press, 1991).

91. Delacourt, *Juggernaut,* 158–159.

92. Taras, *The Newsmakers,* 90.

93. Susan Delacourt, quoted in Turner, "Canadian Journalism," 18.

94. Joel-Denis Bellavance, quoted in Turner, "Canadian Journalism," 7.

95. "Iraq's Weapons of Mass Destruction: The Assessment of the British Government" (London: September 24, 2002), 17; accessed at www.the-hutton-inquiry.org, August 2007.

96. Lord Hutton, *Report of the Inquiry Into the Circumstances Surrounding the Death of Dr. David Kelly C.M.G.* (London: Her Majesty's Stationery Office, January 2004), 12; accessed at www.the-hutton-inquiry.org, August 2007. "Downing Street" is the British equivalent of the Canadian "PMO": shorthand for the prime minister and his or her closest advisors. The British prime minister lives on the upper floors at Number 10 Downing Street in the Whitehall district of London, and his or her offices are located on the lower floors.

97. The Committee members were perturbed by Gilligan's refusal to identify the person on whom he had relied in making a serious allegation against senior Government officials. They noted, in a separate report, that Gilligan enjoyed parliamentary immunity as a witness but that the persons whose reputations might be damaged by his testimony did not. Moreover, if he had named his source, that individual could have been called before the committee with all of the same protections available to him or her. Although the committee members acknowledged that journalists take the need to protect confidential sources very seriously, they called on Parliament to address the conflict between journalistic ethics and Parliament's investigatory duties. House of Commons Foreign Affairs Committee, "Evidence from Mr. Andrew Gilligan to the Committee's Inquiry into The Decision to go to War in Iraq" (London: The Stationery Office, July 17, 2003; accessed at www.the-hutton-inquiry.org, August 2007).

98. Hutton, *Report*, 165–166.

99. Ibid., 329.

100. The BBC insists that a script for the "two-way" between Gilligan and the anchor had been prepared and vetted in advance, "in line with normal production practices in place at the time," but that Gilligan had deviated from it during the 6:07 a.m. broadcast. BBC, "The BBC's Journalism After Hutton: The Report of the Neil Review Team" (London, June 2004), 26; accessed at www.bbc.co.uk, August 2007. For his part, Gilligan insists that the "two-way" was unscripted; see his letter of resignation from the BBC, dated January 1, 2004 (www.newsvote.bbc.co.uk).

101. Hutton, *Report*, 331.

102. Hutton was widely criticized for exonerating government officials of any blame, either in relation to the dossier or to the death of Dr. Kelly. These criticisms are summarized in Dominic Wring, "Politics and the Media: The Hutton Inquiry, The Public Relations State, and Crisis at the BBC," *Parliamentary Affairs*, 58:2 (2005), 380–393. The judge subsequently published a self-defence: Lord Hutton, "The Media Reaction to the Hutton Report," *Public Law* (Winter 2006), 807–832.

103. James Stanyer, "Politics and the Media: A Loss of Political Appetite?" *Parliamentary Affairs*, 55 (2002), 377.

104. "The BBC's Journalism After Hutton," 16; italics in original.

105. Ibid.

106. Taras, *The Newsmakers*, 79–81.

107. Even the most respected media organizations are vulnerable to co-optation by official sources. Former *New York Times* reporter Judith Miller resigned in disgrace after being criticized for her months of uncritical reporting on the Bush Administration's case for invading Iraq.

108. Paul Rhodes, former Communications director for Ontario Premier Mike Harris; quoted in Ira Basen, "Spin Cycles," CBC Radio documentary.

109. Frank Rich, *The Greatest Story Ever Sold: The Decline and Fall of Truth From 9/11 to Katrina* (New York: Penguin, 2006), 166.

110. Daniel Lipinski and Gregory Neddenriep, "Using "New" Media to Get "Old" Media Coverage: How Members of Congress Utilize Their Web Sites to Court Journalists," *The Harvard International Journal of Press/Politics*, 9:1 (2004), 7–21.

111. Stephen J. Farnsworth and S. Robert Lichter, *The Nightly News Nightmare: Network Television's Coverage of U.S. Presidential Elections, 1988–2000* (Lanham, MD: Rowman and Littlefield, 2003), 81.

112. Taras, *The Newsmakers*, 102.

113. Steven Livingston and W. Lance Bennett, "Gatekeeping, Indexing, and Live-Event News: Is Technology Altering the Construction of News?" *Political Communication*, 20 (2003), 370.

114. Tuggle, Huffman, and Rosengard, 70.

115. Livingston and Bennett, 364.

116. Ibid., 376.

117. See, e.g., Good, 63.

118. These statistics are taken from Keown, 12–17.

119. Henry Milner, *Civic Literacy: How Informed Citizens Make Democracy Work* (Hanover, NH: University Press of New England, 2002), Figures 7.2 and 7.3, 99–100.

120. Keown, 17.

121. Kajsa E. Dalrymple and Dietram A. Scheufele, "Finally Informing the Electorate? How the Internet Got People Thinking about Presidential Politics in 2004," *The Harvard International Journal of Press/Politics,* 12:3 (2007), 99–100.

122. Ibid., 101–108.

123. Milner, *Civic Literacy,* Chapter 7; Henry Milner, "Civic Literacy in Comparative Context" (Montreal: Institute for Research on Public Policy, July 2001); available at www.irpp.org.

124. Joseph N. Cappella and Kathleen Hall Jamieson, *Spiral of Cynicism: The Press and the Public Good* (New York: Oxford University Press, 1997), 51.

125. Ibid., 381.

126. Stuart N. Soroka, *Agenda-Setting Dynamics in Canada* (Vancouver: University of British Columbia Press, 2002), 20–21 and 118.

127. Robert A. Hackett, "News Media's Influence on Canadian Party Politics: Perspectives on a Shifting Relationship," in Hugh G. Thorburn and Alan Whitehorn, eds., *Party Politics in Canada,* 8th edition (Toronto: Prentice-Hall, 2001), 382.

128. Aeron Davis, "Investigating Journalist Influences on Political Issue Agendas at Westminster," *Political Communication,* 24 (2007), 181–199.

129. Paolo Mancini, "New Frontiers in Political Professionalism," *Political Communication,* 16:3 (1999), 239.

130. Susan Delacourt, "The Media and the Supreme Court of Canada," in Hugh Mellon and Martin Westmacott, eds., *Political Dispute and Judicial Review: Assessing the Work of the Supreme Court of Canada* (Toronto: Nelson, 2000), 31.

131. Donald J. Savoie, *Breaking the Bargain: Public Servants, Ministers, and Parliament* (Toronto: University of Toronto Press, 2003), 65.

132. On the "digital divide" between rich and poor, see Pippa Norris, *Digital Divide: Civic Engagement, Information Poverty, and the Internet Worldwide* (Cambridge: Cambridge University Press, 2001), especially Chapter 3.

133. Cook, 193; Davis, 190.

134. Susan Delacourt, "The gloves come off," *Toronto Star,* October 6, 2004; accessed at www.thestar.com; Allison Dunfield, "Liberals could fall in evening confidence vote," *The Globe and Mail,* October 7, 2004; accessed at www.globeandmail.com.

135. John Ibbitson, "The madness stops as all sides back off," *The Globe and Mail,* October 8, 2004; accessed at www.globeandmail.com.

136. Giles Gherson, comment on CBC Radio's "This Morning," December 3, 1997; quoted in Savoie, *Breaking the Bargain,* 50.

137. Delacourt, quoted in Turner, "Canadian Journalism," 6.

138. Christopher Dornan, quoted in Turner, "Canadian Journalism," 10.

139. House of Commons, Standing Committee on Procedure and House Affairs, *Nineteenth Report* (November 1998), 1.

140. Bain, 250.

141. Taras, *The Newsmakers,* 108.

142. Quoted in C.E.S. Franks, *The Parliament of Canada* (Toronto: University of Toronto Press, 1987), 159.

143. James R. Robertson, "Television and the House of Commons" (Ottawa: Library of Parliament Research Branch, September 2005).

144. Quoted in Franks, 159; the square brackets were in the original.

145. Taras, *The Newsmakers*, 108–09.

146. Ibid., 108.

147. Ibid., 63.

148. Ibid., 88.

149. Good, 76.

150. Donald J. Savoie, *Court Government and the Collapse of Accountability in Canada and the United Kingdom* (Toronto: University of Toronto Press, 2008), 134.

151. Delacourt, *Juggernaut,* 143.

152. Liane E. Benoit, "Ministerial Staff: The Life and Times of Parliament's Statutory Orphans," Donald Savoie, ed., *Parliament, Ministers and Deputy Ministers,* volume 1 of the collected research studies for the Commission of Inquiry Into the Sponsorship Program and Advertising Activities (Ottawa: Minister of Public Works and Government Services, 2006), 168–169.

153. Stephen Clarkson, "How the Big Red Machine Became the Little Red Machine," in Jon H. Pammett and Christopher Dornan, eds., *The Canadian Federal Election of 2006* (Toronto: Dundurn, 2006), 34.

154. Clarkson suggests that reporters "gleefully [got] back at a communications director they despised for his overbearing behaviour over the previous two years." Ibid., 36.

155. Savoie, *Court Government*, 67.

156. Simon Doyle, "Harper's media strategy not playing well with voters who are aware of it: exclusive poll," *The Hill Times,* June 11, 2007, 25.

157. Abbas Rana, "Government loses eight top ministerial directors of communications in nine months," *The Hill Times*, November 6, 2006, 21.

158. Abbas Rana, "Buckler cancels weekly meetings with top Cabinet ministerial communications staffers," *The Hill Times*, December 4, 2006, 34.

159. Stephen Harper, interview with the *Western Standard*, June 19, 2006; quoted in Tom Korski, "Is Harper's elusive majority because of his fight with Parliament Hill media?" *The Hill Times*, April 30, 2007, 12.

160. Simon Doyle, "Race for Parliamentary Press Gallery presidency heats up, new Hill *Star* reporter Brennan makes it a three-way campaign," *The Hill Times*, February 26, 2007, 23.

161. Simon Doyle, "PM Harper trying to avoid 'dome disease' with media: Conservative," *The Hill Times*, October 30, 2006, 21.

162. Doyle, "Harper's media strategy," 1 and 25.

163. Doyle, "PM Harper trying to avoid 'dome disease,'" 21.

164. In June 2008, shortly before new Chief of Staff Guy Giorno took over from Ian Brodie, the PMO announced Sandra Buckler's resignation. This appeared to be part of an effort to improve relations between the Harper Government and the news media.

165. The executive legal officer's media responsibilities have been well described by a former incumbent. See James W. O'Reilly, "The Supreme Court of Canada and the Media," 42, *St. Louis University Law Journal* (1997–1998), 1189–1200.

166. Delacourt, "The Media and the Supreme Court of Canada," 34.

167. Sauvageau, Schneiderman, and Taras, 200.

168. See, for example, Kent Roach, *Due Process and Victims' Rights: The New Law and Politics of Criminal Justice* (Toronto: University of Toronto Press, 1999), 81 and 83.

169. Sauvageau, Schneiderman, and Taras, 15–17.

170. Ibid.

171. Quoted in Kirk Makin, "Lamer Worries about Public Backlash," *The Globe and Mail,* February 6, 1999, A1.

172. Ian Greene et al., *Final Appeal: Decision-making in Canadian Courts of Appeal* (Toronto: Lorimer, 1998), 184.

173. Robert M. Entman and Susan Herbst, "Reframing Public Opinion as We Have Known It," in Bennett and Entman, eds., *Mediated Democracy,* 207–08.

174. *R. v. Daviault,* [1994] 3 S.C.R. 63.

175. Roach, 178.

176. F.L. Morton and Rainer Knopff, *The Charter Revolution and the Court Party* (Peterborough, ON: Broadview Press, 2000), 136.

177. Sauvageau, Schneiderman, and Taras, Chapter 1.

178. Latimer and his wife defended his action, arguing that it was the only way to end their daughter's physical agony (which they had been told would worsen over the years). For the Crown, Latimer's motive was irrelevant; he had deliberately ended his daughter's life, and he must be convicted of murder.

179. Latimer was released to a halfway house in Ottawa in early 2008, after an adverse ruling by the Parole Board was overturned on appeal. His release received generally favourable news coverage.

180. Andrew Coyne, "The Charter under Attack," *National Post,* May 3, 1999; quoted in Delacourt, "The Media and the Supreme Court of Canada," in Mellon and Westmacott, eds., 36.

181. Sauvageau, Schneiderman, and Taras, 205.

182. Quoted in ibid., 198–199.

183. Ibid., 229.

184. Heather MacIvor, *Canadian Politics and Government in the Charter Era* (Toronto: Thomson Nelson, 2006), 154–155.

185. Ibid., 203.

186. Ibid., 29.

187. Michael Enright, quoted in Turner, "Canadian Journalism," 18.

188. Bill Kovach and Tom Rosenstiel, *The Elements of Journalism: What Newspeople Should Know and the Public Should Expect,* rev. ed. (New York: Three Rivers Press, 2007), 19.

189. Descoteaux, 7:15.

190. Douglas Ahlers, "News Consumption and the New Electronic Media," *The Harvard International Journal of Press/Politics,* 11:1 (November 2006), 48.

191. Lauren Feldman, "The news about comedy: Young audiences, *The Daily Show,* and evolving notions of journalism," *Journalism,* 8:4 (2007), 406–427; Dannagal G. Young and Russell M. Tisinger, "Dispelling Late-Night Myths: News Consumption among Late-Night Comedy Viewers and the Predictors of Exposure to Various Late-Night Shows," *The Harvard International Journal of Press/Politics,* 11 (2006), 113–34.

192. Barry A. Hollander, "Late-Night Learning: Do Entertainment Programs Increase Political Campaign Knowledge for Young Viewers?" *Journal of Broadcasting and Electronic Media* (December 2005), 402–15.

193. Feldman, 410.

194. Jon Stewart, C-Span Newhouse School Forum with Ken Auletta from the *New Yorker,* October 14, 2004; quoted in Young and Tisinger, 115.

195. Hollander, 407; Young and Tisinger, 123.

196. Feldman, 410.

197. Ibid.

198. Ibid., 422–23.

199. Ahlers, 29.

200. Ahlers, 39.

201. Keown, 14–15.

202. Ahlers, 47–48.

203. *Final Report*, 3.

204. Ibid., 48.

205. Stephen D. Reese, Lou Rutigliano, Kideuk Hyun, and Jaekwan Jeong, "Mapping the blogosphere: Professional and citizen-based media in the global news arena," *Journalism*, 8:3 (2007), 240–241. The *Guardian*'s website (www.guardian.co.uk) may well be the best English-language news source anywhere, and a model that other outlets would do well to follow. All of its content is free (the *Guardian* is operated by a charitable trust, so it does not need to raise money from online subscriptions); almost every feature of the site—from the layout to the numerous blogs—is interactive; and it offers an indispensable archive of past articles as well as an outstanding inventory of links to other sites.

206. Starowicz, 7:26.

207. Ahlers, 45 and 48.

208. Andrew Keen, *The Cult of the Amateur: How Today's Internet is Killing Our Culture* (New York: Doubleday, 2007), 9 and 131–132.

209. Kovach and Rosenstiel, 47.

210. Ibid., 48–49.

211. Reese et al., 240.

212. Kovach and Rosenstiel, 18.

213. Keen, 13–16.

214. Harold J. Jansen and Royce Koop, "Pundits, Ideologues and Ranters: The British Columbia Election Online," *Canadian Journal of Communication*, 30 (2005), 613–632.

215. Reese et al., 257.

216. Matt Carlson, "Blogs and Journalistic Authority: The role of blogs in US Election Day 2004 coverage," *Journalism Studies*, 8:2 (2007), 267.

217. Carlson, 272.

218. Kovach and Rosenstiel, 157; Rich, 142–143.

219. Carlson, 269–271.

220. Bea Vongdouangchanh, "Heard on the Hill," *The Hill Times*, January 8, 2007, 2.

221. Kovach and Risenstiel, 181–182.

222. Tim Craig and Michael D. Shear, "Allen quip provokes outrage, apology; name insults Webb volunteer," *The Washington Post*, August 15, 2006, A1; Jeff Jarvis, "Why YouTube gets my vote for political punditry," *The Guardian*, February 5, 2007 (accessed at www.guardian.co.uk).

223. Abbas Rana and Bea Vongdouangchanh, "YouTube 'road warriors' could define the next election campaign," *The Hill Times*, April 2, 2007, 1 and 4.

224. Ibid., 4.

225. Bea Vongdouangchanh, "Parliamentarians using Facebook site to communicate with public," *The Hill Times*, April 2, 2007, 20. As of the end of March 2007, Liberal leader Stéphane Dion listed almost 4000 "friends" on his Facebook page, compared to 847 for the NDP's Jack Layton and 563 for Prime Minister Stephen Harper; this discrepancy can be attributed to the fact that Dion had just won a leadership contest, whereas Layton and Harper had not.

226. Abbas Rana, "PMO's order to get off Facebook angers some Cabinet staffers," *The Hill Times*, June 4, 2007, 1 and 52.

227. Quebec, Commission de consultation sur les pratiques d'accommodement reliées aux différences culturelles, *Final Report* (abridged version) (Gouvernement du Québec 2008), 15–21; accessed at www.accommodements.qc.ca/index.html, May 2008.

228. Ibid., 21.

229. Savoie, *Court Government*, 160.

230. Ibid., 231–232.

231. Savoie, *Court Government*, 68.

Appendix

The Constitution Acts
1867 to 1982

THE CONSTITUTION ACT, 1867

30 & 31 Victoria, c. 3. (U.K.)
(Consolidated with amendments)

An Act for the Union of Canada, Nova Scotia, and New Brunswick, and the Government thereof; and for Purposes connected therewith

(29th March 1867.)

WHEREAS the Provinces of Canada, Nova Scotia, and New Brunswick have expressed their Desire to be federally united into One Dominion under the Crown of the United Kingdom of Great Britain and Ireland, with a Constitution similar in Principle to that of the United Kingdom:

And whereas such a Union would conduce to the Welfare of the Provinces and promote the Interests of the British Empire:

And whereas on the Establishment of the Union by Authority of Parliament it is expedient, not only that the Constitution of the Legislative Authority in the Dominion be provided for, but also that the Nature of the Executive Government therein be declared:

And whereas it is expedient that Provision be made for the eventual Admission into the Union of other Parts of British North America:[1]

---

(1) The enacting clause was repealed by the *Statute Law Revision Act, 1893*, 56-57 Vict., c. 14 (U.K.). It read as follows:

Be it therefore enacted and declared by the Queen's most Excellent Majesty, by and with the Advice and Consent of the Lords Spiritual and Temporal, and Commons, in this present Parliament assembled, and by the Authority of the same, as follows:

I. PRELIMINARY

Short title

1. This Act may be cited as the *Constitution Act, 1867*.[2]

2. Repealed[3]

II. UNION

Declaration of Union

3. It shall be lawful for the Queen, by and with the Advice of Her Majesty's Most Honourable Privy Council, to declare by Proclamation that, on and after a Day therein appointed, not being more than Six Months after the passing of this Act, the Provinces of Canada, Nova Scotia, and New Brunswick shall form and be One Dominion under the Name of Canada; and on and after that Day those Three Provinces shall form and be One Dominion under that Name accordingly.[4]

Construction of subsequent Provisions of Act

4. Unless it is otherwise expressed or implied, the Name Canada shall be taken to mean Canada as constituted under this Act.[5]

Four Provinces

5. Canada shall be divided into Four Provinces, named Ontario, Quebec, Nova Scotia, and New Brunswick.[6]

---

(2) As enacted by the *Constitution Act, 1982,* which came into force on April 17, 1982. The section, as originally enacted, read as follows:

> **1.** This Act may be cited as The British North America Act, 1867.

(3) Section 2, repealed by the *Statute Law Revision Act, 1893,* 56-57 Vict., c. 14 (U.K.), read as follows:

> **2.** The Provisions of this Act referring to Her Majesty the Queen extend also to the Heirs and Successors of Her Majesty, Kings and Queens of the United Kingdom of Great Britain and Ireland.

(4) The first day of July, 1867, was fixed by proclamation dated May 22, 1867.

(5) Partially repealed by the *Statute Law Revision Act, 1893,* 56-57 Vict., c. 14 (U.K.). As originally enacted the section read as follows:

> **4.** The subsequent Provisions of this Act shall, unless it is otherwise expressed or implied, commence and have effect on and after the Union, that is to say, on and after the Day appointed for the Union taking effect in the Queen's Proclamation; and in the same Provisions, unless it is otherwise expressed or implied, the Name Canada shall be taken to mean Canada as constituted under this Act.

(6) Canada now consists of ten provinces (Ontario, Quebec, Nova Scotia, New Brunswick, Manitoba, British Columbia, Prince Edward Island, Alberta, Saskatchewan and Newfoundland) and two territories (the Yukon Territory and the Northwest Territories).

The first territories added to the Union were Rupert's Land and the North-Western Territory, (subsequently designated the Northwest Territories), which were admitted pursuant to section 146 of the *Constitution Act, 1867* and the *Rupert's Land Act, 1868,* 31-32 Vict., c. 105 (U.K.), by the *Rupert's Land and North-Western Territory Order* of June 23, 1870, effective July 15, 1870. Prior to the admission of those territories the Parliament of Canada enacted *An Act for the temporary Government of Rupert's Land and the North-Western Territory when united with Canada* (32-33 Vict., c. 3), and the *Manitoba Act, 1870,* (33 Vict., c.3), which provided for the formation of the Province of Manitoba.

British Columbia was admitted into the Union pursuant to section 146 of the *Constitution Act, 1867,* by the *British Columbia Terms of Union,* being Order in Council of May 16, 1871, effective July 20, 1871.

Prince Edward Island was admitted pursuant to section 146 of the *Constitution Act, 1867,* by the *Prince Edward Island Terms of Union,* being Order in Council of June 26, 1873, effective July 1, 1873.

On June 29, 1871, the United Kingdom Parliament enacted the *Constitution Act, 1871* (34-35 Vict., c. 28) authorizing the creation of additional provinces out of territories not included in any province. Pursuant to this statute, the Parliament of Canada enacted the *Alberta Act,* (July 20, 1905, 4-5 Edw. VII c. 3) and the *Saskatchewan Act,* (July 20, 1905, 4-5 Edw. VII, c. 42), providing for the creation of the provinces of Alberta and Saskatchewan, respectively. Both these Acts came into force on Sept. 1, 1905.

Meanwhile, all remaining British possessions and territories in North America and the islands adjacent thereto, except the colony of Newfoundland and its dependencies, were admitted into the Canadian Confederation by the *Adjacent Territories Order,* dated July 31, 1880.

The Parliament of Canada added portions of the Northwest Territories to the adjoining provinces in 1912 by *The Ontario Boundaries Extension Act,* S.C. 1912, 2 Geo. V, c. 40, *The Quebec Boundaries Extension Act,* 1912, 2 Geo V, c. 45 and *The Manitoba Boundaries Extension Act, 1912,* 2 Geo. V, c. 32, and further additions were made to Manitoba by *The Manitoba Boundaries Extension Act, 1930,* 20-21 Geo. V, c. 28.

The Yukon Territory was created out of the Northwest Territories in 1898 by *The Yukon Territory Act,* 61 Vict., c. 6, (Canada).

Newfoundland was added on March 31, 1949, by the *Newfoundland Act,* (U.K.), 12-13 Geo. VI, c. 22, which ratified the Terms of Union of Newfoundland with Canada.

6. The Parts of the Province of Canada (as it exists at the passing of this Act) which formerly constituted respectively the Provinces of Upper Canada and Lower Canada shall be deemed to be severed, and shall form Two separate Provinces. The Part which formerly constituted the Province of Upper Canada shall constitute the Province of Ontario; and the Part which formerly constituted the Province of Lower Canada shall constitute the Province of Quebec.

Provinces of Ontario and Quebec

7. The Provinces of Nova Scotia and New Brunswick shall have the same Limits as at the passing of this Act.

Provinces of Nova Scotia and New Brunswick

8. In the general Census of the Population of Canada which is hereby required to be taken in the Year One thousand eight hundred and seventy-one, and in every Tenth Year thereafter, the respective Populations of the Four Provinces shall be distinguished.

Decennial Census

III. EXECUTIVE POWER

9. The Executive Government and Authority of and over Canada is hereby declared to continue and be vested in the Queen.

Declaration of Executive Power in the Queen

10. The Provisions of this Act referring to the Governor General extend and apply to the Governor General for the Time being of Canada, or other the Chief Executive Officer or Administrator for the Time being carrying on the Government of Canada on behalf and in the Name of the Queen, by whatever Title he is designated.

Application of Provisions referring to Governor General

11. There shall be a Council to aid and advise in the Government of Canada, to be styled the Queen's Privy Council for Canada; and the Persons who are to be Members of that Council shall be from Time to Time chosen and summoned by the Governor General and sworn in as Privy Councillors, and Members thereof may be from Time to Time removed by the Governor General.

Constitution of Privy Council for Canada

12. All Powers, Authorities, and Functions which under any Act of the Parliament of Great Britain, or of the Parliament of the United Kingdom of Great Britain and Ireland, or of the Legislature of Upper Canada, Lower Canada, Canada, Nova Scotia, or New Brunswick, are at the Union vested in or exerciseable by the respective Governors or Lieutenant Governors of those Provinces, with the Advice, or with the Advice and Consent, of the respective Executive Councils thereof, or in conjunction with those Councils, or with any Number of Members thereof, or by those Governors or Lieutenant Governors individually, shall, as far as the same continue in existence and capable of being exercised after the Union in relation to the Government of Canada, be vested in and exerciseable by the Governor General, with the Advice or the Advice and Consent of or in conjunction with the Queen's Privy Council for Canada, or any Members thereof, or by the Governor General individually, as the Case requires, subject nevertheless (except with respect to such as exist under Acts of the Parliament of Great Britain or the Parliament of the United Kingdom of Great Britain and Ireland) to be abolished or altered by the Parliament of Canada.[7]

All Powers under Acts to be exercised by Governor General with Advice of Privy Council, or alone

---

(7) See the note to section 129, *infra.*

13. The Provisions of this Act referring to the Governor General in Council shall be construed as referring to the Governor General acting by and with the Advice of the Queen's Privy Council for Canada.

Application of Provisions referring to Governor General in Council

14. It shall be lawful for the Queen, if Her Majesty thinks fit, to authorize the Governor General from Time to Time to appoint any Person or any Persons jointly or severally to be his Deputy or Deputies within any Part or Parts of Canada, and in that Capacity to exercise during the Pleasure of the Governor General such of the Powers, Authorities, and Functions of the Governor General as the Governor General deems it necessary or expedient to assign to him or them, subject to any Limitations or Directions expressed or given by the Queen; but the Appointment of such a Deputy or Deputies shall not affect the Exercise by the Governor General himself of any Power, Authority, or Function.

Power to Her Majesty to authorize Governor General to appoint Deputies

15. The Command-in-Chief of the Land and Naval Militia, and of all Naval and Military Forces, of and in Canada, is hereby declared to continue and be vested in the Queen.

Command of Armed Forces to continue to be vested in the Queen

16. Until the Queen otherwise directs, the Seat of Government of Canada shall be Ottawa.

Seat of Government of Canada

IV. LEGISLATIVE POWER

17. There shall be One Parliament for Canada, consisting of the Queen, an Upper House styled the Senate, and the House of Commons.

Constitution of Parliament of Canada

18. The privileges, immunities, and powers to be held, enjoyed, and exercised by the Senate and by the House of Commons, and by the members thereof respectively, shall be such as are from time to time defined by Act of the Parliament of Canada, but so that any Act of the Parliament of Canada defining such privileges, immunities, and powers shall not confer any privileges, immunities, or powers exceeding those at the passing of such Act held, enjoyed, and exercised by the Commons House of Parliament of the United Kingdom of Great Britain and Ireland, and by the members thereof.[8]

Privileges, etc., of Houses

19. The Parliament of Canada shall be called together not later than Six Months after the Union.[9]

First Session of the Parliament of Canada

20. Repealed.[10]

---

(8) Repealed and re-enacted by the *Parliament of Canada Act*, 1875, 38-39 Vict., c. 38 (U.K.). The original section read as follows:

> **18.** The Privileges, Immunities, and Powers to be held, enjoyed, and exercised by the Senate and by the House of Commons and by the Members thereof respectively shall be such as are from Time to Time defined by Act of the Parliament of Canada, but so that the same shall never exceed those at the passing of this Act held, enjoyed, and exercised by the Commons House of Parliament of the United Kingdom of Great Britain and Ireland and by the Members thereof.

(9) Spent. The first session of the first Parliament began on November 6, 1867.

(10) Section 20, repealed by the *Constitution Act, 1982*, read as follows:

> **20.** There shall be a Session of the Parliament of Canada once at least in every Year, so that Twelve Months shall not intervene between the last Sitting of the Parliament in one Session and its first sitting in the next Session.

Section 20 has been replaced by section 5 of the *Constitution Act, 1982*, which provides that there shall be a sitting of Parliament at least once every twelve months.

21. The Senate shall, subject to the Provisions of this Act, consist of One Hundred and five Members, who shall be styled Senators.[11]

22. In relation to the Constitution of the Senate Canada shall be deemed to consist of *Four* Divisions: ——

1. Ontario;

2. Quebec;

3. The Maritime Provinces, Nova Scotia and New Brunswick, and Prince Edward Island;

4. The Western Provinces of Manitoba, British Columbia, Saskatchewan, and Alberta;

which Four Divisions shall (subject to the Provisions of this Act) be equally represented in the Senate as follows: Ontario by twenty-four senators; Quebec by twenty-four senators; the Maritime Provinces and Prince Edward Island by twenty-four senators, ten thereof representing Nova Scotia, ten thereof representing New Brunswick, and four thereof representing Prince Edward Island; the Western Provinces by twenty four senators, six thereof representing Manitoba, six thereof representing British Columbia, six thereof representing Saskatchewan, and six thereof representing Alberta; Newfoundland shall be entitled to be represented in the Senate by six members; the Yukon Territory and the Northwest Territories shall be entitled to be represented in the Senate by one member each.

In the Case of Quebec each of the Twenty-four Senators representing that Province shall be appointed for One of the Twenty-four Electoral Divisions of Lower Canada specified in Schedule A. to Chapter One of the Consolidated Statutes of Canada.[12]

---

(11) As amended by the *Constitution Act, 1915*, 5-6 Geo. V, c. 45 (U.K.) and modified by the *Newfoundland Act*, 12-13 Geo. VI, c. 22 (U.K.), and the *Constitution Act (No. 2), 1975*, S.C. 1974-75-76, c. 53, and the *Constitution Act, 1999 (Nunavut)*, S.C. 1998, c. 15, Part 2.

The original section read as follows:

21. The Senate shall, subject to the Provisions of this Act, consist of Seventy-two Members, who shall be styled Senators.

The *Manitoba Act, 1870*, added two for Manitoba; the *British Columbia Terms of Union* added three; upon admission of Prince Edward Island four more were provided by section 147 of the *Constitution Act, 1867*; the *Alberta Act* and the *Saskatchewan Act* each added four. The Senate was reconstituted at 96 by the *Constitution Act, 1915*. Six more Senators were added upon union with Newfoundland, and one Senator each was added for the Yukon Territory and the Northwest Territories by the *Constitution Act (No. 2), 1975*. One Senator was added for Nunavut by the *Constitution Act 1999 (Nunavut)*.

(12) As Amended by the *Constitution Act, 1915*, 5-6 Geo. V, c. 45 (U.K.), the *Newfoundland Act*, 12-13 Geo. VI, c. 22 (U.K.), and the *Constitution Act (No. 2)*, 1975, S.C. 1974-75-76, c. 53. The original section read as follows:

22. In relation to the Constitution of the Senate, Canada shall be deemed to consist of Three Divisions:

1. Ontario;

2. Quebec;

3. The Maritime Provinces, Nova Soctia and New Brunswick;

which Three Divisions shall (subject to the Provisions of this Act) be equally represented in the Senate as follows: Ontario by Twenty-four Senators; Quebec by Twenty-four Senators; and the Maritime Provinces by Twenty-four Senators, Twelve thereof representing Nova Scotia, and Twelve thereof representing New Brunswick.

23. The Qualifications of a Senator shall be as follows:

(1) He shall be of the full age of Thirty Years:

(2) He shall be either a natural-born Subject of the Queen, or a Subject of the Queen naturalized by an Act of the Parliament of Great Britain, or of the Parliament of the United Kingdom of Great Britain and Ireland, or of the Legislature of One of the Provinces of Upper Canada, Lower Canada, Canada, Nova Scotia, or New Brunswick, before the Union, or of the Parliament of Canada after the Union:

(3) He shall be legally or equitably seised as of Freehold for his own Use and Benefit of Lands or Tenements held in Free and Common Socage, or seised or possessed for his own Use and Benefit of Lands or Tenements held in Franc-alleu or in Roture, within the Province for which he is appointed, of the Value of Four thousand Dollars, over and above all Rents, Dues, Debts, Charges, Mortgages, and Incumbrances due or payable out of or charged on or affecting the same:

(4) His Real and Personal Property shall be together worth Four thousand Dollars over and above his Debts and Liabilities:

(5) He shall be resident in the Province for which he is appointed:

(6) In the case of Quebec he shall have his Real Property Qualification in the Electoral Division for which he is appointed, or shall be resident in that Division.[13]

24. The Governor General shall from Time to Time, in the Queen's Name, by Instrument under the Great Seal of Canada, summon qualified Persons to the Senate; and, subject to the Provisions of this Act, every person so summoned shall become and be a Member of the Senate and a Senator.

25. Repealed.[14]

26. If at any Time on the Recommendation of the Governor General the Queen thinks fit to direct that Four or Eight Members be added to the Senate, the Governor General may by Summons to Four

---

In the case of Quebec each of the Twenty-four Senators representing that Province shall be appointed for One of the Twenty-four Electoral Divisions of Lower Canada specified in Schedule A. to Chapter One of the Consolidated Statutes of Canada.

(13) Section 44 of the *Constitution Act, 1999 (Nunavut)*, S.C. 1998, c. 15, Part 2, provided that, for the purposes of that Part (which added one Senator for Nunavut), the word "Province" in section 23 of the *Constitution Act, 1867,* has the same meaning as is assigned to the word "province" by section 35 of the *Interpretation Act*, R.S.C. 1985, c. I-21, which provides that the term "province" means "a province of Canada, and includes the Yukon Territory, the Northwest Territories and Nunavut."

Section 2 of the *Constitution Act (No. 2), 1975*, S.C. 1974-75-76, c. 53 provided that for the purposes of that Act (which added one Senator each for the Yukon Territory and the Northwest Territories) the term "Province" in section 23 of the *Constitution Act, 1867,* has the same meaning as is assigned to the term "province" by section 28 of the *Interpretation Act*, R.S.C. 1970, c. I-23, which provides that the term "province" means "a province of Canada, and includes the Yukon Territory and the Northwest Territories."

(14) Repealed by the *Statute Law Revision Act, 1893*, 56-57 Vict., c. 14 (U.K.). The section read as follows:

25. Such persons shall be first summoned to the Senate as the Queen by Warrant under Her Majesty's Royal Sign Manual thinks fits to approve, and their Names shall be inserted in the Queen's Proclamation of Union.

or Eight qualified Persons (as the Case may be), representing equally the Four Divisions of Canada, add to the Senate accordingly.[15]

27. In case of such Addition being at any Time made, the Governor General shall not summon any Person to the Senate, except on a further like Direction by the Queen on the like Recommendation, to represent one of the Four Divisions until such Division is represented by Twenty-Four Senators and no more.[16]

Reduction of Senate to normal Number

28. The Number of Senators shall not at any Time exceed One Hundred and thirteen.[17]

Maximum Number of Senators

29. (1) Subject to subsection (2), a Senator shall, subject to the provisions of this Act, hold his place in the Senate for life.

Tenure of Place in Senate

(2) A Senator who is summoned to the Senate after the coming into force of this subsection shall, subject to this Act, hold his place in the Senate until he attains the age of seventy-five years.[18]

Retirement upon attaining age of seventy-five years

30. A Senator may by Writing under his Hand addressed to the Governor General resign his Place in the Senate, and thereupon the same shall be vacant.

Resignation of Place in Senate

31. The Place of a Senator shall become vacant in any of the following Cases:

Disqualification of Senators

(1) If for Two consecutive Sessions of the Parliament he fails to give his Attendance in the Senate:

(2) If he takes an Oath or makes a Declaration or Acknowledgment of Allegiance, Obedience, or Adherence to a Foreign Power, or does an Act whereby he becomes a Subject or Citizen, or entitled to the Rights or Privileges of a Subject or Citizen, of a Foreign Power:

(3) If he is adjudged Bankrupt or Insolvent, or applies for the Benefit of any Law relating to Insolvent Debtors, or becomes a public Defaulter:

---

(15) As amended by the *Constitution Act, 1915,* 5-6 Geo. V, c. 45 (U.K.). The original section read as follows:

> **26.** If at any time on the Recommendation of the Governor General the Queen thinks fit to direct that Three or Six Members be added to the Senate, the Governor General may by Summons to Three or Six qualified Persons (as the Case may be), representing equally the Three Divisions of Canada, add to the Senate accordingly.

(16) As amended by the *Constitution Act, 1915,* 5-6 Geo. V, c. 45 (U.K.). The original section read as follows:

> **27.** In case of such Addition being at any Time made the Governor General shall not summon any Person to the Senate except on a further like Direction by the Queen on the like Recommendation, until each of the Three Divisions of Canada is represented by Twenty-four Senators and no more.

(17) As amended by the *Constitution Act, 1915,* 5-6 Geo. V, c. 45 (U.K.), and the *Constitution Act (No. 2), 1975,* S.C. 1974-75-76, c. 53, and the *Constitution Act 1999 (Nunavut),* S.C. 1998, c. 15, Part 2. The original section read as follows:

> **28.** The Number of Senators shall not at any Time exceed Seventy-eight.

(18) As enacted by the *Constitution Act, 1965,* S.C., 1965, c. 4, which came into force on June 1, 1965. The original section read as follows:

> **29.** A Senator shall , subject to the Provisions of this Act, hold his Place in the Senate for Life.

(4) If he is attainted of Treason or convicted of Felony or of any infamous Crime:

(5) If he ceases to be qualified in respect of Property or of Residence; provided, that a Senator shall not be deemed to have ceased to be qualified in respect of Residence by reason only of his residing at the Seat of the Government of Canada while holding an Office under that Government requiring his Presence there.

Summons on Vacancy in Senate

32. When a Vacancy happens in the Senate by Resignation, Death, or otherwise, the Governor General shall by Summons to a fit and qualified Person fill the Vacancy.

Questions as to Qualifications and Vacancies in Senate

33. If any Question arises respecting the Qualification of a Senator or a Vacancy in the Senate the same shall be heard and determined by the Senate.

Appointment of Speaker of Senate

34. The Governor General may from Time to Time, by Instrument under the Great Seal of Canada, appoint a Senator to be Speaker of the Senate, and may remove him and appoint another in his Stead.[19]

Quorum of Senate

35. Until the Parliament of Canada otherwise provides, the Presence of at least Fifteen Senators, including the Speaker, shall be necessary to constitute a Meeting of the Senate for the Exercise of its Powers.

Voting in Senate

36. Questions arising in the Senate shall be decided by a Majority of Voices, and the Speaker shall in all Cases have a Vote, and when the Voices are equal the Decision shall be deemed to be in the Negative.

The House of Commons

Constitution of House of Commons in Canada

37. The House of Commons shall, subject to the Provisions of this Act, consist of two hundred and ninety-five members of whom ninety-nine shall be elected for Ontario, seventy-five for Quebec, eleven for Nova Scotia, ten for New Brunswick, fourteen for Manitoba, thirty-two for British Columbia, four for Prince Edward Island, twenty-six for Alberta, fourteen for Saskatchewan, seven for Newfoundland, one for the Yukon Territory and two for the Northwest Territories.[20]

Summoning of House of Commons

38. The Governor General shall from Time to Time, in the Queen's Name, by Instrument under the Great Seal of Canada, summon and call together the House of Commons.

Senators not to sit in House of Commons

39. A Senator shall not be capable of being elected or of sitting or voting as a Member of the House of Commons.

---

(19) Provision for exercising the functions of Speaker during his absence is made by Part II of the *Parliament of Canada Act*, R.S.C. 1985, c. P-1 (formerly the *Speaker of the Senate Act*, R.S.C. 1970, c. S-14). Doubts as to the power of Parliament to enact the *Speaker of the Senate Act* were removed by the *Canadian Speaker (Appointment of Deputy) Act, 1895,* 2nd Sess., 59 Vict., c. 3 (U.K.), which was repealed by the *Constitution Act, 1982.*

(20) The figures given here result from the application of Section 51, as enacted by the *Constitution Act, 1985 (Representation)*, S.C., 1986, c. 8, Part 1, and readjusted pursuant to the *Electoral Boundaries Readjustment Act*, R.S.C., 1985, c. E-3. The original section (which was altered from time to time as the result of the addition of new provinces and changes in population) read as follows:

37. The House of Commons shall, subject to the Provisions of this Act, consist of one hundred and eighty-one members, of whom Eighty-two shall be elected for Ontario, Sixty-five for Quebec, Nineteen for Nova Scotia, and Fifteen for New Brunswick.

40. Until the Parliament of Canada otherwise provides, Ontario, Quebec, Nova Scotia, and New Brunswick shall, for the Purposes of the Election of Members to serve in the House of Commons, be divided into Electoral districts as follows:

Electoral districts of the four Provinces

1. — ONTARIO

Ontario shall be divided into the Counties, Ridings of Counties, Cities, Parts of Cities, and Towns enumerated in the First Schedule to this Act, each whereof shall be an Electoral District, each such District as numbered in that Schedule being entitled to return One Member.

2. — QUEBEC

Quebec shall be divided into Sixty-five Electoral Districts, composed of the Sixty-five Electoral Divisions into which Lower Canada is at the passing of this Act divided under Chapter Two of the Consolidated Statutes of Canada, Chapter Seventy-five of the Consolidated Statutes for Lower Canada, and the Act of the Province of Canada of the Twenty-third Year of the Queen, Chapter One, or any other Act amending the same in force at the Union, so that each such Electoral Division shall be for the Purposes of this Act an Electoral District entitled to return One Member.

3. — NOVA SCOTIA

Each of the Eighteen Counties of Nova Scotia shall be an Electoral District. The County of Halifax shall be entitled to return Two Members, and each of the other Counties One Member.

4. — NEW BRUNSWICK

Each of the Fourteen Counties into which New Brunswick is divided, including the City and County of St. John, shall be an Electoral District. The City of St. John shall also be a separate Electoral District. Each of those Fifteen Electoral Districts shall be entitled to return One Member.[21]

41. Until the Parliament of Canada otherwise provides, all Laws in force in the several Provinces at the Union relative to the following Matters or any of them, namely, — the Qualifications and Disqualifications of Persons to be elected or to sit or vote as Members of the House of Assembly or Legislative Assembly in the several Provinces, the Voters at Elections of such Members, the Oaths to be taken by Voters, the Returning Officers, their Powers and Duties, the Proceedings at Elections, the Periods during which Elections may be continued, the Trial of controverted Elections, and Proceedings

Continuance of existing Election Laws until Parliament of Canada otherwise provides

---

(21) Spent. The electoral districts are now established by Proclamations issued from time to time under the *Electoral Boundaries Readjustment Act*, R.S.C. 1985, c. E-3, as amended for particular districts by Acts of Parliament, for which see the most recent Table of Public Statutes and Responsible Ministers.

incident thereto, the vacating of Seats of Members, and the Execution of new Writs in case of Seats vacated otherwise than by Dissolution, — shall respectively apply to Elections of Members to serve in the House of Commons for the same several Provinces.

Provided that, until the Parliament of Canada otherwise provides, at any Election for a Member of the House of Commons for the District of Algoma, in addition to Persons qualified by the Law of the Province of Canada to vote, every Male British Subject, aged Twenty-one Years or upwards, being a Householder, shall have a Vote.[22]

42. Repealed.[23]

43. Repealed.[24]

As to Election of Speaker of House of Commons

44. The House of Commons on its first assembling after a General Election shall proceed with all practicable Speed to elect One of its Members to be Speaker.

As to filling up Vacancy in Office of Speaker

45. In case of a Vacancy happening in the Office of Speaker by Death, Resignation, or otherwise, the House of Commons shall with all practicable Speed proceed to elect another of its Members to be Speaker.

Speaker to preside

46. The Speaker shall preside at all Meetings of the House of Commons.

Provision in case of Absence of Speaker

47. Until the Parliament of Canada otherwise provides, in case of the Absence for any Reason of the Speaker from the Chair of the House of Commons for a Period of Forty-eight consecutive Hours, the House may elect another of its Members to act as Speaker, and the Member so elected shall during the Continuance of such Absence of the Speaker have and execute all the Powers, Privileges, and Duties of Speaker.[25]

Quorum of House of Commons

48. The Presence of at least Twenty Members of the House of Commons shall be necessary to constitute a Meeting of the House for the Exercise of its Powers, and for that Purpose the Speaker shall be reckoned as a Member.

---

(22) Spent. Elections are now provided for by the *Canada Elections Act*, R.S.C. 1985, c. E-2; controverted elections by the *Dominion Controverted Elections Act*, R.S.C. 1985, c. C-39; qualifications and disqualifications of members by the *Parliament of Canada Act*, R.S.C. 1985, c. P-1. The right of citizens to vote and hold office is provided for in section 3 of the *Constitution Act, 1982*.

(23) Repealed by the *Statute Law Revision Act, 1893*, 56-57 Vict., c. 14 (U.K.). The section read as follows:

42. For the First Election of Members to serve in the House of Commons the Governor General shall cause Writs to be issued by such Person, in such Form, and addressed to such Returning Officers as he thinks fit.

The Person issuing Writs under this Section shall have the like Powers as are possessed at the Union by the Officers charged with the issuing of Writs for the Election of Members to serve in the respective House of Assembly or Legislative Assembly of the Province of Canada, Nova Scotia, or New Brunswick; and the Returning Officers to whom Writs are directed under this Section shall have the like Powers as are possessed at the Union by the Officers charged with the returning of Writs for the Election of Members to serve in the same respective House of Assembly or Legislative Assembly.

(24) Repealed by the *Statute Law Revision Act, 1893*, 56-57 Vict. c. 14 (U.K.). The section read as follows:

43. In case a Vacancy in the Representation in the House of Commons of any Electoral District happens before the Meeting of the Parliament, or after the Meeting of the Parliament before Provision is made by the Parliament in this Behalf, the Provisions of the last foregoing Section of this Act shall extend and apply to the issuing and returning of a Writ in respect of such Vacant District.

(25) Provision for exercising the functions of Speaker during his absence is now made by Part III of the *Parliament of Canada Act*, R.S.C. 1985, c. P-1.

49. Questions arising in the House of Commons shall be decided by a Majority of Voices other than that of the Speaker, and when the Voices are equal, but not otherwise, the Speaker shall have a Vote.

Voting in House of Commons

50. Every House of Commons shall continue for Five Years from the Day of the Return of the Writs for choosing the House (subject to be sooner dissolved by the Governor General), and no longer.[26]

Duration of House of Commons

51. (1) The number of members of the House of Commons and the representation of the provinces therein shall, on the coming into force of this subsection and thereafter on the completion of each decennial census, be readjusted by such authority, in such manner, and from such time as the Parliament of Canada from time to time provides, subject and according to the following rules:

Readjustment of representation in Commons

1.   There shall be assigned to each of the provinces a number of members equal to the number obtained by dividing the total population of the provinces by two hundred and seventy-nine and by dividing the population of each province by the quotient so obtained, counting any remainder in excess of 0.50 as one after the said process of division.

Rules

2.   If the total number of members that would be assigned to a province by the application of rule 1 is less than the total number assigned to that province on the date of coming into force of this subsection, there shall be added to the number of members so assigned such number of members as will result in the province having the same number of members as were assigned on that date.[27]

---

(26) The term of the twelfth Parliament was extended by the *British North America Act, 1916,* 6-7 Geo. V. c. 19 (U.K.), which Act was repealed by the *Statute Law Revision Act, 1927,* 17-18 Geo. V, c. 42 (U.K.). See also subsection 4(1) of the *Constitution Act, 1982,* which provides that no House of Commons shall continue for longer than five years from the date fixed for the return of the writs at a general election of its members, and subsection 4(2) thereof, which provides for continuation of the House of Commons in special circumstances.

(27) As enacted by the *Constitution Act, 1985 (Representation),* S.C. 1986, c. 8, Part I, which came into force on March 6, 1986 (See SI86-49). The section, as originally enacted, read as follows:

51. On the Completion of the Census in the Year One Thousand eight hundred and seventy-one, and of each subsequent decennial Census, the Representation of the Four Provinces shall be readjusted by such Authority, in such Manner, and from such Time, as the Parliament of Canada from Time to Time provides, subject and according to the following Rules:

(1) Quebec shall have the fixed Number of Sixty-five Members:

(2) There shall be assigned to each of the other Provinces such a Number of Members as will bear the same Proportion to the Number of its Population (ascertained at such Census) as the Number Sixty-five bears to the Number of the Population of Quebec (so ascertained):

(3) In the Computation of the Number of Members for a Province a fractional Part not exceeding One Half of the whole Number requisite for entitling the Province to a Member shall be disregarded; but a fractional Part exceeding One Half of that Number shall be equivalent to the whole Number:

(4) On any such Re-adjustment the Number of Members for a Province shall not be reduced unless the Proportion which the Number of the Population of the Province bore to the Number of the aggregate Population of Canada at the then last preceding Re-adjustment of the Number of Members for the Province is ascertained at the then latest Census to be diminished by One Twentieth Part or upwards:

(5) Such Re-adjustment shall not take effect until the Termination of the then existing Parliament.

The section was amended by the *Statute Law Revision Act, 1893,* 56-57 Vict., c. 14 (U.K.) by repealing the words from "of the census" to "seventy-one and" and the word "subsequent".

By the *British North America Act, 1943,* 6-7 Geo. VI., c. 30 (U.K.), which Act was repealed by the *Constitution Act, 1982,* redistribution of seats following the 1941 census was postponed until the first session of Parliament after the war. The section was re-enacted by the *British North*

America Act, 1946, 9-10 Geo. VI., c. 63 (U.K.), which Act was also repealed by the *Constitution Act, 1982*, to read as follows:

51. (1) The number of members of the House of Commons shall be two hundred and fifty-five and the representation of the provinces therein shall forthwith upon the coming into force of this section and thereafter on the completion of each decennial census be readjusted by such authority, in such manner, and from such time as the Parliament of Canada from time to time provides, subject and according to the following rules:

(1) Subject as hereinafter provided, there shall be assigned to each of the provinces a number of members computed by dividing the total population of the provinces by two hundred and fifty-four and by dividing the population of each province by the quotient so obtained, disregarding, except as hereinafter in this section provided, the remainder, if any, after the said process of division.

(2) If the total number of members assigned to all the provinces pursuant to rule one is less than two hundred and fifty-four, additional members shall be assigned to the provinces (one to a province) having remainders in the computation under rule one commencing with the province having the largest remainder and continuing with the other provinces in the order of the magnitude of their respective remainders until the total number of members assigned is two hundred and fifty-four.

(3) Notwithstanding anything in this section, if upon completion of a computation under rules one and two, the number of members to be assigned to a province is less than the number of senators representing the said province, rules one and two shall cease to apply in respect of the said province, and there shall be assigned to the said province a number of members equal to the said number of senators.

(4) In the event that rules one and two cease to apply in respect of a province then, for the purpose of computing the number of members to be assigned to the provinces in respect of which rules one and two continue to apply, the total population of the provinces shall be reduced by the number of the population of the province in respect of which rules one and two have ceased to apply and the number two hundred and fifty-four shall be reduced by the number of members assigned to such province pursuant to rule three.

(5) Such readjustment shall not take effect until the termination of the then existing Parliament.

(2) The Yukon Territory as constituted by Chapter forty-one of the Statutes of Canada, 1901, together with any Part of Canada not comprised within a province which may from time to time be included therein by the Parliament of Canada for the purposes of representation in Parliament, shall be entitled to one member.

The section was re-enacted by the *British North America Act, 1952*, S.C. 1952, c. 15, which Act was also repealed by the *Constitution Act, 1982*, as follows:

51. (1) Subject as hereinafter provided, the number of members of the House of Commons shall be two hundred and sixty-three and the representation of the provinces therein shall forthwith upon the coming into force of this section and thereafter on the completion of each decennial census be readjusted by such authority, in such manner, and from such time as the Parliament of Canada from time to time provides, subject and according to the following rules:

1. There shall be assigned to each of the provinces a number of members computed by dividing the total population of the provinces by two hundred and sixty-one and by dividing the population of each province by the quotient so obtained, disregarding, except as hereinafter in this section provided, the remainder, if any, after the said process of division.

2. If the total number of members assigned to all the provinces pursuant to rule one is less than two hundred and sixty-one, additional members shall be assigned to the provinces (one to a province) having remainders in the computation under rule one commencing with the province having the largest remainder and continuing with the other provinces in the order of the magnitude of their respective remainders until the total number of members assigned is two hundred and sixty-one.

3. Notwithstanding anything in this section, if upon completion of a computation under rules one and two the number of members to be assigned to a province is less than the number of senators representing the said province, rules one and two shall cease to apply in respect of the said province, and there shall be assigned to the said province a number of members equal to the said number of senators.

4. In the event that rules one and two cease to apply in respect of a province then, for the purposes of computing the number of members to be assigned to the provinces in respect of which rules one and two continue to apply, the total population of the provinces shall be reduced by the number of the population of the province in respect of which rules one and two have ceased to apply and the number two hundred and sixty-one shall be reduced by the number of members assigned to such province pursuant to rule three.

5. On any such readjustment the number of members for any province shall not be reduced by more than fifteen per cent below the representation to which such province was entitled under rules one to four of the subsection at the last preceding readjustment of the representation of that province, and there shall be no reduction in the representation of any province as a result of which that province would have a smaller number of members than any other province that according to the results of the then last decennial census did not have a larger population; but for the purposes of any subsequent readjustment of representation under this section any increase in the number of members of the House of Commons resulting from the application of this rule shall not be included in the divisor mentioned in rules one to four of this subsection.

6. Such readjustment shall not take effect until the termination of the then existing Parliament.

(2) The Yukon Territory as constituted by chapter forty-one of the statutes of Canada, 1901, shall be entitled to one member, and such other part of Canada not comprised within a province as may from time to time be defined by the Parliament of Canada shall be entitled to one member.

Subsection 51(1) was re-enacted by *Constitution Act, 1974,* S.C. 1974-75-76, c. 13 to read as follows:

51. (1) The number of members of the House of Commons and the representation of the provinces therein shall upon the coming into force of this subsection and thereafter on the completion of each decennial census be readjusted by such authority, in such manner, and from such time as the Parliament of Canada from time to time provides, subject and according to the following Rules:

1. There shall be assigned to Quebec seventy-five members in the readjustment following the completion of the decennial census taken in the year 1971, and thereafter four additional members in each subsequent readjustment.

2. Subject to Rules 5(2) and (3), there shall be assigned to a large province a number of members equal to the number obtained by dividing the population of the large province by the electoral quotient of Quebec.

3. Subject to Rules 5(2) and (3), there shall be assigned to a small province a number of members equal to the number obtained by dividing

(*a*) the sum of the populations, determined according to the results of the penultimate decennial census, of the provinces (other than Quebec) having populations of less than one and a half million, determined according to the results of that census, by the sum of the numbers of members assigned to those provinces in the readjustment following the completion of that census; and

(*b*) the population of the small province by the quotient obtained under paragraph (*a*).

4. Subject to Rules 5(1) (*a*), (2) and (3) there shall be assigned to an intermediate province a number of members equal to the number obtained

(*a*) by dividing the sum of the populations of the provinces (other than Quebec) having populations of less than one and a half million by the sum of the number of members assigned to those provinces under any of Rules 3,5 (1) (b), (2) and (3);

(*b*) by dividing the population of the intermediate province by the quotient obtained under paragraph (*a*); and

(*c*) by adding to the number of members assigned to the intermediate province in the readjustment following the completion of the penultimate decennial census one-half of the difference resulting from the subtraction of that number from the quotient obtained under paragraph (*b*).

5. (1) On any readjustment,

(*a*) if no province (other than Quebec) has a population of less than one and a half million, Rule 4 shall not be applied and, subject to Rules 5(2) and (3), there shall be assigned to an intermediate province a number of members equal to the number obtained by dividing

(i) the sum of the populations, determined according to the results of the penultimate decennial census, of the provinces, (other than Quebec) having populations of not less than one and a half million and not more than two and a half million, determined according to the results of that census, by the sum of the numbers of members assigned to those provinces in the readjustment following the completion of that census, and

(ii) the population of the intermediate province by the quotient obtained under subparagraph (i);

(*b*) if a province (other than Quebec) having a population of

(i) less than one and a half million, or

(ii) not less than one and a half million and not more than two and a half million

does not have a population greater than its population determined according to the results of the penultimate decennial census, it shall, subject to Rules 5 (2) and (3), be assigned the number of members assigned to it in the readjustment following the completion of that census.

(2) On any readjustment,

(*a*) if, under any of Rules 2 to 5 (1), the number of members to be assigned to a province (in this paragraph referred to as " the first province") is smaller than the number of members to be assigned to any other province not having a population greater than that of the first province, those Rules shall not be applied to the first province and it shall be assigned a number of members equal to the largest number of members to be assigned to any other province not having a population greater than that of the first province;

(*b*) if, under any of Rules 2 to 5 (1)(*a*), the number of members to be assigned to a province is smaller than the number of members assigned to it in the readjustment following the completion of the penultimate decennial census, those Rules shall not be applied to it and it shall be assigned the latter number of members;

Yukon Territory, Northwest Territories, and Nunavut

(2) The Yukon Territory as bounded and described in the schedule to chapter Y-2 of the Revised Statutes of Canada, 1985, shall be entitled to one member, and the Northwest Territories as bounded and described in section 2 of the chapter N-27 of the Revised Statutes of Canada, 1985, as amended by section 77 of chapter 28 of the Statutes of Canada, 1993, shall be entitled to one member, and Nunavut as bounded and described in section 3 of chapter 28 of the Statutes of Canada, 1993, shall be entitled to one member.[28]

Constitution of House of Commons

51A. Notwithstanding anything in this Act a province shall always be entitled to a number of members in the House of Commons not less than the number of senators representing such province.[29]

Increase of Number of House of Commons

52. The Number of Members of the House of Commons may be from Time to Time increased by the Parliament of Canada, provided the proportionate Representation of the Provinces prescribed by this Act is not thereby disturbed.

(*c*) if both paragraphs (*a*) and (*b*) apply to a province, it shall be assigned a number of members equal to the greater of the numbers produced under those paragraphs.

(3) On any readjustment,

(*a*) if the electoral quotient of a province (in this paragraph referred to as "the first province") obtained by dividing its population by the number of members to be assigned to it under any of Rules 2 to 5 (2) is greater than the electoral quotient of Quebec, those Rules shall not be applied to the first province and it shall be assigned a number of members equal to the number obtained by dividing its population by the electoral quotient of Quebec;

(*b*) if, as a result of the application of Rule 6 (2) (*a*), the number of members assigned to a province under paragraph (*a*) equals the number of members to be assigned to it under any of Rules 2 to 5 (2), it shall be assigned that number of members and paragraph (*a*) shall cease to apply to that province.

6. (1) In these Rules,

"electoral quotient" means, in respect of a province, the quotient obtained by dividing its population, determined according to the results of the then most recent decennial census, by the number of members to be assigned to it under any of Rules 1 to 5 (3) in the readjustment following the completion of that census;

"intermediate province" means a province (other than Quebec) having a population greater than its population determined according to the results of the penultimate decennial census but not more than two and a half million and not less than one and a half million;

"large province" means a province (other than Quebec) having a population greater than two and a half million;

"penultimate decennial census" means the decennial census that preceded the then most recent decennial census;

"population" means, except where otherwise specified, the population determined according to the results of the then most recent decennial census;

"small province" means a province (other than Quebec) having a population greater than its population determined according to the results of the penultimate decennial census and less than one and half million.

(2) For the purposes of these Rules,

(*a*) if any fraction less than one remains upon completion of the final calculation that produces the number of members to be assigned to a province, that number of members shall equal the number so produced disregarding the fraction;

(*b*) if more than one readjustment follows the completion of a decennial census, the most recent of those readjustments shall, upon taking effect, be deemed to be the only readjustment following the completion of that census;

(*c*) a readjustment shall not take effect until the termination of the then existing Parliament.

(28) As enacted by the *Constitution Act, 1999 (Nunavut)*, S.C. 1998, c. 15, Part 2. Subsection 51(2) was previously amended by the *Constitution Act (No. 1), 1975*, S.C. 1974-75-76, c. 28, and read as follows:

(2) The Yukon Territory as bounded as described in the schedule to chapter Y-2 of the Revised Statutes of Canada, 1970, shall be entitled to one member, and the Northwest Territories as bounded and described in section 2 of chapter N-22 of the Revised Statutes of Canada, 1970, shall be entitled to two members.

(29) As enacted by the *Constitution Act, 1915*, 5-6 Geo. V, c. 45 (U.K.).

53. Bills for appropriating any Part of the Public Revenue, or for imposing any Tax or Impost, shall originate in the House of Commons.

Appropriation and Tax Bills

54. It shall not be lawful for the House of Commons to adopt or pass any Vote, Resolution, Address, or Bill for the Appropriation of any Part of the Public Revenue, or of any Tax or Impost, to any Purpose that has not been first recommended to that House by Message of the Governor General in the Session in which such Vote, Resolution, Address, or Bill is proposed.

Recommendation of Money Votes

55. Where a Bill passed by the Houses of the Parliament is presented to the Governor General for the Queen's Assent, he shall declare, according to his Discretion, but subject to the Provisions of this Act and to Her Majesty's Instructions, either that he assents thereto in the Queen's Name, or that he withholds the Queen's Assent, or that he reserves the Bill for the Signification of the Queen's Pleasure.

Royal Assent to Bills, etc.

56. Where the Governor General assents to a Bill in the Queen's Name, he shall by the first convenient Opportunity send an authentic Copy of the Act to One of Her Majesty's Principal Secretaries of State, and if the Queen in Council within Two Years after Receipt thereof by the Secretary of State thinks fit to disallow the Act, such Disallowance (with a Certificate of the Secretary of State of the Day on which the Act was received by him) being signified by the Governor General, by Speech or Message to each of the Houses of the Parliament or by Proclamation, shall annul the Act from and after the Day of such Signification.

Disallowance by Order in Council of Act assented to by Governor General

57. A Bill reserved for the Signification of the Queen's Pleasure shall not have any Force unless and until, within Two Years from the Day on which it was presented to the Governor General for the Queen's Assent, the Governor General signifies, by Speech or Message to each of the Houses of the Parliament or by Proclamation, that it has received the Assent of the Queen in Council.

Signification of Queen's Pleasure on Bill reserved

An Entry of every such Speech, Message, or Proclamation shall be made in the Journal of each House, and a Duplicate thereof duly attested shall be delivered to the proper Officer to be kept among the Records of Canada.

V. PROVINCIAL CONSTITUTIONS

Executive Power

58. For each Province there shall be an Officer, styled the Lieutenant Governor, appointed by the Governor General in Council by Instrument under the Great Seal of Canada.

Appointment of Lieutenant Governors of Provinces

59. A Lieutenant Governor shall hold Office during the Pleasure of the Governor General; but any Lieutenant Governor appointed after the Commencement of the First Session of the Parliament of Canada shall not be removable within Five Years from his Appointment, except for Cause assigned, which shall be communicated to him in Writing

Tenure of Office of Lieutenant Governor

within One Month after the Order for his Removal is made, and shall be communicated by Message to the Senate and to the House of Commons within One Week thereafter if the Parliament is then sitting, and if not then within One Week after the Commencement of the next Session of the Parliament.

Salaries of Lieutenant Governors

60. The Salaries of the Lieutenant Governors shall be fixed and provided by the Parliament of Canada.[30]

Oaths, etc., of Lieutenant Governor

61. Every Lieutenant Governor shall, before assuming the Duties of his Office, make and subscribe before the Governor General or some Person authorized by him Oaths of Allegiance and Office similar to those taken by the Governor General.

Application of Provisions referring to Lieutenant Governor

62. The Provisions of this Act referring to the Lieutenant Governor extend and apply to the Lieutenant Governor for the Time being of each Province, or other the Chief Executive Officer or Administrator for the Time being carrying on the Government of the Province, by whatever Title he is designated.

Appointment of Executive Officers for Ontario and Quebec

63. The Executive Council of Ontario and of Quebec shall be composed of such Persons as the Lieutenant Governor from Time to Time thinks fit, and in the first instance of the following Officers, namely, — the Attorney General, the Secretary and Registrar of the Province, the Treasurer of the Province, the Commissioner of Crown Lands, and the Commissioner of Agriculture and Public Works, with in Quebec the Speaker of the Legislative Council and the Solicitor General.[31]

Executive Government of Nova Scotia and New Brunswick

64. The Constitution of the Executive Authority in each of the Provinces of Nova Scotia and New Brunswick shall, subject to the Provisions of this Act, continue as it exists at the Union until altered under the Authority of this Act.[32]

Powers to be exercised by Lieutenant Governor of Ontario or Quebec with Advice, or alone

65. All Powers, Authorities, and Functions which under any Act of the Parliament of Great Britain, or of the Parliament of the United Kingdom of Great Britain and Ireland, or of the Legislature of Upper Canada, Lower Canada, or Canada, were or are before or at the Union vested in or exerciseable by the respective Governors or Lieutenant Governors of those Provinces, with the Advice or with the Advise and Consent of the respective Executive Councils thereof, or in conjunction with those Councils, or with any Number of Members thereof, or by those Governors or Lieutenant Governors individually, shall, as far as the same are capable of being exercised after the Union in relation to the Government of Ontario and Quebec respectively, be vested in and shall or may be exercised by the Lieutenant Governor of Ontario and Quebec respectively, with the Advice or the Advice and Consent of or in conjunction with the respective Executive Councils, or any Members thereof, or by the Lieutenant Governor individually, as the Case requires, subject nevertheless (except with respect to such as exist

---

(30) Provided for by the *Salaries Act,* R.S.C. 1990, c. E. 25, c. S-3.

(31) Now provided for in Ontario by the *Executive Council Act*, R.S.C. 1990, c. E.25, and in Quebec by the *Executive Power Act,* R.S.Q. 1977, c. E-18.

(32) A similar provision was included in each of the instruments admitting British Columbia, Prince Edward Island, and Newfoundland. The Executive Authorities for Manitoba, Alberta and Saskatchewan were established by the statutes creating those provinces. See the notes to section 5, *supra.*

under Acts of the Parliament of Great Britain, or of the Parliament of the United Kingdom of Great Britain and Ireland,) to be abolished or altered by the respective Legislatures of Ontario and Quebec.[33]

66. The Provisions of this Act referring to the Lieutenant Governor in Council shall be construed as referring to the Lieutenant Governor of the Province acting by and with the Advice of the Executive Council thereof.

Application of Provisions referring to Lieutenant Governor in Council

67. The Governor General in Council may from Time to Time appoint an Administrator to execute the Office and Functions of Lieutenant Governor during his Absence, Illness, or other Inability.

Administration in Absence, etc., of Lieutenant Governor

68. Unless and until the Executive Government of any Province otherwise directs with respect to that Province, the Seats of Government of the Provinces shall be as follows, namely, — of Ontario, the City of Toronto; of Quebec, the City of Quebec; of Nova Scotia, the City of Halifax; and of New Brunswick, the City of Fredericton.

Seats of Provincial Governments

Legislative Power

1. — ONTARIO

69. There shall be a Legislature for Ontario consisting of the Lieutenant Governor and of One House, styled the Legislative Assembly of Ontario.

Legislature for Ontario

70. The Legislative Assembly of Ontario shall be composed of Eighty-two Members, to be elected to represent the Eighty-two Electoral Districts set forth in the First Schedule to this Act.[34]

Electoral districts

2. — QUEBEC

71. There shall be a Legislature for Quebec consisting of the Lieutenant Governor and of Two Houses, styled the Legislative Council of Quebec and the Legislative Assembly of Quebec.[35]

Legislature for Quebec

72. The Legislative Council of Quebec shall be composed of Twenty-four Members, to be appointed by the Lieutenant Governor, in the Queen's Name, by Instrument under the Great Seal of Quebec, one being appointed to represent each of the Twenty-four Electoral Divisions of Lower Canada in this Act referred to, and each holding Office for the Term of his Life, unless the Legislature of Quebec otherwise provides under the Provisions of this Act.

Constitution of Legislative Council

73. The Qualifications of the Legislative Councillors of Quebec shall be the same as those of the Senators for Quebec.

Qualification of Legislative Councillors

---

(33) See the notes to section 129, *infra*.

(34) Spent. Now covered by the *Representation Act*, R.S.O. 1990, c. R.26.

(35) The Act respecting the Legislative Council of Quebec, S.Q. 1968, c.9, provided that the Legislature for Quebec shall consist of the Lieutenant Governor and the National Assembly of Quebec, and repealed the provisions of the *Legislature Act*, R.S.Q. 1964, c. 6, relating to the Legislative Council of Quebec. Now covered by the *Legislative Act*, R.S.Q. 1977, c. L-1. Sections 72 to 79 following are therefore completely spent.

Resignation, Disqualification, etc.

74. The Place of a Legislative Councillor of Quebec shall become vacant in the Cases, *mutatis mutandis,* in which the Place of Senator becomes vacant.

Vacancies

75. When a Vacancy happens in the Legislative Council of Quebec by Resignation, Death, or otherwise, the Lieutenant Governor, in the Queen's Name, by Instrument under the Great Seal of Quebec, shall appoint a fit and qualified Person to fill the Vacancy.

Questions as to Vacancies, etc.

76. If any Question arises respecting the Qualification of a Legislative Councillor of Quebec, or a Vacancy in the Legislative Council of Quebec, the same shall be heard and determined by the Legislative Council.

Speaker of Legislative Council

77. The Lieutenant Governor may from Time to Time, by Instrument under the Great Seal of Quebec, appoint a Member of the Legislative Council of Quebec to be Speaker thereof, and may remove him and appoint another in his Stead.

Quorum of Legislative Council

78. Until the Legislature of Quebec otherwise provides, the Presence of at least Ten Members of the Legislative Council, including the Speaker, shall be necessary to constitute a Meeting for the Exercise of its Powers.

Voting in Legislative Council

79. Questions arising in the Legislative Council of Quebec shall be decided by a Majority of Voices, and the Speaker shall in all Cases have a Vote, and when the Voices are equal the Decision shall be deemed to be in the Negative.

Constitution of Legislative Assembly of Quebec

80. The Legislative Assembly of Quebec shall be composed of Sixty-five Members, to be elected to represent the Sixty-five Electoral Divisions or Districts of Lower Canada in this Act referred to, subject to Alteration thereof by the Legislature of Quebec: Provided that it shall not be lawful to present to the Lieutenant Governor of Quebec for Assent any Bill for altering the Limits of any of the Electoral Divisions or Districts mentioned in the Second Schedule to this Act, unless the Second and Third Readings of such Bill have been passed in the Legislative Assembly with the Concurrence of the Majority of the Members representing all those Electoral Divisions or Districts, and the Assent shall not be given to such Bill unless an Address has been presented by the Legislative Assembly to the Lieutenant Governor stating that it has been so passed.[36]

3. — ONTARIO AND QUEBEC

81. Repealed.[37]

Summoning of Legislative Assemblies

82. The Lieutenant Governor of Ontario and of Quebec shall from Time to Time, in the Queen's Name, by Instrument under the Great Seal of the Province, summon and call together the Legislative Assembly of the Province.

---

(36) The Act respecting electoral districts, S.Q. 1970, c. 7, s. 1, provides that this section no longer has effect.

(37) Repealed by the *Statute Law Revision Act, 1893*, 56-57 Vict. c. 14 (U.K.). The section read as follows:

81. The Legislatures of Ontario and Quebec respectively shall be called together not later than Six Months after the Union.

83. Until the Legislature of Ontario or of Quebec otherwise provides, a Person accepting or holding in Ontario or in Quebec any Office, Commission, or Employment, permanent or temporary, at the Nomination of the Lieutenant Governor, to which an annual Salary, or any Fee, Allowance, Emolument, or Profit of any Kind or Amount whatever from the Province is attached, shall not be eligible as a Member of the Legislative Assembly of the respective Province, nor shall he sit or vote as such; but nothing in this Section shall make ineligible any Person being a Member of the Executive Council of the respective Province, or holding any of the following Offices, that is to say, the Offices of Attorney General, Secretary and Registrar of the Province, Treasurer of the Province, Commissioner of Crown Lands, and Commissioner of Agriculture and Public Works, and in Quebec Solicitor General, or shall disqualify him to sit or vote in the House for which he is elected, provided he is elected while holding such Office.[38]

Restriction on election of Holders of offices

84. Until the legislatures of Ontario and Quebec respectively otherwise provide, all Laws which at the Union are in force in those Provinces respectively, relative to the following Matters, or any of them, namely, — the Qualifications and Disqualifications of Persons to be elected or to sit or vote as Members of the Assembly of Canada, the Qualifications or Disqualifications of Voters, the Oaths to be taken by Voters, the Returning Officers, their Powers and Duties, the Proceedings at Elections, the Periods during which such Elections may be continued, and the Trial of controverted Elections and the Proceedings incident thereto, the vacating of the Seats of Members and the issuing and execution of new Writs in case of Seats vacated otherwise than by Dissolution, — shall respectively apply to Elections of Members to serve in the respective Legislative Assemblies of Ontario and Quebec.

Continuance of existing Election Laws

Provided that, until the Legislature of Ontario otherwise provides, at any Election for a Member of the Legislative Assembly of Ontario for the District of Algoma, in addition to Persons qualified by the Law of the Province of Canada to vote, every Male British Subject, aged Twenty-one Years or upwards, being a Householder, shall have a Vote.[39]

85. Every Legislative Assembly of Ontario and every Legislative Assembly of Quebec shall continue for Four Years from the Day of the Return of the Writs for choosing the same (subject nevertheless to either the Legislative Assembly of Ontario or the Legislative Assembly of Quebec being sooner dissolved by the Lieutenant Governor of the Province), and no longer.[40]

Duration of Legislative Assemblies

---

(38) Probably spent. The subject-matter of this section is now covered in Ontario by the *Legislative Assembly Act*, R.S.O. 1990, c. L.10, and in Quebec by the *National Assembly Act*, R.S.Q. c. A-23.1.

(39) Probably spent. The subject-matter of this section is now covered in Ontario by the *Election Act*, R.S.O. 1990, c. E.6, and the *Legislative Assembly Act*, R.S.O. 1990, c. L.10, in Quebec by the *Elections Act*, R.S.Q. c. E-3.3 and the *National Assembly Act*, R.S.Q. c. A-23.1.

(40) The maximum duration of the Legislative Assemblies of Ontario and Quebec has been changed to five years. See the *Legislative Assembly Act*, R.S.O. 1990, c. L.10, and the *National Assembly Act*, R.S.Q. c. A-23.1, respectively. See also section 4 of the *Constitution Act, 1982*, which provides a maximum duration for a legislative assembly of five years but also authorizes continuation in special circumstances.

Yearly Session of Legislature

86. There shall be a Session of the Legislature of Ontario and of that of Quebec once at least in every Year, so that Twelve Months shall not intervene between the last Sitting of the Legislature in each Province in one Session and its first Sitting in the next Session.[41]

Speaker, Quorum, etc.

87. The following Provisions of this Act respecting the House of Commons of Canada shall extend and apply to the Legislative Assemblies of Ontario and Quebec, that is to say, — the Provisions relating to the Election of a Speaker originally and on Vacancies, the Duties of the Speaker, the Absence of the Speaker, the Quorum, and the Mode of voting, as if those Provisions were here re-enacted and made applicable in Terms to each such Legislative Assembly.

4. — NOVA SCOTIA AND NEW BRUNSWICK

Constitutions of Legislatures of Nova Scotia and New Brunswick

88. The Constitution of the Legislature of each of the Provinces of Nova Scotia and New Brunswick shall, subject to the Provisions of this Act, continue as it exists at the Union until altered under the Authority of this Act.[42]

5. — ONTARIO, QUEBEC, AND NOVA SCOTIA

89. Repealed.[43]

---

(41) See also section 5 of the *Constitution Act, 1982*, which provides that there shall be a sitting of each legislature at least once every twelve months.

(42) Partially repealed by the *Statute Law Revision Act, 1893*, 56-57 Vict., c. 14 (U.K.), which deleted the following concluding words of the original enactment:

> and the House of Assembly of New Brunswick existing at the passing of this Act shall, unless sooner dissolved, continue for the Period for which it was elected.

A similar provision was included in each of the instruments admitting British Columbia, Prince Edward Island and Newfoundland. The Legislatures of Manitoba, Alberta and Saskatchewan were established by the statutes creating those provinces. See the footnotes to section 5, *supra*.

See also sections 3 to 5 of the *Constitution Act, 1982*, which prescribe democratic rights applicable to all provinces, and subitem 2(2) of the Schedule to that Act, which sets out the repeal of section 20 of the *Manitoba Act, 1870*. Section 20 of the *Manitoba Act, 1870*, has been replaced by section 5 of the *Constitution Act, 1982*.

Section 20 reads as follows:

> **20.** There shall be a Session of the Legislature once at least in every year, so that twelve months shall not intervene between the last sitting of the Legislature in one Session and its first sitting in the next Session.

(43) Repealed by the *Statute Law Revision Act, 1893*, 56-57 Vict. c. 14 (U.K.). The section read as follows:

> **5.** — Ontario, Quebec, and Nova Scotia.
>
> **89.** Each of the Lieutenant Governors of Ontario, Quebec and Nova Scotia shall cause Writs to be issued for the First Election of Members of the Legislative Assembly thereof in such Form and by such Person as he thinks fit, and at such Time and addressed to such Returning Officer as the Governor General directs, and so that the First Election of Member of Assembly for any Electoral District or any Subdivision thereof shall be held at the same Time and at the same Places as the Election for a Member to serve in the House of Commons of Canada for that Electoral District.

6. — THE FOUR PROVINCES

90. The following Provisions of this Act respecting the Parliament of Canada, namely, — the Provisions relating to Appropriation and Tax Bills, the Recommendation of Money Votes, the Assent to Bills, the Disallowance of Acts, and the Signification of Pleasure on Bills reserved, — shall extend and apply to the Legislatures of the several Provinces as if those Provisions were here re-enacted and made applicable in Terms to the respective Provinces and the Legislatures thereof, with the Substitution of the Lieutenant Governor of the Province for the Governor General, of the Governor General for the Queen and for a Secretary of State, of One Year for Two Years, and of the Province for Canada.

Application to Legislatures of Provisions respecting Money Votes, etc.

VI. DISTRIBUTION OF LEGISLATIVE POWERS

Powers of the Parliament

91. It shall be lawful for the Queen, by and with the Advice and Consent of the Senate and House of Commons, to make Laws for the Peace, Order, and good Government of Canada, in relation to all Matters not coming within the Classes of Subjects by this Act assigned exclusively to the Legislatures of the Provinces; and for greater Certainty, but not so as to restrict the Generality of the foregoing Terms of this Section, it is hereby declared that (notwithstanding anything in this Act) the exclusive Legislative Authority of the Parliament of Canada extends to all Matters coming within the Classes of Subjects next hereinafter enumerated; that is to say,—

Legislative Authority of Parliament of Canada

1. Repealed.[44]

1A. The Public Debt and Property.[45]

2. The Regulation of Trade and Commerce.

2A. Unemployment insurance.[46]

3. The raising of Money by any Mode or System of Taxation.

4. The borrowing of Money on the Public Credit.

5. Postal Service.

6. The Census and Statistics.

---

(44) Class I was added by the *British North America (No. 2) Act, 1949*, 13 Geo. VI, c. 81 (U.K.). That Act and class I were repealed by the *Constitution Act, 1982*. The matters referred to in class I are provided for in subsection 4 (2) and Part V of the *Constitution Act, 1982*. As enacted, class I read as follows:

1. The amendment from time to time of the Constitution of Canada, except as regards matters coming within the classes of subjects by this Act assigned exclusively to the Legislatures of the provinces, or as regards rights or privileges by this or any other Constitutional Act granted or secured to the Legislature or the Government of a province, or to any class of persons with respect to schools or as regards the use of the English or the French language or as regards the requirements that there shall be a session of the Parliament of Canada at least once each year, and that no House of Commons shall continue for more than five years from the day of the return of the Writs for choosing the House: provided, however, that a House of Commons may in time of real or apprehended war, invasion or insurrection be continued by the Parliament of Canada if such continuation is not opposed by the votes of more than one-third of the members of such House.

(45) Re-numbered by the *British North America (No. 2) Act, 1949*.

(46) Added by the *Constitution Act, 1940*, 3-4 Geo. VI, c. 36 (U.K.).

7. Militia, Military and Naval Service, and Defence.

8. The fixing of and providing for the Salaries and Allowances of Civil and other Officers of the Government of Canada.

9. Beacons, Buoys, Lighthouses, and Sable Island.

10. Navigation and Shipping.

11. Quarantine and the Establishment and Maintenance of Marine Hospitals.

12. Sea Coast and Inland Fisheries.

13. Ferries between a Province and any British or Foreign Country or between Two Provinces.

14. Currency and Coinage.

15. Banking, Incorporation of Banks, and the Issue of Paper Money.

16. Savings Banks.

17. Weights and Measures.

18. Bills of Exchange and Promissory Notes.

19. Interest.

20. Legal Tender.

21. Bankruptcy and Insolvency.

22. Patents of Invention and Discovery.

23. Copyrights.

24. Indians, and Lands reserved for Indians.

25. Naturalization and Aliens.

26. Marriage and Divorce.

27. The Criminal Law, except the Constitution of Courts of Criminal Jurisdiction, but including the Procedure in Criminal Matters.

28. The Establishment, Maintenance, and Management of Penitentiaries.

29. Such Classes of Subjects as are expressly excepted in the Enumeration of the Classes of Subjects by this Act assigned exclusively to the Legislatures of the Provinces.

And any Matter coming within any of the Classes of Subjects enumerated in this Section shall not be deemed to come within the Class of Matters of a local or private Nature comprised in the Enumeration of the Classes of Subjects by this Act assigned exclusively to the Legislatures of the Provinces.[47]

---

(47) Legislative authority has been conferred on Parliament by other Acts as follows:

1. The *Constitution Act, 1871,* 34-35 Vict., c. 28 (U.K.).

2. The Parliament of Canada may from time to time establish new Provinces in any territories forming for the time being part of the Dominion of Canada, but not included in any Province thereof, and may, at the time of such establishment, make provision for the constitution and administration of any such Province, and for the passing of laws for the peace, order, and good government of such Province, and for its representation in the said Parliament.

Exclusive Powers of Provincial Legislatures

92. In each Province the Legislature may exclusively make Laws in relation to Matters coming within the Classes of Subjects next hereinafter enumerated; that is to say, — | *Subjects of exclusive Provincial Legislation*

1. Repealed.[48]

2. Direct Taxation within the Province in order to the raising of a Revenue for Provincial Purposes.

3. The borrowing of Money on the sole Credit of the Province.

4. The Establishment and Tenure of Provincial Offices and the Appointment and Payment of Provincial Officers.

5. The Management and Sale of the Public Lands belonging to the Province and of the Timber and Wood thereon.

---

3. The Parliament of Canada may from time to time, with the consent of the Legislature of any province of the said Dominion, increase, diminish, or otherwise alter the limits of such Province, upon such terms and conditions as may be agreed to by the said Legislature, and may, with the like consent, make provision respecting the effect and operation of any such increase or diminution or alteration of territory in relation to any Province affected thereby.

4. The Parliament of Canada may from time to time make provision for the administration, peace, order, and good government of any territory not for the time being included in any Province.

5. The following Acts passed by the said Parliament of Canada, and intituled respectively —"An Act for the temporary government of Rupert's Land and the North Western Territory when united with Canada"; and "An Act to amend and continue the Act thirty-two and thirty-three Victoria, chapter three, and to establish and provide for the government of "the Province of Manitoba", shall be and be deemed to have been valid and effectual for all purposes whatsoever from the date at which they respectively received the assent, in the Queen's name, of the Governor General of the said Dominion of Canada.

6. Except as provided by the third section of this Act, it shall not be competent for the Parliament of Canada to alter the provisions of the last-mentioned Act of the said Parliament in so far as it relates to the Province of Manitoba, or of any other Act hereafter establishing new Provinces in the said Dominion, subject always to the right of the Legislature of the Province of Manitoba to alter from time to time the provisions of any law respecting the qualification of electors and members of the Legislative Assembly, and to make laws respecting elections in the said province.

The *Rupert's Land Act, 1868,* 31-32 Vict., c. 105 (U.K.) (repealed by the *Statute Law Revision Act, 1893,* 56-57 Vict., c. 14 (U.K.)) had previously conferred similar authority in relation to Rupert's Land and the North Western Territory upon admission of those areas.

2. The *Constitution Act, 1886,* 49-50 Vict., c. 35, (U.K.).

1. The Parliament of Canada may from time to time make provision for the representation in the Senate and House of Commons of Canada, or in either of them, of any territories which for the time being form part of the Dominion of Canada, but are not included in any province thereof.

3. The *Statute of Westminster, 1931,* 22 Geo. V, c.4 (U.K.).

3. It is hereby declared and enacted that the Parliament of a Dominion has full power to make laws having extra-territorial operation.

4. Under section 44 of the *Constitution Act, 1982,* Parliament has exclusive authority to amend the Constitution of Canada in relation to the executive government of Canada or the Senate and House of Commons. Sections 38, 41, 42, and 43 of that Act authorize the Senate and House of Commons to give their approval to certain other constitutional amendments by resolution.

(48) Class I was repealed by the *Constitution Act, 1982.* As enacted, it read as follows:

1. The Amendment from Time to Time, notwithstanding anything in this Act, of the Constitution of the Province, except as regards the Office of Lieutenant Governor.

Section 45 of the *Constitution Act, 1982* now authorizes legislatures to make laws amending the constitution of the province. Sections 38, 41, 42, and 43 of that Act authorize legislative assemblies to give their approval by resolution to certain other amendments to the Constitution of Canada.

6. The Establishment, Maintenance, and Management of Public and Reformatory Prisons in and for the Province.

7. The Establishment, Maintenance, and Management of Hospitals, Asylums, Charities, and Eleemosynary Institutions in and for the Province, other than Marine Hospitals.

8. Municipal Institutions in the Province.

9. Shop, Saloon, Tavern, Auctioneer, and other Licences in order to the raising of a Revenue for Provincial, Local, or Municipal Purposes.

10. Local Works and Undertakings other than such as are of the following Classes:—

(a) Lines of Steam or other Ships, Railways, Canals, Telegraphs, and other Works and Undertakings connecting the Province with any other or others of the Provinces, or extending beyond the Limits of the Province:

(b) Lines of Steam Ships between the Province and any British or Foreign Country:

(c) Such Works as, although wholly situate within the Province, are before or after their Execution declared by the Parliament of Canada to be for the general Advantage of Canada or for the Advantage of Two or more of the Provinces.

11. The Incorporation of Companies with Provincial Objects.

12. The Solemnization of Marriage in the Province.

13. Property and Civil Rights in the Province.

14. The Administration of Justice in the Province, including the Constitution, Maintenance, and Organization of Provincial Courts, both of Civil and of Criminal Jurisdiction, and including Procedure in Civil Matters in those Courts.

15. The Imposition of Punishment by Fine, Penalty, or Imprisonment for enforcing any Law of the Province made in relation to any Matter coming within any of the Classes of Subjects enumerated in this Section.

16. Generally all Matters of a merely local or private Nature in the Province.

*Non-Renewable Natural Resources, Forestry Resources
and Electrical Energy*

Laws respecting non-renewable natural resources, forestry resources and electrical energy

92A. (1) In each province, the legislature may exclusively make laws in relation to

(*a*) exploration for non-renewable natural resources in the province;

(*b*) development, conservation and management of non-renewable natural resources and forestry resources in the province, including laws in relation to the rate of primary production therefrom; and (*c*) development, conservation and management of sites and facilities in the province for the generation and production of electrical energy.

(2) In each province, the legislature may make laws in relation to the export from the province to another part of Canada of the primary production from non-renewable natural resources and forestry resources in the province and the production from facilities in the province for the generation of electrical energy, but such laws may not authorize or provide for discrimination in prices or in supplies exported to another part of Canada.

Export from provinces of resources

(3) Nothing in subsection (2) derogates from the authority of Parliament to enact laws in relation to the matters referred to in that subsection and, where such a law of Parliament and a law of a province conflict, the law of Parliament prevails to the extent of the conflict.

Authority of Parliament

(4) In each province, the legislature may make laws in relation to the raising of money by any mode or system of taxation in respect of

Taxation of resources

(*a*) non-renewable natural resources and forestry resources in the province and the primary production therefrom, and

(*b*) sites and facilities in the province for the generation of electrical energy and the production therefrom,

whether or not such production is exported in whole or in part from the province, but such laws may not authorize or provide for taxation that differentiates between production exported to another part of Canada and production not exported from the province.

(5) The expression "primary production" has the meaning assigned by the Sixth Schedule.

"Primary production"

(6) Nothing in subsections (1) to (5) derogates from any powers or rights that a legislature or government of a province had immediately before the coming into force of this section.[49]

Existing powers or rights

Education

93. In and for each Province the Legislature may exclusively make Laws in relation to Education, subject and according to the following Provisions:—

Legislation respecting Education

(1) Nothing in any such Law shall prejudicially affect any Right or Privilege with respect to Denominational Schools which any Class of Persons have by Law in the Province at the Union:

(2) All the Powers, Privileges, and Duties at the Union by Law conferred and imposed in Upper Canada on the Separate Schools and School Trustees of the Queen's Roman Catholic Subjects shall be and the same are hereby extended to the Dissentient Schools of the Queen's Protestant and Roman Catholic Subjects in Quebec:

---

(49) Added by the *Constitution Act, 1982.*

(3) Where in any Province a system of separate or Dissentient Schools exists by Law at the Union or is thereafter established by the Legislature of the Province, an Appeal shall lie to the Governor General in Council from any Act or Decision of any Provincial Authority affecting any Right or Privilege of the Protestant or Roman Catholic Minority of the Queen's Subjects in relation to Education:

(4) In case any such Provincial Law as from Time to Time seems to the Governor General in Council requisite for the due Execution of the Provisions of this Section is not made, or in case any Decision of the Governor General in Council on any appeal under this Section is not duly executed by the proper Provincial Authority in that Behalf, then and in every such Case, and as far only as the Circumstances of each Case require, the Parliament of Canada may make remedial Laws for the due Execution of the Provisions of this Section and of any Decision of the Governor General in Council under this Section.[50]

---

(50) An alternative was provided for Manitoba by section 22 of the *Manitoba Act, 1870,* 33 Vict., c.3 (Canada), (confirmed by the *Constitution Act, 1871*), which reads as follows:

22. In and for the Province, the said Legislature may exclusively make Laws in relation to Education, subject and according to the following provisions:

(1) Nothing in any such Law shall prejudicially affect any right or privilege with respect to Denominational Schools which any class of persons have by Law or practice in the Province at the Union:

(2) An appeal shall lie to the Governor General in Council from any Act or decision of the Legislature of the Province, or of any Provincial Authority, affecting any right or privilege, of the Protestant or Roman Catholic minority of the Queen's subjects in relation to Education:

(3) In case any such Provincial Law, as from time to time seems to the Governor General in Council requisite for the due execution of the provisions of this section, is not made, or in case any decision of the Governor General in Council on any appeal under this section is not duly executed by the proper Provincial Authority in that behalf, then, and in every such case, and as far only as the circumstances of each case require, the Parliament of Canada may make remedial Laws for the due execution of the provisions of this section, and of any decision of the Governor General in Council under this section.

An alternative was provided for Alberta by section 17 of the *Alberta Act,* 4-5 Edw. VII, c. 3, 1905 (Canada), which reads as follows:

17. Section 93 of the *Constitution Act, 1867,* shall apply to the said province, with the substitution for paragraph (1) of the said section 93 of the following paragraph:

(1) Nothing in any such law shall prejudicially affect any right or privilege with respect to separate schools which any class of persons have at the date of the passing of this Act, under the terms of chapters 29 and 30 of the Ordinances of the Northwest Territories, passed in the year 1901, or with respect to religious instruction in any public or separate school as provided for in the said ordinances.

2. In the appropriation by the Legislature or distribution by the Government of the province of any moneys for the support of schools organized and carried on in accordance with the said chapter 29 or any Act passed in amendment thereof, or in substitution therefor, there shall be no discrimination against schools of any class described in the said chapter 29.

3. Where the expression "by law" is employed in paragraph 3 of the said section 93, it shall be held to mean the law as set out in the said chapters 29 and 30, and where the expression "at the Union" is employed, in the said paragraph 3, it shall be held to mean the date at which this Act comes into force.

An alternative was provided for Saskatchewan by section 17 of the *Saskatchewan Act,* 4-5 Edw. VII, c. 42, 1905 (Canada), which reads as follows:

17. Section 93 of the *Constitution Act, 1867,* shall apply to the said province, with the substitution for paragraph (1) of the said section 93, of the following paragraph:

(1) Nothing in any such law shall prejudicially affect any right or privilege with respect to separate schools which any class of persons have at the date of the passing of this Act, under the terms chapters 29 and 30 of the Ordinances of the

93A. Paragraphs (1) to (4) of section 93 do not apply to Quebec.[50.1]

Quebec

Uniformity of Laws in Ontario, Nova Scotia, and New Brunswick

94. Notwithstanding anything in this Act, the Parliament of Canada may make Provision for the Uniformity of all or any of the Laws relative to Property and Civil Rights in Ontario, Nova Scotia, and New Brunswick, and of the Procedure of all or any of the Courts in those Three Provinces, and from and after the passing of any Act in that Behalf the Power of the Parliament of Canada to make Laws in relation to any Matter comprised in any such Act shall, notwithstanding anything in this Act, be unrestricted; but any Act of the Parliament of Canada making Provision for such Uniformity shall not have effect in any Province unless and until it is adopted and enacted as Law by the Legislature thereof.

Legislation for Uniformity of Laws in Three Provinces

Old Age Pensions

94A. The Parliament of Canada may make laws in relation to old age pensions and supplementary benefits, including survivors' and disability benefits irrespective of age, but no such law shall affect the operation of any law present or future of a provincial legislature in relation to any such matter.[51]

Legislation respecting old age pensions and supplementary benefits

---

Northwest Territories, passed in the year 1901, or with respect to religious instruction in any public or separate school as provided for in the said ordinances.

2. In the appropriation by the Legislature or distribution by the Government of the province of any moneys for the support of schools organized and carried on in accordance with the said chapter 29, or any Act passed in amendment thereof or in substitution therefor, there shall be no discrimination against schools of any class described in the said chapter 29.

3. Where the expression "by law" is employed in paragraph (3) of the said section 93, it shall be held to mean the law as set out in the said chapters 29 and 30; and where the expression "at the Union" is employed in the said paragraph (3), it shall be held to mean the date at which this Act comes into force.

An alternative was provided for Newfoundland by Term 17 of the Terms of Union of Newfoundland with Canada (confirmed by the *Newfoundland Act*, 12-13 Geo. VI, C. 22 (U.K)). Term 17 of the Terms of Union of Newfoundland with Canada set out in the Schedule to the *Newfoundland Act*, which was amended by the *Constitution Amendment, 1998 (Newfoundland Act)*, (see SI/98-25) and now reads as follows:

17. (1) In lieu of section ninety-three of the *Constitution Act, 1867*, the following term shall apply in respect of the Province of Newfoundland.

(2) In and for the Province of Newfoundland, the Legislature shall have exclusive authority to make laws in relation to education, but shall provide for courses in religion that are not specific to a religious denomination.

(3) Religious observances shall be permitted in a school where requested by parents.

[Publisher's note: The history of amendments to Term 17 of the Terms of Union of Newfoundland with Canada can be found on the Department of Justice Web site at <http://lois.justice.gc.ca/en/const/endnts_e.html>.]

See also sections 23, 29, and 59 of the *Constitution Act, 1982*. Section 23 provides for new minority language educational rights and section 59 permits a delay in respect of the coming into force in Quebec of one aspect of those rights. Section 29 provides that nothing in the *Canadian Charter of Rights and Freedoms* abrogates or derogates from any rights or privileges guaranteed by or under the Constitution of Canada in respect of denominational, separate or dissentient schools.

(50.1) Added by the *Constitution Amendment, 1997 (Quebec)*. See SI/97-141.

(51) Added by the *Constitution Act, 1964,* 12-13 Eliz. II, c. 73 (U.K.). As originally enacted by the *British North America Act, 1951,* 14-15 Geo. VI, c. 32 (U.K.), which was repealed by the *Constitution Act, 1982*, section 94A read as follows:

94A. It is hereby declared that the Parliament of Canada may from time to time make laws in relation to old age pensions in Canada, but no law made by the Parliament of Canada in relation to old age pensions shall affect the operation of any law present or future of a Provincial Legislature in relation to old age pensions.

Concurrent Powers of Legislation respecting Agriculture, etc.

95. In each Province the Legislature may make Laws in relation to Agriculture in the Province, and to Immigration into the Province; and it is hereby declared that the Parliament of Canada may from Time to Time make Laws in relation to Agriculture in all or any of the Provinces, and to Immigration into all or any of the Provinces; and any Law of the Legislature of a Province relative to Agriculture or to Immigration shall have effect in and for the Province as long and as far only as it is not repugnant to any Act of the Parliament of Canada.

VII. JUDICATURE

Appointment of Judges

96. The Governor General shall appoint the Judges of the Superior, District, and County Courts in each Province, except those of the Courts of Probate in Nova Scotia and New Brunswick.

Selection of Judges in Ontario, etc.

97. Until the Laws relative to Property and Civil Rights in Ontario, Nova Scotia, and New Brunswick, and the Procedure of the Courts in those Provinces, are made uniform, the Judges of the Courts of those Provinces appointed by the Governor General shall be selected from the respective Bars of those Provinces.

Selection of Judges in Quebec

98. The Judges of the Courts of Quebec shall be selected from the Bar of that Province.

Tenure of office of Judges

99. (1) Subject to subsection two of this section, the Judges of the Superior Courts shall hold office during good behaviour, but shall be removable by the Governor General on Address of the Senate and House of Commons.

Termination at age 75

(2) A Judge of a Superior Court, whether appointed before or after the coming into force of this section, shall cease to hold office upon attaining the age of seventy-five years, or upon the coming into force of this section if at that time he has already attained that age.[52]

Salaries, etc., of Judges

100. The Salaries, Allowances, and Pensions of the Judges of the Superior, District, and County Courts (except the Courts of Probate in Nova Scotia and New Brunswick), and of the Admiralty Courts in Cases where the Judges thereof are for the Time being paid by Salary, shall be fixed and provided by the Parliament of Canada.[53]

General Court of Appeal, etc.

101. The Parliament of Canada may, notwithstanding anything in this Act, from Time to Time provide for the Constitution, Maintenance, and Organization of a General Court of Appeal for Canada, and for the Establishment of any additional Courts for the better Administration of the Laws of Canada.[54]

---

(52) Repealed and re-enacted by the *Constitution Act, 1960,* 9 Eliz. II, c. 2 (U.K.), which came into force on March 1, 1961. The original section read as follows:

> **99.** The Judges of the Superior Courts shall hold Office during good Behaviour, but shall be removable by the Governor General on Address of the Senate and House of Commons.

(53) Now provided for in the *Judges Act,* R.S.C. 1985, c. J-1.

(54) See the *Supreme Court Act,* R.S.C. 1985, c. S-26, the *Federal Court Act,* R.S.C. 1985, c. F-7 and the *Tax Court of Canada Act,* R.S.C. 1985, c. T-2.

VIII. REVENUES; DEBTS; ASSETS; TAXATION

102. All Duties and Revenues over which the respective Legislatures of Canada, Nova Scotia, and New Brunswick before and at the Union had and have Power of Appropriation, except such Portions thereof as are by this Act reserved to the respective Legislatures of the Provinces, or are raised by them in accordance with the special Powers conferred on them by this Act, shall form One Consolidated Revenue Fund, to be appropriated for the Public Service of Canada in the Manner and subject to the Charges in this Act provided.

Creation of Consolidated Revenue Fund

103. The Consolidated Revenue Fund of Canada shall be permanently charged with the Costs, Charges, and Expenses incident to the Collection, Management, and Receipt thereof, and the same shall form the First Charge thereon, subject to be reviewed and audited in such Manner as shall be ordered by the Governor General in Council until the Parliament otherwise provides.

Expenses of Collection, etc.

104. The annual Interest of the Public Debts of the several Provinces of Canada, Nova Scotia, and New Brunswick at the Union shall form the Second Charge on the Consolidated Revenue Fund of Canada.

Interest of Provincial Public Debts

105. Unless altered by the Parliament of Canada, the Salary of the Governor General shall be Ten thousand Pounds Sterling Money of the United Kingdom of Great Britain and Ireland, payable out of the Consolidated Revenue Fund of Canada, and the same shall form the Third Charge thereon.[55]

Salary of Governor General

106. Subject to the several Payments by this Act charged on the Consolidated Revenue Fund of Canada, the same shall be appropriated by the Parliament of Canada for the Public Service.

Appropriation from Time to Time

107. All Stocks, Cash, Banker's Balances, and Securities for Money belonging to each Province at the Time of the Union, except as in this Act mentioned, shall be the Property of Canada, and shall be taken in Reduction of the Amount of the respective Debts of the Provinces at the Union.

Transfer of Stocks, etc.

108. The Public Works and Property of each Province, enumerated in the Third Schedule to this Act, shall be the Property of Canada.

Transfer of Property in Schedule

109. All Lands, Mines, Minerals, and Royalties belonging to the Several Provinces of Canada, Nova Scotia, and New Brunswick at the Union, and all Sums then due or payable for such Lands, Mines, Minerals, or Royalties, shall belong to the several Provinces of Ontario, Quebec, Nova Scotia, and New Brunswick in which the same are situate or arise, subject to any Trusts existing in respect thereof, and to any Interest other than that of the Province in the same.[56]

Property in Lands, Mines, etc.

---

(55) Now covered by the *Governor General's Act*, R.S.C. 1985, c. G-9.

(56) Manitoba, Alberta and Saskatchewan were placed in the same position as the original provinces by the *Constitution Act, 1930,* 20-21 Geo. V, c. 26 (U.K.).

These matters were dealt with in respect of British Columbia by the *British Columbia Terms of Union* and also in part by the *Constitution Act, 1930.*

Newfoundland was also placed in the same position by the *Newfoundland Act,* 12-13 Geo. VI, c. 22 (U.K.).

With respect to Prince Edward Island, see the Schedule to the *Prince Edward Island Terms of Union.*

Assets connected with Provincial Debts

110. All Assets connected with such Portions of the Public Debt of each Province as are assumed by that Province shall belong to that Province.

Canada to be liable for Provincial Debts

111. Canada shall be liable for the Debts and Liabilities of each Province existing at the Union.

Debts of Ontario and Quebec

112. Ontario and Quebec conjointly shall be liable to Canada for the Amount (if any) by which the Debt of the Province of Canada exceeds at the Union Sixty-two million five hundred thousand Dollars, and shall be charged with Interest at the Rate of Five per Centum per Annum thereon.

Assets of Ontario and Quebec

113. The Assets enumerated in the Fourth Schedule to this Act belonging at the Union to the Province of Canada shall be the property of Ontario and Quebec conjointly.

Debt of Nova Scotia

114. Nova Scotia shall be liable to Canada for the Amount (if any) by which its Public Debt exceeds at the Union Eight million Dollars, and shall be charged with Interest at the Rate of Five per Centum per Annum thereon.[57]

Debt of New Brunswick

115. New Brunswick shall be liable to Canada for the Amount (if any) by which its Public Debt exceeds at the Union Seven million Dollars, and shall be charged with Interest at the Rate of Five per Centum per Annum thereon.

Payment of interest to Nova Scotia and New Brunswick

116. In case the Public Debts of Nova Scotia and New Brunswick do not at the Union amount to Eight million and Seven million Dollars respectively, they shall respectively receive by half-yearly Payments in advance from the Government of Canada Interest at Five per Centum per Annum on the Difference between the actual Amounts of their respective Debts and such stipulated Amounts.

Provincial Public Property

117. The several Provinces shall retain all their respective Public Property not otherwise disposed of in this Act, subject to the Right of Canada to assume any Lands or Public Property required for Fortifications or for the Defence of the Country.

118. Repealed.[58]

---

(57) The obligations imposed by this section, sections 115 and 116, and similar obligations under the instruments creating or admitting other provinces, have been carried into legislation of the Parliament of Canada and are now to be found in the *Provincial Subsidies Act,* R.S.C. 1985, c. P-26.

(58) Repealed by the *Statute Law Revision Act, 1950,* 14 Geo. VI, c. 6 (U.K.). As originally enacted the section read as follows:

118. The following Sums shall be paid yearly by Canada to the several Provinces for the Support of their Governments and Legislatures:

Dollars.

Ontario..Eighty thousand.

Quebec ....Seventy thousand.

Nova Scotia..Sixty thousand.

New Brunswick..Fifty thousand.

Two hundred and sixty thousand;

and an annual Grant in aid of each Province shall be made, equal to Eighty cents per Head of the Population as ascertained by the Census of One thousand eight hundred and sixty-one, and in the case of Nova Scotia and New Brunswick, by each subsequent Decennial Census until the Population of each of those two Provinces amounts to Four hundred thousand Souls, at which Rate such Grant shall thereafter remain. Such Grants shall be in full Settlement of all future Demands on Canada, and shall be paid half-yearly in advance to each Province; but the Government of Canada shall deduct from such Grants, as against any Province, all Sums chargeable as Interest on the Public Debt of that Province in excess of the several Amounts stipulated in this Act.

The section was made obsolete by the *Constitution Act, 1907,* 7 Edw. VII , c. 11 (U.K.) which provided:

1. (1) The following grants shall be made yearly by Canada to every province, which at the commencement of this Act is a province of the Dominion, for its local purposes and the support of its Government and Legislature: —

(a) A fixed grant —

where the population of the province is under one hundred and fifty thousand, of one hundred thousand dollars;

where the population of the province is one hundred and fifty thousand, but does not exceed two hundred thousand, of one hundred and fifty thousand dollars;

where the population of the province is two hundred thousand, but does not exceed four hundred thousand, of one hundred and eighty thousand dollars;

where the population of the province is four hundred thousand, but does not exceed eight hundred thousand, of one hundred and ninety thousand dollars;

where the population of the province is eight hundred thousand, but does no exceed one million five hundred thousand, of two hundred and twenty thousand dollars;

where the population of the province exceeds one million five hundred thousand, of two hundred and forty thousand dollars; and

(b) Subject to the special provisions of this Act as to the provinces of British Columbia and Prince Edward Island, a grant at the rate of eighty cents per head of the population of the province up to the number of two million five hundred thousand, and at the rate of sixty cents per head of so much of the population as exceeds that number.

(2) An additional grant of one hundred thousand dollars shall be made yearly to the province of British Columbia for a period of ten years from the commencement of this Act.

(3) The population of a province shall be ascertained from time to time in the case of the provinces of Manitoba, Saskatchewan, and Alberta respectively by the last quinquennial census or statutory estimate of population made under the Acts establishing those provinces or any other Act of the Parliament of Canada making provision for the purpose, and in the case of any other province by the last decennial census for the time being.

(4) The grants payable under this Act shall be paid half-yearly in advance to each province.

(5) The grants payable under this Act shall be substituted for the grants or subsidies (in this Act referred to as existing grants) payable for the like purposes at the commencement of this Act to the several provinces of the Dominion under the provisions of section one hundred and eighteen of the *Constitution Act, 1867,* or of any Order in Council establishing a province, or of any Act of the Parliament of Canada containing directions for the payment of any such grant or subsidy, and those provisions shall cease to have effect.

(6) The Government of Canada shall have the same power of deducting sums charged against a province on account of the interest on public debt in the case of the grant payable under this Act to the province as they have in the case of the existing grant.

(7) Nothing in this Act shall affect the obligation of the Government of Canada to pay to any province any grant which is payable to that province, other than the existing grant for which the grant under this Act is substituted.

(8) In the case of the provinces of British Columbia and Prince Edward Island, the amount paid on account of the grant payable per head of the population to the provinces under this Act shall not at any time be less than the amount of the corresponding grant payable at the commencement of this Act, and if it is found on any decennial census that the population of the province has decreased since the last decennial census, the amount paid on account of the grant shall not be decreased below the amount then payable, notwithstanding the decrease of the population.

See the *Provincial Subsidies Act,* R.S.C. 1985, c. P-26 and the *Federal-Provincial Fiscal Arrangements and Federal Post-Secondary Education and Health Contributions Act,* R.S.C. 1985, c. F-8.

See also Part III of the *Constitution Act, 1982,* which sets out commitments by Parliament and the provincial legislatures respecting equal opportunities, economic development and the provision of essential public services and a commitment by Parliament and the government of Canada to the principle of making equalization payments.

Further Grant to New Brunswick

119. New Brunswick shall receive by half-yearly Payments in advance from Canada for the Period of Ten Years from the Union an additional Allowance of Sixty-three thousand Dollars per Annum; but as long as the Public Debt of that Province remains under Seven million Dollars, a Deduction equal to the Interest at Five per Centum per Annum on such Deficiency shall be made from that Allowance of Sixty three thousand Dollars.[59]

Form of Payments

120. All Payments to be made under this Act, or in discharge of Liabilities created under any Act of the Provinces of Canada, Nova Scotia, and New Brunswick respectively, and assumed by Canada, shall, until the Parliament of Canada otherwise directs, be made in such Form and Manner as may from Time to Time be ordered by the Governor General in Council.

Canadian Manufactures, etc.

121. All Articles of the Growth, Produce, or Manufacture of any one of the Provinces shall, from and after the Union, be admitted free into each of the other Provinces.

Continuance of Customs and Excise Laws

122. The Customs and Excise Laws of each Province shall, subject to the Provisions of this Act, continue in force until altered by the Parliament of Canada.[60]

Exportation and Importation as between Two Provinces

123. Where Customs Duties are, at the Union, leviable on any Goods, Wares, or Merchandises in any Two Provinces, those Goods, Wares, and Merchandises may, from and after the Union, be imported from one of those Provinces into the other of them on Proof of Payment of the Customs Duty leviable thereon in the Province of Exportation, and on Payment of such further Amount (if any) of Customs Duty as is leviable thereon in the Province of Importation.[61]

Lumber Dues in New Brunswick

124. Nothing in this Act shall affect the Right of New Brunswick to levy the Lumber Dues provided in Chapter Fifteen of Title Three of the Revised Statutes of New Brunswick, or in any Act amending that Act before or after the Union, and not increasing the Amount of such Dues; but the Lumber of any of the Provinces other than New Brunswick shall not be subject to such Dues.[62]

Exemption of Public Lands, etc.

125. No Lands or Property belonging to Canada or any Province shall be liable to Taxation.

Provincial Consolidated Revenue Fund

126. Such Portions of the Duties and Revenues over which the respective Legislatures of Canada, Nova Scotia, and New Brunswick had before the Union Power of Appropriation as are by this Act reserved to the respective Governments or Legislatures of the Provinces, and all Duties and Revenues raised by them in accordance with the special Powers conferred upon them by this Act, shall in each Province form One Consolidated Revenue Fund to be appropriated for the Public Service of the Province.

---

(59) Spent.

(60) Spent. Now covered by the *Customs Act*, R.S.C. 1985, c. 1 (2nd Supp.), the *Customs Tariff*, R.S.C. 1985, c. 41 (3rd Supp.), the *Excise Act*, R.S.C. 1985, c. E-14 and the *Excise Tax Act*, R.S.C. 1985, c. E-15.

(61) Spent.

(62) These dues were repealed in 1873 by 36 Vict., c. 16 (N.B.). And see *An Act respecting the Export Duties imposed on Lumber*, etc. (1873) 36 Vict., c. 41 (Canada), and section 2 of the *Provincial Subsidies Act*, R.S.C. 1985, c. P-26.

IX. MISCELLANEOUS PROVISIONS

General

127. Repealed.[63]

128. Every Member of the Senate or House of Commons of Canada shall before taking his Seat therein take and subscribe before the Governor General or some Person authorized by him, and every Member of a Legislative Council or Legislative Assembly of any Province shall before taking his Seat therein take and subscribe before the Lieutenant Governor of the Province or some Person authorized by him, the Oath of Allegiance contained in the Fifth Schedule to this Act; and every Member of the Senate of Canada and every Member of the Legislative Council of Quebec shall also, before taking his Seat therein, take and subscribe before the Governor General, or some Person authorized by him, the Declaration of Qualification contained in the same Schedule.

Oath of Allegiance, etc.

129. Except as otherwise provided by this Act, all Laws in force in Canada, Nova Scotia or New Brunswick at the Union, and all Courts of Civil and Criminal Jurisdiction, and all legal Commissions, Powers, and Authorities, and all Officers, Judicial, Administrative, and Ministerial, existing therein at the Union, shall continue in Ontario, Quebec, Nova Scotia, and New Brunswick respectively, as if the Union had not been made; subject nevertheless (except with respect to such as are enacted by or exist under Acts of the Parliament of Great Britain or of the Parliament of the United Kingdom of Great Britain and Ireland), to be repealed, abolished, or altered by the Parliament of Canada, or by the Legislature of the respective Province, according to the Authority of the Parliament or of that Legislature under this Act.[64]

Continuance of existing Laws, Courts, Officers, etc.

130. Until the Parliament of Canada otherwise provides, all Officers of the several Provinces having Duties to discharge in relation to Matters other than those coming within the Classes of Subjects by this Act assigned exclusively to the Legislatures of the Provinces shall be Officers of Canada, and shall continue to discharge the Duties of their respective Offices under the same Liabilities, Responsibilities, and Penalties as if the Union had not been made.[65]

Transfer of Officers to Canada

131. Until the Parliament of Canada otherwise provides, the Governor General in Council may from Time to Time appoint such Officers as the Governor General in Council deems necessary or proper for the effectual Execution of this Act.

Appointment of new Officers

---

(63) Repealed by the *Statute Law Revision Act, 1893*, 56-57 Vict., c. 14 (U.K.). The section read as follows:

> **127.** If any Person being at the passing of this Act a Member of the Legislative Council of Canada, Nova Scotia, or New Brunswick, to whom a Place in the Senate is offered, does not within Thirty Days thereafter, by Writing under his Hand addressed to the Governor General of the Province of Canada or to the Lieutenant Governor of Nova Scotia or New Brunswick (as the Case may be), accept the same, he shall be deemed to have declined the same; and any Person who, being at the passing of this Act a Member of the Legislative Council of Nova Scotia or New Brunswick, accepts a Place in the Senate shall thereby vacate his Seat in such Legislative Council.

(64) The restriction against altering or repealing laws enacted by or existing under statutes of the United Kingdom was removed by the *Statute of Westminster, 1931,* 22 Geo. V. c. 4 (U.K,) except in respect of certain constitutional documents. Comprehensive procedures for amending enactments forming part of the Constitution of Canada were provided by Part V of the *Constitution Act, 1982,* (U.K.) 1982, c. 11.

(65) Spent.

Treaty Obligations

132. The Parliament and Government of Canada shall have all Powers necessary or proper for performing the Obligations of Canada or of any Province thereof, as Part of the British Empire, towards Foreign Countries, arising under Treaties between the Empire and such Foreign Countries.

Use of English and French Languages

133. Either the English or the French Language may be used by any Person in the Debates of the Houses of the Parliament of Canada and of the Houses of the Legislature of Quebec; and both those Languages shall be used in the respective Records and Journals of those Houses; and either of those Languages may be used by any Person or in any Pleading or Process in or issuing from any Court of Canada established under this Act, and in or from all or any of the Courts of Quebec.

The Acts of the Parliament of Canada and of the Legislature of Quebec shall be printed and published in both those Languages.[66]

Ontario and Quebec

Appointment of Executive Officers for Ontario and Quebec

134. Until the Legislature of Ontario or of Quebec otherwise provides, the Lieutenant Governors of Ontario and Quebec may each appoint under the Great Seal of the Province the following Officers, to hold Office during Pleasure, that is to say, — the Attorney General, the Secretary and Registrar of the Province, the Treasurer of the Province, the Commissioner of Crown Lands, and the Commissioner of Agriculture and Public Works, and in the Case of Quebec the Solicitor General, and may, by Order of the Lieutenant Governor in Council, from Time to Time prescribe the Duties of those Officers, and of the several Departments over which they shall preside or to which they shall belong, and of the Officers and Clerks thereof, and may also appoint other and additional Officers to hold Office during Pleasure, and may from Time to Time prescribe the Duties of those Officers, and of the several Departments over which they shall preside or to which they shall belong, and of the Officers and Clerks thereof.[67]

---

(66) A similar provision was enacted for Manitoba by section 23 of the *Manitoba Act, 1870,* 33 Vict., c. 3 (Canada), (confirmed by the *Constitution Act, 1871*). Section 23 read as follows:

> **23.** Either the English or the French language may be used by any person in the debates of the Houses of the Legislature, and both these languages shall be used in the respective Records and Journals of those Houses; and either of those languages may be used by any person, or in any Pleading or Process, in or issuing from any Court of Canada established under the British North America Act, 1867, or in or from all or any of the Courts of the Province. The Acts of the Legislature shall be printed and published in both those languages.

Sections 17 to 19 of the *Constitution Act, 1982,* restate the language rights set out in section 133 in respect of Parliament and the courts established under the *Constitution Act, 1867,* and also guarantees those rights in respect of the legislature of New Brunswick and the courts of that province.

Section 16 and sections 20, 21 and 23 of the *Constitution Act, 1982* recognize additional language rights in respect of the English and French languages. Section 22 preserves language rights and privileges of languages other than English and French.

(67) Spent. Now covered in Ontario by the *Executive Council Act*, R.S.O. 1990, c. E.25 and in Quebec by the *Executive Power Act*, R.S.Q. 1977, c. E-18.

135. Until the Legislature of Ontario or Quebec otherwise provides, all Rights, Powers, Duties, Functions, Responsibilities, or Authorities at the passing of this Act vested in or imposed on the Attorney General, Solicitor General, Secretary and Registrar of the Province of Canada, Minister of Finance, Commissioner of Crown Lands, Commissioner of Public Works, and Minister of Agriculture and Receiver General, by any Law, Statute, or Ordinance of Upper Canada, Lower Canada, or Canada, and not repugnant to this Act, shall be vested in or imposed on any Officer to be appointed by the Lieutenant Governor for the Discharge of the same or any of them; and the Commissioner of Agriculture and Public Works shall perform the Duties and Functions of the Office of Minister of Agriculture at the passing of this Act imposed by the Law of the Province of Canada, as well as those of the Commissioner of Public Works.[68]

Powers, Duties, etc. of Executive Officers

136. Until altered by the Lieutenant Governor in Council, the Great Seals of Ontario and Quebec respectively shall be the same, or of the same Design, as those used in the Provinces of Upper Canada and Lower Canada respectively before their Union as the Province of Canada.

Great Seals

137. The words "and from thence to the End of the then next ensuing Session of the Legislature," or Words to the same Effect, used in any temporary Act of the Province of Canada not expired before the Union, shall be construed to extend and apply to the next Session of the Parliament of Canada if the Subject Matter of the Act is within the Powers of the same as defined by this Act, or to the next Sessions of the Legislatures of Ontario and Quebec respectively if the Subject Matter of the Act is within the Powers of the same as defined by this Act.

Construction of temporary Acts

138. From and after the Union the Use of the Words "Upper Canada" instead of "Ontario," or "Lower Canada" instead of "Quebec," in any Deed, Writ, Process, Pleading, Document, Matter, or Thing shall not invalidate the same.

As to Errors in Names

139. Any Proclamation under the Great Seal of the Province of Canada issued before the Union to take effect at a Time which is subsequent to the Union, whether relating to that Province, or to Upper Canada, or to Lower Canada, and the several Matters and Things therein proclaimed, shall be and continue of like Force and Effect as if the Union had not been made.[69]

As to issue of Proclamations before Union, to commence after Union

140. Any Proclamation which is authorized by any Act of the Legislature of the Province of Canada to be issued under the Great Seal of the Province of Canada, whether relating to that Province, or to Upper Canada, or to Lower Canada, and which is not issued before the Union, may be issued by the Lieutenant Governor of Ontario or of Quebec, as its Subject Matter requires, under the Great Seal thereof; and from and after the Issue of such Proclamation the same and the several Matters and Things therein proclaimed shall be and continue of the like Force and Effect in Ontario or Quebec as if the Union had not been made.[70]

As to issue of Proclamations after Union

---

(68) Probably spent.

(69) Probably spent.

(70) Probably spent.

Penitentiary

141. The Penitentiary of the Province of Canada shall, until the Parliament of Canada otherwise provides, be and continue the Penitentiary of Ontario and of Quebec.[71]

Arbitration respecting Debts, etc.

142. The Division and Adjustment of the Debts, Credits, Liabilities, Properties, and Assets of Upper Canada and Lower Canada shall be referred to the Arbitrament of Three Arbitrators, One chosen by the Government of Ontario, One by the Government of Quebec, and One by the Government of Canada; and the Selection of the Arbitrators shall not be made until the Parliament of Canada and the Legislatures of Ontario and Quebec have met; and the Arbitrator chosen by the Government of Canada shall not be a Resident either in Ontario or in Quebec.[72]

Division of Records

143. The Governor General in Council may from Time to Time order that such and so many of the Records, Books, and Documents of the Province of Canada as he thinks fit shall be appropriated and delivered either to Ontario or to Quebec, and the same shall thenceforth be the Property of that Province; and any Copy thereof or Extract therefrom, duly certified by the Officer having charge of the Original thereof, shall be admitted as Evidence.[73]

Constitution of Townships in Quebec

144. The Lieutenant Governor of Quebec may from Time to Time, by Proclamation under the Great Seal of the Province, to take effect from a Day to be appointed therein, constitute Townships in those Parts of the Province of Quebec in which Townships are not then already constituted, and fix the Metes and Bounds thereof.

X. INTERCOLONIAL RAILWAY

145. Repealed.[74]

---

(71) Spent. Penitentiaries are now provided for by the *Corrections and Conditional Release Act*, S.C. 1992, c. 20.

(72) Spent. See pages (xi) and (xii) of the Public Accounts, 1902–1903.

(73) Probably spent. Two orders were made under this section on January 24, 1868.

(74) Repealed by the *Statute Law Revision Act, 1893*, 56-57 Vict., c. 14 (U.K.). The section read as follows:

X. Intercolonial Railway

145. Inasmuch as the Provinces of Canada, Nova Scotia, and New Brunswick have joined in a Declaration that the Construction of the Intercolonial Railway is essential to the Consolidation of the Union of British North America, and to the Assent thereto of Nova Scotia and New Brunswick, and have consequently agreed that Provision should be made for its immediate Construction by the Government of Canada; Therefore, in order to give effect to that Agreement, it shall be the Duty of the Government and Parliament of Canada to provide for the Commencement, within Six Months after the Union, of a Railway connecting the River St. Lawrence with the City of Halifax in Nova Scotia, and for the Construction thereof without Intermission, and the Completion thereof with all practicable Speed.

XI. ADMISSION OF OTHER COLONIES

146. It shall be lawful for the Queen, by and with the Advice of Her Majesty's Most Honourable Privy Council, on Addresses from the Houses of the Parliament of Canada, and from the Houses of the respective Legislatures of the Colonies or Provinces of Newfoundland, Prince Edward Island, and British Columbia, to admit those Colonies or Provinces, or any of them, into the Union, and on Address from the Houses of the Parliament of Canada to admit Rupert's Land and the North-western Territory, or either of them, into the Union, on such Terms and Conditions in each Case as are in the Addresses expressed and as the Queen thinks fit to approve, subject to the Provisions of this Act; and the Provisions of any Order in Council in that Behalf shall have effect as if they had been enacted by the Parliament of the United Kingdom of Great Britain and Ireland.[75]

Power to admit Newfoundland, etc., into the Union

147. In case of the Admission of Newfoundland and Prince Edward Island, or either of them, each shall be entitled to a Representation in the Senate of Canada of Four Members, and (notwithstanding anything in this Act) in case of the Admission of Newfoundland the normal Number of Senators shall be Seventy-six and their maximum Number shall be Eighty-two; but Prince Edward Island when admitted shall be deemed to be comprised in the third of the Three Divisions into which Canada is, in relation to the Constitution of the Senate, divided by this Act, and accordingly, after the Admission of Prince Edward Island, whether Newfoundland is admitted or not, the Representation of Nova Scotia and New Brunswick in the Senate shall, as Vacancies occur, be reduced from Twelve to Ten Members respectively, and the Representation of each of those Provinces shall not be increased at any Time beyond Ten, except under the Provisions of this Act for the Appointment of Three or Six additional Senators under the Direction of the Queen.[76]

As to Representation of Newfoundland and Prince Edward Island in Senate

---

(75) All territories mentioned in this section are now part of Canada. See the notes to section 5, *supra.*

(76) Spent. See the notes to sections 21, 22, 26, 27 and 28, *supra.*

SCHEDULES

THE FIRST SCHEDULE[77]

Electoral Districts of Ontario

A.

EXISTING ELECTORAL DIVISIONS

COUNTIES

1. Prescott.
2. Glengarry.
3. Stormont.
4. Dundas.
5. Russell.
6. Carleton.
7. Prince Edward.
8. Halton.
9. Essex.

RIDINGS OF COUNTIES

10. North Riding of Lanark.
11. South Riding of Lanark.
12. North Riding of Leeds and North Riding of Grenville.
13. South Riding of Leeds.
14. South Riding of Grenville.
15. East Riding of Northumberland.
16. West Riding of Northumberland (excepting therefrom the Township of South Monaghan).
17. East Riding of Durham.
18. West Riding of Durham.
19. North Riding of Ontario.
20. South Riding of Ontario.
21. East Riding of York.
22. West Riding of York.
23. North Riding of York.
24. North Riding of Wentworth.
25. South Riding of Wentworth.
26. East Riding of Elgin.
27. West Riding of Elgin.
28. North Riding of Waterloo.
29. South Riding of Waterloo.
30. North Riding of Brant.
31. South Riding of Brant.
32. North Riding of Oxford.
33. South Riding of Oxford.
34. East Riding of Middlesex.

---

(77) Spent. *Representation Act*, R.S.O. 1990, c. R.26.

CITIES, PARTS OF CITIES, AND TOWNS

35. West Toronto.
36. East Toronto.
37. Hamilton.
38. Ottawa.
39. Kingston.
40. London.
41. Town of Brockville, with the Township of Elizabethtown thereto attached.
42. Town of Niagara, with the Township of Niagara thereto attached.
43. Town of Cornwall, with the Township of Cornwall thereto attached.

B.

NEW ELECTORAL DIVISIONS

44. The Provisional Judicial District of ALGOMA.

The County of BRUCE, divided into Two Ridings, to be called respectively the North and South Ridings:

45. The North Riding of Bruce to consist of the Townships of Bury, Lindsay, Eastnor, Albermarle, Amable, Arran, Bruce, Elderslie, and Saugeen, and the Village of Southampton.

46. The South Riding of Bruce to consist of the Townships of Kincardine (including the Village of Kincardine), Greenock, Brant, Huron, Kinloss, Culross, and Carrick.

The County of HURON, divided into Two Ridings, to be called respectively the North and South Ridings:

47. The North Riding to consist of the Townships of Ashfield, Wawanosh, Turnberry, Howick, Morris, Grey, Colborne, Hullett, including the Village of Clinton, and McKillop.

48. The South Riding to consist of the Town of Goderich and the Townships of Goderich, Tuckersmith, Stanley, Hay, Usborne, and Stephen.

The County of MIDDLESEX divided into three Ridings, to be called respectively the North, West, and East Ridings:

49. The North Riding to consist of the Townships of McGillivary and Biddulph (taken from the County of Huron), and Williams East, Williams West, Adelaide, and Lobo.

50. The West Riding to consist of the Townships of Delaware, Carradoc, Metcalfe, Mosa and Ekfrid, and the Village of Strathroy.

[The East Riding to consist of the Townships now embraced therein, and be bounded as it is at present.]

51. The County of LAMBTON to consist of Townships of Bosanquet, Warwick, Plympton, Sarnia, Moore, Enniskillen, and Brooke, and the Town of Sarnia.

52. The County of KENT to consist of the Townships of Chatham, Dover, East Tilbury, Romney, Raleigh, and Harwich, and the Town of Chatham.

53. The County of BOTHWELL to consist of the Townships of Sombra, Dawn, and Euphemia (taken from the County of Lambton), and the Townships of Zone, Camden with the Gore thereof, Orford, and Howard (taken from the County of Kent).

The County of GREY divided into Two Ridings to be called respectively the South and North Ridings:

54. The South Riding to consist of the Townships of Bentinck, Glenelg, Artemesia, Osprey, Normanby, Egremont, Proton, and Melancthon.

55. The North Riding to consist of the Townships of Collingwood, Euphrasia, Holland, Saint-Vincent, Sydenham, Sullivan, Derby, and Keppel, Sarawak and Brooke, and the Town of Owen Sound.

The County of PERTH divided into Two Ridings, to be called respectively the South and North Ridings:

56. The North Riding to consist of the Townships of Wallace, Elma, Logan, Ellice, Mornington, and North Easthope, and the Town of Stratford.

57. The South Riding to consist of the Townships of Blanchard, Downie, South Easthope, Fullarton, Hibbert, and the Villages of Mitchell and Ste. Marys.

The County of WELLINGTON divided into Three Ridings to be called respectively North, South and Centre Ridings:

58. The North Riding to consist of the Townships of Amaranth, Arthur, Luther, Minto, Maryborough, Peel, and the Village of Mount Forest.

59. The Centre Riding to consist of the Townships of Garafraxa, Erin, Eramosa, Nichol, and Pilkington, and the Villages of Fergus and Elora.

60. The South Riding to consist of the Town of Guelph, and the Townships of Guelph and Puslinch.

The County of NORFOLK, divided into Two Ridings, to be called respectively the South and North Ridings:

61. The South Riding to consist of the Townships of Charlotteville, Houghton, Walsingham, and Woodhouse, and with the Gore thereof.

62. The North Riding to consist of the Townships of Middleton, Townsend, and Windham, and the Town of Simcoe.

63. The County of HALDIMAND to consist of the Townships of Oneida, Seneca, Cayuga North, Cayuga South, Raynham, Walpole, and Dunn.

64. The County of MONCK to consist of the Townships of Canborough and Moulton, and Sherbrooke, and the Village of Dunnville (taken from the County of Haldimand), the Townships of Caister and Gainsborough (taken from the County of Lincoln), and the Townships of Pelham and Wainfleet (taken from the County of Welland).

65. The County of LINCOLN to consist of the Townships of Clinton, Grantham, Grimsby, and Louth, and the Town of St. Catharines.

66. The County of WELLAND to consist of the Townships of Bertie, Crowland, Humberstone, Stamford, Thorold, and Willoughby, and the Villages of Chippewa, Clifton, Fort Erie, Thorold, and Welland.

67. The County of PEEL to consist of the Townships of Chinguacousy, Toronto, and the Gore of Toronto, and the Villages of Brampton and Streetsville.

68. The County of CARDWELL to consist of the Townships of Albion and Caledon (taken from the County of Peel), and the Townships of Adjala and Mono (taken from the County of Simcoe).

The County of SIMCOE, divided into Two Ridings, to be called respectively the South and North Ridings:

69. The South Riding to consist of the Townships of West Gwillimbury, Tecumseth, Innisfil, Essa, Tosorontio, Mulmur, and the Village of Bradford.

70. The North Riding to consist of the Townships of Sunnidale, Vespra, Flos, Oro, Medonte, Orillia and Matchedash, Tiny and Tay, Balaklava and Robinson, and the Towns of Barrie and Collingwood.

The County of VICTORIA, divided into Two Ridings, to be called respectively the South and North Ridings:

71. The South Riding to consist of the Townships of Ops, Mariposa, Emily, Verulam, and the Town of Lindsay.

72. The North Riding to consist of the Townships of Anson, Bexley, Carden, Dalton, Digby, Eldon, Fenelon, Hindon, Laxton, Lutterworth, Macaulay and Draper, Sommerville, and Morrison, Muskoka, Monck and Watt (taken from the County of Simcoe), and any other surveyed Townships lying to the North of the said North Riding.

The County of PETERBOROUGH, divided into Two Ridings, to be called respectively the West and East Ridings:

73. The West Riding to consist of the Townships of South Monaghan (taken from the County of Northumberland), North Monaghan, Smith, and Ennismore, and the Town of Peterborough.

74. The East Riding to consist of the Townships of Asphodel, Belmont and Methuen, Douro, Dummer, Galway, Harvey, Minden, Stanhope and Dysart, Otonabee, and Snowden, and the Village of Ashburnham, and any other surveyed Townships lying to the North of the said East Riding.

The County of HASTINGS, divided into Three Ridings, to be called respectively the West, East, and North Ridings:

75. The West Riding to consist of the Town of Belleville, the Township of Sydney, and the Village of Trenton.

76. The East Riding to consist of the Townships of Thurlow, Tyendinaga, and Hungerford.

77. The North Riding to consist of the Townships of Rawdon, Huntingdon, Madoc, Elzevir, Tudor, Marmora, and Lake, and the Village of Stirling, and any other surveyed Townships lying to the North of the said North Riding.

78. The County of LENNOX to consist of the Townships of Richmond, Adolphustown, North Fredericksburg, South Fredericksburg, Ernest Town, and Amherst Island, and the Village of Napanee.

79. The County of ADDINGTON to consist of the Townships of Camden, Portland, Sheffield, Hinchinbrooke, Kaladar, Kennebec, Olden, Oso, Anglesea, Barrie, Clarendon, Palmerston, Effingham, Abinger, Miller, Canonto, Denbigh, Loughborough, and Bedford.

80. The County of FRONTENAC to consist of the Townships of Kingston, Wolfe Island, Pittsburg and Howe Island, and Storrington.

The County of RENFREW, divided into Two Ridings, to be called respectively the South and North Ridings:

81. The South Riding to consist of the Townships of McNab, Bagot, Blithfield, Brougham, Horton, Admaston, Grattan, Matawatchan, Griffith, Lyndoch, Raglan, Radcliffe, Brudenell, Sebastopol, and the Villages of Arnprior and Renfrew.

82. The North Riding to consist of the Townships of Ross, Bromley, Westmeath, Stafford, Pembroke, Wilberforce, Alice, Petawawa, Buchanan, South Algona, North Algona, Fraser, McKay, Wylie, Rolph, Head, Maria, Clara, Haggerty, Sherwood, Burns, and Richards, and any other surveyed Townships lying North-westerly of the said North Riding.

———————

Every Town and incorporated Village existing at the Union, not especially mentioned in this Schedule, is to be taken as Part of the County or Riding within which it is locally situate.

THE SECOND SCHEDULE

Electoral Districts of Quebec specially fixed

COUNTIES OF —

Pontiac.	Missisquoi.	Compton.
Ottawa.	Brome.	Wolfe and
Argenteuil.	Shefford.	Richmond.
Huntingdon.	Stanstead.	Megantic.
	Town of Sherbrooke.	

THE THIRD SCHEDULE

Provincial Publics Works and Property to be the Property of Canada

1. Canals, with Lands and Water Power connected therewith.
2. Public Harbours.
3. Lighthouses and Piers, and Sable Island.
4. Steamboats, Dredges, and public Vessels.
5. Rivers and Lake Improvements.
6. Railways and Railway Stocks, Mortgages, and other Debts due by Railway Companies.
7. Military Roads.
8. Custom Houses, Post Offices, and all other Public Buildings, except such as the Government of Canada appropriate for the Use of the Provincial Legislatures and Governments
9. Property transferred by the Imperial Government, and known as Ordnance Property.
10. Armouries, Drill Sheds, Military Clothing, and Munitions of War, and Lands set apart for general Public Purposes.

THE FOURTH SCHEDULE

Assets to be the Property of Ontario and Quebec conjointly

Upper Canada Building Fund.
Lunatic Asylums.
Normal School.
Court Houses in ⎱
Aylmer. ⎰
Montreal. ⎱ Lower Canada.
Kamouraska. ⎰
Law Society, Upper Canada.
Montreal Turnpike Trust.
University Permanent Fund.
Royal Institution.
Consolidated Municipal Loan Fund, Upper Canada.
Consolidated Municipal Loan Fund, Lower Canada.
Agricultural Society, Upper Canada.
Lower Canada Legislative Grant.
Quebec Fire Loan.
Temiscouata Advance Account.
Quebec Turnpike Trust.
Education — East.
Building and Jury Fund, Lower Canada.
Municipalities Fund.
Lower Canada Superior Education Income Fund.

THE FIFTH SCHEDULE

OATH OF ALLEGIANCE

I *A.B.* do swear, That I will be faithful and bear true Allegiance to Her Majesty Queen Victoria.

Note. — The Name of the King or Queen of the United Kingdom of Great Britain and Ireland for the Time being is to be substituted from Time to Time, with proper Terms of Reference thereto.

DECLARATION OF QUALIFICATION

I *A.B.* do declare and testify, That I am by Law duly qualified to be appointed a Member of the Senate of Canada [*or as the Case may be*], and that I am legally or equitably seised as of Freehold for my own Use and Benefit of Lands of Tenements held in Free and Common Socage [*or seised or possessed for my own Use and Benefit of Lands or Tenements held in Franc-alleu or in Roture (as the Case may be*),] in the Province of

Nova Scotia [*or as the Case may be*] of the Value of Four thousand Dollars over and above all Rents, Dues, Debts, Mortgages, Charges, and Incumbrances due or payable out of or charged on or affecting the same, and that I have not collusively or colourably obtained a Title to or become possessed of the said Lands and Tenements or any Part thereof for the Purpose of enabling me to become a Member of the Senate of Canada [*or as the Case may be*], and that my Real and Personal Property are together worth Four thousand Dollars over and above my Debts and Liabilities.

THE SIXTH SCHEDULE[78]

Primary Production from Non-Renewable Natural Resources and Forestry Resources

1. For the purposes of Section 92A of this Act,

(*a*) production from a non-renewable natural resource is primary production therefrom if

> (i) it is in the form in which it exists upon its recovery or severance from its natural state, or

> (ii) it is a product resulting from processing or refining the resource, and is not a manufactured product or a product resulting from refining crude oil, refining upgraded heavy crude oil, refining gases or liquids derived from coal or refining a synthetic equivalent of crude oil; and

(*b*) production from a forestry resource is primary production therefrom if it consists of sawlogs, poles, lumber, wood chips, sawdust or any other primary wood product, or wood pulp, and is not a product manufactured from wood.

----

(78) As enacted by the *Constitution Act, 1982.*

SCHEDULE B

CONSTITUTION ACT, 1982[79]

PART I

CANADIAN CHARTER OF RIGHTS AND FREEDOMS

Whereas Canada is founded upon principles that recognize the supremacy of God and the rule of law:

Guarantee of Rights and Freedoms

Rights and freedoms in Canada

1. The *Canadian Charter of Rights and Freedoms* guarantees the rights and freedoms set out in it subject only to such reasonable limits prescribed by law as can be demonstrably justified in a free and democratic society.

Fundamental Freedoms

Fundamental freedoms

2. Everyone has the following fundamental freedoms:

(*a*) freedom of conscience and religion;

(*b*) freedom of thought, belief, opinion and expression, including freedom of the press and other media of communication;

(*c*) freedom of peaceful assembly; and

(*d*) freedom of association.

Democratic Rights

Democratic rights of citizens

3. Every citizen of Canada has the right to vote in an election of members of the House of Commons or of a legislative assembly and to be qualified for membership therein.

---

(79) Enacted as Schedule B to the *Canada Act 1982*, (U.K.) 1982, c. 11, which came into force on April 17, 1982. *The Canada Act 1982*, other than Schedules A and B thereto, reads as follows:

An Act to give effect to a request by the Senate and House of Commons of Canada

Whereas Canada has requested and consented to the enactment of an Act of the Parliament of the United Kingdom to give effect to the provisions hereinafter set forth and the Senate and the House of Commons of Canada in Parliament assembled have submitted an address to Her Majesty requesting that Her Majesty may graciously be pleased to cause a Bill to be laid before the Parliament of the United Kingdom for that purpose.

Be it therefore enacted by the Queen's Most Excellent Majesty, by and with the advice and consent of the Lords Spiritual and Temporal, and Commons, in this present Parliament assembled, and by the authority of the same, as follows:

1. The *Constitution Act, 1982* set out in Schedule B to this Act is hereby enacted for and shall have the force of law in Canada and shall come into force as provided in that Act.

2. No Act of Parliament of the United Kingdom passed after the *Constitution Act, 1982* comes into force shall extend to Canada as part of its law.

3. So far as it is not contained in Schedule B, the French version of this Act is set out in Schedule A to this Act and has the same authority in Canada as the English version thereof.

4. This Act may be cited as the *Canada Act 1982*.

4. (1) No House of Commons and no legislative assembly shall continue for longer than five years from the date fixed for the return of the writs of a general election of its members.[80]

(2) In time of real or apprehended war, invasion or insurrection, a House of Commons may be continued by Parliament and a legislative assembly may be continued by the legislature beyond five years if such continuation is not opposed by the votes of more than one-third of the members of the House of Commons or the legislative assembly, as the case may be.[81]

5. There shall be a sitting of Parliament and of each legislature at least once every twelve months.[82]

Mobility Rights

6. (1) Every citizen of Canada has the right to enter, remain in and leave Canada.

(2) Every citizen of Canada and every person who has the status of a permanent resident of Canada has the right

    (*a*) to move to and take up residence in any province; and

    (*b*) to pursue the gaining of a livelihood in any province.

(3) The rights specified in subsection (2) are subject to

    (*a*) any laws or practices of general application in force in a province other than those that discriminate among persons primarily on the basis of province of present or previous residence; and

    (*b*) any laws providing for reasonable residency requirements as a qualification for the receipt of publicly provided social services.

(4) Subsections (2) and (3) do not preclude any law, program or activity that has as its object the amelioration in a province of conditions of individuals in that province who are socially or economically disadvantaged if the rate of employment in that province is below the rate of employment in Canada.

Legal Rights

7. Everyone has the right to life, liberty and security of the person and the right not to be deprived thereof except in accordance with the principles of fundamental justice.

---

(80) See section 50 and the footnotes to sections 85 and 88 of the *Constitution Act, 1867.*

(81) Replaces part of Class 1 of section 91 of the *Constitution Act, 1867,* which was repealed as set out in subitem 1(3) of the Schedule to this Act.

(82) See the footnotes to sections 20, 86 and 88 of the *Constitution Act, 1867.*

8. Everyone has the right to be secure against unreasonable search or seizure.

9. Everyone has the right not to be arbitrarily detained or imprisoned.

10. Everyone has the right on arrest or detention

(*a*) to be informed promptly of the reasons therefor;

(*b*) to retain and instruct counsel without delay and to be informed of that right; and

(*c*) to have the validity of the detention determined by way of *habeas corpus* and to be released if the detention is not lawful.

11. Any person charged with an offence has the right

(*a*) to be informed without unreasonable delay of the specific offence;

(*b*) to be tried within a reasonable time;

(*c*) not to be compelled to be a witness in proceedings against that person in respect of the offence;

(*d*) to be presumed innocent until proven guilty according to law in a fair and public hearing by an independent and impartial tribunal;

(*e*) not to be denied reasonable bail without just cause;

(*f*) except in the case of an offence under military law tried before a military tribunal, to the benefit of trial by jury where the maximum punishment for the offence is imprisonment for five years or a more severe punishment;

(*g*) not to be found guilty on account of any act or omission unless, at the time of the act or omission, it constituted an offence under Canadian or international law or was criminal according to the general principles of law recognized by the community of nations;

(*h*) if finally acquitted of the offence, not to be tried for it again and, if finally found guilty and punished for the offence, not to be tried or punished for it again; and

(*i*) if found guilty of the offence and if the punishment for the offence has been varied between the time of commission and the time of sentencing, to the benefit of the lesser punishment.

12. Everyone has the right not to be subjected to any cruel and unusual treatment or punishment.

13. A witness who testifies in any proceedings has the right not to have any incriminating evidence so given used to incriminate that witness in any other proceedings, except in a prosecution for perjury or for the giving of contradictory evidence.

14. A party or witness in any proceedings who does not understand or speak the language in which the proceedings are conducted or who is deaf has the right to the assistance of an interpreter.

Interpreter

Equality Rights

15. (1) Every individual is equal before and under the law and has the right to the equal protection and equal benefit of the law without discrimination and, in particular, without discrimination based on race, national or ethnic origin, colour, religion, sex, age or mental or physical disability.

Equality before and under law and equal protection and benefit of law

(2) Subsection (1) does not preclude any law, program or activity that has as its object the amelioration of conditions of disadvantaged individuals or groups including those that are disadvantaged because of race, national or ethnic origin, colour, religion, sex, age or mental or physical disability.[83]

Affirmative action programs

Official Languages of Canada

16. (1) English and French are the official languages of Canada and have equality of status and equal rights and privileges as to their use in all institutions of the Parliament and government of Canada.

Official languages of Canada

(2) English and French are the official languages of New Brunswick and have equality of status and equal rights and privileges as to their use in all institutions of the legislature and government of New Brunswick.

Official languages of New Brunswick

(3) Nothing in this Charter limits the authority of Parliament or a legislature to advance the equality of status or use of English and French.

Advancement of status and use

16.1. (1) The English linguistic community and the French linguistic community in New Brunswick have equality of status and equal rights and privileges, including the right to distinct educational institutions and such distinct cultural institutions as are necessary for the preservation and promotion of those communities.

English and French linguistic communities in New Brunswick

(2) The role of the legislature and government of New Brunswick to preserve and promote the status, rights and privileges referred to in subsection (1) is affirmed.[83.1]

Role of the legislature and government of New Brunswick

17. (1) Everyone has the right to use English or French in any debates and other proceedings of Parliament.[84]

Proceedings of Parliament

---

(83) Subsection 32(2) provides that section 15 shall not have effect until three years after section 32 comes into force.

Section 32 came into force on April 17, 1982; therefore, section 15 had effect on April 17, 1985.

(83.1) Section 16.1 was added by the *Constitution Amendment, 1993 (New Brunswick).* See SI/93-54.

(84) See section 133 of the *Constitution Act, 1867,* and the footnote thereto.

Proceedings of New Brunswick legislature

(2) Everyone has the right to use English or French in any debates and other proceedings of the legislature of New Brunswick.[85]

Parliamentary statutes and records

18. (1) The statutes, records and journals of Parliament shall be printed and published in English and French and both language versions are equally authoritative.[86]

New Brunswick statutes and records

(2) The statutes, records and journals of the legislature of New Brunswick shall be printed and published in English and French and both language versions are equally authoritative.[87]

Proceedings in courts established by Parliament

19. (1) Either English or French may be used by any person in, or in any pleading in or process issuing from, any court established by Parliament.[88]

Proceedings in New Brunswick courts

(2) Either English or French may be used by any person in, or in any pleading in or process issuing from, any court of New Brunswick.[89]

Communications by public with federal institutions

20. (1) Any member of the public in Canada has the right to communicate with, and to receive available services from, any head or central office of an institution of the Parliament or government of Canada in English or French, and has the same right with respect to any other office of any such institution where

(*a*) there is a significant demand for communications with and services from that office in such language; or

(*b*) due to the nature of the office, it is reasonable that communications with and services from that office be available in both English and French.

Communications by public with New Brunswick institutions

(2) Any member of the public in New Brunswick has the right to communicate with, and to receive available services from, any office of an institution of the legislature or government of New Brunswick in English or French.

Continuation of existing constitutional provisions

21. Nothing in sections 16 to 20 abrogates or derogates from any right, privilege or obligation with respect to the English and French languages, or either of them, that exists or is continued by virtue of any other provision of the Constitution of Canada.[90]

Rights and privileges preserved

22. Nothing in sections 16 to 20 abrogates or derogates from any legal or customary right or privilege acquired or enjoyed either before or after the coming into force of this Charter with respect to any language that is not English or French.

---

(85) *Id.*

(86) *Id.*

(87) *Id.*

(88) *Id.*

(89) *Id.*

(90) See, for example, section 133 of the *Constitution Act, 1867,* and the reference to the *Manitoba Act, 1870,* in the footnote thereto.

23. (1) Citizens of Canada

(*a*) whose first language learned and still understood is that of the English or French linguistic minority population of the province in which they reside, or

(*b*) who have received their primary school instruction in Canada in English or French and reside in a province where the language in which they received that instruction is the language of the English or French linguistic minority population of the province,

have the right to have their children receive primary and secondary school instruction in that language in that province.[91]

(2) Citizens of Canada of whom any child has received or is receiving primary or secondary school instruction in English or French in Canada, have the right to have all their children receive primary and secondary school instruction in the same language.

(3) The right of citizens of Canada under subsections (1) and (2) to have their children receive primary and secondary school instruction in the language of the English or French linguistic minority population of a province

(*a*) applies wherever in the province the number of children of citizens who have such a right is sufficient to warrant the provision to them out of public funds of minority language instruction; and

(*b*) includes, where the number of those children so warrants, the right to have them receive that instruction in minority language educational facilities provided out of public funds.

Enforcement

24. (1) Anyone whose rights or freedoms, as guaranteed by this Charter, have been infringed or denied may apply to a court of competent jurisdiction to obtain such remedy as the court considers appropriate and just in the circumstances.

(2) Where, in proceedings under subsection (1), a court concludes that evidence was obtained in a manner that infringed or denied any rights or freedoms guaranteed by this Charter, the evidence shall be excluded if it is established that, having regard to all the circumstances, the admission of it in the proceedings would bring the administration of justice into disrepute.

---

(91) Paragraph 23(1)(*a*) is not in force in respect of Quebec. See section 59 *infra.*

Aboriginal rights
and freedoms not
affected by Charter

25. The guarantee in this Charter of certain rights and freedoms shall not be construed so as to abrogate or derogate from any aboriginal, treaty or other rights or freedoms that pertain to the aboriginal peoples of Canada including

> (*a*) any rights or freedoms that have been recognized by the Royal Proclamation of October 7, 1763; and
>
> (*b*) any rights or freedoms that now exist by way of land claims agreements or may be so acquired.[92]

Other rights and
freedoms not
affected by
Charter

26. The guarantee in this Charter of certain rights and freedoms shall not be construed as denying the existence of any other rights or freedoms that exist in Canada.

Multicultural
heritage

27. This Charter shall be interpreted in a manner consistent with the preservation and enhancement of the multicultural heritage of Canadians.

Rights guaranteed
equally to both
sexes

28. Notwithstanding anything in this Charter, the rights and freedoms referred to in it are guaranteed equally to male and female persons.

Rights respecting
certain schools
preserved

29. Nothing in this Charter abrogates or derogates from any rights or privileges guaranteed by or under the Constitution of Canada in respect of denominational, separate or dissentient schools.[93]

Application to
territories and
territorial
authorities

30. A reference in this Charter to a Province or to the legislative assembly or legislature of a province shall be deemed to include a reference to the Yukon Territory and the Northwest Territories, or to the appropriate legislative authority thereof, as the case may be.

Legislative
powers not
extended

31. Nothing in this Charter extends the legislative powers of any body or authority.

Application of Charter

Application of
Charter

32. (1) This Charter applies

> (*a*) to the Parliament and government of Canada in respect of all matters within the authority of Parliament including all matters relating to the Yukon Territory and Northwest Territories; and

---

(92) Paragraph 25(*b*) was repealed and re-enacted by the *Constitution Amendment Proclamation, 1983. See* SI/84-102.

Paragraph 25(*b*) as originally enacted read as follows:

> "(*b*) any rights or freedoms that may be acquired by the aboriginal peoples of Canada by way of land claims settlement."

(93) See section 93 of the *Constitution Act, 1867,* and the footnote thereto.

(*b*) to the legislature and government of each province in respect of all matters within the authority of the legislature of each province.

(2) Notwithstanding subsection (1), section 15 shall not have effect until three years after this section comes into force. *Exception*

33. (1) Parliament or the legislature of a province may expressly declare in an Act of Parliament or of the legislature, as the case may be, that the Act or a provision thereof shall operate notwithstanding a provision included in section 2 or sections 7 to 15 of this Charter. *Exception where express declaration*

(2) An Act or a provision of an Act in respect of which a declaration made under this section is in effect shall have such operation as it would have but for the provision of this Charter referred to in the declaration. *Operation of exception*

(3) A declaration made under subsection (1) shall cease to have effect five years after it comes into force or on such earlier date as may be specified in the declaration. *Five year limitation*

(4) Parliament or the legislature of a province may re-enact a declaration made under subsection (1). *Re-enactment*

(5) Subsection (3) applies in respect of a re-enactment made under subsection (4). *Five year limitation*

Citation

34. This Part may be cited as the *Canadian Charter of Rights and Freedoms*. *Citation*

PART II

RIGHTS OF THE ABORIGINAL PEOPLES OF CANADA

35. (1) The existing aboriginal and treaty rights of the aboriginal peoples of Canada are hereby recognized and affirmed. *Recognition of existing aboriginal and treaty rights*

(2) In this Act, "aboriginal peoples of Canada" includes the Indian, Inuit and Métis peoples of Canada. *Definition of "aboriginal peoples of Canada"*

(3) For greater certainty, in subsection (1) "treaty rights" includes rights that now exist by way of land claims agreements or may be so acquired. *Land claims agreements*

(4) Notwithstanding any other provision of this Act, the aboriginal and treaty rights referred to in subsection (1) are guaranteed equally to male and female persons.[94] *Aboriginal and treaty rights are guaranteed equally to both sexes*

---

(94) Subsections 35(3) and (4) were added by the *Constitution Amendment Proclamation, 1983. See* SI/84-102.

35.1 The government of Canada and the provincial governments are committed to the principle that, before any amendment is made to Class 24 of section 91 of the "*Constitution Act, 1867*", to section 25 of this Act or to this Part,

> (*a*) a constitutional conference that includes in its agenda an item relating to the proposed amendment, composed of the Prime Minister of Canada and the first ministers of the provinces, will be convened by the Prime Minister of Canada; and

> (*b*) the Prime Minister of Canada will invite representatives of the aboriginal peoples of Canada to participate in the discussions on that item.[95]

PART III

EQUALIZATION AND REGIONAL DISPARITIES

36. (1) Without altering the legislative authority of Parliament or of the provincial legislatures, or the rights of any of them with respect to the exercise of their legislative authority, Parliament and the legislatures, together with the government of Canada and the provincial governments, are committed to

> (*a*) promoting equal opportunities for the well-being of Canadians;

> (*b*) furthering economic development to reduce disparity in opportunities; and

> (*c*) providing essential public services of reasonable quality to all Canadians.

(2) Parliament and the government of Canada are committed to the principle of making equalization payments to ensure that provincial governments have sufficient revenues to provide reasonably comparable levels of public services at reasonably comparable levels of taxation.[96]

PART IV

CONSTITUTIONAL CONFERENCE

37.[97]

---

(95) Section 35.1 was added by the *Constitution Amendment Proclamation, 1983. See* SI/84-102.

(96) See the footnotes to sections 114 and 118 of the *Constitution Act, 1867.*

(97) Section 54 provided for the repeal of Part IV one year after Part VII came into force. Part VII came into force on April 17, 1982 thereby repealing Part IV on April 17, 1983.

Part IV, as originally enacted, read as follows:

> **37.1** (1) A constitutional conference composed of the Prime Minister of Canada and the first ministers of the provinces shall be convened by the Prime Minister of Canada within one year after this Part comes into force.

PART IV.1

CONSTITUTIONAL CONFERENCES

37.1.[98]

PART V

PROCEDURE FOR AMENDING CONSTITUTION OF CANADA[99]

38. (1) An amendment to the Constitution of Canada may be made by proclamation issued by the Governor General under the Great Seal of Canada where so authorized by

General procedure for amending Constitution of Canada

    (*a*) resolutions of the Senate and House of Commons; and

    (*b*) resolutions of the legislative assemblies of at least two-thirds of the provinces that have, in the aggregate, according to the then latest general census, at least fifty per cent of the population of all the provinces.

(2) An amendment made under subsection (1) that derogates from the legislative powers, the proprietary rights or any other rights or privileges of the legislature or government of a province shall require a resolution supported by a majority of the members of each of the Senate, the House of Commons and the legislative assemblies required under subsection (1).

Majority of members

---

(2) The conference convened under subsection (1) shall have included in its agenda an item respecting constitutional matters that directly affect the aboriginal peoples of Canada, including the identification and definition of the rights of those peoples to be included in the Constituion of Canada, and the Prime Minister of Canada shall invite representatives of those peoples to participate in the discussions on that item.

(3) The Prime Minister of Canada shall invite elected representatives of the governments of the Yukon Territory and the Northwest Territories to participate in the discussions on any item on the agenda of the conference convened under subsection (1) that, in the opinion of the Prime Minister, directly affects the Yukon Territory and the Northwest Territories.

(98) Part IV.1, which was added by the *Constitution Amendment Proclamation, 1983* (see SI/84-102), was repealed on April 18, 1987 by section 54.1.

Part IV.1, as originally enacted, read as follows:

37.1 (1) In addition to the conference convened in March 1983, at least two constitutional conferences composed of the Prime Minister of Canada and the first ministers of the provinces shall be convened by the Prime Minister of Canada, the first within three years after April 17, 1982 and the second within five years after that date.

(2) Each conference convened under subsection (1) shall have included in its agenda constitutional matters that directly affect the aboriginal peoples of Canada, and the Prime Minister of Canada shall invite representatives of those peoples to participate in the discussions on those matters.

(3) The Prime Minister of Canada shall invite elected representatives of the governments of the Yukon Territory and the Northwest Territories to participate in the discussions on any item on the agenda of a conference convened under subsection (1) that, in the opinion of the Prime Minister, directly affects the Yukon Territory and the Northwest Territories.

(4) Nothing in this section shall be construed so as to derogate from subsection 35(1).

(99) Prior to the enactment of Part V certain provisions of the Constitution of Canada and the provincial constitutions could be amended pursuant to the *Constitution Act, 1867*. See the footnotes to section 91, Class 1 and section 92, Class 1 thereof, *supra*. Other amendments to the Constitution could only be made by enactment of the Parliament of the United Kingdom.

Expression of dissent

(3) An amendment referred to in subsection (2) shall not have effect in a province the legislative assembly of which has expressed its dissent thereto by resolution supported by a majority of its members prior to the issue of the proclamation to which the amendment relates unless that legislative assembly, subsequently, by resolution supported by a majority of its members, revokes its dissent and authorizes the amendment.

Revocation of dissent

(4) A resolution of dissent made for the purposes of subsection (3) may be revoked at any time before or after the issue of the proclamation to which it relates.

Restriction on proclamation

39. (1) A proclamation shall not be issued under subsection 38 (1) before the expiration of one year from the adoption of the resolution initiating the amendment procedure thereunder, unless the legislative assembly of each province has previously adopted a resolution of assent of dissent.

Idem

(2) A proclamation shall not be issued under subsection 38 (1) after the expiration of three years from the adoption of the resolution initiating the amendment procedure thereunder.

Compensation

40. Where an amendment is made under subsection 38(1) that transfers provincial legislative powers relating to education or other cultural matters from provincial legislatures to Parliament, Canada shall provide reasonable compensation to any province to which the amendment does not apply.

Amendment by unanimous consent

41. An amendment to the Constitution of Canada in relation to the following matters may be made by proclamation issued by the Governor General under the Great Seal of Canada only where authorized by resolutions of the Senate and House of Commons and of the legislative assembly of each province:

(*a*) the office of the Queen, the Governor General and the Lieutenant Governor of a province;

(*b*) the right of a province to a number of members in the House of Commons not less than the number of Senators by which the province is entitled to be represented at the time this Part comes into force;

(*c*) subject to section 43, the use of the English or the French language;

(*d*) the composition of the Supreme Court of Canada; and

(*e*) an amendment to this Part.

Amendment by general procedure

42. (1) An amendment to the Constitution of Canada in relation to the following matters may be made only in accordance with subsection 38(1):

(*a*) the principle of proportionate representation of the provinces in the House of Commons prescribed by the Constitution of Canada;

(*b*) the powers of the Senate and the method of selecting Senators;

(*c*) the number of members by which a province is entitled to be represented in the Senate and the residence qualifications of Senators;

(*d*) subject to paragraph 41(*d*), the Supreme Court of Canada;

(*e*) the extension of existing provinces into the territories; and

(*f*) notwithstanding any other law or practice, the establishment of new provinces.

(2) Subsections 38(2) to (4) do not apply in respect of amendments in relation to matters referred to in subsection (1). **Exception**

43. An amendment to the Constitution of Canada in relation to any provision that applies to one or more, but not all, provinces, including **Amendment of provisions relating to some but not all provinces**

(*a*) any alteration to boundaries between provinces, and

(*b*) any amendment to any provision that relates to the use of the English or the French language within a province,

may be made by proclamation issued by the Governor General under the Great Seal of Canada only where so authorized by resolutions of the Senate and House of Commons and of the legislative assembly of each province to which the amendment applies.

44. Subject to sections 41 and 42, Parliament may exclusively make laws amending the Constitution of Canada in relation to the executive government of Canada or the Senate and House of Commons. **Amendments by Parliament**

45. Subject to section 41, the legislature of each province may exclusively make laws amending the constitution of the province. **Amendments by provincial legislatures**

46. (1) The procedures for amendment under sections 38, 41, 42 and 43 may be initiated either by the Senate or the House of Commons or by the legislative assembly of a province. **Initiation of amendment procedures**

(2) A resolution of assent made for the purposes of this Part may be revoked at any time before the issue of a proclamation authorized by it. **Revocation of authorization**

47. (1) An amendment to the Constitution of Canada made by proclamation under section 38, 41, 42 or 43 may be made without a resolution of the Senate authorizing the issue of the proclamation if, within one hundred and eighty days after the adoption by the House of Commons of a resolution authorizing its issue, the Senate has not adopted such a resolution and if, at any time after the expiration of that period, the House of Commons again adopts the resolution. **Amendments without Senate resolution**

(2) Any period when Parliament is prorogued or dissolved shall not be counted in computing the one hundred and eighty day period referred to in subsection (1). **Computation of period**

48. The Queen's Privy Council for Canada shall advise the Governor General to issue a proclamation under this Part forthwith on the adoption of the resolutions required for an amendment made by proclamation under this Part.

49. A constitutional conference composed of the Prime Minister of Canada and the first ministers of the provinces shall be convened by the Prime Minister of Canada within fifteen years after this Part comes into force to review the provisions of this Part.

PART VI

AMENDMENT TO THE CONSTITUTION ACT, 1867

50.[100]

51.[101]

PART VII

GENERAL

52. (1) The Constitution of Canada is the supreme law of Canada, and any law that is inconsistent with the provisions of the Constitution is, to the extent of the inconsistency, of no force or effect.

(2) The Constitution of Canada includes

    (*a*) the *Canada Act 1982,* including this Act;

    (*b*) the Acts and orders referred to in the schedule; and

    (*c*) any amendment to any Act or order referred to in paragraph (*a*) or (*b*).

(3) Amendments to the Constitution of Canada shall be made only in accordance with the authority contained in the Constitution of Canada.

53. (1) The enactments referred to in Column I of the schedule are hereby repealed or amended to the extent indicated in Column II thereof and, unless repealed, shall continue as law in Canada under the names set out in Column III thereof.

(2) Every enactment, except the *Canada Act 1982,* that refers to an enactment referred to in the schedule by the name in Column I thereof is hereby amended by substituting for that name the corresponding name in Column III thereof, and any British North

---

(100) The amendment is set out in the Consolidation of the *Constitution Act, 1867,* as section 92A thereof.

(101) The amendment is set out in the Consolidation of the *Constitution Act, 1867,* as the Sixth Schedule thereof.

America Act not referred to in the schedule may be cited as the *Constitution Act* followed by the year and number, if any, of its enactment.

54. Part IV is repealed on the day that is one year after this Part comes into force and this section may be repealed and this Act renumbered, consequentially upon the repeal of Part IV and this section, by proclamation issued by the Governor General under the Great Seal of Canada.[102]

Repeal and consequential amendments

54.1.[103]

55. A French version of the portions of the Constitution of Canada referred to in the schedule shall be prepared by the Minister of Justice of Canada as expeditiously as possible and, when any portion thereof sufficient to warrant action being taken has been so prepared, it shall be put forward for enactment by proclamation issued by the Governor General under the Great Seal of Canada pursuant to the procedure then applicable to an amendment of the same provisions of the Constitution of Canada.

French version of Constitution of Canada

56. Where any portion of the Constitution of Canada has been or is enacted in English and French or where a French version of any portion of the Constitution is enacted pursuant to section 55, the English and French versions of that portion of the Constitution are equally authoritative.

English and French versions of certain constitutional texts

57. The English and French versions of this Act are equally authoritative.

English and French versions of this Act

58. Subject to section 59, this Act shall come into force on a day to be fixed by proclamation issued by the Queen or the Governor General under the Great Seal of Canada.[104]

Commencement

59. (1) Paragraph 23(1)(*a*) shall come into force in respect of Quebec on a day to be fixed by proclamation issued by the Queen or the Governor General under the Great Seal of Canada.

Commencement of paragraph 23(1)(a) in respect of Quebec

(2) A proclamation under subsection (1) shall be issued only where authorized by the legislative assembly or government of Quebec.[105]

Authorization of Quebec

---

(102) Part VII came into force on April 17, 1982. *See* SI/82-97.

(103) Section 54.1, which was added by the *Constitution Amendment Proclamation, 1983* (see SI/84-102), provided for the repeal of Part IV.1 and section 54.1 on April 18, 1987.

Section 54.1, as originally enacted, read as follows:

"**54.1** Part IV.1 and this section are repealed on April 18, 1987."

(104) The Act, with the exception of paragraph 23(1)(*a*) in respect of Quebec, came into force on April 17, 1982 by proclamation issued by the Queen. *See* SI/82-97.

(105) No proclamation has been issued under section 59.

(3) This section may be repealed on the day paragraph 23(1)(*a*) comes into force in respect of Quebec and this Act amended and renumbered, consequentially upon the repeal of this section, by proclamation issued by the Queen or the Governor General under the Great Seal of Canada.

60. This Act may be cited as the *Constitution Act, 1982,* and the Constitution Acts 1867 to 1975 (No. 2) and this Act may be cited together as the *Constitution Acts, 1867 to 1982.*

61. A reference to the *"Constitution Acts, 1867 to 1982"* shall be deemed to include a reference to the *"Constitution Amendment Proclamation, 1983."* [106]

---

(106) Section 61 was added by the *Constitution Amendment Proclamation, 1983. See* SI/84-102.

See also section 3 of the *Constitution Act, 1985 (Representation),* S.C. 1986, c. 8, Part I and the *Constitution Amendment, 1987 (Newfoundland Act)* SI/88-11.

INDEX

British model of government, 12–13
British North America Act (1867), 14, 133–34, 173–75. *See also Constitution Act, 1867*
  amendments to, 133–34
  division of powers, 68, 81–82, 86
  federalism, establishes, 81–82
  interpretation by JCPC, 12, 69
  judicial review of, 86–92
  limitations of, 82–83
  no written amending formula, 70, 72–73, 133, 136
  Opposition parties, 72
  Persons case, 69–70
  quasi-federal elements, 87
  vests executive power in Crown, 264
British parliamentary institutions, 207–10
Brodie, Jim, 303
Brokerage or cadre parties, 367, 368, 392
Brokerage politics, 390
Budget, annual, 238, 305
Bureaucracy, government. *See* Permanent executive
Bush, George W., 114
Business interest groups, 487
Business of Supply, 237
By-election, 420

C

Cabinet
  accountability of Ministers, 261, 266–67
  committees, 281–82
  Commons and, 8–9, 12–13, 15, 211–12, 218, 242, 267
  composition, 260–61, 270
  criteria for inclusion, 218, 276, 279–80
  decision-making style, 267
  emergency powers, 19
  evolution in U.K., 209
  full, 284
  fusion of executive and legislative power, 12
  junior ministers, 275
  mandate letters, 271–72
  media and, 281
  ministers chosen by P.M., 270
  operation of Cabinet government, 280–84
  order of precedence, 274
  potential appointees, 276
  regional representation, 277–78, 279
  relationship to the PM, 279–80, 284
  relationships with departmental bureaucracy, 280
  responsibilities of ministers, 261–67, 276, 280–81
  secrecy, 267, 284
  senators in, 276–77

  seniority, 275, 278–79
  solidarity, 93, 94, 267
  voting, 284
Cadre parties. *See* Brokerage or cadre parties
Cairns, Alan, 16, 48, 89
Calgary Declaration (1997), 153
Campbell, Kim, 275
Canada Assistance Plan (CAP), 98, 150
Canada Elections Act, 68, 309, 376, 382, 422, 429–33
Canada Gazette, 311
Canada Health Act, 98
Canada Health and Social Transfer (CHST), 150
Canada Public Health Agency, 116
Canada Round of constitutional reform, 143, 145, 156
Canadian Alliance, 31, 365, 366, 451
  choice of leader, 378
  result of "United Alternative" efforts, 399
  voter support, 401
Canadian Assistance Plan (CAP), 98, 150
Canadian Association of Income Trusts, 425
Canadian Bill of Rights, 68, 175–78
Canadian Broadcasting Corporation (CBC), 508
Canadian Congress of Labour (CCL), 395
Canadian Council of Ministers of the Environment (CCME), 108, 111
Canadian Health and Social Transfer (CHST), 94, 98–99, 150, 485
Canadian Health Transfer (CHT), 100, 148
Canadian Intergovernmental Conference Secretariat (CICS), 109
Canadian Labour Congress (CLC), 395
Canadian Press/Broadcast News, 510
Canadian Public Affairs Channel (CPAC), 536
Canadian Radio-television and Telecommunications Commission (CRTC), 312, 514, 516, 519
Canadian Security Intelligence Service (CSIS), 181, 191–92
Canadian Social Transfer, 100
Canvass, 433
CanWest newspapers, 518
CanWest News Service, 510, 514, 515, 516
Carstairs, Sharon, 141
Carty, Kenneth R., 386, 390, 398
Case law, 69
Casework, 236, 247
Cash transfers, 98
Catch-all party, 368
Categorical ballot, 434–35
Catholics, Liberal supporters as, 450
Caucus, 213, 231, 247, 366

  choice of leaders in early years, 377
  expression of views at meetings, 213
  history, 210
  regional caucuses, 277–78
Caucus parties, 390
CBC/Radio-Canada, 309
CCF-NDP, 396
Central agencies, 285, 296, 297, 298, 315
Certified General Accountants of New Brunswick, 157
Changes and adaptations, 6, 44
Charest, Jean, 48
Charkaoui decision, 192
Charlottetown Accord, 105, 143, 148
  Aboriginal leaders, 147–48, 156
  referendum on (1992), 134, 143
Charter Canadians, 16, 48, 144
Charter of Rights and Freedoms (1982), 13, 14, 36, 135
  application, 180–81
  Charter groups, 16, 48–49, 144
  creation, 178–80
  evolution of *Charter* guarantees, 179–80
  focus for postmaterialism, 144
  impact on politics and policy, 189–90
  key principles of interpretation, 181, 183–86
  limitations clause, 179–80
  media coverage of *Charter* cases, 536–39
  Meech Lake, 11, 146–48
  national security post 9/11, 191–92
  notwithstanding clause, 137, 190
  protection of minorities, 17, 138
  remedies, 185–86
  right to vote, 183–84
  scope, 180–81
  shifts policy-making power to courts, 169–71
  three-stage analysis, 181, 182–86
  transformation of judicial review, 176–78
  voting, 183–84
  equality clause, 180
Chief of Staff (PMO), 302–303
Child-care program, 535
Chong, Michael, 161
Chrétien, Jean, 10, 41, 87, 88, 90, 109, 146, 148, 151, 156
Cities, 112–13
Citizen's constitution, 135, 137, 143, 144–46
Citizen's Forum on Canada's Future, 143
City regions, 112–13
Civil Service Commission Act, 1918, 393
Civil Service employees. *See* Permanent executive
Clarity Act, 68, 151, 154–55